fabulous cookies

SCRUMPTIOUS RECIPES FOR
DELICIOUS HOMEMADE TREATS

Hilaire Walden

LORENZ BOOKS

First published in 2000 by Lorenz Books
an imprint of Anness Publishing Limited
Hermes House, 88–89 Blackfriars Road, London SE1 8HA
© 2000 Anness Publishing Limited

This edition distributed in Canada by Raincoast Books
8680 Cambie Street, Vancouver, British Columbia V6P 6M9

A CIP catalogue record for this book is available from the British Library

Publisher: Joanna Lorenz
Project Editor: Joanne Rippin
Designer: Siân Keogh, Axis Design
Illustrator: Christos Chrysanthou, Axis Design
Cover Artwork: Balley Design Associates
Front cover: William Lingwood, Photographer; Helen Trent, Stylist; Sunil Vijayakar, Home Economist

Also published as part of a larger compendium, *The Great Big Cookie Book*

Printed and bound in Hong Kong/China
1 3 5 7 9 10 8 6 4 2

The recipes in this book were supplied by: Liz Trigg, Patricia Lousada, Carla Capalbo, Laura Washburn, Frances Cleary, Norma MacMillan, Christine France, Pamela Westland, Hilaire Walden, Elizabeth Wolf-Cohen, Janice Murfitt, Carole Handslip, Steven Wheeler, Katherine Richmond, Joanna Farrow, Judy Williams, Sue Maggs, Carole Clements, Jacqueline Clark, Sarah Maxwell, Sallie Morris, Lesley Mackley, Roz Denny, Sarah Gates, Norma Miller, Maxine Clark, Shirley Gill, Judy Jackson, Gilly Love, Janet Brinkworth, Ruby Le Bois, Elisabeth Lambert Ortiz, Sohelia Kimberley.
Photography by: Karl Adamson, Edward Allright, Steve Baxter, James Duncan, John Freeman, Michelle Garrett, Nelson Hargreaves, Amanda Heywood, David Jordan, Patrick McLeavey, Michael Michaels, Polly Wreford.

Notes

For all recipes, quantities are given in both metric and imperial measures and, where appropriate, in standard cups and spoons. Follow one set, but not a mixture because they are not interchangeable. Medium eggs should be used unless otherwise stated.

Recipe for Icing Glaze
15ml/1 tbsp lightly beaten egg white
15ml/1 tbsp lemon juice
75–115g/3–4oz/¼–1 cup icing sugar

Mix the egg white and lemon juice in a bowl. Gradually beat in the icing sugar until the mixture is smooth and has the consistency of thin cream. The icing should coat the back of a spoon.

Recipe for Royal Icing
1 egg white
¼ tsp lemon juice
225g/8 oz/2 cups icing sugar, sieved
2.5ml/½ tsp glycerine

Mix the egg whites and lemon juice in a bowl. Gradually add the icing sugar until the mixture reaches piping consistency. Stir in the glycerine until well blended.

Contents

Introduction

Americans call them cookies and the British traditionally use the term biscuits, although now the word cookie has become quite common all over the world.

Whichever name is used, sweet cookies are delicious to nibble at any time of the day: with a cup of tea or coffee, or to serve with ice cream or other light dessert.

The American word "cookie" is of Dutch origin, from the word *koekje* meaning little cake. The origins of "biscuit" are to be found in the word itself: it comes from the French *bis cuit,* meaning twice cooked, and goes back to the days when bakers put slices of newly-baked bread back into the cooking oven, so that they dried out completely, becoming something like a rusk. This was really a method of preservation for it enabled the cookies to be kept for a long time; so long, in fact that they could be taken as a basic food item, known as "ship's biscuits", on long sea voyages.

For many years housewives continued with the practice of drying their biscuits a second time, and it was not until the beginning of the last century that the habit died out. Then both the quality and variety of biscuits improved dramatically.

A batch of homemade cookies will fill your kitchen with a wonderful aroma when they are ready to come out of the oven. There is a great difference between homemade cookies and the commercial ones sold in shops and supermarkets. Packaged, mass-produced cookies are more concerned with profit and long shelf-life. They are usually too sweet, contain additives and their character and flavour, let alone purity, cannot compare with a tasty cookie from your own store cupboard. Home baked cookies mean you can choose to use only the best ingredients.

There is almost no end to the range of cookies that can be made at home, using recipes that, over the years, have become great favourites the world over, with adults, teenagers and children alike.

This comprehensive collection of recipes suits every occasion and every taste, no matter if the fancy is for something rich and indulgent or traditionally wholesome, delightfully crisp or moist and chewy, satisfyingly chunky or elegantly thin, nutty or chocolatey. This book will inspire you to bake your favourite cookies for high days, holidays and special occasions, keep some dough in the freezer for unexpected guests, and determine never again to resort to the supermarket for your cookies.

▶ *Cookies are not only ideal for everyday eating, or special treats at home; they can also be gift-wrapped and given away as a special gift.*

Cookie Tips
& Techniques

Store Cupboard

The ingredients for cookie making can be found in most people's store cupboards and fridges

Chocolate Buy good quality chocolate with at least 50% cocoa solids for baking. Plain chocolate gives a distinctive strong, rich flavour while milk chocolate has a sweeter taste. White chocolate often does not contain any cocoa solids, and lacks the flavour of true chocolate. It is the most difficult chocolate to melt and has poor setting qualities.

Eggs Eggs should be at room temperature so, if you keep them in the fridge, move the number you want to room temperature at least 30 minutes before making a recipe.

Flours Flour provides the structure that makes the cookies. Always sift flour. Not only will this remove any lumps, which are rare nowadays, but lightens the flour by incorporating air, and makes it easier to mix in.

Self-raising flour has raising agents added and is the type of flour most usually used in straightforward cookies that need to rise.

Plain flour is used when rising is considered a fault, as when making shortbread. Rich or heavy mixtures that should be raised also often call for plain flour plus additional raising agents in the specific proportions required for the particular recipe.

Wholemeal flour adds more flavour than white flour and is the healthier option but does produce denser cookies. When lightness is important extra raising agents should be added. Some recipes work well with a mixture of white and wholemeal flour.

Dried fruits Today, most dried fruits are dried by artificial heat rather than by the sun, and are treated with sulphur dioxide to help their preservation. Oils are sometimes sprayed on to the fruit to give it a shiny appearance and to prevent them sticking together. Try to buy fruit which have been coated with vegetable oils not mineral oils.

Butter and margarine Butter gives the best flavour to cookies and should be used whenever possible, especially when there is a high fat content, as in shortbread. However, it can be used interchangeably with hard block margarine. Butter or margarine to be used for creaming with sugar needs to be at room temperature and softened. For rubbing in, the fat should be at a cool room temperature, not fridge hard, and chopped quite finely.

Soft margarine is really only suitable for making cookies by the all-in-one method and when the fat has to be melted.

Glacé fruits Wash glacé fruits before using them to remove the syrupy coating, then dry thoroughly.

Spices Ground cinnamon, ginger, mixed spice, nutmeg and cloves may be used in cookies. All spices should be as fresh as possible. Buy in small quantities to use within a few months.

Honey Honey adds its own distinctive flavour to cookies. It contains 17% water so you will need to use slightly more honey than sugar, and reduce the amounts of the other liquids used. For easy mixing in, use clear honey.

Sugars Caster sugar is the best sweetener to use for the creaming method because the crystals dissolve easily and quickly when creamed with the fat. Granulated sugar is coarser textured than caster sugar so this is best used for rubbed-in mixtures and when the sugar is heated with the fat or liquid until it dissolves. Icing sugar appears in the ingredients for some cookie recipes where it is important that the sugar dissolves very readily. Demerara sugar can be used when the sugar is dissolved over heat before being added to the dry ingredients. Soft light and dark brown sugars are used when a richer flavour and colour are called for.

Nuts Nuts become rancid if stored for too long, in the light or at too high a temperature, so only buy in amounts that you will use within 1-2 months and keep them in an airtight container in a cool, dark cupboard. Alternatively, freeze them for up to 1 year.

Equipment

A delightful aspect of cookie making is that it requires the minimum

of special equipment.

You can make quite a range of cookies with just a mixing bowl, measures or weights, a wooden spoon, a baking sheet and a wire rack. Only a few items are needed to extend the range much further. Many supermarkets now sell all you will need for cookie making.

Baking tins Used good quality sturdy tins; thin, cheap tins will buckle with time. Cheap tins also heat more quickly so cookies are liable to cook quickly, brown and stick to them more readily. Non-stick tins, of course, save greasing, and lining when called for, greatly reduce sticking and cut down on washing up.

Cannelle knife This tool is great for carving stripes in the skin of citrus fruit. Pare off thin strips before slicing the fruit to make an attractive edge.

Cutters Cutters are available in many different shapes and sizes, ranging from simple plain biscuit circles in various sizes, to small cutters for *petits fours* and savoury cocktail nibbles, to animal shapes, hearts and flowers. For best results, the important criterion that applies to all cutters is that they should be sharp, to give a good clear, sharp outline. This really means that they should be made from metal; plastic cutters tend to compress the cut edges.

To use a cutter, press down firmly on the cutter so that it cuts straight down right through the dough. Then lift up the cutter, without twisting it.

If you want to cut out a shape for which you do not have a cutter, the thing to do is to make a template, or pattern. This is very easy.

Trace or draw the design on to greaseproof paper or card and cut it out using scissors. Lay the template on to the rolled out cookie dough. Use the point of a large, sharp knife to carefully cut around the template, taking care not to drag it. With a thin metal pallette knife or fish slice, transfer the shape to the prepared baking sheet, without distorting the shape.

Food processor Although food processors save time, their drawback is their very speed; they work so fast that you must be careful not to overmix a mixture. Food processors combine rather than beat ingredients together, so they are not so useful for recipes where lightness is important. Also, many models cannot whisk egg whites, and even in those designed for whisking, the whites will not become really stiff.

Knives A round-bladed knife can be used for the initial stages of cutting in the fat before it is rubbed in. Large, sharp knives are needed for cutting cleanly and efficiently through rolled-out dough, or refrigerated dough. Palette knives are invaluable for spreading and smoothing mixtures in cake tins, transferring cut out cookies to baking sheets before baking and then transferring the baked cookies to a wire rack to cool. They can also be used for spreading icing on cookies.

Measures A set of accurate measuring spoons is vital for measuring 15ml/1 tablespoon, 5ml/1 teaspoon and fractions of teaspoons. All the amounts given in recipes are for level spoonfuls unless otherwise stated. For liquids, use a heatproof jug, preferably see-through, that is calibrated for both imperial and metric measures.

Pastry brushes A large pastry brush is very useful for brushing surplus flour from work surfaces and cookie doughs that are being rolled out, and for greasing cake tins. A pastry brush is also needed for brushing on glazes. Buy good quality brushes with firmly-fixed bristles.

Piping bags and nozzles A medium piping bag with a selection of nozzles is very useful to have for piping uncooked cookie dough, and for decorating cookies after baking. Use small disposable piping bags for chocolate or icing, where a fine line is required.

Rolling pin Rolling pins made of
wood are the most common, but you
can now buy marble or even plastic
ones which are considered to be more
hygienic.

Scales A good set of scales is
essential for successful cookie making.
Whether you use spring balance,
modern electronic or old-fashioned
balanced scales with a set of weights,
test them frequently for accuracy by
putting something on them which has
the weight printed on it.

Sieves If possible have a set of strong
sieves in 2 or 3 different sizes.

Skewers and cocktail sticks Either of
these can be used for testing whether
cookie mixtures are cooked.

Spatulas A flexible rubber spatula is
indispensable for scraping every last
morsel from the mixing bowl into the
cake tin.

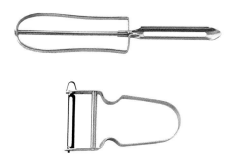

Swivel-blade peelers Both long-
handled and broad-handled peelers are
the best tools for peeling fruit.

Tea strainer A tea strainer will come
in handy for sifting icing sugar over
cookies as last-minute decoration.

Whisk Use either a wire balloon whisk
or a rotary whisk for beating eggs
together. It is a good idea to have two
sizes of balloon whisks, to suit the
amount of mixture.

Zester Ideal for citrus fruit, a zester
has the same function as a cannelle
knife but produces a row of thin
stripes.

Measuring ingredients

Cooks with years of experience may not need to measure ingredients, but if you are a beginner or are trying a new recipe for the first time, it is best to follow instructions carefully. Also, measuring ingredients precisely will ensure consistent results.

1 For liquids measured in pints or litres: use a glass or clear plastic measuring jug. Put it on a flat surface and pour in the liquid. Bend down and check that the liquid is level with the marking on the jug, as specified in the recipe.

2 For liquids measured in spoons: pour the liquid into the measuring spoon, to the brim, and then pour it into the mixing bowl. Do not hold the spoon over the bowl when measuring because some liquid may overflow.

3 For measuring dry ingredients in a spoon: fill the spoon, scooping up the ingredient. Level the surface with the rim of the spoon, using the straight edge of a knife.

4 For measuring dry ingredients by weight: scoop or pour on to the scales, watching the dial or reading carefully. Balance scales give more accurate readings than spring scales.

5 For measuring syrups: set the mixing bowl on the scales and turn the gauge to zero, or make a note of the weight. Pour in the required weight of syrup.

6 For measuring butter: cut with a sharp knife and weigh, or cut off the specified amount following the markings on the wrapping paper.

Making cookies by the rubbing in method

Plain cookies are usually made by rubbing the fat into the flour. For this, the fat, whether butter, margarine or lard, should be neither rock hard from the fridge, nor too warm. It is first chopped into small pieces, then added to the dry ingredients in a bowl. The mixture is lifted high and the lumps of fat rubbed between the fingertips as the mixture is allowed to fall back into the bowl.

1 Sift the flour into a bowl, adding the raising agents, salt and any sugar or spices and mix them evenly.

2 Stir in any other dry ingredients; combine the oats or other cereal, or coconut. Add the butter or margarine, cut into pieces.

3 Sprinkle the liquid ingredients (water, cream, milk, buttermilk or beaten egg) over the mixture.

4 Mix with your fingers or stir with a fork until the dry ingredients are thoroughly moistened and will come together in a ball of fairly soft dough in the centre of the bowl.

5 Press the dough into a ball. If it is too dry to form a dough, add some extra water.

6 Turn the dough on to a lightly floured surface. Knead very lightly, folding and pressing, to mix evenly – about 30 seconds. Wrap the ball of dough in clear film or greaseproof paper and chill it for at least 30 minutes.

Making cookies by the creaming method

To make cookies by the creaming method, the fat and sugar are 'creamed' – or beaten – together before the eggs and dry ingredients are added. The fat (usually butter or margarine) should be soft enough to be beaten so, if necessary, remove it from the refrigerator and leave for at least 30 minutes. For best results, the eggs should be at room temperature.

1 Sift the flour with the salt, raising agent(s) and any other dry ingredients, such as spices or cocoa powder, into a bowl. Set aside.

2 Put the fat in a large, deep bowl and beat with an electric mixer at medium speed, or a wooden spoon, until the texture is soft and pliable.

3 Add the sugar to the creamed fat gradually. With the mixer at medium-high speed, or using the wooden spoon, beat it into the fat until the mixture is pale and very fluffy. The sugar should be completely incorporated.

5 Add the dry ingredients to the mixture. Beat at low speed just until smoothly combined, or fold in with a large metal spoon.

6 If the recipe calls for any liquid, add it in small portions alternately with portions of the dry ingredients.

7 If the recipe specifies, whisk egg whites separately until frothy, add sugar and continue whisking until stiff peaks form. Fold into the mixture.

Making cookies by the all-in-one method

Some cookies are made by an easy all-in-one method where all the ingredients are combined in a bowl and beaten thoroughly. The mixture can also be made in a food processor, but take care not to over-process. A refinement on the all-in-one method is to separate the eggs and make the mixture with the yolks. The whites are whisked separately and then folded in. Soft margarine has to be used.

4 Add the eggs or egg yolks, one at a time, beating well after each addition. Scrape the bowl often so all the ingredients are evenly combined. If the mixture curdles, add 15ml/1 tbsp of the measured flour.

1 Sift the flour and any other dry ingredients such as salt, raising agents and spices, into a bowl.

2 Add the liquid ingredients, such as eggs, melted or soft fat, milk or fruit juices, and beat until smooth, with an electric mixer for speed. Pour into the prepared tins and bake as specified in the recipe.

8 Pour the mixture into a prepared cake tin and bake as specified.

Traditional Cookies

Granola Cookies

Makes 18

INGREDIENTS

*115g/4oz/¹/₂ cup butter or
margarine
75g/3oz/¹/₂ cup light brown sugar
75g/3oz/¹/₃ cup crunchy
peanut butter
1 egg
50g/2oz/¹/₂ cup plain flour
2.5ml/¹/₂ tsp baking powder
2.5ml/¹/₂ tsp ground cinnamon
pinch of salt
225g/8oz/2 cups muesli
50g/2oz/¹/₃ cup raisins
50g/2oz/¹/₂ cup walnuts, chopped*

1 Preheat the oven to 180°C/350°F/
Gas 4. Grease a baking sheet. Put
the butter or margarine in a bowl.

2 With an electric mixer, cream the
butter or margarine and sugar
until light and fluffy. Beat in the
peanut butter, then beat in the egg.

3 Sift the flour, baking powder,
cinnamon and salt over the
peanut butter mixture and stir to
blend. Stir in the muesli, raisins, and
walnuts. Taste the mixture to see if it
needs more sugar, as mueslis vary in
sweetness.

4 Drop rounded tablespoonfuls of
the batter on to the prepared
baking sheet about 2.5cm/1in apart.
Press gently with the back of a spoon
to spread each mound into a circle.

5 Bake for about 15 minutes until
lightly coloured. With a metal
spatula, transfer to a wire rack and
leave to cool.

Crunchy Oatmeal Cookies

Makes 14

INGREDIENTS

*175g/6oz/³/₄ cup butter or
margarine
125g/4¹/₂oz/³/₄ cup caster sugar
1 egg yolk
175g/6oz/1¹/₂ cups plain flour
5ml/1 tsp bicarbonate of soda
pinch of salt
40g/1¹/₂oz/¹/₂ cup rolled oats
40g/1¹/₂oz/¹/₂ cup crunchy
nugget cereal*

Variation For Nutty Oatmeal Cookies,
substitute an equal quantity of
chopped walnuts or pecans for the
cereal, and prepare as described.

1 With an electric mixer, cream the
butter or margarine and sugar
together until light and fluffy. Mix in
the egg yolk.

2 Sift over the flour, bicarbonate of
soda and salt, then stir into the
butter mixture. Add the oats and
cereal and stir to blend. Chill for at
least 20 minutes.

3 Preheat the oven to 190°C/375°F/
Gas 5. Grease a baking sheet.
Flour the bottom of a glass.

4 Roll the dough into balls. Place
them on the prepared baking
sheet and flatten with the bottom of
the glass.

5 Bake for 10–12 minutes until
golden. With a metal spatula,
transfer to a wire rack to cool
completely.

Coconut Oat Cookies

Makes 18

❦

INGREDIENTS

175g/6oz/2 cups quick-cooking oats
75g/3oz/1 cup shredded coconut
225g/8oz/1 cup butter or margarine, at room temperature
115g/4oz/½ cup granulated sugar
40g/1½oz/¼ cup firmly packed dark brown sugar
2 eggs
60ml/4 tbsp milk
7.5ml/1½ tsp vanilla essence
115g/4oz/1 cup plain flour
2.5ml/½ tsp bicarbonate of soda
pinch of salt
5ml/1 tsp ground cinnamon

❦

1 Preheat the oven to 200°C/400°F/ Gas 6. Lightly grease two baking sheets. Grease the bottom of a glass and dip in sugar.

2 Spread the oats and coconut on an ungreased baking sheet. Bake for 8–10 minutes until golden brown, stirring occasionally.

3 With an electric mixer, cream the butter or margarine and both sugars until light and fluffy. Beat in the eggs, one at a time, then add the milk and vanilla essence. Sift over the dry ingredients and fold in. Stir in the oats and coconut.

4 Drop spoonfuls of the dough 2.5–5cm/1–2in apart on the baking sheets and flatten with the glass. Bake for 8–10 minutes. Transfer to a wire rack to cool.

Crunchy Jumbles

Makes 36

❦

INGREDIENTS

115g/4oz/½ cup butter or margarine, at room temperature
225g/8oz/1 cup sugar
1 egg
5ml/1 tsp vanilla essence
175g/6oz/1¼ cups plain flour
2.5ml/½ tsp bicarbonate of soda
pinch of salt
115g/4oz/2 cups crisped rice cereal
1 cup chocolate chips

❦

Variation For even crunchier cookies, add ½ cup walnuts, coarsely chopped, with the cereal and chocolate chips.

1 Preheat the oven to 180°C/350°F/ Gas 4. Lightly grease two baking sheets.

2 With an electric mixer, cream the butter or margarine and sugar until light and fluffy. Beat in the egg and vanilla. Sift over the flour, bicarbonate of soda, and salt and fold in.

3 Add the cereal and chocolate chips. Stir to mix thoroughly.

4 Drop spoonfuls of the dough 2.5–5cm/1–2in apart on the prepared sheets. Bake for 10–12 minutes until golden. Transfer to a wire rack to cool.

Malted Oaty Crisps

These cookies are very crisp and crunchy – ideal to serve with morning coffee.

Makes 18

INGREDIENTS

175g/6oz/1¹/₂ cups rolled oats
75g/3oz/¹/₄ cup light muscovado sugar
1 egg
60ml/4 tbsp sunflower oil
30ml/2 tbsp malt extract

1 Preheat the oven to 190°C/375°F/ Gas 5. Lightly grease two baking sheets. Mix the rolled oats and brown sugar in a bowl, breaking up any lumps in the sugar. Add the egg, sunflower oil and malt extract, mix well, then leave to soak for 15 minutes.

2 Using a teaspoon, place small heaps of the mixture well apart on the prepared baking sheets. Press the heaps into 7.5cm/3in rounds with the back of a dampened fork.

3 Bake for 10–15 minutes, until golden brown. Leave to cool for 1 minute, then remove with a palette knife and cool on a wire rack.

Variation To give these crisp biscuits a coarser texture, substitute jumbo oats for some or all of the rolled oats.

Shortbread

Makes 8

❦

INGREDIENTS

175g/6oz/²⁄₃ cup unsalted butter
115g/4oz/¹⁄₂ cup caster sugar
150g/5oz/1¹⁄₄ cups plain flour
50g/2oz/¹⁄₂ cup rice flour
1.5ml/¹⁄₄ tsp baking powder
pinch of salt

❦

1 Preheat the oven to 160°C/325°F/ Gas 3. Grease a shallow 20cm/8in cake tin.

2 With an electric mixer, cream the butter and sugar together until light and fluffy. Sift over the flours, baking powder and salt and mix well.

3 Press the dough neatly into the prepared tin, smoothing the surface with the back of a spoon. Prick all over with a fork, then score into eight equal wedges.

4 Bake for 40–45 minutes. Leave in the tin until cool enough to handle, then unmould and recut the wedges while still hot.

Oatmeal Wedges

Makes 8

❦

INGREDIENTS

50g/2oz/4 tbsp butter
25ml/1¹⁄₂ tbsp treacle
50g/2oz/¹⁄₃ cup dark brown sugar
175g/6oz/1¹⁄₄ cups rolled oats
pinch of salt

❦

Variation If wished, add 5ml/1 tsp ground ginger to the melted butter.

1 Preheat the oven to 180°C/350°F/ Gas 4. Line a 20cm/8in shallow cake tin with greaseproof paper and grease the paper.

2 Place the butter, treacle and sugar in a saucepan over a low heat. Cook, stirring, until melted and combined.

3 Remove from the heat and add the oats and salt. Stir to blend.

4 Spoon into the prepared cake tin and smooth the surface. Bake for 20–25 minutes until golden brown. Leave in the tin until cool enough to handle, then unmould and cut into eight equal wedges while still hot.

Melting Moments

These cookies are very crisp and light – and they melt in your mouth.

Makes 16–20

INGREDIENTS

40g/1¹/₂oz/3 tbsp butter or margarine
65g/2¹/₂oz/5 tbsp lard
75g/3oz/¹/₂ cup caster sugar
¹/₂ egg, beaten
few drops of vanilla or almond essence
150g/5oz/1¹/₄ cups self-raising flour
rolled oats for coating
4–5 glacé cherries, quartered

1 Preheat the oven to 180°C/350°F/ Gas 4. Grease two baking sheets. Cream together the butter or margarine, lard and sugar, then gradually beat in the egg and vanilla or almond essence.

2 Stir the flour into the beaten mixture, then roll into 16–20 small balls in your hands.

3 Spread the rolled oats on a sheet of greaseproof paper and toss the balls in them to coat evenly.

4 Place the balls, spaced slightly apart, on the prepared baking sheets, place a piece of cherry on top of each and bake for 15–20 minutes, until lightly browned. Allow the cookies to cool for a few minutes before transferring to a wire rack.

Chocolate Chip Hazelnut Cookies

Chocolate chip cookies, with a delicious nutty flavour.

Makes 36

INGREDIENTS

115g/4oz/1 cup plain flour
5ml/1 tsp baking powder
pinch of salt
75g/3oz/¹⁄₃ cup butter or
margarine
115g/4oz/1¹⁄₂ cups caster sugar
50g/2oz/¹⁄₃ cup light brown sugar
1 egg
5ml/1 tsp vanilla essence
125g/4¹⁄₂oz/²⁄₃ cup chocolate chips
50g/2oz/¹⁄₂ cup hazelnuts,
chopped

1 Preheat the oven to 180°C/350°F/ Gas 4. Grease 2–3 baking sheets. Sift the flour, baking powder and salt into a small bowl. Set aside.

2 With an electric mixer, cream together the butter or margarine and the sugars. Beat in the egg and vanilla essence. Add the flour mixture and beat well with the mixer on low speed.

3 Stir in the chocolate chips and half of the hazelnuts, using a wooden spoon.

4 Drop teaspoonfuls of the mixture on to the prepared baking sheets, to form 2cm/³⁄₄in mounds. Space the cookies 2.5–5cm/1–2in apart.

5 Flatten each cookie lightly with a wet fork. Sprinkle the remaining hazelnuts on top of the cookies and press lightly into the surface.

6 Bake for 10–12 minutes until golden. Transfer the biscuits to a wire rack and leave to cool.

Chocolate Chip Oat Biscuits

Makes 60

INGREDIENTS

115g/4oz/1 cup plain flour
2.5ml/¹/₂ tsp bicarbonate of soda
1.5ml/¹/₄ tsp baking powder
pinch of salt
*115g/4oz/¹/₂ cup butter or
margarine*
115g/4oz/¹/₂ cup caster sugar
*90g/3¹/₂oz/generous ¹/₂ cup light
brown sugar*
1 egg
¹/₂ tsp vanilla essence
75g/3oz/³/₄ cup rolled oats
*175g/6oz/1 cup plain chocolate
chips*

1 Preheat the oven to 180°C/350°F/ Gas 4. Grease 3–4 baking sheets.

2 Sift the flour, bicarbonate of soda, baking powder and salt into a mixing bowl. Set aside.

3 With an electric mixer, cream together the butter or margarine and the sugars. Add the egg and vanilla essence and beat until light and fluffy.

4 Add the flour mixture and beat on a low speed until thoroughly blended. Stir in the rolled oats and chocolate chips. The dough should be crumbly. Drop heaped teaspoonfuls on to the prepared baking sheets, spacing the dough about 2.5cm/1in apart.

5 Bake for about 15 minutes until just firm around the edge but still soft to the touch in the centre. With a slotted spatula, transfer the biscuits to a wire rack and leave to cool.

Mexican Almond Cookies

Light and crisp, these biscuits are perfect with a cup of strong coffee.

Makes 24

INGREDIENTS

115g/4oz/1 cup plain flour
175g/6oz/1¹/₃ cups icing sugar
pinch of salt
50g/2oz/¹/₂ cup almonds, finely chopped
2.5ml/¹/₂ tsp vanilla essence
115g/4oz/¹/₂ cup unsalted butter icing sugar for dusting

Variation Try using other nuts such as walnuts, peanuts or pecans.

3 Roll out the dough on a lightly floured surface until it is 3mm/¹/₈in thick. Using a round cutter, stamp out into about 24 biscuits, re-rolling the trimmings as necessary.

4 Transfer the biscuits to non-stick baking sheets and bake for 30 minutes, until browned. Transfer to wire racks to cool, then dust thickly with icing sugar.

1 Preheat the oven to 180°C/350°F/ Gas 4. Sift the flour, icing sugar and salt into a bowl. Add the almonds and mix well. Stir in the vanilla essence.

2 Using your fingertips, work the butter into the mixture to make a dough. Form it into a ball.

Peanut Butter Cookies

For extra crunch add 50g/2oz/¹/₂ cup chopped peanuts with the peanut butter.

Makes 24

INGREDIENTS

115g/4oz/1 cup plain flour
2.5ml/¹/₂ tsp bicarbonate of soda
pinch of salt
115g/4oz/¹/₂ cup butter
125g/4¹/₂oz/³/₄ cup firmly packed light brown sugar
1 egg
5ml/1 tsp vanilla essence
225g/8oz/1 cup crunchy peanut butter

1 Sift together the flour, bicarbonate of soda and salt and set aside.

2 With an electric mixer, cream together the butter and sugar until light and fluffy.

3 In another bowl, mix the egg and vanilla essence, then gradually beat into the butter mixture.

4 Stir in the peanut butter and blend thoroughly. Stir in the dry ingredients. Chill for at least 30 minutes, until firm.

5 Preheat the oven to 180°C/350°F/ Gas 4. Grease two baking sheets.

6 Spoon out rounded teaspoonfuls of the dough and roll into balls.

7 Place the balls on the prepared baking sheets and press flat with a fork into circles about 6cm/2¹/₂in in diameter, making a criss-cross pattern. Bake for 12–15 minutes, until lightly coloured. Transfer to a wire rack to cool.

Tollhouse Cookies

Makes 24

INGREDIENTS

115g/4oz/¹/₂ cup butter or margarine
50g/2oz/¹/₄ cup granulated sugar
75g/3oz/¹/₂ cup dark brown sugar
1 egg
2.5ml/¹/₂ tsp vanilla essence
125g/4¹/₂oz/1¹/₈ cups flour
2.5ml/¹/₂ tsp bicarbonate of soda
pinch of salt
175g/6oz/1 cup chocolate chips
50g/2oz/¹/₂ cup walnuts, chopped

1 Preheat the oven to 180°C/350°F/ Gas 4. Grease two baking sheets.

2 With an electric mixer, cream together the butter or margarine and the two sugars until the mixture is light and fluffy.

3 In another bowl, mix the egg and vanilla essence, then gradually beat into the butter mixture. Sift over the flour, bicarbonate of soda and salt. Stir to blend.

4 Add the chocolate chips and walnuts, and mix to combine thoroughly.

5 Place heaped teaspoonfuls of the dough 5cm/2in apart on the prepared baking sheets. Bake for 10–15 minutes until lightly coloured. With a metal spatula, transfer to a wire rack to cool.

Snickerdoodles

Makes 30

INGREDIENTS

115g/4oz/½ cup butter
115g/4oz/1½ cups caster sugar
5ml/1 tsp vanilla essence
2 eggs
50ml/2fl oz/¼ cup milk
400g/14oz/3½ cups plain flour
1 tsp bicarbonate of soda
50g/2oz/½ cup walnuts or pecans,
finely chopped
For the coating
75ml/5 tbsp sugar
30ml/2 tbsp ground cinnamon

1 With an electric mixer, beat the butter until light and creamy. Add the sugar and vanilla essence and continue until fluffy. Beat in the eggs, then the milk.

2 Sift the flour and bicarbonate of soda over the butter mixture and stir to blend. Stir in the nuts. Refrigerate for 15 minutes. Preheat the oven to 190°C/375°F/Gas 5. Grease two baking sheets.

3 To make the coating, mix the sugar and cinnamon. Roll tablespoonfuls of the dough into walnut-size balls. Roll the balls in the sugar mixture. You may need to work in batches.

4 Place the balls 5cm/2in apart on the prepared baking sheets and flatten slightly. Bake for about 10 minutes until golden. Transfer to a wire rack to cool.

Chewy Chocolate Cookies

Makes 18

INGREDIENTS

4 egg whites
300g/11oz/2½ cups icing sugar
115g/4oz/1 cup cocoa powder
30ml/2 tbsp plain flour
5ml/1 tsp instant coffee powder
15ml/1 tbsp water
115g/4oz/1 cup walnuts, finely
chopped

1 Preheat the oven to 180°C/350°F/ Gas 4. Line two baking sheets with greaseproof paper and then grease the paper well.

2 With an electric mixer, beat the egg whites until frothy.

3 Sift the sugar, cocoa, flour and coffee into the whites. Add the water and continue beating on low speed to blend, then on high for a few minutes until the mixture thickens. With a rubber spatula, fold in the walnuts.

4 Place generous spoonfuls of the mixture 2.5cm/1in apart on the prepared baking sheets. Bake for 12–15 minutes until firm and cracked on top but soft on the inside. With a metal spatula, transfer to a wire rack to cool.

Variation Add 75g/3oz/½ cup chocolate chips to the dough with the chopped walnuts.

Buttermilk Cookies

Makes 15

❧

INGREDIENTS

175g/6oz/1½ cups plain flour
pinch of salt
5ml/1 tsp baking powder
2.5ml/½ tsp bicarbonate of soda
50g/2oz/4 tbsp cold butter or margarine
175ml/6fl oz/¾ cup buttermilk

❧

1 Preheat the oven to 220°C/425°F/ Gas 7. Grease a baking sheet.

2 Sift the dry ingredients into a bowl. Rub in the butter or margarine until the mixture resembles coarse crumbs.

3 Gradually pour in the buttermilk, stirring with a fork until the mixture forms a soft dough.

4 Roll out to about 1cm/½in thick. Stamp out 15 5cm/2in circles with a biscuit cutter.

5 Place on the prepared baking sheet and bake for 12–15 minutes until golden. Serve warm or at room temperature.

Baking Powder Cookies

These make a simple accompaniment to meals, or a snack with fruit preserves.

Makes 8

❧

INGREDIENTS

165g/5½oz/1⅓ cups plain flour
30ml/2 tbsp sugar
15ml/1 tbsp baking powder
pinch of salt
40g/1½oz/5 tbsp cold butter, chopped
120ml/4fl oz/½ cup milk

❧

Variation For Berry Shortcake, split the cookies in half while still warm. Butter one half, top with lightly sugared fresh berries, such as strawberries, raspberries or blueberries, and sandwich with the other half. Serve with dollops of whipped cream.

1 Preheat the oven to 220°C/425°F/ Gas 7. Grease a baking sheet. Sift the flour, sugar, baking powder and salt into a bowl.

2 Rub in the butter until the mixture resembles coarse crumbs. Pour in the milk and stir with a fork to form a soft dough.

3 Roll out the dough to about 5mm/¼in thick. Stamp out circles with a 6cm/2½in biscuit cutter.

4 Place on the prepared baking sheet and bake for about 12 minutes, until golden. Serve these soft biscuits hot or warm, spread with butter for meals. To accompany tea or coffee, serve with butter and jam or honey.

Traditional Sugar Cookies

Makes 36

INGREDIENTS

350g/12oz/3 cups plain flour
5ml/1 tsp bicarbonate of soda
10ml/2 tsp baking powder
2.5ml/¹/₂ tsp grated nutmeg
115g/4oz/¹/₂ cup butter or margarine
225g/8oz/1 cup caster sugar
2.5ml/¹/₂ tsp vanilla essence
1 egg
115g/4oz/¹/₂ cup milk
coloured or demerara sugar for sprinkling

1 Sift the flour, bicarbonate of soda, baking powder and nutmeg into a small bowl. Set aside.

2 With an electric mixer, cream together the butter or margarine, caster sugar and vanilla essence until the mixture is light and fluffy. Add the egg and beat to mix well.

3 Add the flour mixture alternately with the milk to make a soft dough. Wrap in clear film and chill for at least 30 minutes.

4 Preheat the oven to 180°C/350°F/ Gas 4. Roll out the dough on a lightly floured surface to 3mm/¹/₈in thick. Cut into rounds or other shapes with floured biscuit cutters.

5 Transfer to ungreased baking sheets. Sprinkle with sugar. Bake for 10–12 minutes until golden brown. Transfer the cookies to a wire rack to cool.

Brittany Butter Cookies

These little biscuits are similar to shortbread, but richer. Traditionally, they are made with lightly salted butter.

Makes 18–20

INGREDIENTS

6 egg yolks, lightly beaten
15ml/1 tbsp milk
250g/9 oz/2¼ cups plain flour
175g/6oz/¾ cup caster sugar
200g/7oz/scabt 1cup butter

1 Preheat the oven to 180°C/350°F/Gas 4. Butter a heavy baking sheet. Mix 15ml/1 tbsp of the egg yolks with the milk to make a glaze.

2 Sift the flour into a bowl. Add the egg yolks, sugar and butter and, work them together until creamy.

3 Gradually bring in a little flour at a time until it forms a slightly sticky dough.

4 Using floured hands, pat out the dough to about 5mm/¼in thick and cut out rounds using a 7.5cm/3in cutter. Transfer the rounds to the prepared baking sheet, brush each with a little egg glaze, then, using the back of a knife, score with lines to create a lattice pattern.

5 Bake for about 12–15 minutes, until golden. Cool in the tin on a wire rack for 15 minutes, then carefully remove the biscuits and leave to cool completely on the rack.

Cook's Tip To make a large Brittany Butter Cake, pat the dough with well-floured hands into a 23cm/9in loose-based cake tin or springform tin. Brush with egg glaze and score the lattice pattern on top. Bake for 45 minutes–1 hour, until firm to the touch and golden brown.

Toffee Cookies

Makes 36

❧

INGREDIENTS

*175g/6oz/³/₄ cup unsalted butter,
melted
200g/7oz/1³/₄ cups instant
porridge oats
115g/4oz/packed ¹/₂ cup soft light
brown sugar
120ml/4fl oz/¹/₂ cup corn syrup
30ml/2 tbsp vanilla essence
large pinch of salt
175g/6oz/³/₄ cup plain chocolate,
grated
40g/1¹/₂oz/¹/₃ cup chopped walnuts*

❧

1 Preheat the oven to 200°C/400°F/
Gas 6. Grease a 37.5 x 25cm/15 x
10in baking tin.

2 Mix together the butter, oats,
sugar, syrup, vanilla essence and
salt and press into the prepared tin.
Bake for about 15–18 minutes, until
the mixture is brown and bubbly.

3 Remove from the oven and
immediately sprinkle on the
chocolate. Set aside for 10 minutes,
then spread the chocolate over the
base. Sprinkle on the nuts. Transfer to
a wire rack to cool. Cut into squares.

Rosewater Thins

These light, crunchy biscuits are easy to make and bake in minutes.

Makes 60

❧

INGREDIENTS

*225g/8oz/1 cup slightly salted
butter
225g/8oz/1 cup caster sugar
1 egg
15ml/1 tbsp single cream
300g/11oz/2¹/₂ cups plain flour
pinch of salt
5ml/1 tsp baking powder
15ml/1 tbsp rosewater
caster sugar for sprinkling*

❧

1 Preheat the oven to 190°C/375°F/
Gas 5. Line two baking sheets
with non-stick baking paper.

2 Soften the butter and mix with
all the other ingredients until you
have a firm dough. Mould the
mixture into an even roll and wrap in
greaseproof paper. Chill until it is
firm enough to slice very thinly. This
will take 1–1¹/₂ hours.

3 Arrange the cookies on the
prepared baking sheets with
enough space for them to spread.
Sprinkle with a little caster sugar and
bake for about 10 minutes until they
are just turning brown at the edges.

Old-fashioned Ginger Cookies

Makes 60

INGREDIENTS

300g/11oz/2¹/₂ cups plain flour
5ml/1 tsp bicarbonate of soda
7.5ml/1¹/₂ tsp ground ginger
1.5ml/¹/₄ tsp ground cinnamon
1.5ml/¹/₄ tsp ground cloves
115g/4oz/¹/₂ cup butter or margarine
350g/12oz/1¹/₂ cups caster sugar
1 egg, beaten
60ml/4 tbsp black treacle
5ml/1 tsp fresh lemon juice

1 Preheat the oven to 160°C/325°F/ Gas 3. Grease 3–4 baking trays.

2 Sift the flour, bicarbonate of soda and spices into a small bowl. Set aside.

3 With an electric mixer, cream together the butter or margarine and two-thirds of the sugar.

4 Stir in the egg, treacle and lemon juice. Add the flour mixture and mix in thoroughly with a wooden spoon to make a soft dough.

5 Shape the dough into 2cm/³/₄ in balls. Roll the balls in the remaining sugar and place them about 5cm/2in apart on the prepared baking trays.

6 Bake for about 12 minutes until the biscuits are just firm to the touch. With a slotted spatula, transfer the biscuits to a wire rack and leave to cool.

Chunky Chocolate Drops

Do not allow these cookies to cool completely on the baking sheet or they will become too crisp and will break when you try to lift them.

Makes 18

INGREDIENTS

175g/6oz plain chocolate, chopped
115g/4oz/¹/₂ cup unsalted butter, chopped
2 eggs
90g/3¹/₂oz/¹/₂ cup granulated sugar
50g/2oz/¹/₃ cup light brown sugar
40g/1¹/₂oz/¹/₃ cup plain flour
25g/1oz/¹/₄ cup cocoa powder
5ml/1 tsp baking powder
10ml/2 tsp vanilla essence
pinch of salt
115g/4oz/1 cup pecans, toasted and coarsely chopped
175g/6oz/1 cup plain chocolate chips
115g/4oz fine quality white chocolate, chopped into 5mm/¹/₄in pieces
115g/4oz fine quality milk chocolate, chopped into 5mm/¹/₄in pieces

1 Preheat the oven to 160°C/325°F/ Gas 3. Grease two large baking sheets. In a medium saucepan over a low heat, melt the plain chocolate and butter, stirring until smooth. Remove from the heat and set aside to cool slightly.

2 In a large mixing bowl, using an electric mixer, beat the eggs and sugars for 2–3 minutes, until pale and creamy. Gradually pour in the melted chocolate mixture, beating until well blended. Beat in the flour, cocoa powder, baking powder, vanilla essence and salt until just blended. Stir in the nuts, chocolate chips and chocolate pieces.

3 Drop heaped tablespoons of the mixture on to the prepared baking sheets 10cm/4in apart. Flatten each to 7.5cm/3in rounds. Bake for 8–10 minutes, until the tops are shiny and cracked and the edges look crisp; do not over-bake or the cookies will become fragile.

4 Remove the baking sheets to a wire rack to cool for 2 minutes, then transfer to the rack to cool completely.

Orange Shortbread Fingers

These are a real tea-time treat. The fingers will keep in an airtight container for up to 2 weeks.

Makes 18

INGREDIENTS

*115g/4oz/¹/₂ cup unsalted butter
50g/2oz/4 tbsp caster sugar, plus
extra for sprinkling
finely grated rind of 2 oranges
175g/6oz/1¹/₂ cups plain flour*

1 Preheat the oven to 190°C/375°F/
Gas 5. Grease a large baking
sheet. Beat together the butter and
sugar until soft and creamy. Beat in
the orange rind.

2 Gradually add the flour and
gently pull the dough together to
form a soft ball. Roll out the dough
on a lightly floured surface to about
1cm/¹/₂in thick. Cut into fingers,
sprinkle over a little extra caster
sugar and put on the baking sheet.
Prick the fingers with a fork and bake
for about 20 minutes, until the
fingers are a light golden colour.

Double Chocolate Cookies

Keep these luscious treats under lock and key unless you're feeling generous.

Makes 18–20

INGREDIENTS

115g/4oz/¹/₂ cup unsalted butter
115g/4oz/²/₃ cup light muscovado
sugar
1 egg
5ml/1 tsp vanilla essence
150g/5oz/1¹/₄ cups self-raising
flour
75g/3oz/³/₄ cup porridge oats
115g/4oz plain chocolate, roughly
chopped
115g/4oz white chocolate, roughly
chopped

Cook's Tip If you're short of time when making the cookies, substitute chocolate chips for the chopped chocolate. Chopped stem ginger would make a delicious addition as well.

1 Preheat the oven to 190°C/375°F/ Gas 5. Lightly grease two baking sheets. Cream the butter with the sugar in a bowl until pale and fluffy. Add the egg and vanilla essence and beat well.

2 Sift the flour over the mixture and fold in lightly with a metal spoon, then add the oats and chopped plain and white chocolate and stir until evenly mixed.

3 Place small spoonfuls of the mixture in 18–20 rocky heaps on the prepared baking sheets, leaving space for spreading.

4 Bake for 15–20 minutes, until beginning to turn pale golden. Cool for 2–3 minutes on the baking sheets, then transfer to wire racks to cool completely.

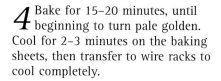

Chocolate and Nut Refrigerator Cookies

The dough must be chilled thoroughly before it can be sliced and baked.

Makes 50

❦

INGREDIENTS

*225g/8oz/2 cups plain flour
pinch of salt
50g/2oz plain chocolate, chopped
225g/8oz/1 cup unsalted butter
225g/8oz/1 cup caster sugar
2 eggs
5ml/1 tsp vanilla essence
115g/4oz/1 cup walnuts, finely
chopped*

❦

Variation For two-tone cookies, melt only 25g/1oz chocolate. Combine all the ingredients, except the chocolate, as above. Divide the dough in half. Add the chocolate to one half. Roll out the plain dough on to a flat sheet. Roll out the chocolate dough, place on top of the plain dough and roll up. Wrap, slice and bake as described.

1 In a small bowl, sift together the flour and salt. Set aside. Melt the chocolate in the top of a double boiler, or in a heatproof bowl set over a saucepan of hot water. Set aside.

2 With an electric mixer, cream the butter until soft. Add the sugar and continue beating until the mixture is light and fluffy.

3 Mix the eggs with the vanilla essence, then gradually stir into the butter mixture.

4 Stir in the chocolate, then the flour followed by the nuts.

5 Divide the dough into four parts, and roll each into 5cm/2in diameter logs. Wrap tightly in foil and chill or freeze until firm.

6 Preheat the oven to 190°C/375°F/ Gas 5. Grease two baking sheets. Cut the dough into 5mm/¼in slices. Place on the prepared sheets and bake for about 10 minutes. Transfer to wire rack to cool.

Double Gingerbread Cookies

Packed in little bags or into a gingerbread box, these pretty cookies would make a lovely gift.

They are easy to make, but will have everyone wondering how you did it!

Makes 25

INGREDIENTS

For the golden gingerbread
mixture
175g/6oz plain flour
1.5ml/¼ tsp bicarbonate of soda
pinch of salt
5ml/1 tsp ground cinnamon
65g/2½oz unsalted butter, cut
in pieces
75g/3oz caster sugar
30ml/2 tbsp maple or
golden syrup
1 egg yolk, beaten
For the chocolate gingerbread
mixture
175g/6oz/1½ cups plain flour
pinch of salt
10ml/2 tsp ground mixed spice
2.5ml/½ tsp bicarbonate of soda
25g/1oz/4 tbsp cocoa powder
75g/3oz/⅓ cup unsalted butter,
chopped
75g/3oz/⅓ cup light muscovado
sugar
1 egg, beaten

1 To make the golden gingerbread
mixture, sift together the flour,
bicarbonate of soda, salt and spices.
Rub the butter into the flour in a
large bowl, until the mixture resembles
fine breadcrumbs. Add the sugar, syrup
and egg yolk and mix to a firm dough.
Knead lightly. Wrap in clear film and
chill for 30 minutes before shaping.

2 To make the chocolate gingerbread
mixture, sift together the flour,
salt, spice, bicarbonate of soda and
cocoa powder. Knead the butter into
the flour in a large bowl. Add the
sugar and egg and mix to a firm
dough. Knead lightly. Wrap in clear
film and chill for 30 minutes.

3 Roll out half of the chocolate
dough on a floured surface to a 28
x 4cm/11 x 1½in rectangle, 1cm/
½in thick. Repeat with half of the
golden gingerbread dough. Using a
knife, cut both lengths into seven long,
thin strips. Lay the strips together, side
by side, alternating the colours.

4 Roll out the remaining golden
gingerbread dough with your
hands to a long sausage, 2cm/¾in
wide and the length of the strips. Lay
the sausage of dough down the centre
of the striped dough.

5 Carefully bring the striped dough
up around the sausage and press
it gently in position, to enclose the
sausage completely. Roll the
remaining chocolate dough to a thin
rectangle measuring approximately
28 x 13cm/11 x 5in.

6 Bring the chocolate dough up
around the striped dough, to
enclose it. Press gently into place.
Wrap and chill for 30 minutes.

7 Preheat the oven to 180°C/350°F/
Gas 4. Grease a large baking
sheet. Cut the gingerbread roll into
thin slices and place them, slightly
apart, on the prepared baking sheet.

8 Bake for about 12–15 minutes,
until just beginning to colour
around the edges. Leave on the
baking sheet for 3 minutes and
transfer to a wire rack to cool
completely.

Spicy Pepper Biscuits

Makes 48

INGREDIENTS

200g/7oz/1³/₄ cups plain flour
50g/2oz/¹/₂ cup cornflour
10ml/2 tsp baking powder
2.5ml/¹/₂ tsp ground cardamom
2.5ml/¹/₂ tsp ground cinnamon
2.5ml/¹/₂ tsp grated nutmeg
2.5ml/¹/₂ tsp ground ginger
2.5ml/¹/₂ tsp ground allspice
pinch of salt
2.5ml/¹/₂ tsp freshly ground black
pepper
225g/8oz/1 cup butter or
margarine
90g/3¹/₂oz/1¹/₃ cups light brown
sugar
2.5ml/¹/₂ tsp vanilla essence
5ml/1 tsp finely grated lemon rind
50ml/2fl oz/¹/₄ cup whipping
cream
75g/3oz/³/₄ cup finely ground
almonds
30ml/2 tbsp icing sugar

1 Preheat the oven to 180°C/350°F/ Gas 4.

2 Sift the flour, cornflour, baking powder, spices, salt and pepper into a bowl. Set aside.

3 With an electric mixer, cream the butter or margarine and brown sugar together until light and fluffy. Beat in the vanilla essence and grated lemon rind.

5 Shape the dough into 2cm/³/₄in balls. Place them on ungreased baking sheets, about 2.5cm/1in apart. Bake for 15–20 minutes until golden brown underneath.

4 With the mixer on low speed, add the flour mixture alternately with the whipping cream, beginning and ending with flour. Stir in the ground almonds.

6 Leave to cool on the baking sheets for about 1 minute before transferring to a wire rack to cool completely. Before serving, sprinkle lightly with icing sugar.

Aniseed Cookies

Makes 24

INGREDIENTS

175g/6oz/1½ cups plain flour
5ml/1 tsp baking powder
pinch of salt
115g/4oz/½ cup unsalted butter
115g/4oz/½ cup caster sugar
1 egg
5ml/1 tsp whole aniseed
15ml/1 tbsp brandy
50g/2oz/¼ cup caster sugar mixed
with 2.5ml/½ tsp ground
cinnamon for sprinkling

1 Sift together the flour, baking powder and salt. Set aside.

2 Beat the butter with the sugar until soft and fluffy. Add the egg, aniseed and brandy and beat until incorporated. Fold in the dry ingredients until just blended to a dough. Chill for 30 minutes.

3 Preheat the oven to 180°C/350°F/ Gas 4. Grease two baking sheets.

4 On a lightly floured surface, roll out the chilled dough to about 3mm/⅛in thick.

5 With a floured cutter, pastry wheel or knife, cut out the biscuits into squares, diamonds or other shapes. The traditional shape for biscochitos is a fleur-de-lis but you might find this a bit too ambitious.

6 Place on the prepared baking sheets and sprinkle lightly with the cinnamon sugar.

7 Bake for about 10 minutes, until just barely golden. Cool on the baking sheet for 5 minutes before transferring to a wire rack to cool completely. The biscuits can be kept in an airtight container for up to one week.

Festive and
Fancy Cookies

Lavender Heart Cookies

In folklore, lavender has always been linked with love, as has food, so make some heart-shaped cookies and serve them on Valentine's Day or any other romantic anniversary.

Makes 16–18

INGREDIENTS

115g/4oz/¹/₂ cup unsalted butter
50g/2oz/¹/₄ cup caster sugar
175g/6oz/1¹/₂ cups plain flour
30ml/2 tbsp fresh lavender florets
or 15ml/1 tbsp dried culinary
lavender, roughly chopped
30ml/2 tbsp superfine sugar for
sprinkling

1 Cream together the butter and sugar until fluffy. Stir in the flour and lavender and bring the mixture together in a soft ball. Cover and chill for 15 minutes.

2 Preheat the oven to 200°C/400°F/ Gas 6. Roll out the dough on a lightly floured surface and stamp out about 18 biscuits, using a 5cm/2in heart-shaped cutter. Place on a heavy baking sheet and bake for about 10 minutes, until golden.

3 Leave the biscuits standing for 5 minutes to set. Using a metal spatula, transfer carefully from the baking sheet on to a wire rack to cool completely. The biscuits can be stored in an airtight container for up to one week.

Vanilla Crescents

These attractively shaped cookies are sweet and delicate, ideal for an elegant afternoon tea.

Makes 36

❦

INGREDIENTS

175g/6oz/1¼ cups unblanched almonds
115g/4oz/1 cup plain flour
pinch of salt
225g/8oz/1 cup unsalted butter
115g/4oz/½ cup granulated sugar
5ml/1 tsp vanilla essence
icing sugar for dusting

❦

1 Grind the almonds with a few tablespoons of the flour in a food processor, blender or nut grinder.

2 Sift the remaining flour with the salt into a bowl. Set aside.

3 With an electric mixer, cream together the butter and sugar until light and fluffy.

4 Add the almonds, vanilla essence and the flour mixture. Stir to mix well. Gather the dough into a ball, wrap in greaseproof paper, and chill for at least 30 minutes.

5 Preheat the oven to 160°C/325°F/ Gas 3. Lightly grease two baking sheets.

6 Break off walnut-size pieces of dough and roll into small cylinders about 1cm/½in in diameter. Bend into small crescents and place on the prepared baking sheets.

7 Bake for about 20 minutes until dry but not brown. Transfer to a wire rack to cool only slightly. Set the rack over a baking sheet and dust with an even layer of icing sugar. Leave to cool completely.

Chocolate Fruit and Nut Cookies

These simple, chunky gingerbread biscuits make a delicious gift, especially when presented in a decorative gift box. The combination of walnuts, almonds and cherries is very effective, but you can use any other mixture of glacé fruits and nuts.

Makes 20

INGREDIENTS

50g/2oz/4 tbsp caster sugar
75ml/3fl oz/¹/₃ cup water
225g/8oz plain chocolate, chopped
40g/1¹/₂oz/³/₄ cup walnut halves
75g/3oz/¹/₃ cup glacé cherries, chopped into small wedges
115g/4oz/1 cup whole blanched almonds
For the Lebkuchen
115g/4oz/¹/₂ cup unsalted butter
115g/4oz/²/₃ cup light muscovado sugar
1 egg, beaten
115g/4oz/¹/₃ cup black treacle
400g/14oz/3¹/₂ cups self-raising flour
5ml/1 tsp ground ginger
2.5ml/¹/₂ tsp ground cloves
1.5ml/¹/₄ tsp chilli powder

Cook's Tip Carefully stack the biscuits in a pretty box or tin, lined with tissue paper, or tie in cellophane bundles.

1 To make the lebkuchen, cream together the butter and sugar until pale and fluffy. Beat in the egg and black treacle. Sift the flour, ginger, cloves and chilli powder into the bowl. Using a wooden spoon, gradually mix the ingredients together to make a stiff paste. Turn on to a lightly floured work surface and knead lightly until smooth. Wrap and chill for 30 minutes.

2 Preheat the oven to 180°C/350°F/ Gas 4. Grease two baking sheets. Shape the dough into a roll, 20cm/8in long. Chill for 30 minutes. Cut into 20 slices and space them on the baking sheets. Bake for 10 minutes. Leave on the baking sheets for 5 minutes and then transfer to a wire rack and leave to cool.

3 Put the sugar and water in a small, heavy-based saucepan. Heat gently until the sugar dissolves. Bring to the boil and boil for 1 minute, until slightly syrupy. Leave for 3 minutes, to cool slightly, and then stir in the chocolate until it has melted and made a smooth sauce.

4 Place the wire rack of biscuits over a large tray or board. Spoon a little of the chocolate mixture over the biscuits, spreading it to the edges with the back of the spoon.

5 Gently press a walnut half into the centre of each biscuit. Arrange pieces of glacé cherry and almonds alternately around the nuts. Leave to set in a cool place.

Black-and-White Ginger Florentines

These florentines can be refrigerated in an airtight container for one week.

Makes 30

INGREDIENTS

120ml/4fl oz/¹/₂ cup double cream
50g/2oz/¹/₄ cup unsalted butter
90g/3¹/₂oz/¹/₂ cup granulated sugar
30ml/2 tbsp honey
150g/5oz/1¹/₃ cups flaked almonds
40g/1¹/₂oz/¹/₃ cup plain flour
2.5ml/¹/₂ tsp ground ginger
50g/2oz/¹/₃ cup diced candied orange peel
65g/2¹/₂oz/¹/₂ cup diced stem ginger
200g/7oz plain chocolate, chopped
150g/5oz fine quality white chocolate, chopped

1 Preheat the oven to 180°C/350°F/ Gas 4. Lightly grease two large baking sheets. In a medium saucepan over a medium heat, stir the cream, butter, sugar and honey until the sugar dissolves. Bring the mixture to the boil, stirring constantly.

2 Remove from the heat and stir in the almonds, flour and ground ginger until well blended. Stir in the orange peel, stem ginger and 50g/2oz/¹/₃ cup chopped plain chocolate.

3 Drop teaspoons of the mixture on to the prepared baking sheets at least 7.5cm/3in apart. Spread each round as thinly as possible with the back of the spoon. (Dip the spoon in water to prevent sticking.)

4 Bake in batches for 8–10 minutes, until the edges are golden brown and the biscuits are bubbling. Do not under-bake or they will be sticky, but be careful not to over-bake as they burn easily. If you wish, use a 7.5cm/3in biscuit cutter to neaten the edges of the florentines while on the baking sheet.

5 Remove the baking sheet to the wire rack to cool for 10 minutes until firm. Using a metal palette knife, carefully transfer the florentines to a wire rack to cool completely.

6 In a small saucepan over a very low heat, melt the remaining chocolate, stirring frequently, until smooth. Cool slightly. In the top of a double boiler over a low heat, melt the white chocolate until smooth, stirring frequently. Remove the top of double boiler from the bottom and cool for about 5 minutes, stirring occasionally until slightly thickened.

7 Using a small metal palette knife, spread half the florentines with the plain chocolate on the flat side of each biscuit, swirling to create a decorative surface, and place on a wire rack, chocolate side up. Spread the remaining florentines with the melted white chocolate and place on the rack, chocolate side up. Chill for 10–15 minutes to set completely.

Jewelled Christmas Trees

These cookies make an appealing gift. They look wonderful hung on a Christmas tree or in front of a window to catch the light.

Makes 12

INGREDIENTS

175g/6oz/1¹/₂ cups plain flour
75g/3oz/¹/₃ cup butter, chopped
40g/1¹/₂oz/3 tbsp caster sugar
1 egg white
30ml/2 tbsp orange juice
225g/8oz coloured fruit sweets
coloured ribbons, to decorate

1 Preheat the oven to 180°C/350°F/ Gas 4. Line two baking sheets with non-stick baking paper. Sift the flour into a mixing bowl.

2 Rub the butter into the flour until the mixture resembles fine breadcrumbs. Stir in the sugar, egg white and enough orange juice to form a soft dough. Knead on a lightly floured surface until smooth.

3 Roll out thinly and stamp out as many shapes as possible using a floured Christmas tree cutter. Transfer the shapes to the prepared baking sheets, spacing them well apart. Knead the trimmings together.

4 Using a 1cm/¹/₂in round cutter or the end of a large plain piping nozzle, stamp out and remove six rounds from each tree shape. Cut each sweet into three and place a piece in each hole. Make a small hole at the top of each tree to thread through the ribbon.

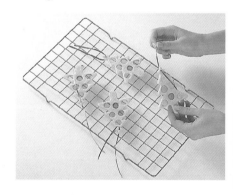

5 Bake for 15–20 minutes, until the biscuits are slightly gold in colour and the sweets have melted and filled the holes. Cool on the baking sheets. Repeat until you have used up the remaining cookie dough and sweets. Thread short lengths of ribbon through the holes so that the biscuits can be hung up.

Christmas Cookies

Makes 30

INGREDIENTS

175g/6oz/³/₄ cup unsalted butter
300g/11oz/1¹/₄ cups caster sugar
1 egg
1 egg yolk
5ml/1 tsp vanilla essence
grated rind of 1 lemon
pinch of salt
300g/11oz/2¹/₂ cups plain flour
For the decoration (optional)
coloured icing and small sweets
such as silver balls, coloured
sugar crystals

1 With an electric mixer, cream the butter until soft. Add the sugar gradually and continue beating until light and fluffy.

2 Using a wooden spoon, slowly mix in the whole egg and the egg yolk. Add the vanilla essence, lemon rind and salt. Stir to mix well.

3 Sift the flour over the mixture and stir to blend. Gather the dough into a ball, wrap, and chill for 30 minutes.

4 Preheat the oven to 190°C/375°F/ Gas 5. On a floured surface, roll out until about 3mm/¹/₈in thick.

5 Stamp out shapes or rounds with floured cookie cutters.

6 Bake for about 8 minutes until lightly coloured. Transfer to a wire rack and leave to cool completely before decorating, if wished, with icing and sweets.

Glazed Ginger Cookies

These also make good hanging biscuits for decorating trees and garlands. For this, make a hole in each biscuit with a skewer, and thread with fine ribbon.

Makes about 20

INGREDIENTS

1 quantity Golden Gingerbread mixture
2 quantities Icing Glaze
red and green food colourings
175g/6oz white almond paste

1 Preheat the oven to 180°C/350°F/ Gas 4. Grease a large baking sheet. Roll out the gingerbread dough on a floured surface and, using a selection of floured cookie cutters, cut out a variety of shapes, such as trees, stars, crescents and bells. Transfer to the prepared baking sheet and bake for 8–10 minutes, until just beginning to colour around the edges. Leave the cookies on the baking sheet for 3 minutes.

2 Transfer the cookies to a wire rack and leave to cool. Place the wire rack over a large tray or plate. Using a dessertspoon, spoon the icing glaze over the cookies until they are completely covered. Leave in a cool place to dry for several hours.

3 Knead red food colouring into half of the almond paste and green into the other half. Roll a thin length of each coloured paste and then twist the two together into a rope.

4 Secure a rope of paste around a biscuit, dampening the icing with a little water, if necessary, to hold it in place. Repeat on about half of the cookies. Dilute a little of each food colouring with water. Using a fine paintbrush, paint festive decorations over the plain cookies. Leave to dry and then wrap in tissue paper.

Easter Cookies

These are enjoyed as a traditional part of the Christian festival of Easter.

Makes 16–18

❧

INGREDIENTS

115g/4oz/¹/₂ cup butter, chopped
75g/3oz/¹/₃ cup caster sugar, plus
extra for sprinkling
1 egg, separated
200g/7oz/1³/₄ cups plain four
2.5ml/¹/₂ tsp ground mixed spice
2.5ml/¹/₂ tsp ground cinnamon
50g/2oz/scant ¹/₃ cup currants
15ml/1 tbsp chopped mixed peel
15–30ml/1–2 tbsp milk

❧

3 Turn the dough on to a floured surface, knead lightly until just smooth, then roll out using a floured rolling pin, to about 5mm/¹/₄in thick. Cut the dough into rounds using a 5cm/2in fluted biscuit cutter. Transfer the rounds to the prepared baking sheets and bake for 10 minutes.

1 Preheat the oven to 200°C/400°F/ Gas 6. Lightly grease two baking sheets. Beat together the butter and sugar, then beat in the egg yolk.

2 Sift the flour and spices over the egg mixture, then fold in with the currants and peel, adding sufficient milk to mix to a fairly soft dough.

4 Beat the egg white, then brush over the biscuits. Sprinkle with caster sugar and return to the oven for a further 10 minutes, until golden. Transfer to a wire rack to cool.

Sultana Cornmeal Cookies

These little yellow biscuits come from the Veneto region of Italy.

Makes 48

INGREDIENTS

*75g/3oz/¹⁄₂ cup sultanas
115g/4oz/1 cup finely ground
yellow cornmeal
175g/6oz/1¹⁄₂ cups plain flour
7.5ml/1¹⁄₂ tsp baking powder
pinch of salt
225g/8oz/1 cup butter
225g/8oz/1 cup granulated sugar
2 eggs
15ml/1 tbsp marsala or 5ml/1 tsp
vanilla essence*

1 Soak the sultanas in a small bowl of warm water for 15 minutes. Drain. Preheat the oven to 180°C/ 350°F/Gas 4. Grease a baking sheet.

2 Sift the cornmeal, flour, baking powder and salt together into a mixing bowl. Set aside.

3 Cream the butter and sugar until light and fluffy. Beat in the eggs, one at a time. Beat in the marsala or vanilla essence.

4 Add the dry ingredients to the butter mixture, beating until well blended. Stir in the sultanas.

5 Drop heaped teaspoons of the mixture on to the prepared baking sheet in rows about 5cm/2in apart. Bake for 7–8 minutes, until the cookies are golden brown at the edges. Transfer to a wire rack to cool.

Amaretti

If bitter almonds are not available, make up the weight with sweet almonds.

Makes 36

INGREDIENTS

*150g/5oz/1¹⁄₄ cups sweet almonds
50g/2oz/¹⁄₂ cup bitter almonds
225g/8oz/1 cup caster sugar
2 egg whites
2.5ml/¹⁄₂ tsp almond essence or
5ml/1 tsp vanilla essence
icing sugar for dusting*

1 Preheat the oven to 160°C/325°F/ Gas 3. Peel the almonds by dropping them into a saucepan of boiling water for 1–2 minutes. Drain. Rub the almonds in a cloth to remove the skins.

2 Place the almonds on a baking tray and let them dry out in the oven for 10–15 minutes without browning. Remove from the oven and allow to cool. Turn the oven off. Dust with flour.

3 Grind the almonds with half of the sugar in a food processor. Use an electric beater or wire whisk to beat the egg whites until they form soft peaks.

4 Sprinkle over half the remaining sugar and continue beating until stiff peaks are formed. Gently fold in the remaining sugar, the almond or vanilla essence and the almonds.

5 Spoon the almond mixture into a piping bag fitted with a smooth nozzle. Pipe out the mixture in rounds the size of a walnut. Sprinkle lightly with the icing sugar, and leave to stand for 2 hours. Near the end of this time, turn the oven on again and preheat to 180°C/350°F/Gas 4.

6 Bake for 15 minutes, until pale gold. Remove from the oven and cool on a wire rack.

Decorated Chocolate Lebkuchen

Wrapped in paper or cellophane, or beautifully boxed, these decorated cookies make a lovely present. Don't make them too far in advance as the chocolate will gradually discolour.

Makes 40

❦

INGREDIENTS

*1 quantity Lebkuchen mixture
115g/4oz plain chocolate,
chopped
115g/4oz milk chocolate, chopped
115g/4oz white chocolate,
chopped
chocolate vermicelli, for
sprinkling
cocoa powder or icing sugar for
dusting*

❦

1 Grease two baking sheets. Roll out just over half of the Lebkuchen mixture until 5mm/¼in thick. Cut out heart shapes, using a 4.5cm/1¼in heart-shaped cutter. Transfer to baking sheet. Gather the trimmings together with the remaining dough and cut into 20 pieces. Roll into balls and place on the baking sheet. Flatten each ball slightly with your fingers.

2 Chill both sheets for 30 minutes. Preheat the oven to 180°C/350°F/Gas 4. Bake for 8–10 minutes. Cool on a wire rack.

3 Melt the plain chocolate in a heatproof bowl over a small saucepan of hot water. Melt the milk and white chocolate in separate bowls.

4 Make three small paper piping bags out of greaseproof paper. Spoon a little of each chocolate into the three paper piping bags and reserve. Spoon a little plain chocolate over one third of the biscuits, spreading it slightly to cover them completely. (Tapping the rack gently will help the chocolate to run down the sides.)

5 Snip the merest tip from the bag of white chocolate and drizzle it over some of the coated biscuits, to give a decorative finish.

6 Sprinkle the chocolate vermicelli over the plain chocolate-coated biscuits that haven't been decorated. Coat the remaining biscuits with the milk and white chocolate and decorate some of these with more chocolate from the piping bags, contrasting the colours. Scatter more undecorated biscuits with vermicelli. Leave the biscuits to set.

7 Transfer the undecorated biscuits to a plate or tray and dust lightly with cocoa powder or icing sugar.

Cook's Tip If the chocolate in the bowls starts to set before you have finished decorating, put the bowls back over the heat for 1–2 minutes. If the chocolate in the piping bags starts to harden, microwave briefly or put in a clean bowl over a pan of simmering water until soft.

Macaroons

Freshly ground almonds, lightly toasted beforehand to intensify the flavour,

give these biscuits their rich taste and texture so, for best results,

avoid using ready-ground almonds as a shortcut.

Makes 12

INGREDIENTS

*115g/4oz/1½ cup blanched
almonds, toasted
165g/5½oz/¾ cup caster sugar
2 egg whites
2.5ml/½ tsp almond or vanilla
essence
icing sugar for dusting*

1 Preheat the oven to 180°C/350°F/ Gas 4. Line a large baking sheet with non-stick baking paper. Reserve 12 almonds for decorating. In a food processor grind the rest of the almonds with the sugar.

2 With the machine running, slowly pour in enough of the egg whites to form a soft dough. Add the almond or vanilla essence and pulse to mix.

3 With moistened hands, shape the mixture into walnut-size balls and arrange on the baking sheet.

4 Press one of the reserved almonds on to each ball, flattening them slightly, and dust lightly with icing sugar. Bake for about 10–12 minutes, until the tops are golden and feel slightly firm. Transfer to a wire rack, cool slightly, then peel the biscuits off the paper and leave to cool completely.

Cook's Tip To toast the almonds, spread them on a baking sheet and bake in the preheated oven for 10–15 minutes, until golden. Leave to cool before grinding.

Madeleines

These little tea cakes, baked in a special tin with shell-shaped cups,

were made famous by Marcel Proust, who referred to them in his novel.

They are best eaten on the day they are made.

Makes 12

INGREDIENTS

*165g/5½oz/1¼ cups plain flour
5ml/1 tsp baking powder
2 eggs
75g/3oz/¾ cup icing sugar, plus
extra for dusting
grated rind of 1 lemon or orange
15ml/1 tbsp lemon or orange juice
75g/3oz/6 tbsp unsalted butter,
melted and slightly cooled*

1 Preheat the oven to 190°C/375°F/ Gas 5. Generously butter a 12-cup madeleine tin. Sift together the flour and baking powder.

2 Using an electric mixer, beat the eggs and icing sugar for 5–7 minutes until thick and creamy and the mixture forms a ribbon when the beaters are lifted. Gently fold in the lemon or orange rind and juice.

3 Beginning with the flour mixture, alternately fold in the flour and melted butter in four batches. Leave the mixture to stand for 10 minutes, then carefully spoon into the tin. Tap gently to release any air bubbles.

4 Bake for 12–15 minutes, rotating the tin halfway through cooking, until a skewer or cake tester inserted in the centre comes out clean. Tip on to a wire rack to cool completely and dust with icing sugar before serving.

Cook's Tip If you don't have a special tin for making madeleines, you can use a bun tin, preferably with a non-stick coating. The cakes won't have the characteristic ridges and shell shape, but they are quite pretty dusted with a little icing sugar.

Tuiles d'Amandes

These biscuits are named after the French roof tiles they so resemble. Making them is a little fiddly, so bake only four at a time until you get the knack. With a little practice you will find them easy.

Makes 24

INGREDIENTS

65g/2¹/₂oz/generous ¹/₂ cup whole blanched almonds, lightly toasted
65g/2¹/₂oz/¹/₃ cup caster sugar
40g/1¹/₂oz/3 tbsp unsalted butter
2 egg whites
2.5ml/¹/₂ tsp almond essence
30g/1¹/₄oz/scant ¹/₄ cup plain flour, sifted
50g/2oz/¹/₂ cup flaked almonds

Cook's Tip If the biscuits flatten or lose their crispness, reheat them on a baking sheet in a moderate oven, until completely flat, then reshape.

1 Preheat the oven to 200°C/400°F/ Gas 6. Generously butter two heavy baking sheets.

2 Place the almonds and about 30ml/2 tbsp of the sugar in a food processor fitted with the metal blade and process until finely ground.

3 Beat the butter until creamy, then add the remaining sugar and beat until light and fluffy. Gradually beat in the egg whites, then add the almond essence. Sift the flour over the butter mixture, fold in, then fold in the ground almond mixture.

4 Drop tablespoonfuls of the mixture on to the prepared baking sheets about 15cm/6in apart. With the back of a wet spoon, spread each mound into a paper-thin 7.5cm/3in round. (Don't worry if holes appear, they will fill in.) Sprinkle with flaked almonds.

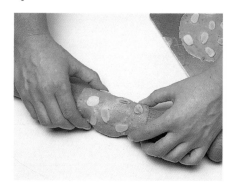

5 Bake the cookies, one sheet at a time, for 5–6 minutes, until the edges are golden and the centres still pale. Working quickly, use a thin palette knife to loosen the edges of one cookie. Lift the cookie on the palette knife and place over a rolling pin, then press down the sides of the biscuit to curve it.

6 Continue shaping the cookies, transferring them to a wire rack as they cool. If they become too crisp to shape, return the baking sheet to the hot oven for 15–30 seconds, then continue as above.

Flaked Almond Biscuits

Makes 30

❧

INGREDIENTS

175g/6oz/³/₄ cup butter or margarine, chopped
225g/8oz/2 cups self-raising flour
150g/5oz/²/₃ cup caster sugar
2.5ml/¹/₂ tsp ground cinnamon
1 egg, separated
30ml/2 tbsp cold water
50g/2oz/¹/₂ cup flaked almonds

❧

1 Preheat the oven to 180°C/350°F/ Gas 4. Rub the butter or margarine into the flour. Reserve 15ml/1 tbsp of the sugar and mix the rest with the cinnamon. Stir into the flour and then add the egg yolk and cold water and mix to a firm dough.

2 Roll out the dough on a lightly floured board to 1cm/¹/₂in thick. Sprinkle over the almonds. Continue rolling until the dough is approximately 5mm/¹/₄in thick.

3 Using a floured fluted round cutter, cut the dough into rounds. Use a palette knife to lift them on to an ungreased baking sheet. Re-form the dough and cut more rounds to use all the dough. Whisk the egg white lightly, brush it over the cookies, and sprinkle over the remaining sugar.

4 Bake for about 10–15 minutes, until golden. To remove, slide a palette knife under the cookies, which will still seem a bit soft, but they harden as they cool. Leave on a wire rack until quite cold.

Mocha Viennese Swirls

Makes 20

INGREDIENTS

*250g/9oz plain chocolate,
chopped
200g/7oz/scant 1 cup unsalted
butter
50g/2oz/¹/₂ cup icing sugar
30ml/2 tbsp strong black coffee
200g/7oz/1³/₄ cups plain flour
50g/2oz/¹/₂ cup cornflour
about 20 blanched almonds*

Cook's Tip If the mixture is too stiff to pipe, soften it with a little more black coffee.

1 Preheat the oven to 190°C/375°F/ Gas 5. Lightly grease two large baking sheets. Melt 115g/4oz of the chocolate in a heatproof bowl over a saucepan of hot water. Cream the butter with the icing sugar in a bowl until smooth and pale. Beat in the melted chocolate, then the strong black coffee.

2 Sift the flour and cornflour over the mixture. Fold in lightly and evenly to make a soft mixture.

3 Spoon the mixture into a piping bag fitted with a large star nozzle and pipe 20 swirls on the prepared baking sheets, allowing room for spreading during baking.

4 Press an almond into the centre of each swirl. Bake for about 15 minutes, until the biscuits are firm and just beginning to brown. Leave to cool for about 10 minutes on the baking sheets, then lift carefully on to a wire rack to cool completely.

5 Melt the remaining chocolate and dip the base of each swirl to coat. Place on a sheet of non-stick baking paper and leave to set.

Chocolate Amaretti

Makes 24

INGREDIENTS

*150g/5oz/1¼ cups blanched whole
almonds
90g/3½oz/scant ½ cup caster
sugar
15ml/1 tbsp cocoa powder
30ml/2 tbsp icing sugar
2 egg whites
pinch of cream of tartar
5ml/1 tsp almond essence
flaked almonds, to decorate*

1 Preheat the oven to 180°C/350°F/
Gas 4. Place the almonds on a
baking sheet and bake for 10–
12 minutes until golden brown. Leave
to cool. Reduce the oven temperature
to 160°C/325°F/Gas 3. Line a large
baking sheet with non-stick baking
paper. In a food processor, process the
almonds with half the sugar until
they are finely ground but not oily.
Transfer to a bowl and sift in the
cocoa and icing sugar. Set aside.

2 In a mixing bowl with an electric
mixer, beat the egg whites and
cream of tartar until stiff peaks form.
Sprinkle in the remaining sugar a
tablespoon at a time, beating well
after each addition, and continue
beating until the whites are glossy
and stiff. Beat in the almond essence.

3 Sprinkle over the almond-sugar
mixture and gently fold into the
beaten egg whites until just blended.
Spoon the mixture into a large piping
bag fitted with a plain 1cm/½in
nozzle. Pipe 4cm/1½in rounds about
2.5cm/1in apart on the prepared
baking sheet. Press a flaked almond
into the centre of each.

4 Bake the cookies for 12–15
minutes, or until crisp. Remove
the baking sheets to a wire rack to
cool for 10 minutes. With a metal
palette knife, remove the amarettis to
a wire rack to cool completely.

Nut Lace Cookies

Makes 18

INGREDIENTS

50g/2oz/¹/₂ cup blanched almonds
50g/2oz/4 tbsp butter
45ml/3 tbsp plain flour
115g/4oz/¹/₂ cup granulated sugar
30ml/2 tbsp double cream
2.5ml/¹/₂ tsp vanilla essence

Variation Add 40g/1¹/₂oz/¹/₄ cup finely chopped candied orange peel to the mixture.

1 Preheat the oven to 190°C/375°F/ Gas 5. Grease 1–2 baking sheets.

2 With a sharp knife, chop the almonds as finely as possible. Alternatively, use a food processor, blender or nut grinder to chop the nuts very finely.

3 Melt the butter in a small saucepan over a low heat. Remove from the heat and stir in the remaining ingredients, including the almonds.

4 Drop teaspoonfuls of the mixture 6cm/2¹/₂in apart on the prepared baking sheets. Bake for about 5 minutes until golden. Cool on the sheets briefly, until the cookies are just stiff enough to lift off.

5 With a metal spatula, transfer the cookies to a wire rack to cool completely.

Oatmeal Lace Cookies

Makes 36

INGREDIENTS

165g/5¹/₂oz/²/₃ cup butter or margarine
175g/6oz/1¹/₂ cups rolled oats
175g/6oz/³/₄ cup firmly packed dark brown sugar
175g/6oz/³/₄ cup granulated sugar
45ml/3 tbsp plain flour
pinch of salt
1 egg, lightly beaten
5ml/1 tsp vanilla essence
50g/2oz/¹/₂ cup pecans or walnuts, finely chopped

1 Preheat the oven to 180°C/350°F/ Gas 4. Grease two baking sheets.

2 Melt the butter or margarine in a small saucepan over a low heat. Set aside.

3 In a mixing bowl, combine the oats, brown sugar, granulated sugar, flour and salt.

4 Add the butter or margarine, the egg and vanilla essence.

5 Mix until blended, then stir in the chopped nuts.

6 Drop rounded teaspoonfuls of the batter about 5cm/2in apart on the prepared baking sheets. Bake for 5–8 minutes until lightly browned on the edges and bubbling. Leave to cool for 2 minutes, then transfer to a wire rack to cool completely.

Raspberry Sandwich Cookies

Children will love these sweet, sticky treats.

Makes 32

INGREDIENTS

115g/4oz/1 cup blanched almonds
175g/6oz/1½ cups plain flour
175g/6oz/¾ cup butter
115g/4oz/½ cup caster sugar
grated rind of 1 lemon
5ml/1 tsp vanilla essence
1 egg white
pinch of salt
40g/1½oz/⅓ cup slivered
almonds, chopped
350g/12oz/1 cup raspberry jam
15ml/1 tbsp lemon juice

1 Finely grind the almonds and 45ml/3 tbsp of the flour.

2 Cream together the butter and sugar until light and fluffy. Stir in the lemon rind and vanilla essence. Add the ground almonds and remaining flour and mix well to form a dough. Gather into a ball, wrap in greaseproof paper, and chill for 1 hour. Preheat the oven to 160°C/325°F/Gas 3. Line two baking sheets with greaseproof paper.

3 Divide the dough into four. Roll each piece out on a lightly floured surface to a thickness of 3mm/⅛in. With a floured 6cm/2½in pastry cutter, stamp out circles, then stamp out the centres from half the circles.

4 When all the dough has been used, check you have equal numbers of rings and circles, then place the dough rings and circles 1cm/½in apart on the prepared baking sheets.

5 Whisk the egg white with the salt until just frothy. Brush only the cookie rings with the egg white, then sprinkle over the chopped almonds. Bake for 12–15 minutes until very lightly browned. Leave to cool for a few minutes on the sheets before transferring to a wire rack.

6 In a saucepan, melt the jam with the lemon juice until it comes to a simmer. Brush the jam over the cookie circles and sandwich together with the rings. Store in an airtight container with sheets of greaseproof paper between the layers.

Chocolate Marzipan Cookies

These crisp little cookies satisfy a sweet tooth and have a little almond surprise inside.

Makes 36

INGREDIENTS

200g/7oz/scant 1 cup unsalted butter
200g/7oz/generous 1 cup light muscovado sugar
1 egg
300g/11oz/2½ cups plain flour
60ml/4 tbsp cocoa powder
200g/7oz white almond paste
115g/4oz white chocolate, chopped

1 Preheat the oven to 190°C/375°F/ Gas 5. Lightly grease two large baking sheets. Cream the butter with the sugar in a bowl until pale and fluffy. Add the egg and beat well.

2 Sift the flour and cocoa over the mixture. Stir in, first with a wooden spoon, then with clean hands, pressing the mixture together to make a fairly soft dough.

3 Roll out about half the dough on a lightly floured surface to a thickness of about 5mm/¼in. Using a 5cm/2in biscuit cutter, cut out rounds, re-rolling the dough as required until you have about 36 rounds.

4 Cut the almond paste into about 36 equal pieces. Roll into balls, flatten slightly and place one on each round of dough. Roll out the remaining dough, cut out more rounds, then place on top of the almond paste. Press the dough edges to seal. Bake for 10–12 minutes until the cookies have risen well. Cool completely. Melt the white chocolate, spoon into a paper piping bag and pipe on to the biscuits.

Cook's Tip If the dough is too sticky to roll, chill it for about 30 minutes, then try again.

Lady Fingers

Named after the pale, slim fingers of highborn gentlewomen.

Makes 18

INGREDIENTS

*90g/3¹/₂oz/²/₃ cup plain flour
pinch of salt
4 eggs, separated
115g/4oz/¹/₂ cup granulated sugar
2.5ml/¹/₂ tsp vanilla essence
icing sugar for sprinkling*

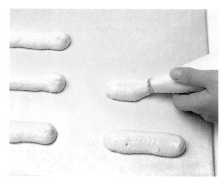

1 Preheat the oven to 150°C/300°F/ Gas 2. Grease two baking sheets, then coat lightly with flour, and shake off the excess.

2 Sift the flour and salt together twice.

3 With an electric mixer, beat the egg yolks with half of the sugar until thick enough to leave a ribbon trail when the beaters are lifted.

4 In another bowl, beat the egg whites until stiff. Beat in the remaining sugar until glossy.

5 Sift the flour over the yolks and spoon a large dollop of egg whites over the flour. Carefully fold in with a large metal spoon, adding the vanilla essence. Gently fold in the remaining whites.

6 Spoon the mixture into a piping bag fitted with a large plain nozzle. Pipe 10cm/4in long lines on the prepared baking sheets about 2.5cm/1in apart. Sift over a layer of icing sugar. Turn the sheet upside down to dislodge any excess sugar.

7 Bake for about 20 minutes until crusty on the outside but soft in the centre. Cool slightly on the baking sheets before transferring to a wire rack.

Walnut Cookies

Makes 60

INGREDIENTS

*115g/4oz/¹/₂ cup butter or margarine
175g/6oz/³/₄ cup caster sugar
115g/4oz/1 cup plain flour
10ml/2 tsp vanilla essence
115g/4oz/1 cup walnuts, finely chopped*

1 Preheat the oven to 150°C/300°F/ Gas 2. Grease two baking sheets.

2 With an electric mixer, cream the butter or margarine until soft. Add 50g/2oz/¹/₄ cup of the sugar and continue beating until light and fluffy. Stir in the flour, vanilla essence and walnuts. Drop teaspoonfuls of the batter 2.5–5cm/1–2in apart on the prepared baking sheets and flatten slightly. Bake for about 25 minutes.

3 Transfer to a wire rack set over a baking sheet and sprinkle with the remaining sugar.

Variation To make Almond Cookies, use an equal amount of finely chopped unblanched almonds instead of walnuts. Replace half the vanilla with 2.5ml/¹/₂ tsp almond essence.

Cookies
for Kids

Lemony Peanut Pairs

For those who don't like peanut butter, use buttercream or chocolate-and-nut spread instead.

Makes 8–10

❧

INGREDIENTS

40g/1½oz/¼ cup soft light brown sugar
50g/2oz/¼ cup soft margarine
5ml/1 tsp grated lemon rind
75g/3oz/¾ cup wholemeal flour
50g/2oz/¼ cup chopped crystallised pineapple
25g/1oz/2 tbsp smooth peanut butter
sifted icing sugar for dusting

❧

1 Preheat the oven to 190°C/375°F/ Gas 3. Grease a baking sheet. Cream the sugar, margarine and lemon rind together. Work in the flour and knead until smooth.

2 Roll out thinly and cut into rounds, then place on the baking sheet. Press on pieces of pineapple and bake for 15–20 minutes. Cool. Sandwich together with peanut butter, dust with icing sugar.

Ginger Cookies

If your children enjoy cooking with you, mixing and rolling the dough, or cutting out different shapes, this is the ideal recipe to let them practise on.

Makes 16

❧

INGREDIENTS

115g/4oz/⅔ cup soft brown sugar
115g/4oz/½ cup soft margarine
pinch of salt
few drops of vanilla essence
175g/6oz/1¼ cups wholemeal plain flour
15g/½oz/1 tbsp cocoa, sifted
10ml/2 tsp ground ginger
a little milk
glacé icing and glacé cherries, to decorate

❧

1 Preheat the oven to 190°C/375°F/ Gas 5. Grease a baking sheet. Cream together the sugar, margarine, salt and vanilla essence until very soft and light.

2 Work in the flour, cocoa and ginger, adding a little milk, if necessary, to bind the mixture. Knead lightly on a floured surface until smooth.

3 Roll out the dough to about 5mm/¼in thick. Stamp out shapes using floured biscuit cutters and place on the prepared baking sheet.

4 Bake the cookies for 10– 15 minutes. Leave to cool on the baking sheets until firm, then transfer to a wire rack to cool completely. Decorate with glacé icing and glacé cherries.

Fruit and Nut Clusters

This is a fun no-cook recipe which children will like.

Makes 24

❦

INGREDIENTS

225g/8oz white chocolate
50g/2oz/¹/₃ cup sunflower seeds
50g/2oz/¹/₂ cup almond slivers
50g/2oz/¹/₃ cup sesame seeds
50g/2oz/¹/₃ cup seedless raisins
5ml/1 tsp ground cinnamon

❦

1 Break the white chocolate into small pieces. Put the chocolate into a heatproof bowl over a saucepan of hot water on a low heat. Do not allow the water to touch the base of the bowl, or the chocolate may become too hot.

2 Alternatively, put the chocolate in a microwave-proof container and heat it on Medium for 3 minutes. Stir the melted chocolate until it is smooth and glossy.

3 Mix the remaining ingredients together, pour on the chocolate and stir well.

4 Using a teaspoon, spoon the mixture into paper cases and leave to set.

Marshmallow Crispie Cakes

Makes 45

❦

INGREDIENTS

250g/9oz bag of toffees
50g/2oz/4 tbsp butter
45ml/3 tbsp milk
115g/4oz/1 cup marshmallows
175g/6oz/6 cups Rice Crispies

❦

1 Lightly brush a 20 x 33cm/8 x 13in roasting tin with a little oil. Put the toffees, butter and milk in a saucepan and heat gently, stirring until the toffees have melted.

2 Add the marshmallows and cereal and stir until well mixed and the marshmallows have melted.

3 Spoon the mixture into the prepared roasting tin, level the surface and leave to set.

4 When cool and hard, cut into squares, remove from the tin, and put into paper cases to serve.

Gingerbread Jungle

Snappy biscuits in animal shapes, which can be decorated in your own style.

Makes 14

INGREDIENTS

175g/6oz/1½ cups self-raising flour
2.5ml/½ tsp bicarbonate of soda
2.5ml/½ tsp ground cinnamon
10ml/2 tsp caster sugar
50g/2oz/¼ cup butter
45ml/3 tbsp golden syrup
50g/2oz/½ cup icing sugar
5–10ml/1–2 tsp water

Cook's Tip Any cutters can be used with the same mixture. Obviously, the smaller the cutters, the more biscuits you will make.

1 Preheat the oven to 190°C/375°F/ Gas 5. Lightly oil two baking sheets.

2 Put the flour, bicarbonate of soda, cinnamon and caster sugar in a bowl and mix together. Melt the butter and syrup in a saucepan. Pour over the dry ingredients.

3 Mix together well and then use your hands to pull the mixture together to make a dough.

4 Turn on to a lightly floured surface and roll out to about 5mm/¼in thick.

5 Use floured animal cutters to cut shapes from the dough and arrange on the prepared baking sheets, leaving enough room between them to rise.

6 Press the trimmings back into a ball, roll it out and cut more shapes. Continue until all the dough is used. Bake for 8–12 minutes, until lightly browned.

7 Leave to cool slightly, before transferring to a wire rack with a palette knife. Sift the icing sugar into a small bowl and add enough water to make a fairly soft icing.

8 Spoon the icing into a piping bag fitted with a small, plain nozzle and pipe decorations on the cookies.

Chocolate Crackle-tops

Older children will enjoy making these distinctive cookies.

Makes 38

❧

INGREDIENTS

200g/7oz plain chocolate, chopped
90g/3¹/₂oz/scant ¹/₂ cup unsalted butter
115g/4oz/¹/₂ cup caster sugar
3 eggs
5ml/1 tsp vanilla essence
215g/7¹/₂oz/scant 2 cups plain flour
25g/1oz/¹/₄ cup unsweetened cocoa
2.5ml/¹/₂ tsp baking powder
pinch of salt
175g/6oz/1¹/₂ cups icing sugar for coating

❧

1 In a medium saucepan over a low heat, melt the chocolate and butter together until smooth, stirring frequently.

2 Remove from the heat. Stir in the sugar, and continue stirring for 2–3 minutes, until the sugar dissolves. Add the eggs one at a time, beating well after each addition; stir in the vanilla.

3 Into a bowl, sift together the flour, cocoa, baking powder and salt. Gradually stir into the chocolate mixture in batches, until just blended.

4 Cover the dough and refrigerate for at least 1 hour, until the dough is cold and holds its shape.

5 Preheat the oven to 160°C/325°F/ Gas 3. Grease two or more large baking sheets. Place the icing sugar in a small, deep bowl. Using a small ice-cream scoop or round teaspoon, scoop cold dough into small balls and, between the palms of your hands, roll into 4cm/1¹/₂in balls.

6 Drop each ball into the icing sugar and roll until heavily coated. Remove with a slotted spoon and tap against the side of the bowl to remove excess sugar. Place on the prepared baking sheets 4cm/1¹/₂in apart.

7 Bake the cookies for 10– 15 minutes, until the tops feel slightly firm when touched. Remove the baking sheet to a wire rack for 2–3 minutes. With a metal palette knife, remove the cookies to a wire rack to cool completely.

Chocolate Dominoes

A recipe for children to eat rather than make. Ideal for birthday parties.

Makes 16

INGREDIENTS

175g/6oz/³/₄ cup soft margarine
175g/6oz/³/₄ cup caster sugar
*150g/5oz/1¼ cups self-raising
flour*
*25g/1oz/¼ cup cocoa powder,
sifted*
3 eggs
For the topping
175g/6oz/³/₄ cup butter
25g/1oz/¼ cup cocoa powder
*300g/11oz/2½ cups icing sugar
a few liquorice strips and
115g/4oz packet M & M's, for
decoration*

Variation To make Traffic Light Cakes, omit the cocoa and add an extra 25g/1oz/3 tbsp plain flour. Omit cocoa from the icing and add an extra 25g/1oz/4 tbsp icing sugar and 2.5ml/½ tsp vanilla essence. Spread over the cakes and decorate with red, yellow and green glacé cherries to look like traffic lights.

1 Preheat the oven to 180°C/350°F/ Gas 4. Lightly brush an 18 x 28cm/7 x 11in baking tin with a little oil and line the base of the tin with greaseproof paper.

2 Put all the cake ingredients in a bowl and beat until smooth.

3 Spoon into the prepared cake tin and level the surface with a palette knife.

4 Bake for 30 minutes, until the cake springs back when pressed with the fingertips.

5 Cool in the tin for 5 minutes, then loosen the edges with a knife and transfer to a wire rack. Peel off the paper and leave the cake to cool. Turn the cake on to a chopping board and cut into 16 bars.

6 To make the topping, place the butter in a bowl, sift in the cocoa and icing sugar and beat until smooth. Spread the topping evenly over the cakes with a palette knife.

7 Add a strip of liquorice to each cake, decorate with M & M's for domino dots and arrange the cakes on a serving plate.

Gingerbread Teddies

These endearing teddies, dressed in striped pyjamas, would make a perfect gift for friends of any age. If you can't get a large cutter, make smaller teddies or use a traditional gingerbread-man cutter. You might need some help from an adult for the decorating.

Makes 6

🌿

INGREDIENTS

75g/3oz white chocolate, chopped
175g/6oz ready-to-roll white sugar paste
blue food colouring
25g/1oz plain or milk chocolate
For the gingerbread
175g/6oz/1¹⁄₂ cups plain flour
1.5ml/¹⁄₄ tsp bicarbonate of soda
pinch of salt
5ml/1 tsp ground ginger
5ml/1 tsp ground cinnamon
65g/2¹⁄₂oz/¹⁄₃ cup unsalted butter, chopped
75g/3oz/¹⁄₃ cup caster sugar
30ml/2 tbsp maple or golden syrup
1 egg yolk, beaten

🌿

1 To make the gingerbread, sift together the flour, bicarbonate of soda, salt and spices into a large bowl. Rub the butter into the flour until the mixture resembles fine breadcrumbs.

2 Stir in the sugar, syrup and egg yolk and mix to a firm dough. Knead lightly. Wrap and chill for 30 minutes.

3 Preheat the oven to 180°C/350°F/ Gas 4. Grease two large baking sheets. Roll out the gingerbread dough on a floured surface and cut out teddies, using a floured 13cm/5in cookie cutter.

4 Transfer to the prepared baking sheets and bake for 10–15 minutes, until just beginning to colour around the edges. Leave on the baking sheets for 3 minutes and then transfer to a wire rack.

5 Melt half of the white chocolate. Put in a paper piping bag and snip off the tip. Make a neat template for the teddies' clothes: draw an outline of the cutter on to paper, finishing at the neck, halfway down the arms and around the legs.

6 Thinly roll the sugar paste on a surface dusted with icing sugar. Use the template to cut out the clothes, and secure them to the biscuits with the melted chocolate.

7 Use the sugar paste trimmings to add ears, eyes and snouts. Dilute the blue colouring with a little water and use it to paint the striped pyjamas.

8 Melt the remaining white chocolate and the plain or milk chocolate in separate bowls over saucepans of hot water. Put in separate paper piping bags and snip off the tips. Use the white chocolate to pipe a decorative outline around the pyjamas and use the plain or milk chocolate to pipe the faces.

Sweet Necklaces

These are too fiddly for young children to make but ideal as novelty Christmas presents.

Arrange in a pretty, tissue-lined box or tin for presentation.

Makes 12

INGREDIENTS

1 quantity Lebkuchen mixture
1 quantity Royal Icing
pink food colouring
selection of small sweets
6m/6 yards fine pink, blue or
white ribbon

1 Preheat the oven to 180°C/350°F/ Gas 4. Grease two large baking sheets. Roll out slightly more than half of the Lebkuchen mixture on a lightly floured surface to a thickness of 5mm/¼in.

2 Cut out stars using a floured 2.5cm/1in star cutter. Transfer to a baking sheet, spacing them evenly. Taking care not to distort the shape of the stars, make a large hole in the centre of each, using a metal or wooden skewer.

3 Gather the trimmings together with the remaining dough. Roll the dough under the palms of your hands, to make a thick sausage about 2.5cm/1in in diameter. Cut in 1cm/½in slices. Using the skewer, make a hole in the centre of each. Put on the second baking sheet.

4 Bake for about 8 minutes, until slightly risen and just beginning to colour. Remove from the oven and, while still warm, re-make the skewer holes as the gingerbread will have spread slightly during baking. Leave to cool on a wire rack.

5 Put half the royal icing in a paper piping bag and snip off a tip. Use to pipe outlines around the stars. Colour the remaining icing with the pink colouring. Spoon into a paper piping bag fitted with a star nozzle.

6 Cut the sweets into smaller pieces and use to decorate the biscuits. Leave to harden.

7 Cut the ribbon into 50cm/20in lengths. Thread a selection of the biscuits on to each ribbon.

Choc-tipped Cookies

Get those cold hands wrapped round a steaming hot drink,

and tuck into choc-tipped cookies.

Makes 22

INGREDIENTS

115g/4oz/½ cup margarine
45ml/3 tbsp icing sugar, sifted
150g/5oz/1¼ cups plain flour
few drops vanilla essence
75g/3oz plain chocolate, chopped

1 Preheat the oven to 180°C/350°F/ Gas 4. Lightly grease two baking sheets. Put the margarine and icing sugar in a bowl and cream them together until very soft. Mix in the flour and vanilla essence.

2 Spoon the mixture into a large piping bag fitted with a large star nozzle and pipe 10–13cm/4–5in lines on the prepared baking sheets. Cook for 15–20 minutes, until pale golden brown. Leave to cool slightly before lifting on to a wire rack. Leave the biscuits to cool completely.

3 Put the chocolate in a small heatproof bowl. Stand in a saucepan of hot, but not boiling, water and leave to melt. Dip both ends of each biscuit into the chocolate, put back on the rack and leave to set. Serve with hot chocolate topped with whipped cream.

Cook's Tip Make round biscuits if you prefer, and dip half of each biscuit in the melted chocolate.

Five-spice Fingers

Light, crumbly biscuits with an unusual Chinese five-spice flavouring.

Makes 28

❦

INGREDIENTS

115g/4oz/¹/₂ cup margarine
50g/2oz/¹/₂ cup icing sugar
115g/4oz/1 cup plain flour
10ml/2 tsp five-spice powder
grated rind and juice of ¹/₂ orange

❦

1 Preheat the oven to 180°C/ 350°F/Gas 4. Lightly grease two baking sheets. Put the margarine and half the icing sugar in a bowl and beat with a wooden spoon, until the mixture is smooth and creamy.

2 Add the flour and five-spice powder and beat again. Spoon the mixture into a large piping bag fitted with a large star nozzle.

3 Pipe short lines of mixture, about 7.5cm/3in long, on the prepared baking sheets. Leave enough room for them to spread.

4 Bake for 15 minutes, until lightly browned. Leave to cool slightly, before transferring to a wire rack with a palette knife.

5 Sift the remaining icing sugar into a small bowl and stir in the orange rind. Add enough juice to make a thin icing. Brush over the biscuits while they are still warm.

Cook's Tip These biscuits are delicious served with ice cream or creamy desserts.

Date Crunch

Makes 24

INGREDIENTS

225g/8oz packet sweetmeal biscuits
75g/3oz/¹/₃ cup butter
30ml/2 tbsp golden syrup
*75g/3oz/¹/₂ cup stoned dates, finely
chopped*
75g/3oz sultanas
*150g/5oz milk or plain chocolate,
chopped*

Cook's Tip For an alternative topping,
drizzle 75g/3oz melted white and
75g/3oz melted dark chocolate over.

1 Line an 18cm/7in square shallow
cake tin with foil. Put the biscuits
in a plastic bag and crush roughly
with a rolling pin.

2 Gently heat the butter and syrup
in a small saucepan until the
butter has melted.

3 Stir in the crushed biscuits, the
dates and sultanas and mix well.
Spoon into the prepared tin, press flat
with the back of a spoon and chill for
1 hour.

4 Melt the chocolate in a heatproof
bowl, over a saucepan of hot
water, stirring until smooth. Spoon
over the cookie mixture, spreading
evenly with a palette knife. Chill until
set. Lift the foil out of the cake tin and
peel away. Cut the crunch into 24
pieces and arrange on a plate.

Peanut Cookies

Packing up a picnic? Got a birthday party coming up?

Make sure some of these nutty cookies are on the menu.

Makes 25

❦

INGREDIENTS

225g/8oz/1 cup butter
30ml/2 tbsp smooth peanut butter
115g/4oz/1 cup icing sugar
50g/2oz/¹/₂ cup cornflour
225g/8oz/2 cups plain flour
115g/4oz/1 cup unsalted peanuts

❦

1 Put the butter and peanut butter in a bowl and beat together. Add the icing sugar, cornflour and plain flour and mix together to make a soft dough.

2 Preheat the oven to 180°C/350°F/ Gas 4. Lightly oil two baking sheets. Roll the mixture into 25 small balls, using your hands and place on the baking sheets. Leave plenty of room for the cookies to spread.

3 Press the tops of the balls of dough flat, using either the back of a fork or your fingertips.

4 Press a few of the peanuts into each of the cookies. Bake for 15–20 minutes, until lightly browned. Leave to cool for a few minutes before lifting them carefully on to a wire rack with a palette knife.

Cook's Tip Make really monster cookies by rolling bigger balls of dough. Remember to leave plenty of room on the baking sheets for them to spread, though.

Apricot Yogurt Cookies

These soft cookies are very quick to make and are useful for lunch boxes.

Makes 16

INGREDIENTS

175g/6oz/1½ cups plain flour
5ml/1 tsp baking powder
5ml/1 tsp ground cinnamon
75g/3oz/1 cup rolled oats
75g/3oz/½ cup light muscovado sugar
115g/4oz/¾ cup chopped ready-to-eat dried apricots
15ml/1 tbsp flaked hazelnuts or almonds
150g/5oz/⅔ cup natural yogurt
45ml/3 tbsp sunflower oil
demerara sugar, for sprinkling

1 Preheat the oven to 190°C/375°F/ Gas 5. Lightly oil a large baking sheet.

2 Sift together the flour, baking powder and cinnamon. Stir in the oats, sugar, apricots and nuts.

Cook's Tip These cookies do not keep well, so it is best to eat them within two days, or to freeze them. Pack into polythene bags and freeze for up to four months.

3 Beat together the yogurt and oil, then stir evenly into the flour mixture to make a firm dough. If necessary, add a little more yogurt. Use your hands to roll the mixture into about 16 small balls.

4 Place the balls on the prepared baking sheet and flatten with a fork. Sprinkle with demerara sugar. Bake for 15–20 minutes, until firm and golden brown. Transfer to a wire rack and leave to cool.

Applesauce Cookies

These fruit-flavoured cookies are a favourite with children.

Makes 36

INGREDIENTS

450g/1lb cooking apples, peeled, cored and chopped
45ml/3 tbsp water
115g/4oz/½ cup caster sugar
115g/4oz/½ cup butter or margarine
115g/4oz/1 cup plain flour
2.5ml/½ tsp baking powder
1.5ml/¼ tsp bicarbonate of soda
pinch of salt
2.5ml/½ tsp ground cinnamon
50g/2oz/½ cup chopped walnuts

1 Cook the apple with the water in a covered saucepan over a low heat until the apple is tender. Cool slightly then purée in a blender or mash with a fork Measure out 175ml/6fl oz/¾ cup.

2 Preheat the oven to 190°C/375°F/ Gas 5. Grease a baking sheet. In a medium-size bowl, cream together the sugar and butter or margarine until well mixed. Beat in the apple sauce.

Cook's Tip If the apple sauce is too runny, put it in a strainer over a bowl and let it drain for 10 minutes before measuring it out.

3 Sift the flour, baking powder, bicarbonate of soda, salt and cinnamon into the mixture, and stir to blend. Fold in the chopped walnuts.

4 Drop teaspoonfuls of the dough on to the prepared baking sheet, spacing them about 5cm/2in apart.

5 Bake the cookies for 8–10 minutes until they are golden brown. Transfer to a wire rack and leave to cool.

Index

Contents

Nursing older people is a major and developing speciality, and is likely to become even more important in the light of demographic projections. Older people are already the major users of health and social care services and therefore, wherever nurses work with adults, the majority of clients are in the older age groups. Each person, nurse or client, is always an individual with 'special' needs, but the distinct needs of older people are not widely recognised in the services provided. Nurses committed to the care of older people have, for many years, sought to understand what older individuals want and need from support services and, through this understanding, to improve what they can offer. Within the last decade, nursing practice with older people has begun to free itself from the shackles of its impoverished heritage and to gradually become an innovative specialty. Through studying gerontology, nurses can learn more about current generations of older people – how they live, what they want from life now and in the future, and how their experiences have influenced their views. Nurses also have the opportunity to 'tune in' to what messages older people want to impart to society in general. When older people experience illness or disability, these messages have particular significance to those working with them who want to offer help, support and care.

This book has materialised as a result of an accumulation of some 40 years between us, of nursing practice and education, the majority of that time seeking ways to articulate what, for us, has always been so 'special' about working with older people. In fact, it came to fruition as a result of a discussion about the need for a comprehensive text which combines a broad base of the gerontological literature with a detailed analysis of the theory and practice of nursing older people in the UK. 'One day, when we retire, we'll adapt Ebersole and Hess for nurses in the UK' was an off-the-cuff remark. As it happened, events overtook our plan for the long-term future and the adaptation became a reality much earlier than we had hoped.

We believe that the strength of this book lies in its ability to bring together the gerontological literature and nursing practice with older people to produce a comprehensive resource for nurses working in a broad spectrum of settings. Some nurses work with fit and active older people towards promoting healthy living. Others work with older people who live in care homes and for whom the complexities of ill-health or disability present major challenges to their desire to live their lives in the manner in which they would choose. In these settings, nurses offering highly informed and expert help can make a considerable contribution towards helping residents achieve their potential.

The book aims to offer a broad scope of literature alongside a detailed discussion of the implications for nursing practice. It includes a comprehensive analysis of foundations for practice in areas which are commonly acknowledged but also in some which have traditionally been neglected, and others not commonly found in UK gerontological nursing texts.

It encompasses consideration of:

- Theoretical foundations for gerontological nursing, including the biographical approach; theories of ageing; perspectives on later life; global, European and UK demography; older people in society; health and social policy; health and wellness in later life; and a range of current and historical influences on care.
- Relevant gerontological literature, particularly new perspectives on psychosocial issues; for example, transitions, self-actualisation and transcendence.
- Detailed discussion of aspects traditionally acknowledged to be at the core of gerontological nursing practice, such as pressure damage prevention, wound care and continence promotion, and also areas of care which are not so well understood, such as person-centred care for people with mental health needs, caring for an older person's feet or teeth, ethical aspects and health promotion.
- Theoretical foundations from which to work towards clinical practice development and higher-level practice, including advanced assessment, laboratory values and emerging nursing roles with older people.

Examples of the content not commonly found in other nursing texts include the following:

- Chapter 5 is written by a geriatrician colleague. It explains in depth about laboratory tests with older people. This understanding could enhance the potential for gerontological nurses to incorporate aspects of physical assessment into their roles.
- Chapter 9 on pain and comfort is written by a palliative care nurse specialist and pulls together what little is understood about how chronic pain is experienced by those older people who are most affected by disabling chronic conditions.
- Chapter 13 on environmental safety and security draws upon a broad range of literature and perspectives. It addresses the continuum of housing options, including a discussion on homelessness. It also addresses travel health specific to older people and the issues related to road safety. The discussion recognises that gerontological nurses will increasingly care for older people with a broad spectrum of lifestyles and in a range of supportive community settings.
- Chapter 20 on self-actualisation is written from the perspective of extensive experience of reminiscence work with older people. While believing that true self-actualisation is beyond the reach of most individuals, the author offers a range of ideas as to how nurses can work with older people towards achieving creativity, self-expression and continuing development.
- The final chapter examines emerging trends which could influence the development of geronotological nursing in the future and, eliciting the views of

Healthy Ageing

Nursing Older People

Hazel Heath

MSc Advanced Clinical Practice
(Care of Older People), BA(Hons),
DipNursing (London), Cert Ed,
FETC, ITEC, RGN, RCNT, RNT

Chair of the Royal College of
Nursing Forum for Nurses
working with Older People

Doctoral Student and
Independent Nurse Adviser

Formerly, Senior Teacher/Subject
Leader in Nursing Theory and
Practice, St Bartholomew School
of Nursing and Midwifery, London
and RCN Adviser in Nursing and
Older People

Irene Schofield

MSc (Gerontology), Cert Hlth Prom
(Open), Cert Ed, CertOncology
Nursing, RGN, RNT

Education Fellow, Royal College of
Nursing Gerontological Nursing
Programme, and Primary Health Care
Nurse, East Lothian.

Formerly, Lecturer in Nursing,
City University St Bartholomew School
of Nursing and Midwifery, London

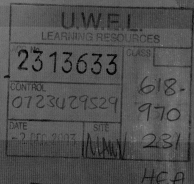
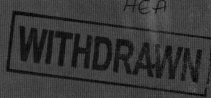
 Mosby

Publisher	**Jill Northcott, Brenda Clark**
Development Editor	**Natasha Dupont, Gillian Harris**
Project Manager	**Dave Burin**
Production	**Susan Walby, Ewan Halley**
Design	**Deborah Gyan**
Layout	**Lara Last**
Cover Design	**Deborah Gyan**
Cover Painting	**Benjamin Warner**
Illustration Management	**Mike Saiz**
Illustrators	**Jo Cameron** **Gisli Thor** **Chris King**

Published in 1999 by Mosby, an imprint of Harcourt Publishers Limited

© Harcourt Publishers Limited 1999

ISBN: 0 7234 2952 9

Printed and bound by Printer Trento, Trento, Italy

For full details of Mosby titles please write to Mosby International Ltd, Lynton House, 7–12 Tavistock Square, London WC1H 9LB, UK.

A CIP catalogue record for this book is available from the British Library.

individual nurses currently working in a range of unusual or innovative roles, it offers a view of how gerontological nurses might best position themselves for the future.

We believe that, through the expertise and commitment of all who contributed to the book, it now encompasses a valuable accumulation of resources and ideas for UK nurses. Some aspects are completely original, some have been adapted from Ebersole and Hess' *Toward healthy ageing* and some sections, which have universal significance and for which there is no substitute in the UK literature, have been retained. We have also retained some of the ideas in the Ebersole and Hess work which, although not necessarily research-based, struck a resonance in the experience of the editors and contributors. These were the types of realities that nurses often witness, that are not necessarily easy to explain, but nevertheless 'strike a chord'; for example, the description of complex family dynamics.

This book uses Maslow's 'Hierarchy of Needs' as a framework for its structure and also to illustrate need within a variety of altered health states. In our view the use of the Maslow framework with its higher-order levels affiliation and self-esteem needs promotes consideration of a truly holistic picture of an older person's needs which are too often neglected in many commonly used nursing models. The framework also allows for consideration of all the very particular aspects which are relevant to ageing, and which can become more important in later life, particularly to a person's viability as an active member of society.

Although Maslow presented his framework as a hierarchy, he did not claim that the hierarchical consequence of needs is either universal or inevitable. Also, although the structure indicates the most usual order of essential needs, Maslow (Maslow A H. *Motivation and personality*, 2nd edn. New York: Harper and Row, 1970) highlighted a number of exceptions. The most common deviation he found was for self-esteem to be more important than love and the reason suggested for this was that those people who are high in confidence and self-esteem are those most likely to be loved. In his original research Maslow found that, in some highly creative people, the need to create may override all other needs and that some people are able to stand up for their ideals and beliefs even in the face of marked deprivation with regard to their 'lower order' needs. He suggested that people who have been made secure and strong in the earliest years, tend to remain secure and strong thereafter in the face of whatever threatens. This may have particular relevance to some older people.

We do not regard any section of the book as being of greater importance or use than any other. Rather, we hope that students and practitioners will dip into sections or chapters according to their own need to know more about a specific issue at a particular time.

We want to thank sincerely all the contributors and reviewers who have willingly given their time and expertise to the project.

Hazel Heath and Irene Schofield
December 1998

Contributors

Hazel Heath
MSc Advanced Clinical Practice (Care of Older People),
BA(Hons), DipNursing(London), Cert Ed, FETC, ITEC,
RGN, RCNT, RNT
Chair of the Royal College of Nursing Forum for Nurses
working with Older People
Doctoral Student and Independent Nurse Adviser
Formerly, Senior Teacher/Subject Leader in Nursing
Theory and Practice, St Bartholomew School of Nursing
and Midwifery, London and RCN Adviser in Nursing and
Older People
Chapters 1, 10, 15, 22

Irene Schofield
MSc (Gerontology), Cert Hlth Prom (Open), Cert Ed,
Cert Oncology Nursing, RGN, RNT
Education Fellow, Royal College of Nursing Gerontological
Nursing Programme, and Primary Health Care Nurse,
East Lothian
Formerly, Lecturer in Nursing, City University
St Bartholomew School of Nursing and Midwifery,
London
Chapters 2, 4, 13, 16

Bernie Arigho
MSc (Gerontology), BA, Cert Ed, RGN, RMN
Freelance Reminiscence Worker and Trainer
(Age Exchange, London) and Doctoral Student with the
Open University School of Health and Social Welfare
Chapter 20

Mary Clay
MSc Advanced Clinical Practice (Care of Older People)
RGN, RM
Matron, Moorlands Nursing Home, Lightwater, Surrey
Chapter 7

Pauline Ford
MA Gerontology, DHMS, CMS, RGN
Royal College of Nursing Adviser on Nursing and Older
People and Co-Director of the RCN Gerontological
Nursing Programme
Chapter 22

Sheila Goff
MSc, RGN, DN
Clinical Nurse Specialist, ICRF Colorectal Family Cancer
Clinic, St Mark's Hospital.
Formerly, Clinical Nurse Specialist, Palliative Care Team,
Royal Hospitals Trust, London
Chapters 9, 21

Michele Hughes
MSc Health Sciences, BSc Nursing, Dip Nursing (London),
Adv Dip Educational Studies for Nursing, RGN RNT
Lecturer in Nursing, University College, Cork
Chapter 8

Andrée Le May
PhD, BSc(Hons), PGCEA, RGN
Deputy Head of Health Studies Department and Senior
Lecturer in Nursing, Brunel University, Isleworth,
Middlesex and Visiting Professor, Canterbury
Christchurch University College
Chapter 12

Abigail Masterson
MN, BSc, PGCEA, RGN
Director of Abi Masterson Consulting Limited,
Southampton
Chapter 14

Mary E McClymont
MSc, BSc(Hons), Qualified Nurse, Midwife and Health
Visitor, Queen's Nurse, Qualified Health Visitor Tutor.
Formerly, Principal Lecturer in Health Studies, Stevenage
College. Currently, Visiting Lecturer, University of
Hertfordshire
Chapter 3

Lynne Phair
MA, BSc(Hons)Nursing, DPNS, PGCCC, RGN, RMN
Nursing and Care Management Adviser, RSAS AgeCare
Chapter 18

Karen Rawlings-Anderson
MSc, BA, Dip N Ed, RGN, RNT
Senior Lecturer – Adult Acute and Critical Care Nursing,
City University St Bartholomew School of Nursing and
Midwifery, London
Chapter 19

Susan Rush
MSc, RGN
Principal Lecturer Clinical Skills, Faculty of Health
Sciences, Kingston University and St George's Hospital
Medical School, London
Chapter 6

Jane Slack
RGN, Dip Health and Social Welfare
Outreach Nurse, Weston Area Health Trust,
Weston-super-mare, North Somerset
Chapter 11

Kevin Somerville
DM, FRCP, FRACP
Medical Consultant to Swiss Re Life and Health
Formerly, Clinical Director of Medicine for the Elderly,
St Bartholomew's Hospital, London
Chapter 5

David Turner
MSc, BA(Hons), RGN
Senior Lecturer, Buckinghamshire Chilterns University
College
Chapter 8

Carole Webster
BSc(Hons) RGN RM, Dip Nursing, Dip Higher Ed
(Biological Sciences) RNT
Welfare/Medical Advice Worker
Formerly, Lecturer in Biological Sciences, St Bartholomew
School of Nursing and Midwifery, London
Chapter 10

Diane Wells
BA(Hons), Dip Social Studies, Cert Ed, RNT, Dip Social
Research, Dip Nursing (Lond), RGN, Cassell Certificate
in Psychosocial Nursing, RGN, RNT
Lecturer, Faculty of Health Sciences, Kingston University
and St George's Hospital Medical School, London
Chapter 17

Acknowledgements

This book has been adapted from a US book – *Toward healthy aging: human needs and nursing response, 4th edition* – published in 1994 by Mosby, and we are indebted to the authors, Priscilla Ebersole and Patricia Hess, for permission to adapt their material.

We would like to thank all our contributors and those people who gave their time to review chapters. We would also like to say a special thank you to Dr Kevin Somerville, formerly Clinical Director of Health Care for the Elderly, St Bartholomew's Hospital, London, who helped us with other chapters besides his own.

Theoretical foundations

1 Perspectives on ageing and older people
Hazel Heath

LEARNING OBJECTIVES
After studying this chapter you should be able to:
- Discuss a variety of perspectives on ageing and older people.
- Discuss the biographical approach to ageing and its usefulness in facilitating intergenerational understanding.
- Discuss the concepts of 'true' and 'false' ageing.
- Discuss demographic trends and some key characteristics of older people in the UK and Europe.
- Discuss how Western societal views of older age impact on the lives of individual older people.
- Discuss health and illness in later life and key influences on the health and social care of older people, including rationing.
- Discuss the historical background to the nursing and medical care of older people, and how this exerts influences on current services.

INTRODUCTION

Each older person is a unique individual. Each has his or her own values, needs, ways of living and perspectives on life. The only factor common to all older people is an accumulation of a variety of different life experiences over a greater period of time than those of younger people. As life experiences interact with individual personalities it could be argued that people in older age represent the epitome of individuality.

This chapter aims to enhance understanding of older people, older age and the processes of ageing. Using a biographical approach it explores the influences of life experiences on how individuals interact, particularly those from different generations, and explores the experiences of older people who have moved from their original homeland. It acknowledges broad characteristics of older populations in the UK, Europe and globally, including health, illness and living standards, and how these might influence the lives of older individuals. It also discusses how older people are viewed and treated in Western societies, and highlights some current debates about their 'value' and needs.

In order to establish a context for discussion about the health and social care of older people today, the chapter traces the development of these services, and specifically of nursing with older people. It then discusses key perspectives on health and social policy and current service provision for older people. Overall, Chapter 1 aims to set a context for the chapters which follow.

AGEING AND OLDER PEOPLE

Ageing is a continuous process which begins at birth. It accompanies each of us on our journey through life. However, as Johnson (1985) highlights, the process of ageing is not a single dimension progression, but a complex of strands, or paths of concern, continuing for differing lengths of time throughout a life's biography and moulding its individuality. These strands may include relationships, occupations or a focus on a particular concern, such as caring for a loved one. According to Johnson, ageing and older age are thus 'the continuing of an intricate pattern of life careers'. Each life is unique, with its experiences, hopes, fears, achievements, failures, fond memories, satisfactions, frustrations and pride in the past. All of these self-estimates are part of each person's cumulative self-image and all are 'non-objective'.

Older age is commonly viewed as a stage in life, and reaching older age as an event. Being 'old' is commonly viewed as a distinct state. These views arise partially from the way in which Western society views ageing, but they are also supported by the research into ageing, which traditionally sought to understand it through objective and observable means. In reality, older age, like any age, is a subjective experience lived by individual people. It is a point on the progression of the journey through life, not the destination. Each individual is the totality of the subjective experiences that have shaped his or her life, and each life is a unique biography. The biographical approach is fundamental to nursing older people. If nurses approach older people as individuals, each within the context of a unique biography that encompasses the person's subjective perceptions of past, present and future, they will more readily be able to understand the older person's self-perceived

3

state, self-image, needs and aspirations at that point in their lives. The potential for a therapeutic relationship and helpful interventions is then considerably enhanced.

A Biographical Approach to Ageing

As individuals evolve throughout their lives, their beliefs, values and self-perceived state are shaped by an interaction of background and culture with the experience of events. Adams (1991a) suggests that the ways in which these interactions impact on individuals, and the individual's responses to the experiences, influence the ways in which these individuals interact with others. The influences can then act as 'filters' through which we view other people. His biographical model suggests three dimensions in which these events may be experienced (**Figure 1.1**).

Events such as the deaths of President John F Kennedy or Diana, Princess of Wales are *public events* in that they are shared with many people. They may or may not have a direct effect on individuals, but they reflect in some way on each personal history. In each person's life, there are also significant events, such as going to school, starting work, developing relationships, moving home, having children or losing a loved one, which are *personal milestones*. The interpretation of events, and the meaning attributed to them are

encapsulated in *personal memories*. This interpretation and meaning can change over time as it is revisited. People may or may not be aware of the meaning of the memories, and they may be pleasant to revisit or difficult to share with others. Therefore, even when public events are shared, they are experienced and interpreted individually. Each person's memories, and the impact on each life, will therefore be distinct. Consider the effects of the experiences shown in **Table 1.1** on the three different birth cohorts.

Intergenerational Understanding

The differences between how a public event is subjectively experienced by an older person and a younger person can be vast, as **Table 1.1** illustrates. Rabbitt (1984, p. 14) described how older people have been fed, housed and educated very differently, have received or failed to receive different medical treatment for different conditions, have been taught to prize different skills and attitudes and have been shaped by dramatically different experiences (Coleman, 1993). Seabrook (1980, p. 118) similarly highlights that 'many of the old grew up in a world where they had to be disciplined, frugal, stoical, self-denying and poor. What this taught them, often in bitterness and pain, appears to be of no use to their children and grandchildren, who have been shaped for different purposes by changed circumstances'. This can cause misunderstanding, or even alienation, between younger and older people, as their respective values and views can be vastly different.

Older people may feel like 'time travellers, exiled to a foreign country which they now share with current 20-year-olds' (Coleman, 1993). However, there are also distinct challenges for younger people, and the author's own experiences over many years of working as a teacher trying to nurture the enthusiasm of young student nurses for working with older people has provided constant reminders of these. As one teenage student wrote in her essay, 'We are taught about the concept of empathy, and I try to empathise with my patients, but this is very difficult to do. How can I as a young person have empathy with a person who has lived for so many more years, and lived through world wars, and had so many experiences that I have not had. It's hard'.

Approaches to Learning About Ageing

Gerontology, the study of ageing, is relatively young compared to other fields of study, and health in later life is inherently complicated to research. No two individuals age physiologically in the same way; the range of 'normal' is greater in older age than younger age, and many factors impact on health, such as genetic, environmental, psychological, social and general lifestyle. This is highlighted in the fact that many people over 80 years of age generally remain physically well, active and contributing to life, while others are more sedentary, either by choice or through ill health. Much of the early gerontological

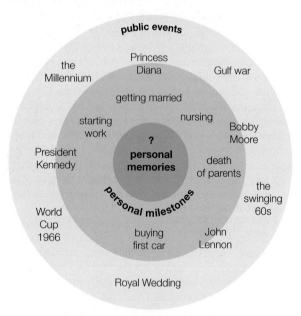

Figure 1.1 A biographical model. (Source: Adapted from Adams J. Human biogrraphy part (i): a personal approach. *Nurs Times* 1991a, 87:1–8. Reproduced by kind permission of *Nursing Times* where this was first published on 19 June 1991; Heath H. *Care of the Older Person*. In: Hinchliff SM, Norman SE, Schober JE eds. *Nursing Practice and Health Care, 3rd Edition*. London: Edward Arnold, 1998. Reproduced by kind permision of Edward Arnold.)

How Different Generations might View World Events				
Decade	World events	Personal memories Born 1915	Personal memories Born 1940	Personal perceptions Born 1975
1920s	Depression/unemployment King George V Jubilee Flappers/charleston Wall Street crash			
1930s	Abdication of Edward VIII Start of the Second World War Depression/unemployment	My family needed food and we had no money. I walked miles with only a cup of tea in my belly to get a job only to be told it had gone. We queued for hours and had to call the counter clerk 'Sir' before we got our dole money. I hope I never again suffer the indignity of having to ask for money!		
1940s	War years Welfare state Rationing Marriage of Princess Elizabeth	I worked as a plater's helper in the docks for most of the war and the East End got its fair share of bombings. We had some laughs in the air-raid shelters and D-day was a great celebration. My daughter had diphtheria but, thanks to the welfare state, she was all right.	My few memories of the war are very vivid. When the air-raid sirens went, my mother would grab me and my baby brother, bundle us under the stairs and crouch over us. The noise was frightening, but my mum always felt so warm and she smelled of soap.	I don't know much about the war – only what I've seen on TV, like on the VE Day celebrations. Granddad says that they never knew who would die next – it might be him or Grandma. I haven't a clue how that was, or why they didn't just go to live somewhere else.
1950s	Coronation End of rationing Suez crisis Korean War			
1960s	President Kennedy assassination Beatlemania/flower power Man on the moon	They sang that the 'times they were a-changing' – they certainly were. Young people seemed to want so much freedom that we hadn't had, but then, with men on the moon, life's horizons seemed endless. Sad about Kennedy – such a young man and with so much promise.	I must have looked ridiculous in all that hippie gear saying 'love and peace man' to everyone I met, and giving them flowers, but it felt like the dawning of a new age ... I was at a psychedelic party when I heard about Kennedy; it was like one of my friends dying – he carried the hopes of our generation.	I've seen pictures of the Beatles but can't really understand what all the fuss was about. Their music's still good though – I'm collecting their CDs. And some of the clothes are really fashionable now – I'm going to a '60s night' next week!
1970s	Three day week/miner's strike Vietnam War Watergate Britain joins the EEC			

Table 1.1 How different generations might view world events. Continued over page.

How Different Generations might View World Events *(cont.)*				
Decade	World events	Personal memories Born 1915	Personal memories Born 1940	Personal perceptions Born 1975
1980s	Margaret Thatcher Falklands War Chernobyl disaster Reagan/Gorbachov			
1990s	Information technology (IT) explosion City crash/recession Genetic engineering HIV and AIDS Channel Tunnel	These computers are marvellous but I must admit I don't know what they're talking about. All this hardware, software, networking, downloading – it's like a foreign language. They use them at the GP surgery now.	I was devastated when I was made redundant. We're really struggling financially and it seems I'm too old to be wanted by another company. They say computer skills will help so the kids are teaching me. I might try to start my own business but it seems so risky.	I loved IT at school. My mate's on the internet and we spend hours on the chat-up lines! Because I haven't got a job I've been placed on a youth scheme. It's not much money but it's better than nothing!

Source: Adapted from Adams J. Human biography part (i): a personal approach. *Nurs Times* 1991a, 87:1–8. Reproduced by kind permission of *Nursing Times* where this was first published on 19 June 1991; Heath H. Care of the older person. In: Hinchliff SM, Norman SE, Schober JE, eds. *Nursing practice and health care, 3rd edition*. London: Edward Arnold, 1998. Reproduced with kind permission of Edward Arnold.

Table 1.1 How different generations might view world events (cont.)

research tended to focus on 'mapping the "problems" of older age, along with their medical, psychological and social correlates' (Johnson, 1985). This resulted in an impression of the process of ageing as progressive physical and mental decline and this is reinforced by the predominant use of cross-sectional, rather than longitudinal, methodologies in the research.

Longitudinal studies take one group or cohort of people over a period of time. For example, the blood pressure (BP) of a group of people could be measured when they reached the age of 50, 60 or 70 years. This would give an indication of how the BP of these individuals changed over time. Longitudinal studies are often avoided because they can be more complex to conduct; for example, it can be difficult to maintain continuity with the research subjects, researchers and research finance. In cross-sectional studies, different age groups, or cohorts, are studied at the same time. For example, the BP of cohorts of people aged 50, 60 and 70 years would be measured within a defined period of time. If the results showed that the BP of the 70-year-old subjects was the highest and that of the 50-year-olds the lowest, it could be concluded that BP increases with age. In fact, this may be due to factors specific to that group of people, such as smoking, eating habits and amount of exercise taken. Recent work using longitudinal methods demonstrates that some of the earlier results suggesting that ageing brought decline were, in fact, characteristics of different lifestyles and illness experiences of the cohort samples used, rather than the true effects of ageing (Grimley Evans *et al.* 1992). What is clear from the research is that chronological age is a poor predictor of either health or functional level in individuals; age, there-fore, is not a useful label when, for example, health and social service entitlement is being decided on that basis.

Ageing – 'True' and 'False'

Ageing is an interaction between intrinsic processes and external factors; but, as Grimley Evans (1994) highlights, other aspects are often falsely assumed to be characteristic of older age. These include the effects of cohort, selective survival and the differential challenges that are presented to people.

- **Intrinsic processes.** In broad terms, genetic inheritance determines the maximum life span of a species; in other words, how long its members could live. The maximum life span for humans is currently around 115 years. Many theories have been developed to explain the intrinsic processes of ageing (*see* Chapter 2).
- **Extrinsic factors.** Environment and lifestyle, interacting with genetic susceptibilities, determine how many years within the maximum life span individuals manage to achieve. Throughout life, factors such as environmental conditions, diet, exercise and smoking influence health. For some conditions, ageing patterns caused by extrinsic factors may be partly determined early in life; for example, dietary calcium intake and physical exercise affect the amount of bone laid down during growth and development, and thus influence the risk of osteoporosis in later life. Other factors can be modified throughout life and still benefit health – giving up smoking or taking more exercise will improve health and fitness and

give increased years of life, even if started after middle age (Grimley Evans, 1994).

- **Cohort effects.** As is highlighted in **Table 1.1**, older people are distinct from younger people because each is a product of his or her life experiences and culture. The characteristics of older people are, therefore, not solely due to biological ageing (*see* Chapter 19).
- **Selective survival.** People who live to older age have undergone a process of natural selection, in that they have survived when their contemporaries have not. There are identifiable physiological 'survivor factors'; for example, very old people have a higher prevalence than younger people of genes that protect against cardiovascular disease. There are also psychological characteristics which may have helped older individuals to surmount the range of personal and social challenges presented throughout this century. Grimley Evans (1994) suggests that 'those people who insist on staying in control of their own lives, the wilful and cantankerous, live longer than the more compliant "sweet old folk" who make the "good patients" favoured by doctors and nurses'.
- **Differential challenge.** In many aspects of life, society presents older people with greater challenges than it does younger people. For example, unless individuals claim for certain disability benefits before reaching pensionable age, they are no longer eligible to claim. Thus, it could be suggested that younger people are deemed worthy of some financial help to cope with disability, while older people have to cope without. Similarly, there are many examples where older people have been discriminated against in access to coronary care or cancer treatment (Medical Research Council, 1994). Older age has also been blamed for inferior treatment outcomes, whereas in reality the older patients have been offered poorer standards of treatment than younger people (Grimley Evans, 1994).

Disadvantage in older age is often viewed as characteristic of older age itself, but older people bring a wide range of resources to their older years. Some bring personal and material resources to support them through any difficulties or hardships. Others who have not accumulated such assets find that the adversities of later life compound their disadvantage, so that later life becomes an even greater struggle. Social class and economic circumstances are a major determinant of the subjective experience of later life, and these influence not only income levels, but education, housing and opportunities. Men in professional occupations have an 80% chance of reaching the age of 65, whereas men in manual occupations have an 80% chance of dying before reaching retirement age (Wilkin and Hughes, 1986). (*See* **Box 1.1** for a summary of the above.)

The Experience of Growing Older

Throughout life, and particularly through personal milestones such as starting school or work, developing relationships, childbirth or job change, individuals make adaptations. Older

1.1 Sources of Differences between Younger and Older People

'True' ageing
- Intrinsic processes – governed by genetic inheritance and individuality (e.g. personality and predispositions).
- Extrinsic factors – environment and lifestyle factors interacting with genetic inheritance and individuality.

'False' ageing
- Cohort effects – differences between generations and generational experiences.
- Selective survival – of the genetically and psychologically resilient.
- Differential challenge – the effects of 'ageist' discrimination against older people, and of differential advantage/disadvantage of older and younger people.

Source: Adapted from Grimley Evans J. Can we live to be a healthy hundred? *MRC Newsletter 64*. London: Medical Research Council, August 1994.

age tends particularly to be linked to loss, and this may derive from the unwanted nature of later-life changes; for example, retirement leading to decreased income, loss of a partner or increasing physical vulnerability. Research suggests that people's capacity to adjust to life changes appears to be enhanced in older age (Coleman, 1993). This is demonstrated in studies such as Bowling and Cartwright's (1982) work on bereavement, and that of Gutmann (1980) in whose work psychiatrists observed that older patients could be maintained in the community with less frequent contact with therapists than younger people.

The enhanced capacity of older people to adapt may be characteristic of the life experience of particular generations or cohorts who are currently older. For example, the war veterans who, as Guttman (1980) highlights, have seen 'a thousand fall', may have become resigned to death in their early years, and therefore appear more stoical about the death of colleagues in later life. Alternatively, or additionally, coping may have been learned through successive experiences of friends or family members dying in middle or older age. Whatever the reason, in surveys older people have expressed much higher rates of satisfaction with life than younger people. For example, older people at home expressed a greater degree of life satisfaction in all aspects of life, apart from health, than any other age group. Expressed self-esteem, contrary to expectations, also remains high in late life (Coleman, 1993). Older people have also been shown to fear death less than younger people. In research studies, older people thought and talked more about death than other age groups, and many referred to it calmly and without anxiety (*see* Chapter 21 for approaches to death, dying and transcendence). Ultimately, as highlighted by the biographical approach, each experience of ageing is individual. (*See* Chapter 17 for further discussion of life transitions.)

Ageing Positively

'Positive ageing' has many dimensions of which health and wellness are two (*see* Chapter 3). Physical and mental fitness, an ability to adapt to changing circumstances, meaningful relationships and self-actualisation are others. (*See* Chapter 20 for full discussion of self-actualisation.) When asked in Grundy's (1994) research 'What makes for a happy old age?', older people identified such aspects as:

- Having nothing wrong with you and being able to do things.
- Companionship and company, somebody to talk to and to tell jokes.
- Knowing that somebody is there to help if you can't help yourself.
- Having someone you can rely on.
- Having services for people who can't get out.
- Being able to adapt.
- Being able to keep your end up.
- Not giving in and waiting for the telegram.

In conducting her research, Grundy was struck by how many of the oldest respondents in good physical and mental shape had outgoing personalities and a strong commitment to making other people's lives better. This strength of personality is highlighted in many other writings. For example:

> *As older women we are a considerable force once we own our strength. We can use it by becoming teachers. Acknowledge that you have a sense of destiny, that you know who you are and have something to say, say it! ... Say I have done something worthwhile with my life and I count.*
>
> Taylor, 1992

Grimley Evans (1994) also links strength of personality with longevity:

> *The first imperative for those wishing to be a healthy hundred is to be informed, to stay in command and to be thoroughly obstreperous in refusing to be fobbed off with second-rate care.*

Self-esteem has been found to be important in achieving quality of life. Sources of self-esteem can be relationships with family members and other people, activities and interests, social responsibilities and the continuing ability to manage life and find meaning in it (Coleman, 1994). Gradually adjusting expectations and accepting the changes that come with growing older can also help to maintain self-esteem. Feeling in control of life and events is crucial in continuing to adjust to life, particularly in an institutional setting.

Much research has shown that the more social ties a person carries into middle or old age, the healthier they are likely to stay. It is thought that social contact may stimulate the body's immune response, but also that social support can act as a buffer against stress. People who have a network of family or friends are also more likely to have help with daily activities when needed, which is likely to lead to better nutrition and hygiene (Grundy, 1994). Having someone in whom one can confide about problems and concerns can also help towards a positive older age. Murphy (1982) found that older people who said that they had no confiding relationships were the most vulnerable to depression when they encountered poor health or adverse life events. (*See* Chapter 16 for further discussion on social networks.)

If people are to experience a positive older age, the maintenance of physical health is a major factor, and nurses have a key role in promoting health, and in detecting and preventing health problems. Older people can and do want to learn more about their health, and health promotion can be effective even into advanced older age (*see* Chapter 3).

Defining Older Age

Applying age-based definitions to people in older age is of limited descriptive or predictive value. Biological ageing is a continuous process with no discontinuity at, say the ages of 60, 65 or 75 years. Similarly, although circumstances may change, such as on retirement from paid work, individuals continue on their unique development path psychologically and socially. There is, therefore, no group who could accurately be labelled as 'the elderly'. People described as 'older', 'old' or 'elderly', may be aged 55 or 105 – a span of five decades! For distinction, older people are sometimes categorised into two sub-groups:

(1) **The third age**. This encompasses people who have retired from mainstream paid employment, those who have completed family raising and some others who do not fall into either of these categories. The third age can begin at around 50 years of age, and generally includes people who are physically and mentally healthy.

(2) **The fourth age**. This usually encompasses people in their eighties and nineties who experience temporary or permanent illness or disability (Grimley Evans *et al.* 1992).

OLDER PEOPLE TODAY – THEIR LIVES AND CIRCUMSTANCES

Global Ageing

Four main factors influence the balance of populations around the world:

(1) The number of people in a specific cohort (for example, those currently old in Britain were born into Victorian and Edwardian families who tended to have large numbers of children).

(2) Specific events which affect the number of people who survive into older age (for example, people killed in

battles, famines or disasters have drastically reduced the numbers of people in some groups).

(3) Trends in death rate (reduced overall death rate means that more people reach older age).

(4) Trends in fertility (for example, the long-term downward trends in Western societies have reduced birth rate, and this results in fewer younger people).

This shift towards population ageing is happening all over the world. Britain has 'aged' earlier that many other industrialised societies and is already managing some of the consequences which other countries have yet to face. By the year 2000, other European countries will have experienced steep rises in the older population, and the UK and Ireland are expected to have the lowest proportions of people over the age of 60 in Europe in 2020, at 24% and 22%, respectively (McGlone and Cronin, 1994). By 2000, Germany (excluding the former East Germany) expects its population of over-sixties to form 30%, and the picture is similar in Italy. These trends are mirrored in Japan where, due to long life expectancy and a low birth rate, the over sixty-fives population, which now makes up 14% of the total, is projected to rise to 25.8% by 2025 (About Japan, 1994). The largest increases in older populations are expected in China and in the 'developing countries'. The over-sixties are set to increase by 201% in Bangladesh and 300% in Brazil (Payne, 1995).

Older Europeans

Of the total European Community (EC) population of 321 million, nearly 100 million people in the EC are over 50 years of age. The EC is also ageing rapidly: one in five of its citizens are over 60 and, by 2020, it will be more than one in four. There is considerable diversity in patterns of growth of older populations in different countries but in all countries there is a significant growth in the number of people aged over 85 years, particularly women. Denmark, Germany and the UK have high proportions of their populations within the 55+, 65+, 75+ and 85+ age groups. France has high proportions of its total population aged over 75 and 85 years. Ireland, Portugal and Spain have much lower proportions of the very old within their populations. Ireland does have an ageing population, although in comparison with the rest of the EC it is ageing at a much slower rate as it still has the youngest population of the Member States, with 25–27% of the total population aged under 14 years (Crosby, 1993).

Older People in Great Britain

The proportions of older people living around the UK varies. In some areas, less than 10% of the population is over pensionable age, while other areas are popular in retirement and people of pensionable age or over comprise up to 35% (Warnes and Law, 1994). The subjective experience of older people will be influenced by the age mix of their local community, but also how well the community recognises and caters for the needs of the older population.

Something like 12.8 million people in Great Britain are aged 55 years and over. Those aged 60 years and over total 11.6 million (21% of the population) and this has increased by 8% since 1981. The increase is almost entirely in the older age groups, where the number of people aged 85 years and over has increased by 50% between 1981 and 1991. Two million people are 80 years of age and over; more than 7000 are more than 100 years old [Office of Population Censuses and Surveys (OPCS), 1993]. In both absolute and relative terms, the increase in the older population is projected to continue. Between 1989 and 2026, the number of people aged 65 years and over is expected to increase by 30%, and the number of people aged 85 years and over by 66% [Department of Health (DoH), 1992]. By the year 2025, the proportion of pensioners in the population is projected to be around 22% (OPCS, 1993), and the number of people aged 75 years and over around 2.9 million (Central Statistical Office, 1991).

The Medical Research Council (MRC) (1994) urges caution in interpreting population projections because of the dearth of research into projection methodologies and detailed analysis of later life trends. However, acknowledging these reservations, the increase in the very old population is set to continue. In the UK, the percentage of people over retirement age is forecast to rise from 18% in 1992 to 20% (11.7 million) in 2010, 22% in 2020 (13.5 million), 26% in 2030 (15.8 million) and 27% (16.3 million) in 2040. However, this growth in the older population, while significant, will only match in percentage terms that which has already taken place over the last 30 years. The balance of the population will change as well. The proportion of children and younger people in the population will fall. Over the period 1992 to 2032, while the total population of England and Wales is projected to rise by only 8%, the proportion of the population aged 45–49 years is projected to rise by 11%, those aged 60–74 years by 51%, those aged 75–84 years by 51% and those aged over 85 years by 126% (OPCS, 1993).

People Who Move Homeland

Geographical mobility is increasing and some people move to a new homeland where they subsequently become older. In Britain, the population of people who are growing older away from their original homeland is small at present, but the proportions will increase within the next 10–20 years (DoH, 1992). Chapter 19 offers full discussion on the diversity of older people living in Britain, specifically those who come from different countries. What is useful here is an acknowledgement of the significance of biography and the experiences of different generations. Adams (1991b) highlights the experiences of people who came to the UK during the Second World War to escape Nazi persecution and others who came from the new Commonwealth during the

1950s. Using Perks' (1984) research, Adams illustrates the acclimatisation of subsequent generations of people who immigrated from the Ukraine.

First generation Ukrainian, aged 74 years:

I born for Ukraine country, I like my country, I want to go back to my country. If my country free.

Second generation Ukrainian, aged 34 years:

Q *You have an English passport and you have got English nationality, do you still see yourself as Ukrainian.*
A *I do, it sounds odd, but I really do. I would never say anything against the British and I mean they have given me everything, and they have given me an education and so on and so forth, but in my heart I just feel Ukrainian.*

Third generation Ukrainian, aged 10 years:

Q *Do you think you will ever go back to the Ukraine?*
A *Yes, when I'm older.... I have never seen it, and I'm kind of part of it, so I'd like to go and see it, and see my relations there.*

Adams (1991b) suggests that the third generation migrant may be influenced predominantly by the British culture in which he spent his formative years, and the second generation migrant by both Ukrainian and British culture. However, the older man still sees himself as being Ukrainian. His lifestyle, and his beliefs about health and health care will likely derive from his own cultural traditions. The older generations from immigrant populations may face particular difficulties if they have spent more formative years in their own culture and have had limited opportunity to socialise and to learn the English language (see Chapter 19).

The Gender Balance

Throughout the world there are generally more women than men in the older age groups. In Britain, women constitute approximately 58% of people aged 60 years and over, 67% of those aged 85 years and over (OPCS, 1993), and 79% of those aged 90 years and over (DoH, 1992). It has been suggested that, because this female predominance in the older age groups is not appreciated, their needs are often neglected in policy and planning, and they are among the most disadvantaged people in our society (Bernard and Meade, 1993). The issues arising from the gender balance are distinct in each country, but particularly in some 'developing' countries such as India and Bangladesh where, despite the expectation that families will support their aged parents, many older women are abandoned. In many countries, such as Senegal, provision for widows and old women with disabilities is

inadequate (Payne, 1995). (*See* Chapter 19 for further discussion of gender issues in older age.)

Older People with Special Needs

Older people with mental health needs can be particularly vulnerable, yet many reports ignore their needs. The incidence of depressive illness is high among some older populations, such as those in care homes, but under-diagnosis and under-treatment are common (*see* Chapter 18 for full discussion of mental health in older age). As with the general population, people with a learning disability are surviving longer. This has not previously been the case, particularly for people with Down's syndrome. These people can have special needs which need a particular type of support. For example, as people with Down's syndrome age, dementia can begin in their forties and fifties, and ageing is accelerated in some cases. As the parents of individuals with a learning disability grow older, this often means that the person with the disability is the sole carer for elderly frail parents. This can place heavy responsibility on someone with a learning disability, particularly if he or she has been protected by the parents throughout their lives.

Living Standards

The 1993 European Observatory Report identified some general trends:

- Rising living standards of older people, particularly the younger elderly (aged 50–74 years), or the group commonly referred to as 'the third age'.
- The persistence of poverty and low incomes among a significant minority in most countries, together with an increased feminisation of poverty in old age.
- The growth of inequalities in income between pensioners, sometimes resulting from income maintenance and pension policies themselves, with gender and generational inequalities being particularly pronounced.
- New developments in pension policy, including the growth of the private pensions sector in the majority of countries.
- Increasing proportions of older people living alone, giving rise in some cases to problems of isolation and loneliness.
- Poor housing conditions among a significant minority in most countries, and the development of progressive housing policies in some (Crosby, 1993).

The economic circumstances of older people vary considerably, and media images tend to highlight the extremes. However, well over half of pensioners in Britain live within, or on, the margins of poverty, and the number of pensioners with an income below half of the national average has nearly trebled since 1979. Older people are more likely than any other age group to live in poverty over a long period of time (Walker, 1990). Currently over 95% of people over 60 years of age in Britain today live in private households, and approximately half of people aged 65 years and over own their own homes (Institute of Actuaries, 1993). The homes of older people, and particularly those aged 75 years and over, are more commonly in poor condition, or even unfit for habitation, lacking in amenities, and with substandard heating. In successive General Household Surveys (GHSs), only about half of elderly households had central heating, and Hunt's (1978) survey found that approximately 8% of older people were not warm in bed or in their living room, and 12% were not warm in their kitchens. This raises concerns about the effects of poor housing on the health of older people, and inadequate housing has been cited as a contributory factor in the admission of older people into residential care (Phillips, 1992). (*See* Chapter 13 for further discussion of the environment.)

There has been an increase in the number of very old people living alone. It is estimated that 41% of older people, some 3.4 million, live alone. In a survey of over 1000 adults aged 65 years and over, Help the Aged (1995) found that although older people chose to live independent lifestyles, thousands had little or no social contact; many also did not receive the help and support they needed to lead fulfilling lives. There are positive aspects in living alone, and people who live alone do not always perceive themselves to be lonely. Indeed some individuals who are married and living with a spouse have described themselves as feeling lonely. However, studies have identified that loneliness can not only be unpleasant, but is linked to various health problems (Holmen *et al.* 1992) and to the need for admission to hospital or entry into long-term care (Laing and Hall, 1991). (*See* Chapter 16 for further discussion of relationships.)

There is a dearth of information on Britain's minority ethnic groups, but what there is suggests that these older people are more disadvantaged than the White population in terms of social class, income, health and housing (Norman, 1985; Hasky, 1989). It is usually the oldest people, those in the lowest socioeconomic groups, and those who are disabled that experience most ill health (McGlone, 1992).

Health and Illness in Later Life

Defining health or ill health is not straightforward. It is now largely acknowledged that, because both the causes and consequences of pathological processes may be multifactorial, the distinction between health and ill health is quantitative, rather than qualitative. Functional ability is increasingly being used as an indicator of general health. Activities of daily living (ADL) scales usually focus on basic activities such as eating and washing. Instrumental ADLs include activities such as shopping and cooking. Sources of statistics on the health of older people include the GHS which reports long-standing illness in the general population, excluding people living in care homes or institutions, and the Office of Population

Censuses and Surveys (OPCS, 1993) surveys on disability in Great Britain, which include more specific details of disability. These surveys generally suggest that the incidences of both chronic illness and disability increase with age. However, the Medical Research Council (MRC) (1994) suggest that, because older people may be excluded from major studies, or the questionnaires structured in such a manner which does not highlight key indicators of their health status or needs, data sources such as the GHS are not adequate for comprehensively monitoring the health of older people. As a result, according to the MRC, the current health status of older people as a group, and changes in their health status over time, remain largely unknown. The MRC, therefore, raises doubts about whether the increase in average life span achieved during this century has, in fact, resulted in an increase in illness and disability in older people, or the total 'burden' of dependence. The MRC urges that the eligibility criteria of studies should ensure that older people are not excluded, and thus services may be more appropriately planned to meet their real health status and needs.

There are many myths and stereotypes about illness, incapacity and dependency in older age. In addition, definitions of dependency vary, which makes direct comparison difficult. Of people aged 60 years and over, about 38% report having a limiting long-term illness (i.e. any health problem or handicap which limits their daily activities). One in eight of these people with limiting long-term illness lives in a communal establishment, such as a communal home (OPCS, 1993). Major causes of limiting long-standing illness are arthritis and rheumatism, which affect around 18% of males and up to 30% of females aged 75 years and over, other bone and joint problems, hypertension, heart problems and cataracts (DoH, 1992). There are estimated to be 6.2 million disabled adults in Great Britain of whom more than two-thirds are over 60 years old. The proportions and severity of disability increase steadily with age, becoming particularly marked over 80 years of age. Over 90% of disabled adults live in private households (McGlone, 1992). GHSs illustrate that the percentage of people unable to perform self-care and household tasks independently increase with age, particularly at ages over 80 years. For most tasks at all ages, the proportion of women unable to do them independently is greater than the proportion of men. This may arise because there are more women than men in the older age groups, but also due to differences in muscle strength (MRC, 1994).

The later a disease develops, the greater the likelihood of it being fatal. This means that the longer a disease can be avoided, the shorter should be the period of disability (MRC, 1994). The MRC also highlights that, although there is an assumption that an increased life span will automatically be accompanied by an increase in disease and dependency, there are, at present, no theoretical or empirical grounds to support this idea. In fact, the data suggest that, in terms of dependency, the longer an individual can live in an independent state, the shorter the period of subsequent dependency (MRC, 1994). This highlights the importance of preventative strategies and their implementation at an early age.

Ageism

In Western society, chronological age is a label that is applied to citizens in order to grant or remove rights, permissions or opportunities:

> People's birthdays are no longer just private affairs: they are public events which they have repeatedly to declare in public to show that they are entitled to go to school, to have sexual intercourse, to buy alcohol, to marry, to vote and much else besides.
>
> Lord Young, 1990

Ageism is pervasive in society. It affects younger people, but the most profound effects are seen in the discrimination against older people, which not only causes them to be treated differently, but robs them of the same rights, responsibilities and opportunities enjoyed by other citizens. The Carnegie Inquiry (Midwinter, 1992) highlighted areas of civic activity where ageism is rife. These include:

- Consumerism, where, in practice, older people are denied rights and access.
- Design, where the arid, grey connotations of design for older age unfailingly label older people in negative, dull styling.
- Crime, where, as victim or offender, the older person is automatically treated differently to the rest of the population, despite the existence of more crucial variables.
- The press and broadcasting, where, frequently, older people are either invisible or deployed negatively – the counterpoint to thrusting, bold, successful younger people.
- Civic and voluntary life, where older people continue to be outlawed by age embargoes in such activities.
- Politics, where little consideration is given to older age, what it is, or older people as social casualties; hardly any reference is made to the broader issue of all-round quality of life in older age.

Myths About Older People

Western cultural images and perceptions of older people have resulted in a number of ideologies that significantly influence not only health and social policy, but the subjective experiences of older people who need health or social care. Common assumptions are:

- That there is a 'rising tide' of older people that could potentially overwhelm other age groups.
- That older people are not economically productive and, therefore, do not contribute to society.
- That there are now fewer younger people to support the non-productive or 'dependent' older population.
- That the majority of older people are ill, disabled and dependent, and therefore consume large amounts of resources.

These perceptions are specific to Western cultures, as distinct from many other societies around the world where older people are venerated as the repositories of cultural heritage and wisdom. Negative Western perceptions arise for many reasons, such as linking older age with physical decline, biological inferiority and a fear of death. In a society which exalts youth and beauty, people who are less youthful or less 'beautiful' may be seen as less valuable.

Structured Dependency

The structure and organisation of modern societies can also contribute to these negative views. For example, rapid developments in industrial and technological processes can render the skills and knowledge of older generations less relevant. In addition, the Western consumer culture renders those with most resources as most powerful. The devaluing and marginalisation can thus become 'structured' into societal functioning. One way in which this works is through mandatory retirement, which removes from older people the opportunity to work and to continue to update their work skills, and reduces their income and thus their consumer power. Society thus forces them into this 'non-productive' category in which they can be viewed as socially dependent. So pervasive and powerful can this process be, that a cycle of dependency is created which becomes a self-fulfilling prophecy.

Kuypers and Bengston (1984) applied Zusmann's concept (Victor, 1989) of a social breakdown syndrome to older people (**Figure 1.2**). Examples of this structurally-induced dependence abound in many aspects of health social policy, alongside the assumption that it is acceptable for older people to be offered lower standards of service than younger people. For example, because older people are expected to be ill and disabled, they are denied benefits such as mobility allowance and other disability benefits unless they claim for these before reaching pensionable age. If they become disabled after retirement age, they are not eligible to claim. Thus, younger people are deemed worthy of some financial help to cope with disability while older people have to cope without (Evandrou and Falkingham, 1989). It could be argued that a society which offered ill or disabled people of any age an average income and housing, and good access to education, employment, leisure and transport, for example, would minimise the need for specialist services and create a much greater equality of opportunity and social and economic integration (Harding *et al.* 1996).

Partially due to the negative assumptions and prejudices which underpin much of Western society's treatment of older people, the undervaluing and marginalisation of older people has historically continued largely unchallenged. Ageing itself can be associated with a loss of the social and economic

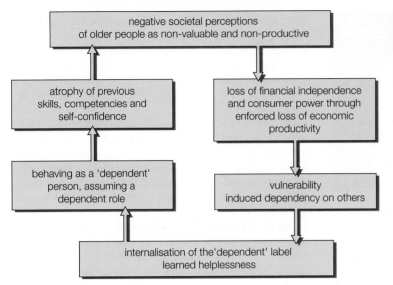

Figure 1.2 The cycle of structurally induced dependence (Source: Adapted from Kuypers JA, Bengston VL. Perpectives on the older family. In: Quinn WH, Hughston GA, eds. *Independent ageing*. Rockville: Aspen Publications, 1984).

resources available to younger people. This has direct implications for the extent to which older people are able to cope with illness or disability, and it is generally the oldest and most disabled who are the poorest (McGlone, 1992). Poverty in older age arises partly from the economic redundancy enforced on older people by retirement, and partly from the progressive reduction of the relative value of the state pension on which a high proportion of older people are dependent. It has been suggested that, because poverty in older age has gone unchallenged it has thus become accepted as an inevitable part of growing older. This has reinforced society's view of older people as economically and socially redundant, and has legitimised their marginalisation. (*See* Chapter 14 for further discussion of poverty.)

The Value of Older People in Society

Harding *et al.* (1996) contend that it makes little sense to label one-fifth of the population as a burden as soon as it reaches the age of 65 years, indeed the ageing population should be seen as an indication of success, of improved living standards, better housing, better public health and better medical care. Views of older people as a 'burden' on society ignore the contributions that older people make to society. Contrary to being 'economically inactive' older people have paid, and do pay taxes, own and maintain property, consume goods and services, handle savings and investments, and may do so increasingly in the future. They also form a large proportion of carers, and are major contributors both financially and in kind to the voluntary sector. In 1991, Bury and Holme's study of people aged 90 years and over clearly demonstrated that older age did not inevitably bring greater dependence and suggested that it was not older age as such, but death, that was the resource consuming event in later life.

The Future 'Dependency' Scenario

In 1986, Falkingham re-examined the impact of an increasing number of older people on society and concluded that 'it is not necessarily the case that a change in the age profile of the population will lead to a greater burden of dependency'. Falkingham suggested that, in fact, a breathing space exists with respect to increasing age dependency until around the year 2020, and that current and short-future problems regarding dependency levels are likely to relate to the state of the economy rather than to age pyramids. She added 'that is not to say that we should be complacent over future dependency levels, but rather that the degree of scaremongering over the ageing of the population that has been prevalent in the last few years has been unfounded' (Falkingham, 1986, p. 230).

Older People as a Political Force

If older people were able to speak with a strong and united political voice, this would help to reinforce their citizenship and publicise their role and status in society. However, older people in the UK remain 'steadfastly unpoliticised'. In their analysis of the 1987 election, Midwinter and Tester (1987) found that, although well over one-quarter of the electorate were aged 60 years and over, little campaign emphasis was given to 'older people' issues and 'politicians did not seem over-anxious to woo them as a specific voting mass'. The authors highlight that, unlike the American Grey Panthers, older people in Britain have not formed themselves into any kind of political 'gerontocratic mission'. One reason for this is the diversity of individuals within the older age groups – in social class, living conditions, income – and thus the lack of any similarity in their priorities and political outlooks.

1.2 European Senior Citizen's Charter

This stresses the rights of older people to:
- Autonomy, security and dignity in terms of income, housing, residential, health and community services.
- Safe environments in which to live.
- Pursue leisure, cultural and educational activities.
- Responsible citizenship.
- Participation in decision-making through effective participation on administrative bodies.

Groups representing the interests of older people at a policy level exist in Belgium, Denmark, France, Ireland, Luxembourg and Portugal. In the UK, there are representative organisations such as Age Concern. In Germany, there is a 'grey' political party – Die Grauen. In 1992, a meeting of over 500 senior citizens from European Union member states took place in Luxembourg. One of the results was that a European Senior Citizen's Charter was adopted (**Box 1.2**).

Issues of ageing and older people are increasingly becoming an important topic on the political agenda. This has become particularly evident in recent years in Belgium, France, Germany, Italy, Luxembourg and The Netherlands (Crosby, 1993).

THE HEALTH AND SOCIAL CARE OF OLDER PEOPLE

The History and Development of Services

The health care, social care and nursing services offered to older people today are influenced not only by aspects such as societal perceptions, which are discussed in this chapter, but also by the way in which these services have developed. Many of the traditional perceptions about nursing older people do not derive from older people themselves, and are not intrinsic to nursing them. Aspects such as chronic underfunding, inferior care environments, inadequate equipment, low staffing levels, the lack of educational preparation and updating, the low priority given to the service by others and the general perceptions of older patients as inferior in some way have profoundly influenced the way in which many, including health and social care professionals, think about nursing older people. Additional influences on these perceptions arise when inadequately prepared staff are given responsibility for dealing with chronic illness, disability, dependency and death.

In order to set the context for the following chapters in this book, it is important to acknowledge the foundations on which services for older people were built, the factors that influenced their development and the influences that still remain today. By understanding these influences, for example

that they derive from traditional but outdated perceptions of nursing older people, nurses and others will be more able to identify the real and current influences on their practice. Thus, they will be more equipped to deal with them and move the services forward.

The Early History

Until early Tudor times, society was predominantly rural, with the physical, social and welfare needs of older people met from within the family circles or small communities. Following changes in rural economy, the dissolution of the monasteries, and the discharging of soldiers and monastery staff, poverty and vagrancy became national problems as the numbers of homeless, unemployed and sick 'paupers' increased. Various poor law acts were passed in an attempt to control the problem and, as early as 1536, consideration was given to the separate categorisation of the 'impotent' who needed help. This category, which included older people and those who were sick, 'lame', or 'feeble', were considered as 'deserving' of charitable help.

Although under the poor laws, the mutual responsibility of parents and children was emphasised, ultimately each parish had to provide for its own poor from rates levied on parishioners, collected by appointed overseers and distributed via the relieving officer. Local workhouses were established to provide paupers with basic shelter, food and clothing but also to give them work. Workhouse staff overlooked the expediency of treating old people 'with the kindness that was in every sense their due' and Crabbe's poem *Village* written in 1783 describes the average workhouse as being a 'higgledy-piggledy conglomeration of idiots, children, sick poor, senile cases, unmarried mothers and unemployed'. He refers to some inmates as 'dejected widows with unheeded tears, and crippled age with more than childhood fears' (cited in Gibson, 1981).

The legacy:
- Older people labelled as 'impotents' and 'deserving' cases for charity.
- Sick, older people cared for in units with other 'impotents'.
- Units for older people as low status places of misery and hopelessness with little money and very poor facilities.

The Development of a Class System in Health Care

From the twelfth century, the Royal Hospitals of London began to develop, St. Bartholomew's and St. Thomas's being the first. These were highly selective in the patients they would take, preferring those they knew they could cure and those who were clinically interesting. Even hospitals originally intended to care for the 'sick poor', such as Guy's, The London, Westminster, St. George's and the Middlesex, gradually rejected those deemed chronically sick and 'incurable', many of whom were older people. The large, voluntary hospitals were flourishing as centres of excellence in practice, teaching and research. Thus was born the 'two-tier' hospital system. The workhouses were the lowest class of establishment and continued to take the majority of 'the needy', including older people and those with chronic illness. The voluntary hospitals would reinforce the low status of the workhouses by using them as 'dumps' for the patients they had failed to cure. Patients were sent to the workhouses to die and the resulting pauper funeral became greatly feared.

Any 'nursing' in the workhouses was given by the more able paupers but none were trained and few were paid. Thus, two distinct classes of 'nurse' were evolving. At the time when the matron of St. Thomas's hospital was being described as 'superior female of the establishment', the status of a paid nurse in a workhouse was extremely low. Their patients, the paupers, were third-class citizens, despised and disenfranchised, and those who cared for them were given similar status. The conditions of work were far below those of the voluntary hospitals and the trainee nurse or probationer in a workhouse was not in the same social class as their hospital counterpart. Women applying for workhouse jobs tended to those who had failed in their work in the higher status in institutions. Doctors in workhouses were similarly viewed as second class.

The legacy:
- Acute hospitals as high status – undertaking interesting work, rejecting older people.
- Older people labelled as 'chronic', 'irremediable' and 'clinically uninteresting'.
- 'Cure' much more highly valued and a higher status than 'care'.
- Nurses and doctors working with older people viewed as 'second class' and less skilled than the nurses who worked with the more highly valued patients.

The Development of the Specialism

The speciality of 'geriatrics', as it was called, began in the 1930s when Dr. Marjorie Warren was appointed as a deputy medical superintendent at the West Middlesex Hospital in London and took charge of the associated workhouse infirmary with its predominantly older sick and bedbound population. She substituted her philosophy of 'old age is not a disease' for the previously existing 'infirmary decubitus' and pioneered assessment, diagnosis and rehabilitation. For the first time, the acute and curative aspects of care for older people began to develop.

During the Second World War, many older people, along with other previous workhouse inmates such as young people with a chronic illness, were moved out of city centres into peripheral hospitals. It was in these facilities that the specialism continued to develop, although many of them were far from ideal in terms of environment and facilities. As the infectious disease hospitals, and later the maternity units, became under-used, older people and other previous workhouse inmates were moved in.

The legacy:
- Hospital services for older people were housed in old buildings, often run down and not designed for the care of older people.
- The specialist service for older people developed largely outside the mainstream acute services and away from the main hospital sites.

- There were few diagnostic or treatment facilities on site.
- They were viewed as being of secondary importance to acute sites.

The Influence of the Medical Model

The development of nursing with older people needs to be considered alongside that of geriatric medicine. From the early days doctors who worked in the workhouses were viewed as inferior in status and skills but this was compounded by the prevailing values in medicine generally. Cure was the highly valued ultimate goal of the medical model, and particularly a cure that was effected quickly or involved the use of state-of-the-art technology.

As Isaacs (1981) describes, older, sick people do not easily fit into the standard medical paradigm. A single diagnosis is not always possible, as their disease manifestations may be multiple and complicated by the effects of the ageing processes. Likewise, the most appropriate treatment for an older person may be that which enables him or her to function in everyday life, rather than treatment for each separate disease process. Isaacs suggests that it is from the achievement of cure that the doctor derives his professional fulfilment and that 'the standard medical encounter (with an older person) may seem to offer little scope for this, resulting in feelings of frustration and failure'. In this circumstance, he suggests, 'there is a tendency to blame the victims, or to abrogate responsibility for them by labelling them for "removal and storage" '. In other words, remove them from the acute setting and refer them to the geriatricians.

The legacy:
- Geriatricians labelled as second-class doctors with inferior skills doing less important work than other doctors.
- Units for older people seen as a 'dumping ground'.
- Nursing according to a medical model tends to ignore aspects of the patient that do not offer an apparent cure, and views aspects needing care as lower priority.

The Development of Nursing Older People

The first major study into nursing older people was the pioneering, multidisciplinary work of Norton, McClaren and Exton-Smith in the 1960s. This highlighted the routinised and ritualistic practice that has featured in much of the subsequent research into 'geriatric nursing'. However, what is not usually recognised is that in those days the nursing of older people was still in its infancy, and its identity or potential had generally not been recognised. Units 'specialising' in the care of older people did not become widespread until the 1950s or early 1960s in some areas, and at that stage routinised and ritualistic practice was the norm for nursing. (Norton *et al*, 1975).

There were no other major research studies into the care of older people until the late 1970s and early 1980s with the work of Wells (1980), Evers (1981) and others. These offered recurring themes of what Baker (1978) termed 'routine geriatric style', with its emphasis on meeting physical needs and 'getting through the work'. What is not so often highlighted but what, in retrospect, is very apparent is that during this period units for the care of older people were systematically disadvantaged. Although this does not excuse poor nursing practice, it does go some way towards explaining it. A parallel could be drawn with an individual or family systematically disadvantaged in society by inadequate finance, substandard education, impoverished and unsuitable housing and the only available support being from untrained or uncommitted personnel.

The legacy:

- Nursing older people disadvantaged to the majority of other specialities, with the poorest facilities, unsuitable equipment and receiving little priority and chronic underfunding.
- The predominant image of nursing older people as 'just basic custodial-type care'.
- Nurses in older people units offered little or no updating or education.
- No finance offered for research or development.
- Many staff 'relegated' to 'elderly care' because they were considered unsuitable for 'more important' areas.
- The general trends in nursing separating 'basic' and 'technical' tasks, with the technical aspects being highly valued and the fundamental care devalued.

Nursing older people has now largely cast off the shackles of its legacy and has overcome the majority of the challenges presented by these. Through overcoming these challenges, it is becoming one of the most pioneering, courageous and innovative areas of practice. Nurses have had to fight for recognition of their skill and what they can offer to the lives and health of older people. They have had to be open to the realities and challenges, be flexible and responsive to the needs, and creative in finding new ways of working to develop their practice and the services within which they work. As the following chapters in this book demonstrate, the potential for nurses working with older people is enormous and the future is exciting. (The book concludes with Chapter 22 offering a full discussion of the potential for the future.)

Current Health and Social Policy for Older People

European Policy

Keighley (1996) emphasises that the UK is a part of Europe and that all its social policy, including health policy, needs to be considered within that framework. Key policy areas affecting older people are consistent across Europe. These include the general move towards care in the community, with the increased emphasis on family care and the more cost-effective use of resources. Key concerns remain the provision of long-term care, particularly the coordination and regulation of services, and there are other broad concerns such as the high levels of service utilisation by older people and the general inadequacy of information available to service users.

In 1990, the European Council of Ministers decided to institute its first programme of 'Actions' for older people, to

1.3 Key Policy Issues of the European Observatory Report

- Community care. The observatory reported a general consensus that this is the most appropriate policy for the care of older people but, in a number of countries, there is severe under-supply of community care services.
- The high level of institutional and organisational fragmentation of health and social services. This causes serious problems in coordination.
- Marked variations in the supply of both residential and domiciliary care services.
- The use of services. While the observatory acknowledged that the majority of older people are living in fairly good health, there was concern that, as a group, they remain heavy users of health services.

run from 1991 to 1993. In taking this decision, the Council recognised the significant demographic developments over the 33 years since the Treaty of Rome in 1957, the general desire to promote solidarity between generations and to integrate older people more fully into society, the demands for action with regard to older people by the European Parliament, and various commitments concerning this group given in the Social Charter. The programme of actions included information exchanges, meetings, seminars and conferences, a network of innovatory projects, cross-nation research studies and the designation of 1993 as the European Year of Older People and Solidarity Between the Generations.

The Council decision also called for the establishment of an 'observatory' (or network of experts) to monitor the impact of social and economic policies on older people. Thus the Observatory on Ageing and Older People was created in January 1991. The European Observatory (1993) report identified key policy issues for older people across Europe (**Box 1.3**).

During the last 15–20 years, many European Community (EC) countries have experienced a decentralisation of services (particularly the UK, France, Germany, Denmark and Greece), and in some countries decentralisation is linked to deregulation and privatisation of public services. Despite this, in these countries, central government is still significant in the funding and legislation of services. Privatisation of services has frequently meant an increase in the need for informal care provision and less public intervention. This is particularly the case if the cost of private care is too high for many older people to benefit. Some EC countries that are pursuing decentralisation in favour of more local level community services (particularly UK, France, Germany, Ireland and Denmark) are also encouraging the development of the voluntary, informal and private sectors. In this way, services are provided at the most decentralised level, that of the older person, his or her family, or a private or voluntary organisation.

Some EC countries are experiencing problems in the

regional coordination of public, private and voluntary provided services, and a lack of collaboration between health, community and residential services. The wide regional variation in service provision for older people in many EC countries will greatly affect those currently pursuing the development of services at a local level (again, particularly in the UK, France, Germany, Ireland and Denmark). Regions with high levels of very old people are making higher demands and local governments are finding difficulty in affording the rising costs of care. In the future, there may be large differences in terms of organisation and availability of local government funding for care provision for older people, and this will inevitably affect the extent and quality of local care available.

There are still many gaps in information available to service users on service provision, particularly in Portugal, Spain and Greece but also in several northern EC countries. There is also an urgent need for better quality information about care provision throughout the EC, specifically on the private and voluntary sector provision, and for the collection of basic data, both qualitative and quantitative, on factors that facilitate the family care of older people (socioeconomic situations, housing, income and informal networks). The ageing of the population of individual EC Member States, and across the EC as a whole, has wide implications for future development and costs of the provision of health and social services for older people. Although the structure and composition of service provision, and the emphasis on the various forms, differs widely across the EC countries, the issues involved in the need for care for the older population are similar. This need will inevitably increase as older populations increase (Crosby, 1993).

Policy in the UK

Health policy, and the planning and provision of health and social care services, have undergone a period of accelerated change, particularly in the last 5–10 years. Decentralisation has been a feature of this but, with increased emphasis on local assessment, planning, provision and evaluation of services, there is a wide variety of methods of assessing, quantifying and recording health and social need around the UK, as each locality plans and delivers its services according to its own priorities. The priority given to older people in the planning and delivery of services similarly varies considerably around the UK and this leads to marked inequity in the services that older people receive (House of Commons Health Select Committee, 1995).

Health-Care Utilisation

It has been suggested that something like 60% of National Health Service, and 50% of social services budgets are for older people services (McGlone, 1992), but estimating the use of services by older people is not straightforward. As the Medical Research Council (MRC) (1994) highlights, health-care utilisation depends not only on levels of ill health, but also on levels of provision of services, advances in treatment and care, expectations of individuals for their own health,

individual's thresholds for self-referral and professionals' thresholds for referral and use of specialist services. Thus, a rise in health-care utilisation does not automatically reflect an increase in disease, disability, morbidity and self-reported illness, but rather individuals expectations about their health and the services available.

Family Care

The willingness and abilities of families, friends and neighbours to provide care for people who would otherwise need support from the state or private agencies, is a key factor, if not *the* key factor, in the planning and provision of health and social services. Carers, sometimes called 'informal' carers to distinguish them from those who are paid to give care, provide an enormous service to people in need. Estimates suggest that 80% of the care given to people who are sick or disabled is given by unpaid family members, friends of neighbours, with only 20% given by the state or other 'formal' services. There are about 6.8 million carers in Great Britain. A high percentage of carers are aged 65 years and over. Around 1 million carers provide care for at least 35 hours a week, and many have dependent children in addition to their caring role. About half of the people receiving care are aged 65 years or over, and the main problems experienced include 'neurological conditions' (strokes, Parkinson's disease), physical disabilities, and mental illness such as dementia. The potentially enormous cost of caring includes loss of income, additional expenditure and changes in family or social life. Caring can also be very detrimental to the carers themselves, about two-thirds have said in surveys that their own health has suffered as a result of their caring responsibilities. Approximately half of the carers in one survey said that they had been caring for their dependent person for at least 5 years, and 13% had not had a break from caring for 15 years or more (Warner, 1994).

Some commentators question the willingness of families to continue to provide care, but there is no clear evidence for this at present. What is known is that social and economic changes may well impact on families' abilities to care, and this is so throughout Europe. Working patterns have become more unstable, with an increase in contract, temporary and part-time work. With rising divorce rates, families are becoming more complex. There is also increased geographical mobility and family members may live many miles apart. Newly developing policies will also impact on family budgets in the future, including increased individual responsibility for health insurance, personal pensions, paying for long-term care and paying tuition fees for higher education. Harding *et al.* (1996) suggest that these may well affect families' abilities to provide financial support, time and energy towards caring.

The Carers (Recognition and Services) Act 1995 formally acknowledges that carers have their own needs. However, no new resources were allocated to provide extra help that may be needed as a result of assessments of carers' needs under this act.

The Rationing of Services

Debates about rationing are a constant, if not always apparent, feature of today's health and social care. Some commentators deny that it exists, others claim that it is inevitable. Older people usually feature somewhere in the rationing debates, either explicitly or implicitly, and age-based rationing is widespread, despite explicit government statements that withholding treatment on the basis of age is not acceptable (Smith, 1996).

A number of arguments are put forward for age to be used as a criterion for choosing who should be offered services, care and treatments, and who should not. These arguments were debated between Professor Alan Williams and Professor John Grimley Evans in 1997 and a selection of the arguments from the debate are discussed briefly here:

Younger people derive more benefit from treatment than older people. This argument is based on the assumption that health-care outcomes are directly linked to age and that a 50-year-old derives greater benefit from a treatment than an 80-year-old. This is not so. The physiological variability between individuals is considerable at any age, but this variability becomes markedly more pronounced with increasing age. It is true that, because of the increasing prevalence of impairments the risk to benefit ratio adversely increases with age so that, if physiological measurements are used to assess ability to benefit from treatment, more older people would be excluded than younger people. However, many older individuals function physiologically within the normal range for people much younger and therefore if the decision about ability to benefit is based on physiological (and one could argue psychosocial) variables, age ceases to become a criteria.

One of the major problems in assessing 'ability to benefit from treatment' is that many research studies, for example testing new drugs, exclude older people; protocols and treatment regimes are, therefore, recommended on studies of young fit people. So in many fields there is limited evidence on how best to treat older people. Despite this, as the MRC highlights (1994), what evidence we have suggests very positive, and sometimes even improved outcomes than younger age groups, for example in the treatment of cancers, high blood pressure, and myocardial infarctions.

The fact that older people receive a lower standard of treatment than younger people, because it is assumed that they will not derive equal benefit, is well documented. This is widespread and includes acute care, rehabilitation, and palliative and hospice care. It is particularly well documented in coronary units where older people are deprived of thrombolytic treatments, in cancer care and in renal transplantation (Grimley Evans, 1997). Older people are also denied access to routine breast screening, despite evidence that more cancers are detected (Horton-Taylor *et al.* 1996). In all of these areas, research has clearly demonstrated that older people actually derive greater benefit than younger people, yet age discrimination prevents them from doing so. Grimley Evans (1997) argues that this age-based rationing leads to premature deaths and unnecessary disability.

Younger people have a future, older people have had a 'fair innings' The 'fair innings' argument was used by Williams (1997), who described himself as a 'self-confessed oldie'. He said that 'a reasonable limit has to be set upon the demands we can properly make on our fellow citizens in order to keep us going a bit longer' and he argued that 'a lot more life is saved by treating a fit 50-year-old than a fit 80-year-old'. This argument assumes that the value of life is directly linked to the quantity of it, but how can the value of a life be quantified? This is the basis of quality adjusted life years (QUALYs) measurement.

If the 'fair innings' argument were to prevail, the decision in an accident and emergency department on which survivor of a road traffic accident should be the priority – the 18-year-old or the 68-year-old – would be straightforward. The priority would be given to the patient with the most life left to live – the value of life equated to its quantity. However, as Grimley Evans (1997) highlights, the decision seems less straightforward when it becomes apparent that the 18-year-old, whose blood alcohol was well over the legal limit, had driven head-on into three cars, and one survivor was the 68-year-old, a gifted scientist involved in important cancer research.

Decisions about the value of life are far too complex to be made on an age basis alone. It could be argued that the only person who can really place value on a life is the person living it and, contrary to some expectations, surveys have demonstrated that many older people value their lives highly (see above section on positive ageing).

Rationing saves money. This argument assumes that withholding treatment saves money, but this can be false economy. If thrombolytic drugs or coronary artery bypass surgery are not offered to an older woman, money will be saved. However, if she later requires to live in a nursing home for months, or years, because of her continuing angina, this money will be spent several times over. The same argument could be made for many of the new drugs being developed to limit long-term disability in people with arthritis, Alzheimer's disease or Parkinson's Disease. Palliative care can be as expensive, if not more expensive, than therapeutic treatment. Withholding treatment may save money in the short term – it will not necessarily do so in the long term.

Rationing debates and daily rationing decisions will continue. Rationing is an ethical and emotive issue but, as Grimley Evans (1997) argues, it is important to treat older people as individuals with equal rights and opportunities to others in society. He argues that patients should be not automatically viewed as if they conform to the generalisations accepted for that group and suggests that we could draw a parallel with social class or skin colour. Should we withhold health care from members of particularly groups in society on the basis of a poorer average outcome for their group. Rather, he contends, most of us would suggest that extra attention should be paid to vulnerable members of each group to try to compensate for their disadvantage. Why should older people not be viewed similarly?

SUMMARY

This chapter has explored a variety of perspectives on ageing and older people, and has set a context for the other chapters in the book. The chapter has emphasised that older people are unique individuals, each within a biography. Older age, like any other, is a subjective experience lived by individual people and each life history is influenced by personal memories and milestones within the experience of public events shared with others. The chapter has drawn distinctions between ageing that derives from genetic inheritance and environment or lifestyle, and aspects falsely attributed to ageing that derive from cohort characteristics, selective survival and the effects of differential challenge. It highlights the experiences of some individuals as they grow older, specifically those from different lands, and explores their ideas on age-

ing positively. The chapter reviews definitions of older age and demographic patterns within the UK and Europe. It explores aspects of the lives of older people, such as housing and economic resources, and highlights processes in Western Society which lead to disadvantage, such as ageism and structurally induced dependency. The chapter presents an analysis of health and social policy for older people in the UK and in Europe and, within this, highlights the emerging debate about age-based rationing. It also includes a review of the legacy of the development of services for older people, specifically in terms of the challenges that the speciality has overcome.

Working with older people is arguably the most important practice area for nurses in the future. The following chapters in the book demonstrate how nurses can work with older people in a way which is helpful, empowering, enriching, rewarding and enjoyable for both the older person and the nurse.

KEY POINTS

- Each older person is a unique individual within a unique biography.
- Older age is a period of experience along the journey through life, it is not the destination.
- Ageing is commonly viewed objectively, whereas, in reality, ageing is a subjective experience unique to each individual.
- Life experiences build into personal biographies, which act as 'filters' through which we view and interact with others.
- The vastly different life experiences of old and young people can present challenges to intergenerational understanding, particularly for younger people.
- Gerontology is a relatively young discipline and much early research has focused on ageing as decline and older age as a range of problems. Methodological challenges remain.
- Older people are heterogeneous individuals, but each generation or cohort of older people brings distinct characteristics that derive, for example, from lifestyles, or because they are the survivors of their generations. These characteristics are often wrongly assumed to be an aspect of the ageing process.
- Older people today are widely diverse individuals from all social groups, backgrounds, social classes and income levels, and ranging in age from 50 to over 100 years.
- The living circumstances of older people vary but many live alone, commonly in poorer housing than younger people, and receive much lower incomes. These factors can adversely affect their health and ability to remain independent.
- The older population from minority ethnic groups is small at present but will increase within the next 10–20 years. These people are often particularly disadvantaged in income, housing and health.
- Many older people feel positive about their ageing.
- Many of the negative Western perceptions of older people derive not from factors intrinsic to them as a group, but rather from the way in which society disadvantages and marginalises them.
- There is a degree of scaremongering about increasing numbers of older people. More older people does not necessarily mean a greater burden of dependency, and there is a 'breathing space' with respect to increasing age dependency until around 2020.
- Because of the dearth of research including older people, and the multiplicity of factors which influence statistics on health, illness and service utilisation in older age, these should be interpreted with caution.
- Older people, largely because of their diversity, have not formed a unified political force in the UK, as they have in some other countries.
- Age-based rationing is widespread in the UK but is based on false premises such as those which assume that rationing saves money, that younger people derive greater benefit, and that the value of life can be measured by its quantity.
- Nursing older people has overcome many fundamental challenges in its development and it is now poised for a bright future.

REFERENCES

About Japan Series. *Japanese families*. Tokyo: Foreign Press Centre, 1994.

Adams J. Human biography part (i): a personal approach. *Nurs Times* 1991a, 87:1–8.

Adams J. Human biography part (ii): different lives, different perspectives. *Nurs Times* 1991b, 87:1–8.

Baker D. *Attitudes of nurses to care of the elderly*, PhD Thesis, University of Manchester, 1978.

Bernard M, Meade K, eds. *Women come of age: understanding the lives of older women*. London: Edward Arnold, 1993.

Bowling A, Cartwright A. *Life after a death: a study of elderly widows*. London: Tavistock, 1982.

Bury M, Holme A. *Life after ninety*. London: Routledge, 1991.

Central Statistical Office. *Social trends 21*. London: HMSO, 1991.

Coleman PG. Adjustment in later life. In: Bond J, Coleman P, Peace S, eds. *Ageing in society: an introduction to social gerontology, 2nd edition*. London: Sage Publications, 1993.

Coleman PG. Assessing self-esteem and its sources in elderly people. *Ageing in Society* 1994, 4:117–135.

Crosby G, *European directory of older age*. London: Centre for Policy on Ageing, 1993.

Department of Health. *The health of elderly people: an epidemiological overview*. Central Health Monitoring Unit, Epidemiological overview series, Vol. 1. London: HMSO.

Evandrou M, Falkingham J. Benefit discrimination. *Community Care Supplement* 1989, 25 (May):3–4.

Evers HK. Tender loving care? Patients and nurses in geriatric wards. In: Copp LA, ed. *Care of the elderly*. Edinburgh: Churchill Livingstone, 1981.

Falkingham J. Dependency and ageing in Britain: a re-examination of the evidence. *J Soc Policy* 1986,18(2):211–233.

Gibson R, Little grains of sand, *British Medical Journal* 1981, 283:1647.

Grimley Evans J, Goldacre MJ, Jodkinson M, Lamb S, Savory M. Health: abilities and well-being in the third age. *The Carnegie inquiry into the third age: results paper No. 9*. Dunfermline: The Carnegie United Kingdom Trust, 1992.

Grimley Evans J. Can we live to be a healthy hundred? *MRC Newsletter 64*. London: Medical Research Council, August 1994.

Grimley Evans J. Rationing health care by age: the case against. *British Medical Journal* 1997, 314:11–23.

Grundy E. Live old, live well. *MRC Newsletter 64*. London: Medical Research Council, August 1994.

Gutmann DL. Psychoanalysis and ageing: a developmental view. In: Greenspan SI, Pollock GH, eds. *The course of life: psychoanalytic contributions towards understanding personality development Vol. III: adulthood and the ageing process*. Washington DC: US Department of Health and Human Science, 1980.

Harding T, Meredith B, Wistow G. *Options for long-term care: economic, social and ethical choices*. London: HMSO, 1996.

Hasky J. Families and households of the ethnic minority and white populations of Great Britain. *Popul Trends* 1989, 57:8–19.

Heath H. Caring for the older person. In: Hinchliff SM, Norman SE, Schober JE, eds. *Nursing practice and health care, 3rd edition*. London: Edward Arnold, 1998.

Help the Aged. *Living alone – sharing responsibility*. London: Help the Aged, 1995.

Holmen K, Ericsson K, Andersson L, Winblad B. Loneliness among elderly people living in Stockholm: a population study. *J Adv Nurs* 1992, 17:43–51.

Horten-Taylor *et al*. Response of Women Aged 65–74 to invitations for screening for breast cancer by mammography. *Journal of Epidemiology and Community Health* 1996, 50:77–80.

House of Commons. *Long-term care: NHS responsibilities for meeting continuing health care needs*. First Report, Session 1005–1996, HC19–1 Annexe 2. London: HMSO, 1995.

Hunt A. *The elderly at home: a study of people aged sixty-five and over living in the community in England*. London: Office of Population Censuses and Surveys, 1978.

Institute of Actuaries. *Financial long-term care in Great Britain*. Oxford: Institute of Actuaries, 1993.

Isaacs B. Is geriatrics a speciality? In: Arie T, ed. *Health care of the elderly*. London: Croom Helm, 1981.

Johnson MJ. That was your life: a biographical approach to later life. In: Carver V, Liddiard P, eds. *An ageing population*. Milton Keynes: Open University Press, 1985.

Keighley T. European perspectives. In: Wade L, Waters KA. *Textbook of Gerontological Nursing: Perspectives on Practice*. London: Bailliere Tindall, 1996.

Kuypers JA, Bengston VL. Perspectives on the older family. In: Quinn WH, Hughston GA, eds. *Independent ageing*. Rockville: Aspen Publications, 1984.

Laing W, Hall M. *The challenges of ageing: a review of the economic, social and medical implications of an ageing population*. London: The Association of the British Pharmaceutical Industry, 1991.

McGlone F. *Disability and dependency in old age: a demographic and social audit*. London: Family Policy Studies Centre, 1992.

McGlone F, Cronin N. *A crisis in care? The future of family and state care for older people in the European Union, occasional paper 19*. London: Centre for Policy on Ageing and Family Policy Studies Centre, 1994.

Midwinter E. Citizenship: from ageism to participation, *The Carnegie Enquiry into the Third Age, Research Paper Number 8*. London: Carnegie UK Trust and Centre for Policy on Ageing, 1992.

Midwinter E, Tester S. Poll's apart? Older voters and the 1987 General Election. London: Centre for policy on aging, 1987.

MRC. *The health of the UK's elderly people*, London: Medical Research Council, 1994.

Murphy E. Social origins of depression in old age. *Br J Psychiatry* 1982, 141:135–142.

Norman A. *Triple jeopardy: growing old in a second homeland*, London: Centre for Policy on Ageing, 1985.

Norton D, McLaren R, Exton-Smith AN. *An investigation of geriatric nursing problems in hospital, 2nd edition*. Edinburgh: Churchill Livingstone, 1975.

Office of Population Censuses and Surveys. *General Household Survey*. London: HMSO, 1980.

Office of Population Censuses and Surveys. *1991 Census: persons aged 60 and over in Great Britain*. London: HMSO, 1993.

Payne K. Global feminisation of care. *Elderly Care* 1995,7(6):96.

Perks RB. A feeling of not belonging: interviewing European immigrants in Bradford. *Oral History* 1984, 12(2):64–67.

Phillips J. *Private residential care: the admission process and reactions of the public sector*. Aldershot: Avebury Press, 1992.

Rabbitt PMA. Investigating the grey areas. *The Times Higher Education Supplement* June 1st 1984, 14.

Seabrook J. *The way we are*. Mitcham: Age Concern England, 1980.

Smith R. Rationing health care: moving the debate forward. *British Medical Journal* 1996, 312:1553–4.

Taylor A. *Older than time*. London: Harper Collins Publishers, 1992.

Victor CR. *Old age in modern society: a textbook of social gerontology*. London: Chapman and Hall, 1989.

Walker A. Poverty and inequality in old age. In: Bond J, Coleman P, eds. *Ageing in society*. London: Sage Publications, 1990.

Warner N. *Community care: just a fairy tale?* London: Carers National Association, 1994.

Warnes A, Law C. Elderly population distributions and housing prospects in Britain. *Town Planning Review* 1994, 56:292–313.

Wells T. Nurse/patient verbal communication in a geriatric ward. In: *Problems in geriatric nursing care*. Edinburgh: Churchill Livingstone, 1980.

Wilkin D, Hughes B. The elderly and the health service. In: Phillipson C, Walker A, eds. *Ageing and society: a critical assessment*. Aldershot: Gower, 1986.

Williams A. *Rationing health care by age: The case for, British Medical Journal* 1997, 314:8–20.

Young,M (Lord Young of Dartington). Dawn with age. *London Review of Books,* October 1990. Cited in Midwinter E, 1992.

2 Theories of ageing
Irene Schofield

LEARNING OBJECTIVES

After studying this chapter you will be able to:

- Describe the major biological, sociological and psychological theories of ageing.
- Formulate your own definition of ageing and be prepared to present it for discussion.
- Describe the major problems encountered in attempting to articulate a coherent, all-encompassing theory of ageing.
- Differentiate between life expectancy and life span.
- Describe the factors which contribute to the achievement of longevity.
- Discuss the influence of ageing processes on stability of personality.

INTRODUCTION

The subject of human ageing is a complex phenomenon and as the title of this chapter suggests, there is no single theory which explains how, why and at what rate ageing takes place. Rather there are many theories embracing the different disciplines that study human life and social interaction. In simple terms, ageing is used to describe changes in living organisms that are time dependent. The only certainty about human ageing is that the older person is more advanced in terms of time on the life-span continuum. Bernice Neugarten (1968) suggested that one of the most reliable observations about ageing in humans is the vast difference between individual older people, to the extent that they are the least homogeneous group in society. As people age, they become more differentiated and more unique. This uniqueness has often been overlooked, as biologists and social scientists have grappled with the 'problems' of ageing as they saw it, rather than from the point of view of older people themselves. This is gradually being addressed as gerontologists from many disciplines have begun to adopt study methods that reflect the lived experience of older people. This chapter aims to provide an overview of the most prominent and accepted theories of ageing. It is then up to the reader to attempt to combine them into a holistic view of the individual.

The following influences, acting singly or in combination, affect and describe the way individuals age:

Chronological Ageing

This denotes movement from one point in time to another. It is marked by annual birthdays. It is to some extent predictive as to how a person will age but it is by no means a definite indicator. It may be tempting to make assumptions about a persons physical and mental condition from knowing their chronological age, but this may well turn out to be incorrect.

Biological Ageing

This describes an individual's present position with respect to potential life span. It dominates people's ideas of what getting old is about. The emphasis tends to be on decline and deterioration, but a person can learn to make some compensatory adjustments. An individual's biological age can be younger or older than chronological age.

Psychological Ageing

This relates to mental capacities to adapt to a changing environment in order to achieve needs and wants. It requires effective functioning of cognitive, emotional and motivational processes.

Functional Ageing

This refers to a person's coping and practical skills. Mental and physical abilities are put to practical use.

Social Ageing

This refers to age-graded behaviours. People of a certain age are expected within a particular culture or society to fulfil certain roles and behave in particular ways. This might apply to type of dress, language and membership of institutions.

Definitions of Ageing

There appears to be few comprehensive definitions of human ageing. Most definitions have a biological focus and describe the gradual decline of cellular replication and function based upon either stochastic or non-stochastic theories. Stochastic theories propose error catastrophes in control mechanisms such as ribonucleic acid (RNA) that cannot be predicted but occur randomly. Non-stochastic theories involve those changes biologically 'intrinsic' to human beings and genetically programmed. Ebersole and Hess (1994, p. 25) suggest their own comprehensive definition:

> Ageing is an energy process beginning at conception that is directed by genetic endowments and impelled by perceived phenomenologic events, which sustain the process until the biologic mechanism ceases to function.
>
> (Ebersole and Hess, 1994, p.25)

Although the prospect of longevity may be attractive to some individuals, few scientists admit to seeking the key to extending the life span for its own sake. Rather the interest lies in gaining a clearer understanding of the biological ageing processes so as to find ways of preventing the onset of age-related disease. Rowe and Schneider (1990) describe this as the quest for 'successful ageing', which refers to older individuals demonstrating age-determined changes uncomplicated by disease, environmental exposures and lifestyle factors.

Anthropology and Ethnography of Ageing

Anthropological studies of older people in remote places have been published occasionally since the early nineteenth century. They are rarely exclusive studies of older people but rather are a part of a general cultural study. Titbits of information about how older people have been treated in other societies, cultures and subcultures have sometimes filled us with guilt, wonder or horror. In some less industrialised societies in the past, older people were treated with reverence and supreme care. Often there were few of them and only the very hardy and unusual lived to be very old. Also, these tended to be societies where food was not in short supply. On the other hand, the myth that older people were always revered in primitive societies is soon dispelled on reading Chapter 2 in de Beauvoir's book *Old Age*.

During the next decade, many members of ethnic minority groups living in the UK will reach retirement age. There is increasing interest among researchers to understand the experience of ageing amongst ethnic minority elders. Whilst researchers need to inquire about origins and customs, it is important that they do not lose sight of the fact that socioeconomic status and educational opportunities have much more to do with present lifestyle than origins of forbears. Ethnicity and ageing is discussed in detail in Chapter 19.

The basis of human life begins with the cell and cell division (meiosis and mitosis). This continues to shape the human organism with its varied systems at different rates of generation and regeneration throughout the life span. Theories of biological and physiological ageing relate to three different cell types:

(1) Cells that multiply clonally (meiosis) throughout life, such as white blood cells and epithelial cells.
(2) Cells that are incapable of division and renewal, such as neurones.
(3) Noncellular material with little turnover, that is under integrated physiological control, such as collagen and intercellular substances.

These cellular ageing processes result in mechanical failure of non-replaceable parts in organ systems, accumulation of metabolites, depletion or exhaustion of body reserves, and morphological problems of the cell development that gives organs size, shape and structure.

Different biological theories of ageing have held sway at different times. The theories described in this chapter are those which are most current and reflect the consensus views that ageing is caused by factors that damage the body, including radiation, toxic by-products of metabolism and random everyday damage by genes. The damage is not properly repaired and this may be due to lack of metabolic energy, hormone deficiencies, lack of genetic support or failure of the immune system (IS) (Kyriazis, 1994a). The theories which relate to endocrine and IS functioning are discussed in detail as they connect more readily with many nursing functions.

Stochastic Theories of Ageing

Stochastic theories suggest that ageing events occur randomly and accumulate with time. These theories include the gene theory, the disposable soma theory, the free radical theory and the cross-link theory.

Gene Theory

Supporters of this theory believe that we have a pool of advantageous and disadvantageous genes at birth. Natural selection protects individuals from the harmful effects of disadvantageous genes prior to reproduction, but, once this has taken place, disadvantageous genes cause deleterious effects almost without control, causing ageing, disease and death (Kryriazis, 1994b).

There is a second variation on the theory which suggests that certain genes (pleiotrophic genes) play a dual role: the juvenescent aspects function in early life and promote survival of the organism, and the senescent aspects have a deleterious effect and are activated in later life. This mechanism is known as antagonistic pleitropy. An example of the second variety is the female menopause. During the reproductive years oestrogen facilitates the normal reproductive cycle. At the time of perimenopause and menopause the oestrogen level declines, increasing the risk of arteriosclerosis and hypertension in women (Hayflick, 1987). The genetic theory is similar to the disposable soma theory in that ageing occurs as a result of natural evolution. For this reason they are classified as 'evolutionary theories of ageing'.

The most important recent discovery in genetics has come from the simple worm *Caenorhabditis elegans*. Researchers have succeeded in prolonging life in this species by generating random genetic mutations. A single gene, *age-1*, can increase the average life span of C. elegans by about 70%. Researchers are systematically mapping the involved genome with the expectation that it will lead to the discovery of genes controlling life span in humans. It is also hoped to be able to identify the genes that cause chronic and debilitating diseases such as Alzheimer's disease, Parkinson's disease (PD), arthritis and osteoporosis, with a view to finding a treatment through gene therapy.

Disposable Soma Theory

This theory advocates that immortality would waste energy better used for sexual reproduction and that senescence, therefore, is the price to be paid for sexual reproduction. The theory was proposed by Tom Kirkwood (1977) on the basis that human organisms have a fixed amount of physiological energy, which is divided between sexual reproduction and maintenance of the body cells (somatic cells). The somatic cells have capacities for repair until the end of the reproductive period, up to about 40 years of age. Once reproduction has occurred, the somatic cells become expendable, defects in cells accumulate and senescence begins.

The disposable soma theory lends support to the idea that ageing results from the destruction caused by molecules in the normal course of living, including the havoc caused by oxygen free radicals, and Cerami's glycosylation theory. Cerami (1986) postulated that glucose and other non-reducing sugars react with proteins over time in a non-enzymatic reaction to produce substances which cross-link with proteins. The accumulation of these altered proteins might account for conditions associated with ageing. It is thought that lens proteins undergo this process leading to cataract formation.

Free Radical Theory

The free radical theory, proposed by Harman in 1956, emphasises the importance of the mechanism of oxygen use by the cell. Free radicals are charged molecules that are produced during normal cell metabolism. They are also powerful oxidants and can destroy cellular components, particularly the lipids and proteins that make up the cellular membrane.

The greatest source of free radicals is the metabolism of oxygen, which produces the superoxide radical O_2^-. Oxygen is a highly reactive gas both inside and outside the human body. Internally, oxidation of protein, fat and carbohydrate results in free radical formation and unusable end products or compounds. Oxidation of polyunsaturated fats, for example, forms lipid peroxides that cross-link protein, lipids and deoxyribonucleic acid (DNA).

In the course of normal living, oxidation continually causes body destruction and produces a biological dichotomy. The body needs oxygen for metabolic survival but it also causes gradual self-destruction through the release of free radicals from perioxidation. Although body cells possess the capacity to eliminate unwanted waste and materials, neutralise by-products and repair damage, free radical accumulation is thought to be faster than the repair process of the organism. Scientists who favour the free radical theory consider the cell membrane to be the key to survival and think that the greatest damage is perpetuated by free radicals at this level.

Within the cell, metallic ions, enzymes and cellular materials combine with oxygen to form free radicals and compounds. Oxidation of cellular waste provides an additional source of radicals and electrons. In arterial walls, oxygen interacts with lipoprotein (a substance in the artery wall), forming free radicals. This plays an important part in the pathogenesis of atherosclerosis (Kyriazis, 1994a). When DNA, the genetic component of the cell, is irradiated, it also responds with free radical formation and establishes aberrant cellular growth and development, which bring about ageing. Copper, iron and magnesium in the body increase free radical activity by catalytic action in the oxidation process.

Free radical activity is also introduced into the body from the environment. The best-known source is air pollution. Other environmental sources thought to cause harmful cumulative breakdown effects in cells are oxidation of petrol in car engines, by-products in the plastics industry, drying linseed oil paints and atmospheric ozone.

In order to prevent damage from free radicals, mammals have developed defence mechanisms in the form of free radical scavengers. These are enzymes and other chemicals that circulate in the blood stream and attack free radicals. Several dietary supplements known as antioxidants are thought to increase the action of free radical scavengers. The mitochondria, major sites of cellular oxidation, are thought to be protected from the hazards of free radical activity by vitamin E (Walford, 1983). Studies exploring vitamin E's effectiveness as an antioxidant demonstrate that vitamin E deficiencies increase excessive lipid oxidation. At normal cellular levels of vitamin E, a slower oxidation rate occurs. Research continues into the role of vitamin E as an anti-oxidant and as a binding agent in the antioxidation process. Other anti-oxidants are vitamin C, beta-carotene, and the mineral selenium.

Certain enzymes degrade, neutralise or detoxify free radicals that attack the cell membrane. These free radical scavenging enzymes include superoxide dismutase, catalase and glutathione peroxidase. Reduced levels of glutathione peroxidase are frequently found in the brains of patients with PD and it is thought that increased free radical damage in the brain may be a causative factor. Free radicals are also linked to other age-related diseases, such as atherosclerosis, cataracts, diabetes and rheumatoid arthritis. Research at the

National Institute of Aging in the USA has found that the enzyme dismutase increases proportionally to metabolic rate with increased life span of various species. Individuals who enjoy high levels of protection against oxygen metabolism by-products (free radicals) should live longer than those with lower levels (Walford, 1983).

The body seems to be bombarded by both internal and external sources of free radicals. If this theory is as fundamental to ageing as proponents believe, monitoring the kind of food consumed and the environment should play an important role toward healthier ageing in the future. Food selection might be directed toward intake of items with high antioxidant properties and low potential for stimulating free radical activity.

Advocates of the free radical theory point to the fundamental microscopic nature of the theory and its relationship to the cross-link and chromosomal mutation theories. Research continues to determine the significance of an ageing pigment, lipofuscin, which accumulates in ageing tissue (predominantly in heart and brain cells). Lipofuscin is thought to be a by-product of lipid and protein fragmentation from perioxidation of the cell membrane. The significance of lipofuscin and the role of free radical scavengers and antioxidants continue to be explored in their relationship to the ageing process. **Figure 2.1** illustrates the dynamics of the free radical theory.

Cross-Link or Connective Tissue Theory

The cross-link theory is based on the internal and external behaviour of collagen, elastin and the ground substance in cells, tissues and extracellular substances. These materials are widespread and are involved in the transport and exchange of material for cell function.

This theory suggests that chemical reactions create strong bonds between molecular structures that are normally separate. Cross-link agents are so numerous and varied in the diet and in the environment that they are impossible to avoid. Aldehydes, minerals (copper and magnesium) and oxidising fats serve as biological reservoirs of cross-link-inducing agents. Lipids, proteins, nucleic acid and carbohydrates are major body chemicals that exist in repetitive, linear structural patterns and are capable of cross-linkage.

Saccharides are important ingredients in collagen, elastin and DNA. Collagen makes up about 25–30% of body protein and is important in physiological function and in some pathological processes (Sharma, 1988). Collagen forms the gelatinous cell matrix that is responsible for maintaining structural form, support and strength of tissues. High concentrations of collagen appear in the skin, tendons, bones, muscle, blood vessels and the heart.

Discovering the relationship between cross-linkage and ageing remains a scientific challenge. Cross-linkage is most rapid between 30 and 50 years of age but it is not yet known

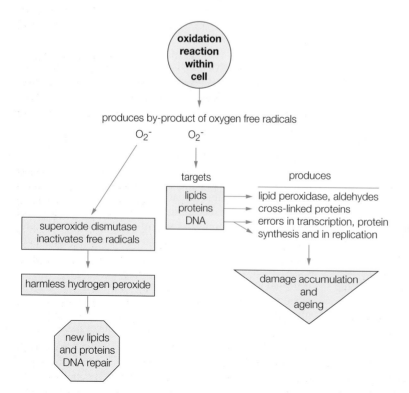

Figure 2.1 Free radical theory of ageing.

how to prevent this from occurring. The concept of cross-linkage can best be defined in terms of the behaviour and characteristics of collagen and elastin, components of connective tissue. Changes in connective tissue indicate that cross-linkage has occurred. Synthesis of new collagen reveals minimum signs of cross-linkage. With age, collagen develops an increased number of cross-links in both intracellular and intercellular structure. Ageing collagen becomes increasingly insoluble, chemically stable and progressively rigid as a result of the cross-link phenomenon. Consider agar or gelatin as an example of what possibly happens in cross-linkage. Gelatin, likened to collagen, loses its sheen, becomes firmer, cracks, and dries out when exposed to air, heat or sunlight for several days. Its original resilience and elasticity disappear. The sheen turns to a cloudy dullness. Likewise, collagen molecules dehydrate and develop a bonding pattern that links the molecules together.

Elastin in connective tissue mirrors collagen behaviour and is equally prone to cross-linkage. Old elastin is frayed, fragmented and brittle. Extracellular water diminishes and produces a concentration of calcium, sodium and chloride. Deposits of calcium salts are found throughout the cardiovascular system: in the epicardium and endocardium, in the valves of the heart and in the major blood vessels. Amino acids are considered to be part of elastin and also cross-link agents. Skin is one of the best examples of what happens in the cross-linkage of elastin. The change in skin texture and response with age is familiar to most people. Skin that was once smooth, silky, firm and soft becomes drier, saggy, and less elastic. Cross-linkage of skin tissue has been compared to the changes that occur in the tanning process of animal hides; chemicals applied to hides cause cells or molecules to stick together and transform soft stretchy skin into a shiny stiff leather. Connective tissue cross-linkage has a deleterious effect on cell permeability, fibril flexibility of muscles and heart contractility. The passage of gases, nutrients, metabolites, antibodies, and toxins throughout the vessels are all affected. Tendons become dry and fibrous, teeth may loosen, arterial walls lose elasticity and the lining of the lungs and gastrointestinal tract decreases in efficiency. DNA also is capable of cross-linkage (Hayflick, 1987). Linkage is attributed to free radicals that bind DNA molecules together somewhere in their chemical makeup. This raises the question of the possible relationship between the free radical and cross-link theories.

Non-stochastic Theories

Non-stochastic theories consider ageing to be predetermined. These theories include the neuroendocrine theory and immune theory, suggesting genetic programming of a specific time for the life span of an organism and programmed senescence, which brings about ageing of the entire organism.

Neuroendocrine Control Theory

The neuroendocrine control theory focuses on ageing as part of the life span programme regulated by neurohormonal signals that begin at the time of fertilisation and continue until death. Common neurones in the high brain centres act as pacemakers that regulate the biological clock during development and ageing.

Ageing is manifested in slowing down or activity imbalance of the pacemaker neurones in the hypothalamus that connect with the pituitary gland. The pituitary gland is considered to be in direct control of the thyroid, adrenals and gonads. With increasing age, some signal efficiency of the pituitary–hypothalamus connection is lost or changed, resulting in decreased function and an increase in pathology of most organ and tissue systems. Decline in function is brought about by a decrease in secretion of the following hormones:

(1) Oestrogens, which result in ending the reproductive capacity of the female.
(2) Growth hormone, which is essential to growth and development. It is thought to decline from the 'somatopause', which begins after sexual maturity.
(3) Melatonin secreted by the pineal gland, which interprets how the body perceives the passage of time.
(4) Thymosine produced by the thymus gland, which itself involutes in the first decade of life, gradually declining from the age of 20 years. Thymosine is necessary for the maturation and development of the immune system.

The performance of an organism relies on a variety of control mechanisms that regulate the interplay between different organs and tissues. With time, homeostatic adjustment declines – with consequent failure to adapt – and this is followed by ageing and death. Rudman among others has demonstrated that administration of growth hormone can reverse the effects of ageing by increasing lean body mass and decreasing fat. However, this has not been achieved without side effects. Current thinking suggests that understanding the age changes affecting the reproductive cycle due to the interconnectedness of so many neurotransmitters, may contribute to a better understanding of biological ageing in general (Wise and Krajnak 1996). **Figure 2.2** provides a visual schematic of the neurohormonal theory.

Immunological Theory

Studies of cell division in many vertebrate animals suggest that the cells of the immune system (IS) become increasingly more diversified with age. It has also been demonstrated that there is a progressive loss of self-regulatory patterns between the body and it own cells (Walford, 1983). The result is impaired surveillance by antibody cells or an autoaggressive phenomenon in which cells normal to the body are misidentified as alien and are attacked by the body's IS.

Control of the immunity is shared by the humoral (B-cell) and cellular (T-cell) systems. In brief, the humoral system provides protection for the body against bacterial and viral infection. This function occurs through activity of the plasma cells, tonsillar tissue, abdominal mesentery Peyer's patches and the peripheral lymph system. Cellular immunity delays hypersensitivity, causes rejection of foreign tissue cells and organ grafts, and provides protection against tumour formation through the activity of the thymus gland and its associated organs. The primary organs in cell-mediated immunity are the bone marrow and the thymus. The spleen and lymph nodes are also important but play a secondary role in cellular immunity. Lymphocytes produced by the thymus and bone marrow serve as precursor cells because they evolve through embryonic development in the organ tissue. **Figure 2.3** illustrates the sources and movement of the thymic-independent (B-cell) humoral system and the thymic-dependent (T-cell) cellular immune system.

Autoaggression

Lymphocytes generated and released by the lymph nodes are considered to be sensitised to specific antigens. These white blood cells are thought to develop a programmed self-recognition by the time an individual is 1 year of age. It has been hypothesised that regulatory cells, particularly the suppressor cells, diminish with age, allowing previously suppressed clones of autoactive cells to respond. Any antibodies that are not programmed by this time are identified by the body as foreign and treated as invading organisms. Antibodies of the cell-mediated (T-cell) immunity system are dispatched from the lymph nodes to engulf and break down the invasive antigens by phagocytosis. B and T cells are able to regulate the differential events of humoral and cell-mediated responses. The immune response of the cell-mediated system, although major, does receive immune assistance from the humoral system. However, cell-mediated reactions take place before

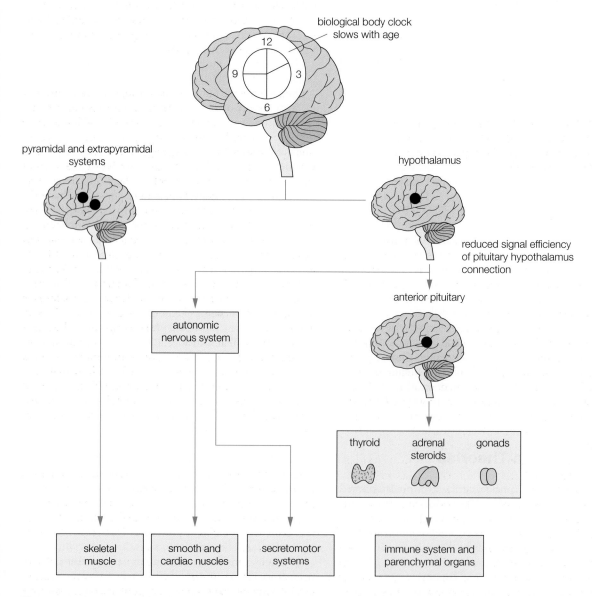

Figure 2.2 The neuroendocrine theory of ageing.

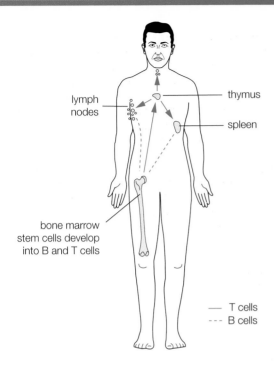

lymph nodes

thymus

spleen

bone marrow stem cells develop into B and T cells

— T cells
- - - B cells

Figure 2.3 Cellular traffic of the immune system (Source: Adapted from Finch C, Hayflick L, eds. *Handbook of the biology of aging*. New York: Van Nostrand Reinhold, 1977).

Graft-versus-host reaction experiments with mice have demonstrated significantly higher rejection rates of tissue grafts in older mice than in younger mice. This has lead to the postulation that greater cell aberration occurs with age and that cell self-regulation is greatly lacking (Makinodan, 1990). This might be one reason that wound healing and generation of healthy tissue seem to progress more slowly in older people, despite a healthy diet, rest and care.

Immunoglobulins, which contain two or more antigen-binding sites and other unique structures, are part of the humoral system and are responsible for the antibody activity of globulins. There is evidence that gamma globulin, rhesus factor, and antithyroid and anti-insulin antibody activity accelerates with increasing age (Rowe and Schneider, 1990). The possibility of IS exhaustion as a cause of ageing has been considered and may eventually explain the number of cases of adult-onset diabetes mellitus and rheumatoid arthritis exacerbations, as well as the development of other conditions among older individuals.

Depletion

Immunodeficient conditions such as infection, autoimmunity and cancer are thought to be the body's response to several types of events. Studies of newborn mice with slow virus infections showed a suppression of normal immune function. Mice infected with leukemogenic virus also responded with suppression of the IS. In long-lived mice the onset of the decline of immune function began early in life. Correlations can be made to human responses in similar situations, since the responses of laboratory animals give some indication as to what might occur in human tissue reactions.

The question arises whether all vertebrates harbour slow viruses that can induce the gradual decline in the IS with advancing age. It is reasonable to consider that a decline in IS function would occur since the function of all systems seems to diminish with age, and age-dependent anatomical and physiological changes (e.g. decreased secretions, dry skin and collagen changes) add to the disruption of the host's defence mechanisms. In addition, there is a simultaneous decline in the IS and increase in the autoimmune response. A decline in immunity would, therefore, allow malfunctioning immune cells to have an adverse effect. Decreased efficiency of the IS certainly increases vulnerability to disease and malignancy (Makinodan, 1990). **Figure 2.4** depicts the IS process of ageing.

humoral ones. Antibodies of the humoral system (B cells) circulate in the blood and attach themselves to antigens in sufficient numbers to dilute the antigens in a neutralising effect. Specific B and T cells respond to specific antigens by antibodies or by developing a tolerance so that re-exposure does not elicit a destructive reaction. Imbalance of B and T-cell activity gives rise to an increased production of autoantibodies. Cytotoxic effects occur in host tissue when thymic-deprived lymphoid cells are transferred to the peripheral lymphoid circulation. B and T-cell imbalance results in a compromise of the humoral mechanism, decreasing the body's immune surveillance capability and causing hypersensitivity to the autoimmune phenomenon. The cell-mediated T cells are responsible for hastening the age-related changes attributed to autoimmune reactions; the body battles against itself.

Haptens (low molecular weight compounds) in combination with natural body proteins form hapten–protein units. Antibodies mistake these hapten units for antigen and thus attack their own body protein (Guyton, 1986). The release of abnormal protein products during infectious episodes or the release in later life of particular antibodies, which have been dormant or sequestered in various immune system organs from the early development of the individual, is an additional cause for autoimmune responses. Research has shown instances of age-related autoimmune and immune-deficient responses.

Immune System, Disease And Ageing

Viruses and/or their antigens and corresponding antibodies comprise some of the antigen–antibody complexes. When these lodge in specific body sites, such as kidneys and arteries, factors damaging to the tissue are released and begin the process of deterioration. This may be instrumental in triggering or causing normal ageing and disease.

Autoimmune disorders and ageing may be correlated, as evidenced by several shared characteristics. Both processes exhibit lymphoid depletion and hypoplasia, thymic atrophy and increased plasma cells in lymphoid organs. The most relevant pathological change in the IS is thymic atrophy and that T cell-dependent immunity is probably related to decreased circulating thymic hormone levels (*see* **Figure 2.4**). Thymic transplants, as well as the administration of young thymocytes or thymic extract, were shown to be able to correct several age-dependent immunological impairments, such as antibody formation. In older people, hypergammaglobulinaemia is present, and tests for antibodies are positive. The alloantigen response (which requires B and T-cell cooperation) is also decreased. Two types of autoimmune and immunodeficient diseases exist: those that affect the young person and those that affect the older adult. Autoimmune and immunodeficient diseases in older adults illustrate the impact of the immunological theory on ageing. Cell-mediated immunity decreases in older persons and may be responsible for decreased survival.

Decline in the immunological state increases susceptibility to infection, autoimmune disease and cancer. Amyloidosis, cancer and adult-onset diabetes mellitus have been considered diseases of ageing that occur as a result of immunodeficiencies. Fibres that appear in amyloidosis are identified as chains of immunoglobulins and are present in various body organs of older individuals. The islets of Langerhans in the pancreas show signs of amyloidosis and complement-fixing anti-insulin antibodies. Cancer appears to be strongly influenced by immunodeficiencies, particularly those associated with immunosuppressant drugs. Individuals who require immunosuppressants are 80 times more vulnerable to cancer than those who do not receive such therapy (Makinodan, 1990).

Autoimmune mechanisms also contribute to atherosclerosis, hypertension and thromboembolism in certain susceptible people. Cardiovascular disease, allergic angiitis and rheumatic heart disease are considered partially the result of IS dysfunction. Senile plaques, found in ageing, degenerating human brain tissue, contain a large quantity of amyloid fibre. Studies of mice suggest that the cause of neuronal degeneration may lie in the neurone-reactive antibodies in the sera of older mice.

There is a growing interest in the effects of age on the mucosal IS. Evidence suggests that the secretory IS may be affected by the ageing process. It is known that secretory antibodies play an important part in protection of mucosal surfaces from a variety of pathogens. The complexity of the ageing regional IS suggests that factors (e.g. IgA antibody production) in local ocular, salivary, nasal and intestinal sites play a pivotal role in the larger immune response (Makinodan, 1990). The acute antibody response to extrinsic antigens, such as pneumococcal and influenza vaccines, is considerably reduced in older people. It is thought that circulating immunoglobin levels reflect increased response to intrinsic antigens (autoantibodies).

Cellular immunity most clearly exhibits an age-related decrease in functional ability. The decline of cell-mediated immunity with increasing age correlates with an increasing frequency of reactivation tuberculosis. However, while reduction in the levels of thymic hormones is clearly age related it is unclear if thymic involution is associated with increased susceptibility to infection.

Challenging the Immunological Theory of Ageing

No theory is without counter arguments. Studies at Duke University showed through cross-analysis and longitudinal analysis of immune changes that immunoglobulins increased with age in about two-thirds of the study population. A correlation was made between low blood levels of immunoglobin and failure to survive. However, normal to high levels of immunoglobulins were noted in the blood of long-lived individuals with various immunodeficiencies. This raises the question, 'To what extent do immunoglobulins affect ageing?' Cell-mediated immunity, presented earlier as a primary factor in immunity, was found to remain relatively intact for the whole life span in long-lived strains of experimental mice.

Biologists are looking at the field of immunoengineering for possible approaches to control the decline of the IS and to retard the ageing process. Through immunoengineering, the manipulation of the IS for the purpose of maintaining normal function might be achieved. The reasonable success of manipulation of some conditions in organ transplants may have been the impetus for attempts to pursue its benefits in ageing. A number of years ago, it was shown that the complicated IS was regulated by an aggregate of genes on a single chromosome. This cluster of genes was called the major histocompatibility chromosome (MHC), and is like a super blood-grouping system. Part of the responsibility of the MHC is self–antiself recognition. Susceptibility to many

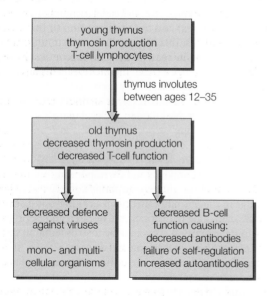

Figure 2.4 Immune system process of ageing.

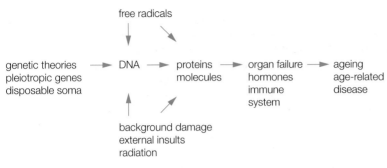

free radicals

genetic theories → DNA → proteins → organ failure → ageing
pleiotropic genes   molecules   hormones   age-related
disposable soma   immune   disease
                                   system

background damage
external insults
radiation

arrows indicate damaging influence

Figure 2.5 The interrelationship between the different theories of ageing. (Source: Kyriazis M. Age and reason. *Nurs Times* 1994b, 90(18):60–63. Reproduced by kind permission of *Nursing Times*.)

diseases of ageing, such as Alzheimer's disease, is influenced by the MHC type of the affected person, and organ graft survival rate is noted to be better when both donor and recipient have the same MHC type (Walford, 1983). Two approaches on which immunoengineering is focused are:

(1) Selective alteration by diet, temperature regulation and drugs in conjunction with surgery.
(2) Replenishment or rejuvenation.

Selective alteration is an attempt to suppress abnormal immune function through such actions as moderate protein restriction. This would depress the humoral system while leaving the cellular system intact. Severe diet restriction can delay or extend maturation of both humoral and cellular immune activity. High-fat diets have demonstrated an increase in autoimmunity, a propensity for autoimmune diseases and a decrease in cell-mediated immunity and life span (Makinodan, 1990). Immune factors have also been found to be temperature dependent. Diet restriction and mild hypothermia appear to enhance survival and alter patterns of immunity in test animals. Immunosuppressants have at this point provided marginal effectiveness in life span extension because of loss of autoimmune reactions. Surgical removal of the spleen in test animals before manifestation of immunodeficiencies occurred has shown limited results. Replenishment or rejuvenation of the human IS is based on the idea of injecting immune cells of a compatible young donor into older recipients. The intent is to return the IS of the ageing individual to its normal effective state.

In summary, immune responses are thought to affect age-related changes. Clues to this are offered through accumulated data that show that the IS begins to decline when the following effects occur:

(1) Thymic atrophy and possibly a decrease of thymic hormone (thymosine) in the blood.
(2) A significant increase in plasma cell activity.
(3) Circulating lymphocytes with an abnormal number of chromosomes are increased.
(4) An increase in immunoglobins in the blood.

Research has identified various diseases that may be linked to immunity and ageing. Selective alteration and replenishment or rejuvenation are immunoengineering challenges to control, moderate or eliminate the effects of autoimmunity, immunodeficiencies and perhaps, one day, the ageing process.

Towards a Unified Theory of Ageing

A unifying theory does not yet exist that explains the mechanics and causes underlying the biological phenomenon of ageing. It is apparent that some theories emerge from others and that one or more theories could be superimposed on others. Each theory in its own right provides a clue to the ageing process. Many unanswered questions still remain. **Figure 2.5** shows the interrelationship between some of the different biological theories of ageing contained in this chapter.

LONGEVITY

Longevity encompasses life span, life expectancy and healthy life expectancy. Life span potential is determined by genetic characteristics of a given species. It appears to be slowly lengthening in humans, reflecting changes in their genetic make up. Maximum life span for humans is governed by the age at death of the longest surviving member. This has now been recorded as 120 years.

Life expectancy in broad terms strongly reflects the severity of the environment and is defined by the age at which 50% of a birth cohort are found as survivors. Life expectancy in developed countries is continuing to rise; over the last 20 years life expectancy in the UK has risen from 76 to 79 years for females and from 70 to 74 years for males. **Figure 2.6** illustrates the changing pattern of survival. High infant mortality and deaths throughout the life span (A) have changed dramatically to the present situation of increased survival into later life (B). Curve (C) represents a future scenario where life expectancy is equal to maximum life span potential. This is sometimes referred to as squaring the rectangle of survival.

Although there have been gains in life expectancy, there is concern that healthy life expectancy has not grown with

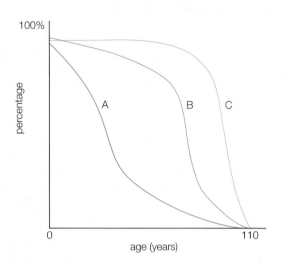

Figure 2.6 The changing pattern of survival. (Source: Hampton J. *The biology of human aging.* Dubuque, IA: Wm C Brown, 1991.)

months with a synthetic version of human growth hormone, a potent secretion of the pituitary gland. The dosage used remained within the limits of that naturally secreted in younger men. The variance between the two groups was significant. Those taking the hormone therapy regained 10% muscle mass, 9% skin thickness, and lost 14% of their body fat. While there were some side effects, Rudman indicated that, the treatment reversed body composition changes that would occur in 10–20 years of ageing.

Exceptional Longevity

Data gathered from these groups have been important in pursuit of maximum life span. Common factors influential to longevity are given in **Box 2.1**:

The value of under-nutrition as a means of extending life span seems to arise from lifelong patterns of minimum intake. High altitudes and decreased temperature may also be important factors. The claims of exceptional longevity from people living in the Caucasus and Andes mountains have proved questionable because of unverified birth records. In the case of the Caucasus, it was observed that as population and life expectancy were increasing, the number of centenarians was decreasing. It is now believed that at one time people falsified their birth records in order to avoid the army, thus claiming that they were older than in fact they were.

Animal studies have shown that a decrease of a few degrees centigrade in body temperature could add approximately 15–25 years to human life. One must be careful not to assume that a decrease in measured temperature means a decrease in metabolic rate. It is the core temperature that makes the difference. If the substance that triggers hibernation in animals could be isolated and transferred, researchers might seek ways to trick the human body into periods of torpor or hibernation, thus extending the life span. Drugs, biofeedback and yoga are other means that are also being explored as methods of lowering body temperature to extend life span.

Heredity

The most provocative studies of the influence of genetics on ageing adaptation come from the seminal work of Kallman and Sander and the Swedish Adoption/Twin Study of Ageing.

this rise. It has remained more or less constant at 59 years for men and 62 years for women (Office of National Statistics, 1997). This situation contradicts the two hypotheses put forward by Fries (1980). He suggested that there is a natural limit to human life span. He also proposed that a general improvement in health would lead to a reduction in the period of infirmity and illness associated with later life, (in his terms a compression of morbidity). However, in considering the statistics on morbidity, and hence healthy life expectancy, one must recognise that they are self-reported. As such, they probably reflect the increased expectations of people that they should remain in good health for longer. Increasingly, chronic disease and disability are less readily accepted as an inevitable consequence of the ageing process; however, in a US study by Mitteness (1987), older people reported symptoms of incontinence which they believed to be a consequence of ageing. Moreover, this view was reinforced by the doctors, of those who sought consultations.

The studies of life extension through food restriction have been conducted on rats. Not only do they live almost twice as long as the projected life span, but also they do not develop the disorders common to ageing rats. The theory is that life is prolonged by restricting food and thus increasing metabolic efficiency.

Some believe that humans may extend their physical and mental capacity in later years by continued use and stimulation. Brain dendrites grow when the brain is stimulated; muscles remain strong and resilient when used. Gradual physical decline begins early in youth but remains gradual if the lifestyle is not abusive. In 1990, Rudman, in a 6-month experiment, was able to reverse some symptoms of ageing in a group of men in their sixties and seventies. A comparable control group was also used (Darrach, 1992). The experimental group injected themselves three times a week for 6

2.1 Common Factors Influential to Longevity

- Dietary restrictions: low in fat, high in vegetable protein and fibre.
- Limited calorie intake.
- Exercise.
- Sociability.

The Kallman–Sander study surveyed cognitive similarities of 1000 pairs of twins over 60 years of age residing in the state of New York. Similarities for disease, life span and time of death were significant for identical twins, more so than fraternal twins. The authors concluded that genetic influences are primarily responsible for individual differences in ageing. The Swedish Adoption/Twin Study on Ageing includes a comparison of identical twins reared apart, which has added a strong component to the study of genetics and behaviour in later life. This ongoing, longitudinal study indicates at this time that, though remaining strong, the significance of genetics on behaviour in late life is probably less than earlier in life. However, there appears to be a similarity in life experiences between identical twins, and this may have a genetic basis.

Heredity, once thought to have a great influence on life span, is not considered as important today. An individual born of long-lived parents may live a very long life, but heredity is only partially influential in this process. The major developmental theorists of ageing (Baltes *et al.* 1980) propose that the older one gets the more one is influenced by non-normative life events. The last third of life requires very different adaptive capacities than the first two-thirds. Ordinarily, one is consumed with and measured by performance until the later years. In older age, existential issues move to the forefront: losses, transitions to roles not yet understood by society, living in the moment, defining meanings in existence and learning the measure of one's mettle. In addition, it has always been a problem to sort cohort variances and their influence on adaptation to given situations and life stages (Schaie, 1965).

Nutrition

Nutrition is receiving considerable attention as a major influence on longevity. Walford (1986), from his ongoing research, advocates the 'high/low' diet, a diet that provides the greatest concentration of nutrients with the least amount of calories. In the laboratory, Walford began restricted diets on rats at the time of weaning and found significant extension of life span. Restricted diets at weaning are not feasible for humans because they tend to decrease the ultimate body size. Studies conducted on adolescent rats found that restricting diets at this point in time was just as effective on life span extension as was weaning-initiated restriction.

Calorie-restricted diets for rats have received considerable attention in research. Findings show that dietary restriction hastens DNA repair. The theory of ageing based on the accumulation of DNA damage in somatic cells is an old one, but it was unknown whether repair of DNA was gradually diminished in the ageing process. These studies have shown that DNA repair processes are involved in ageing and not only does restricted calorie intake slow DNA error accumulation during ageing but also it facilitates the repair process, resulting in longer-lived mice.

Socio-economic Status

There is ample evidence to demonstrate the positive correlation between socioeconomic status and longevity. The Black Report emphasises the effect of continuity of circumstances throughout the life span. It suggests that in later life 'the relationship between income and the capacity to protect personal health is stronger than at any other time in the life cycle' (Townsend and Davidson, 1986, p. 133). Those people who are able to make financial provision for their later years, through savings or contributions to index-linked pension schemes, lead the healthiest and longest lives after retirement.

Statistics have shown that marital status influences longevity, particularly for men. Whether it is the result of mutual caring by the spouse that occurs in the relationship or because of a more regulated life-style has not been definitely established, but those who are married have a longer life expectancy than those who are single (Askham, 1995).

In the 25-year follow-up of the first Duke University longitudinal study on ageing, intelligence, health, activities, sexual relations and life satisfaction were all factors that contributed directly to longevity of the study group. Some of the questions yet to be addressed in order to understand factors influencing longevity are:

- What factors account for individual longevity?
- How can predisposition for diseases be determined?
- What accounts for the increasing longevity of women as compared to men?
- What are the effects of social class?
- What are the ultimate differences accrued by habits of smoking, exercise and diet?
- How are wisdom and creativity cultivated and demonstrated in older age?

The most critical questions do not concern how long we live, but for what reasons and in what conditions. Human progress can be measured by the total percentage of individuals who achieve longevity while maintaining a life of meaning and purpose. An integrative matrix, drawing from the psychologists, biologists and sociologists, to organise the considerable quantities of data and fragmented bits of information is still needed (Birren and Birren, 1990).

PSYCHOLOGICAL ASPECTS OF AGEING

The psychology of ageing is the study of changes in behaviour that characteristically occur after young adulthood. Behaviour in this sense includes the following (Birren and Birren, 1990):
- Sensation.
- Perception.
- Learning.
- Memory.
- Intellect.

- Motivation.
- Emotion.
- Personality.
- Attitudes.
- Motor movement.
- Social relationships.

The psychology of ageing attempts to 'discern laws governing the way humankind grows up and grows old' (Birren and Birren, 1990, p. 12). Several theoretical approaches describe psychological change in later life: cognitive and behavioural theories centre on age-related changes in intellectual functioning, cognitive ability and personality. Theory is developed as a result of experimental methods in laboratory conditions. Results tend to show a gradual increase in ability during the early years, reaching a peak in early adulthood, followed by variable but inevitable decline in later life. More recently, cognitive psychologists have come to recognise that it is performance in the real world that matters, and studies have been designed to take account of this (Rabbitt, 1988) (*see* Chapter 4 for in-depth discussion of cognitive change). Developmental theories, which describe human development as a series of qualitative leaps from one stage to another, began with the work of Piaget, who described discrete stages of cognitive development in children and the notion that each stage must be evaluated by tools appropriate to the stage and task. His methods and interpretations were later used by others to propose further stages of cognitive development in adulthood. The theories selected for discussion in this section are in the view and experience of the author to be the most useful in understanding ageing from a psychosocial perspective.

The most well-known developmental theory in the field of personality study came from Sigmund Freud. He described early stages of development with the basic nature of personality and sense of identity being established finally in adolescence and remaining stable thereafter. Freud did, however, acknowledge that how issues were dealt with in earlier life could have major repercussions later. Jung, a contemporary of Freud, was one of the first psychologists to define the last half of life as having a purpose of its own, quite apart from species survival – the development of self-awareness through reflective activity.

Jung's Theory of Individuation

Jung made a distinction between the first half of life, which is orientated to biological and social issues, and the second half of life, which is characterised by inner discovery. This midlife transition takes place at around the age of 40 years when 'individuation' occurs. Jung describes this as a developmental process by which the person becomes more unique and better able to use inner resources to pursue personal aims. The development of the psyche and the inner person is accompanied by a search for personal meaning and the spiritual self. Jung believed that a person who denies the validity of unconscious experience and the existence of the psyche is in self-conflict, consciously denying the relevance of the psyche because it reaches into obscurities beyond understanding. This denial of an aspect of one's nature results in restlessness, uprootedness, disorientation and meaninglessness.

Life Span Developmental Psychology

The life span developmental approach is concerned with issues of continuity and change across the life span. It assumes that developmental change can occur at any point in the life-course. This is contrary to the cognitive and behavioural theories derived from experimental studies, which seem to indicate that the attainment of adulthood is the end stage of a developmental change process, after which change is seen as decline. The following ideas are integral to the concept of psychological development:
(1) The organism is a dynamic system.
(2) Time is a quantifying element.
(3) Movement in time is toward complexity of organisation.
(4) Parts are incorporated into the whole.
(5) The highest state of organisation is self-regulatory.

Erikson's Developmental Stages

Erik Erikson is the best known exponent of the life span approach. He applies the theory of epigenesis to the total life span. This theory is based on the principle that 'anything that grows has a ground plan, and out of this ground plan the parts arise, each part having its time of special ascendancy, until all forms have arisen to form a functioning whole' (Erikson, 1980, p.53). Erikson formulated eight stages of ego development from infancy to older age. The development of the ego concerns an individual's experience of himself and it is this which determines behaviour throughout life. Each stage represents a choice or crisis and how that choice or crisis is dealt with affects all subsequent stages, the development of future personality and success in adapting to the world. The two final stages are most relevant to a discussion of later life concerns. The stage for middle adulthood is the development of generativity (expansion of ego interests and a sense of having contributed to the future) versus a sense of ego stagnation.

Generativity takes place through guiding the next generation. These might be one's own children, younger work colleagues or perhaps students. Ebersole and Hess (1994) describe the findings of an Institute of Human Ageing longitudinal study in north America, whereby Erikson and his wife interviewed the octogenarian parents of the original study subjects, who were at that time in their sixties. The older parents seemed to demonstrate all the stages identified by Erikson in his early work. The stage most obvious was caring, and although not as actively generative as in the earlier adult years, it was the most visible. For many, caring remained focused on children and grandchildren and seemed a vicarious way of continuing vital involvement in living. Others had grown beyond the central focus of the family, and their caring had more universal and altruistic components. For most of these older people, in spite of the multiple facets of generativity, concern for their children dominated their thoughts. In reflecting on the successes of their children they confirmed their own success as parents. The aspect of caring, so predominant in the adult years, is the quality that provides the greatest sense of continuity. As individuals nurture their young and watch their descendants nurture their young, they experience a connectedness, the repetitious nature of life cycles and at times an opportunity to revisit their youth. As the dialectic around caring is cultivated the older person is challenged 'to accept from others that caring which is required, and to do so in a way that is itself caring' (Erikson, Erikson and Kivnick, 1986, p. 74). Continuity and vicarious fulfilment are experienced as the older person sees qualities in grandchildren that are identified in the self, and their own parents, or grandparents. As many as six generations may be viewed in continuous progression in this way.

Although the life history data at the disposal of the Eriksons was rare and of an exceptionally longitudinal nature, they did not explore the dynamics of any individual lives over time but rather used the collective themes to support conclusions regarding the dynamics of older age, which in their view reiterated the issues of development earlier identified as continually providing the essence and meaning of life in the later years. Achieving each of the eight stages of psychosocial development produces the necessary strength for extension of the self in vital involvement with an ever-increasing social radius. The basic theme identified in this study is 'the remaining or new potentials of the last interactions and the vital (if paradoxical) involvement in the necessary disinvolvements of old age' (Erikson, Erikson and Kivnick, 1986, p. 33).

Integrity Versus Despair

Erikson postulated that the final task of later life is concerned with seeking a sense of integrity. As in other stages of his life span theory, he suggests there is a continuum of experience; in this last stage of life, the continuum lies between the experiences of integrity and despair.

Integrity is concerned with a sense of wholeness, uniqueness and worthwhileness, a feeling that one's life has been of value. Erikson is at pains to point out that integrity is not the same as achievement. Those older people who are unable to feel a sense of worthwhileness about their lives, he suggested may feel bitter, frustrated and hopeless about there being little time left to make amends. Like Butler (1963), Erikson suggests that there is a tendency to 'review' life in the later years. It is in this process of review that the individual may come to an evaluation of their life, struggling for a sense of wholeness or integrity. Nurses may witness this process of taking account, which may be spurred by health and social crises. Interestingly, questions have been raised as to whether integrity is indeed the highest development in older age.

Erikson's concept of integrity in older age and the concomitant ego attribute, wisdom, may not be attainable by many elders. The wisdom of older age is an adaptive perception of reality to elicit new meanings from prior experience. The wisdom of age paradoxically means a mode of knowledge beyond time or age. Unlike ordinary knowledge, wisdom leads to an apprehension of reality in its fullest. Wisdom of older age becomes a crisis of explanation in which the ordinary structures are shaken and the meaning of life is re-examined. It may include the wisdom of unknowing in the search for meaning in the last stage of life. It has been questioned whether it is necessary to attain wisdom to achieve integrity in older age and whether the epigenetic steps from young adulthood onward are ever fully achieved in a lifetime.

More recently, Erikson's wife Joan has extended her husband's original work to describe a ninth stage. This stage takes account of the increasing numbers of very old people who live long into their eighties and nineties and who face the challenges of daily life encumbered by frailty and disability. Joan Erikson (1997) uses the dichotomy of disgust versus wisdom to describe this final stage.

Balance

Erikson et al. (1986) propose that each of the major stages of development involves a balance of the 'syntonic' and 'dystonic' modes of coping if a person is to remain vitally involved. In other words, trust must be balanced with mistrust to achieve a vital adjustment that proceeds toward higher levels of development.

Too much trust results in maladaptation, which is considered neurotic, and too much mistrust results in malignant adaptation, which has the potential for psychoses. Trust is mandatory for development, but it can exist positively only in juxtaposition with a sensible mistrust. The balance of trust versus mistrust results in a sense of hope. The notion of too much and too little is vague and variable, but the contention is that if an appropriate individual balance has been achieved the individual is hopeful. Likewise, for each of the other stage dichotomies the balance must be achieved.

The process of bringing into balance feelings of integrity and despair involves a review of and a coming to terms with the life one has lived thus far.

(Erikson *et al.* 1986, p. 70)

All individuals have a central mental tendency to organise experience, a function of the ego.

Erikson and associates found that many informants refrained from mentioning any former discontent with their lives, although the data indicated periods of profound discontent. The researchers speculate that the omissions may be from a desire to construct a satisfactory life view by 'pseudo-integration'; the need to maintain their privacy; a lifelong process of recasting and finding new meanings in events; denial; or putting traumatic events over the years into perspective. Those who seemed best adapted were able to draw sustenance from the past but remained vitally involved in the present (Erikson *et al.* 1986).

Although Erikson's theory can be useful in helping nurses to understand the behaviour, priorities and aspirations of older individuals, it is not without criticism. For example, the dialectic concepts are difficult to measure and give no clues to the central issues of a person's life. The concepts are culturally and socially specific, implying the need for conformity to particular age-related roles. As a result, the theory does not allow for alternative self-created routes to the achievement of integrity. Social environments may prohibit development through epigenesis and Erikson himself later acknowledges that favourable conditions are needed for the attainment of wisdom. Coleman (1993) cites the work of Gutmann, who suggests that modern Western societies do not provide favourable conditions in which older people can flourish. Gutmann claims that 'a coherent culture with well defined traditions is the necessary context for the development of wisdom in later life'. Nurses, particularly those working in care homes, have the potential to create microenvironments conducive to individual resident's psychological development.

Erikson is to human development what Maslow is to motivation. Each has provided the depth and clarity of concepts that provide an organisational framework for nurses to categorise behaviours and understand dynamics of individuals. Eagerly, gerontologists have awaited further refinements of Erikson's thoughts regarding old age. Each of the epigenetic stages of psychosexual development occupies a progressively increasing period of one's life until the last two, which may last decades, but clearly there must be distinctive and characteristic psychosexual issues that emerge periodically throughout maturity and into very late life.

Erikson and his wife (1986) have reconsidered his seminal work from the perspective of their own ageing and from the experience of a select group of their cohort, 29 surviving parents of the subjects from the Institute of Human Development study already referred to above.

Peck's Psychological Developments for the Second Half of Life

Robert Peck (1968) carried forward Erikson's work, to produce quite specific psychological developments for the second half of life, related to the establishment of identity (see **Box 2.2**). It is clear that to achieve integrity by Peck's model the older person must develop the ability to redefine self. In middle age, this means no longer relying on outward physical attributes for acceptability, relying on the companionship aspects of relationship rather than the sexual, having the ability to shift emotional attachments as losses may begin to occur, and being open to new ideas and new learning opportunities. In older age, key tasks are to let go of occupational identity, to rise above bodily discomforts and to establish personal meaning that goes beyond the scope of self-centredness. Peck's theory can prove valuable in helping nurses assess clients' adjustments to inevitable changes. However, in part, it appears to have been made obsolete as a result of environ-

2.2 Psychological Developments in the Second Half of Life

Middle age
- Valuing wisdom versus valuing physical powers.
- Socialising versus sexualising in human relationships.
- Cathectic (emotional) flexibility versus cathectic impoverishment.
- Mental flexibility versus mental rigidity.

Older age
- Ego differentiation versus work role preoccupation.
- Body transcendence versus body preoccupation.
- Ego transcendence versus ego preoccupation.

Source: Peck R. Psychological developments in the second half of life. In: Neugarten B, ed. *Middle age and aging*. Chicago: University of Chicago Press, 1968.

mental change. Expectations of mid life are such that the areas Peck designated for adjustment are perhaps more relevant to older age.

Havighurst's Tasks for Later life

Robert Havighurst (1972) defines a developmental task as 'a task which arises at or about a certain period in the life of the individual, successful achievement of which leads to his happiness and to success with later tasks, while failure leads to unhappiness in the individual, disapproval by the society, and difficulty with later tasks'. Havighurst's developmental tasks are also based on the epigenetic principle and though they echo the concerns of Erikson and Peck, they are more concrete. The tasks arise at a certain point in time, determined by physical maturity, social expectations and individual aspirations. The influencing factors may operate singly or in combination, depending on the nature of the task. The tasks span six life stages but only those for later maturity will be illustrated here (**Box 2.3**). Nurses will readily recognise areas which involve transition and adjustment, for their older clients.

Levinson's Eras

Levinson *et al.* (1978) proposed a stage theory based on data from an in-depth study of 40 middle-aged, middle-class men. The informants were asked to give retrospective descriptions of their own lifecourse. Levinson *et al.* described the stages of overlapping transition periods as 'eras'; a new era is under way as the previous one is being terminated. The researchers described four stages then added a fifth, though the final stages could not be based on the experience of their original informants (**Box 2.4**). The changes within each era consist of biological, psychological and social aspects of the 'character of living'. The sequences of eras give structure to the life cycle, and provide a framework for developmental periods.

Readers should note that the final stages are not based on observation or report and might ask do they truly reflect the late-life experiences of the majority of older people. It is also important to acknowledge that the data describes the lifecourse experience of men only, when in fact women are the majority of late-life survivors. Nurses who are interested in reading more about theories of life-span development could look at the work of Charlotte Buhler (1964) and Roger Gould (1978). Birren and Birren (1990) believe that as more theorists and investigators mature who have their primary training in the field of gerontology we can expect more theories to emerge that are seminal rather than borrowed from other life stages or disciplines (**Figure 2.7**).

Influences on Life-span Development

The contribution of Baltes *et al.* (1980) to the field of life-span development is a more flexible model and unlike the theories so far described, it is not culturally specific. Three sets of influences act and interact during the passage of an individual's lifecourse to produce life-span development: Normative age-graded events exert their peak effects in childhood and to a lesser extent in later life. Examples of normative events are learning to walk, leaving school or retiring from paid work. Normative history-graded events occur to most members of the same cohort: examples are economic depressions causing severe social hardship, wars and social change associated with modernisation, such as the development of the motor car. Non-normative life events are the unexpected or events which are out of synchronisation with what is considered to be normal for one's cohort (**Figure 2.8**). Such events can have a biological cause such as the onset of dementia, or an environmental cause such as a divorce. They might also be determined by a combination of both factors, such as the older woman with osteoporosis who falls and fractures her hip who then requires institutional care.

Baltes *et al.* (1980) speculated that non-normative events take on an increasingly important role in determining the course of human development in adulthood and older age. Non-normative events are responsible for the increased heterogeneity and plasticity (capacity for change) in later life (**Figure 2.9**). The dynamic relationship between the individual and the environment in this model, provide a much more integrated account of the human life span.

The Life Review Process

Butler described the growth potential for older individuals through the 'life-review' process (1963). His hypothesis was that approaching death prompts review, as a response to the biological and psychological fact of death. This looking back process is set in motion by looking forward to death. Butler

2.3 Tasks for Later Maturity

- To adjust to decreasing physical strength.
- To adjust to retirement and decreased income.
- To adjust to death of one's spouse.
- To establish links and friendships with one's age group.
- To adopt and adapt to social roles in a flexible way.
- To establish satisfactory living arrangements.

Source: Havighurst R. *Developmental tasks and education*. New York: David McKay, 1972.

2.4 4th and 5th Stages

Late adulthood

In the early sixties, middle adulthood ends and the transition to late adulthood begins. Illness and retirement may shape transitional processes. The individual is less interested in obtaining rewards offered by society and more interested in utilising his or her own inner resources. The approach of death is contemplated, but a broader perspective on the human race may develop. Levinson *et al.* along with Erikson (1986) and Butler (1963) believe that there is a need to review life and make reparation.

Late late adulthood

Levinson *et al.* later proposed a fifth stage, as more people are living into their late eighties At this time, they concede that most people have infirmities, and the process of decline is more evident than growth. Life structure tends to be confined to a small territory, and a small number of significant relationships. Their main preoccupation is with immediate bodily needs and personal comforts. Under conditions of severe personal decline and social deprivation, life in this era may loose all meaning. Under more favourable conditions, however, development can take place.

Sources: Levinson DJ, Darrow DN, Klein EB, Levinson MH, McKee B. *The seasons of a man's life*. New York: AA Knopf, 1978; Butler RL. Life review: an interpretation of reminiscence in the aged. *Psychiatry* 1963, 26:65; Erikson EH, Erikson JM, Kivnick HQ. *Vital involvement in old age: the experience of old age in our time*. New York: Norton, 1986.

believed that by reviewing the past, unresolved conflicts might be surveyed and reintegrated into a present acceptance. However, if these conflicts remain very intense, the process of integration may be hard; integration may never happen for some people who may experience severe depression. More positively, meanings of past experiences might be revised and the person may reach a deeper understanding of past events. Hidden themes may emerge and change the quality of lifelong relationships. These can assist in 'the evolution of candour,

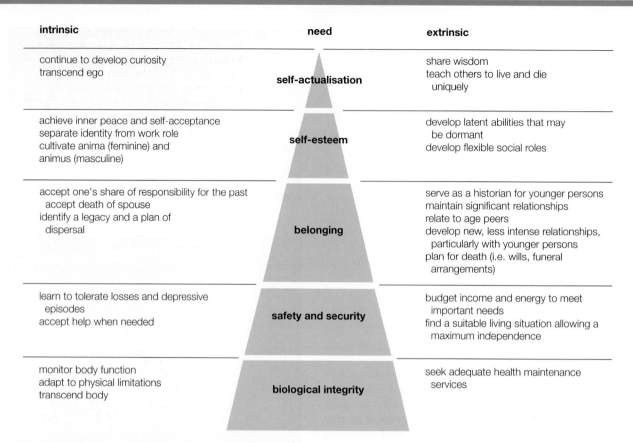

intrinsic	need	extrinsic
continue to develop curiosity transcend ego	**self-actualisation**	share wisdom teach others to live and die uniquely
achieve inner peace and self-acceptance separate identity from work role cultivate anima (feminine) and animus (masculine)	**self-esteem**	develop latent abilities that may be dormant develop flexible social roles

accept one's share of responsibility for the past
accept death of spouse
identify a legacy and a plan of
  dispersal
	belonging	serve as a historian for younger persons
		maintain significant relationships
		relate to age peers
		develop new, less intense relationships,
		  particularly with younger persons
		plan for death (i.e. wills, funeral
		  arrangements)

learn to tolerate losses and depressive
  episodes
accept help when needed
	safety and security	budget income and energy to meet
		  important needs
		find a suitable living situation allowing a
		  maximum independence

monitor body function adapt to physical limitations transcend body	**biological integrity**	seek adequate health maintenance services

Figure 2.7 Developmental tasks of later life in hierarchical order (Source: Peck R. Psychological developments in the second half of life. In: Neugarten G, ed. *Middle Age and aging*. Chicago: University of Chicago Press, 1968; Havighurst R. *Developmental tasks and education*. New York: David MacKay, 1972; Ebersole, 1976; Butler, Lewis, 1977.)

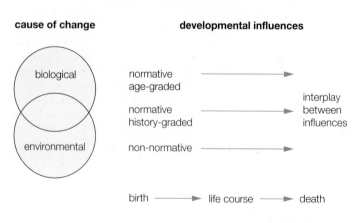

Figure 2.8 Baltes, Reese and Lipsitt's multicausal and interactive model of life-span development (Source: Baltes PB, Reese HW, Lipsitt LP. Life-span developmental psychology. *Annu Rev Psychol* 1980, 31:65–110). With permission, from the Annual Review of Psychology, Volume 31, ©1980, by Annual Reviews.

serenity and wisdom' (Butler, 1963, p. 65) for some people. Nurses who are caring for older people at this time are often present when they begin this review process. With understanding, nurses can respond positively by giving time to listen and helping the older person complete any unfinished business. Butler's observations confirmed Jung's views that reflective activity is intense and healing for many elders. Butler wrote:

The old are not only taking stock of themselves as they review their lives, they are trying to think and feel through what they will do with the time that is left and with whatever emotional and material legacies they may have to give others.

(Butler, 1975, p. 412.)

The task of transmission may be made more urgent in the presence of vulnerability or recent trauma (Fitch, 1992).

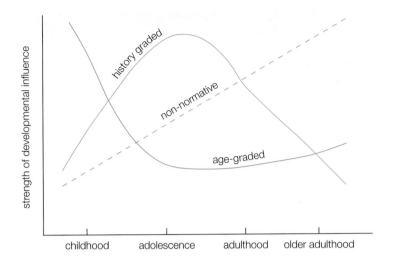

Figure 2.9 Influences of history-graded, non-normative and age-graded events throughout the life span (Source: Baltes PB, Reese HW, Lipsitt LP. Life-span developmental psychology. *Annu Rev Psychol* 1980, 31:65–110). With permission, from the Annual Review of Psychology, Volume 31, ©1980, by Annual Reviews.

Achieving Transcendence

Fitch (1992) points out that when we visit our older relatives we see the same old house, same old furniture and sometimes we may believe the people are as unchanging as their surroundings. Very little is known about the developmental issues and phases of the very old. With encouragement, older people will share their understanding of life and forge additional links in the chain of understanding that grows with each generation. Fitch (1992) suggests that the psychological tasks of older age are:

- Slowing.
- Life-review.
- Transmission.
- Letting go.

These describe activities rather than issues of development. Developmental tasks certainly include arrival at a personally acceptable philosophy of existence that transcends the limitations of the ageing body and its systems.

The task of letting go may sound deteriorative but perhaps it really means letting go of the non-essentials, the facades and charades, the need to conform and please, of long held hurts and slights, of the need to brood over injustice. Nirvana? Perhaps it is a Western version of an Eastern concept that is poorly understood in the West. Older age may hone a person to the essential simplicity of existence in its most penetrating sense. The pace of this process is unique to each individual. We can support or undermine these developments by the attitudes we hold and the environment we create (Fitch, 1992). Fitch says the last phase of life involves a shift from conceptual thought to a more intuitive, emotional mode. She suggests:

There is an organic, evolutionary dynamic in the elderly that happens even in the midst of confusion, and which
is tremendously potent and valid. There is some real victory and celebration possible even in the midst of existential decrepitude. We must do all that we can to see that everyone has that final and crowning opportunity.
(Fitch, 1992, p. 106.)

Morality

The classic theory of Kohlberg proposes that crises and turning points of adult life are moral dilemmas and he postulates that these form structural stage changes analogous to Piaget's cognitive operations in youth. The last stage of moral development is defined as 'universal ethical principle orientation'. This fits nicely into the Eriksonian model of development because integrity is built on morality and ethics. However, Kohlberg subsequently had reservations that few older people would reach this level of moral development.

Moral reasoning in later life may take on a very pragmatic function corresponding to changes associated with one's position in the life span. The nature of moral decisions in older age may be characterised by a shift from purely logical justification to a dialectic resolution between justice and personal caring.

Competence

The founders of ego psychology recognised the importance of stimulating experiences and mastery of new situations. According to them, the ego is continually striving for more challenges rather than a state of rest or satisfaction. An invigorating environment is needed to maintain an energising level of stress. Accordingly, individuals do not seek homeostasis (a steady state) but rather stimulation. This has important implications for older people. Most older people have had many experiences, and new situations occur with less frequency. Some are isolated from the mainstream of life and may deteriorate from boredom and lack of stimulation (*see* Chapter 12). Experiments with sensory deprivation seem to confirm this notion. Perhaps the most challenging stimuli for older people are maintaining autonomy and independence.

Commitment to mastery or competence is critically linked to motivating drives, incentives, needs and the degree of control over one feels. Satisfaction can arise from several channels, although opportunity for mastery relates to social class, health, life stage and gender. In older age, it seems that sense of control is an important precursor of successful coping.

Personality

The concepts of personality are based on several theoretical viewpoints:
(1) Psychoanalytic.
(2) Psychometric.
(3) Behaviourist.
(4) Environmental.

These viewpoints determine the expectations of personality in older age. The neopsychoanalytic viewpoint looks to childhood for the formation of lifelong personality traits. The psychometric view is related to the identification and measurement of specific personality traits, such as extroversion–introversion, neuroticism and psychoticism traced through the life cycle. Descriptive studies of personality traits and age are of considerable interest to psychometricians. The behaviourist concern is more focused on what older people do that is observable and can be measured. Motivation is not of major interest to behaviourists. The environmentalists contend that traits and situations are both potent predictors of adaptation in later life and that in some persons personality traits predominate and for others situations are more influential to development. It is difficult to sort out personality traits that are developed or suppressed because of experience rather than age. To further complicate the issues, certain personality traits tend to emerge strongly in particular situations and with particular persons.

Personality under ordinary conditions is assumed to remain quite stable across the adult life span. Such personality traits as stability, sociability, imaginativeness, neuroticism and openness to experience do not seem to change when studied longitudinally and cross-sequentially. However, the use of personality inventories does indicate a slight shift towards introversion in the extroversion–introversion domain (Coleman, 1993).

Personality stability seems to be a central belief of most life span psychologists. They have grouped traits into three domains that may be measured with some degree of validity and reliability using various instruments. The domain divisions are:
(1) Neuroticism (evidenced by anxiety, hostility, depression,

Meeting Psychological Needs

Florence Maxwell, a long-standing resident in the care home where you work as a primary nurse, has just celebrated her 100th birthday. She is a little hard of hearing and needs to use a wheelchair as a result of severe arthritis. Mrs Maxwell says, 'I'm like an old motor that's falling to bits'. However, for her years she seems physically robust and is very determined. Her slight deafness results in limited interactions and puts her at risk of isolation. However, she has a loud booming voice and readily 'barks' out precise instructions to ensure that her needs are met. Mrs Maxwell has never had children, and her husband died many years ago. She willingly talks about her marriage, saying that it was very unhappy. Her husband drank away his wages and never gave her any money. She has little association with other residents and seems to have kept her distance from potential friendships in the past. Mrs Maxwell does, however, seem to have a soft spot for you, and regards you as her only friend.

- **What are Mrs Maxwell's comments that provide subjective evidence of her psychological development and her attitude to life in general?**
- **What theoretical approaches might you draw on to help you understand Mrs Maxwell's motives and aspirations at this time?**
- **Suggest two areas for nursing intervention that have the potential to be most helpful to Mrs Maxwell at this time.**
- **Suggest the nursing aims for each area of intervention, reflecting outcomes and using concrete and measurable terms.**
- **Suggest one or more interventions for each chosen area of unmet need, justifying your choice of intervention.**

self-consciousness, impulsiveness and vulnerability to stress).
(2) Extroversion (evidenced by warmth, gregariousness, assertiveness, activity, excitement seeking and positive emotions).
(3) Openness (manifested in fantasy, aesthetics, feelings, actions, ideas and values).

Empirically, it would seem that all of these components of personality exist in each individual. Some are nurtured by various families and societies, and some are squashed. Recent studies confirm that even minor personality characteristics may be genetically predetermined or at least are strongly dis-positional. Personality influences the adaptation of the indi-vidual at any given stage. The following questions need to be investigated:

- How do the lives of introverts differ from the lives of extroverts?
- Do neuroticism and poor coping styles interfere with an orderly life plan?
- What personality dispositions influence adaptation to stressful life events?

The question that has not been addressed by gerontologists is 'what happens to persons who have unstable personalities as they age?' Stability of personality over time is in itself a personality characteristic. In other words, some persons will act in very predictable ways throughout their life and others seem to have a thread of inconsistency in their life patterns and actions. Age as a developmental variable does not appear to be strongly related to most personality traits in healthy, community residents, although serious disease states, brain pathological conditions and institutional living may bring about major personality changes.

Personality factors, cultural age norms and expectations interact in undetermined ways to affect the individual life course. In short, the uniqueness, the highly prized fruit of a long life well lived, is the very factor that belies our efforts to predict norms for the later years.

SOCIOLOGICAL THEORIES OF AGEING

It has been suggested that sociological theorists have focused on the activities and lifestyles of older people and neglected to describe how ageing fits into the mainstream of social, political and psychological theory. There remains much scope for theory development in this area.

The development of social gerontology occurred in the early 1950s in response to compulsory retirement, accelerat-ing technological change, increased social and geographical mobility and growing numbers of older people surviving beyond retirement age. The issue of how older people could be accommodated into this rapidly changing social world was the main preoccupation. Adjustment to loss of role and suc-cessful ageing were, therefore, major themes in this early work.

Many of the social theories of ageing are underpinned by the idea of structural functionalism, in that behaviour, attitudes and values are formed by the organisation and struc-ture of the society in which we live. The following theories are all cast in this mould:

Role Theory

Status and role are the concepts around which norms, rela-tionships, conformity and deviance, and stability and change are organised. Rosow (1985) considers four problems involved in applying role concepts to older people:

(1) Is there a role?
(2) What are the boundaries?
(3) What are the interactions with other roles?
(4) What are the levels of the role performance?

When considering the role of older people in our society we might examine the regard in which they are esteemed as a measure of role relevance, boundaries and performance. Rosow identifies the major issues in role theory as applied to older people:

- Loss of roles excludes older people from significant social participation and devalues their contribution.
- Older age is the first stage of life with systematic status loss for the entire cohort.
- Persons in our society are not socialised to the fate of ageing.
- Because there is no specified role for older people, their lives may become unstructured.

Informal and tenuous roles are identified by Rosow as those lacking structure and stability and not linked to social status. In late life, it is expected that institutionalised roles will decrease in number and significance while the tenuous roles will increase in significance if not in number. Tenuous roles are those that embody a definite social position but with vague or insubstantial role expectations (Rosow, 1985).

The principle exponent of role theory in the UK was Parsons. Role theorists saw cessation of paid work as an enor-mous loss for older people, who were made to take compul-sory retirement. Much has been written about the presumed negative effects of being in this state of rolelessness in a soci-ety which views the production of goods and services as inte-gral to its survival. The theory emphasised the impact of roles in determining behaviour, though to a great extent this has been contested. However, the need to prepare for retirement was seen as important and it has been suggested that prep-aration for retirement courses have evolved as a result of role theorists, who stressed the need for a positive means of man-aging the transition (Fennell et al. 1988).

Disengagement Theory

The disengagement theory of Cumming and Henry (1961, p. 2) stated that 'ageing is an inevitable, mutual withdrawal or disengagement, resulting in decreased interaction between the ageing person and others in the social system he belongs to'. The authors contended that disengagement was a uni-versal, inevitable and healthy process. Society retracts because of the need to fit younger people into slots once occupied by older people, who are no longer dependable as they were, in order to maintain the equilibrium of the system. Individuals choose to retract because of an awareness of their diminish-ing capacities and the short time left before death. The authors stress that this is a harmonious arrangement between the individual and society, which did not lead to any loss of morale, wellbeing or life satisfaction for the older person. The theory was seen as universal and applicable to older people in all cultures, although there were expected variations in timing and style.

Although the theory was controversial, it did attempt to counteract the wholly negative view of later life at that time (Coleman, 1991). Subsequent studies challenged the view of disengagement as inevitable; the Health and Lifestyles Survey (Blaxter, 1990) and Getting Around After 60 (The Gerontology Data Service, 1996) provide evidence that older people continue active participation in all aspects of living, well into older age. Reasons for withdrawal are ill health and other stresses associated with ageing, such as bereavement and caring responsibilities. Other critics have suggested that the theory encourages negative aspects of social policy and attitudes towards older people by providing a rationale for retirement, a low level of state pension (as older people's needs are seen as less), poor transportation facilities and custodial residential institutions, as opposed to community care (Coleman, 1991). It marginalises older people by giving support to ageist policies as well as giving the message that older people have little to offer.

Activity Theory

The activity theory (Havighurst, 1963) supports the maintenance of regular actions, roles (formal and informal) and solitary as well as social pursuits for a satisfactory old age. Activists began to champion the notion that older age was only an extension of the middle years and could be abolished by keeping active. The activity theory may make sense when individuals live in a stable society, have access to positive influences and significant others, and have opportunities to participate meaningfully in the broader society if they continue to desire to do so. Attempts at clarifying activity theory as a general concept of satisfactory ageing have not been supported.

The theory is idealistic in the sense that activity may eventually be limited for some older people by the onset of ill health and chronic disease. It may be unrealistic because the economic, political and social structure of society prevents the older person from maintaining the major activity of adult life, that of paid employment. Alternatively, some people may be looking for a more leisured lifestyle in later life.

Continuity Theory

The continuity theory, proposed by Neugarten (1968), focused on the relationship between life satisfaction and activity as an expression of enduring personality traits. Personality was considered the important factor in determining the relationship between role activity and life satisfaction, and personality was seen to be not only enduring but also becoming more clearly delineated with ageing. Three ideas important to this perspective, remain fundamental to beliefs about the ageing individual:

(1) In normal ageing, personality remains consistent in men and women.
(2) Personality influences role activity and investment in same.
(3) Personality influences life satisfaction regardless of role activity.

Political Economy Theory

This UK theory, first described by Townsend (1981), proposes that peoples' experience and status in later life is the direct consequence of political and economic policies. He gives the following examples:
• Older people are forced into a structured dependence as a result of compulsory retirement, thus having to live on a much reduced income.
• Others then may enter residential care homes, where any attempt to remain independent is discouraged by staff and deemed unnecessary.
• For older people living in their own homes, community care services are laid on without asking clients about their real needs.

Johnson (1987), among others, has criticised the political economy theory on the grounds that the research supporting its development has focused on the small number of people resident in care homes. Also, rather than constricting older people's lifestyles, the state retirement pension and development of welfare has brought a security of income and a range of choices to a large number of people.

Any future development of theory will take place in the chaotic context of a post-structuralist modern world, where the continued rapid pace of change, the absence of moral certainty, the enormous proliferation of information and the drive to create new markets for consumer goods provide the opportunity for most members of society to create new identities and roles.

ADDITIONAL APPROACHES

The Biographical Approach

For the most part, social gerontologists have tended to concentrate their research efforts on needs assessment with a view to determining social policy. To this end, retirement, social networks, disability, carers and older people's living arrangements have been the subjects of many surveys. The use of predetermined survey questionnaires may collect hard facts but do not always capture the individual's true needs. This was recognised by Johnson (1978) who advocated the use of biography as a means of data collection in the research domains of health and welfare. Johnson argues that studies of needs assessment have concentrated on dependency needs, disabilities and problems rather than strengths and abilities. Central to the approach is the biographical interview, whereby the client is encouraged to tell their life story. Salient aspects of the story are then used to interpret the client's personal meanings and motivations, with a view to determining current needs (Johnson, 1978). The biographical approach has applications in nursing assessment and reminiscence and will be revisited in Chapters 1, 4, 17 and 20.

Life Transitions

Transitional periods are a major focus of understanding ageing from a sociological perspective. The transitions throughout the lifecourse include major shifts attributed to age, role, occupation, family and economics (Cunningham and Brookbank, 1988). (*See* **Figure 2.10** for distribution of these transitions.)

Changes are stressful but often provide opportunities for growth because they require development and application of distinctly different adaptive skills. For many of the major transitions in life we receive little preparation, and in those cases they may be especially traumatic. In cases of role accumulation, such as that of grandparent, the experience of having been a parent will be applicable, with modification, to the new role. Likewise, the shifts in filial relationships are often gradual and do not require complete role deletion or role reversal. Those transitions that make use of past skills and adaptations may be least stressful. Some shifts, such as from functional independence to functional dependence, cut across many aspects of life and require several transitional shifts. Chapters 14, 16 and 18 address some of these issues.

From a lifecourse perspective, the transitions and adaptations required produce both stability and change in individual preferences, capacities, expectations and behaviour. Age-related transitions are socially created, shared and recognised. A transition is socially recognised and entails a reorientation of perceptions and expectations of and by the individual. It is also important to remember that cohort and gender differences are inherent in all of life's major transitions. Chapter 17 discusses in detail some of the major later life transitions (see **Figure 2.10**).

Social Supports

Social support is derived from the assurance of love, esteem and belonging to a network involving common and mutual concerns. This certainly sounds like the ideal social support a person would wish from intimates and family. However, the social support derived from informal ties may be much less intense but every bit as vital in older age. Friendships, neighbours and spontaneous social ties may increase in later life. Social gerontologists are interested in these types of social supports and how such interpersonal ties contribute to the health and wellbeing of older individuals. Chapters 16 and 17 refer to the work of key UK researchers whose work emphasises the importance of sustaining social networks in later life.

SUMMARY

The complexities of ageing and the numerous predictable and unpredictable events that occur in an individual lifetime have made many theorists conclude that ageing in adulthood is a random process of change with no discernible patterns or

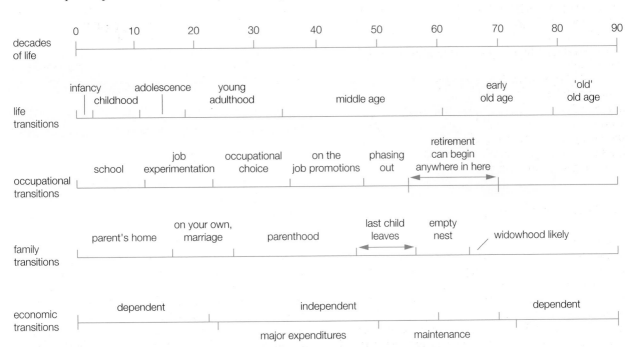

Figure 2.10 Life transitions (Source: Cunningham W, Brookbank J. *Gerontology: the physiology, biology and sociology of aging*. New York: Harper & Row, 1988).

underpinning theory. From this viewpoint, the individual organism progresses through the ordered state of programmed development to the chaotic state of later life in which patterns are no longer discernible; when the undefined, and perhaps individually developed, critical thresholds of function are exceeded and incapacity results. However, even though at this time there is not sufficient conceptual sophistication to embrace the intricacies of adult development, we continue to try to organise our expectations of the ageing process into predictable, or at least foreseeable, patterns.

There are still many areas of adult development and ageing that have been minimally explored and may be the essence of development in maturity and older age. The development of love, compassion, creativity and wisdom are areas that need considerably more attention and may in the future yield specific patterns in older people. Tentative theories of ageing recognise changes in conception of time, self-concept, hope, and future orientation as the individual grows older. The sense of inner control has important ramifications in terms of how a person ages. Living well in older age is an art, a science and a challenge. These first two chapters have attempted to introduce the reader to an overview of ageing as it is seen in our society today. The body of the text will consider the relevance of all these views to health-care provision and explore them in depth in further chapters.

KEY POINTS

- Ageing is a gradual process of change over the course of time. Chronological age is only one indication of how an individual will age.
- Biological theories of ageing can be categorised as stochastic theories, where ageing events occur randomly and accumulate over time, or non-stochastic theories, which consider ageing to be predetermined. No single theory accounts for the age changes which occur at all levels of structure.
- Each species has an expected life span and that of humans is at present limited to 120 years.
- There is widespread agreement that personality remains relatively stable with ageing, though there may be some tendency towards introversion.
- Psychological theories of ageing can be useful in helping nurses understand the behaviour, priorities and aspirations of older people in their care. However, it is important to remember that theories may be cohort and culture specific.

AREAS AND ACTIVITIES FOR STUDY AND REFLECTION

In the case study on page 38:
- What factors would you consider important in determining Mrs Maxwell's longevity?
- Discuss Mrs Maxwell's physical changes as they relate to theories of ageing.
- Which of the psychological and/or sociological theories of ageing seem most relevant in Mrs Maxwell's case?
- Discuss the factors in longevity that have already been identified and whether these are evident in the cases of individuals you have cared for.

REFERENCES

Askham J. The married lives of older people. In: Arber S, Ginn J, eds. *Connecting gender and ageing*. Buckingham: Open University Press, 1995.

Baltes PB, Reese HW, Lipsitt LP. Life-span developmental psychology. *Annu Rev Psychol* 1980, 31:65–110.

Birren J, Birren B. The concepts, models and history of the psychology of aging. In: Birren J, Schaie KW, eds. *Handbook of the psychology of aging, 4th edition*. San Diego: Academic Press, 1990.

Blaxter M. *Health and lifestyles*. London: Routledge, 1990

Buhler C. The human course of life in its goal aspects. *J Hum Psychol* 1964, 4:1.

Butler RL. Life review: an interpretation of reminiscence in the aged. *Psychiatry* 1963, 26:65.

Butler R, Lewis M. *Ageing and Mental Health: positive psychosocial approaches, 2nd edition*. St Louis: Mosby, 1977.

Butler R. *Why survive? Being old in America*. New York: Harper & Row, 1975.

Cerami A. Aging of proteins and nucleic acids: what is the role of glucose? *TIBS* 1986, 11:311–314.

Coleman P. Retrospective Reviews. *Ageing and Society* 1991, 11:217–220.

Coleman P. Psychological Ageing. In: Bond J, Coleman P, Peace S, eds. *Ageing in Society*. London: Sage, 1993.

Cumming E, Henry W. *Growing old*. New York: Basic Books Inc, 1961.

Cunningham W, Brookbank J. *Gerontology: the physiology, biology and sociology of aging*. New York: Harper & Row, 1988.

Darrach B. The war on aging. *Life* 1992, 15:38.

Ebersole P. Developmental Tasks in Late Life. In: Burnside I, ed. *Nursing and the Aged*. New York: McGraw-Hill, 1976.

Ebersole P, Hess P. *Toward healthy aging, 4th edition*. St. Louis: Mosby, 1994.

Erikson EH. *Identity and the lifecycle: a reissue*. New York: Norton, 1980.

Erikson EH, Erikson JM, Kivnick HQ. *Vital involvement in old age: the experience of old age in our time*. New York: Norton, 1986.

Erikson J. *The life cycle completed: extended version with new chapters on the ninth stage of development*. New York: Norton, 1997.

Fennell G, Phillipson C, Evers H. *The sociology of old age*. Milton Keynes: Open University Press, 1988.

Finch C, Hayflick L. (eds) *Handbook of the Biology of Ageing*. Van Nostrand Reinhold, 1977.

Fitch V. The psychological tasks of old age. *Naropa Inst J* 1992, 8:91.

Fries JF. Aging, natural death, and the compression of morbidity. *N Engl J Med* 1980, 303:130.

Gould RL. *Transformations: growth and change in adult life*. New York: Simon & Schuster, 1978.

Gerontology Data Service. *Getting around after 60: a profile of Britain's older population*. London: HMSO, 1996.

Guyton AC. *Textbook of medical physiology, 7th edition*. Philadelphia: WB Saunders, 1986.

Havighurst RL. Successful aging. In: Williams RH, Tibbitts C, Donahue W, eds. *Processes of aging, Vol.1*. New York: Atherton, 1963:299–320.

Havighurst R. *Developmental tasks and education*. New York: David McKay, 1972.

Hayflick L. Biologic aging theories. In: Maddox G, ed. *The encyclopedia of aging*. New York: Springer, 1987.

Johnson M. That was your life: a biographical approach to later life. In: Carver V, Liddiard P, eds. *An ageing population*. Milton Keynes: Open University Press, 1978.

Johnson P. *Structured dependency of the elderly: a critical note*. London: Centre for Economic Policy Research, 1987.

Kirkwood TBL. Evolution of ageing. *Nature* 1977, 270:301–304.

Kyriazis M. Free radicals and ageing. *Care of the Elderly* 1994a, 6:260–262.

Kyriazis M. Age and reason. *Nurs Times* 1994b, 90:60–63.

Levinson DJ, Darrow DN, Klein EB, Levinson MH, McKee B. *The seasons of a man's life*. New York: AA Knopf, 1978.

Makinodan T. Gerontologic research. In: Beck J, ed. *The year book of geriatrics and gerontology*. St Louis: Mosby, 1990.

Mitteness LM. So what do you expect when you're 85: urinary incontinence in later life. *Res Sociol Health* 1987, 6:177–219.

Neugarten B. Adult personality: toward a psychology of the life cycle. In: Neugarten G, ed. *Middle age and aging*. Chicago: University of Chicago Press, 1968.

Office of National Statistics. *Social Trends*, 1997.

Peck R. Psychological developments in the second half of life. In: Neugarten B, ed. *Middle age and aging*. Chicago: University of Chicago Press, 1968.

Rabbitt PMA. Social psychology, neuroscience and cognitive psychology need each other; (and gerontology needs all three of them). *The Psychologist: Bulletin of the British Psychological Society* 1988, 12:500–506.

Rosow I. Status and role change through the life cycle. In: Binstock R, Shanas E, eds. *Handbook of aging and the social sciences, 2nd edition*. New York: Van Nostrand Reinhold Co, 1985.

Rowe J, Schneider E. Aging processes. In: Abrams W, Berkow R, eds. *Merck manual of geriatrics*. Rahway: Merck Sharp and Dohme Research Laboratories, 1990.

Sharma R. Theories of Ageing. In: Timirus PS, ed. *Physiologic Basis of Geriatrics*. New York: Macmillan, 1988.

Schaie KW. A general model for the study of developmental problems. *Psychol Bull* 1965, 64:92.

Townsend P. The structured dependency of the elderly: creation of social policy in the twentieth century. *Ageing and Society* 1981, 1:5–28.

Townsend P, Davidson N, eds. *Inequalities in health: the Black report*. Harmondsworth: Penguin, 1986.

Walford RL. *Maximum life span*. New York: Norton, 1983.

Walford RL. *The 120 year diet: how to double your vital years*. New York: Pocket Books, 1986.

Wise PM, Krajnak ML. Menopause: the aging of multiple pacemakers. *Science* 1996, 273:67.

BIBLIOGRAPHY

Binstock R, George L, eds. *Handbook of aging and the social sciences, 4th edition*. San Diego: Academic Press, 1995.

Birren J, Schaie K, eds. *Handbook of the psychology of aging, 4th edition*. San Diego: Academic Press, 1995.

Olshansky SJ, Carnes BA, Cassel CK. The aging of the human species. *Sci Am* 1993, 268:18–24.

Ricklets RE, Finch CE. *Aging a natural history*. New York: Scientific American Library, 1995.

Rusting RL. Why do we age? *Sci Am* 1992, 267:87–95.

Saul H. Can we grow younger? *New Scientist* 1994, 1913:22–24.

Schneider E, Rowe J, eds. *Handbook of the biology of ageing, 4th edition*. San Diego: Academic Press, 1995.

Slater R. *The psychology of growing old*. Buckingham: Open University Press, 1995.

Health and wellness
Mary McClymont

LEARNING OBJECTIVES

After studying this chapter you will be able to:

- Define and discuss the concepts of health and wellness, explaining the dimensions of wellness.
- Recognise and value the central part that older people have played, and continue to play, in promoting their own health and wellness, and support this.
- Compare and contrast the medical model and the wellness model, with particular reference to older people.
- Identify and explain the multidimensional nature of health promotion, with its components of health education, health protection and disease prevention, clarifying its relevance for older people.
- Give a brief overview (citing recent research) of the current health status of older people within the UK, describing the screening and health maintenance services available to them, with particular reference to the needs of social and ethnic minority groups.
- Examine and discuss the current strategies for promoting and maintaining the health and wellness of older persons, with particular reference to their implications for nurses and health visitors.

INTRODUCTION

The last three decades have been characterised by marked demographic changes, so that the UK population is now slowly but steadily ageing. Statistical predictions indicate that this trend will continue, with the current 16% of persons aged 65 years and over rising to 20% by the year 2025. The most marked increase will be among those aged 75 years and upwards. Life expectancy from birth has risen, currently being 74 years for men and 79.5 years for women. This highlights several points. Firstly, that premature death is being reduced, so that more people are now achieving longevity – surely cause for celebration. Secondly, indicating the statistical risks which older persons face, now that over 78% of all deaths occur in persons aged 65 years or more. However, such figures mask the fact that the indices currently used to measure the health status of population groups, are entirely negatively stated. That is, they focus mainly on the three Ds, Death, Disease and Disability, but give little indication about how those who survive and are not diseased or disabled fare. Hence, they disregard the large numbers of older people who now enjoy long periods of good health, experience heightened wellbeing, and are finding their later years times of personal growth and great fulfilment.

Does this mean that in any discussion of health in later years we should ignore these negative but vital statistics? The answer is 'certainly not', for they tell us important facts concerning past achievements, present problems and future challenges. For example a study of current mortality statistics indicates that women have significantly lower death rates than men in each of the age groups from 65 years onwards. This causes us to pause and ask 'why' and 'can this be redressed?' Additionally, analysis by social class reveals marked differentials, with those in the three lower socioeconomic groups experiencing 60% greater risk of earlier death than those in the two higher groups (Victor, 1991). Surely indicating the scope for further research and improvement. For instance Goldblatt (1990) points out that women over 75 years, living in local authority housing and without access to a car, have a standardised mortality ratio 20 per cent higher than those owner occupiers of comparable age with cars. Facts such as these confirm that material advantage is critical for an older person's sense of wellbeing, and prompt calls for appropriately designed policies to reduce inequalities in health among older age groups.

Furthermore, although the major causes of mortality for those 65 years and over remain broadly similar between groups (namely ischaemic heart disease, stroke, malignant diseases and respiratory diseases), there are distinct ethnic variations. Indians demonstrate greater risk of death from coronary heart disease, while Bangladeshi elderly show almost twice the normal risk for stroke. The pattern also changes slightly with advancing years, for all racial groups, so that stroke and respiratory diseases tend to predominate more in those aged 85 years and upwards. Elements of prevention can clearly be seen in relation to many of these conditions.

Cohort differences concerning the causes of mortality also present. For example, the rising lung cancer rates among males aged 65 years and above reflect the prevalence of smoking among men in the first 70 years of this century. This can change dramatically in the future if smoking is effectively prevented.

Grimley Evans *et al.* (1992, 1993) point out that mortality in later life will likely continue to fall, as efforts to prevent premature deaths throughout the life span continue. However, the impact of conditions such as AIDS upon older people has yet to be determined and it is possible that female deaths from lung cancer may rise for a period, as cohort effects show their increased rates of smoking from the 1930s onwards. Optimistic forecasts may be confounded by further variations in mortality within ethnic groups and the damaging effects of deprivation and unemployment which have prevailed within the middle-aged population in the past few years. Nevertheless, this brief review of the mortality picture indicates not only the opportunities for improvement which exist, but serves as a timely reminder concerning the impact made upon families, friends and society, through the loss of experienced older people.

Morbidity in the Later Years

Although as noted, the majority of older people are living active lives and contributing to their communities, the years with long-standing illness that limit daily activities currently stand at a mean of 15 years for men and 17.5 years for women, indicating a further challenge still facing society and particularly those in the health-care professions. The relationship between disability and age was confirmed by The National Disability Prevalence Studies [Office of Population, Censuses and Surveys (OPCS), 1988] which revealed that 69% of all disabled adults were aged 60 years or over (4.2 million persons) with rates rising within each age group and for each severity category, so that the 'oldest old' are at greatest risk. Even so, one must be aware that two out of three persons aged 60 years and over are not disabled. There is increasing evidence that these rates may well improve, given timely and effective intervention. This means people can remain active, disability-free, socially engaged and productive throughout the majority of their life span (Bone *et al.* 1995; Colvez, 1996). Moreover, many older individuals who are presently chronically sick or disabled triumph over their incapacities to live abundant and contributing lives, especially when they receive facilitative and supportive help in health maintenance, as Sidell (1997) records.

Understanding the extent of morbidity among older people, and hence enabling persons to deal appropriately with it, is a highly complex matter. Partly because in the past data have not been comprehensive and were not always linked, and partly because UK research has been limited, particularly regarding longitudinal studies. However, more recently, much useful information has been provided by The Carnegie Inquiry into the third age (Carnegie UK Trust, 1990), which studied persons in the age range 50–74 years and, among various aspects, examined their health, abilities, function and wellbeing. These reports indicate that there are important conditions which call urgently for attention, because of the suffering they cause. Conditions such as osteoarthritis, osteoporosis, incontinence, depression and dementia, together with

vision and hearing difficulties. Many of these are amenable to preventive action (Grimley Evans *et al.* 1992, 1993). All raise issues about improving the quality of life for older individuals.

Quality of Life

The term quality of life has gained currency over the past few years, but tends to be used interchangeably and often without being well defined. Farquhar (1995) has reviewed this. Her research with older people showed that, for those living at home, meanings of quality of life included good health and the opportunity to maintain family relationships, social contacts and activities. Her conclusions highlight the need for health personnel to use tighter definitions when considering quality of life for older people, and when assessing their wellbeing, to focus as much on their ability to maintain social contacts as they do to their functional competence. In fact, to use a truly holistic approach. This raises the need for more positive health indicators to be used when measuring health status in older people.

Catford (1983) recognised such a need and suggested some indicators relevant to individuals, their physical environment and their socioeconomic conditions. Few as yet have been introduced, demonstrating just how far we still have to go in health promotion! Meantime, we note that ill health and disability not only spawn a greater interest in self-care among the older population (so calling for greater awareness of their needs among health personnel), but accelerate demands upon health and social services. So there is a strong case on personal, professional and socioeconomic grounds for robust action to promote the health of older people [Health Education Authority/Centre for Policy on Ageing (HEA/CPA), 1996].

The Impact of Consumerism on Health in Later Life

Coupled with these trends, a burgeoning interest in health matters in all sections of society and the rise of consumerism have led to the growth of the self-health movement and an increasing focus upon holistic health. Cumulative client reactions to a prevailing sense of loss of control over their health, together with the increasing medicalisation of health problems, has led people of all ages to seek greater autonomy in health care and a more participative role in decision-making. Older people with years of experience in exercising responsibility for their own, and often their family's, health are no exception. Many of them do not want to passively accept situations and services, preferring instead to take an active part in their own ageing. Eager for further information in order to discover the various options available to them, they are ready to question and to use a range of services, rather than rely solely on professional direction, so fostering a partnership approach to health promotion and health care. This was confirmed in research undertaken by Young (1996). Those within a public health setting, such as health visitors, who work mainly with the well population, and community nurses who recognise that they work as guests in their clients' homes, are highly aware of the need for a shared approach to health promotion, conscious that the final decision rests always with their clients. There are increasing indications that more nurses within other settings, such as hospitals, also regard themselves as patients' partners. Meutzel (1988) observes this when arguing that it is one of the duties of the nurse to establish a contract of shared power, control and responsibilities acceptable to both. Mackintosh (1995) advocated greater empowerment of clients and patients, as a means of securing effective partnerships, and this is in line with the current thinking expressed in recent documents such as the White Paper on the new National Health Service (NHS) [Department of Health (DoH), 1998a] and the Green Paper on public health (DoH, 1998b). However, Wright (1995) questions whether some nurses are yet ready to change their attitudes. The extent to which this shift in the balance of power and equality is being achieved has been reviewed by Latter *et al.* (1992) and by Ward (1997), whose research indicates that a much wider understanding of the concept of health promotion is required among nurses, and that the activity needs to be practised more by those working with older people.

The Impact of Organisational Change on Health in Later Life

Throughout the 1990s, organisational changes within the NHS have added impetus to moves to involve health service users in their health care. Examples include the Patients' Charter, with its named nurse system and the shift of emphasis to primary care led services. Now new proposals advance this notion of contract whereby the Government, local communities and individuals will join in partnership to improve all our health (DoH, 1998b). This builds on the growing awareness that responsibility for health is everybody's business. Health promotion is now visible on the UK government agenda. Beginning with the publication of the *Health of the Nation* strategy for England and other similar initiatives in Scotland, Wales and Northern Ireland [DoH, 1991; Welsh Office, 1989; Scottish Office, 1991; Department of Health and Social Services (DHSS) Northern Ireland, 1991], it is developing further direction with the strategy *Our Healthier Nation*, which emphasises a broader public health approach and increases the number of stakeholders. Even so, whether the concept of health promotion activity is fully grasped is open to question, and the degree of commitment from the various government sectors remains a matter of some debate. It is against this background that we now turn to the meaning of health and wellness for older people and discuss the relevance of health and wellness promotion for them.

CONCEPTS OF HEALTH AND WELLNESS

Lay Views

Although individuals of all ages have strong ideas about health , there is no general consensus among lay persons about its meaning. Some regard health as a resource for living, a valuable asset to be sought and held. To others it represents a means of fulfilling roles and responsibilities. A number perceive it as synonymous with 'coping', which implies an adaptive response to the pressures of life. But how do older people regard health, bearing in mind their great heterogeneity and the fact that later life spans a period of some 40 or more years? Are their views determined by reference to their prior health history? By comparing themselves with their peers, with previous generations, or with the general population with its youth productivity focus. Studies of older people show that they frequently regard health as 'possessing strength', as functional fitness or independence. Some see it as the capacity to enjoy life, or an ability to enable others to enjoy it, as Sidell found in her work (1997). The notion of health as freedom from disease and disability is also commonly stated, as is the idea of soundness, bearing some similarity to the old English term 'hoelth' meaning wholeness. Gender differences regarding its meaning are reflected in the work of Calnan (1987), while Victor (1991) reminds us that perceptions of health are not only age but also social class related. Cultural perceptions also impinge upon ideas about what constitutes health in later life, affecting responses to health-care initiatives. Distinctions between health and wellness can also be detected .

Professional Views

An exploration of professional definitions reveals similar diversity. For those espousing the rational-scientific perspective, the perception of health as a disease-free state appears as a logical conclusion. This idea has formed the basis of the traditional medical model for many years. It gave rise to professional medical strategies concerned with diagnosis and treatment of disease each with cure as a goal. Consequently, this led to a strong focus upon classification of disease and to the development of specific therapies. In turn, this notion resulted in the development of epidemiology – the science concerned with the distribution and determinants of disease. Some have argued that it also fostered paternalistic attitudes towards those seeking medical care and permeated the thinking of some other health workers such as nurses and members of the professions allied to medicine.

By contrast, The World Health Organisation's (WHO) definition, first introduced in 1948 and frequently reiterated, emphasised the positive aspect of health by saying:

Health is a state of complete physical, mental and social wellbeing, and not merely the absence of disease or infirmity.

Criticised by some as being too idealistic and hence unattainable, and by others as suggesting a static state, this definition nevertheless stresses the multidimensional nature of health and places the individual in the socio-environmental context. It is more fully discussed by writers such as Lafaille (1993) and Seedhouse (1997).

Dubos (1959) was the forerunner of those who regard health not as a state but as a dynamic process, with the organism striving to achieve homeostasis in the face of a constantly changing environment. This notion underlies several nursing models, such as Roy's adaptation model (Riehl and Roy, 1983) and the wellness model of Neumann where all subsystems of the organism are seen as working towards balance, while a strong flexible line of defence enables individuals to resist disequilibrium (Neumann, 1980). Ideas such as these are considered to be useful when applied to older people (cf. McClymont *et al.* 1991, p. 108–111).

The idea of health as a fluctuant, dynamic experience, with wellness as its goal, was postulated by Dunn (1961). He envisaged health and illness as an upwardly directed continuum, ranging from a peak of high level wellness at one end, to very poor health and possible death at the other, but with the individual constantly endeavouring to move upwards along it, in spite of occasional setbacks. This notion became the bedrock of the wellness movement in the 1970s, thus making the link between positive health and wellness.

Maslow (1962) built upon this perception, when he introduced the term self-actualisation as the peak of his 'hierarchy of needs' model, postulating that it is the drive towards the fulfilment of cherished personal aspirations and potential which provides the motivational force towards wellness. His model was later adapted for older people by Ebersole and Hess (1985) and McClymont *et al.* (1991). **Figure 3.1** illustrates the application of this concept. Maslow's stance has some similarity with the views currently expressed by Seedhouse (1997 who proposes health as the foundation for achievement.

Other Viewpoints

Several other ideas of health and wellbeing have been propounded by nursing theorists, which are discussed by Pender (1987). In general, they regard health positively, defining it 'as soundness of structure and optimum biopsychosocial functioning: a balance between one's internal and external environment'. Wellness is depicted as experienced wholeness – as growth and a moving towards maturity and personal development, while contending with adversity in an manner appropriate for each individual. Such traits frequently characterise older people, who have often learned through experience that they are the experts on their own wellness status.

Downie *et al.* (1996) extended these various ideas of positive/negative health and wellness/illness, pointing out that while the negative side of health may include disease, injury,

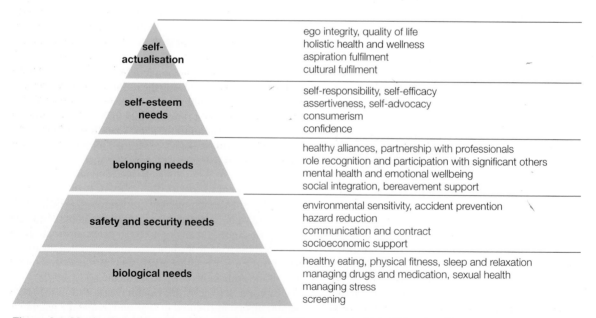

Figure 3.1 Maslow's model of human needs showing dimensions of health and wellness promotion. (Source: McClymont ME, Thomas SE, Denham MJ. *Health visiting and elderly people: a health promotion challenge, 2nd edition*. London: Churchill Livingstone, 1991.) Reproduced by kind permission of Churchill Livingstone, London.

disability or handicap, either singly or in various combinations, disease and illness are not synonymous. Hence, they argue it is possible to have a diagnosed disease without manifesting illness, and conversely someone can look and feel ill without having a diagnosed disease. This is because illness and wellness are largely subjective, qualitative-related perceptions, while disease and negative health are objectively defined, hence quantitative-related. This means older persons with chronic disease or disability can, and often do achieve high level wellness within their limitations, as also can those in terminal states. Rijke (1993) supports these views, demonstrating from general population research that subjectively good health often coexists with objectively defined pathology.

The Meaning of Wellness

Wellness, therefore, is more an attitude, an aspect of one's life-philosophy. It embodies a zest for living, a desire for 'becoming', which involves one's whole being. It subsumes both perceived quality of life and behavioural competence. Characterised by the exercise of autonomy to the highest level possible within one's circumstances, it represents interest and involvement which is oriented towards maximum function and development. Ebersole and Hess (1993) define it as 'a balance between one's environment, internal and external, and one's emotional, spiritual, social, cultural and physical processes'. It is not an artificially contrived or spurious condition, but a state of being which takes account of realities and works within them to achieve potential. Many older people are successfully striving towards their wellness goal without recourse to any professional help. However, nurses can enable older people who fall within their purview for care to achieve further wellness through participative effort. Working with them in an empowering manner to regain their health, develop competent self-care and greater self-efficacy, enhance their fitness, extend their life skills and make informed choices about their wellbeing. The various dimensions of wellness are elaborated on later in the chapter.

Differences Between the Traditional Medical Model and the Wellness Model

The Traditional Medical Model

Under the traditional medical model, the individual is regarded as possessing good health if free from disease. Hence, if an individual develops a condition it is expected that he or she will take steps to resolve the ailment. Entry into the health-care system, therefore, classifies the person as sick and, as already mentioned, entitled to the services of doctors and other caregivers for diagnosis and treatment. The severity of the condition dictates length of recovery and the degree of dependency and restricted activity. Major conditions may require institutionalisation and may lead to death. Such a model was appropriate when the majority of illness was unicausal (e.g. infectious diseases) and doctors possessed the knowledge for cure. It has less relevance when chronic diseases develop which are multi-causal and cures are less certain; examples include arthritis, diabetes mellitus, cancer and heart disease.

Older persons frequently experience chronic conditions, which may be multiple and sometimes progressive. Under the traditional medical model, therefore, they may be perceived as negating the doctor's goal of cure, and this can give rise to a stereotype of old age as a time of decrepitude, creating negative attitudes concerning treatment. In the extreme, such views can generate behaviour which treats older diseased or disabled individuals as unlikely to benefit from anything beyond simple ameliorative care. Nothing could be further from the truth, as many doctors and nurses now recognise. This is why some medical care is changing and why therapeutic nursing is beginning to develop a health focus, directed more towards participative care, rehabilitative and restorative measures, quality of life and optimum functioning.

The Wellness Model

By contrast the wellness model, assuming some wellbeing can be attained by everyone despite incapacities, focuses not on deterioration and a downward path, but upwards in a positive direction. However, it allows for plateaux *en route* to higher levels of wellbeing, as well as for regression should infection or other illness intervene (considering these may be but temporary stages, and that the climb upwards will be resumed when the individual is ready). **Figures 3.2a and 3.2b** represent these ideas pictorially, allowing for comparison.

Thus wellness becomes an exciting though complex concept offering much to those working with older people. However, it requires further refinement, and its evaluation calls for different and more sophisticated health indicators than are currently employed under the traditional medical model. Wellness also provides a basis for developing a range of health promoting activities. Achieving the goal of wellness with older people requires effort on the part of both client/patient and the professional practitioner, since relevant individual risk factors need to be addressed; motivation harnessed and broader individualised interventions explored. Paramountly, wellness recognises that choice and decision-making concerning proposed action rest with the older person.

CONCEPTS OF HEALTH PROMOTION

Just as variation occurs when defining health, so there is no one universally acceptable definition of health promotion. The term has different meanings when viewed from medical, educational, economic, political or philosophic perspectives, hence a brief exploration of the various conceptual frameworks is needed (*see* Bunton and Macdonald, 1992; Benzeval *et al.* 1995; Downie *et al.* 1996; Seedhouse, 1997).

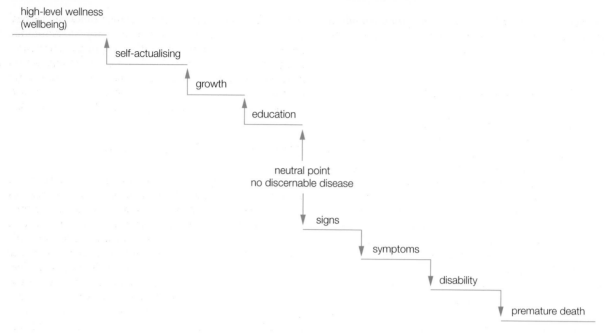

Figure 3.2a The positive side of health.

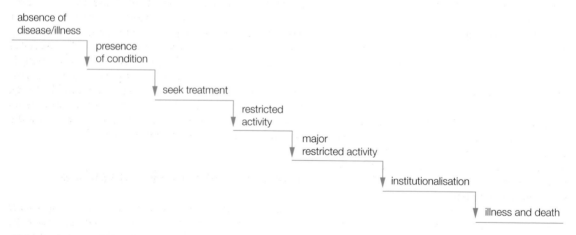

Figure 3.2b The negative side of health.

The Medical Perspective

Since from this stance health is seen as an absence of disease, health promotion is regarded as utilising those measures which attack disease, so safeguarding health. Hence, it incorporates diagnostic and treatment measures, plus risk reduction (preventive) strategies. While many consider this as laudable action [and indeed this is the idea underpinning our National Health Service (NHS)], critics regard this approach as necessary but restrictive, placing medicine in a dominant position when decisions are made about how and which conditions should be 'attacked'. Opponents argue that an imbalance of expenditure may occur favouring 'cure' rather than prevention (as is presently the case), while conditions selected may not be those which older people regard as most important. Conversely, those which do bother older people may be dismissed as 'trivia' or 'inevitable concomitants of ageing'. Nevertheless, essential health promoting activities are conducted from this stance. These include those interventions earlier in the life span which impact on pathological ageing, as well as the various screening measures which detect latent conditions in older persons, with a view to presymptomatic remedial action.

The Educational Perspective

This view considers that lack of awareness about the dimensions and determinants of health leads to poor levels of well-being. Hence, adherents judge, raising the levels of health literacy will give individuals, groups and communities opportunity to apply this knowledge to their own situations, so bringing about improved health. Proponents are, therefore, concerned with personal development, methods of effective presentation, effective learning strategies and the clarity and appeal of the messages communicated. Aware of individual differences in rates and styles of learning, they endeavour to deal with hindrances to health learning and its application, aiming to help individuals of all ages, as well as groups and communities, become 'knowledgeable doers' in matters pertaining to health. However, until recently, older persons were largely disregarded in official health education efforts, despite evidence that many are eager for health knowledge and ready to make appropriate lifestyle changes in consequence. This is changing and both at individual, group and community levels and via the mass media, education for health in later life has a higher profile. However, there is still scope for improving the presentation of health messages to older people, as well as identifying particular barriers that may hinder them accepting health knowledge and acting upon it.

The Economic Perspective

Those espousing this viewpoint, regard ill health as a drain on individual and national resources. Therefore, for them health promotion is judged to be prudent. Inputs are then considered as investments that should reap dividends in the form of health gain and increased productivity – a view which underpins NHS managerial thinking (Piggot, 1994). It places great emphasis on cost-effectiveness and cost–benefit, aiming to obtain the very best returns on outlay. In the context of health care or health promotion, the focus is on outcomes and value for money. Critics argue that health gain targeting is reductionist; that it concentrates effort in narrow directions only, leaving wider issues untouched, as well as failing to recognise the importance of structure and process in relation to the delivery of health care. Others fear that if productivity is used as a main criteria for determining priorities for health gain, this might work against vulnerable groups, including older people.

Already there are indications that rationing in health care is occurring. For example, older persons being denied access to services such as coronary care or thrombolysis, even though research shows they can benefit greatly (Dudley and Burns, 1992). It is also reflected in cuts in the availability of continuing care, in the subtle removal of the older person's right to free health care within nursing homes and in legal decisions which threaten to remove their right to home-care services (Williams, 1997). Nevertheless, positive NHS commissioning, which has health gain for older persons within its remit, can be health promoting, holding great promise for the future. Nurses who play a part in commissioning are, therefore, urged to act positively on behalf of older people.

The Political Perspective

Those approaching health promotion from this standpoint argue that many of the determinants of health involve issues such as poverty, inequitable distribution of resources, deprivation, adverse vested interest and pollution. This may lead to poor housing, unhealthy environments, inadequate nutrition, poor transport services or social support, and hence reduce health. Such conditions frequently impact upon older people. Proponents, therefore, look for radical policies from national Government and local authorities which will reduce inequalities in health and deal effectively with these various determinants, so making it easier for all people to choose healthy lifestyles (Benzeval et al. 1995; Wilkinson, 1997). Critics regard their proposals as somewhat naive and idealistic – emphasising collectivism at the expense of individual aspirations. They fear that 'those who have' may suffer in an attempt to improve the health of 'those who have not'. However, there has been mounting pressure for a greater health promotion onslaught on inequalities, as evidenced by a number of writers (Savage, 1988; Markus, 1993; Majeed et al. 1994). With the changing political scene, this thinking is coming to the forefront and is incorporated in documents such as Our Healthier Nation [Department of Health (DoH), 1998b]. Nurses and health visitors supporting these views may, therefore, be afforded greater scope to influence the political agenda in favour of health promotion.

The Philosophical Perspective

Those approaching health promotion from this viewpoint are concerned with health ethics and values. They emphasise the importance of the individual, for whom they advocate empowerment, holism, participation and personal autonomy. Deploring the prescriptive generalised approach shown in some other stances, they stress the need for respect and trust as part of an egalitarian relationship between older persons and health workers. Ethical health promotion they consider, starts by eliciting the individual's thoughts and feelings about their health, their aspirations, needs and goals. It involves the professional in working with clients in exploring solutions with them, finding acceptable balances and seeking to enhance the view of health as a resource for living, rather than an end in itself; this is a means by which individuals and communities are enabled to achieve their potential (Caraher, 1994, 1995; Thomas and Wainwright, 1996; Seedhouse, 1997). Clearly there is a need for ethical considerations affecting health promotion with older people to be brought to the fore. Such individuals may be highly vulnerable to coercive programmes and the advocacy and interpretative roles of the nurse may well have to be strengthened. Those nurse readers wishing to explore this further are referred to Campbell (1993) and Cribb (1993).

Health Promotion Perceived as 'the New Public Health'

From this perspective, health promotion is seen as synonymous with a resurgence of public health, that is a collective approach which has much in common with the political perspective. Proponents advocate strengthening community responsibility, development and involvement, pointing to the achievements of the nineteenth century public health movement, which reduced mortality and raised levels of health and personal dignity by organised community measures (involving sanitary engineering, slum clearance, factory legislation, mutual aid, improved education and targeted personal health services). It is ideas like this which underlie the Healthy Cities Project, first launched by the World Health Organisation (WHO) in 1986, which has several pilot schemes in the UK. They are discussed by writers such as Thornley (1992), and Davies and Kelly (1993). The public health/health promotion contribution of nurses and health visitors was stressed by the WHO in its Alma Ata declaration *Health for All - by the year 2000*, (1978) and more recently was recognised by SNMAC (1995), who emphasised 'all that is required is that we make it happen'. Older people stand to benefit from such ventures as much as other age groups. They rely heavily on healthy caring communities to complement their personal health promotion efforts.

With the advent of new Government thinking, public health measures are being reviewed and incorporated into new national strategies. Healthy living centres are being encouraged, health action zones are setting up and health improvement programmes are being launched. The ideas underlying the Healthy Cities Project are being reflected in the concepts of healthy schools, healthy workplaces and healthy neighbourhoods, the latter focusing particularly on older people. It is to be hoped that this specific focus will place greater emphasis on the value of older persons' views being sought and heeded from the outset. Increasingly their views are being raised through such organisations as pensioners federations and Age Concern.

HEALTH PROMOTION WITH OLDER PEOPLE: A COMPLEX MULTI-PERSPECTIVE CONCEPT

These various diverse viewpoints each have much to contribute. Taken together they suggest that health promotion is no longer solely an individual responsibility (important though this will continue to be), nor is it to be regarded as largely a health service responsibility (although the NHS will continue to play a major role and adopt an increasingly proactive stance), rather it applies to every sector of life. Health promotion is a positive and purposeful activity, concerned with increasing the level of health and wellbeing of individuals, groups and communities. Hence, it is of paramount importance for everyone, including older people. Encompassing work at both micro and macro levels, it includes inputs from various statutory and voluntary agencies, and from private and public sectors. Involving industry, commerce and education as much as it does environmental and personal health services or social care, it has a place in every aspect of life. When operationalised in projects such as the Rotherham venture (Steinke, 1992), it challenges the health professions in a new way, requiring them to adopt a broad health focus instead of the disease focus they have traditionally held; to become more flexible and collaborative, ready to recognise the contribution of others, as well as that of the professions.

Applying these Various Concepts to Health and Wellness Promotion with Older People

Amalgamating these varying concepts and applying them to our topic, one suggests that at the heart of the matter are older individuals with their unique heredity, varying ages, race and gender. Each older individual is seen as a bio-psycho-spiritual being, with each part contributing to the whole person, who in turn is essentially socially interactive. However, older individuals must be placed in their bio-socio-cultural environmental context, as **Figure 3.3** shows, because influences from these environments impact constantly upon them. As each older individual progresses through the life span, the interplay of their heredity with their distinctive cultural and life experiences (resulting from their specific internal and external environments), produces their lifestyle, develops their personality and dictates both their age changes and age differences. It also brings about each rich biography, which then constitutes a heritage for others. It is at the level of the older individual that an emphasis can be placed upon the need for healthy personal behaviours, such as personal hygiene, physical fitness, greater nutritional awareness, self-efficacy, self-empowerment, the maximising of functional ability and the development of self-care and stress-reduction competencies. Such topics are pertinent to nursing and health visiting, because many practitioners engage with older people at the individual level. However, before exploring these in greater detail, we first need to examine the drive towards wellness and stability which characterises these older individuals.

the older individual

Figure 3.3 The older individual at the core of wellness promotion.

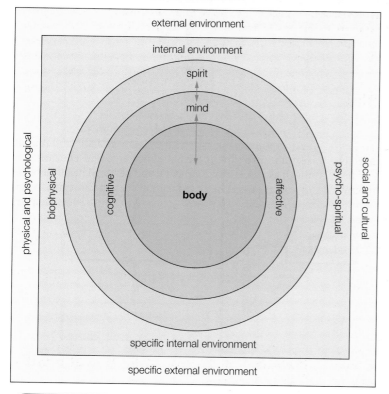

external environment

internal environment

spirit

mind

body

cognitive

affective

biophysical

psycho-spiritual

physical and psychological

social and cultural

specific internal environment

specific external environment

interplay between unique heredity and specific internal
and external environments produces
  a) personality
  b) lifestyle
and determines the rate and character of ageing

Wellness and Health Promotion Seen as a Dynamic and Integrative Process

Both Pender (1987) and Ebersole and Hess (1993) point out that throughout the life span individuals are engaged in a dynamic integrative process, which is aimed at creating a balance between their striving towards high level wellbeing in all domains on the one hand, and the mechanisms to achieve stability on the other (**Figure 3.4**). Many older persons have become adept at such balancing, although with advancing age the scope for imbalance increases. It should be noted that the thrust individuals make towards wellness is both tension-producing and change-creating.

Proceeding in sequence, it passes through the levels of awareness-raising, via health education, to personal growth and development (particularly in the psycho-spiritual domains), eventually reaching self-actualisation. It is this last level which incorporates need-satisfaction, the fulfilment of personal aspirations and the realisation of potential; it in turn

leads to high-level wellness. Working with older people in an empowering fashion to help them achieve this peak, constitutes wellness promotion. It is only achieved through comprehensive, holistic assessment of each older person's aspirations, needs and potential, and by personalised health education being subsequently offered on the basis of mutual trust and respect. Conversely the drive towards stability is non-thrusting, embodying tension reduction and steadying.

Here the sequence passes through biological homeostasis, emotional tranquillity, and stress reduction to personal adaptation, through the use of effective coping strategies. Therefore, this side of the integrative process is concerned more with health protection measures, risk reduction and with the prevention of disease, injury, disability and deprivation. Of course, each part of such health protection and prevention needs to be accompanied by relevant health education.

Even though in this model health/wellness promotion and health protection/disease prevention have been depicted separately, readers will realise they are essentially two sides

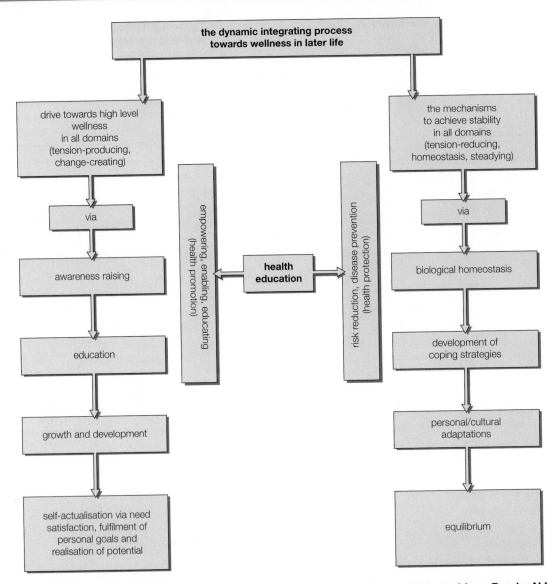

Figure 3.4 The dynamic integrating process towards wellness in later life. (Source: Adapted from Pender NJ. *Health promotion in nursing practice, 2nd edition.* **Norwalk: Appleton and Lange, 1987; McClymont ME, Thomas SE, Denham MJ.** *Health visiting and elderly people: a health promotion challenge, 2nd edition.* **London: Churchill Livingstone, 1991; Ebersole P, Hess P.** *Towards healthy aging, 4th edition.* **St Louis: Mosby, 1994.**

of the one coin. One employs the health promoting activities of empowering, enabling and educating older people when facilitating their thrust toward high level wellness, while utilising risk reduction measures, disease prevention strategies and health protection actions when assisting them towards stability and the steady state. However, adaptive and 'tailored' health education provides the bridge as it were between both. Helping older individuals successfully integrate these two different drives into one dynamic process is what nursing with a health focus is all about. It is an exciting, challenging activity. The various strategies used to bring this about form much of our subsequent discussion.

Health and Wellness Promotion in Later Life, as Related to Group, Community and Society

Just as no individual can exist in a vacuum, so older people's health cannot be promoted without reference to their social context. This means we need to take account of their families and other relevant groups, their local communities and the wider society of which they form part. Aware that each level influences the health behaviours older people adopt and the health choices they can and do make. Conversely, the degree of involvement and type of demands older persons generate, will

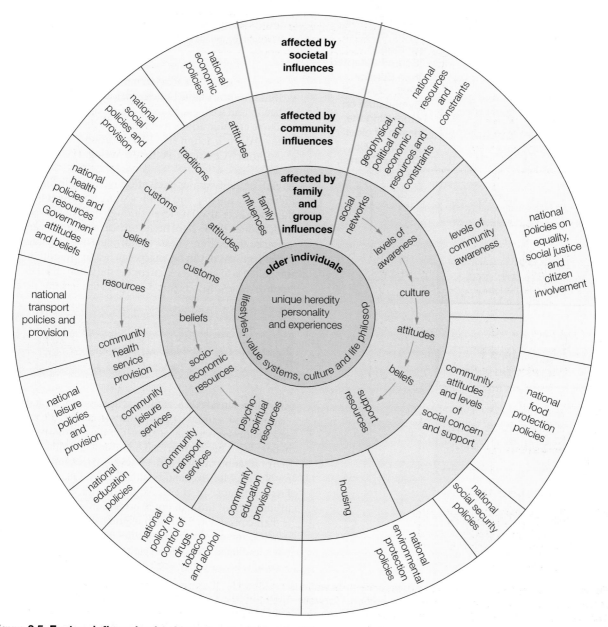

Figure 3.5 Factors influencing health and wellness in later life.

impact upon the attitudes, responses and subsequent policies of each successive level. Older people are unlikely to be able to realise their aspirations for fulfilling and creative leisure if their personal resources are insufficient to provide for these; if family attitudes or group cultural beliefs frown upon their engaging in certain pursuits; if community facilities are non-existent; or if transport difficulties make existing facilities inaccessible. Similarly national health policies concerning eligibility for screening, will likely be a major determining factor in whether an older person engages in secondary prevention. This also means that if we seriously intend to promote health and wellness for older people, a concerted effort has to be made to conduct health promotion efforts at all these levels simultaneously,

although not necessarily by the same workers!

Healthy, integrated intergenerational or older families, who practice health promoting behaviours, will impact favourably on community wellness. Similarly, strategies aimed at community wellness can, in turn, make it possible for families and smaller social groups to practice health promoting behaviours. Examples include community provision for healthy leisure; parks, gardens and safe cycle-ways; provision for swimming, sport and physical activity; education, libraries and information centres; advice agencies; luncheon clubs; and social groups of all types. Healthy neighbourhoods and communities, when aggregated, make up healthy societies. However, it is policies adopted at society level which make it possible, or not, for individuals,

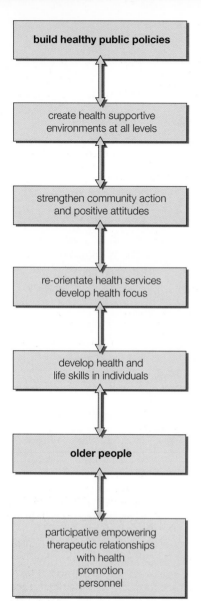

Figure 3.6 The layers of health promotion (Source: Adapted from Eurolink, 1996; HEA/CPA. Symposium on promoting the health of older people, 1996; Ottawa Charter, 1986.)

involvement and participation, improving resources and inculcating positive attitudes, especially towards older people.
- Create health-supportive environments that make it easier for people of all ages to make healthy choices.
- Build healthy public policies that work to promote health and wellness, prevent disease and reduce risk.
- There are indications that Europe is slowly moving towards such action (Health Education Authority/Centre for Policy on Ageing, 1996).

At each of these various levels affecting the wellbeing of older individuals, nursing and health visiting is represented. From those working at WHO level, through national government level, through the levels of health service management and education, to the delivery of care to individual older persons, these professions are, or can be, engaged in health promotion. What is required is to grasp the concept, see the vision and then work towards achieving it. **Figure 3.7** depicts this in some detail.

THE PIVOTAL ROLE OF NURSING IN HEALTH AND WELLNESS PROMOTION

As we have already seen, at the practice level nurses and health visitors have a unique opportunity to contribute to health and wellness promotion at all ages, but particularly for those in later life. This is confirmed on several grounds, as a number of documents and articles testify (UK Central Council for Nurses, Midwives and Health Visitors, 1983; Ward, 1997). Firstly, because of their recognised and valued expertise brought about through initial professional education, which is then consolidated through ongoing experience, reflective practice and continuing educational development, the latter often leading to specialist preparation or advanced level work. Secondly, because they work at individual client/patient level. At best this provides an intimate personalised service, based upon holistic health assessment and jointly negotiated personal health-care plans, the implementation of which calls for careful monitoring, outcome evaluation, review and reformulation. Thirdly, because their frequent and continuing contact with client/patients and their significant others, is often on a longer-term basis and takes place in a variety of primary and secondary care settings. Where this involves institutional care, such as inpatient, hospital or nursing home care, then the contact is available over 24 hours and throughout the year. Few professions can claim this intimate, close and often continuing contact. Nevertheless, while this confers great benefits it also constitutes a strong challenge, not just in respect of the nature of the relationship (important as this is), nor even in regard to the teaching, counselling, communicating and leadership skills involved (vital as these are), nor the quality of care delivered (paramount though this be), but largely because of the responsibility it brings to serve as health promotion role models. It is all too easy for professionals to

groups and communities to successfully engage in health and wellness promoting activities. **Figure 3.5** sets out the interlocking relationship between these levels. Furthermore, international concerns demonstrate that health issues which begin at the individual level eventually have global aspects. **Figure 3.6** demonstrates the WHO *Health for All* strategies, which policy makers everywhere have been urged to adopt in the wake of the Ottawa Charter for Health Promotion 1986. These are to:
- Develop health and life skills in all individuals including older people.
- Re-orientate health services so that they develop participative approaches and health focused strategies instead of disease-centred ones.
- Strengthen community action by increasing

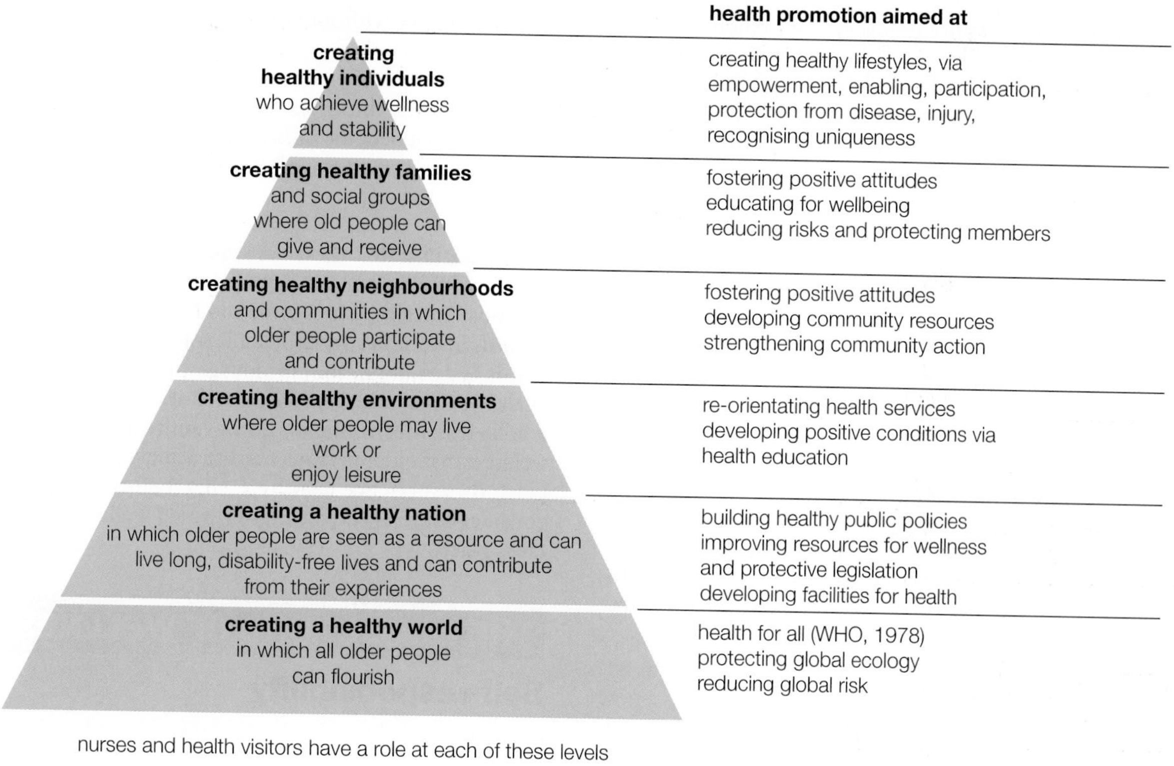

The health promotion pyramid.

	health promotion aimed at
creating healthy individuals who achieve wellness and stability	creating healthy lifestyles, via empowerment, enabling, participation, protection from disease, injury, recognising uniqueness
creating healthy families and social groups where old people can give and receive	fostering positive attitudes educating for wellbeing reducing risks and protecting members
creating healthy neighbourhoods and communities in which older people participate and contribute	fostering positive attitudes developing community resources strengthening community action
creating healthy environments where older people may live work or enjoy leisure	re-orientating health services developing positive conditions via health education
creating a healthy nation in which older people are seen as a resource and can live long, disability-free lives and can contribute from their experiences	building healthy public policies improving resources for wellness and protective legislation developing facilities for health
creating a healthy world in which all older people can flourish	health for all (WHO, 1978) protecting global ecology reducing global risk

nurses and health visitors have a role at each of these levels

Figure 3.7 The health promotion pyramid.

become so involved in promoting the health of others, that they fail to take on board the relevance of the wellness message for themselves.

Additionally, those nurses and health visitors working in primary care settings, have responsibility for developing their activities not only with individuals but with groups and population aggregates as well, hence becoming involved in community development programmes affecting older people. Here their role-modelling is even more relevant.

Building Healthy Alliances

We have already mentioned the need to build healthy alliances, as part of the overall health promotion strategy. Such alliances are designed to develop partnerships between individuals, teams and organisations, each contributing different expertise, viewpoints and interests, so enabling them to work together with common purpose. Team work is particularly relevant to the care of older people, whose needs often straddle both primary and secondary health-care services, housing, education and social services. Higginbottom and Simpson (1996) address this matter in relation to nursing, setting out a conceptual framework for networking, which draws in a wide range of statutory and voluntary work-

ers. This indicates the breadth of collaboration necessary to promote the health and wellbeing of older people at individual, group and community level.

Nevertheless, it follows that if this collaboration is to happen, and older persons are to be enabled to 'achieve their aspirations, meet their needs and cope with or change their environments' as the Ottawa Charter sets out (1986), then nurses, other professionals, planners and policy makers need to listen to and heed what older people are saying. Many of them are highly articulate, politically conscious and socially aware. Most old people, by reason of their experience over many years, are usually highly realistic. They have often learned to accept their limitations and consequently are unlikely to have unduly high aspirations. Nevertheless, some may, on occasions, require help to articulate their needs and represent themselves if only because, in the past, they have felt their views to be disregarded or invalidated. Wherever this is so, there are implications for nurses regarding how best to elicit such aspirations, and then subsequently build upon them, in order to promote the drive towards self-actualisation and wellness. This may involve assisting older individuals to develop a higher internal health locus of control (Wallston, Wallston and Devellis, 1978); as well as encouraging them to examine their strengths as a means to fulfilling their potential.

The implications regarding need-satisfaction, however,

57

are different. They require that very comprehensive needs-assessment be undertaken by skilful, sensitive practitioners working with older people, so that they can be enabled to choose those options which best meet their needs. Nurses will appreciate it is often easier to assist individuals and groups to meet their biological, safety and security needs, than it is to help them meet their belonging and esteem needs. The reason being that these latter call for acceptance, affiliation, a clear personal identity, control over one's own affairs, opportunity for social integration and meaningful roles, each of which may be denied to older people. Yet such enabling should not be disregarded just because it is challenging.

Enabling older people to change or cope with their environments is possibly most demanding of all. Especially is this so when frail or sick older individuals are living in deprived or adverse conditions in the community or find themselves residents in care settings or nursing homes where others make major decisions. At the immediate environment level small changes may be readily achieved through the application of a little imagination. However, those changes needed to improve adverse socio-environmental conditions, are often outside the direct remit of either older persons or nurses, as Thomas and Wainwright (1996) state. Nevertheless, as citizens, nurses can become more socially aware, and as a powerful and informed professional group nurses can, given the will, raise issues on behalf of older people and exert pressure for change. Advocacy represents a core nursing skill.

Helping older persons improve and extend their coping skills by increasing their knowledge about self-care management, the sources of help available to them and the measures to reduce stress, can often be highly effective. However, one needs to be aware that failure to bring about change or adopt more adaptive coping strategies, may sometimes lead older persons to resign themselves passively to adverse circumstances, which can lead to 'learned helplessness' and depression, attitudes which militate against self-efficacy, independence and wellness.

Are Nurses and Health Visitors at Practice Level Exploiting their Health Promotion Opportunities with Older People?

In spite of the many exhortations given and the clear opportunities open to nurses, as well as the evident enthusiasm of some practitioners, there is considerable evidence to suggest that many are still not exploiting their chances to promote health and wellness with older persons as they might (Pursey and Luker, 1993). Various reasons have been advanced for this including:
- Inadequate preparation and lack of confidence.
- Insufficient grasp of the breadth of the concept.
- Poor mentoring or inadequate role models.
- Negative attitudes towards older people resulting from stereotypes and images of ageing generated by exposure to the 5% highly dependent, sick, disabled or demented

older people, without balancing exposure to the 95% of well older people.
- The pressured social environment within the various settings in which nurses work causing them to regard the longer-term benefits of health promotion as less tangible or important than the physical and clinical nursing tasks which lie to hand.

It is important that these various reasons are addressed by nurses at all levels of practice as well as by those in both pre and post-nursing education, and that research is directed towards investigation and possible solution of such problems. If this is not done, the immense opportunity nurses and health visitors have to promote wellness with older persons, will be lost. Meantime, we now examine the dimensions of wellness that older persons need to achieve if they are to successfully experience healthy ageing, before we move on to consider some of the settings in which wellness promotion takes place.

THE DIMENSIONS OF WELLNESS

Self-responsibility

This issue of self-responsibility is not introduced as a political expediency, intended to solve the problem of extra demands on health services, by 'passing the buck' as it were back to old people, but rather is set out as a liberating experience for them. It forms an opportunity for them to learn that their wellness promotion lies equally with themselves. That they can exercise some choice about how they will maintain their body, exercise their mind and develop their spirit, even if they are heavily dependent upon others for their needs, such as those who are in continuing care.

Many older individuals, of course, have already developed such plans of self-care. They know the importance of adequate sleep and rest, balanced with exercise and body movement. They understand the value of creative leisure and mental stimulation, as well as the importance of a healthy diet, weight control and appropriate personal hygiene. Many are cognisant of the principles of medication management, complying carefully with prescribed treatments. They also often know the place of self-treatment and of the helpful advice that community pharmacists can offer when simple over-the-counter remedies may be needed. Some have a knowledge of first-aid and others regularly carry out health techniques such as testing urine or blood for glucose and acetone, in the case of those with diabetes mellitus; prepare special diets; adopt measures designed to improve continence; or carry out asthma-control measures. Some have learned to cope with stoma care; are well aware of the need for follow-up and monitoring; and take steps to carry out regular health screening, such as checks on hearing, vision, blood pressure and dental state. Many attend regularly for chiropody, recognising the importance of foot care in maintaining mobility and amiability. Some derive benefit from complementary therapies, although these techniques can prove expensive and beyond the reach of other older individuals. Some regularly practice breast or testicular/prostate self-examination, attending at recommended times for measures such as mammography or cervical screening. They also exercise responsibility for prophylactic immunisation, such as annual influenza vaccination, tetanus 'boosters' at 10-yearly intervals, pneumonia vaccination, or the range of inoculations advised before travelling abroad. Others, of course, may be less well informed and for them awareness-raising is an essential prelude to wellness promotion.

Nurses can enhance and support older persons' moves towards greater self-responsibility, by recognising the degree of competence they may already possess and building on this, exploring with them further areas of wellness imbalance and discussing options available to them. Older persons are mostly able to make meaningful decisions if unbiased information is given them and if they recognise that support is available for them, regardless of the decisions made.

However, some aged persons may choose not to be fully responsible for their own wellness. Illness causes some individuals to regress, seeking attention that may otherwise be denied them. Such behaviour can sometimes provide escape from unpleasant situations, and may represent one form of coping when overwhelmed by problems such as intense weakness or pain. It is important for nurses to exercise understanding in such situations, recognising that although such action may be contrary to the wellness ideal, it is the individual's choice. Our society makes provision for aged illness-behaviour, recognising that such situations often prove temporary and the move to wellness is then renewed, given a period for restoration and recovery.

Enlisting the Help of Significant Others

We have already noted how vital it is to involve significant others in the care and wellbeing of older individuals. Now we see that families and friends can often help older individuals further their self-responsibility by facilitating their responses; perhaps acting on occasions for them; discussing with them their health-care needs; helping them decide on the most appropriate plans of action for them; and identifying the health-related steps relevant for them to take. This type of action can be undertaken also by older peers. An example is seen in the trained Senior Health (Peer) Mentors being used in the UK Ageing Well Programme, which comes under the EuroLink Age, Ageing Well initiative (Ageing Well UK Programme, 1996). Each senior health mentor, when given simple training, can assist another older individual to move towards greater wellness and exercise self-responsibility for healthy behaviours by befriending them and showing them how healthy practices can make a difference. This type of

Target number	Timescale	Target statement
\multicolumn{3}{l}{**World Health Organisation Targets for Europe which Apply Particularly to Older People (1985)**}		
1	By year 2000	Inequalities in health within/between countries should be reduced by at least 25%
3	By year 2000	Disabled persons should have the opportunity to develop their health potential and live fulfilling lives
4	By year 2000	There should be a 10% improvement in the average number of years a person is free from major disability
6	By year 2000	Life expectancy in the European region should be at least 75 years and there should be a sustained and continuing improvement in the health of all people aged 65 years or over
11	By year 2000	Accident mortality should be reduced by at least 25% from the base year
12	By year 2000	Current trends/rises in suicide and parasuicide rates should be reversed
32	By year 2000	Research must be developed to support *Health for All*, particularly in the following areas: • descriptions of the health of the older population • ascertainment of the biological factors that determine health in older people • the effects of lifestyle in old age • the effects of environment on health • the best ways to deliver appropriate care to older people • improvements needed in policy making, planning and management

Source: World Health Organisation. *Targets for Health for all*. Geneva: WHO, 1985.

Table 3.1 World Health Organisation targets for Europe which apply particularly to older people.

3.1 Aims of the Ageing Well Programme

- Working with others in healthy alliances.
- Increasing the expectation of good health in later life among older people and those who work with them.
- Enabling older people to take a lead role in improving and maintaining their own health, including the involvement of senior health mentors.
- Promoting effective models of healthy ageing in line with national and international strategies.
- Establishing Ageing Well UK as a major national programme of health promotion for and with older people.

activity complements the WHO *Health for All* principles, and is in line with WHO's *Healthy Ageing* targets. **Table 3.1** sets out the main WHO targets for Europe, which apply to older persons, although other of the total 38 targets have an application to older individuals as well. In England, the *Health of the Nation* strategy adopted some of these targets. With changing policies, these targets are expected to undergo further modification but will remain in line with WHO principles. Nurses can help in the training of such senior health mentors and can facilitate their work.

The mission statement of the Ageing Well Programme states that it 'aims to improve and maintain the health of older people, recognising that they can be an important resource to themselves and others' (**Box 3.1**).

Since 1993, this programme has initiated nine major projects, all now being evaluated (Ageing Well UK Programme, 1996). Several of these initiatives involve nurses and health visitors, but the programme manager is keen to encourage further interest and action.

Other examples of community-based programmes which support self-responsibility in older individuals include the Look After Yourself/Look After Your Heart Programmes, introduced by the Health Education Authority in 1991, which a number of health visitors have successfully used. These cover education concerning safe physical activity; healthy eating; coping with stress; smoking cessation; sensible drinking and weight control, and encourage older individuals to become accountable for such actions.

Nutritional Awareness

While self-responsibility is a somewhat over-arching concept, other dimensions of wellness refer to more specific focused activity; one concerns nutritional awareness. In general, persons of all ages in the UK risk obesity by overconsuming calories, yet sometimes tend to remain malnourished because of imbalanced diet. Nutrition in the older population often reflects cultural attitudes and dietary practices. Each successive cohort may have been educated differently, as general

nutritional advice has varied considerably over the years. Raising nutritional awareness, therefore, means encouraging older people not only to learn about healthy, nutritionally dense diets, but to recognise where inappropriate long-standing and current practices need to be changed. Specific cultural preferences may not always be the most nutritious. With increasing age, older people may rely on convenience or processed foods, which may have high sodium content, excess fat (especially saturated fatty acids) or sugars. Soft foods may be chosen because of chewing problems; therefore, there may be less inclination to select 'hard', fresh vegetables or fruit. Fatty fish such as herrings, rich in essential fatty acids, may be excluded for fear of bones. Valuable pulses may be neglected because they need careful preparation. Wholemeal bread and other complex starches may have less appeal for diminished appetites than sugary cakes and biscuits. Hence, older individuals may fail to follow the recommended healthy balanced diet which is given in **Box 3.2**.

Recent research has centred on the important function of antioxidants, particularly the role of beta-carotene, vitamin C and vitamin E in both prevention and treatment of various conditions affecting older people, such as cataract (Wynn and Wynn, 1996), osteoporosis; cancer and heart disease (Lachance, 1996). The value of fibre in aiding intestinal health and preventing constipation is also well known.

Raising nutritional awareness in older persons is best undertaken through appropriate education, personal counselling and group work. For those living at home, sessions covering creative menu planning and the health and economic

3.2 Recommended Healthy Balanced Diet for an Older Individual

(1) An energy intake within the range 1,200–1,600 Kilocalories daily, derived mainly from carbohydrate, in the form of complex starch. Fats, making up not more than 35% of the total energy requirement. Saturated fat should be kept at or below 11% of the total fat intake, greater reliance being placed on foods containing polyunsaturated fatty acids.

(2) Protein, in the form of meat, fish or meat alternatives such as eggs, cheese, pulses, nuts and mycoprotein items, making up 10% of the total energy requirements.

(3) Recommended amounts of vitamins, mineral salts and trace elements are likely to be available to the body if the overall daily dietary intake includes:

- 6 portions carbohydrate, mainly complex starches.
- 5 portions fruit and vegetables.
- 2–3 portions dairy produce.
- 2 portions meat, fish or protein alternatives

Source: Department of Health. *Eat well: an action plan from the Nutrition Task Force to achieve the Health of the Nation targets on diet and nutrtion*. London: HMSO, 1994a; Health Education Authority. *Nutrition briefing papers 'Dietary Facts'*. London: HEA, 1994; Ministry of Agriculture, Food and Fisheries. *Manual of nutrition, 10th edition*. London: HMSO, 1995.

benefits of healthy diet can prove stimulating and fun. Those living in continuing care settings such as nursing homes, should be offered opportunity to make informed choices not only from the menus offered, but through participation with other residents and appropriate staff in overall menu planning. Those whose appetite levels are low, may find they benefit from a daily vitamin and mineral supplement, but care should be taken to ensure this only provides up to 100% of recommended nutritional intake, in order to avoid the risk of toxic effects. Nutrition is dealt with in greater detail in a subsequent chapter. Its relevance for those striving for wellness applies equally to those living at home and those in hospital or long-term care (*see* Chapter 6 for further detail).

Physical Fitness

High-level wellness, independence within the community and coping abilities in later life depend largely upon physical fitness, stamina, flexibility and the strength to perform a range of physical activities in daily living. Yet personal attitudes and some cultural expectations have projected retirement as a 'time to take things easy', causing older people often to assume sedentary lifestyles. This results in 'disuse atrophy' and is thought to be responsible for up to 50% of the physiological decline associated with ageing (McClymont *et al.* 1991; Uittenbroek, 1996, p. 21). Exercise benefits both physical and psychosocial health, bringing about significant changes such as:

- Decreases in blood pressure.
- Improved neuromuscular function, particularly in heart muscle tone.
- Increases in high-density lipoproteins, which help protect against coronary heart disease.
- Decreases in body fat.
- Greater joint flexibility.
- Increased energy and vitality.
- Reduced tension and increased self-esteem (Fentem, 1994; HEA, 1997a; HEA, 1997b; Sharp, 1997).

Skelton (1993, 1994) discusses the beneficial effects exercise brings to older people, in relation to the prevention of falls, fractures and osteoporosis. Exercise:

- Heightens alertness.
- Improves insomnia.
- Alleviates depression.
- Avoids constipation.
- Aids continence.
- Assists in the treatment of diabetes mellitus through reducing need for insulin.
- Is helpful in the case of those suffering from Parkinson's disease.

Through her research, Skelton found older women aged 75–93 years improved the strength of their thigh muscles by approximately 25% in only 12 weeks of gentle exercise – a bonus equal to the rejuvenation of strength by some 16–20

years! Her exercise programme for older people across the later age span (available from Research into Ageing), is being used by a number of nurses and health visitors working with older people to promote independence in living.

Yet, in spite of all these benefits which exercise can confer, what is the stark reality? Further analysis by Young *et al.* (1997), of the physical activity and fitness data for adults aged 50 years and over, collected in The Allied Dunbar Fitness Survey and the HEA National Survey of Activity and Health (1992) shows:

- Only 26% of men and 17% of women of this age group participated in enough physical activity to benefit their health; that is, they undertook moderate intensity exercise such as walking, gardening, stair-climbing or heavy housework, at least five times per week.
- Of the 74% of men and 83% of women who did not exercise sufficiently, 29% and 42%, respectively, were sedentary; that is, they participated in less than 30 minutes moderate exercise less than once per week. Yet over half of both men and women who were inactive thought they participated in sufficient exercise to keep fit and well!
- Furthermore, a quarter of all women and 7% of men aged 70–74 did not have sufficient strength in their legs to rise from a chair without using its arms, and 35% of men and 80% of women did not have the physical ability to walk comfortably at 20 minutes-a-mile pace.
- In consequence of these findings, the Health Education Authority has mounted a campaign designed to encourage those aged 50 years and over to become active in order to stay healthy.

What is Involved in Achieving Fitness in Later Life?

Fitness involves several elements, including aerobic capacity, body structure and composition, muscle strength and flexibility and balance. Aerobic activity fortifies the body against stress, and is well within the reach of many older persons in the form of brisk walking, swimming, gardening, dancing, cycling or tennis. What is important is:

- Sustaining the activity long enough to accelerate the respiratory and cardiac rate sufficiently to reap benefit.
- Ensuring that the activity is undertaken safely: wearing suitable clothing and footwear; avoiding jerky movements.
- Allowing time for warming up and cooling down before and after strenuous activity.

Those with established medical conditions are advised to seek medical guidance before undertaking particular regimens, as a few conditions may be worsened by inappropriate activity. They may need adapted programmes in order to obtain benefit. Those older individuals who are currently limited in functional ability or confined to chair/wheelchair should not be precluded from active participation. Specially designed exercise programmes can be conducted from a sitting position equally well as from an ambulatory one. Group activi-

Meeting Health and Wellness Needs

Kathleen Nicholson, a 77-year-old former middle-level business executive, widowed for 3 years, had recently moved into a bungalow within a sheltered housing complex, when she sustained a right-sided cerebrovascular accident. Hospitalised for 10 weeks, she was then transferred to the care of the Elderly Care Team and two weeks later referred to the Community Nursing Services.

When visited initially by the community nurse, Kathleen said that she had had asthma for many years and was fully accustomed to managing her respiratory problems and medication, including a nebuliser. She expressed concern about the effects of her recent stroke, saying she felt very unsteady when walking and was scared of falling. Furthermore, she was worried because she sometimes had difficulty finding the correct words to express what she wished to say and was aware that this led to others sometimes thinking she was confused and rather odd. This made her feel angry at times and at other times rather depressed. This upset her because she was very happy in her new home and wished to continue to live there, independently, for as long as possible – attending her church and keeping in touch with friends in the locality. Her only son and his family now lived in the south of England, but she did not feel she could uproot herself to move nearer to them. They visited her whenever they could. Two elderly cousins lived some 7 miles away and called to see her regularly, often dealing with her laundry because since her stroke she was sometimes incontinent, particularly at night.

On observing Kathleen, the nurse noted that she was a neatly dressed individual, rather thin for her height, with a somewhat anxious expression. She demonstrated tension movements with her fingers and moved restlessly on her seat while speaking. Speech was generally articulate, measured with occasional hesitations. The well-appointed home environment was warm, clean and comfortable. Furniture and flooring did not appear to present specific hazards and Kathleen negotiated the short journey to the kitchen using her walking frame correctly and successfully made a cup of tea, under covert observation. She did, however, become a little breathless with this activity. On examination, Kathleen was apyrexial and her respirations were rather 'wheezy'. Her gait was somewhat uncoordinated and she had several large bruises and one abrasion on her right leg which she attributed to knocking herself on the furniture while trying to walk. The skin over her upper limbs, back and buttocks was intact, but there was some vulval excoriation. Kathleen wore a hearing aid in her left ear and on being questioned produced reading glasses which she said 'no longer appeared as effective to her since her stroke'.

- What subjective data did the community nurse obtain from Kathleen's proffered information?
- What information did the nurse obtain from her observations and examination that provided objective data for an holistic nursing assessment?
- What other information might the community nurse seek to obtain in order to appropriately formulate a nursing care plan participatively with Kathleen?
- What behaviours did Kathleen display which might indicate her level of health awareness, self-care competency, functional ability and degree of self-efficacy?
- What strengths, demonstrated by Kathleen, might the community nurse seek to build upon in order to assist this client in her drive towards high level wellness and stability?
- What factors might the nurse need to take into account when assessing risk, reducing risk and formulating preventative strategies for incorporation into Kathleen's health-care plan?
- Which health alliances might appropriately be forged in order to fully promote Kathleen's health?
- List possible client and professional outcome criteria in respect of Kathleen's care plan and relate these to the drive toward health and wellness.

ties often increase enjoyment and exercise that is fun is more likely to be regularly sustained. Nurses and health visitors are in a prime position to encourage activity in older people and to educate individuals about the positive benefits. Many have already availed themselves of the courses run by the voluntary society EXTEND, which was formed with the expressed goal of encouraging older persons to participate in and enjoy regular exercise.

Nursing home residents and those attending day centres may find pleasure from trying to walk round specially designed 'round the world' circuits, set up to provide interest within their setting, or from participating in music and movement activities. Imagination and innovation can create enjoyable programmes, which will enable older persons to obtain the extra oxygen and movement so vital for them (*see* Chapter 6 for further discussion).

Environmental Sensitivity

The importance of the physical and social environment in relation to health has already been emphasised. The influence of air, light, water, terrain, temperature, climate and season upon wellbeing is well known. However, even knowledgeable older individuals may have limited control over their physical environments, especially when forced to leave their own homes and relocate into residential or nursing home care. Then specified standards for the physical environment, designed to facilitate coping and easy movement, as well as to provide attractive, comfortable and homely surroundings, are vital. Examples include those set out by the City and Hackney Health Authority (King's Fund, 1987). However, it is the quality of relationships that older persons experience, whether in their own homes or in institutional care, which promotes true healing and wellness (Royal College of Nursing, 1996).

The personal environment should offer older people the requirements shown in **Box 3.3**.

A rehabilitative and restorative focus within such an environment can help rekindle motivation within tired, dejected and sick old people, enabling them to regain physical, psychosocial and spiritual functioning, thereby aiding self-care competence. It often falls to the nurse to help older individuals learn about ways to create healthier, happier personal environments, instead of watching them languish in situations devoid of the ingredients that encourage wellness. Such intervention is important because, directly or indirectly, all of one's senses are both affected by and affect the environment (*see* Chapter 13 for further discussion on environment).

3.3 The Older Person's Requirements of their Personal Environment

- The chance to experience nature.
- Space and time to be with family and friends, with abundant chances to give and receive affection.
- A supportive network which facilitates and reinforces wellness behaviour.
- Personal space which gives scope for increasing self-development and for establishing roles judged to be important.
- A culturally sensitivity atmosphere where psychosocial, spiritual and ethnic needs are considered.

Emotional and Mental Wellbeing: the Management of Stress

Not only do environmental influences help determine one's enjoyment or conversely cause displeasure, one's attitudes towards various life-happenings and the often uncontrollable events of daily life can precipitate similar reactions. Emotional wellness depends largely on a person's perception of their self-worth, their awareness of group acceptance and belonging and their sense of security. However, change and stress seem inevitable in modern life, and older individuals are often subjected to multiple stresses, leading to overload. Selye (1956), recognising the relationship between stress and wellbeing, defined it as ' the non-specific response by the body to demands made upon it, pleasurable or not'.

Eustress he regarded as an agreeable and healthy experience, whereby as stress increases, health and performance do likewise. Distress, however, is a disagreeable, pathogenic state whereby, as stress heightens, health and performance decrease. The process is well known. Stressors initiate stimulation, elevating enzymes in the adrenal glands to produce the major stress hormones, adrenaline, noradrenaline and adrenal corticoids. In turn, these hormones activate biochemical changes in the nervous, endocrine and immune systems, thereafter rippling out to affect all organs and systems. This forms part of the general adaptation syndrome (fight or flight mechanism), designed to eventually create a balanced state. However, adaptive energies are finite and prolonged stress taxes adaptive capacity, depleting adaptive reserves, affecting homeostasis, and eventually leading to exhaustion and possibly death. Because of their generally decreased adaptive capacity, older individuals need longer time to recover and return to pre-stress levels than when they were younger. Hence, nurses need to be alert to signs of increased tension among their older clients.

Stress-reduction Measures

The essence of promoting psychological wellbeing and reducing stress in older persons is to:
(1) Reduce the frequency and intensity of stress-creating situations.

This is done by exploring sources of heightened stress; helping persons to recognise and then avoid unnecessary pressures; developing appropriate routines so conserving energy; marshalling resources more effectively, including external support services; and providing time for individuals to focus on particular problems which generate stress for them, e.g. an older person newly diagnosed as diabetic needs time to acquire information about their condition and to make plans for adjustment to dietary and other changes.
(2) Strengthen the individual's psycho-physiological ability to resist stress.

This may be achieved by enhancing self-esteem; assisting older individuals to develop more effective problem-solving and coping strategies; and teaching them to re-orientate their cognitive perceptions of individuals and events, by analysing demands more objectively, so defusing potential stressors.
(3) Counter-condition older individuals to avoid undue

physiological arousal.

Various techniques exist for this latter mode of stress reduction, conducted at both individual and group levels. They include the promotion of healthy sleep; the use of creative leisure activities, which provide for emotional release; physical activity; psychosocial stimulation; the use of progressive relaxation techniques, such as autogenic training and biofeedback; visualisation; meditation; assertion education and self-advocacy. Detailed examination of many of these is beyond the scope of this chapter. However, some are dealt with here and others later in the book.

Healthy Sleep

With advancing age, the quality of sleep often reduces, becoming fragmented and creating some concern. Older individuals with disturbed cycles of orthodox or paradoxical sleep are often left lethargic and unrefreshed. The adverse effects of sedatives or hypnotics not only heighten stress but can cause confusion, falls and agitation. Teaching simple measures for healthy sleep to older persons and their carers, therefore, aids wellness. Measures include:

- Attention to bedtime rituals: to adequate quiet, temperature regulation and ventilation.
- Adequate daytime stimulation, including moderate-intensity exercise, with soothing wind-down activities pre-rest (King *et al.* 1997).
- Warm baths before retiring and foot massage sometimes have a soporific effect.
- The provision of beverages that contain the pre-cursors of serotonin.

(*See* Chapter 6 for further discussion.)

Relaxation Techniques

These may take the form of deep breathing and muscle relaxation exercises, practised singly or in groups. (Information on suitable exercises can be obtained from organisations such as Relaxation for Living.). Certain complementary therapies, soothing music, the use of visual imagery, autogenic training, biofeedback, prayer or meditation are also helpful, as is the use of absorbing, creative hobbies which are personally congenial to the individual. These are particularly helpful if undertaken at times on a group basis so increasing social interaction. The value of physical activity in stress reduction and relaxation promotion with older people is well documented and has already been mentioned.

Assertion Education: Self-advocacy and Self-efficacy

Empowering older people often involves improving their communication and self-presentational skills. Educating them in assertiveness without aggressiveness and assisting them to present their aspirations and needs appropriately is, therefore, pertinent. It can reduce stress and facilitate negotiation. Most important is the strengthening of self-efficacy within older individuals. This situation-specific concept relates to an individual's or group's belief about their level of ability and competence to perform adequately in particular ways in specific situations, e.g. to retain or regain mobility after a stroke through following a specific exercise regime. Two conditions are necessary:

- Persons must have confidence in their personal competence (this equals high self-efficacy).
- Persons must believe the particular advocated behaviours will bring about desired results.

The relevance is that those older people with high levels of self-efficacy, who perceive related behavioural outcomes as beneficial, are more likely to produce the specific behaviour, so achieving their goals, reducing stress and promoting wellness. Staff can assist in the promotion of high self-efficacy by:

- Demonstrating the particular behaviour in clear, related stages (modelling).
- Verbally encouraging the individual to attempt the behaviour.
- Offering spaced 'reinforcements' designed to encourage continuance of the behaviour and feedback, and rewards for endeavour.
- Reducing anxiety through reassurance and continuing encouragement within a relaxed atmosphere.
- Using the Health Locus of Control Construct to encourage older individuals to develop greater 'internality' (McClymont *et al.* 1991, p. 178–183).

Bereavement Counselling

One of the most important sources of stress for older persons is bereavement. Multiple loss is a prevalent theme in later life, partly because many older persons had large families of origin, causing them to have widely dispersed kinship networks, and partly because of loss of contemporaries now that the majority of deaths occur in the older age groups. Concomitant losses can often arise, especially after the death of a spouse or partner, such as loss of home, transport, cherished possessions, income, changes in social identity and some friendships. 'Bereavement overload' (the overwhelming grief precipitated by a rapid succession of multiple losses) can lead to confusion, disorientation, a pervasive sense of helplessness, loneliness and risk of suicide. 'Older old' (85 years of age and upwards) and widows are most at risk. The symptomatolgy accompanying bereavement is well documented (Parkes, 1972). The adverse impact on health can, however, be eased if interventions are appropriate.

The stages of grief need to be recognised, from the immediate shock and numbness, through defensive retreat and eventually the sad acknowledgement of reality, to adaptation and change and hopefully integration and reorganisation. This process can take over a year, and sometimes much longer, so it is necessary for nurses to be patient and to realise the time healing may need. Health promoting interventions range from initial comforting and strengthening; guidance concerning procedures such as registering the death and contacting undertakers; mobilising help to ensure basic needs are met; obtaining spiritual support if client requests this; recognising the importance of cultural rituals and giving support via continuing surveillance. Health promotion measures need to be continued, especially between the third to ninth month when grief is most heightened. Health visitors are in a prime position to provide this continuing support, and referral to organisations such as Cruse can be helpful, but all nurses have much to offer in the support of older bereaved people, if the process is to be healthy (*see* Chapters 17 and 21 for further discussion).

These then constitute the main dimensions of wellness which older persons and their professional carers need to address. They are frequently discussed under the term primary prevention. Health visitors are regarded as major workers in this field, but increasingly other professionals recognise its importance. We turn next to consider the various settings within which strategies for wellness can be employed.

SETTINGS AND STRATEGIES FOR PROMOTING HEALTH AND WELLNESS

Health and Wellness Promotion within Hospital Settings

Within the professional context many nurses are likely to encounter older people during their admission to hospital. Admission rates, which earlier remain fairly constant, begin to rise from 50 years of age, the rate increasing for each succeeding 5-year age band, with the rate for males surpassing that for females for each age group. This increase in admissions is greater in the specialities of general medicine, general surgery, trauma and orthopaedic surgery, and ophthalmology. Within mental health there are slight increases for admission due to dementia (Grimley Evans *et al.* 1992).

Of course these figures represent not merely the prevalence of morbidity, but the availability of treatments, so when nurses encounter older patients within these settings it will often be in the context of amelioration of symptoms. For some older persons, such as those admitted for hip arthroplasty or lens extraction, treatment may prove restorative and markedly health promoting.

Admission to hospital can be anxiety-provoking for all older individuals, posing threat to health, so it is a responsibility of nurses to see that the hospital environment is conducive not merely to recovery but to promoting wellness. The altered presentation of illness in old age may affect the older individual's drive towards stability (see **Figure 3.4**), causing

it to slow or even be thrown off course for a time, depending on the nature and severity of the condition. Therefore, allowing older people time to settle in and become adjusted to routines forms part of creating positive experiences for them. It is all too easy for staff to become over-familiar with techniques and procedures and to lose sight of their impact upon older individuals.

The holistic assessment, upon which any plan of care is based, requires one to take comprehensive account of health promotion needs, whether these be for specific health education, prevention in the form of individualised risk reduction, or health protection measures. The subjective element of the systematic assessment, which encapsulates the patient's thoughts and feelings about his or her health, is as important as the more objective comprehensive functional review undertaken by the nurse. A deliberate effort has to be made to work out the learning objectives for each patient in relation to wellness and the associated teaching aims for the nurse, making these explicit, so that they can be incorporated into the plan of care along with other goals.

Involving Significant Others

As already emphasised, health promotion means far more than patient education. It is concerned with creating a participative relationship, built upon mutual respect and trust, which has wellness as its focus and is as much directed towards involving family and friends in plans of care as it is in increasing the older individual's self-efficacy and self-care competence. From the outset, therefore, older individuals and their significant others need to feel comfortable to ask questions and discuss their concerns freely. Time constraints are a constant for all staff and it is all too easy to appear too busy to answer enquiries or offer explanations, especially when older individuals or their relatives may have difficulty articulating their worries. Professional involvement needs to be clearly demonstrated and health guidance requires to be very specific. Older individuals need to know exactly what they should do to promote their wellbeing, especially in relation to their particular condition, and require time to assimilate this knowledge, so the material given should be clear, concise, unambiguous and presented in logical sequence. Inviting the older individual to rehearse the material via spaced repetition is helpful.

Drugs and Medication

Particularly important is guidance regarding medication. Polypharmacy is a common phenomenon among older people, with some individuals taking six or more drugs daily. The most common include antihypertensives, anti-arthritic preparations, anxiolytics, diuretics and heart drugs such as digoxin. The scope for drug interactions or reactions is, therefore high, especially when altered pharmacokinetics apply, or the older person uses additional over-the-counter remedies as well. A number of hospital admissions are due to either poor compliance with prescribed medication or adverse drug reactions, so care is needed to ensure a comprehensive drug history is taken at admission, and in devising ways of simplifying drug self-administration. Strategies include:

- Checking that older individuals can read medicine labels, or identify drugs correctly by other means; can open containers (many of these intended to protect children prove too difficult for older fingers to manipulate); and are clear about correct dosages.
- Educating older individuals and their significant others in the correct methods and timing of drug-administration, by utilising dose-dispensers, written instructions, memory aids and mnemonics.
- Explaining the reasons for particular drug use and potential expected benefits.
- Impressing upon older persons and their carers the advisability of carrying a written list of current medications with them, and always to tell health professionals about the same.
- Teaching and confirming that older individuals and their caregivers know the common symptoms associated with drug side-effects/reactions, and the action to take if these occur.
- Explaining about the avoidance of alcohol where this applies in drug use.
- Ensuring at discharge that adequate supplies of needed medication are available and that professionals who may be taking over responsibility for care are appropriately informed about drug regimes (*see* Chapter 10 for further discussion).

Health Education Related to Specific Conditions

Nurses often find it helpful to collect or develop written and pictorial health education packages for the more common conditions met within their settings, possibly creating a ward resource. These serve as valuable reinforcement for individualised teaching and also help older persons realise they are not the only ones coping with a particular condition. Where local self-help groups are available, it is often helpful to involve them in providing material and in assisting with follow-up support. Local Health Promotion Units are also valuable sources of help. Those older individuals admitted for acute care will of course require different health promotion approaches from those coping with chronic and progressive illnesses, while particularly sensitive handling is needed for those facing mutilating procedures and disfigurement. Clearly those admitted with life-threatening or terminal illness have special needs. Yet as we have seen, wellness can be achieved, even in dying, if the older individual has a sense of control and is able to express their wishes and any anxieties without fear of censure, participating fully in decision-making.

Palliative care has a holistic approach and is as much concerned with psychological and spiritual needs as it is with biological and medical ones. Pain-relief is of paramount importance and older individuals frequently need reassurance that this will receive high priority (*see* Chapter 9 for further discussion).

Particular care may need to be exercised should relatives collude in keeping prognoses from patients, so affecting discussion of any related aspects. Nurses may find they need to offer appropriate health promotion guidance to significant others in order to allow the older person with terminal illness to achieve a dignified and pain-free death. The model offered by hospice care is valuable here, especially as a number of deaths now take place within institutional settings (*see* Chapter 21 for further discussion).

Although bereavement counselling is longer-term and, therefore, inappropriate for most hospital staff, the health promotion needs of the just-bereaved do need to be considered. Frequently, those affected are themselves elderly. Hence, sensitive empathetic care offered in an unhurried manner can enable bereaved persons to feel positively supported.

Transferring Patients to Intermediate, Outpatient and Community Care

Leaving hospital can sometimes generate anxiety in older individuals, so nurses with a positive health focus will take time to check that instructions for care are well understood both by the older person and significant others, and that community care arrangements are in place. Those nurses in intermediate care settings have particular scope for encouraging rehabilitation and promoting self-efficacy and self-competence, while allowing older individuals to make the needful transition between hospital and home. Examples include an account by Davis (1994) of a research-based, self-empowerment programme utilised within a neurorehabilitation unit. Hardman *et al.* (1995) describe a specialist health visitor/hospital liaison scheme, whereby elderly people were followed-up after hospital discharge, leading to contacts with 19 other services for additional help for these individuals in order to further their wellness. Twenty carers were also identified within this group, who needed support and help to protect their own health.

Outpatient settings also provide special opportunities for health education and prevention, which are often neglected. Quantock (1994) outlines a programme offered to 23 older people waiting in an outpatient department. As a result of her research this author recommends health promotion, particularly in the form of health education, be incorporated into planned care within outpatient clinics and that staff receive further training to fulfil this role. Lindsay *et al.* (1995) describe how they set up a telephone help line for those older adults discharged from coronary care units, which proved highly successful in allowing queries to be quickly resolved and appropriate health education given, while Monks and Illesley (1995) give an account of close coordination of health and social services input for older persons discharged back into the community, which has proved to be health promoting. Illesley and her colleague McKnight also marketed their services to general practitioners, explaining what they could offer to older individuals on discharge from hospital, or needing surveillance and help. This too has extended their health promoting role (Illesley and McKnight, 1997).

Accident and emergency departments afford particular opportunity for intervening in a health promoting manner for older persons. Among similar schemes, Pengelly (1997) (personal communication) outlines an initiative whereby all persons of 65 years of age and over who attend A & E are referred to a health visitor; he or she then carries out a follow-up visit with particular reference to accident prevention and other relevant health education, assessing need and marshalling resources as necessary. This has proved a much valued contact, well received by clients as helping to restore confidence and relieve anxiety. Evaluation will determine if the accident re-attendance rate subsequently falls.

So from health promoting hospitals to health enhancing community care, the scope for nurses to engage in imaginative innovative health promotion ventures with older people appears endless. What is needed is the will to engage.

Health and Wellness Promotion within Primary Care

While the nuclear primary health-care team (PHCT) tends to consist of general practitioners (GPs), practice nurses, district nurses and health visitors, the wider team includes community psychiatric nurses, community learning disability nurses, MacMillan nurses, and a range of supporting specialist and outreach nurses. Sometimes social workers are also attached members. While some have district-wide duties, others are responsible for the care of a defined general medical practice population. Additionally, a number of health visitors carry public health responsibilities, so widening their remit potentially with older people (Standing Nursing and Midwifery Advisory Committee, 1995). For example, they may have designated responsibility for the health visiting care of homeless older persons (approximately 1000 households containing older persons come within local authority purview annually and are accommodated either in hostels or bed and breakfast accommodation), for older travellers and for older vagrants, who are highly unlikely to be registered with any medical practice.

In 1996, as a result of the publication of three White Papers [Department of Health (DoH), 1996a, 1996b, 1996c], the NHS became primary care led, with the intention of:
- Creating a more flexible, seamless and responsive service.
- Assuring greater consistency in high-quality provisions across the country.
- Generating a greater contribution from community nursing staff, including nurse-prescribing.
- Providing increased multidisciplinary education.
- Improving needs-assessment, clinical effectiveness and audit; research and development; developing

partnerships between different agencies.
- Devoting attention to the use and distribution of resources.

Although legislative changes take some time to filter through, these provided great challenges for community nursing staff. Now newer developments under the White Paper *NHS: Modern and Dependable* (DoH, 1998a) are extending the scope for primary health-care groups still further. The Queen's Nursing Institute has already set up a primary health-care resource centre.

The Need for Interdisciplinary and Multidisciplinary Alliances to Meet the Community Health Needs of Older People

We have already seen that the population is ageing. Over 5 million households in England and Wales (one in four) now consist of only older people and one-third of all pensioners live alone. Although nationally, the proportion of overcrowding in households is 5%, in some areas such as Tower Hamlets it reaches 27%, with ethnic minority households, which frequently contain older members, rising to 30%. Hence, the distinct health needs of older people are assuming greater importance, highlighting the requirement for systematic needs-assessment community-wide. This implies nursing staff within individual practices forging alliances, across localities, in order to comprehensively represent the needs of the older population, shown against the current sources of help. Without such community-wide profiling there is little hope of appropriate solutions. It is only when the full extent of need is determined that the importance of health promotion, with its components of health education, disease prevention and health protection, will be recognised and the activity afforded time and financial support.

Health Promotion within General Practice

Since 1993, health promotion within general medical practice was tied more closely to the Key areas outlined in the *Health of the Nation* strategy (DoH, 1992) and similar national initiatives in Scotland, Wales and Northern Ireland. The key areas for health promotion in England were:
- Heart disease.
- Stroke.
- Cancers.
- Accidents.
- Mental health.
- Sexual health.

GPs were urged to focus particularly on the first three areas, since as we have seen they currently constitute greater mortality. Readers will note the sharply increased risk for both these conditions incurred by persons aged over 65 years, thus re-emphasising the need for health promotion both for and in later maturity. Revised proposals under the new strategy (*Our Healthier Nation* (DoH Green Paper). London: HMSO, 1998b) carry these targets forward with the aim of reducing deaths from heart disease, stroke and circulatory disorders for those aged under 65 years by at least a further one-third by the year 2010. Two strategies are mainly used within general practice to achieve these targets:

(1) **Whole population strategy**, whereby individuals in the selected age groups are either invited for screening (specific risk factors being hypertension, obesity, body mass index, cholesterol levels, alcohol intake and smoking behaviour), or are picked up opportunistically when attending a GP for any reason.

(2) **High-risk groups targeting**, whereby those with familial history of heart attack or stroke are particular invited to attend for risk reduction appraisal and 'tailored' health education.

Population screening, by invitation, generally leads to greater response from those less likely to be at risk (some GPs regard these as 'the worried well'). The reason for this appears to be that such responders are often better informed, possibly due to higher levels of education; they may be more health aware and most importantly they may have fewer barriers to overcome in responding. For this reason, focusing on those at highest risk appears to carry some distinct advantages, appearing a more egalitarian approach. However, both approaches are needed if the targets are to be achieved. Both approaches need to be applied with rigour and conscientiousness.

Searching for and Preventing Cardiovascular Disease in Older People

It is important to recognise that cardiovascular disease (CVD) can be prevented among older people. Furthermore, their intrinsically higher risk means they may gain more benefit from prevention programmes than do younger people. Effectiveness reviews indicate that those older persons who have already shown signs of CVD should in future be better targeted [Health Education Authority (HEA), 1996b].

Examples of initiatives involving nurses and health visitors include an account of a multidisciplinary project in Chester which offers rehabilitation and a 9-week health education and follow-up programme to individuals who have sustained either a myocardial infarction or cardiac surgery. Audited via users and the PHCT, the programme has not only improved bed turnover and smoothed discharge arrangements, but has helped individuals successfully reorient their lifestyles and improve their health (Evans, 1994). A second example is an intergenerational programme for 'maintaining healthy hearts' set up by nurses and others in Sheffield. Here the 488 client contacts have ranged in age from 20–78 years, and the project demonstrates a health promotion service, tailored to specific need and taken to clients by professionals working with a broad spectrum of agencies, does confer benefit (Thomas, 1993). A third example of the value of personalised health education for those already experiencing heart disease is given by O'Neill *et al.* (1996). Here a randomised

controlled trial was conducted of persons aged up to 75 years, known to have had angina for at least 6 months. All were assessed at the start and end of the study in relation to their disease status, coronary heart disease (CHD) risk factors, self-assessed quality of life, medications and current use of health services. Those assigned to the intervention group had three visits per year from a health visitor who focused on more effective ways of living with angina and reducing further risks. Findings showed significant improvements in survival and self-assessed quality of life among those in the intervention group. Drug usage was reduced and the authors concluded it proved a cost-effective intervention, reducing risk factors and conferring benefits on older persons (Cupples *et al.* 1996). We now examine some advocated preventative approaches.

Advocated Preventative Approaches

Smoking Control

Smoking is arguably the most crucial single preventive measure that can be taken, not only in relation to CVD, but chronic respiratory disorder, cancer and osteoporosis as well. Attempting to reduce smoking by whatever target is no mean goal (**Table 3.1**). It implies that the PHCT already know the smoking habits of their older practice population, or that they can easily obtain such information. This is often a fallacy, although with computerisation the task is made easier. Moreover, some argue on ethical grounds against the obtaining of such personal data so readers should be aware of this. Once the smokers from within the older population have been identified, it next means contacting them and making a concerted effort to encourage them to quit smoking, either through attending smoking cessation groups, or via personalised programmes. Success depends on:

(1) Convincing individuals of the benefits of not smoking, so creating strong incentives to quit.

(2) Simultaneously identifying those barriers to individuals giving up smoking that exist and reducing these hindrances where possible, so making 'giving up' easier.

(3) Providing encouragement to persevere until the outcome is achieved.

Helpful information on smoking cessation is given by Wilson (1997).

Older smokers have taken the brunt of smoking-related diseases. Encouraged by persuasive social attitudes in their younger years and by certain political incentives (having been supplied with free or subsidised cigarettes in two world wars), they have become habitually physiologically and psychologically dependent (addicted) to tobacco. It is no light thing, therefore, for them to quit smoking and those aiming to help them should recognise the struggle that many go through in endeavouring to quit. Yet findings indicate that health workers often hold negative attitudes towards older people and many rarely use health promotion to encourage older smokers to stop smoking (Young, 1996). The fact is that older persons often can and do quit, and it is never too late to obtain some benefit from smoking cessation, though obviously the longer one has been a smoker the greater the risk incurred.

Diet and Nutrition

Trying to reduce an older person's intake of saturated fatty acids by 35%, and their overall fat intake by 12%, obviously means discovering the dietary habits of the older practice population. This calls for stringent, comprehensive assessment and careful documenting when contact is made. Individuals then have to be convinced of the benefits of healthy eating and the part diet can play in the prevention of illness. Very low-fat diets can bring down cholesterol levels, but depend upon how strictly the diet is maintained.

Obesity

Readers are, of course, aware that obese individuals of any age are at high risk of mortality from CHD and stroke. It is, therefore, important for nurses to identify those older individuals with a Body Mass Index of 30 or more (BMI = weight in kilogrammes divided by square of the height in metres). They can then be given appropriate information, dietary advice and supportive help, as requested.

Blood Pressure

Attempting to reduce the mean systolic pressure in the adult population by at least 5 mmHg implies that some baseline data must be available from which to make comparison. This again emphasises the need for local targets to be set – a factor strongly emphasised in *Our Healthier Nation*. The most effective ways of reducing blood pressure in older people appear to be:

- Increasing their levels of physical activity.
- Taking fish oil supplements.
- Reducing salt intakes, alcohol consumption and smoking.
- Increasing potassium intakes.

There is strong evidence to support medical treatment of even mild degrees of hypertension up to 85 years, with a 25–33% reduction in cardiovascular risk. Moreover, the absolute benefits are greater for older than younger people, with the exception of those suffering from other serious conditions for whom antihypertensive drugs may be hazardous (HEA, 1996b).

Alcohol Intake

Traditionally, health education regarding alcohol has not been directed towards older persons, yet, if the recommendations of an overall reduction of 4% reduction are to be met, then it suggests drinking behaviour will need to be identified and specific guidance given as required.

Cancer Prevention: The Place of Screening

Cancers account for one in five of all deaths among older individuals. The following cancers are listed in order of fatality:

(1) Men
   - Lung.
   - Large bowel.
   - Prostrate.
   - Stomach.
   - Bladder.
   - Leukaemia/lymphomas.
   - Pancreas.
(2) Women
   - Breast.
   - Lung.
   - Large bowel.
   - Ovarian.
   - Leukaemia.
   - Cervical.
   - Bladder.

Skin cancer is assuming greater importance due to greater sun exposure. Among preventive strategies smoking cessation is to the fore. Thereafter, a diet rich in anti-oxidants, pollution control, skin protection, and improved general health and safety measures are thought to be important. Apart from these, primary prevention is limited at present, since causes of cancers have not yet been fully identified. Secondary prevention must, therefore, be employed.

Secondary prevention means the prompt effective identification of latent disease within individuals, preferably at the presymptomatic stage. For this to happen, effective, simple, accurate, precise, sensitive and specific screening tests need to be available. Sensitivity and accuracy are vital, because they indicate positive results will be demonstrated if the disease is present. Specificity and precision are vital, meaning the test has the ability to give negative results if the condition being screened for is not present. However, screening will not be successful unless tests are acceptable. Which means non-invasive painless procedures being available that are neither time-consuming nor threatening. Ethical issues dictate that the condition being screened for is important and that beneficial treatment is available. In the case of cancers, cervical cytology and mammography are the two national screening procedures currently available to women in the UK. At present, there is no screening programme for prostatic cancer, although this is becoming a current issue.

Cervical Cancer

England and Wales have one of the highest death rates from this condition in the developed world. Its relevance for older people is that it mostly presents in women in their early sixties. Risk factors for cervical cancer are given in **Box 3.4**.

Cervical cancer in the pre-invasive stage is amenable to treatment, therefore it is worthwhile to screen for this condition. The population target for screening currently comprises women aged 20–64 years, with older women being followed up in certain cases to 74 years. However, a substantial proportion of women 65 years and more have not been screened, nor under current policies are they likely to be. Fletcher (1990), pointing out that older women often present

3.4 Risk Factors for Cervical Cancer

- Sexual activity (risk being particularly related to age at first intercourse; multiple partners for the women; and risk is increased for women if male partners have multiple sexual contacts).
- Lower socioeconomic class.
- Parity (risk increases with multi-parity).
- Smoking.

3.5 Risk Factors for Breast Cancer

- Early onset of menstruation.
- Late menopause.
- Age at first pregnancy (older women at greater risk).
- Obesity.
- Excessive alcohol consumption.
- Benign breast disease.
- Socioeconomic factors (condition is commoner in socioeconomic groups 1 and 2).
- There also appears to be some link with those who have not breast fed children, those who have taken oral contraceptives (slight risk) and genetic predisposition (DoH, 1995).
- At present the National Breast Screening Programme (NBSP) is coordinated within the National Health Service. It routinely covers women between the age of 50 and 64 years. Older women are entitled to breast screening on request, but this fact is not advertised and a recent survey on behalf of Age Concern (Age Concern, 1996) found:
  - 55% of those interviewed (over 1000 respondents in different regions of the country), aged 65 years or more, had never had a breast scan at any time in their lives.
  - 76% had not requested screening since they were 65 years.
  - Only 30% thought their age group was eligible for screening.

with late-stage disease and, therefore, have a poorer survival rate, advocates their opportunistic screening within general practice, with a regular recall schedule of 3–5 years. She considers on a crude estimate basis, that women over 65 years could benefit with a 65% improvement in mortality from this disease, if screened regularly.

The present aim is to screen at least 80% of the 20–64 age group, if the *Health of the Nation* target of a 20% fall in incidence from 1990, is to be reached by 2000 AD. Women in metropolitan areas tend to respond less readily to cervical cytology screening programmes, possibly for socioeconomic reasons, so nurses working in these areas are particularly challenged to target those at risk and present relevant health education more effectively. Such health education directed towards those most at risk is a main plinth of the strategy and nurses and health visitors can reinforce the message whenever they have contact with women. However, some older women fallaciously assume that after menopause they are no longer at risk. It is important that explanations about regular screening into old age are given.

Breast Cancer

A foremost target in the *Health of the Nation* strategy was to reduce the rate of breast cancer deaths among women invited for screening by 15% by the year 2000 – a saving of some 1,250 lives per year. The new strategy *Our Healthier Nation* aims to further reduce all cancer deaths in persons aged 65 years and under by a further one-fifth.

At present one in fourteen women in the UK develops breast cancer at some time in her life, but the incidence is more common in those aged 50 years and over. Some 13,000 deaths occur annually, of which 89% (11,500) are in women over 50. Survival rates for operable breast cancer are around 70% after 5 years, with comparable rates for locally advanced breast cancer standing at 35%. There is no known way of preventing breast cancer at present. Identified risk factors include those given in **Box 3.5**.

Major reasons for not requesting screening appear to be:

(1) **The belief that older women are not eligible for screening (70%).** Findings show the older the age of the respondent the less likely they were to think they were eligible.

(2) **The belief that older women are either at no risk or very little risk of developing the condition.** This belief is fallacious.

(3) **The belief that they were not at risk because they did not have a family history of breast cancer.** The fact is that most women who develop breast cancer have no family history of the disease.

By contrast to this there is a good deal of research evidence supporting the likely benefits of breast screening for older women. An estimated 2000 lives annually could be saved if routine screening was adopted for all women over 50 years of age. The present detection rate for breast cancer in the UK is 5.5 per 1000 in women aged 50–64 years compared to 13.3 for women aged 65 years or more (indicating greater cost-effectiveness). In Guernsey, where breast screening has been offered to all women over 50 years of age since 1990, the detection rate is 12 cancers found per 1000 women screened aged 50–64 years and 19 cancers per 1000 women screened age 65 years and upwards. This indicates the work that still remains to be done.

Age Concern is currently mounting a campaign for routine screening to be offered to all women aged 50 years and more. Meantime, all nurses and health visitors are urged to raise breast awareness among all women 50 years of age and upwards, pointing out their eligibility for screening on request.

Mental Health

Under the *Health of the Nation* strategy (see **Table 3.1**) each of the three targets had application to older people, although progress on the first target 'to improve significantly the health and social functioning of mentally ill persons' could not be accurately measured since indicators were not set. This is because, as yet, comprehensive data are lacking on the prevalence and severity of mental illness in the community. We do, however, know that the conditions mostly affecting older individuals are depression and dementia.

Depression in Later Life

For a variety of reasons, older persons may be prone to depression. A community-based study by Murphy *et al.* (1988) found 29% of older adults, living in private households were frank or borderline depressives, not all known to their GP or receiving treatment. Further studies by Dewey (1994) have demonstrated increased mortality rates in relation to later-life depression. It is important to be aware of such statistics, not only to help ameliorate the personal misery they reveal, but also because late recognition of depression increases suicide risk. In this connection, it should be appreciated that the document *Our Healthier Nation* (DoH, 1998b) aims to reduce the suicide rate by a further one-sixth. A joint campaign has recently been mounted by The Royal Colleges of Psychiatry and GPs to 'defeat depression', designed particularly to increase professional awareness. Also, the University of Exeter is producing audit packages on the primary care of those suffering from depression, which may well prove helpful in improving therapeutic approaches to older persons and their families.

Nurses and health visitors can do much to help detect incipient depression among older individuals through careful assessment and monitoring, and can help reduce the adverse effects of the condition through a variety of preventive, teaching and social support techniques. Liaison with voluntary agencies working in the mental health field extends their health promotion activities. Armstrong (1995, 1996), working as a mental health facilitator across several GP practices, describes her work in facilitating PHCT members to identify, treat and support older individuals with anxiety and depression. She offers practical guidance to nurses. The project is being evaluated.

Older men in particular are at risk of suicide or parasuicide (attempting to take one's own life). Nurses need to be aware of those at greater risk, e.g. those recently bereaved (especially loss of a partner), those who have recently relocated (particularly if they have lost close social networks), those who are isolated (especially if they are also coping with protracted, painful or debilitating illness), those suffering from depression, low self-esteem and role loss. All this points to the ability of nurses within the primary care setting being able to carry out regular surveillance of their older clients, either through home visiting, clinic contact or being in touch with older people in groups such as Horizon Clubs, Independent Living Groups or Look after Yourself groups. Nor should the benefits of exercise on mental health be forgotten (Biddle,

1997). Possibly in the future more surveillance can be given through increased numbers of older persons attending physical activity groups. Regular monitoring of carers is also essential because they have been shown to be prone to depression (Krause *et al.* 1992). Careful profiling of all the older individuals within the practice or locality setting and regular review of same, can help to keep a needs-based overall care plan fresh and relevant, while maintaining health alliances enables jaded staff to renew interest and motivation.

Dementia and Older People

Dementia will be dealt with in Chapter 18, but its prevalence is pertinent here, in relation to the promotion of wellness. At present, approximately 2% of those 60 and over are affected, rising to 22% for those aged 80 years and more. This means some 500,000 older persons with dementia are being cared for at home. Significantly improving the health and social functioning of persons with dementia living in the community, rests upon staff having positive attitudes, recognising the individuality of each affected person, fostering their dignity and independence as much as with other older persons, and seeking to meet their physical and psychosocial needs in creative ways.

Promoting the health of those caring for persons with dementia is another area where the primary health-care team will be closely involved. The need for respite requires to be recognised and staff alerted to signs of undue stress.

Accidents in Relation to Older People

Currently some 6000 deaths occur annually among older people due to accidents, with some 50% occurring in and around the home. The largest number occur on steps, stairs or in the kitchen. An estimated 300,000 serious but not-fatal accidents happen per year, so community nursing staff of all types will frequently encounter older persons who have had an accident. They should be aware of the long-standing impact of disability resulting from serious but non-fatal accidents in later life. It is noteworthy that the *Health of the Nation* target for those 65 years and over aimed to reduce the death rate from accidents by at least 33% from a base rate in 1990 from 55.8 per 100,000 to no more than 37.4 per 100,000 by 2005. Interestingly, the thinking under the proposed new strategy (DoH, 1998b) is to focus on reducing the incidence of serious accidents by at least one-fifth.

Evidence suggests that most accidents are preventable [Royal Society for the Prevention of Accidents (RoSPA), 1996]. The largest number result from falls in and around the home (Oakley *et al.* 1996). Members of the PHCT are ideally placed to carry out opportunistic advice and to contribute to accident prevention groups, through close collaboration with those from other disciplines. A study among older people in the UK revealed that accidents were significantly associated with poor mobility, disabilities, giddiness and poor vision, indicating the need for comprehensive assessment at regular intervals and appropriate intervention to control or relieve these conditions (Bennett, 1997). Older persons living in terraced houses or flats were more frequently involved in accidents, indicating to community staff those more vulnerable who need health protection and education. However, older people who had participated in regular exercise, had attended a retirement club, or who had used safety equipment, had significantly fewer accidents. As the majority of accidents in the home were due to falls, those wishing to successfully intervene require to understand the complexity of causes for falls in older people. Contributory environmental factors relate to poor design of buildings, poor maintenance of older property, lack of maintenance of pavements, faulty equipment and inadequate lighting (Morgan and Carter, 1996). RoSPA recommend that members of the PHCT:

- Incorporate accident prevention issues whenever they see older clients at home or in surgeries.
- Introduce the topic of accident prevention as a routine component of the over seventy-five's assessment.
- Disseminate the knowledge more widely when their practice facilities are available for the treatment of minor accidents.
- Develop greater multi-agency collaboration at local levels, in order to prevent accidents.

They also urge that older people are given opportunity to participate in the planning of homes; that design features in future include walk-in showers fitted with seats; second stair rails on steps and stairs; and that the training needs of the PHCT in respect of accident prevention are recognised both in more multidisciplinary courses and specific courses, such as those arranged by National Boards. (Safety needs are more fully addressed in Chapters 11 and 13.)

Sexual Health

None of the *Health of the Nation* targets related particularly to persons over 65 years of age. Nevertheless, contrary to popular belief, older persons are as sexually active as those of other age groups. The general objectives to reduce the incidence of HIV infection and the incidence of other sexually transmitted diseases in the population, therefore, have relevance for them. Developing local profiles as part of the base for a comprehensive needs assessment of the local older population can help identify particular groups who may be at increased risk, hence indicating the services required to meet their needs.

The full impact of HIV/AIDs has yet to be demonstrated among older people, but Marr (1994a,b) considers the issue is under-researched, probably because of lack of awareness among health professionals of HIV issues in this age group. Misdiagnosis and underdiagnosis can place individuals at risk of premature death, and HIV dementia in particular is likely to be misdiagnosed as Alzheimer's disease or Parkinson's disease. On the psychosocial level, older people may be significantly affected as either caregiving spouses, partners, parents or grandparents of a person with HIV/AIDs. Hence,

members of the PHCT may wish to reconsider the most effective ways of offering health education to older persons, especially concerning 'at risk' behaviour, routes of transmission and sources of supportive care. One example of good practice is provided by Baker (1994) who discusses a district-nurse-led project in Edinburgh, which is making an impact (*see* Chapter 15 for further discussion).

WELLNESS PROMOTION WITH PERSONS FROM ETHNIC MINORITIES

Britain has traditionally catered for a range of ethnic minority groups, and many have been assimilated into the host country, adding richness to the overall culture. More recently Black and Asian people have settled in the UK, making up a more substantial part of the population, especially in some larger conurbations. Additionally, smaller groups of refugees have arrived from further cultures, so that there is a diversity of ethnicity. According to 1991 census data, there are an estimated 175,500 persons from these groups, aged 60 years and over; with the numbers expected to rise considerably over the next two decades (Pharoah, 1995). Studies in the 1980s revealed considerable level of health need and social deprivation among certain ethnic minorities, with a particularly low uptake of health and social services among ethnic elders. Misconceptions of need and use of services were common among service providers (Badger *et al.* 1989; Boneham, 1989; Chiu, 1989).

Stereotypical assumptions led to the belief that as older ethnic elders are mostly highly revered, even in Britain they will be totally supported and cared for within their extended family, needing little or no help from community health or social services. Such assumptions disregarded those older people who had no family in the UK or whose families were unable to provide this 'ideal' caring situation, however culturally desirable (Donaldson, 1993). With further research the needs of ethnic minorities are being identified and the plight of ethnic elders highlighted (Ahmed, 1993; Hopkins and Bahl, 1993; Askham *et al.* 1995).

Health Needs among Ethnic Minority Elders

Surveys show older individuals from Black and ethnic minorities often have similar patterns of illness and disability to the older indigenous population, although their specific risks must also be borne in mind. However, their illness experience frequently appears more severe, they consult general practitioners more often, and have a generally higher mortality, which has shown less tendency to improve than that of indigenous elders (Balarajhan *et al.* 1989).

When considered in relation to the key areas within the *Health of the Nation* strategy, older persons from ethnic minorities aged 65–74 years showed the following:

- **Coronary heart disease**. Indians aged 65–74 years have a 37% increased mortality risk, Pakistanis and Bangladeshis an 18% higher risk, and Irish a 16% greater risk than comparable older persons in England and Wales. Conversely, East Africans, some other African Commonwealth elders, Caribbeans and those from other European countries tend to have lower mortality rates.
- **Stroke**. Bangladeshis aged 65–74 years, especially males, have significantly higher mortality risk (two and a half times greater than the rate for England and Wales of comparable age). Commonwealth Africans and Carribeans also have increased risk, showing rates twice and one and a half times higher, respectively.
- **Breast cancer**. Mortality rates for breast cancer are lower among all ethnic group women aged 65 years and upwards, than is the case for women in England and Wales. The lowest rates are found among Indian and Pakistani women.
- **Lung cancer**. Irish men and women have a 44% greater mortality risk from this disease than the indigenous older population. Bangladeshis have only a 13% less risk than those of comparable age in England and Wales. Caribbeans, Indians and Pakistanis currently have lower mortality rates.
- **Accidents**. In relation to accidents, older Irish and Indians (65–74 years) have higher rates than indigenous older persons, but Carribeans and Africans demonstrate lower rates.
- **Mental health**. For reasons given earlier, mental health experience is less well defined. However, the suicide rate among Irish older persons is 17% and among Indians 15% higher than for those of comparable age from England and Wales. Carribeans have a suicide rate comparable to the indigenous population (Balarajhan, 1995).

The Need for Culturally Sensitive Health Promotion

These figures highlight the problems which still have to be faced and point to the preventive health education needed. Pharoah (1995), who conducted research particularly into primary health care for ethnic elders in London and other large conurbations, found a range of problems which PHCTs need urgently to address. For instance, because of considerable communication difficulties the needs of different ethnic groups appear not to be adequately represented to health professionals, but neither does it seem that staff take steps to adequately elicit them.

There are interpreting problems and an urgent need for link and health liaison workers to assist in improving communication and promoting wellbeing. Low levels of literacy among older women in particular, mean written health education materials are not always appropriate. Yet it seems few among community nursing staff have urged the use of videoed material, or audio tapes in ethnic languages. For cultural reasons, many older women wish only to be treated by female staff, yet as many general practitioner practices in London and some of the large conurbations tend still to be single-handed, this choice is often denied them. Furthermore, in such situations, practice nurses may not always be employed, again denying users their services, although evidence suggests nursing services are highly valued by ethnic elders.

Perceptions of health and illness differ between ethnic groups, and these may affect compliance with prescribed treatments, or recommended regimes may conflict with traditional alternative health care. Orwin (1996) considers primary nursing to be particularly helpful in setting patients from ethnic minorities at ease. She also stresses the importance of understanding attitudes and cultural values; for example, some older Muslim men may be embarrassed by women in positions of authority and may hesitate to articulate their needs.

Nurses will realise that very positive efforts have to be made in order to offer culturally sensitive health education which meets the needs of older people from different ethnic minorities, and that this is an urgent and challenging problem. Help is available from local health promotion units and many self-help groups are now producing ethnically appropriate material. The Health Education Authority has helpful suggestions to offer, culled from its research into Black and ethnic minority health and lifestyles. Examples of innovative ventures, such as that shown by Redmond (1993) and Goodburn (1994, 1995), also have much to commend them. There is necessity to engage in sensitive local needs-assessment, and in research to identify particular problems and to determine more effective solutions.

The wishes of ethnic elders for health education need to be respected. Research shows they particularly wish to learn how to manage certain illnesses, such as diabetes or tuberculosis, more effectively; want information on accessing health and social services; are concerned about the effects of social deprivation, loneliness and isolation upon health; and are looking for information about how best to change lifestyles within their cultural framework, particularly in relation to nutrition and physical activity (Elliott, 1994). In responding, nurses need to adopt more innovative approaches, formulating tailored health promotion care plans. At the population level, commissioning strategies need to be more focused, multidisciplinary education and training for health professionals extended, and particular attention paid to the over seventy-five's annual assessment, which currently appears to be working less well among ethnic elders (Pharoah, 1995).

HEALTH ASSESSMENT FOR THOSE AGED 75 YEARS AND OVER

The idea of regular health checks for older people has been mooted for some time, and some health authorities have set up projects, mainly directed towards the younger elderly (65–74 years). However, in 1990 the health assessment of those aged 75 years and more became mandatory, as part of the general practitioner's (GP's) contract (Department of Health, 1989). Since then it has proved a somewhat controversial issue, with enthusiasts pointing to the many advantages it confers and those who are sceptical arguing that it is as yet unproven, is costly in terms of manpower and time and may not be cost-effective. It is important to appreciate the background to this issue in order to understand if this assessment is relevant to health promotion.

Background

Early in the life of the National Health Service (NHS) a series of studies of older people were undertaken, which revealed a level of illness and disability unknown to the health service: this became known as ' the iceberg of morbidity'. The reasons were that prior to the NHS older persons had tended to accept much ill health as a concomitant of ageing and the costs of obtaining medical care acted as a deterrent to their seeking health care. Since then older persons have learned how to use the existing services, preventive care has increased and attitudes have begun to change. Although under-reporting of illness still exists, more recent studies have indicated that the 'iceberg' is smaller than first thought. (Ebrahim *et al.* 1984; Perkins, 1991; Garrett, 1992). Nevertheless, difficulties older persons experience with continence, sight, hearing, mobility, foot health, dental care, anxiety or depression may still not be revealed to health-care professionals, largely because of social reasons. Lack of attention to these problems can, however, lead to functional difficulties, which in turn impact on the quality of an older person's life. It is now recognised that such 'case-finding', especially in the early stages, can lead quickly to improvement, so reducing both time and more costly treatments. Accordingly, a scheme was launched to deal with the more vulnerable section of the older population, employing a mixture of assessment and screening techniques. Hence, under the terms of the 1990 contract (DoH, 1989), for an increased capitation fee for each patient, GPs are required to:

- Invite each patient 75 years or over to attend for a consultation.
- Offer to make a home visit to assess suitability of service provision.

GPs are allowed to delegate this activity to another competent person, but remain responsible for the activity. The areas for review are determined and include:
- Social environment and relationships.
- Sensory functioning.
- Mental health status.
- Physical condition, including continence.
- Use of medicines.

Certain prerequisites are necessary, including an age/sex register for easy identification of persons aged 75 years and upwards, appropriate assessment sheets (there is as yet no standardised form) and an appropriate record system to deal with both personal and aggregated data. Williams and Wallace (1993) have set out detailed proposed assessment schedules and many GPs utilise these frameworks, encouraging nursing

staff to do so. In practice, approximately one-third of initial assessments are carried out by GPs, the remainder being undertaken mostly by practice nurses or health visitors.

In one or two instances, GPs have used 'trained' volunteers, a practice which Williams and Wallace deplore on both professional and ethical grounds. It is expected that staff carrying out the health checks will have a wide understanding of the processes of normal and abnormal ageing; knowledge of medical, paramedical and social services, both statutory and voluntary; are familiar with the organisation of general practice; and have positive attitudes towards older persons and their problems. They also require a range of skills to undertake effective assessment, elicit relevant information, refer appropriately, monitor and follow-up. Communication ability is paramount, as is a knowledge of relevant screening techniques, health education, preventive measures and the principles of anticipatory care.

In her study, Tremellen (1992) found nurses with extra qualifications identified the highest number of unmet needs (400 per 1000 visits). Several studies indicate that approximately 64% of those older persons invited accept the assessment. However, few refused if they were subsequently followed-up (Brown *et al.* 1992). Approximately 43% of those assessed have unreported need, the majority of referrals being for chiropody and occupational therapy, (Wormald *et al.* 1992; Nocon, 1993).

Nurses appear to make wider referrals than do GPs (Littlewood *et al.* 1990; May, 1992). The latter explains how the use of a personalised invitation, a specific appointment and a franked envelope for reply, led to a 98% response rate within her practice. She found the assessment gave opportunity to check when glasses if worn, were last renewed, if spectacles still fit, if dentures are used and are in good condition and if hearing aids are being worn appropriately. In making a full physical assessment, chance is afforded not just to check blood pressure or test urine, but to note levels of self-care ability, skin state, muscle tone and vitality. In keeping with the Patients' Charter, which stresses the need to involve patients and their families in decision-making, May finds the health assessment offers opportunity to consider use of relevant services or additional aids to daily living as part of the health promoting role. This is borne out by Whitely and Brittain (1993), who describe their experiences with older persons in Glasgow.

However, studies also show considerable difference in thoughts concerning the value of the activity. Older people in general favour the procedure, as do nurses and health visitors. GPs are less convinced of their value, arguing that as 90% of older people consult annually the specific check is unnecessary (Chew *et al.* 1994). Against this must be set the identified level of unreported need. Furthermore, the benefits of routine assessment are not merely related to the identification of unmet need. For the apparently well older person they also provide an opportunity to:
- Explain that the primary health-care team is concerned about older persons.
- Confirm levels of wellness.
- Provide information about existing and new relevant services that the older person might wish to use in future.

- Offer relevant health promotion via 'tailored' health education and primary, secondary and tertiary prevention.
- Explore social and environmental circumstances and establish degree of vulnerability.
- Undertake a medication and therapeutic review.
- Review with older person health care goals and care plan.
- Meet with and review needs of caregivers/carers.
- Establish a more comprehensive data-set for future contact.
- Use the assessment for audit purposes.

This latter may cover:
- Length of time health checks take (currently estimated as 1 hour per person).
- Amount and type of need found.
- Adequacy of resources available to meet such need.
- Improvements required or possible.
- The type and frequency of referrals made.
- Changes made by older person as a result of the health assessment.
- Changes in health status following the assessment.
- Time expenditure and costs incurred in carrying out assessments (Williams and Wallace, 1993).

These authors consider those older persons resident in nursing homes should also receive an annual assessment from 75 years and upwards. This in spite of some dissent from staff, who consider they are well covered. The point is that one can sometimes become blunted to the needs of persons in long-term care, so failing to perceive short-falls in provision. The over seventy-five's health check can provide the opportunity for a detached review to be given and relevant health promotion provided. The health promotion opportunities within nursing homes are great, but are mostly related to the preservation and restoration of function, rehabilitation, health maintenance and to quality of life measures. All the measures suggested above under hospital settings have their application to those working with nursing homes. Additionally, these nurses have the responsibility of creating a home-like atmosphere in which older persons can continue to flourish and contribute.

SUMMARY

In concluding our consideration of health and wellness in later life, we have established that this is an increasingly important area as the population ages. While great improvements have been made in the longevity and health of older people there is still much room for further prevention of illness, and for offering focused health education and health and wellness promotion (McCarthy, 1995). As the new shape of the National Health Service emerges, nurses and health visitors will continue to play a vital role, increasing their input into the promotion of health and wellness among older individuals, their families and communities. They will be afforded still greater scope under the new thinking contained in the strategy *Our Healthier Nation* with its key aims of:
- Promoting the health of the population as a whole by increasing the length of people's lives and the number of years people spend free from illness.
- Improving the health of the worst-off in society and narrowing the health gap.

Under a new national target the Government, health and local authorities, voluntary bodies, communities and individuals will be invited to join in partnership to reduce inequalities and improve wellbeing. The wider socioeconomic determinants of health and disease are being recognised and emphasised. Those engaged in professional practice, education and research now have the opportunity and the responsibility to see the vision realised.

KEY POINTS

- As the UK population ages, health and wellness are becoming increasingly important. Although people are living longer, there is room for improvement in the the health of people in later life.
- The concepts of 'health' and 'wellness' are complex and multidimensional. Lay views and professional views may contrast.
- Older people have a central role in promoting their own health and wellness.
- Perspectives on health promotion can be medical, educational, economic, political and philosophical.
- Key dimensions of wellness include self-responsibility, enlisting the help of significant others, nutritional awareness, physical fitness, environmental sensitivity, emotional wellbeing and the management of stress, healthy sleep, relaxation techniques, assertion, self-advocacy and self-efficacy, and bereavement counselling.
- New strategies towards *Our Healthier Nation* aim to promote the health of the population as a whole and reducing inequalities by improving the health of the worst-off.
- There are distinct considerations for health and wellness promotion within different settings.
- A wide range of preventative approaches are being utilised, specifically for smoking control, diet and nutrition, avoiding obesity, blood pressure or excessive alcohol intake, and towards mental and sexual health. Screening for cancer can be highly effective in older age, particularly as the majority of cancers occur in later life.
- Nurses and health visitors have a vital role in the promotion of health and wellness with individuals, their families, and within communities.

AREAS AND ACTIVITIES FOR STUDY AND REFLECTION

- Ask older persons with whom you come into contact what they mean by the terms 'health' and 'wellness'. Discover what they include as components of wellness. Compare these with your own personal perceptions. Analyse and explain any differences.
- Study the integrative dynamic process of wellness and health promotion in later life, represented in Figure 3.3b. As you do so, think of some of the older individuals with whom you have worked, endeavouring to relate your experiences with them to the two prongs of this process. Try to think of the different activities you engaged in with them, identifying and listing those which were directed towards helping them maintain equilibrium and the steady state and then those which formed part of helping them in their thrust towards high-level wellness. Consider too the values, ideas and skills which you brought to the partnership-activity, both as a person and as a nurse. Think how these various qualities may have influenced the older person and the situation.
- In your work setting, identify and list the particular opportunities for health and wellness promotion with older persons which present to you. Are these opportunities being exploited? If they are not, consider what can be done to utilise these opportunities.
- Identify the opportunities within your work setting for the building of intradisciplinary and interdisciplinary health alliances in order to facilitate health promotion with older people. Make a list of the stages necessary to reach out and make these alliances, considering how best these might be achieved by discussing ideas with your peers and managers.
- Consider how in your practice setting you might help to reduce inequalities in health within and between groups of older people with whom you come into contact. Identify ways in which those older persons who are more vulnerable, or at greater risk, might be more effectively helped to achieve higher levels of wellness.

REFERENCES

Age Concern England. *Not at my age: why the present breast screening system is failing women aged 65 years or over*. London: Age Concern England, 1996.

Ageing Well UK Programme. *Guidelines for partnership*. London: Age Concern England/Health Education Authority, 1996.

Ahmed WIU, ed. *Race and health in contemporary Britain*. Buckinghamshire: Open University Press, 1993.

Allied Dunbar National Fitness Survey. *Activity and health research*. London: Sports Council and Health Education Authority, 1992.

Armstrong E. Challenging Depression. *Nursing Stand* 1995, 20 September 1995, 9:55.

Armstrong E. Depression in primary care:– knowledge for practitioners. *Nursing Times* (Professional Development Section) 1996a, 27 November 1996, 92:1–4.

Armstrong E. Depression: The role of the nurse. *Nursing Times* (Professional Development Section) 1996b, 4 December 1996, 92:5–8.

Armstrong E. Depression: professional issues. *Nursing Times* (Professional Development Section) 1996c, 11 December 1996, 92:9–12.

Askham J, Henshaw L ,Tarpey M. *Social and Health Authority services for elderly people from Black and minority ethnic communities. Studies in ageing*. Age Concern Institute of Gerontology, King's College. London: HMSO, 1995.

Badger F, Atkin K, Griffiths R. Why don't GPs refer their disabled Asian patients to district nurses? *Health Trends* 1989, 21:

Baker V. Supporting patients with HIV/AIDS. *Community Outlook* 1994, 4:19–20.

Balarajhan R. Ethnicity and variations in the nation's health. *Health Trends* 1995, 21:114–119.

Balarajhan R, Yuen P, Raleigh V. Ethnic differences in general practice consultations. *Br Med J* 1989, 299:958–960.

Bennett G. *Falls and balance*. Health Education Authority conference session 'Active in Later Life'. London: HEA, 1997.

Benzeval M, Judge K, Whitehead M. *Tackling inequalities in health: an agenda for action*. London: King's Fund, 1995.

Biddle S. *The psychology of physical activity and ageing*. Lecture proceedings at Health Education Authority conference 'Active in Later Life'. London: HEA, 1997.

Bone MR, Bebbington AC, Jagger C, Morgan K, Nicolas G. *Health expectancy and its uses*. London: HMSO, 1995.

Boneham M. Ageing and ethnicity in Britain: the case of elderly Sikh women in a Midland town. *New Community* 1989, 15:447–459.

Brown K, Williams EI, Groom L. Health checks on patients 75 years and over in Nottinghamshire, after the new GP contract. *Br Med J* 1992, 305:619–621.

Bunton R, MacDonald G, eds. *Health promotion: disciplines and diversity*. London: Routledge, 1992.

Calnan M. *Health and illness: the lay perspective*. London: Tavistock Publications, 1987.

Campbell AV. The ethics of health education. In: Wilson-Barnett J, Macleod Clark J, eds. *Research in health promotion and nursing*. Basingstoke: MacMillan, 1993.

Caraher M. Nursing and health promotion practices: the creation of victims and winners, in a political context. *J Adv Nurs* 1994, 79:465–468.

Caraher M. Nursing and health education: victim blaming. *Br J Nurs* 1995, 4:1190–1211.

Carnegie UK Trust. *The Carnegie inquiry into the third age*. Dunfermline: Carnegie UK Trust, 1990.

Catford JC. Positive health indicators: towards a new information base for health promotion. *Comm Med* 1983, 5:125–132.

Chew A, Wilkin D, Glendinning C. Annual assessments of patients aged 75 years and over: views and experiences of elderly people. *Br J*

Gen Pract 1994, 44:567–570.

Chiu S. Chinese elderly people: no longer a treasure at home. *Social Work Today* 1989, (10 Aug):15–17.

Colvez A. Disability-free life expectancy. In: Ebrahim S, Kalanche A, eds. *Epidemiology in old age*. London: BMJ/WHO Publications, 1996.

Cribb A. Health promotion: a human science. In: Wilson-Barnett, Macleod Clark J, eds. *Research in health promotion and nursing*. Basingstoke: MacMillan, 1993.

Cupples ME, McKnight A, O'Neill C, Normand C. The effect of personal health education on the quality of life of patients with angina, in general practice. *Health Educ J* 1996, 4:75–83.

Davis SM. An investigation into nurses' understanding of health education and health promotion within a neuro-rehabilitation setting. *J Adv Nurs* 1994, 21:951–959.

Davies J, Kelly M, eds. *Healthy cities: research and practice*. London: Routledge, 1993.

Department of Health. *Terms of service for doctors in general practice*. London: HMSO, 1989.

Department of Health. *A consultative document for health in England*. London: HMSO, 1991.

Department of Health. *A strategy for health in England*. London: HMSO, 1992.

Department of Health. *Eat well: an action plan from the Nutrition Task Force to achieve the Health of the Nation Targets on diet and nutrition*, London: HMSO, 1994a.

Department of Health. *Fit for the future. A health of the nation review: 2 years on*. London: HMSO, 1994b.

Department of Health. *The health of the nation. Key area handbook: CANCERS*. London: HMSO, 1995.

Department of Health. *Choice and opportunity: primary care – the future* (White Paper). London: HMSO, 1996a.

Department of Health. *The NHS: a service with ambitions* (White Paper). London: HMSO, 1996b.

Department of Health. *Primary care: delivering the future* (White Paper). London: HMSO, 1996c.

Department of Health. *New NHS – modern and dependable*. London: HMSO, 1998a.

Department of Health. *Our healthier nation* (Green Paper). London: HMSO, 1998b.

Dewey ME. Mortality and mental disorder. In: Copeland JRH, Abou-Saleh M, Blaxter DG, eds. *Principles and practice of geriatric psychiatry*. Chichester: Wiley, 1994.

DHSS (NI). *A regional strategy for the Northern Ireland Health and Personal Social Services 1992–1997*. Department of Health and Social Security (NI), 1991.

Donaldson LJ. Health and health care of elderly people: some current issues. In: *Central Health Monitoring Unit. The health of elderly people: an epidemiological overview, Companion papers to Vol. 1 overview series*. London: Department of Health/HMSO, 1993.

Downie RJ, Tannahill C, Tannahill A. *Health promotion: models and values, 2nd edition*. Oxford: Oxford University Press, 1996.

Doyle Y. Aiming for health gain in the UK. *Irish Med J* 1994, 87:82–83.

Dubos R. Mirage of health: Utopias, progress and biological change. In: Ansen R, ed. *World perspectives*. New York: Harper and Row, 1959.

Dudley NJ, Burns SE. The influence of age on policies for admission and thrombolysis in CCUs in the UK. *Age and Ageing* 1992, 21:95–98.

Dunn M. *High-level wellness*. Arlington: RW Beatty Ltd, 1961.

Ebersole P, Hess P. *Towards healthy aging, 2nd edition*. St. Louis: Mosby, 1985.

Ebersole P, Hess P. *Towards healthy aging, 4th edition*. St Louis: Mosby, 1993.

Ebrahim S, Hedley R, Sheldon ML. Low levels of ill-health among elderly non-consulters in general practice. *Br Med J* 1984, 289:1273–1275.

Elliott K. Working with Black and minority ethnic groups. In: Webb P, ed. *Health promotion and patient education: a professional's guide*. London: Chapman and Hall, 1994.

Evans P. The Chester Cardiac Rehabilitation Project. *Community Outlook* 1994, 4:31–32.

Farquhar M. Elderly people's definitions of quality of life. *Soc Sci Med*

1995, 41:1439–1446.

Fentem P. Benefits of exercise in health and disease. *Br Med J* 1994, 308:1291–1295.

Fletcher A. Screening for cancer of the cervix in elderly women. *Lancet* 1990, 335:97–99

Garrett G. Health screening for elderly people. *Nurs Stand* 1992, 6:255–257.

Goldblatt P. Mortality and alternative social classifications. In: Goldblatt P, ed. *Longitudinal study in mortality and social organization 1971–1981*. OPCS Series LS No. 6. London: HMSO, 1990.

Goodburn A. A place of greater safety. *Nurs Times* 1994,13 July 1990 90:46–48.

Goodburn A. A health centre for refugees. In: Ross F, Elliott M, eds. *Innovations in primary health care nursing*. Edinburgh: Community and District Nursing Association, 1995.

Grimley Evans J, Goldacre MJ, Hodkinson HM, Lamb S, Savory M. *Health: abilities and well-being in the third age*. Papers presented for The Carnegie Inquiry into the third age, research paper 9. Dunfermline: Carnegie Trust UK, 1992.

Grimley Evans J, Goldacre M, Hodkinson HM, Lamb S, Savory M. *Health and function in the third age*. London: Nuffield Provincial Hospitals Trust for Carnegie Trust UK, 1993.

Hardman C, Guy PM, Dunn R, Lewis PA, Vetter NJ. Health visiting elderly people after discharge from hospital. *Health Visitor* 1995, 68:370–371.

HEA/The Sports Council. *National Survey of Activity and Health: main findings (The Allied Dunbar National Fitnesss Survey, commissioned by The Sports Council and HEA)*. London: Health Education Authority/The Sports Council, 1992.

HEA. *Nutrition Briefing Papers 'Dietary Facts'*. Sanders T, ed. London: Health Education Authority, 1994.

HEA/Center for Policy on Aging. *Towards a framework for promoting the health of older people. Draft report of a symposium held by the HEA in collaboration with the CPA*. Dalley G, Howes K, Killoran A, Seal H, eds. London: Health Education Authority, 1996.

HEA. *Health promotion in older people, for the prevention of coronary heart disease and stroke*. Ebrahim S, Davey-Smith G, eds. London: Health Education Authority, 1996b.

HEA. *Health promotion effectiveness reviews. Summary report on health promotion in older people, for the prevention of coronary heart disease and stroke. The burden of cardio-vascular disease*. London: Health Education Authority, 1996c.

HEA. *Proceedings of the 'Active for Later Life' conference, Birmingham February 1997*. London: Health Education Authority, 1997a.

HEA. *Physical activity at our age. qualitative research among people over the age of 50*. London: Health Education Authority, 1997b.

Higginbottom C, Simpson C. Developing alliances for health. *Health Visitor* 1996, 69:108–109.

Hopkins A, Bahl V, eds. *Access to health care for people from Black and ethnic minorities*. London: Royal College of Physicians, 1993.

Illesley L, McKnight L. *The health visitor role in caring for the elderly, in the Malvern and Upton area: (01684 612660) (01684 612806)*. Worcestershire Community Healthcare NHS Trust, 1997.

King A, Oman RF, Brassington MA *et al*. Moderate-intensity exercise and self-related quality of sleep in older adults. A randomised controlled trial. *JAMA* 1997; 271:32–37.

King Edward's Hospital Fund for London/King's Fund Centre for Health Services Development, and City of Hackney DHA. *Achievable standards of care for elderly patients cared for in the acute assessment wards, continuing care wards, nursing homes and day hospitals within the city and Hackney DHA*. London: King's Fund, 1987.

Krauze M, Herzog AR, Baker E. Providing support to others and well-being in later life. *J Gerontol* 1992, 47:300–311.

Lachance PA. Future vitamin and anti-oxidant recommended daily allowances, for health promotion. Prev Med 1996, 25:46–47.

Lafaille R. Towards the foundations of a new science for health. In: Lafaille R, Fulder S, eds. *Towards a new science for health*. London: Routledge, 1993.

Latter S, Macleod Clark J, Wilson-Barnett J, Maben J. Health education in nursing: perceptions of practice in acute settings. *J Adv Nurs* 1992, 17:164–172.

Lindsay S, Hinney J, Gaw A. Setting up a help line on heart disease. *Nursing Standard* 1995, 29 November, 10:27–30.

Littlewood J, Scott HR. Screening the elderly. *Health Visitor* 1990, 63:268–270.

Mackintosh N. Self-empowerment in health promotion: a realistic target? *Br J Nurs* 1995, 4:1273–1278.

Majeed A, Cook D, Anderson S, *et al*. Monitoring and promoting equity in primary and secondary care. *Br Med J* 1994, 308:1426–1429.

Markus T. Cold, condensation and housing poverty. In: Burridge, Ormandy, eds. London: E&FN Spon, 1993.

Marr J. The impact of HIV/AIDS on older people: part I. *Nurs Stand* 1994a, 8:28–31.

Marr J. The impact of HIV/AIDS on older people. Part II. *Nurs Stand* 1994b, 8:25–27.

Maslow AH. *Towards a psychology of being*. New York: Harper and Row, 1962.

May A. Implementing an annual screening programme. *Health Visitor* 1992, 65:240–241.

McCarthy M. The health of the nation (England): the way forward. In: Harrison H, Bruscinis, eds. *Health care UK, 1994–5*. London: King's Fund, 1995.

McClymont ME, Thomas SE, Denham MJ. *Health visiting and elderly people: a health promotion challenge, 2nd edition*. London: Churchill Livingstone, 1991.

Meutzel PA. Therapeutic nursing. In: Pearson A, ed. *Nursing in the Burford and Oxford development unit*. London: Croom Helm, 1988.

Ministry of Agriculture, Fisheries and Food. *Manual of Nutrition, 10th edition*. London: HMSO, 1995.

Monks J, Illesley L. Working together for the care of elderly people. *Health Visitor* 1995, 68:195–196.

Morgan SA, Carter YH. *A study of accidents among older people in the UK. Accident prevention in primary care*. Birmingham: Royal Society for the prevention of accidents (RoSPA), 1996.

Murphy E, Smith R, Lindesay J, Slattery J. Increased mortality rates in late-life depression. *Br J Psychiatry* 1988, 152:347–353.

Neumann B. The Betty Neumann health care systems model: a total person approach to viewing patients' problems. In: Rhiel J, Roy C, eds. *Conceptual models for nursing practice*. New York: Appleton-Century-Crofts, 1980.

Nocon A. GP's assessment of people aged 75 years and over: identifying the need for occupational therapy services. *Br J Occup Ther* 1993, 56:123–127.

Oakley A, Dawson MF, Holland J *et al*. Preventing falls and subsequent injury in older people. *Quality in Health Care* 1996, 5:243–249.

Office of Population, Censuses and Surveys. *The prevalence of disability among adults: Report No. 1*. London: HMSO, 1988.

O'Neill C, Normand C, Cupples M, McKnight A. Cost-effectiveness of personal health education in primary care, for persons with angina in the Greater Belfast area of Northern Ireland. *J Epidemiol Community Health* 1996, 50:538–540.

Orwin R. Health promotion for Asian patients with coronary heart disease. *Prof Nurse* 1996, 12:170–172.

Ottawa Charter for Health Promotion. *The charter: Health Promotion, Vol. 1, No. 4*. Oxford: Oxford University Press; 1986: 3–5.

Parkes CM. *Bereavement: studies of grief in adult life*. London: Tavistock, 1972.

Pender NJ. *Health promotion in nursing practice, 2nd edition*. Norwalk: Appleton and Lange, 1987.

Perkins ER. Screening elderly people: a review of the literature in the light of the new General Practitioner Contract. *Br J Gen Pract* 1991, 41:382–385.

Pharaoh C. *Primary health care for elderly people from Black and minority ethnic communities. Studies in ageing*, London: Age Concern Institute of Gerontology, King's College/HMSO, 1995.

Piggot CS. The health gain cycle. In: Piggot CS, Roe P, eds. *Health gain and how to achieve it*. Uxbridge: Glaxo Pharmaceuticals UK Ltd, 1994.

Pursey A, Luker K. Assessment of older people at home: a missed opportunity. In: Wilson-Barnett J, Macleod Clark J, eds. *Research in health promotion and nursing*. Basingstoke: MacMillan, 1993.

Quantock C. Promoting health in elderly people. *Nurs Stand* 1994, 8:30–33.

Redmond E. Reaching out to the Asian community. *Community Outlook* 1993, 3(7):13–16.

Riehl J, Roy C, eds. *Conceptual models for nursing practice, 2nd edition*. New York: Appleton-Century-Crofts, 1983.

Rijke R. Health in medical science: from determinism towards autonomy. In: Lafaille R, Fulder S, eds. *Towards a new science of health*. London: Routledge, 1993.

RoSPA. *Accident prevention in primary care*, Birmingham: Royal Society for the Prevention of Accidents 1996.

Royal College of Nursing. *Nursing Homes:– Nursing Values*. London: RCN, 1996.

Savage A. *Warmth in winter: re-evaluation of an information pack for elderly people*. Cardiff: University of Wales College of Medicine, Research Team, 1988.

Scottish Office. *A frame-work for action: the NHS in Scotland*, Edinburgh: Scottish Office, 1991.

Seedhouse D. *Health promotion: philosophy, prejudice, and practice*. Chichester: Wiley and Son, 1997.

Selye H. *The stress of life*. New York: McGraw-Hill, 1974.

Sharp C. *The human potential of older people. Achievements of older people – lest we limit our thinking*. 'Active for Later Life' Conference. London: Health Education Authority, 1997.

Sidell M. *Health in old age: myth, mystery and management*. London: Open University Press, 1997.

Skelton D. Muscle power and strength after strength training by women aged 75 years and over: a randomised controlled study. *J Physiol* 1993, 473:83.

Skelton D. *Exercise for healthy ageing*. London: Research into Ageing, 1994.

SNMAC. *Making it happen. Public health: the contribution, role and development of nurses, midwives and health visitors*. Report of the Standing Nursing and Midwifery Advisory Committee. London: Department of Health, 1995.

Thomas S. Multidisciplinary health promotion in Sheffield. *Nurs Times* 1993, 23:63–67.

Thomas J, Wainwright P. Community nurses and health promotion: ethical and political perspectives. *Nursing Ethics* 1996, 3:97–107.

Thornley P. Liverpool healthy city: investing in community empowerment. *Community Health Action* 1992, 23:7–9.

Townsend P, Whitehead M, Davidson N, eds. *Inequalities in health: the Black report and the health divide*. London: New Edition Penguin Books, 1992.

Tremellen J. Assessment of patients aged 75 years and over in general practice. *Br Med J* 1992, 305:621–624.

Uittenbroek DG. A new public health model and ageing: the example of primary prevention by way of exercise and physical activity. *Health Care in Later Life* 1996, 1:5–27.

United Kingdom Central Council for Nurses, Midwives, and Health Visitors (UKCC). *The Nurses' Midwives' and Health Visitors' Act 1979: Rules Approval Order*. London: HMSO, 1983.

Victor CR. Continuity or change: inequalities in health in later life. *Ageing and Society* 1991, 11:25–39.

Wallston KA, Wallston BS, Dvellis R. Development of the multidimensional Health Locus of Control. *Health Education Monographs* 1978, 6(2):160–171.

Ward M. Student nurses' perceptions of health promotion: a study. *Nurs Stand* 1997, 11:34–40.

Welsh Office/Welsh Health Planning Forum. *Intent and direction for Wales*. Cardiff: The Welsh Office, 1989.

Whitely S, Brittain O. Assessing the health needs of elderly people. *Health Visitor* 1993, 66:133–135.

Wilkinson R. Hierarchy harms health. *Nurs Stand* 1997, 11:15.

Williams EI, Wallace P. *Health checks for people aged 75 years and over, Occasional Papers No. 59*. London: Royal College of General Practitioners,1993.

Williams K. Legal threat to home care. *Nurs Stand* 1997, 11:15.

Wilson M. Don't give up on it: smoking cessation (repeat). *RCN Nurs Update* (Learning Unit 039). *Nurs Stand* 1997, 11:1–27.

Wormald RPL, Wright LA, Courtney P, Beaumont B, Haines AP. Visual problems in the elderly population. Implications for services. *Br Med J* 1992, 304:1226–1229.

Wright J. Can patients become empowered? *Prof Nurs* 1995, 10:599.

Wynn M, Wynn A. Can improved diet contribute to the prevention of cataract? *Nutr Health* 1996, 11:87–104.

Young A *et al*. *Physical activity in later life*. London: Health Education Authority, Expected 1999.

Young K. Health promotion and the elderly. *J Clin Nurs* 1996, 5:241–248.

USEFUL ADDRESSES

Age Concern: England. Astral House, 1268 London Road, London SW16 4ER. Tel: 0181 679 8000.

Age Concern: Scotland. 113 Rose Street, Edinburgh EH2 3DT.

Centres of information, policy, research and social advocacy for older persons. Publish a range of relevant literature.

Centre for Policy on Ageing. 25–31 Ironmonger Row, London EC1V 3QP. Tel: 0171 253 1787.

Encourages improved services for older individuals through informed debate, research and good practice. Has a reference library, an information service and publications.

Ageing Well UK. 12 Craneswater Park, Southsea, Hants PO4 0NT. Tel: 01705 293 203.

A programme linked with the European Ageing Well Network, developed by The Health Education Authority in association with Age Concern England. Provides information on a flexible non-prescriptive programme for maintaining the health and independence of older persons. Addresses health issues affecting those of 50 years and over: encourages older people to 'volunteer' to be Senior Health Mentors and be positively involved in developing health programmes to suit the needs of older people. Provides information on striking up 'healthy alliances' with other local agencies/professional groups; on resources and current research.

EXTEND, (Exercises for Elderly People and the Disabled). 22 Maltings Drive, Wheathampstead, Herts AL4 8QJ. Tel: 01582 832 760.

Specialises in exercises to music for older persons.

Health Education Authority. Hamilton House, Mabledon Place, London WC1H 9TX. Tel : 0171 383 3833.

Responsible for health promotion within England. Produces a range of health information material, has extensive library facilities, conducts and publishes research; launches campaigns. Has a large data-base and acts as a resource for health professionals.

Health Education Board for Scotland. Woodburn House, Cannan Lane, Edinburgh EH10 4SG. Tel: 0131 447 8044, Fax: 0131 452 8140.

Relaxation for Living Trust. Fox Hill, 30 Victoria Avenue, Shanklin, Isle of Wight PO37 6 LS. Tel: 01983 868 166.

Provides a range of self-help material, runs 4-day residential Courses, has a range of classes across all regions, offers teacher training in relaxation (credited by The University of Greenwich). Publishes a newsletter.

Research into Ageing. Baird House, 15–17 St Cross Street, London EC1N 8UN. Tel: 0171 404 6978.

A national medical charity committed to improving the health and quality of life of older people, through funding and supporting medical research.

The Beth Johnson Foundation. Parkfield House, 64 Princes Road, Hartshill, Stoke on Trent ST4 7JL. Tel: 01782 844 036, Fax: 01782 746 940.

A voluntary sector foundation involved in self-health care and maintaining older people's health. The foundation has been at the forefront of developments in self-health care for older people and influenced the national Ageing Well initiative. It offers superb examples of how an organisation can work with older people in the community and has produced valuable publications and resources, many in partnership with older people (such as the resource for seniors on sexual health). Projects include a telephone service for people not in contact with social services, citizen advocacy and intergenerational work bringing together younger and older people towards counteracting ageist attitudes.

4 Age-related changes
Irene Schofield

LEARNING OBJECTIVES

After studying this chapter you will be able to:

- Identify and discuss the common age-related changes that occur in the body systems.
- Distinguish between normal age-related physiological change and pathology, and discuss their influence on functional ability.
- Describe the contribution that diminished homeostatic control makes to the altered presentation of illness in older people and give examples from your nursing practice.
- Critically evaluate the assessment tools that are commonly used to measure general health and physical and mental function in older people.
- Utilise knowledge of gerontology in carrying out holistic health assessments.
- Adapt teaching and learning strategies to take account of age-related changes in cognition.

NORMAL AGE CHANGES AND PATHOLOGY

It is fundamental that nurses working with older people can differentiate between the major physiological changes which occur with normal ageing and the common age-related pathologies that affect increasing numbers of adults as they grow older. Many people, including health-care professionals and older people themselves, are unable to appreciate that there is a difference. The ability to differentiate between the two is important, as the following examples will illustrate. Both an older person and the nurse who is caring for him/her may believe that a pathological symptom such as incontinence is an inevitable and irremediable consequence of ageing and that little can be done about it. For the older man, failure to maintain a penile erection without manual stimulation may be viewed as pathological when in fact it is known to be a normal consequence of ageing. Lack of such knowledge by the practice nurse he is currently consulting about his problem might lead to the premature curtailment of sexual activity. It is the intention of this chapter to examine some of the major age-related changes at the level of organ systems (others will be dealt with in specialist chapters) and to evaluate the tools that are commonly used to assess physical function in older people. With the advent of increasing interest in rehabilitation and the requirement for interdisciplinary working in this area, specialist nurses need to be aware of the strengths and weaknesses of such tools. The requirements of a comprehensive and holistic nursing assessment will also be addressed.

Ageing and Homeostasis

Linnane *et al.* (1989, p. 643) describe ageing as 'a biological process with a progressive decline in the performance of most organs, culminating in the inability to meet the environmental demands for continued existence'. The decline in functional capacity can be ascribed to 'a progressive loss with age of functional tissue cells'. Under normal circumstances, homeostatic mechanisms maintain a steady state in response to changes in both the internal and external environment. Younger adults have considerable reserve functional capacity in all organ systems, but with ageing reserve capacity is gradually lost (**Figure 4.1**). This tends to occur slowly and insidiously, so that most physiological processes function quite adequately in older individuals under resting conditions. However, when the older person is subject to a

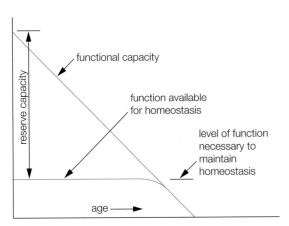

Figure 4.1 Age-related changes in functional and reserve capacity. (Source: Herbert R. The biology of ageing: maintenance of homeostasis. *Geriatr Nurs* 1986 May/June:14.) Reproduced with kind permission of RCN Publishing, Harrow, Middlesex, UK.

physiological stressor, such as infection, extremes of temperature or strenuous exercise, the reduction in functional reserve capacity results in homeostatic mechanisms that are less efficient in re-establishing a steady state. Deviations from the equilibrium of homeostasis tend to be greater and return to a steady state tends to take longer. Disturbance of fluid and electrolyte balance resulting in dehydration is a common feature of acute illness in older people. This is due in part to the following age-related changes:

- Reduction in total body water.
- Loss of nephrons in the kidney leads to loss of ability to produce concentrated urine.
- Sense of thirst diminishes, even when dehydration is present.

In conditions of extreme ambient temperatures, an impaired homeostatic response leads to difficulty in controlling core body temperature with a risk of hypo or hyperthermia. When changing position from lying to standing, a decline in baroreceptor activity can result in orthostatic hypotension and an increased risk of falls. Finally, systems failure followed by death occurs when functional capacity is depleted to the point when the ability to maintain a steady state can no longer by met. Such events are most likely to take place in advanced old age.

What Constitutes an Age Change?

In the 1960s, Strehler described four concepts integral to the definition of a biological age change:

(1) It must be universal, in that it affects all members of a species (in this case, man). However, the degree of effect varies between individuals.

(2) It is intrinsic, in that the change must come from within, but the rate of change can be influenced from outside.

(3) It is progressive with increasing age.

(4) It is deleterious, in that it weakens individuals and makes them more vulnerable.

One of the most remarkable aspects of ageing is the enormous variability in the rate at which individuals age. Every nurse can cite examples of very fit and active older people, such as the man who is still flying a glider at 77 years of age, whilst others of the same age can barely walk down the street or get upstairs. This variability is governed by our genetic makeup together with the influence of environmental or lifestyle factors (*see* Chapter 2). Physical activity without causing undue stress on body systems is an important contributor to healthy ageing (*see* Chapter 6) and lack of even gentle exercise can result in age-related detraining. This is not a true age change but contributes further to overall decline; the cardiovascular and musculoskeletal systems are most at risk. Simple questioning on activity levels and observation of performance can assist nurses in their estimation of the extent of age-related detraining. There has been some recent debate on the practicality and feasibility of assessing biological age with a view to

predicting morbidity or mortality (Bulpitt, 1995). Indeed, if it were possible to do so we would have a more logical way of predicting a person's health status. This type of information could assist in deciding who would gain most benefit from an expensive health intervention. Fitness rather than chronological age would be the relevant criterion.

Not only are there large differences between individuals in the rate of ageing but also ageing does not occur as a uniform process across all systems of the body. The renal system can decline to almost half of its original function, yet there is only minimal reduction in the rate of nerve conduction velocity. However, it is rather misleading to consider the ageing effects of each body system separately. They are almost all interconnected in some way and ageing effects in one system can cancel out the effects in another. One such example is in the gut, where there is a reduced surface area for absorption due to the loss of villi and reduced secretion of gastrointestinal fluids. These changes have the potential to hinder absorption; however, they coincide with a reduction in tone and nervous stimulation of the intestinal smooth muscle, which slows peristalsis and allows more time for absorption. **Figure 4.2** shows changes in biological function with age.

The Baltimore Longitudinal Study, which began in 1958, continues to follow a group of 1000 men as they age, with the objective of identifying normal changes of ageing not associated with disease. Finally, lifelong use and abuse of the body through accidents, athletic injuries and other physical trauma are responsible for some of the changes thought of as wear and tear. In youth, it is difficult to realise that neglect of skin, teeth or nutrition will not necessarily produce visible or significant changes until later life, at which time the effects of earlier neglect become more apparent and important to a person's health.

Structure and Posture

An adult loses 1.5 cm of height every 20 years after the age of 40 years. Obvious manifestations, which are an interaction of many factors such as age, sex, race and environment, occur in the fifth decade of life. Long-bones take on the appearance of disproportionate length as stature decreases. Intervertebral disks become thin due to dehydration, causing a shortening of the trunk. Many very old people assume a stooped, forward-bent posture, with hips and knees somewhat flexed and arms bent at the elbows, raising the level of the arms. These changes are caused by decreases in ligamental flexibility. To maintain eye contact, the head is tilted backward, which makes it appear that the individual is jutting forward. In addition, shoulder width may narrow due to shrinkage of the deltoid muscles and acromions. Abdominal length also decreases, contributing to the overall picture of a disproportionate individual who needs to be stretched out a bit. One must keep in mind that these changes involve multiple developmental factors: skeletal, muscular, subcutaneous tissue, fat and dermal changes. Regular physical activity may forestall development of these conditions.

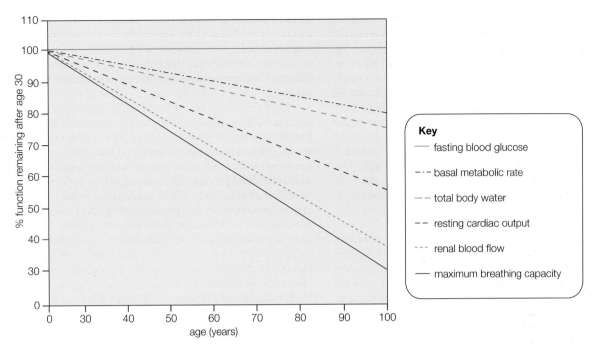

Figure 4.2 Changes in biological function with age. (Source: Adapted from Shock NW. In: Carlston AL, ed. *Nutrition in old age*. Tenth symposium of the Swedish Nutrition Foundation. Uppsala: Almquistand Wilksell, 1972.)

Bone mass is constantly undergoing cyclic resorption and renewal. Disequilibrium of this process with greater resorption and less calcium deposition is characteristic of ageing bone. Posture and structural changes occur primarily because of calcium loss from bone and as a result of atrophic processes of cartilage and muscle. Such changes can produce increased curvature of the lower spine, lordosis, kyphosis or hump back, and scoliosis, a lateral curvature of the spine. They also contribute to the shortening of stature in the older person. Excessive leaching of calcium from the bone matrix creates the condition called osteoporosis. This type of degeneration is four times more prevalent in women, becoming apparent as oestrogen declines in older women. Maintaining muscle use and bone stress, for example, by walking, can slow the process.

Resorption of the bone leads to poor-fitting dentures and painful sensations when chewing or biting. Bone demineralisation affects the jaw or alveolar bone of the lower jaw, especially in individuals who are edentulous. Degeneration of underlying cartilage appears to decrease intervertebral distance. The forward-leaning posture is attributed to muscle shrinkage, and breasts that were full and firm begin to sag and become pendulous as the glandular envelope of fat atrophies. Nipples may also invert because of shrinkage and fibrotic changes.

Lack of use, known as disuse atrophy, is thought to be a major cause of reduced muscle bulk in later life. There is a progressive loss of muscle tissue brought about by a decrease in both the number and diameter of muscle fibres. This is evident by the appearance of clefts in the long-bones of the hands and the flabby appearance of the lower leg muscles. Atrophy is greater in the lower extremities, largely as a result of self-imposed exercise restriction (Carnegie UK Trust, 1990).

Muscle tone or tension of particular muscle groups decreases steadily after 30 years of age. Possible causes are attributed to neurone loss and the loss of sensory and motor elements of spinal nerves of the muscles. Nerve cells in the spinal cord are lost after 80 years of age. Strength and stamina decrease to 65–85% of the maximum strength an individual had at 25 years of age.

Ligaments, tendons and joints show the results of cellular cross-linkage over time, resulting in hardened, more rigid, less flexible movement and predisposing these structures to tears. Worn-down cartilage around joints produced by continuous flexing over the years coupled with stray pieces of cartilage and diminished lubricating fluid in the joints can lead to slower and painful movement at times. Landmarks become more prominent, and muscle contours are easily identified. Skin-fold thickness, a measure of subcutaneous fat content, is markedly reduced in the forearm with age. Women over 45 years of age begin to see the skin folds on the back of their hands rapidly diminish, even if there is a substantial weight gain. Areas such as the pubis, umbilicus and waist do not change appreciably.

Skin, Hair and Nails

Numerous changes affect the skin as it ages. Changes are characterised by wrinkling, fragility, irregular pigmentation, dryness and a variety of skin lesions. The severity of these changes are governed by heredity and exposure to the sun's ultraviolet rays. Light-skinned people have smaller amounts of protective melanin and are most at risk. Melanocyte distribution is more uneven, producing both areas of hypopigmentation and brown pigment spots known as solar lentigo. Epidermal cell renewal time increases by one-third after 50 years of age. The normal young adult renews epithelium every 20 days, whereas an older person requires 30 or more days because of diminished mitotic epidermal activity. Because of this slow replacement of epidermal cells, wound healing is approximately 50% slower than at 35 years of age. The amount of collagen decreases approximately 1% per year, causing the skin to 'give' less under stress and tear more easily. Vascular hyperplasia results in more pronounced varicosities, benign cherry angiomas and venous stars.

Race, sex, sex-linked genes and hormonal influences determine the quantity and quality of hair and the changes that will occur with it throughout life. Greying occurs as a result of loss of pigment and cellular material. Grey hairs are usually more fragile and may become kinked. Greying usually begins at the temples and spreads toward the crown of the head. Hair loss from the scalp is more prominent in men than women. Greying of underarm, pubic and other body hair tends to lag behind that of the scalp and loss may be total. Paradoxically, women may experience the growth of bristly facial hair. In men, there may be an increase in coarse hair in the ears, nose and eyebrows. Such changes have the potential to threaten self-image and perceptions of attractiveness. Nails of the fingers and toes develop longitudinal striations and growth declines with age. Toenails grow at a 15% slower rate than fingernails in older people. The nail plate may thicken and become distorted. Toenails lose their translucency and turn yellow. With ageing the cuticle becomes less thick and wide. Vigorous manipulation of the cuticle may lead to retardation of the already slowed nail growth.

Facial Changes

Facial changes occur as a result of altered subcutaneous fat, dermal thickness, decreased elasticity and lateral surface compression of underlying muscle contractions. Loss of bone mass, particularly the mandibular bone, accentuates the size of the upper mouth, nose and forehead. Indented 'loss of lip' appearance of the mouth occurs with tooth loss when uncorrected by dentures or other oral prostheses. Eyelids appear swollen as a result of the redistribution of fat deposits. Conversely, eyes that look sunken are the result of the loss of orbital subcutaneous fat. Loss of elasticity accentuates jowls and elongated ears and contributes to the formation of a double chin.

Loss of Tissue Elasticity

Elastin and collagen fibres become progressively more coarse and inelastic as they become cross-linked (*see* Chapter 2).

This decreases the flexibility and thickness of the skin and promotes wrinkling. Other factors that contribute to wrinkling are reduced moisture content of skin cells, loss of skeletal and muscle mass, and redistribution of subcutaneous fat. Chapter 7 will discuss skin integrity and maintenance in more detail.

Elasticity affects blood-vessel integrity, particularly the arteries. With ageing, elastic fibres fray, split, straighten and fragment. Calcium that leaves the bone is deposited in the vessels. This chemical and anatomical alteration decreases the lumen size of the major arteries and may result in a rise in systolic blood pressure (SBP). Blood flow to various organs becomes uneven. There is little flow change to the coronary arteries and the brain, but perfusion of the liver and kidneys shows significant reduction in the amount of blood brought to these two organs. In the liver blood flow is reduced by 35%, and there is a 50% decrease in liver size (James, 1992). In the kidneys, blood flow decreases by 10% per decade. Peripheral resistance due to arteriosclerosis leads to a greater increase in diastolic blood pressure (DBP) with advancing age. In some parts of the world, for example Ethiopia, Delhi, India and the Kenyan frontier, there appears to be no association between age and SBP. Parameters for the diagnosis and treatment of older people with hypertension are discussed in Chapter 6.

Body Composition

Body weight changes because of a decline in lean body mass (a measure of muscle mass) and a loss of body water [54–60% in men; 46–52% in women; (*see* **Figure 4.2**)]. At the same time, basal metabolic rate decreases, possibly as a result of loss of muscle tissue. The rate of decline increases in later years and is greater in men than women. Fat-free weight falls significantly with age and deposition of subcutaneous fat in the region of the upper thighs increases through middle age. Abdominal girth measurement increases as a result of enlargement or sagging of the abdominal organs. In a cross-sectional study, the weight of total body fat remained relatively constant. In the extremities, the diameter of the calf and arm decline due to loss of muscle tissue rather than fat. Cellular solids and bone mass decline; extracellular water, however, remains relatively constant. Cellular sodium increases 20% from 30 to 70 years of age. The intercellular matrix (collagen and elastin) cross-link, reducing resilience. Intracellular concentrations of structural proteins, enzymes and chromosomal components, including deoxyribonucleic acid (DNA) and ribonucleic acid (RNA), change. Lipofuscin, or 'ageing pigment', increases in the nervous system and other nonrenewing tissues (e.g. the heart).

Cardiac Changes

Several changes occur in the ageing heart, but it is difficult to determine whether these changes are due to normal physiological change, lifestyle changes or pathology. There is general consensus that the following are characteristic of normal ageing. Interstitial fibrosis and collagen cross linking result in a decrease in elasticity of the heart muscle. Motility is further compromised by the accumulation of altered proteins – lipofuscin and amyloid in the heart muscle cells. Despite these changes, a study of 7000 human hearts at autopsy showed no evidence of atrophy in overall heart size. Calcification and fibrosis of the cusps of the mitral and aortic valves were observed in individuals aged 70–90 years. Stiffening of the valve cusps can result in systolic ejection murmurs. Within the heart, the left and right atrium increase in size while the left ventricle decreases. Cell loss in the conductive tissue leaves heart rate at rest unchanged, but there is a greater than normal increase in response to activity. Paradoxically however, there is a decline in maximal heart rate with increasing age.

Catecholamines and other enzymes also influence the effect of the force and speed of heart contractions. Catecholamine levels are decreased in older people, and produce a longer interval between contractions, a weakened cardiac force, and a greater energy demand on the heart muscle. Maximum O_2 consumption decreases in men and women and persists even after physical conditioning. The decline in cardiac output occurs at rest in healthy men between 20 and 90 years of age when supine but remains the same when sitting upright. This change may be related to the action of reflexes which increase cardiac output when the heart pumps against gravity. Reduced contractile strength, smaller cardiac output (though this is now under debate) and reduced enzymatic stimulation together cause the heart to respond to the work demand with a less efficient performance and a greater energy expenditure than would be required by the younger individual.

Although the changes described so far have a deleterious effect on heart function, there are adaptive and compensatory mechanisms. The heart attempts to compensate for decreased contractibility by delaying diastolic filling and developing a longer relaxation phase (Rodeheffer *et al.* 1985). In addition, although the increase in cardiac output with exercise may not be as great in older people, there are some gains to be made by training. The lower O_2 uptake with exercise in sedentary older people can be increased by physical training but not to the level of fit young people. Although these changes are not overtly visible, the nurse should be aware of them and their importance to the state of wellness for older people in pursuit of a healthy lifestyle.

Vascular Changes

Arteries
The term arteriosclerosis or stiffening of the arteries occurs with increasing frequency in older people. This is because collagen cross-linking reduces elasticity in the arterial walls. Loss of elasticity in large vessels such as the aorta increases the 'after load' on the heart because the aorta and other large vessels are less able to expand in response to the surge of

blood leaving the heart. This results in a slight rise in SBP. Recoil is also less effective, so that DBP may decrease or remain the same. Decreased elasticity of arteries and arterioles is partly responsible for a decrease in blood flow to organs such as the heart, liver, kidneys and pituitary gland. Atherosclerosis more accurately describes a disease process common in industrialised societies.

Veins
Venous elasticity also declines and veins become more tortuous. Semilunar valves are rendered incompetent by a genetic deficiency or from excessive high pressure as a result of constriction in pregnancy or the wearing of tight garters or corsets.

Renal Changes

Kidneys are the primary organs responsible for regulation of blood and fluid volume and the chemical composition of the body. Studies indicate several age-related changes in the structure and function of the kidney. Loss of as much as 50% of the millions of nephrons (each kidney has at least 1 million) leads to little change in the body's ability to regulate body fluids and the ability to maintain adequate fluid homeostasis in later life. A decrease in kidney weight of 20–30% occurs primarily in the cortex, where entire nehprons are replaced by scar tissue; it loses about one-fifth of its size. With increasing age, the glomeruli and their associated nephrons are damaged by scar tissue (5–37% between 40 and 90 years of age). These changes result in an accelerating decline in glomerular filtration rate (GFR) after the age of 40 years, equivalent to 1% per year. Furthermore, in the presence of decreased cardiac output the elimination of nitrogenous waste is also impaired. The rate of excretion of creatinine acts as a measure of GFR. Earlier results from the Baltimore Longitudinal Study on Ageing suggested that creatinine clearance declines from 140 ml/minute at 29 years of age, to 97 ml/minute at 80 years of age. More recent results show no change in the rate for 30% of subjects, 65% showed variable decline and 5% showed an increase. It is surprising how little such changes affect the wellbeing of fit older people. However, this may be due in part to the overestimation of the extent of age-related change, as the more recent longitudinal work suggests that decrements are not so universal (*see* Chapter 5 for further exposition of urea and creatinine estimation).

Decline in renal function has been a major factor in the need to exercise caution in the prescription and administration of medication for older people. These new findings reinforce the importance of basing dosages on individual clinical information, rather than age alone.

Pulmonary Changes

The respiratory system is vulnerable to a variety of extrinsic agents that take their toll on its structure and function throughout life. Daily continued exposure to atmospheric pollutants and cigarette smoke make it difficult to separate their effects from normal intrinsic age-related change. Changes in the respiratory tract and pulmonary performance occur gradually, enabling the older person to continue to breathe effortlessly at rest and in the absence of disease states. Confronted with a little exertion or stress, however, dyspnoea and other symptoms usually appear.

The Thoracic Cavity and Airways

Lungs are limited in expansion by alterations in the structural configuration of the thorax. Lung function is restricted by ribs that do not move as freely with inspiration as a result of costal cartilage calcification, osteoporosis and loss of elasticity of pleural tissue. The speed of muscle contraction, as in the period between stimulus and relaxation, increases with age and requires more conscious effort being applied to inspiration. In addition, older adults may be seen to use accessory muscles of respiration, such as the abdominal, sternocleidmastoid and trapezius. Kyphosis increases the anterior–posterior dimension of the thorax and decreases the thoracic transverse measurement further limiting thoracic movement. Obesity, chronic poor posture and weakness of respiratory muscles as a result of inactivity cause shallow breathing and contribute to poor respiratory performance. Calcification of cartilage in the airways themselves leads to dilatation of the trachea and bronchi. These structures are normally dead space in that no gas exchange takes place within them; they are just channels for the movement of air. Their increase in size results in a slight increase in dead space.

Changes Within the Lung and their Effect on Function

Changes also occur within the lung. Loss of elastin and collagen cross-linking decreases the distensibility of the alveoli and the alveolar ducts. The alveoli undergo similar changes to those seen in emphysema in that there is progressive loss of the supporting structures, thinning of the alveolar walls and fewer capillaries available for gas exchange. The alveoli and respiratory bronchioles increase in size with the net effect of decreasing their surface area in relation to volume and resulting in a smaller area for gas absorption. The surface area of the alveoli is reduced to 65–70 square metres in the 70-year-old compared to the normal of 80 square metres at the age of 20 years. The loss of elastic recoil as a result of increased rigidity leads to decreased expansion of the lungs within the chest cavity when the ribs are raised and the diaphragm is lowered. On expiration the loss of elastic recoil causes the small airways to close, trapping air that would otherwise have been exhaled. The effect of such changes on lung function leads to a reduction in vital capacity on inspiration and an increase in residual volume on expiration. Incomplete lung expansion does not provide for inflation of the lung bases and can lead to basilar lung collapse. The changes that have occurred in the anatomic structure of the chest and the altered muscle strength do not lend themselves to the forcefulness needed to expel material that accumulates or causes

an obstruction. These changes result in a less effective cough response. The lack of basilar inflation, inefficient cough response, and a less efficient mucociliary escalator and immune system pose potential problems for those older people who are sedentary, bedridden or limited in activity by disease states.

Gas Exchange and Altered Responses

The above changes in lung function also influence gas exchange. The diffusion capacity of O_2 from alveoli to blood is reduced and occurs more rapidly in males than females. A normal oxygen pressure (PO_2) for a 70-year-old is 75–80 mmHg; a normal PO_2 for a 20-year-old is 90–100 mmHg (Pierson, 1992). Haemoglobin is reduced resulting in a decrease in O_2 carrying capacity of the blood. There is little change in the transfer of carbon dioxide (CO_2) from the plasma to the alveoli.

There is some evidence to suggest that older adults exhibit a blunted response to hypoxaemia and hypercapnia. They may not respond to hypoxaemia with the usual increase in rate and depth of respiration and increase in heart rate and blood pressure. Older individuals with PO_2 levels as low as 40 mmHg have little or no immediate compensatory response in cardiac function. Young people with the same blood gas level show a marked increase in cardiac rate as an attempt to compensate and deliver more O_2 to body tissues. Also there is less increase in heart rate and a slower response to rising CO_2. These altered responses are thought to be due to reduced sympathetic nervous system response. Compensatory responses are significantly hindered when the older person is experiencing moderate amounts of stress. The most sensitive indicator for hypoxaemia and hypercapnia are changes in mental status such as forgetfulness that cannot be explained by other factors, confusion when awakening from sleep and complaints of occipital headache. The response to hypoxaemia and treatment are also less sensitive. A small increase in O_2 demand can result more quickly in hypoxic symptoms in the older person. Decreased physical fitness further limits the availability of additional gaseous exchange. Kinney (1989) cites the fourth decade and retirement as the two periods of time when the decrease in physical fitness adds to the limited availability of gaseous exchange.

Alterations in Endocrine Function

The pituitary gland, with its diverse functions and central role in the complex hormonal feedback system, begins to atrophy after middle age but continues to maintain adequate hormonal secretions.

Antidiuretic Hormone

Ability to concentrate urine decreases with age and this may be due to increased renal tubular resistance to antidiuretic hormone (ADH). However, when there is excessive production of ADH the decrease in sensitivity may result in relatively normal urine concentration.

Growth Hormone

It has now been established that there is a marked difference in growth hormone (somatotropin) production with age. It falls to about 50% of the levels of early adulthood by the age of 65 years and can be absent in the very old. Growth hormone stimulates the release of IGF-1 (somatomedin-C) which appears to be its effector hormone. IGF-1 is produced in cyclical fashion and release is pulsed. There are lower concentrations in each pulse and overall levels are lower in older people. It is thought that this reduction in the production of growth hormone could account for the increase in fat and decrease in lean muscle seen with ageing. Preliminary studies with older males have shown some benefit from growth hormone treatments in that they appeared to develop an increase in lean body mass, skin thickness and bone density.

Insulin

Older people exhibit a decreased ability to metabolise glucose, with the result that glucose tolerance declines with age. Following a glucose load, the rise in blood glucose is greater and returns to normal more slowly. This may happen because the pancreas fails to release sufficient insulin in the presence of a rise in blood glucose, despite there being little age-related change in the islets of Langerhans and the quality of insulin produced. In addition, cell sensitivity to insulin may decrease because there are fewer receptors either as a result of reduced cell sensitivity or because there is a post-receptor deficit.

As a consequence of these changes, older people with normal fasting blood glucose levels may have raised postprandial glucose levels (*see* Chapter 5 for an interpretation of laboratory results). Glucagon, which is synthesised by the alpha cells of the islets of Langerhans, reverses the action of insulin. The liver cells respond with increased sensitivity to glucagon with increasing age.

Thyroid Hormones

The function of the thyroid is to control metabolic rate and this remains adequate with age, despite evidence of atrophy and a decrease in glandular function. The thyroid in older women is also susceptible to autoimmune disease. There is little change in iodine uptake. Secretions of thyroid-stimulating hormone (TSH) continue unchanged as does the serum concentration of thyroxine (T4). There is some evidence of decline in tri-iodothyronine (T3), which is thought to reflect reduced conversion of T4 to T3 in extrathyroidal locations (*see* Chapter 5 for an in-depth description of test results). These changes bring about a slowing of the metabolic rate and O_2 use by the body with increasing age. However, as the metabolic effect of T4 primarily involves muscle tissue, which is itself reduced, the net effect may be negligible.

Collective signs, such as a slowed basal metabolic rate, thinning of the hair and dry skin, are characteristic of hypothyroidism in younger people but are normal manifestations of ageing in those who have no history of thyroid deficiencies. Many drugs interfere with the protein binding of T4 and T3, thus distorting the results of thyroid function tests.

T4 levels may be raised during treatment with levodopa, digoxin or cotrimoxazole. Hypothyroidism is more common in later life and thyroid disorders are generally more common in older women. Disease presentation may be atypical and symptoms such as cold intolerance, slow thought processes, obesity and depression are characteristic.

Cortisol

Corticosteroids produced by the adrenal are either glucocorticoids that have a major role in glucose metabolism (e.g. cortisol, which also has some mineralocorticoid activity) or mineralocorticoids that act on salt and water balance (e.g. aldosterone). Cortisol is produced by the adrenal cortex in a characteristic diurnal pattern in response to adrenocorticotrophic hormone (ACTH) produced by the anterior pituitary. Secretion of ACTH is maximal immediately prior to waking and is at its lowest overnight. This diurnal pattern continues into old age but may be reduced in amplitude and delayed (Van Cauter *et al.* 1996). In general, both cortisol and ACTH levels are unaffected by age (Tietz *et al.* 1992), although elevation of cortisol with ageing, which is more marked in women, has been reported (Van Cauter *et al.* 1996).

Adrenalin and Noradrenalin

Both basal and stimulated levels of the catecholamines adrenalin and noradrenalin increase with age, although their effects on tissues (e.g. the cardiovascular system) decline. This is thought to be due to a decrease in the numbers of receptor binding sites and a decrease in affinity. Nerve ending production of noradrenalin may decline in some older people, producing a delayed blood pressure (BP) response to moving to an upright posture (orthostatic hypotension).

Sex Hormones

Gonadotrophic hormones undergo secretory and stimulatory changes. From the menopause, there is loss of response in the ovary to circulating gonadotrophic hormones and the production of oestrogen and progesterone declines. Any remaining ovarian follicles degenerate and die and the female menstrual cycle ceases. Gonadotrophic hormones increase with age due to lack of oestrogen and progesterone feedback. Diminished oestrogen levels lead to atrophy of the ovaries, uterus and vaginal tissue. It is after the menopause that the effects of oestrogens on non-reproductive organs is most evident. Calcium loss from bone tissue is no longer suppressed, leading to an increased risk of osteoporosis. The protective effects of oestrogen in the prevention of atherosclerotic heart disease is also lost. There is some evidence that testosterone levels in women decrease with age and this may bring about a corresponding decrease in libido.

In the male, testosterone production decreases over the years in tandem with the loss of the Leydig cells that produce it or possibly due to the loss of receptors for pituitary hormones. This process is mediated by a decline in renal clearance of testosterone, so that in healthy older men there is little change in testosterone levels. This enables older men to remain sexually active and fertile until well into later life. However, the number of active testis tubules engaged in sperm production does diminish with age, with the effect of decreasing the sperm count until it reaches infertile levels. Older men develop firmer testes and a tendency for prostatic hypertrophy, which is a benign condition in most instances (*see* Chapter 5 for explanation of laboratory results).

Alterations in Gastrointestinal Function

The Mouth and Teeth

Food entering the mouth is prepared for digestion by the action of the saliva and the teeth. Many older people continue to be edentulous, dependent on dentures. In the future, as a result of better dental hygiene, fluoride in present-day water systems and the conservation techniques of modern dentistry, older people may retain their own teeth for longer. However, according to Todd and Lader (1991) it will take more than 50 years before the whole population retain some of their natural teeth for life.

With age the teeth darken or become more yellow. The chewing surfaces may become mechanically worn down, so that chewing is less efficient. In addition, the gums may recede (hence the expression 'long in the tooth'), as a result of periodontal disease and accompanying infection. Many gum conditions can be prevented with proper tooth brushing and oral hygiene. Chapter 7 discusses dental health. Resorption of bone occurs in the jaw, causing loosening of the teeth and pockets between gum and teeth. Bone loss in the jaw results in a poorer fit for denture wearers. The cumulative effects of caries as a result of a diet high in sugar and age changes in the teeth and jaw lead to the loss of teeth. Adequate dentition is not only important to nutrition but also to appearance and communication. (These aspects will be addressed in Chapters 6 and 16, respectively.) There is atrophy of the buccal mucosa and degeneration of the underlying tissues. Saliva production can be decreased as 25% of the secretary cells are replaced by fibrous or fatty tissue. From the age of 50 years, ptyalin in the saliva, which is responsible for starch breakdown, is diminished, and this slows the initial digestion of complex carbohydrates.

The Oesophagus and Stomach

Decreased peristaltic action and a failure to relax by the lower oesophageal sphincter slow the emptying of the oesophagus. Insufficiently masticated food exacerbates this situation. The sluggish emptying of the oesophagus also forces the lower end to dilate, sustain greater stress in this area and cause an uncomfortable feeling of fullness below the sternum. At about 60 years of age, the gastric mucosa shows atrophic changes and fewer parietal cells result in a reduction of gastric acidity. The reduction in stomach acidity also diminishes the rate of digestion by enzymes such as pepsin.

Absorption is affected by gastrointestinal (GI) motility, the degree of digestion that takes place, the condition of the absorption surface, the blood flow to the GI tract, and the efficiency of the transport mechanism. Xylose and dextrose are absorbed more slowly, and fat absorption tends to be delayed. Calcium use is affected by the lack of adequate gastric acid and slower active transport in the body. The absorption of drugs is largely unaffected by age. Chapter 6 discusses nutrition for older people in depth.

The Small and Large Intestine

Some atrophy is seen in the small and large intestine but often less than in the stomach. Normal function of the colon is maintained in later life in spite of structural atrophy of the muscle and mucosal layers, and mucous glands. Diverticula or pouches develop and affect 50% of people aged over 70 years, though this tends to be a Western phenomenon. The internal sphincter of the large intestine loses its muscle tone and can create difficulty in bowel evacuation. The external sphincter, which retains much of its original tone, cannot by itself control the bowels. Slower transmission of nerve impulses dulls the need to defaecate. The elimination need is presented in Chapters 6 and 8.

Alterations in Sensory Perception

A number of sensory changes occur with age due to the intrinsic ageing process in sensory organs and their association with the nervous system. Other changes are extrinsic and linked to the environment (*see* **Appendix 1**). Taste, smell, sight, sound and touch are all affected to a greater or lesser degree. There is a lack of consistent evidence that taste buds decline in number. The belief that taste sensitivity fades dramatically has been shown to be generally false. Studies indicate that only 10% of healthy subjects report taste loss. Thirty percent who were taking medication reported taste loss. Men showed no loss to ordinary concentrations of taste materials, but women indicated a diminished ability to taste sweet and salty items. The threshold necessary to relay flavours rises for the four primary taste qualities: sweet, salty, bitter and sour. External factors such as smoking and medications, as well as more viscous saliva, contribute to altered ability to taste. Decline in sense of smell is attributed to loss of cells in the olfactory bulb of the brain and a decrease in the number of sensory cells in the nasal lining. It may contribute to any decrease in the perception of taste. Individuals with keen olfactory sensitivity in youth are purported to retain this sense. A decrease in ability to taste and smell may interfere with the anticipation and enjoyment of food and also the detection of food that smells bad.

Pain, Touch and Proprioception

At times, caregivers have been amazed by an older person's lack of response to pain. Conditions that are normally painful may occur with an absence of pain or create only minor discomfort or a sense of pressure. Life-threatening myocardial and abdominal infarctions are often experienced this way and catastrophies may occur with missed symptoms. This does not mean that elders do not experience postoperative pain, for example. The diminution of normal pain signals creates some potentially dangerous situations for older people and their state of wellness. Persons with limited activity, confined to a wheelchair or to bed, may not feel the pressure on bony prominences or the body messages to change position. Transmission of hot and cold impulses may be delayed just long enough for the older individual to sustain significant tissue damage to some part of the body. Contact with such items as heating pads, hot water bottles, radiators and iced items can result in serious consequences and lengthy hospitalisation for older people (see Chapter 9 for in-depth discussion of pain). Tactile sensitivity in the palms of the hands and soles of the feet declines with age because of a decrease in the number of Meissner's and Pacinian corpuscles. The kinesthetic sense or proprioception (position of the body in space) is altered with age. Older people may have more difficulty orientating their body in space when externally induced changes in body position are made. Slowed movements and altered position in space can lead to considerable difficulty with balance and spatial orientation. They may not be able to avoid obstacles as quickly in ordinary situations such as those that occur on a crowded street, nor are they as able as they once were to prevent an accident from happening to themselves or to others when fast movement might be essential. The automatic response to protect and brace oneself when falling is slower. This is partly the reason why hip fractures occur as a result of falls in older people, while a Colles' fracture is more likely to occur in younger adults whose reflexes are yet unimpaired. In addition, older people may be observed making more precise and deliberate movements, such as placement of the feet when walking. Conditions such as arthritis, stroke, some cardiac disorders or damage to the structures of the inner ear may affect peripheral and central mechanisms of mobility. Further discussion of sensory alterations appears in Chapters 12 and 13, as these changes affect safety and security of the older person.

The Ageing Eye

All persons will eventually experience some decline in visual capacity with age. Weale (1989, p. 39) grimly reminds us 'that prolonging life implicitly tends to promote blindness'.

Age Changes in Structure

The cornea, which is responsible for refraction of light, is among the first eye structures to be affected by ageing. A flatter, less smooth and thicker cornea is noticeable by its lacklustre appearance or loss of sparkling transparency and leaves the older individual more susceptible to astigmatism. More light must pass through the eye in order to achieve the same intensity of image. Pupil size diminishes thus decreasing the amount of light to reach the retina. This is of particular consequence at night when more time is needed to adapt vision in dim light or darkness. The surrounding iris becomes paler

due to loss of the black pigment which provides the intensity of colour, so that the eyes of a blue-eyed individual appear paler. The arcus senilis, a milky or grey ring made up of fat deposits, encircles the periphery of the iris as a partial arc or complete circle. Pigmentary particles may block the drainage channel through which aqueous humour leaves the eye. The rise in intraocular pressure may eventually lead to glaucoma. The anterior chamber of the eye decreases due to the thickness of the lens. The sclera may yellow and lose opacity, permitting stray light to enter the eye. As a result, images tend to appear washed out, necessitating more striking colour contrasts for satisfactory visual perception.

Presbyopia

A major age change affects the lens and causes the condition known as presbyopia, whereby close vision becomes blurred. With ageing, the lens becomes thicker, stiffer and more dense, due to biochemical changes within both the nucleus and capsule. As a consequence, the accommodating power of the lens is reduced, so that it becomes progressively less able to shorten its focal length to produce a sharp image on the retina. Changes in the suspensory ligaments, ciliary muscles and parasympathetic nerves contribute to the decreased accommodation that occurs. In the UK, the average age-of-onset of presbyopia is around 45 years, whereas in warmer countries, such as those near the equator, the age-of-onset can be as early as 30 years. The yellowing and darkening of the lens as a result of protein changes alter colour perception, particularly for shades of brown, beige, blue and violet. Reds, oranges and yellows are more easily seen. Colour clarity diminishes by 25% in the sixth decade and by 50% in the seventh decade.

The vitreous humour loses some of its water and fibrous skeletal support with age and produces harmless floaters within the field of vision. This is a benign condition but the presence of increasing numbers can be an early sign of a detached retina. Arterial and venous occlusions occur in retinal blood vessels and the retina and optic pathways lose some of their cells, making it harder to see detail, contrast and colour. Decreases in the number of cells within the visual cortex of the brain contribute to an increase in the time required to discriminate light stimuli and movement both in space and frequency. Peripheral vision is reduced, limiting the size of the visual field and depth perception may also be impaired. **Figure 4.3** shows age-related changes within the eye. A decrease in visual acuity in bright light, known as glare sensitivity, is thought to be due to light scattering by the lens and cornea. Glare is a major problem for older people, not only glare created by sunlight outdoors but also the reflection of light on any shiny object and especially light striking polished or linoleum floors. Older people require three times as much light to see things as they did when they were in their twenties. There is a need for more light for all visual perception. It is more effective to improve direct illumination of the object or surface under view than to increase the intensity of light in the entire area or room. For example, it would be more effective to focus the light directly on the newspaper that the person is trying to read than to increase the lighting

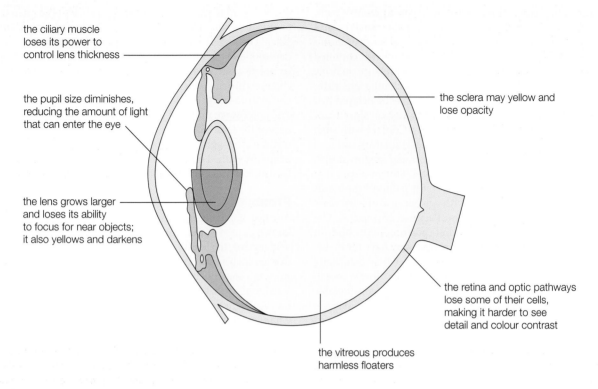

the ciliary muscle loses its power to control lens thickness

the pupil size diminishes, reducing the amount of light that can enter the eye

the lens grows larger and loses its ability to focus for near objects; it also yellows and darkens

the sclera may yellow and lose opacity

the retina and optic pathways lose some of their cells, making it harder to see detail and colour contrast

the vitreous produces harmless floaters

Figure 4.3 Age changes affecting the eye. (Source: Adapted from Weale R. In: Warnes AM, ed. *Human ageing and later life*. London: Edward Arnold, 1989.)

in the whole room. (*See* Chapter 12 for the effects of major eye diseases.)

Age Changes in External Structures

Changes may take place in the external structures of the eye, though these are not universal. Loss of periorbital fat and a decrease in the muscle tone of the upper eyelid can result in drooping known as ptosis. This can interfere with vision if the lids sag far enough over the eyes. The lubrication and cleansing action of the lacrimal secretions diminish. Eyes take on a dull appearance, and there is a sensation of dryness, scratchiness or tightness. Depending on the severity of discomfort of this situation, artificial tears are an available lubricant. Paradoxically, tearing of the eyes appears to increase and this is due to an overflow of tears from a loose lower lid.

Changes in Hearing and Vestibular Function

Hearing loss is a common but not inevitable accompaniment to ageing. Presbycusis is the term used to describe hearing loss that is brought about by age-related sensorineural changes. Hearing loss is thought to be caused by loss of hair cells and nerve fibres within the organ of Corti near the oval window, where high-pitched sound is converted to nerve impulses. The process is bilateral and starts from around the

age of 40 years. Presbycusis is characterised by hearing loss for high-frequency sounds, and one result is that sufferers experience poor speech discrimination for consonants. Reduced hearing acuity is exacerbated by high levels of background noise. Normal or slightly louder than normal speech may be perceived as unpleasant or even painful. This hypersensitivity is known as loudness recruitment and may affect a person's ability to tolerate a hearing aid. Impaired sound localisation makes it difficult for the older person to detect where sound is coming from. Tinnitus, a constant or recurring high-pitched clicking, buzzing, roaring, ringing or other sounds in the ear, may be unilateral or bilateral and becomes most acute at night or in quiet surroundings. Tinnitus may also be caused by medications, infection, cerumen accumulation or a blow to the head. A decline in central nervous system function may slow auditory processing. Excessive wax accumulation in the ear canal will intensify presbycusis. Impacted wax is a common temporary cause of hearing loss in older people. Atrophic changes in the sebaceous and apocrine glands lead to drier cerumen. This coupled with a narrowed auditory canal and stiffer, coarser hairs lining the canal can lead to cerumen impaction. Conductive hearing loss is caused by otosclerosis or arthritic conditions, which affect the joints between the malleus and stapes to cause joint fixation or reduced vibration of these bones. Older people with impaired hearing may have a combination of problems resulting from sensorineural and conductive causes. Asymmetrical

Types and Causes of Presbycusis		
Types	Description	Cause
Sensory	A sharp hearing loss at high frequencies with little effect on speech understanding	Degeneration of hair cells and atrophy of the organ of Corti
Neural	Hearing loss reduces speech discrimination	Widespread degeneration of cochlea nerve fibres and spiral ganglia
Metabolic or stria	Hearing loss that initially reduces sensitivity to all sound frequencies; it later interferes with speech discrimination	Degeneration of the stria vascularis and interruption in essential nutrients
Mechanical	Hearing loss that gradually increases from low to high frequencies and affects speech discrimination when high frequency hearing loss occurs	Mechanical changes in the inner ear

Table 4.1 Types and Causes of Presbycusis

or sudden hearing loss is not characteristic of presbycusis and needs referral. There is moderate degeneration in the vestibular system with age. Cell loss occurs in both the organs detecting the movement, position and acceleration of the head and those detecting movement in all directions. These changes are brought about by decreases in both the hair cell receptors in the vestibular apparatus and nerve fibres in the eighth cranial nerve. (*See* **Table 4.1** for summary.)

Immunological Changes

It is thought that infections, cancer and autoimmune disease occur more commonly in later life, in part as a result of decreased efficiency in the immune system. The protection of both cell-mediated and humoral immunity declines with age and there is loss of lymphoid tissue from the thymus, spleen, lymph nodes and bone marrow. Although the number of T cells remains the same, they seem to have a decreased ability to produce the cytokines needed to promote the growth and maturation of B cells. Furthermore, T-cells appear less likely to proliferate in the presence of an antigen. B-lymphocytes also respond less readily to stimulation by antigens with age, and it is thought that the poor response is due to lack of functional T-helper cells and a reduced number of B-cell precursor units (*see* Chapter 5 for further discussion). Age-related changes in immunity mean that the response to vaccination may be attenuated.

Nervous System Changes

It is a popular myth that we are losing millions of nerve cells each day. The consensus now appears to be that we do not lose cells throughout life and that when losses do occur, they are confined to specific areas of the brain. Net cell loss occurs in the caudate nucleus. The brain atrophies and can decrease in weight from 1.4 kg in a young male to as much as 1.2 kg in the very old. The ventricles increase in size, due to atrophic changes that are concentrated in the frontal cerebral cortex. These changes also result in a widening of the sulci and a decrease in the size of the gyri. Changes in brain morphology can be seen readily with magnetic resonance imaging or computerised tomography. Amyloid and lipofuscin are altered proteins found in ageing brains, and in small quantities appear to have little effect on normal brain function. Amyloid is found in increased amounts in some dementias. As yet the evidence for a decline in the levels of neurotransmitter substances remains inconclusive, but a decrease in the speed of nerve transmission suggests that changes do occur.

COGNITIVE FUNCTION

Age-related Change in Cognition

Consideration of age-related change in adult cognition can be viewed from a variety of perspectives. Pratt and Norris (1994) describe three major theoretical frameworks:
(1) Psychometric.
(2) Information processing.
(3) Developmental.

Because of the variability in cognitive performance in later life, no single approach can provide a satisfactory explanation of this complex area.

Measuring Intelligence Using Psychometric Tests

Cognitive ability encompasses intelligence, memory and learning and enables individuals to cope with environmental change. Intelligence can be defined as a general ability to think rationally, solve problems, learn new tasks and deal effectively with the environment. Much of the early work to measure age-related changes in intelligence took place in the USA. Cross-sectional studies were used to compare the performance in standardised assessment procedures of groups of young adults, with different age groups up to 60 years of age. Invariably, older people performed less well than the younger ones and this finding was interpreted as a decline in mental faculties across the life span. Early tests by Wechsler in the 1940s showed that intellect peaked between 20 and 30 years of age, and by 75 years subjects were functioning at only one-third of their original capacity. It was later realised that the methodology was flawed, in that no account had been taken of differences in culture, environment and social circumstances between the different age groups. For example, older people would have been subject to a wide variety of influences on cognitive performance. In the UK, education was disrupted by war and economic depression, people might not have completed their education and there were differences in education in urban and rural environments. Other factors such as nutrition, medical care, differences in child rearing practices and occupational opportunities are also thought to have influenced results. In essence, the cross-sectional study reflected cohort differences rather than a true maturational change.

It is now acknowledged that these early studies grossly underestimated older people's cognitive ability. However, the generalisation of such results to the older population as a whole may have contributed to the stereotype of inevitable decline in later life. Subsequently, cohort effects were reduced using longitudinal studies. However, environmental changes do occur both over lifetimes and over the time span of studies, so that age changes are not easily separated from environmental effects. Longitudinal studies may overestimate cognitive ability: subjects may become ill or die, remaining subjects may become test-wise and poor performers may drop out, leaving only an elite. Eventually, through the implementation of cross-sequential studies, which combined the features of the two previous methods, Schaie (1989) was able to distinguish between age effects, cohort effects and the time of measurement effects. He concluded that cohort effects can be as large as age differences for most of the life span. Schaie found that there was no uniform pattern of age-related changes across all intellectual abilities, and no reliably detectable decrements in ability below the age of 60 years. This means that on average, intellect is preserved throughout a person's working life and challenges the view that older workers are less able. He also found varying rises and falls in different abilities throughout adulthood. These intra-individual differences demonstrate the concept of plasticity and challenge the view of cognitive ability developing in childhood and adolescence and being fixed through life. More recent work by Rabbitt (1994) demonstrates the substantial gains that can be made by a period of practice, when adults aged 50–82 years were asked to identify and classify letters of the alphabet.

Overall, studies have demonstrated that there is decline is some areas of cognitive ability, but these remain small in absolute terms and can often be compensated for by knowledge or skills acquired over a lifetime. A 75-year-old lawyer illustrated this point admirably, when comparing his performance with that of much younger colleagues: 'They work more quickly than I do but I know the law like the back of my hand, so I don't have to look it up and that saves time.' This example also illustrates the concepts of fluid and crystallised intelligence, and their differences. Fluid intelligence stems from qualities inherent in the central nervous system and reflects a person's ability to solve novel problems with speed and accuracy. The speed of performing simple tasks does decrease more markedly from the age of 60 years upwards and there is a positive correlation with scores in intelligent quotient (IQ) tests (Rabbitt, 1994). Crystallised intelligence, which reflects acquired bodies of knowledge, vocabulary and ways of dealing with the world (such as social skills), remain relatively intact and may improve with age. Many authors have commented on the inappropriateness of using IQ tests that were originally designed for school students to determine cognitive change in mature adults, who may perceive them as trivial and meaningless.

They recommend that tests which are more relevant to older people's everyday lives, known as ecologically valid tests, are employed wherever possible. 'Use it or lose it' is an adage that describes many aspects of age-related change and applies equally to cognition. Cognitive performance is less likely to decline with involvement in a complex and intellectually stimulating environment. With this in mind, nurses can play a useful role in encouraging older people to continue with intellectual pursuits at times when they are perhaps feeling less needed, at retirement for example. Continuing-care nurses can play their part by ensuring that residents have access to newspapers and books of their choice, while a regular general knowledge quiz can be both mentally stimulating and a great source of fun.

Memory and Information Processing

Current thinking suggests that poor memory is not an inevitable feature of ageing but memory decline describes more and more people as they grow older. However, those affected tend to develop their own strategies to counteract memory loss, so that lapses may only minimally interfere with daily living (Maylor, 1990). In unfamiliar, stressful or demanding situations, such as during admission to hospital, these lapses may be more marked.

According to the information processing (IP) model of adult cognition, memory is the process of storing and retrieving information. The computer is the metaphor for human

Meeting Age-related Change Needs

Fred Hollins is an active man in his mid seventies. His hobbies are leather tooling and restoration of classic cars. He has a wide circle of international acquaintances with similar interests. His retirement from a senior post in an engineering firm has not been easy but he does 'get a lot out of his friends and hobbies'. He often talks about his postings during the war years, which he says 'were the best years of my life ... things have never been quite the same since ... the sense of comradeship you see'. Mr Hollins is similar to many men who reached maturity during the last war and enlisted for active military service. His legacy is a generation of 'survivors' with some unique experiences.

Separating the age-related influences from the generational and environmental ones can be very difficult. The first sign of growing older that Mr Hollins noticed was the loss of hearing, especially in situations that are loud with multiple sources of noise. A nurse friend told him that it is likely to be related to his years in the war, when the unnatural noises of shelling had affected his hearing. Then he gradually became aware that his eyesight was impaired so that he could only focus on distant objects but near objects were fuzzy. More frustrating than these, however, is his inability to write to his acquaintances with the same fluidity as in earlier years. Sometimes the words are on the tip of his tongue but simply will not come. Another thing that troubles him is the decreasing strength of his grip. Recently it has become more difficult for him to work on his cars because of his weaker grip strength. He does not know whether these are normal age-related changes that he must adjust to or whether they are indications of failing health that required active medical intervention.

- What are Mr Hollins's comments that provide subjective evidence of his needs?
- What theoretical approaches can the nurse draw on in order to provide objective data for an holistic nursing assessment?
- Suggest two unmet needs that may be the most significant to Mr Hollins at this time.
- What might be the nursing aims for each unmet need, reflecting a realistic outcome and using concrete and measurable terms?
- Suggest one or more interventions for each area of unmet need.

- **What are Mr Hollins's comments that provide subjective evidence of his needs?**
- **What theoretical approaches can the nurse draw on in order to provide objective data for an holistic nursing assessment?**
- **Suggest two unmet needs that may be the most significant to Mr. Hollins at this time.**
- **What might be the nursing aims for each unmet need, reflecting a realistic outcome and using concrete and measurable terms?**
- **Suggest one or more interventions for each area of unmet need.**

cognition and this relies on the methods of experimental psychology. Cognitive psychologists using the IP model describe three kinds of memory ability:

- Primary memory, which can maintain a literal copy of a stimulus for up to 2 seconds and is affected little by age.
- Secondary memory, which requires attention and retention of information from 30 seconds to 30 minutes.
- Remote memory, which stores and retains information for long periods. The slower speed of information processing affects the laying down (encoding) of new information and retrieval of information from both the secondary and remote memory.

It is a myth that healthy older people can remember events from the distant past better than those from the recent past. Holland and Rabbitt (1991) compared the abilities of three groups of older people to recall early and recent autobiographical events. The first group lived independent lives in the community, the second group were physically disabled and had lived in an institution for over 2 years, and the third group were mentally impaired and living in an institution. The community dwellers rehearsed more memories from recent years than early years, whilst the reverse was true of the institutionalised physically disabled group. Group three produced few memories, and these were mainly early ones. The results of this study emphasise the importance of context and the opportunities for rehearsal of memories. For the community dwellers, active management of daily life requires continued referencing of the recent past in order to plan for the future.

In a study of self-reported memory ability by both younger and older people, Cohen and Faulkner (1984) found that both groups had difficulty remembering the same things and that this seemed to get even harder with increasing age. There is no sign of any change in ability to remember before the age of 60 years and only moderate decline in memory beyond the age of 60 years but not across the board. Older people in particular find telephone numbers, postcodes and names of acquaintances difficult to remember. Temporary retrieval blocks in which a previously known proper name cannot be recalled are reported as occurring with increasing frequency by older individuals (Cohen, 1994). However, memory for meaningful factual information remains unimpaired and older people are well able to keep track of personal plans and actions. Rabbitt (1981) suggests that older individuals sometimes have more difficulty in remembering who said what in group conversations. This is important information for nurses who are engaged in facilitating groups with older people. He concludes that it is helpful if older group participants can be tactfully drawn into the conversation, reminded of what has been said and by whom, proceeding at a slower pace and providing pauses for their remarks.

The Effects of Pathology

Hearing loss is thought to compound memory ability in that cognitive resources are directed into more effortful listening (Rabbitt, 1988). Other pathologies have been found to produce cognitive decrements. Results from more recent studies, however, would appear to challenge the 'terminal drop theory', which suggests that there is a steep decline in cognitive performance some 2 years before death and that this is accelerated towards the point of death.

The Developmental Perspective

There are many questions which remain to be answered in relation to adult cognition. While there are known patterns of decrement, it is thought that there are adaptive features too. Labouvie-vief and Blanchard-Fields (1982) argue that there could be a developmental approach to cognition, whereby there is a final reintigrative stage that is not characterised by decrement and which is not readily measured by psychometric tests. Baltes and Willis (1982) describe selective optimisation, whereby individuals choose to expend energy on things that are important to them at the expense of performance in psychometric tests. The phenomenon of encapsulation is thought to exist where, for some people, particular areas of ability develop and improve over time.

Finally, the practicality of these distinctions in everyday life is that even though older subjects show some decrements in processing information, reaction time, perception and attentional tasks, the majority of older people adapt successfully to changing environmental demands. Familiarity, previous learning, life experience, and possibly strategies that are so far little understood, compensate for the minor loss of efficiency in the basic neurological processes. Nurses can be supportive to older people by applying their knowledge of cognitive change in adapting teaching strategies and ensuring that at times of assessment of competence, whenever possible, appropriate supports are in place to facilitate optimal performance.

PHYSICAL AND MENTAL HEALTH ASSESSMENT

Altered Presentation of Illness in Later Life

One of the essential differences between the presentation of disease in early and later life is the atypical responses often observed in older adults, which are due in part to impaired homeostasis. Presentation may be less dramatic, so that acute chest pain and shock is often absent in an older person suffering a myocardial infarction. Instead, the person may present with heart failure, an episode of confusion or a 'queer turn'. The presence of a high temperature with fever is less marked and is probably due to an altered immune response. The reduced perception of visceral stimuli together with a grossly impaired immune response contribute to an atypical presentation of appendicitis in some older people. In a study by Horattas *et al.* (1990) only 20% of 96 patients suffering from appendicitis presented with the classic signs of nausea, vomiting, fever, right lower quadrant pain and an increased white blood cell count. The symptoms and diagnostic test results of the remaining 80% failed to result in an initial definitive diagnosis.

It is generally accepted that older people, particularly those over 75 years of age, present with one or more of the following symptoms when they are ill:
(1) Mental confusion.
(2) Falls.
(3) Incontinence.
(4) Immobility.

These areas are major domains for nursing intervention in the care of older people, and comprehensive assessment and management strategies will be covered in detail in later chapters. However, the presence of any one of the above symptoms should alert the nurse and her medical colleagues to seek out treatable causes in the first instance. (*See* **Appendix 1** for normal physical assessment findings in older people.)

Multiple Pathology

A further complicating factor in the physical assessment process is the likelihood of multiple pathology, making it more difficult to link signs and symptoms in order to establish a diagnosis in the presence of several disease conditions. If some, or all, of these conditions are being treated with medication, there is the added complexity of polypharmacy with the associated hazards of drug interaction and compliance.

The Importance of Function

The biological status of the human organism as it reaches the latter end of the life span is one of increasing complexity.

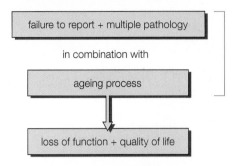

failure to report + multiple pathology

in combination with

ageing process

loss of function + quality of life

Figure 4.4 Equation of diminishing function. (Source: Williams I. *The healthcare of older people in the community*. Radcliffe Medical Press.)

In practical terms, it is difficult to assess the contribution of normal age-related changes, age-related detraining, multiple pathology (which is often age associated) and polypharmacy to the current physical state of an older person who is in need of health care. It is generally agreed, therefore, that assessment of function is the most meaningful method of assessing their combined effects (Williams, 1993). (*See* **Figure 4.4** for the equation of diminishing function.)

A state of independent social wellbeing is governed by the ability to perform activities of daily living (ADLs). These can be considered at three different levels: sociability or ability to take part in life outside the home, ability to carry out domestic tasks sometimes known as instrumental ADLs (IADLs) and personal care ADLs. Threats to personal autonomy as a result of the above combined age-related insults tend to occur in sequence, so that there is decline or complete cessation of activity outside the home, followed by inability to carry out domestic tasks, while personal self-care activities are affected last of all. Williams (1986) illustrates these levels in diagrammatic form as concentric rings, with the older adult in the centre, so that the dynamic relationship between the levels can be appreciated (**Figure 4.5**). The model can provide a particularly useful framework for practice nurses who perform over seventy-fives' health assessments. Decline can be detected at each level and steps taken to halt or reverse the process either by treatment alone or referral for social service support.

ASSESSMENT TOOLS

It is well established that an interdisciplinary team approach to the care of older people is most likely to achieve the best outcome. In practice, such teams achieve varying degrees of cohesiveness and effectiveness. It is widely acknowledged that the most successful care outcomes are achieved when all team members, including the patient, have agreed and are working towards mutual goals. Integrated care pathways are being adopted as a means of improving joint working. In essence, this means that all members of the interdisciplinary care team

have agreed a treatment schedule based on available scientific evidence or best practice. The total care process, which includes initial assessment, is documented in a joint record. The use of such schemes of care may require that nurses have a working knowledge of assessment tools which have traditionally been the domain of other therapists. Feeling comfortable with an assessment method requires practice using the tool and refinement so that it is appropriate for use with older clients. It will be of concern to some nurses that the use of integrated care pathways conflicts with a desire to base care on a nursing model. This is particularly so when the preferred model seems to accommodate all the aspects specific to an older person. In this instance, the challenge remains for nurses to negotiate their requirements on behalf of their client group. *See* Chapter 22 for an example of a recently developed assessment tool, categories of which can be used as the basis of a nursing care plan.

Functional Assessment

Tools that assess ability in activities of daily living (ADLs) are designed to provide qualitative data regarding an individual's capacity to be or remain independent. Bowling (1997) raises a number of issues on the measurement of functional ability:

- One of their major drawbacks is that they tend to be either too broad in that they miss specific aspects of disease, such as breathlessness, or they concentrate on a narrow range of tasks, which do not include financial, social or emotional needs.
- The scales have been developed on the basis of professionals' judgements about essential aspects of daily living and do not always reflect the client's priorities.
- Scales may also lack sensitivity in that they do not allow for degrees of impairment.
- Nurses should make certain that the rating scale is appropriate for the intended client group, in terms of age and location, i.e. community dwellers or residents in a care home.

The Index of Activities of Daily Living

The Katz index of ADLs (*see* **Appendix 2**) provides a basic framework to evaluate an older person's ability to live independently and is used in rehabilitation facilities to measure response to therapy. Its lack of detail precludes it from community use as it does not take into account adaptation to the environment. Scoring of the Katz index is based on a 3-point scale and allows the scorer to rate client performance abilities as independent, requiring assistance or dependent. The value of the Katz index is that it can be administered by anyone, with minimum training, and it can provide data that identify the kind of services that might be needed. It is a popular test and has proved successful in predicting the long-term course and social adaptation of patients with strokes and hip fractures. Despite its widespread use, there is little evidence to support its validity and reliability.

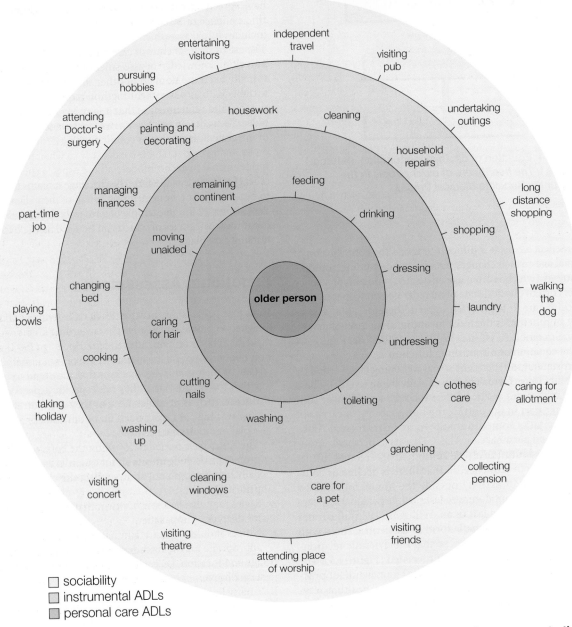

Figure 4.5 Social performance levels. Threats to autonomy of the older person tend to occur in sequence starting with the outer ring. (Source: Williams EM. A model to describe social performance levels in elderly people. *J R Coll Gen Practit* 1986, 36:422–423.)

The Barthel Index

This was originally designed for use with long-term care patients with neuromuscular or musculoskeletal disorders. The Barthel index provides data to determine the amount of personal care required, and can serve in rehabilitation settings as a method of documenting improvement of a patient's ability.

The index is divided into two categories: independent and dependent. Under each of these headings, activities are rated as independent (intact and limited ability) or depen-

dent (requiring a helper or unable to do an activity or activities at all) (*see* Chapter 8). Scoring can be carried out in approximately 30 seconds, so it is exceedingly quick to use. Bowling (1997) states that validity has been confirmed by studies where its use has successfully predicted mortality among stroke patients, length of stay and independent rating by a physician. More recent tests of its reliability support its continued use with patients with neuromuscular disability (Collin *et al.* 1988).

The Crichton Royal Behaviour Rating Scale (CRBRS)

Developed and tested for use with institutionalised older people who have physical and mental deficits, the CRBRS was the tool chosen to evaluate the experimental National Health Service nursing home projects of the mid 1980s. The modified version contains 10 items, five relating to functional ability (mobility, feeding, dressing, bathing, continence) and five relating to mental disturbance (memory, orientation, communication, cooperation, restlessness). The confusion sub-scale can be used independently of the functional ability scale, and has been used to confirm a diagnosis of dementia. Interviewers require training as its use involves subjective classifications of behaviour. Structured questions which have been tested for reliability are available as a result of the previously mentioned work by Bond *et al.* (1989). Overall, there is limited evidence for its validity and reliability.

The Clifton Assessment Procedures for the Elderly (CAPE)

According to Bowling (1997), this is the most extensively tested measure of dependency in widespread use in the UK. It was developed and tested for validity for older people with mental infirmity in institutional care. The assessment consists of two schedules designed to measure behaviour and cognition. Its main advantage is that it is short and takes little time to complete, although some interviewer training is required. More evidence is required to confirm validity and its reliability is weak.

Mental Assessment

Abbreviated Mental Test Score (AMTS)

The Royal College of General Practitioners (RCGP) recommends the use of the AMTS to check for cognitive impairment and to discriminate between organic and functional mental impairment. It consists of a 10-item questionnaire that is administered by an interviewer and which covers among others factors, age, date, place, person and recognition. The maximum score is 10 and cut-offs range from >6 to <10, though >8 has been reported as being the most sensitive value. Validity and reliability is reported to be good (Bowling, 1995).

The Mini-mental State Examination (MMSE)

The MMSE is a short and convenient measure of the types of deficits found in the dementias; it is administered by an interviewer. It is composed of two parts: one requires verbal response and assesses orientation, memory and attention, and the other component requires the ability to write a sentence, draw a complex polygon, respond to written and oral commands and name objects. The total score is 30 and the cut-off score is 23–24. Validity is reported to be good and reliability satisfactory (Bowling, 1995). A General Medical Council (1997) clinical bulletin on the diagnosis and management of Alzheimer's disease recommends the MMSE as the preferred adjunct to diagnosis.

The Geriatric Depression Scale (GDS)

The GDS comprises part of the assessment package recommended for the over seventy-five's health assessment by the RCGP. The test is administered by an interviewer and respondents are required to give yes/no answers to 15 questions related to feeling states over the last week. A score of >5 indicates probable depression.

Integrated Assessments

Recommended batteries of tests for use with older community dwellers have been published by a combined working group from the Royal College of Physicians and the British Geriatrics Society (RCP/BGS, 1992), and separately by the RCGP. The latter are for specific use in the annual over seventy-five's health check, for which nurses working in general practice may have delegated responsibility. Interestingly, both groups recommend different instruments. Bowling (1995) gives in-depth assessments of many of these and suggests that more work needs to be carried out into devising more sensitive measures for use with older people.

The Nottingham Health Profile (NHP)

This is a useful tool for nurses carrying out community studies and wishing to estimate the patient's self-perception of health status. It is not an index of disease, illness or disability but enables people to express how they feel when they are experiencing more severe states of ill-health. The profile has two parts. Part one asks for yes/no responses to 38 simple statements covering mobility, pain, energy, sleep, emotional reactions and social isolation. Part two asks about the effects of health on seven areas of daily life: work, looking after the home, social life, home life, sex life, interests, hobbies and holidays. Bowling (1997) cites evidence of its validity for a variety of groups, including people over 65 years of age. Reliability has been partly tested. In summary, it is short and easy to administer but provides only a limited measure of function.

The Short Form-36 (SF-36)

The SF-36 and its shorter version, the SF-12 are alternatives to the NHP and are gaining in popularity in the UK as core measures of disease-specific health-related quality of life (Bowling, 1995). The longer version consists of 36 questions covering eight dimensions. Physical functioning forms the major component, together with social functioning, role limitations due to both physical and emotional problems, mental health, energy and vitality, pain and general health perception. Moderate validity and reliability has been demonstrated, but further testing is required prior to recommending widespread use with older people. There is evidence that it is not suitable for use in postal questionnaires with older people (Brazier *et al.* 1992), however, this does not exclude it from use in interview surveys.

Recording of Data

Problem-oriented medical recording (POMR) is also known as Weed's problem-oriented system. It was designed primarily for use by medical staff but it can be adapted to the needs of nurse practitioners who work with older clients. The database can be broadened to encompass a multidimensional assessment of a client. The components of the problem-oriented system are database, problem list, initial plan and progress notes, which assume the SOAP format (subjective data, objective data, assessment or diagnosis, and plan).

The database is usually derived from patients themselves. To obtain an initial database from well elders, however, the nurse should consider obtaining information from the physical, psychological, social and economic domains. A database can be obtained through various assessment tools presented in this book or from those designed by other organisations and which are validated for use with older people. When there is no tool available, the nurse will need to create one geared to assessment of functional ability or disability in the physical, mental, social, economic and ADL spheres of the older person's life.

Once data are collected, a problem and potential problem list can be generated, that portrays a holistic picture of the person's lifeworld. The initial plan includes diagnosis (if appropriate), treatment (if appropriate) and education, as well as progress notes that stem from the problem list. Findings and conclusions from the assessment should be discussed with the client so that responsibility for the health programme can be appropriately delegated. This ensures that the client is an active participant in health care and is encouraged to adopt a healthy lifestyle as presented in Chapter 3. Given sufficient information, the older client should be capable of making decisions about his or her health status and needed resources. The goal of preventive health care is aimed at maintenance of the present health status and maximising function.

THE NURSE'S ROLE

In health care settings that provide care for older people, it is crucial that nurses have expertise in the assessment of the older adult. Older people can experience a variety of unique physical, mental and social problems that often coexist and are interrelated. Age-related changes alter norms and illness presentation is often atypical. In addition, poor memory, stress or the effects of illness may prevent the older person from recalling significant aspects of health history (Eliopoulos, 1990). Comprehensive and holistic assessment of an older person requires a thorough physical examination together with the collection of subjective and objective data

encompassing biological, psychosocial and functional domains. In contexts where the caring period is likely to be longer term, such as in a care home or in the person's own home, the inclusion of biographical knowledge can explain beliefs and behaviour and strengthen the relationship between patient and nurse (Schofield, 1994). Proper assessment requires that nurses possess a knowledge base covering aspects of gerontology, skills in interviewing, observation and physical assessment techniques (Heath, 1995). Inadequate preparation can lead to inaccurate assessment of need based on stereotypical assumptions about the lifeworld and aspirations of the older people. *See* **Figure 4.6** for Maslow's hierarchy as a template for assessment.

Questions regarding genetic background, although important, have less significance for older people because genetic consequences usually appear in earlier phases of life. However, concern for genetic inheritance cannot entirely be eliminated since latent changes do occur and affect physical and mental wellbeing, for example the inherited form of Alzheimer's disease.

There is evidence to suggest that older people do not usually seek assistance from health care professionals until there is obvious physical and emotional difficulty (Blaxter and Paterson, 1982) and that there is some dissatisfaction with general practitioner (GP) consultations (Sidell, 1992). Despite this, GP consultations rates are higher for people over 75 years of age, with an average of six GP consultations per annum compared with an average of four for adults under 65 years of age (Office of Population Censuses and Surveys, 1988).

The client may find giving certain types of health information stressful and may be reluctant to discuss changes or problems that might confirm fears of illness, limitations or old age. Any illness may be seen as a threat to independence and viewed as leading to eventual institutionalisation. Sometimes an initial health questionnaire can be completed by the client before coming to the surgery, or prior to a planned hospital admission. The client may feel more comfortable in responding to the printed question, it saves time, and it provides a background from which the interview can develop. The nurse can clarify questionnaire answers, and the client can elaborate with details.

In addition, the ethnic mix of elders is rapidly changing. Many of our present assessment tools do not provide for the collection of accurate data. Assessment must utilise ways to elicit health care beliefs from older people in ethnic minority groups. Cultural sensitivity of the care provider is important in order to disentangle cultural normative behaviour from behaviour that mimics pathology. The tools are very limited that can facilitate this type of assessment data. Pfeifferling and Kleinman both have developed tools that assist a caregiver in gleaning pertinent assessment information to provide appropriate health promotion, prevention, maintenance and interventions (*see* **Appendix 3**).

Any health history form or interview should include personal details, the chief complaint and documentation of present illness (if applicable), family history, nutritional state, the use of prescribed medications and over-the-counter

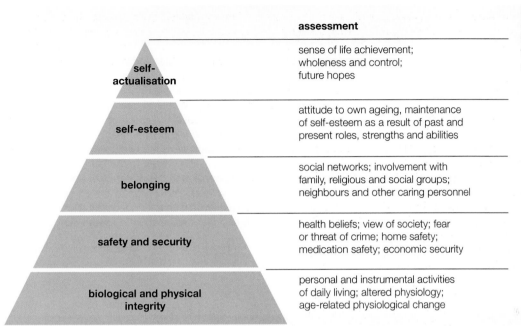

assessment

Level	Assessment
self-actualisation	sense of life achievement; wholeness and control; future hopes
self-esteem	attitude to own ageing, maintenance of self-esteem as a result of past and present roles, strengths and abilities
belonging	social networks; involvement with family, religious and social groups; neighbours and other caring personnel
safety and security	health beliefs; view of society; fear or threat of crime; home safety; medication safety; economic security
biological and physical integrity	personal and instrumental activities of daily living; altered physiology; age-related physiological change

Figure 4.6 Maslow's hierarchy as a template for assessment.

preparations, and a review of systems. Additional data should consider the functional and instrumental activities of daily living, psychological parameters such as cognitive and emotional wellbeing, the individual's self-perception, and social parameters such as economic resources and concerns, pattern of health and health care, education, family structure, plans for retirement and living environment. Much of this information is obtained orally, but it can also be evaluated by observation of personal grooming, facial expression, responsiveness to the interview and physical examination. Information about involvement with the surrounding community and group participation should reveal additional information about the emotional state and feelings of self-worth of the older person. A home visit assessment compliments or provides information that is difficult to gauge in a clinic, surgery or other formal setting. Especially difficult to ascertain are such areas as nutrition, use of alcohol, actual level of function on a daily basis and suitability and safety of the environment. Even when the individual is relatively independent, an appreciation for any difficulty encountered in food preparation, use of the lavatory, bathing and heating the home can be acquired.

SUMMARY

Many changes that occur with ageing have been discussed here and will be expanded in subsequent chapters. Biological age changes are universal, progressive, decremental and intrinsic. In addition, it can be concluded that complex functions of the body decline more than simple body processes; that coordinated activity, which relies on interacting systems such as nerves, muscles and glands, has a greater decremental loss than single system activity; and that a uniform and predictable loss of cell function occurs in all vital organs. Most older individuals are able to function within the physical dictates of their body and continue to live to a healthy old age.

KEY POINTS

- Age-related physiological changes affect most major organ systems but there is wide inter and intra-individual variation in the degree of change.
- Change in homeostatic mechanisms is a common feature of the biological ageing process.
- The extent of age-related cognitive change is often overestimated. Decline is minimal until 60 years of age, after which there is variable decline in mental activities with those requiring speed and visuospatial manipulation most affected.
- Modified teaching and learning strategies can compensate for cognitive and sensory impairments.
- Illness states in older people often present in an atypical manner. Common presentations are immobility, confusion, incontinence and falls.
- Functional ability is a more important indicator of general wellbeing in older people than the presence of age-related change and pathology. Interdisciplinary working requires that nurses have a working knowledge of assessment tools.
- A comprehensive holistic health assessment of an older adult can only be achieved with the underpinning gerontological knowledge. Stereotypical beliefs about ageing are more likely to lead to inaccurate assessment of need.

 AREAS AND ACTIVITIES FOR STUDY AND REFLECTION

- Monitor admissions to your unit (or new referrals if you are a community nurse) and make a note of 'atypical' presentations of disease states characteristic of later life.
- Select a client and where possible differentiate between signs and symptoms of age-related change and pathology.
- For nurses working in assessment and rehabilitation settings, consider the use of a functional assessment tool and discuss its potential to enhance team working towards common goals.
- Select a topic for client education and draw up a teaching plan appropriate to your client group.

REFERENCES

Baltes PB, Willis SL. Enhancement (plasticity) of intellectual functioning in older age: Penn States Adult Development and Environment Project (ADEPT). In: Craik FIM, Trehub S, eds. *Ageing and cognitive process*. New York: Plenum, 1982.

Blaxter M, Paterson L. *Mothers and daughters: a three-generational study of health, attitudes and behaviour*. Oxford: Heinemann Educational, 1982.

Bond J, Gregson B, Atkinson A et al. *Evaluation of continuing care accommodation for elderly people, Vol. 2. The randomised controlled trial of experimental NHS nursing homes and conventional continuing care wards in NHS hospitals*, Report No. 38. Newcastle upon Tyne: University of Newcastle upon Tyne Health Care Research Unit, 1989.

Bowling A. *Measuring disease*. Milton Keynes: Open University Press, 1995.

Bowling A. *Measuring health: a review of quality of life measurement scales, 2nd edition*. Milton Keynes: Open University Press, 1997.

Brazier J, Harper R, Jones NMB et al. Validating the SF-36 health survey questionnaire: new outcome measures for primary care. *Br Med J* 1992, 305:160–164.

Bulpitt CJ. Assessing biological age: practicality? *Gerontology* 1995, 41:315–321.

Carnegie Trust UK. *The Carnegie inquiry into the third age*. Dunfermline: Carnegie Trust UK, 1990.

Cohen G. Age-related problems in the use of proper names in communication. In: Hummert ML, Wiemann JM, Nussbaum JF, eds. *Interpersonal communication in older adulthood*. Sage, 1994.

Cohen G, Faulkner D. Memory in old age: 'good in parts'. *New Scientist* 1984, (October 11):49–51.

Collin C, Wade DT, Davies D. The Barthel ADL index: a reliability study. *International Disability Studies* 1988, 10:61–63.

Eliopoulos C. *Health assessment of the older adult*. Redwood City: Addison-Wesley, 1990.

General Medical Council. *Setting standards for the diagnosis and management of Alzheimer's disease in primary and secondary care*. Sevenoaks: Medpress, 1997.

Heath H. Health assessment of people over 75. *Nursing Standard* 1995, 9:30–37.

Horattas M, Guyton D, Wu D. A reappraisal of appendicitis in the elderly. *Am J Surg* 1990, 160:291–293.

Holland CA, Rabbitt PMA. Ageing memory: use versus impairment. *Br J Psychology* 1991, 82:29–39.

Kinney RA. *Physiologic aging, 2nd edition*. Chicago: Mosby, 1989.

Labouvie-vief G, Blanchard, Fields F. Cognitive ageing and psychological growth. *Ageing and Society* 1982, 2:183–209.

Linnane AW, Sungkot M, Takayaki O, Masushi T. Mitochondrial DNA Mutations as an Important Contributor to Ageing and Degenerative Diseases. *The Lancet* 25 March 1989, 642–645.

Maylor EA. Age and prospective memory. *Q J Exp Psychol* 1990.

Office of Population Censuses and Surveys. *General household survey*. London: HMSO, 1988.

Pierson DJ. Effects of aging on the respiratory system. In: Pierson DJ, Kacmarek RM, eds. *Foundations of respiratory care*. New York: Churchill Livingstone, 1992.

Pratt MW, Norris J. *The social psychology of aging*. Cambridge: Blackwell, 1994.

Rabbitt PMA. Talking to the old. *New Society* 1981, (January 22):140–141.

Rabbitt PMA. Social psychology, neuroscience and cognitive psychology need each other; (and gerontology needs all three of them). *The Psychologist: Bulletin of the British Psychological Society* 1988, 12:500–506.

Rabbitt P. Declining years? *Care of the Elderly* 1994, Nov/Dec 6(6):407–411.

RCP/BGS. *Standardised assessment scales for elderly people*. Report of Joint Workshops. London: Royal College of Physicians Research Unit and British Geriatrics Society Research Unit, 1992.

Rodeheffer RJ, Gerstenblith G. In: *Relations between normal ageing and disease*. HA Johnson, ed. Raven Press, 1985.

Schaie KW. The hazards of cognitive aging. *Gerontologist* 1989, 29:484–493.

Schofield I. A historical approach to assessment. *Elderly Care* 1994, 6:14–15.

Sidell M. The relationship of elderly women to their doctors. In: George J, Ebrahim S, eds. *Health care for older women*. Oxford: Oxford University Press, 1992.

Strehler BL. *Time, Cells and Aging*. New York and London: Academic Press, 1962.

Tietz NW, Shuey DF, Wekstein DR. Laboratory values in fit aging individuals – sexagenarians through centenarians. *Clin Chem* 1992, 38:1167.

Todd JET, Lader D. *Adult dental health UK 1988*, London: HMSO, 1991.

Van Cauter E, Leproult R, Kupfer DJ. Effect of gender and age on the levels of circadian rhythmicity of plasma cortisol. *J Clin Endocrinol Metab* 1996, 81:2468.

Weale R. Eyes and Age: views on visual health promotion. In: Warnes AM, ed. *Human ageing and later life*. London: Edward Arnold, 1989.

Williams EM. A model to describe social performance levels in elderly people. *J R Coll Gen Practit* 1986, 36:422–423.

Williams EM, Wallace P. *Health checks for people aged 75 and over*. London: Royal College of General Practitioners, 1993.

BIBLIOGRAPHY

Brookbank JW. *The biology of aging*. New York: Harper & Row, 1990.

Christianson JL, Grzybowski JM. *Biology of aging*. St. Louis: Mosby, 1993.

Cullinen T. *Visual disability in the elderly*. Beckenham: Croom Helm, 1986.

Dellasega C, Clark D, McCreary D, Helmuth A. Nursing process: teaching elderly clients. *J Gerontol Nurs* 1994, 20:31–38.

Villar MA, Wiggins J, Evans TO. The structure and function of the ageing lung. *Care of the Elderly* 1991, 3:129–132.

Weinrich SP, Boyd M, Nussbaum J. Continuing education: adapting strategies to teach the elderly. *J Gerontol Nurs* 1989, 15:17–21.

Weinrich SP, Boyd M. Adapting and Evaluating Teaching Tools. *J Gerontol Nurs* 1992, 18:15–20.

Laboratory values and implications
Kevin Somerville

LEARNING OBJECTIVES

After studying this chapter you will be able to:
- Explain in detail altered physiological change that may be indicative of disease states in older people.
- Appreciate that established normal laboratory values require cautious interpretation when applied to older people.
- Discuss the rationales for collecting, storing and transporting specimens for clinical measurement under specific conditions.
- Begin to develop a knowledge base for specialist practice in nursing older people.

INTRODUCTION

Adequate care of the older patient often requires clinical investigations because of the vagaries of illness in later life. The older patient is more likely than their younger adult counterpart to present with vague or nonspecific symptoms such as confusion, falls and immobility, and may have complex multiple pathologies. However, the results of investigations may be difficult to interpret in older people. There is greater heterogeneity (increased coefficient of variation) among the old than in younger adults, marked as a wider 'normal' range for some laboratory values. Some parameters change with normal ageing and some do not. Age-related changes in organ function occur such as a loss of functioning nephrons within the kidney and reduction in hepatic size and blood flow. However, the magnitude of these changes varies between individuals, which makes the concept of 'the elderly' problematic with regard to laboratory values.

At menopause, ovarian secretion of oestrogens ceases, with implications for the maintenance of bone mass and clinical chemistry laboratory values that relate to bone turnover. There are alterations in body composition, a consequence of an increasingly sedentary lifestyle, with reduced muscle mass and changes in diet, while the ageing process itself produces changes in metabolism and reduced adaptation to stress (homeostasis). These may alter baseline laboratory tests and blunt or accentuate changes with disease. Circadian and circumannual variation of some tests occurs, but is clinically important in few circumstances. Cortisol is an exception, with marked diurnal variation that continues into old age but in blunted form (Van Cauter *et al.* 1996); timing of blood sampling is crucial. Gender differences may be greater than those observed with ageing (Whitehead *et al.* 1994; Beregi *et al.*, 1995)

Establishing Normal Laboratory Values for Older People

Since the 1970s, many studies have been done to establish age-related normal laboratory values. Normal laboratory values are usually determined from a random sample of 'healthy' individuals aged 20–40 years by obtaining the mean and setting as normal a range of two standard deviations on either side of the mean. However, the concept of a normal range may be difficult when trying to develop age-related norms in the elderly population. It is hard to define a healthy elderly population, particularly in the oldest old, and unrecognised disease in those selected for such studies may distort the data. Thus, the raised erythrocyte sedimentation rate reported in some apparently healthy older people could be the result of chronic occult disease. Many older people have one or more diseases and are taking one or more medications which may act as confounding factors.

It has been suggested that it is more appropriate to refer to laboratory values as reference values or reference intervals. Rock (1984) suggested the use of reference intervals as a better approach to laboratory values in older people. Reference intervals can be further stratified by age and gender. Whitehead *et al.* (1994) used this approach by applying non-parametric statistics to the results obtained by the British United Provident Association (BUPA) Health Screening Centre in London from 1983 to 1990. The results of testing over 85,000 adults (some of whom may have had unrecognised disease) were used to develop percentile reference intervals. Although only 1402 tested were over 71 years of age (1.6% of the total), this represents the largest comparative analysis of laboratory testing in older people to date. Tietz *et al.* (1992) compared laboratory values in 327 volunteers over the age of 60 years screened for disease and medication use; 69 individuals were over the age of 100 years. Ranges, medians, means and central 95 percentile ranges were compared with those from younger adults. Both these data sets are useful referents when considering changes in laboratory values and are referred to throughout. Reference values, a term recommended by the International Federation of Clinical Chemistry, will be used synonymously with reference intervals throughout this chapter.

Use of any laboratory test, especially in screening for disease, raises the issue of its overall clinical usefulness. Firstly, as the reference range includes 95% of normal individuals, when multiple tests are carried out in an individual patient the chances are that at least one result will lie outside the reference range, while the patient being studied is actually normal for that parameter. For a single test, the chance of this happening is 1 in 20 (5%), or conversely if 20 normal people are screened then on average the result of one individual will be 'abnormal'. The possibility of this occurring increases with the number of tests carried out both within and between individuals. Secondly, laboratory tests themselves have a coefficient of variation, although in modern laboratories with good quality control this is an unlikely source of error. Thirdly, not all abnormal results have the same clinical relevance. A raised alkaline phosphatase in a healthy older person does not carry the same urgency as a high potassium in a patient with renal failure. Fourthly, although some measures have been shown to change with age, these may be of little clinical relevance. Haemoglobin may decline with age in men but age-adjusted reference ranges are unnecessary in clinical practice. Finally, spurious abnormal results can occur. The blood specimen may have been mislabelled. Changes in the sample may have occurred as a result of traumatic venepuncture or the specimen remaining at room temperature overnight, allowing haemolysis of red cells and thereby producing spurious elevation of potassium (potassium is the predominant cation in cells). If the result does not fit the clinical picture the test may need to be repeated. In general, laboratory tests need to be interpreted in their clinical setting.

Sensitivity and Specificity

These are important concepts. Sensitivity is the ability of a test to identify cases with the disease under investigation (the true positive rate). Specificity is the ability of a test to identify people without the disease as normal (the true negative rate).

An example of how these work can be gained from considering the use of the serum prostate specific antigen (PSA) level to screen for prostate cancer. Altering the cut-off level in an attempt to distinguish between normal (i.e. those unlikely to have the disease) from abnormal men (i.e. those with the disease) has effects upon both sensitivity and specificity. As prostate cancer is associated with elevated PSA levels, the higher the cut-off value the greater the sensitivity (i.e. there will be fewer men selected as abnormal because of a high PSA, but their chances of having prostate cancer are higher than with a lower cut-off level; this is because proportionally more men with prostate cancer will be included

5.1 Laboratory Values that are Essentially Unchanged with Ageing

- Haemoglobin – clinically insignificant decline in both genders.
- Red cell indices.
- Coagulation tests – suggestion of a prothrombotic state in some older people.
- Red cell and serum folate.
- Thyroid function tests.
- Cortisol and adrenocorticotrophic hormone (ACTH).
- Creatinine kinase.
- Lactic dehydrogenase.
- Bilirubin.
- Aspartate aminotransferase.
- Alanine aminotransferase.
- Glutaryl transpeptidase (GTP) – an increase has been reported. Male levels greater than female.
- High-density lipoprotein (HDL)-cholesterol.
- Serum sodium – wider normal range among the oldest old.
- Serum potassium – a slight increase has been noted.
- Serum ionised calcium.
- Serum phosphate – women, some studies show a small increase.
- pH.

in the 'abnormal group'). However, increasing the cut-off level will lower the specificity, as more men with the disease will be falsely regarded as normal because their PSA lies below the cut-off level. The normal range for PSA increases with age, which makes interpretation of a borderline result more difficult, as does uncertainty about the best method of treating the disease.

For any test, clinicians can set cut-off values according to whether they wish to detect all true cases (a 100% sensitivity) or a predetermined proportion of cases. This is because complete ascertainment of those with the disease means that a greater proportion of normal people will be misclassified as having the disease by the test. If this happens then there are resource implications (usually further expensive and sometimes invasive tests) and needless distress for the misclassified individual. Lowering the sensitivity in these circumstances means that not all cases will be picked up but fewer false positives (i.e. a higher specificity) will occur. If a disease is easily treated when diagnosed but lethal later, then a policy of high specificity may be prudent. This may be at the expense of a lowered sensitivity, as the disease will be regarded as too important not to miss. There are very few tests with 100% sensitivity and specificity.

The remainder of this chapter discusses the laboratory values that significantly change with ageing. Since normal

5.2 Laboratory Values that Alter with Ageing

Decrease

- Leucocyte count.
- Serum iron.
- Serum cobalamin (vitamin B$_{12}$).
- Testosterone – men.
- Oestrogens and progestagens – women.
- Albumin.
- Serum calcium – but some increase in women post menopause.
- Serum phosphate – men.
- Creatinine clearance.
- PO$_2$.

Increase

- Erythrocyte sedimentation rate (ESR).
- Luteinising hormone (LH) and follicle-stimulating hormone (FSH) (both men and women).
- Alkaline phosphatase.
- Low-density lipoprotein (LDL)-cholesterol – an earlier peak in men compared with women with a decline in the 9th decade.
- High-density lipoprotein (HDL)-cholesterol.
- Triglycerides.
- Parathyroid hormone.
- Serum urea.
- Serum creatinine.
- Uric acid – women greater than men.

value ranges will vary with institutions, depending on the instrumentation used for performing tests, reference ranges produced by the local laboratory should be used. (*See* **Box 5.1** for laboratory values that remain unaltered and **Box 5.2** for values that change with ageing.)

HAEMATOLOGY

Haemoglobin

Haemoglobin (Hb) is the main component of the red blood cell. It is a conjugated protein containing iron, whose main function is to transport oxygen to the tissues. Hb concentration decreases in men after 65 years of age and remains the same in elderly women, although some studies have shown a slight decline. The decrease in males is probably related to the reduction in androgen production. In healthy young adults, male Hb levels are normally higher than female ones and this appears to continue into later life (Whitehead *et al.* 1994).

Anaemia is a condition indicated by lower than normal Hb concentration, red cell count or haematocrit levels. Signs and symptoms of severe anaemia, such as apathy, depression, confusion and general fatigue, are often attributed to old age instead of anaemia (Nardone *et al.* 1990). Anaemia may be a common problem in older people, but it is not caused by normal ageing. Evaluation of Hb for levels below normal is necessary at any age. Decrease in Hb concentration may indicate reduced red cell production (the most frequent causes in older people are iron, folate or vitamin B$_{12}$ deficiency, chronic disease, disease of the bone marrow or renal failure), increased red cell destruction due to haemolysis, and bleeding. Anaemia is associated with an increased risk of pressure ulcers in acutely unwell patients and a delay in wound healing.

Red Blood Cells, Haematocrit, Mean Cell Volume and other Haematological Indices

There is inconsistent evidence of age-related differences in red blood cells. There may be changes in red cell enzymes that affect the life span of the cell, but the significance is uncertain. The red cell count, quoted as the number of red cells per litre of blood, remains constant in women while declining in men over the age of 65 years (Whitehead *et al.* 1994).

The haematocrit is the ratio of the volume of red blood cells (packed cell volume) to that of whole blood. Haematocrit values in men have been shown to decrease slightly with age (Htoo *et al.* 1979; Whitehead *et al.* 1994) with an increased negative skew in older as compared with younger men. Studies also show that women maintain their haematocrit levels throughout life, although at a lower level than men (Htoo *et al.* 1979; Whitehead *et al.* 1994). In practice, age-adjusted ranges are not required, as the 5% of elderly men who have a haematocrit below the 1% range for young men will require further investigation (Cavalieri *et al.* 1992; Whitehead *et al.* 1994).

The mean cell volume (MCV) is derived from the packed cell volume divided by the red cell count. It measures the average size of the erythrocytes in the sample analysed. It is expressed as femtolitres (10^{-15} litre). The median values are similar in both men and women and at all ages. The terms microcytosis and macrocytosis apply to a reduction (i.e. the red cells are smaller on average) and an increase in MCV, respectively. Macrocytosis occurs in a wide range of disorders affecting old people, the most important being folate and vitamin B$_{12}$ deficiency (see below), alcohol abuse, liver disease, hypothyroidism, haemolysis and the myelodysplastic syndromes. The commonest cause of microcytosis in older people is iron deficiency, although the anaemia associated with chronic diseases may be microcytic but is usually normocytic.

Mean cell Hb concentration (MCHC) is the concentration of Hb in 100 ml (1 dl) of red cells. There is no change with age among women but, as for Hb, there is a small decline in older men. MCHC is reduced in iron deficiency where the classic presentation is with a hypochromic (low MCHC) microcytic anaemia. By microscopy, the erythrocytes appear small and irregular with a pale rim of pigment around the margin of the cell. With reduced erythropoiesis, the reticulocyte count (erythrocytes newly released into the circulation, which have a reticular appearance on staining) is reduced, but increased erythropoiesis with haemolysis (premature destruction of red cells) increases the number of reticulocytes in circulation (normally around 1–2% of red cells). There is no change in the reticulocyte count with ageing.

Other laboratory tests such as iron, folate and vitamin B_{12} should always be evaluated along with the results when making a diagnosis. However, careful review of the haematological indices in the clinical context are often strongly predictive of the cause of the anaemia. High Hb levels are observed with primary polycythaemia vera and secondary to chronic hypoxic states (chronic pulmonary disease). Polycythaemia may increase blood viscosity and increase the risk of stroke.

Erythrocyte Sedimentation Rate

When well-mixed venous blood is placed in a vertical tube, erythrocytes remain suspended while drifting towards the bottom. The distance from the upper border of the red cell layer to the top of the column achieved after 60 minutes is the erythrocyte sedimentation rate (ESR). This reflects the relative specific gravities of the red cells and plasma and whether the red cells clump together (rouleaux formation), the latter affected by fibrinogen and globulins in plasma. Many pathological conditions show an increase in ESR, particularly those that alter globulins, such as multiple myeloma. Studies have been reported on the effect of age on the ESR. These studies suggest that higher values are normal in older age. Bottiger and Svedberg (1967) and Hayes and Stinson (1976) found increased ESRs in healthy older adults. Both sexes show skewed distributions at all ages, which is more marked in older men (Whitehead *et al.* 1994).

There is evidence of reduced plasma albumin and increased plasma fibrinogen in later life, which increase the ESR. However, Gambert *et al.* (1982) and Sharland (1980) suggest that ESR determination may have a limited diagnostic value with older people and greater use of an acute phase protein, C-reactive protein, as a nonspecific marker of inflammation has been advocated. An ESR above the accepted normal range may or may not be an indication of disease and can be consistent with good health. Forty-five per cent of men aged 71 years or over had ESRs between 5 and 50 (Whitehead *et al.* 1994). However, ESRs greater than 80 are associated with underlying disease such as neoplasia, infection or rheumatic disease (Cavalieri *et al.* 1992). Sox and Liang (1986) found that ESR is often normal in patients with connective tissue disease, cancer and infection. A thorough history and physical examination is paramount before excluding these diseases by ESR values alone.

White Blood Cells

Overall, the formation and development of leucocytes are affected by age, but the changes in the white blood cell count (WBC) do not follow consistent trends in both sexes. In men, there is a slight increase in those aged over 71 years, whereas for women, there is a decline until the sixth decade with a small increase thereafter (Whitehead *et al.* 1994). Very elderly people have a comparable WBC to those in the seventh decade (Beregi *et al.* 1991). Older people have a greater risk of infection than young adults, although nutrition, socioeconomic differences and so-called immunosenescence (a decline in the function of immunoregulatory cells such as lymphocytes) may be relevant. It is suggested that tetanus, influenza and pneumococcal vaccines be considered (Jeppesen, 1986; Kelso, 1990), particularly in the frail older people at high risk in institutions. However, antibody responses to vaccination may be poor and unsustained (Haeney, 1994). Furthermore, WBC may provide only an indirect measure of resistance to infection as leucocyte numbers and function in infected tissue is the crucial issue.

Drug toxicity and sepsis are the most likely explanations for a reduced WBC in an older person, and a low WBC in an older patient with pneumonia carries an increased risk of death. Pneumonia and urinary tract infections are two conditions that are frequently seen in the older patient which may increase WBC. The signs of inflammation, such as fever, swelling, pain and lymph node enlargement, may be reduced or absent (Andres *et al.* 1985).

Leucocytes

Leucocytes are of two main types: phagocytes, which ingest and kill bacteria, and lymphocytes, which mediate the immune response. The phagocytes include neutrophils, monocytes, eosinophils and basophils.

Phagocytes

The largest number of circulating phagocytes are neutrophils, which are produced in the bone marrow. Age does not appear to change the neutrophil count in older adults and variable results have been reported with eosinophils and basophils. However, there does appear to be an age-related increase in monocytes (Rochman, 1988). Some data suggest that the rate of release of neutrophils from the bone marrow may be reduced in older persons and that the number of neutrophils stored in the marrow may be fewer (Andres *et al.* 1985).

Lymphocytes

Lymphocytes 'are a heterogeneous population of cells which can make immunoglobulins proliferate in response to many antigenic and mitogenic stimuli, and modulate immune responses through cell–cell interactions and secretory products' (Andres *et al.* 1985, p. 379). Lymphocytes are of two types: T cells, which are produced by the thymus and are concerned with cell immunity, and B cells, which are bone marrow related, have antibodies on their surface and are precursors of plasma cells which produce antibodies.

B lymphocytes are activated by a combination of antigen exposure and T helper-(CD4+) lymphocytes.

An effect of age on total lymphocyte counts is not evident, but studies suggest an increased number of B cells in older people and an age-related decline in T cells, especially CD4+ function (Wedelin *et al.* 1982; Lokhorst *et al.* 1983; Thompson *et al.* 1984). This decrease in T cell function is in part a consequence of thymic involution with age. T lymphocytes have surface markers which identify sub-populations with different functions. The two most commonly referred to are CD4+ associated with inducer (helper) properties, and CD8+ associated with cytotoxic and suppressor functions. There is data suggesting that both CD4+ and CD8+ levels decline with ageing and that the way in which CD4+ lymphocytes respond to infection is different.

SERUM CHEMISTRY

Serum Iron

The most common cause of anaemia in older people is iron deficiency, especially among those with low incomes and chronic disease. In both sexes, there is a progressive decrease in serum iron levels with age (Tietz *et al.* 1992). In those aged over 71 years, levels are 80% of that of young adults (Whitehead *et al.* 1994), although there is considerable overlap. It is important to distinguish between age-related iron level decreases and disease-related iron deficiency causing anaemia. Iron deficiency is a result of poor diet, malabsorption or occult bleeding.

In plasma, iron is transported bound to a protein called transferrin. In older adults, a low serum iron may not reflect low body iron stores but reduced levels of transferrin in the blood, as bioassay for iron measures total iron in plasma. Thus, the anaemia of chronic disease is associated with a combination of a low serum iron and low iron binding capacity (low transferrin), whereas true iron deficiency has the pattern of a low serum iron and high iron binding capacity. Estimation of serum ferritin, one of two iron storage compounds, may give a better estimate of body iron levels. Ferritin levels decline in iron deficiency and increase with chronic disease states as part of the acute phase response to inflammation. Iron overload may occur following repeated transfusions and, if severe, tissue damage will occur causing haemochromatosis.

Serum iron level appraisal is important for older adults. Inadequate consumption of iron-rich foods, poor appetite, chronic blood loss and reduced absorption of iron are commonly found in older patients both within and outside long-term care facilities.

Vitamin B$_{12}$

Vitamin B$_{12}$ is found in foods of animal origin and is added to some cereals. Serum vitamin B$_{12}$ has been shown to decrease with advancing age (Kane *et al.* 1989; Tietz *et al.* 1992) but this may not reflect reduced tissue levels of the vitamin but changes in transcobalamin, the B$_{12}$ binding protein. As body-stores of the vitamin are sufficient for up to 2 years, dietary deficiency is uncommon. Atrophic gastritis is more common in older people and eventually vitamin B$_{12}$ deficiency will occur as a result of reduced intrinsic factor (IF) produced by the stomach, with resulting anaemia – pernicious anaemia (PA). IF binds B$_{12}$ in the gut lumen, which enables absorption in the terminal ileum. The other major cause of B$_{12}$ deficiency is malabsorption. In addition to anaemia, vitamin B$_{12}$ deficiency can cause major neurological problems, such as subacute combined degeneration of the spinal cord, which becomes irreversible if not promptly treated. It has been reported that low levels of vitamin B$_{12}$ may rarely cause reversible dementia (Gambert *et al.* 1982) but many of these cases do not show reversibility and are probably Alzheimer's disease occurring at the same time as PA.

Folic Acid

Folic acid is found in green vegetables, yeast and liver. Serum folate levels may be lower in younger elderly people while being at the level of or exceeding those of younger adults in the oldest old (Tietz *et al.* 1992). However, serum folate is labile and changes quickly with altered folate in the diet. Red cell folate levels provide a better estimate of body folate stores and do not appear to decline with a poor diet or disease. However, some older people have elevated homocysteine levels and folate is important in its metabolism (Koehler *et al.* 1997). Not only does this point to subclinical deficiency of folate but also elevated homocysteine blood levels are a powerful predictor of cardiovascular risk. Fortification of flour with folate has been advocated to prevent neural tube defects in neonates and may reduce the risk of vascular disease by reducing homocysteine.

Unlike B$_{12}$, folic acid deficiency is usually dietary in origin although malabsorption may also reduce folic acid levels. Folate deficiency is commonly observed in alcoholics who have a poor diet. Other causes of folic acid deficiency are coeliac disease and inflammatory bowel disease. Clinical features of folic acid deficiency include glossitis, reduced cognition (in part a reflection of poor diet in general with or without alcohol abuse) and megaloblastic anaemia (Riggs *et al.* 1996).

ENDOCRINE

The normal ageing process is associated with a number of alterations in hormone production, secretion and biological effect (Winger and Hornick, 1996). In practice, substantial changes to the reference ranges with age are unnecessary except with gonadotrophins. Age-related changes in renal, pulmonary, gastrointestinal and hepatic

Meeting Endocrinological Needs

Following an episode of pneumonia, Doris Clarke has been experiencing disturbing symptoms for several months. These include mental clouding, anorexia, episodes of weakness and unsteadiness of gait, general lethargy, sensitivity to cold and constipation. She is resigned to the inevitability of such problems and comments, 'Oh, this is just part of getting old. My own mother had these problems, too. Mrs Clarke's daughters persuade her to visit her general practitioner (GP), who orders a biochemical profile [including urea, electrolytes, liver enzymes (aspartate aminotransferase, alanine aminotransferase, glutamyl transpeptidase) and a base profile (calcium, phosphate, alkaline phosphatase)], thyroid function testing, full blood count and urinalysis. The blood test and urinalysis are carried out by the practice nurse who is told by Mrs Clarke, 'I don't like these tests. It's just my age, but I'll go along with what's found.' All are within normal limits with the exception of a slightly low serum thyroxine concentration and an elevated TSH. The GP immediately diagnoses hypothyroidism and starts 0.05 mg of L-thyroxine daily for Mrs Clarke, planning to review (and increase if possible) the dose in a fortnight.

- **What are Mrs Clarke's comments that provide subjective evidence?**
- **What is the basis of the physiological evidence provided by the results of the diagnostic test?**
- **Suggest two areas for nursing intervention.**
- **Suggest the nursing aims for each intervention, reflecting realistic outcomes and using concrete and measurable terms.**
- **Suggest one or more interventions for each of your chosen areas, justifying the choice of intervention.**

organs may complicate endocrine test result interpretation (Demers, 1988).

Thyroid

The thyroid gland produces three hormones: thyroxine (T4), tri-iodothyronine (T3) and calcitonin. The last is secreted by the parafollicular cells and has a minor role in calcium metabolism. T4 and T3 are dependent upon iodine for synthesis and are the effector hormones of the hypothalamic–pituitary–thyroid axis. These hormones influence metabolism and the growth and development of tissues. Conventionally, thyroid function tests (TFTs) assess the status of the pituitary–thyroid system and do not include measurement of calcitonin.

Thyroxine

Measurement of T4 is the standard test of thyroid status. Over 10 times the quantity of T4 is secreted each day compared with T3. Both hormones are transported strongly bound to proteins in plasma of which the most important is thyroid-binding globulin (TBG). Laboratory measures of total T4 (TT4) quantify both bound and unbound hormone, so that changes in TT4 levels may reflect alterations in thyroid hormone binding to plasma proteins in the plasma. As it is the unbound (or free) T4 which is biologically active and which also participates in feedback to the pituitary (see below), it is important to assess this fraction either directly or indirectly.

Measurement of both thyroid hormone binding capacity of plasma and measurement of TT4 (bound and unbound) can be used to calculate indirectly the level of free (or unbound) T4 in plasma, known as the free thyroxine index (FTI). Thyroid hormone binding capacity is estimated either by means of the T3 uptake tests (thyroid hormone binding ratio), which calculate the capacity of plasma to bind radiolabelled T3, or by direct measurement of TBG. However, in recent years direct assay of free T4 has been available. Free T4 is measured in picomols per litre (10^{-10} mol/litre) whereas TT4 is present in nanomolar (10^{-9} mol/litre) concentrations.

Tri-iodothyronine

T3 is produced by the peripheral deiodination of the T4 molecule. About 20% is directly secreted by the thyroid gland. Although T3 is bound to TBG, it is not bound to other plasma proteins to the same extent as T4 so that there is a greater proportion of free T3 in plasma than T4 (although T3 is still over 95% plasma-protein bound). As T3 has three times the potency of T4, it is metabolically more important. Direct estimates of free T3 are available in some laboratories, though calculation of the free T3 index is rarely carried out. Rarely, T3 levels are elevated in hyperthyroidism without change in T4.

Thyroid-stimulating Hormone (TSH)

TSH is produced by the anterior pituitary and stimulates both thyroid hormone synthesis and secretion. It is subject to negative feedback from thyroid hormones so that indirectly these hormones regulate their own production and release. Thyrotrophin releasing hormone (TRH), produced by the hypothalamus and passed down the portal vascular system of the pituitary stalk to the anterior pituitary, stimulates TSH secretion. As the thyroid gland begins to fail because of intrinsic disease (primary hypothyroidism), TSH levels rise due to reduced negative feedback from thyroid hormones. Thus, the most sensitive indicator of hypothyroidism is elevation of TSH. In contrast, with increasing concentrations of circulating T3 and T4 as a result of hyperthyroidism, TSH levels fall. Recent improvements in the sensitivity of the laboratory tests of TSH now enable low levels to be assayed down to 0.01 ml U/l (the bottom of the normal range is about 0.4 ml U/l). Low TSH levels also occur in primary pituitary failure but, in this case, thyroid hormone levels are low. If there is doubt about the integrity of the pituitary or whether the pituitary–thyroid axis no longer has a feedback mechanism (as occurs when an overactive thyroid has 'escaped' from control by the pituitary), then a TRH test can be carried out. This measures the TSH response to injected TRH: a rise in TSH (positive response) excludes hyperthyroidism, no change excludes primary hypothyroidism but suggests an overactive autonomous thyroid (hyperthyroidism).

The Thyroid and Disease

Thyroid dysfunction is more common in older as compared with younger adults, and observed changes in thyroid function tests with age may be a result of occult disease. In fact, no change in TT4 and TSH have been reported in some studies, which is consistent with this view (Tietz *et al.* 1992; Kabadi and Rosman, 1988), although an increase in TSH has been observed (Rochmann, 1988). The latter could be a result of increased subclinical hypothyroidism as anti–thyroid antibodies occur more frequently in older people. Excluding older people with circulating anti–thyroid antibodies from datasets suggests that the TSH normal range is the same for old and young adults. A slight reduction of free T4 with age in older patients in hospital has also been noted, but no age-related adjustment to the free T4 range appears necessary (Szabolcs *et al.* 1993). By contrast, with any age-related changes the clinical condition of the patient and any concomitant medications appear more likely to increase free T4, so that estimation of free T4 alone may be of reduced value in sick old people. With the new sensitive assays for TSH it has been suggested that TSH alone could be an adequate screening test for primary hypothyroidism and hyperthyroidism (Bauer and Brown, 1996). However, most laboratories measure both TSH and free T4 when TFTs are requested.

It seems likely that production of thyroid hormone does decline with age, possibly as a result of changes in thyroid gland morphology which have been reported in older people. However, this is matched by a reduction of metabolic clearance from plasma, leaving plasma concentration unaffected (Sowers and Felicetta, 1988). Both a slight reduction and no change in total T3 has been reported in healthy older people (Tietz *et al.* 1992) and a reduction of free T3 has been observed in extreme old age (Mariotti *et al.* 1993). Reduced metabolism of T4 to T3 would be consistent with the former (Feit, 1988). Certainly, a marked reduction in the conversion of T4 to T3 occurs in a variety of clinical situations, both acute and chronic – the so-called 'sick euthyroid syndrome'. In this, the TSH is normal and T4 is normal or slightly elevated with a reduced T3 in an unwell patient. Repeat testing after recovery shows return of the T3 to within the normal range. In general, age adjustment of the normal range for TFTs appears unnecessary (Tietz *et al.* 1992; Mooradian, 1995).

Screening for Thyroid Dysfunction

Both hyperthyroidism (thyrotoxicosis) and hypothyroidism are more common in older people. However, the classic clinical manifestations of these disorders may not be present. In common with many diseases among older adults, presentation is often nonspecific or occult with symptoms sometimes attributed to 'old age' (Bemben *et al.* 1994; Helfand and Crapo, 1991). Attempts to detect unrecognised dysfunction can take place as screening (apparently healthy older people are invited to have tests to determine thyroid status), or case-finding (testing thyroid function in those who already present with a problem), as sometimes the thyroid dysfunction would not be suspected from the patient's presentation. General screening for thyroid disorders in older adults is not advocated (Wiersinga, 1995), whereas there is a strong argument for case-finding. The symptoms of up to 50% of patients admitted to acute elderly care wards would be consistent with thyroid dysfunction (failure to thrive, mental slowing or confusion), so that checking TFTs would be clinically indicated. Whether all admissions to an elderly care unit should have TFTs carried out is debated by Helfand and Crapo (1991). They suggest that case-finding in outpatient clinics is more likely to produce a positive result in women who have nonspecific complaints. The most common abnormality of TFT detected by screening or case-finding is subclinical hypothyroidism. This is where both free T4 and T3 are normal, but TSH is elevated consistent with reduced thyroid function compensated by increased pituitary TSH production. In this situation, it is uncertain whether the 'patient' should be 'treated' with thyroid replacement therapy or monitored.

Cortisol

Appropriate timing of blood sampling for cortisol is important. Samples are normally obtained between 8 a.m. and 9 a.m. However, with cortisol excess caused by disease (Cushing's syndrome), the normal diurnal variation is lost and suppression of cortisol by exogenous steroids such as dexamethasone is no longer apparent. This is the basis of the dexamethasone suppression test when a dose of dexamethasone (usually starting at 2 mg) is given the night before blood sampling at 9 a.m. Failure of suppression of cortisol production suggests either excess adrenocorticotrophic hormone (ACTH) production (e.g. a pituitary adenoma producing ACTH) or disease of the adrenal (e.g. an adenoma or carcinoma producing glucocorticoids when ACTH will be suppressed). Twenty-four hour urine collection for urinary free cortisol or 17-hydroxycorticosteroids (which includes other glucocorticoids as well as cortisol) can be carried out as a screen and can be combined with a prolonged dexamethasone suppression test when the 24-hour response to exogenous steroid is measured. The dexamethasone suppression test is unaffected by age. (*See* Chapter 4 for discussion of age-related changes to cortisol production.)

Deficiency of both glucocorticoid and mineralocorticoid from primary disease of the adrenal (Addison's disease) is more common in older people. This can present surreptitiously with weight loss, lassitude, postural hypotension and abdominal symptoms. Addisonian crisis can develop, which is life threatening due to cardiovascular collapse. A low potassium level in an older person with fatigue and postural hypotension is suggestive of the diagnosis. Baseline cortisol is low and fails to respond to administered synthetic ACTH (the Synacthen® test). Treatment with mineralocorticoids and glucocorticoids is life saving.

Sex Hormones

Androgens

Testosterone is produced in a pulsed manner from the testis in response to luteinising hormone (LH) production by the pituitary. There is a feedback mechanism. Testosterone is transported in plasma bound to proteins such as albumin and sex hormone-binding globulin. From the age of 60 years, both total and free testosterone levels decline in men, but remain within the normal range, with some older men having values in the upper percentiles of the normal range (Tietz *et al.* 1992). Gonadotrophin [LH and follicle-stimulating hormone (FSH) from the pituitary] levels increase perhaps as a secondary respond to reduced feedback from testosterone. Testosterone is metabolised to dihydrotestosterone, an active metabolite which can also be measured, and to oestrogens. The latter appears increased in older men.

Oestrogens and Progesterone

The climacteric is a result of a marked decline in ovarian function. Both the production of ova (which ceases) and secretion of oestrogens are affected. Oestrone and oestradiol concentrations decline markedly (Tietz *et al.* 1992). As a result, feedback by oestrogens to the hypothalamic–pituitary axis reduces and gonadotrophin levels increase, especially FSH (Tietz *et al.* 1992; Kenny and Fotherby, 1984), while changes in neurotransmitter activity and hypothalamic hormone release, including alterations in the periodicity of hormone secretion, occur with age (Wise, 1994). Following the menopause, production of oestrogens outside the ovaries assumes a greater role. This physiological process is associated with a progressive decline in bone mass and an increased risk of osteoporosis. Progesterone decreases with age in women (Tietz *et al.* 1992).

BLOOD CHEMISTRY

Glucose

Glucose metabolism changes with increasing age (Andres *et al.* 1985) and both a consistent increase in serum glucose and a wider normal range have been observed (Tietz *et al.* 1992; Whitehead *et al.* 1994). Fasting plasma glucose increases 0.06–0.11 mmol/litre with each decade of life (Morrow *et al.* 1992). Insulin resistance increases because of a relative

increase in body fat alongside a decrease in lean body mass, and decreased numbers of insulin receptors (Tietz *et al.* 1992). Reduced physical activity has been observed among older people, and exercise is known to enhance insulin sensitivity. Insulin levels do not appear to rise with increasing age, but there is a delay in glucose uptake by cells (Morrow *et al.* 1992). However, there remains the possibility that some of these changes are a consequence of disease in a sub-group of older people [i.e. a mild form of noninsulin-dependent diabetes mellitus (NIDDM)] rather than a physiological response to ageing. Low normal insulin levels have been reported in healthy, very old people, which would be consistent with this hypothesis. The glucose tolerance test measures plasma glucose before and after a defined amount of glucose is taken orally (Rock *et al.* 1986). This produces a glucose peak 1–2 hours later, which is higher in older when compared with younger adults; the 1-hour post-ingestion concentration of glucose increases 0.33–0.78 mmol/litre with each decade (Morrow *et al.* 1992).

In theory, as there is an overlap between the changes that are observed with age and NIDDM, a definitive diagnosis of diabetes in the older adults might be difficult. However, the World Health Organisation criteria for the diagnosis of diabetes and impaired glucose intolerance (defined by abnormal response to a glucose load, for example with the glucose tolerance test, see below) are not age-adjusted (*see* **Box 5.3**). Laboratories do not quote different normal ranges for older people. In a frail elderly person, it should be determined on an individual basis not only whether an elevated blood glucose indicates glucose intolerance or diabetes but also whether treatment should be commenced and what the defined therapeutic goals are. Over-aggressive treatment increases the chances of hypoglycaemia, which could be disastrous in an older person living alone. Treatment to alleviate symptoms such as glycosuria, producing troublesome polyuria and nocturia or recurrent urinary tract infection, is always indicated, even when anti-diabetic therapy to prevent future vascular complications is not thought worthwhile.

Creatinine Kinase

Creatine kinase (CK, also known as creatine phosphokinase – CPK), is predominantly an enzyme of skeletal and cardiac muscle, although it is also found in the brain. CK levels are determined when myocardial infarction (MI) or skeletal muscle disease is suspected (e.g. polymyositis), as an increased amount of the enzyme is released from these tissues into the bloodstream. CK levels are slightly higher in younger elderly people than younger adults but begin to decline in the eighth decade. CK is significantly lower in men and especially women in their nineties. This is probably a result of reduced total muscle mass as well as reduced amounts of CK in muscle tissue (Tietz *et al.* 1992).

The diagnosis of MI may be difficult in older people, as presenting symptoms such as intense dyspnoea, syncope and weakness may be different from those of younger patients,

5.3 WHO Criteria for Diabetes Mellitus and Glucose Intolerance

Diabetes
- Fasting plasma glucose >7.8 mmol/l (two occasions),
- or fasting glucose <7.8 mmol/l but glucose tolerance test
- >11.1 mmol/l at 1 and 2 hours,
- or non-fasting hyperglycaemia with symptoms.

Impaired glucose tolerance
- Fasting glucose <7.8 mmol/l but glucose tolerance test
- >11.1 mmol/l at 30, 60 or 90 minutes and glucose
- 7.8–11.1 mmol/l at 2 hours.

Source: World Health Organisation. *Diabetes mellitus*. Technical Report Series 727. Copenhagen: WHO, 1985.

where chest pain is more common (Kannel and Abbott, 1984). Also, when an older person has lain for some hours on the floor because of a heart attack, CK levels may be difficult to interpret because of pressure-related skeletal muscle trauma releasing CK into the circulation. As measurement of CK (total CK) is of all the three distinct forms (or isomers) found in the body, CK-B (found in brain), CK-M (found in skeletal muscle) and CK-MB (found mostly in cardiac muscle). A specific assay for CK-MB is useful to distinguish skeletal from cardiac muscle damage. The CK-MB isoenzyme concentration in healthy older people is much lower than in younger adults. As it is the rise in CK-MB that may be important rather than the absolute level, interpretation of CK-MB levels in an older person suspected of a MI can be difficult when the electrocardiogram is equivocal. CK-MB levels increase within 6 hours after a MI, with a peak at 24 hours; changes in other enzymes are slower. The amount of CK-MB released reflects the size of the infarct. In general, total CK does not increase when neurological diseases cause muscle abnormalities.

Alkaline Phosphatase and Gamma-Glutamyl Transpeptidase

Alkaline phosphatase (ALP) is found in most tissues, with high levels in bone and the bile ducts of the liver. ALP increases with age in women and less so in men. In healthy older women, normal values may be up to 50% higher than the average for younger women (Whitehead *et al.* 1994). The rise in women is most marked at the menopause (Tietz *et al.* 1992; Whitehead *et al.* 1994). It is also probable that there is a substantial contribution to the rise with age from subclinical disease such as renal insufficiency, hepatic dysfunction, bone disorders and malabsorption.

An elevated ALP is suggestive of either biliary tract or bone pathology. ALP is produced by osteoblasts, which are responsible for bone regeneration, whereas osteoclasts, responsible for bone destruction, do not have ALP. Thus, destructive bone disorders that do not involve remodelling of bone (e.g. multiple myeloma) do not alter ALP. However, secondary tumours of bone from prostate and breast for example, and more commonly Paget's disease of bone, produce bone remodelling and the ALP is elevated. The ALP may be increased in osteomalacia (deficient mineralisation of bone) with reductions of serum calcium and phosphate, but this is not always the case. Biliary tract disease [intrahepatic (drug induced, tumour-related or primary biliary cirrhosis) or extrahepatic cholestasis (gallstones or tumour blocking the common bile duct)] is usually associated with an increase of ALP.

When the distinction between bone and biliary pathology can not be made from the clinical presentation, quantification of the isoenzymes of ALP can be useful to determine the source (whether bone or liver in origin). Gamma-glutamyl transpeptidase (GTP) estimation is a frequently used alternative to this. GTP may be elevated in hepatobiliary disorders, including secondary malignancy of the liver, but is unchanged in bone disease. Some reports suggest GTP increases with age, although there are some studies showing no change (Tietz *et al.* 1992). Male GTP levels are higher than those of women with double the distribution range. GTP is also increased in alcohol abuse and alcoholism and this may account for an increased distribution spread within the higher percentiles with age in both genders.

Lactate Dehydrogenase

Lactate dehydrogenase (LDH) is involved with glucose metabolism and is present in all organ cells but at higher levels in heart, liver, kidney, brain, red blood cells and skeletal muscle. Damage to any of these tissues will cause release of the LDH enzyme. Highest values are seen with MI, with a maximum 48 hours after onset, haemolytic disorders and pernicious anaemia. LDH levels increase only slightly with age (Tietz *et al.* 1992).

LDH consists of four sub-units of two different types and has five isoenzymes: LDH1–5. Heart muscle and red cells are richest in LDH-1; liver and skeletal muscle in LDH-5; other tissues have a majority of LDH-2 or 3. LDH-2 is the isoenzyme most commonly found in normal plasma and there is no change in the isoenzyme pattern with age (Tietz *et al.* 1992).

Aspartate Aminotransferase

Serum aspartate aminotransferase (AST), also known as glutamic oxaloacetic transaminase (SGOT), is found primarily (in descending order) in heart, liver, skeletal muscle and kidney. Increased values indicate MI (peak at 24–36 hours); hepatocellular disease, such as hepatitis, malignancy, drugs and toxins, and liver necrosis, and skeletal muscle damage, such as polymyositis and pressure necrosis. Either no or only slight increases in AST have been reported with ageing (Tietz *et al.* 1992; Whitehead *et al.* 1994).

Alanine Aminotransferase

Alanine aminotransferase (ALT), also known as serum glutamic pyruvic transaminase (SGPT), is found mainly in the liver. In hepatocellular disease, it responds in similar fashion to AST but is more sensitive. Values in men tend to be higher than in women (Whitehead *et al.* 1994) with a peak in men around 35 to 54 years of age followed by a decline. ALT in women increases slightly at the menopause with little decline thereafter (Tietz *et al.* 1992; Whitehead *et al.* 1994).

Serum Albumin

Albumin is a vital constituent of plasma. This protein is important in regulating the distribution of extracellular fluid by an effect on oncotic (osmotic) pressure. It also acts as a reservoir of amino acids as part of the amino acid pool and as a carrier protein for drugs, such as warfarin, and naturally occurring substances, such as calcium. Albumin declines with age, with the most marked change in the lower limit of the distribution range; values in men are higher than in women at all ages (Tietz *et al.* 1992; Whitehead *et al.* 1994). These age changes are probably a result of decreased liver size, enzyme function and hepatic blood flow (Garner, 1989), but subclinical disease may play a part. Low levels of albumin are caused by increased loss (e.g. nephrotic syndrome, protein losing gastrointestinal disorders or burns); reduced synthesis (e.g. liver disease); increased tissue breakdown or catabolism (e.g. disease states); or malnutrition.

LIPIDS

Cholesterol and triglycerides are transported within lipoprotein particles in plasma. This is because lipids are insoluble in water. Lipoproteins have a lipid core surrounded by a surface coat consisting mostly of phospholipids but also some cholesterol and protein (apoprotein). The major lipoproteins are high-density and low-density lipoprotein (HDL and LDL, respectively), which are the major carriers of cholesterol, and very low-density lipoprotein (VLDL), which mostly carries triglycerides. In general, the lower the density the larger the lipoprotein particle, so that chylomicrons, which transport dietary lipids from the small bowel, are the largest lipoprotein particles and also have the lowest density.

Quantification of chylomicrons, VLDL, LDL and HDL can be carried out, but most laboratories measure HDL and LDL cholesterol, and triglycerides. A rise in lipoprotein concentration produces hyperlipidaemia. Whether this is cholesterol or triglyceride provides indirect evidence as to whether VLDL (triglycerides) or LDL (cholesterol) levels are indicated. Usually a raised total cholesterol indicates raised LDL. A discussion of the types of hyperlipidaemia is beyond the province of this chapter, but quantification of both LDL and HDL is important (see below). The apolipoproteins are a heterogeneous group; a subtype of apolipoprotein E4

(ApoE4) appears to increase the risk of Alzheimer's disease (Corder *et al.* 1993).

Cholesterol

Total cholesterol is similar in both men and women under 25 years of age (Whitehead *et al.* 1994). Thereafter, the pattern diverges. In men, there appears to be a rapid rise during the decade after the age of 25 years to a maximum around the sixth and seventh decades of life. After this, the total cholesterol declines. In women, the rise in early and middle adult life is more gradual with a peak in the eighth decade followed by a small decline. Values for men and women are similar in the sixth decade. The fall in men (and women) is usually attributed to differential survival: men with elevated total cholesterol levels being less likely to live into old age (Tietz *et al.* 1992).

LDL levels make up 70–80% of the total cholesterol so that the observed changes with increasing age are the changes of LDL cholesterol. HDL increases very slightly with age (Tietz *et al.* 1992), which could be survival effect, but limited change has also been observed (Whitehead *et al.* 1994). Both an elevated LDL cholesterol and a low HDL cholesterol increase the risk of arteriosclerosis and cardiovascular disease (CVD) in younger adults. But there is limited evidence of a link between raised serum lipids and CVD in people over the age of 70 years. Screening for hyperlipidaemia in the older adult has not shown to be of value even as secondary prevention.

Triglycerides

Triglyceride values increase with age but there is a decrease in the very old (Tietz *et al.* 1992). In women, levels increase at the menopause but are always lower than for men at any age (Whitehead *et al.* 1994). Raised triglyceride levels increase the risk of coronary disease in older people, particularly when LDL cholesterol is elevated; there is no evidence of therapeutic benefit of lowering triglycerides in those over 80 years of age (Bonita, 1996).

ELECTROLYTES

Sodium

Sodium and chloride concentrations in plasma are remarkably stable during adult life (Whitehead *et al.* 1994). A wider normal range of serum sodium (132–146 mmol/litre) for centenarians has been observed (Tietz *et al.* 1992). However, older people are susceptible to electrolyte imbalances because of medications (either directly, as with diuretics, or indirectly, through effects on renal function); poor fluid intake, with a blunted response to dehydration; and changes in renal function, including a reduced renal response to sodium deficiency.

The plasma sodium concentration is a poor indicator of total body composition of sodium: it is changes in water balance which usually alter sodium concentration.

Hyponatraemia (low serum sodium) is the most common electrolyte disturbance in older people and is frequently iatrogenic. Symptoms arising from dehydration and electrolyte abnormalities such as hyponatraemia are nonspecific and a high index of suspicion is needed in the sick elderly patient. Treatment with diuretics is often a clue. Hypernatraemia (raised serum sodium) most commonly occurs with water deprivation. In hyperglycaemic hyperosmolar nonketotic coma, plasma sodium may be elevated despite total body depletion of sodium because of severe water loss and reduced intake.

Potassium

Potassium is predominantly an intracellular cation. Serum potassium levels remain constant until the sixth decade, when a small age-related increase occurs but no adjustment to the reference range is necessary (Whitehead *et al.* 1994). Abnormal potassium levels are often observed in older people taking diuretics. Additional factors such as reduced dietary intake of potassium rich foods (e.g. fruit) and use of laxatives increase the chances of potassium depletion, especially in long-term care institutions.

Hypokalaemia is important as it is associated with cardiac arrhythmias (particularly if digoxin is being taken) and may cause glucose intolerance, postural hypotension and renal tubular dysfunction. In hypokalaemia, there is a shift of potassium from the extracellular to the intracellular compartment, which decreases in potassium plasma concentration. Nonspecific symptoms such as apathy and weakness may occur. Confusion and mood changes (in particular an increased tendency towards aggression, with a time delay of several weeks before return to premorbid personality) have been reported. Use of potassium-sparing diuretics such as amiloride combined with loop or thiazide diuretics does not guarantee that hypokalaemia will be avoided and may result in hyperkalaemia.

Hyperkalaemia usually involves a shift of potassium from the intracellular to the extracellular compartment. A decrease in pH (acidosis) causes potassium to migrate out of cells, resulting in an increase in plasma potassium concentration. An increase in pH (alkalosis) causes the potassium to migrate into the cells, resulting in a decrease in plasma levels. Diabetic ketoacidosis may be associated with hyperkalaemia despite a depletion of total body potassium. Treatment of the acidosis allows potassium to return to the cells and hypokalaemia may occur rapidly. Close monitoring of potassium and adequate replacement is as critical as regular estimation of glucose in this situation. Hyperkalaemia occurs in renal failure when there is also elevated serum creatinine (see below). Marked hyperkalaemia produces severe neuromuscular and cardiac dysfunction.

Calcium and Phosphate

Most calcium in the body (99%) is within the skeleton. In plasma, calcium is present both free (ionised) and bound (to albumin, other proteins and anions such as phosphate). Approximately equivalent amounts are present as both forms. Laboratory measurement of total calcium assays both, although it is ionised calcium which is biologically active. An increase of calcium in women after the menopause has been noted. However, in general there is a decline of total calcium with age (Tietz *et al.* 1992; Whitehead *et al.* 1994). In part, this has been attributed to the reduction of serum albumin. Both an increase (Tietz *et al.* 1992) and decrease (Wiske *et al.* 1979) in ionised calcium with age have been noted. The former would be consistent with an increase in parathyroid hormone noted in older people. In a patient with an abnormal total calcium, it is worthwhile estimating the ionised calcium from a calculation involving the serum albumin (*see* **Box 5.4**). Some laboratories will measure ionised calcium directly. Phosphate levels decline with age in men but not in women (Whitehead *et al.* 1994).

Parathyroid hormone (PTH) produced by the parathyroid glands and a metabolite of vitamin D [1,25(OH)D] are the two most important regulators of serum calcium. Calcitonin inhibits bone resorption but plays limited part in the physiological regulation of calcium. PTH secretion increases serum calcium and decreases phosphate resorption by the kidney. Vitamin D comes from the diet and exposure of skin to sunlight. It requires conversion in the liver to 25-hydroxyvitamin D, which is in turn metabolised in the kidney to 1,25 (OH)2D, the active form. Vitamin D promotes absorption of calcium and phosphate from the gut. There appears to be an age-related decline in the synthesis of 1,25 (OH)2D and reduced formation of vitamin D in skin following exposure to sunlight.

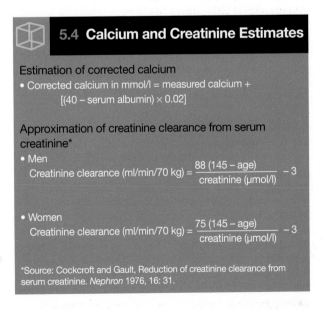

5.4 Calcium and Creatinine Estimates

Estimation of corrected calcium

- Corrected calcium in mmol/l = measured calcium + [(40 – serum albumin) × 0.02]

Approximation of creatinine clearance from serum creatinine*

- Men

$$\text{Creatinine clearance (ml/min/70 kg)} = \frac{88\,(145 - \text{age})}{\text{creatinine (μmol/l)}} - 3$$

- Women

$$\text{Creatinine clearance (ml/min/70 kg)} = \frac{75\,(145 - \text{age})}{\text{creatinine (μmol/l)}} - 3$$

*Source: Cockcroft and Gault, Reduction of creatinine clearance from serum creatinine. *Nephron* 1976, 16: 31.

Hypercalcaemia occurs when the ionised serum calcium is greater than 1.3 mmol/litre. In general, this correlates with a total calcium of 2.6 mmol/litre, but in older people a low albumin may mask true hypercalcaemia. The two most common causes of hypercalcaemia in older people are primary hyperparathyroidism (characterised by a high calcium, low phosphate, and inappropriately high PTH level) and malignancy. The latter raises serum calcium in two ways: direct invasion of bone or secretion of PTH-like substances by the tumour. Hypocalcaemia has many causes in older people of which osteomalacia, either because of deficiency of vitamin D (malabsorption, poor diet, no sunlight exposure) or because of reduced formation of the active metabolite, is most important. Osteomalacia is suggested by hypocalcaemia, low serum phosphate and raised ALP, but all these parameters may be normal. Chronic renal failure is associated with a low serum calcium, raised phosphate and elevated PTH levels.

Blood Urea and Creatinine

Blood urea and creatinine levels are used as indirect markers of renal function. Glomerular filtration rate (GFR) declines with age (Rowe, 1992), although there are some older people who have well-preserved renal function, including the ability to maintain salt and water balance and concentrate the urine (Lubran, 1995; Hodkinson, 1992). As a result of overall age-related changes in renal function, urea increases with age in both genders, although female mean and reference range values are lower than those of males (Hale *et al.* 1983; Whitehead *et al.* 1994). Urea levels are also influenced by protein intake and protein turnover, both of which may be altered in older people.

Serum creatinine more closely follows GFR and the rise with age is not as marked as with urea. However, creatinine is derived from skeletal muscle so that thin elderly women with moderate renal failure may have a creatinine concentration at the upper limit of the normal range. Creatinine clearance (see below) will give a closer estimation of GFR than serum creatinine, although change in serum creatinine over time is a useful method of following renal function. Creatinine is sometimes plotted as the reciprocal for this purpose (1/creatinine).

Creatinine Clearance

Mean creatinine clearance declines at about 8 ml/min for each decade of life over the age of 40 years (Rowe *et al.* 1976). Measurement of creatinine clearance requires a blood sample during a timed urine collection (usually 24 hours) for assay of creatinine. However, a complete urine collection may be difficult to achieve in older people. Nurses should be aware of this, as the amount of medication prescribed may need to be reduced to compensate for the decrease in renal function seen with age (Drusano *et al.* 1988). This is important with drugs such as digoxin and gentamicin which are cleared by renal excretion. Creatinine clearance can be calculated approximately from the serum creatinine (*see* **Box 5.4**).

Acid–Base Balance

The plasma pH may decrease slightly with increasing age (Tietz *et al.* 1992) but it is unlikely that this is of clinical relevance. There is at least one report of no change in acid–base balance with age (Gillibrand *et al.* 1980) and no adjustment of the normal range is necessary. The kidney appears less responsive to an acid load (Lubran, 1995).

Arterial Blood Gases

There appears to be a small decline in oxygen pressure (PO_2) with age. This is because age-related changes occur in the lungs (Jeppesen, 1986; Cavalieri *et al.* 1992). There is no consistent trend with PCO_2: both minor elevations and decreases have been noted in older subjects (Rock, 1984).

Uric Acid

Serum uric acid shows no age-related change in men, but there is a perimenopausal increase in women. Males at all ages have higher uric acid levels than females, as a consequence of gender differences in renal clearance (Tietz *et al.* 1992; Whitehead *et al.* 1994). Thiazide diuretics are a common cause of increased uric acid levels in older adults (Jeppesen, 1986) and are a risk factor for gout. Gout is very unlikely with uric acid values lower than 420 µmol/litre unless the serum uric acid has been recently lowered.

Urinalysis

Most urinalysis values do not change with advancing age. Specific gravity is a simple test that compares the density of urine relative to the density of water. Specific gravity declines with age, which reflects reduced concentrating ability of the kidney. This decline has been related to the 33–50% decline in the number of nephrons with ageing (Garner, 1989). Estimation of specific gravity testing is often not carried out because of its limitations. For example, the presence of abnormal solutes such as glucose and protein may produce a falsely elevated reading (Rock *et al.* 1986). Quantification of solutes such as electrolytes, glucose and protein is carried out when indicated clinically. Urine osmolality has been shown to be raised in nursing-home residents, which could reflect mild dehydration in institutionalised older people.

Use of dipsticks to detect and quantify protein, blood, glucose and nitrates is useful as part of clinical assessment. Albumin is more often detected in the urine of apparently healthy elderly than in young adults (Tietz *et al.* 1992); the significance of this is uncertain. The presence of glucose and blood is always abnormal at any age. The test for nitrates is to determine whether nitrate-reducing bacteria are present in the specimen of urine, indicating a urinary tract infection, but the test has low sensitivity.

SUMMARY

Nurses are in a pivotal position to note and interpret laboratory values, which are more likely to be abnormal in older people who are unwell. This may reflect normal ageing as well as disease states, although in practice abnormalities are much more likely to arise from the latter. As presentation of disease in older people is nonspecific, the importance of laboratory testing cannot be overemphasised (Steen, 1990). Usually quoted normal reference ranges for laboratory values for younger adult are satisfactory for older people with some exceptions (Kelso, 1990). However, laboratory values are tools to assist with the diagnosis and treatment of disease in older patients and not an end in themselves. The nurse should perform a comprehensive baseline assessment of the older adult, obtaining the relevant, nursing and psychosocial history. This will indicate which tests would be useful to carry out so that clinical assessment and laboratory testing are integrated. The goal is to provide quality care for old people.

KEY POINTS

- The nonspecific presentation of disease in older people makes laboratory assessment vital.
- The clinical heterogeneity of older people (older adults show greater individual differences than younger adults) also applies to some laboratory values in older people.
- There are some laboratory values that have a different normal range in older people as compared with younger adults.
- Interpreting laboratory values in older people requires caution.
- Screening for disease by use of laboratory tests has limitations in older people.

AREAS AND ACTIVITIES FOR STUDY AND REFLECTION

- Discuss the special considerations relevant to clinical investigations in older adults.
- Identify the common laboratory tests undertaken in your work area, that have a different normal range in older people.
- Look out for an older person newly diagnosed with hypothyroidism. How did that patient present and what were the clinical findings?
- How might diabetes present in later life? Discuss how clinical diagnosis is affected by age-related change?

REFERENCES

Andres R, Bierman E, Hazzard W. *Principles of geriatric medicine*. New York: McGraw-Hill, 1985.

Bauer DC, Brown AN. Sensitive thyrotropin and free thyroxine testing in outpatients. Are both necessary? *Arch Intern Med* 1996, 156:2333.

Bemben DA, Hamm RM, Morgan L *et al*. Thyroid disease in the elderly. Part 2. Predictability of subclinical hypothyroidism. *J Fam Pract* 1994, 38:538.

Beregi E, Regius O, Rajczy K. Comparative study of the morphological changes in lymphocytes of elderly individuals and centenarians. *Age* 1991, 20:55.

Beregi E, Regius O, Nemeth J *et al*. Gender differences in age-related physiological changes and some diseases. *Gerontol Geriatr* 1995, 28: 62.

Bonita R. Classical cardiovascular risk factors. In: Ebrahim S, Kalache A, eds. *Epidemiology in old age*. London: BMJ Publishing Group, 1996.

Bottiger L, Svedberg C. Normal erythrocyte sedimentation rate and age. *Br Med J* 1967, 2:85–87.

Cavalieri T, Chopra A, Bryman P. When outside the norm is normal: interpreting lab data in the aged. *Geriatrics* 1992, 7:66.

Cockcroft & Gault. Prediction of creatinine clearance from serum creatinine. *Nephron* 1976, 16:31.

Corder EH, Saunders AM, Strittmatter WJ *et al*. Gene dose of apolipoprotein E type 4 allele and the risk of Alzheimer's disease in late onset families. *Science* 1993, 261:921.

Demers L. The aging endocrine system. *Lab Management* 1988, 26:24.

Drusano G, Muncie H, Hoopes J *et al*. Commonly used methods of estimating creatinine clearance are inadequate for elderly debilitated nursing home patients. *J Am Geriatr Soc* 1988, 36:437.

Feit H. Thyroid function in the elderly. *Clin Geriatr Med* 1988, 4:151.

Gambert S, Osuka M, Duthie E *et al*. Interpretation of laboratory results in the elderly. *Postgrad Med* 1982, 72:147.

Garner B. Guide to changing lab values in elders. *Geriatr Nurs* 1989, 10:144–145.

Gillibrand D, Grewal D, Blattler DD. Chemistry reference values as a function of age and sex, including pediatric and geriatric subjects. In: Dietz AA, ed. *Aging – its chemistry*. Proceedings of the Third Arnold Beckman conference in clinical chemistry. Washington: AACC, 1980.

Haeney M. Infection determinants at extremes of age. *J Antimicrob Chemother* 1994, 34:1.

Hale W, Stewart R, Marks R. Haematological and biochemical laboratory values in an ambulatory elderly population: an analysis of the effects of age, sex and drugs. *Age Aging* 1983, 12:275.

Hayes G, Stinson I. Erythrocyte sedimentation rate and age. *Arch Ophthalmol* 1976, 94:939.

Helfand M, Crapo LM. Screening for thyroid disease. In: Eddy D M, ed. *Common screening tests*. American College of Physicians, 1991.

Hodkinson HM. Reference values for biological data in older persons. In: Grimley Evans J, Williams TF, eds. *Oxford textbook of geriatric medicine*. Oxford: Oxford Medical Publications, 1992.

Htoo MSH, Kofkoff R, Freedman M. Erythrocyte parameters in the elderly: an argument against new geriatric normal values. *J Am Geriatr Soc* 1979, 27:547.

Jeppesen M. Laboratory values for the elderly. In: Carnevali D, Patrick M, eds. *Nursing management for the elderly, 2nd edition*. Philadelphia: J B Lippincott, 1986.

Kabadi UM, Rosman PM. Thyroid hormone indices in adult healthy subjects: no influence of aging. *J Am Geriatr Soc* 1988, 36:312.

Kane R, Ouslander J, Abrass I. *Essentials of clinical geriatrics, 2nd edition*. New York: McGraw-Hill, 1989.

Kannel WB, Abbott RD. Incidence and prognosis of unrecognized myocardial infarction. *N Engl J Med* 1984, 311:1144.

Kelso T. Laboratory values in the elderly. *Emerg Med Clin North Am* 1990, 8:241–255.

Kenny RA, Fotherby K. The sex hormones and trophic hormones. In: Hodkinson HM, ed. *Clinical biochemistry of the elderly*. London: Churchill Livingstone, 1984.

Koehler KM, Pareo-Tubbeh SL, Romero LJ *et al*. Folate nutrition and older adults: challenges and opportunities. *J Am Diet Assoc* 1997, 97:167.

Lokhorst H, Linden J, Vander Schurman H *et al*. Immune function during aging in man: relation between serological abnormalities and cellular immune status. *Eur J Clin Invest* 1983, 13:209.

Lubran MM. Renal function in the elderly. *Ann Clin Lab Sci* 1995, 25:122.

Mariotti S, Barbesino G, Caturegli P *et al*. Complex alteration of thyroid function in healthy centenarians. *J Clin Endocrinol Metab* 1993, 77:1130.

Mooradian AD. Normal age-related changes in thyroid hormone economy. *Clin Geriatr Med* 1995, 11:159.

Morrow LA, Herman WH, Halter JB. Diabetes mellitus. In: Grimley Evans J, Williams TF, eds. *Oxford textbook of geriatric medicine*. Oxford: Oxford Medical Publications, 1992.

Nardone D, Roth K, Mazur D *et al*. Usefulness of physical examination in detecting the presence or absence of anemia. *Arch Intern Med* 1990, 150:201.

Riggs KM, Spiro III A, Tucker K, Rush D. Relations of vitamin B_{12}, vitamin B_6, folate and homocysteine to cognitive performance in the Normative Aging Study. *Am J Clin Nutr* 1996, 63:306.

Rochman H. *Clinical pathology in the elderly*. New York: Karger, 1988.

Rock R. Interpreting laboratory tests: a basic approach. *Geriatrics* 1984, 39:49.

Rock R, Walker G, Jennings C. Nitrogen metabolites and renal function. In: Tietz NW, ed. *Textbook of clinical chemistry*. Philadelphia: WB Saunders, 1986.

Rowe J. Nephrology and the genitourinary system. In: Grimley Evans J, Williams TF, eds. *Oxford textbook of geriatric medicine*. Oxford: Oxford Medical Publications, 1992.

Rowe JW, Andres R, Tobin JD *et al*. The effect of age on creatinine clearance in man: a cross sectional and longitudinal study. *J Gerontol* 1976, 31:567.

Sharland D. Erythrocyte sedimentation rate: the normal range in the elderly. *J Am Geriatr Soc* 1980, 28:346.

Sowers JR, Felicetta JV, eds. *Endocrinology of aging*. New York: Raven Press, 1988.

Sox H, Liang M. The erythrocyte sedimentation rate. *Ann Intern Med* 1986, 104:515.

Steen B. The importance of diagnostic procedures to ensure quality of health care in geriatric medicine. Examples from recent studies. *Qual Assur Health Care* 1990, 2:387.

Szabolcs I, Ploenes C, Beyer M *et al*. Factors affecting the serum free thyroxine levels in hospitalised chronic geriatric patients. *J Am Geriatr Soc* 1993, 41:742.

Tietz NW, Shuey DF, Wekstein DR. Laboratory values in fit aging individuals – sexagenarians through centenarians. *Clin Chem* 1992, 38:1167.

Thompson J, Wekstein D, Rhoades J *et al*. The immune status of healthy centenarians. *J Am Geriatr Soc* 1984, 32:274.

Van Cauter E, Leproult R, Kupfer DJ. Effect of gender and age on the levels and circadian rhythmicity of plasma cortisol. *J Clin Endocrinol Metab* 1996, 81:2468.

Wedelin C, Bjorkholm M, Holm G *et al*. Blood T-lymphocyte function in healthy adults in relation to age. *Scand J Haematol* 1982, 28:45.

Whitehead TP, Robinson D, Hale AC, Bailey AR. *Clinical chemistry and adult reference values*. London: BUPA Medical Research, 1994.

Wiersinga WM. Subclinical hypothyroidism and hyperthyroidism. Part 1. Prevalence and clinical relevance. *Neth J Med* 1995, 46:197.

Winger JM, Hornick T. Age-associated changes in the endocrine system. *Nurs Clin North Am* 1996, 31:827.

Wise P. Nathan Shock Memorial Lecture 1991. Changing neuroendocrine function during aging: impact on diurnal and pulsatile rhythms. *Exp Gerontol* 1994, 9:13.

Wiske PS, Epstein S, Bell NH *et al*. Increases in immunoreactive parathyroid hormone with age. *N Engl J Med* 1979, 300:1419.

Basic biological needs

Biological support needs
Susan Rush and Irene Schofield

LEARNING OBJECTIVES

After studying this chapter you will be able to:

- Identify age-related changes that affect the basic biological support needs of cardiovascular and respiratory function, nutrition, elimination, sleep and physical activity.
- Discuss the role of the nurse in the maintenance of optimal cardiac function for older people.
- Identify key areas for assessment of respiratory function and explain their significance.
- Describe the factors that influence nutritional status in older people and discuss how nurses can work with them to promote healthy eating.
- Identify the causes of constipation in later life and suggest strategies to alleviate it.
- Identify common sleep disorders experienced in later life and discuss how older people can be helped to sleep well.
- Describe the benefits of physical activity in later life and discuss the nurse's role in promoting exercise.

INTRODUCTION

Changes in homeostasis in later life make achievement of life-support needs more precarious. Assessment and monitoring of survival functions are, therefore, a means of ensuring that the older person reaches an optimum state of health and wellness. This chapter looks at these crucial functions in the context of the biological needs of Maslow's hierarchy. Attention is given to nutrition, elimination, rest and sleep, and exercise because these are areas of function in which the nurse can practice more independently and can make a difference between health and illness. Age changes affecting elimination in general are discussed in Chapter 4 while in this chapter the focus is on bowel elimination. Chronic problems relating to urinary and faecal elimination are discussed in Chapter 8.

The nurse's role in the maintenance of neurological, renal and cardiopulmonary function in the older person is more indirect. Nurses cannot directly change the existing pathophysiology of the heart, lungs, nervous system or kidneys, but they can promote rest and sleep, exercise and nutrition, which affect the function of these systems. Two important questions should be considered in assessing the life-support needs of the older adult: what worries or concerns the client, and what threatens his or her life or health? Keeping these two questions in mind will assist the nurse in providing the most appropriate and realistic approaches to the survival needs of the older person.

CARDIOVASCULAR SYSTEM

Cardiovascular Disease

For centuries, the heart, which must function continuously to maintain life, was considered the centre of life, until the technological redefinition of death included the cessation of brain activity as well as heart function. Cardiovascular disease (CVD) is a major cause of death worldwide in people aged 60 years and over. In the UK, CVD accounted for nearly 300,000 deaths in 1995 (British Heart Foundation, 1997). One in seven men and one in 17 women die from coronary heart disease (CHD) before 75 years of age. The premature death rate from both heart and cerebral vascular disease is much higher in the Asian and the Afro-Caribbean populations. The British Heart Foundation suggests that survival rate depends upon place of residence, socioeconomic circumstances and ethnic background.

One out of every two persons aged 60 years and over may have some severe narrowing of the coronary arteries, but only about 50% of these have clinical signs of coronary artery dysfunction. This occult manifestation may contribute to the variability of cardiac reserve reports that appear in different studies. It is difficult to know whether widespread disease exaggerates the functional decline that is considered to be the result of age-related decline.

Physiological Changes

Under normal conditions, the older person's heart is able to sustain adequate function to maintain daily living activities. Mechanisms that determine cardiovascular (CV) function depend on the interaction of intrinsic cell performance, heart rate, coronary blood flow, cardiac filling (pre-load), and cardiac after-load. All of these are governed by autonomic tone and a negative feedback system. Decreased overall energy demands and a moderate degree of body atrophy place less demand on cardiac function. Sudden demands for more oxygen and energy brought on by various physiological, psychosocial and environmental stress are poorly tolerated. Regardless of the type of stress, physiological manifestations will eventually appear. General risk factors that can cause stress and strain on the heart include the following:

- Cigarette smoking.
- Obesity.
- Inactivity.
- Air pollution.
- Continued high intake of dietary animal fats, salt and calories.
- Internalising emotions.
- Existing chronic conditions.

Other physical conditions that impose added demands on the older adult's heart include arrhythmias, surgery, fever, diarrhoea, hypoglycaemia, malnutrition, avitaminosis, circulatory overload, and drug-induced and non-cardiac illnesses such as renal disease and prostatic obstruction.

Even though the death rate from heart and vascular disease is declining, the older person today is a reflection of their previous health practices. Some damage can be lessened by modifying behaviour (*see* Chapter 4 for age-related changes in cardiac function).

Peripheral Vascular Function

Hypertension

It is well documented that in industrialised countries blood pressure (BP) tends to rise with age. Some authors suggest that 25–50% of the over-65s are hypertensive (Pascual, 1997). Ethnic background is also significant in the development of hypertension. Law *et al.* (1991) suggest that people of African origin have a racial predisposition to hypertension due to a hypersensitivity to salt. Hypertension occurs as a result of age-related changes in the structure of the heart and blood vessels. These include enlargement of the heart due to increased work load, increased diameter and thickness of the aorta, increased resistance to blood flow and decreased numbers or increased sensitivity of receptors concerned with relaxation of the arterial wall (The Association of the British Pharmaceutical Society, 1991).

In 1995, 30% of men and 45% of women aged over 75 years were found to be either taking antihypertensive drugs or had a measured BP that was classified as hypertensive (Joint Health Surveys Unit, 1997). A further 29% of men and 28% of women over 75 years of age were classified as normotensive but were treated with medication that affected BP. Prior to the menopause the incidence of hypertension and CVD is much less in women than in men. However, with the onset of the menopause there is a marked increase in morbidity and mortality from CVD that accompanies an increase in hypertension. A 10 mmHg rise in systolic blood pressure (SBP) is associated with a 20–30% increase risk of CVD in women after the menopause (Prelevic, 1996).

In recent years, treatment of hypertension in older people has had a significant impact on reducing morbidity [Medical Research Council Working Party, 1992; Society of Health Education Professionals (SHEP) Cooperative Research Group, 1991]. Despite this, there has been some reluctance to treat and often a higher treatment-threshold is given to older people prior to treatment. This may be due to an uncertainty of what constitutes a normal BP for the older person, together with concerns about compliance, side effects and drug interactions (Pascual, 1997).

Defining Hypertension

In the UK, current guidelines published by the British Hypertension Society (1997) recommend that the aim of treatment should be to reduce diastolic blood pressure (DBP) to below 90 mmHg and SBP to below 160 mmHg. Sever *et al.* (1993) advise that patients aged 60–80 years should be treated if there is evidence of sustained SBP above 160 mmHg and DBP above 90 mmHg. However, these guidelines deal only with BP (**Box 6.1**). It is suggested that all CV risk factors should be taken into account when deciding on future treatment (Scott and Roomi, 1997). A form of hypertension often seen in older people is isolated systolic hypertension (ISH). This type of hypertension occurs when DBP is normal but SBP is elevated above 160 mmHg. It is known that ISH is even more strongly associated with stroke, cardiac events and deaths than diastolic hypertension. In females, the risk of stroke is doubled and in men, the risk increases fourfold (Pascual, 1997).

Non-pharmacological Treatments

It is recommended that non-pharmacological treatments are used in all people with mild hypertension (i.e. SBP 140–159 mmHg and DBP 90–99 mmHg). In people with more severe hypertension, non-pharmacological measures can reduce the need for high doses and multiple drugs (British Hypertension Society, 1997). Nurses working in a variety of settings with older people have a key role in informing them of measures that they can take to improve their own health, and working with them to determine what might be the best way forward for the individual.

Weight reduction nearly always leads to a lowering of BP. Each kilogram of weight loss can be expected to reduce SBP by 2 mmHg, and DBP by 1 mmHg. Dietary restriction in 'salt-sensitive' individuals can also be effective. A reduction of 3 g salt per day (half a teaspoonful) is estimated to lower BP by 5 mmHg (Lakin *et al.* 1996). Alcohol may increase BP in sensitive individuals and adherence to the recommended

6.1 Blood Pressure and the Older Person

Benefits of blood pressure lowering in the older person with hypertension have been confirmed in six trials (*see* Society of Health Education Cooperative Research Group, 1991; Medical Research Council, 1992).

60–80 years
Treat if systolic blood pressure (SBP) >160 mmHg or diastolic blood pressure (DBP) > 90 mmHg or both. This includes isolated systolic hypertension; i.e. SBP >160 mmHg and DBP <90 mmHg.

80 years
Stay on existing treatment – little evidence for benefit from initiating treatment, although trial data are awaited.

Source: Sever P, Beevers C, Bulpit C *et al.* Management guidelines in essential hypertension a report of the Second Working Party of the British Hypertension Society. *Br Med J* 1993, 306:983–987.

6.2 Cardiac Assessment

- Blood pressure.
- Pulse – rate, rhythm and strength.
- Cough or wheeze.
- Haemoptysis.
- Distension in neck veins.
- Shortness of breath after exercise.
- Waking with sudden breathlessness at night.
- Peripheral oedema.
- Apex/radial pulse check.
- Chest pains.

6.3 Blood Pressure (BP) Measurement

- Patient seated.
- Using conventional mercury manometer with an appropriate bladder size.
- Diastolic reading taken at disappearance of sound (phase V).
- Record to nearest 2 mmHg.
- At least two BP measurements at each visit.
- Four separate visits to determine BP thresholds.
- In mild hypertensives and older patients with isolated systolic hypertension, but no target organ damage, take BP measurements over 3–6 months.
- In severe hypertensives, take BP measurements more often (e.g. weekly for 1 month).
- Standing BP measurements important for older people and diabetic hypertensives in whom orthostatic hypotension is common.
- The routine use of ambulatory blood pressure measurement (ABPM) is not yet established but may be helpful in identifying white coat effect.

Source: The British Hypertension Society. *Management guidelines in essential hypertension*. London, 1997, Modified recommendations based on the report by the Second Working Party of the British Hypertension Society.

intake is thought to be helpful. Taking regular moderate exercise can reduce DBP by 10 mmHg and it is thought that regular exercise may prevent the age-related increase in BP. In addition, training sessions on handling stress and use of relaxation techniques have both been shown to be effective in the management of hypertension. Weber *et al.* (1983) studied older individuals who were on a high-complex carbohydrate, low-fat diet and taking daily exercise that involved walking approximately 3.1 miles (5 kilometres) daily, for 26 days. Following this closely monitored programme, half were able to reduce hypertension, discontinue hypertensive medication and reduce cholesterol levels. The older people's work capacity and health status was significantly improved with this dietary programme and daily walking.

Assessment

Assessment of a client's CV status requires knowledge of that system and the signs and symptoms indicative of adequate or inadequate CV function. **Box 6.2** contains the basic observations related to a nursing assessment of CV function. Major nursing and health texts explore in extensive detail the pathological conditions of the heart and vessels. However, discussion concerning the skill of accurately recording a client's BP does warrant some expansion. Success in confirming an accurate diagnosis of sustained hypertension in the older person is dependent on reliable BP measurement. The move to utilising electronic methods of recording BP will reduce the potential for errors. The British Hypertension Society (1997) guidelines on the accurate measurement of BP should be adhered to (**Box 6.3**). An accurate record of the apical/radial pulse rate and evidence of peripheral oedema should be considered when undertaking a CV assessment on the older person.

Nurse's Role in the Maintenance of Cardiac Function

Key functions of the nurse are to assist the older person to conserve energy and to prevent oxygen demand from exceeding the functional capacity of the cardiac system. Examination of the older person's activities and environment includes indications of wasted activity, location of objects and other necessities frequently used, distances that must be walked and stairs that must be climbed. If the older person does not do so already, the nurse is in the best position to help the person

Age-related Cardiovascular Changes, Outcomes, and Health Prevention, Promotion and Maintenance Approaches		
Age-related changes	Outcomes	Health prevention, promotion and maintenance
Decreased cardiac output	Dyspnoea	Seek medical evaluation for sudden onset of shortness of breath or dyspnoea
Decreased stroke volume	Fatigue	Seek medical evaluation if change in mental status, confusion, restlessness or irritability occurs
Endocardium and left ventricle fibrosis and sclerosis (thickening of left ventricle wall)	Postural hypotension	Rest when tired
		Arrange items for accessibility and to decrease fatigue for elders at home and in care facilities
		Sit down at a table to do meal preparation such as peeling vegetables
		Heavy items throughout home should be at waist level or below to decrease strain and oxygen required to get them
		For elders in care facilities, place chairs in convenient places to enable rest stops
		Seek medical evaluation for respiratory infections and change in urinary pattern that does not improve in a 2–3-day period
Stiffening of vasculature	Hypertension	Have blood pressure (BP) checked regularly and in case of dizziness and headache
Increased peripheral resistance	Isolated systolic hypertension	Keep a BP record
		Limit salt, sodium, fat and cholesterol intake
		Lose weight if overweight or obese
		Stop smoking
		Learn how to take apical or radial pulse
Altered conduction tissue	Slowed heart rate	
Altered response to adrenergic stimulation	Palpitations	
	Arrhythmias	
Decline in baroreceptor response	Varicosities	Increase walking tolerance
Veins thicken, fibrose and dilate	Peripheral oedema	Avoid tight clothing on lower body
		Avoid sitting and standing for long periods of time
		Wear support hose
		Elevate feet when sitting
		Monitor pulse and respiration to guide cardiac status when involved in activity

Table 6.1 Age-related cardiovascular changes, outcomes, and health prevention, promotion and maintenance approaches.

pace daily activities. **Table 6.1** provides additional interventions based on age-related CV changes, outcomes of age changes, and health prevention, promotion and maintenance approaches that the nurse or the older person can initiate.

Nurses are increasingly responsible for managing cardiac rehabilitation programmes post-myocardial infarction, both in hospital and in primary care. Working with patients to increase physical activity, adjust dietary intake and monitoring medications are part of the nurse's role in such programmes. The nurse must be able to assess the therapeutic effect, and possible side effects and toxicity of medications used. Nurses play a vital role in educating clients on the benefits of exercise, supporting the individual in establishing a personal exercise programme and maintaining a positive attitude toward achievement of goals. Group and individual support and counselling are often used. Strategies to promote

compliance with an exercise rehabilitation programme include:
- Involving patients in the decision-making process and in setting short and long-term goals.
- Drawing up a contract that will encourage the individual's adherence to the programme and sense of self-responsibility.
- Teaching groups and individuals about the benefits of an exercise programme.
- Involving family or significant others in the rehabilitation programme.

Prescribed and carefully controlled exercise reduces resting heart rate, reduces SBP/DBP, improves stroke volume and cardiac output, increases maximal oxygen consumption and increases anginal pain threshold. Improved tolerance to activity promotes the individual's return to a more normal lifestyle. In addition, those people with vascular problems will experience decreased peripheral vascular resistance. Hormonal levels, especially the catecholamines, are decreased after exercise. As a result, the person has a less pronounced reaction to stress and is better able to cope with stressors. In general, mood states and emotional stability are improved with an exercise programme. Most studies agree that individuals improve their sense of wellbeing, improve their outlook on life, have more energy and zest for life and generally feel better when participating in an exercise programme.

There appear to be some distinct differences in the responses of men and women. Women begin light household activities soon after discharge and tend to increase them gradually until fully resuming household duties. During the period of convalescence, many express guilt related to an inability to perform all their usual and expected duties. Women are slow to resume sexual activity, and many remain celibate. Men tend to rest and relax longer than women and do not express feelings of guilt; they also return to sexual activity more rapidly. Twice as many men in their 70s are likely to attend a rehabilitation programme than women in their seventies. McGee and Morgan (1992) found that women were more likely to drop out of programmes.

These differences highlight the need for individualised programmes and for particular attention to be given to the potential problems women may experience during recovery. Because of their feelings of guilt and low participation rate in such schemes, women may require special education concerning the benefits of rehabilitation programmes. Any type of exercise should be introduced gradually to prevent sudden cardiac stress and should involve rhythmic repetition of movements of the arm and leg muscles.

Devising an Exercise Programme

Prior to embarking on an aerobic, CV-conditioning exercise programme, a medical history will be taken and a physical examination that includes assessment of the CV, pulmonary, musculoskeletal and neurological systems will be carried out. Laboratory analysis usually includes a haematocrit ratio and a haemoglobin level. A low haematocrit ratio and haemoglobin level will increase the workload on the heart to maintain an adequate oxygen supply. Analysis of electrolyte and fluid balance are necessary to evaluate conductivity and contractility of the cardiac muscle and its ability to function adequately. A treadmill test will measure the cardiac response to exercise. The exercise should be sufficient to exert a training effect but not high enough to overtax the ageing musculoskeletal system. Level of exertion is usually expressed as target heart rate (THR). A THR of 60% of maximum heart rate is given as the minimum required to improve CV endurance. Activity tolerance can be monitored through pulse rate. An accurate resting pulse is the baseline of activity and should increase to approximately 60–80% of the cardiopulmonary capacity (Kligman and Pepin, 1992). Those individuals 65 years of age and over who are certified medically healthy can safely attain a pulse rate of 165 beats per minute (bpm) during sustained activity for a training effect. A sustained pulse rate of 99–132 bpm is the expected. Individuals with a resting pulse of 100 bpm and who after a rest period maintain a pulse of 120 beats require less demanding activity. A pulse rate greater than 130 bpm indicates excessive stress to the cardiac system. In severe cardiac conditions, the heart should not be stressed more than 20 beats above the baseline pulse and should return to normal in 5 minutes.

The nurse can establish the safe activity pulse for the healthy person by subtracting the individual's age from 220 then multiplying the answer by 60% for the lower heart rate and by 80% for the upper heart rate limit. Alternatively, the resting pulse is multiplied by 60% and by 80%, and the results added to the resting pulse value to obtain the parameters for the safe level of function. For example, if a resting pulse is 72, multiply by 60% and add the result (43) to the resting pulse for the lower limit (115). Then multiply 72 by 80% and again add the result (57) to the resting pulse for the upper limit of (129) safe cardiac function. In this instance, the activity should be kept so that the heart rate is between 115 and 129 bpm. Above this limit, excessive demands on cardiopulmonary function could be problematic. A rule of thumb is the ability to talk whilst doing exercise. The nurse should consider the increase in pulse rate from the baseline before, during, and at 3–5 and 10-minute intervals after activity. Baseline values can be obtained anytime during a resting state, except in rapid eye movement sleep, when physiological activity is erratic.

The respiratory system indicates intolerance to activity when dyspnoea is evident or when a decrease in respiratory rate occurs during the activity. The cheeks, lips and nailbeds become flushed, pallid or cyanotic with intolerance. Fatigue, tiredness and a request to sit down are additional signs of inability to tolerate the activity. Tightness and heaviness in the chest and tightness in the legs are indicative of diminished capacity for activity. If nothing occurs within the expected tolerance level, but the nurse notices that the older person is slowing down, shows signs of decreased dexterity or coordination and needs frequent rests, then the person is not able to tolerate that level of activity.

The work of the heart is relieved by the action of large muscles. As they contract, the venous blood is propelled toward the heart. This auxiliary cardiac function is important and is frequently neglected in older adults. Even when movement is restricted, the large muscles can be exercised.

The general principles for any exercise programme are as follows:
- Mode.
- Intensity.
- Frequency.
- Duration.
- Rate of progression.
- Strength training.

It must be recognised, however, that in older people functional capacity is reduced due to age-related changes and decreased physical activity levels that may have occurred over time. Coats *et al.* (1995) suggest that in this group exercise programmes can also be complicated by the increased incidence of osteoporosis, hypertension, orthostatic hypotension and diabetes mellitus. They also point out the increased risk of musculoskeletal injury as a result of muscle atrophy. As a result, endurance training should exclude high impact activities, and resistance training should be carried out with lighter weights and with more repetitions than for the younger clients. Endurance training is safe for the older person if initiated at a low percentage of peak work capacity. Coats *et al.* (1995) suggest that functional capacity can be increased with training initiated as low as 30–40% peak oxygen consumption. In the older individual, the heart rate will take longer to return to pre-exercise rates and there is a tendency for venous pooling due to age-related slowing of baroreceptor responsiveness. It is important, therefore, that older people have a longer cooling down period.

Suitable Types of Exercise

Older adults have varied capacities for exercise. Those who have taken some form of exercise throughout life usually continue into later life. It is less easy for older people who have led a more sedentary lifestyle to suddenly take up exercise. Many people find a daily programme of walking acceptable. As stamina improves, distances may be increased. A walk of 1–2 miles a day for 45 minutes, four to five times a week should be the goal. Walks should be on level ground, as hills make the heart work harder. During winter months, walking in the late morning and early afternoon is suggested, since these times are the warmest periods of the day. Walks in the wind should be avoided, since this also forces the heart to work harder and beat faster. In the hot summer months, walks should be taken early in the morning and late afternoon or early evening to avoid heat exhaustion.

Some older people enjoy dancing, which is an excellent exercise activity. Those who are able continue their lifelong enjoyment of regular swimming sessions or progress to a version of tennis or golf that is easier than that played when they were younger. Other people become adventurous and discover yoga and other exercises that are popular today. Those who can pursue unlimited exercise will improve their cardiopulmonary function, endurance, flexibility and balance. Jogging, cycling, walking and swimming facilitate these benefits. Running, skipping, lifting weights or participating in isometric exercises are not recommended because they increase the heart rate and SBP/DBP too rapidly. Suggested exercise should suit the individual's interest and capacity. Activity should not produce shortness of breath, angina or tachycardia. Adequate periods of rest should be provided when exercise is attempted. Regular exercise is known to reduce CV risk, improve lipid profile, increase insulin sensitivity and decrease resting BP (McMurdo and Rennie, 1992).

Dietary Modification

Giving older people information about a healthy diet and helping them make healthy food choices is a key role for the nurse. Education about cholesterol and fat consumption as a major factor in heart disease is important. Cholesterol levels increase with age and peak in men around 60 years old, declining thereafter. Women's levels tend to be higher than men's after the age of 50 years and continue to rise at least until the age of 70 years. White *et al.* (1993) recommends a plasma cholesterol concentration no higher than 5.2 mmol/litre. However, over 80% of older British men and 95% of older British women are in excess of this value. Severely elevated or frank hypercholesteroaemia, where plasma cholesterol concentration is above 7–8 mmol/litre is present in about a quarter of older British women and 2% of older British men (Webb and Copeman, 1996). In the UK, a measurement of 8 mmol/litre is diagnostic of hypercholesteroaemia (Hughes *et al.* 1995). Webb and Copeman (1996) point out that an intervention trial which attempted to lower cholesterol levels only benefited those older individuals who were at the highest risk of dying from CHD. Therefore, caution should be adopted when advising older people to alter the composition of their dietary fats. Restricting cholesterol-rich foods may not be acceptable, as often these foods are rich in essential nutrients. Eating a variety of foods is advocated to ensure that a healthy diet is achieved.

Education about any medication taken to improve cardiac and circulatory efficiency supports the medical regimen and assists in the maintenance of optimum function. The nurse should be able to discuss the information with the older person and to use illustrations and pamphlets that might facilitate understanding. The nurse should ascertain that the individual understands and can comply with the medication directions. Simple, non-alarmist information helps in the presentation of the signs and symptoms of side effects and toxicity. Periodically, the nurse should review the medication knowledge with the older person. Individuals taking potassium-depleting drugs require information and perhaps a list of foods that can supply adequate amounts of potassium. Together, the nurse and the older client can work out dietary variations to incorporate sufficient potassium into the diet or establish the feasibility of dietary supplements rather than drug forms of potassium supplements. For an individual taking a potassium-depleting drug, three servings daily (1800 mg) should be sufficient. Meat, fish and poultry contain plenty of potassium but they are also high in calories and fat. Fruits and vegetables contain as much or more potassium with fewer calories.

Stress Management

Teaching relaxation techniques to cope with stress is also a nursing function. It is not necessary to teach transcendental meditation but self-selected imagery such as pleasant scenes or memories can be suggested. Time spent developing images or pictures takes the mind and body off stresses and provides a respite. The nurse can help the person plan a specific time to stop for 10 minutes and find a comfortable place to sit and practise a relaxation technique. The client can learn to identify when periods of stress are most intense. Tensing and relaxing the major muscle groups (arms, legs, neck) is another approach to achieving relaxation. The individual gets comfortable in a chair or lays on the bed; muscles are tightened from the toes to the buttocks in one leg and relaxed, then the other leg is tensed and relaxed, followed by each arm. The person concentrates on relaxing each part of the body; it feels as if the body is sinking past the individual into the chair or mattress. Breathing should be rhythmic, with slow inspirations and expirations. In a sitting position, the chin should fall to the chest and the head rotate from front to side, to back to side, several times in a rhythmic, slow movement.

In summary, the well-informed nurse can play an important part in the assessment of CV status and assist the client to meet and maintain optimal CV function. Interventions are focused on helping to reduce cardiac workload, supporting medical protocols, and providing education in the areas of diet, relaxation/stress reduction and exercise. The nurse's direct involvement in interventions will depend on the extent to which the older person is unable to independently achieve optimum CV function.

RESPIRATORY SYSTEM

Respiratory changes, as a result of normal physiological changes and the superimposed consequences of acute and chronic illness, can be sufficiently debilitating to limit life enjoyment. The prominent effect of physiological and functional changes in the respiratory system of the older adult is reduced efficiency in air expulsion. It is accepted that exercise tolerance declines and that breathlessness leads to varying degrees of fatigue, but under usual or resting conditions the older person has little difficulty accomplishing and participating in their customary life activities. However, when confronted with unusual and stressful circumstances, the demand for oxygen surpasses the available supply and establishes a significant reduction in respiratory function deficit, which must be resolved. Stable respiratory function is also affected by a lowered resistance to infection, engendered by a diminished immune system response and less effective self-cleansing action of the respiratory cilia.

Physiological Changes

Normal physiological changes can resemble pathological change. It has been observed that the lungs of 'healthy' older people who are non-smokers show evidence of small, scattered areas of lung destruction similar to those with emphysema. It has been suggested that the normally reduced efficiency of air expulsion found in the general older population resembles significant findings in those diagnosed with emphysema. In both instances, the extent of change is the critical factor in determining normality or pathological conditions (*see* Chapter 4 for a detailed description of age-related changes in respiratory function).

Meeting Cardiovascular Needs

Jim MacIntosh is a successful lawyer and at 75 years of age he is still working part-time. He visits his general practitioner for his health check with the practice nurse. A mild myocardial infarction the year before has initially frightened him, but he soon returns to his usual lifestyle. However, he notices every twinge of pain or indigestion and is generally bordering on hypochondria. He has become an insomniac and says, 'I'm really frightened that one night I'll go to bed, fall asleep and never wake up again.'

You reassure him that his weight is ideal and his diet exemplary but you believe that Mr MacIntosh might be under too much emotional stress and suggest he might want to think about retiring. You also recommend that Jim refrain from drinking too much alcohol. Mr MacIntosh enjoys wine with his meal and also takes whisky as a nightcap.

Psychosocial factors significant to this case include that Mr MacIntosh is widowed and harbours a great deal of resentment about the medical mismanagement (as he had perceived it) of his wife's last illness. Also, two of his best golfing friends have recently died.

- **What are Mr MacIntosh's comments that provide subjective evidence?**
- **What objective data can you use to inform your assessment of the situation?**
- **Suggest two unmet needs that may be the most significant to Mr MacIntosh at this time.**
- **Suggest the nursing aims for each unmet need, reflecting realistic outcomes using concrete and measurable terms.**
- **Suggest one or more interventions for each area of unmet need, justifying the choice of intervention.**

Lung Function Tests

Reliable pulmonary function measurement in older people is difficult to obtain. There are few published values on respiratory function tests for older adults, particularly test values for older women. Many values considered normal for older people have been derived from studies using small numbers of patients, often highly selected, under specific testing conditions. The absence of reliable pulmonary function values on which to evaluate the respiratory status of older people requires that the nurse uses other methods to assess their respiratory ability and needs. Structural changes, diminished immune response and environmental factors predispose the older adult to respiratory problems.

Common Respiratory Diseases

Conditions that affect the respiratory system are among the most common life-threatening disorders affecting older people and are considered to be among the leading causes of death. Pneumonia was responsible for 52,000 deaths in those aged 65 years and over in 1994 (Office of National Statistics, 1996). The mortality rate dramatically increases in older adults over 75 years of age. Pnuemococcal pneumonia is the most common bacterial respiratory infection in older people. Other less common bacterial pneumonias occur from infection with *Haemophilus influenzae*, *Staphylococcus aureus* and *Klebsiella pneumoniae* (Office of National Statistics, 1996). Signs and symptoms of pneumonia which manifest in the young are not commonly seen in older adults. The tendency toward atypical responses can easily lead to an incorrect diagnosis made too late in the progress of the disease. Aspiration pneumonia is a high-risk condition for a person with swallowing difficulty or oesophageal disease, a person who regurgitates food, a person with an endotracheal tube or tracheostomy, and a person who is heavily sedated. Chronic obstructive pulmonary disease (COPD) includes bronchitis, asthma, emphysema and bronchiectasis. COPD and lung cancer constitute the major medical conditions from which respiratory problems develop.

Assessment

In addition to having knowledge of normal physiology and anatomy of the thorax and respiratory system, the nurse should develop the ability to assess the respiratory system by using inspection, palpation, percussion and auscultation. These skills can be developed through attending physical assessment courses now offered as part of post-registration specialist practice courses.

Assessment of the pulmonary needs of older adults should include past and present history of smoking. For the present generations of older people, smoking in their youth was considered fashionable, sociable and a sign of maturity. Little was known then about the adverse effects of smoking. Changes as a result of smoking occurred subtly and gradually over time and generally were not noticed until major symptoms and lung damage had already occurred. For this reason, the age at which the individual began to smoke is as important as the number of cigarettes smoked per day and the brand of cigarettes used. Education of young people today concerning the hazards of smoking will perhaps help to maintain better respiratory function for future generations of older people. However, there is evidence that more younger people are smoking, in particular girls and young women. In the future, therefore, more females than males may go on to develop respiratory problems.

Exposure to various air pollutants should be explored. Communities located near industrial areas may receive higher emission levels than other locations in the same city. Present and past occupations and hobbies may also provide clues to pulmonary irritants. Certainly, any older person who has been exposed to coal or asbestos dust is at high risk of developing cancer or pneumoconiosis. A history of any cough should be obtained:
- Is the cough dry or moist?
- Is it phlegm producing?
- If phlegm is present, are the secretions from the chest or the back of the throat?
- How long has the cough persisted and what colour is the phlegm?

The degree of breathlessness can be established by identifying the level of shortness of breath experienced by the older person. The following is a gradation of breathlessness:
(1) Shortness of breath when hurrying on a level surface or when walking up hills or stairs.
(2) Shortness of breath when walking on a level surface with people of the same age.
(3) Shortness of breath when walking on a level surface at one's own pace.
(4) Shortness of breath when washing or dressing.
(5) Shortness of breath when sitting quietly.

Another indicator of the extent of breathlessness is the distance the older person can walk on a flat surface without stopping to rest. Observation of the individual's pace is also a good index of respiratory efficiency. The older adult should be asked if shortness of breath is experienced during the night or at other specific times and if it interferes with the individual's lifestyle. If chest pain is experienced, questions should be asked to differentiate between pain originating from respiratory or cardiac problems.

Information not frequently obtained includes data about wheezing and the effect of weather conditions on the chest. Foggy, cold and damp weather conditions increase coughing and usually worsen breathlessness. Air conditioning, hot weather and high altitudes also aggravate breathing problems. Vital signs will indicate respiratory rate, rhythm and depth. Chest and accessory muscles of the thorax and neck should be observed to determine if they are being used to compensate or aid in difficult breathing. The neck and back should be assessed for structural defects such as deviations of the trachea, kyphosis or scoliosis, which interfere with and limit chest expansion (*see* **Box 6.4** for an outline of respiratory assessment).

6.4 Respiratory Assessment Outline

History
Respiratory diseases.
History of smoking.
Exposure to pollutants.

Symptoms of shortness of breath
Cough.
Breathlessness.
Wheezing.
Orthopnoea.
Haemoptysis.

Physical examination
Inspection.
Skin colour.
Posture.
Chest shape and symmetry.
Chest expansion.
Respiratory rate.
Capillary fill of fingers.
Sputum (if any).

Palpation
Rib tenderness.
Skin temperature, turgor, moisture.

Percussion
Lung fields (bilaterally).

Auscultation
Breath sounds (particular to the bases).

6.5 Effects of Giving Up Smoking

After 20 minutes
Blood pressure and pulse return to normal.

After 8 hours
Nicotine and carbon monoxide levels in the blood reduce by half, oxygen levels return to normal.

After 24 hours
Carbon monoxide will be eliminated from the body.
Lungs start to clear out mucus and other smoking debris.

After 48 hours
There is no nicotine left in the body.
Ability to taste and smell is greatly improved.

After 72 hours
Breathing becomes easier.
Bronchial tubes begin to relax and energy levels increase.

After 2–12 weeks
Circulation improves.

After 3–9 months
Coughs wheezing and breathing problems improve as lung function is increased by up to 10%.

After 5 years
Risk of heart attack falls to about half that of a smoker.

After 10 years
Risk of lung cancer falls to half that of a smoker.
Risk of heart attack falls to the same as someone who has never smoked.

Source: Royal College of Nursing. *Nurses against tobacco*. London: Royal College of Nursing, 1997.

Nursing Interventions

Assessment will reveal a number of care problems, but all will revolve around these issues:
- Preventing respiratory complications.
- Attaining adequate oxygen by the body.
- Minimising energy expenditure and obtaining maximum function.

Preventing respiratory complications begins with prophylactic measures to lessen the susceptibility to respiratory infections. It is now acknowledged that benefits can be gained from smoking cessation even in later life. This is the single most important method of affecting outcomes at all stages of COPD. Nurses can counteract the response that it is too late to stop because the damage has already been done, with the responses that the rate of deterioration can be slowed and that more benefit can be gained from treatments (British Thoracic Society, 1997). **Box 6.5** gives benefits of smoking cessation in detail.

The older adult who is susceptible to respiratory illness because of debility and chronic cardiac and respiratory conditions should be immunised against influenza. Vaccines exist that are capable of preventing pneumonial infection from 14 strains of pneumococcal organisms. Use of vaccines can help reduce the mortality and morbidity caused by this type of pneumonia. Early detection of upper respiratory infections can help limit the severity of illness in some instances. Early stages of respiratory insufficiency may only be indicated by excessive yawning and anxiety following engagement in activity.

An adequate intake of fluids will keep mucous membranes hydrated and help keep secretions liquid for easier expectoration. Attainment of adequate oxygen by the body and conservation of energy can be achieved through pacing activities. Pacing will help to conserve energy and limit additional demands for more oxygen by the body. Non-productive coughing consumes energy needed for other tasks, and can be controlled with hard sweets such as lemon drops.

Breathing Exercises

Use of maximum breathing ability can be facilitated by daily breathing exercises. These will help to relieve breathlessness and lead to improved gaseous exchange in the lungs. Those who are immobile and do not get adequate oxygen exchange can benefit from these exercises when carried out several times a day. One exercise requires that the individual breathes slowly and fills the lungs as completely as possible, followed by a forceful expiration through pursed lips. A second exercise can be done separately or together with the first. This breathing routine requires that the individual relaxes the abdomen on inspiration and contracts the abdominal muscles on expiration. The effectiveness of this exercise can be checked by the person by placing one hand on the abdomen and the other on the chest. On inspiration, the abdominal hand should rise; likewise, on expiration, the chest hand should rise with the chest movement. The exercise can be performed in a sitting, lying or standing position, but the most effective position is recumbent with knees flexed.

Posture

Good posture can improve use of the lung space that currently exists. A stooped or hunched position resulting from muscle weakness decreases the space available for lung expansion within the thoracic cavity. Walking, in addition to being good exercise, can help improve posture; arms swing at the sides naturally and stretch and contract the muscles of the back and chest. In addition, walking facilitates deeper breathing. Humidification of the immediate environment helps keep the respiratory tract moist; mucous membranes remain intact so as to resist microbial invasion, which often occurs through dry and irritated membranes.

Emotional stress and fear accelerate respirations and the demand of oxygen. Attention should be given to the individual who exhibits anxiety, and ways should be explored to alleviate or reduce stress. The older person who takes to their bed when not feeling well should be encouraged to take a short daily walk around the bedroom or home, if this is tolerable. Confinement to bed causes generalised weakness, fainting when attempting to get up and sudden onsets of mental confusion. Hypoxia is apparent in many older people who maintain a recumbent position for an extended period, even as short as a night's rest. The full respiratory capacity for oxygen becomes diminished to the extent that the balance between blood flow and ventilation distribution is minimal.

Positioning

Persons confined to bed should be optimally positioned to facilitate the best chest expansion possible. Sitting positions do facilitate free movement of the diaphragm, but frequently the older person slides downward in the bed and is found in a 'scrunched' position that impedes, rather than benefits, respiratory exchange. An anti-slip sheet can help to prevent this. Those confined to bed should also be changed from sitting to lying positions in an attempt to aerate tissues that do not receive adequate distribution of oxygenated blood. At times it may be necessary to employ positive pressure breathing apparatus to assist those who are too debilitated to exchange air more effectively. The respiratory system action matches that of the cardiac system. When working with older adults with special respiratory needs, nurses should be aware that there will be special cardiac needs as well.

Many of the actions suggested in the preceding cardiovascular section apply equally to those people with respiratory problems. The nurse can help by teaching the client to pace activities, to breathe more effectively, and to be aware of exposure to specific environmental pollutants. In the event of acute and chronic respiratory disease, the nurse's role is to support and maintain the medical treatment and to assist the client in fulfilling the prescribed plan of care within their chosen lifestyle (*see* **Table 6.2** for a summary of this section).

 Meeting Respiratory Needs

Winnie Jackson is in her mid-seventies and has smoked heavily from the time of her late teens, when it was expected of sophisticated women. Ten years ago, on experiencing such shortness of breath that she could not walk up the stairs in her home, she gave up smoking cigarettes. Initially this proved difficult, as her husband continued to smoke in her presence, but she has been able to persist. Now she finds that in spite of her winning struggle with the habit, breathing is becoming more laboured. Mrs Jackson is angry and disheartened, and feels helpless. She remarks, 'All that struggle to give up cigarettes doesn't seem to have done a bit of good. You know, that's really the only vice I have; I've always been careful about my diet, I don't drink, and I faithfully go for my annual check up'.

A district nurse comes each week to monitor Mrs Jackson's bedridden husband. One week the nurse finds the home in a mess and Mrs Jackson still in bed at 10 a.m. – she says that she simply doesn't have the energy to get up.

- **What information can the nurse herself obtain from observations and examination that will provide objective data for a holistic nursing assessment?**
- **Suggest two unmet needs that may be the most significant to Mrs Jackson at this time.**
- **Suggest nursing aims for each unmet need, reflecting realistic outcomes and using concrete and measurable terms.**
- **Suggest one or more interventions for each area of unmet need, justifying your choice of intervention.**

Age-related Respiratory Changes, Outcomes, and Health Prevention, Promotion and Maintenance Approaches		
Age-related changes	Outcomes	Prevention, promotion and maintenance approaches
Anterior–posterior diameter increase Diminished chest wall movement Weakened chest wall muscles Calcification of costal cartilage Decreased elastic recoil of lungs Pulmonary walls thicken Increased residual volume} tidal volume Decreased vital capacity} unchanged Enlarged alveoli Diminished number of capillaries to alveoli Thinning of alveoli walls Bronchioles enlarge Reduced cilia movement Altered neuromuscular functions and reflexes of breathing Early airway closure	Barrel chest Fatigue Dyspnoea Ineffective cough Kyphosis	Senile emphysema is normal Systemic muscle toning exercises as tolerated Deep breathing exercises Diaphragmatic rather than chest breathing Avoid irritants, cigarettes, dust and polluted air Use air purifier Stay inside at peak hours of environmental pollution Seek medical attention for respiratory infections that last more than 2–3 days Avoid people with upper respiratory infections Get flu and pneumonia immunisations Adequate fluid intake to keep secretions liquified

Table 6.2 Age-related respiratory changes, outcomes, and health prevention, promotion and maintenance approaches.

NUTRITIONAL NEEDS

Good nutritional status helps to maximise significantly the functional capacity, wellbeing and independence of older adults. Ill health can be avoided or managed more effectively if the older person has a well-balanced diet. The need to eat and drink is essential to life, but it also provides an important social component.

Older people's eating and drinking patterns have been established over many years. From early childhood, individuals develop preferences for some foods and dislike of others. Individuals learn early on the importance of meals as social events, and a preference for the atmosphere and environment in which to eat is established. These factors and preferences remain with individuals as they age and will affect the older person's view of nutrition. For example, Mr. Franks, a patient in a rehabilitation ward where patients were encouraged to eat communally, said that he would not eat if he had to go to the dining area. It turned out that although he lived with his sister and she cooked all of their meals, they ate in their separate rooms.

The variances in nutritional requirements throughout the life span are now well established for older people. Increased amounts of calcium and vitamins A and C are important in later life but tend to be deficient in the average diets of older adults. In addition, they can be affected by alterations in storage, use and reabsorption. Total calorific intake should decline in response to corresponding changes in metabolic rate and a general decrease in physical activity. A Department of Health (DoH) report (1992) suggests average daily energy requirements for well, older people as follows:

Men
65–74 years	71 kg	2330 kcal per day
75+ years	69 kg	2100 kcal per day

Women
65–74 years	63 kg	1900 kcal per day
75+ years	60 kg	1810 kcal per day

The common nutritional education tools utilised in the UK to aid individuals to select their diet are the Four Food Groups, the Food Guide Pyramid and the Food Guide Plate.

In most industrialised countries, if the individual consumes a varied diet which has sufficient calories they will generally meet the minimum needs for essential nutrients without much effort. However, this is not necessarily true of older people, where a large minority of over seventy-fives are underweight, inactive and have a low basal metabolic rate. This may reduce energy requirements so that the amount of food eaten is less than adequate to meet other nutrient needs, unless the diet is high in nutrient density (Webb and Copeman, 1996).

Nutritional education has made a priority of moving from a point of ensuring adequacy in an individual's diet to the promotion of a dietary pattern which is expected to reduce or delay the degenerative, diet-related diseases such as coronary heart disease. To reflect this change, the Food Guide Pyramid, has emerged from the USA (**Figure 6.1**). It provides a clear visual message that can be used to transcend cultural and speech barriers and educational limitations. The individual is provided with information relating to the quantitative contribution from the food groups.

The British version of this pyramid is essentially the same except that the fruit and vegetables are presented as a simple grouping on the second tier with combined 5–9 servings and potatoes are included with the bread and cereals. The specific recommendations about portion numbers are considered by some people as confusing and potentially misleading, given that energy requirements are essentially individualised. The estimated energy requirements of older UK adults utilising the Food Guide Pyramid is provided in **Table 6.3**.

Dietary Reference Values

In the UK, an individual's nutritional status is calculated by the use of standards called dietary reference values (DRVs) [The Committee on the Medical Aspects of Food Policy (COMA), 1991]. These standards have been set by national and international experts in the field of nutrition and are regularly updated. They attempt to establish the daily minimum amount of essential nutrients required for each age and sex sub-group. Some adjustment is required for different individuals. DRVs are based on the healthy individual and do not consider additional nutrients in the presence of infection, metabolic disorders and chronic illness. In the case of the older adult with a chronic condition and taking regular medication, the effects upon nutrient needs have not been estimated and are rarely considered (*see* **Table 6.4** for foods that play a role in disease).

Using the Food Guide Pyramid to Provide the Estimated Energy Requirements of Older UK Adults		
	Men	Women
EER (kcal)	2100–2330	1810–1900
EER (MJ)	8.77–9.71	7.61–7.96
Bread group	9	7
Vegetable group	4	3–4
Fruit group	3	2–3
Milk group	2–3	2–3
Meat group	2	2

These figures are intended only to be an approximate guide: the exact calorie content would be very dependent upon extent to which fats, sweets and oils are consumed and factors like the fat content of any milk used, the leanness of meat, whether white fish or oily fish is used and whether vegetables are boiled or fried.

Portions
(as in United States Department of Agriculture, 1992)
- 1 slice bread, 1/2 cup cooked rice, pasta or cereal, 25 g ready-to-eat cereal
- 1/2 cup chopped raw or cooked vegetables, 1 cup leafy raw vegetables
- 1 piece fruit, 1/2 cup canned fruit, 1/2 cup dried fruit, 1/2 cup fruit juice
- I cup milk or yoghurt, 40–50 g cheese
- 70–80 g cooked lean meat, poultry or fish; an egg or 1/2 cup of cold beans counts as about 1/3 of a serving.

Source: Webb GP, Copeman J. *The nutrition of older adults*. London: Edward Arnold, 1996.

Table 6.3 Using the food guide pyramid to provide the estimated energy requirements of older UK adults.

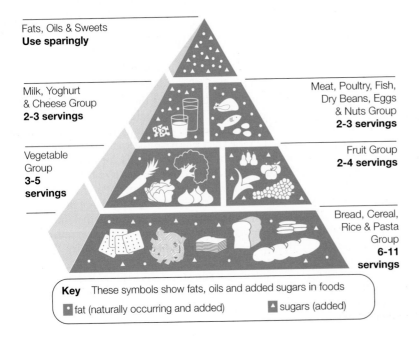

Figure 6.1 Food Guide Pyramid. (Source: United States Department of Agriculture.)

Many studies on nutrient requirements have been carried out on the young and the estimations for older people have been based largely on extrapolation. However, the dynamic changes which occur with ageing influence nutrient and energy requirements. Webb and Copeman (1996) report that there is a lack of studies into the nutritional needs of older adults and this has culminated in general uncertainty as to their requirements. A report by COMA has recommended that more research must be aimed at estimating the energy requirements of older people, in particular those who are thin; determining the effects of health status on the energy requirements of older adults; and determining the protein requirements of older adults.

Factors Affecting Fulfilment of Nutritional Needs

Fulfilment of nutritional intake in later life depends on an individual's dietary history as well as present food practices. Lifelong eating habits are developed out of tradition, ethnicity and religion, all of which collectively can be called culture. Eating habits do not always coincide with fulfilment of nutritional needs. Rigidity of food habits may increase with age as familiar food patterns are sought. Ethnicity determines if traditional foods are preserved, whereas religion affects the possible choice of foods. Throughout an individual's life, therefore, preferences for particular foods bring deep satisfaction and often possess emotional significance. Lifelong habits of dieting or eating fad foods also echo through the later years. Some older adults may be taken in by food fads that profess to partially or completely cure various ailments or increase vitality. Meals may be missed; the person may eat less resulting in an inadequate intake of basic nutrients. It is very difficult to reach an adequate nutritional intake if the total calories are fewer than 1200 a day. Individuals who are on self-imposed diets of 1000 calories or less a day are inviting malnutrition.

The expansion in the use of ready-to-eat foods has also affected the way older people select and cook foods. These foods are often seen by older adults living alone as a way of making food preparation easier, though they are often expensive. Some of the products can be used in restricted salt, fat, cholesterol or calorie-controlled diets. The foods often comprise complete meals and provide a variety of meat, fish and poultry dishes. These foods require little preparation or no heating before eating; they are palatable because the freshness and flavour are sealed in; and there are few preservatives. However, these are not without disadvantages for use by older people. Package and storage guidelines may be confusing since some of these foods resemble non-refrigerated, shelf-stable products. Also, unless older adults pay attention to expiry dates on packaging, there could be the risk of food-borne illnesses, which could be life threatening.

The Food Selection Model

Older adults are affected by a variety of factors which influence dietary intake. These factors include lack of car ownership,

Food Ingredients that Play a Role in Disease		
Condition	Dietary factor	Food ingredients
Stroke	Adverse	Sodium, alcohol (dose-related)
	Protective	Potassium, vitamin C, magnesium, fruit and vegetables
Coronary heart disease	Adverse	Saturated fat, trans fatty acids, dietary cholesterol
	Protective	Omega-3 fatty acids, non-starch polysaccharides, starch, certain elements, phyto-oestrogens, anti-oxidants, flavonoids, carotinoids, folate/riboflavin
Osteoporosis/fractures	Adverse	Caffeine, animal protein, sodium, alcohol (high dose)
	Protective	Calcium, vitamin D, omega-3 fatty acids, alcohol (low dose), phyto-oestrogens
Osteoarthritis	Adverse	Saturated fat, meat
Rheumatoid arthritis	Protective	Omega-3 fatty acids
Respiratory disease	Protective	Fruit and vegetables, vitamin C
Cataracts	Protective	Anti-oxidants, riboflavin, vitamin B_{12}
Dementia	Adverse	Aluminium
	Protective	Anti-oxidants, e.g. vitamin E, B vitamins
Large bowel disease	Adverse	Sulphite, meat, fat
	Protective	Non-starch polysaccharides, starch
Diabetes	Adverse	Non-milk extrinsic sugars
	Protective	Omega-3 fatty acids, anti-oxidants, soluble non-starch polysaccharides

Source: Kay-Tee Khaw. In search of the clues to healthy old age. In: *Medical Research Council News*, Autumn, No 75, 1977.

Table 6.4 Food ingredients that play a role in disease.

which precludes access to the out-of-town supermarkets, lack of finances and the expense of some packaged items. Webb (1995) has suggested a hierarchy of constraints upon food availability (**Figure 6.2**) which provides a comprehensive model of food selection. This will be used to discuss further the factors which influence dietary intake in later life.

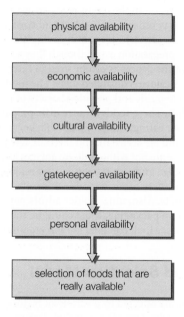

Figure 6.2 **A model of food selection based upon the concept of a hierarchy of constraints upon food availability. (Source: Webb GP.** *Nutrition: a health promotion approach.* **London: Edward Arnold, 1995.)**

Physical Availability

As mentioned previously, older adults have an increased prevalence of cardiovascular disease, and often with increasing age there can be a decrease in the individual's ability to get about. Loss of mobility can reduce the older adult's ability to ensure a balanced and varied diet. Many small long-standing corner shops selling groceries have been closed in the wake of the larger supermarkets normally located on the outskirts of towns. It may have become impossible for the older person to walk to the supermarket, so those that can have to use public transport. Older people who have difficulty with walking and use a stick or walking frame find the carrying of groceries extremely difficult. Convenience foods, often devoid of many essential nutrients, are lighter to carry or pull along in a trolley than are fresh fruit and vegetables.

Organisations such as Help the Aged and Dial-a-Ride provide transport for older adults and the disabled. Webb and Copeman (1996) identify that older people are less likely to own a car than younger ones, and access to a car declines with increasing age. However, some large retailers are now offering a delivery service for groceries, but again some older

adults may find the extra cost unacceptable. Those older people who are housebound may have to rely on others for help in buying groceries; this further reduces their ability to exercise choice. The opportunity to walk around the supermarket choosing items on special offer, new items and fruits in season should not be overlooked; this is an important factor in maintaining interest in food.

Webb and Copeman (1996) also examine the lack of ability to prepare a main meal. The DoH (1992) suggests that a quarter of people over 85 years of age find this difficult and have inadequate facilities to keep food fresh. Cooking for one can be viewed as time consuming and less rewarding by some older people. For some people, it may be easier to 'make do' with tea and biscuits. Healthy eating guides produced by Help the Aged in conjunction with the Nutrition Advisory Group for the Elderly (NAGE) encourages older people to spend a little more time and thought in food preparation. NAGE provides many helpful leaflets to encourage older adults with small appetites. In addition, publications by Louise Davis and Delia Smith suggest nutritious recipes when cooking for one or two people.

Economic Availability

Inflation is constantly eroding the purchasing power of older adults, forcing them to buy foods that satiate hunger but provide many empty calories. These foods may or may not be expensive. Some older people may eat only once a day in an attempt to make their income last through the week. Older people accustomed to eating meat, fish and poultry as their main sources of protein have watched the cost climb to heights beyond their purchasing power.

Inexpensive, alternative protein sources such as tofu and quorn are foreign to the diets of older people in Western society, but are slowly becoming more acceptable. The development of a taste for alternative protein sources, and an understanding of what foods to include in order to obtain complete dietary protein, requires some knowledge and practice to ensure adequate protein intake and to prevent monotony. Vegetable protein can be suggested as an alternative source of protein to meet daily needs. This is a more economical form of protein, which may help older people conserve their income for other necessities, unexpected bills or special treats. Poverty may force many older people to choose between adequate heating or adequate food. Older adults may 'feel the cold' more than younger individuals, and may well choose to keep warm. Combinations such as milk or cheese with bread or pasta; cereal with milk; rice and cheese or rice and bean casseroles; whole-wheat bread with baked beans; and bean soup with bread are sources of protein. There is a tendency for retailers to apply special offers to bulk buy foods. This may not be appropriate for those who are single or widowed, as buying food in small quantities is often more expensive. Webb and Copeman (1996) point out that over 80% of older adult households in the UK consist of either one or two persons.

At times, it is difficult to purchase foods in small quantities; therefore, the single older person may have to deal with more wastage or spoilage of foods. Careful planning is important to ensure that the required amounts of nutrients are obtained. Ideally, one meal that consists of protein (generally meat, fish or poultry), potato, vegetable, salad and dessert should be eaten daily. Other snacks can be prepared and eaten with minimum effort. **Box 6.6** provides suggestions for a basic stock of foods. The purchase of some convenience foods can leave the older person without some essential nutrients. However, for many people the purchase of such foods is more economical than having to prepare raw vegetables, and there is less wastage. For many of the above reasons, there is a dramatic contrast between younger and older adults in the economic availability of food. Webb and Copeman (1996) conclude that it is expensive for older people to eat a healthy well-balanced diet. The diet may be less varied, and for those who are unable to cook and do not have support, cold food may be the only option.

Cultural Availability

This is covered in detail by Webb and Copeman (1996), who provide examples of how cultural factors affect the availability of some foods. Although food may be available, it may be culturally unacceptable; for example, pork is not acceptable to Jews nor beef to Hindus. The significance of these examples should not be underestimated. In the UK, there has been a nutritional education programme to reinforce the importance of wholemeal bread. Webb and Copeman (1996) point out that in earlier years this type of bread was seen as inferior, and older people may continue to regard it as such.

Gatekeeper Availability

This term refers to the person who controls the planning, purchasing and preparation of food. In the majority of families, this role is undertaken by a female member, who continues this role into later life, unless she is prevented from doing so by illness or disability. For many older men, the traditional role of the woman as the gatekeeper can mean that the loss of a spouse is very difficult to cope with. The older man may have never developed the skills required for food preparation and cooking, and this may have a significant impact on his dietary intake.

For older people receiving meals-on-wheels, attending a luncheon club or living in a care home, the gatekeeper role will be taken by the service manager or caterer. High on the list of concerns for the latter will be cost, ease of preparation, low wastage of food and minimal staffing for the serving and feeding of clients. These priorities will obviously impact on the nutritional status of the older person.

Personal Availability

Webb and Copeman (1996) suggest three factors which are long-lasting and influence personal acceptance of particular foods:

(1) Personal preferences: the dislike of some foods.
(2) Individual intolerance: unable to manage some foods without physiological or psychological reaction.
(3) Personal beliefs about foods: influences that may be positive or negative, often not based on rational decisions; can be based on prejudice.

Other factors that affect the personal availability of food are as follows:
- Poorly fitting dentures.
- Reduced sense of taste and smell.
- Therapeutic diets, e.g. diabetes mellitus.
- Avoidance of some foods because they cause indigestion or heartburn.
- Lack of appetite due to depression, illness, boredom, drug therapy or a large intake of alcohol.

Problems in Nutrition

Adequate Hydration

Older adults are vulnerable to fluid and electrolyte imbalance. Acidosis and alkalosis are potential consequences. Dehydration can also cause confusion because of electrolyte imbalance. Increased amounts of fluid not only prevent confusion associated with dehydration but are also necessary for individuals who are receiving specific medications. Lithium, for example, requires that the person drinks as much as 3 litres of fluid a day. Use of diuretics requires that a normal fluid intake be maintained, unless specifically ordered to the contrary. Coffee has a diuretic effect that requires fluid intake

6.6 Basic Four Food Stocks

Dairy products	Box of dry skimmed or whole milk. Small can evaporated milk. Instant cocoa. Instant pudding to use with dry milk. Small pieces of cheese (if wrapped air tight and kept in cool place). Cottage cheese.
Meat + other protein products	Small can of tuna fish, sardines, salmon. Canned or potted meat. Peanut butter. Hard boiled eggs.
Fruit and vegetables	Small cans of any fruit and vegetables. Dried fruit (raisins, apricots, dates). Fresh apples, oranges, seasonal fruits.
Miscellaneous foods	Instant coffee. Instant cocoa. Tea. Sugar. Condiments of choice.

to compensate for fluid loss through diuresis. In hot weather, increased perspiration and evaporation deplete the individual of essential body fluid. Fever and upper respiratory infections also cause dehydration in older people. Adequate fluid intake is as important to total nutrition as food. Under normal circumstances, a healthy adult needs 1.5 litres of oral fluids; additionally, 700 ml comes from solid food and 300 ml from oxidation of food during metabolism (Reedy, 1988).

Those older people in either acute or long-term care settings are most prone to becoming dehydrated. When scheduled procedures prohibit eating and drinking for a period, fluid intake is rarely equalised by the end of the day. Those who eat a late lunch may also eat an early dinner. They then might not drink fluids after the evening meal and as a result become dehydrated overnight. Some patients go for as long as 15 hours without fluid and not complain of thirst. Older adults who cannot obtain fluids by themselves should be offered hourly drinks and have sufficient fluids with their meals. Routine and regular prompts may be necessary for frail older people. Water should be situated in the most accessible place and favourite drinks should be offered to break the monotony of drinking only water. For those who can reach out for their own fluids, the container should be light enough to lift and manipulate. The use of iced drinks can encourage people to take more fluid.

Gasper (1988) has identified seven variables that affect fluid intake for older adults in care homes. She noted that with increasing age, fluid intake decreased. Other factors that influenced fluid intake were speech, the ability to request fluids, visual impairment, functional ability, gender, opportunity to obtain water and the time taken to reach the fluid dispenser. The findings suggest that those who are semi-dependent are at greater risk of inadequate fluid intake than those who are independent (able to obtain their own fluids) and dependent (care needs are anticipated). Gasper concluded that nursing care plans for those who are semi-dependent, female and over 85 years of age should include nursing interventions clearly stating the need to increase the number of times water and other fluids are offered. **Box 6.7** contains measures to prevent dehydration in acute care settings.

It appears that older adults who feel well and have access to a variety of acceptable fluids have no trouble in maintaining fluid balance, while those who feel unwell or have had fluid intake restricted, may develop dehydration due to diminished thirst perception (*see* Chapter 4). Older adults should be made aware of how much fluid they drink and to keep it fairly constant at a recommended amount.

Adequate Fibre

Fibre is an important dietary component that some older adults do not consume in sufficient quantities. Fibre, the indigestible material that gives plants their structure, is abundant in raw fruit and vegetables, and unrefined grains and cereals. Fibre facilitates the absorption of water, increases bulk and improves intestinal motility. It prevents constipation, haemorrhoids and diverticulosis. Fibre also helps reduce calorie intake, aids in the control of obesity and is thought to play a

role in the prevention of 'diseases of civilisation' such as heart disease and colon cancer.

Various types of fibre exist, but all possess the common characteristic of indigestibility. Individuals who can chew foods well can benefit from eating increased amounts of fresh fruit and vegetables daily or combining unsweetened bran with other types of food. Twelve to eighteen grams per day of non-starch polysaccharides (fibre) is recommended for an older person (DoH, 1992). Care must be taken when adding bran to foods such as cereals or soups. If the amount is not gradually increased the older person will experience bloating, wind, diar-

6.7 Measures to Help Prevent Dehydration in Acute Care Settings

- Assure a 24-hour intake of at least 1500 ml of oral fluid.
- Food intake and metabolic oxidation should provide additional fluid for hydration.
- Offer fluids hourly during the day. Include fluids with an evening snack.
- Ask the doctor to order intravenous fluids if the patient is not able to take oral fluids.
- Accurately record intake and output for all older patients (24-hour urine volume should be 1–1.5 litres).
- Note the urine colour and specific gravity.
- Listen to bowel sounds. Note any change in activity (extra soft or loose stool means losing water and hard stool means dehydration).
- Be familiar with tests or examinations that the patient may have had. If enemas or laxatives were given prior to the tests, there will be a fluid loss.
- Replace fluids when the patient has been nil-by-mouth or fluids have been lost through test preparation.
- Obtain a drug history.
- Provide cups, glasses and jugs that are not too big or heavy for the older person to handle (help those who can't help themselves to fluids).
- Offer other fluids in addition to water. Find out the types of beverages liked and fluid temperature preferred.
- Remember that coffee acts as a diuretic. Fluid loss by coffee should be supplemented to compensate for the fluid loss.
- Note skin turgor and mucous membranes.
- Note increases in pulse and respiration and decrease in blood pressure (suggestive of dehydration).
- Check laboratory values for changes: sodium, blood urea nitrogen, haematocrit, haemoglobin, urine and serum osmolarity, and creatinine. Also check for signs of acidosis.
- Weigh the patient daily at the same time and on the same scales.

Source: Gasper PM. Fluid intake: what determines how much patients drink? *Geriatr Nurs* 1988, 9:221.

rhoea and other colon discomforts. Cooked dried beans are a good source of fibre; kidney beans, split peas and peanuts can be served in casseroles and soups. These are all relatively inexpensive and nutritious, in addition to having high fibre content (*see* **Box 6.8** for examples of foods containing fibre).

Osteoporosis

Osteoporosis is the most common skeletal disorder in the world, second only to arthritis in older adults. This often debilitating and painful metabolic disorder affects four times as many women as men and has been linked to various causative factors among which are dietary deficiencies, specifically an inadequate intake of calcium and vitamin D.

The menopause causes an accelerated rate of bone loss in women, and they are likely to reach the fracture threshold well before men. A study by Wickham *et al.* (1989) found that women over 85 years of age were four times more likely to suffer a hip fracture compared with women in the 65–74 years age band. Spector *et al.* (1990) also found a female-to-male ratio of 4:1 in the incidence of hip fractures. The sedentary lifestyle of some older adults is also believed to increase the risk of osteoporosis (*see* Chapter 11). The evidence is that very few older adults continue with exercise. This low level of fitness and lack of activity is discussed later in the chapter.

Other factors which are thought to affect bone density include being underweight, a body mass index below 20 and cigarette smoking. The dietary link with osteoporosis is open to much debate. It is accepted that heavy alcohol consumption affects bone density, and to some extent being a vegetarian increases bone density. However, Webb and Copeman (1996) suggest that interpretation of this data is complex and controversial. Controversy also surrounds the relationship between calcium nutrition and bone health. Some studies have shown that there is little evidence that dietary calcium has much impact on bone density. Vitamin D is required for efficient absorption of calcium from food and deposition in the bone. The main source of vitamin D is exposure to sunlight, and there is evidence that older adults in care homes can lack this exposure. Webb and Copeman (1996) reiterate the need for architects of care facilities to address this problem. Although the debate continues, there is a strong case for ensuring that older adults receive an adequate intake of calcium and vitamin D.

Malnutrition

Malnutrition encompasses more than pathological states that result from a deficiency of essential nutrients and calories. It also refers to significant deviations in dietary patterns, which may produce undesirable risk factors. These can be detected in physical examinations, biochemical studies and physiological tests. Included in malnutrition are specific nutrient deficiencies, nutritional imbalances and obesity (*see* **Figure 6.3** for a trajectory of malnutrition).

Protein calorie malnutrition (PCM) is the inadequate intake of calories and protein at the expense of a high carbohydrate, low-protein diet (Gupta *et al.* 1988). Symptoms include weight loss, pallor, dry flaky skin and loss of muscle mass. Biochemical analysis reveals low serum albumin and transferrin levels if the malnutrition has been long term. Otherwise, there is no evidence of hypoproteinaemia. Normochromic or normocytic anaemia is present and older people are also susceptible to infection. Older people who spend longer than 2 weeks in hospital are at high risk from this nutritional problem. PCM also occurs in the presence of poor nutritional intake due to socioeconomic status, loss of dentition, gastrointestinal (GI) malabsorption and functional disorders. Generally, older adults complain of fatigue, weakness, dyspnoea on exertion and ankle oedema. All of these complaints can be attributed to anaemia and congestive heart failure, when in reality the symptoms may be due to PCM. If PCM occurs in the presence of congestive heart failure, it is important to be on the look out for digitalis toxicity. This is because the symptoms of anorexia, nausea and vomiting associated with this form of toxicity are also precipitators of PCM. Because PCM may coexist with other disorders, it is important to have a medical evaluation and imperative that a complete nutritional history is included (see **Table 6.5** for clinical signs of nutritional status).

Malnutrition in hospitals is well documented. Older adults who are at high risk of malnutrition include those who have psychosocial and mechanical difficulty. In **Box 6.9** are examples of situations that increase the risk of malnutrition in older people.

Nutrition guidelines for hospital catering attempt to address some of the problems related to poor nutrition in hospital. However, a person need not be ill or hospitalised to have or develop one or more mechanical or psychosocial nutritional risk factors. Nutritional deficiencies develop from diets that are monotonous, destructive and low in energy and nutrient/calorific ratio.

6.8 High Fibre Choices

- Dried beans (kidney, split peas, limas, garbanzo, pinto, black peas, others: baked beans).
- Bran cereals. Whole-wheat and other whole-grain products: cereals – rye, oats, buckwheat, stone-ground wholemeal; breads, pastas, pizzas, pancakes, rolls made with whole-grain flour.
- Dried apricots, figs, prunes, dates, raisins.
- Fresh or frozen beans; peas.
- Greens: cabbage, kale, collards, Swiss chard, turnip tops, Brussel sprouts
- Sweetcorn.
- Baked potato with skin; also mashed or boiled.
- Broccoli.
- Carrots.
- Green beans.
- Raspberries, blackberries, cranberries, strawberries
- Bananas.
- Apples, pears, plums.

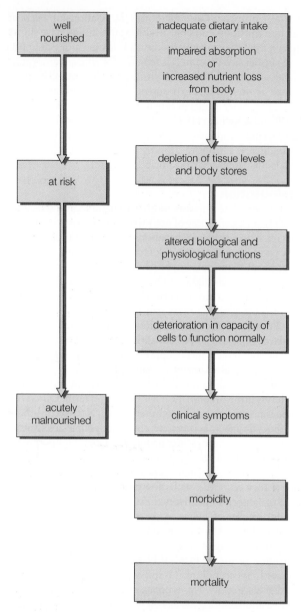

Figure 6.3 A trajectory for malnutrition. (Source: adapted from Prodabsky M. In: Mahan LK, Arlin MT, eds. *Krause's food nutrition and diet therapy*, ed 8. Philadelphia: WB Saunders, 1992.)

6.9 Factors that Increase Risk of Malnutrition in Older People

- Psychosocial risk factors.
- Limited income.
- Abuse of alcohol and other central nervous system depressants.
- Bereavement, loneliness or living alone.
- Removal from usual cultural patterns.
- Confusion, forgetfulness or disorientation.
- Working toward intentional or subintentional death.
- Mechanical risk factors.
- Decreased or limited strength and mobility.
- Neurological deficits, arthritis, handicap, impairment of hand-arm coordination, loss of tongue strength and dysphagia.
- Decreased or diminished vision or blindness.
- Inability to feed self.
- Pressure sores.
- Loss of teeth, poor-fitting dentures or chewing problems.
- Difficulty breathing.
- Polypharmacy.
- Surgery, nil-by-mouth for extended periods of time or intravenous therapy only.

(1) Assessment of past and/or potential difficulties in eating and drinking.
(2) Enabling the client to eat and drink.
(3) Monitoring and evaluating the nutritional status and nutritional care of the client.

Tierney (1996) provides a review of the literature and reiterates that slow acquisition and application of available knowledge are responsible for lack of progress in tackling the problem of malnutrition in hospital. Publication of The Community Health Council (1997) paper Hungry in Hospital clearly identifies the problems, some of which fall within the remit of nurses. The report suggests that guidelines do not seem to be implemented and that in some hospitals, no one is taking responsibility to ensure patients are eating. It appears that much remains to be done to ensure that this basic biological need is met.

Ethics of Nutrition

Food Fads
Older adults are not immune to food faddism and some people may fall prey to advertisements that claim specific foods maintain youth and vitality or treat chronic conditions. Fad foods are often more costly than a balanced diet and can sometimes only be obtained in health-food stores or by mail order. Even if the food is easily obtained in a supermarket, such large quantities may be called for that some nutrients are obtained in excess, whilst others are excluded.

Megavitamin therapy, or the ingestion of large amounts

In 1993, The Royal College of Nursing highlighted the level of malnutrition suffered by older adults and suggested that this problem is widespread in hospitals. Health-care professionals do not appear to view nutrition as a priority and there is a failure to recognise the specific nutritional needs of older adults. In the light of these findings, a set of comprehensive standards have been developed for use by registered nurses which aim to reinforce existing knowledge. The following three standards form the basis of the document:

Clinical Signs of Nutritional Status

Features	Good nutritional status	Poor nutritional status	Signs of malnutrition
General appearance	Alert, responsive	Listless, apathetic, cachectic	—
Hair	Shiny, lustrous, healthy scalp	Stringy, dull, brittle, dry, depigmented	—
Face			Swollen: dark cheeks and dark areas under eyes; skin on nose and mouth lumpy or flaky; enlarged parotid glands
Neck (glands)	No enlargement	Thyroid enlarged	Thyroid enlarged
Eyes	Bright, clear; no fatigue circles beneath	Dry, signs of infection, increased vascularity, glassiness, thickened conjunctiva	Dull; membranes dry and either too pale or too red; triangular, shiny grape-like spots on conjunctiva; bloodshot ring around cornea
Lips	Good colour, moist	Dry, scaly, swollen, angular lesions (stomatitis)	Red, swollen, especially corners of mouth
Tongue	Good pink colour, surface papillae present, no lesions	Papillary atrophy, smooth appearance; swollen, red, beefy (glossitis)	Swollen, appears raw, purple; abnormal papillae
Gums	Good pink colour; no swelling or bleeding, firm	Marginal redness or swelling, receding, spongy	Same as poor nutritional status; bleed easily
Teeth	Straight, no crowding, well-shaped jaw, clean, no discoloration	Unfilled cavities, caries, absent teeth, worn surfaces, mottled malposition	Same as poor nutritional status
Skin (general)	Smooth, slightly moist; good colour	Rough, dry, scaly, pale, pigmented irritated, petechia, bruises	—
Face and neck	Smooth, slightly moist; good colour, reddish pink mucous membranes	Greasy, discoloured, scaly	More extensive than in poor nutritional status
Nails			Spoon shaped, brittle, ridged
Physique (musculoskeletal system)	Well developed, firm; no malformations. Erect, arms and legs straight; abdomen in, chest out. No tenderness, weakness, or swelling; good colour of legs	Flaccid, poor tone; undeveloped, tender. Bow legs, knock-knees, chest deformity at diaphragm, beaded ribs, prominent scapulas. Sagging shoulders, sunken chest, humped back. Oedema, tender calf, tingling, weakness of legs	Same as for poor nutritional status but more extensive; muscles wasted; bow legs, knock-knees, bumps on ribs, swollen joints
Weight	Normal for height, age, body build	Overweight or underweight	—
Abdomen	Flat	Swollen	
Nervous system	Good attention span for age; does not cry easily, not irritable or restless	Inattentive, irritable	Irritable and confused; burning and tingling sensation of hands and feet; loss of sensation of position, decreased ankle and knee reflexes
Internal function			Heart rate above 100; abnormal rhythm; enlarged spleen and liver; high blood pressure
Gastrointestinal function	Good appetite and digestion; normal regular	Anorexia, indigestion, constipation or diarrhoea Easily fatigues, no energy, falls asleep during the day, looks tired, apathetic	—

Sources: Russel RM *et al.* In Calkins E, Davis PJ, Ford AB, eds. *The practice of geriatrics.* Philadelphia: WB Saunders, 1986; Ebert NJ. Nutrition in the aged. In: Yurick AG, Spier BE, Ebert NJ *et al. The aged person and the nursing process,* 3rd ed. Norwalk: Appleton Lange, 1989; Podrabsky M. In: Mahan LK, Arlin MT, eds. *Krause's food nutrition and diet therapy,* 8th ed. Philadelphia: WB Saunders, 1992.

Table 6.5 Clinical signs of nutritional status.

of a specific vitamin or many different vitamins, can also be considered a fad. Unless the individual is severely depleted of vitamins that can usually be obtained in an adequate diet, megavitamin therapy is nonessential and dangerous. Risks exist in megavitamin therapy: bone meal, a source of calcium, may contain lead and thus cause lead poisoning; high doses of zinc causes zinc toxicity; and kelp, with its high iodine content, can cause goitre in those with pre-existing thyroid enlargement. High intake of niacin is discouraged because of increased incidence of cardiac arrhythmias, abnormal biochemical findings and GI problems. Increased intake of vitamin D has the potential for toxicity and for vitamins C and E there is insufficient data to warrant recommendation. The money spent on food fads and unneeded vitamins by older adults could buy more economical foods that benefit the individual's health. Megavitamin therapy has a role in maintaining nutrition when illness, malnutrition or excessive demands are placed on body function.

Feeding the Impaired Older Adult

Studies carried out in institutions have shown that feeding a patient is viewed by qualified staff as time consuming and having a low priority; often this task is given to the most junior members of staff. Feeding older adults who do not respond intelligibly becomes mechanical and devoid of conversation and feeling. Depending on the time the caregiver is allotted for feeding the patient, the feeding process may be too rapid or too slow, and in the latter case the meal may be ended abruptly. Any pleasure that could be derived through socialisation and eating is destroyed and dignity that should be maintained while depending on others for food is lost. Food should be given with variety throughout the meal; that is, serve a bite of one item, then another, and so forth. This not only eliminates the monotony of eating all of one food before being given another, but by changing textures, eating enjoyment is enhanced.

Watson's work (1993) revolves around the characteristic eating difficulties experienced by older people suffering from dementia. These include refusal to eat, spitting out food and dysphagia. Watson emphasises the importance of detailed observation and assessment, so that the most appropriate interventions are employed. Anytime a patient has not eaten a meal, or has refused as few as three consecutive meals, it is essential that a nutritional assessment be done to prevent malnutrition and its complications. In the acute care hospital setting it is equally important to give consideration, care and attention to the feeding of the dependent older patient. Sufficient time should be provided to accommodate the older person who has a slow eating pace. It is crucial that mealtimes are supervised by a first level nurse who is responsible for ensuring that the patient receives a meal, that they are given any assistance required to eat it and that food is not removed until the patient has finished eating.

Intentional Starvation

Refusal of food can be an acceptable means of suicide to the older person. Some older adults have given up and wish to die. Not eating is one last bastion of control over life and dignity. It is essential for the nurse to differentiate between the individual who is refusing food because it is unpalatable and the person who is depressed and really wishes to die. Intentional starvation is easier and more successful when the person is not living in an institution. The institutionalised person may be denied this right and robbed of the option by forced feeding via nasogastric tube. Watching someone starve is difficult for all members of the caring team and it is essential that ethical dilemmas such as this are discussed openly with the patient's point of view central to the discussion. There is no easy answer but it can be helpful if the rights and responsibilities of patient and carers are discussed and documented. Some large hospitals now have clinical ethics committees which can help clinicians assess the situation, and facilitate their ethical decision making. If the patient is intent on refusing to eat the nurse can demonstrate a duty of care by continuing to order meals and taking them to the patient, in the acknowledgement that the individual has the right to eat or not eat. It is important to leave the tray so that the person can exercise the option to change his or her mind. If the person is unable to feed him/herself, check soon after the first offering of food has been refused to see if the person now wishes to eat.

An empathetic and nonjudgmental approach by the nurse to the older person who demonstrates starvation behaviour will convey that the individual is still in control, and if for some reason the older person decides to exercise the option to eat again, this too is all right. Either way, the nurse has provided support and respect for that individual.

Assessment

Weight alone is an inaccurate measurement of nutritional status, since it does not indicate the adequacy of the diet. An individual can meet the correct weight value for height, but the weight may be the result of fluid retention, oedema or ascites. The adequacy of muscle mass and body fat are not assessed, yet these are the two measurements that can provide accurate information about body nutrition. A nutritional assessment that provides the most conclusive data about a person's actual nutrition state consists of four steps: interview, physical examination, anthropometric measurements and biochemical analysis. The collective results provide the data needed to identify the immediate and potential nutrition problems of the client. The nurse can then begin to establish plans for supervision, assistance and education in the attainment of adequate nutrition for the older person.

The Interview

The interview provides background information and clues to the nutritional state and actual and potential problems of the older person. Questions should be asked about the individual's state of health, social activities, normal patterns and changes that have occurred. The nurse must explore the individual's needs, the manner in which food is obtained and the client's ability to prepare food. Information concerning the relationship of food to daily events will provide clues to the meaning and significance of food to that person. Older adults who eat alone are considered candidates for marginal malnutrition. Information about occupation and daily activities will suggest the degree of energy expenditure and calorific intake most correct for the overall activity. Financial status will have a direct bearing on nutrition. It is, therefore, important to explore the client's financial resources to establish available income for food. Knowledge of medications taken should be included in the nutrition history; additional medical information should be included in the interview.

The presence or absence of mouth pain or discomfort, visual difficulty, bowel and bladder function, and food intake patterns should be explored. When the older person cannot provide all the information requested, it may be possible to obtain data from a family member or another source. There will be times, however, when information will not be as complete as the nurse would like, or the older person, too proud to admit that he or she is not eating, will furnish erroneous information. The nurse will still be able to obtain additional data from the other three areas of the nutritional assessment.

Keeping a dietary record for 3 days is another means of assessment. Careful recording of when food is eaten, what is eaten and amounts eaten must be made. This approach can only be attempted with a dependable and motivated client. Portion size and the depth of information should be discussed beforehand; for example, slices of bread or serving spoons of a vegetable.

Physical Examination

Physical examination provides clinically observable evidence of the existing state of nutrition. Data such as height and weight; vital signs; condition of the tongue, lips and gums; skin turgor, texture and colour are assessed. The general overall appearance is observed for evidence of wasting. Close inspection of the weight scale shows that there is a gradual decline in weight with increasing age. This is different from the values presented on standard weight charts used to assess the weight of most adult people. The standard charts suggest that persons of different ages, such as a 20-year-old woman and a 40-year-old woman of comparable height, should also weigh about the same. The nurse should be sure that assessment of weight for older adults is based on schedules specifically developed for older adults and not those that were created for individuals under 51 years of age. Irrespective of care context, it is important that weight is checked at regular intervals so as to monitor changes over a period of time.

Weight, however, is not the only issue; fat distribution needs to be considered. Dr William Castelli, head of the Framingham Heart Study, indicated that fat stored above the waist is associated with hypertension and raised cholesterol levels. Lower body weight is benign. A man's waist should not exceed the hips at its largest diameter, and a woman's waist

Meeting Nutritional Needs

Willie Grace has been a widower for 10 years. After retirement, he worked as a messenger for a city firm until his wife died. He lives alone in a one-roomed flat in the city centre. He has a son who lives on the coast who visits once or twice each fortnight. His son keeps trying to persuade him to move in with him because he realises that his father's accommodation is no longer suitable for his needs. However, Mr Grace is reluctant to leave the area where he has spent most of his life saying, 'I've lived in this city all my life and this is where I belong'.

During his working life, Mr Grace was employed as a chef in some of the grandest hotels of the time and had even grilled steak for King George VI. He can normally manage the two flights of stairs but only slowly, as his knees are stiff and painful, particularly first thing in the morning. He can get to the post office, local shops, laundrette, pub, betting shop and local café, which he uses weekdays in order to get a hot meal. He says, 'I enjoy a good fry-up at the weekend'.

The kitchen consists of a cooker and sink at the top of the stairs, and the kitchen area looks particularly unclean. Mr Grace appears overweight. You are able to check his waist measurement, which confirms that he is at risk. You are visiting him to undertake the over seventy-fives' health assessment.

- **What are Mr Grace's comments that provide subjective evidence?**
- **What information can the nurse herself obtain from observations and examination that will provide objective data for a holistic nursing assessment?**
- **Suggest two unmet needs that may be the most significant to Mr Grace at this time.**
- **Suggest the nursing aims for each unmet need, reflecting realistic outcomes and using concrete and measurable terms.**
- **Suggest one or more interventions for each area of unmet need, justifying your choice of intervention.**

should not exceed 80% of her hip diameter. Men with a waist measurement greater than 102 cm. and women with a waist measurement greater than 88 cm. are considered to be at substantial risk of coronary heart disease and noninsulin dependent diabetes mellitus (Scottish Intercollegiate Guidelines Network, 1996).

Anthropometric Measurements

Anthropometric measurements should include height, weight, mid-arm circumference and triceps skin-fold thickness. These measurements provide information about the status of the person's muscle mass and body fat in relation to height and weight. However, Lehmann (1992) points out that skin-fold measurements are subject to error, as these are increased in older people due to the changing composition of body compartments. Also, in some instances, an individual is bedridden or confined to a chair, or the individual has a spinal curvature preventing accurate height measurement. In these situations, the arm span from mid sternum to fingertips (demi-span) can be used as a surrogate for height. The measurement is then related to weight, in a formula which provides an alternative approach to the calculation of nutritional status (Kwok and Whitelaw, 1991).

Biochemical Examination

Biochemical examination includes an analysis of the pH; the presence or absence of protein, glucose and acetone in the urine; and the levels of haemoglobin, total protein, serum albumin, serum transferrin (tends to be a more accurate reflection of protein status than serum albumin), cholesterol and the haematocrit ratio in the blood. Data directly related to the present nutritional state can be gathered and evaluated. When the older person cannot provide information or tolerate a full nutritional assessment, some information is obtainable from other sources. Based on the nurse's assessment, it may be necessary to refer the older person to a dietitian. However, in most cases the nurse should be able to educate older adults about their nutritional needs and how to meet them effectively.

Interventions

Interventions are formulated around the identified nutritional problem or problems. **Table 6.6** summarises age-related GI changes and health maintenance through diet. Perhaps the most significant intervention for the older person living

Age-Related Gastrointestinal Changes, Outcomes, and Health Prevention, Promotion and Maintenance Approaches		
Age-related changes	Outcomes	Health prevention, promotion and maintenance
Decreased acuity of taste	Diminished taste, food tastes bland, over-seasons food, decreased appetite	Encourage social dining, use herbs for seasoning, lemon, spices (non-salty)
Decreased saliva production with increased alkalinity	Dry mouth, coughing or choking	Suck on ice chips or hard sweets
Brittle teeth/retracted gingiva	Atrophy of gums with loss of teeth or decay, difficulty chewing	Good oral care, use soft bristled tooth brush and dental floss. For dentures, brush to clean between teeth. Consult dentist once or twice a year
Decreased oesophageal and intestinal motility	Dysphagia	Cut food into small pieces, chew thoroughly, hold cold water in mouth before swallowing
Decrease in gastric secretions	Heartburn/indigestion	Have abdominal pain evaluated
Decreased blood flow to intestines, reduced blood flow to liver	Nausea/vomiting	Have a regular meal pattern
Weaker neural impulses to lower bowel, loss or diminished anal sphincter control	Diarrhoea, constipation, faecal impaction, malnutrition, drug toxicity	Increase dietary fibre, fluids and exercise. Respond promptly to the urge to defecate. Report any change in bowel routine. Recognise signs of drug toxicity

Table 6.6 Age-related gastrointestinal changes, outcomes and health prevention, promotion and maintenance approaches.

in the community is nutrition education. Problem solving, as how best to resolve the potential or actual nutritional deficit, also has significant benefits. For older people in hospital or living in a care home, it is crucial that they receive appropriate supervision at mealtimes, so that they are able to eat their food. In addition, the creation of an environment and atmosphere which promotes social interaction at mealtimes is likely to contribute to the enjoyment of food.

BOWEL ELIMINATION

Normal Frequency

It has been suggested that normal frequency of bowel action varies between 2–3 movements daily to only 2–3 per week (Kassianos, 1993; Irvine, 1996). Norton (1996) cites a large-scale prospective study in which less than one-third of women defecated daily. However, Irvine (1996) reminds us that what is considered normal on taking a Western refined diet, high in animal fat and low in fibre, is far from optimal as evidenced by the high rate of bowel cancer. Normal elimination should be an easy passage of stool, without undue straining or a feeling of incomplete evacuation on defecation.

Constipation

According to Norton (1996), there is no universal or accepted meaning of constipation. Constipation has different meanings to different people. Some individuals consider constipation as infrequent bowel action, others perceive it as difficulty in passing faeces and others consider both to be indicative. Williams and Roe (1995) refer to constipation as the infrequent passage of stool or excessive straining on defecation. It has been suggested that 20% of people over 65 years of age are affected by constipation (Rouse *et al.* 1991). Kassianos (1993) estimates that constipation accounts for 13 consultations per year for every 1000 patients on a general practitioner's list. As constipation or altered bowel habit and bleeding are the most common symptoms of bowel cancer, it is important that the cause of constipation is properly investigated. In the UK, bowel cancer is the third most common cancer (Imperial Cancer Research Fund, 1996). Generally, simple constipation (that which has no underlying bowel pathology – Irvine, 1996) appears to be more of a problem for older people, as evidenced by increased laxative use with age (Barrett, 1993). It is thought that the extensive use of laxatives by older people is related to upbringing. During their formative years, today's older people consumed weekly doses of rhubarb, cascara and other types of laxatives, in the belief that a daily bowel action rid the body of toxins and was, therefore, paramount to maintaining good health.

Surveys of older people in hospital suggest a higher incidence of constipation in those who are in poor health. A survey involving over 1,500 older patients in Oxford hospitals found that 44% were suffering from constipation (Williams

6.10 Causes of Constipation

- Insufficient dietary fibre.
- Inadequate fluid intake.
- Laxative abuse, diminished muscle tone and motor function.
- Blunting or loss of the defecation reflex.
- Environmental factors resulting in postponement of defecation.
- Lack of food intake or anorexia associated with depression.
- Use of drugs that slow intestinal motility or increase the excretion of body water.
- Organic illness such as hypothyroidism or hypocalcaemia.
- Tumours or strictures.

and Roe, 1995). In an earlier survey in 1992, from a group of hospitals in Leeds, it was found that on admission 50% of patients were receiving some form of regular treatment for constipation (Webb and Copeman, 1996). **Box 6.10** lists the causes of constipation.

Assessment

A thorough history should be obtained from the client. An assessment which incorporates biographical knowledge is helpful in establishing what approaches would be acceptable to the client. Questions should be asked that shed light on the possible cause or causes of altered bowel function (**Box 6.11**). The frequency of bowel action, stool consistency and need to strain should be assessed (Williams and Roe, 1995). The activity level and eating patterns, including fluid intake, are all important segments of the assessment. The older person should be asked whether they feel any sensation concerning the need to defecate. The presence of haemorrhoids or anal fissures should be noted together with the presence of blood on defecation. Laxative use and type should be documented. A rectal digital examination will reveal cases of faecal impaction with hard stools but may be unreliable if stools are soft (Barrett, 1993). Biochemical tests should include calcium and potassium levels, complete blood count and thyroid studies.

Intervention

Although many older people regularly use laxatives, more natural methods of relieving constipation can be recommended. Acceptable lifestyle changes which involve an increase in exercise, dietary fibre and fluid intake are likely to be helpful. Increasing dietary fibre will increase the bulk of the stool and reduce transit time through the bowel. Recommended foods that can prevent constipation are whole-grain breakfast cereals; wholemeal bread; brown rice; fruit and vegetables, especially with edible skins; pulses such

6.11 Constipation Assessment Questions and Rationale

Question	Rationale
When did constipation begin?	Lifelong history of constipation is likely to be a functional disorder; sudden changes may be an organic lesion such as carcinoma
Has anything in bowel function recently changed?	A sudden change even in constipation may signal an underlying disorder.
How often do bowel movements occur?	Frequency of defecation may actually be normal. The question may also unknowingly describe their use of uperients.
Is the urge to defecate lacking or the stool difficult to expel?	Absent urge may indicate chronic suppression of normal function or neurological disorder. Difficult passage of stool may be due to fibre or fluid deficit, medication use or thyroid disorder.
Is pain associated with defecation?	Pain implies faecal impaction of rectum, anorectal fissures or intestinal obstruction.
Is blood evident in bowel movement?	Witnessed, usually is haemorrhoid bleeding, tear or fissure.
What medications are taken, including over-the-counter drugs?	Multiple drugs are capable of causing constipation.

ical position for passing stool, a position closer to a squat, and enables the use of abdominal muscles. This may ease evacuation if there is difficulty and straining. **Box 6.12** summarises the interventions for prevention of constipation.

Faecal impaction

Faecal impaction is most common in those who are mentally and physically debilitated and need to rely on others for toileting. The causes are similar to constipation. Unrecognised, unattended or neglected constipation eventually leads to faecal impaction and faecal incontinence (spurious diarrhoea), which occurs as a result of a ball-valve effect that allows liquid stool to seep around the obstructing faecal mass during normal colon contractions. Barrett (1993) has also described a type of faecal loading that consists of soft putty-like stool. He suggests that this may be caused by laxatives and excess fibre.

Intervention

Management of faecal impaction requires the removal of the hard, compacted or putty-like stool from the rectum. An oil-retention enema may be used to soften hard faeces, prior to the use of evacuation enemas or in preparation for manual removal. An alternative is a dioctyl sodium (stool softener) enema. Use of suppositories is not very effective, since their action is blocked by the amount and size of the stool in the rectum as compared with the capacity of the sphincter to dilate. Suppositories do not facilitate the removal of stool in the sigmoid colon, which may continue to ooze once the rectum is emptied. Seven to 10 days may be required to totally empty the sigmoid colon and rectum of impacted faeces. The

6.12 Types of Interventions for Constipation

- **Dietary manipulation**
  6–8 glasses of fluid daily.
  High fibre.

- **Postprandial use of toilet**

- **Sitting on toilet for at least 10 minutes**

- **Exercise**

- **Pharmacological**
  Bulk-forming laxatives.
  Stool softeners.
  Stimulant laxatives.
  Osmotic laxatives.
  Rectally administered: enemas and suppositories.

as baked beans, kidney beans and lentils; dried fruit; and nuts. However, Webb and Copeman (1996) suggest exercising caution in adding bran to the diet of an older person who normally has a diet low in dietary fibre. The addition of bran must be carried out slowly otherwise the client may complain of abdominal pains, diarrhoea and flatulence. Other problems can also occur, in particular a reduction in the absorption of calcium and iron by the body. Extra fluids must be taken if iron has been prescribed.

Exercise is important as an intervention to stimulate colon motility and bowel evacuation. Daily walking, pelvic tilt exercises and range of motion (passive or active) exercises are beneficial for those who are less mobile. Sometimes the lavatory pedestal or commode is too high, so that the person is unable to push down with their abdominal muscles. Placing the feet on a foot stool aligns the colon in the normal anatom-

Meeting Bowel Elimination Needs

Maud Dixon, at 80 years old, can truthfully say to her visiting community nurse that she has never had problems with her bowel movements. They have always been regular each morning, about 30 minutes after breakfast. In fact, she hardly thinks of them at all as they have been so consistent. Following a period in hospital for a fractured hip last year she has never regained her reliable pattern of bowel function. She is greatly distressed by this, as bowel function is a symbol to her of good health.

Admittedly, Miss Dixon does not move about as much now and uses a walking frame. She has heard that painkillers sometimes cause constipation, but uses such medication sparingly. She has even re-established her pattern of attempting a bowel movement every morning after breakfast, but begins to worry considerably about her constipation and to use laxatives almost routinely. She says, 'This constipation really upsets me. I just don't feel like myself if I don't have a bowel movement every day'.

- What are Miss Dixon's comments that provide subjective evidence?
- What information can the nurse herself obtain from observations and examination that will provide objective data for a holistic nursing assessment?
- Suggest two unmet needs that may be the most significant to Miss Dixon at this time.
- Suggest the nursing aims for each unmet need, reflecting realistic outcomes and using concrete and measurable terms.
- Suggest one or more interventions for each area of unmet need, justifying your choice of intervention.

emphasis should be on gentleness, any bleeding or pain should be noted and the patient observed for shortness of breath or perspiration. A plain abdominal X-ray will confirm that the bowel has been cleared. Once this is achieved, attention should be directed to the preventive measures already described. The provision of privacy and time to defecate without feeling rushed will facilitate easy and regular bowel function.

REST AND SLEEP

Human beings need rest and sleep to restore the body and its functions and to maintain energy and health. Rest depends on the degree of physical and mental relaxation. It is often assumed that lying in bed constitutes rest, but worry and anxiety cause muscles to remain tense, even though physical activity has ceased. Achievement of rest depends on the interrelationship between body and mind. During later life, personal resources may be taxed by bereavement, chronic ill health and the demands of caring for others. Persistently disturbed sleep can further erode health and progressively wear away the morale and stamina necessary to cope. This section will consider the factors which affect sleep in later life, and how nurses working in a variety of settings can make a proper assessment of sleep and help older people get a better night's rest.

Circadian Rhythms and Sleep

Circadian rhythms affect almost all living creatures. They are continuous cycles of fluctuating activity of physiological, biochemical and behavioural functions. Body temperature, pulse, blood pressure, neurotransmitter, excretion and hormonal levels change significantly and predictably in a circadian rhythm. These internally controlled (endogenous) rhythms are thought to be synchronised to the 24-hour cycle of light and dark. Cues in the external environment such as the change from day to night and vice versa, are known as exogenous cues (Armstrong-Esther and Hawkins, 1982). The hormone melatonin secreted by the pineal gland at the base of the brain is thought to control the sleep–wake cycle. Through neuronal links with the retina, melatonin secretion is stimulated by the effects of bright natural light. Age changes in the eye, the neural pathways and calcification of the pineal gland itself might all contribute to a less efficient response to the light–dark cycle.

When natural cues are missing, they can be compensated for by social cues and routines, such as mealtimes, watching television programmes or listening to the radio. It may be that older people who lose their responsiveness to light and dark come to rely more on social synchronisers, and when these are disturbed, such as on admission to hospital or a care home, sleep disturbance occurs (Armstrong-Esther and Hawkins, 1982). Attention to the older person's routines can help establish the normal sleep–wake cycle and identify the best times to introduce activities, periods of rest and therapeutic measures (see **Table 6.7**). According to Haimov *et al.* (1994), as melatonin secretions decrease in later life and its time of secretion is delayed, there may be a case for melatonin replacement therapy to resynchronise circadian rhythms. Circadian rhythms can also be disrupted by time-zone changes, shift work and physical conditions. Alterations in the usual sleep–wake cycle, sleeping during the day and being wakeful at night can signal serious illness.

Normal Sleep Patterns

Normal sleep pattern consists of rapid eye movement (REM) sleep and non-rapid eye movement (NREM) sleep. NREM sleep consists of four stages. Stages 1 and 2 consist of lighter

Insomnia in Older People	
Problem	**Care and treatment**
Sleep cycle changes	Educate the patient Encourage daytime activity
Stress overload	Teach relaxation measures Encourage deep breathing
Pain/discomfort	Provide comfort measures
Anxiety	Explore fears Provide emotional support Suggest physical outlet.
Affective disturbance	Identify problems accurately Educate the client Suggest bedtime tricyclic antidepressant use
Physiological diurnal disturbances	Identify and discuss problem. Clearly demark daytime/night-time differences in activity Suggest energy discharge in daytime Safety measures in environment if night time waking occurs

Table 6.7 Insomnia in older people.

6.13 Phases of the Sleep Cycle

Stage 1 (light sleep)
Drops off to sleep.
Relaxed.
Fleeting thoughts.
Easily awakened.
Remembers being drowsy but not asleep.

Stage 2 (medium deep sleep)
Enters within minutes of stage 1.
More relaxed.
Vague, dreamlike thoughts (fragmentary dreams).
Slow eye movement under eyelids can be observed.
Unmistakably asleep, but easily roused.

Stage 3 (medium deep sleep)
About 20 minutes after stage 1.
Muscles relaxed.
Slower pulse.
Decreased body temperature.
Undisturbed by moderate random stimuli (closing doors, etc.).

Stage 4 (deep sleep)
Restorative sleep.
Very relaxed.
Rarely moves.
Awakens only with vigorous stimuli.
Period during which most sleepwalking, screaming, nightmares and bed-wetting occurs.

REM Sleep (active sleep)
Relieves tensions.
Drifts up from stage 4 every 90–100 minutes (REM sleep resembles stage 1 by electroencephalogram monitoring).
Rapid eye movement.
Head and neck lose tonus, body feels flaccid.
Increased and fluctuating pulse, blood pressure and respirations.
Most dreaming and sleep talking occurs.
When medical crisis occurs (i.e. angina, dyspnoea), most often because of anxiety or fear induced by dreams.

sleep, and stages 3 and 4 involve a deeper sleep known as slow-wave sleep. NREM sleep is predominantly a quiet period when:
- Body secretions in the nose, mouth, throat, eyes, stomach and bile tract are minimal.
- Small-intestine motility is reduced.
- Heart rate slows and systolic pressure is diminished.
- Basal metabolic rate is low.
- There is generalised muscle relaxation.
- Body temperature falls.
- Breathing is slower and more shallow.
- There is no definite eye position, just notable constriction of the pupils (see **Box 6.13**).

Healthy people have a reasonably short sleep latency (time taken to enter stage 1 sleep) of 15–20 minutes, which begins with nodding or dropping off to sleep. This stage is characterised by easy arousal as a result of noise, touch or other stimuli. If awakened, the individual does not realise that dozing has occurred and would describe the state as being similar to daydreaming. At times, as stage 1 sleep is entered, the individual is awakened by muscle jerks or by the sensation of falling which is a phenomenon attributed to initial muscle relaxation. If

undisturbed, stage 2 sleep is quickly entered followed by stage 3, a period of medium deep sleep; stage 4 deep sleep, from which arousal is extremely difficult, soon follows. Individuals deprived of stage 4 sleep have reported feelings of depression, general malaise, apathy and general lethargy. Stage 4 sleep (considered the restorative stage) is markedly reduced in older adults, but the significance of this has not been established.

After about 90 minutes, from the onset of dropping off to sleep, the first episode of REM sleep follows stage 4. This alternating cycle of REM and NREM sleep continues at 90-minute intervals, four to six times a night. The density of REM periods increases as the night progresses, so that REM sleep is most prominent in the early morning hours (Moon, 1991). Dreams during REM sleep tend to be more vivid and elaborate and if an individual is wakened during this time, they can usually recall their dreams. Sleeping in new and unaccustomed surroundings or being exposed to constant loud noise reduces REM sleep. REM sleep appears to be more important for psychological restoration. Bowman (1997) describes a study whereby REM sleep is needed to be able to remember a repetitive task.

Age-related Changes in Sleep Patterns

The structure of sleep changes with age. The sleep latency period may last up to 30 minutes, so it may take longer to fall asleep. It is estimated that the amount of wake time for older adults after sleep onset is approximately two to three times greater after 60 years of age for stage 1 sleep with little change in REM and stage 2 sleep time. REM sleep remains fairly constant across the adult life span, but the periods of deep slow-wave sleep are reduced considerably and may be nonexistent for some older people. This slow wave activity is three to four times greater in a 13-year-old than in a 64-year-old. A small but significant number of females continue to display sustained periods of stage 4 sleep but males over 60 years of age show very little. Stage 4 sleep time is reduced 50% by the age of 50. It is thought that slow-wave sleep decline may be a close correlate of the ageing process in the central nervous system (CNS) across the adult life span. An increase in stage 1 and sometimes stage 2 sleep is experienced and this appears to be characterised by increased sleep fragmentation with more frequent awakening (Morgan, 1987). The number of awakenings increase from one or two to six per night (Bixler and Vela-Bueno, 1987). For the most part, age-related sleep changes are minor and do not interfere with the restorative function of sleep (Foreman and Wykle, 1995). **Figure 6.4** shows a comparison of sleep patterns across the life span.

Quality of Sleep in Later Life

'Good' or 'poor' sleep is a subjective judgment based on body position, movement and personal opinion. A patient or resident may appear to sleep 'well', as nurses' notes (based on closed eyes and no movement in the bed) frequently record. Yet other factors are significant in determining sleep quality. Good sleepers have been described as registering a normal body temperature on awakening and less of a temperature drop in stage 4 sleep than do poor sleepers. Those who sleep poorly have body temperatures that do not rapidly return to normal by the time the individual awakens.

The question arises whether those who are poor sleepers have a different time sequence or rhythm, which is longer than

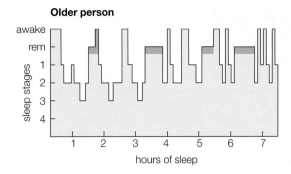

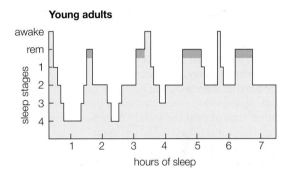

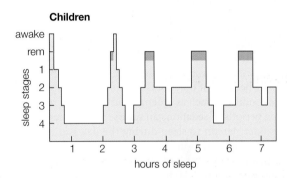

Figure 6.4 Comparison of sleep patterns across the life span. (Source: Kales JC, Carvell M, Kales A. Sleep disorders. In: Castell CK, Riesenberg DE, Sorensen LB, *et al*, eds. *Geriatric Medicine*, ed 2. New York: Springer-Verlag, 1990.)

the established circadian rhythm. Those people with a physiological rhythm not synchronous with the local time clock may sleep longer and arise later than is socially convenient. This is true in residential settings that have specific routines; thus, an individual's body time may lag behind clock time. In a US study, Ancoli-Israel *et al.* (1989) found that nursing-home residents' sleep is more fragmented and on average lasted 1 hour longer than for older people living independently in their own homes. Sleep patterns can be disturbed when REM sleep is altered or stopped through the administration of sedatives and hypnotics or by repeated awakening.

Gall *et al.* (1990) studied the nocturnal activity patterns of hospitalised older adults and found a decreasing amount of sleep over a period of 3 days of the study. These were mainly due to procedural monitoring of vital signs and administration of medicines. The authors concluded that while sleep patterns varied from person to person, the environment was not conducive to sleep. The most common causes of sleep deprivation are difficulty in falling asleep, anxiety or over activity of the mind and intermittent waking because of poor sleep habits, nightmares, or unpleasant dreams. Early morning waking with an inability to return to sleep is viewed as a symptom of depression. Often when asked about the quality of sleep, the older person responds with remarks or complaints that they hardly 'slept a wink'. Frequent and long periods of wakefulness occur during the night. The interruptions may be a result of nocturnal micturition, leg cramps (usually in men), nightmares (more characteristic of women), and mental stimulation through worry, bereavement or extraneous noises in the environment. Women tend to go to bed earlier than men, but both rise later in the morning. Monk *et al.* (1991) noted that older people had an earlier habitual time of awakening and a circadian orientation associated with longer sleep in the morning.

Older people spend more total time in bed to achieve the same amount of restorative sleep that they had in their younger years. Ancoli-Israel *et al.* (1989) found that older people living in nursing homes spent substantially more time in bed to obtain the same amount of sleep as those living independently. It was thought at one time that the older person needed more sleep, but this is not necessarily true. Older people seem to sleep less; if an older person sleeps more, it is usually because of boredom, sedation or a symptom of disease conditions such as uraemia and cardiac or renal failure. Long periods of sedation can reverse sleep patterns, causing the older person to sleep during the day and be awake at night. Discontinuation of sedation can re-establish the older person's sleep pattern. Those older people who are lonely, cold and bored may go to bed about 6 p.m. or 7 p.m. in the evening. When they awaken in the early morning hours, they do not understand why sleep does not return. To them this constitutes insomnia.

Sleep–Wake Disorders

Disorders of Initiating and Maintaining Sleep and Disorders of Excessive Somnolence

Generally speaking, insomnia describes disturbed sleep with impairment of either its quantity or quality, and frequently leads to tiredness the following day (Jago, 1995). The older person will complain of daytime drowsiness which they attribute to a poor night's sleep. Insomnia affects approximately 35% of those over 65 years of age. Although older women are more likely to report dissatisfaction, sleep disturbance is actually increased in older men. Older men wake more frequently and have a slightly shorter sleep time than older women (Morgan, 1987). The prevalence increases in a linear fashion with age and there is no clear social class gra-

dient (Lader, 1992). Insomnia is a symptom; successful resolution depends on understanding and addressing the individual's special mix of contributing factors. These factors may be biological, medical, emotional or bedtime routines which do not promote sleep.

Insomnia can be transient or persistent (Moon, 1991). Transient insomnia occurs as a result of environmental changes, stress, anxiety or some kind of conflict, and lasts for up to 3 weeks. Resolution occurs without medical intervention when the individual adapts to the changes or removes them. Persistent insomnia describes sleep problems which last over 3 weeks and those which recur throughout life. Persistent insomnia occurs most frequently in people with mental health problems, chronic drug and alcohol dependency, dementia or serious physical illnesses or conditions. This form of insomnia requires concentrated medical and psychiatric attention.

Those older people who experience disorders of initiating sleep and disorders of excessive somnolence will have delayed sleep onset and increased residual muscular activity (due to anxiety) that will cause them to awaken frequently. Sleep will be fragmented, and where anxiety is a major factor there is decreased REM and slow-wave sleep. Frequent daytime drowsiness follows (Moon, 1991).

Sleep Apnoea

Sleep apnoea is thought to affect up to 5% of 40–60 year olds (Moon, 1991). In a US study comparing episodes of sleep apnoea for nursing-home residents with those of older community dwellers, 42% of nursing-home residents had five or more episodes of apnoea per hour of sleep, whilst 4% of 427 community dwellers had 20 or more apnoea episodes per hour (Ancoli-Israel *et al.* 1989). Recognition of this disorder is usually through the symptoms of snoring, interrupted breathing of at least 2 seconds and unusual daytime sleepiness.

Nurses are very likely to observe episodes of sleep apnoea in older people admitted to hospital with congestive cardiac failure. Sleep apnoea syndrome can lead to chronic heart failure, pulmonary hypertension and death during sleep. It is particularly hazardous for people who have this syndrome to take hypnotic medications to induce sleep. Sleep apnoea may occur in individuals who may not have any respiratory problem while awake. During sleep, breathing may be interrupted as many as 30 times and apnoeic episodes may last at least 10 seconds (Moon, 1991). At least 30 apnoeic episodes in 7 hours of nocturnal sleep is diagnostic of sleep apnoea syndrome (Morgan, 1987). It is thought that sleep apnoea occurs for two reasons:

(1) CNS mechanisms in which thoracic breathing movements cease, cause a complete absence of ventilatory effort and a constant intrathoracic pressure. Respiration resumes when a person is aroused. Central apnoea is associated with brainstem disorders and bulbar damage, or it is idiopathic.

(2) Oropharyngeal membranes collapse or are obstructed by excess tissue. Individuals make increasingly greater attempts to breathe against the obstruction until air is

forced through the upper airway with a loud snorting sound. Obstructive apnoea is associated with hypertrophy of adenotonsillar or buccal tissue, or it may be idiopathic.

Those most likely to have sleep apnoea are adult men with a long history of loud intermittent snoring. Hypertension and cardiac arrhythmias are common and people who have had a stroke may be at increased risk. Commonly these individuals are obese and have short, thick necks. Symptoms of sleep apnoea include loud and periodic snoring, broken sleep with frequent nocturnal waking, and unusual night-time activity such as sitting upright, sleep walking and falling out of bed. It seems that additional symptoms such as memory changes, depression, excessive daytime sleepiness, morning headaches, nocturia and orthopnoea result from sleep apnoea. Assessment includes information from the sleeping partner as well as observation of signs and symptoms noted above. Sleep assessment will be detailed later in this section. Specific treatment of sleep apnoea may involve weight loss, surgery to remove redundant tissue or medical management. It is suggested that the sufferer avoids drugs with analeptic effects, particularly alcohol. Anything that interferes with the arousal response is exceedingly dangerous. Extra pillows or sleeping in a chair are sometimes helpful. Ordinarily, the individual has quite spontaneously made compensatory adjustments during sleeping time.

Naps

Napping is a sequence of sleeping and waking from less deep sleep. It is a normal pattern that seems to increase with age and is indicative of a different distribution of sleep. Moon (1991), cites a US study in which 25–33% of older people take a nap during the day. There tends to be a correlation between age and the length of napping: the older the person the longer the nap. An increased frequency of daytime napping in older adults indicates a change in circadian rhythm (Buysse et al. 1992). Naps tend to peak in late afternoon. Napping is not an attempt to compensate for lost sleep at night; sleep and napping are independent from each other. Naps augment sleep and increase the total amount slept. Afternoon naps provide the deeper slow-wave sleep, a necessity for physical rest. It is speculated that the individual may need napping to restore energy. Napping may be based more on physical health, psychological health and volitional factors, which may mediate daytime sleepiness (Buysse et al. 1992). The average nap lasts from 15–60 minutes; this usually occurs several times a day. If older adults do not nap during the day, they may take several rest periods.

Nocturnal Myoclonus and Restless-leg Syndrome

The syndrome of periodic leg jerks caused by the unconscious contraction of leg muscles during sleep is called nocturnal myoclonus. Contractions may affect one or both legs. A contraction lasts about 0.5–10 seconds and is repeated every 20–40 seconds. Because of the repeated awakenings from this con-

dition, the older person is likely to complain of insomnia and excessive daytime sleepiness. Sometimes the condition is seen in association with chronic renal failure, sleep apnoea and tricyclic antidepressant use. The restless-leg syndrome is characterised by unpleasant sensations in the calf and thigh, which is relieved by movement of the legs. Exercise during the day may help relieve the movements (Johnson, 1994).

Sundown Syndrome/Night Confusion

Sundown syndrome or sundowning (an American term) describes behaviour characterised by recurring confusion and agitation in the late afternoon or early evening. It is thought that psychosocial stressors in conjunction with impaired cognitive function may account for night confusion. Sundown syndrome usually accompanies dementia. Whether this behaviour really increases in the evening or is more noticeable at that time is not known. It is thought that night confusion is the result of brain hypoxia due to the following:

- Biological or biochemical factors such as the effects of drugs, cardiovascular (CV) disorders and dehydration.
- Sensory overload or deprivation.
- Circadian rhythm disruption.
- Psychological stress.
- Isolation.
- Fear.
- Influence of the lunar cycle.
- The weather.

Sundowning is a temporary condition but can be dangerous when it occurs. People may walk out of their own home or care home, or the caregiver may become sleep deprived trying to cope with the night behaviour. The behaviour can also present enormous challenges to nurses. (Evans, 1987) refers to a small study where people with dementia were more than twice as likely to exhibit sundowning. The individuals were 74 years of age and older, 91% of whom had CV or cerebrovascular disorders. Urine odour in the evening but not in the morning (suggestive of dehydration) and frequent wakening for routine nursing care were significantly associated with sundown syndrome. In addition, the individuals were relatively isolated, had fewer visitors and were engaged in fewer activities in the afternoon. Moving an older resident within a care home setting may make adaptation to the new environment and identification of new or missing social cues difficult.

Lower light levels have been previously been linked to sundowning. Satlin et al. (1992) found that pulsating bright light improved the sundowning behaviour of some people with Alzheimer's disease. The authors speculated that the pulsating bright light changed the sleep–wake cycle disturbance. The effect may be attributed to mediation in the chronobiological mechanism. Evans' sample (1987) were observed to be in dim light in the afternoon. Although no definitive conclusions can be drawn from such a small sample, the possibility of melatonin replacement to improve response to the light–dark cycle has already been discussed.

Assessment of an individual for risk factors includes age,

history of delirium or sundowning, cardiovascular disease or dementia, polypharmacy and electrolyte imbalance. Nursing measures might include providing environmental-orientating cues, minimising the relocation of a person within a nursing care setting, frequent night-time monitoring, turning on the lights before dark, and offering soft music or social stimulation in the late afternoon. Restriction of daytime sleep, and exposure to bright light may lead to better night sleep. If all else fails, the use of neuroleptics such as haloperidol or thioridazine is recommended. However, long-term use of these drugs has major complications and side effects require close monitoring.

Sleep and Medications

Older people are often prescribed hypnotics. This may occur in care home and hospital settings when a change in environment, perhaps combined with ill health or other life events, disrupts sleep patterns. There is now much greater understanding of pharmacokinetics in older individuals (*see* Chapter 10). This, together with the dependence, tolerance and rebound insomnia that occur as a result of long-term use of hypnotics, indicates the need for judicious prescribing of hypnotics for older people. Few hypnotic drugs are compatible with the normal sleep cycle. Instead, these drugs depress the necessary REM sleep for the relief of tension and anxiety. When medication is discontinued, normal sleep patterns usually return, but dreaming and nightmares are increased until natural sleep cycles are re-established. Some researchers believe this compensates for dreams that have been depressed or obliterated by REM sleep suppression. Hypnotic drugs often induce night terrors; hallucinations; and paradoxical responses such as agitation instead of relaxation, hangover, depression, and changes in memory, balance and gait. In a study of three different elderly care homes, Clapin-French (1986) found that residents were more likely to be currently taking hypnotics than prior to admission. Seventy-one per cent of patients were taking sleeping medications. It is interesting to note that patients had an earlier bedtime than most had been used to at home and some patients had significant shifts in sleep patterns following admission.

Ideally, prescribed sleeping medication should not change the normal sleep pattern or continue to have an effect after the waking period. Sleep medication should be prescribed sparingly and on a short-term basis. Only when the insomnia is severe and disabling should older people be given hypnotics. Life changes such as bereavement or relocation to a care home, may be the cause of poor sleep patterns and loss of quality sleep. Assessment is crucial to determine the level of insomnia. If hypnotic drugs are necessary, those that are least disruptive to the sleep cycle should be employed. Drug accumulation due to a reduced ability to metabolise the drug quickly (*see* Chapter 10), can be avoided by recommending that medication is taken every 2–3 nights in order to help complete its metabolism. The choice of medication is crucial and prescribers should ensure that medication has a short

half-life and that the lowest effective dose is given. Short-acting benzodiazepines such as chlormethiazole and triazolam have been found useful where rapid sleep induction is necessary but rebound anxiety the following day has been reported. Medium-acting benzodiazepines such as temazepam and lormetazepam are the drugs of choice but for 2 weeks at a time only (Moon, 1991). Jago (1995) suggests that treatment should be for a maximum of 28 days and that professionals should emphasise to the individual that treatment is on a short-term basis. Patients can be weaned off hypnotics after long-term use by a gradual reduction in dose and alternate day use. Nurses can have a supportive role during this time by raising awareness that rebound anxiety and insomnia will occur, and that sleep pattern will improve with time.

Assessment

Nurses are in an excellent position to assess sleep, to improve the quality of the older person's sleep and to study sleep or assist in sleep research by being available at customary sleep times. Sleep history interviews are important and should be obtained from all older clients. Biographical material such as past occupation involving shift work or early rising, is useful here as the older person may adhere to the same sleep–wake routines even in retirement. The nurse can calculate a sleep efficiency score by dividing total sleep time by the total time spent in bed. If the score is less than 0.6, with substantial periods spent awake before getting up, then an earlier getting up time may be beneficial (Morgan and Gledhill, 1991). It is important to enquire about rituals or routines which occur at bedtime. In a small study by Johnson (1991) of community dwelling older people, those with a bedtime routine had fewer complaints about sleep. Men's rituals tended to involve food, drink, television and walking, while women prayed, read and listened to music. Failure to carry out these rituals is likely to interfere with the individual's ability to fall asleep. Other assessment data should include the amount and type of daily exercise; favourite position when in bed; room environment, temperature, ventilation and illumination; and activities engaged in several hours before bedtime.

The lifestyle factors described above can affect sleep quality and are known as sleep hygiene factors. Occasionally, such factors represent the sole major cause of poor sleep patterns or, more typically, interact with and exacerbate a more fundamental cause (Morgan and Gledhill, 1991). For example, drinks containing caffeine such as tea or coffee can delay the onset of sleep. Alcohol may help to induce sleep but in certain quantities can disturb sleep in the latter part of the night; it also has a diuretic effect. Sensitivity to a number of 'sleep antagonists' can change with age, so that determinants such as drinks containing caffeine, noise or keeping irregular hours which previously had minimal effect on sleep now produce a disturbing effect. The older person may not have recognised this influence.

The use of hypnotics as well as other medications taken routinely should be documented. Some medications taken regularly produce side effects that interfere with the ability to sleep. The following common medications are sources of sleep interference:

- Diuretics.
- Anti-parkinsonian medications.
- Certain antidepressants and antihypertensives.
- Steroids.
- Decongestants.
- Medications for the treatment of asthma.

Information about involvement in hobbies, life satisfaction and perception of health status are also important to establish possible depression. The history can be confirmed with the caregiver and family members. An important part of assessment and necessary for the implementation of appropriate intervention is the maintenance of a sleep diary. This information will provide an accurate account of the person's sleep problem and identify any sleep disturbances. If the older person is living communally, a family member or caregiver records specific behaviours on a flow sheet. Ten to fourteen

6.14 Assessing Sleep

- The number of occurrences of a call for assistance to the bathroom, pain medication or subjective symptoms of inability to sleep, such as anxiety.
- If the person is out of bed.
- Whether the person appears to be asleep or awake on rounds.
- Episodes of confusion or disorientation.
- If sleep medication is given and if repeated.
- Time the person awakens in the morning (approximation).
- Whether naps are taken during the day and for how long.

days is required to obtain a clear picture of the sleep problem (Morgan and Gledhill, 1991). Important items to record are listed in **Box 6.14**. With this information, the nurse is ready to initiate a mutually developed plan to enhance the quality of the older person's sleep.

Intervention

Sleep hygiene factors can be manipulated to minimise their disruptive effect on sleep and to optimise the conditions for improving sleep quality. Clients should be warned that changes in bedtime routines or environmental modifications need to be practised every night and that they are unlikely to produce benefits in less than 2 weeks (Morgan and Gledhill, 1991).

Morgan (1987) describes the process of stimulus control as an intervention. Stimulus control is brought about by pre-sleep routines and rituals and the physical aspects of the sleeping environment. The goal of stimulus control is to re-establish or reinforce the association between the sleep environment and sleep itself. An example would be not to use the bedroom for any activity other than for sleeping.

Then if lying awake for longer than 30 minutes to get up and go to another room and to perhaps knit or read for a while before trying once more to fall asleep. Mornhinweg and Voignier (1995) tested the effect of music on the promotion of sleep. Subjects who had some sleep disturbance listened to classical and New Age music before bedtime. All but one of the 25 subjects reported improved sleep using this self-administered intervention. The majority believed that the music helped them fall asleep, return to sleep quicker if awakened during the night, or sleep longer in the morning. Music enabled them to 'turn off' their mind so that they could relax enough to fall asleep.

The use of bright light has also been found to be beneficial. Campbell *et al.* (1993) evaluated the use of bright light

Meeting the Need for Rest and Sleep

Jack Fellows has a sleep disorder and consequently is lethargic during the day and lonely at night. His wife of 35 years has recently insisted on moving into the spare room as she can no longer cope with his loud snoring and periods of interrupted breathing. Mr Fellows suffers from obstructive sleep apnoea. In recent years, he has often awoken abruptly with a feeling of drowning and gasping for air. However, he simply tolerates this discomfiture as he thinks nothing can be done about the problem. Now that it has become a threat to his marriage he has become more motivated to investigate possible solutions. Jack says, 'This doesn't amount to anything, but it annoys my wife'.

Although reluctant to admit to it, Mr Fellows is also worried, as he is beginning to feel rather sleepy during the day. On consulting the practice nurse, he finds that there are some very practical means of dealing with sleep apnoea and, if these prove ineffective, there are additional medical interventions that can be helpful.

- **What are Mr Fellows's comments that provide subjective evidence?**
- **What information can the nurse herself obtain from interview and observations that will provide objective data for a holistic nursing assessment?**
- **Suggest two unmet needs that may be the most significant to Mr Fellows at this time.**
- **Suggest the nursing aims for each unmet need, reflecting realistic outcomes and using concrete and measurable terms.**
- **Suggest one or more interventions for each area of unmet need, justifying your choice of intervention.**

Causes, Reasons and Potential Interventions for Sleep Alterations in Older People

Causes	Reasons	Potential interventions
Arthritis	Pain builds; joints stiffen during periods of activity; pain relief medicine may wear off	Provide comfortable pillows; offer pain medication before pain becomes too intense
Angina pectoris	Pain likely to occur during REM sleep	Keep nitroglycerine at bedside
Chronic obstructive pulmonary disease	Abnormal increases in alveolar tension: decrease in oxygen saturation; prone position causes dyspnoea and stasis of mucus	Patient education regarding self-care Toilet before bedtime; bronchial dilators; prevent fatigue; rest during day; no diuretics in late afternoon; caution to avoid coke, coffee, tea, chocolate; use sedatives and over-the-counter medication with caution
Heart failure	Nocturnal dyspnoea Nocturia	Appropriate cardiotonic regimen; extra pillows; do not take diuretics late in day or in the evening
Diabetes	Inadequate regulation of blood sugar may lead to glycosuria and nocturia; overly tight control of blood sugar Hypoglycaemic attacks (can mimic anxiety attacks)	Control by diet, insulin or oral medication Adjust diabetic regimen Teach regular, adequate caloric intake; bedtime snack
Disturbed sensory perception	Poor environmental lighting; visual difficulties; nocturnal hallucinations; alterations in REM–NREM cycle	Modify environment; check hearing aid; put glasses nearby; reduce noise at home or in hospital; orientate frequently
Alzheimer's disease (AD)	AD patients' sleep shows reduction in stages 3 and 4 sleep early in disease; late in AD these stages disappear; daytime sleepiness increases as disease progresses	Assist staff and family with wandering behaviour and sundown syndrome; major tranquillisers may be needed; be sure person has comfortable chair in which to rest; strict scheduling of night-time bed hours, day naps, and activity periods and needs; for wanderers and behaviour problems, stop all drug treatment to see if normal sleep rhythm returns
Depression	Disturbed sleep pattern: problem falling asleep early morning awakening, decreased total sleep time; barbiturate use can cause fragmented sleep and nightmares	Assess sleep; check for recent discontinued drugs; frequent reassurance; have same caregiver relate to client; tricyclic antidepressants if depression diagnosed
Congestive heart failure	Fluid build up produces symptoms	Restrict fluids at bedtime; prop up on pillows
Peptic ulcers	Gastic juices and stomach acid increases during REM sleep	Provide nightly ulcer medicine
Alcoholism	Abnormal EEG pattern results; as effects wear off, sleeper may awaken with withdrawal symptoms and a hangover	No alcoholic beverages; explain that reformed alcoholics may experience insomnia for 1 year after withdrawal of alcohol
Parkinsonism	Total wake time increase; decreased REM	L-Dopa at bedtime may help decrease rigidity that occurs during the night
Surgical procedures	Premature arousal related to early preparation; anxiety and worry about outcome; pain	Analyse rituals and routines in place. Can they be changed? Keep pain free; monitor vital signs frequently, and promote rest
Cardiac	Discomfort due to environment (noise, temperature, lights); postoperative psychosis (usually follows 24-hour lucid interval)	Modify environment Establish therapeutic rapport early; instruct patient preoperatively; orientate frequently when postoperative; elicit family support
Situational insomnia	On admission to care home or hospital; after visit by relative; after move to new residence; after recent loss or death	Establish one-to-one relationship; provide short-term use of hypnotic

Sources: Wagner D. On sleep and Alzheimer's disease. *Alzheimer's Disease and Related Disorders Newsletter* 1985, 5; Pacini C, Fitzpatrick J. Sleep patterns of hospitalized and non-hospitalized aged individuals. *J Gerontol Nurs* 1982, 8:327; de Brun S. Insomnia: the common sense approach. *Occup Health Nurs* 1981, 29:36; Hemenway J. Sleep and the cardiac patient. *Heart Lung* 1980, 9:453; Raskind M, Eisdorfer C. When elderly patients can't sleep. *Drug Therapy* 1977, 7:44.

Table 6.8 Causes, reasons and potential interventions for sleep alterations in older people.

Age-Related Sleep Changes, Outcomes, and Health Prevention, Promotion and Maintenance Approaches		
Age-related changes	Outcomes	Health prevention, promotion and maintenance
Total sleep time decreases until 80 years of age, then increases slightly. Time in bed increases after 65 years of age, presumably an effect of the free time of retirement Onset to sleep is lengthened (>30 minutes in about 32% of women and 15% of men) Awakenings are frequent, increasing after 50 years of age (>30 minutes of wakefulness after sleep onset in over 50% of older subjects) Naps are more common, although only about 10% report daily napping Sleep is subjectively and objectively lighter (more stage I, less stage 4, more disruptions)	Insomnia Chronic fatigue Extensive napping	Maintain same daily schedule of waking, resting, sleeping Avoid staying in bed beyond waking time If bedtime changes temporarily, keep awake time as close to normal as possible Daytime napping is healthy; however, total napping should not exceed 2 hours Establish bedtime ritual Eliminate caffeine in afternoon and evening (coffee, tea, chocolate) A light snack prior to bedtime may help Maintain room temperature between 21°C and 24°C If there is pain, take an analgesic; be careful of over-the-counter preparations, as they can contain caffeine Use relaxation methods: deep breathing, progressive relaxation, mental imagery Use non-pharmacological measures to promote sleep, e.g. soft music, warm milk Use the bedroom only for sleeping Get up at the regular time even if did not sleep well **Hospital Interventions** Schedule treatments and procedures for times when patient is awake Keep a clear path to and from bathroom. Keep urinals, bedpans and commodes near bed if bathroom is some distance Do not waken patient unnecessarily

Table 6.9 Age-related sleep changes, outcomes and health prevention, promotion and maintenance approaches.

exposure in the treatment of sleep maintenance insomnia among 16 elderly men and women who had experienced sleep disturbance for at least 1 year. Exposure to bright light resulted in substantial changes in sleep quality. Waking time within sleep was reduced by 1 hour, and sleep efficiency improved by just over 10% without altering the time spent in bed. As already mentioned, a bedtime routine tends to be conducive to better sleep. For those nurses working in care homes or hospital, it is important to remember that the bedtime routine is that which is established by the client and not by the institution. Johnson (1993) found that progressive whole-body relaxation using controlled breathing and alternate contractions improved the self-reported sleep patterns of older people living independently. Foreman and Wykle (1995) suggest non-pharmacological measures that the nurse or other caregivers can institute to aid quality sleep for the older person. **Table 6.8** provides information on common age-related diseases that can contribute to sleep disturbance and **Table 6.9** contains age-related sleep changes, outcomes and interventions.

Evaluation

Usually nurses observe patients when they are awake. Sleep can also be a time of observation to evaluate if sleep is restful. Physiological changes are observable during sleep, which gives clues to the phases of the sleep cycle (listed previously in **Box 6.12**). The older person's complaints of restlessness, daytime sleepiness and other types of sleep problems may be thought inconsequential unless their significance is known. Understanding the stages of sleep can provide the nurse with the basis for assessment of physical and mental states during the night or sleeping hours.

PHYSICAL ACTIVITY

The ability to perform physical activity usually declines with age; however, it is still not clear how much this occurs as a result of disuse atrophy (sometimes referred to as age-related detraining) or the biological ageing processes within the body systems (Christianson and Grzybowski, 1993).

The Benefits of Activity

It is now well established that exercise and physical fitness protect health and increase life expectancy. Regular physical activity provides protection against cardiovascular disease (CVD). Donahue *et al.* (1988) examined the relationship of physical activity to the development of coronary heart disease (CHD) in males aged 45–69 years. A 12-year follow-up indicated that increased levels of activity reduced the risk of CHD by 30% compared to those with lower levels of activity. In men over 64 years, the rate of diagnosed CHD in active individuals was less than half the rate experienced by those who led more sedentary lifestyles. This study upholds earlier observations that physical activity is beneficial to middle-aged and older men. It is now well established that engaging in exercise increases the high density lipoprotein (HDL) cholesterol concentration in the blood. HDL appears to provide some protection against heart disease; it is not readily increased by changes in the diet. Regular physical activity also slows down the decline in aerobic power, muscle strength, muscle mass and bone density. Older people who engage in moderate exercise reap benefits in terms of an improved quality of life, increased stamina, strength and suppleness (Royal College of Physicians, 1991).

Emery and Blumenthal (1990) demonstrated that adults aged 60–83 years perceived positive changes in their lives as well as improved physiological outcomes following a 4-month aerobic training programme. Exercise, in general, facilitates efficient gaseous exchange; maximum oxygen consumption, which usually declines with age as a result of loss of oxygen-consuming muscle, can be slowed down by regular participation in aerobic exercise. Christiansen and Grzybowski (1993) report a 30% rise in maximum oxygen consumption in a group of sedentary older people who enrolled in an endurance training programme. According to McMurdo and Rennie (1992) it is possible to increase aerobic capacity or muscle strength by 15% with only a few weeks of training. A 10–20% improvement in strength provides an additional 10–20 years in which to reach the critical threshold level of aerobic power whereby a person would no longer be capable of self-care. The authors continue, not only is regular physical activity important in preventing CVD but of equal importance is the potential for regular exercise to preserve function and prolong active life.

Older adults often wonder whether exercise is safe, in particular after cardiovascular (CV) problems. Such fears are misplaced; emphasis must be placed on the importance of physical activity and that the body is in a constant state of renewal, unlike manufactured materials which degenerate over time. In fact, physical exercise encourages this renewal and vitality is thus enhanced.

The Fitness Level of Older People

The Allied Dunbar National Fitness Survey (Sports Council and Health Education Authority, 1992) has drawn attention to the low level of fitness of the UK population, in general, and older people, in particular. In a further analysis of the data relating to people over 50 years of age, 39% of men and 42% of women are sedentary. Only 26% of men and 17% of women over 50 participate in enough physical activity to benefit their health. The effects of lack of physical activity have repercussions on daily living activities, with the effect that one-quarter of women aged 70–74 years do not have sufficient strength in their legs to get out of a chair without using their arms. Lack of strength and power in the leg muscles makes it difficult to climb stairs, particularly for older women. Physical ability to walk is also affected, in that one-third of men in the 70–74 year age group and four out of five women do not have the physical ability to walk comfortably at a 20 minute-a-mile pace. In comparison to these findings, over half of men and women aged 50 years and older who were inactive thought they participated in enough physical exercise to keep fit (Health Education Authority, 1997).

Older People's Attitudes to Physical Activity

In an earlier study of self-rated activity, the vast majority of older people felt they were leading a healthy life and cited taking exercise as one of the important components, alongside having a good diet and being moderate of habits (Victor, 1991). According to Ebersole and Hess (1994), older adults themselves may underestimate their own capacity to engage in activity; they often use the justification that vigorous activity is a great risk, emphasising that light and sporadic exercise is physiologically better, or that they garden, shop, and do household chores, which are adequate activity. The benefits of exercise on chronic conditions are shown in **Table 6.10**.

Although physical fitness programmes focused on older adults are becoming more common in the UK, the recent interest in physical fitness by younger age groups has not been particularly helpful to older people. The false premise communicated is that if a little exercise is useful then a great deal more must be better, and that to gain anything from exercise it must involve pain. Scrutton (1992) suggests that this approach has discouraged older people from taking up exercise, as they believe they are unable to usefully participate. He also surmises that by reinforcing the idea that physical exercise is only for the young, this becomes a major psychological hurdle for older people who then view even the mildest form of exercise as daunting and worthless.

Qualitative methods both in the USA and UK have attempted to discover more about older people's views and attitudes towards physical activity. Mellilo *et al.* (1997) identified themes of functional independence 'being able to do', holism 'mind and body working together', and age reference 'for people of my age' as being key considerations for the 23 self-selected older respondents in their study. All carried out activities such as walking, swimming, dancing, gardening and heavy housework on a regular basis. Some had learnt the benefits of exercise from the media and most

Benefits of Exercise on Chronic Conditions		
Conditions	Types of exercise	Benefits
Cognitive dysfunction	Aerobic	Improve cerebral function Increase cerebral perfusion Increase beta-endorphin secretion
Coronary heart disease	Aerobic Endurance type	Reduce blood pressure Increase HDLs and reduce body fat Increase maximal oxygen consumption
Diabetes mellitus	Aerobic Endurance type	Fat loss Increase insulin sensitivity Decrease glucose intolerance risk
Hypertension	Aerobic Endurance type	Decrease systolic blood pressure Decrease total peripheral resistance
Osteoarthritis Osteoporosis	Leisure-time activity Resistance Stretching Endurance type Weight-bearing	Maintain range of motion; muscle mass Increase muscle strength Strengthen postural muscles Stimulate bone growth Decrease rate of bone loss

Sources: Kligman EW, Pepin E. Prescribing Physical activity for older patients. *Geriatrics* 1992, 47:33; Elward K, Larson EB. Benefits of exercise for older adults. *Clin Geriatr Med* 1992, 8:35.

Table 6.10 Benefits of exercise on chronic conditions.

of the group saw health status as contributory to physical activity, so that those perceived to be in poor health were less inclined to participate. It was important to interviewees that exercise was something that they wanted to do for themselves. Motivation was increased if it was an activity they enjoyed.

In a UK focus group study Stead *et al.* (1997) found that older people were unlikely to participate in exercise for its own sake or for health reasons. The older people's priority was for activities which afforded regular opportunities to socialise and make friends. This reinforces earlier work which suggests that compliance with an exercise programme is often linked with the social benefit gained from attending such sessions. The researchers learnt that the older focus group participants tended to read local papers, free sheets, direct mail and used word of mouth as a means of finding out about local activities. This information is useful in considering how best to publicise physical activity groups. The study identified people who had already incorporated physical activity into their lifestyle and those who had not. The challenge for health professionals and allied agencies is seen as reinforcing and maintaining motivation for the former group and encouraging the incorporation of physical activity into the lifestyles of the latter.

The Nurse's Role

Kligman and Pepin (1992), suggest that exercise is not commonly recommended or incorporated into health prevention care for most older adults. However, in the light of increasing evidence as to the health benefits of exercise, it is paramount that nurses coming into contact with older people take up the challenge of promoting physical activity as a key to healthy ageing. Practice nurses are able to enquire about current levels of activity in a general health check consultation and the over seventy-fives' assessment, whilst hospital nurses might do so opportunistically. Exercise levels should be assessed under the headings of frequency, intensity and duration. There is increasing information on the benefits of gentle exercise for the residents of care homes and nurses are actively involved in devising and leading programmes of activity (Sobczak, 1997).

The Sports Council and Health Education Authority recommend 12 occasions of moderate activity lasting 20 minutes on each occasion during a 4-week period, as a target level for healthy adults aged 55–74 years. Biographical information on physical activity is likely to reveal past and current attitudes to increasing or engaging in exercise. In addition, nurses need to be mindful of the research findings described in earlier sections, in exploring with clients what might be acceptable. Attention should be paid to the simplicity, effectiveness and adaptability of a programme for older adults in whatever setting they may live.

Special Considerations

Those older people who express the intention to begin a moderately intense or vigorous exercise programme should be advised to consult their doctor for a complete medical examination before they begin. This is crucial if there are known risk factors for CHD. Comprehensive assessment and nursing support during a CV conditioning programme are discussed earlier in this chapter in the section on CV status. Acceptable exercise programmes for older adults should have realistic objectives. Activities should provide for improvement and maintenance of endurance, strength, flexibility, balance and coordination, whilst minimising the risk of injury. Nurses can capitalise on activities of daily living such as encouraging older adults to use bath brushes to wash their own backs in the shower or bath and to dry body parts or rub the back dry with a towel. Reaching for objects while cleaning the house can be included in an activity programme, along with washing dishes in warm water to provide finger exercises.

Walking

Walking, if acceptable, is an easy and convenient form of exercise and it requires no special equipment. Those who have done little walking can be encouraged to start slowly by first walking for 10–15 minutes a day, and gradually increasing the distance. Residents in care homes can also be encouraged to increase the amount of walking. First it may only be from bed to the bathroom, then with time down the hall, and perhaps eventually around the building, depending of course on individual capacity.

Dancing

For those accustomed to it, ballroom, folk or square dancing should be encouraged. This form of activity done properly can have as much aerobic benefit as workouts to videotapes. Dancing is kind to the joints and can burn as many calories as swimming, cycling or walking. Line dancing is currently very popular. Dancing provides a means of obtaining pleasant, sociable and vigorous exercise which tones the body and benefits cardiopulmonary and mental health. A disadvantage of dancing as the sole form of exercise is that it does not develop upper body strength.

Swimming

Swimming is popular and improves muscle tone, muscle strength, circulation, endurance, flexibility and weight control. In addition, it can be relaxing and act as a mood elevator. The benefits of aquatic activity or exercise therapy allow arm and leg movements against water to be less painful. Movements do not seem to require as much effort due to the buoyancy of the water. Some older people maintain a swim-

ming programme begun earlier in life; others enjoy this as a relaxing new way to get exercise and socialise. Those who are non-swimmers or who do not want to swim might well benefit from water exercise classes held in the shallow end of the pool. Most recreation centres offer water exercises or 'aquarobics', and often at suitable times such as late morning. Swimming may be hazardous to those with ischaemic heart disease (IHD) because horizontal water immersion can increase central blood volume thus stressing the limited cardiac reserve of the individual. Those with IHD who want to swim should first consult their doctor.

Yoga

Yoga is another form of exercise that can be practised by most people. The word yoga means union and this form of exercise promotes the union of body, mind and spirit. This discipline focuses on positions, methods of breathing and activity, which is beneficial for both physical and mental health. The exercises are simple, encouraging the stretching and gentle releasing and relaxing of the body to enhance flexibility. There are now books on yoga aimed specifically at older adults. Basic postures are adapted and increased time given to accomplish the exercises. Scrutton (1992) suggests that there is evidence that yoga contributes to the physical and psychological wellbeing of the client and can help osteoporosis. The breathing exercises contribute to the expansion of lung capacity. Yoga relaxation is also useful in the management of hypertension.

Modifying Activities

Many individuals who conduct aerobic exercise programmes and classes do not consider differences between the abilities of younger and older people. Classes are generally taught by young fit persons who become so involved in what they are doing that they are unaware that the older participants may not be able to carry out the number of repetitions they consider necessary for toning muscles. These programmes can damage the muscle tendons, ligaments and joints of the older person. Often when beginning a physical exercise programme muscles may be sore. Warm, but not hot, baths or soaks are excellent as a way of alleviating the soreness. Another way to minimise muscle soreness is a 5–10 minute cooling down period of slow walking or stretching. This keeps the primary muscle groups active, decreases venous pooling, increases venous return to the heart and prevents vagal responses. Marsiglio and Holm (1988) suggest guidelines for prescribing exercise for older adults (**Box 6.15**).

A selection of exercises for bed, chair and standing are presented in **Appendix 4a–d**. Other activities can be done whilst watching television or whenever there are a few spare minutes during the day, like rolling a pencil between the hand and a hard surface, exaggerating the chewing motion of the jaw, holding the stomach in, tightening the buttocks, flexing the fingers and rotating the head and the ankles.

Activity, in general, should be paced and ideally carried out on a daily basis. Activities that will help eliminate stiff-

6.15 Guidelines for Exercise for Older Adults

- Be alert to conditions for which exercise is contraindicated and the presence of underlying disease.
- Assess present activity level.
- Establish medication status.
- Establish mutual goals.
- Begin programme at a very slow level (40–50% of maximum heart rate).
- A minimum of 10 minutes warm-up to maximise flexibility and decrease risk of muscle injury.
- Assess ability to tolerate low-level activity without signs and symptoms of muscle fatigue, shortness of breath, angina, arrhythmias, abnormal blood pressure or intermittent claudication.
- Increase activity slowly by intensity (workload), duration (time) and frequency (time intervals or length of time).
- Cool-down until heart rate returns to resting level.
- Provide longer rest periods between exercises.
- Modify exercise programme to meet individual's capacity.

ness should be planned for the morning when stiffness is most prevalent. Warm water aids in the relief of stiffness and enables the fingers to move more easily without discomfort. **Table 6.11** shows age-related musculoskeletal changes and approaches to health maintenance. Relaxation exercises could be carried out before bedtime to help induce sleep. With any activity in which older people are involved, sufficient intermittent rest periods should be provided. Those who are frail should not engage in strenuous activity nor should their joints be forced past the point of resistance or discomfort. If the frail person has regularly participated in activity that the nurse believes to be too stressful to the skeletal system, it is important to keep in mind that an activity done for many years is not as difficult as if it were just introduced. When the activity is new, serious consideration should be given to levels of stress produced.

Care homes with recreational programmes can make exercise a social and pleasurable period and help promote fine and gross motor movement. Range-of-motion exercises can be choreographed to music and those who like to keep busy might wish to lay tables or carry out light dusting.

The progression should be from smaller, more personal movements to larger ones that may involve communication with the rest of the group. Movements should begin slowly

Age-Related Gastrointestinal Changes, Outcomes, and Health Prevention, Promotion and Maintenance Approaches		
Age-related changes	Outcomes	Health prevention, promotion and maintenance
Bones become more porous (osteoporosis) Demineralisation of vertebral trabecular bone Intervertebral discs dehydrate and narrow Reduced height Erosion of cartilage through exposure and wearing Subchondral bone becomes hyperdemic and fibrotic Synovial membranes become fibrotic Synovial fluid thickens Muscle wasting of hand dorsum Diminished protein synthesis in muscle cells Glucose mobilises slowly in response to exercise Diminished muscle mass decreases glucose stores Bone–muscle weakness changes the centre of gravity	Dowager's hump (kypohosis) Risk of hip fracture Tremors Back pain Joint swelling Ankylosis Crepitation Decreased range of motion Stiffness Muscle wasting Reduced muscle strength Night leg cramps Gait problems Smaller steps Wider stance base Poor posture	Have good lighting, dry floors, non-slip rugs Diet high in calcium Calcium supplements as necessary Do moderate exercise; walking or swimming Use assistive devices: stick, walking frame, if needed Do range of motion activity Seek medical evaluation of back pain Wear shoes with low heels, non-slip soles and support Use leg muscles rather than back muscles when lifting Rest joints when pain occurs Lose weight when necessary Allow for rest periods Break big jobs into small parts Adjust activities to periods of day when energy is high Remove scatter rugs Use non-slip rubber mats in tub and shower Take stretch breaks Eat more potassium and calcium-rich foods Coordinate and balance exercise

Table 6.11 Age-related musculoskeletal changes, outcomes and health prevention, promotion and maintenance approaches.

and later develop speed. The amount of balance required should be minimal at first, increasing when the participants feel more secure and uninhibited. A sample class might be as follows:

- Scratch the small of your back against the chair. Now, try your upper back, too.
- Begin by pretending to wash your face, then your arms and shoulders and neck.
- Stretch up as high as you can; now sink down as low as you can. Now try to reach as far forward as possible, now out to each side.
- Can you nod your head up and down as if to say 'yes'? Now try 'no' out to each side.
- Let's try marching in place to the music. You may use one or both feet.
- Let's try making circles with different parts of our body. Start with one shoulder. Try both shoulders. Try one hand, now the other hand. Can you reverse directions?
- How about kicking one leg at a time up in the air as the music gets louder?
- Let's have one half of the group kick while the other half stomps. Now let's reverse.
- Can you now reach out as if you're trying to shake hands with the person across the circle from you?
- Now try actually shaking hands with the person next to you. How about the person on the other side?

- Now, let's all take a huge deep breath stretch as tall and as long as possible. Now let the air out slowly and let your head, back and arms deflate slowly as a balloon. Try it again, take in even more air. Now deflate even more slowly.

The above is a simple example of what can be done with a small group of 6–10 people. It is advisable, if possible, to have one assistant present to help encourage participants and monitor safety. The goals that may be achieved include increased range of motion and strength, increased balance and coordination, and increased cardiovascular function if the class takes place for at least 20 minutes on a regular basis. Non-physical goals may be greater social interaction, communication with others who are limited in function or disabled in the same or different ways, and greater self-awareness.

SUMMARY

This chapter has looked at individual life support needs where it is apparent that each area influences the function of others. Older people would not continue to survive if these needs could not be met independently or with assistance from others. Nurses working in a variety of settings can contribute to improving overall quality of life for older people by monitoring these specific functions and providing support or assistance according to identified problems.

KEY POINTS

- Age-related changes affect the achievement of basic biological support needs in relation to cardiovascular and respiratory function, nutrition, elimination, sleep and physical activity.
- Nurses can work with older people to maintain optimum cardiac function by advising on exercise, nutrition and medication regimens.
- Following comprehensive assessment, environmental modification, breathing exercises and positioning can improve respiratory function.
- Holistic assessment encompassing lifetime habits, and present financial and physical status is required prior to interventions aimed at improving nutritional status for older people.
- Constipation is a particular and preventable problem for older people living in care homes.
- Sleep disorders are more common in later life and nurses can advise on strategies to improve sleep.
- Physical activity confers many benefits and increasingly nurses are involved in the promotion of physical activity for older people.

AREAS AND ACTIVITIES FOR STUDY AND REFLECTION

- How might you include health maintenance strategies for clients suffering from cardiovascular disease into your way of working?
- Give information about the benefits of smoking cessation to an older client and use it as an area for reflection.
- Give information on the dietary prevention of constipation to an older client and use it as an area for reflection.
- Observe day and night-time sleep behaviour of a client who complains of 'poor nights' and devise some helping strategies.
- Liaise with medical and physiotherapy colleagues and devise an exercise routine appropriate to a client or client group.

REFERENCES

Ancoli-Israel S, Prarker L, Sinaee R *et al.* Sleep fragmentation in patients from a nursing home. *J Gerontol* 1989, 44:M18.

Armstrong-Esther CA, Hawkins LH. Day for night circadian rhythms in the elderly. *Nursing Times* 1982, 78:1263–1265.

Barrett JA. *Faecal incontinence and related problems in the older adult*. London: Edward Arnold, 1993.

BHF. *Coronary heart disease statistics: death by cause*. London: British Heart Foundation, 1997.

BHS. *Management guidelines in essential hypertension*, London, 1997, Modified recommendations based on the report by the Second Working Party of the British Hypertension Society.

Bixler EO, Vela-Bueno A. Normal sleep: physiological behaviour and clinical correlates. *Psychol Ann* 1987, 17:437.

Bowman AM. Sleep satisfaction, perceived pain and acute confusion in elderly clients undergoing orthopaedic procedures. *J Adv Nurs* 1997, 26:550–564.

de Brun S. Insomnia: the common sense approach. *Occup Health Nurs* 1981; 29:36.

BPI. *The Challenges of Ageing*, London: The Association of the British Pharmaceutical Industry, 1991.

BTS. *Guidelines for the management of chronic pulmonary disease*, London: British Thoracic Society, 1997.

Buysse BJ, Browman KE, Monk TH *et al.* Napping and 24-hour sleep/wake patterns in healthy elderly and young adults. *J Gerontol* 1992, 40:779.

Campbell SS, Dawson D, Anderson MW. Alleviation of sleep maintenance insomnia with timed exposure to bright light. *J Am Geriatr Soc* 1993, 41:779.

Christiansen JL, Grzybowski JM. *Biology of aging*. St Louis: Mosby, 1993.

Clapin-French E. Sleep patterns of aged persons in long-term care facilities. *J Adv Nurs* 1986, 11:57–64.

Coats AJS, McGee HM, Stokes HC, Thompson DR, eds. British Association for Cardiac Rehabilitation. London: Blackwell Science, 1995.

Committee on the Medical Aspects of Food Policy (COMA). Dietary reference values for food energy and nutrients for the United Kingdom. Report on health and social subjects, No. 41. London: HMSO, 1991.

Community Health Council. *Hungry in hospital*. 1997.

Department of Health. *The nutrition of elderly people*, London, 1992, HMSO.

Donahue R, Abbott R, Reed D *et al.* Physical activity and coronary heart disease in middle aged and elderly men. The Honolulu Program. *Am J Public Health* 1988, 78(6):683–685.

Ebersole P, Hess P. *Toward healthy aging: Human needs and nursing response*, 4th edn. St Louis: Mosby, 1994.

Ebert NJ. Nutrition in the aged and the nursing process. In: Yurick AG, Spier BE, Ebert NJ *et al.* eds. *The aged person and the nursing process*, 3rd edition. Norwalk: Appleton-Lange, 1989.

Elward K, Larson EB. Benefits of exercise for older adults. *Clin Geriatr Med* 1992, 8:35.

Emery CF, Blumenthal JA. Perceived change among participants in an exercise program for older adults. *Gerontologist* 1990, 30:516.

Evans, LK. Sundown syndrome in institutionalized elderly. *J Am Geriatr Soc* 1987, 35(2):101–108.

Foreman MD, Wykle M. Nursing standard of practice protocol: sleep disturbances in elderly patients. *Geriatr Nurs* 1995, 16:238–243.

Gall K, Petersen T, Riesin SK. Night life nocturnal behaviour patterns among hospitalized elderly. *J Gerontol Nurs* 1990, 16:31.

Gasper PM. Fluid intake: what determines how much patients drink? *Geriatr Nurs* 1988, 9:221.

Gupta K, Dworkin B, Gambert SR. Common nutritional disorders in the elderly: atypical manifestations. *Geriatr Nurs* 1988, 43:87.

Haimov I, Laudon M, Zisapel N *et al.* Sleep disorders and melatonin rhythms in elderly people. *Br Med J* 1994, 309:167.

HEA. *Physical activity in later life*. London: Health Education Authority, 1997.

Hemenway J. Sleep and the cardiac patient. *Heart Lung* 1980, 9:453.

Hughes J *et al.* The British National Diet and Nutrition Survey of people aged 65 years or over: feasibility study. *Proc Nutr Soc* 1995, 643.

ICRF. Fact Sheet, *Bowel cancer*. London: Imperial Cancer Research Fund, 1996.

Irvine L. Faecal incontinence. In: Norton C, ed. *Nursing for continence*. Beaconsfield Publishers; 1996.

Jago W. Does insomnia matter in older people? *Geriatr Med* 1995, (May):12–15.

Johnson JE. A comparative study of the bedtime routines and sleep of older adults. *J Community Health Nurs* 1991, 8:129–136.

Johnson JE. Progressive relaxation and sleep of older men and women. *J Community Health Nurs* 1993, 10:31.

Johnson JE. Sleep problems in the elderly. *J Am Acad Nurs Pract* 1994, 6:161.

Joint Health Surveys Unit. *Health survey for England*, London: The Stationary Office, 1997.

Kassianos G. Constipation. *Care of the Elderly* 1993, 5:444.

Kay-Tee Khaw. In search of the clues to a healthy old age. In: *Medical Research Council News*, Autumn, No.75, 1977.

Kligman EW, Pepin E. Prescribing physical activity for older patients. *Geriatrics* 1992, 47:33.

Kwok T, Whitelaw M. The use of armspan in nutritional assessment of the elderly. *J Am Geriatr Soc* 1991, 39:492–496.

Lader M. *The medical management of insomnia in general practice*. Round table series No. 28. London: Royal Society of Medicine Services, 1992.

Lakin V, Gill T, James W. Diet and coronary heart disease. *Cardiol Update* 1996, (Oct):314–329.

Law MR, Frost CD, Wald NJ. By how much does dietary salt reduction lower blood pressure? III - Analysis of data from trials of salt reduction. *Br Med J* 1991, 302:819–824.

Lehmann A. Measuring the nutritional status of old people. In: Morgan K, ed. *Gerontology: responding to an ageing society*. London: Jessica Kingsly Publishers Ltd, 1992.

Marsiglio A, Holm K. Physical conditioning in the aging adult. *Nurs Pract* 1988, 13:33.

McGee HM, Morgan JH. Cardiac rehabilitation programmes: are women less likely to attend? *Br Med J* 1992, 305:283–284.

McMurdo MET, Rennie L. Don't underestimate the power of exercise. *Care of the Elderly* 1992, 4(4): 171–173.

Medical Research Council Working Party: 1992 Medical Research Council trial of treatment of hypertension in older adults: principal results. *Br Med J* 1992, 304:405–411.

Mellilo KD, Futrell M, Chamberlain C *et al.* Perceptions of physical fitness and exercise activity among older adults. *J Adv Nurs* 1996, 23:542–547.

Monk TH, Reynolds CF, Buysse DJ *et al.* Circadian characteristics of healthy 80-year-olds and their relationship to objectively recorded sleep. *J Gerontol* 1991, 46:171.

Moon CAL. Insomnia: advice on managing this all-too-common complaint. *Care of the Elderly* 1991, 3:361–366.

Morgan K. *Sleep and ageing*. London: Croom Helm, 1987.

Morgan K, Gledhill K. *Managing sleep and insomnia in the older person*. Bicester: Winslow Press, 1991.

Mornhinweg GC, Voignier RR. Music for sleep release in the elderly. *J Holistic Nurs* 1995, 13(3):248–254.

Norton C. The causes and nursing management of constipation. *Br J Nurs* 1996, 5:1252–1258.

Office of National Statistics, 1996. *Mortality statistics – cause*. London: Stationery Office.

Pacini C, Fitzpatrick J. Sleep patterns of hospitalized and nonhospitalized aged individuals, *J Gerontol Nurs* 1982, 8:327.

Pascual J. The Problem – hypertension in the elderly. *Geriatr Med* 1997, (July):1–3.

Podrabsky M: In: Mahan LK, Arlin MT, eds. *Krause's food nutrition and diet therapy*, 8th edn. Philadelphia: WB Saunders, 1992.

Prelevic G. Hypertension: an important problem in postmenopausal women. *Geriatr Med* 1996, (March):47–53.

Raskind M, Eisdorfer C. When elderly patients can't sleep. *Drug Therapy* 1977, 7:44.

RCN. *Nurses against tobacco*. London:The Royal College of Nursing, 1997.

Reedy DF. Fluid intake: how can you prevent dehydration? *Geriatric Nurs* 1988, 9:224.

Royal College of Physicians. Medical aspects of exercise: benefits and risks. *J Royal Coll Physicians* London 1991, 25(3):193–196.

Rouse M, Mahapatra M, Atkinson S *et al*. An open randomised parallel group study of lactulose verus ispaghula in the treatment of chronic constipation in adults. *Br J Clin Pharmacol* 1991, 45:28–30.

Russel RM *et al*. In: Calkins E, Davis PJ, Ford AB, eds. *The practice of geriatrics*. Philadelphia: WB Saunders, 1986.

Satlin A, Volicer L, Ross V *et al*. Bright light treatment of behaviour and sleep disturbance in patients with Alzheimer's disease. *Am J Psychiatry* 1992, 149(8):1028–1032.

Scott A, Roomi J. Hypertension: An evidence-based approach. *Geriatr Med* 1997, (March):47–49.

SC/HEA. *Activity and health research: Allied Dunbar National Fitness Survey*, London: Sports Council and Health Education Authority, 1992.

Scottish Intercollegiate Network. *Obesity in Scotland: Integrating prevention with weight management*. National guidelines recommended for use in Scotland by the SIGN, Edinburgh, 1996.

Scrutton S. *Ageing, healthy and in control. An alternative approach to maitaining health of older people*. London: Chapman Hall, 1992.

Sever P, Beevers C, Bulpitt C *et al*. Management guidelines in essential hypertension: a report of the second working party of the British Hypertension Society. *Br Med J* 1993, 306:983–987.

Sobczak J. Music and movement to exercise older people. *Nursing Times* 1997; 93:46–49.

Society of Health Education Professionals Cooperative Research Group. Prevention of stroke by antihypertensive drug treatment in older persons with isolated systolic hypertension. *J Am Med Assoc* 1991, 265:8255–8264.

Spector TD, Cooper C, Fenton Lewis A. Trends in admissions for hip fracture in England and Wales 1968–1985. *Br Med J* 1990, 300:1173–1174.

Stead M, Wimbush E, Eadie D, Teer P. A qualitative study of older people's perceptions of ageing and exercise: the implications for health promotion. *Health Educ J* 1997, 56:3-16.

Tierney AJ. Undernutrition and elderly hospital patients: a review. *J Adv Nurs* 1996, 23:228–236.

Victor C. *Health and health care In later life*. Milton Keynes: Open University Press, 1991.

Wagner D. On sleep and Alzheimer's disease. *Alzheimer's Disease and Related Disorders Newsletter* 1985, 5.

Watson R. Measuring feeding difficulty in people with dementia: perspectives and problems. *J Adv Nurs* 1993, 18:25–31.

Webb GP. *Nutrition: a health promotion approach*. London: Edward Arnold, 1995.

Webb GP, Copeman J. *The nutrition of older adults*. London: Edward Arnold, 1996.

Weber F, Bernard R J, Ray D. Effects of a high complex carbohydrate low fat diet and daily exercise on individuals years of age and older. *J Gerontol* 1983, 38:155.

White A, Nicolaas G, Foster K, Browne F, Carey S. *Health survey for England 1991*. London: HMSO, 1993.

Wickham CAC, Walsh K, Baker DJP, Margaretts BM, Morris J, Bruce SA. Dietary calcium, physical activity and risk of hip fracture: a prospective study. *Br Med Bull* 1989, 299:8899–8892.

Williams K, Roe B. Developments in continence care. *Elderly Care* 1995, 7:5.

USEFUL ADDRESSES

Cardiac
British Heart Foundation,
14 Fitzhardinge Street,
London W1H 4DH.
Tel 0171 935 0185

Sleep
Sleep Matters,
PO Box 3087,
London W4 4ZP.
Helpline 0181 994 9874, 2–10 p.m., Mon–Fri

Activity
Extend (Exercise Teachers for Elderly and/or Disabled),
22 Maltings Drive,
Wheathampstead,
St Albans,
Hertfordshire AL4 8QJ.
Tel 01582 832760

Aquarobics
391 Clarence Lane,
London SW15 5QB.

Research into Ageing
Baird House,
15/17 St Cross Street,
London EC1N 8UN.

For 35 min videotape: 'More active, more often' - chair-based activities set to music.

Excel 2000
1A North Street,
Sheringham NR26 8LW.

Neglected areas: Dental health, foot care and skin care
Mary Clay

LEARNING OBJECTIVES

After studying this chapter you will be able to:

- Identify normal age changes of the oral cavity, feet and skin.
- Identify common dental, foot and skin problems in older people.
- Identify preventative, maintenance and restorative measures for dental, foot and skin health.
- Carry out assessments of the mouth, feet and skin.

- Plan care for the prevention and maintenance of dental, foot and skin health.
- Plan care for the treatment of dental, foot and skin problems.
- Identify when older people need to be referred for medical, dental or chiropody assessment, in relation to dental, foot and skin problems.
- Carry out health promotion with older people and their carers relating to teeth, feet and skin.

INTRODUCTION

The maintenance needs discussed in this chapter affect not only the physical health of older people but also their psychosocial wellbeing. The mouth, feet and skin are areas in which nurses have a key role in assessment, health promotion, treatment, care and referral to specialists, yet they are often neglected.

The status of a person's mouth and teeth can affect their wellbeing in a variety of ways. Acute dental problems can put the older person at risk of systemic problems. The mouth is an important zone for communication between people through speech and smiling. Much socialisation and pleasure is derived from food and drink. Poor oral function, hygiene and chronic oral problems can lead to loss of life satisfaction and raise concern with self-presentation and fear of embarrassment that affects socialisation and self-esteem.

Foot health is also vitally important to physical health and psychosocial wellbeing. Foot problems can severely limit an older person's ability to move around. This can lead into a downward spiral whereby they become more sedentary, leading to joint and muscle stiffness, inability to shop, undernutrition and reduced social contact.

A great deal of emphasis has been given to the care of skin in terms of preventing pressure problems and treating wounds, but there are many other aspects of care and health promotion in which nurses have a key role. These include the care of hair and nails, dry skin, allergic reactions, pruritis and recognising skin changes, particularly skin cancer. By addressing these neglected areas in detail, this chapter attempts to redress the balance.

THE MOUTH AND TEETH

In cannot be stated too strongly that a functional and healthy mouth has strong psychological implications throughout life. It influences such activities as smiling, eating, drinking and sexual pleasure throughout adulthood. These activities contribute directly or indirectly to one's self-esteem. The ability to communicate, socialise and maintain adequate nourishment depends on dental health, which concerns the whole oral cavity, teeth, gums, lips, tongue and mucous membranes. Fulfilment of dental needs as a psychological requirement influences the attainment of successive levels of Maslow's hierarchy of needs.

Dental Health

Lack of teeth alters articulation of speech, jaw alignment and general appearance. People without teeth may be reluctant to smile, they may feel embarrassed and cover their mouths or withdraw from social contacts. The type and consistency of food becomes limited and monotonous. Unless great care is taken, food eaten by those who are edentulous is inadequate and deficient in nutritive value.

The dental health of older people is a basic need which is often neglected. Those caring for older people should be aware of the value of oral hygiene and oral health. Older people themselves may consider the loss of teeth to be a natural consequence of ageing and this attitude is one which can foster neglect. The percentage of edentulous (toothless) people over 65 years is decreasing. In 1968, 37% of the adult population were edentulous. By 1983, this figure had dropped to 25%, and the estimated figure for the turn of the century is 10% (Social Trends, 1986).

The Adult Dental Health Surveys of 1968, 1978 and 1988 illustrate that tooth loss is strongly correlated with age. The 1988 survey found that, on average, the number of 65–74-year-olds in the UK who were edentulous was just under 60%, whereas the percentage of over 75-year-olds was just over 80%. Although there has been an overall reduction, there has been a shift in the relative proportion of edentulousness to the older population (Office of Population Censuses and Surveys, 1990). The majority of this group own, even if they do not wear, full dentures (Fiske *et al.* 1986). There are still about 9 million edentulous denture wearers in the UK and several million people wearing partial dentures (Taylor, 1991).

Tooth loss is not necessarily related to the ageing process but is rather a problem that accrues over time and is, therefore, most evident in older people. Older people who still have teeth have the right to have help in the maintenance and preservation of their remaining teeth. Dental disease is largely preventable and nurses working with older people can make a major contribution to dental health education and promotion [Health Education Authority (HEA), 1996]. Community nurses

have a central role in health promotion and their important contribution has been well documented [Department of Health (DoH), 1989; Clarke, 1991], but few studies have addressed their attitudes to dental health promotion. One such study (Sweeney and Zoitopoulos, 1995), found that although they had positive attitudes to disease prevention, their own knowledge was lacking. Training to enable them to see the relevance and benefits of good oral health for themselves was suggested as a means of making them more likely to appreciate its significance for their clients. Factors contributing to periodontal problems in older adults are shown in **Box 7.1**.

Since 1991, dentists have been required to provide patient information leaflets (Taylor, 1991). The combined public and private outlays on dental care is over £1.5 billion a year in Britain, the great majority of which is spent on minimising the consequences of dental caries and periodontal disease. There appears to be a lack of service use by older people, with just over one-fifth of over 75-year-olds registered with dentists for continuing care (Taylor, 1991). [Continuing care registration with a National Health Service (NHS) dentist now only lasts 15 months before renewal is necessary.] Older people received only 4.6% of courses of treatment instead of the 15%, which their proportion in the overall population would suggest (Steele, 1984). This could be due to expectations and attitudes, inaccessibility of dental services or fear of the dentist.

Older people are eligible to pay NHS dental charges unless they are receiving income support or are on a low income (DoH, 1997). Those who are not eligible for free or reduced cost treatment must contribute 80% of the cost. The most which can be charged for a course of NHS treatment is £325 (April, 1996) (HEA, 1996).

There are two primary care dental services in the UK, the general or family dental practice and the community dental service. Both provide preventative advice and care. The availability of NHS dental services may be difficult in some areas of the UK. Although nationally, only 10–20% of dental treatment is carried out privately, a DoH survey (1991) confirmed that about half of all London dentists were not accepting NHS patients. This proportion rises to 70% in some localities (Taylor, 1991). The local health authority or health board will provide a list of practices providing some NHS care and information on exemption from patient charges.

The community dental service is operated by the local community health authority and based in health centre dental clinics, often with mobile surgeries. Their services include caring for disabled people and in some areas may provide an NHS general dental service for adults who cannot find an NHS dental practice to accept them. The provision of specialist domiciliary dental care to older people, who have limited mobility and are unable to go to a dental surgery, may be provided, either by the local community dental service or by local dentists. A list of dentists prepared to make domiciliary visits is available from local health authorities (Health Education Authority, 1996).

Domiciliary visits, as well as having the obvious advantage in that there are no transport difficulties for the person, mean that they are likely to be more relaxed and better able to communicate their problems in the security of their own homes. Referral to a community dental service may be made by any

7.1 Factors Contributing to Periodontal Problems in Older People

Anatomical
- Tooth malalignment.
- Thinning gingival mucosa.

Mechanical
- Calculus.
- Retention of impacted food.
- Moveable and spreading teeth.
- Ragged edged fillings and crown overhangs.
- Poorly designed or poorly fitting dentures.

Bacterial
- Plaque accumulation.
- Invasion of organisms at or below gumline.
- Food impaction.
- Drugs, metallic poisons.
- Allergic responses.
- Phenytoin.
- Cytotoxins.
- Heavy metals (lead, arsenic, mercury).

Intrinsic (Systemic)
- Endocrine.
- Metabolic.
- Altered immune system.

Emotional and psychomotor
- Bruxism.
- Mental impairment.

health-care worker who identifies a need in an older person (Steele, 1984).

Changes in the Oral Cavity during the Ageing Process

Ageing teeth become brittle, drier and darker in colour, may lose some of the enamel covering, and may loosen from bone loss (reabsorption) or breakdown of the supporting tissue and gum recession. Years of crushing and grinding wear down the chewing surfaces (attrition), causing teeth to become uneven, fracture and develop jagged edges. Vascularity of the gums is reduced, limiting or decreasing the ability of the tissue to heal after injury. Gum recession occurs in part from the loss of tissue elasticity or the periodontal tissue, atrophy of the alveolar bone and periodontal disease.

Periodontal changes should be minimal in healthy older people, but the attention given to oral care by health care professionals and by older people themselves is inadequate. Inattention to periodontal conditions results in inflammation, swelling, pain of dental structures, and discomfort from mouth taste and odours. Periodontal disease does not appear to be a specific disease of older people but the result of chronic periodontitis from young and middle adulthood (*see* Chapter 4 for further discussion).

Gum disease is believed to be almost pandemic in the older population; for example, a study of older people in Scottish residential homes found that, of the 10% who still had some of their own teeth, 95% required periodontal treatment (Manderson and Ettinger, 1975). Inflammation of the gums (gingivitis) may occur due to gums being irritated by partial dentures and faulty bridges. A predisposition to gingivitis may also occur when the mucous membranes are irritated by dryness of the mouth from habitual mouth breathing. Systemic problems such as endocrine dysfunction, the use of certain drugs and nutritional deficiencies may be additional causes of gingivitis.

However, the most prevalent cause of gum inflammation and disease is the inadequate removal of dental plaque, which accumulates at the gum line between the teeth. (Plaque is the name given to the film of microbes embedded in sticky products of microbial and salivary origin, which adheres to the teeth and surrounding tissues.) Dental experts concur that most tooth loss is due to periodontal disease. **Figure 7.1** illustrates gingival and root decay and **Figure 7.2** illustrates the progression of periodontal disease.

The advent of fluoridation and overall dental health improvements have helped. People are keeping their teeth longer, but additional factors contribute to the condition and retention of teeth (**Box 7.2**).

Friability of the oral mucosa may be caused by the shift of intracellular and intercellular fluid. This is seen in progressive dehydration or decreasing kidney function in older people. The transitional mucosal border is not covered with keratinising cells and is vulnerable to mild stress. Since most oral cancers occur in older people it is significant that the mucosa be maintained intact and free from chronic irritation. Tobacco from smoking insults the oral cavity. Although all mucous membranes are susceptible to cancer, the lips and the sides of the tongue are particularly vulnerable.

Diminished vascularity may lead to nutritional deficiencies of the cells. Dietary deficiencies of vitamins A, B and C,

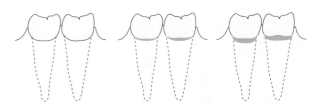

Figure 7.1 Gingival and root decay.

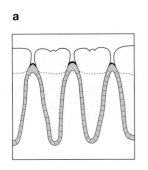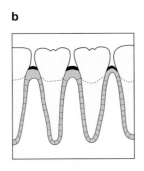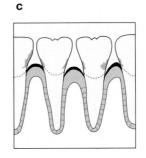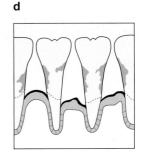

| a | b | c | d |

Figure 7.2 Progression of periodontal disease. (a) Normal, healthy gingivae (gums): healthy gums and bone anchor teeth firmly in place; (b) Gingivitis: plaque and its by-products irritate the gums, making them tender, inflamed and likely to bleed; (c) Periodontitis: unremoved, plaque hardens into calculus (tartar). As plaque and calculus continue to build up, the gums begin to recede (pull away) from the teeth, and pockets form between the teeth and gums; (d) Advanced periodontitis: the gums recede further, destroying more bone and the periodontal ligament. Teeth – even healthy teeth – may come loose and need to be extracted.

- Excessive wear (attrition).
- Loosening of teeth by night grinding (bruxism).
- Habitual consumption of abrasive foods, which accelerates wear and loss of tooth height.
- Diminished salivary secretions and chemical erosion by substances such as fruit acids, particularly lemon juice and soft drinks.

folic acid and zinc are added factors that affect tissue integrity and susceptibility to periodontal disease. Insufficient vitamin A reduces the cohesion and intactness of the epithelial layer, lack of vitamin B interferes with cell metabolism, and an inadequate amount of vitamin C, folic acid and zinc is responsible for poor differentiation of the connective and fibrous tissue. This delays the healing process by prolonging the period of gum oedema after tooth extraction. A deficiency of calcium, which is usually related to osteoporosis of bones, can be seen in the mandible and maxilla.

Minor salivary gland activity diminishes in response to age changes and to the effects of systemic conditions and medication. Many drugs commonly taken by older people, for example diuretics and antidepressants, are thought to cause a dry mouth (xerostomia) and this can predispose to caries and irritation of sensitive mucous membranes. Most older people experience some dryness of the mouth, which interferes with adequate moisture to wet food in chewing. It may be for this reason that some older people like to 'dunk', for example biscuits in tea before eating them. An increase in mucin causes saliva to become thicker and ropy in texture and reduces the natural cleaning and washing action of saliva present in earlier years. Inadequate saliva is also responsible for diminished action to protect gums from irritation. Alterations in pH seem to be influenced by the number of natural teeth an individual has. The more natural teeth the older person retains, the better the pH acidity and the maintenance of it's protective properties.

Common Oral and Dental Problems

Xerostomia

Dry mouth is a condition often found in older people as a result of salivary gland dysfunction. In addition to medication, possible causes of this annoying and uncomfortable condition are radiation therapy of the head and neck for tumours, chemotherapeutic agents for cancer and immunosuppression therapy, physiological disorders, blockage of salivary ducts and fibrosis of the parotid glands.

Depending on the severity of dry mouth, older people may complain of a burning sensation or difficulty chewing or swallowing, speaking or retaining upper dentures. Decreased sense of taste, which occurs as a result of dry mouth, leads to loss of appetite and the lack of saliva results in an increase in caries and tooth sensitivity. When necessary, a variety of prescription and over-the-counter saliva substitutes are available either in sprays or rinses.

Dental Caries

Tooth decay is the progressive destruction of the teeth by acid generated in the bacterial plaque of the tooth surface. The bacteria produce acid by metabolism of dietary sugars and the plaque holds the acid in contact with the tooth surface like a piece of blotting paper. Therefore, to produce tooth decay three factors are needed: a susceptible tooth, bacteria and sugar [Health Education Authority (HEA), 1996].

Root caries occurs on any tooth surface where periodontal attachments from the mentoenamel junction. Most root caries are found on the proximal and buccal surfaces of the teeth, appearing initially as small, round, shallow pigmented defects at the root surface. As these caries advance, they usually spread laterally and may undermine the tooth crown.

Gingivitis and Periodontitis

With the increasing retention of teeth in older people, there has been an increase in gum disease. Signs of periodontal disease include:

- Gums bleeding when the teeth are brushed.
- Red, swollen or tender gums.
- Detachment of the gums from the teeth.
- Chronic bad breath or bad taste.

As the condition progresses, pus may appear from the gum line when the gums are pressed, and teeth may become loose or change their position.

Thrush

This is a very common condition found in denture wearers, caused by *Candida albicans* infection. In this often painless condition, the palate is inflamed and there could be white plaques on the surface. Candida can also infect the deep folds at the angles of the mouth which form when old dentures are worn. It may also be precipitated by a course of broad spectrum antibiotic, anaemia or systemic condition. Antifungal treatment will clear this infection but denture hygiene is also important (Health Education Authority, 1996).

Oral Cancers

About 3000 new cases of malignant tumours of the oral cavity are reported in the UK each year. Many involve older and edentulous people, and are smoking or alcohol related (Health Education Authority, 1996). Eighty-five per cent of sufferers are aged over 50 years and about 1000 deaths per year in the UK are caused by oral cancers (Taylor, 1991).

Leukoplakia is a precancerous lesion that presents as a slightly raised, slightly circumscribed patch or patches, which are generally found on the lips, tongue, gums or oral mucosa. It may also appear as a velvety red patch which does not rub off (erythroplakia). Basal cell carcinoma is a malignant tumour that begins as a papule and enlarges peripherally. It develops a central crater which erodes, crusts, and bleeds. Local invasion destroys the underlying and adjacent tissue, and if ignored can be very disfiguring. A common site for this type of cancer is the upper lip. Tumours of the salivary glands or bone usually present as swellings.

Assessment

Assessment of the oral cavity should be a regular part of dental hygiene. It is much better for older people to periodically have their mouth inspected than wait until there is a problem. It is recommended by the British Dental Association and Health Education Authority that everyone has a dental checkup at least once a year.

Gums should be inspected for colour and palpated for lesions and swelling. Ill-fitting dentures are responsible for ulcerations, which resemble cancerous lesions. Generalised inflammation, or sore mouth, is demonstrated by a reddened mucosa and a granular looking outline of the denture bases along the gingival borders. Papillary hyperplasia is a warty papular type of condition of the palate created by the suction of the upper denture. Ill-fitting dentures can also cause a breakdown of the angle of the mouth – skin folds overlap and crack and resemble the lesions seen in vitamin B deficiency, infection such as candidiasis and cold sores.

Teeth, if present, should be checked for jagged edges, fractures, lost fillings, caries, the number of teeth and adequate occlusion. Dentures (partial or full) should be checked for excessive wear, breakage and rough spots. The tongue should be inspected for colour, swelling and lesions, and palpated on all surfaces for tenderness and lesions. It cannot be emphasised too strongly how vital dental care is to the wellbeing of older people.

Assisting Older People

It is essential that daily oral care is provided for any older people who are unable to carry out their own oral hygiene. They are at greater risk of developing oral disease. They take more medications, have decreased saliva production, lack resistance to bacterial toxins that cause periodontal disease, eat softer food, more liquids and foods with a higher sugar content, which tend to remain in their mouths longer than elders who are healthier.

Caregivers should be provided with written instructions to reinforce verbal instructions and demonstration. (**Box 7.3** provides guidance for caregivers.) To ensure that the older person receives thorough oral hygiene, this may be written in the individual's care plan and evaluated daily.

Interventions

Oral Care

Holmes (1996) suggests that, at present, mouth-care procedures carried out by nurses for frail older people appear to be largely based on tradition with little reference to existing research. The existence of dehydrating stressors must be recognised, such as

7.3 Dental Care: Guidance for Caregivers

- If the person is in bed, elevate their head by raising the bed or propping it with pillows and have the patient turn their head to face you. Place a clean towel across the chest and under the chin, and place a basin under their chin.
- If the person is sitting in a stationary chair or wheelchair, stand behind the patient and stabilise their head by placing one hand under the chin and resting the head against your body. Place a towel across their chest and over the shoulders. (It may be helpful to secure it with a safety pin.) The basin can be kept handy in the patient's lap or on the table placed in front of or by the side of the patient. A wheelchair may be positioned in front of the sink.
- If the lips are dry or cracked, apply a light coating of Vaseline or lipsalve.
- Brush and floss the teeth as you have been instructed, using toothpaste containing fluoride.
- Provide mouthwashes, as indicated, for persons who are conscious.

Source: Papas AS, Niessen LC, Chauncey HH. *Geriatric dentistry, aging and oral health*. Mosby: St Louis, 1991.

oral breathing, oxygen therapy and poor fluid and dietary intake. Care is needed when using oral antiseptics since they disrupt the normal microflora. There are two types of mouthwashes that individuals can use:

(1) **Cosmetic.** The primary function of cosmetic rinses is to refresh the mouth, but there are major disadvantages. Depending on the brand, cosmetic rinses contain between 6 and 29% alcohol by volume, which can be an oral tissue irritant as well as exacerbate or create xerostomia. Their use may mask underlying causes of oral disease such as halitosis.

(2) **Therapeutic.** These rinses contain an agent that is beneficial to the surface of teeth and the oral environment. Some, for example chlorhexidine, which contains alcohol as well as a broad spectrum antimicrobial agent that helps control plaque, are prescription only medicines. Listerine, which is in the same category, is an over-the-counter product that contains a high quantity by volume of alcohol (26.9%). Gooch (1985) suggests tap water as the ideal mouth wash. Foam swabs are widely used to remove plaque, although tooth brushing has been shown to be more effective. It appears that the frequency of oral care is more important than the method used. Lanolin, Vaseline or other lip salves will keep the lips moist (Holmes, 1996).

Care of the Teeth

The basic cause of caries is sugars in the diet, with the frequency of consumption being the most important factor, as even a tiny intake can cause acid to be generated in the plaque for up to 2 hours. This leads to the demineralisation of tooth enamel. The most important preventative measure against dental caries is reduction in the frequency of sugar intake (Macgregor, 1987).

Older people should be encouraged to brush their teeth to reduce plaque formation, which causes periodontal disease, and to prevent halitosis. Fluoride toothpastes, which entered wide-scale use in the UK in the early 1970s gives a major benefit.

Their use is the single most effective personal means of improving dental health and is largely the reason why caries rates have fallen by half in many areas of the UK.

(HEA, 1996)

Water fluoridation, that is adjusting the fluoride content of the water supply to the optimal level of one part per million, is a safe and powerful dental health intervention.

A soft-to-medium toothbrush with a small head and a straight handle should be used twice daily, preferably after meals. Many older people find it useful to have a thickened handle. Foam attached with waterproof tape is a simple yet effective method. An electric toothbrush is very useful for those who are less dextrous as they have thick handles which are easier to grasp, require little or no arm or wrist movement, and provide a constant motion. They can be used by the older person or their carers to achieve an otherwise impossible degree of oral hygiene.

The method of brushing recommended is referred to as a modified scrub method and is generally considered the most satisfactory. This consists of very short backwards and forwards vibratory or small circular strokes (not more than half the length of the brush) followed by a short twist to the bristles to sweep the plaque away from the embrasures between the teeth. The biting surfaces of the back of the teeth are brushed with a short scrubbing stroke (Geissler and McCord, 1986). **Figure 7.3** Demonstrates correct tooth brushing routine.

As well as teeth being brushed for 2 minutes, it is recommended that teeth are flossed at least once a day. The person should use about a 46 cm length of lightly waxed or unwaxed floss. A seesaw motion places the floss between the tooth surfaces and the removal of plaque requires an up and down movement under the gum line and side surfaces of teeth. **Figure**

7.4 shows the correct method of flossing. Disclosure tablets or drops will stain the plaque that collects at the gum line red or pink and can help the person see the plaque accumulation, which otherwise may not have been visible on inspection.

Care of Dentures

It is important that the gums and soft tissues of edentulous older people are kept clean. Bland mouthwashes are useful in removing debris from the mucosa and keeping the mouth fresh and well lubricated in cases of xerostomia. If necessary, the gums, tongue and palate should be cleansed using a soft bristled brush. Dentures should be rinsed carefully after meals and cleaned once a day. They should always be removed at night so as to allow the gums to relax, and soaked in cold or lukewarm water with a proprietary denture-soaking solution. If dentures are allowed to dry out or are immersed in very hot water, they are likely to distort. Dentures, like natural teeth, require brushing to remove plaque, followed by thorough rinsing before being placed in the mouth.

Occasionally denture stomatitis, caused by *C. albicans*, affects the denture-bearing surfaces of the mouth. It occurs in people who have ill-fitting dentures and poor hygiene, and both the buccal mucosa and dentures will need to be treated in order to cure the condition (Davis, 1989). Sometimes loose-fitting dentures can be held in place using a proprietary fixative, although relining or rebasing of dentures may be necessary.

Many older people expect their dentures to last a lifetime and visits to the dentist to be no longer necessary. A study by Manderson and Ettinger (1975) found that only half of older people with dentures had been seen by a dentist in the previous 10 years and that only 12% of dentures were satisfactory. Dentures may get broken or damaged, often by being accidentally dropped. They should be professionally repaired by a dentist or a dental laboratory. When a new set of dentures is required, clients are advised to take the old set to the dental consultation so that the best features of the previous dentures can be copied. This usually reduces the number of visits involved in making new ones (Fiske, 1992). An annual dental inspection for a whole mouth examination is recommended as well as for an examination of dentures (HEA, 1996). Nurses have a role in guiding and supporting older people through dental surgery

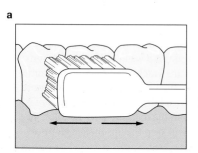
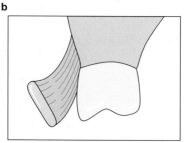
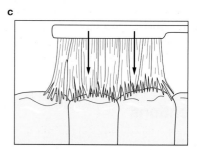

Figure 7.3 Correct toothbrushing routine. (a) brush sides of teeth, (b) angle brush to clean along gum line. (c) brush chewing surface.

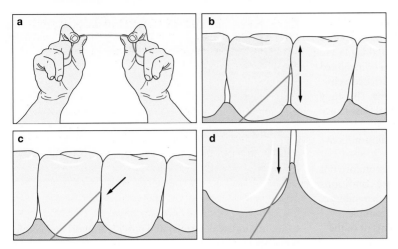

Figure 7.4 Effective flossing technique. (a) Take a 46 cm piece of floss. (b) Slide floss between teeth. (c) Move floss up and down. (d) Make sure floss goes below gum line.

and in enabling them to adjust to wearing dentures. In order to achieve this detailed information needs to be given with empathy and tact.

A full set of dentures obtained through the NHS cost from £86.16 (Age Concern, 1997). Although, unlike some other countries, there is no legal requirement in the UK for dentures to be marked, the practice is widely recommended (Whittle *et al.* 1985). The commercially available system is the 'Identure kit' by (3M), which is simple and quick to use, the drawback being the cost (£45). Dentures may be marked by writing the name or the initial on the buccal flange or on the palate and then covering it with two coats of clear nail varnish. This is likely to last for at least a year.

Most older people will communicate painful oral health problems. However, nursing staff need to observe aphasic and confused patients, who may be unable to communicate such problems. Indications may include refusal to eat, facial grimaces during mastication or persistent touching, pushing or pulling at a certain area of the mouth or face.

It is anticipated that in the future most people surviving into later life will be able to retain most or all of their teeth. In the meantime, much more traditional restorative dentistry will be required. Expectations are likely to be that they will not wish to wear dentures. For this group, dental implants may prove attractive. Older people are undoubtedly vulnerable to declining oral health status, so good oral care will help maintain self-esteem and improve general wellbeing and quality of life.

FOOT CARE

Feet influence the physical, psychological and social wellbeing of an individual. Feet carry one's body weight, hold the body erect in an upright and stationary position, coordinate and maintain balance in walking, and must be rigid yet loose and adaptable enough to conform to surfaces underfoot, all the while holding the legs and body in an upright position.

Foot discomfort can cause irritability, fatigue and chronic complaints. Socrates is thought to have said 'to him whose feet hurt, everything hurts'. Older peoples' feet are subjected to functional and physical neglect and traumatic stresses over the years. Ability to adequately inspect feet requires good vision and joint mobility, both of which tend to decline with age. Feet often reflect systemic disease or give clues to physical ailments before their actual appearance (Echevarria *et al.* 1988).

Foot care is undoubtedly one of the most important aspects of health care (Help the Aged, 1994). As people get older, they tend to have more trouble with their feet. People over the age of 75 years report themselves that they are frequently unable to manage toenail cutting (General Household Survey, 1985) and uncomfortable and painful feet may force older people to become sedentary and deprived of social contacts. Feet undergo a great deal of use, trauma, misuse and neglect as part of everyday living, yet adequate care of the feet can alleviate disability, pain and the propensity for falling. Often little attention is given to these valuable appendages until the feet interfere with walking and the ability to maintain independence. Health care records suggest that feet are not considered a priority. Nurses may have strong negative reactions to contact with feet, they often adopt the attitude that feet care is not part of nursing practice.

Foot Problems in Older People

A major study of people over 65 years of age, undertaken for the Department of Health and Social Security, found that over 52% reported some trouble with feet. Examining chiropodists assessed that 84% had some foot problems, describing 4% as major, 22% as moderate and 58% as minor. Only one in six had feet which were entirely trouble free (Cartwright and Henderson, 1986).

Difficulty cutting toenails, hard skin or calluses, thickened or other nail problems, corns, aching or swollen feet, and bunions or enlarged big toe joints were the most common conditions reported by the older people interviewed. The conditions most frequently diagnosed by examining chiropodists were corns and calluses, lesser toe deformities, ingrown or involuted toenails, thickened toenails, hallux valgus, varicose veins, osteoarthritis, valgus or pronated foot, and oedema. The study found no differences with their indicator of social class in age or sex of older people, in the nature and extent of reported or assessed foot problems, or in the proportions needing or receiving chiropody treatment.

Major abnormalities occur gradually with discomfort, not pain. Without proper care and treatment, these conditions become disabling and a threat to the person's independence. Specific pathologies may also affect the feet, for example:

- Deformities resulting from diseases of the joints or of the central nervous system.
- Inadequate blood supply resulting from disease of the blood vessels of the feet or legs.
- Damage to the skin of the feet as a result of altered sensation due to peripheral nerve disease.
- Swelling due to abnormal fluid balance.

The problems posed by each of these main groups are different. (**Box 7.4** lists age-related foot changes.)

Diseases of the Joints or Central Nervous System

Osteoarthritis is almost entirely a disease of joints and the deformities which it produces are cumulative as age advances. Destruction of articular cartilage is followed by a deforming process affecting the bone ends. Weight bearing joints are particularly affected and may be very painful. The main foot problems caused are likely to be stiffness in the back of the foot and hallux rigidus, a condition in which the big toe becomes stiff at the metatarso-phalangeal joint. Dorsiflexion (the movement of the foot and ankle upwards towards the leg) is restricted making walking difficult and painful.

Chiropody appliances and footwear adjustments to modify the way in which weight is taken can help to relieve the pain. Physiotherapy can also be helpful by mobilising a painful joint. People with degenerative joint disease often find walking easier in the morning and activities could be planned with this in mind.

Rheumatoid arthritis is a condition in which inflammation of the joints occurs as part of a widespread systematic process. The joint space becomes narrow, erosions occur in the ends of the bones and the tissues become thickened. Movement becomes stiff and painful, particularly after resting. Disease in the joints of the forefoot results in a clawing deformity of the toes, which may progress to subluxation (partial dislocation). When the disease affects the back part of the foot it is the joint beneath the talus which is affected, causing the heel to twist outwards on the ankle and the front part of the foot to roll inwards. People suffering from rheumatoid arthritis will already be under the care of medical practitioners who will control drug treatment and be a source of advice. Chiropodists and physiotherapists can help control symptoms. Footwear of suitable depth

7.4 Age-related Foot Changes

- The skin tends to become dry, inelastic and cool.
- Subcutaneous tissue on dorsum and sides of the foot thins.
- Plantar fat pads shrink and degenerate.
- Toe nails become brittle and thicken with decreased resistance to fungal infections.
- Degenerative joint diseases diminish range of motion.

to accommodate deformity and provide support and comfort is essential.

Of all the joint diseases, gout is the one most dramatically associated with the foot. It most commonly affects the metatarso-phalangeal joint of the big toe. It is really a metabolic disease in which there is an abnormally high quantity of uric acid in the blood which leads to the deposition of uric acid crystals in the synovial fluid. Gout causes excruciating pain, which may be relieved by modern drug treatment. Footwear must be chosen to suit the symptoms, for example wide fitting with soft uppers.

Diseases of the Blood Vessels

These may endanger the feet either by depriving parts of it of blood supply (ischaemia) or by making the tissues particularly susceptible to injury as a result of inflammation of the blood vessels (vasculitis).

Atherosclerosis is a disease of the arteries in which fatty deposits (plaques) occur on the inner surface of the wall of the artery, and may harden or afford a basis for the formation of blood clots. These may then block the artery or bits may break off forming emboli which block small arteries. Atherosclerosis is said to be a disease of the Western industrial society and is associated with cigarette smoking, lack of exercise and a diet high in saturated fats. It causes pallor and coldness in the foot, flaking and thinning of the skin and thickening of the nails. In more serious cases, actual tissue death occurs (necrosis and gangrene).

Gangrene is due to the total depravation of blood, so it begins at the furthest part away from the heart. Initially, it may only affect the tip of one toe and then progress to affect the larger part of the front of the foot. The characteristic changes begin with an area of redness, which is rapidly followed by white and blue appearance and eventually the dead tissue becomes black. Ischaemia may be associated with pain, at first during exercise, later at rest and often during the night. Gangrene may sometimes be prevented by arterial bypass surgery, but once it has occurred it is irreversible. Care of the feet is important; to keep the skin healthy and clean, well-fitting hosiery and footwear are essential to prevent external constriction and to minimise the possibility of trauma to the thinned skin. Treatment for corns and calluses should only be undertaken by a chiropodist as otherwise accidental damage may allow infection to take hold quickly due to diminished blood supply. Narrowing of the arteries occurs more extensively in older people with diabetes. Cold feet and cramps in the legs may be experienced due to this vascular disease. (Foot ulcers, which are vascular in origin, will be addressed later in this chapter under integument.)

Peripheral Nerve Disease

Motor nerve deficits cause muscle weakness and paralysis with or without abnormalities in muscle tone. Tone may increase (hypertonicity or spasticity) making the muscle stiff or it may decrease (hypotonicity or flacidity) causing floppiness. As a result of this, there may be a loss of selected movement patterns or disorders of the postural reflex mechanism. Whatever the cause of the weakness or paralysis the symptoms in the foot are similar. The most common problem is foot drop, which is associated with difficulty in bending the foot up (dorsiflexion) and in turning it outwards (eversion). This makes walking difficult as the toes drag on the ground and the foot turns in. As a result of the foot drop, the posture and control of the rest of the leg and trunk is often affected during standing and walking. Slow passive movement of the Achilles' tendon should be practised regularly to maintain a full range of movement at the ankle. A bed cradle should be used to relieve the foot of the weight of the bed clothes. A variety of adaptations to footwear and appliances can help to maintain a normal walking pattern. All treatment should be directed towards the cause of the problem, for example spasticity or muscle weakness in the leg or the trunk as well as in the foot.

Sensory nerve deficits cause disorders in sensation (anaesthesia and paraesthesia) by disrupting the body's awareness and response to impulses on their way to the brain. This can affect not only skin and joint sensation but also coordination and perception of the body's awareness in space. Loss of sensation can occur with paralysis or as a result of other conditions, for example diabetes. The most common form of diabetic neuropathy is a peripheral involvement of the nerves of the lower part of both legs. Sensory impairment involves gradual loss of all types of sensation. Motor impairment starts with loss of ankle jerks and weakness of the intrinsic muscles follows. The major danger of diabetic neuropathy combined with vascular disease is neuropathic ulcers, which will be addressed in the integument section.

The danger of absent or reduced sensation is that trauma and infection can occur without pain and, therefore, may not be noticed by the older person. Other problems associated with sensory nerve damage is the inability to feel the foot and leg when standing or to know where it is in space when walking. This makes walking very slow and laborious, and reduces confidence. In the case of hemiplegia, sensory deficit may improve and during rehabilitation ordinary biofeedback techniques, for example a heel pressure sensor under the heel in the shoe, can help people know where their heels are on the ground and thereby improve their confidence in walking. Scrupulous attention to foot care is needed in all cases.

Abnormal Fluid Balance

Swelling of the ankles and feet occurs as a result of many different medical conditions and may make foot care difficult and

Meeting Oral/Foot Needs

George Raymond has lived alone for some years but, following his annual over seventy-fives' health check, the community nursing team had begun to visit regularly. When Mr. Raymond moved into a nursing home, he told the nurse that he was diabetic and controlled this with the diet given to him by his community dietician. He had become quite accustomed to what he could eat and what he could not. Eating didn't bother him too much anymore, because his dentures made his mouth sore and they seemed to be too large now. His community nurse had obtained for him some treatment for 'thrush', but both the dentures and the cream were in a drawer at home. He said that his niece could bring them in if necessary. He also admitted to 'some difficulty getting about' because he 'couldn't get comfortable shoes any more'.

When the nurse in the home examined Mr. Raymond, she found oral thrush. His toenails were long and his feet were very cold to the touch, but the skin was intact.

- What information did Mr. Raymond give to the nurse in the home that offered subjective data for the nursing assessment?
- What information did the nurse collect that provided objective data for the assessment?
- What strengths does Mr. Raymond demonstrate that could be used as a basis for his plan of care?
- What interventions could the nurse make regarding his oral and dental problems?
- What interventions could the nurse make regarding his foot discomfort, and what advice could she offer Mr. Raymond in this regard?
- What criteria might the nurse use to decide when Mr. Raymond should be advised that referral to a specialist dentist or podiatrist might be necessary?
- List possible outcome criteria for the plan of care regarding Mr. Raymond's oral and foot health. His own desired outcomes, and assessment of the achievement of these, should be included.

necessitate special shoes. Pitting oedema may occur in renal and hepatic disease or as a response to tissue damage through injury, for example a sprained ankle. The most common cause of ankle and foot swelling in frail older people is congestive cardiac failure. Diuretics affect the body's fluid balance and may be used to treat pitting oedema. Physiotherapy treatments are likely to reduce swelling in some cases. Low and lacing footwear (or other fastening that allows for adjustment) to cope with fluctuations in swelling will be needed. Putting shoes on immediately on rising, before swelling increases, has been suggested. Lying with the feet higher than the hips will allow gravity to reduce swelling (Hughes, 1983).

Common Foot Problems

Corns and Calluses

Corns are the most common of all foot problems. They are conical shaped layers of compacted skin, usually on the toes, which occur as a result of friction and pressure on the skin rubbing against bony protuberant areas of the toes when shoes are worn. Once the small, hard, white corn is established, continued pressure causes pain. Unless the cause is removed, it will continue to enlarge and cause increasing pain. Soft corns form in a similar manner but occur between opposing surfaces of the toes. Both corns and calluses interfere with the ability to walk comfortably and wear shoes.

Over-the-counter preparations for corns damage normal tissue as well as removing the corn. Oval corn pads, which seem to aid the relief of corns, actually create greater pressure in the toes and can decrease circulation to the tissue within the oval pad (in much the same way as a rubber ring at the coccyx for a pressure sore will damage surrounding tissue). It is suggested that the corn pad is cut so that it resembles the letter u and is placed around three aspects of the corn protecting it from pressure without restricting circulation to healthy tissue. If such foot-care treatments do not deal with the problem, treatment by a chiropodist is recommended (Help the Aged, 1994), and a change of footwear (Hughes, 1983). Older people are more prone to corns as their skin tends to loose its elasticity and the fibro-fatty padding under the skin gets thinner. Therefore, activities or pressure that cause no symptoms to young skin may cause painful problems in older people.

Calluses are layers of compacted skin that usually occur on the soles and heels of the feet due to chronic irritation and friction from shoes. They grow over any bony area, usually on the ball of the foot. They may not cause any pain nor need any special attention, but can be kept under control by regular careful use of a pumice stone or chiropody sponge after bathing. Alternatively, calluses can be extremely painful or give a burning sensation on the soles of the feet due to hard skin pressing on the nerves. This type of callus may be removed by the chiropodist, but undoubtedly it will reoccur unless the cause is removed. Again, the chiropodist will be able to pinpoint the cause and advise on prevention. Commercial preparations should only be used with extreme caution as some contain caustic substances which will destroy normal skin and be slow to heal.

Decreased sebaceous activity, dehydration of the horny layer and environmental influences are responsible for the majority of dry and scaly foot problems found in older people. Metabolic or nutritional alterations and dysfunctions of keratin formation are considered other possible causes of dry foot

problems. Dryness leads to fissures in the soles of the feet, particularly the heels. Feet itch and are scratched to relieve discomfort. It is necessary to lubricate the feet with lotion at least twice a day to maintain tissue hydration. A moisturising lotion or oil should be massaged into the feet.

Bunions

Clinically called hallux valgus, these are bony prominences that occur over the medial aspect of the first metatarsal head (the joint of the great toe). The cause is not clear, although hereditary factors may play a part. It is more common in women than men; this may be due to their different bone structure (wider hips applying a lateral force to the knees and feet) or it may be related to the wearing of fashion footwear (Hughes, 1983).

Shoes that properly support, protect and provide comfort for the foot are essential. Shoes should provide enough forefoot space laterally and dorsally, have a wide toe box and generally fit well. Custom made shoes, although expensive, are still available for the older person with bunions. Less expensive are ultralight walking and running shoes. Fabric shoes are perhaps the most comfortable for the older person with bunions because the fabric stretches more than leather and synthetic materials. Cloth shoes should have a good quality walking surface.

Hammertoe

This is a permanently flexed and rotated toe or toes that have a claw like appearance. It is often seen in the second toe associated with hallux valgus as the pressure from a short shoe can cause both these deformities. Balance and comfort are affected. Painful corns develop on the fixed joint and sometimes a bursa (small fluid filled sack) forms as a result of pressure from footwear.

Buying shoes becomes difficult as extra depth is required to accommodate the bent toes. Chiropody appliances can be made to hold the toe in a good position while it is still flexible and chiropody treatment can help control the resulting corns and calluses. If the only problem is the toe rubbing on footwear, the shoes can be made comfortable by inserting a balloon patch. This modification involves cutting a large enough hole in the upper to allow the deformity to protrude through the hole. A leather patch is then placed over the hole and ballooned out so that the area is enclosed but not constricted (Hughes, 1983).

Metatarsalgia

Metatarsalgia is pain in the ball of the foot and may be due to any of the following causes:
- A narrow high arched foot, which focuses stress on the ball of the foot.
- Legs that are unequal in length, thus adding stress to the metatarsal joints of the shorter leg.
- Rheumatoid arthritis.
- Stress fractures.
- Fluid accumulation, muscle fatigue, flat feet or overloaded feet as in the case of obesity.
- Morton's metatarsalgia, caused by swelling of a nerve in the interface between either the second and third or third

and forth metatarsal bones, may also be responsible for this foot problem.

Relief is often obtained by foot freedom, that is when the foot is not restricted by footwear or tight bed clothes. Again shoes must be wide and hold the foot back in the shoe so that the toes are not squashed together. Orthotics and the use of non-steroidal anti-inflammatory medications are also helpful.

Fungal infections of the feet are common in older people, particularly athlete's foot. The skin in the webs between the toes becomes white and sodden in appearance; scaling occurs and the skin may also itch. Anti fungal ointment is an effective treatment, but the prevention of the spread of the infection is important. Fungal infections which occur under the nail are characterised by dirty yellow streaks or total nail discoloration. The nail becomes opaque, scaly and hypertrophied. A fine powdery substance forms under the centre of the nail and pushes it up, casing the sides of the nail to dig into the flesh. Systemic treatment (griseofulvin) takes a period of approximately 9 months, as it only effects new nail growth. Commonly, topical treatments are used with or without prior removal of the nail plate (Kemp, 1988).

Deformed Toenails

Involuted nails are a problem, as the edges curve towards the nail bed. This can be a painful problem caused by tight hose or footwear putting pressure on the nail plate and inducing malformed growth. Involuted nails are likely to be difficult to cut, particularly as the edges are likely to be thickened. Chiropody treatment can help thin the edges.

Ingrown toenails (onychocryptosis) are a cause of pain in the big toes, as the edges of the nail become embedded in the surrounding skin as the nail grows. This may result in inflammation and swelling which can lead to infection. The main causes are faulty nail cutting and narrow footwear. Chiropody techniques can be employed to correct the problem and education on correct nail cutting may be necessary to prevent recurrence.

Ram's horn nail (onchogryphosis) is a condition where the nail becomes thickened and deformed, and is due to one side of the nail growing faster than the other. It is likely to occur due to injury, like severe stubbing of the nail or to infrequent nail cutting in older people whose self-care has been neglected. If untreated, pain will ensue and footwear will not fit. Chiropody treatment will provide immediate relief. **Figure 7.5** illustrates some common foot problems.

Skin Conditions Affecting the Feet

Rashes can cause intense irritation and itching. The most likely causes are allergies, psoriasis and eczema. They are fairly easily distinguished by their distribution. For example, allergies to shoe uppers are likely to cause redness and scaling to the areas of the feet in contact with the fabric. Psoriasis pustules are likely to present on the instep of the foot and the skin in the area will be reddened. Eczema is likely to cause redness and scaling in the area of the big toe. Any skin condition affecting the feet will be aggravated by poor foot hygiene and hosiery, and footwear must be chosen with great care to provide comfort to sensitive

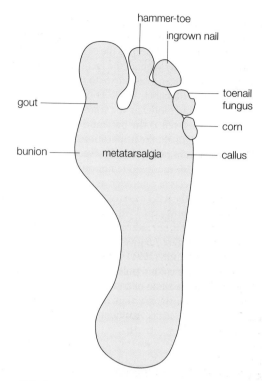

Figure 7.5 Common foot problems.

areas. Chilblains are red and swollen areas on the toes and heels and can be very itchy. They are caused by an abnormal reaction of the blood vessels to changes in temperature. They are a much less common problem nowadays, with the increase in the use of central heating. The best means of prevention is for the whole body to be kept warm by wearing warm clothing. Cold feet should be warmed up gradually rather than by the application of direct heat.

Care of the Feet

Foot care is a prime factor in determining mobility and retaining independence.

Nursing care of the feet of older people should be directed towards maintaining and enhancing comfort and function, removing possible mechanical irritants and decreasing the likelihood of infection.

Assessment

The nurse has the important function of assessing the feet of older people, not just bathing and applying lotion to the feet. Assessment is the key to maintenance of the older person's highest level of function and ability. Nurses can identify potential and actual problems and refer to medical and chiropody staff as appropriate.

Various foot nursing assessment tools are available (King, 1978; Kelechi and Lucas, 1991) but are not perceived to be widely used by nurses working with older people in the UK.

Instead, elements of foot-care assessment are likely to be included in a holistic assessment of the older person. Regardless of where nursing takes place, it is the concept of seeing people as individuals, together with all the factors that may influence their wellbeing which enables nurses to make a unique contribution to foot care (Hughes, 1983). Foot care can benefit from the use of a nursing model as the framework can be used to include the feet as well as the patient overall. The use of the model helps to highlight the implications of present or potential foot problems in relation to the everyday life of the older person. It also helps to integrate not only specific treatments but also other aspects of care, such as the management of predisposing factors, the relief of symptoms and the prevention of further associated problems. With this approach the feet are not dealt with in isolation, but rather as part of individually planned, total nursing care. **Box 7.5** gives essential data for foot assessment. Kelechi and Lucas (1991) suggest that assessment includes a description of the colour, pulses, structure and temperature of the feet, and the location of any problems, for example, corns, calluses, cracks/fissures, dry skin, oedema, lesions/ulcerations and long or thick toenails. Ambulation, gait, foot hygiene and footwear should be closely observed. Echevarria *et al.* (1988) combined foot assessment with patient education.

Interventions

Ability to adequately inspect feet requires good vision and joint mobility, both of which tend to decline with age (Pelican *et al.* 1990). Half of older people surveyed have reported difficulty cutting their own toenails (Cartwright and Henderson, 1986). Hand tremors and obesity are other significant factors. It is, therefore, often necessary for inspection and interventions to be carried out for the older person.

Care of the Toenails

Feet should be soaked in warm water for 20–30 minutes to soften the nails before they are cut (**Figure 7.6**). They should be cut straight across and even with the top of the toe. Nails which have become thickened should be brought to the attention of a chiropodist, as attention by nursing staff may result in further damage to the matrix or precipitate infection. Assessments by chiropodists indicated that although almost half of older people should be referred to a chiropodist for treatment, only 20% were receiving chiropody services (Cartwright and Henderson, 1986). In order to receive chiropody every 6 weeks through the National Health Service, a state registered chiropodist is required for every 1000 older people. Numbers available are grossly inadequate, leading to some older people being provided with a considerably reduced service and others paying for private provision.

Foot Massage

This is a means of reducing oedema, stimulating circulation and improving pedal flexibility. It not only relaxes the feet but also stimulates relaxation in the rest of the body. The nurse will find that foot massage can easily be modified to incorporate a range of motion exercises for the toes and ankles (**Figure 7.7**). Older people may also benefit from aromatherapy and reflexology.

Footwear

Shoes should be worn that cover, protect, provide stability for the foot and minimise the chance of falls. Ideal footwear fulfils the criteria given in **Box 7.6**.

A major study found that 1 in 25 older people felt that trouble with their feet caused or contributed to disability. This suggests that half a million people aged over 65 years in England are restricted in some way because of foot problems (Cartwright and Henderson, 1986). Attention to this neglected area is likely to make a difference.

CARE OF THE SKIN

Skin Structure and Function

The skin is the largest and most visible organ in the body. **Figure 7.8** gives details of the structure and function of integument with some associated conditions. The skin's main functions are (Onselen, 1997):
- Protection.

7.5 Essential Data for Foot Assessment

Observations of mobility
- Gait.
- Ambulation.
- Foot hygiene.
- Footwear.

Past health history
- Systemic diseases.
- Musculoskeletal problems.
- Vascular/ulcerations/peripheral vascular disease.
- Vision problems.
- Falls.
- Trauma.
- Smoking history.
- Pain.

Bilateral assessment of:
- Colour.
- Circulation.
- Pulses.
- Structures (hammertoe, bunion, overlapping digits).
- Temperature.
- Dermatological aspects – skin lesions (fissures, corns, calluses, warts, excoriation).
- Oedema.
- Itching.
- Rash.
- Toenails – long, thick, discoloration.

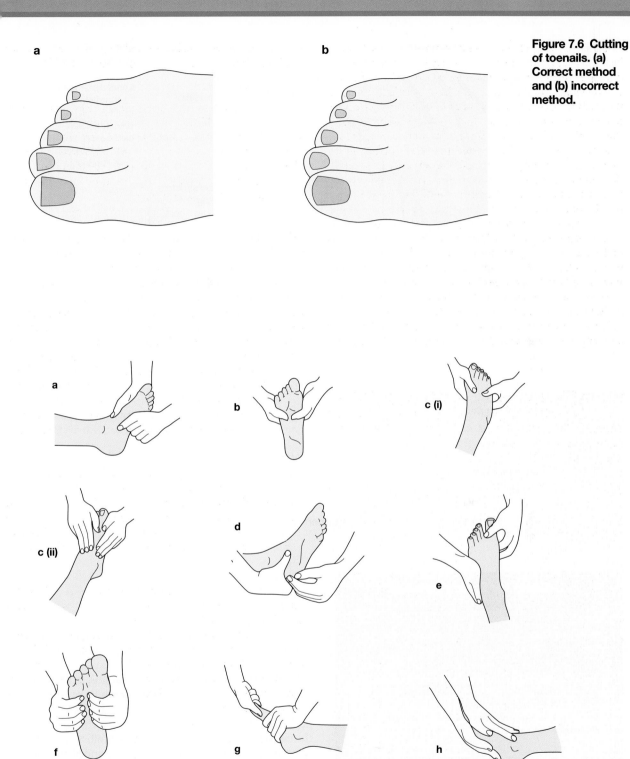

Figure 7.6 Cutting of toenails. (a) Correct method and (b) incorrect method.

Figure 7.7 Foot massage. (a) With knuckles make small circles over sole of foot. (b) and (c) With thumbs and fingers make circles over entire foot. (d) With tips of fingers make circles on heel. (e) Gently run thumb between tendon grooves from ankle to toes. (f) As if breaking a cracker, move the foot back and forth. (g) Gently stretch and rotate each toe. (h) End by placing foot between hands.

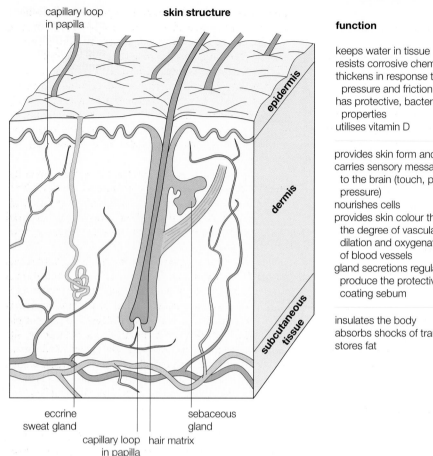

skin structure

function	skin condition in the aged individual
keeps water in tissue resists corrosive chemicals thickens in response to pressure and friction has protective, bacterial properties utilises vitamin D	dry skin keratosis: actinic, seborrheic pruritus pressure sores skin cancer: basal and squamous cell carcinoma
provides skin form and structure carries sensory messages to the brain (touch, pain, heat, pressure) nourishes cells provides skin colour through the degree of vascular dilation and oxygenation of blood vessels gland secretions regulate heat, produce the protective coating sebum	pressure sores
insulates the body absorbs shocks of trauma stores fat	advanced pressure sores

Labels on diagram: capillary loop in papilla; epidermis; dermis; subcutaneous tissue; eccrine sweat gland; capillary loop in papilla; hair matrix; sebaceous gland

Figure 7.8 Correlation of structure and function of integument with some associated conditions.

7.6 Criteria for Ideal Footwear

- Length. There should be a 1.25 cm gap between the end of the largest toe and the shoe front.
- Width. This must be adequate both across the ball of the foot and the toes. Some shops specialise in wide-fitting shoes.
- Depth. The uppers must not press down on any toes. The Drushoe is an example of extra depth shoes which are easily available.
- Fastenings. These should be adjustable, such as laces, buckles or Velcro. Any limited finger dexterity should be taken into account.
- Heels. These should be thick and no higher than 3.75 cm.
- Material. Leather is preferable, unless contraindicated.

Source: Adapted from Helfrand AE. Focus on geriatric care and rehabilitation. Rockville, MD: Aspen, 1989.

- Sensory perception.
- Preservation of water balance.
- Regulation of temperature.

The epidermis is the non-vascular, relatively impermeable outer layer that consists of four layers of cells which protect the dermis. The basal layer contains cells that produce melanin, the pigment responsible for skin colour.

The dermis, lying beneath the epidermis, is a supportive layer of connective tissue composed of a matrix of yellow elastic fibres that provide stretch and recoil, white fibrous collagen fibres that provide tensile strength and an absorbent gel between the two fibres. The dermis supports hair follicles, sweat and sebaceous glands, nerve fibres, muscle cells and blood vessels.

The subcutaneous tissue that lies beneath the dermis is composed of loose adipose tissue. Subcutaneous tissue insulates and cushions the body, it varies at different body sites and between individuals. Most weight gain is due to an increase in subcutaneous fat. With ageing, the distribution of subcutaneous fat changes. Fat deposits begin to disappear from the extremities, particularly the upper arms, and accumulate on the abdomen and hips. In the face, fat shifts from the upper to the lower part (Porth and Kapke, 1983).

The epidermis, dermis and subcutaneous layers of skin have specific functions:

- Epidermis – keeps water in tissues, thickens in response to pressure and friction, has protective bacterial properties and utilises vitamin D.
- Dermis – provides skin form and structure, carries sensory messages to the brain (touch, pain, heat, pressure), nourishes cells, provides skin colour through the degree of vascular dilation and oxygenation of blood vessels. Gland secretions regulate heat and produce the protective coating sebum.
- Subcutaneous tissue – insulates the body, absorbs shocks of trauma and stores fat. In older people, the epidermis produces varying cell shapes and sizes. The previously textured skin becomes thin, fragile, shiny and flat resulting from the loss of cone like projections called rete ridges.

Age-related Changes

With age the dermis elasticity and suppleness is lost because of cross-link changes of the elastin and collagen components. Blood flow diminishes, dermal cells are replaced more slowly causing delayed wound healing, and sensory receptors do not transmit sensations as rapidly.

The rate at which skin ages is proportional to the degree of exposure to environmental factors such as wind and the irradiation of the sun. The face and hands being the most constantly exposed areas of the body show more immediate signs of ageing than those which are rarely exposed. Visible changes of the skin, for example quality of colour, firmness, elasticity and texture, all indicate ageing.

Skin colour varies with blood flow. Pallor is apparent with diminished blood flow and flushing occurs when blood flow increases. Decreased haemoglobin in capillary blood flow that has lost most of it's oxygen produces cyanosis. Circulatory disorders cause skin to loose its colour and blood vessels become more fragile.

Pigmentation changes occur in response to hormone activity. Melanocytes increase in size but decrease in number over time and it is the degree of activity that creates uneven pigmentation. Pigmented moles and levi are thought to be benign neoplasms or melanocytes. The development of lentigines, commonly called 'age spots' or 'liver spots', and seen on the back of the hands and wrists of light-skinned races, is also thought to be from uneven melanin production. From the sixth decade on, they are thought to be sun related.

Eccrine, apocrine and sebaceous gland activity is influenced by the hormonal and nervous systems. Therefore, if the effectiveness of hormonal and nervous stimulation decreases, glandular activity diminishes significantly. There are two types of sweat glands:

- The apocrine glands – these are mainly present in the axillary, genital and perianal areas as well as in the external ear canal. They produce sweat and ear wax, which are odourless until bacteria begin to act on the moisture to produce odours. Deodorants and antiperspirants are often used to suppress such odours and it is suggested that dusting powder could also be effective. Aprocrine sweating may be induced by emotion but not by temperature changes.
- The eccrine glands – these are located all over the body. They produce a watery secretion whose composition can vary according to the body's excretory needs and normally includes a weak sodium chloride solution that contains lactate and potassium. Eccrine sweating occurs in response to heat and emotion and is usually more profuse on the hands and feet.

With ageing there is a general decrease in eccrine sweating, which may be due to a decrease in the number of sweat glands or in their activity. Older people should, therefore, avoid spending long periods in the sun and should wear a hat, light cool clothing and drink adequate fluids. Apocrine sweating, however, remains unchanged.

The sebaceous glands empty their secretions into the canal of the hair follicles, which are found in all parts except the palms of the hands and the soles of the feet. Sebum is not water soluble, does not form emulsions and may act as an emollient. It may also act as a bacteriostatic and fungistatic agent. As an example, the soles, which have no sebaceous glands, are the primary site of the fungal infection, athletes foot. The activity of the sebaceous glands usually decreases with age. Although there is not a reduction in the actual number of glands, their secretory activity decreases and this leads to dryness of the skin and hair.

Hair

Hair has a biological, psychological and cosmetic value for both men and women. Hair is tightly fused horny cells that arise from the dermal layer and obtain colour from melanocytes. Hair colour correlates with skin; the darkest races have the darkest hair.

The hormone testosterone influences hair distribution in both men and women. Axillary and pubic hair tends to diminish with age in women and in some instances disappears. Hair on the head becomes thinner and depleted of melanin, giving it its characteristic grey colour. Older women are inclined to develop facial hair due to decreased oestrogen production. Men become bald or develop a receding hair line. Hair growth may also be affected by diet, radiation, physical condition and drug therapy.

Nails

Older people often complain about the splitting and breaking of their nails. Their nails become harder and thicker, more brittle, dull and opaque. The nail changes in shape, at times becoming flat or concave instead of convex. Vertical ridges appear due to decreased water, calcium and lipid content. The blood supply decreases as well as the rate of nail growth. Photoageing is the result of environmental damage to the skin by sunlight and many of the changes are preventable.

Skin Problems

Skin conditions are common place in the UK, approximately 10% of all consultations in primary health care are skin related, and studies estimate that 75% of skin conditions in the community are not seen by a doctor (British Association of Dermatologists, 1993).

Dry Skin

Dry skin (xerosis) is perhaps the most common problem. Diminished amounts of sebum secreted by the sebaceous glands lessen the availability of the protective lipid film that retards the evaporation of water from the horny layer. The thinner epidermis allows more moisture to escape from the skin. Inadequate fluid intake has a systemic effect; it pulls moisture from the skin to assist in the overall hydration of the body.

Exposure to the environmental elements, decreased humidity, use of harsh soaps, frequent hot baths and nutritional deficiencies also contribute to drying of the skin. Dry skin may just be dry skin or it may be a symptom of more serious systemic disease, for example diabetes. Itching frequently accompanies dryness; scratch marks may be visible at affected areas.

Treatment of dry itchy skin is to rehydrate the dermis. The use of super fatted soaps helps to restore the protective lipid film to the skin surface. Incorporation of bath oils into the bathing routine helps hold moisture and retards its escape from the skin. Hot baths should be discouraged and the number of baths and showers each week limited to two or three. Oil may be applied directly on to moist skin and the application of lotions or emollients to the body several times a day is another way to keep the epidermal layer lubricated and hydrated. The pH of skin ranges between 4.5 and 6. A moisturising lotion with a pH in the range of 6–7 will soften the skin as the skin absorbs beneficial ingredients more easily when a product has a neutral pH.

Older people should be encouraged to have an adequate intake of fluids including a few glasses of water a day and to maintain an environment with adequate humidity. They should wear soft non-abrasive clothing and in cold or windy weather a warm hat, gloves and scarf to protect the extremities. They should also avoid direct sunlight for extended periods, wear a brimmed hat to shade from the sun and use a sun-screen lotion on all exposed areas.

Pruritus

Pruritus (itching) is a symptom rather than a diagnosis or a disease; as well as being an unpleasant sensation, it is an additional threat to skin intactness. Pruritus is the most common complaint of older people, which is aggravated by heat, sudden temperature changes, sweating, contact with articles of clothing, fatigue and emotional upheavals. It may accompany systemic disorders such as chronic renal failure, metabolic disease, iron deficiency anaemia, leukaemia, lymphomas and Hodgkin's disease, and other malignant conditions. It often presents with primary skin disorders like dermatitis, eczema, pemphigoid, prickly heat, psoriasis and infestations such as scabies and lice.

Lichen (a group of inflammatory affections of the skin in which the lesions consist of papular eruptions), infectious diseases such as chickenpox, as well as fungal infections, for example candidiasis, all cause itching.

Allergic reactions such as urticaria (nettle rash or hives) and adverse drug reactions, for example to antibiotics, can also cause severe irritation.

The urge to scratch is an inefficient response to remove the irritant from the skin. When one scratches, a counter-stimulus is introduced, which is stronger than the original stimulus. The nerve messages become confused or eliminate the itching sensation by the intensity of the scratching stimulus. Itching is akin to pain. The nerve endings that produce cutaneous pain also respond to itching. When rehydration of the stratum corneum (outer horny layer of epidermis) is not sufficient to control itching, cool compresses of saline solution may be helpful. Other suggestions for dealing with pruritus are given in **Box 7.7**.

Keratoses

Keratosis or seborrhoeic warts are the commonest benign tumours found in older people. It is a horny growth that occurs due to an abnormal growth of the keratinising cells of the epidermis. They are sharply circumscribed wart-like lesions which appear to sit on the top of the skin like a blob of wax. They usually begin as yellow or brown flat lesions of less than 1 cm and may become larger, dark brown to coal black lesions with a greasy appearance. These benign growths appear mainly on the trunk, face or scalp either as single or multiple lesions.

Although sebaceous keratoses are benign, they must be differentiated from nevi or moles, which are formed from clusters of melanocytes, since a change in the colour, texture or size of a nevus may indicate malignant transformation to a melanoma. These lesions can at times be removed by a fingernail but they tend to return unless treated by dermatologists – for cosmetic reasons only. Other benign neoplasms include skin tags. They are soft, pedunculated, brown or flesh coloured papules, appearing on the front or side of the neck or in the axilla. They range in size from a pin head to the size of a pea and have the normal colour and texture of the skin.

Actinic or solar keratosis, unlike the seborrhoeic keratosis has the potential to become a cancerous lesion. It is the result of years of overexposure to the sun and occurs more frequently in older men. Common sites include the surface of bald heads, hands and faces. Actinic keratosis is characterised by localised thickening of the skin and a hard keratin build-up, which begins as reddish, scaly patch or patches on superficial areas.

Early diagnosis and removal of the lesion are important to prevent serious problems which may occur later on.

Skin Cancers

A seven-point checklist for skin cancer is given in **Box 7.8**. Squamous cell carcinoma resembles actinic keratosis and is the second most common skin cancer. It is most prevalent in fair-skinned older men who live in sunny climates. It begins as a flesh coloured nodule, then like the actinic keratosis it becomes reddened and scaly. It may be hard and wart-like with a grey top and horny texture, or it may be ulcerated with raised defined borders. Squamous cell carcinoma is less common and more aggressive than basal cell carcinoma; it has a higher incidence of metastasis and cannot be ignored.

Basal cell carcinoma or rodent ulcer is a slow growing, locally destructive tumour. Although it does not usually metastasise, this can occur, and can be quite disfiguring. Early detec-

7.7 Dealing with Pruritus

- Take tepid baths with bath oil added so as not to further dehydrate the skin, apply soothing creams or emollients several times a day, especially to hands, feet and face.
- Wear soft absorbent clothing such as cotton.
- Caution in the use of topical steroid creams is advised as the absorption is unpredictable. The use of low-dose systemic steroids should be avoided as they are likely to lead to complications.
- Older people using antihistamines should be aware of the possibility of sudden, severe side effects, such as excessive drowsiness or even confusion.

tion and treatment is, therefore, recommended. This neoplasm is waxy and shiny in appearance, but may ulcerate. They are very common in older people (the most common malignant lesion of epithelial tissue) and although often appearing in light-exposed skin, and hence thought to be sun induced, they may appear on covered sites.

Melanoma is a fast spreading, malignant skin tumour which will metastasise rapidly and become life threatening. The legs and backs of women and the backs of men are the most common sites for this neoplasm. Melanoma is a neoplasm of melanocytes that can spread throughout the body through lymph and blood. Two-thirds of melanomas develop from pre-existing moles. While it is less common than squamous or basal cell carcinomas, it has a high mortality rate, and although it can be a result of sun exposure, non-exposed areas of the body are not exempt.

Sun Protection

In order to avoid skin cancer, it is advised that intense sunlight is avoided between 11 a.m. and 3 p.m. The use of a sun-screen of sun protection factor 15 or above should be applied liberally to the face and neck 20 minutes before going out in the sun-

7.8 Seven-Point Checklist for Skin Cancer

Major skin signs
- Change in a mole or lesion.
- Change in mole shape.
- Change in colour of mole.

Minor skin signs
- Change in sensation, does it itch, is it painful?
- Is the mole inflamed?
- Is there bleeding, crusting or oozing?
- Is it larger than 6 mm?

Source: Mackie R. *Skin Cancer*. London: Martin Dunitz, 1996.

light and reapplied every 2–3 hours and after swimming (Onselen, 1997).

Skin cancer is the second most common cancer with more than 40,500 new cases a year in the UK (Imperial Cancer Research Fund, 1996). The incidence of malignant melanoma is doubling every 10–15 years (British Association of Dermatologists, 1993).

Skin Assessment

Patient assessment must always be holistic and include examination of the whole body. Ensuring privacy, time and understanding are important considerations when conducting assessment. Essential aspects of a nursing assessment are given in **Box 7.9**.

Most dermatology patients will feel embarrassed about their appearance as they are coping with changes in their body image and an often unsympathetic public response.

Intervention

People with skin problems need:
- Understanding and realistic expectations of their condition.
- Skilled nurses who have had dermatology training and are constantly improving their professional knowledge.
- Help in finding ways of coping and adapting to their skin conditions.
- Educational sessions that are practically based.
- Information should be given verbally, with additional written information and personalised care plans on all aspects of skin care.
- Family members may need additional support, understanding and education (Onselen, 1997).

Pressure Damage

In 1992, the Department of Health (DoH) estimated that 6.7% of the adult hospital population were affected by pressure sores. Although not exclusively a problem for older people, 70% of pressure sores are believed to occur in the older age group (Young and Dobrzanski, 1992). It has been suggested that 95 % of all pressure sores are preventable if there is early prediction of an individual's susceptibility and an active prevention programme is implemented. This claim is well documented in the nursing literature, for example Hibbs (1988) and Waterlow (1988a, 1988b). Improved primary care and community support increasingly enable frail older people to be cared for at home. The necessary expertise and equipment for pressure sore prevention, therefore, also needs to be available in the community.

A pressure sore can cost the individual pain, misery, systemic illness, increased length of hospital stay, reduced self-esteem, altered body image and may sufficiently delay rehabilitation measures to preclude return to independence

7.9 Essential Aspects of Nursing Assessment

(1) History of skin condition
- What is the skin problem, when did it first appear and where ?
- How is the skin affected today, where are the affected sites (body, scalp, flexures, feet and hands)?
- Past skin condition – severity and contributing factors.
- Family history.
- Additional systems, e.g. itch, pain and signs of infection.

(2) Health status
- Past health history, hospital admissions.
- Allergies.
- Oral/inhaled medications.

(3) Psychosocial patient and family perspectives
- Coping mechanisms.
- Level of knowledge on skin conditions and treatments.
- Expectations regarding nursing care and treatment.

(4) Topical skin management
- Assess previous and current treatments, and reasons for change.

(5) Contributing environmental factors
- Occupational factors.
- Recreational factors.
- Recent foreign travel.
- Household triggers: clothing, washing, housework and bedding.
- Animals and pets.
- Diet and fluids.
- Psychological support and education.

(Hibbs, 1988). There is no doubt that pressure sores are accompanied by increased mortality. The financial implications of pressure sores are enormous. The annual cost to the National Health Service is somewhere between 60 and 200 million pounds (DoH, 1993). The total cost of hospital care for one patient with a severe pressure sore in 1988 was calculated to be in excess of £25,000 (Hibbs, 1988). Litigation can increase the cost of pressure sores – damages in excess of £100,000 have been awarded for the development of a hospital-acquired pressure sore (Robertson, 1987). Health-care purchasers consider pressure sore prevalence and incidence data to be key indicators of the quality of care delivered in a provider unit (Audit Commission, 1991).

Risk Assessment

It is recommended that an individual's pressure sore risk status should be documented within 12 hours of admission and then at appropriate intervals as dictated by the overall state of the patient's health. Risk assessment tools should be used as they provide the basis of a systematic approach to the risk of pressure sore development. Tools have limitations and should be used as an adjunct to, rather than the basis of, a nursing assessment (Simpson *et al.* 1996). The pressure sore risk assessment tools most commonly used in the UK are British in origin – Norton *et al.* (1962) and Waterlow (1988a, 1988b): **Tables 7.1 and 7.2**, respectively.

The Norton Risk Assessment Tool

This was the first pressure sore risk assessment tool of its kind and is well known and widely used. It was developed as a result of systematic observations of elderly hospital patients and sought to establish which of a patient's health characteristics were relevant in relation to the development of pressure sores. It showed that the most important characteristics were general physical condition, mental state, activity, mobility and incontinence. These factors form the basis of the tool.

This tool has received widespread critical review. It has been shown to both under and over-predict pressure sore risk (Flanagan, 1993). Some users have reported difficulty in determining the internal ratings of the tool items and problems of assessor subjectivity are apparent in this relatively simple tool. (Alternatively, student nurses were slightly better able to agree on the patient's risk score using this tool than the Waterlow scale.)The tool has been subjected to repeated reliability and validity testing, but results have been inconsistent. In its favour, this tool was developed specifically for use with frail older people in continuing care settings and is both simple and quick to complete.

The Waterlow Risk Assessment Tool

This tool was developed following a review of the research into pressure sores and discussions with medical colleagues. It was designed specifically as an aide-mémoire for nurses working within medical and surgical settings. It aims to provide guidelines on the selection of preventative aids and equipment as well as on the management of established pressure sores. It also aims to promote the user's awareness of the causes of pressure sores and provide a means of determining the risk of pressure sore development. The scoring system identifies six main areas of risk:
- Build and weight.
- Continence.
- Skin type.
- Mobility.
- Sex and age.
- Appetite.

This tool has enjoyed widespread popularity due to the fact that it is accompanied by preventative and treatment guidelines and offers an educational component. Consequently, it has been incorporated into many health-care providers' pressure sore prevention strategies. However, the fact that Waterlow did not undertake any data collection to support the developmental stage of her work, and little has been achieved with regard to the formal evaluation of this tool, reduces the scientific credibility. Gross over-prediction of patients at risk using this tool have been reported

The Norton Score									
(A) Physical condition		**(B) Mental state**		**(C) Activity**		**(D) Mobility**		**(E) Incontinence**	
Good	4	Alert	4	Ambulant	4	Full	4	None	4
Fair	3	Apathetic	3	Walks with help	3	Slightly limited	3	Occasional	3
Poor	2	Confused	2	Chairbound	2	Very limited	2	Usually urinary	2
Very bad	1	Stuporous	1	Bedfast	1	Immobile	1	Double	1

Instructions for use:

1. Assess the patient's condition and score accordingly (1–4) under each heading (A–E).
2. Total the scores together.
3. A total of 14 and below indicates a patient is at risk and preventative measures should be taken.
   The lower the total, the higher the risk.
4. Assess the patient regularly.

Table 7.1 The Norton Score. (Source: Simpson A, Bowers K, Weir-Hughes D. *Pressure sore prevention*. Whurr Publishers, 1996, page 31.) Reproduced with kind permission of Churchill Livingstone.

Waterlow Pressure Sore Risk Assessment					
Build/weight for height	**Skin type – visual risk areas**	**Sex Age**	**Continence**	**Mobility**	**Appetite**
Average Above average Obese Below average	Healthy Tissue paper Dry Oedematous Clammy (temp ↑) Discolored Broken/spot	Male Female 14–49 50–64 65–74 75–80 81+	Occasionally incontinent Catheterised/incontinent of faeces Doubly incontinent	Complete/catheterised Fully Restless/fidgety Apathetic Restricted Inert/traction Chairbound	Average Poor Nasogastric (NG) tube Fluids only NBM/anorexic
Special risks:	**Tissue malnutrition**		**Neurological deficit**	**Major surgery/trauma**	**Medication**
	Terminal cachexia Cardiac failure Peripheral vascular disease Anaemia Smoking		Diabetes, Muscular Sclerosis (MS), Cerebrovascular accident (CVA) Motor/sensory Paraplegia	Orthopaedic Below waist, spinal On table >2 hours	Cytotoxics High-dose steroids Anti-inflammatory
Score:	10+ At risk	15+ High risk	20+ Very high risk		

Table 7.2 Waterlow Pressure Sore Risk Assessment. The Waterlow Pressure Sore Risk Prevention/Treatment Policy is reproduced with the permission of Judy Waterlow SRN RCNT. Copies of the card and her Pressure Sore Prevention Manual can be obtained from 'Newtons', Curland, Taunton TA3 5SG

by various authors (e.g. Dealey, 1989), and reliability of the tool compares unfavourably with Norton's.

This scale encompasses a broad range of important risk factors, such as nutritional status and tissue tolerance, which other scales exclude. Another advantage is the inclusion of preventative strategies and choice of equipment based on scored level of risk.

The Braden Risk Assessment Tool (Bergstrom *et al.* 1987)

This tool is based on the conceptualisation of the aetiological factors relating to pressure sore formation. It is composed of six categories:

- Sensory perception.
- Moisture.
- Activity.
- Mobility.
- Nutrition.
- Friction and shear.

It originated in the USA, is widely utilised there and recommended by the Agency for Health Care Policy and Research for use in predicting pressure sore development. Evaluation of the tool's reliability and validity have been predominately favourable. The view that this tool confers good reliability is supported by Bridel (1994) who considers it to be the most reliable tool of those described in the literature. Flanagan (1993) considered that this tool demonstrated greater sensitivity and specificity than any other published scale. It is less well known in the UK, but is considered to have greater reliability and validity than either the Norton or Waterlow tools, although no comparative work has been undertaken (Simpson *et al.* 1996).

Nursing Documentation

Nursing documentation is a major medium through which nurses demonstrate their accountability. The document *Guidelines for records and record keeping* (1998) by the United Kingdom Central Council for Nursing, Midwifery and Health Visiting (UKCC) states that, where possible, records should be written in terms that the patient will be able to understand. (This may also be helpful for unqualified health-care workers who use the documentation to guide patient care.) Plans of care formulated by first-level nurses, in relation to the prevention and management of pressure sores, should be patient focused and include patient education where appropriate.

Nurses caring for older people have responsibility for the prevention, assessment and management of wounds, and are accountable for their acts and omissions (UKCC, 1992). Accurate and ongoing assessment is essential for selecting appropriate preventative strategies, planning wound management and for evaluating its effectiveness. This may benefit from the use of a nursing model, which can be used as a framework for the overall care of the individual. Using a model, such as activities of living (Roper *et al.* 1980), may help to communicate pressure sore prevention strategies and highlight the implications of wounds in relation to the everyday life of the patient. It helps not only to integrate specific treatments but also other aspects of care like predisposing factors, the relief of symptoms and the prevention of further associated problems. Thus, pressure sore prevention and wound care are not dealt with in isolation but as part of the overall planned care for the patient.

Aetiology of Pressure Sores

A pressure sore is 'a localised area of cellular damage resulting either from direct pressure on the skin causing ischaemia, or from shearing forces causing mechanical stress on the tissues' (Chapman and Chapman, 1986): **Figure 7.9**.

Reduced mobility, activity and sensory perception can all lead to increased pressure. Extrinsic factors such as moisture, friction and shear and intrinsic factors such as nutrition, age, arteriolar pressure, interstitial fluid flow changes, emotional stress, smoking and skin temperature all impact on tissue tolerance and potentially contribute to pressure sore development (Braden and Bergstrom, 1987).

Tissue damage from friction occurs when the epidermis rubs against another surface, for example elbows and heels rubbing against a sheet. It may be as a result of poor patient handling techniques and, therefore, avoidable. Shear occurs when tissues are wrenched in opposite directions, resulting in disruption or angulation of capillary blood vessels. Shear most commonly occurs in individuals who spend long periods in a semi-recumbent position, for example when a patient slips down the bed and the outer layer of skin remains static but the underlying tissues are pushed forward. Shear can cause full thickness tissue damage and can be prevented by good positioning.

Pressure sores most commonly occur over bony prominences that support the body during lying, sitting and standing. Seating as well as lying surfaces, therefore, need to be considered in relation to pressure sore prevention.

Prevention of Pressure Sores

The preventative management of pressure sores should focus on controlling or alleviating identified predisposing factors in addition to minimising exposure to precipitating factors of pressure, shear and friction. Encouraging frail older people to sit in chairs as opposed to remaining in bed during the day, so-called 'chair nursing', is widely thought to prevent pressure sores and the other complications of prolonged bed rest (e.g. venous thrombosis, chest infection, urinary tract infection and constipation). A study by Gebhardt and Bliss (1994) does not support this theory, but found that the development of pressure sores was strongly correlated with the length of time individuals spent sitting. By sitting for less than 2 hours they were less fatigued and developed fewer complications. It is suggested that

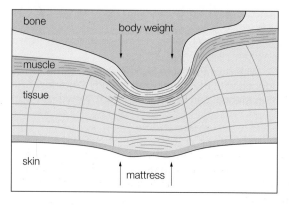

Figure 7.9 Tissue under pressure.

sitting time should not exceed 2 hours for vulnerable individuals and that a good comfortable seating position is essential (Simpson *et al.* 1996).

Nutritional assessment is of paramount importance. Older people have been shown to have a greater protein requirement. Anaemia may result from a dietary deficiency in either iron or vitamin B_{12}, which results in poor blood oxygenation and predisposes to tissue death when exposed to pressure (Livesley, 1990). Vitamin deficiency leads to a reduced integrity of cell walls, decreased enzyme activity for cellular development and reduced tissue restoration. Vitamin C can assist in protein use and it's deficiency has been identified as a factor in pressure sore development, (Goode *et al.* 1992). Supplements of vitamin B help in the metabolism of carbohydrate.

Poor hydration through low fluid intake or high fluid loss reduces tissue resistance, elasticity and, therefore, viability (Livesley, 1990). As well as being part of an initial nursing assessment, the nutritional status of all frail older people should be reassessed regularly. **Appendix 6** shows the decision-making guide for the selection of pressure-relieving equipment (Simpson *et al.* 1996).

Classification of pressure sores
See **Figure 7.10** for pressure sore development.

Treatment of Pressure Sores
The general principles of pressure sore management are:
- To remove extrinsic factors which delay healing, such as unrelieved pressure, shearing and frictional forces.
- To alleviate the effects of the intrinsic factors which contribute to tissue breakdown, such as malnutrition, incontinence and recurrent illness.
- To provide the optimum local environment for healing at the wound site (Morison, 1990).

Dressings should be carefully selected to suit the wound, following local protocols based on current knowledge. For a summary of wound care products available in both the community and in hospital and their uses *see* **Appendix 7** Wound Management (Monthly Index of Medical Specialities, 1997). Manufacturers of wound care products, for example Coloplast, Convatec, Johnson and Johnson, and Smith and Nephew all provide case studies illustrating the clinical effectiveness of their products.

Leg Ulcers

Leg ulcers are found more frequently in older people (Awenat, 1996) and may be either venous or arterial in origin. There are local indications as to their type. For example, in the case of venous ulcers the surrounding skin is liable to be stained and pigmented, with signs of eczema, oedema, and ankle flare (caused by dilated small veins around the ankle). They occur in the gaiter region, usually medial or lateral malleolus and tend to be shallow, flat ulcers. Pain is variable and is exacerbated by cellulitis and oedema.

In the case of arterial ulceration, the skin may be thin, shiny and hairless due to the malnourishment of the tissues. Toenails are likely to be thickened and the affected limb cold and pale. Both legs and the skin surrounding the ulcers should be examined for signs of ischaemia. Ulcers may occur anywhere on the legs or feet and tend to be deep ulcers with adherent slough that may expose bone or tendon. Pain is severe, unremitting and worse on elevation and exercise as well as at night.

Anyone presenting with leg ulceration should have their foot pulses checked. They should be palpable in the case of venous ulcers and absent or diminished in the case of arterial ulcers. If this cannot be recorded, either due to their absence or to oedema, then referral should be made for the measurement of the brachial-to-ankle pressure ratio using the non-invasive Doppler technique. In the case of deep diabetic foot ulcers, X-rays should be taken as part of assessment. The thorough assessment of all leg ulcers to diagnose their type is vital before treatment is commenced. Inadequate assessment could lead to hazardous regimes; for example, compression therapy is likely to have a disastrous effect on an ischaemic limb.

Leg ulcers tend to be chronic wounds that form where a predisposing condition impairs both tissue integrity and healing. Common examples are impaired venous damage due to venous hypotension, and impaired arterial blood supply due to peripheral vascular disease. Leg ulcers are difficult to prevent and the management of predisposing factors and underlying disease is possibly the most important preventative measure. For example, anyone who has evidence of peripheral vascular disease should be referred for vascular assessment. Individuals with varicose veins should be encouraged to avoid sitting or standing for long periods. Foot and leg elevation is essential when resting. Particularly important is the activation of the calf muscle pump, which should be achieved by ankle movement and exercise. The wearing of tight socks and garters should be discouraged as well as the crossing of legs when sitting. Leg ulcers may be prevented by giving up smoking, eating a well-balanced diet,

---

7.10 The UK Consensus Pressure Sore Classification

- Stage 0. No clinical evidence of pressure sore.
- Stage 1. Discoloration of intact skin – light finger pressure applied to the site does not alter the discoloration.
- Stage 2. Partial thickness skin loss or damage involving epidermis and or dermis.
- Stage 3. Full thickness skin loss involving damage or necrosis of subcutaneous tissue but not extending to underlying bone.
- Stage 4. Full thickness skin loss with extensive destruction and tissue necrosis extending to underlying bone, tendon or capsule

Source: Ried J, Morison M. Classification of pressure sore prevention. Nurs Times 1994, 90:46–49).

stage 1

erythema not resolving within 30 minutes of pressure relief. epidermis remains intact reversible with intervention

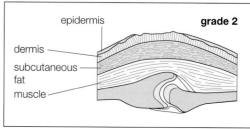

stage 2

partial thickness loss of skin layers involving epidermis and possibly penetrating into but not through dermis. May present as blistering with erytherma and/or induration; wound base moist and pink; painful; free of necrotic tissue

stage 3

full-thickness tissue loss extending through dermis to involve subcutanoeus tissue. presents as shallow crater unless covered by eschar.* may include necrotic tissue, undermining, sinus tract formation, exudate, and/or infection. wound base is usually not painful

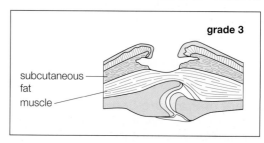

stage 4

deep tissue destruction extending through subcutaneous tissue to fascia and may involve muscle layers' joint and/or bone. presents as a deep crater.* may include necrotic tissue, undermining, sinus tract formation, exudate and/or infection. wound base is usually not painful

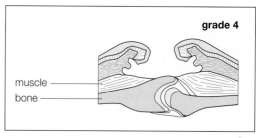

Figure 7.10 Pressure sore development.

avoiding obesity and undertaking suitable exercise, especially if mobility is impaired.

Leg Ulcer Treatments

Experience suggests that an activity of living framework modified to include assessment of the leg and the wound, as well as pain and special health education, works (Awenat, 1996). In addition to appropriate local wound management, high compression bandaging and elevation are recommended for venous ulcers. Arterial ulcers require appropriate local wound management, and possibly surgery, for example revascularisation or angioplasty.

A critical review of the research into the management of leg ulcers in the community (Cullum, 1994) found there was good evidence that a moist environment is the optimum for wound healing. Modern dressings such as hydrocolloids, hydrogels and semipermeable films provide such an environment. Although no study directly examined the role of compression versus no compression in ulcer healing, physiological considerations, expert opinion and clinical experience imply that compression is beneficial.

Once a venous ulcer has healed, it is important to prevent recurrence. High quality, class II compression stockings are available on prescription. Careful measurements are essential to ensure correct fit and hosiery should be replaced at 3-monthly intervals.

SUMMARY

Older people are particularly vulnerable to declining oral health, although tooth loss is not necessarily related to the ageing process but rather a problem that accrues over time. Older people are also at risk of developing foot problems, and these may not become apparent until the person enters the 'downward spiral' of limited movement, leading to deteriorating physical health and declining social contact. Due to age-related changes in the skin, older people need special attention from nurses in order to identify potential problems such as dryness, pruritis, keratoses and skin cancers. The prevention of pressure damage, and the prevention, care and treatment of leg ulcers is also a key area for nursing practice. The health of older people's mouths, feet and skin have tended to be neglected by health care professionals, but by addressing the areas discussed in this chapter they can profoundly affect wellbeing, functioning and quality of life.

KEY POINTS

- Nurses have a vital role in the maintenance of oral, foot and skin health.
- The assessment of neglected areas is an important nursing function.
- Tooth loss is avoidable – it is not a part of normal ageing.
- All older people have the right to access appropriate dental care and are entitled to treatment under the NHS.
- Oral care should not be based on tradition but on existing research which is as strongly evidence-based as possible.
- All older people have the right to access the services of podiatrists.
- Pressure sores can almost always be prevented by appropriate nursing assessment and interventions.

AREAS AND ACTIVITIES FOR STUDY AND REFLECTION

- Do you know when all the older individuals in your care last had a dental checkup?
- Do you know how long each older person has had their current dentures?
- Have care staff you supervise been given verbal and written guidance on oral care?
- How can you help prevent skin cancer in the older people in your care?
- Do all older people in your care wear suitable footwear?
- Do you use foot massage as part of the care of older people?
- Can you differentiate between leg ulcers that are arterial or venous in origin?
- How could you improve patient education on neglected areas?
- Is the assessment of the neglected areas adequately addressed in your assessment procedures?

REFERENCES

Adult Dental Health Surveys, Office of population censuses and surveys. Adult Dental Health 1988. *Br Dental J* 1990, 168:270–281.

Age Concern. *Dental care in retirement factsheet*. London: Age Concern England, 1997.

The Audit Commission For Local Authorities and the National Health Service. *The virtue of patients: making the best use of ward nursing resources*. London: London Audit Commission, 1991.

Awenat Y. Advanced practice: the case of leg ulcers. In: Wade L, Waters KA, eds. *Textbook of gerontological nursing: perspectives on practice*. London: Balliere Tindall, 1996.

Bergstrom N, Braden B, Laguzza A *et al*. The Braden scale for predicting pressure sore risk. *Nurs Res* 1987, 36:205.

Braden B, Bergstrom B. A conceptual scheme for the study of the etiology of pressure sores. *Rehabilitation Nursing* 1987, 12:9.

Bridel J. Risk assessment. *J Tissue Viability* 1994, 4:84–85.

British Association of Dermatologists. *Dermatology – a service under threat*, Position Paper. London: Schering Plough, 1993.

Cartwright A, Henderson G. *More trouble with feet. A survey of foot problems and chiropody needs of the elderly*. Institute for Social Studies in Medical Care, Department of Health and Social Services. London: HMSO, 1986.

Chapman EJ, Chapman R. Treatment of pressure sores: the state of the art. In: Tierney A, ed. *Clinical nursing practice*. Edinburgh: Churchill Livingstone, 1986.

Clarke AC, Nurses as role models and health educators. *J Adv Nursing* 1991, 16:1178–1184.

Cullum N. *The nursing management of leg ulcers in the community: a critical review of the research*. Liverpool: Department of Nursing, 1994.

Davis J. Oral answers. *Nursing the Elderly* July 1989, 1(2):9, 11.

Dealey C. Risk assessment of pressure sores. A comparative study of the Norton and Waterlow scores. *CARE – Science and Practice* 1989, 7:5–7.

Department of Health. *A strategy for nursing*. Report of the Steering Group, Nursing Division. London: HMSO, 1989.

Department of Health. *Pressure sores: a quality indicator*, London: Department of Health Publication Unit, HMSO,1993.

Department of Health. *Are you entitled to help with health costs?* HC11, London: HMSO, 1997.

Echevarria KH, Bezon J, Black JR *et al.* A team approach to foot care. *Geriatr Nurs* 1988, 9:338.

Fiske J. *Dental care for elderly people, Occasional Paper 1*. London: British Dental Association,1992.

Fiske J, Graham T, Gelbier S. Denture identification for elderly people. *Br Dent J* 1986, 161–448.

Flanagan M. Pressure sore risk assessment scales. *J Wound Care* 1993, 2:162–167.

Gebhardt K, Bliss MR. Preventing pressure sores in orthopaedic patients – is prolonged chair nursing detrimental? *J Tissue Viability* 1994, 4:51–54.

Geissler P, McCord F. Dental care for the elderly. *Nurs Times* 1986, 14:53–54.

Gooch J. Mouthcare. *Professional Nurse* 1985, 3:77–78.

Goode HF, Burns E, Walker BE. Vitamin C depletion and pressure sores in elderly patients with femoral neck fracture. *Br Med J* 1992, 305:925–927.

Health Education Authority. *Handbook of dental health for health visitors, midwives and nurses*. London: HEA, 1996.

Help the Aged. *Fitter feet. A help the aged advice leaflet*. London: Help the Aged, 1994.

Hibbs P. Action against pressure sores. *Nurs Times* 1988, 84:68–73.

Holmes S. Nursing management of oral care in older patients. *Nurs Times* 1996, 92:37–38.

Hughes T. *Footwear and footcare for adults*. London: Disabled Living Foundation, 1983.

ICRF. *Melanoma skin cancer, fact sheet*. London: Imperial Cancer Research Fund, 1996.

Kelechi T, Lucas K. Nursing footcare for the aged. Clinical outlook. *J Gerontol Nurs* 1991, 17:40–43.

Kemp J. Feet and footwear of older people. Squires J, ed. In: *Rehabilitation of the Older Patient, A handbook for the multi-disciplinary team*. London: Chapman and Hall, 1988.

King PA. Foot assessment of the elderly. *J Gerontol Nurs* 1978, 4:47.

Livesley B. Pressure sores: clinical aspects of their cost, causation and prevention. In: Bader DL, ed. *Pressure sores – clinical practice and scientific approach*. London: Macmillan Press, 1990.

Manderson RD, Ettinger RL. Dental status in the institutionalised elderly population of Edinburgh. *Community Dent Oral Epidemiol* 1975, 3:100.

MacGregor I. Some facts about tooth-brushing and dental care. *Education and Health* 1987, 5:9–13.

Mackie R. *Skin cancer*. London: Martin Dunitz, 1996.

Monthly Index of Medical Specialities (MIMS). Duncan C, ed. Loughborough: Walsh Mander, February 1997.

Morison MJ. *Pressure sore blue print: aetiology, prevention and management*. Ickenham: Convatec, 1990.

Norton D, McLaren R, Exton-Smith AN. *An investigation of geriatric nursing problems in hospital*. London: National Corporation for the Care of Old People, 1962.

Office of Population Censuses and Surveys. Adult dental health 1988. *Br Dent J* 1990, 168:270–281.

Onselen JV. *Pocket guide to skin care*. Nurs Times, 1997.

Pelican P, Barbiera E, Blair S. Toe the line: A nurse run well foot care clinic. *J Gerontol Nurs* 1990, 16(12):6.

Porth C, Kapke K. Ageing and the skin. *Geriatr Nurs* 1983, 4:158–162.

Ried J, Morison M. Classification of pressure sore severity. *Nurs Times* 1994, 90:46–49.

Robertson JC. £100,000 damages for a pressure sore. *CARE – Science and Practice* 1987, 5(2).

Roper N, Logan W, Tierney A. *The elements of nursing*. Edinburgh: Churchill Livingstone, 1980.

Simpson A, Bowers K, Wier-Hughes D. *Pressure sore prevention*. London: Whurr Publishers, 1996.

Social Trends, No. 12. London: Central Statistical Office, 1986.

Steele L. Provision of dental care for elderly handicapped people: a community dental officer's view. *J R Soc Health* 1984, 104:208–209.

Sweeney PC, Zoitopoulos L. A survey of district and community nurses: assessing their attitudes to oral and dental health and basic dental knowledge. *J Inst Health Educ* 1995, 33:55–61.

Taylor D. Dental health care in the 1990's. Fewer pickings in healthier teeth? *Health Care UK* 1991, 78–103.

Todd JE, Walker AM. *Adult dental health, Vol. 1, England and Wales 1968–1978*. London: HMSO, 1980.

UKCC. *Code of professional conduct*. London: United Kingdom Central Council for Nursing, Midwifery and Health Visiting, 1992.

UKCC. *Standards for records and record keeping*. London: United Kingdom Central Council for Nursing, Midwifery and Health Visiting, 1998.

Waterlow J. The Waterlow card for the prevention and management of pressure sores: towards a pocket policy. *CARE – Science and Practice* 1988a, 6:8–12.

Waterlow J. Prevention is cheaper than cure. *Nurs Times* 1988b, 84:69–70.

Whittle JG, Sarll DW, Grant AA. Marking dentures. *Br Dent J* 1985, 159:359.

Young JB, Dobrzanski S. Pressure sore: epidemiology and current management concepts. *Drugs and Ageing* 1992, 2:42–57.

USEFUL ADDRESSES

Dent-O-Care Limited, 7 Cygnus Business Centre, Dalmayer Road, London NW10 2XA. Tel: 0181 459 7550, Fax: 0181 451 0063, Mail Order and Helpline.

Age Concern England, Astral House, 1268 London Road, London SW16 4ER. Tel: 0181 679 2832.

Health Promotion Information Centre, Hamilton House, Mabledon Place, London WC1H 9TX. Tel:0171 413 1995.

British Dental Association, 64 Wimpole St, London W1M 8AL. Tel: 0171 935 0875.

British Dental Health Foundation, Eastlands Court, St Peter's Road, Rugby, Warwickshire CV 21 3QP.

Society of Chiropodists (publications on foot wear and foot care), 8 Wimpole St, London W1M 8AX. Tel: 0171 580 3228.

Disabled Living Foundations (operates a foot wear advisory service), 380/384 Harrow Rd, London W9 2HV. Tel: 0171 289 6111.

Arthritis Care (information on foot problems and foot care related to arthritis), 18 Stephenson Way, London NW1 2HD. Tel: 0171 916 1500.

British Diabetic Association (offers guidance on foot care to diabetics), 10 Queen Anne St, London W1M 0BD. Tel: 0171 323 1531.

County Foot wear (Drushoe, made to measure specialist footwear by mail order), Unit 4, Bective Rd, Kingsthorpe, Northampton NN2 7TD. Tel: 01604 791 917.

Bury Boot and Shoe Co Ltd, Brandlesholme Rd, Bury, Lancashire BL8 1BG. Tel: 0161 764 5317.

Help the Aged, St James Walk, London EC1R 0BE.

The Tissue Viability Society, c/o Wessex Rehabilitation Association, Salisbury District Hospital, Salisbury, Wiltshire SP2 8BJ. Tel: 01722 336 262.

The Wound Care Society, PO Box 263, Northampton NN3 4UJ.

Melanoma and Related Cancers of the Skin Patient Support Group. Tel: 01703 794 573.

8 Common chronic problems and their management
David Turner and Michele Hughes

LEARNING OBJECTIVES
After studying this chapter you will be able to:
- Describe the impact of chronic illness on the individual and his or her family.
- Explain the trajectory concept and its relationship to chronicity.
- Explain lifestyle factors that are frequently impinged upon by chronic disorders.
- Discuss activities of daily living (ADLs) in relation to chronicity.
- Discuss the impact of several of the most common chronic disorders and their consequences for older people.
- Explore strategies that have been used successfully to maintain maximum function and comfort for a person experiencing a chronic disorder.
- Discuss the concept of rehabilitation and its relevance to chronic illness.
- Describe a range of services that can be offered to older people experiencing chronic disease.

INTRODUCTION

Chronic illness is difficult to define. Many acute disorders have ongoing effects, and many of the disorders that tend to flare up intermittently and then go into remission are as yet poorly understood. Lubkin provides possibly the most inclusive and appropriate definition.

Chronic illness is the irreversible presence, accumulation, or latency of disease states or impairments that involve the total human environment for supportive care and self-care, maintenance of function and prevention of further disability.

(Lubkin, 1995, p. 8)

Orem's self-care movement has become popular in nursing, based partially on the increasing awareness of the individual's direct impact on disease, but also on the feelings of impotence in nurses, therapists and others trying to help an individual to feel positively about life when they see themselves as declining. A self-care deficit is experienced when an individual is unable to carry out basic functions without assistance. These deficits are primarily the result of pathophysiological disorders that impinge upon neuromuscular, musculoskeletal or sensory integrity. The interruption in function may also stem from current situation or the consequences of treatment. Thus, when all three situations coalesce, it may require more adaptive capacity than an individual has at the time. The appropriate approach is very individual and may involve changing the situation, modifying the treatment or retraining the individual to compensate for the pathophysiological changes. The impact of chronic illness is also very individual and may include identity erosion, expectation of death, dependency conflicts, and feelings of failure and fatalism.

This chapter explores the concept of chronic illness and its impact on older people and their families. It discusses a range of chronic problems and the care that could be offered.

CHRONIC ILLNESS

Chronic illnesses are frequently composed of multiple diseases. They follow a long-term and often an unpredictable course. They can sap economic resources, be intrusive into an individual's and their family's life, threaten self-esteem and may require extensive palliative care.

The prevalence of chronic illness increases markedly with age: 13% of those aged 0–4 years were reported to have long-standing illness compared with 63% of those aged 75 years or over [General Household Survey (GHS), 1995]. For all age groups, long-standing illness decreases markedly in relation to higher socioeconomic status. According to the GHS, the prevalence of chronic diseases has risen from 20% in 1972 to 30% in 1995 (of all ages), although prevalence has stabilised since the mid 1980s. Much of this rise is probably a consequence of increases in longevity and improvements in health care. Occasionally, the aggressive treatment of one disorder may result in the emergence of additional disabilities, iatrogenically induced. The relative prevalence of the most common chronic conditions are listed in **Table 8.1**.

Strauss and Corbin (1988) emphasise the changing nature of health care needed for an ageing population in which chronic disorders are by far the most prevalent forms of illness. Until the late 1930s, prevailing illnesses were predominantly caused by bacteria or parasites. These diseases have decreased markedly

Condition	Men			Women		
	Age group (years)			Age group (years)		
	65–74	75 and over	All ages (16 and over)	65–74	75 and over	All ages (16 and over)
Musculoskeletal						
Arthritis and rheumatism	124	116	52	194	264	84
Back problems	34	15	47	44	21	38
Other bone and joint problems	61	91	45	48	92	36
Heart and circulatory	59	55	26	72	82	33
Hypertension	92	54	25	45	73	18
Heart attack	20	31	6	19	35	7
Stroke	79	79	27	44	77	20
Other heart complaints	30	33	40	57	34	46
Respiratory	30	30	10	18	20	8
Asthma	20	22	10	12	22	8
Bronchitis and emphysema						
Other respiratory complaints						
Bases = 100%	985	541	8585	1136	907	9502

Table heading: **Chronic Sickness: Rate per Thousand Reporting Long-standing Conditions**

Source: General Household Survey. *Living in Britain*. London: Office of National Surveys, 1995.

Table 8.1 Chronic sickness: rate per thousand reporting long-standing conditions.

in the industrialised nations, primarily as a result of improvements in sanitation, housing and living standards. In their place, cancers, arthritis and cardiovascular conditions have become the most common health problems. Because of these changes, Strauss and Corbin (1988) contend that new modes of thinking and a complete restructuring of the health-care system are necessary to realistically care for and treat the large numbers of chronically ill. Indeed, much of the acute care delivered in hospitals is in response to acute episodes of chronic illness. A system that attends only to acute stages of illness neglects the complex, long-term nature of most disorders. The explosion of chronic illness could be a catalyst for change. The vast majority of disabled adults live in private homes. Only approximately 7% live in institutional settings (Martin *et al.* 1988).

There is a growing recognition that chronic illness is the major area of health concern and that health-care professionals and the public generally have inadequate knowledge of chronic illness and its management.

Wellness in Chronic Illness

Although the prevalence of chronic illness and disability increases with advanced age, many older people do not experience these. Moreover, as Sidell (1995) points out, of those that do suffer from chronic illness many claim to be in good health. Sidell argues for the need to go beyond a purely biomedical description of health and adopt an holistic and psychological account of health which relates to self-esteem and life satisfaction. Hence, "It is possible to suffer from chronic illness and disability and still 'feel good'" (Sidell, 1995, p. 7). **Figure 8.1** shows how the wellness continuum and Maslow's hierarchy of needs can complement each other in the presence of chronic illness.

Physical manifestations of chronic illness are not always the predominant factors in an older person's experience of health or wellness, and an important factor can be adaptation. (*See* Chapter 3 for full discussion of the illness–wellness continuum.)

Chronic Illness Trajectory

Corbin and Strauss (1988) present a view of chronic illness as a trajectory that traces a course of illness through eight phases, which may be upward, downward or plateaued. In its entirety, a chronic illness may include the following phases:
- Preventative.
- Definitive.
- Crisis.
- Acute.
- Comeback.
- Stable.
- Unstable.
- Deterioration.
- Death.

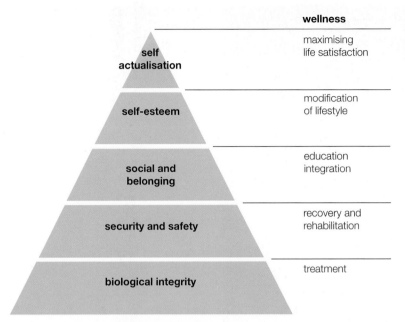

wellness

maximising
life satisfaction

self
actualisation

modification
of lifestyle

self-esteem

education
integration

social and
belonging

recovery and
rehabilitation

security and safety

treatment

biological integrity

Figure 8.1 Correlation between illness–wellness continuum and Maslow's hierarchy of needs in the presence of chronic illness

 8.1 Theoretical Assumptions Regarding Chronic Illness Trajectory

- The prevalent form of disease at this time is chronic illness.
- These presumably incurable illnesses may appear at any time in the life span but are most frequent in later life.
- Chronic illnesses are lifelong and entail lifetime adaptations.
- Those with chronic illnesses are likely to experience the trajectory phases identified by Strauss and Corbin (1988).
- The acute phase of illness management is designed to stabilise physiological processes and promote a comeback from the acute phase.
- Other phases of management, except the severely deteriorating, are primarily designed to maximise and extend the period of stability in the home with the help of family and augmented by visits to physicians or clinics.
- Maintaining stable phases is central in the work of managing chronic illness.
- Chronic illness and its management often profoundly affect the lives and identities of the afflicted and the family members.
- The management in the home by the family, self or significant other is central to care and is not peripheral to medical management (Strauss and Corbin, 1988).
- Recommended actions require appropriate timing and patience of the family and the practitioner.
- A primary care nurse able to coordinate multiple resources is needed.
- Finally, creativity and ability to use what is available are essential to successful management.

This model, originally conceptualised by Strauss and Glaser, has aided innumerable health-care providers to a better understanding of the realities of chronic illness. Key points of the model are based on the theoretical assumptions in **Box 8.1**.

Maslow's concept of five major levels of need that affect function and self-perception dovetails with the Corbin and Strauss model in that the person's perceptions of needs met and basic biological or functional limitations are paramount in predicting movement within the illness trajectory (Woog, 1992). In this respect, a wellness approach assists an individual to meet as many of the Maslovian defined needs as possible at any given time. These efforts can then help the person to enhance their potential for remaining on a plateau or gaining ground in any of the trajectory phases (**Table 8.2**).

Corbin and Strauss (1988) focused particularly on the impact of chronic illness on self-concept and self-esteem.

There are a host of biographical consequences, which in turn cycle back to affect to some degree the trajectory work and the illness itself. These include the changing relationships of body, self and sense of biographical time.

(Corbin and Strauss, 1988, p. 2)

Table 8.2 Definitions of phases and goals.

Phase	Definition
1. Pre-trajectory	Before the illness course begins, during the preventative phase no signs or symptoms present
2. Trajectory onset	Signs and symptoms are present, includes diagnostic period
3. Crisis	Life-threatening situation
4. Acute	Active illness or complications that require hospitalisation for management
5. Stable	Illness course/symptoms controlled by regimen
6. Unstable	Illness course/symptoms not controlled by regimen but not requiring hospitalisation
7. Downward	Progressive deterioration in physical/mental status characterised by increasing disability/symptoms
8. Dying	Immediate weeks, days, hours preceding death

Definitions of Phases and Goals

Source: Woog P. *The chronic illness trajectory framework: the Corbin and Strauss nursing model*. New York: Springer, 1992.

The trajectory of chronic illness varies with the individual and the disorder. It may progress slowly, relentlessly or unpredictably through exacerbations and remissions, or the superimposition of other disorders and treatments may change the projected course of the disability.

Perceived Uncertainty of Illness Trajectory

It has been proposed that there is a relationship between effectiveness of coping and the degree of perceived uncertainty in chronic disease and functional disability. Uncertainty and unpredictability are recurrent themes in accounts of chronic illness (Bury, 1991). This can add to the disruption to peoples' lives caused by chronic illness and at times render treatment plans ineffective.

It has already been shown in previous research that the types and quality of social supports and the perception of purpose in life influence one's adaptation to chronic disorders (McNett, 1987; Mishel and Braden, 1988). Research to untangle and understand the relationships among these factors is progressing. In the meantime, it is important for nurses to learn about the potential influence of these factors on the person's adaptation and to encourage expression of perceptions related to uncertainty, quality, and durability of support networks and purpose in life. Knowledge of disease processes may assist in coping with even those diseases that have an unpredictable course. Knowledge and information are certainly necessary if individuals and their families are to maximise their control over their lives (Sidell, 1995).

Fatigue from Living with Chronic Disorders

The reality of the fatigue experienced by many people living with chronic disorders is seldom considered in its full significance. Fatigue is variable and unpredictable, yet may be relegated to a consequence of growing older. The work and effort involved in managing a chronic illness at different phases in their trajectory will also vary enormously. Zest for life may be reduced, to the extent that every action can seem to involve such energy that it is hardly worth the effort. Individuals may also have fluctuating internal and external resources, including motivation, physical and emotional strength, family and friends, and finance and knowledge (Corbin and Strauss, 1988). Nurses may need to validate the reality and debilitating effects of the patterns of fatigue and to help identify the precipitants. Keeping a log of the low points of energy may prove useful and individuals may need encouragement to move in 'lower gear' and to rest periodically.

Individuals tend to make decisions about where to expend energy and in which situations to conserve it. For instance, an individual may wish to have assistance in dressing in order to save the energy for playing the piano or to use a wheelchair rather than a walking frame to avoid fatigue during dinner. Direct assistance by caregivers or families may be necessary to assist an individual to explore lifestyle adaptations that decrease energy expenditure and permit continued involvement in valued interests. Throughout the process, the older disabled person must remain involved in decision making on every level of need. The older person may have different priorities to the caregiver, and may relegate health needs to a lower priority to fulfil other needs or life demands. For older people who have disabling chronic conditions, more time might be required to allow a slower pace of activity. Slower movements and the response to physiological stress may require more time for care activities, with rest periods in between.

Activities of Living and Disability

A strong association has been demonstrated between advancing age and the prevalence of ill health and disability, with sharp increases occurring after the age of 80 years (Martin *et al.* 1988). It is the oldest old people who are most likely to experience difficulty with self-care and domestic tasks (*see* **Table 8.3** and **Figure 8.2**). The survey by Martin *et al.* selected a sample of 100,000 addresses, both private households and

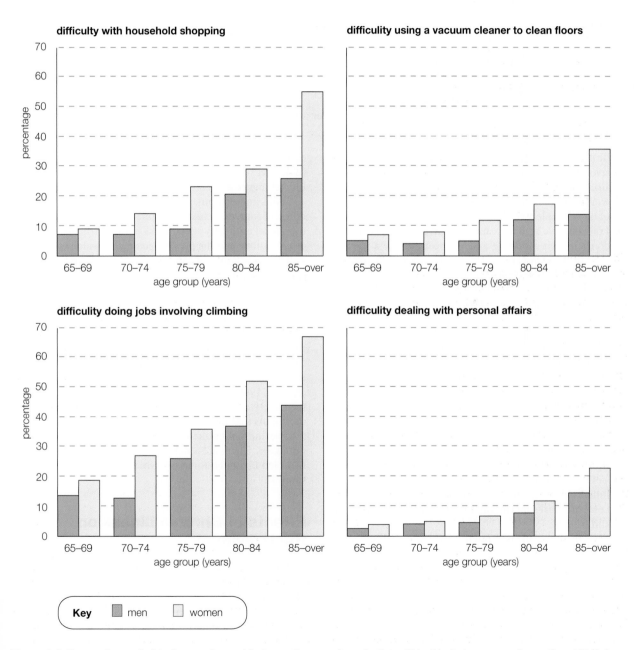

Figure 8.2 Percentage of elderly people unable to perform various tasks without help by age and sex: Great Britain, 1994. (Source: General Household Survey. *Living in Britain.* **London: Office of National Surveys, 1994.)**

Type of disability	In private households		Total (including institutions)	
Age group (years)	60–74	75 and over	60–74	(E) 75 and over
Locomotion	195	464	198	496
Reaching and stretching	52	129	54	149
Seeing	52	225	56	262
Hearing	108	307	110	328
Communication	38	112	42	140
Eating, drinking, digesting	11	18	12	30
Personal care	93	263	99	313
Continence	38	120	42	147

Estimates of Prevalence of Disability Among Older Adults in Great Britain (Rate per Thousand Population)

Source: Martin J, Meltzer H, Elliot D. *The prevalence of disability among adults, OPCS surveys of disability in Great Britain, Report 1*. London: HMSO, 1988.

Table 8.3 Estimates of prevalence of disability among older adults in Great Britain (rate per thousand population).

institutional settings. It found that more than two-thirds of disabled adults (an estimated 4.2 million of the general population) are aged 60 years and over (McGlone, 1992). However, most are not severely disabled, and only a minority of older people are unable to cope. The GHS (1994) found that of all people aged 65 years and over, only 16% are unable to do their own shopping and 10% cannot use a vacuum cleaner. In Bury and Holme's survey of nearly 200 men and women aged 90 years and over (from private household and institutional settings), 'difficulty and dependence' were experienced, particularly in relation to mobility and sensory impairments. However, they did not find this group 'facing a major burden of disease and illness' (Bury and Holme, 1990, p. 145). They found considerable diversity in functional capability and dependency which should, they argue, act as a warning against overgeneralisation even among those aged 90 years and over.

Chronic disorders may only become problems when they involve pain or self-care deficits in activities of daily living (ADLs). The goal is obviously to sustain or improve all functions as much and as long as possible with a minimum of discomfort. However, a number of factors may mediate this process. These may include:

- Individual personality and motivational characteristics.
- Level of social support and informal care from relatives and friends.
- Level of care available from the formal sector.
- Financial limitations.
- Access to adaptive devices, as discussed below.

Adaptive Devices

A wide range of adaptive devices are available to compensate for deficits in functional capability. Liaison with other health disciplines, such as occupational therapists, physiotherapists and speech therapists may be required before the provision of devices to assist individuals to reach their highest level of independence and comfort.

Aids and equipment can be obtained from a number of different sources including hospital trusts and health authorities, local authority social services departments, voluntary organisations and the private sector. This patchwork of provision can be confusing and poorly coordinated, and obtaining aids and equipment can be time-consuming and frustrating (Beardshaw, 1988). The 1990 Community Care Act was an attempt to streamline and improve community services by giving local authority social service departments, as the lead agents in community care, responsibility to assess the needs of individuals and implement care packages within the community. However, the range and availability of what is on offer may vary significantly between local authorities (Adams, 1996; Heywood Jones, 1994a). For private purchase the variety can be bewildering. Heywood Jones (1994b) recommends that professional advice should be sought and a trial period undertaken, to avoid unsuitable and expensive purchases. There are a number of associations, such as The Disabled Living Foundation, which can provide advice and support.

Effects of Chronic Illness on the Individual

Bury (1982) found that withdrawal from social relationships and increased social isolation are major features of chronic illness. Increasing ill health may lead to difficulties in performing ADLs and maintaining social contacts, and this inevitably affects an individual's satisfaction with life (Bowling *et al.* 1993). There is also commonly a greatly increased effort required for everyday life, including maintaining social networks (Bury, 1982; Strauss *et al.* 1984). Widowed, disabled and housebound people are most at risk (Qureshi and Walker, 1989), and the loneliness brought on by social isolation is most visible in those chronically ill persons who live alone.

In addition to loneliness, diminished control and independence can lead to loss of self-esteem. This can be aggravated by visible symptoms which can be stigmatising and embarrassing (Strauss *et al.* 1984). The whole process can be made worse given the unpredictability associated with many chronic illness trajectories and the uncertainty that it produces. Even minimal contacts with health professionals can assume tremendous significance. Self-esteem can be bolstered by affording an individual full adult status and respect, emphasising positive aspects of current existence and, as discussed later, maximising independence and autonomy.

Grieving the loss of function and comfort may occupy much of one's time initially, particularly if the loss interferes directly with a major source of an individual's pleasure (MacElveen-Hoen, 1985). Grief reactions will be highly individual depending upon the significance of the loss to the person concerned. This may be compounded by other losses that the individual might be experiencing.

Chronic illness and pain often go hand in hand and one of the major management issues is the control of pain (*see* Chapter 9 for further discussion). Moderate alcohol consumption may not cause any harm (unless medically contraindicated); there is evidence to suggest it can even offer positive health benefits (David and Redfern, 1991). However, alcohol abuse may be a consideration when looking for factors associated with unstable chronic health problems.

Effects of Chronic Illness on the Family

Despite some popular representations of the demise of familial ties, there is little evidence to support the claim that families are failing to care for their older members (Allen, 1985; Qureshi and Walker 1989). The modern family is, however, undergoing change: families are more geographically mobile than they were in the past; families are smaller, female employment has risen and so have divorce rates. Nonetheless, according to Bulmer (1987), kinship ties are still the most important source of informal care. Although older generations are increasingly living on their own, two-thirds to three-quarters of older people see at least one relative at least once a week. This is not to say that the long-term burden of caring for those with chronic need cannot produce enormous levels of stress and take their toll on the familial relationships (Bulmer, 1987; Strauss *et al.* 1984; Anderson, 1992). This can produce deleterious effects on the health and emotional well-being of carers. Writing of multiple sclerosis (MS) Robinson (1988) quotes Burnfield (1985, p. 95), "MS is not a disease which affects people in isolation. When one person in the family has MS then the whole family 'has MS' as well".

The management of chronic illness may not only require a great deal of work and effort, but also skill and ingenuity. Strauss *et al.* point out that although help from health professionals may be crucial, 'the sick person spends most of the time away from medical facilities, so he or she and the family must rely on their own judgement, wisdom, and ingenuity for controlling symptoms' (Strauss *et al.* 1984, p. 49). (*see* Chapter 16 for discussion about relationships). Heywood Jones (1994a) points out that while much attention may be directed to offering services to the disabled client, health staff may overlook the needs of the carers. She recommends services such as the Crossroads Care Attendant Scheme which offer relief for full-time carers by supplying replacement carers to undertake their role. Institutional respite care may also be on offer from some local authorities.

Becoming a burden on others, in particular family and friends, is certainly not what most disabled people want (Bulmer, 1987). People are very reluctant to give up personal care despite great difficulties; commitment to independence is valued very highly (Qureshi and Walker, 1989). Adequate input and support from the formal care sector will not be able to meet all of a client's needs, but it could provide the regular routine 'tending' that is required (Allen, 1985). Although Qureshi and Walker (1989) point to a long-standing gap in community care provision for an increasing number of older people, they also remind us that many older people are themselves providing care, help and support to others. Nonetheless, as Nolan suggests, 'as the significant majority of long-term care is currently and is likely to continue to be provided by family carers, potentially the most influential nursing contribution will be the support of these individuals' (Nolan, 1996, p. 836).

Along with physical, social and psychological costs, chronic illness can also bring economic hardship to the individual and their family (Qureshi and Walker, 1989). Individual sufferers and carers may be forced to abandon employment. Bury (1982) and Sidell (1995) point out that the economic resources at an individual or family's disposal can help compensate for the effects of disability and help determine how well people cope and manage chronic illness.

CARE AT HOME FOR PEOPLE WITH CHRONIC ILLNESS OR DISABILITY

Older people with chronic illnesses and disabilities primarily reside in their homes (Martin *et al.* 1988). There is evidence, at least in the recent past, to indicate a significant gap between need and care provision (Allen, 1985; Qureshi and Walker, 1989). The 1994 General Household Survey found that, for those over the age of 65 years who needed help with mobility and self-care tasks, those living alone generally received help from the local authority or National Health Service. People living with their spouse only usually received help from their spouse. The survey also found that the self-care tasks which caused the most problems were bathing, showering or washing all over and cutting toenails. The need for help with self-care rose with age; from 4% of those aged 65–69 years, to 21% among those over 85 years.

Strauss and Corbin (1988) suggest that assisting

individuals and their support persons to view chronic disorders as having a 'trajectory' may help them cope with the ups and downs and the acute exacerbations that may require hospitalisation. If they are able to better understand the phases of a disorder, they are likely to weather the difficult periods without undue discouragement. Often it must be seen as a lifetime situation that passes through stages in which resources must be tailored accordingly. In summary, they suggest the following points for practitioners to consider:

(1) Chronic illness must be seen through the eyes of the persons experiencing it.
(2) The illness is often a lifelong course that passes through many phases.
(3) Biographical, medical, spiritual and everyday needs must be considered.
(4) Collaborative, rather than purely professional relationships may be most effective.
(5) Lifelong support may be necessary, although the type, amount and intensity of such support will vary.

The goal of care of people with chronic illness may be to slow the pace of decline, relieve discomfort and support preferred lifestyle with as few restrictions as possible (**Box 8.2**). Not all chronic conditions require nursing service. The ability of the individual and the family to manage and cope with the problems encountered determines the need. Carers may need help (**Box 8.3**).

Progress may be measured in maintenance of a steady state, or regression of the condition.

In his study of adults under 65 years of age suffering from chronic illness, Bury found that 'the presence or absence of a supportive social network may make a significant difference in the course of disablement' (Bury, 1982, p. 175). This was not significantly reaffirmed in a larger UK study of people aged over 85 years (Farquhar *et al.* 1993), although there did exist a positive association with number of friends and level of functional

8.2 Goals in Management of Chronic Problem

- Stabilise the primary problem.
- Prevent and manage medical crisis.
- Control symptoms.
- Encourage compliance with regimen.
- Prevent secondary disabilities.
- Prevent social isolation.
- Treat functional deficits.
- Promote adaptation – person to disability;
  – environment to person;
  – family to person.
- Adjust to changes in progression of problems.
- Normalise interactions.

Sources: Brummel-Smith K. Geriatric rehabilitations. *Generations* 1992, 16:27; Corbin JM, Strauss A. *Unending work and care: managing chronic illness at home.* San Francisco: Jossey-Bass, 1988.

8.3 Help Needed by Carers

- Improving function.
- Managing the existing illness.
- Preventing secondary complications.
- Delaying deterioration and disability.
- Facilitating death with peace, comfort and dignity.

ability. The latter study also found that one-fifth of those in the most disabled group had no informal helper (a non-professional, such as a relative, friend or neighbour) and relied totally on formal (local authority and health authority) services.

Maintaining a Health Diary

A health diary can assist in the assessment and management of chronic disorders. There is no standard format or structure and it is thus designed according to individual preference. The entries will describe the individual's experiences. Over time the diary reveals progression or remission of the condition and assists longitudinal assessment. It may also be useful in facilitating individual release of thoughts and feelings, while highlighting coping mechanisms.

HOSPITALISATION AND CHRONIC FUNCTIONAL DISABILITIES

Nurses are well aware of the potentially detrimental iatrogenic effects of hospitalisation superimposed upon the acute illness that required treatment. Simple interventions have proved helpful in retaining functional status during episodic illness (Wanich *et al.* 1992). **Box 8.4** suggests a number of interventions which may prove helpful in minimising the effects of hospitalisation on functional capacity. Effective rehabilitation facilitates optimum personal development and function for older people. The penalty for lack of accessibility to appropriate rehabilitation is increased dependence on family, nursing homes, or other care providers at an even greater cost to individuals and society. In the early phases of disability, individuals require rehabilitation-orientated care in order to achieve maximum wellness potential.

Transfer of Care (Discharge Planning)

As with rehabilitation, the process of planning the return of a client back into the community needs to start as soon as possible after admission, or even before a planned admission, and is based on a thorough assessment. This and other criteria associated with 'good practice' in relation to discharge

8.4 Minimising the Effects of Hospitalisation on Functional Capacity

Staff education
- Mental and functional status assessment.
- Management of sensoriperceptual function.
- Mobility.
- Environment modification.

Orientation and communication
- Use of cues and repetition.
- Continuation of usual routines.
- Providing anticipatory guidance regarding procedures.
- Reassurance regarding likelihood of delirium.

Mobilisation
- Encouraging movement and activity.
- Involving physiotherapy and occupational therapy in exercise.

Environment modifications
- Glasses and hearing aids available and working well.
- Calendars.
- Favourite programmes on radio and TV available.
- Increased lighting, night lights from dusk until dawn.

Caregiver education and consultation
- Families asked to bring in significant items.

Medical management
- Daily medication review; discouraged use if not clearly necessary; particularly discouraged neuroleptics and anticholinergics, which tend to exacerbate delirium.

Discharge planning
- Weekly, or more frequent, case conferences with primary nurse, social worker, physiotherapist, occupational therapist, dietician.

8.5 Criteria Associated with 'Good Practice' in Relation to Discharge Planning

1. On admission to hospital, a thorough assessment of a patient should include: a detailed account of the home environment; level of formal and informal support received; and ability to perform activities of daily living (ADLs) (Waters, 1987).

2. Discharge planning should begin as soon as possible.

3. Rehabilitation with a view to discharge to begin as soon as possible, including necessary assessments by other members of the multidisciplinary team.

4. Regular and ongoing communication between members of the multidisciplinary team, and effective coordination of their activities (Bowling and Betts, 1984; Edwards, 1991).

5. Patients/relatives/carers involved in the discharge planning process, including any necessary education and training inputs.

6. Adequate notice of discharge date given to patient/relative/carer (Bowling and Betts, 1984).

7. Sufficient notice and adequate information given to general practitioner and community services. Involvement, if necessary, of these services in the discharge planning (Bowling and Betts, 1984; Waters, 1987).

8. Once at home, all the planned services are in place and the transition from hospital to home is 'seamless' (Bowling and Betts, 1984; Department of Health, 1989).

* Most of these criteria are mentioned in the Department of Health Circulars, HC (89)5 and HSG (95)8/LAC (95)5.

planning are listed in **Box 8.5**. Nursing staff may need to ensure that rehabilitation is a philosophy and a continuous process which underpins all aspects of a client's care. It is insufficient to consider, for example, physiotherapy once or twice in a week day as 'rehabilitation'.

REHABILITATION

Defining Rehabilitation

The term 'rehabilitation' has various meanings. Following an extensive literature review and curriculum analysis, Nolan

(1997) identified a number of trends:
- A lack of consensus on the definition of rehabilitation.
- Emphasis on the physical and functional components.
- Rehabilitation generally presented as a finite, time-limited process confined largely to the acute and sub-acute phase.
- An emphasis on outcome measurement, often not appropriate to chronic illness.
- Rehabilitation confined largely to hospital settings.
- Liaison and follow-up arrangements post-discharge generally poorly developed and ad hoc.
- User and carer involvement discussed frequently in the literature but markedly different perceptions between

professionals, and users and carers.
- Generally, a lack of information, and failure to involve users/carers.
- The International Classification of Impairment, Disability and Handicap (ICIDH) exerting considerable influence over rehabilitation practice, but most of the attention paid to impairment and disability with little attention paid to handicap (World Health Organisation, 1980).
- Multi and interdisciplinary team working presented as the best way of organising care but considerable barriers to effective team working.
- A number of areas receive scant attention in the literature including gender, race, ethnicity, culture, ethical dilemmas and the role of community rehabilitation.

Nolan suggests that there is now 'widespread recognition that chronic illness represents one of the greatest health challenges faced by modern society', yet the majority of the literature defines rehabilitation as a finite, time-limited process largely confined to the acute phase of an illness. In his review, rehabilitation was also seen largely as the province of the therapists, with nursing have little rehabilitative input. With the developments in intermediate care and the work of the Royal College of Nursing (RCN) Rehabilitation Forum, this is now beginning to change.

Rehabilitation is defined by Dudas:

Rehabilitation is the dynamic process directed toward the goal of enabling persons to function at their maximum level within the limitations of their disease or disability in terms of their physical, mental, emotional, social and economic potential.

(in Maclaren, 1996, p. 492)

Rehabilitation in the UK

The nature of the provision of rehabilitation services in the UK is varied [Medical Research Council (MRC), 1994; Young, 1996] and it is necessary for health staff to become familiar with local resources and service arrangements. Rehabilitation services are available usually both in hospital or in the community. Community rehabilitation can be organised by referral to an outpatient therapy department, a day hospital for older people or a domicilliary rehabilitation team. Some considerations for opting for either inpatient or outpatient rehabilitation are listed in **Box 8.6**.

Compared with younger people, recovery may be more problematic and take longer, and older generations may have more functional consequences. All the more reason that rehabilitation should be central to the care of older people (Fielding, 1991) and, moreover, should be commenced as soon as possible (MRC, 1994). Older people with long-standing physical disabilities to which they have adapted quite well may find that the adaptation sustained earlier may be more

8.6 Considerations for Inpatient and Outpatient Rehabilitation

Inpatient rehabilitation
- High dependency/high care needs (especially night-time care).
- Complex or multiple disability.
- Rapid response needed.
- Poor housing or unsuitable domestic circumstances.
- No community rehabilitation available.

Outpatient rehabilitation
- Low or modest dependency.
- Less complex disability.
- Slower response acceptable.
- Appropriate housing and domestic circumstances.

Source: Young J. Rehabilitation and older people. *Br Med J* 1996, 313:677–681.

difficult in late life because of generally decreased functional ability and energy to cope. The normal changes of ageing must be incorporated into life patterns.

Assessment

Crucial to the rehabilitation process is an adequate holistic assessment of current and previous capabilities. It may be that if a client is in a crisis, and personal strengths are not easily visible or easily assessed, staff may only see one portion of a patient's biography. They urge that staff develop effective methods for discovering biographies and utilising this information to the full. To help achieve this they recommend that nurses have a system of organised accountability, and that interviewing skills are reviewed. Strauss *et al.* (1984) recognise that there are limitations in time so they suggest that nurses use 'action interviews', which can take place whilst a nurse is working with a patient and can take place over a number of occasions.

If the aim of rehabilitation is to restore (hospital inpatients) to their home environment, adequate knowledge of that environment including their social networks and social support is essential and fundamental to the process of discharge planning (discussed earlier). Measures of functional capability may be used (such as the 'Barthel Index' – *see* **Box 8.7**) to establish a baseline from which to systematically monitor progress and help in setting goals. Although as Williams (1987) points out, this may only tell us what a client can do as opposed to what they actually will do once home. It must also be remembered that the impact and significance of a given impairment can vary greatly between individuals, including the perception of that impairment (Robinson, 1988). A thorough grounding in a client's home situation and if necessary a home visit with the

8.7 Original Barthel Index

Bowels
0 = Incontinent (or needs to be given enema).
1 = Occasional accident (once a week).
2 = Continent.

Bladder
0 = Incontinent, or catheterised and unable to manage
    alone.
1 = Occasional accidents (maximum once per 24 hours).
2 = Continent (for more than 7 days).

Grooming
0 = Needs help with personal care: face, hair, teeth,
    shaving.
1 = Independent (implements provided).

Toilet use
0 = Dependent.
1 = Needs some help but can do something alone.
2 = Independent (on and off, wiping, dressing).

Feeding
0 = Unable.
1 = Needs help in cutting, spreading butter, etc.
2 = Independent.

Transfer
0 = Unable – no sitting balance.
1 = Major help (physical, one or two people); can sit.
2 = Minor help (verbal or physical).
3 = Independent.

Mobility
0 = Immobile.
1 = Wheelchair independent, including corners, etc.
2 = Walks with help (verbal or physical) of one person.
3 = Independent (but may use aid).

Dressing
0 = Dependent.
1 = Needs help but can do about half unaided.
2 = Independent (including buttons, zips, laces, etc.).

Stairs
0 = Unable.
1 = Needs help (verbal, physical, carrying aid).
2 = Independent up and down.

Bathing
0 = Dependent.
1 = Independent (or in shower).

Source: Young J. Rehabilitation and older people. *Br Med J* 1996, 313:677–681.
The original Barthel Index requires supplementation with items reflecting domestic activities (e.g. cooking, shopping and cleaning) if used in a community setting (see Bowling, 1995).

client and the health practitioners may be required. Young (1996) argues for the advantage of a home-based assessment over departmental-based assessments. The former can highlight the real daily life problems experienced by the client (and the carers). There is also a greater opportunity to involve the family and carers, and the community health-care staff. Community follow-up could help to maintain independence and prevent further readmission to hospital or admission to hospital in the first instance (Williams, 1994).

A Team Approach

The expertise of a number of disciplines is required for the comprehensive rehabilitation of the client with chronic illness, and it is established practice to use a 'team' approach (Lubkin, 1995). Communication between and coordination of team members' efforts is important. Coordination between individual disciplines can be considerably more difficult to achieve in the community compared to hospital settings (Young, 1996). In general hospitals, team members include the nurse, physician, physiotherapist, occupational therapist, speech therapist, dietician and social worker. The client and

their family and carers are integral members of the rehabilitation team.

Empowerment

The aim of rehabilitation is to enable clients to become good 'self-managers' and regain control over their lives. A prevalent theme in relation to all aspects of chronic illness is lack of control. This is reinforced by a lack of involvement in management decisions, which can further promote regression into unwarranted dependency. Empowering clients involves an equal partnership between clients and professionals, and Maclaren (1996) argues that this empowerment can, moreover, increase a client's ability and motivation to sustain involvement in a rehabilitation programme. Both Coates and Boore (1995), and Maclaren (1996) argue that if increased independence and autonomy are the goals of rehabilitation then clients must as far as possible be equal members of the multidisciplinary team. This involves a move away from a more 'paternalistic' attititude by health-care professionals where treatment regimes are prescribed and clients are expected to adhere to them (*see* section below on health beliefs and discussion of 'compliance' in Chapter 10).

Both the client and the rehabilitation practitioner make important contributions to the partnership. The client brings his or her unique experience of disability and illness. Other members of the multidisciplinary team bring past experiences of disability and illness, and expert knowledge about current advances in treatment and rehabilitation techniques (Maclaren, 1996).

Communication

Communication is a key factor in facilitating empowerment and rehabilitation.

> *It is important that clients receive the information they require to make decisions about their health care, regardless of how trivial these are assumed to be.*
>
> (Maclaren, 1996, p. 496)

Maclaren cites *The Patient's Charter* (Department of Health, 1992) which states that patients should be able to expect a clear explanation of treatment and its benefits, risks and alternatives in order to make decisions about that treatment.

Young (1996) suggests it is easy to focus on predominantly physical functioning, yet successful rehabilitation requires social and psychological problems to be addressed. Communication skills are obviously needed for this. Young further states that 'talking to, listening to, understanding and counselling' are greatly valued by the client (Young, 1996, p. 678). Resnick (1996) found in a small qualitative study of older women in a US rehabilitation setting that factors associated with increased client motivation included: receiving encouragement, humour, caring, kindness and non-dominating power with relationships between staff and clients.

Young (1996) reminds us that rehabilitation is not a 'quick fix' but requires considerable patience, perseverance and energy. He suggests that some commonly found barriers to rehabilitation progress are:

- Unidentified medical problems (e.g. anaemia, heart failure, hypothyroidism).
- Occult depression (commonly associated with physical disease in older people, yet often overlooked).
- Occult dementia (sometimes masked by preserved social skills).
- Communication problems (impaired hearing or eyesight).

Rehabilitation and the Future

The MRC are concerned 'that rehabilitation for older people may not always be provided; the inadequacy of rehabilitative provision within health services will result primarily in increased disability and dependency in the elderly population, with economic and social consequences' (MRC, 1994, p. 46). Ebersole and Hess (1994) argue that this is a result of

lack of education in rehabilitation among health-care professionals, and that the potentials of rehabilitation are poorly understood.

Lubkin (1995) and Strauss *et al.* (1984) contend that there is a lack of interest by health-care professionals in rehabilitation and chronic illness, and a lower status is attached to these fields. Strauss *et al.* argue that the split between acute and chronic, and between care and cure, are characteristic constraints of contemporary health care. Waters and Luker (1996) found in their UK study that even staff working in two rehabilitation settings for older people, viewed nursing as separate from rehabilitation, and hence concluded that nurses were an under-utilised resource in this field. This last point is especially important given that nurses, if necessary, have the opportunity to deliver care with a rehabilitative focus over 24 hours, 7 days a week.

Rehabilitative care providers often have difficulty demonstrating precise outcomes, since services are provided through multiple disciplines: medicine, physical and occupational therapy, speech therapy, nursing and psychology. Consequently, outcome measures are extremely difficult to develop. This can make research into rehabilitation difficult and complex, which is perhaps important reason why evidence remains patchy (Young, 1996). The MRC suggest that consequently there is little guidance at present for both purchasers and providers regarding the best approaches to rehabilitation. They argue that more research on modes of rehabilitation specific to older people will help remedy perceived 'current uncertainty and widespread scepticism regarding the effectiveness and cost-effectiveness of rehabilitation techniques among elderly people, which has led to barriers in access to this type of care' (MRC, 1994, p. 47).

There is a current and growing emphasis on rehabilitation by all professionals and increased integration of its principles into all health and social activities. Greater accountability will be expected of all professionals and institutions. This accountability will seek a balance between the resources expended and the practical outcomes achieved.

COMMON CHRONIC DISORDERS

In this chapter, a small number of conditions have been selected in order to illustrate the effects of differing trajectories on older people and their families. The discussion in each section highlights specific aspects. It is not intended to be a comprehensive discussion of the effects of each condition.

The following extracts from Pinder's work (1988) vividly describes some of the day-to-day realities:

> *Patients are engaged in constant revisions as perceptions of disability and handicap change and life options are modified or reduced. New trade-offs are made as symptoms are redefined, but periods of disequilibrium when subjects are off-balance are common. Information plays a crucial role in deciding what is to be assessed. Balancing problems generally become more complex as*

new symptoms emerge. Yet despite this, a certain conti-nuity of strategy management seems to emerge over time. Strategies of acquiescence, avoidance, covering combat-ing and accommodation are recurrent themes at differ-ent stages in people's illness careers. Where one might have expected a change in direction as the perceived severity of symptoms increased, patients' major concerns were largely geared to preserving some core of normality, even though room for manoeuvre was often radically reduced.

Individuals can find themselves living their lives around their treatment regimes. They may feel they are living life by the clock, unable to go too far from where treatment is available, and every activity punctuated by thoughts of the next treatment.

Patient: 'Nothing could interfere with the taking of pills. They structure my life. Pill-taking, if you like, has ruled my life … for example this morning (when she slept through the alarm) my first thought was I've got to get those tablets down me before you come … I've got to take medicines at different times to enable me to do things. It's not a case of 'take one tablet twice a day'.

Talks with her were punctuated by pauses to consult the clock, calculate to the nearest five minutes the timing of her next dosage and decide what topics we could accom-plish in the intervening time. Although defining herself as only moderately disabled and handicapped, the intru-siveness of the regime was the price she was prepared to pay to achieve some of the things she wanted and to sus-tain some semblance of a normal lifestyle.

Over time, patients can become highly knowledgeable and skilled in managing their lives and their conditions. They know what works and what does not. This is not only an important aspect of achieving good disease management, but also in helping the person to retain control over his or her life.

What they are nice about, they say in their letter 'this lady is intelligent, she knows what she's doing, will adjust her own dose'. So they just put one of the doses on the bottle, but I don't necessarily follow that.

Older patients may experience difficulty in assuming total day-to-day management of their illness, particularly if they have coexisting health problems such as visual or hearing changes. Support and education must be geared to their indi-vidual circumstances, abilities, needs and wishes.

The dependence of doctors on patients' own evaluations of what is going on in their bodies is perhaps one of the more equivocal considerations involved in managing the drug regime. As with other older patients, few subjects had been socialised into expecting to share with their doc-tors in any decision-making process. Patients such as Mr R were ill-prepared for such a role. It was felt that doc-tors were rarely explicit in guiding subjects towards a modus vivendi where their own daily knowledge and experience would be the linchpin in future illness and drug management.

Diabetes Mellitus

Diabetes mellitus requires of a patient that he or she man-ages and monitors health every day of their lives. It requires a detailed understanding not only of how the condition can be managed but also how the individual person responds and how an optimum individual lifestyle can be achieved.

The risk of diabetes increases with age, and older people represent almost half of the diabetic population. In people over the age of 65 years, the prevalence may be as high as 15%, and about 90% of older diabetics have noninsulin-dependent diabetes mellitus (NIDDM). The morbidity asso-ciated with NIDDM in older people is high, particularly associated with coronary heart disease (CHD), cerebrovas-cular disease (CVD) and gangrene (Richmond, 1995).

Although the classical diabetic presentation of weight loss and polyuria can occur in old age, it is not the norm, and screening for elevated blood sugar should be part of the phys-ical check on any older person who exhibits a deterioration in health, mental changes, incontinence, worsening of mobil-ity or any other cause of increased dependency (Bates, 1987). Blood glucose, both fasting and after food, rises with age and a diagnosis of impaired glucose tolerance is so common in old age as to be of little practical value.

Diabetes in older people is usually not their only health problem, and coexisting multiple pathology, particularly deficits in sight or hearing, may exacerbate the effects of the diabetes and make managing it more difficult for the patient. In addition, many will have had diabetes for up to 10 years before diagnosis, and complications such as blindness, foot ulceration or gangrene of the lower limb are not uncommon. Merely relieving the symptoms of hyperglycaemia and pre-venting hypoglycaemia is now outmoded. Normal blood glucose levels are 4–8 mmol/litre, but the World Health Organisation suggests that overenthusiasm to achieve nor-mal metabolic control in older people can be distressing and dangerous (Richmond, 1995). Tattersall and Gale (1990) sug-gest that the aims of treatment should be to:

- Do more good than harm.
- Promote a good quality of life.
- Make the patient feel well.
- Avoid hypoglycaemia.
- Prevent or delay the progression of long-term complications.
- Achieve and maintain an agreed level of blood glucose.
- Maintain a keynote of simplicity.

Nutritional guidance for older people is similar to that for the general population, but carbohydrate tolerance declines with age. Many older diabetics are overweight and dietary fat restriction is indicated. The British Diabetic Association rec-ommends that half of the diet should be made up of carbo-hydrate, mostly from complex sources, i.e. polysaccharides. The fibre content of the diet should be increased as 15 g of soluble fibre tends to improve blood glucose levels by 10%. Sugar should be limited to 25 g per day. The daily fat intake should be limited to 30% of the diet made up from 10%

polyunsaturates, 1% monounsaturates and 1% saturates, leaving a daily intake of protein of 15%. Food should be taken at regular interval with no long fasts. Salt intake should be limited to 6 g per day, 3 g if the patient is hypertensive. Alcohol guidelines recommend no more than 3 units per day for men and 2 units per day for women. Exercise at an appropriate level will also be beneficial.

If glycaemic control is not achieved within 2 or 3 months, oral hypoglycaemics may be indicated. When deciding on an oral hypoglycaemic agent for an older person, the duration of action of the drug is important. Up to about one-fifth of older diabetics will require insulin therapy, possibly during acute illness, trauma or surgery. If concurrent illness or disability prevents the older person injecting their own insulin, a pen injector may be easier to handle. Monitoring should be based on individual need, but testing for urinary glucose can be misleading because renal thresholds tend to rise with age and an older person can, therefore, have a raised blood glucose but no glycosuria. If the person is unable to undertake his or her own blood glucose monitoring, a relative or friend, or the local community nurses may be willing to help. Hypoglycaemia usually occurs at levels lower than 3 mmol/litre and can lead to falls at home resulting in serious fractures. Severe hypoglycaemia may result in coma, hypothermia and death. Older people living alone, or those with mental health needs, are particularly at risk (Richmond, 1995). Long-term complications can be particularly serious for older people, the most common are eye and foot problems (*see* Chapters 7 and 12 for more detail). They should be offered regular review, and referred to appropriate specialists.

Parkinson's Disease (PD)

The initial diagnosis will probably provoke shock, depending on the individual's experience and understanding of PD. Support is vital in this period and the person must be reassured that, although not a cure, treatment is available. Contact numbers for the PD Society, who run local groups in many areas, could be offered to provide access to practical advice and information.

Like other chronic illnesses which are of unknown aetiology, progressive and incurable, the trajectory of PD in any individual is uncertain and unpredictable. Its manifestations vary considerably from person to person. The classic symptoms – tremor, rigidity and slowness of movement – are supplemented by a host of others which may affect some patients but not others. These include:

- Chronic fatigue.
- Early morning immobility.
- 'Mumbly' if not incomprehensible speech.
- Stooping gait.
- Freezing or start/hesitation episodes.
- Mask-like facial immobility.

All of the above symptoms may be thoroughly disconcerting socially (Pinder, 1988).

Superimposed on these symptoms, and often difficult to distinguish from them, are medication side effects. Drugs may help to mask some of the symptoms some of the time, they can produce others, such as mood and memory disturbances, involuntary movements, end-of-dose deterioration and various forms of fluctuations, most dramatically the 'on/off' syndrome, where a patient changes from mobility to total immobility, often many times a day and with startling rapidity. In its extreme form this is known as 'yo-yoing'. Levodopa does not halt the underlying progression of the illness itself and tends ultimately to lose its efficacy.

Pinder's (1988) research highlights the effects of living with PD on individual lives:

Mr I's life was characterised by unpredictable and often

Meeting Chronic Illness Needs

Merle Holder is a devout Christian and attends the New Testament church in Hackney, where she is popular with her many friends. Mrs Holder has developed diabetes mellitus recently, but she is learning to manage her diet and tablets fairly well. Her seventieth birthday is approaching and she is increasingly losing her sight; she also has two small infected ulcers on her feet. Mrs Holder tries to keep active by walking to the shops in Mare Street but is becoming 'fed up' with the dietary restrictions and is generally feeling 'under the weather'. She is sorely tempted to try one of the 'miracle cures' that she suspects are probably fraudulent, but might offer an alternative to the tablets. Mrs Holder's daughter, who lives in the neighbourhood, has contacted the nurse to explain how her mother is feeling and to invite the nurse to call. The daughter said she was happy to see her mother daily until she was feeling better.

- **List aspects of Mrs Holder's situation that provide objective data for your nursing assessment.**
- **List comments that she has made that provide subjective data.**
- **Identify her needs for nursing intervention.**
- **Devise a health education plan to help Mrs Holder learn about, and manage, her diabetes.**
- **List two strengths displayed by Mrs Holder that could assist this.**
- **State outcome criteria for your care and education plan, including outcomes which Mrs Holder might want to evaluate.**
- **State how you could evaluate the effectiveness of the care.**

violent 'yo-yoing'. Arriving one morning to talk I found him glued in frozen immobility in his chair. Enjoined by his wife to tell him a story, it was like watching a butterfly emerge from its chrysalis as he retrieved his speech, loosened up, flexed his muscles and came to life before my eyes. Within an hour he was conversing animatedly and then performed his 'party trick', running up and down the stairs to his flat. An hour later, darkness descended again and he was reduced to total dependence on his wife. He described this as 'the Lazarus effect'.

Another interviewee said:

I cram in to the periods when I'm flexible all the things I would have liked to have done the rest of the day. It doesn't always work that way though. One day I may be nine-tenths of the day free, although that's very rare and another much less. There's nothing I can do about it.

(Pinder, 1988)

As the disease progresses, the individual may become very disabled. However, persons with PD can experience great functional problems with mobility, communication and home management. The loss of dexterity in the fingers can result in problems with counting change and daily activities such as washing and dressing, which in turn reduces the person's level of independence. Tremors may also produce embarrassing moments. Socialising can also be particularly difficult as they may be embarrassed about their condition, concerned about its unpredictability. An added problem is that the 'mask-like' facial expression can prevent them from conveying the facial messages, such as smiling, that are so fundamental for enjoyable interpersonal exchanges. The expressionless face, slowed movement and soft, monotone speech can give the impression of apathy, depression and disinterest. An inability to cope with their adjusted life circumstances and changed roles can result in depression.

Local PD groups can be of enormous personal support as individuals meet with others sharing some of their difficulties. However, many PD sufferers are reluctant to attend group sessions because they fear that seeing other's disabilities, particularly those in whom the disease is advanced, will destroy their faith in any potential for their own future.

Chronic Obstructive Pulmonary Disease (COPD)

COPD is a chronic slowly progressive disorder characterised by airways obstruction that does not change markedly over several months. Most of the lung function impairment is fixed, although some reversibility can be produced by bronchodilator (or other) therapy (British Thoracic Society, 1997). It is a condition in which acute exacerbations can leave the patient fighting for breath, and many patients describe their terror at wondering if this is to be their last breath. COPD limits lifestyle and activities considerably, and it may affect nutritional state if the person is unable to eat adequately due

to breathlessness. It also carries stigma. Patients may become socially embarrassed by other people's reactions to their noisy breathing, coughing and phlegm production. There can also be a perception that, particularly if the person has smoked, that the condition is self-induced. This attitude can be particularly unfair on older people as smoking was the norm in their younger years, and the dangers of the habit were not fully appreciated. In addition, many of them may have worked or lived within polluted environments, the long-term effects of which were similarly not understood.

The aim of treatment is to preserve and prevent further damage to the functioning lung tissue. Smoking and exposure to other respiratory irritants is the area first targeted to prevent further lung deterioration. Bronchodilator medication, which is normally administered through inhalation, is used to preserve the lung function. When the individual does not respond to 'conventional doses' of the bronchodilators a nebuliser may be suggested:

- In patients aged over 65 years, nebulisers are mostly used to deliver high-dose bronchodilator medication to those with severe chronic obstructive pulmonary disease (COPD) or asthma, but they will also occasionally be needed for patients with milder disease who are unable to use hand held inhalers.
- Older patients who might benefit from treatment with nebulisers should be assessed and managed as indicated in the current guidelines (e.g. British Thoracic Society 1997).
- Older patients who do not have cognitive impairment can keep peak flow records just as well as younger patients and these should be used in a similar manner.
- A relatively high proportion of older patients may not be able to use metered dose inhalers satisfactorily due to impaired cognitive function or memory loss, weak fingers, or poor coordination.
- It is recommended that the use of alternative devices to a metered dose inhaler by the patient or his or her carer should then be assessed – for example, a metered dose inhaler with spacer and tight fitting face mask; a Haleraid or breath-activated inhaler; a dry-powder inhaler; or a nebuliser.
- With advancing age, the response to beta-agonists declines more rapidly than the response to anticholinergics. For this reason, anticholinergic treatment by hand-held inhaler or nebuliser should also be considered.
- Ischaemic heart disease (IHD) is increasingly prevalent with advancing age. High dose beta-agonist treatment with nebulisers or other devices should be used with caution in older patients with known IHD in whom the first dose may require electrocardiogram monitoring at a hospital.
- Beta-agonists are especially likely to cause tremor in older people. High doses should be avoided unless necessary.
- Prostatism and glaucoma are more common in older people. Treatment by mouthpiece rather than face mask

should be considered when high doses of anticholinergics are used to avoid the risk of acute glaucoma or blurred vision.

(British Thoracic Society, 1997)

Long-term oxygen therapy may be prescribed for people with chronic hypoxia.

Due to the difficulties caused by changed breathing pattern it may be helpful to offer an assessment of the person's home environment. Developing strategies to cope during anxious periods of acute dyspnoea can also help. They will need to balance activity with rest, and specific postures can help to decrease the effort of breathing.

Older persons with reductions in manual dexterity may have problems using inhalers, which can sometimes be resolved by the use of 'spacer' devices or changing to a dry powder device or one that is activated by a breath. Pharmaceutical companies as well as charities such as Breath Easy Club, at the British Lung Foundation, provide concise information booklets that clearly reinforce the necessary information needed for successful inhaler techniques.

Cerebral Vascular Accident (Stroke)

The World Health Organisation (WHO) definition of stroke is that of 'rapidly developing clinical signs of focal or global disturbance of cerebral function with symptoms lasting over 24 hours due to a vascular incident' (WHO, 1989). The stroke produces various impairments according to location within the brain, from mild weakness' to paralysis on the opposite side of the body, impairments of sight, speech, swallowing and sensation, spatial deficits, neglect of the opposite side of the body, personality changes and incontinence of urine.

Stroke is the third most common cause of death. Around 20% of all stroke victims die in the first 4 weeks, with most dying within the first week from the direct neurological effects of the stroke; a further 10% die within a year. Up to 75% of patients who suffer a stroke are admitted to hospital and these tend to be the worst affected, although not always. Some of them will require intensive nursing care until they improve sufficiently to begin active rehabilitation or up to their death. Most survivors of stroke recover rapidly during the first 3 months but after this time, the rate of improvement diminishes and it is unusual to continue after 1 year. Fifty per cent, however, will have some significant disability. Stevens *et al.* (1984) suggested an average duration of 6 weeks hospital stay, for stroke rehabilitation and in an average health district up to 30 beds at a time might be occupied by stroke sufferers.

The majority will return to the community, unless cared for at home from the outset. These people may need regular and substantial support from carers, often spouses or adult offspring. According to Legh-Smith *et al.* (1986) the most used resources in their study of 383 stroke survivors in an average health district, were district nurses, (81%), home help (81%), meals-on-wheels (92%) and day centre (89%). The

same research team also studied the effects of stroke on the mood of the chief carer. Carers showed anxiety and emotional stress unrelated to the patients' physical disability after 2 years. These results highlight the need for support groups and respite care, to enable carers to cope and continue caring.

Wade (1992) suggests that 10% of stroke survivors are unable to live in the community and will need long-term nursing care. These people lack social support and are moderately or severely disabled, both physically and mentally. Stroke consumes 4% of the total National Health Service bill without including long-term and respite care and its cost to patients and their families is incalculable. The costs and burdens can be reduced by setting targets, which could result in improved quality of life, prevention of further disability and unnecessary suffering.

Around one-third of strokes survivor experience speech difficulties (University of Leeds, 1992) and ability to communicate essential needs is a continuous frustration for both patient and carers, thus affecting quality of life for both. Dysphagia is one of the indicators for admission to hospital and avoidance of complications such as aspiration pneumonia is a desirable outcome for the acute phase; an early assessment is advisable.

Stroke thus has a distinct trajectory. The onset is sudden and acute. The person may be unconscious for some time, which can be an enormous strain on relatives. When the reality of the disabilities dawns, the threat to body image and self-esteem can be overwhelming, particularly for an older person who may have pre-existing illnesses of disabilities. Stroke can affect perception, cognitive functioning, communication, coordination, control and every aspect of functioning in life. Following the acute trauma and shock, the person may face a long battle to regain functioning accompanied by ever-present doubts as to what functioning can be regained.

Urinary Incontinence

Urinary incontinence is one of the most prevalent symptoms encountered in the care of older people. Many families cannot cope with incontinent relatives. It is, therefore, not surprising that incontinence is judged to be a leading precipitating cause of older people moving into a care setting.

A large survey by Thomas *et al.* (1980) revealed that over the age of 65 years, 6.9% of men and 11.6% of women living at home, reported regular urinary incontinence (twice or more per month). In a review of 10 studies investigating prevalence of incontinence in individuals over 65 years of age in acute and long-term institutional setting, Mohide (1994) found a range of 19–55%. Prevalence rates vary widely due to differences in definitions of incontinence used, sample composition, setting and methods of data collection. In the same study by Thomas *et al.* (1980), only 1.3% of men and 2.5% of women (over 65 years of age) who reported regular urinary incontinence were known to be incontinent to either the health, social or voluntary services.

The International Continence Society defines urinary incontinence as 'the involuntary loss of urine, which is objectively demonstrated and is a social or hygienic problem' (Andersen *et al.* 1988). It is not a result of advancing age nor is it a disease. It is a symptom of existing environmental, psychological, drug, or physical disturbances and can become a catastrophic event when it interferes with mobility, sociability and the ability to remain in one's home. It can exact an enormous social, psychological and economic burden on individuals and their families or carers, and lead to social isolation and depression (Mohide, 1994).

If it is assumed that all older people eventually become incontinent, a resolution of the problem will not be sought, and it will become a self-fulfilling prophecy. A study by Goldstein *et al.* (1992) points out that older people generally did nothing about incontinence because they considered it a normal part of ageing, did not realise that treatment existed, did not think that treatment would help, worried about the cost or were too embarrassed to discuss it. This could be the reason why the study by Thomas *et al.* (1980) found such a disparity between self-reported incontinence and incontinence 'known' to the health and social services. Norton *et al.* (1992) investigated distress and delay in seeking help associated with urinary incontinence. They found that lack of information was a major factor, along with acceptance of symptoms as normal, and fear that surgery was the only available treatment option.

With a comprehensive assessment leading to a correct diagnosis and the appropriate treatment, incontinence can often be cured and, if not cured, at least better managed. Simple nursing interventions can achieve cure rates of up to nearly 70% (O'Brien and Long, 1995).

Urinary incontinence may be differentiated into four different types (Norton, 1992):
- Bladder instability.
- Genuine stress incontinence.
- Outflow obstruction.
- Underactive bladder (**Table 8.4**).

Types of Urinary Incontinence

Description	Causes	Symptoms
UNSTABLE BLADDER Bladder muscle (detrusor) contractions are not under perfect voluntary control and contract unpredictably with relatively small volumes	Often no obvious bladder or neurological pathology However, does occur with neurological conditions such as multiple sclerosis and stroke	Urgency, frequency and urge incontinence Common precipitants include: standing, rain, cold, proximity to toilet, and bumpy journeys Symptoms usually confined to certain times of the day
STRESS Increased intra-abdominal pressure, which causes leakage of a small amount of urine	Coughing, laughing, vomiting or lifting with a full bladder; obesity; full uterus in third trimester; incompetent bladder outlet; weak pelvic musculature	Dribbling of urine with pressure increased intra-abdominal pressure, urinary urgency and frequency
OUTFLOW OBSTRUCTION Outflow of urine from the urethra is impeded, causing residual urine to accumulate in the bladder	Most common cause in men is an enlarged prostate Can be caused by faecal impaction in both sexes Some may experience a feeling of incomplete emptying of the bladder	Dribbling overflow or stress incontinence Frequency and double voiding, i.e. voiding twice in quick succession
LOSS OF BLADDER TONE A hypotonic bladder which will not contract effectively to empty-residual urine accumulates and overflows	Common in diabetic patients/clients, and others with neurological problems	Dribbling overflow or stress incontinence Frequency and double voiding, i.e. voiding twice in quick succession Some may experience a feeling of incomplete emptying of the bladder

Source: Heath HBM, ed. *Potter and Perry's foundations in nursing theory and practice*. London: Mosby, 1995.

Table 8.4 Types of Urinary Incontinence

One problem can coincide with another, hence the need for an accurate assessment and diagnosis. For example, outflow obstruction due to an enlarged prostate in an older man can also lead to the development of an unstable bladder. Bladder function and conscious control of its function can also be influenced by other factors such the environment, infection, drug therapy, functional capability and the attitudes of carers.

Assessment

Assessment is multidimensional. It includes a health history, physical examination and a urinalysis. There are numerous assessment guidelines and check lists in the literature that can be utilised to help ensure a systematic approach (e.g. **Table 8.5**). Urinary symptoms, together with a comprehensive history and examination, can provide clues as to the likely

---

Incontinence Assessment Checklist

Note: These headings will elicit the basic information needed for an assessment. The reader should construct a checklist using these headings (and any others found necessary and relevant for specific circumstances), leaving adequate space for filling in the answers and any comment.

PERSONAL DETAILS
Name:
Date of Birth:
Address:
General Practitioner:
Assessed by:
Date:
Referred by:

URINARY SYMPTOMS
Frequency:
Nocturia? (?woken)
Urgency:
Average warning time:
Urge incontinence:
Stress incontinence:
Passive incontinence:
Nocturnal enuresis:
Number of nights per week:

Symptoms of voiding difficulty
Hesitancy:
Poor stream:
Straining:
Manual expression:
Post-micturition dribble:
Dysuria:
Haematuria:

Incontinence
Onset – when?
Circumstances:
Is incontinence improving/static/
  worsening?
How often does incontinence occur?
How much is lost?
Are aids or pads used?
Type of aid:
Number per day:
Source of supply:
Are aids effective?
Problems:
How wet are pads at each change?
Average cost of pads if brought
  privately:
Type and amount of fluid intake:
Fluid restriction:

Other urinary symptoms:

MEDICAL HISTORY
Neurological problems:
Previous illnesses/operations:
Parity:
Difficult deliveries?
Current medication:
Any previous treatment for incontinence?

BOWELS
Usual bowel habit:
Constipation?
Laxatives or diet regulation used?
Faecal incontinence?

PHYSICAL ABILITIES
Problems with mobility:
Aids used?
Needs assistance?
Who is available?
Difficulties in transfer to/onto lavatory?
Comments:
Foot problems:
Manual dexterity:
Clothing suitability:
Eyesight:
Observe self-toileting and comment on
  problems:
Problems with personal hygiene:

PSYCHOLOGICAL STATE
Attitudes to incontinence:
Anxiety?
Depression?
Impaired mental abilities?

SOCIAL NETWORK
Usual activities:
Are these restricted by incontinence?
Who does patient live with?
Who visits regularly?
Relationship problems because of
  incontinence?
Sexuality issues?
Official services received:

ENVIRONMENT
Lavatory facilities:
Are urinals or commode used?
Obstacles to using lavatory:
Washing/laundry facilities:
Comments on general physical and social
  environment:

RESULTS OF PHYSICAL EXAMINATION:
Skin problems:
Prolapse (women):
Atrophic changes (women):
Rectal examination:
Post-micturition residential urine volume:
MSSU/urine test result.
Other findings:

RESULTS FROM CHART

SUMMARY OF PROBLEMS

AIMS/GOALS

PLANNED ACTION

REFERRED TO

URODYNAMIC RESULTS

REVIEW DATE

FOLLOW UP

Source: Norton C. *Nursing for Continence, 2nd ed.* Beaconsfield: Beaconsfield Publishers Ltd, 1996.

Table 8.5 Incontinence Assessment Checklist

diagnosis for incontinence. However, symptoms alone are notoriously unreliable indications of underlying bladder problems (Norton 1996) and those older people with a complex mixture of symptoms will require urodynamic tests in order to provide an accurate diagnosis.

In order to gain accreditation from the Health Services Accreditation Unit, a service must demonstrate that a comprehensive assessment is always carried out either by the continence advisor or by another qualified health professional. Special investigations (such as urodynamics) may be required and referral onto the specialist expertise of a urologist, gynaecologist, neurologist or physician (Health Services Accreditation, 1997).

The character of the urine (odour, colour, sedimentary or clear) and difficulty starting and stopping the urinary stream should be recorded. Activities of daily living such as ability to reach a toilet and use it and finger dexterity for clothing manipulation should be documented. Use of medications such as sedatives, hypnotics, anticholinergics and antidepressants should be assessed. Frusemide (Lasix), diazepam (Valium), amitriptyline (Elavil) and phenothiazines are among the common drugs prescribed. In addition, the nurse should not forget to ask about vaginal discharge and constipation or faecal impaction. The nurse may also do all or part of the physical examination, which includes evaluation of mental status; mobility; dexterity; and a neurological, abdominal, rectal and pelvic examination.

Intervention

The nurse may need to coordinate and combine efforts with other disciplines to maximise a client's functional capabilities. Improving mobility, for example, could enable an individual with urgency to reach the toilet before becoming incontinent. Successful treatment of a transient confusional state or faecal impaction may have an equally dramatic effect (Tobin, 1992). An individual's environment also needs to be taken into consideration. Providing a bedside commode or urinal may facilitate nocturnal continence. Appropriate siting and signposting of toilets in institutional settings may be required.

Accessibility to the toilet is an intervention that is often not considered in providing assistance for the incontinent patient. Environmental circumstances can contribute to incontinence. If the distance that an individual must either walk or travel by wheelchair to reach the toilet is longer than the time between the onset of the desire to micturate and actual micturition, incontinence is certain to occur. An absolute last resort in dealing with incontinence is the use of urinary appliances.

Toilet Substitutes

Toilet substitutes for the sick have been around for hundreds of years. Four types are used:

- Commodes for the bedside.
- Overtoilet chairs for transport.
- Bedpans for beds or commodes.
- Urinals for both men and women that can be used in bed, chair or a standing position.

The criteria for use of a commode is that the toilet is too far for the individual's mobility capability or requires too much energy for the older person to get to the toilet. It can also substitute for an inadequate number of available toilets. Overtoilet chair criteria is similar to that for a commode. However, it should not be used as a substitute for available toilets. Urinals are generally used by men but bottle-shaped urinals for females have been designed and are used on occasions.

Protective Undergarments

There are numerous continence aids and appliances available, thousands of different items are listed in the Continence Products Directory, published by the Continence Foundation (1997). Absorbency pads and pants remain the most common form of management (Norton, 1992). It is important that the most appropriate type and size of garment or padding is used. When helping a client choose an item to suit individual requirements (including dignity and self-esteem) expert knowledge and advice should be sought.

Penile Sheath

Some men will be able to use penile sheaths, which are soft and pliable. They are an externally applied device and, therefore, pose less of a urinary tract infection risk and are not traumatic to the urethra. They can also be fairly easily applied by the client or their carers, although they are unsuitable for men with a very small or retracted penis. Sheaths can be used for men not only with continual incontinence but also as an aid to men suffering from symptoms of urgency in situations where they may not easily be able to reach a toilet. The selection of sheath and type of adhesive will depend on the client's preference and possible skin sensitivity. The penile sheath should be removed daily to allow the penis to be cleansed, dried and aired to help prevent irritation and possible skin breakdown. For comfort and to facilitate adhesion Norton (1996) recommends that long pubic hairs around the base of the penis should be trimmed short.

Behavioural Techniques

Behavioural techniques such as bladder training, habit training, biofeedback and hypnotherapy are utilised for the treatment of symptoms of urgency and urge incontinence which are usually associated with bladder (detrusor) instability. Bladder training may also be useful for people suffering from genuine stress incontinence, as clients may indirectly strengthen their pelvic floor muscles when trying to increase periods between voidings (Kennedy, 1994). Pelvic floor muscle exercises are the main mode of treatment for genuine stress incontinence. These methods are free of side effects and do not limit future options. Bladder training, biofeedback and pelvic floor exercises do, however, require time, effort and practice by an individual who is highly motivated.

Habit training, and timed and prompted voiding are useful for the treatment of functional incontinence in clients who are mentally and physically impaired. Timed voiding may also help people with spinal cord lesions suffering from underactive bladders. For all three techniques motivated staff (working as a team in institutional settings) are essential. Copperwheat (1985) emphasises that staff need to be aware of the aims and objectives of these programmes, and that they are offered ongoing support and training.

- **Bladder training** (bladder re-education, bladder drill). This involves the progressive extension of the interval between voidings. Concomitant interventions are often used such as anticholinergics, sedatives, and psychotherapy and counselling, either initially or throughout the programme. Improvement may take place from a few weeks after commencement to a few months. Follow-up is necessary. Cure and improvement rates can be up to 90% (Kennedy, 1994).
- **Habit training.** Baseline patterns are established and then a toileting schedule is adjusted to fit a client's pattern. In care settings for older people, Copperwheat (1985) achieved a 100% cure rate; Colling *et al.* (1992) with a much larger population achieved a 86%

improvement, but cited staff compliance as a problem.
- **Timed voiding.** This involves a fixed voiding regime. For people with spinal cord lesions the regime can involve techniques to stimulate voiding and allow complete emptying of the bladder (Kennedy, 1994). Evidence is limited and patchy in relation to timed voiding.
- **Prompted voiding.** Clients and residents are asked at regular intervals if they need to void, and are assisted to use the toilet only if the response is affirmative. Prompts can also be accompanied by social approval if the client is dry and social disapproval if the client is wet. Improvement rates ranged from 10.4% to 97%. A large study by Schnelle *et al.* (1989) obtained a 97% improvement rate (36% or which improved by 75% or more) with residents who were severely debilitated.

For all techniques, voiding diaries (e.g. **Figure 8.3**) are required to act as a baseline observation; to plan and monitor the pro-

Figure 8.3 Voiding diary. (Source: Conveen Teaching Resource Kit.)

| name _____ | | week beginning _____ | | | | |
| key ☐ _____ | | ☐ _____ | | | | |
	sunday	monday	tuesday	wednesday	thursday	friday	saturday
6am							
7am							
8am							
9am							
10am							
11am							
12am							
1pm							
2pm							
3pm							
4pm							
5pm							
6pm							
7pm							
8pm							
9pm							
10pm							
11pm							
12pm							
1am							
2am							
3am							
4am							
5am							
total							

gramme, and evaluate progress. If possible, voiding diaries should be completed by the clients themselves. This has been demonstrated to offer therapeutic value in itself by providing a simple form of biofeedback (Mahady and Begg, 1981).

Pelvic floor exercises strengthen the periurethral and pelvic floor muscles. The contractions exert a closing force on the urethra. These exercises are one approach to the problem of stress incontinence. They can be either slow or rapid. The muscle contraction is held for 3 seconds then relaxed. This is repeated 10 times working up to 20 times. The exercise is repeated five times a day. Quick pelvic floor exercises begin with tightening and relaxing the pubococcygeal muscle without a pause between. These are done as fast as possible beginning with a count of 15 seconds and working up to 2 minutes. Initially it is difficult to identify, tighten, and relax this muscle but with repeated work becomes easier (Jette et al. 1990). Exercises can be performed standing, sitting or lying. The anal sphincter is tightened (as if to control the passage of flatus or faeces) and then the urethra and vaginal muscles are tightened (as if to stop the flow of urine). This should be done at least four times each hour.

Pelvic floor exercises can be very effective in the treatment of mild-to-moderate genuine stress incontinence, but it can take from 6 weeks to 1 year for some to attain continence (Laycock, 1994), hence a high degree of motivation and support is required. They have traditionally been taught by physiotherapists but Norton (1996) suggests that there is no reason why skilled nurses should not teach them. Weighted vaginal cones are a very effective alternative (or supplementary) method strengthening pelvic floor muscles (Laycock, 1994). They can also be used as a teaching aid, for the assessment of muscle capability. Neuromuscular stimulation of the pelvic floor muscles can be used for those with very weak or absent voluntary muscle contraction on initial assessment (Dolman, 1997).

Biofeedback employs both visual or auditory instruments to give the individual immediate feedback on how well he or she is controlling the sphincter, the detrusor muscle and abdominal muscles. Those who are successful learn to contract the sphincter and relax the detrusor and abdominal muscles automatically. Complete continence can occur in 20–25% of individuals and improvement in an additional 30%. Biofeedback requires sophisticated equipment.

Drugs

Drugs to eliminate or improve incontinence include bladder relaxants and bladder stimulants. Bladder relaxants include anticholinergic agents that delay, decrease or inhibit detrusor muscle contractions, especially the involuntary contractions, and may increase bladder capacity. They can be used alone or as adjunctive therapy in the treatment of bladder instability. The most commonly used drug is propantheline (Pro-Banthine). Undesirable side effects such as dry mouth, dry eyes, constipation, confusion or the precipitation of glaucoma may occur with high doses of this drug.

Smooth muscle relaxants such as flavoxate (Urispas), oxybutynin (Ditropan) and dicyclomine (Bentyl) work directly on the bladder detrusor muscle. These drugs exert mild anticholinergic side effects. Calcium channel blockers, also used for cardiovascular problems, have a depressant effect on the bladder. More study is needed to determine if there is a significant benefit for their use in urge incontinence. Imipramine (Tofranil), a tricyclic antidepressant, exerts both anticholinergic and direct relaxant effects on the detrusor muscle, as well as a contractile effect on the bladder outlet, thus enhancing continence. Two important side effects to be aware of in older people are hypotension and sedation.

Bladder outlet stimulants include alpha-adrenergic agonist agents and oestrogen replacement preparations. Alpha-adrenergic agonists, pseudoephedrine and ephedrine, cause contractions of smooth muscle at the bladder outlet and improve stress incontinence. Oestrogen replacement therapy, while not definitively used for stress incontinence, has been effective in improving postmenopausal urgency, frequency and urge incontinence.

Surgery

Surgical intervention might be considered for some conditions of incontinence. Suspension of the bladder neck in women has proved effective in treating women with genuine stress incontinence. Outflow obstruction incontinence due to prostatic hypertrophy is generally treated by prostatectomy or transurethral resection of the prostate. Sphincter dysfunction due to nerve damage following surgical trauma or radical perineal procedures is repairable through sphincter implantation. Complications for this type of surgery are greater than 20% and may require an additional surgery (Ebersole and Hess, 1998). Bladder augmentation is more specific and limited to neurological disorders such as a contracted bladder. A segment of the bowel has been used to increase bladder capacity and to facilitate release of excess pressure.

Catheters

As a last resort, appliances may need to be used, particularly in cases of long-term intractable incontinence and terminal care. Although not without some potentially serious complications, they may add greatly to the quality of life of an individual, and help restore an individual's dignity and comfort.

Indwelling Urethral Catheters

The three main complications of long-term urethral catheterisation are infection, encrustation and tissue damage.

Significant bacteriuria will occur in 90% of individuals within 17 days of catheterisation (Crow et al. 1986). Treatment is, however, only indicated when there is evidence of significant infection (Tobin, 1992). Nonetheless, 40% of nosocomial infections are urinary tract infections (UTIs) and 70% of these are associated with indwelling catheters (Norton, 1996). Efforts to minimise risks of catheter-associated infection are best aimed at reducing risks of cross infection. The introduction of the closed drainage system has helped towards this end, but care must be taken when emptying the system to wash hands before and after and wear disposable gloves. Receptacles used for this purpose must be sterile or disposable (Mulhall *et al.* 1993). Back flow and reflux of urine should be prevented and the drainage bag kept off the floor (Mullhall *et al.* 1988). Research regarding meatal cleansing is contradictory and ambivalent (Roe, 1994). The use of antiseptic has not been found to be effective and they can be irritant, and encourage the emergence of multiresistant organisms. Roe recommends the maintenance of meatal hygiene with soap and water, and clean disposable wash cloths. A high fluid intake (2 litres or more) has been traditionally recommended to help flush microorganisms from the bladder but, along with cranberry juice, more evidence is needed to prove its efficacy (Getliffe, 1997).

Infection by some microorganisms leads to alkaline urine, which in up to 50% of catheterised individuals encourages the precipitation of mineral deposits leading to encrustation and eventual blockage of the catheter (Roe and Brocklehurst, 1987). Getliffe (1994a) recommends that individuals who habitually suffer from blocked catheter (due to encrustation) are identified so that planned replacement of catheters can occur. An *in-vitro* study by Getliffe (1994b) found that bladder instillations (20–30 ml) of an acidic reagent can promote the dissolution of encrustations and prolong catheter life.

Catheterisation involves the blind introduction of a foreign body along a delicate urethra, hence trauma can result (Slade and Gillespie, 1985). If continued tension is applied to the catheter then pressure necrosis can occur (Getliffe, 1997). This can occur if a urine drainage bag is left hanging over the side of a mattress; or if a patient turns over in bed forgetting his or her catheter drainage. Clients with impaired pain sensibility or cognition are particularly at risk (Lowthian, 1989). Distally fixing a drainage tube to a patient may help.

It is very important that the correct catheter material is chosen – all silicone, silicone coated latex or hydrogel coated latex are indicated for long-term use. There has been found to be a significant association between catheter size and experience of pain and discomfort (Crow *et al.* 1986; Roe and Brocklehurst, 1987). Small catheters allow the free drainage of urethral secretions (Norton, 1996) and reduce the incidence of bladder spasm (Kennedy *et al.*, 1983). Getliffe (1994a) found that long-term catheterisation was rarely trouble free and that patients need ongoing support and education. This is particularly important, given that catheterisation also involves psychological and social implications, particularly in relation to sex and sexuality (Pomfret, 1996) (*see* Chapter 15 for further discussion of sexual activity for people with catheters).

Suprapubic Catheterisation

This involves the insertion of a catheter suprapubically, into the bladder through the abdominal wall. This method can be use for long-term urine drainage, and has been found by one controlled trial to significantly reduce rates of infection when compared with urethral catheters (Horgan *et al.* 1992). People who are chair and wheelchair bound, who are sexually active, or experience problems with urethral catheters (such as leakage or rejection) may benefit from a suprapubic catheter. It is associated with greater patient satisfaction and comfort (Kelly *et al.* 1995; Barnes *et al.* 1993), and there is no risk of urethral trauma. The catheter insertion site is more easily accessible for cleansing and catheter change (Getliffe, 1997). Although initial catheter insertion is a surgical procedure, catheters can be routinely changed by an experienced nurse

With all types of catheters, careful and informed consideration should be given to the type of urine collection device used. There are a multitude of devices available and the client needs to be able to choose a device which is discrete, and which they and their carers can easily operate. A female client, for example, may need a urine collection bag which can be attached to the leg above the dress line, which has correspondingly shorter urine collection tubing (attached to a shorter female catheter).

Intermittent Catheterisation

This technique is particularly valuable for people suffering from an underactive bladder. It is only considered necessary if a residual urine is persistently greater than 100 ml (Norton, 1996). Frequency of insertion can range from 2 hourly to once every other day depending on the needs of the individual. Getliffe (1997, p. 326) lists the following advantages:

- There is greater opportunity for patients to reach their own potential in terms of self-care and independence.
- The risks of urethral trauma and urinary tract infection are reduced. The risk of encrustation is removed.
- The upper urinary tract is protected from reflux.
- There is a reduced need for equipment and appliances.
- There is greater freedom for expression of sexuality.

A certain degree of manual dexterity and motivation is required in order for this technique to be successful, but age is no bar to self-catheterisation. In a client's own home environment a clean rather than sterile technique is required. Unhurried counselling and advice, as well as ongoing support, are essential (Norton, 1996).

Faecal Incontinence

Faecal incontinence is defined as the inability to control the passage of stool or gas via the anus (Basch, 1992). The prevalence of faecal incontinence is estimated to be approximately 3–4% of the community dwelling older people and 10% of those living in institutions (Tobin and Brockelhurst, 1986). Often faecal incontinence is associated with urinary incontinence, and like urinary incontinence it has devastating social ramifications to the individuals and families who experience it. Consequently, it is probably a significantly under-reported symptom, with the majority of sufferers receiving no pro-

8.8 Factors that affect Incontinence

- Intestinal transit time.
- Rectal factors (sensory).
- Pelvic floor and sphincter tone.
- Musculature.
- Medications.
- Muscular flaccidity.
- Inability to get to the toilet when the urge to eliminate is present.

fessional help (Thomas *et al.* 1984). Factors affecting faecal incontinence are given in **Box 8.8**.

This translates into such causes as sphincter dysfunction, anatomical disarrangement, neurological impairments and sufficient bulk in diet, insufficient fluid intake, lack of exercise, haemorrhoids and depression. Many instances of faecal incontinence result from constipation leading to faecal impaction and 'spurious diarrhoea' (Norton, 1996). Serious illness accompanied by delirium and excessive doses of iron, antibiotic and digitalis preparations may precipitate incontinence. Sedatives, too, can account for incontinence through depression of cerebral awareness and control over sphincter response.

Assessment

Assessment should include a complete client history, as in urinary incontinence. The following questions should be included in a bowel incontinence assessment (**Box 8.9**).

A rectal digital examination can identify faecal impaction, although this is not always the case and the rectum may be empty. A straight abdominal X-ray will reveal higher inpaction, if this is suspected (Norton, 1996). Severe constipation with impaction of faeces is the most common cause of faecal incontinence and it certainly predominates as a cause among older people and those living in institutional care (Norton, 1996).

8.9 Bowel Incontinence Assessment

(1) What is the availability of the toilet or commode and the time required to get to them?
(2) What medications, if any, are being taken that might influence peristaltic action, lucidity or fluid balance?
(3) How much bulk is provided in the food (pureed food does not help)?
(4) What is the manual dexterity in removing clothing?
(6) Is there any neurological or circulatory impairment of the cerebral cortex?

Intervention

The nurse's attitude in assisting the person who is incontinent of faeces should be sensitive. Faecal incontinence is a symptom. It requires that the patient be accepted as a person, that the incontinence problem not be advertised or ridiculed, and that the person is not made to feel ashamed or guilty. A great deterrent to successful intervention in incontinence is inconsistency in implementing the planned strategy and unrealistic expectations of rapid, full recovery (Ebersole and Hess, 1998). Time and patience are essential ingredients of success.

Nursing interventions should include several days' surveillance of the patient's bowel function. A chart similar to that used to monitor urinary incontinence can be constructed. Nurses should work with other professionals and with the client and carers, to manage and restore bowel continence through environmental manipulation, dietary alterations, bowel training, sensory re-education, sphincter training exercises, medication and surgery to correct underlying defects. Instituting a diet adequate in dietary fibre will add bulk, weight and form to the stool and may improve colon evacuation of the sigmoid and rectum rather than produce a continuous or intermittent oozing of faecal material. This may assist in the attainment of more controlled and complete bowel movements. Some of the evidence relating to the efficacy of increasing fibre intake is contradictory (*see* Chapter 6). It may help some individuals but may worsen symptoms in others (e.g. in cases of idiopathic slow-transit constipation). The intervention, therefore, needs to be carefully evaluated on an individual basis.

When the incontinence has a cerebral neurological cause, it is often necessary to identify triggers that initiate incontinence. For example, eating a meal stimulates defecation 30 minutes following the completion of the meal, or defecation occurs following the morning cup of coffee. If the faecal incontinence is only once or twice a day, it might be controlled by specific preparation. Offering the toilet, commode or bedpan at a given time following the trigger event can facilitate defecation in the appropriate place at the appropriate time. If incontinence is continual, a regimen of planned defecation could be implemented. Defecation is stimulated once to three times a week by the use of an enema and, to prevent possible leakage in between, a constipating drug may be needed such as loperamide or codeine phosphate (Barrett, 1994). Bowel management of this type allows for less embarrassment and more predictability for the individuals and carers concerned.

Continence in People with Mental Health Needs

Reasons for, and Manifestations of, Incontinence

Norton (1996) points out that incontinence (faecal and urinary) is not an inevitable feature of dementia and memory loss and should not preclude the investigation and exclusion of other causes. Many people with dementia are not incontinent. Continence is deeply ingrained in individual socialisation and it is often one of the last social skills to be lost (Norton, 1996).

Familiar surroundings can be vital to the functioning of people with mental health needs, and incontinence may arise when surroundings change. Individuals can become disorientated in new surroundings. They may be unable to locate the lavatory, particularly if there are no recognisable signposts. They may be unfamiliar with the equipment, for example may identify a commode as an armchair and seek a recognisable lavatory.

Incontinence is very rarely a consequence of a deliberate, conscious choice but it is important for nurses to be alert to staff practices which may reinforce the positive consequences of an episode of incontinence, for example if this is the only time a person receives attention. Cheater (1987) researched nurses' attitudes to incontinence and found that some patients were only incontinent when specific staff were on duty.

People with advanced dementia may lose social realisation, become uninhibited and pass urine or faeces as the desire arises. Familiarity of routine can be maximised, for example by assessing the times at which the person usually voids, and taking them to the lavatory. Privacy and comfort are also important to facilitate voiding. In this way, the usual routine is maintained and incontinence is likely to occur less frequently. It is important that caregivers do not give inappropriate cues, such as taking the person to the toilet at regular intervals but when their bladder may not be full, or removing their underclothes and sitting them onto a pad. This can be extremely confusing for the person with impaired mental capacity who may not be able to pass urine after being taken to an uncomfortable toilet but, once relaxing in a comfortable chair, can pass urine quite easily. This can cause frustration in caregivers but the situation arises because they have inadvertently given the patient the wrong messages. Some people with advanced dementia may become distressed by incontinence as they genuinely do not understand what is happening. Some are aware of their incontinence, are embarrassed by it and may try to conceal the evidence by hiding soiled clothes, putting clean clothes over soiled ones, or blaming someone or something else, such as the cat. Some may become angry and aggressive about being discovered. Other people may be oblivious to incontinence.

Assessment

A comprehensive assessment, including a behavioural assessment, is important; for example, there may be a particular prompt or behaviour that occurs prior to passing urine or faeces, such as become fidgety, picking at clothing, getting up and walking around. These cues may be verbal or non-verbal. The ABC Assessment of Behaviour is useful in this context. (*see* Chapter 13). For full discussion of assessing someone with mental health needs *see* Chapter 18.

Intervention

An appropriate environment with orientation cues is important. Following the person's usual daily routine can also prevent episodes of incontinence. For people who don't recognise that they need to go to the toilet, verbal prompts at appropriate times may help.

Maintaining a healthy lifestyle is also vital, for example in drinking sufficient fluid, eating sufficient fresh foods and dietary fibre (*see* Chapter 6), and maintaining physical activity can all help preserve muscle strength and bodily functioning. It is very important that good skin care is provided because self-esteem and skin integrity depend on it.

Protective garments may be necessary (many of the garments used for incontinence of urine may be suitable and can facilitate greater mobility and participation in daily activities. Continence goals should be realistic, but simple interventions can be very effective (Tobin and Brocklehurst, 1986).

HEALTH BELIEFS IN CHRONIC ILLNESS

People with chronic illness make constant decisions about how to manage their lives and their difficulties. These are based on individual beliefs and values, including those relating to the effectiveness of health advice that has been offered by professionals. Volumes of research into the extent to which a person's behaviour coincides with health or medical advice has been conducted under the heading of 'compliance' or, more recently 'adherence'. There has been a growing dissatisfaction with these terms, with their suggestions of paternalism and of 'wilful disobedience'. (The term compliance and its alternatives, particularly in relation to taking prescribed medications, are fully discussed in Chapter 10.) Patients choose not to follow recommendations for a wide range of reasons but the incidence of 'non-compliance' is generally estimated at about 50% in people with chronic disorders generally, but this figure varies with different disorders, at different stages of the illness and disability progression, and with different elements of the recommended regimes.

It is important to be aware of the potential for 'client blaming strategies' where a lack of 'recovery' is attributed to an individual's failure to follow health professionals' recommendations. Social stigma may accompany a chronic disorder if an individual is seen by others to have 'given in' to the disease and not given sufficient effort to fight the disease (Robinson, 1988). This might be especially the case for conditions with symptoms of low social visibility (e.g. lethargy), or with conditions characterised by relapse and remission ('why is the person in a wheelchair one week and not the next?').

Treatment regimes may be rejected because of the possible discomfort they might produce and further disruption to already disrupted lives. The regime may add to the already great effort that individuals and their families invest into the management of the chronic illness. Adherence to a treatment programme has to be qualified with social and cultural demands placed on an individual (Bury, 1991). The demands of long-term illness may conflict with values and needs developed over a lifetime. Health professionals must appreciate the interpersonal, cultural, situational and other factors that underlie what may appear to be simple resistance and negativity. Individuals also have different physical, psychological, social and economic resources at their disposal.

For health professionals to give appropriate and effective care a sensitive and informed approach is required. 'Without understanding a great deal about how the chronically ill get through their days outside of health facilities (and inside them, too), health personnel will never understand what they really need to know to give effective care' (Strauss *et al.* 1984, p. 9). As already mentioned above (see section on 'empowerment'), for a treatment programme to be successful the client (and family) must be given sufficient information and be involved in the formulation of the programme. The aim is for the client, as far as possible, to be enabled to take control over his or her life. Failure to do this may result in high rates of 'non-compliance'.

The health belief model investigated by Redeker (1988) was developed to explain response to preventive health behaviours. The major belief factors are the value to the individual of a particular outcome and the individual's estimate of the likelihood of a particular outcome associated with compliance or noncompliance. Belief in the efficacy of an action implies belief that that action will reduce the threat to health. The requirements of compliance must not outweigh the benefits, or the client will rarely feel it is worth the effort. Careful assessment of the client's belief in outcomes and energy needed to comply with the regimen are essential. Questions to be addressed are given in **Box 8.10**.

Emphasis on the importance of the client's perception of health is consistent with Orem's concept (1980) that education, experience, attitudes and knowledge all colour one's response to health requirements.

SUMMARY

This chapter has studied the increasingly important, yet often underemphasised, area of chronic illness in older people. It has analysed some of the relevant statistics and discussed the chronic illness trajectory. Throughout, the chapter has emphasised the reality for older people of living with chronic illness or disability, for example in terms of lifestyle adjustment. The impact of a sample of chronic conditions has been examined, and the potential for rehabilitative services reviewed. Nurses have an increasingly important role working with people with chronic illness and disability. The nurse needs to assess the knowledge base of the client in relation to the regimen prescribed and keep on balance an awareness that resistance to direction may be a form of autonomy and personality strength. Nurses can assist by:

- Identifying and stating strengths the individual demonstrates.
- Discussing healthy lifestyle modifications.
- Encouraging the reduction of risk factors in the environment.
- Assisting the individual to devise methods of improving function, halting disabilities and adapting lifestyle to reasonable expectations of self.
- Providing access to resources when possible.
- Referring appropriately and when needed.
- Organising interdisciplinary case conferences and informing the individual of insights gained in management of disorders.

In summary, management of chronic problems of the older person must be centred around that individual, and viewed from his or her standpoint. Nurses are resource persons, advisors, teachers, and at times assistants, but individuals are ultimately in control of their adaptation and their lives.

8.10 Health Belief's Assessment

- Do health beliefs remain stable over time?
- Is there a difference in the response of individuals recently diagnosed and of those with a long history of chronic disorders?
- How important is symptom severity in compliance?
- What relationship exists between social support and maintenance of health benefits?

KEY POINTS

- Chronic illness is the irreversible presence, accumulation or latency of disease states or impairments that involve the total human environment for supportive care and self-care, maintenance of function and prevention of further disability.
- One of the most difficult aspects of chronic disease is the unpredictability of the trajectory.
- The management in the home by the family, self or significant other is central to care.
- Adaptations and assistance with ADLs and IADLs can considerably assist day-to-day functioning.
- The goals of rehabilitation for older people are to ensure opportunity for optimum personal development and function.
- Fundamental to nursing an older person with chronic progressive disease and disability is trying to understand that person's reality, goals for life and ways of coping.

AREAS AND ACTIVITIES FOR STUDY AND REFLECTION

- Select some older people with chronic illness or disability, and with whom you have developed a good relationship. Discuss the reality of their everyday lives with them. What did they feel when they first learned of their illness, and how did they react? How did those around them react? How have they coped since? How do they see their future?
- What is your understanding of the term 'rehabilitation'? Review the care plans in your patient caseload and identify the aspects of rehabilitative and restorative care. How could this be improved? What are the distinct aspects of the nursing role in rehabilitation?
- In the light of the chapter contents, review the prevention and management of incontinence in your clinical area. How could this be improved?
- Review the structures and mechanisms for interagency working in your area? Is this effective and how could it be improved? In particular, could communication be achieved more effectively and, if so, how?

REFERENCES

Adams J. Adapting for community care. *Br J Occup Ther* 1996, 59:115–118.

Allen G. *Family Life*. London: Blackwell, 1985.

Andersen J, Abrams, P, Blaivas JG, Stanton SL. Standardisation of terminology of lower urinary tract function. *Scand J Urol Nephrol Suppl* 1988, 114:5–19.

Anderson R. *The aftermath of stroke: the experience of patients and their families*. Cambridge: Cambridge University Press, 1992.

Barnes DG, Shaw PJR, Timoney AG, Tsokos N. Management of the neuropathic bladder by suprapubic catheterisation. *Br J Urol* 1993, 72:169–172.

Barrett JA. Faecal incontinence. In: Roe, ed. *Clinical nursing practice. The promotion and management of continence*. London: Prentice Hall, 1994.

Basch A. *Continence control: vision for the future*, Senior Focus, Mills-Peninsula Hospitals Conference, San Francisco, Ca, USA, October 26–27, 1992.

Bates A. The elderly diabetic with multiple problems. *The Practitioner* 1987, 231:1475–1478 (9 November 1987).

Beardshaw V. *Last on the list. Community service for people with physical disabilities*. London: Kings Fund, 1988.

Bowling A. *Measuring disease*. Milton Keynes: Open University Press, 1995.

Bowling A, Betts,G. Communication on discharge. *Nurs Times* 1984, 80(32)31–33.

Bowling A, Farquhar M, Grundy E, Formby J. Changes in life satisfaction over a two and a half year period among very elderly people living in London. *Soc Sci Med* 1993, 36:641–655.

British Thoracic Society. *Guidelines for the Management of COPD*, London, 1997, British Thoracic Society.

Brummel-Smith K. Geriatric Rehabilitation. *Generations* 1992, 16:27.

Bulmer M. *The social basis of community care*. London: Allen & Unwin, 1987.

Bury M. Chronic illness as biographical disruption. *Sociol Health Illness* 1982, 4:167–181.

Bury M. The sociology of chronic illness: a review of research and prospects. *Sociol Health Illness* 1991, 13:451–468.

Bury M, Holme A. The challenge of the oldest old. In: Bury M, Macnicol J, eds. *Aspects of ageing*. Surrey: Department of Social Policy, Royal Holloway and Bedford New College, 1990.

Cheater F. Incontinence: a nursing perspective. *Nurs Times* 1987, 18:46.

Coates VE, Boore JRP. Self-management of chronic illness: implications for nursing. *Int J Nurs Stud* 1995, 32:628–640.

Colling J, Ouslander J, Hadley BJ, Eisch J, Campbell E. The effects patterned urge-response toiletting (PURT) on urinary incontinence among nursing home residents. *J Am Geriatr Soc* 1992, 40:135–141.

Continence Foundation. *Continence products directory, 2nd edition*. London: Continence Foundation, 1997.

Copperwheat M. Putting continence into practice. *Geriatr Nurs* 1985, 5:4.

Corbin JM, Strauss A. *Unending work and care: managing chronic illness at home*. San Francisco: Jossey-Bass, 1988.

Crow RA, Chapman R, Roe B, Wilson J. *A study of patients with an indwelling catheter and related nursing practice*, Report from the Nursing Practice Research Unit, University of Surrey, 1986.

David JA, Redfern SJ. Drugs and elderly people. In: Redfern S, ed. *Nursing elderly people, 2nd edition*. London: Churchill Livingstone, 1991.

Department of Health. *Discharge of patients from hospital*. Circular HC (89)5, 1989.

Department of Health. *NHS responsibilities for meeting continuing health care needs*. Circular HSG (95)8/LAC(95)5, 1995.

Dolman M. Mostly female. In: Getliffe K, Dolman M, eds. *Promoting Continence*. London: Balliere Tindall, 1997.

Ebersole P, Hess P. *Toward healthy aging: human needs and nursing response, 4th edition*. London: Mosby, 1994.

Edwards D. Discharge home. *J District Nurs* 1991(August)4–7.

Farquhar M, Bowling A, Grundy E, Formby J. Functional ability of very elderly people. *Nurs Stand* 1993, 7:31–36.

Fielding P. Nursing old people in hospital. In: Redfern S, ed. *Nursing elderly people*. London: Churchill Livingstone, 1991.

General Household Survey. *Living in Britain*. London: Office of National Surveys, 1994.

General Household Survey. *Living in Britain*, London: Office of National Surveys, 1995.

Getliffe K. The characteristics and management of patients with recurrent blockage of long-term urinary catheters. *J Adv Nurs* 1994a, 20:140–149.

Getliffe K. The use of bladder wash-outs to reduce urinary catheter encrustation. *Br J Urol* 1994b, 73:696–700.

Getliffe K. Catheters and cathetersiation. In: Getliffe K, Dolman M, eds. *Promoting continence*. London: Balliere Tindall, 1997.

Goldstein M, Hawthorne ME, Engeberg S *et al*. Urinary incontinence: why people do not seek help. *J Gerontol Nurs* 1992, 18:15.

Health Services Accreditation. *Standards for continence services*, 1997.

Heath HBM, ed. *Potter and Perry's, foundations in nursing theory and practice*. London: Mosby, 1995.

Heywood Jones I. Meeting personal care needs. *Community Outlook* 1994a, (September):30–32.

Heywood Jones I. Maintaining Independence. *Community Outlook* 1994b, (May):23–24.

Hilton P, Stanton SL. Algorithmic method for assessing urinary incontinence in elderly women. *Br Med J* 1981, 282:940–942.

Horgan A, Prasad B, Waldron D, O'Sullivan D. Acute urinary retention: a comparison of suprapubic and urethral catheterisation. *Br J Urology* 1992, 70:149–151.

Jette AM, Branch LG, Berlin J. Musculoskeletal impairments and physical disablement among the aged. *J Gerontol* 1990, 45:203.

Kennedy AP, Brocklehurst JC, Lye MDW. Factors related to the problems of long-term catheterisation. *J Adv Nurs* 1983, 8:207–212.

Kennedy AP. Bladder re-education for the promotion of continence. In: Roe B, ed. *Clinical nursing practice. The promotion and management of continence*. London: Prentice Hall, 1994.

Laycock J. Pelvic floor re-education for the promotion of continence. In: Roe B, ed. *Clinical nursing practice. The Promotion and management of continence*. London: Prentice Hall, 1994.

Legh-Smith J, Wade DT, Langton-Hewer R. Services for stroke patients one year after stroke. *J Epidemiol Community Health* 1986, 40:161–165.

Lowthian P. Preventing trauma. *Nurs Times* 1989, 85:21.

Lubkin IM. *Chronic illness: impact and interventions*. Boston: Jones and Bartlett, 1995.

MacElveen-Hoehn. The impact of chronic illness on the family. In: King K, ed. *Long-term care*. New York: Churchill Livingstone, 1985, 150–170.

Maclaren JA. Rehabilitation through advocacy and empowerment. *Br J Ther Rehabil* 1996, 3:492–497.

Mahady IW, Begg BM. Long-term symptomatic and cystometric cure of the urge incontinence syndrome using a technique of bladder re-education. *Br J Obstetr Gynaecol* 1981, 88:1038–1043.

Martin J, Meltzer H, Elliot D. *The prevalence of disability among adults, OPCS surveys of disability in Great Britain, Report 1*. London: HMSO, 1988.

McNett, S. Social support and coping effectiveness in the functionally disabled. *Nurs Res* 1987, 6(2):98–103.

Mishel M, Braden C. Finding meaning: antecedents of uncertainty in illness. *Nurs Res* 1988, 37:98.

Mohide EA. The prevalence of urinary incontinence. In: Roe B, ed. *Clinical nursing practice. The promotion and management of continence*. London: Prentice Hall, 1994.

MRC. *The health of the UK's elderly people*. London: Medical Research Council, 1994.

Mulhall A, Chapman R, Crow R: Catheters. The acquisition of bacteriuria. *Nurs Times* 1988, 84:4.

Mullhall A, King S, Lee K, Wiggington E. Maintenance of closed urinary drainage systems: are practitioners more ware of the dangers? *J Adv Nurs* 1993, 2:135–140.

Nolan M. Supporting family carers: the key to successful long-term care? *Br J Nurs* 1996, 5:836.

Nolan, M. The nursing contribution to rehabilitation within the multidisciplinary team: literature and curriculum analysis. London: English National Board for Nursing, Midwifery and Health Visiting, 1997.

Norton C. Incontinence in old age. *Nurs Elderly* 1992, 4:4.

Norton C. *Nursing for continence, 2nd edition*. Beaconsfield: Beaconsfield Publishers Ltd, 1996.

O'Brien J, Long H. Urinary incontinence: long term effectiveness of nursing intervention in primary care. *Br Med J* 1995, 311:1208.

Orem D. *Nursing: concepts of practice, 2nd edition*. New York: McGraw-Hill, 208.

Pinder R. Striking balances: living with Parkinson's disease. In: Anderson R, Bury M, eds. *Living with chronic illness*. London: Unwin Hyman, 1988.

Pomfret IJ. Catheters: design, selection and management. *Br J Nurs* 1996, 5:4.

Qureshi H, Walker A. *The caring relationship, elderly people and their families*. London: Macmillan, 1989.

Redeker N. Health beliefs and adherence in chronic illness. *J Nurs Scholarship* 1988, 29:31.

Resnick B. Motivation in geriatric rehabilitation. *IMAGE: J Nurs Scholarship* 1996, 28:41–45.

Richmond J, Diabetes mellitus in old age. *Elderly Care* 1995, 7(3):25–30.

Robinson I. Reconstructing lives: negotiating the meaning of multiple sclerosis. In: Anderson R, Bury M, eds. *Living with chronic illness, the experience of patients and their families*. London: Unwin Hyman, 1988.

Roe B. Use of indwelling catheters. In: Roe B, ed. *Clinical nursing practice. The promotion and management of continence*. London: Prentice Hall, 1994.

Roe B, Brocklehurst JC. Study of patients with indwelling catheters. *J Adv Nurs* 1987, 12:713–718.

Schnelle JF, Traughber B, Sowell VA, Newman DR, Petrilli CO, Ory M. Prompted voiding treatment of urinary incontinence in nursing home patients. *J Am Geriatr Soc* 1989, 37:1051–1057.

Sidell M. *Health in old age, myth, mystery and management*. Birmingham: Open University Press, 1995.

Slade W, Gillespie WA. *The urinary tract and the catheter*. Chichester: John Wiley and Sons, 1985

Stevens *et al*. Stroke rehabilitation units in the United Kingdom. *Health Trends* 1984, 16(3):61–63.

Strauss A, Corbin J. *Shaping a new health care system*. San Francisco, Jossey-Bass, 1988.

Strauss AL, Corbin J, Fagerhaugh S *et al*. *Chronic illness and the quality of life, 2nd edition*. St Louis: Mosby, 1984.

Tattersall RB, Gale EAM. *Diabetes: clinical management*. Edinburgh: Churchill Livingstone, 1990.

Thomas TM, Plymat KR, Blannin J, Meade TW. Prevalence of urinary incontinence. *Br Med J* 1980, 281:1243–1246.

Thomas TM, Egan M, Walgrove A, Meade TW The prevalence of faecal incontinence. *Community Medicine* 1984, 6(3):216–220.

Tobin GW, Brocklehurst JC. Faecal incontinence in residential homes for the elderly: prevalence, aetiology and management. *Age Aging* 1986, 15:292.

Tobin GW. *Incontinence in the elderly*. London: Edward Arnold, 1992.

University of Leeds. *Effective health care: stroke rehabilitation*, 1992.

Wade DT. Strokes: rehabilitation and long-term care. *Lancet* 1992, 339:791–793.

Wanich K, Sullivan-Max EM, Gottlieb GL *et al.*, Functional status outcomes of a nursing intervention in hospitalised elderly. *Image* 1992, 24(3):201.

Waters K. Discharge planning. *J Adv Nurs* 1987, 12:71–83.

Waters KR, Luker KA. Staff perspectives on the role of the nurse in rehabilitation wards for elderly people. *J Clin Nurs* 1996, 5:105–114.

WHO, *The health of the elderly*. Geneva: World Health Organisation, 1989

Williams J. The rehabilitation process for older people and their carers. *Nurs Times* 1994, 90:33–34.

Woog P. *The chronic illness trajectory framework: the Corbin and Strauss nursing model*. New York: Springer, 1992.

Young J. Rehabilitation and older people. *Br Med J* 1996, 313:677–681.

USEFUL ADDRESSES

Disabled Living Foundation
Display equipment and offer advice. Provide a telephone help-line (same number).
Adaptive devices
Gadgets for easier living include such things as talking clocks, stocking pullers, sound-operated light switches, and jumbo-size push-button telephones.
Tub benches assist a person into and out of the bathtub and are designed according to individual needs and degree of mobility.
Helping hands, and reachers assist in grasping items when bending is difficult. There are many other useful items to compensate for deficits in function.
380–84 Harrow Road, London W9 2HU. Tel. 0171 289 6111

Keep Able Ltd.
Large store and showroom - advice by in-store therpists. Can arrange domicillary assessments and advice.
11–17 Kingston Road, Staines, Middlesex TW18 4QX. Tel. 01784 440044

Continence
The Continence Foundation
A national resource centre for information, education and research. Provides an information helpline staffed by nurse continence advisors.
The Continence Foundation, 2 Doughty Street, London WC1 2PH. Tel: 0171 404 6875. Information helpline: 0171 213 0050.

The Association for Continence Advice (ACA)
A multidisciplinary professional body for anyone with a special interest in continence.
Association for Continence Advice, 2 Doughty Street, London WC1N 2PH. Tel:0170 404 6821.

Royal College of Nursing Continence Care Forum
A continence special interest group for RCN members, c/o Royal College of Nursing, 20 Cavendish Square, London W1M OAB. Tel: 0171 409 3333.

General
Crossroads
Offers domicillary respite care for full-time carers.
10 Regent Place, Rugby, Warwickshire CV21 2PN. Tel. 01788 573 653.

Royal Association for Disability and Rehabilitation (RADAR)
Information resource and campaigning organisation.
12 City Forum, 250 City Road, London EC1V 8AF. Tel. 0171 250 3222

Association to Aid the Sexual and Personal Relationships of People with a Disability (SPOD)
Offer information and advice, publications, counselling and training.
286 Camden Road, London, N7 OBJ. Tel. 0171 607 8851.

Arthritis Care
Arranges activities, transport, clubs , holiday accommodation for people with arthritis.
18 Stephenson Way, London NW1 2HD. Tel. 0171 916 1500.

Multiple Sclerosis Society
Offer advice, information, telephone councelling, produce publications, respite care and holiday homes. Network of local branches and support groups.
25 Effie Road, Fulham, London SW6 1EE. Tel. 0171 610 7171
Telephone help-line: 0171 371 8000

Parkinsons Disease Society
Offer information and welfare advice. Run local support groups.
22 Upper Woburn Place, London WC1H ORA. Tel. 0171 383 3513, Telephone help-line: 0171 388 5798

Spinal Injuries Association
Newpoint House, 76 St James Lane, London N10 3DF. Tel. 0181 444 2121.

Stroke Association
Run support groups, Free publications regarding stroke and hypertension. Telephone help-line.
Stroke House, 123–127 Whitecross Street, London EC1 8JJ. Tel. 0171 490 7999

Pain and comfort
Sheila Goff

LEARNING OBJECTIVES

After studying this chapter you will be able to:
- Define pain and factors influencing pain experience in the older person.
- Understand common misconceptions about pain and its management in the older person.
- Understand current thinking on pain theory.
- Differentiate between acute and chronic pain.
- Describe methods of assessing pain in older people, especially those unable to respond verbally.
- Describe a variety of pain management strategies appropriate to older people.
- Have an understanding of the pains particularly prevalent in older people.

INTRODUCTION

In recent years, there has been a huge amount of research interest from many different disciplines into aspects of pain. There has been increasing recognition that pain is much more than a physical phenomenon. Dame Cicely Saunders first used the term 'total pain' to emphasise that pain has emotional, social and spiritual components as well as physical, and all of these need attention if pain relief is to be achieved. This burgeoning interest has not encompassed the particular problems of pain in later life. Melding (1991) found that a mere 1% of over 4000 papers published annually addressed these issues. Yet, it is likely that problems associated with both acute and chronic pain are most prevalent in later life (Closs, 1994). Details on the prevalence of pain in older people within the UK are sparse, but Closs (1994) cites a London-based survey by Bowling and Browne (1991) in which 70% of a sample of 662 people over the age of 85 reported aches, pains, and muscle and joint stiffness. Studies in long-term residential care settings have also found significant pain problems (Ferrell *et al.* 1990; Yates *et al.* 1995).

Pain can have a very negative effect on the quality of later life; the scarcity of specific research into the effects of age on the meaning of pain to the sufferer, on pain perception, assessment and treatments has tended to allow erroneous beliefs about these issues to be formed.

This chapter will first examine the concepts of comfort and pain and the effects of acute and chronic pain on the sufferer. Some of the misconceptions about pain in the older person will then be highlighted. The effect of age on pain perception will be considered, as will some of the many factors that influence response to pain. A brief review of the physiology of pain will be followed by a look at the challenges of pain assessment in later life. Finally, pain control interventions will be examined, highlighting treatments of common pains to which older people are particularly susceptible.

Pain, whatever its source, erodes personality, saps energy, and manifests itself in an ever-intensifying cycle of pain, anxiety, and anguish until the cycle is broken. 'Pain is whatever the person experiencing pain says it is' (McCaffery and Beebe, 1989).

COMFORT

Comfort seems to be an intrinsic balance of the physiological, emotional, social and spiritual essence of the individual and can be perceived as synonymous with wellness. By definition comfort is 'a state of ease and satisfaction of the bodily wants and freedom from pain and anxiety'. The absence of physical pain is not always sufficient to provide comfort. The older person may have their biological or bodily needs satisfied but may be emotionally distressed. Conversely, physical needs may be the priority and no comfort is possible until need fulfilment is accomplished.

Nurses use the word comfort to describe goals and outcomes to nursing measures, but the meaning remains vague and essentially abstract to the person who is the recipient of the nursing intervention. Hamilton (1989) studied the meaning and attributes of comfort from the point of view of chronically ill older people in hospital. Questions were asked about the older patient's definition of comfort; contributors and detractors of comfort; and how to increase the person's comfort. The findings identified several themes:
- Disease process (pain, bowel function and disability).

		Summary of Comfort Findings	
Comfort themes	Contributors to comfort	Distractors of comfort	Adds to comfort
Disease process	Achieving relief from pain; regular bowel function	Physical disabilities; being in pain most of time	Better pain management
Self-esteem	Faith in God; being independent; feeling relaxed; feeling useful	Adjust to change; being afraid	Being informed; taking part in decision-making
Positioning	Individually adjusted seating; sitting correctly; independent movement in chair	Unsuitable wheelchairs; sitting too long; sliding down in chair; being in unfavourable position arrangements	Return to bed when requested; better seating in bed
Staff approach and attitudes	Friendly, kind people; empathetic nurses; reliable nurses	Lack of caring and understanding; inaccessible nurses	Caring and understanding; encouraging patients to help themselves
Hospital life	Homelike surroundings; social and family contacts; informal pastimes; occupational and physiotherapy	Fragmented care; routinized care; boredom with activities; lack of privacy; unpleasant meal atmosphere	Staff continuity. New content in activities; continuation of personal pastimes; improved patient mealtimes; some privacy

Source: Adapted from Hamilton J. Comfort and the hospitalized chronically ill. *J Gerontol Nurs* 1989, 15(4):28.

Table 9.1 Summary of Comfort Findings

- Self-esteem (feelings, adjustment, independence, usefulness, faith in God).
- Positioning (if the older person could carry out activities in bed, chair or wheelchair).
- Approach and attitude of staff (relationships, encounters).
- Hospital life (surroundings and environment – feeling at home, well fed, pleasant surroundings).

Table 9.1 summarises each of these themes and includes contributors and distracters to comfort and patients' suggestions for facilitating more comfort.

Hamilton's definition, 'comfort is multidimensional and means many things to different people' parallels McCaffery's definition of pain, 'pain is whatever the person experiencing pain says it is' (McCaffery and Bebee, 1989). This raises the issue of whether there is a way to identify comfort–discomfort zones outside that of acute or chronic pain in a manner similar to the pain assessment measures that are presently used. This is definitely a fruitful area for research.

ACUTE AND CHRONIC PAIN

Acute, temporary pain has been controlled easily by analgesic preparations for many years. Almost everyone has experienced this type of pain and knows that it is a temporary, time-limited situation with attainable relief. Chronic pain is not that simple. It has no time frame; it is continually persistent at varying levels of intensity, and it manipulates the individual and can manipulate the person attempting to give care. *See* **Table 9.2** for a summary of the differences in causes and effects on life of acute and chronic pain.

Chronic pain can manifest itself as depression, eating disturbances or sleep disturbances. Chronic pain is categorised as:

(1) Chronic pain caused by uncontrolled neoplastic disease.
(2) Chronic benign pain (non-neoplastic), which usually lasts over a period of months and is coped with adequately.
(3) Chronic intractable benign pain that erodes an individual's coping ability. The International Association for the Study of Pain (IASP) gives 3 months as the time period that generally distinguishes chronic from acute pain.

The consensus definition of chronic pain developed by IASP is:

An unpleasant sensory and emotional experience associated with actual or potential tissue damage or described in terms of such damage.

(Merskey and Bogduk, 1994)

Chronic pain may be due to the following:
- **Muscle and joint pain**, which includes low back pain, arthritis and bursitis.
- **Causalgia**, which is a searing type of pain experienced

Comparison of Acute and Chronic Pain

Characteristic	Acute pain	Chronic pain
Experience	An event	A situation, state of existence
Source	External agent of internal disease	Unknown, or if known, changes cannot occur or treatment is prolonged or ineffective
Onset	Usually sudden	May be sudden or develop insidiously
Duration	Transient (up to 6 months)	Prolonged (months to years)
Pain identification	Pain versus non-pain areas generally well identified	Pain versus non-pain areas less easily differentiated, intensity becomes more difficult to evaluate (change in sensations)
Clinical signs	Typical response pattern with more visible signs	Response patterns vary, fewer overt signs (adaptation)
Meaning	Meaningful (informs person something is wrong)	Meaningless, person looks for meanings
Pattern	Self-limiting or readily corrected	Continuous or intermittent, intensity may vary or remain constant
Course	Suffering usually decreases over time	Suffering usually increases over time
Actions	Leads to action to modify pain	Leads to actions to relieve pain experience
Prognosis	Likelihood of eventual complete relief	Complete relief usually not possible

Source: Adapted from Karb, 1991. In: Phipps W, Long B, Woods N, eds. *Medical-surgical nursing: concepts and clinical practice, 4th edition,* St Louis: Mosby, 1991; Forest J. Assessment of acute and chronic pain in older adults. *J Gerontol Nurs* 1995, 21:10.

Table 9.2 Comparison of Acute and Chronic Pain

after sudden systemic shock and would be comparable to placing a lighted cigarette to the skin. It may dissipate in 6 to 12 months, but at least 25% of individuals who experience this pain continue to suffer from it for a much longer time.

- **Neuralgia** arising from peripheral nerves, with the most devastating of this type of pain being tic douloureux, which is similar to the pain that occurs in conjunction with shingles (herpes zoster).
- **Phantom pain**, which begins as a pins and needles sensation seemingly arising from an amputated part and possibly developing into cramping, burning or shooting pains that last for years. These are similar types of sensations that persons paralysed with spinal cord injuries experience.
- **Vascular pain**, which is most dramatically evident in migraine headaches.
- **Diabetic pain** arising from neuropathy and peripheral vascular occlusion combine together in people with advanced diabetes to produce a constant or intermittent burning pain, similar to the pain of frostbite, or a deep aching in the extremities.
- **Terminal cancer pain**, which produces fear and anxiety in the patient and distress in the staff.

- **Central post-stroke pain** occurs in at least 2% of people with stroke (The Stroke Association, 1997). It is often experienced as deep boring or crushing sensations, or superficial burning, lacerating or pricking and cold sensations. It may affect half, or only a small part of the body, sometimes hands and feet are more severely affected than arms and legs. Ordinary sensation is always abnormal in the affected area. Movement of the side and other sensations to the affected side such as touch, sound, bright light and air increase this kind of pain. The situation in which a normally non-painful stimulus is perceived as painful is known as allodynia (Wittink and Michael, 1997). Hyperalgesia, an increased response to a stimulus that is normally painful, can also occur. People with diabetic neuropathy and shingles sometimes experience altered pain sensation in this way.

Misconceptions about Pain in the Older Person

Some of the many pitfalls that the nurse can experience when assessing and helping any patient in pain are summarised in Box 9.1.

9.1 Nurses' Misconceptions about the Pain Experience

- Patients should expect to have pain in hospital.
- Obvious pathology, test results, and/or type of surgery determine the existence and intensity of pain.
- Patients who are in pain always have observable signs.
- Chronic pain is not as serious a problem for patients as acute pain.
- Patients are not the experts about their pain – health professionals are.
- Patients will report that they are in pain and will use the term 'pain'.

Source: Watt-Watson JH, Donovan MI. *Pain management nursing perspective*. St Louis: Mosby, 1992.

There are a number of misconceptions about the pain experience that are particularly relevant to the older person. Many of these were investigated in a study by Closs (1996) in which over 200 qualified hospital nurses were surveyed for their knowledge about pain and pain control in patients aged 70 years and over.

(1) Misconception that pain is an unavoidable consequence of growing older. Closs (1996) found that one-third of nurses believed this to be the case and points out that it is a sad assumption as it can lead to the neglect of otherwise treatable pain. This myth is not just attributable to health professionals but seems to be a prevalent view held by older people themselves. Yates *et al.* (1995) sought views about the pain of older people living in long-term residential care in Australia and found that many had become resigned to pain, believed that nothing would help to alleviate it and consequently saw little point in expressing how it felt.

(2) Misconception that the perception of a given painful stimulus decreases with age. There was some confusion in the responses of the nurses in Closs's study to this issue. In fact, the literature is inconsistent as will be shown later in this chapter.

(3) Misconception that the analgesic effect of a given dose of drug increases with age. One-third of the nurses in Closs's study believed this to be the case. Although there are some situations, which will be dealt with later, where analgesic dose should be reduced in the older person, a general assumption could lead to under-treatment of pain in older people.

(4) Misconception that opioid drugs are too dangerous to use in treatment of pain in older people. Opioids have a vital part to play in the alleviation of pain in this group of patients and may be safely used if the pharmacokinetics are recognised (Twycross, 1994; Forman *et al.* 1992) (*see* Chapter 10). However, Closs (1996) found that nurses tended to exaggerate the risk

of respiratory depression. Such a tendency could again lead to under-treatment.

Pain Perception

Clinical observations that pain decreases with age remain inconclusive. Portenoy (1990) reports pain reduction at all anatomic sites except the joints. The literature has revealed instances of serious abdominal and cardiac conditions that should elicit severe pain but that have produced little or no pain in older people. It is not uncommon for acuity of symptoms or severity of pain to be less dramatic than in younger persons. Other studies have been carried out with inconsistent findings (Tucker *et al.* 1989).

One factor which may make pain perception appear lower in older people is that of under-reporting because they consider it to be a normal part of ageing. Behavioural changes or manifestations such as confusion and restlessness are possible indicators of painful stimuli in older people. However, the potential for lowered pain tolerance exists with diminished adaptive capacity in old age. Changes in peripheral vascular function, skin and transmission of pain impulses through the central nervous system may actually place them at high risk from damage as a result of diminished pain sensation.

Studies of pain threshold have been difficult to evaluate because of the methodological problem that age-related threshold changes may vary as a function of body location. Another factor affecting pain research on humans is the refusal of relatives to allow patient participation in a study (Duffy *et al.* 1989). Differences in the interpretation of pain also arise from caregivers' own experience with acute rather than chronic pain. In addition, questions are now arising about how to discern pain in older people who are cognitively impaired and without speech. Thus, evidence to support long-held assumptions that pain perception decreases with age is contradictory.

Pain Behaviour

Many different factors affect how pain is experienced by individuals and the way in which they respond. Pain is much more than merely a biological response to a noxious stimulus. The psychological, social and cultural biography of a person will have input into their total pain experience. The nurse, too, has a definition or interpretation, as well as the patient. These interpretations are formulated from experiences and are influenced by the unique history of the individual and the meaning ascribed to the pain. Some of the factors influencing an individual's response to pain are summarised in **Box 9.2**.

The influence of cultural background of both professional and patient is important to consider in any therapeutic encounter. This is an area of study of interest to anthropologists (Helman, 1994) and a famous study examining the role of ethnicity on pain expression was carried out

9.2 Factors Influencing Clients' Response to Pain

- Past pain experience.
- Culture.
- Gender.
- Significance of pain.
- Depression.
- Fatigue.
- Physiological age changes.
- Altered pain stimulus transmission.
- Decrease in inflammation response.

Source: Adapted from Eland JM. Pain management and comfort. *J Gerontol Nurs* 1988, 14(4):10.

by Zborowski in the 1950s. He observed and interviewed male veterans of the world wars at a hospital in New York. They were of Jewish, Italian and 'Old American' origins. He noted big differences in pain behaviour with the Italians and Jews openly and emotionally expressing their pain in words, gestures, crying and groaning while the 'Old Americans' did not publicly express their pain but factually reported it to health professionals. He then went on to show that the meaning of the pain was different in all three groups even though the expression was similar amongst Jews and Italians. The Italians were very anxious and concerned about the pain experience itself and their expression of this pain reflected their intense desire to obtain relief from it. The Jews' response to the pain seemed to reflect more of their worry about the meaning and significance of it for their future health and prognosis of their illness. Thus, unlike the Italians they were unwilling to accept analgesia because of worries about side effects. The 'Old Americans' were more like the Jews in that their anxieties about pain were focussed on their future health. Zborowski's work and other similar studies have since been criticised for tending to create ethnic stereotypes in pain behaviour, but such work was important in opening up the study of pain and suggesting that meanings attributed to pain can influence behaviour. The importance of the meaning of the pain is taken up by Lanceley (1995) who points out that the Western view of the body as distinct from thoughts and emotions results in particular meanings associated with pain which cannot necessarily be generalised cross-culturally.

Physiology of Pain

Several early theories of pain were used to explain the pain phenomenon and the interventions for pain control.

The specificity theory was among the first explanations as to why an individual experienced pain. In essence, the specificity theory proposed that single, specialised peripheral nerve fibres were responsible for pain transmission. The discovery of the myelinated delta-A fibres, which transmit sensations that localise the source of pain and detect pain intensity, and

the unmyelinated C fibres, which relay impulses of a deeper and more diffuse nature, lent credence to this theory.

The pattern theory, also an early theory, stated that excessive stimulation of all nerve endings produces a pattern that was interpreted as pain by the brain cortex. In phantom limb pain, for example, the pain experienced before amputation of the limb leaves a memory tracing that is recalled after amputation. However, this theory does not provide concepts useful for interventions.

The gate theory, introduced by Melzack and Wall in the mid 1960s integrated the specificity and pattern theories and proposed that an anatomical gate regulates or blocks the pain experience. The suggested location of the gates is in the dorsal horn of the spinal cord. When gates are open, pain impulses flow freely, but when gates are closed, impulses become blocked. Partial opening of the gates may also occur.

Excitation of the delta-A and C fibres inhibits the gating mechanisms so that pain stimuli reach the cortical centres of the brain. Larger beta-A fibres share the same gating mechanisms. A bombardment of beta-A fibre sensory impulses, such as those from the pressure of a massage or from the heat of a hot pad, has the effect of closing the gates to painful stimuli. It is also believed that the reticular formation in the brainstem can send inhibitory signals to gating mechanisms. When there is excess sensory input (for example, from pain), the reticular formation can close gates. The gate theory also suggests that 'higher central nervous system' activities such as anxiety, attention, suggestion, past experiences and the meaning of the pain experience can influence the opening and closing of the gate. Bates (1996) explores such interactions further in her biocultural model of pain. Auditory or visual stimulation can also be used as a distraction to help make pain more tolerable. Neural memory, however, is not explained within the context of the gate theory.

ASSESSMENT

Assessment of pain in the older person is important for several reasons as shown in **Box 9.3**. (Watt-Watson and Donovan, 1992).

Jacox (1979) noted that 70% of patients studied did not like to discuss their pain with others or were ambivalent when they did talk about it. Two-thirds of patients remained calm and did not show their pain experience. No verbal communication occurred until the pain was severe.

Assessment Strategies

Question the patient about the pain. Do not rely on the word 'pain' alone; use other synonyms: discomfort, sore, ache, hurt, and so on (Watt-Watson and Donovan, 1992). Jacox (1979) found that 80% of patients considered itching (a form of pain) as discomfort. The experience of pain can be described as sharp and throbbing or as sensations of pressure, dullness and aching. It can manifest in acute physical signs. Psychosocial

9.3 Importance of Pain Assessment in the Older Person

- They will often have more than one pain.
- An accurate assessment with attention to detail will lead to accurate diagnoses.
- Assessment facilitates evaluation of the effects of therapy.
- Assessment can help differentiate acute, endangering pain from long-standing chronic pain.
- Successful pain management begins with an accurate assessment.

9.5 Nursing Questions about Pain in the Older Person

- Is the person concerned about the pain sensation itself or about the future implications of pain?
- Is there a worry that the pain indicates fatal illness or that the pain does or will deprive him or her of some specific pleasures of life?
- Does the person seem to want to be asked about the pain or not be reminded of it?
- Does the person want to be alone for fear of showing an emotional response, or does he or she want to be alone because of having their own method of handling pain?
- Does the person want visitors to share the pain or to use visitors as a distraction?
- Is immediate relief or a period of suffering expected?
- Does it matter to the person if relief is palliative or curative?
- Does the person believe drugs are unnatural pain-relief measures or fear the consequences of addictive drugs?

pain or discomfort was identified as occurring from unkindness by caregivers or while awaiting new procedures.

Observe the patient for physical and psychological signs (**Box 9.4**). Acute pain can precipitate restlessness, grumbling, and audible moans, groans, and crying, to mention a few. The individual in chronic or acute pain decreases movement; movements are quiet, controlled and deliberate. Vital signs may be unstable, or there may be an increase in pulse rate and an elevation in blood pressure; however, if pain persists for some time, vital signs stabilise and are not a reliable indicator of pain. Ask questions and discuss the situation you observe.

In addition, several questions may be helpful for the nurse to think about when helping an older person with pain (**Box 9.5**).

Assessment should also consider how the pain interferes with the patient's ability to meet the needs of security, belonging, socialisation and self-esteem. The person who considers him or herself strong and courageous may find it very humiliating to be forced to whimper or cry out with pain.

- What does the person want to be able to do?
- How does the person feel about himself or herself?
- Is the pain a mask for depression, of which the nurse is unaware?
- Does the person feel useless, dependent, isolated?
- Has the pain changed interpersonal relationships?
- Can you, the nurse, help control the pain so that the individual can do what is most important to him or her?

The nurse may not be overtly aware of the influence that the patient's pain experience has upon him or her as a participant and observer in the care. If the patient is in control of the pain, it has a calming effect on the caregiver. If the patient's pain is uncontrollable, it can make the caregiver agitated and irritated (Watt-Watson and Donovan, 1992), thus colouring the ability to accurately assess pain. Another possible impediment to accurate pain assessment is the discrepancy between perception of pain by the patient and by the health professional. This is illustrated in a study by Walker *et al.* (1990) involving the management of pain in older people by district nurses. They found little use of formal assessment tools by the nurses and a tendency for nurses to underestimate levels of greatest pain and overestimate levels of least pain.

Patients Unable to Verbalise their Pain

The cognitively impaired and nonverbal patient is the most difficult to assess and requires astute observation. Most assessment tools rely on verbal or written reports of pain. Attempts have been made to devise more suitable assessment tools for this challenging group in whom pain may well be undertreated. Marzinski (1991) studied five patients with dementia and pain. She found significant behaviour changes. Hurley *et al.* (1992) used the observations of nurses caring for patients with Alzheimer's disease to devise a discomfort scale. Nine items remained on the scale after reliability tests and these were: noisy breathing, negative vocalisation, looking content, looking sad, looking frightened, frown, relaxed body posture, tense body posture and fidgeting. Although the research indicated that the scale was accurate in the assessment of discomfort, it was not specific enough for pain.

Simons and Malabar (1995) developed a menu of 25 observable pain behaviours for nurses to refer to when car-

9.4 Nursing Observations of Pain in the Older Person

The older person in pain may:

- Not be mobilising.
- Have changes in continence.
- Not be eating.
- Be restless.
- Have poor chest expansion postoperatively.
- Push the examining hand away.
- Pull at tubes, even those distant from the operative site.

rying out pain assessments. Their pilot study involved 105 patients on whom pain behaviours were observed and interventions carried out 246 times. Ninety-six per cent of interventions resulted in a change of exhibited pain behaviours to non-pain behaviours. The study needs replication but seems an encouraging addition to the limited tools available for the assessment of pain in cognitively impaired patients.

Assessment Tools

Assessment tools have been developed to help clinicians and researchers measure, document and communicate a client's pain experience more accurately. Qualitative tools attempt to describe the client's pain using recording devices such as: pain diaries, pain logs, pain graphs and observation. The diary and graph are particularly helpful in determining adequacy of pain management. The pain log or diary is a record written and kept by the client. For these methods to be effective, the client should carry a notebook and pencil to record pain as soon as possible after the pain episode. Such items as activity, intensity and duration of the pain during daily activities, and medications taken, and when, should be recorded. The diary should be reviewed with the caregiver to assess the relationship between pain, medication use and activity. The pain graph provides a visual picture of the highs and lows of the client's pain. The caregiver can assist the client when necessary in the plotting of the pain experience.

Quantitative assessment tools including the pain rating scales, visual analogue scales (VAS) and verbal descriptor scales (VDS) help to measure pain severity. The McGill Pain Assessment Questionnaire is a comprehensive tool that is useful for initial pain assessments, if the client is not in acute distress. The questionnaire asks about past pain experience, medications used, other treatments tried, current pain episode, pain effect on activity and work, and quality and location of pain. The tool relies heavily on verbal and cognitive capacity and takes a long time to administer.

McCaffery and Beebe (1989) present an initial pain assessment tool that can be completed by the client or with the help of the caregiver (**Figure 9.1**). It obtains similar information to the McGill questionnaire but uses a different format. An alternative popular pain assessment tool is the London Hospital Pain Assessment Chart (Raiman, 1981). There are several versions of the VAS that can be used. The scale utilises a 10-cm long line that at the left end has a zero (no pain) and at the right end 10 (worst pain). Clients are asked to indicate where on the line they would place their pain. The numeric version of the VAS places the numbers 0 to 10 along the baseline at the intervals of 1 cm apart. Zero indicates no pain, 5 is labelled moderate pain and 10 remains the worst pain. The Descriptive Pain Intensity Scale uses the same principle and graduates the description of pain from no pain to mild, moderate, severe and very severe to worst possible pain. **Figure 9.2** illustrates the VAS scale and its variations.

A pain colour scale is another approach to learning a client's quantity of pain. A colour variation designed for chil-

dren that can be used with adults as well. The scale goes from yellow-orange to red-black with verbal descriptors of no pain at the yellow end and worst pain at the black end. Providing a body outline and coloured markers is another approach to learning the intensity of a client's pain. Four marker pens or crayons are used to pinpoint the pain on a body outline. Each colour represents a degree of pain: none, mild, moderate and worst pain. This is a useful tool for an individual who has difficulty with language. Using these tools the nurse can obtain a fairly accurate idea of the degree of discomfort or pain. When the client is unable to tolerate lengthy questioning, a quick assessment should be done, illustrated by the example presented in **Box 9.6**. Ascertain the location, quality, intensity and chronology of the pain. Rather than ask questions, have the patient describe the pain. Leading questions often give the nurse inaccurate information. Patients often answer according to what they think the nurse expects to hear. **Box 9.7** indicates some points to consider in the complex process of assessing pain.

INTERVENTION

There are a variety of strategies to help control different types of pain. These include both pharmacological and non-pharmacological methods.

Pharmacological Pain Control

General principles of pain control apply to the older person as well as to the young but with some adaptations. The well-established and validated World Health Organisation's guidelines for the management of cancer pain (WHO, 1986; Hanks *et al.* 1996) can be more widely applied to the management of chronic non-malignant pain. The aim of treatment is to prevent pain by administering appropriate doses of analgesic drugs on a regular basis, preferably by the oral route. The guidelines advise a step-by-step approach to the choice of drug based on the system of the 'analgesic ladder' (**Figure 9.3**). The first step of the ladder is a non-opioid drug such as aspirin, paracetamol or a non-steroidal anti-inflammatory drug. If the maximum dose of such a drug is ineffective in controlling pain, a drug from the second step of the ladder is added. Second step drugs are weak opioids and include codeine and coproxamol. If this proves inadequate at maximum daily dose, a strong opioid is substituted. Morphine is the preferred opioid in cancer pain and is the standard against which all other opioids are measured. The dose of morphine is titrated up to gain pain relief. There is no upper limit. The analgesic ladder approach recommends the use of adjuvant analgesics in conjunction with the conventional analgesic at any step of the ladder.

Fears associated with morphine

The public and health professionals alike have generally feared the use of morphine for many years but there seems

initial pain-assessment tool

date _____

date _____

age _____ ward _____

patient's name _____

diagnosis _____

doctor _____

nurse _____

I. location patient or nurse mark drawing

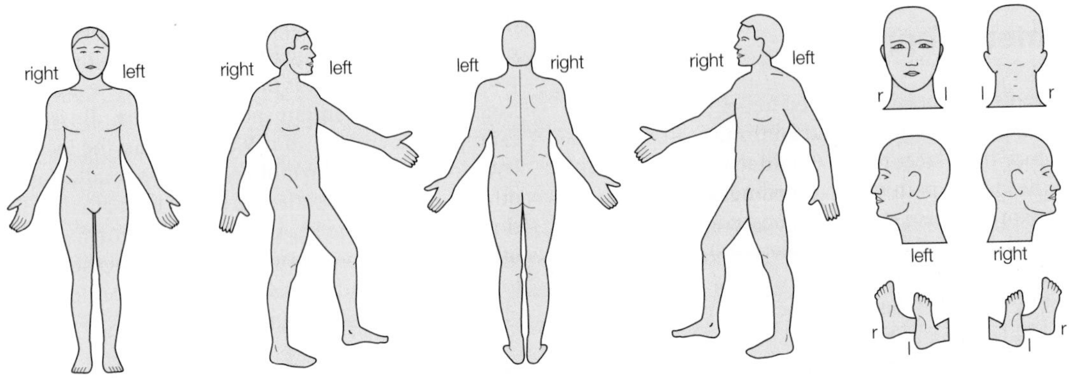

right   left   right   left   left   right   right   left

r   l   l   r

left   right

r   l   r   l

II. intensity : patient rates the pain - scale used _____
present _____
worse pain gets _____
best pain gets _____
acceptable level of pain _____

III. quality (use patient's own words, e.g. prick, ache, burn, throb, pull, sharp) _____

IV. onset, duration variations, rhythms _____

V. manner of expression of pain _____

VI. what relieves the pain _____

VII. what causes or increases the pain _____

VIII. effects of pain (note decreased function, decreased quality of life)
accompanying symptoms (e.g. nausea) _____
sleep _____
appetite _____
physical activity _____
relationship with others (e.g. irritability) _____
emotions (e.g. anger, suicidal, crying) _____
concentration _____
other _____

IX. other comments _____

X. plan _____

Figure 9.1 Pain assessment form (Source: McCaffrey M, Beebe A. *Pain: clinical manual for nursing practice.* **St Louis: Mosby, 1989.)**

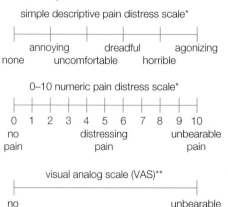

pain distress scales

simple descriptive pain distress scale*

none / annoying / uncomfortable / dreadful / horrible / agonizing

0–10 numeric pain distress scale*

0 1 2 3 4 5 6 7 8 9 10
no pain / distressing pain / unbearable pain

visual analog scale (VAS)**

no distress / unbearable distress

* if used as a graphic scale, a 10-cm baseline is recommended

** a 10-cm baseline is recommended for VAS scales

Figure 9.2 Example of pain distress scale. (Source: *Clinical practice guideline: acute pain management.* **US Department of Health and Human Service, Public Health Services Agency for Health Care Policy and Research, No 92-0032, 116–117. Rockville, Md, 1992**

 9.6 Nursing Observations of Pain in the Older Person

Quick Assessment in Situations where Patients are Unable to Tolerate Lengthy Questions

Time involved: Reading time, 5 minutes; implementation time, about 10 minutes.

Sample situation: Mr M, 65 years old, with lung cancer and widespread metastasis is admitted to your ward. He is not able to concentrate long enough to answer many questions. He grimaces frequently and cries out saying 'It hurts, please give me something'. His wife states that he is not swallowing anything by mouth.

Possible solution: Assess pain with minimal number of questions in order to give initial analgesic safely.

Expected outcome: Patient states he is comfortable. Further pain assessment is completed at a later time so that a detailed plan of care may be implemented. Tell the patient that you are going to work to get him comfortable as quickly as possible but that you must get some information first:
1. Point (on his body) to where the pain is.
Mr M. points to his lower back.
2. Is this the same location for the pain over the last several days?

Mr M. says that this is the same area that has bothered him over the last week, but it has got much worse since yesterday evening.
3. On a 0 to 10 scale (0=no pain, 10= worst pain), what number would you give your pain right now?
Mr M becomes very agitated and yells 'It is unbearable'. This is a good enough answer under the circumstances.
4. What medication were you taking at home, and did it help the pain?
Mrs M tells you that her husband was taking morphine 90 mg 4 hourly with Ibuprofen 800 mg 6 hourly. He has not been able to swallow anything since late last night, so he has had nothing for pain since then. Prior to this, the medication was keeping the pain well controlled.
Due to Mr M's condition, it was appropriate to ask only the most essential questions to initiate an analgesic regimen. The above four questions give you important baseline data and establish an initial opioid dose.
Using a flow sheet, the immediate goal is to establish pain control quickly. Using Mr M's words ask 'Is the pain more bearable now?' Once Mr M is comfortable, additional questions from the initial pain assessment tool may be filled in, and a long-term plan of care may be reviewed with the patient and his wife.

Source: McCaffery M, Beebe A. *Pain: clinical manual for nursing practice.* St Louis: Mosby, 1989.

9.7 Content for Assessing Pain in the Older Patient

- **Pain description**: identify location, quality, intensity (present, worst, best), onset, duration, pattern of radiation or variation, manner of expressing pain, relationship to movement or position, time of occurrence and related motor or sensory complaints.
- **Observations**: note vocalisations such as grunting or groaning and facial expressions including wrinkled forehead, tightly closed or widely opened eyes or mouth, or other distorted expressions. Observe body movements noting guarding, rocking, pulling legs into abdomen, increased hand/finger movements, inability to keep still, pacing behaviours, or other restrictive motions.
- **Alleviating or aggravating factors**: explore what intensifies or decreases the pain and what treatments, remedies or activities relieve the pain.
- **Impact**: identify any changes in daily activities, gait, behaviours. Note onset of new behaviours such as confusion, irritability, increased activity; accompanying symptoms such as nausea, dizziness, sweating, fatigue; any changes in sleep, appetite, emotions, concentration, physical activity, relationships with others, social interactions and common routines.
- **Social history**: explore functional status prior to onset of symptoms, marital status, family/community resource network, social and leisure activities and environmental barriers to social activity.

Source: Herr KA, Mobily RR. Complexities of pain assessment in the elderly: clinical considerations. *J Gerontol Nurs* 1991, 17(4) 12.

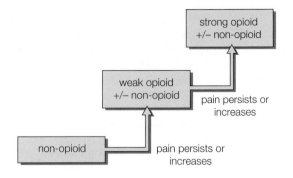

Figure 9.3 An adaptation of the WHO analgesic ladder (Source: Hanks GW *et al.* 1996. Adapted from World Health Organization. Cancer pain relief and palliative care. A report of a WHO Expert Committee, WHO Tech Rep Series No 804, Geneva, 1990. Reproduced by kind permission of BMJ Publishing Group.)

Anxieties about opioid-induced respiratory depression are common but there is little evidence to suggest that this is any more prevalent in older people than those who are younger. Closs (1994) points out that it is not uncommon for older people to exhibit Cheyne-Stokes breathing patterns whilst sleeping, so this should not be an indication for stopping effective opioid medication.

Other side effects of morphine, such as drowsiness, mental clouding and nausea, commonly occur when treatment is started but usually resolve within the first few days and should not be the reason for stopping treatment. Unfortunately, the constipating and mouth-drying effects of morphine do not resolve and need careful explanation and treatment.

If possible, the preferred route of administration of morphine is by mouth. Two types of oral preparation are used. Immediate release morphine in liquid or tablet form for dose titration and controlled release morphine in suspension or tablet form for maintenance treatment, which can be given in once daily or twice daily preparations. If the oral route is impossible, the equivalent dose may be given rectally. Alternatively, the subcutaneous route may be considered. This is particularly useful in the care of patients who are terminally ill when small, battery-operated syringe driver machines may be used to deliver a variety of palliative drugs. In Britain, the preferred opioid for subcutaneous administration is diamorphine because of its greater solubility. The subcutaneous dose of diamorphine is one-third of the oral morphine dose (Hanks *et al.* 1996). (See Appendices 7–9.)

Managing Postoperative Pain with Opioid Analgesia

There are indications that postoperative pain in older people is under-treated, possibly as a result of the fears about use of morphine discussed above. Duggleby and Lander (1994) carried out a study investigating the effect of age on postoperative pain, mental status and analgesic intake and concluded

to be a particular fear associated with administering morphine to older people. It does seem that the morphine requirements of older people are less. Twycoss (1994) cites a study carried out by Forman *et al.* (1992) in which the morphine requirements of a group of patients over the age of 60 years were compared with a younger group. The older patients required about half the dose. These smaller dose requirements were found to correlate with decreased creatinine clearance in the older group. Consideration of renal function would be advisable before starting to titrate the dose of morphine in an older person.

Other worries about the use of morphine concern the side effects. Fears about addiction are unfounded. Morphine can be safely given in regular doses over periods of months or years for chronic pain (McCaffery and Beebe, 1989). Alternatively, if a pain either changes or becomes unresponsive to morphine or goes away, the dose may be reduced and then discontinued without difficulty (Hanks *et al.* 1996).

that poor pain management can lead to an acute decline in cognitive status which possibly explains acute confusion experienced by some older people following surgery. The use of patient controlled analgesia (PCA) systems gets around the problem of under-treating due to patients unwillingness to ask for relief and professionals reluctance to give adequate doses. A study by Egbert *et al.* (1990) compared PCA with on demand intramuscular opioid injections in older male post-operative patients. Those using PCA had better analgesic effect with less confusion and pulmonary impairment.

Non-opioid Analgesia

Non-steroidal Anti-inflammatory Drugs NSAIDS

These are analgesic drugs very commonly used by older people because they form the mainstay of treatment for the painful condition of osteoarthritis, which is most common in older women. Aspirin, voltarol, naproxen, ibuprofen and indomethacin are frequently used oral NSAIDs. Unlike morphine, they do have maximum doses beyond which no further analgesic effect occurs. The side effects of gastric irritation and renal insufficiency limit their use in some people. When topical NSAID creams such as Ibuleve and Feldene (which can be bought over the counter) are used in conjunction with oral NSAIDs, there is an increased risk of gastric bleeding. This occurs because people have not been informed that creams can be absorbed into the system, thus increasing the dose of NSAID. Creams should not be used at the same time as taking oral NSAIDs.

Other Drugs with an Analgesic Effect

Conventional analgesic drugs are known to have little effect upon certain types of pain, particularly neuropathic pain. This includes painful conditions that particularly affect people in later life such as postherpetic neuropathy, diabetic neuropathy and post-stroke allodynia. Co-analgesic drugs are those which have been developed to treat specific conditions but have subsequently been found to have an analgesic effect which is particularly effective in the control of chronic pain. Tricyclic antidepressants such as amitriptyline are effective in doses far lower than those given to treat depression. A dose of 10–25 mg once a day will often relieve pain within days of commencing treatment; it is particularly effective on 'burning' pain (McQuay, 1988). Side effects of dry mouth, constipation and dizziness are reported and the sedative effect is overcome by taking medication at bedtime (Pain Concern, 1994). Anticonvulsant drugs such as carbamazepine (Tegretol), sodium valproate (Epilim) and clonazepam have been found to be effective in treating facial neuralgia, shooting type pains as a result of nerve damage, and diabetic neuropathy. Sometimes people who are prescribed these drugs, on learning about their use as anticonvulsants, may believe that they are being treated for epilepsy and have not been told (Pain Concern, 1994). Nurses will need to inform patients of their alternative uses, if this situation arises.

Non-pharmacological Pain Control

There is a range of complementary therapies, which may be helpful in relieving pain in older people when used alone or in combination with drug therapy. Unfortunately, research evidence to support the claims of effectiveness of these therapies is scarce particularly in the case of older people. Some training or experience is required in all of the therapies, as there are risks attached if they are carried out inappropriately. (Rankin-Box, 1988).

Cutaneous Nerve Stimulation

Stimulation of the skin for the purpose of pain relief has been practised for centuries. Massage, vibration, heat, cold and ointments have been a part of nursing interventions for years. However, cutaneous stimulation is not suitable for people with neuropathic pain, associated with allodynia or hyperalgesia, as it may increase rather than relieve pain. People who have had a stroke may be unable to verbalise this.

Massage is perceived to alleviate stress by relaxing muscles and so can be helpful in reducing pain that has a component of muscle tension or spasm, for example headache and backache. (Mason, 1988). Fakouri and Jones (1987) demonstrated the positive effects of a 3-minute, slow-stroke back rub on both sides of the spinous processes from the crown of the head to the sacrum as a means of promoting relaxation in older people. Physiological effects that occurred were a decrease in heart rate and blood pressure and an increase in skin temperature.

More recently a small study on older people in long-term care indicated a reduction in anxiety scores following back massage (Fraser and Kerr, 1993). Twenty-one residents were divided into three groups. The first group received a back massage with normal conversation in contrast to the second group who simply received the same type of conversation only. The third group had no intervention. The researchers found that the first group had statistically less anxiety than the no intervention group. The difference between the groups who received massage and conversation and conversation alone approached statistical significance. Similar studies with larger numbers would be useful in validating the anecdotal and perceived benefits of massage and lead to more widespread but appropriate use.

Heat is effective for musculoskeletal disorders such as rheumatic conditions. It is contraindicated with occlusive vascular disease. Intermittent cold packs are helpful in low back pain and radicular disturbances, although they may be less comforting. They serve to negate or delay the transmission of pain impulses to the cerebral pain centre. Pathophysiological conditions should be taken into consideration when using heat and cold with older people. Care must be taken when applying heat and cold to the skin to prevent damage from extended periods of heat and cold applications.

Transcutaneous Nerve Stimulation

Another method of cutaneous stimulation is transcutaneous electrical nerve stimulation (TENS). Electrodes, applied and taped to the skin over the pain site or on the spine, emit a mild electric current that is felt as a tingling, buzzing or vibrating sensation. The patient operates the stimulator and starts the electric impulses, which then activate the large A-beta nerve fibres that transmit impulses to close the hypothetical gate in the spinal cord and prevent pain signals from reaching the brain. TENS has been helpful in phantom limb pain, postherpetic neuralgia and low back pain.

Touch

Touch is a natural comfort mechanism, although its therapeutic properties are still not clearly understood. Sometimes considered a cutaneous stimulation technique, 'therapeutic touch' used in experimental laboratory and clinical settings showed that placing hands on or near the body might result in healing or improvement (Kreiger, 1975). Relaxation and proper sensory stimulation decrease anxiety, reduce muscle tension and help provide distraction from pain, thereby relieving pain. Perceptual tendencies and sensory dimensions influence pain reactions and tolerance. Persons who were sensory deprived exhibited low pain tolerance, but those who received adequate or a high degree of sensory stimulation possessed a high pain tolerance. Laying on of hands employed by Kreiger (1975) and the Touch for Health Movement has proved beneficial, but the reasons behind its effectiveness have not been fully established.

Acupuncture and Acupressure

Acupuncture is based on a series of meridians (energy pathways) in the body, which 'flow' from the head towards the feet or hands, and return to the head. The meridians connect with the inner organs and form channels through which energy can pass. Penetration of the skin at specific points (acupuncture points) by small needles helps the body to correct itself by realigning or redirecting the energy. For pain relief, the acupuncture needles are inserted into areas overlying tender regions (Trevelyn and Booth, 1994). As yet, no Western scientific theory has proved wholly satisfactory in explaining how acupuncture works.

Acupressure is acupuncture without needles. Pressure is applied to the traditional acupuncture points with the thumbs, tip of the index finger, palm of the hand, or by pinching and squeezing.

Reflexology

The basis of this therapy is that the application of pressure to one part of the body produces an effect in another part of the body (Trevelyan and Booth, 1994). Pressure is usually applied to the feet but the hands can also be used. Reflexologists work to a body map in which there are 10 longitudinal zones, which correspond to 10 zones on the feet and hands. When pressure is applied in one of these zones on the feet or hands, all of the organs lying within that zone are affected. There are anecdotal reports of the benefits of this therapy in many chronic painful conditions.

Autogenics: Biofeedback, Meditation and Imagery, and Hypnosis

Biofeedback

An individual can learn voluntary control over some body processes and alter them by changing the physiological correlates appropriate to them. Response to certain types of pain can be controlled. Boczkowski (1984) found that biofeedback decreased chronic pain of rheumatoid arthritis. Another study demonstrated no appreciable effect of biofeedback on migraine headaches in older people. Training and often time and equipment of some type are needed to learn how to alter one's body responses. Biofeedback results have provided conflicting data. In some instances, it has proved successful in the reduction or elimination of pain.

Meditation and Imagery

Imagery uses the client's imagination to focus on settings full of happiness and relaxation rather than on stressful situations. Several studies using guided imagery have shown there was a decrease in pain perception in foot pain and abdominal pain. It was suggested that a strong image of a pain-free state effectively alters the response of the autonomic nervous system to pain (Pearson, 1988; McCaffery and Beebe, 1989).

Hypnosis

Hypnosis has been used to help to alter pain perception through positive suggestions. Research has demonstrated hypnotic analgesia reduces what are called 'overreactions' to pain when apprehension and stress are apparent.

Some people have the ability to induce self-hypnosis, and some do not. Most of the population, however, has some capacity for hypnosis and with training can increase their control in this area. There are three recognised modes of hypnosis:
(1) Spontaneous, which is what most of us do when we daydream.
(2) Self-induced trance.
(3) Formal hypnosis, which requires the services of a hypnotist.

Intense concentration is required for hypnosis. Hypnosis can be used to:
- Alter pain perception, thus blocking pain awareness.
- Substitute another feeling for a painful one.
- Displace pain sensation to a smaller body area.
- Alter the meaning of pain so that it is viewed as less important and less debilitating.

(Thomas, 1990).

EVALUATION

Whatever intervention methods are used to help a patient in pain, careful review of the effectiveness of each is essential. This requires reassessment using appropriate tools mentioned earlier. Treatments can then be continued or changed accordingly.

PAIN CLINICS

When the usual standard measures to relieve pain, particularly chronic pain, are unsuccessful, referral of the patient to a pain clinic may be helpful. Such clinics specialise in the management of complex and intractable pain problems and usually have a multidisciplinary approach to treatment including the use of specialised anaesthetic techniques such as nerve blocks (Latham, 1987). *See* **Appendix 10** for some of the available procedures and their indications.

PAINS MORE COMMON IN LATER LIFE

Osteoarthritis

Osteoarthritis is one of the most common forms of joint disease with its prevalence increasing into the eighth decade. It is the leading cause of disability in persons 65 years of age and older. Joint pain and stiffness is initially intermittent and then can become constant. Pain is characterised by aching in the joints, surrounding muscles and soft tissue, usually relieved by rest and exacerbated by activity. Such joints as the distal and proximal interphalangeal, cervical and lumbar spine, hips, knees and toes are affected. Many older adults have other medical conditions in addition to osteoarthritis, which require that the total picture be considered when the arthritic pain is treated. Generally, treatment consists of anti-inflammatory preparations such as non-steroidal anti-inflammatory medications with the caution that these drugs are particularly irritant to the gastrointestinal lining. This effect is reduced if the drugs are taken with food or if medication that has a gastric protective action is taken concurrently. Newer drugs are meloxicam (Mobic), which produces a much lower incidence of gastric irritation and is indicated for the short-term treatment of acute osteoarthritis, and Arthrotec, a combination of diclofenac sodium and misoprostol, which also protects the gastric mucosa. Paracetamol, while not as effective as anti-inflammatory preparations, is preferred to salicylates. Effective pain relief can be achieved without the risk of gastric irritation or potential for gastric haemorrhage. Non-pharmacological pain management includes application of moist heat to relieve pain, spasm, and stiffness; orthotic devices such as braces and splints to support painful joints; weight reduction if overweight or obesity is a contributing factor; and occupational and physiotherapy. Severe arthritis with unrelieved pain and extensive disability may require surgical intervention resulting in a period of acute pain.

Postherpetic Neuralgia (PHN)

Herpes zoster (shingles) is a common condition in later life affecting half of people over 85 years of age (McKendrick, 1993). Postherpetic neuralgia, the painful sequel to herpes

Meeting Pain Management Needs

Katy Sims is 66 years old and has diabetes mellitus. Following a stroke, her diabetes rapidly becomes out of control. Her blood sugar ranges from 3 mmol/litre to 25 mmol/litre. Some of this is due to erratic eating habits, almost no exercise, frequent urinary tract infections, and considerable stress related to her condition and her future. She has bumped her toe while receiving assistance to transfer into her wheelchair after occupational therapy. Within a few days the bruise develops sloughed skin and a non-adherent dressing protects the open sore. The sore becomes necrotic and is debrided with a topical preparation. The debridment of necrotic tissue removes half of her left great toe. Miss Sims, who rarely complains, begins to moan while she is sleeping and to cry a lot during the day. She complains of a continuous burning sensation, and it feels as if her toe is 'on fire'. One day Miss Sims throws her coffee cup across the room, simply unable to bear the discomfort without expressing her frustration and anger. Various pain medications are given by mouth on an inconsistent basis but the relief she experiences is minimal. She begins to beg to die.

- What are Miss Sims' comments that provide subjective evidence?
- What information can you as a new primary nurse obtain from your observations and examination that provides objective data for a holistic nursing assessment?
- State two unmet needs that may be the most significant to Miss Sims at this time.
- Suggest the nursing aims for each unmet need, reflecting realistic outcomes and using concrete and measurable terms.
- Suggest one or more interventions for each area of unmet need, justifying your choice of intervention.

zoster will occur in at least 50% of patients over 60 years of age; at 80 years of age the incidence will be more than 75% (Budd, 1993). Postherpetic neuralgia is experienced because of irritation of the nerve roots that leave the spinal cord. The stinging, burning pain, with or without an underlying sharp, jabbing sensation, continues for weeks, months and for some older people indefinitely after the initial skin lesions have healed. Sleep disturbance, depression and an overall deterioration in quality of life are characteristic features of the condition. In a study by McKendrick *et al.* (1986), 15% of patients over the age of 60 years had pain persisting 6 months after the acute illness. Budd (1993) recommends a two-stage approach. Initial therapy to treat the symptoms of herpes zoster and also to prevent the occurrence of postherpetic neuralgia consists of oral and topical antiviral chemotherapy, analgesia, sympathetic blockade of the affected dermatomal area of the body and the use of transcutaneous electrical nerve stimulation (TENS). For those who go on to develop postherpetic neuralgia, treatment may consist of tricyclic antidepressants alone, or in combination with carbamazepine or phenytoin, to achieve a synergistic effect. The topical agent capsaicin cream may be applied to the dermatomes in which the pain is felt. The cream should be used for at least 2 months before assessment is carried out. The major side effect is the burning and stinging at the initial application, although this generally resolves over the first few days or weeks. If patients find this unacceptable, lignocaine ointment can be applied prior to using capsaicin. Topical treatment can be used alone or in combination with the oral therapies described above (Budd, 1996). **Box 9.8** suggests some non-pharmacological interventions.

Pain from Venous Ulceration

Despite the prevalence of this condition in later life, this seems to be yet another under-researched area. Walshe (1995) reports that the whole issue of pain in the leg ulcer assessment and treatment literature is neglected because ulceration is generally regarded as pain free. Yet in her study of 13 patients' experience of living with a leg ulcer, the overwhelming feature of the experience was of it being painful. Treatments often exacerbated the pain and analgesics were frequently ineffective. Patients developed their own coping mechanisms to deal with the pain and avoided activities that made the pain worse. In some cases, this meant restricting going out. Pain is often alleviated by treatment with the four-layer compression bandaging (Franks *et al.* 1992).

Terminal Cancer Pain

Cancer is an illness that predominantly affects people in later life. Pain from cancer is probably one of the better-researched areas, although much of the research does not relate specifically to older people. Nevertheless, the knowledge gained about cancer pain and its treatment has in many ways formed the basis on which to treat non-cancer pain. Principles such as careful assessment to distinguish and diagnose each pain, remembering that not every pain will necessarily be related to the cancer, have been well documented by those working in the now well-established field of palliative care. An example often cited is that of a patient receiving regular doses of morphine for abdominal pain due to secondary liver cancer who complains of a headache. The assumption should not be made that the morphine will alleviate the headache. Rather the headache should be assessed as a new pain and treated appropriately. In fact, morphine is not generally a helpful

 9.8 Some Non-Pharmacological Interventions for Postherpetic Neuralgia in the Older Person

Neuroaugmentation
- Counter-irritation.
- Transcutaneous electrical nerve stimulation (TENS).
- Percutaneous nerve stimulation.
- Acupuncture.

Physiotherapy
- Mobilisation of affected areas and joints.
- General conditioning exercises.

Psychological approaches
- Cognitive:
  relaxation training;
  distraction techniques;
  hypnosis;
  biofeedback.
- Behavioural.
- Activities diary to set goals.

Source: Adapted from Portenoy RK. Postherpetic neuralgia: a workable treatment plan. *Geriatrics* 1996, 41(11): 34.

analgesic for headache and the patient should be offered some paracetamol in addition to the other medication being taken.

Other principles, such as a systematic and regular method of administering analgesia, have been referred to above. Expertise has developed in administering analgesia and other palliative medications via the subcutaneous route. More recently, the transdermal route has been used to administer the opioid fentanyl. The system developed provides for continuous sustained release of the drug from a patch applied to the skin for 72 hours (Portenoy *et al.* 1996; Zech *et al.* 1992).

The palliative care and hospice field has taken a lead in practising a multidisciplinary approach to the care of patients and their families and has advocated a holistic approach to pain and symptom management (Twycross, 1997). Dame Cicely Saunders first used the term 'total pain' to indicate that a patient's pain had physical, psychological, social and spiritual components. This concept has been adopted by the World Health Organisation (1990) as part of their guidelines for the management of cancer pain.

SUMMARY

The experience and treatment of pain in later life is a neglected area. While general principles of assessment, treatment of pain and evaluation of the outcome do apply to everyone regardless of age, there are some special considerations when applying these to older people.

Assessment is crucial and may be more challenging with older people who may have more complex chronic pain with many components and who may have difficulty describing their pain according to conventional assessment tools that rely on full cognitive function. Pharmacological treatments may have different effects on older people and nurses should have a thorough understanding of the principles behind such differences. More work is needed on the benefits of complementary treatments for pain in older people and the knowledge should be disseminated so that nurses may receive appropriate training.

Finally, Ferrell (1991) put forward 10 principles of pain management in older people that serve as a useful summary (**Box 9.9**).

9.9 Principles of Pain Management in Older People

(1) Always ask patients about pain.
(2) Accept the patient's word about pain and its intensity.
(3) Never underestimate the potential effects of chronic pain on a patient's overall condition and quality of life.
(4) Be compulsive in the assessment of pain. An accurate diagnosis will lead to the most effective treatment.
(5) Treat pain to facilitate diagnostic procedures. Don't wait for a diagnosis to relieve suffering.
(6) Use a combined approach of drug and non-drug strategies when possible.
(7) Mobilise patients physically and psychosocially. Involve patients in their therapy.
(8) Use analgesic drugs correctly. Start doses low and increase slowly. Achieve adequate doses and anticipate side effects.
(9) Anticipate and attend to anxiety and depression.
(10) Reassess responses to treatment. Alter therapy to maximise functional status and quality of life.

KEY POINTS

- Pain is a multidimensional phenomenon, not merely a physical event.
- Pain can have a very negative effect on quality of life.
- The debate on age-related changes in pain perception continues.
- Pain accompanies many of the diseases prevalent in later life, yet has largely been neglected in the literature.
- There are many misconceptions surrounding pain in later life.
- There is a need for adaptation of assessment methods in order to be relevant to older people.
- Effective pain control can be achieved by a step-by-step approach as illustrated by the analgesic ladder.
- Fears about morphine addiction or side effects are commonly exaggerated.
- A combination of therapies is often the most effective approach to treatment.

AREAS AND ACTIVITIES FOR STUDY AND REFLECTION

- What aspects of your own cultural background do you bring to the assessment process of an older person's pain?
- Reflect on the underlying lay and professional attitudes to pain in later life and how these can influence assessment and treatment.
- How can general principles of pain assessment and management be applied individually to each patient?
- What factors might influence how a patient expresses their pain?
- How might you help a patient who is very frightened about starting morphine?
- What techniques might you use to assess the pain of:
  (1) Someone unable to respond verbally?
  (2) Someone cognitively impaired?
- In your own practice, how often are combined approaches to treatment used?
- When would you consider it appropriate to refer a patient to another professional for help with their pain and which specialists would you collaborate with?

REFERENCES

Bates MS. *Biocultural dimensions of chronic pain*. Albany: University of New York Press, 1996.

Boczkowski JA. Biofeedback training for the treatment of chronic pain in the elderly arthritic female. *Clin Gerontol* 1984, 2:39.

Bowling A, Browne PD. Social networks, health and emotional well-being among the oldest old in London. *J Gerontol* 1991, 46:20.

Budd K. Value of topical therapy for post-herpetic neuralgia. *Care of the Elderly* 1993, 5:326.

Budd K. Post-herpetic neuralgia: what treatment protocol? *Med Dialogue* 1996, 455:

Closs SJ. Pain in elderly patients: a neglected phenomenon? *J Adv Nurs* 1994, 19:1072–1081.

Closs SJ. Pain and elderly patients: a survey of nurses' knowledge and experiences. *J Adv Nurs* 1996, 23:237–242.

Duffy LM, Wyble SJ, Miles SH. Obtaining geriatric patient consent. *J Gerontol Nurs* 1989, 15:21.

Duggleby MN, Lander J. Cognitive status and post-operative pain: older adults. *J Pain Symptom Manage* 1994, 9:19–27.

Egbert LD, Battit GE, Welch CE, Barlett MK. Randomised trial of postoperative patient controlled analgesia vs intramuscular narcotics in frail elderly men. *Arch Int Med* 1990, 150:1897–1903.

Eland JM. Pain management and comfort. *J Gerontol Nurs* 1988, 14:10.

Fakouri C, Jones P. Slow stroke back rub. *J Gerontol Nurs* 1987, 13:32.

Ferrell BA. Pain management in elderly people. *J Am Geriatr Soc* 19991, 39:64–73.

Ferrell BA, Ferrell BR, Osterweil D. Pain in the nursing home. *J Am Geriatr Soc* 1990, 38:409.

Forman B, Portenoy RK, Yanagihara RH, Hunt WC, Kush R, Shepard K. Elderly cancer patients with pain: response to oral morphine (ms) dose, pain and toxicity. *J Am Geriatr Soc* 1992, 40:26.

Franks P, Moffat C, Connolly M *et al.* Quality of life during leg ulcer treatment. *Phlebologie* 1992, 9:275–277.

Fraser J, Kerr JR. Psychophysiological effects of back massage on elderly institutionalised patients. *J Adv Nurs* 1993, 18:238–245.

Hamilton J. Comfort and the hospitalized chronically ill. *J Gerontol Nurs* 1989, 15:28.

Hanks GW *et al.* Morphine in cancer pain: modes of administration. *Br Med J* 1996, 312:823–826.

Helman C. *Culture, Health and Illness, 3rd edition*. Oxford: Butterworth-Heinemann, 1994.

Herr KA, Mobily RR. Complexities of pain assessment in the elderly: clinical considerations. *J Gerontol Nurs* 1991, 17:12.

Hurley AC, Volicer BJ, Hanrahan PA, Houde S, Volicer L. Assessment of discomfort in advanced Alzheimer patients. *Res Nurs Health* 1992, 15:369–377.

Jacox AK. Assessing pain. *Am J Nurs* 1979, 79:895.

Karb V, Phipps W, Long B, Woods N, eds. *Medical-surgical nursing: concepts and clinical practice, 4th edition*. St Louis: Mosby, 1991.

Kreiger D. Therapeutic touch: the imprimatur of nursing. *Am J Nurs* 1975, 75:784.

Lanceley A: Wider issues in pain management. *Eur J Cancer Care* 1995, 4:153–157.

Latham J. *Pain Control, 2nd Edition*. Lisa Sainsbury Foundation. Reading: Austen Cornish, 1987.

Marzinski LR. The tragedy of dementia: clinically assessing pain in the confused, nonverbal elderly. *J Gerontol Nurs* 1991, 17:25.

Mason A. Massage. In: Rankin-Box DF, ed. *Complementary health therapies: a guide for nurses and the caring professions*. Beckenham: Croom Helm, 1988.

McCaffery M, Beebe A. *Pain: clinical manual for nursing practice*. St Louis: Mosby, 1989.

McKendrick MW, McGill J, White G, Wood MW. Oral acyclovir in acute herpes zoster. *Br Med J* 1986, 293:1529–32.

McKendrick M. Encircled by pain. *Care of the Elderly* 1993, 5:330–332.

McQuay HJ. Pharmocological treatment of neuralgic and neuropathic pain. *Cancer Surveys* 1988, 7:141–159.

Melding PS. Is there such a thing as geriatric pain? *Pain* 1991, 46:119–121.

Merskey H, Bogduk N, eds. *Classification of chronic pain, descriptors of chronic pain syndromes and definitions of pain terms, 2nd edition*.

Seattle: International Association for the Study of Pain Press, 1994.

Pain Concern. Newsletter: Autumn, Canterbury, 1994.

Pearson BD. Pain control: an experiment with imagery. *Geriatr Nurs* 1988, 13:28.

Portenoy RK. Pain. In: Abrams WB, Berkow R, eds. *The Merck manual of geriatrics*. Rahway: Merck Sharp & Dohme Research Laboratories, 1990.

Portenoy RK, Southam MA, Gupta SK: Transdermal fentanyl for cancer pain: repeated dose pharmacokinetics. *Anaesthesiology* 1993, 78:36–43.

Portenoy RK. Postherpetic neuralgia: a workable treatment plan. *Geriatrics* 1996, 41:34.

Raiman J. Responding to pain. *Nursing* 1981, 31:1362–1365.

Rankin-Box DF. *Complementary health therapies: a guide for nurses and the caring professions*. Beckenham: Croom Helm, 1988.

Simons W, Malabar R. Assessing pain in elderly patients who cannot respond verbally. *J Adv Nurs* 1995, 22:663–669.

The Stroke Association. *Central post-stroke pain*, London: The Stroke Association, 1997.

Thomas BL. Elder care: pain management for the elderly: alternative interventions, Part I. *Am Operat Room Nurses J* 1990, 52:1268.

Trevelyan J, Booth B. *Complementary medicine for nurses, midwives and health visitors*. Basingstoke: Macmillan, 1994.

Tucker MA, Andrew MF, Ogle SJ, Davison JG. Age associated change in pain threshold measured by transcutaneous neuronal electrical stimulation. *Age Ageing* 1989, 18:241–246.

Twycross R. *Pain relief in advanced cancer*. Edinburgh: Churchill Livingstone, 1994.

Twycross R. *Symptom management in advanced cancer*. Oxford: Radcliffe Medical Press, 1997.

Walker JM, Akinsanya JA, Davis BD, Marcer D. The nursing management of elderly patients in the community: study and recommendations. *J Adv Nurs* 1990, 15:1154–1161.

Walshe C. Living with a venous leg ulcer: a descriptive study of patients' experiences. *J Adv Nurs* 1995, 22:1092–1100.

Watt-Watson JH, Donovan MI. Pain management nursing perspective. St Louis: Mosby, 1992.

Wittink H, Michael T. *Chronic pain management for physical therapists*. Oxford: Butterworth Heinemann, 1997.

WHO. *Cancer pain relief*, Geneva: The World Health Organisation, 1986.

WHO. Cancer pain relief and palliative care, Geneva: The World Health Organisation, 1990.

Yates P, Dewar A, Fentiman B. Pain: the views of elderly people living in long-term residential care settings. *J Adv Nurs* 1995, 21:667–674.

Zech DFJ, Grond SUA, Lynch J. Transdermal fentanyl and initial dose-finding with patient controlled analgesia in cancer pain. A pilot study with 20 terminally ill cancer patients. *Pain* 1992, 50:293–301.

USEFUL ADDRESSES

The Intractable Pain Society of Great Britain and Ireland
c/o The Association of Anaesthetists, 9 Bedford Square
London WC1B 3RA.

National Benevolent Fund for the Aged,
1 Leslie Grove Place, Croydon CRO 6TJ.
Tel 0181 688 6655.
Donates TENS machines to older people in the UK in receipt of income-related benefit.

Pain Association Scotland,
Cramond House, Cramond Glebe Road, Edinburgh EH4 6NS.
Tel 0131 312 7955.

Pain Concern (UK),
PO Box 318, Canterbury, Kent CT2 0GD.
Information Line: 10am–4pm Monday to Friday

Shingles Support Society,
41 North Road, London N7 9DP.
Tel 0171 607 9661; Helpline Tel 0171 609 9061

Pharmacology and medications
Hazel Heath and Carole Webster

LEARNING OBJECTIVES

After studying this chapter you will be able to:

- Describe the pharmacokinetic and pharmacodynamic changes that occur in older age.
- Identify the altered effects of drugs on older people.
- Discuss the potential benefits and risks of drug therapy in older people.
- Discuss special considerations for medications in continuing care settings.
- Discuss the role of the pharmacist in medication for older people.
- Discuss the role of information technology in drug prescribing and monitoring.
- Discuss the role of the nurse in assessing, administering and monitoring medications for older people, and in preventing and recognising adverse drug reactions.

INTRODUCTION

In the last 10–20 years, developments in pharmacology have been prolific, especially in the field of cardiovascular drugs, non-steroidal anti-inflammatories (NSAIDs) for arthritic conditions, treatments for gastrointestinal problems and in the development of at least a dozen new antibiotics. New forms of more traditional drugs or new delivery methods, such as transdermal patches, have also proliferated. Recombinant DNA technology has also produced biosynthetic preparations such as 'human' insulin. There are obviously tremendous benefits to be derived from new developments in pharmacology and drug delivery, but the pace of development can also make the reality of optimal prescribing and monitoring of drug therapy progressively more difficult in terms of the decisions about which drug to prescribe, and the discussions with the patient about what is being recommended and why. The choice is not only about which drug will optimally treat that individual for his or her specific problem. It also concerns deciding between a drug that may have been on the market for many years, with well-documented side effects, and a new drug which, although approved, has been used by far fewer people.

Although the majority of older people are independent and would describe themselves as healthy, older people are prescribed many more drugs than younger people. This potentially means that they are not only the greatest beneficiaries of appropriate and optimal drug treatment but also potentially the group that experience the most problems.

Nurses who work with older people have a key role in the following:

- Recognising when older people might need treatment.
- Instigating lifestyle changes or nursing measures (such as to relieve constipation or insomnia) that can avoid the need for medication.
- Administering medications, monitoring their effects and reporting adverse drug reactions. Helping older people understand the medications they have been prescribed and making positive choices about taking them.

From a Maslovian perspective, drugs impinge on many levels of human needs. When used appropriately, drugs can enhance; when used inappropriately, they threaten all levels of the hierarchy of needs. **Figure 10.1** illustrates the possible problems that can be avoided by optimal prescribing and medication use.

PATTERNS OF PRESCRIBING AND MEDICATION USE

In 1996, prescriptions for older people were estimated to account for 48% of all prescriptions, compared with 45% in 1995 and 40% in 1986 [Department of Health (DoH), 1997; Royal College of Physicians (RCP), 1997]. Older people receive more prescriptions per head than any other group, and the figures have increased from an average of 15 per head in 1986 (based on fees) to 21.2 in 1996 (based on items). Unfortunately, trends over time are difficult to estimate accurately as during 1995 the category of 'older people' changed from covering men aged 65 years and over and women aged 60 years and over, to both men and women aged 60 years and over.

Data for England show that in 1996 the number of prescription items for older people was 213 million. This cost

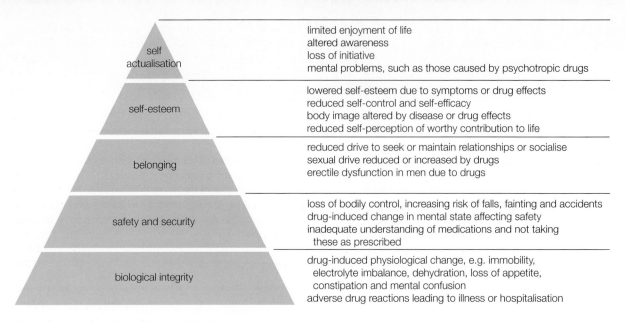

self
actualisation
- limited enjoyment of life
- altered awareness
- loss of initiative
- mental problems, such as those caused by psychotropic drugs

self-esteem
- lowered self-esteem due to symptoms or drug effects
- reduced self-control and self-efficacy
- body image altered by disease or drug effects
- reduced self-perception of worthy contribution to life

belonging
- reduced drive to seek or maintain relationships or socialise
- sexual drive reduced or increased by drugs
- erectile dysfunction in men due to drugs

safety and security
- loss of bodily control, increasing risk of falls, fainting and accidents
- drug-induced change in mental state affecting safety
- inadequate understanding of medications and not taking these as prescribed

biological integrity
- drug-induced physiological change, e.g. immobility, electrolyte imbalance, dehydration, loss of appetite, constipation and mental confusion
- adverse drug reactions leading to illness or hospitalisation

Figure 10.1 Problems which can be avoided by optimal drug use.

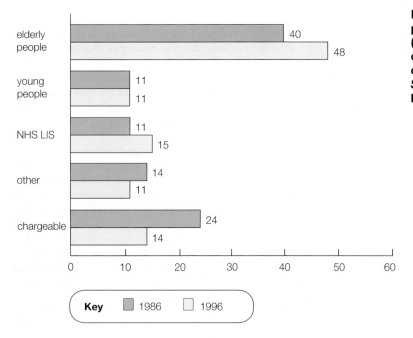

Figure 10.2   Percentage of total prescriptions by category, 1986 and 1996 (Source: Department of Health. Statistics of presciptions dispensed in the community: England 1986 to 1996. *Statistical Bulletin.* London: 1997, HMSO).

£1723.7 million, an average of £8.09 per item (DoH, 1997). During the 10 years from 1985 to 1995, this average net ingredient cost to older people rose from £4.10 to £7.55 and, according to the DoH (1997), this accounted for some 45% of the increase in the drugs bills of health authorities for this period. In 1985–1986, the drugs bill of health authorities in England was £1275 million. In 1995–1996 it was £3498 million. This constitutes an increase of 73% in real terms, around £60 per head of population. The number of prescription items for older people is, therefore, not only rising but constitutes a significant and increasing proportion of the spending on drugs (**Figure 10.2**).

Most of the medications prescribed to older people are long term. The number of first prescriptions is relatively small and is comparable with other adult age groups. However, prescribing patterns vary considerably between practices and between individual doctors, suggesting that treatment guidelines are not uniformly adopted. For example, there is considerable variation in prescribing rates for cardiovascular drugs for hypertension and angina in older patients (Roberts and Bateman, 1994). The variations are, however, likely to reduce gradually as audit and information systems become more efficient. Systems are already well developed in many areas and, although these may be primarily cost-focused, they provide valuable feedback of what drugs are being prescribed. The role of pharmacists in monitoring and advising general practitioners (GPs) and hospital doctors is also developing. However, the RCP suggests that too many or inappropriate drugs are still being prescribed and repeat prescribing does not receive the attention it merits (RCP, 1997).

One important factor contributing to the complexity and problems within the whole sphere of medications and older people has been the exclusion of older people, and particularly ill older people, from the majority of the trials for the drugs that would ultimately be prescribed to them. This even includes drugs for which they are the major client group (MRC, 1994).

The interaction of individual drugs with the distinct and individual characteristics of older people, such as those which derive from age-related changes, have been largely unknown when drugs are prescribed. However, the RCP report that, when older persons are likely to be significant users of a therapy, pharmaceutical companies now usually extend their trials to both fit and ill older people. As a result, there have been significant advances in knowledge concerning pharmacokinetics and pharmacodynamics of drugs in older age.

The whole field of medications and older people is thus highly important within today's health-care system, in both human and financial terms. However, it is important to retain a balanced perspective, for example to remember that at least one-third of older people take no regular medication (Duggan *et al.* 1996).

Influences on Prescribing for Older People

Many factors influence prescribing decisions, and these can be summarised as follows:
* Doctor's perception of patient expectations: the patient's expectations, health beliefs and understanding of the illness.
* Doctor's knowledge, prescribing experience and training: postgraduate experience and training, previous experience of managing a particular condition or using a specific drug.
* Influences on the doctor: pharmaceutical industry marketing, scientific publications, formularies and guidelines, peer group pressure, pharmacists, nurses, audit, drug costs and time available for the consultation.
* Doctor's attitude to older people: attitude to older people generally, to the efficacy of prescribing for older people, and priorities between younger and older people.

Specialist Knowledge
The distinct and special considerations in prescribing for older people are still not always appreciated. The RCP reports

that some doctors still do not appreciate the importance of assessing individual capacity to benefit based on biological age. Rather they continue to fix on the concept of chronological age and thus have higher thresholds for initiating treatment in older patients, for example myocardial infarction and hypertension, despite evidence that older patients experience greater benefits of treatment than younger patients (Beard *et al.* 1992).

Evidence-based Prescribing
With increasing emphasis on evidence-based practice, information and guidance available to assist in accurate diagnosis and appropriate treatment is now much more readily available. District-based and hospital-based formularies can assist doctors to prescribe drugs which have been shown by clinical research to be most efficacious, and nationally developed guidelines, such as those published by the British Thoracic Society on chronic obstructive pulmonary disease (1997), are now widely used in primary and secondary care. Improved information technology has also assisted the widespread dissemination and updating of evidence-based information (see section on information technology below).

Rationing
Rationing is a highly emotive subject and there are further discussions in Chapters 1 and 22. Various terms are used to describe rationing but cost constraints are now an ever-present reality and decisions about who will or will not be offered treatment present constant dilemmas for health-care professionals. Historically, doctors made decisions about prescriptions based solely on clinical judgement but, with the emphasis on achieving maximum health gain within limited resources, there are now financial constraints on prescribing.

Methods of allocating prescribing budgets to primary health-care practices, and the terms within these, have changed in recent years, particularly during the period of GP fundholding. In situations where savings made on prescribing could be transferred to other categories of the budget and used to develop other areas of the practice, this could potentially disadvantage older patients. The RCP has called for careful monitoring in order to ensure that older people are not being denied effective therapies in order that the savings achieved can be used for other services.

Real dilemmas are being faced by doctors in their prescribing between different client groups, different disease groups and different types of drugs; for example, a patient may not respond as well to a generic preparation as to a more expensive brand-named drug. Particular dilemmas arise when new drugs come onto the market. For example, new preparations for Parkinson's disease (PD) or rheumatoid arthritis may be much more expensive than more traditional treatments, but the safety and efficacy in preventing disability has been demonstrated in clinical trials and using the drug can reduce the consumption of other drugs such as antidepressants. From the evidence, it is likely that the new drugs would be considerably more effective in reducing disability in the long-term, thus considerably enhancing the patient's quality of life. However, because trials have not been conducted over a period of perhaps 15–25 years, the long-term effects, both in terms of effects and side effects, remain conjectural. Does the GP prescribe for the long-term quality of life of patients with PD or rheumatoid arthritis, or look at the practice spending in all categories, such as cardiovascular or gastrointestinal (GI) drugs, for all age groups, and for other aspects of care such as acute hospital admissions, and decide there are greater priorities?

The Nurse's Influence

The prescribing decisions of doctors are greatly influenced by nursing staff. Nurses who work closely with older people can identify when treatment might be needed and assist in the prescribing by encouraging the patient to provide relevant personal and lifestyle information. They have a key role teaching the patient about his or her medications, in monitoring the effects of medications and reporting any problems to the doctor in order that the prescription can be changed. This was demonstrated by Coomber *et al.* (1992) following a review of the community team skill mix. The loss of high-grade district nurses reduced the team's ability to monitor the effects of prescribed medications and identify adverse drug reactions.

Prescribing decisions are particularly influenced by nurses with specialist expertise. The number and range of nurse specialists is gradually increasing not only in the traditional fields of diabetes, continence and stoma care but also in disease-specific specialities such as PD, epilepsy, rheumatology, cardiology and respiratory care, and also with client-specific groups, including older people. These nurses develop high levels of understanding of the treatments appropriate for their client groups. Because they work closely with more people with, for example, PD than the GP, they develop high levels of understanding about the treatments used with their client groups. They also often liaise with representatives of drug companies in order to gain information about a particular treatment, or report adverse effects for the drug company's records. As a result of this expertise, many GPs are happy to accept the advice of specialist nurses on prescribing and changing medications. Some local areas, or groups such as the PD Nurses forum at the Royal College of Nursing, have developed protocols to enable nurses to alter prescribed medications within pre-agreed guidelines. Specialist nurses and GPs generally work in partnership in the care of their clients, and the nurse liaises with or advises the GP about any change in medication.

Many specialist nurses are now developing nurse-led clinics within primary health-care practices, and medication review is a key aspect of their work.

Polypharmacy, Under-treatment and Inappropriate Prescribing

Older people are often treated with multiple drugs. This occurs because they generally experience more chronic disorders and their health problems are multiple. Polypharmacy is common. It occurs when several conditions are treated at the same time or when the side effects of one drug are mistakenly treated as a new disorder with another drug. This produces what has been called the 'prescribing cascade'. For example, anticholinergic drugs may produce constipation, for which laxatives are prescribed; metoclopromide may produce parkinsonism for which levedopa is then prescribed inappropriately.

Studies have shown that, when the prescriptions of older people admitted to hospital were checked, one-third of the drugs could be stopped without detriment to the patient, either because they were unnecessary or because they were expressly contraindicated. Diuretics were the most common of these. Ten per cent of prescriptions were contraindicated, either for use with their specific clinical diagnosis or in the light of the findings of laboratory tests (Gosney and Tallis, 1984).

The RCP report that, despite repeated advice, studies continue to show that polypharmacy, inappropriate treatment and under-treatment continue in both primary and secondary care settings. Older people receive inappropriate therapy particularly if the underlying cause of the problem has not been adequately assessed, or if inappropriate treatment is chosen for a correctly diagnosed problem. A common example of under-treatment is hypertension, where the RCP report that many older people remain undetected and untreated.

Self-prescribed and Over-the-counter (OTC) Treatments

Self-medication has assumed a new emphasis as part of the general movement towards consumer choice and self-responsibility in promoting and protecting individual health. The 1995 World Health Organisation's *Report on National Drug Policies* stated explicitly that responsible self-medication could both enable patients to control their own chronic conditions and reduce the increasing pressure on medical services for the relief of minor ailments. In the UK in recent years, the range of choice in self-medication has been enhanced with the re-categorisation of many proven and valuable medications from prescription-only medicine (POM) status to pharmacy (P) medication, or that which can be purchased over the counter (OTC). Medicines switched from POM to OTC status since 1983 include ibuprofen, isosorbide dinitrate, loperamide, paracetamol/dihydrocodeine, cimetidine, ranitidine and various topical preparations including hydrocortisone. More than 40 products were reclassified from POM to OTC status in the 5 years since 1992, when the procedure for changing drug status was streamlined.

The OTC market in 1996 was £1275.8 million – a growth of 1.5% on figures for 1995. These figures include sales from pharmacies, health food stores, drug stores and grocery shops but do not include own label products (Proprietary Association of Great Britain, 1997). Successful self-medication through the patient making OTC purchases is facilitated

Meeting Medication Needs

Viola Thompson has lived in an Abbeyfield home for many years and is now in her late seventies. Her brother and two sisters died some years previously and she has lost touch with other members of the family. She enjoys living in the home and has found great companionship with the other residents and the members of the committee who run the home on a voluntary basis. Her special friend is Peggy who chairs the committee and selflessly gives most of her time to managing the home and helping individual residents with their problems. Miss Thompson particularly enjoys the times when Peggy visits her room and they sit for hours drinking tea while she recounts the many experiences she has enjoyed during her years as an actress in repertory theatres around the country.

Miss Thompson enjoys shopping in the local high street but has never enjoyed robust health. She takes prescribed medication for arthritis and hypertension, but is regarded by some of the other residents as a hypochondriac because they say she constantly complains to them about various aches and pains, her knees that 'give out', her 'dizziness' and her 'sensitive stomach'. Miss Thompson has not been well for some weeks and during a 'tea and chat' session, Peggy notices that one of her cupboards is full of medicine bottles. When Peggy asked what they were all for, Miss Thompson said that she wasn't absolutely sure but she took some whenever she felt dizzy or her pain became worse. Peggy has persuaded Miss Thompson to ask the community nurse (who is visiting the home to see one of the other residents the following day) for advice.

- What subjective data should the nurse collect from Miss Thompson?
- What objective data could help the nurse in undertaking her assessment?
- What strengths does Miss Thompson demonstrate that could be used as the basis for a plan of action?
- What advice should the nurse give to Miss Thompson?
- What further action could and should the nurse take?
- What type of information should the nurse report to Miss Thompson's general practitioner?
- What ongoing help could the nurse offer to Miss Thompson?
- What outcome criteria could the nurse use to evaluate her work with Miss Thompson?
- Suggest two areas for nursing intervention.
- Suggest the nursing aims for each intervention, reflecting realistic outcomes and using concrete and measurable terms.
- Suggest one or more interventions for each of your chosen areas, justifying the choice of intervention.

by cooperation between the patient, the pharmacist and the GP. This emerging model has been described as collaborative care.

The increasing emphasis on self-medication is also reinforced by the potential savings in GP consultation time that could be achieved if patients self-medicated for minor ailments, when necessary asking the advice of pharmacists. The Audit Commission identified that if only one-quarter of the current number of consultations for minor ailments could be avoided under the concept of collaborative care, that would equate to 24 million consultations per year, potentially valued at over £380 million (Audit Commission, 1994).

Older patients are major users of OTC medications, despite the fact that prescription drugs are free to people of pensionable age. Cough and cold remedies, laxatives and antacids are the most commonly requested preparations. McElnay and Dickson (1994) suggest that the reasons why older people purchase OTC medicines include:

- Convenience.
- Previous usage of that particular OTC medicine.
- Advertisement.
- Usage recommended by a friend.
- Usage recommended by a pharmacist or GP.
- Unavailable on prescription.
- Did not want to bother the GP.
- Felt that the condition was not sufficiently serious to bother the GP.
- Unable to obtain an appointment with the GP.
- Too embarrassed to ask the GP.

Many OTC drugs contain ingredients that, in larger amounts, would require a prescription and could potentially be dangerous.

Older people naturally have the same rights to consumer power as any other group in society and if they choose to buy OTC rather than consult a doctor or nurse, this is their right of choice. Pharmacists, doctors and nurses must nevertheless be alert to recognising when that choice might compromise the health of the individual and alerting them to this. For example, McElnay and Dickson (1994) demonstrated that 25% of the OTC purchases made by older people were for conditions for which they had already been prescribed a medicine. Their survey also showed that nearly 75% of older patients did not discuss their OTC medicine with their GP.

Some older people also use traditional medications such as folk medicine, herbs and homeopathic remedies. These may have been an aspect of their culture for many generations (*see* Chapter 19 for further discussion of cultural and ethnic influences on health practices). Even seemingly innocuous substances could potentially react with other medications and, again, health professionals need to be alert to recognising when they should advise the patient of potential problems.

Achieving Therapeutic Alliances (Formerly Known as 'Compliance')

Terminology

For decades the term 'compliance' has been a prominent feature of the literature related to how patients put into practice prescribed medication or lifestyle regimes but, for many commentators, there has been a growing dissonance with the connotations of the term. The dissatisfaction stems from its suggestions of paternalism – of the disobedience of patients in the face of medical wisdom. It seems to undervalue the patient's right to self-determination and potential for choice in self-management.

'Non-compliance' was agreed as a nursing diagnosis in the USA in 1982. It was defined as 'a person's informed decision not to adhere to a therapeutic regime'. Subsequent to that it was decided that non-compliance was not, in fact, a nursing diagnosis but a component of other nursing diagnoses such as lack of family support, lack of self-esteem or 'ineffective coping'. More recently, the term 'adherence' has been favoured, for example in the recent systematic reviews undertaken for the Cochrane Database (Haynes *et al.* 1997).

Nurses searching the literature will need to use the terms 'compliance' and 'adherence' in order to seek evidence for their practice, and there is a great deal of literature on the subject, even when the additional keywords of older people (or alternatives) and medications (or alternatives) are used in conjunction. We suggest, however, that it is important to retain an awareness of the connotations of some of the terminology. In particular, that which inherently infers blame on the older person for something on which they may have been offered no information on or had no choice (i.e. terms such as 'non-comprehension', 'confusion', 'ineffective coping').

Because the authors value older people as citizens, consumers and autonomous individuals, the term 'therapeutic alliances' is preferable. The key to this is negotiation based on the prescriber learning to understand the individual patient, the patient learning to understand what the prescriber is recommending and ultimately mutual agreement about the best regime in the circumstances.

The Scale of 'Non-compliance'

There are various estimates of the numbers of older people who do not take medications in accordance with prescriptions. In 1984, the RCP estimated that 75% of older people do not 'comply' with prescribed regimes and that, in 25% of these cases, the consequences could be serious. Col *et al.* (1990) assessed 'compliance' in ambulatory patients and concluded that 29–59% make errors in self-administration of prescribed medicines. Hussey (1991) estimated the rate of 'non-compliance' in older people to be 50–75%.

However, as Wade and Bowling (1986) highlight, measures of 'compliance' and 'non-compliance' vary considerably from one study to another. Therefore, the true incidence of 'non-compliance' is unknown, and it cannot be confidently stated that the incidence is higher among older people than for the general population.

Reasons Why Older People Do Not Take Medicines as Prescribed

Older people do not to take the medications prescribed according to the recommended regime for a number of reasons. These are well documented in the extensive literature. They include:

(1) Decision not to take the medications. Lamy (1986) estimated that 75% of older people intentionally do not adhere to their drug regimen either by altering the dose because it is ineffective or because of the uncomfortable side effects. Others stop taking medications because they feel they are not needed anymore. Pendleton (1992) reviewed the research on compliance and concluded that one reason was because the drugs interfered with the older person's activities of daily living.

(2) The complexity of drug regime. The more drugs prescribed and the more frequently that these need to be taken, the greater the difference between the regime and what is actually taken (Burns *et al.* 1992; Cargill, 1992).

(3) Patient's understanding of the drug regime. If older people are to take their medications as prescribed, they must first understand the regime, and it is important to distinguish between 'non-compliance' and 'non-comprehension'. Estimates of non-comprehension vary, but difficulties with comprehension are obviously compounded by sensory loss, impaired memory, and difficulties in interpreting complex language (Burns *et al.* 1992). Studies suggesting a strong link between lack of understanding and 'non-adherence' include Pendleton (1992). Steele *et al.* (1986) found that 36% of the older people in their research did not know what their drugs were for, and 91% could not list frequent side effects or side effects that should be reported to the doctor. In Madhy and Seymour's (1990) study, older patients were asked to give details of their usual medications without reference to drug bottles or written lists. They were then asked to give

the names of the drugs, the reason why it was prescribed, the dosage and frequency of administration. The patients' accuracy was low in all four categories but particularly in respect of the drug name where only 10% were able to give a complete list of their drugs. The mean number of drugs in the regimes was 3.8, and the incidence of errors correlated with increasing age, decreasing mental score and, to a lesser extent, number of drugs prescribed. Generic prescribing has achieved savings in drug costs but can be highly confusing for a person who receives different formats of the same drug on different occasions.

(4) Sensory impairments which interfere with learning. Impaired hearing or sight interfere with a person's abilities to hear or read explanations of medications and regimes (Lewis and Crossland, 1992). If labels are particularly small, or the person has difficulty distinguishing colour coding, this can further hamper their abilities to follow regimes. (*See* Chapter 12 for full discussion of sensory changes.)

(5) Not remembering to take medications. Davis (1991) showed that 'forgetfulness' was a key factor in 'non-adherence', and Leirer *et al.* (1991) showed that memory failures associated with non-adherence to medication regimens were of two general types: forgetting the way to correctly take medications and failure to remember to take medication at the correct times. This latter type of 'non-adherence' was reported to increase with the number of different prescriptions taken.

(6) Difficulties with packaging. Reduced manual dexterity can make many drug containers difficult to use. One study found that almost half of newly supplied medications were issued in child-proof containers, and one-fifth of the container labels were nonspecific with instructions such as 'take as directed' (Burns *et al.* 1992).

(7) Inadequate support. Living arrangements and support systems of older people can increase the likelihood of not taking medicines as prescribed. Such factors as living alone, problems with mobility, social isolation and inability to obtain help have been cited. However, the availability of family and friends who are in regular contact need not guarantee more accurate taking of medicines.

Professional Support

Wade and Bowling (1986) reviewed the literature on drug therapy 'compliance' in older people and concluded that many of the factors associated with 'non-compliance' are within the control of health-care professionals. They identify issues related to doctors' awareness of what the patients are taking but supporting older people in 'healthy therapeutic alliances' is obviously the responsibility of the health-care team, and particularly when the patient is transferred between secondary and primary care or vice versa. Quilligan (1990,

p. 568) concluded that her review of the literature had shown that 'many of the factors that influence medication compliance have been recognised for as long as a decade. It is suggested that in many clinical areas the importance of this information is being ignored and that nurses now need to consider the significance of their role in this important aspect of care'.

PHARMACOKINETICS AND PHARMACODYNAMICS

Pharmacokinetics refers to those aspects of a drug involved in the distribution of the drug in the body from the point of administration through absorption, metabolism and excretion. Pharmacodynamics refers to the processes involved in the interaction between a drug and the effector organ, ending in a response of the organ.

Absorption

Absorption is the uptake of a drug into the body. Drugs enter the circulation via the oral, sub-lingual, rectal or parenteral routes. Not all the administered drug enters the body (apart from via parenteral administration); bioavailability is the term used to describe the proportion of the drug which does.

For most drugs, maximum absorption occurs in the small intestine when medications are given by mouth. Parenteral routes of administration enter circulation either immediately by intravenous administration or more slowly through intramuscular injection.

Sublingual administration allows direct absorption via the sublingual veins. This bypasses the liver, the site of uptake and metabolism of most drugs, and the drug (e.g. sublingual nitrates for angina) directly enters the systemic circulation.

In older people, there does not seem to be conclusive evidence that there is an appreciable change in the absorption process. However, delayed stomach emptying and delivery of the drug to the vast absorption surface of the small intestine may delay the onset of action of drugs.

Some enteric-coated medications, which are specifically meant to bypass stomach acidity, may be delayed so long that their action begins in the stomach and may produce undesirable effects such as gastric irritation or nausea.

Increased motility of the small intestine or increased intestinal transit from diarrhoeal diseases may reduce the time available for absorption and optimal drug levels may not be attained especially if the drug is enteric coated.

Conversely, slowed intestinal motility can increase the contact time and increase drug efficiency because of prolonged absorption or can cause adverse reactions to occur.

Antispasmodic drugs, if taken as part of a multiple medication regimen, have the propensity for slowing gastric and intestinal motility. In some instances this drug action may be useful but when there are other medications involved it is necessary to consider the problem of drug absorption. Impaired or slowed mesenteric (splanchnic) blood flow definitely interferes with absorption. Sluggish blood flow lengthens the absorption time and increases the amount of drug absorbed. However, many authorities agree that the quality of the absorption process is unchanged even though it may be slowed.

Diminished gastric secretions in older people will retard the action of acid-dependent drugs. Antacids or iron preparations affect the availability of some drugs for absorption by binding the drug with elements and forming compounds.

Distribution

Distribution of any drug depends on the adequacy of the circulatory system and the binding of the drug to tissue receptors. Altered cardiac output and sluggish circulation delay the arrival of medication at the target receptors, retard the release of a drug from storage tissue, and the excretion of the drug, or its by-products, from the body. In addition, distribution influences the amount of free and bound drug in the circulation system. This depends on the availability of plasma protein, especially plasma albumin, on which many drugs are transported in the circulation (as bound drug). In the younger adult, adequate quantities of plasma albumin are present to bind with drugs. In older people, the concentration of plasma albumin available for binding with drugs diminishes. This means that more free active drug circulates in the older person's blood and becomes a contributing factor in overdose and toxicity. The pharmacological effect perceived originates from the free drug. Unbound or free drugs circulate and can be filtered through cell and organ membranes, excreted unchanged by the kidney or metabolised to a less active inert form.

Changes in body composition during ageing influence drug distribution. Total body water decreases, altering cellular distribution of drugs that are water-soluble such as cimetidine, digoxin and ethanol. These drugs will be reflected in a higher than usual blood level in older people. Adipose tissue, or fat content of the body, nearly doubles in older men and increases one and a half times in older women. Highly lipid-soluble drugs may be stored in the fatty tissue, thus extending and possibly elevating the drug effect. This potentially occurs in such drugs as Lorazepam, Diazepam, Chlorpromazine, Phenobarbitone and Haldol. These medications can be stored in fatty tissue, which can increase and prolong their effect.

Free drug concentration is an important factor in distribution and elimination of a drug. Serum albumin may be much lower in older people when there is chronic illness and poor nutrition. Distribution of the drug may be altered by changes in the plasma protein concentration, red blood cells and other body tissue. **Box 10.1** lists drugs that, when given to the frail, chronically ill old person, have a greater potential for more circulating free drug than bound drug, creating a risk of toxicity. When prescribing drugs, attention should

10.1 Highly Protein-bound Drugs

Aspirin
Chlorothiazide (Saluric)
Chlorpromazine (Largactil)
Chlorpropamide (Diabinese)
Diazepam (Valium)
Frusemide (Lasix)
Haloperidol (Haldol)
Ibuprofen (Brufen)
Indomethacin (Indocid)
Naproxen (Naprosyn)
Nifedipine (Adalat)
Phenobarbitone
Phenytoin (Epanutin)
Sulindac (Clinoril)
Thioridazine (Melleril)
Tolbutamide (Rastinon)
Verapamil (Cordilox)
Warfarin (Marevan)

Source: Santo-Novak D, Edaeds RM. Rx: Take caution with drugs for elders. *Geriatr Nurs* 1969, 10(2):72.

be given to whether the patient is young or old, frail or chronically ill, fat or lean, male or female. All these factors have a marked influence on drug action.

Metabolism

The microsomal enzyme system of the liver is the primary site of drug metabolism (biotransformation). Some studies using a drug, which under normal circumstances should be totally metabolised by the liver, show a diminished metabolism in older people. Studies are conflicting in identifying universal age changes in the liver. The studies report differences in rates of metabolism but there is consensus that there is a decreased blood flow to the liver whether from disease or normal ageing or both. This results in decreased hepatic clearance and thus the half-life of a drug – the time required for the excretion process to reduce the plasma concentration of a drug by half – increases as a result of diminished rate of metabolism in older people. The duration of drug action is determined by the metabolic rate. Slow metabolism suggests that the drug will remain in the body longer and produce a prolonged half-life.

Sensitivity of the central nervous system alters receptor activity and produces greater receptor variation because of physiological decline in autonomic nervous function such as exaggerated or idiosyncratic reactions to hypotensive drugs or a hypothermic effect from phenothiazines.

A drug has a specific affinity for receptor sites, which are designated areas inside or outside particular cells. When the drug reaches the receptor, it is translated into a chemical action that affects the body. This alteration at the receptor site, and associated metabolic changes, is called pharmacodynamics.

Excretion

Under normal circumstances when a drug is taken by mouth, it is absorbed through the walls of the GI tract into the bloodstream, which facilitates distribution to various tissues of the body. Degradation, breakdown of the drug into intermediate compounds, may occur with some drugs to produce a more excretable form. Elimination is primarily effected through the kidneys in urine; some, however, is eliminated through bile, faeces, sweat and saliva.

Administration, supervision, evaluation and education of the patient, in part, depend on this knowledge. **Figure 10.3** illustrates the intricate relationship between physiological age changes and the pharmacokinetics and pharmacodynamics of drugs with the age population. These interrelated processes are the basis for many of the positive and adverse responses of older people to medications. Only a brief discussion of important issues is presented here. Specific and more detailed information on the pharmacokinetics and pharmacodynamics of drugs can be found in numerous pharmacology textbooks.

Biological half-life, the time required for half of the drug to be excreted, is affected by the degree of kidney function. Altered filtration and decreased plasma volume, which occur in dehydration, are common in older people. These prolong and elevate blood levels of drugs. This can occur with penicillin. In some instances this situation can be beneficial, but with drugs such as streptomycin, toxic effects can overshadow the therapeutic value. Other drugs are ineffective in the presence of a low creatinine clearance.

Creatinine clearance (CrCl) can be used as an index of renal function in older people, but most doctors tend to use serum creatinine as a guide for prescribing.

DRUG INTERACTIONS

Drug interactions are the result of two or more medications, given simultaneously or in close sequence, with an outcome response of drug synergism, which is rare, or more frequently drug potentiation or antagonism. Interactions may be precipitated by drug–drug, drug–nutrient, drug–disease, and social or psychological factors that influence drug response.

These interactions can occur within or outside of the body. Many of the interactions are the result of pharmacokinetic activity. A variety of interactions occur. Within the body, absorption can be delayed by drugs exerting an anticholinergic effect. Tricyclic drugs (antidepressants) act in this manner to decrease gastrointestinal (GI) motility and interfere with absorption of other drugs. Several drugs simultaneously compete to bind with protein before metabolism; one drug will bind and occupy the binding sites needed by the other drug, creating a varied bioavailability of one or both of the drugs. Interaction may be blocked at the receptor site, preventing the drug from reaching the cells. Interference with enzyme activity may alter metabolism and cause drug deficiencies, or toxic and adverse responses may develop from altered tubular function. Outside the body, interactions can occur any time two medications are mixed before administration. An example of this is insulin.

Concern with older people's total response to drug therapy and its effect on the ability for activities of daily living and functional capacities such as vision, hearing, memory and mobility is a substantial reason for a drug assessment of each older person under the supervision of the nurse. **Table 10.1** indicates the manner of administration of drugs to reduce or prevent interactions.

Adverse Drug Reactions (ADRs)

The 'Yellow Card' adverse reaction reporting scheme has been useful in determining the patient groups at risk of some adverse effects. The total number of ADR reports received by the Committee on Safety of Medicines confirm an increase in the number of reports of serious reactions with increasing age, although the relationship is complex and subtle. Factors associated with an increase of ADR in older people include multiple drug therapy, female gender, small body size, hepatic or renal insufficiency, cognitive impairment and previous ADR.

ADRs remain an important cause of morbidity, even mortality, in older people, especially those who are frail with an acute illness. Many studies have demonstrated an increased incidence of ADRs in hospitalised older patients, with an up to three-fold greater rate in patients of aged 60 years and over, compared to those under 30 years. Approximately 1 in 10 older patients are admitted to hospital because of an ADR or develop an ADR during hospital admission (Nolan and O'Malley, 1989). Lack of recognition of ADRs is common and the incidence of ADRs in older patients in community settings is not well described.

One study found that nearly 20% of all prescriptions involved a risk of drug interactions, although only a small proportion of interactions were likely to be of clinical significance (Adams *et al.*, 1987). However, some drugs show increasing evidence of severe, or fatal, reactions with age, these include Co-trimoxazole. Lamy (1986) estimated that approximately 40% of older people in the community experienced adverse drug reactions, 80% of which occurred with well-known drugs given at usual dosages. The most common drugs that produce adverse reactions include warfarin, digoxin, prednisone, diuretics, antihypertensives, insulin, aspirin and antidepressants (Nolan and O'Malley, 1989).

The most common reactions have been identified as sedation, lethargy, confusion and falls (Palmieri, 1991). Mental confusion perhaps is the most striking. Confusion in an individual who previously had not been confused may be interpreted as a

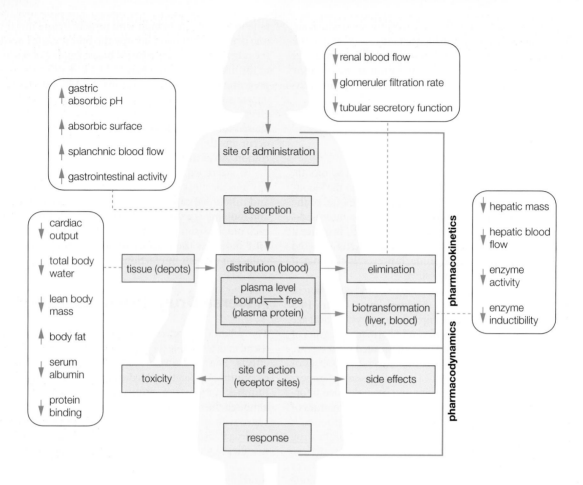

Figure 10.3 Physiological age changes and the pharmacokinetics and pharmacodynamics of drug use. (Source: Adapted from Lamy PP. Hazards of drug use in the elderly. *Postgrad Med* 76(1):50, 1982; Kane RL, Ouslander JG, Abrass JB. *Essentials of clinical geriatrics*. New York: McGraw-Hill, 1984;

new symptom of some disease yet unidentified and a new medication is inappropriately prescribed. Lethargy can also be misinterpreted as a symptom connected with cardiac, respiratory or neurological conditions rather than a medication response. Polytherapy with several psychoactive drugs exerting anticholinergic action is perhaps the greatest precipitator of confusion as an adverse reaction. In addition, while the potential for an adverse drug reaction or interaction is only 6% when two drugs are taken, it rises to 50% when five drugs are ingested and to 100% when eight or more medications are taken together

(Shaughnessy, 1992). and **Boxes 10.2–10.5** highlight the drugs which commonly cause adverse reactions.

Drug Toxicity

Drug toxicity is a condition that occurs when the amount of a drug in the body exceeds the amount necessary to bring about a therapeutic effect, exceeds the therapeutic level or becomes a harmful agent in the body, producing adverse effects.

Some Preventable Drug Interactions through Proper Administration						
Drug	Take with food, milk, meals	Do not take with milk or its products	May impair nutrient and electrolyte uptake and use	Do not take with alcohol	Do not take with fruit juice	Take on empty stomach
Alcohol			X			
Aminophylline and derivatives	X					
Ampicillin					X	
Antacids						X
Antihistamines				X		
Anti-infectives			X	X		
Atropine			X			
Benzathine penicillin G					X	X
Bisacodyl (Duco-Lax)		X	X	X		
Chloral hydrate				X		
Chlorpropamide (Diabinese)				X		
Cholestyramine (Questran)			X			
Clindamycin (Cleocin)			X			
Cloxacillin					X	X
Corticosteroids (oral)	X					
Dioctyl sodium sulphosuccinate (Colace, Surfak)			X			
Diphenoxylate (Lomotil)			X			
Diuretics	X		X			
Erythromycin (oral)					X	X
Folic acid inhibitors			X			
Ibuprofen (Motrin)	X					
Indomethacin (Indocin)	X					
Iron salts						X
Monoamine-oxidase inhibitors				X		
Metronidazole (Flagyl)	X			X		
Mineral oil			X			
Narcotics				X		
Neomycin			X			
Nitrofurantoin (Furadantin)	X					
Penicillin (oral)						X
Phenazopyridine (Pyridium)						X
Phenylbutazone (Butazolidin)	X					
Phenytoin	X					
Potassium chloride solutions		X				
Tolbutamide (Orinase)				X		
Trimeprazine (Temaril)	X			X		

Source: Knoben JE, Anderson PO. *Handbook of clinical data*, 6th edition. Hamilton: Drug intelligence Publications, 1988; Long JW. *Essential guide to prescription drugs*. New York: Harper Collins, 1991.

Table 10.1 **Some drug interactions preventable through proper administration.**

10.2 Outcomes of Interactions that Occur during Absorption, Distribution, Metabolism, and Excretion of Some Drugs

Substance	Effect
Altered absorption	
Magnesium antacids + oral anticoagulants	Enhance possible bleeding episodes
Antacids + antibiotics	Possibility of infection not responding properly to therapy
Milk + enteric coated tablets (bisacodyl)	Premature disintegration and irritation in stomach: nausea, vomiting
Mineral oil + stool softeners	Absorbed by body and may be carried by lymph, spleen, liver; may react as foreign body
Mineral oil + oral anticoagulants	Unpredictable anticoagulation possible with large doses of mineral oil
Altered distribution	
Oral anticoagulants + Anti-inflammatory agents and anticholesteremics	Labile anticoagulation: sudden episodes of bleeding possible
Oral hypoglycaemic agents (sulphonylurea type) + Aspirin, sulphonamides, oral anticoagulants,	Enhancement of hypoglycaemic response
Methotrexate + Aspirin, sulphonamides, penicillin	Severe toxic reaction, nausea, vomiting diarrhoea; bone marrow depression to pancytopaenia
Altered metabolism	
Anticoagulants + barbiturates, carbamazepine (Tegretol) phenytoin	Less therapeutic effect: possibility of precipitating bleeding if drugs discontinued, except anticoagulant
Phenytoin + para-aminosalicylic acid	Motor incoordination; nystagmus; lethargy
Oral hypoglycaemic agents (chloropropamide) + anticoagulants	Patient with diabetes predisposed to severe hypoglycaemic reactions; coma
Altered excretion	
Cimetidine + anticoagulants	Increased anticoagulation
Phenytoin + anticoagulants	Reduced anticoagulation
Diuretics (ethacrynic acid, frusemide, thiazides) + Digoxin	Reduced potassium and increased toxicity unless supplement given

A drug that has a cumulative effect has the potential for drug toxicity. Other drugs may produce drug toxicity under such circumstances as polypharmacy, slowed metabolism, altered excretion, dehydration, drug overdose due to self-medication errors, or excessive prescribed dosage.

THE NURSE'S ROLE

Assessment

Nurses have an important role in identifying when there might be a need for assessment and treatment, in encouraging the older person to agree to assessment and seek treatment, and in facilitating this. Physical or mental health problems should not be dismissed as being due to age alone, and older age should not be a barrier to adequate assessment and treatment. Low expectations of health by older people should not lead to under-treatment.

Considerations for undertaking an assessment are shown in **Box 10.6** and a medication assessment worksheet is offered in **Figure 10.4**.

A full nursing assessment would note all medications currently being taken, including over-the-counter (OTC) medications, also previous drug history, particularly of any adverse drug reactions (ADRs). Through questioning and observation, the nurse will identify further areas for investigation, such as particular problems for which OTC treatment may be taken [e.g. headaches, eye problems, ear problems, gastrointestinal (GI) problems]. Additional information about drug management can be gathered by asking about how drugs are taken, the frequency of administration, dosage, purpose and potential side effects. Assessment will provide information about:

- The beliefs and motivations of the person for taking the medications.
- Understanding of what they are taking and why.

10.3 Drugs with the Potential to Cause Intellectual Impairment

- Alcohol.
- Analgesics.
- Anticholinergics.
- Antidepressants.
- Antipsychotics.
- Antihistamines.
- Anti-Parkinsonism agents.
- Cimetidine.
- Digitalis.
- Diuretics.
- Hypnotics.
- Sedatives.
- Sudden withdrawal of benzodiazepines.

Source: Adapted from Nolan L, O'Malley K. Prescribing for the elderly: Part I, Sensitivity of the patient to adverse drug reactions. *Am Geriatr Soc* 1988, 36(2):142; Lamy PP. Drug interactions and the elderly, *J Gerontol Nurs* 1986b,12(2); Lamy PP. Adverse drug effects. *Clin Geriatr Med* 1990, 6(2).

- Level of sensory, mental and physical ability.
- General lifestyle and routine.
- Support at home.
- Willingness to go to the general practitioner for help and advice.

The nurse should actively seek information that might indicate side effects or adverse drug reactions. These are not always obvious, but may be revealed by seemingly minimal lifestyle changes. For example:

- Has the person's functional ability changed?
- Has their mental functioning changed?

10.4 Effects of Systemic Drugs on Vision

Drug	Effect
Frusemide (Lasix)	Blurred vision, decreased tolerance to contact lenses, photophobia, allergic reactions to eyelids and conjunctivae
Propranolol (Inderal)	Transient blurred vision with diplopia, decreased accommodation
Brompheniramine maleate	Mydriasis (contradicted in glaucoma), blurred vision, intolerance to contact lenses
Diazepam (Valium)	Allergic conjunctivitis
Digoxin (Lanoxin)	Diplopia, blurred vision, changes in colour perception (warnings of toxicity)

Source: Adapted from Osis M. Drugs and vision. *Gerontion* 1986, 1(5):15.

10.5 Toxic Characteristics of Specific Drugs Prescribed for Older People

Drugs	Signs and symptoms
Benzodiazepines *Diazepam (Valium)* *Flurazepam (Dalmane)* *Lorazepam (Ativan)*	Confusion, psychomotor retardation, instability
Cimetidine (Tagamet)	Confusion, depression
Digoxin	Confusion, headache, anorexia, vomiting, arrhythmias, blurred vision or other visual changes, paraesthesia
Frusemide (Lasix)	Electrolyte imbalance including hypokalaemia, dehydration
Levodopa	Confusion, hallucinations, dyskinetic movements, postural hypotension
NSAIDs *Ibuprofen (Brufen)* *Indomethacin (Indocid)* *Naproxen*	Peptic ulcer, gastrointestinal bleeding, fluid retention, anaemia, visual changes, photosensitivity, nephrotoxicity
Phenothiazines	Confusion, anticholinergic effects, postural hypotension
Phenytoin(Epanutin)	arrhythmias, neuroleptic malignant syndrome
Sulphonyl ureas *Chlopropamide (Diabinese)* *Tolbutamide (Orinase)*	Hypoglycaemia, hepatic changes, congestive heart failure bone marrow depression, jaundice
Tricyclic antidepressants *Amitriptyline (Tryptizol, Lentizol)* *Imipramine (Tofranil)*	Confusion, arrhythmias, seizures, agitation, tachycardia, jaundice, hallucinations, postural hypotension, anticholinergic effects

Source: Skidmore-Roth L. *Nursing drug reference*. St Louis: Mosby, 1992; Oradell NJ. *Physician's desk reference*. Medical Economics, 1992; Salzman C. Basic principles of psychotropic drug prescriptions for the elderly. *Hosp Comm Psychiatr* 1982, 33:133; Todd B. Identifying drug toxicity. *Geriatr Nurs* 1985, 4:231.

- Do they find difficulty arising in the morning?
- Are their spectacles as effective as they were?
- Is their appetite as good as it was before starting the medication?
- Has leakage of urine started to become a problem more recently?
- Do they 'get around' as well as they did?

The local pharmacist will be a valuable resource in answering queries.

The use of vitamins, herbal preparations and 'folk' remedies should also be noted. Many preparations contain ingredients that, particularly if an individual is taking several preparations that contain the same ingredients, could interact with OTC or prescription drugs to reach toxic levels. Because many drugs take 2–4 weeks to be completely excreted, recently discontinued drugs as well as the reason for discontinuation may be significant.

Intervention

Once the nurse has undertaken a comprehensive assessment, they can minimise the need for some medications by health advice or therapeutic interventions. Some medicines can be avoided by measures such as those given in **Box 10.7**.

The type of information given in this box can be relayed to the doctor in order that the person's individual and lifestyle needs can be incorporated in the treatment regime from the outset.

10.6 Drug Use in Older Adults: Principles of Assessment

Assessment of drug use in older adults should:

- Focus upon the older person's perceptions and aspirations as to their own health status.
- Be a multidisciplinary activity involving collaboration between nursing, medical and pharmacy staff, and others where appropriate.
- Be conducted as soon as possible to determine baseline knowledge of prescribed medication regime.
- Involve the introduction of self-medication programmes to encourage people to take responsibility for administering their own medications.
- Precede the introduction of an individualised teaching programme to educate older people about safe self-administration of medication.
- Incorporate both written and verbal communication strategies.
- Ensure that medication education programmes incorporate strategies to compensate for the sensory and motor changes associated with the ageing process, the alteration in cognitive function and the situational differences among older adults.
- Be tailored to meet educational needs of individual participants.
- Include the views of family/carer.
- Be conducted at regular intervals, particularly in continuing care settings.

Source: Ryan A, Jacques I. Medication compliance in older people. *Elderly Care* 1997, 9:16.

10.7 Measures Taken to Reduce Need for Medication

General health measures and lifestyle changes, such as the following, can reduce the need for medication:
- Adequate nutrition.
- Fluid and movement, rather than laxatives.
- Relaxation therapies rather than night sedatives.
- Weight loss and salt reduction rather than medication for hypertension.
- Weight loss and diet rather than medication for diabetes mellitus.

Once these aspects are addressed, there are additional questions that can be asked before recommendations are made:
- Is medication really necessary?
- If not, what might be the alternatives for this person?
- If medication is needed, what type of administration methods would the person find easiest (e.g. are there swallowing difficulties)?
- What type of regime would be most appropriate (e.g. if the patient shops on Tuesdays and Thursdays, diuretics on alternative days would likely be preferable).
- If the patient has physical needs, how can the medication be prescribed so that it facilitates maximum independence (e.g. easy-open bottles can be requested for people with arthritic hands).
- Are there religious or cultural considerations (e.g. if a Muslim person wishes to fast for Ramadan, and this is imminent, it is preferable not to prescribe medications that need to be taken over a 24-hour period with food).

Helping an Older Person to Take Medicines According to the (Mutually) Agreed Regime

Assisting Understanding

Studies have shown that older people want to know more about their medicines. It is important to work with them as individuals, in terms of their pre-existing knowledge base, preferred ways of learning, individual pace of learning (Esposito, 1995). This could include names of drugs, dosages, times and methods of administration (e.g. that taken 'three times a day' means 8-hourly), side effects to watch for. Particular attention needs to be given to people:

- Whose first language is not English, or whose cultural or religious practices may be compromised by medication regimes.
- Who have difficulties with hearing, sight, speech, comprehension or information processing.
- Who have physical weakness or disability and are unable to take medication without help.

The nurse may want to offer consistent support for a period of time, and a series of short discussions about medications are likely to be more effective than one comprehensive session (Haynes *et al.* 1987).

A skilled nurse will recognise when a person is not ready to expend mental focus or energy on learning about what medications they should be taking. Times of anxiety, physical distress or fatigue are not appropriate for teaching about medication. The nurse can offer a 'first aid kit', reinforced by a clearly written 'action' sheet of each item that needs to be taken, until additional support is available or the nurse can visit again.

It is important that the person understands that the need for medication will not necessarily cease because they begin to feel better.

Assisting the Practicalities of Taking Medication

The simpler the regime, the more straightforward it will be to administer. Reducing the number of medications and

General considerations : what is the client/patient's:

1. ability to understand _____
_____

2. visual acuity & ability to read labels _____

3. hand/muscle coordination (to pour, uncap/cap bottle) _____

4. ability to swallow without difficulty _____

5. level of ADLs: independent ( ) needs help ( ) _____

6. life style patterns (alcohol, smoking, activity) _____
_____

7. beliefs and attitudes toward: _____
    self _____
    illness _____
    treatments _____
    prescribing physician or nurse _____
_____

8. living conditions: alone ( ) with others ( ) _____
    relationship with others _____
_____

9. ability to afford cost of any additional medications _____

Specific medication history

10. medications currently taking: (ALL prescribed and non-
    prescribed)

    prescribed   over-the-counter
    _____   for pain _____
    _____   constipation _____
    _____   sleep _____
    _____   vitamins _____
    _____   health food products _____

11. knowledge: (reason for taking drug) _____

    times and frequency of self medication _____
_____
_____

12. are medications shared with: family ( ) friends ( )
    if so who _____

13. ADR (adverse drug reaction(s)):
    has experienced ADR(s) yes ( ) no ( )
    if yes, how was it handled _____
_____
_____

14. incidence of over-use or under-use of medication:
    yes ( ) no ( ) describe _____
_____

15. storage:
    how is medication stored _____
    where stored _____
    reason kept that way _____

16. disposition of old drugs (how handled): _____

*if medications administered by a carer, the assessment should include his/her understanding

Figure 10.4 Medication assessment and history worksheet.

developing a schedule appropriate or compatible with the individual's lifestyle can help.

The person's ability to open containers, to read labels, to administer the medication (particularly with routes other than oral) and to recognise problems if they occur should be assessed. Self-administration of medications is ideal. The nurse can then observe, support, and intervene if or as necessary.

Memory aids such as a weekly calendar with pockets for medications indicating day, time and date, or a daily tear-off calendar, can assist. After the medication is taken, the date page is torn off. Larger calendars are helpful when multiple drugs must be taken; a tick can be placed in the date square each time a medication is taken. A variety of 'memory aids' are available.

Other ideas include colour coding, circling the hours on a clock face affixed to the container, or setting an alarm clock to remind the person when to take the medication. There are electronic pill containers that audibly let the person know when it is time to take his or her medication. These methods can be of tremendous assistance to the older person who is having difficulty managing medications. The use of cueing, for example linking daily events such as brushing teeth or dentures or watching a particular television programme, can also be useful (Hussey, 1991).

When medications are dispensed, the pharmacist should be informed if a patient might have difficult reading a small-print label. Alternative arrangements can be made. The use of Braille labelling for people who are severely visually impaired is also being developed.

Written Information

The relationship between supportive written information and increased knowledge has been well documented. In a study by Culbertson *et al.* (1988), 62% of patients preferred a combination of written and oral information and 45% indicated that information leaflets had altered their medication use.

As Miselli and Tognoni's (1990) work demonstrated, regardless of age, gender or educational level, patients prefer written information which is simple and straightforward. Some written information is written at a level which is not comprehended by the majority of people for whom it is intended (Estey *et al.* 1991; Meade and Smith, 1991). Written information should also be appropriate for people with visual difficulties, particularly bearing in mind the age-related changes in vision (*see* Chapter 12). **Box 10.8** offers guidance on taking medications at home.

Drug Administration

Professional Responsibilities

Nurses work within professional guidelines from the United Kingdom Central Council for Nursing, Midwifery and Health Visiting. Guidance of Standards for the Administration of Medicines was issued in 1992 and is likely to be revised within the current UKCC agenda.

Methods of Administration

Most medications are taken orally. Some tablets and capsules may be difficult for older people to swallow because of their size or because they stick to the buccal mucosa. In these circumstances, administration of a drug in liquid form is preferable and facilitates flexibility.

Crushing tablets or emptying the powder from capsules into fluid or food should not be done unless specified by the pharmaceutical company or approved by a pharmacist because it may interfere with the effectiveness of the drug or create problems in administration, as well as injure the mouth or GI tract.

Enteric coatings are used to protect the stomach against irritating substances or to protect certain drugs from breakdown by stomach acid. Some pharmaceutical companies coat the drug beads in extended-action capsules with different types of coatings to allow some of the medication to be released immediately and the remainder at predetermined intervals. Some tablets are made of an inert porous plastic matrix that is impregnated with the active drug. As the drug passes through the GI tract, it is slowly leached out and absorbed into the body, which is a timed-release effect. Coated beads, plastic matrix tablets, and layered tablets should not be crushed, since all the medication would be released at one time or inactivated by stomach acid. This is tantamount to administering higher doses of medication than prescribed or none at all. A particularly noteworthy example is slow-release potassium tablets which, if crushed, can lead to bowel wall injury, GI irritation, bleeding, obstruction and perforation.

It is important that adequate fluid is taken, particularly for older patients. Walker's study (1982) highlighted the dangers of oesophageal ulceration when insufficient fluid was

10.8 Taking Medicines at Home: Guidance for Older People

Ask the doctor or nurse the following:
- Name of medicine.
- Amount to take.
- Best time to take it.
- How often to take it.
- How to take it.
- How long to take it for.
- Reason for taking it.
- Most common side effects.
- Whether any foods or other drugs should or should not be taken with it.
- Take all the medicine prescribed unless the physician states otherwise. Stop taking the medicine and report symptoms to the physician immediately, should any new or unusual problems such as the following happen:
  Shortness of breath.
  Nausea, vomiting or diarrhoea.
  Sleepiness.
  Dizziness.
  Weakness.
  Skin rash.
  Fever.
- Never take a medicine prescribed for another person.
- Do not take any medicine more than 1 year old or past the expiry date on the container.
- Store medicines in a safe place, preferably the kitchen rather than the bathroom where moisture from bathing, especially showers, may affect the medicine.
- Do not keep medicines, especially sedatives or hypnotics, by your bedside because when you are sleepy, you may forget that you have already taken the medicine earlier.
- Do not place different medicines in the same container.
- Take a sufficient supply of all medicines in their individual containers when travelling away from home.
- Use a chart to keep track of medications.

ingested with tablets or capsules. Approximately half of the patients ingested less than 30 ml of fluid and were at high risk of oesophageal retention and damage. Walker recommends that at least 40 ml of fluid should be taken and 200 ml offered to the patient.

Preventing Toxicity

The nurse is a key person in the prevention of drug toxicity. As part of an interdisciplinary approach, the nurse works with the physician, pharmacist, dietitian and speech therapist, if appropriate, to teach, monitor and promote the actions necessary to prevent drugs from becoming toxic and to treat toxicity promptly should it occur.

Monitoring is the most effective way to prevent or minimise drug effects. The nurse's role includes knowledge of the characteristics indicative of toxicity and education of older people about drugs.

The advocacy role of the nurse includes awareness of the older person's overall functioning in order to influence the plan of treatment, clarify the treatment goals, and coordinate the activities of physician and other clinicians to keep them focused on the goals of the client and family.

Drug holidays are another intervention that may be used to decrease the potential of drug toxicity. A drug holiday is a planned omission of a specific drug or drugs for one or more days or weeks. The benefits of drug holidays include increased alertness of the individual, a decreased use of medication and subsequent reduction in overall medication cost, and easier scheduling of activities that can be restricted when certain medications are taken. For example, an individual who is taking a diuretic might not be able to leave home until noon for fear there will not be a toilet accessible or that they cannot hold their urine long enough to find a toilet. Although a drug holiday may be beneficial, questions arise regarding the length of time of a drug holiday. A variety of drugs taken by older people accumulate in body fat and take much longer to be depleted below therapeutic levels than other drugs. For those medications, a one or two day holiday may be ineffective. Perhaps, rather than a drug holiday, reducing the number of medications prescribed and implementing a drug holiday from specific medications would be more appropriate. Whatever the approach is, the nurse assumes a major assessment and intervention role (*see* **Box 10.9**).

THE PHARMACIST'S ROLE

Pharmacists have a valuable role in advising health professionals and older patients in addition to their traditional service of supplying medication. There are over 12,500 registered pharmacists in the UK with around six million visits made per day by the general public. Around one million of these visits will be related to medication enquiries either to have prescriptions dispensed or to seek advice. Their role in identifying and advising on drugs-related problems in care homes has also increased (Gammie and Luscombe, 1995; Taylor *et al.* 1995). Computer-based records can facilitate the ready access of pharmacists to patient's medication records should review be necessary, particularly across the primary and secondary care interface.

The NHS report *Primary Care: The Future* has suggested potential areas of service development for community pharmacists which are highly relevant in the care of older people. The document suggests greater liaison between pharmacists and general practitioners, pharmacist review and management of repeat prescriptions, and the monitoring of treatment. The Royal College of Physicians recommend that the community pharmacists' role in providing advice on therapy of minor illness, monitoring drug therapy and reviewing

10.9 Administration of Medications to Older People: Nursing Responsibilities

- Take a complete medication history including:
  - Past medications.
  - Present medications (prescription and OTC).
  - Allergies of all kinds.
- Patient's understanding of medications being taken (name, purpose, dosage, method, times).
- Space oral medications so that not more than one or two are taken at one time.
- Encourage patient to drink a little fluid before taking oral medications (to ease swallowing).
- Encourage the patient to drink at least 40 ml of fluid after taking medications (to assure that the medications have left the oesophagus and are in the stomach and to speed absorption of the medication).
- Be cautious about regular analgesics. Because of the delayed absorption and distribution and the half-life of the medication, there may be an adverse cumulative effect. Be observant for cumulative effects but do not leave the person in pain.
- If the patient has difficulty swallowing a large capsule or tablet, ask the physician to substitute a liquid medication if possible (cutting the tablet in half or crushing it and placing it in jam or fruit juice may distort the action of some medications, reduce the dose or cause choking or aspiration of particles of medication or jam).
- Teach alternatives to medications, such as the following:
- Proper diet instead of vitamins.
- Exercise instead of laxatives.
- Bedtime measures/activities instead of hypnotics.
- Decrease in weight, salt, fats, stress and smoking, and increased exercise instead of hypertensive agents (may need to check with the doctor).

repeat prescriptions in older people should be evaluated.

For many years, hospital pharmacists have had a major role advising on the selection and rational use of medication. More recently they have played a key role in providing the background information which has enabled decisions to be made regarding the inclusion of drugs in hospital formularies, and in developing specific guidelines for prescribing medication for older patients.

THE DOCTOR'S ROLE

The Royal College of Physicians offer recommendations to doctors (**Box 10.10**).

INFORMATION TECHNOLOGY (IT)

Computers are rapidly becoming an essential tool in monitoring drug use. Computers are now common in general practice since the Department of Health in England supported computerisation through the reimbursement system and introduced an accreditation system for computers in primary care. Information technology facilitates the monitoring, costing and rationalisation of prescribing and enhances the informational exchange between physicians and pharmacists in the surveillance of drug compatibilities. The Royal College of Physicians is recommending that IT should be developed for secondary care to provide drug information systems similar to primary care, e.g. prescribing analysis and cost (PACT), general practice research database (GPRD), and that the National Health Service network should be developed to allow easy transfer of patient and prescribing information between primary and secondary care.

The British National Formulary is now available in electronic form on CD-ROM and has direct links from each drug entry to interactions associated with that drug.

Patient held 'smart' cards, like credit cards, hold information of prescribing records and these are being developed in some areas.

DRUG USE IN CARE HOMES

There are particular considerations in the care home sector, housing the most vulnerable older people who need continuing care. Over 90% of older people living in continuing care receive medication. Polypharmacy is frequent and combinations of prescribed drugs may be inappropriate or hazardous (Adams *et al.*, 1987). Prescribing and dispensing patterns are varied and more than one doctor or more than one pharmacist may be involved in prescribing or dispensing within one home. There are particular concerns around sedation, and one study of private nursing homes in the UK found that nearly half the patients were prescribed major tranquillisers or benzodiazepines (McGrath and Jackson, 1996).

In homes where registered nurses (RN) dispense medications, their practice is governed by standards set by the United Kingdom Central Council for Nursing, Midwifery and Health Visiting. Registered nurses also have a professional responsibility to monitor medication effects and to report problems to the patient's doctor.

Under the Registered Homes Act 1984, however, in residential care homes, where there is no RN to supervise and monitor medication use, there may be particular problems. Studies show that the prevalence of chronic illness requiring multiple and long-term drug therapy is high (Gosney *et al.* 1991). Under the Registered Homes Act, the health care of people in residential homes remains the responsibility of the primary health-care team. Staff dealing with medications need adequate training and it is also important that policies and standards protect both residents and staff.

10.10 Recommendations to Doctors from the Royal College of Physicians

- Think carefully before prescribing. Make every effort to establish an accurate diagnosis. Consider whether drug treatment is appropriate, and review prescriptions at regular intervals.
- Prescribe with maximum knowledge about the patient. Take a thorough history of drugs taken including over-the-counter therapies, previous adverse drug reactions and social support to assist compliance. Where the patient's history appears incomplete, seek information from relatives, the general practitioner, primary care nurses and any other relevant source.
- Base your decisions on best available evidence. Understand the clinical pharmacology of the drug prescribed, especially the effects of ageing and disease on drug effects in older patients. In general, use as few drugs as possible and keep regimens simple.
- Monitor for the efficacy and side effects of medication. 'Start low and go slow'.
- Help the patient to make better use of their medication by giving clear information, reinforcing this with written information, use compliance aids.
- Agree responsibility for prescribing across the primary and secondary care interface.

The Royal College of Physicians (RCP) recommends that health and local authorities should develop national guidelines for the administration of medication in nursing and residential homes, including the monitoring of medications and particularly psychotropic drugs. The RCP is urging health and local authorities to liaise with managers of care homes to identify a lead geriatrician or general practitioner with expertise in the medical problems of older people in order to develop clinical standards, improve the prescribing and monitoring of medication and ensure appropriate training of nursing and other staff in observing patients for potential drug-related problems.

It also recommends that the medical and pharmaceutical advisers of the health authorities should have special training and knowledge of prescribing in older age. Where several doctors visit a home, the RCP recommends that one should be the 'lead' clinician and that he or she should have expertise in the medical and mental health care of frail older people. There should be a low threshold for referral for the opinion of a geriatrician or psychiatrist of old age, particularly if there is a need for the frequent or continued use of psychytropic medication. Medications should be reviewed regularly. Polypharmacy should be avoided and the need for sedatives or tranquillisers should be questioned.

Community pharmacists have an increasingly important and influential role to play for older people in care homes.

Pharmaceutical advice and services are provided to residential and nursing homes where pharmacists check the handling of drugs, records, stock levels and the security, particularly of controlled drugs (Gammie and Luscombe, 1995; Taylor *et al.* 1995). Although payment is made for providing services to care homes, there is no charge for a pharmacy providing advice or delivery service for older patients living at home.

Nurses in nursing homes obviously have the key role in administering and monitoring medications, as described above. Community nurses have a key role in monitoring and, as far as possible, supervising medication use in residential care homes.

Self-administration of medicines may present difficulties for care homes in providing storage facilities which the individual resident can easily access, but will not put other residents at risk. However, care home residents should be encouraged and facilitated to administer their own medications whenever possible.

NURSE PRESCRIBING

The Prescription of Medicinal Products by the Nurses Act 1992 permits nurses with appropriate expertise in areas such as wound and stoma care to prescribe specific items in order to offer a complete nursing service. Nurse prescribing could improve the management of chronic conditions in older people who live at home. *see* **Figure 10.4** for one form of a medication assessment tool.

COMPLEMENTARY AND ALTERNATIVE THERAPIES

The use of complementary or alternative therapies is gaining popularity and their use by nurses is becoming more widespread. The United Kingdom Central Council for Nursing, Midwifery and Health Visiting (UKCC) (1996) stresses the importance of ensuring that the use of these therapies is always in the best interests and safety of patients. They emphasise that the registered practitioner must be convinced of the relevance of the therapy being used and must be able to justify using it in a particular circumstance, especially when this is part of professional practice. It should also be part of professional teamwork to discuss the use of complementary therapies with medical and other members of the team caring for the particular patient.

The UKCC also reminds practitioners that they are personally accountable for their practice and, should a complaint be made against them, the UKCC can call them to account for any activities carried out outside conventional practice.

SUMMARY

Medication use by older people is a high priority area of health care. Advances in recent years offer enormous potential for the enhancement of the lives and health of older individuals but, when medicines are not used optimally, the potential for damage to health is similarly enormous. The financial expenditure on prescriptions to older people has increased markedly over the last 10 years and, largely through the use of information technology, detailed information is now readily available on which doctors can base their prescribing decisions. The role of the pharmacist in offering over-the-counter advice, working closely with doctors in both community and hospital, advising and monitoring in care homes, and developing formularies, has developed considerably in recent years. This chapter has demonstrated that nurses have a key role in working with older people and other members of the health-care team in order to ensure the optimum use of medications by older people. Nurses must ensure that their understanding of the distinct considerations with medication use in older age, and specifically the altered pharmacokinetics and pharmacodynamics, is sound and up-to-date. Nurses have a particular role in assessing the medication needs of older people, in preventing unnecessary medication use by lifestyle changes or nursing measures. They have a vital contribution to make to the education and ongoing support of older people who take medications, and in recognising early when problems arise. Optimal medication use not only uses resources cost-effectively, it can considerably enhance the health, functioning and quality of life of the majority of older people.

KEY POINTS

- The range of medications has increased considerably within the last 10–20 years and many more preparations are now available 'over-the-counter'.
- Older people are major beneficiaries of optimal medication use, receiving approximately 48% of all prescriptions and more prescriptions per person than any other group, mainly for long-term medications.
- There are particular considerations when prescribing for older people including specialist knowledge, evidence-based practice and 'rationing' decisions. Nurses are having an important and potentially increasing influence on prescribing decisions.
- Nurses have a key role in recognising when an older person might need treatment and in suggesting lifestyle changes or nursing measures which can avoid the need for medications.
- Administering, monitoring and reporting adverse reactions to medications is a fundamental aspect of the nursing role.
- Nurses can considerably help older people to understand the medications they have been prescribed and to make positive choices about taking them.
- Pharmacists in both the hospital and community, offer valuable advice, support and monitoring services.
- Developments in the use of information technology have considerably assisted towards optimal drug use.
- There are special considerations for the use of medications in care homes.
- Nurses who use complementary therapies must be clear about their appropriateness for each individual and are accountable for their practice.

AREAS AND ACTIVITIES FOR STUDY AND REFLECTION

- How do you assess older patients who might be at risk of adverse drug reactions? What do you look for and how do you obtain the information needed to undertake a full assessment?
- How are older people given information about their medications and who tends to do this?
- What actions do nursing staff in your area undertake in order to ensure that older people can and do take their medications according to the prescribed regime?
- What guidelines or protocols exist in your area regarding medications? Are they comprehensive and effective and, if not, how could they be improved?
- How much do you understand about altered pharmacokinetics and pharmacodynamics in older age?
- What is the role of the pharmacist in your area? Could the pharmacist's knowledge be used more effectively, for example in reviewing medication administration, storage or reordering protocols?
- How could information technology be used in your area in order to increase access to medication records?
- If complementary therapies are used in your area, what training have the nurses undergone? How are patient assessments made? Are they aware of their responsibilities and accountability within the United Kingdom Central Council for Nursing, Midwifery and Health Visiting regulations?

REFERENCES

Adams KRH, Al Hamonz S, Edund E, Tallis RC. Inappropriate prescribing in the elderly. *J Roy Coll Phys* 1987, 21:39–41.

Audit Commission Health and Personal Social services Report, No. 1. London: HMSO, 1994.

Beard K, Bulpitt C, Mascie-taylor *et al.* Management of elderly patients with sustained hypertension. *Br Med J* 1992, 302:412–416.

British Thoracic Society. COPD Guidelines. *Thorax* 1997, 52 (Suppl):1–32.

Burns JMA, Sneddon I, Lovell M. Elderly patients and their medication: a post-discharge follow-up study. *Age Ageing* 1992, 21:178–181.

Cargill JM. Medication compliance in elderly people: influencing variables and interventions. *J Adv Nurs* 1992, 17:422–426.

Col N, Fanale JE, Kronholm P. The role of medication noncompliance and adverse drug reactions in hospitalization of older people. *Arch Intern Med* 1990, 150:1.

Coomber R, Cubbin J, Davison N, Pearson P. *Nursing skill mix review*. Newcastle: Newcastle Community Health, 1992.

Culbertson VL, Arthur TG, Rhodes PJ, Rhodes RS. Consumer preferences for verbal and written medication information. *Drug Intelligence and Clinical Pharmacy* 1988, 22:533–538.

Davis S. Self -administration of medicines. *Nurs Stand* 1991, 5:29–31.

Department of Health. Statistical Bulletin. *Statistics of prescriptions dispensed in the community: England 1986 to 1996*. London: HMSO, 1997.

Duggan S, Eccles M, Ford GA. Audit of prescribing in 65–80 year-old patients in primary care practices in Northern Region 1996 (unpublished observations) cited in RCP. *Medications for older people, 2nd edition*. London: Royal College of Physicians, 1997.

Esposito L. The effects of medication education on adherence to medication regimes in an elderly population. *J Adv Nurs* 1995, 21:935–943.

Estey A, Musseau A, Keehn L. Comprehension levels of patients reading health information. *Patient Education and Counselling* 1991, 18:165–169.

Gammie SM, Luscombe DK. Pharmaceutical care of the elderly: continuing education. *Pharm J* 1995, 254:578–582.

Gosney M, Tallis RC. Prescription of contraindicated and interacting drugs: elderly patients admitted to hospital. *Lancet* 1984, 564.

Gosney M, Tallis RC, Edmond E. The burden of chronic illness in local authority residential homes for the elderly. *Health Trends* 1991, 22:153–158.

Haynes RB, Wang E, Gomez MD. A critical review of interventions to improve compliance with prescribed medications. *Patient Educ Counsel* 1987, 10:155.

Haynes RB, McKibbon KA, Kanani R. Interventions to assist patients to follow prescriptions for medications. In: Bero L, Grilli R, Grimshaw J, Oxman, eds. *A collaboration on effective professional practice module of The Cochrane Database of Systematic Reviews* [updated 03 March 1997]. Available in The Cochrane Library [database on disk and CD-ROM]. The Cochrane Collaboration; Issue 2, Update Software; 1997. Updated quarterly.

Hussey LC. Overcoming the clinical barriers of low literacy and medication noncompliance among older people. *J Gerontol Nurs* 1991, 17:27.

Knoben JE, Anderson PO. *Handbook of clinical data*, 6th edition. Hamilton: Drug Intelligence Publications, 1988.

Lamy PP. Drug interactions and older people. *J Gerontol Nurs* 1986, 12:36.

Leirer VO, Morrow DG, Tanke ED *et al.* Nonadherence: its assessment and medical reminding by voice mail. *Gerontologist* 1991, 31:514.

Lewis R, Crossland M. Organisation of a medications group for older patients with mental illness. *Geriatr Nurs* 1992, 13:187–191.

Long JW. *Essential guide to prescription drugs*. New York: Harper Collins, 1991.

Mahdy HA, Seymour DG. How much can elderly patients tell us about their medications? *Postgrad Med J* 1990, 66:116–121.

McGrath AM, Jackson GA. Survey of neuroleptic prescribing in residents of nursing homes in Glasgow. *Br Med J* 1996, 312:611–612.

McElnay JC, Dickson FC. Purchases from community pharmacies of OTC medicines by elderly patients. *Pharm J* 1994, 253:15.

Meade C, Smith CF. Readability formulas: caution and criteria. *Patient Educ Counsel*1991, 17:153–158.

Miselli M, Tognoni G. What information for the patient? Large scale pilot study on experimental package inserts giving information on prescribed and over the counter drugs. *Br Med J* 1990, 301:1261–1265.

MRC. *The health of the UK's elderly people*. London: Medical Research Council, 1994

Nolan L, O'Malley K. Adverse drug reactions in older people. *Br J Hosp Med* 1989, 41:446.

Palmieri DT. Clearing up confusion: adverse effects of medications in the elderly. *J Gerontol Nurs* 1991, 17(10): 32.

Pendleton D. Knowledge and compliance – not linked after all? *Pharm J* 1992 (February):196.

Proprietary Association of Great Britain. *Annual report*, London: Proprietary Association of Great Britain, 1997.

Quilligan S. Tablets to take away: Why some old people fail to comply with their medication. *Professional Nurse* 1990, (August):568.

RCP. *Medication for older people, 2nd edition*, London: Royal College of Physicians, 1997.

Roberts SJ, Bateman DH. The use of nitrates, calcium channel beta-blockers and ACE inhibitors in primary care in the Northern Region: a pharmacoepidemiology study. *Br Jr Clin Pharmacol* 1994, 38:489–497.

Ryan A, Jacques I. Medication compliance in older people. *Elderly Care* 1997, 9:16.

Shaughnessy AF. Common drug interactions in the elderly. *Emerg Med* 1992, 24:21.

Steele J, Bettesworth L, Ruzicki D. Uses of survey information to develop a hospital-based medication teaching programme. *Patient Educ Counsel* 1986, 86:40.

Taylor B, Rihal D, Iles C. Nursing homes: An inspector calls or a pharmacist visits. *Pharm J* 1995, 254:367.

UKCC. *Guidelines for professional practice*, London: United Kingdom Central Council for Nursing, Midwifery and Health Visiting, 1996.

Wade B, Bowling A. Appropriate use of drugs by elderly people. *J Adv Nurs* 1986, 11:47–55.

Walker R. A study of the fluid intake with tablets and capsules in geriatric patients. *Br J Pharm Prac* 1982, (December):6–7.

Safety and security needs

11 Mobility
Jane Slack

LEARNING OUTCOMES

After studying this chapter you will be able to:

- Describe the age-related changes in bones, joints and muscles that may predispose the older person to falls and accidents.
- Describe the effects of ageing on mobility.
- Describe the disease processes that affect mobility in older people.
- Discuss the effects of immobility on general function.
- Discuss the risk factors for immobility.
- Discuss measures to prevent falls and identify those at high risk.
- Discuss the nurse's role in maintaining mobility.

INTRODUCTION

Mobility is the capacity for moving within an area, be that a room, a chair or a bed, or from one area to another. Throughout life, moving about is a way of interacting with the environment and with others. Movement remains a significant means of personal contact, exploration, sensation, pleasure and control. Movement is integral to the attainment of all levels of need as conceived by Maslow.

Older people have identified their needs to include maintaining pride, dignity, social contacts and activity. All of these are facilitated by mobility. Thus, in terms of Maslow's hierarchy and the needs identified by older people, maintaining mobility is an extremely important issue.

In older age, and particularly advanced older age, a person tends to move more slowly and more purposefully, and often with more forethought and caution. This may result from many factors including societal perceptions and expectations of older people, older people's reduced confidence in a specific environment or their reduced confidence in the reliability of their own functional capacity. Images of how older people move around include the road sign depicting stooped people holding a walking stick. However, reduced mobility is not an inevitable consequence of growing older. Physical decline is likely to be a combination of the consequences of societal expectations that older people should 'take things easy' and some age-related detraining. It has been suggested that only 26% of men and 17% of women over the age of 50 participate in sufficient physical activity to benefit their health (Young *et al.* 1997).

Although growing older does not mean an inevitable slide towards functional decline, it does result in changes in anatomical, physiological and psychological functions that may impose impairments on individuals. These impairments may lead to disabilities that represent restrictions in the manner or range of activities considered normal within the context of the physical and social environment (Pendergast *et al.* 1993). For many older people, these mobility difficulties have been a major factor in determining their ability to live independently, or within a care setting. Yet, even for the more able bodied older person living at home, difficulties with walking outside, accessing transport, standing to do the cooking or cleaning; or washing and dressing can increasingly cause problems (Farquhar *et al.* 1993).

EFFECTS OF AGEING ON MOBILITY

These physiological changes can affect older people to different degrees, such as disturbance of gait, decrease in hand-grip strength, and vision. Nurses must not overlook the effect of age-related changes in vision on an individual's ability to move freely with confidence.

Range of motion or movement (ROM) refers to the range through which a joint can move or be moved, and is measured in degrees of a circle. A range of motion may become limited or unequal due to joint stiffness, swelling or pain. ROM exercises are designed to restore motion in a joint, or to keep joints functioning normally. These exercises may be performed by the person themselves, or be passive, and be performed by the nurse or therapist who moves the body part through the possible range of movement.

Body alignment refers to the positioning of the joints, tendons, ligaments and muscles while standing, lying and sitting. The nurse needs to look at how the older person stands,

11.1 Gait Disorders

Ataxia
- Wide-based gait with frequent side stepping.

Normal pressure hydrocephalus
- Step height reduced.
- Shuffling gait as if feet stuck to floor.
- Unsteady speed.
- Ataxia.

Parkinson's disease
- Stooped posture.
- Short rapid shuffling gait.
- Uncontrollable propulsion or retropulsion.
- 'Freeze' walk, when feet abruptly halt while body continues to move forward.

Spondylotic cervical myelopathy
- Spastic, shuffling gait.
- Deep tendon reflexes below level of compression increase muscle tone.
- Sometimes nonspecific, e.g. clumsy feet, legs gave way.

'Senile' gait
- Associated with stooped posture, hip and knee flexion, diminished arm swing, stiffness in turning.
- Broad based, small steps with poor gait intention.

Hemiplegia
- Poor arm and leg swing.
- Affected limb does not bend at knee.
- Ankle fixed and inverted as leg swings in wide circle.
- Foot tends to drag.

Osteomalacia
- Ill-defined skeletal pain.
- Pain on weight bearing.
- Unstable waddling gait.

whether they are off balance. Ageing produces changes in muscles and joints, particularly to the back and legs, while strength and flexibility decrease markedly.

Gait refers to the manner or style of walking. Normal gait involves the vestibular system of balance, proprioception (sensitivity to body in motion), neurophysiological integrity and vision. Some normal gait changes in later life include a narrow standing base, wider swaying when walking, the appearance of a 'waddle', bowing of legs and less muscular control of the lower extremities. Steps taken are shorter, and with a decreased stepping motion. These changes are less pronounced in those who remain active and at a desirable weight.

The nurse must observe how the older person walks: is their gait shuffling, do they lift the foot off the floor adequately, is it hesitant or slower than normal, does it become slower the further they walk. **Box 11.1** describes gait disorders and **Box 11.2** gait description and assessment. Exercise or activity tolerance also changes. Significant decreases in metabolism, endurance and contraction velocity and muscle strength occur in the older person leading to loss of function. Postural instability increases, often accompanied by dizziness, and is exacerbated by some medications. It is thought that about 15% of older people are particularly susceptible to orthostatic hypertension.

The musculoskeletal tissue changes that affect the body with time include changes to the ligaments and soft tissue structures that hold the bones of the foot in alignment. Connective tissue changes are noticeable in the skin, and many older people have problems with dry skin, which causes the foot to be itchy. Combined with a diminished circulation this can lead to the development of cracks and fissures, culminating in a serious bacterial infection.

MOBILITY AND THE DEPENDENCY CYCLE

Nurses work with older people with varying levels of dependency in many different settings. Dependency does not always occur when physical ability is lost, it may be fostered by the nurse who is unable to facilitate the person in carrying out the activity themselves, such as walking to the bathroom rather than being pushed in a chair. Many nurses carry out tasks for the older person using the rationale that it helps them, it's too difficult a task or it is quicker for the nurse to do it. This dependency may be fostered as easily in the patient's own home as in an institutional setting such as hospital or nursing home. It is suggested that nurses cause dependency simply by using a task-oriented care system rather than a patient-centred model such as primary nursing (Miller, 1985).

This can be demonstrated by looking at the negative effect a nurse can have on an older person by reinforcing dependency. An elderly man known to suffer from Parkinson's disease is admitted to hospital for assessment of his reduced mobility, mental disorientation, dehydration and a urinary tract infection. He has been living alone at home, and until admission, has been able to live independently. He is placed in the centre of noise and activity in the ward quite a distance from the toilets. The external environmental stimuli exacerbate his disorientation, and increase his continence problem, as he is unable to orientate himself to reach the toilet in time. A commode is placed by his bed, and he is discouraged from walking around the ward on his own. As a result, he sits for longer periods during the day, becomes more withdrawn and begins to lose interest in his surroundings. His self-esteem becomes lowered, due to his increased incontinence and decreased mobility. As he is moving less, his joints become stiffer. This makes walking more difficult, so he moves less. The patient's sleep pattern becomes disturbed due to dozing, and results in a state of confusion. His mood sinks

11.2 Gait Description and Assessment

Pain in back and lower limbs
- Antalgic gait.
- Short steps flexed towards affected side.

Contracture or ankylosis
- Short-leg gait.
- Wide outward swing of affected side.
- Unaffected knee flexed.
- Body bent forward.

Foot deformities
- Loss of spring and rhythm in step.
- Toes inward or outward bilaterally or unilaterally.

Footdrop
- Foot slap heard due to knee raised higher than usual.
- Gluteus medius weakness
- Waddle gait.
- Drop and lag in swing phase of unaffected side (seen in osteomalacia and senile gait in women).

Stroke
- Wide, open, flinging foot on affected side.
- Uncoordinated.

Cerebroarteriosclerosis
- Bilateral involvement manifested by extremely short steps.

Parkinsonism
- Festinating gait; short, hurried, often on tiptoe.
- Rigid, tremorous, slow gait, tends toward retropulsion, mincing.

État lacunaire
- Similar to Parkinson's gait.
- Irregular footsteps.

Dementia
- Slow, shuffling apraxic, short steps.

Peripheral neuropathy
- Difficulty lifting feet.
- Stumbles easily.

Subdural haematoma
- Ataxic.
- Prominent feature is gait disturbance.

Cerebellar ataxia
- Staggering.
- Unsteady, irregular wide-based gait.
- Inappropriate foot placement.

Vitamin B$_{12}$ deficiency
- Paraesthesias.
- Unsteadiness.
- Foot dragging.

Endocrine disorders
- Gait ataxia, particularly with hypothyroidism.

Medications
- Ataxia.
- Parkinsonian gait.
- Imbalance.

as he feels he has no value, with a resultant deterioration in appetite. As his nutritional status decreases, his sleep pattern becomes more disturbed, mobility decreases, immobility increases, and dependency level increases. This is illustrated in **Figure 11.1** – the dependency cycle.

Physical and psychological activity assists the older person to remain at their potential. It encourages feelings of value and motivation, and helps the older person retain a sense of dignity, despite the restrictions imposed upon them by disease or ageing.

THE NURSE'S ROLE IN MAINTAINING MOBILITY

Nurses working with older people, both in primary and secondary care, are often faced with the long-term, damaging effects of chronic illness. Practising at different levels in a variety of clinical settings, nurses have a major role in the management of symptoms and ensuring optimum mobility for the older person. The term 'reduced mobility' is often used to loosely describe a whole range of problems that the individual may be experiencing. They may have difficulty turning over in bed, or be unable to walk safely carrying a plate of food. The definition and description of the older person's mobility must be specific and based on accurate observation and assessment.

Good practice dictates that, wherever possible, the assessment should include the physiotherapist and occupational therapist team members and encompass a review of medication as well as the older person's physical ability. The physical assessment must include vision, blood pressure, range of motion, muscle strength, balance, posture, neurological and cognitive assessment, and examination of the foot.

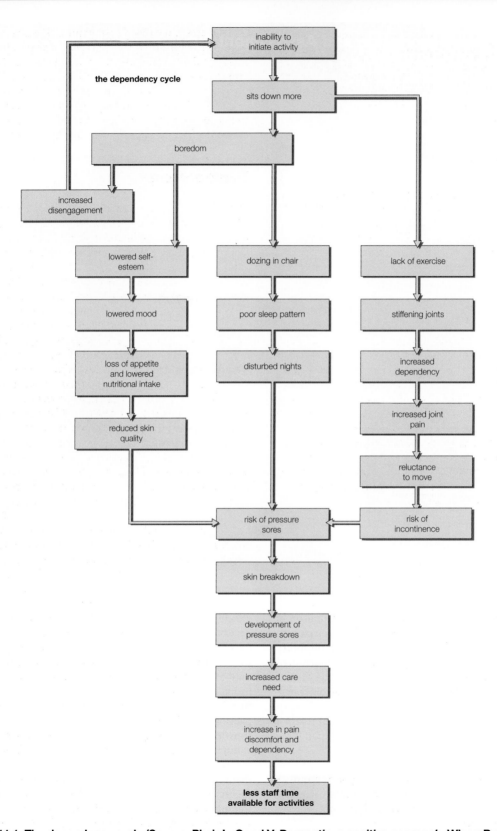

Figure 11.1 The dependency cycle (Source: Phair L, Good V. *Dementia: a positive approach*. Whurr Publications 1997).

COMMON DISEASE PROCESSES AFFECTING MOBILITY IN OLDER PEOPLE

Figure 11.2 shows some common conditions affecting mobility (Cohen, 1984).

Gait Disorders

Gait disorders make one vulnerable to tripping and falling. In addition, they impede activity and increase anxiety in an older person who is aware of instability in their gait. A mnemonic device for remembering the common causes of gait disorders is CANE (cardiovascular, arthritic, neurosensory and aetiology unknown).

Arthritic Conditions

Osteoarthrosis or chronic arthritis and rheumatoid arthritis are acknowledged to be a major cause of impaired mobility in older people. Arthritis is characterised by degenerative changes particularly to the weight bearing joints of the hip, knee or foot and is the most common cause of instability. Arthritis of the knee may result in ligamentous weakness and instability causing legs to give way or collapse. Rheumatoid arthritis is a chronic disease of unknown aetiology, characterised by polyarthritis affecting mainly the smaller peripheral joints, accompanied by general ill health and resulting in varying degrees of ankylosis, disabling joint deformities, and associated muscle wasting.

Hemiplegia

For many older people, the consequences of a cerebral vascular accident (CVA), or stroke, on their ability to move and function independently are profound. Some individuals may be left completely immobile, unable to initiate any voluntary activity, with the complete loss of independence, while others can continue to function independently with only moderate mobility problems. A hemiplegic gait is characterised by poor arm and leg swing. The affected limb does not bend at the knee, ankle remains fixed and inverted, as the leg swings round in a wide circle.

Other Causes

Muscle weakness is often experienced in hyperthyroidism and hypothyroidism, hypokalaemia, hyperparathyroidism, osteomalacia, hypophosphataemia, and in some cases is brought about by various drug therapies.

Diabetes, alcoholism and vitamin B deficiencies may cause neurological damage and resultant gait problems. Vestibular dysfunction causes unsteadiness in walking and listing to one side or another when eyes are closed. The individual cannot focus well on a fixed target while moving or on a moving object while standing still. Older people suffering from diabetes, and individuals on certain medications may experience dizziness, unsteadiness and light-headedness.

Osteoporosis

Osteoporosis is a common disease that is often associated with pain, disability and death. Osteoporosis is symptomless until it produces complications such as fractures or spinal deformities, thus impinging on mobility. It becomes more common with advancing age, so that 70% of women in the UK aged 80 years or over have osteoporosis, and 60% of this group have experienced one or more fractures (Royal College of Physicians, 1996). It is estimated that osteoporosis results in approximately 60,000 hip fractures per year in the UK, 90% of which are in people of 50 years of age, and 80% of which are in women (Department of Health, 1994).

The lack of mobility, pain, loss of independence, loss of self-esteem and the personal and financial burden it places on the individual and their carers are incalculable. The common perception of both the general public, and indeed many health professionals, is that osteoporosis is untreatable, and, therefore, a normal, expected, process of ageing. It is accepted that older women lose height and develop stooped posture as they become older. However, osteoporosis is a preventable and treatable disease that can be objectively diagnosed at an early stage, before fractures occur, by the measurement of bone mass.

The World Health Organisation defines osteoporosis as 'a disease characterised by low bone mass and microarchitectural deterioration of bone tissue, leading to enhanced bone fragility and a consequent increase in fracture risk'. The health of the skeleton is maintained by the continuous processes of bone removal (resorption) and bone replacement (formation). These normally remain in balance, but imbalance between resorption and formation over a period of time results in osteoporosis. Bone mass at any age is determined by the peak bone mass achieved during growth and adolescence, the age at which bone loss starts and the rate at which it proceeds.

The categories of the disease are defined in terms of bone mass density (BMD):

(1) Normal – a value for BMD or bone mineral content (BMC) within 1 SD of the young adult reference mean.

(2) Low Bone Mass (osteopaenia) – a value for BMD or BMC more than 1 SD below the young adult reference mean but less than 2.5 SD below this value.

(3) Osteoporosis – a value for BMD or BMC 2.5 SD or more below the young adult mean.

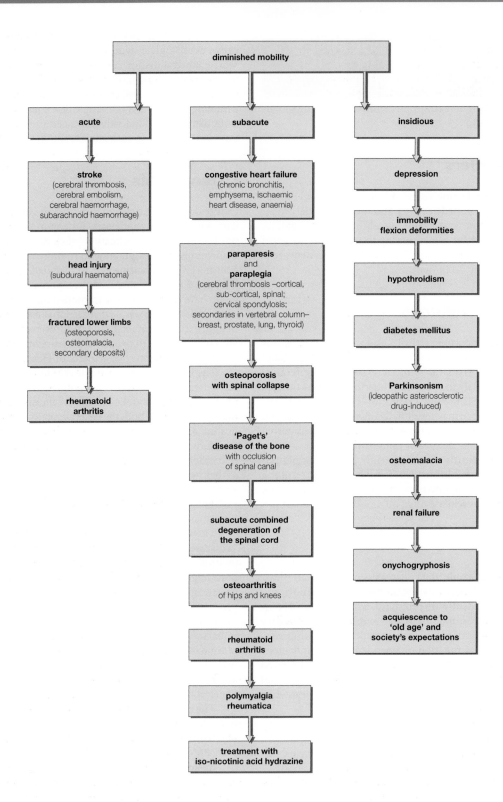

Figure 11.2 Common conditions affecting mobility. (Source: Cohen C. Diminished mobility is never inevitable. *Geriatrics* **1984(October):22.)**

Osteoporosis can result from:

- Prolonged steroid therapy and other medications, such as thyroxin, heparin, tetracycline, frusemide, anticonvulsants and aluminum-containing antacids.
- Endocrine disorders, notably Cushing's syndrome, hyperparathyroidism, hyperthyroidism, premature menopause and hyperadrenocorticism.
- Gastrointestinal disorders, such as malabsorption syndrome, peptic ulcer, lactase deficiency and subtotal gastrectomy.
- Infection, injury and synovitis, which may cause localised bone loss in affected areas.

Successful management of osteoporosis requires a comprehensive and flexible management programme, with patients becoming 'bone aware' and able to contribute to their own 'bone health'. The two main aims of management, using a combination of dietary advice and medical treatment are to build bone and to prevent fractures occurring (*see* Chapter 6 for further discussion of dietary aspects).

Over recent years, there has been relatively good progress in understanding the use of drug interventions in the management of osteoporosis, such as hormone replacement therapy, and how drugs such as biphosphonates and calcitonin can affect the bone metabolism, thus reducing the incidence of fractures.

Exercise

Recent research indicates that the promotion of exercise through brisk walking advice given by nursing staff may have a small, but clinically important, impact on bone mineral density, but that it is associated with an increased risk of falls. Further work is needed to evaluate the best means of safely achieving increased activity levels in different groups, such as older women and those at high risk of fractures (Ebrahim *et al.* 1997).

The Nurse's Role

The major symptom for older people suffering from osteoporotic fractures and vertebral deformities that affects the older person's ability to mobilise is pain. It is crucial to provide adequate pain relief to allow mobility to continue, thus preventing further bone loss and loss of coordination. The nurse has an important role to play in the assessment of pain using pain charts and in the education of the older person about medication in order to ensure compliance (*see* Chapter 10 for further discussion of medication 'compliance').

Although the nurse does not prescribe medication, he or she may aid compliance by clear and simple explanations on the commencement of therapy and ongoing monitoring during the treatment period. It is not uncommon for the older person to presume that treatment will result in pain control, and therefore it is vital that the nurse explains the need to continue with appropriate analgesia. The nurse has the knowledge to monitor the side effects of analgesia, such as constipation, confusion and loss of balance, which will also impinge on the ability to mobilise (*see* Chapter 9 for further discussion of pain control).

The nurse is able to access other members of the multi-disciplinary team to ensure the older person's potential is reached and maintained. The physiotherapist can participate in the management of osteoporosis in older people by assessing pain, muscle power, mobility function and other measures of quality of life. Approaches such as exercise, hydrotherapy, relaxation techniques and transcutaneous electrical nerve stimulation (TENS) may also be considered. Individuals who have experienced these therapies support their use, but unfortunately to date there have been few evaluations of their effectiveness.

There are a number of clinical triggers that should lead the nurse to the recognition of this condition. Nurses working in accident and emergency departments, practice nurses and community nurses are all in key areas where nursing assessment combined with routine health checks may reveal osteoporosis is present. An older person presenting with a fracture following minimal or no trauma, and back pain, particularly associated with height loss and kyphosis, should always be referred for further medical investigation.

The psychological effects of pain, disability, loss of height and poor self image can lead to severe depression. The older person who has suffered an osteoporotic fracture can become frightened of falling or of being knocked, which will increase their reluctance to mobilise or venture outdoors, and thus increase their social isolation. The nurse is in a key position to access both health and social services, such as day care, meals-on-wheels and community dietitian home care in order to restore feelings of self-worth and reduce the negative psychological effects of this disease process.

Parkinson's Disease (PD)

PD is an ageing-related neurodegenerative disease associated with difficulty of movement that is becoming more common in our ageing society. PD affects about 120,000 people in the UK. Around two-thirds of patients suffering from this debilitating disease are over 70 years of age, and at least half are severely disabled.

The three main features of this movement disorder are slowed or reduced voluntary movement, rigidity or stiffness of muscles, and tremor. Loss of motor skills and expression, difficulty in swallowing and characteristically small handwriting are also major features. Cognitive problems may include short-term memory loss, depression and hallucinations. Older patients with PD are more likely to complain initially about tremor, bilateral signs and difficulty in walking. **Figure 11.3** shows the typical stance of a person with Parkinson's disease (Pentland, 1988).

The terms hypokinesis and bradykinesis are used synonymously when describing the effect on movement experienced by a sufferer of PD; a delay in initiation of movement, slowness, poverty and imprecision of the movement and reduction in spontaneous movement overall.

Akinesia describes the absence of movement or 'off' or freezing. The individual experiences difficulty walking through doorways and along corridors. The nurse needs to be aware of what strategies to employ to reinitiate movement when this occurs, such as placing a stick on the floor for the patient to step over, or to verbally prompt the individual. **Figure 11.4** illustrates stages for correcting the freezing stance of PD.

There is a wide variability in how the symptoms present to each individual person. Some will have difficulty in commencing an activity, such as getting up from a chair, beginning to walk or rolling over in bed, while others will be very slow, restricted or clumsy in movements, and will be unable to complete the activity. In some individuals, their gait

disturbance is characterised by an involuntary hastening of walking, known as festination. The individual is unable to maintain their heel on the floor, leans forward and moves into a run rather than walking.

Tremor is the symptom most commonly associated with this illness, and can be a major factor in the older person becoming withdrawn from social life. It is often worse at rest, and may be aggravated by stress or tension. It can often disappear in sleep. In most cases, it is lessened by purposeful movement and so may not interfere with physical function.

Rigidity describes the stiffness of muscles on examination, affecting all striated muscle, and it is this that leads to the stooped flexed posture typical of advanced parkinsonism. It can be felt either as a fairly even stiffness, likened to bending a lead pipe, called lead pipe rigidity or as a regularly interrupted resistance called cog wheel rigidity.

One of the most intractable functional difficulties experienced is that of rolling over in bed. When rolling over in bed the uppermost hip may not be flexed enough to pull the lower trunk into side lying, thus preventing the arms and upper trunk from helping to complete the movement. Physiotherapy can assist the individual and their carer to perform this movement, as well as the use of gliding sheets, or nylon sheets, that slide, thus aiding the manoeuvre.

PD is an important cause of falls and reduced mobility in older people. Many of the most severely affected patients have frequent falls, the main cause of which is postural instability. A high proportion of these falls result in hip fractures, possibly due to a combination of abnormal gait and a tendency to fall backwards or to the side (Taggart and Crawford, 1995). The typical shuffling, stumbling gait experienced by sufferers also predisposes to falls.

Figure 11.3 The typical stance of the Parkinson's disease sufferer, with rounded shoulders and bent limbs (Source: Pentland B. The management of Parkinson's disease. *Geriatr Nurs Home Care* 1988(January):133).

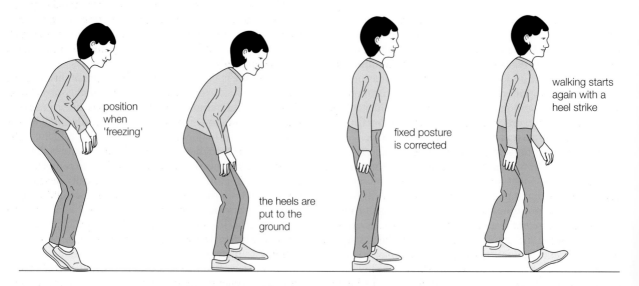

Figure 11.4 Stages for correcting the freezing stance of a Parkinson's disease patient.

Treatments for Parkinson's Disease

The principal lesion in PD is the degeneration of the nigrostriatal pathways in which the dopamine is the neurotransmitter. This leads to a depletion of striatal dopamine and treatment is aimed at correcting this.

The main drug of choice in managing the symptoms of PD, which primarily affect mobility, is levadopa, a precursor of dopamine, although it has no effect on the natural progression of the disease. Current first-line treatments combine levadopa with a dopa-decarboxylase inhibitor, such as benserazide. This helps block one set of enzymes and so improve the availability of levadopa in the brain. Many patients receiving continuous levadopa treatment develop response fluctuations or dyskinesia, which can become as disabling as their PD. The patient is often faced with a dilemma, whether to continue with medication despite the gross involuntary movements that the drug causes, in order for them to be able to carry out any activities of daily living, or to choose to stop and be relieved of the side effects, but be unable to move independently.

Further problems often occur with long-term drug therapy relating to the fluctuating level of effectiveness. As the drugs wear off, the duration of effect of each dose appears to get shorter and shorter, while in the on–off syndrome the person rapidly alternates between being 'on' when he is mobile, and 'off' when immobile. This on–off effect can have devastating impact on the individual, and it is crucial that both the sufferer and formal and informal carers understand the nature of the disease, as well as the aims of the treatment. As each individual responds differently to the medication regimes, the timescale of effectiveness of these drugs are extremely variable.

Catechol-O-methyltransferase (COMT) inhibitors help to block COMT so enhancing the efficacy of levadopa, thus enabling a reduced dose with a significant decrease in side effects.

Seligiline inhibits monoamine oxidase B, which metabolises dopamine. It is often used as an adjunct to levadopa to reduce end-of-dose effects. However, a recent study has raised serious doubts about its efficacy and the possibility that it may be associated with excess mortality (Fogarty, 1997).

Dopamine agonists act by stimulating dopamine receptors and generally have a longer duration than levadopa. Common agonists are Apomorphine, Pergolide, Ropinorole, Cabergoline, Lisuride and Bromocriptine. Apomorphine is mainly used for reversing disabling and unpredictable 'off' periods. It can only be given by subcutaneous injection by intermittent or continuous infusion. It is a quick acting, short duration therapy commonly referred to as 'rescue therapy'.

Anticholinergic agents lessen the effects of acetylcholine, but are associated with unpleasant side effects, such as dry mouth, confusion and urinary retention. Anticholinergic agents are not recommended for people over the age of 50 years.

Surgical intervention is also an option. Pallidotomy is sometimes used in late stage PD patients for severe dyskinesia, for whom drug therapy has become ineffective. A small number of hospitals in the UK perform the operation, although there are issues regarding funding from health authorities. The operation is carried out with the patient awake in the 'off' state after overnight drug withdrawal. A sterotactic frame is attached to the patient's head in theatre and a CT scan is performed, under a short-acting anaesthetic. A small hole is made in the skull through which the surgeon passes a fine probe and takes electrical recordings from it, to identify an area in the globus pallidus. A second electrode is then inserted into this area, and using an electric current burns away a cluster of neurones which can become over-active in the absence of dopamine.

Thalamic stimulation is also used, particularly for reversing the effects of severe disabling tremor. A stimulator is implanted in the upper part of the chest, which can be activated externally by means of a magnet. This in turn triggers an impulse via an electrode situated in the thalamus of the brain and arrests tremor.

In Sweden and the USA, surgeons have transplanted fetal brain tissue into the basal ganglia of PD sufferers. In the few patients treated this way there has been remarkable improvement, but the technique is still in its early stages and open to considerable ethical controversy.

The Nurse's Role

The impact of PD on an individual and their family can be psychologically devastating. The nurse is able to support the older person and must be aware of how emotional factors such as anxiety, grief and depression can significantly affect the symptoms, and thus the individual's capacity to mobilise safely. PD is known to cause clinical depression (Burn and Dearden, 1990).

Major mobility problems often occur when a PD sufferer is admitted to hospital and requires medication outside the drug round times, possibly hourly throughout the day. If medication is not given on time, as the individual requires, then their condition will deteriorate, causing significant distress. It is important that the nurse understands how the medication works, and is able to develop policies that enable self-medication where possible.

In the UK, there has been the development of specialist disease clinics, where the specialist nurse plays a pivotal role. Education of professionals and sufferers and their carers is a major responsibility of the specialist nurse, who will visit the patients in their own homes, and see them regularly in the PD or movement disorder clinics. Other aspects of the specialist nurse's role include coordinating the care between community health-care trusts and nursing homes, developing services, promoting specialist skills within the multidisciplinary team through education and research, and acting as a resource for other professionals, including physiotherapists, doctors, dieticians, speech therapists, chiropodists and occupational therapists.

Assessment and treatment of the variable level of mobility of a PD sufferer can be immeasurably aided by the completion of a diary (by the sufferer or caregiver), which

Patient diary

date _____

patient's name _____

your next appointment is _____

doctor's name _____

Instructions

mark the description which best describes your level of mobility for each 30-minute period. If you are resting but not asleep during the day, try to engage in some activity such as standing or walking in order to accurately record your level of mobility. Your carer may help you to complete this chart if necessary

Definition of terms:

1. On - useful mobility.

2. On with dyskinesia - able to move but troubled by involuntary or unintentional movements (write in mild, moderate or severe).

3. Off - only able to move slowly or not at all.

circle your meal times	medication taken	asleep	on	on with dyskinesia	off	circle your meal times	medication taken	asleep	on	on with dyskinesia	off	circle your meal times	medication taken	asleep	on	on with dyskinesia	off
midnight						8:30						4:00					
:30						:30						:30					
1:00						9:00						5:00					
:30						:30						:30					
2:00						10:00						6:00					
:30						:30						:30					
3:00						11:00						7:00					
:30						:30						:30					
4:00						noon						8:00					
:30						:30						:30					
5:00						1:00						9:00					
:30						:30						:30					
6:00						2:00						10:00					
:30						:30						:30					
7:00						3:00						11:00					
:30						:30						:30					

Figure 11.5 Patient diary.

describes the level of mobility throughout the day. **Figure 11.5** shows a patient diary.

Systemic factors such as atherosclerosis and diabetes can also impair the delivery of nutrients to the tissue, thus reducing their ability to repair.

COMMON FOOT DISORDERS

Common foot problems include :

- Arthritic foot disorders, resulting from rheumatoid arthritis.
- Osteoarthritis.
- Osteoporosis.
- Gout.
- Atrophy of the plantar pads that lead to loss of shock absorption and metatarsalgia with increased difficulty in walking.
- Onychogryphosis (thickening and deformity of the nail plate) results in overgrown, claw-like toenails that cause difficulty in walking, pain, immobility and falls.
- Hallux valgus, with an angle of greater than 16 degrees, will in many cases impair the function of the adjacent toes.

Care of the feet is an important aspect of comfort, stable gait and mobility, and is one that is often overlooked. It is impossible to maintain normal gait in an older person if their feet are painful or deformed. Mobility can be severely restricted by relatively minor foot problems, such as corns (helomas) and calluses, trouble with toenails and foot deformities resulting from badly fitting shoes in youth.

The Nurse's Role

The nurse must not only assess the state of the older person's feet, and initiate the appropriate intervention, such as referral to a registered chiropodist, but must also assess their ability to carry out the required foot care, concurrent illnesses allowing. Routine nail care is often difficult for many older people, not only because of limitations in flexibility, grip strength and eye sight, but because they may feel embarrassed to ask friends or family to perform what they view as a menial task. They will often not mention any problems to a health professional, deeming it too trivial. In one study of 100 patients in geriatric and rehabilitation wards, only 11 were able to cut their own toenails (Ebrahim *et al.*, 1981) (*see* Chapter 7 for full discussion of the nurse's role in foot care).

FALLS CAUSES AND CONSEQUENCES

Older people who fall present a complex diagnosis challenge to both medical staff and nurses. Nursing observations may be essential to establishing an accurate diagnosis. The nurse may be the only professional who has been into the home and seen the older person functioning in a familiar setting. The nurse may also have knowledge of the older person's usual lifestyle and needs, and is often most likely to view the older person holistically and advocate for appropriate intervention.

A fall may best be described as a person unintentionally coming to rest on the ground or at some lower level *not* as a result of a major intrinsic event or an overwhelming hazard (Kellog International Working Group, 1987). This definition excludes major medical events such as a stroke, syncope, seizure and environmental hazards that would cause even a young healthy person to fall, such as being pushed or being hit by a vehicle.

Why Do Older People Fall?

Falling is one of the most serious and frequent problems associated with the ageing process, and can be attributed to extrinsic or intrinsic factors, or may be a combination of both. **Table 11.1** shows fall factors (*see* Chapter 13 for discussion of extrinsic or environmental factors).

A consistent pattern is emerging from the multiple research studies into falls and older people, which identifies older people at risk as those taking multiple medications, especially sedatives, those with dementia, weakness from arthritis or neurological disease, and those with gait or foot abnormalities.

The risk of falls and injuries because of a failure to see obstacles or a changed environment are much higher due to age-related changes in the eye (*see* Chapter 4 for full discussion of eye changes). Visual impairment may be transient, as a symptom of other problems such as hypotension, cardiac arrhythmia, temporal arthritis or vertebrobasilar artery insufficiency. When there is a sudden unexpected visual problem, these become major fall risks. Additionally, new glasses or recent cataract surgery may initially be a handicap, until the older person readjusts to their new improved vision.

Intrinsic Factors

Vertigo and Dizziness

These are the result of dysfunction in balance control systems and vestibular apparatus. Benign positional vertigo is very common in older people. This may be precipitated by ear infection or head trauma.

Labrynthitis

This is an infectious or toxic process that results in dizziness and gait ataxia. Certain medications can be ototoxic (affecting the organs of balance and hearing, or on the eighth cranial nerve), particularly the aminoglycosides such as gentamycin, netilmicin. These cause tinnitus and hearing loss, which may become permanent. Treatment of the infection and discontinuation of the drug often resolves the problem.

Transient Ischaemic Attacks (TIAs)

These attacks affect the perfusion of the brain and cause intermittent dizziness. It is estimated that up to 25% of falls are associated with TIAs. The older person may not have a loss of consciousness, but will feel as if the legs give way. Faulty evaluation of spatial relationships resulting from neural deficiencies may also precipitate a fall event.

Syncope

Syncope or a brief loss of consciousness due to cerebral ischaemia has many causes. Vasodepressor syncope typically occurs during emotional upset, injury, excessive fatigue or during prolonged standing in a warm environment. Orthostatic syncope is a compensatory response to rapid rising to a standing position when depletion of body fluids or medications interfere with rapid venous return and dynamic homeostatic responses. Postprandial reductions in blood pressure may also occur sufficiently to produce syncope. Older patients should be cautioned against sudden rising from sitting or supine positions, particularly after eating. Carotid sinus syncope occurs frequently in older people who have sinus node disease. This hypersensitivity to pressure or mechanical obstruction makes the individual vulnerable to syncope when applying pressure to the carotid when shaving, turning sharply or wearing tight collars. Drugs such as digoxin and propanolol may produce carotid hypersensitivity. Cardiac arrhythmias are a common cause of syncope, particularly supraventricular tachycardia.

Fall Factors		
Psychogenic	Physiological	Environmental
Dementia Alterations in gait and vitamin B$_{12}$ level; poor evaluation of ability and environment	Neurological Dementias Somnolence Normal pressure hydrocephalus Neurosensory and visual deficits: loss of proprioception; peripheral neuropathy; vestibular dysfunction; dizziness; vertigo; syncope; seizures; brain tumours or lesions; Parkinson's disease; cervical spondylosis	Slippery floor: urine or fluid on the floor, loose throw rugs Uneven and obstructed walking surfaces: types, furniture, pets, children, uneven doorsteps or stair risers, loose boards, cracked pavements

Depression
 	
Disinterest in surroundings, no concern for safety, subliminal suicide
	Cardiovascular disorders
	  Cerebrovascular insufficiency
	  Strokes and transient ischaemic attacks
	  Syncope
	  Arrhythmias:
	  Vertebral artery insufficiency
	  Stokes-Adams valvulopathies
	  Congestive heart failure
	Hypotension
	  Postural hypotension
	  Postprandial drop in blood pressure
	  Medication induced
	  Male micturation when urethral obstruction present
	  Hypovolaemia (dehydration, haemorrhage)
	  Impaired venous return (venous pooling, valsalva)
	  Impaired vasoconstriction (autonomic disorders, vasovagal)
		Inadequate visual supports: glaring; low-watt bulbs; lack of night lights for bathroom, stairs and halls; poor marking of steps and other hazards

Fear/anxiety
 	
Distraction, scattered perceptions
	Metabolic disorders
	  Anaemia
	  Hypoxia
	  Hypoglycemia
	  Hyperventilation
	Debilitating disease
	  Cancer
	  Pulmonary disease
	  Immunosuppressant disorder
		Inadequate construction: absence of railing, lack of grab bars on shower or tub, poorly designed stairs and walkways. (See Chapter 13)

Table 11.1 Fall Factors

Disequilibrium

This may arise from many disorders, including Parkinson's disease (PD), Alzheimer's disease (AD) and peripheral neuropathy caused by diabetes, alcoholism or pernicious anaemia. PD particularly affects the gait, causing stumbling, shuffling, stiffness and slowness of movement. Once threatened, the older person is unable to regain balance to prevent falling.

Drop Attack

When an older person falls 'just because my leg went out from under me', we often call them drop attacks. These falls often cause hip trochanter cracks or femur fractures, or sometimes both. This is thought to be due to osteoporotic bone erosion that often accompanies old age, and in some women with a high-risk profile it reaches pathologic proportions.

When osteoporosis of this magnitude occurs, the bone can no longer bear the weight of the individual in walking. It is sometimes difficult to determine whether the fall creates the fracture or the fracture creates the fall. It is of little consequence as to which precedes the other. In fact, numerous conditions may precipitate a drop attack. Many neurological disorders may lead to syncope and drop attacks. Seizures, sleep and arousal disorders, vagotonic and several other central autonomic disorders are sometimes culprit; even psychogenic seizures must be considered. Cerebrovascular disorders account for a high incidence of drop attacks.

Medication

Medication is a major risk factors in causing falls. Multiple pathology requiring polypharmacy increases the risk of destabilising drug interactions as well as altered handling of drugs (including alcohol) by the ageing body systems. Resultant toxic effects can affect equilibrium. Drugs may affect postural control either through a direct therapeutic action or side effects to the brain (e.g. hypnotics, sedatives, tranquillisers, antidepressants and anticonvulsants). Benzodiazepine-induced psychomotor impairment may be manifested as ataxia, delayed reaction time, increased body sway and decreased proprioception. Drugs can also have indirect effect on the brain arising from their pharmacological action on other body systems (e.g. hypoglycaemic agents, anti-arrhythmics and those affecting cardiac output, and antihypertensives). Digoxin and benzodiazepines, combined with psychoactive agents such as antipsychotics, antidepressants and narcotics, administered to hospitalised older patients suffering from congestive cardiac failure have been shown to be a major factor in causing falls of hospitalised patients (Gales and Menard, 1995).

Alcohol

Although there is little data on the influence of ageing on the effects of alcohol on the central nervous system, alcohol is known to considerably accentuate the effects of any concurrently administered sedative drug and has been associated with falls in an institutional population (Pentland, 1986).

Continence

Urinary frequency and urgency, leading to unsafe manoeuvring when getting to the toilet, and incontinence or dribbling of urine, leading to slipping on a wet floor, can also be factors causing an older person to fall.

Cognitive Impairment

AD and multi-infarct dementia have also been associated with an increased risk of falls.

Accidents

Accidents affect all age groups, but children, young adults and older people are particularly vulnerable. The absolute number of accidental deaths is greatest in people over 65 years and over. Accidents, such as falls, are an important cause of disability and use of the health service in older people.

Older people are more likely to live in houses that are unfit, lack amenities or are in poor conditions. However, many older people have considerable experience negotiating their environment, and have survived many dangerous situations. They are usually more aware of potential dangers and exert more caution than younger people. (*See* Chapter 13 for further discussion of accidents.)

Fear of Falling

Some older people develop symptoms or behaviours in response to a fall, regardless of the physical trauma (or lack of it). The fear of falling can become more disabling to an older person than the physical consequences of an actual fall. Loss of confidence in one's ability to carry out daily living activities can create a scenario in which anxiety and fear precipitate an actual fall, rather than any other intrinsic or extrinsic factor. Individuals who are afraid of falling tend to stiffen their posture when walking. This postural change can actually induce more falls.

Rehabilitation programmes must take into account that it is estimated that up to one-third of older people can develop a fear of falling after an incident, with older women particularly at risk. Gait abnormalities, and poor self-perception of physical health, cognitive status and economic resources have shown to be significantly associated with fear of falling (Vellas *et al.* 1997). **Figure 11.6** illustrates what older people can do if they fall.

Consequences of Falling

Regardless of the cause of an older person falling, the end result is often immobility, restrictions in movement, institutional living and all of the physical ailments that tend to follow immobility, especially in the very frail older person. Falls are the most important cause of hospitalisation for older people. Over 85% of all fatal falls in the home in England and Wales are in people aged over 65 years (Lilley *et al.* 1995).

Apart from the physical injury sustained when an older person falls, one consequence can be measured by the destination of the patient following discharge from hospital. Individuals who fall on more than one occasion were found to be 2.5 times more likely to be transferred to a long-term care setting from hospital. By comparison, people who fell once are twice as likely to be discharged home (Gaebler, 1993).

The most common serious injuries are fractures, which account for 40% of deaths from injury admissions to hospital and two-thirds of bed days for injury (Cryer *et al.* 1993)

Reducing Injury From Falls

Dietary Intervention

Studies have shown that body levels of vitamin D decline with age, and that the lowest levels occur in winter when there is least sunlight and in people who are artificially deprived of sunlight for an extended period of time, such as those who have been housebound. There is potential to prevent fractures in older people by vitamin D and or calcium supplementation, perhaps by promoting exposure to sunlight and increased consumption of dairy products. There is currently no data to assess the cost-effectiveness of vitamin D and calcium supplementation in older people .

Hip Protectors

Most hip fractures seem to be related to trauma near the hip. The protector is designed to divert a direct impact away from the greater trochanter during falls from standing heights, and offers nearly full protection to this region. The outer shield

What to do if you have a fall

Don't panic: you will probably feel a little shocked and shaken, but try to stay calm.
Assess the situation: if you are hurt or feel unable to get up, follow the rest and wait plan, if you are unhurt, and know you are able to get up, follow the up and about plan.
See your GP: all falls are potentially serious and you should see your general practitioner afterwards.

The rest and wait plan

If you are hurt or unable to get up, wait for help.
try to summon help : use a pendant alarm if you have one, bang on the wall, call out for help, crawl towards your telephone, (keep it at a low level).

Move to a soft surface: if you have fallen on a hard floor try to move to a carpeted area.

Keep warm: try to reach for something to cover yourself with. Try to move out of drafts.

Keep moving: do not lie in one position for too long, as you may get cold and suffer from pressure sores, roll from side to side and move arms and legs if possible.

If you need to empty your bladder while on the floor, use a newspaper or item of clothing to soak up the wet, and try to move from the wet area.

The up and about plan

Before you attempt to get up, make sure that you are not hurt. The method below is one safe way to get up from a fall but there are others. We strongly recommend that you ask for an assessment from a physiotherapist who can advise you on the most appropriate way to get up.

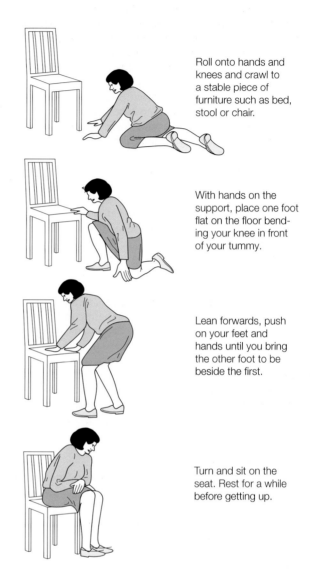

Roll onto hands and knees and crawl to a stable piece of furniture such as bed, stool or chair.

With hands on the support, place one foot flat on the floor bending your knee in front of your tummy.

Lean forwards, push on your feet and hands until you bring the other foot to be beside the first.

Turn and sit on the seat. Rest for a while before getting up.

Figure 11.6 What to do if you have a fall.

is made of polypropylene, and is attached to special underwear. Introducing the use of hip pad protectors for high-risk people in care settings has been demonstrated to significantly reduce the risk of hip fractures (Lauritzen, 1993). However, the extent to which protection pads are generally acceptable and would be worn in the community is not presently clear, and further research is ongoing. An Australian study elicited the views of women aged over 75 years in a rehabilitation unit using focus group technique. In the main, the protection pads were seen as unacceptable (Quine and Cameron, 1995).

FALL PREVENTION

Systematic Reviews of the Research Evidence

Falls experienced by older people are usually multifactorial in nature, which means that they are difficult to predict and prevent. A systematic review of research, which was undertaken by the University of York National Health Service (NHS) Centre for Reviews and Dissemination and the University of Leeds, Nuffield Institute for Health (1996), sought to evaluate the effectiveness of programmes designed to prevent falls and subsequent injury in older people. The review included 36 randomised controlled trials and the results of a newly completed Cochrane Collaboration meta-analysis of trials of vitamin D and calcium supplementation. It identified over 400 variables that have been investigated as potential risk factors in older people. The authors concluded that:

- Exercise, particularly that involving balance training, is effective in reducing the risk of falls in older people.
- Home visiting to identify and remedy environmental and personal risks for falling may reduce the risk of falling.
- Hip protectors for high-risk people in institutional care may significantly reduce injury due to falls, but the acceptability of such protectors needs to be assessed.
- Vitamin D and calcium supplementation have the potential to prevent fractures in older people.
- Any new programme to prevent falls and subsequent injury in older people should be developed as part of controlled evaluations (Sowden and Dickson, 1997).

The findings were published in the Effective Health Care Bulletin (1996).

Another review to determine if short-term exercise reduces falls and fall-related injuries in older people was undertaken by Province *et al.* (1997). From the best available evidence, a protocol of interventions to reduce the incidence of falling in older people was published by Gillespie *et al.* (1997). Recommended measures include the following:

- A retrospective analysis of accidents (only by auditing falls and examining the circumstances can an initial fall or reoccurrence be prevented).
- Use of a risk assessment tool.
- Defining organisational policy on patient safety.
- Defining corporate monitoring processes and necessary equipment.
- Identifying 'at-risk' patients, by taking detailed medical and drug history, and identifying frequent fallers.
- Staff education and awareness raising.
- Promoting active rehabilitation.

An example of a patient interview following a reported fall is given in **Figure 11.7**.

The Use of Bedrails

Prevention of falls is a commonly reported reason for the use of bedrails in this country, particularly when an older person labelled as 'confused' is involved, despite there being little evidence that the use of a bedrail actually prevents a fall (O'Keefe *et al.* 1996). Indeed, it is suggested that the use of bedrails actually increases the number of falls, as the individual clambers over the top in an attempt to get out of bed, usually to reach the toilet. It has also been suggested that bedrails have the potential to worsen aggression or mental confusion (Gray and Gaskell, 1990). Bedrails will increase the distance a patient will fall, and hence increase the risk of seri-

ous injury. Asphyxial deaths attributable to bedrail use have been reported in the USA.

As a result of the sparse data available, one NHS Trust in Leeds undertook a review of accident reports in order to establish the extent of the problem. Three types of incidents specific to bedrails were analysed:

- Falls from height.
- Becoming trapped.
- Becoming caught in the equipment.

The authors concluded from their review that bedrails do not necessarily prevent falls from bed and can cause serious injury if they are used inappropriately. They suggest the development of local guidelines (Everitt and Bridel-Nixon, 1997).

Beds of adjustable height are essential for all older people who need assistance to move and to enable ambulant people to sit with their feet on the floor when transferring from bed to chair. Alternative strategies to the bedrail include placing the bed at its lowest setting or placing the mattress on the floor.

HIP FRACTURE

The number of people who fracture their hips is rising, because both the population of older people and the rate of fracture are increasing. Estimates of numbers expected in 20 years time vary between 60,000 and 117,000 hip fractures a year (Audit Commission, 1995). Significant progress has been made in the treatment of hip fractures, and almost all can now be repaired surgically. Most patients can walk again within a day or two, and be home in a few weeks, unless frailty or medical complications cause delay. The Audit Commission has used hip fractures in older people as a 'marker' condition for identifying the effectiveness of treatment within the overall movement towards evidence-based health care, and it's recommendations for good practice can be applied to older people with other conditions. These recommendations include developing a closer relationship between surgeons and physicians – known as orthogeriatric liaison. The role of a gerontology nurse specialist to advise on the complex nursing needs of these patients has yet to be evaluated.

The Nurse's Role

Because of their complex needs, an older person with a hip fracture requires a comprehensive nursing assessment, which should start when they arrive at the accident and emergency department. This assessment must be completed when they reach the ward and forms the basis for planning treatment and care. An incomplete assessment may fail to identify problems that subsequently may cause delays during rehabilitation and discharge planning. The assessment should utilise a range of tools, and should include items given in **Box 11.3**.

Listed below are two examples of schemes to support the rehabilitation and return home of older people following hip fracture:

Patient interview following a reported fall

name _____ date _____ time _____

admission date _____ age _____ ward _____

Objective data:

room lighting: light _____ dark _____ lights on _____ lights off _____

safety assessment: yes _____ no _____ current _____ not current _____

Pt. care plan indicates safety problem present:

yes _____ no _____ current _____ not current _____

ADL sheet indicates follow-up safety assessment:

yes _____ no _____ always _____ most of the time _____ sometimes _____ rarely _____

Relevant problems

visual _____ auditory _____

urinary _____ mobility _____

hypotension _____ hypertension _____

general debility _____ diuretics _____

hypnotics/tranquilisers _____ pain medications/barbiturates _____

mental status _____

proper fit of shoes/slippers: _____ yes _____ no _____ n/a _____

Subjective data:

when you fell, what happened? _____

what do you think caused you to fall? _____

were you unfamilar with the area where you fell? _____

was there anything in your way when you fell? What was it? _____

were you barefoot? yes _____ no _____

if no, wearing: hospital slippers _____ socks _____ TEDS _____ own shoes _____ own slippers _____

did you feel dizzy? faint? _____

have you ever been dizzy and fallen before in the hospital? _____

have you ever been dizzy and fallen at home? _____

how many times would you estimate that you have fallen in the past? _____

have you ever hurt yourself when you fell at home? _____

fractures _____ other injuries _____

do you know what you can do to prevent this from happening? _____

avoid tilting head back _____ sit up slowly _____

stand up slowly _____ eat soon after awakening _____

wear sturdy shoes _____ other _____

did you try to get help before you fell? _____

if yes, how? call bell _____ called out _____ asked another patient _____ asked visitor _____

what happened then? no one came _____ took too long to come _____

didn't know if they heard me _____ couldn't wait to go to the bathroom _____

tired/ not feeling well, wanted to return to bed _____

if no, why not? thought staff was too busy _____ could see staff was busy _____

didn't want to bother them/be nuisance _____ thought I could do it myself _____

wanted privacy _____ prefer to do things myself _____ didn't want female nurse in bathroom with me _____

other _____

do you think that you can prevent this from happening again? _____

what can the nurses do to prevent this from happening again? _____

other comments _____

Figure 11.7 Patient interview form following a repeated fall. (Source: Barbieri EB. Patient falls are not patient accidents. *Gerontol Nurs* 1983, 9:171.)

(1) The Peterborough 'hospital-at-home' scheme.
The service is district-wide and has been running for 17 years. Responsibility for medical care lies with the patient's general practitioner (GP), who has immediate access to a hospital bed if there are problems. For hip fracture patients, hospital-at-home offers:
• Discharge soon after surgery.

• Assessment by a district nurse.
• Support according to the patient's needs, nursing care may initially be available 24 hours a day.
• Physiotherapy.
• Occupational therapy.
• Patient aides to provide help and support.

11.3 Key Aspects of Nursing Assessment

- Pressure sore risk
- Pain
- Continence
- Mental state
- Previous mobility
- Functional ability
- Social circumstances
- Nutritional status (see **Table 11.2**)

Meeting Mobility Needs

Isaac Schiffman had been hospitalised several times during the past year due to problems managing his diabetes, urinary retention and chronic heart failure. At 79 years of age, he is physically quite frail, but alert and very strong minded. Mr Schiffman admits that he never takes his medications as prescribed because he resents being what he called a 'pill popper'. He generally eats healthy foods but his eating patterns are very sporadic. Mr Schiffman's wife worries about 'his insistence on doing things for himself' because she feels that he puts himself at unnecessary risk, such as on the occasion when he decided he would climb a high step ladder to clean the upstairs windows. One night Mr Schiffman got up to urinate, as usual. His wife heard him fall and found him in the bathroom unconscious. He was taken into hospital immediately and thoroughly assessed. Mr Schiffman suffered no broken bones but there was a great deal of concern about the cause of his fall and how to prevent him falling in the future.

- What information did Mr Schiffman and his wife give to the nurse that offered subjective data for the nursing assessment?
- What information could the nurse collect that would provide objective data for the nursing assessment?
- What strengths do Mr Schiffman and his wife demonstrate that could be used as a basis for the nursing care plan?
- What interventions should the nurse make to help Mr Schiffman to mobilise safely again?
- What other professionals or specialists should be involved in Isaac's care?
- List possible outcome criteria for plan of care. Mr Schiffman's own desired outcomes, and assessment of the achievement of these, should be included.
- What advice should be offered, and what actions should be taken to prevent further falls?

(2) The Edinburgh early supported discharge scheme. The Royal Infirmary, Edinburgh, has established an early supported discharge scheme for fitter hip fracture patients. The aim is to enable them to be discharged directly home from acute orthopaedic care, with rehabilitation and reliable post-discharge support.

A liaison occupational therapist and a liaison nursing sister have been appointed to work with the orthopaedic nursing and rehabilitation staff and an elderly care doctor. The team promotes and monitors early rehabilitation, carries out pre-discharge assessment and home visits, liaises with community health and social services, and monitors progress after the patient has gone home.

The proportion of hip fractures going straight home from acute care has risen, and satisfaction is high among patients, their carers, GPs and community health and social services staff. Economic evaluation has shown that the scheme has brought considerable savings by reducing length of stay (Audit Commission, 1995, p. 45).

IMMOBILITY

Immobility occurs when an individual loses the ability to move separate parts of the body (especially the limbs or whole body) easily and without pain. For many older people, the presence of chronic illnesses leads to an increased risk of complications which consequently can become life threatening.

Complications of Immobility

Complications of Immobility include:
- Bronchial pneumonia.
- Mental confusion.
- Constipation.
- Contractures.
- Deep vein thrombosis.
- Dehydration.
- Depression.
- Disability.
- Disorientation.

Some of the Main Components of an Assessment for Older Patients	
Component	Assessment
Pressure sore risk	Age-related changes in the skin increase the risk of skin breakdown. A frail older person may experience damage in as little as 30 minutes. A validated risk assessment tool highlights the risk factors for pressure sores: • female, aged 75 years or over • trauma and surgery • dehydration • reduced mobility • underweight • pain • debilitating disorders • discoloured or broken skin • poor nutrition • poorly managed continence The specific risk factors can then be addressed through a plan of care.
Hydration and nutrition	In addition to a straightforward assessment of hydration, the patient's nutritional risk factors should be considered. Nutritional status can be affected by physical, social and economic constraints: • impaired taste and smell can lead to loss of appetite • ill-fitting dentures or oral infections can cause soreness of the mouth and gums • Parkinson's tremor, poor sight and poor coordination make it difficult for people to feed themselves in unfamiliar surroundings • poverty limits the food that people can afford • depression, bereavement, social isolation and loneliness may take away the motivation to prepare food and eat • confusion and dementia may cause the patient to forget to eat
Pain	In the past, assessment of pain has often been based on the subjective judgement of nurse and patient (and many older patients do not like to 'make a fuss'), but a variety of pain assessment tools now exist which aim to provide a more objective measure of pain. The benefits include: • more accurate information on the level of pain • information to help establish the pattern of pain • evaluation of the effects of medication • a framework for setting specific goals For some elderly patients the pain of the fracture may add to chronic pain associated with other conditions. Each problem should be assessed carefully, as different care may be required.
Continence	Incontinence is a symptom of an underlying problem, and a thorough assessment is needed. The causes of incontinence can include constipation, urinary infection, pelvic floor damage or neurological disease, and each requires a different plan of care.
Coexisting medical problems	The patient's past medical history may include illness that could affect anaesthesia, including respiratory and cardiac disorders. A drug history is also useful. Patients and carers should both be involved in this assessment; useful information can also be obtained from the general practitioner or district nurse and, perhaps, social services. The assessment should also cover the patient's overall wellbeing. Vague symptoms may indicate problems with long-term use of sedatives or other drugs, or undiagnosed medical problems.

(cont.)

Table 11.2 Some of the main components of an assessment for older patients.

• Hypothermia.
• Iatrogenic complications.
• Institutionalisation.
• Loss of independence.
• Pressure sores.
Whatever disease process is prevalent, pain is often the major barrier to prevent normal movement. When it hurts to move, the most natural reaction is to stop the activity. When immobility occurs, either as a direct consequence of the disease process or as a result of the medication or other intervention, further complications then arise, thus impacting on the individual's ability to be independent. Many older people are reluctant to admit feeling pain or to request adequate pain relief for fear of exacerbating their problems.

Component	Assessment
	Some of the Main Components of an Assessment for Older Patients (*cont.*)
Mental function	Poor cognitive function is closely associated with poor outcome following a hospital stay. Confusion due to pain, dehydration or simple disorientation can be misdiagnosed as dementia, so a careful assessment is necessary to ensure that the right care is provided. Simple tools are available which give a guide to cognitive function, such as the geriatric depression score and the mini-mental state examination. The person's lifestyle and past history are important; someone who has recently developed acute confusion requires very different care from an elderly person with long-term memory loss. Early (and full) involvement of the person's carer is important.
Previous mobility	In older people, mobility is often more important than diagnosis in predicting outcomes. Assessment of previous mobility provides a baseline against which realistic goals can be set and progress measured: • how far could the patient walk? • could the patient climb the stairs? • what aids were required? • did they become breathless? Again, consultation with somebody who knows the person well may produce more realistic and reliable results.
Functional abilities	This includes an assessment of how an individual carries out the activities that fitter people take for granted. The assessment should include: • the patient's normal routine • what they do for recreation • how they wash and dress • their interests and hobbies • how they prepare food • any paid employment Things the patient is no longer able to do should be considered, such as visiting friends, bathing or cooking. This allows the development of a plan to address problems.
Social circumstances	The assessment should include: • the condition of the patient's home and their ability to function in that environment • their financial circumstances; including any problems with pensions or bills • support from family, friends and others such as district nurses or home helps. The discussion should include the individual's preferences for the future, the views of carers and relatives, and what they think they can cope with realistically.

Table 11.2 Some of the main components of an assessment for older patients (*cont.*). Source: Audit Commission. United they stand: coordinated care for elderly patients with hip fracture. London. HMSO. 1995)

THE NURSE'S ROLE IN REHABILITATION FOR MOBILITY

Rehabilitation is concerned with lessening the impact of disabling conditions. These are particularly common in older people and considerable health gain can be achieved by successful rehabilitation. The nurse needs to be aware that rehabilitation involves a complex set of processes. These usually involve several professional disciplines and are aimed at improving the quality of life older people facing daily living difficulties caused by chronic disease. The key purposes of rehabilitation may be summarised as:
· Realisation of potential.
· Reablement.
· Resettlement.
· Role fulfilment.
· Readjustment.

(*See* Chapter 8 for further discussion of the nurse's role in rehabilitation.)

There are now over 40 different types of assessment tools available to assess functional ability. A variety of these are discussed in Chapters 4 and 8.

It is essential to establish, through regular assessment, not only what physical care and rehabilitation can be undertaken, but the psychological and interpersonal care required. Motivation is necessary to maintain independence, but this can be very difficult to achieve without continual support and involvement from the nurse, whether the older person is in an acute hospital setting, their own home or within a care setting.

DEVICES TO ASSIST MOBILITY

A walking stick or other supportive device may be required to support and balance the older person, thus aiding movement and reducing the risk of a fall. The occupational therapist and physiotherapist are able to assess and provide the appropriate walking aid, such as a Zimmer frame, or Delta frame, a three wheeled tripod with wheels, that is extremely manoeuvrable.

It is important that the nurse ensures the appropriate device is available for use, and that access to therapists for reassessment is available. Enabling an older person to remain mobile is just as significant when a wheelchair is required. Awareness of the risks of immobility, particularly relating to pressure sores and the appropriate prevention strategy is vital. There is an increased risk of falls for the individual when transferring to and from a wheelchair, and continued assessment by both physiotherapist and occupational therapist as to the most appropriate method of transferring is necessary. **Figure 11.8** shows a Delta frame.

However the older person is able to mobilise, the one common denominator is that they will be moving slower than the nurse. This statement may seem very obvious, but many falls are precipitated by haste. The older person does not want to keep the nurse waiting, and verbal and non-verbal signals from the nurse reinforce that message. Allowing the older person time is perhaps the most important aid to mobility the nurse can contribute. An older person needs time to manoeuvre in bed so that they are in a position to sit up, time to position their feet correctly so they can stand up from being seated and time to start to walk along the corridor, stopping when necessary. In this way, they can reach their destination calm not breathless, and motivated that they have achieved a goal. If an older person lacks confidence in their ability, or is frightened, they may react by grasping onto the nurse or holding a piece of furniture tightly. Calm reassurance by the nurse, bending down if necessary so that the nurse and patient are in eye contact, allowing the person to hold on to their hand or arm for support and refraining from holding on to them too closely are all strategies that assist confident movement. If an older person is not feeling in control of their movements, or the situation they are in, then a panic response is initiated and a fall is waiting to happen.

Physical inactivity has been demonstrated to be a significant predictor of fracture risk. Preservation of the ability to go shopping is associated with lower rates of hip fracture (Cooper, 1988). The question of whether short-term exercise reduces fall and fall-related injuries in older people is being actively researched in randomised controlled trials (RCTs), mainly in the USA. To date there is little evidence about the likely effectiveness of prescription for exercise schemes in the UK. Few of the RCTs have been carried out in the UK, and this may be an important limitation, since sociocultural factors can have an important influence on health promotion, particularly on the acceptability of and likely adherence to recommended intervention.

Improving balance, strength and flexibility through exercise might make falls less likely. Small studies involving the effects of exercise in older women in relation to bone density and falls indicate that the women taking exercise and calcium experienced fewer falls than those taking calcium supplements only (McMurdo, 1997). The medical focus on improving bone density using medication alone addresses only part of the problem; prevention of falls might contribute substantially to reducing fracture rates. Older people should be offered access to exercise classes or home exercise routines that include, for example, balance training such as Tai Chi, although to date little is known as to how best to implement such programmes in the UK.

It has been observed that some frail older people stop walking when they start a conversation with a walking companion, presumably because walking demands attention and they stop when they are expected to do two things at once (Lundin-Olsson, 1997). This could be a self-activated method of preventing a fall. The observation 'stops walking when talking' could be utilised as part of the assessment process by nurses involved in assessing the risk of falls in an older person.

During the planning, evaluation and implementation of any interventions designed to enhance the older person's mobility and reduce the risk of falls and their possible consequences, it is essential that the perspectives of the older person should be taken into account.

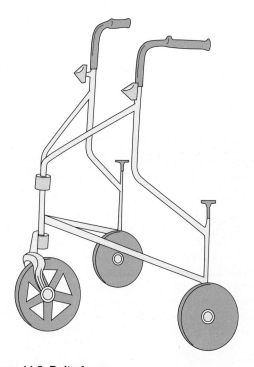

Figure 11.8 Delta frame.

SUMMARY

Movement is a way of interacting with the environment and with others. Nurses have a key role in helping older people to maintain their abilities and minimise mobility problems by identifying those older people who are at risk of developing a particular disease, such as osteoporosis or of falling. The nursing assessment should include vision, blood pressure, range of motion, muscle strength, balance, posture, neurological assessment, cognitive assessment and examination of the feet. The assessment should also encompass a review of medication and, wherever possible, include the physiotherapist and occupational therapist team members. Nurses also have a key role in:

- The care of people with mobility difficulties.
- Health promotion based on the best available evidence of effectiveness (e.g. exercise programmes, particularly those which involve balance training).
- Identifying and remedying environmental risks.
- Promoting active rehabilitation.
- Staff education.

Older people are particularly at risk of problems resulting from immobility and the cycle of dependence through limiting mobility should be avoided at all costs.

KEY POINTS

- Mobility is integral to the attainment of all levels of need as conceived by Maslow.
- Ageing does bring changes in anatomical, physiological and psychological functioning that may affect mobility, but they do not bring inevitable decline.
- Common conditions affecting mobility include gait disorders, arthritic conditions, hemiplegia, and a range of other causes.
- Osteoporosis can severely limit mobility and lead to fractures. The emphasis is on the prevention of bone loss, dietary advice, exercise, limiting disability and pain control.
- Parkinson's disease can devastate the life of a person and their family. A range of treatments and care measures are available.
- Falls are a major cause of morbidity in older people. There are many causes which may be extrinsic or intrinsic.
- The prevention of falls and consequent injury is a major aspect of nursing practice.
- The Audit Commission work on hip fractures produced recommended protocols, tools of assessment and example models of service provision.
- A variety of devices are available to assist mobility.
- Nurses have a fundamental role in rehabilitation for mobility.

AREAS AND ACTIVITIES FOR STUDY AND REFLECTION

- Record the movement activity of several of the older people in your care during the course of one day. What percentage of the day are they immobile and what could be the consequences of this immobility to their health? What could be done to increase the amount of time they move around and remain active?
- How well does your work area facilitate older people moving around? Are there physical or environmental barriers to movement? What could be done to facilitate greater movement around the area?
- Undertake an audit of your falls and accident records? Are there any particular trends that could signpost the way to improved practice?
- How closely do your local policies reflect those discussed in the chapter, particularly with regard to falls, hip fractures and the use of bedrails?
- Review the sections on osteoporosis and Parkinson's disease. How could you improve the care you give to people with these diseases?
- What 'active rehabilitation' measures are promoted within your service and system of work? How effective is working between the disciplines, particularly nursing–medical–physiotherapy–occupational therapy? Are the patient's goals for their own rehabilitation used as the basis for the care and treatment plan?
- Review Figure 11.1, the dependency cycle. Can you identify this in any of the older people with whom you work? What could you do to prevent this deterioration progressing?

REFERENCES

Audit Commission. *United they stand: coordinating care for elderly patients with hip fracture.* London: HMSO, 1995.

Burn W, Dearden T. Physical aspects of depression. *Geriatri Med* 1990, (May): 61–64.

Cohen C. Diminished mobility is never inevitable. *Geriatrics* 1984, (October):22.

Cooper C, Barker DJ, Wickham C. Physical activity, muscle strength and calcium intake in fracture of the proximal femur in Britain. *Br Med J* 1988, 297:1443–1446.

Cryer C, Davidson L, Styles C. *Injury epidimiology in the South and East: identifying priorities for action,* prepared by the Southeast Institute of Public Health, 1993, South Thames Regional Health Authority.

Department of Health. *Advisory group on osteoporosis.* London: HMSO, 1994.

Ebrahim SB, Sainsbury S, Watson S. Foot problems of the elderly: a hospital survey. *Br Med J* 1981, 283:949–950.

Ebrahim SB, Thompson PW, Baskaran V, Evans K. Randomised placebo-controlled trial of brisk walking in the prevention of postmenopausal osteoporosis. *Age Ageing* 1997, 26:253–260.

Effective Health Care Bulletin. *Preventing falls and subsequent injury in older people.* London: Churchill Livingstone, 1996.

Everitt V, Bridel-Nixon J. The use of bedrails: principles of patient assessment. *Nurs Stand* 1997, 12:44–47.

Farquhar M, Grundy E, Formby J. Functional ability of very elderly people. *Nurs Stand* 1993, 7:31–36.

Fogarty M. Are we rationing Parkinson's care? *Medical Interface* 1997, (March):

Gaebler S. Predicting which patient will fall again ... and again. *J Adv Nurs* 1993, 18:1895–1902.

Gales BJ, Menard SM. Relationship between the administration of selected medications and falls in the hospitalized elderly patients. *Ann Pharmacother* 1995, 29:354–358.

Gillespie LD, Cumming R, Gillespie WJ, Lamb S, Rowe B. Interventions to reduce the incidence of falling in the elderly [protocol]. In: Gillespie WJ, Madhok R, Swiontkowski M, Robinson CM, Murray GD, eds. *Musculoskeletal injuries module of the Cochrane database of systematic reviews [updated 3 March 1997].* Oxford: The Cochrane Collaboration, 1997.

Gray CS, Gaskell D. Cot sides: a continuing hazard for the elderly. *Geriatr Med* 1990, 20:21–22.

Kellog International Work Group. The prevention of falls in later life. *Dan Med Bull* 1987, 34:1–24.

Lauritzen JB, Petersen MM, Lund B. Effect of external hip protectors on hip fractures. *Lancet* 1993, 341:11–13.

Lilley JM, Arie T, Chilvers CED. Accidents involving older people: a review of the literature. *Age Ageing* 1995, 24:346–365.

Lundin-Olsson L, Nyberg L, Gustafson. 'Stops Walking when Talking' as a predictor of falls in elderly people. *Lancet* 1997, 349:617.

McMurdoM, Mole PA, Paterson C. Controlled trial of weight bearing exercise in older women in relation to bone density and falls. *Br Med J* 1997, 314:569.

Miller A. Nurse/patient dependency. Is it iatrogenic? *J Adv Nurs* 1985, 10:63–69.

O'Keefe S, Jack C, Lye M. Use of restraints and bedrails in a British hospital. *J Am Geriatr Soc* 1996, 44:1086–1088.

Pendergast DR, Fisher NM, Calkins E. Cardiovascular, neuromuscular and metabolic alterations with age leading to frailty. *J Gerontol* 1993, 48:61–67.

Pentland B, Jones P, Roy C, Miller J. Head injury in the elderly. *Age Ageing* 1986, 15:192–202.

Pentland B. The management of Parkinson's disease. *Geriatr Nurs Home Care* 1988, (January):133.

Phair L, Good V. *Dementia: a positive approach.* Whurr Press, 1997.

Province M, Hadley E, Hornbrook M *et al.* The effects of exercise on falls in elderly patients. A pre-planned meta-analysis of the FICSIT

trials *J Am Med Ass* 1995, 273:1341–1347.

Quine S, Cameron I. The use of focus groups with the disabled elderly. *Qual Health Res* 1995, 5:454–462.

Sowden A, Dickson R. Preventing falls and further injury in older people. In: *Systematic reviews: examples for nursing,* Nursing Standard and the University of York NHS Centre for Reviews and Dissemination, RCN Publishing Company, February 1997.

Taggart H, Crawford V. Reduced bone density of the hip in elderly patients with Parkinsons disease. *Age Ageing* 1995, 24:326–328.

University of York NHS Centre for Reviews and Dissemination and University of Leeds Nuffield Institute for Health. Preventing falls and subsequent injury in older people. *Effective Health Care* 1996, 2:16.

Vellas BJ, Wayne SJ, Romero LJ, Baumgartner RN, Garry PJ. Fear of falling and restriction in mobility in elderly fallers. *Age Ageing* 1997, 26:189–193.

Young A *et al. Physical activity in later life,* London, 1997, Health Education Authority.

FURTHER READING

Darnborough A, Kinrade D. *The directory for older people: a handbook of information and opportunities for the over 55's.*

Department of Trade and Industry *Home accident surveillance system* London, 1987.

National Osteoporosis Society and Royal College of Nursing, Osteoporosis Resource Pack: For Nurses, Midwives and Health Visitors, 1996; National Osteoporosis Society, PO Box 10, Radstock, Bath BA3 3YB
  Tel: 01761 432472

USEFUL ADDRESSES

The Arthritis and Rheumatism Council, Copeman House, St Mary's Court, St Mary's Gate, Chesterfield, Derbyshire S41 7TD. Tel: 01246 558033

The Society of Chiropodists, 53 Welbeck Street, London W1M 7HE. Tel: 0171 486 3381

Disabled Living Foundation, 380–384 Harrow Road, London W9 2HU Tel: 0181 289 6111

Mobility Information Service, National Mobility Centre, Unit 2A Atcham Estate, Shrewsbury SY4 4UG

The Motor Neurone Disease Association, PO Box 246, Northampton NN1 2PR. Tel: 01604 250505

The National Osteoporosis Society, PO Box 10, Radstock, Bath BA3 3YB. Tel: 01761 432472

The Neurological Alliance, 41 Frewin Road, London SW18 3LR Tel: 0181 875 0282

The Parkinson's Disease Society, 22 Upper Woburn Place, London WC1H 0RA. Tel: 0171 383 3513

Royal College of Nursing, 20 Cavendish Square, London W1M 0AB Tel: 0171 409 3333

The Stroke Association, CHSA House, Whitecross Street, London EC1Y 8JJ. Tel: 0171 490 7999

12 Sensory and perceptual issues of ageing
Andrée Le May

LEARNING OBJECTIVES:

After studying this chapter you will be able to:

- Describe the sensory and perceptual channels related to maintaining feelings of safety and security in later life.
- Identify sensory changes accompanying ageing that alter the perceptions of an older person and may impinge on feelings of safety and security.
- Describe several factors that affect sensory function and awareness.
- Relate sensory changes to perceptual and environmental insecurity and behavioural disturbances.

- Describe a range of conditions that may alter communication.
- Identify several interventions that may enhance sensory function and perceptual integration.
- Identify the nursing concerns associated with assisting an older person with a perceptual and communication disorder in order to develop a sensitive individualised plan of care.
- Appreciate the complexity of nursing older people experiencing sensory or perceptual challenges and the impact that skilled nursing can make to restore feelings of safety and security.

INTRODUCTION

Throughout life, human senses help the development and maintenance of safety and security. These feelings may be threatened when sensory and perceptual channels are in some way interrupted, for instance during later life. In older age, when people have completed their working lives outside the home and have more time to communicate for pleasure, they often develop sensory or perceptual difficulties that challenge the communication process. When sensory disturbances and motor disabilities thwart interactions, isolation and withdrawal may follow with resultant alterations to our feelings of physical, psychological and social safety and security. When this does occur, many people are able to overcome or adapt to these limitations with the skilled help of a range of healthcare professionals. In the main, this process is facilitated by focusing attention on the person's ability, rather than solely on their disability, as well as minimising that disability.

This chapter focuses on the major areas of communication and sensory organ alterations experienced in later life, and how these affect the individual and his or her ability to make satisfactory contact with the environment; these are critical factors in the maintenance of safety and security. While suggestions for nursing interventions are woven throughout this chapter and related to specific problems, it is important to remember the need to work in partnership with older people and their carers, focusing on them holistically rather than as a collection of varying 'parts' or 'problems'. In this way, nursing can be therapeutic by using creative methods to assist the older person in negotiating challenges to communication. The nurse's role is central to identifying and minimising deficits in the sensory and perceptual channels needed for communication. It also involves helping older people to find ways of maintaining or enhancing their quality of life through skilled care and empowering support.

THE SENSES – AN OVERVIEW

Senses help us to understand the world in which we live. They allow the collection of information about factors which influence feelings of safety and security as well as filtering out superfluous information, thereby protecting from an overwhelming bombardment of environmental messages. The highly developed human sensory and perceptual apparatus filters out extraneous messages and lets in those that increase adaptability. However, when defences are lowered, through illness, fatigue or stress, it may be harder to keep irrelevant information at bay. This can result in increased feelings of anxiety, fragmented thoughts, distractibility, insecurity or mood swings. Senses order our lives but, when they are under or overstimulated, or we interpret their message incorrectly, we become vulnerable.

During life, vulnerability can occur at any age but, as we get older, it is generally accepted that our senses decline in their acuity. The gradual diminution of the senses throughout the ageing process is usually well accommodated by experience, and normal sensory loss is not detrimental to safety and security. However, in some instances this is not the case, and it is this that forms the basis for the consideration of the senses in this chapter.

The senses are generally acknowledged as being taste, smell, sight, hearing and touch. Although they can be described individually when considering the capacities and changes in various sensory and perceptual mechanisms, it must be understood that they can, in some instances, all work together. Situations can be experienced through sight, sound, taste, smell and feel simultaneously (Sacks, 1989), so it is not unacceptable to suggest that the senses form a tightly inter-woven perceptual base to our world. In many instances, when one sense is undermined another works in a compensatory way, thus emphasising the interrelationship between the senses. Whether they are working in concert or individually, they provide a protective net that allows us to feel safe and secure through the recognition of situations which put us, or those close to us, at risk. In order to sustain this, we frequently rely on these five senses and speech to help us to communicate with ourselves, through our thoughts, and with others, through verbal and nonverbal channels.

Age-related changes to sensory and perceptual mechanisms are, however, variable and cannot be generalised to all people. Many of the changes related to the usual process of ageing have been described in Chapter 4, and **Table 12.1** provides a summary. In many of these situations, skilled nursing assessment and referral, use of appropriate equipment and attention to the environment will help to maintain safety and maximise feelings of security related to sensory, perceptual and communicative losses. Details of health prevention, promotion and maintenance strategies are provided in **Table 12.1**.

When the senses are understimulated or overloaded, perception and reactions may become distorted and the world may become an alien, confusing place. In these circumstances, fear and anxiety increase and withdrawal from reality may occur. Altered sensory experience may significantly affect one's view of oneself and one's ability to relate to others (*see* Chapter 16 for further discussion of relationships).

Emotional responses to altered sensory input may be far ranging and include boredom, diminished concentration, incoherent thoughts, anxiety, fear, depression, emotional lability or hallucinations. Significant research on the range of older peoples' responses to sensory losses is limited at present since most attention has been focused on the development and evaluation of well-designed communication aids and their fitting. However, research is beginning to understand that sensory input is essential to continued cognitive development and that some of the cognitive clouding attributed to 'ageing' may well be due to the absence of sufficient mental stimulation resulting from diminished sensory input. This reduction of sensory input may occur as a result of impaired sensory apparatus and a boring environment, or the rigidity of others' demands on and expectations of the older person.

We are all subject to alterations in our sensory experience, and with increasing age it is likely that these circumstances will occur more frequently and perhaps be more devastating. They result from a variety of alterations to our lives, which may be environmental, organic or perceptual in nature.

(1) Environmental alterations.
  • Isolation within the home, leading to extreme loneliness and self-neglect.
  • Protective isolation (e.g. in hospitals during an acute illness).
  • Environmental overload (e.g. lack of opportunities for privacy and solitude).
  • Noxious agents, including noise, glare or temperature.

(2) Organic alterations.
  • Illness (e.g. alterations in the ability to smell and taste due to a cold).
  • Physiological changes.
  • Psychological changes.

(3) Perceptual alterations.
  • Selective inattention.
  • Habituation.
  • Expectations derived from past experience.
  • Conflicts.

With the passage of time all senses gradually lose some of their acuity (*see* Chapter 4). Although the normal changes of age do not result in any abrupt awareness of sensory loss, the accumulated atrophy of sensory receptors in the eye, ear, nose, mouth and nervous system substantially reduce our impressions of the vividness of our environment. This natural blunting may be compounded by sensory or perceptual impairment, having far-reaching effects on an individual's sense of self-esteem and quality of life. Given a chance, we adapt to some of these minor alterations without help from others. However, for some, greater assaults affecting the senses will leave lasting effects that require skilled interventions from the entire multidisciplinary team of health-care professionals. In these more catastrophic situations, nursing care focuses on helping the older person to maintain an appropriate level of independence, which retains their safety and enhances their feelings of security and confidence.

TASTE AND SMELL

The senses of taste and smell are intertwined and can, when acute, provide great pleasure as well as protection from harm. Four basic tastes have been identified (sweet, sour, salt and bitter) and are detected by approximately 9000 taste buds. Scientists believe there are more yet to be identified and an unknown number of basic and subtle odours.

Overall, enjoyment of taste is complex consisting of the experience of temperature, texture, smell, appearance and flavour, together with the ability to choose what to eat or drink and, for some people, having the opportunity to shop and cook. Ordinarily, subtle changes may occur during the ageing process that usually do not interfere with one's pleasure or safety. However, for some people, significant, rapid and noticeable changes in smell and taste may occur as a result of medication or organic brain disease and warrant immediate attention.

Age-Related Sensory Changes, Outcomes and Prevention, Health Promotion and Maintenance Approaches

Age-related changes	Outcomes	Health prevention, promotion and maintenance
Vision Lid elasticity diminishes Loss of orbital fat Decreased tears Arcus senilis becomes visible Sclera yellows and becomes less elastic Yellowing and increased opacity of cornea Increased sclerosis and rigidity of the iris Decrease in convergence ability Decline in light accommodation response Diminished pupillary size Atrophy of ciliary muscle Night vision diminishes Yellowing of lens Lens opacity Increased intraocular pressure Shrinkage of gelatinous substance in the vitreous Vitreous floaters appear Ability to gaze upward decreases Thinning and sclerosis of retinal blood vessels Atrophy of photoreceptor cells Degeneration of neurones in visual cortex	Pouches under the eyes Excessive dryness of eyes Lack of corneal lustre Presbyopia Lessened acuity Decline in depth perception Diminished recovery from glare Night blindness Diminished colour perception (blues and greens) Cataracts Rainbows around lights Altered peripheral vision	Use isotonic eye drops as needed Have eyes examined at least once a year Use magnifying glass and high-intensity light to read Increase light to prevent falls Clip on sunglasses, visors, sunhat, non-glare coating on prescription glasses/sunglasses Don't drive at night Keep nightlight in bathroom and hallway Paint first and last step of staircase and edge of each step between with a bright colour Surgical removal of lens Have a yearly eye examination including tonometer testing
Hearing Thinner, drier skin of external ear Longer and thicker hair in external ear canal Narrowing of auditory opening Increased cerumen Thickened and less resilient tympanic membrane Decreased flexibility of basilar membrane Ossicular calcification Diminished neurone, endolymph, hair cells and blood supply to inner ear and auditory nerve Degeneration of spiral ganglion and arterial blood vessels Weakness and stiffness of muscles and ligaments	 Difficulty hearing high-frequency sounds (presbycusis) Gradual loss of sound	 Check ears for wax or infection Formal hearing test Consultation for proper hearing and speaking tone-shouting distorted
Smell Decreased olfactory cells	Decreased appetite Decreased protection from noxious odours and tainted food	Encourage social dining
Taste Possible decrease in size and number of taste buds	Poor nutrition	Nutritional supplementation Use of stronger flavours

Table 12.1 Age-related Sensory Changes, Outcomes and Prevention, Health Promotion and Maintenance Approaches

Taste

The taste buds that seem most affected by ageing are those for sweet and salt at the tip of the tongue since they are exposed to more contact during life and thus may deteriorate slightly quicker than others. The sensory pleasure of food combined with the symbolic nurturance inherent in eating and feeling satiated are important ways in which one maintains security, so any alteration in this may result in altered perceptions of quality of life. Indeed, when feeling insecure, many people notice alterations in their eating habits. Taste acuity is known to be dependent on the olfactory sense, so that any alteration in the sense of smell coupled with diminished taste may profoundly affect enjoyment of food as well as one's quality of life, since eating is often associated with meeting others and sharing experiences.

Assessing changes in taste is best done through individual questioning, since this will also help the nurse to determine external factors that may impinge on the person's appreciation of flavours (e.g. smoking, medication or food habits). Questions about appetite, weight, enjoyment of food, problems related to chewing or swallowing, and sudden or unusual changes in taste are good starting points. Any sudden or unusual changes should be reported to a doctor for further assessment.

Olfaction

A decreased sensitivity to odours may at times be dangerous for the older person, for instance failure to detect leaking gas, a smouldering cigarette or tainted food. Most people, however, lose some ability to discriminate between smells, resulting in a slightly lowered capacity to enjoy subtle scents and fragrances and placing a stronger reliance on texture and visual cues.

In order to determine the reason for olfactory changes, the nurse may find it useful to make an assessment of the nose with the older person and consult his or her relatives. A framework for this, adapted from the work of Knapp (1989), is given in **Box 12.1** and should be used in conjunction with the detailed diagram of the nose shown in **Figure 12.1**.

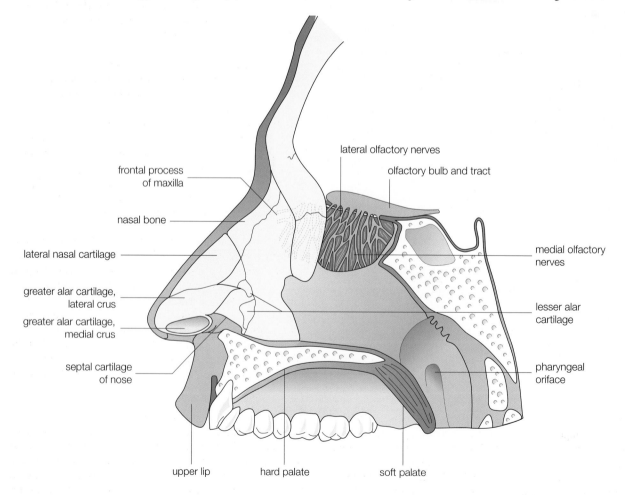

Figure 12.1 Key structures of the nose (Source: Knapp, MT. A rose is still a rose: how does losing the sense of smell affect an elder's life. *Geriatr Nurs* **1989, 10(6): 290.)**

12.1 Knapp's Assessment of the Nose

(1)   Ask the older person and his or her relatives if any alterations in smelling or breathing have been noticed. Try to determine the nature of these and the length of time over which they have occurred.

(2)   Look at the nose noting any asymmetry that could interfere with breathing or smell as well as the colour and texture of the nose and its membranes.

(3)   Palpate the nose feeling for raised bumps along the frontal bone at the base and hard nodes in the cartilage. Changes may suggest either new or old fractures that may require medical attention.

(4)   Occlude each nostril, one at a time, and ask the person to close his or her mouth and breathe through the open nostril. This will help to determine any obstructions that may be affecting smell and breathing.

(5)   Test his or her ability to discriminate between smells by asking the person to identify various smells. If any cannot be distinguished, try to find out if these alterations are long-standing, and if not, when they occurred and if there were any factors associated with their development.

Any unusual features should be discussed with the doctor. Nurses may also find it useful to combine assessments of the olfactory sense with those of taste to gain a comprehensive overview of these two closely interlinked senses.

VISION

Vision has been described as the most important of the senses since it tells us so much about the world around us. Naturally then, any alteration in our visual acuity and accommodation (regardless of its 'normality') will affect our lives and our feelings of security. Having said this however, it is fair to state that the normal changes in vision associated with ageing cause little more that inconvenience to many people and can, in the main, be easily rectified. For some, however, more profound visual changes, such as the development of cataracts or glaucoma, will impact significantly on not only the person's quality of vision but also his or her quality of life.

The normal changes associated with the ageing visual system have been detailed in Chapter 4. This section will focus on some of the more commonly occurring visual problems that may present themselves during older age (glaucoma,

cataracts and macular degeneration) and how the nurse may be alerted to these, assess vision and offer support to those who find themselves visually compromised.

Glaucoma

Glaucoma can be categorised as both an acute and a chronic condition resulting from increased intraocular pressure, usually bilateral, which can lead to permanent damage to the optic nerve. Several risk factors associated with this disease have been identified and should be noted by all health-care professionals providing care and advice to older people. This includes nurses working in hospitals, nursing homes and the community, practice nurses and health visitors who may be responsible for regular health assessments for older people, and those working in specialised eye clinics and wards. These risk factors include:

- Elevated intraocular pressure (greater than 22 mmHg).
- Age (over 50 years).
- Family history.
- Associated conditions (diabetes mellitus, thyroid disease, near-sightedness, hypertension and cardiovascular disease) (Ralson *et al.* 1992).

There are two distinct types of glaucoma:
(1) **Open-angle glaucoma**. This is asymptomatic and is a common cause of blindness, probably due to its insidious nature.
(2) **Angle-closure glaucoma**. This is caused when the natural fluids of the eye are blocked by ciliary muscle rigidity and the resultant pressure build-up damages the optic nerve. It is characterised by a rapid rise in intraocular pressure accompanied by redness and pain in and around the eye, severe headache, nausea, vomiting, as well as blurring of vision.

Usually medication can control glaucoma, but when surgery is necessary it is only successful if scar tissue does not subsequently obstruct the drainage channel. The catastrophic results of glaucoma have prompted heightened awareness of this visual disease amongst opticians and other health-care workers. All those concerned with screening older people, for example in the over seventy-fives' health check, should pay particular attention to this potential problem and alert the client to the risk factors and possible manifestations of the condition so that prompt action can be taken if these occur.

Cataracts

Another prevalent disorder among older people is the development of cataracts – opacities within the lens. The Royal National Institute for the Blind (RNIB) (1996a) suggested that over half of those aged 65 years and over would have some cataract development. Cataracts are usually recognised by the clouding of the usually clear lens. Their formation is normal in the ageing process but may be worsened by diabetes, hypertension, kidney disease, and injuries or exposure to toxic situations. Common symptoms of cataracts are:

- Painless, progressive loss of vision usually reported as, 'I'm not seeing as well as I used to'.
- Seeing halos around objects as light is diffused.
- Blurring.
- Seeing double images.
- Decreased perception of light and colour.
- Poor vision in bright light.
- Change of colour vision (RNIB, 1996a).

Treatment involves the surgical substitution of the lens for an artificial lens and is undertaken once the visual loss impedes the individual's daily life. In the past, cataracts were only operated on when they were described as 'ripe', meaning that they had reached the point of greatest deterioration; in the main, people no longer have to wait for this but find surgery is available as soon as vision becomes significantly impaired. This procedure is usually straightforward and involves only a short period of time in hospital (usually a day) with careful skilled nursing care following discharge from hospital. The substitution of the lens is usually carried out using a local anaesthetic and lasts less than an hour in most cases. After surgery the following simple precautions should be taken to avoid unsettling the lens:

- Avoid rubbing the eye.
- Avoid heavy lifting and strenuous exercise.
- Take care in windy weather in case foreign bodies blow into the eye.
- Wash hair leaning backwards not forwards.
- Avoid eye make-up for about six weeks.
- Avoid driving until you are told you may (RNIB, 1996a).

Sight is gradually regained with a resultant increased quality of life being experienced due to increased mobility, renewed opportunities to meet others and increased ability to see and enjoy more involvement in leisure activities which rely on sight.

Macular Degeneration

The macula is the central visual point of the retina and as such is the source of central visual clarity. Age-related macular degeneration (ARMD) results from systemic changes in circulation, accumulation of cellular waste products, tissue atrophy and growth of abnormal blood vessels in the choroid layer beneath the retina (**Figure 12.2**).

ARMD is the most common visual impairment associated with later life, which leads to permanent visual incapacitation characterised by loss of central visual acuity. Interestingly, peripheral vision is unaffected and so it does not lead to complete loss of sight. The aetiology is unknown. Presentation often includes:

- Blurred or distorted central vision.
- Things beginning to look unusual in size and shape.
- Sensitivity to light.
- Seeing lights that are not there.
- Seeing blank patches or dark spots in the centre of the visual field.

All of the symptoms listed above are painless (RNIB, 1996b).

Macular degeneration can be detected early in its development by the use of an Amsler grid (**Figure 12.3**), which determines clarity of central vision. A perception of wavy lines on the grid is diagnostic of the beginnings of macular degeneration. Treatment, if diagnosed early, may include laser treatment or the use of a variety of visual aids tailored to the condition as it presents and develops.

Diabetic Retinopathy

Some visual disabilities are acquired through the harmful effects of elevated blood sugar due to diabetes mellitus, which creates haemorrhaging and exudates in the retina. Diabetic retinopathy accounts for only a small percentage of blindness in the UK, but it is the commonest cause of blindness in older age and accounts for about 40% of sight problems associated with being an older person with diabetes (Cullinan, 1991).

Symptoms depend on the location and extent of the haemorrhaging or exudate deposits. Since this complication of diabetes is well known and the consequences so marked, annual eye tests are required to monitor this condition and any alterations in vision should be followed up immediately.

Other Visual Challenges

For some people, visual disturbance may occur as a result of a stroke or other cerebral trauma. This may result in a variety of consequences associated with seeing and recognising objects and people, which include the following:

- Problems associated with recognition (what is it?). These include visual agnosia (inability to tell what an object is by looking at it) and prosopagnosia (impaired recognition of faces).
- Problems of spatial awareness (where is it?). These include unilateral neglect (one side of the body, the opposite side to their lesion, is unrecognised), impaired depth perception and optic ataxia (difficulty coordinating movement and vision; for example, being unable to accurately reach out for something).
- Problems related to using the objects seen (what do I do with it?) or visual apraxia.

These visuoperceptual problems present a challenge to nurses who need to be alert to their possibility and manifestation since nurses are often in the best position to notice changes that might be suggestive of these problems. Subsequent treatment and rehabilitation will be determined through consultations between the patient, his or her carers and the multidisciplinary team.

General Assessment of Vision

Various problems with vision are common in ageing and nurses may make a preliminary assessment prior to referral for further evaluation. There are certain signs and symptoms of visual problems that should alert the nurse. These fall into

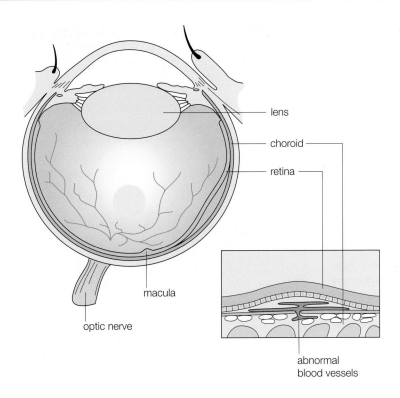

- lens
- choroid
- retina
- macula
- optic nerve
- abnormal blood vessels

Figure 12.2 Age-related macular generation (ARMD) results if abnormal blood vessels grow in the choroid layer beneath the retina, or if any part of the retina fails to receive proper nutrients. (Source: Mayo Health Clinic Health Letter. *Macular degeneration.* **Rochester, MN, September 1990.)**

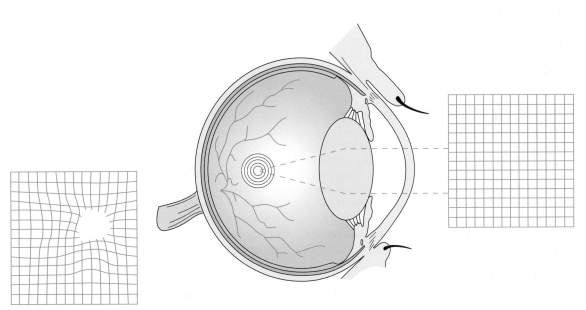

Figure 12.3 Macular degeneration: distortion of central vision; normal peripheral vision. (Source: Illustration by Harriet R. Greenfield, Newton, MA.)

two categories – those reported by the patient and those observed by the nurse.

(1) The older person may report:
  - Pain in the eyes.
  - Difficulty seeing in darkened areas.
  - Double vision.
  - Flashes of light.
  - Distorted vision.

(2) The nurse may notice that the older person:
  - Gets lost.
  - Bumps into things.
  - Strains to read or no longer reads.

279

- Stumbles and falls.
- Spills food.
- Withdraws.
- Suffers from severe headaches accompanied by blurred vision.
- Uses less eye contact during conversations.
- Has placid facial expression.
- Watches television at close range.
- Has a decreased sense of balance.
- Wears mismatched clothing.

Any of these, either noted in isolation or in conjunction with another, should alert a nurse to seek more expert advice. A more standardised approach may be taken to assessment through the completion of a simple assessment form that presents triggers for the nurse to evaluate with the person. The ENB (1990) produced such a form designed to help nurses undertaking the over seventy-fives' health screening advocated by the Department of Health in 1989. Questions related to vision are simple but may form an appropriate starting point to begin exploring this sense with the older person:

- How well can you see?
- Do you need glasses?
  - reading?
  - distance?
- When did you last have an eye test? (ENB, 1990, p. 109).

The findings from these questions may then lead the nurse to perform a preliminary eye test and suggest the person seeks appropriate advice elsewhere if need be.

Caring for an Older Person with Visual Impairment

Visual impairments are likely to significantly affect the safety of an older person, particularly when living in a strange environment. Nurses are in an ideal position to create and maintain environments that promote safety and enhance feelings of security. This can be achieved by focusing on the criteria displayed in **Boxes 12.2 and 12.3** as well as paying attention to the following:

Environmental Lighting

The pupil of the aged eye admits less light to the retina. To compensate for this, careful attention needs to be paid to environmental lighting (Kolanowski, 1992). To achieve a safe environment more light needs to be made available but at the same time glare should be avoided. During later life, sensitivity to glare is markedly increased due to the clouding of the lens and vitreous humour that results in scattering of light as it passes through the lens.

The quality of artificial light becomes exceedingly important for older people, particularly those living in institutions, as they often spend a great deal of their time indoors and may have less control over lighting than if they lived in their own

12.2 Caring for Visually Challenged People

- Remember there are many degrees of blindness; allow as much independence as possible.
- Speak normally but not from a distance; do not raise or lower voice, and continue to use gestures if that is natural to your communication. Do not alter your vocabulary; words such as 'see' and 'blind' are parts of normal speech. When others are present, address the blind person by prefacing remarks with his or her name or a light touch on the arm.
- When entering the presence of a blind person, speak promptly, identifying yourself and others with you. State when you are leaving to make the person aware of your departure.
- Speak descriptively of your surroundings to familiarise the blind person. State the position of people who are in the room.
- Do not change room arrangements without explanation.
- Speak before handing the person an object. Describe positions of food on plate in relation to clock position (e.g. 3 o'clock, 6 o'clock).
- When walking with a blind person, offer your arm. Pause before stairs or curbs; mention them. In seating, place the person's hand on the back of the chair. Let him or her know position in relation to objects.
- Blind people like to know the beauty that surrounds them. Describe flowers, scenery, colours and textures. People who have been blind since birth cannot conceive colour, but it adds to their appreciation to hear full descriptions. Older people most frequently have been sighted and can enjoy memories of beauty stimulated by descriptive conversation.

home. The type of lighting used also appears to affect sight; Kolanowski (1992) suggests the use of broad-spectrum fluorescent lighting since it simulates natural sunlight. There is some evidence that these types of lighting also produce calmness and relaxation, which may add to feelings of safety and security.

Nurses are largely responsible for the types of lighting that older people are subjected to. Therefore, it is worthy of careful consideration since nursing care involves the creation of hospitable environments in which to deliver care.

Clarity of Notices

Using large clear print for notices and displaying them prominently will facilitate reading and help people with compromised sight to recognise strategic parts of their new environment, thus promoting safety and feelings of security.

Clarity of Speech and Instructions

Speak clearly, facing the person, if possible ensuring that there is good light on your face. This will help the older person to

12.3 Suggestions for Communication with and Caring for a Visually Challenged Nursing-Home Resident

1. Always identify yourself clearly.
2. Always make it clear when you are leaving the room.
3. Make sure you have the resident's attention before you start to talk.
4. Try to minimise the number of distractions.
5. Whenever possible, choose bright clothes with bold contrasts.
6. Check to see that the best possible lighting is available.
7. Assess your position in relation to the resident.
8. One eye or ear may be better than the other.
9. Try not to move items in resident's room.
10. Staff members should try to narrate their actions.
11. Try to keep resident between you and the window, or you will appear as a dark shadow.
12. Use some means to identify residents who are known to be visually impaired.
13. Use the analogy of clock hands to help locate objects.
14. Keep colour and texture in mind when buying clothes.
15. Be careful about labelling a resident as confused. He or she may be making mistakes due to poor vision!

Source: McNeely E, Griffin-Shirley N, Hubbard A. Diminished vision in nursing homes. *Geriatr Nurs* 1992, 13(6): 332.

see your facial expression and your lips, which may in turn help with the interpretation of the message being conveyed. Communicating with older people is an important way of making them feel safe and secure, explanations need to be clear and fully understood if empowering partnerships are to be developed and sustained.

Orientating the Visually Challenged Person

Methods to assist the visually impaired person are not generally taught in nursing curricula. McNeeley *et al.* (1992) suggest three simple strategies:

(1) The clock method in which the individual is simply told where the food or item is as if it were on a clock face.
(2) The sighted guide, who accompanies the older person enhancing safety and security. The following steps may help anyone using this approach to care:
   • Find out if the older person would like you to guide them.
   • If they do, offer your elbow or arm and ask the older person to hold it above the elbow (if need be, physically assist the person to do this).
   • Walk half a step ahead and slightly to the side of the person who you are guiding. If the person is frail, place a hand on their forearm.

   • Relax and walk at a comfortable pace.
   • Tell the person when you are approaching doors or other obstacles, particularly those that necessitate a change in direction.

The RNIB produce a leaflet detailing their advice on how to guide people (*see* end of Chapter 12 for contact address).
(3) Colour contrast for accented visual impact may be a useful way of helping people with impaired sight. A simple example of this is the bright towel set against a cream background or a change in floor colour to denote different rooms within a hospital or nursing home.

Most visually impaired people have enough residual vision to use their eyesight with proper aids or training to read, write and move around safely. Unfortunately, many older people with serious visual impairments consider themselves 'blind' and are usually treated as if they are. However, adequate training in using residual vision and the correct use of aids to enhance remaining sight may prevent partially sighted older people from falling into unnecessarily dependent lifestyles.

Impact of Visual Impairment on Safety and Security

Ross *et al.* (1991) found that a direct relationship existed between functional status and low vision with regard to correctly identifying objects, reading and participating in general activities of daily living. Enriched communication may keep a visually impaired older person in contact with the environment and foster increased feelings of security and safety. Several aids are available to increase safety and to help the person become more secure in their environment and lifestyle. Some of these are listed below, however the interested reader is referred to the RNIB to ensure up-to-date information since there remains huge potential for development. They will also give advice about paying for aids such as the following:

(1) Magnifiers. These come in a variety of different sorts ranging from hand held ones to ones attached to spectacles.
(2) Varying types of spectacles.
(3) Illuminated aids (e.g. a hand-held magnifier with a built in light).
(4) Closed circuit television.
(5) Typoscope. This is a card with a central opening which can be laid over the sentence being read to provide a clear framework around these words and eliminate glare (RNIB, 1996c).

Older people should also be advised to take care over trailing wires, rugs, slippery surfaces (e.g. getting into or out of the bath), leaning over gas or halogen rings and badly positioned objects. For those people being discharged home following an alteration to their sight, a home visit guided by an occupational therapist would be beneficial.

Common Causes of Hearing Loss in Older People

Disorder	Characteristics
Hypothyroidism	Slowly progressive sensorineural and conductive hearing loss; affects all frequencies equally
Ototoxic drugs	Hearing loss with or without vestibular dysfunction, following treatment with known ototoxic drugs
Noise-induced	History of prolonged exposure to loud continuous noise or brief hearing loss exposures to loud impulse noise
Presbycusis	Gradual, progressive loss of hearing after 20 years; affects reception of high-frequency sounds

Hearing loss from any of these disorders may be improved with hearing aids; in cases of profound sensorineural loss, a cochlear implant may be considered.

Table 12.2 Common Causes of Hearing Loss in Older People. (Source: Adapted from Anderson R, Meyerhoff W. In Calkins E, Davis P, Ford M eds. *The practice of geriatrics.* Philadelphia: WB Saunders, 1986.)

HEARING AND HEARING IMPAIRMENT IN OLDER AGE

The ear has two major functions – hearing and maintaining balance. Both are major concerns for the nurse caring for an elderly person. Hearing loss may be an imperceptible, but much feared, accompaniment to older age, which has several far-reaching consequences. Some people are aware of a hearing loss and are disturbed by misperceptions and distortion of sounds; often they imagine derogatory remarks are said about them. However, knowing that one has a hearing loss is not sufficient on its own; careful treatment and management are essential components of skilled care and the promotion and maintenance of independence.

It is estimated that over 8 million people have a hearing loss in the UK. The chances of hearing loss increases with age and it is estimated that 33% of people in their sixties have some loss rising to 70% of those over the age of 70 years (Hearing Concern, 1996). Hearing loss after 65 years of age varies according to the degree and type of loss being considered (**Table 12.2**) but, despite this variability, it is often seen as a stigma associated with growing older and becoming isolated from others.

Common problems associated with the ageing ear are cerumen impaction, presbycusis and tinnitus. These need to be considered when providing care to older people whether within their own homes, residential homes, nursing homes or hospitals. All too often those receiving care (nursing or social) are not adequately assessed in relation to their hearing ability (Tolson and MacIntosh, 1992; Department of Health, 1997).

Cerumen Impaction

Cerumen impaction is the most common and easily corrected hearing problem associated with growing older. The reduction in the number of cerumen-producing glands and activity of the glands results in a tendency towards cerumen impactions in older age. These tend to occur more frequently in older men as the hairs in the ear (tragi) become entangled with the wax preventing its dislodgement (Anderson and Meyerhoff, 1986). Long-standing impactions become hard, dry and dark brown in colour. Although wax is easily removed by ear syringing, some older people occasionally use foreign objects to clean their ears and in so doing have perforated the tympanic membrane resulting in severe hearing loss in the injured ear.

People at particular risk of impaction are those with large amounts of ear canal hair, those who habitually wear hearing aids, those with benign growths that narrow the external ear canal and those who have a predilection to cerumen accumulation.

Presbycusis

Presbycusis is a common form of hearing impairment due to wear and tear on the mechanisms for hearing. It is deemed to be a natural consequence of ageing and is detailed in Chapter 4.

Presbycusis is a progressive condition which tends to worsen with age, leaving some people feeling very disabled by compromised hearing. Anybody noticing and reporting increased deafness should be referred to an audiologist for assessment, which may result in the fitting of a hearing aid. In many instances, older people do not notice this progressive change in their hearing and as such community nurses, practice nurses and health visitors have a role in assessing hearing changes through routine health screening.

Tinnitus

Tinnitus, ringing or swishing sounds arising in the ear, is a condition that can cause great distress as well as interfering with hearing. The incidence of tinnitus peaks between the ages of 65 and 74 years and then seems to decrease. The impact of tinnitus was shown by Stouffer and Tyler (1990) who found that in 528 elderly people suffering from this disorder, it was present almost continuously (26 days a month), thereby impacting heavily on their quality of life. A variety of treatments are available, ranging from transtympanal electrostimulation and tinnitus maskers to the use of hearing aids. In a study investigating the success of various techniques, von Wedel *et al.* (1990) attributed varying levels of success to the available treatment approaches. After a 1-year follow-up, hearing aids were found to be helpful in the study group and 3% of patients were helped by tinnitus maskers.

Further details of this problem may be obtained from the British Tinnitus Association or the Tinnitus Helpline run by the Royal National Institute for Deaf People (RNID). Details are provided at the end of Chapter 12.

Assessment of those with Impaired Hearing

Assessment of a hearing disability may be done in a superficial manner by almost any observant practitioner; however, the responsibility for the initial identification of hearing problems usually falls upon the nurse and therefore rapid, reliable, effective screening methods must be available to them. Nurses are reminded that the best judge of adequate hearing capacity is the older person themselves so asking if the person thinks that they may have a hearing problem is the best place to start. Clark *et al.* (1991) found high levels of accuracy of self-reported hearing loss among older women if it hampered their daily life. However, older people are often unaware of mild-to-moderate hearing loss because of the gradual manner in which it usually develops.

Awareness and acceptance of the deficit are the precursors to accurate assessment and coping with the presenting problem. To this end, the following useful points for consideration are given in **Box 12.4**.

The answers to questions posed in **Box 12.4** will give you a lot of useful information. For a more in-depth evaluation you may decide to use a standardised check list like the one presented in **Figure 12.4**. This type of evaluation needs to be handled with the utmost care since many older people are reluctant to admit that they have a problem. When there is any doubt, referral should be made to a doctor or audiologist.

Physical examination, interview, self-assessment, relative or friend assessment and audiometric findings are all neces-

12.4 Assessment of those with Impaired Hearing

(1) Ask relevant questions related to the ear, hearing and balance. For example, in the last 3 months:
  - Have you had discharge from your ears?
  - Have you experienced dizziness?
  - Have you had pain in your ears?
  - Have you noticed a sudden or rapid change in your hearing?

(2) Observe the person. Consider if the person:
  - Seems to be inattentive to others.
  - Believes people are talking about him or her.
  - Fails to respond to sounds in the environment.
  - Has difficulty following clear directions.
  - Appears to be withdrawn or alone much of the time.
  - Asks for things to be repeated.
  - Turns one ear towards the speaker.
  - Has a monotonous voice or unusual voice quality.
  - Speaks unusually loudly.

(3) Once you have established a hearing problem is present you may delve deeper by asking the person to:
  - Describe the problem.
  - Discuss the history of the problem.
  - Describe the extent of the problem and how it interferes with communication and the quality of the person's life.

sary to arrive at a meaningful recommendation for the hearing impaired older person. The nursing assessment forms a small but vital part in this whole process since further testing must be done to determine the nature of the loss, how much it interferes with communication, whether it is treatable and whether a hearing aid will be useful.

Impact of Deafness on Safety and Security

Hearing loss can impact on a person's life in a variety of different ways leading to feelings of insecurity, suspicion and isolation. These may be manifested through:
- Exclusion from conversation.
- Exclusion from day-to-day life (the hubbub of life may be muffled or unnoticed).
- Exclusion from information.
- Exclusion from leisure activities.
- Exclusion from family and friends (Hearing Concern, 1996).

Hearing Handicap Scale

Rating	Scoring	Scores	
always or 2	raw score – 29 x 1.25 = %	no handicap	0% to 20%
frequently or 4		mild hearing handicap	21% to 40%
never or 5		moderate hearing handicap	41% to 70%
		severe hearing handicap	71% to 100%

1. At 2 to 4m from radio or television, do you understand speech?
2. Can you converse on telephone easily?
3. Can you carry on conversation comfortably in a noisy place?
4. Can you understand speech when in a noisy bus, on an airplane, at a movie, on the street corner?
5. Can you understand a person when seated beside him and you cannot see his face?
6. Can you understand speech if someone is talking to you while chewing crunchy food?
7. Can you understand a whisper when you cannot see a person's face?
8. Can you carry on a conversation across a room with someone in normal tone of voice?
9. Can you understand women when they talk?
10. Can you carry on conversation outdoors when it is reasonably quiet?
11. When in a meeting or a large dinner would you know what speaker said if lips were not moving?
12. Can you follow conversation at a large dinner or in a small group?
13. When seated under balcony of a theatre or auditorium, can you hear what is going on?
14. When in church or a lecture hall can you hear if speaker does not use a microphone?
15. Can you hear telephone ring when it is located in another room?
16. Can you hear warning signals such as car horns, railway crossing bells, or emergency vehicle sirens?
17. Can you carry on conversation in a car with windows open?
18. Can you carry on conversation in a car with windows closed?
19. Can you hear when someone calls from another room?
20. Can you understand when someone speaks to you from another room?
21. Can you carry on conversation with someone who speaks quietly?
22. When you ask for directions, do you understand what is said?
23. When you are introduced, do you understand the name the first time it is spoken?
24. Can you hear adequately when conversing with more than one person?
25. When seated in the front of an auditorium, can you understand most of what is being said?
26. Can you carry on everyday conversations with family members without difficulty?
27. When seated in the rear of an auditorium, can you hear most of what is said?
28. When in a large formal gathering, can you hear what is said if the speaker uses a microphone?
29. Can you hear night sounds, such as dogs barking, distant trains, cars passing, etc.?

Figure 12.4 Hearing handicap scale (Source: Modified from High *et al. J Speech Discord* 1964, 29: 215).

Clearly each of these may impact on a person's feelings of security and safety resulting in depression, isolation, reduced feelings of wellbeing and increased dependence on others (Gilhome Herbst, 1991). These psychological consequences may also affect the friends and carers of the deaf person, resulting in uncertainty surrounding the extent of the person's deafness; this in turn may lead to them thinking that the older person can hear more than he or she acknowledges. This is particularly the case when others are discussing the older person who is hard of hearing within earshot. The older person naturally concentrates more fully in order to hear what is being said, hence the comment from others that they can hear when they want to. When the name is mentioned, they concentrate in case what is being said is relevant to them. In order to minimise misunderstandings, the carer also requires careful explanation of the extent and effects of deafness and how they can best help to maximise hearing.

Overcoming Deafness

Several approaches to overcoming deafness have been advocated. Some are listed below, however the interested reader is referred to the RNID for further information.

Hearing Aids

A hearing aid is a personal amplifying system that includes a microphone, an amplifier and a loud speaker. In this era of highly sophisticated, personalised and computerised hearing aids, almost anyone can find some hearing enhancement. Hearing aids have changed dramatically in recent years, but many individuals, having tried one several years ago, have decided against using them on the basis of out-of-date information. There are two main types of hearing aid in use:

(1) The 'behind the ear aid', which looks like a shrimp and fits around behind the ear.
(2) The 'in the ear aid', which is small and fits in the concha of the ear.

There are many different manufacturers of hearing aids and several different outlets involved in the assessment for and fitting of hearing aids so that the informed consumer now has a broad selection from which to choose.

Suggestions for the care and use of hearing aids are given in **Table 12.3** and will be useful for nurses when caring for someone with a hearing aid, or in advising someone about how to obtain one or caring for a relative or friend with one. In order to adapt to hearing aids, of whatever type, the individual will require motivation. Therefore, sensitive nursing and the passage of accurate, helpful information are important.

Other Technical Aids

Many environmental and technical aids have been designed to help people who are deaf or hard of hearing. Some are listed below, however more detailed up-to-date information may be obtained from the RNID.

(1) Listening devices (including head sets and neck loops to help people to hear the radio or television).
(2) Teletext.
(3) Amplified telephones, fax machines.
(4) Alerting devices (especially adapted alarm clocks with flashing lights and vibrating pads that can be placed under a pillow, doorbells, smoke and fire alarms).
(5) World Wide Web.

Helping the Deaf Person

In **Box 12.5** are pointers that may be helpful when you consider ways in which you can generally help a deaf person.

The aim of skilled nursing care is to enhance the person's quality of life since hearing loss may result in depression, cognitive dysfunction, social isolation and overall reductions in health status. In order to do this, the nurse needs to be visible, clear, concise and patient (Deaf and Hard of Hearing UK, 1996).

TOUCH

For many older people using and receiving touch is an important component of their lives. However, this primary form of communication is principally used in infancy and childhood and may be perceived as inappropriate in later life despite the suggestion by some that adults have an increased need for touch when they are in situations of danger, sickness or incapacity (Bowlby, 1958). Hence the need for nurses to consider their use of touch when caring for older people. Touch is obviously a central component of nursing care not only during physical tasks but also as a means of affective communication, for instance to convey acceptance, empathy and friendship. For older people suffering from challenges to their sensory, perceptual and communicative channels, the judicious use of touch may be one way of enhancing their feelings of being accepted, reassured and encouraged to continue to work towards greater independence. Receiving touch may enhance feelings of safety and security when other senses are compromised (*see* Chapter 15 and 16 for further discussion).

The Care and Use of Hearing Aids	
Hearing aid use	Care of the hearing aid
• Initially, wear aid 15–20 minutes daily • Gradually increase time until 10–12 hours • Hearing aid will initially make client uneasy • Insert aid with canal portion pointing into ear, press and twist until snug • Turn aid slowly to third or half volume • A whistling sound indicates incorrect ear mold • Adjust volume to a level comfortable for talking at a distance of 1 metre • Do not wear aid under heat lamps, hair dryer or in extreme heat or cold • Do not wear aid while bathing • Sit close to speaker in noisy situations • Continue to be observant of nonverbal cues • Be patient although the process of adaptation is difficult it will ultimately be rewarding	• Insert battery when hearing aid is turned off • Store hearing aid in a dry, safe place • Remove or disconnect battery when not in use • Clean cerumen from tip weekly with pipe cleaner • Common problems include: switch turned off, clogged ear mold, dislodged battery, twisted insertion tubing between ear mold and aid • Ear molds need replacing every 2 or 3 years • Check ear molds for rough spots that will irritate ear • Avoid exposing aid to very wet cold weather • Clean batteries occasionally to remove corrosion; use a sharpened pencil eraser and gently scrape • Concentrate on conversation, request repeat if necessary

Table 12.3 The Care and Use of Hearing Aids

12.5 Helping the Deaf Person

(1) Ask the person if there are any things that they use to help their hearing.
(2) If the person wears a hearing aid, encourage its use.
(3) Use charts, pictures or models to explain medications and procedures.
(4) Make sure that you face the person and that there is adequate light so that they can clearly see your face.
(5) When speaking keep your hands away from your face.
(6) Use facial and hand expressions freely to facilitate understanding.
(7) Face the person and stand or sit on the same level.
(8) Gain the person's attention before beginning to speak. This could be achieved by touching the person's shoulder or shaking their hand to signify the beginning and end of the interaction.
(9) Avoid speaking from another room or while walking away.
(10) Articulate carefully and moderate the speed of your speech. Pause between sentences to confirm understanding.
(11) Restate with different words when you are not understood.
(12) Reduce background noise.
(13) Ensure that the call button is within easy reach.
(14) Make sure that you don't restrict both arms of the deaf person with, for instance, intravenous infusions, as they may need their hands for communication.
(15) Communicate to the multidisciplinary team that the person is deaf.
(16) Consider alternative strategies to enhance 'hearing' for instance Hearing Dogs for the Deaf. This approach may be particularly appropriate when safety is considered, since these dogs are trained to warn the deaf person about impending dangers (e.g. fire and smoke) as well as increasing quality of life and independence (e.g. through notifying the owner that a phone or door bell is ringing).

 Meeting Hearing Impairment Needs

Minnie Cooke, now 73 years of age, lives in a nursing home. She had worked as a weaver in a textile mill for most of her working life but she stopped working at a time before ear protectors were recommended and health and safety regulations were enforced. She really enjoys the social life in the home, particularly the musical evenings or when a party goes out to the local entertainment centre. She also has a number of friends who visit regularly. Minnie is quite hard of hearing, and this frustrates her. She also often appears disorientated by what is going on around her. The nurses in the home have tried to talk with her about a hearing aid but Minnie says that she has friends who have them but 'just can't get on with them'. Eventually she agrees to try a hearing aid, provided the nurses help her to use it. By the end of the first week, Minnie is even more frustrated. She finds the cocophony of sounds overwhelming at times, and is worried that other residents will hear it humming. She is talking of giving up with using it.

- **What subjective data is Minnie offering that will assist with the nursing assessment?**
- **What objective data can the nursing team collect that will assist their assessment?**
- **What strengths does Minnie demonstrate on which the plan of care can be based?**
- **What actions should be included on the care plan?**
- **What would be the desirable outcomes of the plan of care for Minnie?**
- **How could these outcomes be evaluated?**
- **What other professionals should be involved in her care?**

Watson (1975) proposed two main types of touch – instrumental (a deliberate physical contact initiated as part of a task) and expressive (relatively spontaneous, affectionate contact which may not necessarily be task oriented). Several researchers have observed this difference in the care which older people receive (le May and Redfern, 1989) and noted, empirically and anecdotally, positive benefits to patients of the latter type (Copstead, 1980; Langland and Panicucci, 1982).

Feeling sensations also forms a central component of protecting oneself from harm; for example, feeling heat from a fire or cold when environmental temperatures put older people at risk of hypothermia. For some older people these safety mechanisms do not function effectively and put them at risk of harm. Nurses need to be aware of this and warn older people and their carers of any potential risks to their safety and security.

SPEECH

Speech is a major means of organising and maintaining environmental security and personal safety. Having spent a lifetime relying on speech as the principle means of communicating with others any alteration in this ability may be isolating and dehumanising. Verbal communication is the single most important definition of humanity and security. Caring for a person with speech impairment is complex and requires the involvement of and close liaison with a speech and language therapist.

There are three main categories of impaired verbal communication; these are associated with:

(1) Reception.
(2) Perception.
(3) Articulation.

Reception may be impaired by anxiety, hearing deficits and altered levels of consciousness. Stroke, dementia and delirium may distort perception. Dysarthria, respiratory disease, destruction of the larynx and cerebral infarction may hamper articulation.

Specific difficulties associated with language disorder in older people include:

- **Anomie.** This is difficulty in retrieving words during spontaneous speech and naming tasks.
- **Aphasia.** This is an acquired impairment of the language processes underlying receptive and expressive modalities caused by damage to areas of the brain that are primarily responsible for language processes.
- **Apraxia.** This is an impairment in the ability to carry out voluntary movements because of brain damage.
- **Dysarthria.** This is an impairment as the result of damage to the central or peripheral nervous system.

Difficulty in articulating words or selecting and comprehending appropriate words is caused by neuromotor disturbances that may be transient, long-standing, reversible or irreversible. Prophylactic or primary prevention of these disorders is poorly understood, but much can be done in speech retraining programmes through the involvement of speech and language therapists.

Aphasia

In old age the most common language disorder is aphasia following stroke. The importance of Broca's and Wernicke's areas of the left cerebral cortex in the expression and understanding of language has been recognised for over a century (Geschwind, 1965). These lie within the distribution of the left cerebral artery surrounding the sylvian fissure. Broca's area is associated with the posteroinferior frontal lobe. Wernicke's area lies adjacent to the primary auditory cortex. The right hemisphere, unlike the left, cannot be compartmentalised into discrete functional roles. The more diffuse organisation appears to adapt the right hemisphere to a more holistic, global processing of information. The skills of the right hemisphere include selective attention, visual perceptions, orientation to time and place, and understanding of the subtleties of communication. Research is increasingly emphasising the importance of the right hemisphere and the subcortical structures in language processing.

There are several types of aphasia (**Figure 12.5**) that the nurse may encounter with elderly persons:

- Wernicke's aphasia is the result of a lesion in the superior temporal gyrus. People with Wernicke's aphasia speak easily but in a repetitive jargon that is poorly understood. Unrelated words may be strung together or syllables repeated. They also have difficulty understanding spoken language.
- Broca's aphasia typically involves damage to the posteroinferior portions of the dominant frontal lobe. People with Broca's aphasia understand others but speak very slowly and use minimum words. They often struggle to articulate a word and seem to have lost the ability to voluntarily control the movements of speech. This is often called 'apraxia of speech'.
- People with conductive aphasia understand speech and may speak fluently but may substitute sounds and words for the ones they wish to use.
- Anomic aphasia is associated with lesions of the dominant temporoparietal regions of the brain, although no single locus has been identified. People with anomic aphasia understand and speak readily but may have severe problems finding a word.

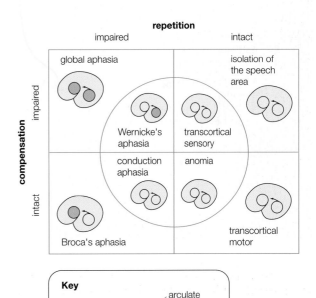

Figure 12.5 Aphasia diagram: the three components of language function to be tested are comprehension, fluency and repetition. Aphasias depicted within the circle are the fluent aphasias (Source: Modified from Gallo JJ, Reichel W, Anderson L.. *Handbook of geriatric assessment* Aspen Publishing: Gathersburg, MD, 1988.)

• Global aphasia is the result of large left hemisphere lesions and affects most of the language areas of the brain. People with global aphasia are unable to understand words or speak intelligibly. They may use meaningless syllables repetitiously.

These types of aphasia can be broken down into two categories – receptive and expressive aphasia (see **Figure 12.6**):

(1) Receptive aphasic patients cannot understand language; it is as if they are in a foreign land but they may recognise objects and their uses.

(2) Expressive aphasic patients can understand verbal and written communication but cannot organise concepts into words or meaningful expressions.

Communicating with aphasic patients is a skilled component of nursing. Some suggestions for enhancing this process are provided in **Box 12.6**.

Nurses are responsible for accurate observation and recording of the speech and word recognition patterns of the client and for consistently implementing the recommendations of the speech and language therapist. The speech and language therapist may be able to identify the areas of language that remain relatively unimpaired and capitalise on these remaining strengths. The prognosis for recovery of speech is summarised in **Table 12.4**.

Additional techniques have been developed to assist us in communicating with those who have temporarily or permanently lost their verbal skills, for example, electro-mechanical boards, electronic boards, sentence structure boards and computer programs. Various types of communication boards, for example **Figure 12.7**, have been developed for patients with several levels of disability. For some, a particularly sensitive pressure switch can be activated by the touch of an ear, nose or chin. To be generally useful, devices must be simply constructed, inexpensive, portable and connected to a signalling device to attract attention when the individual wishes to communicate. In situations in which electronic devices are not available, game boards with pointers and appropriate pictures may be developed.

Dysarthria

Dysarthria is a condition arising from central or peripheral neuromuscular disorders in which there is interference with the clarity of speech and pronunciation. Dysarthria is second only to aphasia as a communication disorder of old age and may be due to neuromuscular flaccidity, spasticity, ataxia, hypokinesia or hyperkinesia. Dysarthria may be a mixture of any of these and will often involve several mechanisms of speech, such as respiration, phonation, resonance, articulation

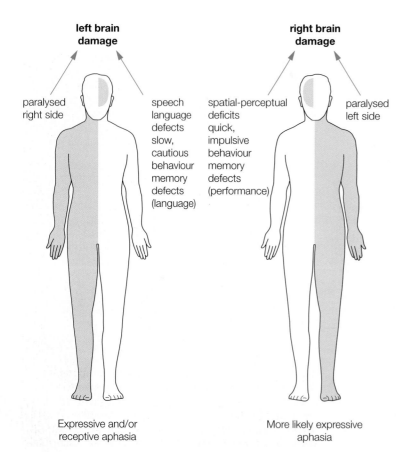

left brain damage

paralysed right side

speech language defects slow, cautious behaviour memory defects (language)

right brain damage

spatial-perceptual deficits quick, impulsive behaviour memory defects (performance)

paralysed left side

Expressive and/or receptive aphasia

More likely expressive aphasia

Figure 12.6 Receptive and expressive aphasia arising from right and left brain damage (Source: Adapted from: Fowler R, Fordyce W. *Stroke: why do they behave that way?* American Heart Association: Dallas, 1974.)

Prognostic Variables in Aphasia	
Variable	Summary
Age at outset Premorbid education, intelligence, and language abilities	Younger patients have a better prognosis Undetermined influence on prognosis
Associated defects and health during recovery Social milieu Cause	Patients with no associated deficits or illness have a better prognosis Undetermined influence on prognosis Non-penetrating trauma has a better prognosis than penetrating trauma, vascular accident, tumour and infection
Size and site of lesion	Small lesions not in temporoparietal area have a better prognosis
Time after outset	Patients with brief duration of aphasia have a better prognosis
Severity and type of aphasia	Mild aphasia and the absence of significant auditory comprehension deficits and severe apraxia of speech are favourable prognostic signs
Non-language behaviour Length and intensity of signs	Awareness, high motivation, and high aspirations are favourable prognostic signs Participation in a longer, more intense treatment Treatment programme is more likely to achieve prognosis

Table 12.4 Prognostic Variables in Aphasia

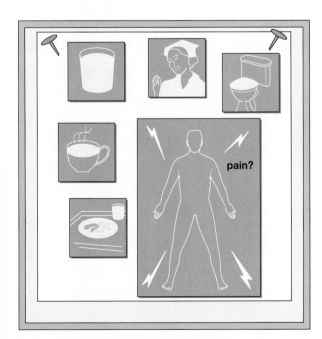

Figure 12.7 Communication board. (Source: Adapted from illustration by Joseph Pierre.)

12.6 Communicating with Aphasic People

- Explain situations, treatments and anything else that is pertinent to the patient as he or she may understand; the sounds of normal speech tend to be rehabilitative even if the words are not understood. Talk as if the person understands.
- Avoid patronising and childish phrases.
- The aphasic patient may be especially sensitive to feelings of annoyance; remain calm and patient.
- Speak slowly, ask one question at a time and wait for a response.
- Ask questions in a way that can be answered with a nod or the blink of an eye; if the patient cannot verbally respond instruct him or her in nonverbal responses.
- Speak of things familiar and of interest to the patient.
- Use visual cues, objects, pictures and gestures as well as words.
- Organise environment to be as predictable as possible.
- Encourage articulation, even if words convey no meaning.
- Show interest in the patient as an individual.

Source: McNeely et al. 1992.

and prosody (the meter, rhythm of speech). It is characterised by one or more of the following:

(1) Organic voice tremor produces a quavering articulation arising from tremors of the larynx muscles, lips, tongue and diaphragm.
(2) Transient tremulous articulation may be the result of tranquillisers, particularly phenothiazines.
(3) A slow, unsteady speech pattern may be the result of cerebellar degeneration. In this case, the gait will also be halting and wide based.
(4) Uncontrolled movement of lips, face and tongue may be an indication of Parkinson's disease. Speech may be slurred and jumpy, the expression flat and the voice tone monotonous, sometimes hardly audible.
(5) Spastic dysarthria is found in 12% of stroke patients. Words are correct, but flow of speech is tight, constrained and laborious.

Treatment after an acute episode, such as stroke or surgery, requires a speech and language therapist to develop a treatment programme to retrain muscular coordination. In a progressive neurological disease, the treatment begins early and is ongoing as the person is encouraged to maintain speech as long as possible. The speech and language therapist will assist in modifying speech patterns when necessary to maintain articulation (Lee and Itoh, 1990) and advise on suitable equipment to complement or substitute for speech (see above).

Verbigeration

Some older people develop a tendency to communicate via a series of apparently meaningless repetitions of words or sounds. Sounding is a conscious or subconscious need to express oneself, often associated with dementia, occurring when meaningful communication has been interrupted. This type of communication, it is proposed, has several purposes among older people:

· To reaffirm their presence.
· To test the caregiver's reaction to the sounds of need.
· To discharge tension.
· Self-stimulation.
· To establish one's personal space or territorial boundaries.

Sounding has been coined as a word to cover all the meaningless babbling that often occurs in settings providing skilled care for older people suffering from dementia. Zachow (1984) reported work with a very old lady (Helen) with dementia who constantly repeated 'wa, wa, wa, wa' in a loud voice. A common and significant problem of communication in people with dementia is their seeming inability to control their repetitious utterances. Zachow assumed that Helen wanted to communicate and planned multisensorial stimulation daily for 6 weeks to achieve this. She used touch, talk, baroque music, body movement, and a combination of

validation and fantasy to give meaning to all of Helen's actions. With continued work, Helen was eventually able to feed herself and to speak a few words that could be understood. This emphasises the importance of acknowledging that skilled, innovative care can be therapeutic and impact significantly on a person's quality of life.

Nursing Actions which may Promote Feelings of Safety and Security

Nursing actions which may promote feelings of safety and security are given in **Box 12.7**.

12.7 Nursing Actions which may Promote Feelings of Safety and Security

The following suggestions summarise important nursing actions which may help to promote feelings of safety and security by communicating with those suffering speech and language disorders:

• Establish rapport and demonstrate interest in the person's attempts to communicate.
• Establish a climate of acceptance and worth.
• Avoid artificial praise.
• Reduce the person's anxiety by a relaxed approach and consistent expectations.
• Reassess the person often and increase expectations as improvement is noted.
• When with the client, talk about what you are doing, name the act and talk about the events in the daily routine.
• Involve the family in the care plan to ensure a consistent approach and family involvement.
• Share realistic gains and expectations with the client and his or her family.
• Use the family as a source of information when the person is unable to provide information.
• Use varied stimuli (touch, odours, tastes, colours and sounds) to emphasise ideas and stimulate thoughts and conversation.
• Convey information verbally and nonverbally.
• Ask questions occasionally to verify comprehension.
• Use alternative words when the individual does not seem to understand.
• Give adequate time for response.
• Ask yes and no questions if that is all the person can respond to.
• Encourage choices and decisions.
• Anticipate occasional loss of control of words and emotions; reassure the person that this is normal.
• Keep a familiar and predictable environment if possible.
• Encourage any attempts to communicate and give feedback about that which is understood.
• Work towards establishing a therapeutic, empowering partnership.

SENSORY DEPRIVATION

Sensory deprivation can occur at any age; however, older age, with its frequent accompaniments of challenged sensory and perceptual mechanisms coupled with loss of independence, may make some people more vulnerable to sensory deprivation than others. The effects of sensory deprivation are as follows:

- Sensory deprivation tends to amplify existing personality traits. Vernon *et al.* (1961) believe sensory deprivation generates a great need for socialisation and physical stimulation.
- Perceptual disorganisation occurs in visual/motor coordination, colour perception, apparent movement, tactile accuracy, ability to perceive size and shape, and spatial and time judgement. Sensory deprivation brings about temporary loss in colour perception, motor coordination and weight loss.
- Affectual changes include boredom, restlessness, irritability, anxiety and panic.
- Sensory deprivation alters mechanisms of attention, consciousness and reality testing, resulting in general disorganisation of brain function similar to that produced by anorexia.
- Marked changes of behaviour occur, such as inability to think and solve problems, affectual disturbance, perceptual distortions, hallucinations and delusions, vivid imagination, poor task performance, increased anxiety and aggression, somatic complaints, temporal and spatial disorientation, emotional lability, and confusion of sleeping and waking states.
- Monotony produces a disruption of the capacity to learn and the ability to think. In the absence of varied stimulation, brain function becomes less efficient; an electroencephalogram shows slowed alpha waves maintained by constant sensory flux.
- Illness often increases the perceptual confusion, particularly among the aged, although studies show that adults of all ages experience distortion and depersonalisation when environmental stimuli are bland.

There are three main types of sensory deprivation:
(1) Reduced sensory input.
(2) Elimination of order and meaning from input.
(3) Restricting the environment to a dull monotony.
These may occur in any situation lacking varied environmental stimuli and consequently put an older person at risk of sensory deprivation. This is an important consideration in the assessment and planning of nursing interventions for older people and their carers, as well as the environments in which they live and are cared for.

Problems of environmental boredom may be exacerbated by poor vision, decreased energy, poor hearing, extended periods in a supine position, debilitating illness and chronic disorders, little pleasant sound, little meaningful contact with others, the existence of monotonous institutional decorations or inadequate indoor lighting. There are simple nursing actions that will alleviate this barren existence (**Box 12.8**).

12.8 Nursing Actions that Alleviate Sensory Deprivation

(1) Keeping curtains and windows open; sights, sounds and smells of outdoors and life can be enjoyable and reassuring.
(2) Ensure plenty of light – natural or artificial.
(3) For those restricted to bed or their immediate environment, raise the bed or assist the person into a chair bolstered comfortably with pillows; sit down; speak, touch and listen to the person's feelings and perceptions.
(4) Encourage them to bring personal possessions and mementoes to add variety and familiarity to their environment.
(5) Find out each person's interests in order to create a more stimulating environment.

It is essential to plan activities with the older person, not for them, whilst remembering to discuss meaningful activities which contribute to the maintenance of daily living activities. The older person needs to feel that he or she is working in partnership with the carer and therefore feels able to have control over the choice of activities that will be participated in. At all times, however, it is important to respect the older person's choice, since some older people may have led a life of solitude or not had hobbies which they enjoyed and so do not wish to pursue them. Someone deciding not to take part in activities should be allowed this choice just as someone wishing to participate is. Increasingly the provision of activities is being seen as a central element of care in continuing care environments. In many instances, activity coordinators are being appointed explicitly to facilitate tailored activity programmes. These coordinators, some of whom are nurses, play a large part in enhancing quality of life of an individual and at a collective level within the institution. They may work very closely with nurses and occupational therapists.

SENSORY OVERLOAD

Sensory overload, in contrast to sensory deprivation, is a very individual matter. The amount of stimuli necessary for healthy function varies with each individual. Any overloading of this system may be recognisable in a number of different ways, for example racing thoughts, attention deficits or increased activities.

Sensory overload cannot always be avoided especially when one is extremely stressed and bombarded with many demands. Older people in hospital or cared for in nursing and residential homes may be particularly vulnerable to sensory overload due to lack of privacy and opportunities for solitude. In order to minimise this threat to security, time must be arranged for peacefulness and rest. The nurse can facilitate this by getting to know the older person, discussing this aspect of care openly and facilitating a plan to minimise sensory overload that is appropriate for each individual.

DISORIENTATION

Disorientation is not an inevitable accompaniment to older age and, when it does occur, it is very distressing for older people and their families since it threatens their innermost feelings of safety and security. Disorientation may be expressed in a variety of ways, which may present themselves singly or in conjunction with one another. These include disoriented perceptions of time, place and person.

Perception of Time

The first level of disorientation to emerge is often related to the timing of events. Time disorientation may be a result of several factors, including organic impairment, personal crises and loss, and a colourless and boring institutional environment. Being unclear about time measurement puts one out of step with the world at large. Illness, loss and crises are frequently accompanied by an expanded, contracted or muted sense of time passing. When stress is severe enough, personal time may remain out of synchronisation with the world of clocks and dates or become totally submerged. Older people living in monotonous environments may be particularly vulnerable since they may lack contrasting events and experiences that mark progression in most peoples' lives. Those in this situation may eventually lose interest and pay little attention to the flow of time, seeming disengaged from the world in which they live.

In order to restore an element of time awareness our interventions may focus on capturing the elderly person's attention by direct, personalised communication and through provision of cues in the form of cards, name tags, calendars, clocks, reality boards and schedules. Daily living patterns should remain as constant as possible. Meaningful stimulating events introduced into a consistent supportive atmosphere may produce feelings of enhanced wellbeing, security and safety.

Perception of Place

The second level of orientation is interrupted when a person is uncertain of territory. Chapter 13 discusses several kinds of territories that influence the security of an individual. Distortion of perception relating to one's place may occur following relocation, for example from home to hospital or hospital to nursing home or during an episode of acute illness. It is important at these times to establish a degree of security and frequently the nurse has an important role in achieving this. For those moving from hospital or home to a nursing home, this may be achieved by helping each person to bring their own possessions into the environment retaining an element of continuity (Millard and Kist, 1997) and making the environment as accommodating as possible to each person's individual needs.

If the person consistently insists he is not in the place he should be or repeatedly calls for someone who is not there, interventions aimed toward increasing security and orientation may be helpful; some of these are listed in **Box 12.9**.

Perception of Person

The third level of disorientation is to person and is often closely tied to confusion about one's whereabouts, for instance a patient who believes he or she is at home may expect a family member to enter the room. Quite often health-care workers resemble a significant person in one's past and are naturally believed to be that person. Sometimes it is not disorientation but rather longing that precipitates identity confusion.

Disorientation Resulting from Traumatic Events

It is common to encounter patients who have transient periods of disorientation related to abrupt interference with

12.9 Increasing Security and Orientation

(1) Tailor activity to suit the patient's level and reduce or increase stimulation toward a more normal range because either in the extreme will increase psychological stress and the need to hold onto delusion.

(2) See the person frequently, introduce yourself each time, and explain why you are there, why he or she is there and what you would like to do.

(3) Obtain some objects that provide comfort or familiarity, for example, pictures or sentimental objects. If the person has no family, try to find out personal routines, such as drinking a glass of warm milk at bedtime, how many pillows are used or if a particular brand of toothpaste or denture cleanser is preferred. It is imperative that every effort is made to alter the environment to meet the individual's personal needs and thereby contribute to feelings of safety and security.

body integrity; for example, cardiac surgery can be a precipitant of disorientation and hallucinatory experiences. With the rapidity of day surgery and home recovery this problem is, in the main, being alleviated.

Disorientation is a feature of acute confusional states, which occur at all ages but most frequently in older people. Common causes of disorientation are detailed below:

- Drug intoxication.
- Circulatory disturbances.
- Metabolic imbalances.
- Fluid imbalance.
- Major medical and surgical treatments.
- Neurological disorders.
- Infection.
- Nutritional deficiencies.

Exacerbating factors may be:

- Abrupt loss of significant person.
- Multiple losses in short span of time.
- Moves to radically different environments.

The nurse has a key role in identifying these predisposing factors and providing a supportive environment in which care is provided (*see* Chapter 13 for further discussion of environmental issues). *See* Chapter 18 for further discussion of mental-health issues.

The Experience of Disorientation

Disorientation may be expressed in the following ways:

(1) **Illusions.** These are visual misinterpretations of the environment. They are often concomitant with disorientation and may arise from similar sources. A classic example of an illusion seen by one older lady was her perception of a huge spider on the wall; actually it was an oxygen outlet but was very real to her before careful explanation. If this occurs, nurses need to repeatedly explain the source of the illusion and reassure the patient regarding the temporary nature of the misperception.

(2) **Hallucinations.** Hallucinations are best described as a sensory perception of a nonexistent object stimuli and may be precipitated by the internal stimulation of any of the five senses (Sprinzeles, 1992). People who develop hallucinations must be assessed in terms of threats to security, physical or psychological, withdrawal symptoms and overload of stimuli. They will need a subdued environment with staff continuity as well as comprehensive assessment and care.

(3) **Delusions.** Delusions are intellectual mechanisms for maintaining a sense of power and control when security is threatened. They are beliefs that guide one's interpretation of events and make sense out of

disorder. The delusions may be comforting or threatening but nearly always form a structure for understanding what otherwise might seem unmanageable.

(4) **Defences.** Defences are unconscious mechanisms to ward off insecurity. Remember that while they may be obvious to others, they are not so to the person using them. If they are conscious, they are no longer defence mechanisms but have become coping strategies. Some common strategies are denial and projection.

Denial of illness, ageing, loss, death or incapacity all help to ease one through some of the difficulties of life. Denial may be difficult to assess because many older people avoid discussion of major concerns and losses, not because they are unaware but rather because they have a strong enculturation to stoic endurance or have great courage.

Fear, anxiety and anger accompanying uncertainty about one's situation are often not perceived as part of one's repertoire of feelings but rather are projected into others with whom one comes in contact. Older people often become suspicious of others' intentions toward them because they may be vulnerable and may have been used to total independence. Rather than feeling the vulnerability or precariousness of their existence, they may be wary and untrusting of others. This may progress to a pathological paranoia and feelings that specific people are biased against them. Assessing and managing older people suffering from these disorienting conditions is critical to appropriately provided care.

SUMMARY

A person's ability to pass on and receive messages about their world is central to helping them to maintain safety and security. For many older people, this does not present problems but for some, due to altered sensory and perceptual mechanisms, these problems are so intense that they require professional intervention. This may take several forms that vary in their effectiveness and appropriateness depending on the individuals concerned. These range from:

- Helping someone to use a hearing aid, spectacles, a wheelchair, dentures or a walking aid.
- Providing skilled communication that empowers older people to make informed choice and feel confident that the care that they are receiving is appropriate to their needs.
- Simply 'being there' with or for the person.

The central tenet of this chapter is that skilled nursing can make a difference to the restoration, maintenance and improvement of an older person's health and wellbeing through focusing on safety and security.

KEY POINTS

- Feelings of safety and security rely on the senses, and may be threatened when sensory and perceptual channels are interrupted in some way.
- Age-related changes to sensory and perceptual mechanisms are highly variable between individuals.
- Decline in sensory acuity is common in later life, but the majority of older people adapt to or overcome limitations and can continue to function independently.
- Changes in taste and olfaction can affect enjoyment of eating and the safety of the environment.
- Normal age-related changes in vision can, in most cases, be rectified but pathological change leading to glaucoma, cataracts, macular degeneration or diabetic retinopathy need investigation and treatment.
- Common problems associated with the ageing ear are cerumen impaction, presbycusis and tinnitus.
- Nurses have an important role with visually or hearing impaired people in assessment, creating and maintaining a suitable environment, orientation, communication and support.
- For older people whose sensory, perceptual and communicative channels are challenged, the judicious use of touch by nurses may be one way of enhancing their feelings of being accepted, reassured and encouraged to continue their interest in life.
- Speech disorders in later life may impair the reception, perception and articulation of information. Having relied on speech as a principle means of communicating throughout life, impairment can be dehumanising and isolating.
- Most people remain orientated in time, place and person but disorientation can occur from a variety of causes and requires urgent investigation, diagnosis, treatment and skilled nursing care.
- The nurse's role is central to identifying and minimising deficiencies in the sensory and perceptual channels needed for communication, as well as helping older people to find ways of maintaining or enhancing their quality of life through skilled care and empowering support.

AREAS AND ACTIVITIES FOR STUDY AND REFLECTION

- Review your caseload of nursing home residents. How many people have you identified who are hard of hearing and in what ways do you offer help to them?
- How thoroughly could you explain and demonstrate how to use and care for a hearing aid?
- In the light of the chapter content, review your work environment with regard to how effectively it can help to compensate for age-related changes in sight and hearing?
- How long is it since the older people with whom you work had their spectacles checked?
- Observe your colleagues at work. How often do they touch the older people with whom they work? What type of touch is it? In your view, is it effective?
- What kinds of speech difficulties do the patients in your care experience and how effectively are they helped?
- What facilities exist in your environment to minimise disorientation?

REFERENCES

Anderson R, Meyerhoff W. Otologic disorders. In: Calkins E, Davis P, Ford M, eds. *The practice of geriatrics*. Philadelphia: WB Saunders, 1986.

Bowlby J. The nature of the child's tie to his mother. *Int J Psychoanal* 1958, 39:350.

Clark K, Sowers MF, Wallace RB et al. The accuracy of self-reported hearing loss in women aged 60–85 years. *Am J Epidemiol* 1991, 134:704.

Copstead L. Effects of touch on self-appraisal and interaction appraisal for permanently institutionalised older adults. *J Gerontol Nurs* 1980, 6:747.

Cullinan T. Sight. In: Redfern S, ed. *Nursing elderly people*. Edinburgh: Churchill Livingstone, 1991.

Deaf and Hard of Hearing UK. Total communication, 1996, http://www.netlink.co/www_communication.htm.

Department of Health. *Inspection report of social services for deaf and hard of hearing people*, Wetherby, 1997, HMSO.

ENB. *Health promotion with older people*, London, 1990, ENB.

Fowler R, Fordyce W. *Why do they behave that way?* Dallas, 1974, American Heart Association.

Gallo JJ, Reichel W, Anderson L. H*andbook of geriatric assessment*. Garthesburg: Aspen Publications, 1988.

Geschwind N. Disconnection syndromes in animals and man. *Brain* 1965, 88:237.

Gilhome Herbst K. Hearing. In: Redfern S, ed. *Nursing elderly people*. Edinburgh: Churchill Livingstone, 1991.

Hearing Concern. *Understanding deafness*. http://web.ukonline.co/...concern/fdeaf.htm.

High WS *et al. J Speech Disord* 1964, 29:215.

Knapp M. A rose is still a rose. How does losing the sense of smell affect an elder's life? *Geriatr Nurs* 1989, 10:290.

Kolanowski AM. The clinical importance of environmental lighting to the elderly. *J Gerontol Nurs* 1992, 18:10.

Langland R, Panicucci C. Effects of touch on communication with elderly confused clients. *J Gerontol Nurs* 1982, 8:152.

Lee MH, Itoh M. General concepts of geriatric rehabilitation. In: Abrams WB, Berkow R, eds. *Merck manual of geriatrics*. Rahway: Merck Sharp & Dohme Research Labs, 1990.

le May A, Redfern S. Touch and elderly people. In: Wilson Barnett J, Robinson S, eds. *Directions in nursing research*. London: Scutari, 1989.

Mayo Clinic Health Letter *Macular degeneration*. Rochester, MN. September 1989.

McNeely E, Griffin-Shirley N, Hubbard A. Diminished vision in nursing homes. *Geriatr Nurs* 1992, 13:332.

Millard P, Kist P. The Bollingbroke Hospital long-term care project. In: Denham M, ed. *Continuing care for older people*. Cheltenham: Stanley Thornes Ltd, 1997.

Ralston ME, Choplin NT, Hollenbach KA *et al*. Glaucoma screening in primary care. The role of noncontact tonometry. *J Family Pract* 1992, 34:73.

RNIB. *Understanding cataracts*, 1996a, http://www.rnib.org.uk.../eyeimpoi/cataract.htm, Royal National Institute for the Blind.

RNIB. *Understanding age-related macular degeneration*, 1996b, http://www.rnib.org.uk.../eyeimpoi/macdegen.htm, Royal National Institute for the Blind.

RNIB. *Low vision – aids and gadgets*, 1996c, http://www.rnib.org.uk.../fctsheet/fctshet3.htm, Royal National Institute for the Blind.

Ross CK, Stelmack JA, Stelmack TR *et al*. Preliminary examination of the reliability and relation to clinical state of a measure of low vision patient functional status. *Optom Vis Sci* 1991, 68:918.

Sacks O. *Seeing voices: a journey into the world of the deaf*. Berkeley: University of California Press, 1989.

Sprinzeles, 1992

Stouffer JL, Tyler RS. Characterization of tinnitus by tinnitus patients. *J Speech Hearing Disord* 1990, 55:439.

Tolson D, MacIntosh J. Hearing impairment in elderly hospital residents. *Br J Nurs* 1992, 1:705.

Vernon et al., 1961

von Wedel H, von Wedel UC, Zorowka P. Tinnitus diagnosis and therapy in the aged. *Acta Otolaryngol Suppl* 1990, 476:195.

Watson W. The meaning of touch. *J Communication* 1975, 25:104.

Zachow K. Helen, can you hear me? *J Gerontol Nurs* 1984.

USEFUL ADDRESSES

Alzheimer's Disease Society
Gordon House
10 Greencoat Place
London
SW1P 1PH

British Tinnitus Association
Room 6
14-18 West Bar Green
Sheffield
S1 2DA

Disabled Living Foundation
380-384 Harrow Road
London
W9 4HU

Royal National Institute for the Blind
224 Great Portland Street
London
W1N 6AA

Royal National Institite for Deaf People
19-23 Featherstone Street
London
EC1Y 8SI

RNID Tinnitus Helpline - 0345 090210

Stroke Association
Stroke House
Whitecross Street
London
EC1Y 8JJ

13 Environmental safety and security
Irene Schofield

LEARNING OBJECTIVES

After studying this chapter you will be able to:
- Identify a range of factors in the micro and macroenvironment that ideally contribute to the safety and security of older people.
- Explain the significance of personal space and environmental demands on adaptation in later life.
- Explain why older people are at risk from extremes of temperature and describe methods of risk reduction.
- Compare and evaluate the continuum of housing options available to older people.
- Discuss ways in which environments can be built or modified to compensate for the disabilities of older clients with dementia or confusional states.
- Describe strategies for preventing accidents and injury to older clients both in the home and while moving around in the community.

INTRODUCTION

Personal space is defined by geographical and perceptual boundaries, which are subject to expansion and contraction at various points throughout the life span. In later life, life space – that beyond personal space – may extend to regular travel overseas, perhaps to remote destinations. In extreme disability and frailty, the physical life space may be the home, and near to death, the bed space may become the person's physical world. At such times, however, it is important that nurses acknowledge that the older person's mental and spiritual world has no such boundaries and possibly extends beyond the scope of our comprehension. In her novel, *The Stone Diaries*, which chronicles the life of Daisy Goodwill-Flett, Carol Shields describes this process. As Mrs Goodwill-Flett grows increasingly more frail in her Florida nursing home, 'Pictures fly into her head, brighter by far than those she sees on the big TV screen in the patients' lounge. A sparkling subversion. Murmurings in her ears. She can tune in any time she likes.' (Shields, 1993, p. 337).

This chapter, however, will concentrate on the physical environment, while the mental and spiritual aspects of being will be discussed in depth in later chapters. It will include selected environmental hazards that are particularly dangerous to the vulnerable older person. Suggestions and nursing interventions throughout are designed to restore balance and environmental predictability, and a sense of safety and security. There are several areas of concern where gerontological nurses can contribute to the improvement of the environment for older people. For example, nurses may act in their capacity as private citizens to lodge objections to urban projects, where planning proposals might prohibit the free and safe movement of older citizens. In a professional capacity, nurses should be involved in the planning of health-care facilities, and advising and supporting older people themselves to adopt safe and healthy behaviours in new and changing environments. Consideration of environment becomes increasingly more important in later life. Impairment of homeostatic mechanisms through age-related change and pathology affect an older person's ability to adapt to a rapidly changing environment.

Environmental Competence

Lawton and Nahemow presented a classic transactional model in the 1970s as a means to examine the relationship of an individual to the environment:
- Degree of competence in specific areas: cognition, psychological adjustment, physical health and other qualities.
- Intensity of environmental press, including the forces in the environment that evoke a response. At various times environmental press will fluctuate in accordance with individual needs and competence. Environment is only positive or negative as it can or cannot support individual needs.
- Adaptive behaviour: the manifestation of competence within the environment, not only in terms of maintaining social norms but also in demonstrating creative and self-actualising behaviour.
- Affective responses, including feeling reactions to the environment.
- Adaptation level: range of stimuli that is tolerable for individual adaptive behaviour. Beyond those limits of

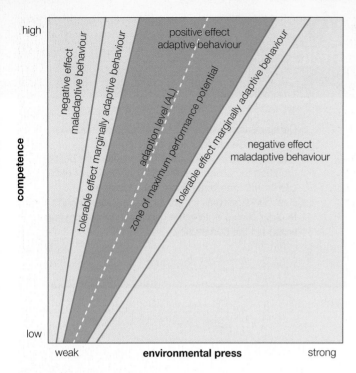

Figure 13.1 Lawton's environmental press (Source: Lawton MP, Nahemow L. Ecology and the aging process. In: Einsdorf C, Lawton MP, eds. *Psychology of adult development and aging*. Washington: American Psychological Association, 1973).

high or low stimulus, maladaptive behaviour becomes noticeable.

Lawton and Nahemow advanced an ecological model of ageing which highlighted the importance of the environment for an older person attempting to maintain a sense of wellbeing. The person and their environment interact to produce a successful outcome of adaptation and wellbeing, but as individual competence declines, the environment exerts a stronger effect on the person.

In Lawton's environmental press diagram (**Figure 13.1**), the middle diagonal line indicates mean adaptation level and implies comfort and competence. It has been observed that feelings of wellbeing will increase as stimulus departs from the mean, but discomfort is conveyed when the limits of effective performance are reached. This model clearly shows that in situations of low competence and weak stimulus there is a narrow latitude of effective responses, whereas individuals with high competence can tolerate a wide range of strong stimuli. A weak, bland or monotonous environment in the presence of high competence can be managed relatively well, but an environment consisting of strong stimuli in the presence of low personal competence will provoke a wide range of abnormal behaviours.

Competence can be increased by health interventions, prostheses and behavioural modifications by the older individual, while environments may be designed or modified to facilitate adaptation and reduce environmental stress. It is the intention of this chapter to raise awareness of key environmental issues which impact on the health and wellbeing of older people. These vary in scope from the respect of personal space within high dependency nursing environments

such as care homes to the provision of advice and preventive health treatments to intrepid older travellers. This chapter, therefore, will cover the following aspects of environment:

- Personal space.
- Life space.
- Relocation stress.
- Migration patterns.
- Moving.
- Travel.
- Transport and mobility.
- Driving.
- Road traffic accidents.
- Crime.
- Extremes of temperature.
- The Continuum of housing options.
- Environments and management of people with dementia and confusional states.
- Accidents.

PERSONAL SPACE

Personal space embodies two main concepts: privacy and periphery. In the study by Sixsmith (1986) on the concept of home, the older interviewees referred to these as 'inside', and 'outside'. Each person needs an inviolable space for solitude, intimacy, anonymity and reflection. The amount of time needed and the boundaries of this private space vary according to individual preference. Likewise, an individual needs personalised boundaries, which define their limits of control. An older person with no opportunity for privacy may cease to care about the activities on the perimeter. This person may erect psychological barriers for self-protection from personal invasion and may no longer care about seeking to enlarge their life space. Insufficient personal space and lack of privacy are known to cause stress and anxiety. Problems such as sensory overload (related to loss of environmental control), medication haze, isolation from significant others, pain and pathological conditions can all affect an individual's sense of personal space. A skilful nurse will respect territorial boundaries, and will not move into private space or thought too rapidly. Such measures are of crucial importance when older people are being cared for in institutional settings. **Box 13.1** suggests ways to promote a sense of personal security in institutional settings.

LIFE SPACE

The remainder of this chapter examines life spaces and how these may or may not enhance feelings of safety and security. Life space can be conceived as physical and psychosocial, the temporal and the imagined. Here we will deal with the various temporal life spaces (time space). The psychological space will be discussed in Chapters 16 and 17, and imagined potential will be considered in Chapter 20. Most of us are immersed in a range of microenvironments in which we routinely participate with little thought as to their effects. We become accustomed to the usual sounds, odours, shifting temperatures and vegetation patterns. It is only when these change noticeably that we become aware that environment has meaning to us. Older people in restricted living situations, those that are homebound or institutionalised, suffer a type of deprivation that is not well understood. We sense that quality of life is somehow diminished but do not know the impact on the individual. Friedman and Ryan (1986) conclude that 'many of the challenging behaviours observed in the care home setting can be viewed as attempts on the part of the resident to actively re-establish a sense of control, dignity and self-worth in the face of an ecological crisis' (p. 268). In all situations where the older person is at the mercy of an unnatural environment, thought must be given to the artificial aspects of the surroundings.

RELOCATION

In view of the strong instinctual nature of territorial needs, it is not surprising that much attention has been given to the crisis of relocation. Regardless of the type of move and its desirability or undesirability, some degree of stress will be experienced. An early seminal review of studies on relocation by American psychologists Schulz and Brenner (1977) acknowledges the importance of relocation as a major life event and the attention given to the crisis of relocation. The relocation may be from institution to institution, such as hos-

13.1 Promoting Personal Security in Institutional Settings

- Residents' rooms need a 'please do not disturb' sign that can be hung on the door when the resident chooses.
- Transfer residents from one room to another infrequently or not at all.
- Include objects of personal significance in the environment.
- Respect the arrangement of the residents' space; do not move things without permission.
- Prepare people for intrusive procedures, even though these may be routine to nursing staff, and verbally assure them you are aware of intruding into their space. Respect residents' dignity and modesty. Do not leave body exposed.
- Ask whether resident wants door open or shut and curtains closed or open.
- Avoid direct eye contact during care of intimate body areas.
- Be alert to cues. Touching may increase or decrease anxiety.
- Communicate territorial preferences of resident to other health-care team members.
- Confer with residents regarding arrangement of public space.
- Give choices as much as possible, which in turn will give you territorial clues about residents' preferences.

pital to care home, it may be from home to care home or home to home. In the latter case, the older person may be moving from a family home to a smaller flat or sheltered housing complex. Schulz and Brenner give key principles for the management of relocation based on the studies in their review:

- The greater the choice, the less negative the effects of relocation.
- The more predictable, the less negative the effects of relocation.
- Prelocation preparation programmes appear to increase predictability of a new environment and effectively contribute to improved health.

Both hospital and community nurses can make use of such findings by ensuring that prospective residents either visit or have access to publicity material on the new home and that they have the opportunity to meet staff members who will be their future carers. Written care plans should contain details of an imminent move, together with regular evaluations as to its acceptability by the older person. Thus, the continuing need for psychological support is communicated to the nursing team.

Relocation between Institutions

The continuing closure of long-stay National Health Service hospitals and the transfer of patients to private sector-run nursing homes make relocation an important issue for nurses working in these areas. In view of the anecdotal reports that patients have died as a result of relocation, such moves need to be managed with care and attention to detail. A study by Grant *et al.* (1992) measuring the impact of relocating individuals from an old institution to a newer one with the same level of institutional care, confirms previous findings that prior preparation, anticipation and involvement in the process make for a smooth, non-stressful move. Profiles of residents' physical, social and emotional needs, as well as careful inventories of personal possessions and specific needs, contribute to more comfortable relocation. Nurses' concerns are on assessing the impact of relocation and finding ways of alleviating negative reactions. **Box 13.2** lists the questions that must be asked to assess the impact on the individual following a move.

13.2 Assessment of Impact on the Individual Following a Move

- Are significant persons as accessible in the new location as they were before the move?
- Is the individual developing new and reciprocal relationships in the new setting?
- Is the individual functioning as well, better or not as well in the new location? This determination cannot be made immediately but must be assessed at least 6 weeks after the move.
- Was the individual given options before the move?
- Was the individual given the opportunity to assess the new environment before making a decision to move?
- Has the individual been able to move important items of furniture and memorabilia to the new setting?
- Has a particular individual who is familiar with the environment been available to assist with orientation?
- Was the decision to move made hastily or with inadequate information?
- Does the new situation provide adequately for basic needs (food, shelter, and physical maintenance)?
- Are individual idiosyncratic needs recognised, and is there the opportunity to actualise them?
- Does the new situation decrease the possibility of privacy and autonomy?
- Is the new living situation an improvement over the previous situation, similar or worse?

Migration

According to Warnes and Ford (1995) the majority of older people's long distance moves are to coastal and rural areas. In reviewing studies of post-retirement migration over the last decade, the authors found that motivations and triggers for moving depended on age. Immediately post-retirement, moves were connected with social networks and environmental preferences linked with past associations, for example the new location had been a favourite holiday place. One-third of moves had been made to move nearer children. In older age, housing type and social factors became more important considerations. Older people who own their own homes have greater flexibility and choice deciding whether to move long distance. Those renting their home from a local authority are at a disadvantage, due to a lack of national tenancy exchange schemes. However, moving house in later life, albeit a short distance, is common among the one-third of older people who rent their home from a local authority.

Moving

Older people who are contemplating a move to a new home or area may turn to nurses for advice and support during their decision-making. Nurses may help older clients to articulate their reasons for moving, to realistically appraise the potential benefits and liabilities of the new situation and what supports they will need and expect, and to consider all their options. The following aspects are worthy of consideration:

- Closeness to friends, family, local shops and services, and social activities.
- A move may entail giving up valued possessions and furniture.
- A new home may be easier to manage, cheaper to maintain and heat.
- A move to the seaside or country may seem idyllic, but how accessible are shops and services, especially in winter? How good are local health and welfare services?
- Is this really the best time to move? Sometimes people who are recently bereaved make a quick decision to move and then regret it afterwards.
- If the move is to a sheltered housing complex, will they welcome daily visits by the warden or will they regard it as an intrusion?

HOLIDAY TRAVEL

Many older people now take regular holidays both at home and abroad. However, increasing age and the presence of chronic disease can make long-distance travel, in particular, a hazardous undertaking. Practice nurses are well placed to give specific advice to older people, in addition to the usual precautions given to other travellers. Modes of travel merit particular attention.

For the most part, coach tours are a convenient and popular method of getting about, involving minimal physical exertion. However, long periods of sitting can cause venous stasis and swollen ankles. Travellers should be advised to walk about at stopping points, and encouraged to take any prescribed diuretic medications on the day of travel.

Older people are now travelling more frequently by air to long-haul destinations. Long periods of sitting promote venous stasis, and older travellers are at more risk of developing a deep vein thrombosis or pulmonary embolism. They should be advised to carry out ankle exercises at least every hour and to take walks when the aisles are clear. It is also important to avoid dehydration in the dry atmosphere of the cabin by taking regular fluids but avoiding alcohol. People with arthritic hips and knees should also be advised to move around during the flight. Cabin air pressures are lower than those on the ground, so those older travellers with chronic respiratory or cardiac disease are at more risk of becoming hypoxic. Pressure in body cavities is increased, so that the older person may experience gastric distension or pain in the sinuses. On arrival, the impact of jetlag can be greater for older travellers, particularly for Far East flights that cross four or five time zones. Resynchronisation after eastward flights can take 11 days or more for older people, with sleep disturbance being one of the main problems. People with limited cognitive reserves may experience difficulty in making decisions and may even have episodes of confusion.

Taking a cruise is also popular with older people, however facilities on board ship may not cater for the needs of people with some instability or disability. For example, a cabin five decks down, with no lift and a rolling swell may destabilise the fittest person. Prospective travellers should be advised to check out the location of their cabin, nearness of toilet facilities, availability of lifts and methods of summoning help from their cabin. Advice on managing seasickness may also be needed.

One other environmental issue worthy of mention is that of climbing to high altitude, although age is no barrier to acute mountain sickness, which can affect all people who venture above 3000 metres. The individual may experience weakness, headache, fatigue, nausea, vomiting, vertigo and poor balance. Slow acclimatisation to altitude is recommended, and symptoms disappear on return to a lower altitude. Those with existing respiratory or cardiac problems should be advised of the risks of visiting high altitude locations.

PUBLIC SPACE: TRANSPORTATION

Available, accessible and affordable public transport is central to the lives of most older people. This is particularly so for the 53% of people over 65 years of age who do not own a car (Office of Population Censuses and Surveys, 1991). The trend towards out-of-town shopping centres makes suitable transport vital. Older people may be less able to afford taxis or to bulk buy in order to cut down on the number of shopping trips. The benefits system discriminates against older

people in that the mobility component of the Disability Living Allowance is not paid to people over the age of 65. In isolated communities there may be no public transport facilities. For example, in Scotland 16% of the rural population are aged over 65 years. Where public transport exists, the design of vehicles and associated facilities may preclude their use by older people with disabilities. Transport planners must be urged to consider easy access to vehicles, the provision of shelters and seating at bus stops. Managers of services should ensure that timetables are large enough to be read by those with less than perfect vision and that wherever possible, stations have staff to give help and advice.

Figure 13.2 shows the changes in use of public transport with increasing age. Reasons given for non-use of public transport were car-ownership, access to another car and ill health or disability. People living alone, women and the very old most often cited ill health and disability as the main reason for non-use of public transport. Furthermore, 28% of the over sixty-fives did not have a car and did not use public transport (Office of Population Censuses and Surveys, 1986).

In many areas, local transportation schemes have been developed for disabled people of all ages. The schemes tend to range from small voluntary car services to the more well-known Dial-a-Ride service. All these schemes have been set up by organisations aware of the gaps in public transport provision, and some of the larger initiatives receive financial support from local councils and other statutory bodies. However, choice and spontaneity open to able-bodied transport users may be compromised by the planning required to use such services.

DRIVING AND OLDER PEOPLE

In the UK, there is no age limit to holding a driving licence. At present every driver from the age of 70 years submits a health self-declaration of fitness to drive at 3-yearly intervals. In addition, some insurance companies require general practitioner (GP) certification of fitness to drive for those people over the age of 65 years. Driving should be considered an instrumental activity of daily living because it is vital to the independence and wellbeing of those individuals who live in rural areas.

Studies of functional capacity neglect this important area of ability. Primary care nurses who carry out the over seventy-fives' health assessment should ask whether the individual drives and feels safe driving. Depending on the response, the nurse should be prepared to give information on safe practice. A useful leaflet is available from the Automobile Association. Normal age changes in vision such as decreased dark adaptation, decreased depth perception, susceptibility to glare, and the general slowing of reflexes and cognitive processes, together with a reduction in physical agility, make driving hazardous for some older people. Older people are also more susceptible to pathological changes which render them unsafe to drive. Those with bilateral cataracts can fail the compulsory test to read a numberplate at a distance of 20.5 metres because of increased sensitivity to the glare from ambient daylight. However, remedial surgery

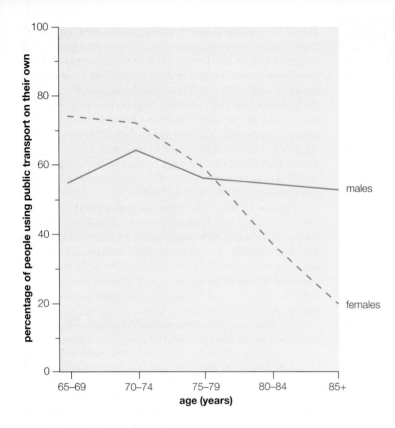

Figure 13.2 Elderly people using public transport on their own. (Source: General Household Survey, 1986. In: *The health of elderly people: an epidemiological overview.* London: Central Health Monitoring Unit, HMSO, 1992.) Crown copyright is reproduced with permission of the Controller of Her Majesty's Stationery Office.

may restore vision. It is estimated that 40% of 85-year-old drivers fail this test (Taylor, 1995).

Glaucoma and strokes, which affect visual and perceptual function (*see* Chapter 12), can also impair ability to drive. An American study found that out of 25 new stroke sufferers, 13 were able to resume driving and at 6 months follow-up had not been involved in any accidents or driving offences. Epilepsy often occurs as a result of stroke, and epileptic seizures in older people have been mistaken for transient ischaemic attacks or drop attacks. An individual with epilepsy must be seizure-free for 1 year before they can hold a driving licence.

Many older people experience insomnia and take hypnotics to help them sleep at night. Medications with a long half-life can cause drowsiness, which is a threat to road safety. Kline *et al.* (1992) found that most problems experienced by older drivers involved:

- Unexpected vehicles.
- Moving too slowly for the flow of traffic.
- Problems reading road signs.
- Problems seeing the roadway clearly enough.

In addition, Rabbitt (1994) suggests older motorists find it increasingly difficult to estimate the relative speeds at which they and other vehicles are travelling, as a result of the combined effects of ageing in both the sense organs and the brain. When these occur, the older person's abilities no longer meet the demands of the environment, and only those people who

elect to drive at quiet periods on familiar routes are unlikely to experience any problems. Unfortunately, when judgement is impaired, an individual may believe and insist he or she retains the capacities for safe driving even though objective assessment shows this is not true. Donnelly and Karlinsky (1990) found that individuals diagnosed with mild-to-moderate Alzheimer's disease do have more car crashes than age-matched controls. It is therefore incumbent on the GP to determine when the individual should no longer drive.

Driving is a symbol of freedom, autonomy and independence and it is very hard to relinquish the privilege. This position is supported by Kapust and Weintraub (1992), who found that patients with the same level of mild-to-moderate dementia performed quite differently on actual road tests. Some were deemed safe to drive. The authors recommend that a road competency test be given, before making a decision of such importance to an individual as the revoking of a driver's license. The older person, if continuing to drive, should be advised to follow the advice listed in **Box 13.3**.

These tips are particularly critical for older drivers.

Driving Safety

Most driving accidents occur in drivers under the age of 25 years. The risk of being involved in an accident falls progressively until the age of 65 years and then starts to climb slowly. The highest accident rate per mile travelled is in women over

13.3 Driving Advice for Older People

- Avoid night driving.
- Wear hearing aids and glasses to increase sensory awareness.
- Avoid driving under the influence of medications or alcohol.
- Avoid driving in fog, heavy rain, snow and ice.
- Plan relief periods if driving for long distances.
- Keep the car in good repair.

the age of 74 but this is probably due to lack of practice. The women involved are thought to be those who take up regular driving again after the death or illness of a spouse. Good advice to couples is that they share the driving. Alternatively, Saga offers residential driver confidence courses. Overall, older drivers tend to drive less as the years go by. In a study by Persson (1993) of 56 former drivers aged between 66 and 96 years, the main reasons for cessation were advice from a doctor, increased nervousness behind the wheel, trouble seeing pedestrians and cars, and medical conditions. Very few health-care professionals other than doctors discussed driving. Older people are less likely to survive the trauma of road traffic accidents on account of having more fragile bodies.

THE IMPORTANCE OF NEIGHBOURHOOD

The idea of neighbourhood is a smaller concept than community and is more attuned to the convenience and friendliness of daily contacts. It usually includes local shops, post office, bank, hairdressers and general practitioner surgery. Low morale and isolation are inversely correlated with the older person's sense of 'neighbourhood'. The neighbourhood seems to be a most important environmental unit for older people. The character of a neighbourhood may be an important source of satisfaction or alienation. Many older people who once belonged in their neighbourhood have been left behind by migration to the suburbs and find themselves in a neighbourhood that has evolved into an alien, unsatisfactory and sometimes frightening milieu. A significant contributor to fear of crime among older people is the socioeconomic deterioration of the neighbourhood.

Safety in the Community and Neighbourhood: Crimes against Older People

Crime is of particular concern to many older people. Crimes against their person or property are magnified because of their sense of vulnerability. Although crime is no more frequent or severe against older adults, the resultant distur-

bance and consequences are often more devastating. For instance, an attack resulting in a fall and broken leg may end in death for an older person but only a few weeks of limited activity for a young adult. Many older people live alone, have a lower income, and fewer sources of material and social support, and will take longer to recover if they are a victim of crime. Fear of victimisation has been studied and identified frequently as more predominant in older than younger people; however, in reality, they are less likely to be victims. A recent study in south London challenges the findings of earlier studies. The researcher found no evidence that older people in general are overwhelmingly afraid of crime. Eighty per cent of older people were unafraid to walk alone in the neighbourhood during the day and 77% did not feel at risk from crime indoors; 68% did not feel that their daily activities were restricted by fears for personal safety or property (Lindesay, 1997). Nurses need to be aware of the true picture in order to reassure older people.

Street Crime

Surveys indicate that older people are no more likely to suffer physical injury or financial loss from crime than other age groups, although this has been a common assumption. Age Concern (1995) cite the findings of The British Crime Survey, which found that those who felt most unsafe on the streets were least often the victims. The 1993 figures on victims of offences against the person show that the highest rate of victimisation was in the 16–29 years age group, while the lowest rate was in the 60 years and over age group [Office of Population Censuses and Surveys (OPCS), 1996]. Location and income are often far more significant than age in predicting crime rate. In fact, with age as the variable, older people are the least likely to be victims of crime. However, there is still much national attention paid to crimes against older people because of the recognised serious consequences. Such media attention may have the effect of augmenting the fear of crime among older people, to the extent that they may refuse to go out, even during the day, refuse to admit visitors, take excessive security measures, keep guard dogs and even move house. Older people's sense of personal safety and security appears to depend on the extent to which they view themselves as part of the local community.

Burglary

The older the head of the household, the less likely it is to be burgled. Compare 91 burglaries per 1000 households where the head is aged 16–29 years and 35 per 1000 households where the head is aged over 65 years (OPCS, 1993).

Crime Prevention

Crime prevention programmes, such as the neighbourhood watch scheme, help to increase security conscious behaviours that will decrease vulnerability to crime. Positive aspects of security consciousness should be emphasised. Nurses can be instrumental in reducing fear of crime, and assisting older clients in exploring ways they may protect themselves and feel more secure. The information contained in **Box 13.4** may be useful.

White-collar Crime'

Muggings and robbery involving older people are frequently brought to public attention, but a larger, less socially visible problem is the numerous fraudulent schemes victimising older people on a daily basis. Bogus callers, door-to-door salespersons, 'cowboy' builders and unethical business persons are among those that prey on older people. News media sometimes alert people to fraud and protective actions.

Older widows are particularly vulnerable if they have always relied on their husbands to manage household affairs. Grief and inexperience in making business decisions combine to create many problems stemming from naivety and poor judgement. Although nurses are not often in a position to assist in such decisions, they can alert older people to local helping organisations.

13.4 Crime Reduction Suggestions

Outdoor precautions

- Bag and purse snatchers are usually not interested in injuring anyone. People can be advised to carry only a little money and personal items in a purse or bag; house keys, larger amounts of money and credit cards should be kept in an inside pocket of clothing. Money belts can be worn under clothing. When accosted, hand over purse or wallet readily.
- Some older persons travel about in groups of three and feel quite secure.
- Some people wear an alarm around their neck.
- Pensions and income support payments are a prime target for muggers, and older people should be encouraged to have their cheques sent directly to their bank.

Indoor precautions

- Have a secure lock fitted to outer doors. A 5-lever mortice lock can only be opened with a key. A spy hole and door chain help in screening callers.
- Check the identity of a caller before admitting anyone, even if they appear to be 'official' or authentic.
- Use the chain to secure the door until you have checked the pass of an official caller.
- Children with criminal intentions may attempt to gain admittance by asking to collect a ball from the garden, asking for a drink of water or to use the toilet.
- Property marking and listing serial numbers of property may help with recovery of stolen items.
- Keep large sums of money in a bank, building society or post office account.
- Clients who have been victims of bogus callers may feel embarrassed about it. Offer to support them by calling the police.

EXTREMES OF TEMPERATURE

Changes in response to thermal stress become evident after 70 years of age and contribute to the excessive deaths of older people during heat waves and cold spells. This is due to age-related decline in the mechanisms controlling temperature homeostasis, which in some cases results in a less efficient response to changes in ambient temperature. Decreased ability to regulate blood flow is thought to occur as a result of loss of elasticity in the blood vessels and less efficient autonomic control (*see* Chapter 4); this is exacerbated by pathological changes such as peripheral vascular disease.

Cold

Between 37,000 and 44,800 extra deaths occur in the winter months (Age Concern, 1998), most of these are older people suffering from respiratory and circulatory diseases; it is rare to record hypothermia as a primary cause of death. The increase in death rate is higher than for countries with comparable climates and is thought to be due to a combination of physiological, social and economic factors. With increasing age, the thermoregulatory mechanism that maintains a constant core body temperature declines in efficiency; this is accompanied by reduced thermal perception. Collins *et al.* (1981) have demonstrated that some older people are less able to discriminate between temperatures than younger subjects are, and show a lower temperature preference for comfort than the average. As a consequence, some people at risk of hypothermia (i.e. with low, deep-body temperatures below 35°C) do not necessarily report feeling cold. The proportion of body mass made up of actively functioning cells is smaller, resulting in an overall decrease in total metabolic heat production. This is likely to be the reason why older people who are less active prefer a temperature higher than that for younger and more active people. Also, heat is lost any time the air temperature falls below 37°C and accounts for the more rapid decline in skin temperature. Windy, dry weather can accelerate loss of body heat by evaporation. In low temperatures, poor vasoconstriction results in unwanted heat loss. The shivering response is frequently suppressed (Collins and Exton-Smith, 1983).

In a study to compare the effects of cold stress on young and older adults in controlled conditions, after 6 hours, core temperature fell by 0.4°C in older adults but was maintained in the younger subjects. In the older subjects, the rise in blood pressure (BP) exceeded that of the young; this was thought to be due to reduction in sensitivity of the baroreflex (Collins *et al.* 1995). Some medical conditions put older people at increased risk of hypothermia; these include confusional states, endocrine disorders, strokes and heart attacks. Immobility as a result of a sedentary lifestyle or medical conditions such as severe arthritis and Parkinson's disease cause a decrease in heat production as a result of reduced muscular activity. Some groups of drugs, particularly phenothiazines, hypnotics and antidepressants impair thermoregulation.

13.5 Advising on the Prevention of Cold-Related Disease

- A daily hot meal and hot drinks throughout the day. A vacuum flask could be made up by a helper.
- Thermal underwear and several layers of light clothing are more efficient than one heavy layer. Hat, gloves and scarf will minimise heat loss from the extremities when outdoors.
- Keep active. Alternate physical activity with rest periods.
- Consider living and sleeping in warmest room during winter months, and place the bed on an inside wall.
- Keep windows closed, but ensure there is adequate ventilation for coal, gas and oil burning appliances.
- Means-tested grants are available to retired people through the Home Energy Efficiency Scheme, for home insulation and draught proofing. Local advice centres will have further information.
- Gas and electricity suppliers have budget schemes to help people pay for their fuel more easily.
- The Cold Weather Payments scheme provides additional payments to help vulnerable people already claiming income support, with extra heating costs during exceptionally cold weather. The payments are made for each period of seven consecutive days when the average daily temperature is 0°C or below.

13.6 Managing Hypothermia

Recognition
- The client is sitting in a cold room but does not complain of being cold.
- The client is unusually apathetic, confused and becomes increasingly drowsy.
- The voice sounds husky and speech is slurred.
- The face is swollen and pallid.
- The skin feels cold to touch, especially in the axillae and over the abdomen.
- The client's respirations are slow and shallow.
- The presence of arrhythmia, bradycardia and hypotension.

Action
- Inform the general practitioner.
- Warm the client slowly, by warming the room and placing blankets under and over the them.
- Do not apply direct heat of any kind since this will cause peripheral vasodilation and bring about even more heat loss (giving alcohol will also have this effect).
- Give the client a warm drink if sufficiently alert to swallow.

Psychosocial Factors

Retired people generally spend more time at home than those who are out at work and, therefore, need to spend more money on heating. Poorer pensioners tend to spend twice as much (as a percentage of their total income) than the rest of the population on heating. It has been suggested that fuel costs should not exceed 10% of the total household income, and that poor housing standards together with inefficient and expensive heating systems contribute significantly to excess winter deaths. Boardman, (1991, p. 219) uses the term 'fuel poverty', which she defines as 'the inability to afford adequate warmth because of the energy efficiency of the home'. In particular, people in private rented accommodation are less likely to have central heating, home insulation and warm homes than those people living in their own or local authority homes. Although 79% of older people live in centrally heated homes (Office of Population Censuses and Surveys, 1991), a survey by Salvage (1993) found that many older people were living in low temperatures in winter and that this was due in the main to lack of money.

Cold-related Illness

The World Health Organisation (1982) recommends a minimal indoor temperature of 18°C with an increase of 2–3°C for rooms occupied by sedentary older people, young chil-

dren and the handicapped. Below 16°C, resistance to respiratory infections may be diminished and both low and high relative humidities promote respiratory conditions. At temperatures below 12°C, cold extremities and a slight drop in core body temperature can bring about short-term increases in BP. In temperatures as low as 6 °C, cardiovascular (CV) reflexes can be stimulated by cold air on the face or hands that result in changes in heart rate and blood pressure and increased CV strain (**Box 13.5**).

Raised BP and an increased blood viscosity in moderately cold conditions are thought to be important causal factors in the increase in morbidity and mortality from myocardial infarction (MI) and stroke. The length of time which passed between the onset of the cold weather and an increase in mortality was 1–2 days for MI and 3–4 days for stroke (Collins, 1986).

Older people who live alone, particularly those over 75 years of age who do not receive regular visitors and who are on the lowest incomes, are thought to be most at risk of developing hypothermia (**Box 13.6**).

Nursing Interventions

Nurses have a role to play in preventing hypothermia and cold-related disease, particularly in the high-risk group. The over seventy-fives' health check provides an ideal opportunity to explore housing conditions as part of the assessment of the social environment (Williams and Wallace, 1993). The authors suggest that clients should be asked whether they have had any difficulty keeping their home warm during the last year and about adequacy of heating and problems with damp. Those nurses who carry out home visits in cold weather should be equipped with thermometers to check room temperatures, both in the living room and bedroom, as the latter are often underheated or not heated at all (Salvage, 1992). Information on the cold weather risks to health and immediate measures to promote warmth can be given both verbally and by printed leaflets. Referral to social services may be necessary if the nurse suspects that the person is not claiming the financial and material benefits to which they are entitled. Problems with the fabric of the home or the heating system may need to be brought to the attention of the housing authority, landlord or energy supplier. In some areas, there are local schemes that give information and advice to vulnerable people in cold weather conditions.

Heat

Morbidity and mortality as a result of high ambient temperatures rarely occur in the UK because of its temperate climate. However, older people are increasingly taking trips abroad and may therefore be exposed to hot and humid conditions. Those practice nurses who run travel clinics are well placed to advise older travellers on specific precautions to keep healthy in hot climates. The mechanisms that lower body temperature, such as perspiration, blood vessel dilation and thirst, are affected by the ageing process. Older people are not as sensitive to thirst, and the reduction in the number of sweat glands and an increase in the threshold temperature for the start of sweating lead to a rise in core body temperature. Ability to perspire declines and the presence of arteriosclerosis makes it harder for the older person to increase cardiac output and decrease systemic vascular resistance in hot weather. In addition, humid climates slow evaporation from the skin and interfere with the effectiveness of perspiration as a cooling mechanism.

Older people with cardiovascular disease, diabetes, peripheral vascular disease and those on certain medications (anticholinergics, antihistamines, diuretics, beta-blockers, antidepressants and anti-parkinsonian drugs) are more at risk of hyperthermia. These findings also, emphasise the need to carefully evaluate the basal temperature of older people and recognise that even low-grade fevers may signify illness.

To prevent hyperthermia when the temperature exceeds 39°C:

- Drink 2–3 litres of fluid daily.
- Take plenty of rest at first and avoid mid-day exposure.
- Alternate periods in heat with cooling periods.
- Stay in air-conditioned hotels and use air-conditioned vehicles or use fans when possible.
- Wear a hat and loose clothing of natural fibres.
- Use cold wet towels or dampen clothing in extreme heat.
- Avoid alcohol.

THE CONTINUUM OF HOUSING OPTIONS

Introduction

Havighurst identifies the establishment of satisfactory living arrangements as one of the key developmental tasks for later life (*see* Chapter 2). Its achievement depends not only on personal resources but also on the availability of a range of housing type. Given the choice as to where they would wish to live in later life, with few exceptions older people opt to remain in their own home (Salvage *et al.* 1989; Roberts *et al.* 1991). The government White Paper *Caring for People* referred to the importance of housing for the health and welfare of older people and stressed the need for inter-agency collaboration. However, Means (1993) suggests that progress has been slow and that increasing provision of specialist housing such as sheltered accommodation, often by private developers and housing associations, has overshadowed the possibility of staying put after modifications to the present home. Housing provision has developed piecemeal rather than through a coordinated effort between housing, health and social services.

It is important that nurses working with older people have an appreciation of the housing options and constraints in later life. Many nurses may have experienced frustration at working with patients to achieve optimum function, only to find that the patient's home environment will not support their present level of functional ability. This is not surprising, considering that older people tend to live in the oldest housing stock. It is a well-established belief that quality of housing impacts upon the health and wellbeing of all age groups. However, this perhaps becomes increasingly more important in later life, beginning at retirement when home rather than work becomes the focus of people's lives, and later becomes even more crucial for those older people who are incapacitated by chronic illness. In these circumstances, a home, which is warm, secure and adapted to facilitate independence, can provide an appropriate 'prosthetic' environment thus enabling the person to remain in the setting of their choice. Tinker (1987) suggests that home adaptations such as the installation of a downstairs lavatory, a stair lift or an efficiently heated and insulated home can be carried out by local authorities under the Chronically Sick and Disabled Persons Act, 1970. Measures such as these may provide greater long-term benefit than visits by professional carers or meals-on-wheels. Professionals need to be knowledgeable about what is available from departments other than their own. The problems faced by older people in relation to housing, therefore, revolve around the provision of suitable housing to meet their changing needs.

Housing Condition

Although 90% of older people do live in their own homes in the community, some live in less than desirable housing. According to the English House Condition Survey (Department of the Environment, 1988), older people generally tend to live in the oldest housing stock. Households with a head over 75 years of age often live in homes which lack basic amenities or are unfit for habitation. Ten per cent of heads of households aged over 75 years live in dwellings which lack amenities and 16% in unfit dwellings. Half of older households rent their accommodation and older people are the largest group occupying private rented accommodation. In a study of older people living in private rented accommodation, Smith (1986) found that steps and stairs, uneven floors and badly lit areas presented a major obstacle to getting around. The increased risk of falls (Department of Trade and Industry, 1990a) and age-related changes in eyesight added to their vulnerability. However, 81% said that they preferred to stay where they were rather than move to unfamiliar surroundings.

Owner-Occupiers

Sixty-three per cent of people over 60 years of age now own their homes (Office of Population Censuses and Surveys, 1991). However, an older person's capacity and resources to carry out home improvements may be limited. The 1980 Housing Act enabled more owner occupiers to become eligible for grants to improve, adapt or heat their own homes, and more recently, the 1989 Housing Act introduced a new mandatory system to bring properties up to a new standard of fitness. However, a savings and income threshold restricts entitlement, so that not everyone in need will benefit. Schemes known as home improvement agency services are now available, which give advice on sources of funding and also give practical help to oversee the work. An example of such a scheme is Anchor Housing Association's Staying Put, which operates in partnership with local authorities in some areas.

Housing Supply

Housing supply is also changing and this too affects older people. Although the new stock tends to consist of more manageable one and two-bedroomed housing, there is less of it. A person may wish to move to somewhere more compact but the opportunity to do so, in the desired location, may be infrequent. This prolongs the period of under-occupation and the attendant difficulties of managing and heating a home that is too large. An additional factor is the decrease in building by local authorities and the increase in provision by housing associations and private builders (Tinker, 1995). This may restrict choices even more for those on limited income, who are occupying council and private rented accommodation.

Income from Housing

Owner-occupiers may be 'house rich' and 'income poor'. Home equity release schemes enable people to release some of the value of the house to provide a lump sum or regular income. People should be advised to take financial advice before doing this, as rises in interest rates and slumps in the property market have meant that some older people have benefited very little from doing so.

Homesharing

Homesharing is an innovative scheme managed by the Community Care Trust, and as yet is only available in some parts of the UK. It enables frail older people and the younger disabled to be supported in their own home by a live-in homesharer, as an alternative to institutional care. The householder offers free accommodation in return for about 10 hours of help each week. In addition, some householders receive daily care from social services or a community health team. Such schemes obviously require close professional monitoring and support.

Home Improvement Agency Schemes

It is important that nurses are aware of the alternatives to sheltered housing, which allow frail older people to remain in their own homes. These include agency schemes to carry out much needed renovations, the use of alarms and extra care packages. Tinker (1984) evaluated a variety of care and alarm schemes for a sample of over 1300 older people who were on average more dependent than those in sheltered housing. Nearly all the people wanted to stay in their own homes and the innovations enabled them to do so. Later, Tinker (1989) demonstrated that staying at home with a package of innovatory and other statutory services was £1000 cheaper per annum than very sheltered housing.

Amenity Housing

Describes homes (often flats) that are purpose built or adapted, and which contain design features for ease of living and management. They are often sold specifically as retirement homes. Sometimes the flats are linked to a central source to provide an alarm system.

Almshouses

Almshouses were the first type of social housing for older people. Most of those occupied today were provided from trusts set up by philanthropists in the last century. The occupants are known as beneficiaries and approximately 30,000 older people still live in almshouses.

Retirement Communities

Community can be defined as any group sharing common characteristics or interests. Retirement communities usually have a lower age limit of 55 years, and set out to attract affluent retirees. Those who argue against the seclusiveness of these senior communities may not be fully aware of the advantages. Social events, friendships and social support is readily available in these exclusive and secure settings.

Speakers, entertainers and services are available in the community, and persons rarely need to leave the compound unless they wish. Although retirement communities, the most famous of which is Sun City in New Mexico, appear to be flourishing throughout the USA, there appears to have been much less interest in the UK. One such retirement village is that set up for retired publicans by the Licensed Victuallers Association, but few others have followed. Jefferys (1997) reports on a visit to Bradeley retirement village in Staffordshire, which is unusual in that it is a Housing Association project. She questions the appropriateness of providing such enterprises through communal resources, suggesting instead that money is better spent in providing care services that enable people to stay in their own home in age-mixed communities. At the time of the visit, many of the residents were mainly fit and healthy over fifty-fives who run the village's own shop, pub and hairdressing salon. Jefferys reflects on the viability of this community in 20 to 30 years time when the present residents become more frail.

Supportive Housing

This describes the type of housing for which the Abbeyfield Society is perhaps the best known. A large house is occupied by several older residents who rent and furnish their own room. There is a resident housekeeper who cooks a main meal, which can be taken communally. This model provides for a balance of privacy and companionship, security and independence.

'Lifetime Homes' for the Future

A recent publication by the Joseph Rowntree Foundation (1997) describes an innovative approach to housing design, whereby features cater for the changing needs of individual occupants over a lifetime. These 'lifetime homes' incorporate 16 design standards, which apply to outside access, layout within the home, and fixtures and fittings. The authors claim that the homes can be provided at very little additional cost and recommend that the standards are included in new homes, with modernisation programmes to existing social housing. In the long term this would cut down on the cost of future adaptations for disabled occupants and possibly delay a move into institutional care.

Older People Living in Tied Accommodation

Those in tied accommodation may be forced to move on termination of employment. Alternative affordable accommodation is increasingly difficult to find because of the problems already discussed and the general rise in rents.

The Housing Needs of Ethnic Minority Elders

Ethnic minority elders may have special needs in relation to cooking and worship and may also wish to be grouped with people who share the same language and culture. Orthodox Jews tend to be well organised in this respect, but so far there is little provision by mainstream providers. In some areas, voluntary groups have set up schemes or made deals with housing associations. The Gharana Housing Association operating in the Midlands is an example of such a scheme.

Sheltered Accommodation

Sheltered housing is often viewed by professionals and family as an ideal solution to the needs of frail older people, enabling them to remain in self-contained units but with support. It consists of grouped housing, usually flats or bungalows with a warden on hand, who acts as a good neighbour in case of emergencies. Some wardens may help to organise social activities. The dwellings themselves have special design features for the less agile, and are small, easy to run and heat. There is the possibility of companionship from other tenants or owners, yet there is privacy too. In some schemes, there are also communal facilities such as lounges, hairdressing, laundry rooms, showers and assisted bathing. Sometimes these are made available to people living outside and, according to Anchor House Association, this can help residents to maintain contact with the community and provides a community resource. However, this may also pose an additional threat to the security of those residents who expected to be more secure in a communal scheme. Anchor has expanded the role of the warden to include identification of needs, liaising with social services and providing hands-on care in case of emergencies.

Five per cent of older people live in sheltered housing. Most provided by local authorities, some by housing associations and an increasing number over the past 10 years by private developers. Up to the early 1980s, sheltered housing was considered to be a useful housing option, particularly by professionals concerned with the health and welfare of frail older people. However, the study by Butler *et al.* (1983) cast doubt on its acceptance by the very people for whom it was intended to benefit and also questioned its cost-effectiveness. It suggested that sometimes professionals and relatives put pressure on older people to move into sheltered housing, without fully exploring the alternatives which may enable them to remain in their present home. In addition, it found enormous variation in schemes throughout the country. Residents expressed more satisfaction with the dwelling being small, easy to manage and heat rather than the extra features of the warden and communal facilities. Twenty-three per cent had been persuaded to move there by family or professionals and had regretted it. There was also much misunderstanding among professionals about the warden's role, believing that it was much more extensive and involved direct care.

However, the schemes are not without advantages to society and service providers. They may help under-occupation, as people vacate large houses more suitable for families, and it is easier to provide services to people who are grouped together. Butler *et al.* (1983) found that residents received more domiciliary services than people of equal need outside did. The study concluded that the chief aim of sheltered housing was to prolong active life and prevent people from going into institutions, but there was no evidence of this. The findings challenged many of the views on sheltered housing and for some people an ordinary small flat would have done just as well.

A final point about sheltered housing, which may contribute to its popularity with professionals, is that care given in people's homes is less visible to the community at large than the obvious provision of a sheltered dwelling. Studies are beginning to suggest that it is not the universal panacea in preventing entry to institutional care but, on the other hand, it looks as though something is being done. A report by Tinker *et al.* (1995) finds instances of hard to let sheltered housing, which provides further evidence of its shortcomings.

Very Sheltered Housing or Extra Care Schemes

These are aimed at physically frail older people and those with dementia. They are more likely to meet with the expectations which professionals seem to have of supportive housing, although even then expectations sometimes remain unrealistic. This is sheltered housing with extra care, such as meals, domestic help, personal care, extra communal rooms and 24-hour cover. They are offered by the spectrum of housing providers and provision by local authorities and housing associations is increasing rapidly. Tinker (1989) carried out a national survey of 10 local authorities and 10 housing associations to ask how good were the schemes and how much did they cost? All those involved expressed satisfaction, though again 25% of tenants had not wanted to move. The schemes tend to be cheaper than local authority residential care (part III accommodation), but any substantial rise in salaries in the future will make care altogether more expensive. Thirty-eight per cent had no disability whatsoever, which again casts doubt on the selection process.

Care in the Community

For those people who are adamant about remaining in their own homes, there are now other schemes such as alarms. These are usually body worn and enable people in difficulty, such as having fallen, to summon assistance. However, these are only successful if backed up by support services with good channels of communication. The aim of the National Health Service and Community Care Act 1990 is to provide tailor-made packages of care for frail older people who wish to remain in their own homes. Despite the acknowledgement that housing is often the key to independent living, Lund and Foord (1997) found that joint planning between social services and housing authorities did not always reflect the needs of local residents. Midgley *et al.* (1997) echo some of their findings and suggest an innovative model of multi-agency working and user involvement. There remains much scepticism as to how successful it is in achieving this aim. There is continued concern over underfunding and the lack of proper structures, which will enable agencies such as housing and health and social services to provide the promised 'seamless' service.

Older Homeless People

A report by Age Concern (1991) highlights the plight of older people who are without a permanent home. The report estimates that of the total populative living on the streets or in hostels in London 25–30% are people over the age of 50. Tinker (1995) suggests there are two ways of ascertaining homelessness among older people:

(1) Those who are found accommodation by local authorities. In 1991, 4% of homeless households were found accommodation by local authorities, as they were considered vulnerable because of age.
(2) Those sleeping rough or in squats. Little is known about this group, although there is increasing interest (Crane, 1992). Family breakdown, loss of family and death of spouse, or the carer becoming homeless after the death of the person being cared for, are some of the reasons given for the plight of this second group.

Older homeless people tend to be in poor health, often with multiple pathologies related to ageing and as a result of living on the streets or in hostels for many years. Homeless people often lack access to mainstream services. This precludes them from receiving appropriate levels of health and social service support enabling them to resettle in ordinary housing. Their needs are given low priority, support is patchy and inevitably falls on the voluntary sector.

In conclusion, appropriate and affordable housing is essential to the continuing health and wellbeing of older people, particularly in the event of increasing frailty. A home of one's own, whether owned or rented, remains a goal for the majority, and knowledgeable health-care professionals can support older people in their decision to stay put, if this is what they want.

Living in a Care Home

A number of studies have explored the concept of home with a view to being able to continue to provide the essence of 'home life' within a care home. The findings of these studies are of particular significance to nurses working in care homes, as the nursing philosophy contributes to the creation of a homely care environment. Studies indicate that feeling at home is a complex concept with many meanings. The older people in Sixsmith's study (1986) described the importance of good neighbours, memories associated with home, particularly for those who had been bereaved, and their need for privacy and security. People liked to return home and for some the outside world was geared up for younger people. Most of the concepts were not connected with fabric or buildings. More recently, Pat Parkinson carried out an exploratory study on behalf of The Abbeyfield Society on the meaning of assisted independent living options have been explored, older people often need time to come to the realisation that to continue living alone is beyond the realms of possibility in the light of available resources. Relatives may experience guilt at pushing ahead with a plan, which they know is unwanted by the older person. A proactive approach that involves frequent and sensitive exploration of the views of both parties is likely to ease the transition.

Development in the Care Home Sector

At the present time, the need for high-dependency, long-term care for older people is increasingly being met by the private care home sector. New purpose-built homes tend to be in the region of 120 beds, in order to achieve economies of scale. However, there has been some criticism that such large units are little better than the long-stay hospitals they have replaced. There is concern that such large units preclude the provision of individualised care in a 'homely' environment. A code of practice covering all aspects of care provision for use in residential and nursing homes, sheltered accommodation and long-stay wards is enshrined in *A Better Home Life* (Centre for Policy on Ageing, 1996). This is essential reading for nurses working in any of the above care settings and should underpin the organisation's care philosophy and practice. Other considerations for the purchasers of care home places are identified by Ebrahim *et al* 1993 (**Box 13.8**). All new purpose built homes, and extensions to existing homes, should be built with single occupancy accommodation; research suggests that most residents prefer this (Association of Directors of Social Services, 1995).

home to community dwelling older people, some of whom were on the list for very sheltered accommodation with the Abbeyfield Society. She found that emerging themes demonstrated the common thread that people wished to keep their existing life as intact as possible. Autonomy and the need to have it recognised by others, retaining social networks and the feeling of still being in the mainstream of life were the dominant preoccupations of those interviewed. Sinclair (1988) reviewed the research for evidence of satisfaction from older people already resident in care homes and identified five priorities for care (**Box 13.7**)

Many other studies have explored life from within the home, most notably Wilcocks *et al.* (1987), Dixon (1991) and Allen *et al.* (1992). All the authors came up with similar themes surrounding the loss of autonomy and lack of continuity with previous lifestyle. The guidelines published by the Centre for Policy on Ageing (1996) are based on the results of these studies and form a useful framework for the development of a local care-home philosophy.

Factors Influencing a Move into a Care Home

A move into a care home tends to take place as a last resort when it is physically impossible for the older person or their relatives to cope using all the services available. In the review by Sinclair (1988), poverty, inadequate housing, increasing disability and lack of appropriate community services were the main factors necessitating admission to residential care. Furthermore, two-thirds of the older people in the studies reviewed were transferred direct from hospital or someone else's home. There is some disturbing evidence to suggest that the older person is not always involved in this crucial decision. Roberts *et al.* (1991) found this is particularly so when the person is perceived to be frail or mentally impaired. The older person was barely consulted in the decision-making in that they were neither presented with information nor involved in any discussion about the transfer. This is also supported by Reid and Payton (1996).

Herein lies one of the key advocacy roles that gerontological nurses can adopt with older patients and their carers. Nurses can encourage and foster open and honest communication between patients and their carers. When all other

The recommended minimum size for a single room is 10 square metres, though the code recommends 12 square metres in order to accommodate the resident's own furniture. In addition, en suite toilet and washing facilities should be provided for each room. If a home is to cater solely for the needs of a particular ethnic group or to house a culturally mixed clientele, then building requirements may need to take account of the following:

• Washing and toilet facilities of particular specifications.
• Segregated male and female quarters.
• Areas for prayer and meditation.
• Requirements relating to food storage and preparation.

Some care homes are also used as a community resource and are open to nonresidents, for example to people attending a day centre. In such cases, the concept of progressive privacy protects that of residents while allowing the building to be used in other ways. The day care facility would become a semi-public area, and those spaces for the exclusive use of residents would be semi-private. Private accommodation would be open to individual residents only.

A suitable environment is essential to maintaining optimal function for older people. Those living in a care home may have restricted mobility, sensory deficits and dementia, so a prosthetic environment will compensate for deficits and maximise competence. The code acknowledges the challenges inherent in designing a building which must meet standards relating to design and fabric, provide a supportive environment for residents and serve as a functional and safe workplace for staff to provide quality care. The need to take advantage of economies of scale is recognised, while at the same time unit or group living centred around small communal facilities is more likely to achieve the desired domestic scale of living.

Effects of the Environment on Patients with Confusional States

The role of the environment is even more important in the care and function of older people with dementia than in others (Roberts and Algase, 1988). Furthermore, some of the more simple measures that are to be discussed could also be adopted as design features in acute hospital settings, bearing in mind Lipowski's (1990) estimation that between a third and a half of older patients are admitted with, or go on to develop, acute confusional states in these areas.

Kitwood and Benson (1995) describe a new functional approach to people with dementia, which acknowledges that people with dementia function at different levels depending on the degree of neurological damage, previous personality, social and physical or built environment. Marshall (1997) suggests that dementia is characterised by the combined disabilities of impaired memory, impaired ability to learn, impaired ability to reason and high levels of stress. As with other types of disability, the built environment needs to be able to compensate for the deficits of the service user, while

at the same time providing a healthy workplace for staff and a welcoming place for visitors. People with dementia are unlikely to remember why they are not living in their own homes but yet may be able to remember the houses they have lived in. It is thought that providing small, homely units with a person's own or a familiar type of furniture is more likely to make the individual feel more confident and secure. Siting the building in a familiar locality where people can go out or look out on old familiar territory also provides continuity.

Impaired ability to learn prevents the person from locating essential amenities such as lavatories, and finding their way to the dining room or their own room. The use of colour coding, pictures and large signs on doors are all useful reinforcement strategies. Others include the placement of doors so that when they are opened, the inside of the room and its function, are clearly visible. Long corridors with many doors are very confusing to the person with dementia. The best designs are where people can see the door to their room from public areas, and where their own door has particular features that distinguish it from that of other residents. In addition, well-lit areas present people with maximum information in order to assist remaining learning abilities.

It is important that buildings are designed to make sense to their occupants. Roberts and Algase (1988) use the term legibility of the environment, which refers to quantity, quality and stability of cues. People with dementia may have impaired ability to access and appraise their environment, for example they might not be able to work out the way to the lavatory or dining room, so that the building should be structured so that important places are made familiar and visible. Redundant cueing (Taira, 1990), whereby multiple cues are combined to compensate for losses, can be used to help people with dementia make sense of their environment. The author gives the example of the sound of activity, and the smell of food from a kitchen, situated next to the dining room in which tables are laid with cutlery and crockery. These features combine to indicate that it will soon be time to eat a meal. Age changes affecting visual ability can alter depth perception, and increase glare (see Chapter 4). At the same time, neurological damage as a result of the dementia prevents the person from using other information to work out what is happening. As a consequence, the person tries to negotiate a step that doesn't exist, and falls, or sees reflections in polished floors which resemble ice or water and becomes fearful. Floor coverings and furnishings need to be chosen with care so as to avoid such misperceptions. Safety for people with dementia is paramount as they may lack the ability to understand that they are at risk. Windows with restricted opening, thermostats on taps and guards on radiators are standard safety features in care facilities. Residents can be discouraged from entering particular areas by painting doors the same colour as the surrounding wall.

High levels of stress are experienced by people who are struggling to make sense of an unfamiliar world. Many of the features already discussed will help to decrease stress. Age changes in hearing (see Chapter 4), such as increased sound recruitment, may combine with the effects of the dementia to cause the individual to feel stressed. Design features that absorb sound such as acoustic ceiling tiles and carpets are helpful, so too is the provision of quiet areas. Staff can make an important contribution by controlling 'meaningless' noise from radios and televisions.

Nurses are key workers in the care of people with dementia, and should press to be part of any planning team set up to upgrade existing facilities or to commission new ones. However, they should be aware that there is still some resistance to the idea that design features can make a difference to the experience of people with dementia living in care homes (Marshall, 1997).

Wandering or Walking Behaviour – an Environmental and Behavioural Approach

One of the most common and challenging behaviours to manage in older people with mental impairment is that of persistent and apparently meaningless wandering or walking. The person has a tendency to keep on the move, either in what appears to be an aimless or confused fashion or in pursuit of an indefinable or unobtainable goal. In part, wandering occurs as a result of deteriorating memory and declining ability to think and reason. These cognitive deficits affect the person's ability to explain and communicate where they are going, or maybe even why they started to move in the first place. We have all had the experience of going into another room to collect something but once there are unable to remember what it was we had come for. Try to imagine what this might feel like when it happens several times a day.

Marshall (1993) expresses strong views about the use of the word wandering to describe what is mostly purposeful movement for the person suffering from dementia. In many instances, the wanderer is unable to articulate where they want to go or why they are on the move. However, it is important to listen carefully to what may seem on the surface to be inappropriate speech, as this may give a clue to the person's agenda (Rader *et al.* 1985). For example, Mr X, with a diagnosis of moderate dementia, was waiting in an acute ward to take up residence in a care home. His constant preoccupation while heading towards the door was his need to go to the post office. There had been some discussion with the social worker about the financing of his placement from his personal savings. He was obviously very anxious and agitated about what was happening to his post office savings book, his money and about his own future. The nurse asked the social worker if she could talk with him again and maybe show him the post office book to reassure him that it was safe.

In the absence of explanations from individual patients, a number of authors have suggested reasons that might underpin wandering behaviour. It has been found that those older people most prone to wandering had participated in high levels of social and leisure activities and had experienced more stressful life events prior to the deterioration in their health. These individuals had previously coped with stress by

regular participation in physical activity. In the present, wandering may be a reaction to a change in routine or living arrangements.

Separation anxiety is thought to be a major cause of wandering (Rader *et al.* 1985; Stokes, 1988). The old person at home may wander looking for their carer, or while in hospital or a care home, looking for a friend or relative. This may occur even if the visitor has just left or is expected shortly. The person is unable to remember the visit because of short-term memory loss but the feelings of insecurity surrounding the departure or absence of the loved one remain. Loneliness is most common in those who have lost a spouse. The person may not remember that the spouse has died and, therefore, begins to search for the deceased. Searching may also extend to other loved ones who have long gone, such as parents or places such as old haunts (previous homes, places of work or those associated with happy memories).

A US study of institutionalised older people found this type of wandering to be most often exhibited in new residents, and described it as 'exit-seeking behaviour'. Statements reflecting a desire to go home, often for the reasons already discussed, accompany the behaviour. Distracting activities may be temporarily useful. Exit-seeking behaviour is highly motivated and may persist until the individual finds some gratification in the present environment that reduces the desire to leave. The worry for carers is that the person may come to harm in attempting to seek out these people and places.

The self-stimulatory behaviour that takes the form of wandering is often seen in people with advanced dementia and is associated with other repetitive actions such as furniture rubbing, hand clapping and repetitive vocalisations. The behaviour may be connected to past occupation, such as laundry or cleaning work. Continuous self-stimulation may indicate a lack of external sensory stimulation in the environment. Modelling occurs when a person with severe dementia shadows a staff member or carer and will follow him or her everywhere. Engagement in other activities has proved a useful deterrent to the shadowing. The interruption of these behaviours may cause more distress for the individual and is usually not necessary. When any behaviour is negated or discouraged it is important to provide something to take its place. It is also most essential to modify the environment so that the wandering is not likely to be hazardous.

Discomfort as a result of unmet physiological needs, such as thirst, hunger and pain, or the desire to urinate, may trigger wandering in order to ease discomfort and serve as a distraction. It may be that the person is simply disorientated. Wandering might occur initially following arrival in a new situation. The person may roam around looking for the toilet, dining room or bedroom. Failure to find what is needed can result in inappropriate urinating, or entry into the wrong bedroom, much to the concern of staff and fellow residents. Wandering due to disorientation is often worse at night. This is partially related to decreasing sensory stimulation; darkness, decreased sounds and fewer people greatly reduce the person's sensory input. This is exacerbated by diurnal changes in hormone levels, which reduce blood pressure which in turn

13.9 The ABC Analysis of Behaviour

A – Activating Event of Situation
- When and where did wandering start?
- What was the person doing immediately before they started to wander?
- What was happening around them at the time?

B – Behaviour
- What form did the wandering take?
- Was the person agitated, distressed or happy while wandering?
- Did they appear to be searching?
- Did they roam about the building or did they attempt to go outside?
- Were they talking while wandering?

C – Consequences
- What was the response of carers to the wandering?
- Was the person told off, ignored, restrained, sedated or guided back to where they had started from?

Source: Stokes G. *Managing disruptive behaviour: wandering*. Winslow Press, 1988.

13.10 Strategies to Manage and Guide Walking in Care

- On initial entry, significant items from own home may help the individual feel more comfortable in the unfamiliar setting.
- Walking and exercise are healthy activities. Those residents who have been used to high levels of physical activity should be enabled to continue. Environmental modification through innovative building and garden design, using pictorial signs, colour cues and accompanying residents around to learn the route (cognitive mapping), may help those with mild to moderate impairment.
- Use of night lights to guide residents towards the toilet.
- Interesting activity programmes to meet varied needs, which include activities that utilise energy.
- Continuing contact with significant others. Relatives and friends may need encouragement to visit especially when they feel that the older person no longer recognises them. They may also require support during visits.
- Use of risk assessment (*see* Chapter 14).
- Personal identification, which could be a name band or a discreet label sewn in a jacket.
- Use of electronic tagging systems (See RCN, 1994).
- Use of baffle locks.
- Continuity of staff and use of 'named nurse' system.
- Use of interpersonal communication which maintains self-esteem of resident.
- Use of therapeutic approaches such as validation and reality orientation.

results in decreased tissue perfusion, particularly to the brain. Another factor to consider is that older people may normally only sleep for 5–6 hours per night. Wandering may be a means of relieving the boredom of lying awake in bed. Stokes (1988) suggests that, in some cases, wandering may serve as a means of attention seeking, in that the person receives more attention from carers when carrying out perceived disruptive behaviour.

Stokes (1988) advises that although the nature of wandering can be ascribed to any of the reasons already discussed, it must be interpreted as behaviour unique to a particular client at a specific point in time. He points out that wandering is not a continuous activity – even the most active wanderer roams for only one-third of waking time. He recommends the use of a simple behavioural analysis tool known as the ABC analysis of behaviour (**Box 13.9**), where A is the activating event or situation, B the behaviour and C the consequences of the behaviour. There are questions to be asked for each level of analysis whenever the wandering takes place. This approach provides an accurate and detailed description of actual behaviour in terms of how often it occurred, the circumstances in which it arose and consequences for the wanderer. It is essential to use it in tandem with information on the person's present situation and past life history. **Box 13.10** suggests strategies for managing what might appear to be aimless wandering within a care home setting.

The suggested series of steps to manage an individual who is trying to leave a protected setting (**Box 13.11**) reinforces your interest in the resident's feelings and needs and may relieve their distress.

 ## 13.11 Managing Wandering and Walking

- Observe from a distance first, the wanderer may return.
- Never confront or argue, or adopt an aggressive stance, your motive is to increase trust.
- If there is a likelihood of violence do not invade the resident's personal space.
- Fall into step and begin a non-threatening conversation. Use eye contact.
- Speak calmly and slowly with a voice which expresses concern.
- Listen and maintain eye contact. Repeat the resident's key words and validate feelings.
- When a decrease in tension is observed, orientate with a general statement.
- Cajole, humour and befriend. Your aim is to keep the resident safe and at the same time maintain their confidence and self-esteem.

Source: Adapted from Heim K. Wandering behaviour. *J Gerontol Nurs* 1986, 12:4–7.

ACCIDENTS

Older people appear more likely than younger adults to have accidents because of sensory and cognitive impairment, pre-existing medical conditions and their associated drug treatments. Slower reaction times in the event of a fire or car accident increase vulnerability, as accident victims are less able to escape easily and quickly. Death rates tend to be higher for older adults, as they are less able to survive the effects of trauma. For those who sustain an injury, the recovery process may be delayed due to slow healing, secondary infection and complications (Lilley *et al.* 1995).

As accidents are a significant cause of death and ill health among older people, they are identified in the national strategy for health gain as a target area for improvement (Department of Health, 1992). The target for England and Wales is 'to reduce the death rate for accidents among people aged 65 and over by at least 33% by 2005 (from 56.7 per 100,000 population in 1990 to no more than 38 per 1,000,000)'. Over 85% of all fatal home accidents in the UK occur in people aged 65 years and over (Office of Population Censuses and Surveys, 1992); nearly 57% of all home deaths are in the over seventy-fives. More than 300,000 people aged 65 years and over attend accident and emergency (A&E) departments each year as a result of a home accident (Department of Trade and Industry, 1990b).

Falls

Falls account for the majority of both fatal and nonfatal accidents involving older people. A review of falls among elderly people (Askham *et al.* 1990) gives compelling reasons as to why there is a need to reduce the incidence of falls among older people:

- Falls are devastating experiences leading to death or protracted disability. This may also lead to a lack of confidence and social isolation for the older individual.
- The risk of falling is a worry to carers, both family and professional carers.
- The cost to the National Health Service for attendance at A&E departments, inpatient and outpatient treatment and general practitioner (GP) treatment is estimated at £90 million.
- Falls may be a sign of unmet or undetected medical need.
- The sufferer may not regain the same level of function as before the fall, and may need social service support to remain independent or to be cared for in a care home. Falls occur more frequently in older women.
- The prevalence of falls will increase as the numbers of very old people increase, as they are the group most likely to fall.

Falls in older people are often associated with intrinsic factors such as physiological age changes and instability associated with impaired general health (*see* Chapter 11) and extrinsic factors such as environmental influences and the type of activity being undertaken at the time of the fall. GPs Graham and Firth (1992) who set out to determine the incidence and nature of reported and unreported home accidents in older people, and to investigate associated environmental factors, had difficulty in attributing a fall to any one factor. Most falls resulted from a combination of environmental hazards, physical disability, carelessness or excessive risk taking. However, intrinsic factors are thought to play the major part in falls for the over 75 years age group, while environmental aspects are viewed more as contributory factors (Askham *et al.* 1990). The most significant environmental hazards in and around the home are described under the following categories, though, in general, there is a dearth of research on the role of environmental factors:

(1) **Accidents on one level.** Accidents to older people occur in any part of the house, with the kitchen, living/dining room, inside stairs and garden the most common accident locations for the 65–74 year age group. For people aged 75 years and over, the most common locations are the living

room, dining room and bedroom (Department of Trade and Industry, 1988). Poyner (1986) suggests that loose rugs and mats can contribute to falls, particularly where the individual has some disability and is trying to hurry. Tripping over objects usually involved small objects that were not easily seen, such as a cushion or stool. A study by Campbell *et al.* (1990) concluded that although 20% of falls involved trips or slips, most occurred over normal household objects in an uncluttered environment. Intrinsic factors, such as poor balance and lack of prompt correcting action were thought to be major factors contributing to the fall. Falls outside the house account for one in three domestic accidents to older people living in ordinary houses. Poyner (1986) found that uneven paths and loose stones were implicated in virtually every fall.

(2) **Falls on stairs**. Older people tend to live in the oldest, and often least suitable, housing stock (see p. 308 of this chapter). A substantial proportion of both fatal and nonfatal accidental falls happen on stairs, the majority of these older houses have stairs. Home Accident Surveillance System data on nonfatal accidents for 1992 show that, for older people living in ordinary housing, one in four falls are from stairs. Ideally, an older person is safer in single storey accommodation. A 1989 World Health Organisation (WHO) document drawing attention to the growing evidence on the environmental contribution to falls, focused on why stairs might be so hazardous:

> Stairs are particularly hazardous to the old and care should be taken that stairways used by older people are well lit, have clearly visible step edges and do not have repetitive carpet patterns that may produce a false perception in those that have defective visual fixation. Stairways can also be hazardous if there are irregularities in the height or depth of treads or any other features that require a change in the natural rhythm of walking.
>
> (WHO, 1989, p. 37.)

Stairs have been subject to specific building regulations since 1965 but many houses occupied by older people will predate this.

(3) **Falls while climbing to reach up**. These are reported in detail by Poyner (1986) and are thought to be due to use of platforms (ladders, stools and chairs) which are inadequate for the task and older people misjudging their fitness for the task in hand.

There is some evidence to suggest that home visits and surveillance to modify personal and environmental risk factors contribute to a reduction in falls (*see* Chapter 11 for discussion on prevention of falls).

Falls in Institutional Care

In care homes, falls are virtually the only type of accident occurring. Falls in institutional care might be thought to occur as a result of negligence on the part of the staff who are charged with ensuring the safety of the older people in their care. A low incidence of falls could be used as a performance indicator of safe care within the institution. In the light of this, many hospitals and homes are developing risk management strategies in an attempt to prevent accidents and reduce litigation, while encouraging individual autonomy for a course of action. However, the tendency of some medical conditions to present as instability or to make older people more vulnerable to falls renders this almost impossible to achieve without use of restraint. In addition, active rehabilitation involves the commencement of mobility at a time when the patient is still unsteady. A degree of risk needs to be taken if progress is to be made.

Nurses and carers can play their part in reducing falls by knowing how to facilitate safe movement, by correct use of aids, ensuring that the manoeuvre or the distance is achievable and that the environment is free from hazards. A study by Gluck *et al.* (1996) attempts to evaluate the risk factors for falls on specialist acute medical and rehabilitation wards for older people. A previous history of falls, the presence of confusion or disorientation and the need for assistance with toileting, incontinence of urine or diarrhoea were the most significant characteristics of fallers. However, these were not typical of every faller. They conclude that it is difficult to predict who is at risk of falling and that in the case of falls, it is important to convey to hospital managers that risk assessment has its limitations. A study by Bowling *et al.* (1992) found that nursing-home residents had more falls than those in long-term hospital care. They suggest that this could be due to the nursing-home residents being encouraged to be more independent in their homely surroundings. They conclude that while exercising choice to move around freely is thought to be positive in relation to quality of life, it can have negative consequences in terms of health. Nurses can begin to tackle this difficult issue by discussing rights, benefits and risks with the client, medical colleagues and perhaps relatives, and documenting how progress is to be made in the individual care plan. This at least demonstrates a commitment to accident prevention in a high-risk area. Additional risk factors for falls and prevention of falls are discussed in Chapter 11, which covers mobility.

Fire-related Accidents

For older people, accidents due to fire and flames are the second most important cause of accidental death in the home. Around 340 people over the age of 60 years die each year in fires to which brigades are called (Office of Population Censuses and Surveys, 1989). It is estimated that brigades attend only a fraction of household fires and that householders deal with the majority themselves. Approximately 50% of fire deaths affect people aged 60 years and over, with 20% over 80 years of age. Poor mobility, poor sense of smell and a reduced tolerance of smoke and burns contribute to fatalities. Major sources of ignition include smoker's materials, candles, cookers, coal fires, heaters and electric blankets.

The Nurse's Role in Home Accident Prevention

Nurses can play a key role in raising older people's awareness of environmental hazards. This is much easier to accomplish if care includes a home visit by a community nurse, when most observations can be made without invading privacy. A systematic risk assessment might be carried out by room. Printed checklists are available for such an assessment such as that produced by The Royal Society for the Prevention of Accidents (RoSPA). Practice nurses carrying out the over seventy-fives' health assessment and hospital nurses who are caring for those who have suffered a fall can also play a part by addressing risky areas and supporting discussion with suitable printed information. RoSPA and local health promotion departments are good sources of material.

Safety messages should be kept short and simple. An older person occupying a home with stairs or outside steps can be informed of the following hazards and precautions:
- Keep climbing stairs to a minimum.
- Never leave trip hazards on the stairs.
- Two easy grip handrails give more stability.
- Make sure there is good lighting. Two-way switches are an advantage.

Sometimes the older person may lack awareness that a piece of equipment is wearing out or needs servicing, perhaps believing that if it works it must be alright. Also, the person may be reluctant to take action over faulty equipment because it will cost money. A survey commissioned by the Consumer Safety Unit of electric blanket users found that older people, particularly those over 75 years of age, owned the oldest and least reliable blankets and used them more frequently than younger people. They were also more likely to leave them on while in bed and to delay replacing old models. Clients can be tactfully reminded to have electric blankets serviced regularly according to manufacturer's instructions or at least

every 2 years, and to buy new blankets fitted with overheat protection. Gas cookers and fires also require regular checks; Gas suppliers will usually carry out a free annual safety check.

Road Traffic Accidents

Road traffic accidents are the leading cause of accidental death in the 65–74 year age group, and after falls is the second highest cause of accidental death for those aged 75 years and over. A Department of Transport Survey in 1993 found that 25% of older road-user casualties were injured while walking, compared to 9% of other adults (Office of Population Censuses and Surveys, 1996). However, as more regular drivers move into the older age groups, this is likely to change. At the present time, the continuing high level of pedestrian accidents are of concern, as older people rely on walking as an important means of getting around. Approximately 95% of casualties affecting older pedestrians occur in built-up areas, where traffic is moving relatively slowly.

SUMMARY

Personal territory and life space are integral to human existence. How people cluster together, where they establish their roots and personally define the limits of their range influences all other aspects of adaptation. In later life, environmental response is strongly rooted in experience and the emotional impact of certain houses, areas and events connected with them. When relocation is essential, the environment should be matched as carefully as possible to previous desirable aspects. The most positive outcomes occur when support is given with adaptation and the individual regains a sense of control in the new environment.

KEY POINTS

- Environments can be modified and the older person's competence increased, so as to deal more effectively with their environment.
- Relocation is less stressful when the older person chooses it. Nurses can actively assist older people to prepare for the move.
- Ability to use public and private transport is integral to remaining fully engaged in society.
- Changes in response to thermal stress put some older people at risk when exposed to extremes of temperature.
- The provision of housing appropriate to changing need contributes greatly to the health and welfare of the older person.
- Older people are at increased risk of accidents, particularly falls in and around the home. Nurses can play an important role in risk assessment.

AREAS AND ACTIVITIES FOR STUDY AND REFLECTION

- If you care for older people in an institutional setting, consider the environment in terms of its suitability for older people with mobility, sensory and cognitive deficits. Is there anything you can do to make it more suitable?
- Wherever you work, do you provide discussion time for the older client who is considering or being persuaded by others to move into a care home? Do you document care needs surrounding this issue in the care plan?
- If you are a practice nurse working in a rural area, how do you address the issue of driving during the over seventy-fives' assessment?
- Identify opportunities for giving advice on accident risk reduction in you day-to-day nursing practice with older clients.

REFERENCES

Age Concern Greater London, Older Homeless People in London. Age Concern, 1991.

Age Concern. *Feeling safer at home and outside*, Factsheet No. 33, London, June 1995, Age Concern.

Age Concern. *Information circular*, p. 11, London, January 1998, Age Concern.

Allen I, Hogg D, Peace S. *Elderly people, choice, participation and satisfaction*, London, 1992, Policy Studies Institute.

Askham J, Glucksman E, Owens P, Swift C, Tinker A, Yu G. *A review of research on falls among elderly people*, London, 1990, Age Concern Institute of Gerontology, King's College.

Association of Directors of Social Services. *A room of one's own*, 1995, London.

Boardman B. *Fuel poverty: from cold homes to affordable warmth*. London: Belhaven Press, 1991.

Bowling A, Formby J, Grant K. Accidents in elderly care: a randomised controlled trial, part III. *Nurs Stand* 1992, 6:25–27.

Butler A, Oldman C, Greve J. *Sheltered housing for the elderly: policy practice and the consumer*. London: Allen and Unwin, 1983.

Campbell AJ *et al*. Circumstances and consequences of falls experienced by a community population 70 years and over during a prospective study. *Age Ageing* 1990, 19:136–141.

Central Health Monitoring Unit. *The health of elderly people: an epidemiological overview*, London, 1992, HMSO.

Centre for Policy on Ageing. *A better home life*, London, 1996.

Collins KJ. Low indoor temperatures and morbidity in the elderly. *Age Ageing* 1986, 15:212–220.

Collins KJ, Exton-Smith AN. Thermal homeostasis in old age. *J Am Geriatr Soc* 1983, 31:519–524.

Collins KJ, Abdel-Rahman TA, Goodwin J, McTiffin L. Circadian body temperature and the effects of a cold stress in elderly and young subjects. *Age Ageing* 1995, 24:485–489.

Collins KJ, Exton-Smith AN, Dore C. Urban hypothermia: preferred temperature and thermal perception in old age. *Br Med J* 1981, 282:175–177.

Crane M. Elderly homeless and mentally ill: a study. *Nurs Stand* 1992, 7:35–38.

Department of the Environment. *English house condition survey 1986*, London, 1988, HMSO.

Department of Health. *Caring for people: community care in the next decade and beyond*, London, 1989, HMSO.

Department of Health. *The health of the nation*, 1992, London, HMSO.

Department of Trade and Industry, Home and Leisure Accident Research including Special Reports Accidents and Elderly People, DTI, 1988.

Dixon S. *Autonomy and dependence in residential care*, London, 1991, Age Concern.

Donnelly RE, Karlinsky H. The impact of Alzheimer's disease on driving ability: a review. *J Geriatr Psych Neurol* 1990, 3:67.

DTI. *Home and leisure accident research* including Special Reports: Accidents and Elderly People. DTI, 1988

DTI. *Accidents and elderly people*, Special report (1988 data), London,1990a, Department of Trade and Industry.

DTI. *Home and leisure accident research*, London, 1990b, Consumer Safety Unit, Department of Trade and Industry.

Ebrahim S, Wallis C, Brittis S *et al*. Purchasing for quality: the provider's view. *Quality in Health Care* 1993, 2:198–203.

Friedman S, Ryan LS. A systems perspective on problematic behaviours in nursing homes. *Family Therapy* 8(3):265, 1986

Gluck T, Wientjes H, Rai G. An evaluation of risk factors for inpatient falls in acute rehabilitation elderly care wards. *Gerontology* 1996, 42:104–107.

Graham HG, Firth J. Home accidents in older people: role of primary care team. *Br Med J* 1992, 305:30–32.

Grant PR, Skinkle RR, Lipps G. The impact of interinstitutional relocation on nursing home residents requiring a high level of care. *Gerontologist* 1992, 32:834.

Heim K. Wandering behavior. *J Gerontol Nurs* 1986, 12:4–7.

Jefferys M. Bradeley retirement village: a good or bad thing? *Generations Review* 1997, 6:2–4.

Joseph Rowntree Foundation. *Foundations: building lifetime homes*, February,York, 1997.

Kapust LR, Weintraub S. To drive or not to drive: preliminary results from road testing of patients with dementia. *J Geriatr Psych Neurol* 1992, 5:210.

Kitwood T, Benson S, eds. *The new culture of dementia care*. London: Hawker Publications, 1995.

Kline DW, Kline TJG, Fozard JL *et al*. Vision, aging, and driving: the problems of older drivers. *J Gerontol* 1992, 47:27.

Lawton MP, Nahemow L. Ecology and the aging process. In: Eisdorfer C, Lawton MP, eds. *Psychology of adult development and aging*. Washington: American Psychological Association, 1973.

Lilley JM *et al*. Accidents involving older people: a review of the literature. *Age Ageing* 1995, 24:346–365.

Lindesay J. Fear of crime in England. *Aging Mental Health* 1997,1:

Lipowski ZJ. *Delirium:acute confusional states*. New York: Oxford University Press, 1990.

Lund B, Foord M. *Towards integrated living? Housing strategies and community care*. Bristol: The Policy Press, 1997.

Marshall M. Wandering is a myth. *J Dementia Care* 1993, 1:11.

Marshall M. Therapeutic design for people with dementia. In: Marshall M, ed. *State of the art in dementia care*. :CPA, London, 1997.

Means R. Housing and community care. In: Johnson J, Slater R, eds. *Ageing and later life*. London: Sage, 1993.

Midgley G, Munlo I, Brown M. *Sharing power, integrating user involvement and multi-agency working to improve housing for older people*. Bristol: Community Care and The Policy Press, 1997.

Office of Population Censuses and Surveys. *General Household Survey*, London, 1986, HMSO.

Office of Population Censuses and Surveys, 1989

Office of Population Censuses and Surveys. *General Household Survey*, London, 1991, HMSO.

Office of Population Censuses and Surveys. *Mortality statistics*, London, 1992, HMSO.

Office of Population Censuses and Surveys, *Social trends*, London, 1993, HMSO.

Office of Population Censuses and Surveys. *Social trends*, London, 1996, HMSO.

Persson D. The elderly driver: deciding when to stop. *Gerontologist* 1993; 33:88–91.

Poyner B. *Accidents to the elderly*, London, 1986, Consumer Safety Unit, Department of Trade and Industry.

Rabbitt P. Declining years? Care of the Elderly 1994, November/December, 6:407–411

Rader J, Doan J, Schwab M. How to decrease wandering, a form of agenda behavior. *Geriatr Nurs* 1985, 6:196.

Reid J, Payton VR. Constructing familiarity and managing the self: ways of adapting to life in nursing and residential homes. *Ageing and Society* 1996, 16:567–578.

Roberts B, Algase D. Victims of Alzheimer's disease and the environment. *Nurs Clin North Am* 1988, 23:83.

Roberts S, Steele J, Moore N. *Finding out about residential care*, working paper 3, London, 1991, Policy Studies Institute.

Salvage AV. *Energy wise? Elderly people and domestic energy efficiency*, London, 1992, Age Concern Institute of Gerontology.

Salvage AV. *Cold comfort: a national survey of elderly people in cold conditions*, London, 1993, Age Concern Institute of Gernotology.

Salvage AV, Vetter NJ, Jones DA. Opinions concerning residential care. *Age Ageing* 1989, 18:380–386.

Schulz RD, Brenner G. Relocation of the aged: a review and theoretical analysis. *J Gerontol* 1977, 32:323–333.

Shields C. *The stone diaries*. London: Fourth Estate, 1993.

Sinclair I. The client reviews: elderly. In: *Wagner report: the research reviewed*. London: HMSO, 1988; 241–292.

Sixsmith AJ. Independence and home in later life. In: Phillipson C, Bernard M, Strang P, eds. *Dependency and interdependency in old age: theoretical perspectives and policy alternatives*. London: Croom Helm, 1986; 338–347.

Smith K. *I'm not complaining*, London, 1986, Shelter Housing Advice Centre.

Stokes G. *Managing disruptive behaviour: wandering*. : Winslow Press, 1988.

Taira ED. Adaptations of the physical environment to compensate for sensory changes. In: *Aging in the designed environment*. New York and London: The Haworth Press, 1990; 5.

Taylor J. Safely assessing which patients must give up driving. *Care of the Elderly* 1995, 7:32–34.

Tinker A. *Staying at home: helping elderly people*, London, 1984, HMSO.

Tinker A. A review of the contribution of housing to policies for the frail elderly. *Int J Geriatr Psychiatry* 1987, 2:3–17.

Tinker A. *An evaluation of very sheltered housing*, London, 1989, HMSO.

Tinker A. Housing and older people. In: Allen I, Perkins P, eds. *The future of family care for older people*. London: HMSO, 1995.

Tinker A, Wright F, Zeilig H. *Difficult to let sheltered housing*, London, 1995, HMSO.

Warnes A, Ford R. Migration and family care. In: Allen I, Perkins P, eds. *The future of family care for older people*. London: HMSO, 1995.

Wilcocks D, Peace S, Kellaher L. *Private lives in public places: a research-based critique of residential life in local authority old people's homes*. London: Tavistock, 1987.

Williams EI, Wallace P. *Health checks for people aged 75 and over*, London, Royal College of General Practitioners, 1993.

WHO. *The effects of indoor housing climate on the health of the elderly*, Graz, September 1982, World Health Organisation.

WHO. *Health of the elderly*, technical report series 779, 1989, World Health Organisation, Geneva.

USEFUL ADDRESSES

'Homesharing'
The Community Care Trust,
St. Mary Abbots Church Hall,
Vicarage Gate,
London, W9 4HN.

The Brendoncare Foundation,
Brendon,
Park Road, Winchester,
Hampshire SO23 7BE.

The Abbeyfield Society,
St. Albans,
Hertfordshire.

Anchor Trust,
Fountain Court,
Oxford Spires Business Park,
Kidlington,
Oxfordshire OX5 1NZ.

Care & Repair,
22a, The Ropewalk
Nottingham NG1 5DT.

Criminal Injuries Compensation Board,
Blythswood House,
200 West Regent Street,
Glasgow G2 4SW.

Gharana Community Care Services Ltd.,
23 Oxford Street, Wellingborough,
Northamptonshire NN8 4JE.

The Royal Society for the Prevention of Accidents,
Edgbaston Park,
353 Bristol Road,
Birmingham B5 7ST.

Victim Support,
Cranmer House,
39, Brixton Road,
London SW9 6D2.

USEFUL PUBLICATIONS

Advice for older drivers, Automobile Association, Fanum House, Basingstoke, Hants RG21 2EA.

Medical aspects of fitness to drive. A guide for medical practitioners. London: The Medical Commission on Accident Prevention, 1995.

Royal College of Nursing (1996) *Nursing homes: nursing values*. RCN, London. A collection of papers highlighting the development needs of nurses working in care homes, with recommendations to purchasers, managers and clinicians as to how these might be achieved.

Counsel and Care,
Twyman House,16 Bonny Street,
London, NW1 9PG.

McIntosh IB: *Travel and health in the elderly – A medical handbook*, Lancaster: Quay Publishing, 1992. A comprehensive textbook, covering all aspects of travel health in relation to older travellers. Most useful to practice nurses who are regularly involved in preparing and advising older people for leisure travel.

Directories of retirement housing

14 Frail and vulnerable older people
Abigail Masterson

LEARNING OBJECTIVES

After studying this chapter you will be able to:

- Identify demographic and economic factors that influence the lives of older people.
- Describe and explain legal and ethical issues of concern to older people and their nursing implications.
- Discuss advance statements and living wills and their significance to the lives of older people and in clinical practice.
- Describe the role of the nurse in relation to patients' rights.
- Relate essential aspects about power of attorney and court of protection and the nursing responsibilities in relation to these.
- Explain the dynamics of elder abuse and situations that may trigger it.
- Discuss the nurse's responsibility with regard to assessing, intervening and reporting in cases of suspected elder abuse.
- Discuss key considerations when undertaking an assessment of an older person's risk, and the influences that may lead nurses to be overprotective of older vulnerable people.

INTRODUCTION

Living into very old age brings its own challenges, particularly for those whose self-determination is compromised by illness, disability, physical frailty or life circumstances. There are also particular considerations as individuals approach death. For some older people, remaining in charge of their lives is a real and daily issue. For the nurses and others who work with these people, supporting them in exerting choice, control and rights of citizenship can present complex challenges. When faced with images of vulnerability, frailty or dependence, the rights of these people can easily be eroded if not preserved and exerted by all concerned. It is important to remember that people who have lived the longest have quantitatively, and probably qualitatively, the greatest accumulation of life experiences. These people are the survivors, and potentially those who have learned most about life. They have overcome life challenges, taken risks, developed means to cope with and overcome challenges, and found new ways of living. This chapter discusses issues concerning the UK's oldest people and how they live. It explores legal and ethical challenges surrounding the exercising of their rights and choices. It also considers abuse and neglect, rights and risks, and offers principles for working with vulnerable older people.

THE OLDEST OLD

The oldest old are the most rapidly growing group in the population. Among the oldest old, women vastly outnumber men. There were approximately 2500 centenarians in the UK in the early 1980s (Bury and Holme, 1991). Very old persons are often much less vulnerable than they appear. They may attribute their health to exercise, religion and a positive attitude, but genetics, good health practices and a certain degree of luck are probably involved. The very process of enduring beyond the average life span indicates personal survival capacities beyond those of the ordinary person, so much so that achieving a century is marked in the UK by a telegram from the Queen.

However, there is also a small but increasing group of very old people who would have died of various disorders but have been kept alive through sophisticated medical technology. Therefore, among the very old we find two distinct groups: those hardy souls genetically meant to endure for a century and the extremely frail who walk a tightrope between survival and death. Researchers have for more than a decade investigated the concept of 'hardiness' in relation to survival and coping among the oldest old with chronic illness and multiple stressors. Hardiness has been defined as a personality style characterised by three elements: feelings of control, deep commitment to something or someone, and enjoyment of challenge (Wagnild and Young, 1991).

The origins of the characteristics identified in the oldest old are difficult to identify. They may derive from generational or cohort factors, from survival traits or from an interaction between these and the ageing process itself (*see* Chapter 1 for further discussion).

The oldest of the old are little known or understood other than in relation to their degrees of dependency. The element they all share is the recognition that they are old, although many still feel the essence of self is not old only the outer trappings. The major traumas of life, such as widowhood and retirement, are long since past for many of these older people. They have reckoned with all the significant life transitions except those that entail their own dependency and death. Others with whom they have been close have doubtless provided models for those events. These are definitely the elite, the survivors. For example, an American doctor (Perls, 1995, p. 50) reflects on the challenge to stereotyping posed by this group. He stated, 'when I became a fellow in geriatrics, I was surprised to find that the oldest old were often the most healthy and agile of the senior people under my care'. He concludes that the common idea that advancing age inevitably leads to extreme deterioration and escalating need for health care requires revision. Some have termed this 'the fourth age': the time when issues of retirement are long past and the dominant theme of life is self-determination versus dependence.

The family relationships of the oldest old tend to be characterised by cross-generational assistance, affection and association (Troll and Bengtson, 1992). Phone calls, letters, gifts, visits and other evidence of concern and caring are highly valued. Relationships with children are significant but those with grandchildren sometimes weaken perhaps to save energy for the most important relationships. Some very old people serve as the 'kin-keeper' or family member who arranges get-togethers, develops the family history, rituals and in other ways promotes solidarity and unity among the kin (Rosenthal, 1985).

There are four times as many women as men over 90 (Bury and Holme, 1991). But 40% of 105-year-olds are male (Perls, 1995). There are marked differences between the lives of men and women in this group. Half of the oldest-old men are married, but only 8% of the women. The caretaking role invariably belongs to the woman, and when the spouse dies women are far poorer than men of equivalent age. A very old mother has a 1 in 4 chance of surviving her son and of living with her married daughter. Before 85 years of age, marriage is a protection against institutionalisation, but after 85 years of age it cannot be relied on as a buffer unless the spouse is much younger (Stone *et al.* 1987). A national survey of caregivers for the functionally disabled oldest old found that 30% were neither spouses or children. Other relatives and siblings were significant participants in caregiving arrangements. Obviously, more attention needs to be given to these other care providers who are critical to sustaining the very old.

Although many of the oldest old live alone or with family, many are in institutions. The key concern of these very old people is remaining in charge of their own lives within their limited economic resources and community supports. Perls (1995) notes that US researchers have shown that although the death rates for Black Americans are higher than for White Americans up to 75 years of age, the trend is reversed after that age. This change has been explained by suggesting that Black Americans died earlier because they were economically disadvantaged and had less access to health care. Those who survive, therefore, are an unusually vigorous group able to overcome obstacles which defeat others. Among the oldest old, minority populations at present form a small group who are in some ways a very select group of survivors, having overcome the effects of poorer education, poverty and discrimination. These patterns may change in the coming decades.

The Over-Nineties

Bury and Holmes' seminal study of the over nineties in England generated the following findings concerning the lives of older people in their nineties and over. Arthritis was a common problem which seriously affected half of the people in their study and proportionately more women than men. Half reported having trouble with their vision and hearing. There was a relatively low prevalence of dementia (5%) and of serious confusion (14%). The great majority reported from one to four chronic health conditions, a small but important minority reported five or more and a very small group none. Mobility for the majority was restricted. Nevertheless, just over 40% were able to go out mostly without help. Individuals living in private households tended to be more self-caring than those in communal establishments.

Bury and Holmes warn that although it may be reasonable to presume that worsening health or disability may precipitate a move into institutional care it is also possible that life in an institution fosters dependency. Significantly more men had full mobility and a lower level of disability. The great majority of the sample were middle class and reported that they had not suffered severe hardship in life. Most had a positive attitude but women were more likely to report boredom and loneliness. Personal relationships meant a lot and there was only a tiny minority who never saw their relatives or had none living. Many had had long-lived parents and long-lived siblings. Being a non-smoker also appeared to be associated with longevity but there were not clear associations with diet and alcohol consumption. Positive perceptions of earlier achievements and feelings of self-worth appeared to promote feelings of wellbeing and helped to compensate for current difficulties.

Perls (1995) suggests that men who survive into their late nineties become less and less likely to develop Alzheimer's disease with each passing year. Men who are over 90 years of age generally have better mental function than their female peers. Women seem to live with their dementia rather than to die from it. Very elderly men are also physically healthier than their female peers. Finally upholding Fries theory of compression morbidity, Perls (1995) notes that robust centenarians often have a relatively short period of infirmity before death. Usual causes of death in this group are acute illnesses such as pneumonia rather than chronic long-standing conditions.

Frailty

Buchner and Wagner describe frailty as:
A state of reduced physiological reserve associated with increased susceptibility to disability. Reduced physiological capacity in neurological control, mechanical perfor-

mance and energy metabolism are the major components of frailty. Although disease is an important cause of frailty, there is sufficient epidemiological and experimental evidence to conclude that frailty is also due to the additive effects of low-grade physiological loss resulting from a sedentary lifestyle and more rapid loss due to acute insults (illness, injuries, major life events) that result in periods of limited activity and bed rest. The pathogenesis of frailty involves a complicated interaction of factors that block recovery from rapid physiologic loss.

(Buchner and Wagner, 1988, p. 1)

Individuals may be mentally or physically frail or both. Jones (1990) found that frailty was evidenced by increased susceptibility to disease and accident, diminished physiological function and compromised host-defence mechanisms. Often the frail and vulnerable are seen when they are incontinent, dementing or immobilised. Nurses know the hazards of immobility and its effect on reserve capacities (*see* Chapter 11 for additional discussion). These vulnerable individuals frequently develop urinary tract infections, skin infections and wounds, pneumonia and gastroenteritis.

Growth hormone is under investigation currently as a possible factor in preventing frailty. Normally, growth hormone diminishes during ageing. A National Institute on Ageing (NIA) study is aimed at determining whether administration of growth hormones on an ongoing basis will keep people strong and fit. In a previous small study, it was shown that administration of growth hormone increased strength, muscle mass and skin integrity in healthy men over 65 years of age. This larger NIA study is aimed at increasing healthy ageing and reducing frailty.

Very old people may often experience decreasing energy levels. Wells (1986, p. 21) offers an enlightened perspective on energy use. He argues, for example, that older people may be able to walk but prefer to use a wheelchair in order to travel a greater distance in less time and have more energy remaining. Although the ability to walk should be maintained, the desire to be more mobile should be respected and a wheelchair provided to permit a wider range of social opportunities. Similarly a person may prefer the privacy of self-toileting and may wish to use considerable energy in that activity but wish assistance with dressing. Such choices in energy expenditure should be supported and encouraged. Although very old people should not be viewed as helpless, neither should they be forced individually inappropriate self-care. The goal of maximising function and delaying decline while using and building on personal strengths and desires is the goal of wellness-oriented rehabilitation for this group.

Researchers have questioned whether there are similarities between marasmus babies that could not survive without human stimulation and the very old, isolated, frail older people who lack companionship and caring. Research has shown that failure to thrive in adults had many corollaries with this syndrome in infants and symptomatically presented a mirror image. Failure to thrive (FTT) is, however, a rather indiscriminate diagnosis. FTT generally describes a person with unexplained weight loss, nutritional deficits, unexplained decline in physical and cognitive function, and depressive symptoms such as remaining in bed, giving up and feeling helpless. There are many possible causes for these symptoms, so they must be evaluated carefully. For example, Newbern (1992) suggests the necessity of a thorough nutritional assessment first as many of the symptoms of FTT may be related to serious malnutrition. Mental assessment must be made to determine cognitive and depressive status. Suggested interventions include reminiscence, life-review; physical stimulation through stroking, touching and rocking. Assistance to re-establish personal and social ties may be needed.

DEMOGRAPHIC AND ECONOMIC FACTORS

The average life span is increasing by an average of 2 years every decade (Social Trends, 1995). Survival beyond the age of 65 years to extreme old age has become more usual. The Office of Population Censuses and Surveys (1992) suggest that, by 2001, 16% of the total population will be 65 years of age or more and 2% will be aged at least 85 years. During the 1990s, the numbers of young elderly is expected to decline slightly, reflecting the small birth cohorts of the 1920s and 1930s. This will be followed by a renewed increase when the post-war baby boomers attain 65 years of age.

Population ageing is not uniform across the UK. For example, Wales has a large elderly population: 17.3% are aged 65 years and over compared to the UK figure of 15.7%. The highest levels of need occur in the very elderly. The 85+ population is projected to increase by 15% between 1995 and 2001 and by 44% between 1995 and 2019.

The General Household Survey (GHS) compared data from 1974 and 1993 and found that a higher proportion of both men and women in all age groups reported chronic sickness in 1993. Nearly half of all social security payments in 1993–1994 were made to older people (Social Trends, 1995). In Britain in 1993 there were 264,000 residents living in homes for the elderly and 8000 living in homes for the physically disabled. The District Nursing Service has many older patients: over two-thirds are aged over 65 years. The over 65s received 5.2% of health visitor visits, 35% of community psychiatric nurse visits and 3.7% of community mental handicap nurse visits (Welsh Office, 1996). The 1990 GHS found that 15% of people aged 16 years and over were carers – 17% of women and 13% of men. The peak age for caring is 45–64 years, presumably because at this age a person's parents may become in need of care (Social Trends, 1995).

Demographic projections have caused concern about the dependency ratio. The dependency ratio in a society is affected by the distribution of age and work. The dependency ratio (number of workers in relation to non-workers) is continually rising, fuelling fears about the cost burden of care for frail and vulnerable older people, but the lower birth rate and thus reduction in child welfare payments, education costs and so on is seldom considered in this equation. In reality, the ratio of children under 18 years of age to the number of working adults is continually decreasing. Discussing the US context, Bengtson (1992) adds the costs of education for the young and the transfer of an estimated $7 trillion of assets to the middle aged on the deaths of their parents (the present generation of elders) to the equation of dependency. This complicates the predictions and tends to balance the picture of cost projections that is secured when pension and care costs are viewed in isolation. Similarly, the volume of care needed depends on health status, marriage patterns, household composition and living arrangements.

In many respects, the older population of the future will be advantaged in comparison with preceding cohorts. Fewer will be unmarried, childless or widowed; more will have occupational pensions and property; and there will be a significant increase in people aged 45–64 years, the peak age for providing informal care (Raleigh, 1997). Also as the BMA and RCN (1995, p. 3) note, 'Regrettably, the attitudes perpetuated portray the increasing population of older people as a social problem or a demographic disaster rather than as a positive asset. The majority of older people enjoy good health and contribute to society in many ways'.

ASPECTS WHICH LINK WITH VULNERABILITY

Gender

In 1992, women accounted for 60% of the whole elderly population and 62% of those aged 75+. Within the general population aged 60 years or more, women outnumbered men by 6 to 4, rising to 7.5 to 2.5 for people aged 85 years or more [Office of Population Censuses and Surveys (OPCS), 1993]. It has been suggested that the marital status composition of the elderly population is extremely important in the context of family support for older people. A spouse can be a potential source of practical help and emotional support and the never married are unlikely to have the potential support of children. Marital status also has a major impact on living arrangements, which in turn influences service use and, particularly in men, reported wellbeing and other indicators of health (Grundy, 1995).

Older women, particularly those aged 75 years and over, are more likely than men in the same age group to be living alone. Differences in marital status and living arrangements largely account for the higher use made by women of institutional care (Grundy, 1995). The OPCS disability services showed that 45% of women over 75 years of age in the most severely disabled groups were living in institutions compared with only 30% of men of the same age and level of disability. However, Sinclair (1990) reported that widowed or single men were more likely to apply for residential care compared with single or widowed women of the same age. This may be associated with the reluctance of many men to engage in household domestic tasks and society's expectations that they cannot or should not do this (Warburton,

1994). Available evidence suggests that elderly people in Britain and other Western countries prefer to maintain their own households wherever possible.

In 1981, widows comprised half the female population at the age of 75 years and increasing proportions in older age groups. This is a reflection of sex differences in mortality and women tending to marry men older than themselves. The proportion of never married women is declining but the proportion of divorced older people is projected to reach 5% by the year 2000. The effects of divorce and remarriage on intergenerational relationships is largely unknown. (For further discussion of gender issues *see* Chapter 19.)

Ethnicity

The UK has a multiracial, multicultural population, yet there is a paucity of research literature concerning the health experience of minority ethnic groups. Several studies have examined chronic illness, disability, self-assessed health or physical characteristics of South Asian and Caribbean elders. Chronic illness has been found to be higher among Gujaratis aged 54 years and over than an age-matched sample of Whites from the same practice. Donaldson (1986) identified high levels of disability in a sample of south Asian over sixty-fives resident in Leicester. Other researchers have identified problems with hypertensive disease and diabetes among elderly Caribbean populations (Fenton, 1985). Calder *et al.* (1994) have suggested that hip fracture in elderly South Asians is exacerbated by Vitamin D deficiency. Little attention has been paid to the impact of social isolation and poor social support on older people from minority ethnic groups.

Williams (1990) highlighted the under-use of health and social services by older people from minority ethnic groups. She attributed this under-use to:

- The low priority accorded to meeting the needs of Black elders by statutory agencies.
- Language problems.
- Lack of information in appropriate languages about services.
- Hostile or incomprehensible responses by staff to requests for help.
- Organisational passive racism and cultural ignorance, including the belief of White staff that Black families look after themselves.
- Concerns of Black elders and families being seen as burdens to society.
- The (often accurate) perceptions of Black communities that services are neither relevant to them nor culturally sensitive.
- A lack of planning information on the needs and numbers of Black older people.

Norman (1985) and Hek (1991) found that fewer Caribbean and south Asian older people received care from district nurses than would be expected on the basis of population estimates, which they attributed to lack of information and knowledge about the service among older people from minority ethnic groups and the attitudes of the nurses themselves.

Research has cast doubt on the simple stereotype of South Asian older people living in large and supportive extended families (Bhalla and Blakemore, 1981) and Caribbean older people in particular appear to have access to less domestic support than White populations. It cannot be assumed that such findings are static; patterns of social interaction are highly varied and there is some evidence of changes in intergenerational relationships upon migration (Mays, 1983; McFarland et al. 1989).

A preoccupation with ethnicity can lead to simplistic 'cultural' explanations of health differentials which ignore the wider socioeconomic context. The 1991 census contained two new questions that dealt with ethnicity and long-term illness. However, findings do have to be treated with caution for the following reasons:

- They rely on self-report.
- They do not allow for cultural differences in understanding of the concept of long-term illness and its translation into different languages.
- The form possibly being completed by someone other than the claimant (Stott, 1994).

Nevertheless, 1991 Census data indicate that the structure of all the minority ethnic groups is younger than that of the White group so there is likely to be a large increase in demand for services in the future by older people. McFarland et al. (1989) suggested that minority ethnic elders had low expectations of services. The 'triple jeopardy' described by Norman (1985) of old age, racism and inaccessible services which has so far been inadequately addressed will undoubtedly form an increasingly prominent issue in service provision (see Chapter 19 for further discussion of ethnicity issues).

Poverty

The evidence linking poor health among older people and low social class is very strong (Phillipson, 1990). For example, Evandrou and Victor (1989) noted how homeowners experienced better health than those in council or private rented accommodation and Blakemore (1989) reported that the relatively low employment status and poor pay of Black and minority ethnic groups created multiple hazards to health in later years. The present cohort of elderly Black people have been disadvantaged in education and income throughout their lives and thus are poor in old age. There is also some evidence that mental-health problems in old age, compounded by discrimination and lack of support from statutory agencies may be more serious among Black and minority ethnic groups (Bhalla and Blakemore, 1981). Policies that promote better distribution of services are essential for the present group, and more effective means of improving socio-economic status throughout life must be considered for the future.

In spite of the gradually increasing economic status of older people, many older people are existing below the poverty level. People from minority ethnic groups are poorer than Whites in all age categories and older Black women are the poorest. Poverty rates among very old women living alone have remained high in the last three decades. Holden (1988) suggests that the high poverty rates are caused not only by income differences between cohorts of women but also by their increasing propensity to live alone and the higher costs associated with this. Throughout the UK, there are great discrepancies in the costs of goods and services in relation to income. One person may live in abject poverty in a house in central London while another may manage well in a 'granny-flat' in Scotland on the same income. Housing, fuel and health are the major expenditures of older people. Nurses will become increasingly involved in discussions about and provision of resource materials on benefits.

Assets and Income

Often the major asset of an older person is a home that has increased immensely in value. Taxes and maintenance costs have also risen. If monthly income is low, a deprived state of existence may be chosen over selling one's home. Many older people are homeowners who have paid off their mortgages. Until recently, it has not been possible to spend these assets without selling the home and moving or making monthly payments on a loan. Several plans now exist to take advantage of home equity to the benefit of the individual who is presently experiencing financial need. The most common are reverse mortgages, and sale and lease back arrangements. Reverse mortgages are designed to provide monthly income that is to be paid back in a lump sum with interest at a designated time. It is often to be paid from the estate on the death of the loan recipient. Sale and lease back is a method whereby an investor purchases the home at 15–25% below current market value and leases it to the elderly residents for the remainder of their lives.

HEALTH CARE

The National Health Service has been under scrutiny since its inception when it was realised that costs were spiralling. Health care consumes an increasing percentage of the Gross National Product (GNP). Lifestyle changes and self-care have become popular ideas in the attempt to reduce costs and can certainly improve health status over time but, realistically, most older people have accrued the dividends from decades of healthy or unhealthy habits. Case management has been seen as a possible solution to provide more comprehensive, individualised and economic care.

Many people will need nursing-home care at some time for themselves or a parent. The cost is often devastating. Home care is often preferred to institutional care. Sometimes conditions may be less than desirable from professional standards but by the standards of the individuals are much more acceptable than institutionalisation. An array of public and privately financed services has developed across the UK to support the desire of older people to live out their lives in the comfort and independence of their own homes.

Ideally, the services provide a combination of health care, day-care supervision, housekeeping, counselling, meal deliveries, transportation, visits from friendly companions, home repairs and other services as needed. The cost of such services has been the subject of much debate and thus all services are often not available to those who need them. In many cases, a wide range of services is available to those who can afford them, but older people and their carers may be unaware of what is needed or where it can be obtained. It is estimated that something like 10–20% of persons in nursing homes could have remained in their own homes if appropriate services had been available to them. However, cost-effectiveness has been difficult to establish.

In day-to-day nursing work with older people, particularly those who are vulnerable, there is the potential for the rights and choices of the older person to be eroded.

It is important for nurses to be aware of the factors that may influence this (for example, the British Medical Association (BMA) and the Royal College of Nursing (RCN), 1995):

- Nurses know that a person is vulnerable and that she/he has a legal duty of care and a professional responsibility to protect them from harm. This can lead to an over-emphasis on protecting.
- Because the older person is, to a degree, dependent on the nurse, the balance of power in the relationship is unequal. Nurses may, usually unintentionally, reinforce this power balance, particularly in the use of controlling language.
- Health-care professionals have traditionally expected people who are ill and dependent on them, to comply with their advice. In fact, it is often when patients do not comply that their mental competence is first questioned.
- People who are dependent and disempowered may tend to comply without questioning.
- Professionals may make decisions based on their own personal values, including values about ways of living, ways of dying, the importance of religion or the appropriateness of sex in older age. These values may be totally different to those of the older person, and there may thus be covert pressure.
- Particularly when working with very vulnerable older people, nurses often consult the family or carers about a decision. The family may even be seen as the 'customer' of the service, such as when they pay for care in a nursing home. The values of family members may be very different to those of the older person, particularly with regard to risk taking and, again, there is pressure for the vulnerable person to conform to the wishes of others.

LEGAL AND ETHICAL ISSUES

Many people who need protection do not come to the attention of authorities, particularly if they are old and alone and their behaviour is not bizarre. Some people may appear alert and competent during formal assessments but are a danger to themselves and others in their daily lives. The courts currently seem to be reluctant to judge people incompetent. Although this is a great improvement from 25 years ago, when old people were 'railroaded' into institutions, it is sometimes detrimental to the client and family.

Nurses would do well to familiarise themselves with the laws that specifically affect older people so that they can assist their patients, clients and their carers. For instance, knowing about power of attorney and court of protection law would enable the nurse to guide appropriate individuals or family members through the process of filing for power of attorney or court of protection when necessary. Older people are more likely than most other adults to experience an erosion of their rights (BMA/RCN, 1995). The ability to be heard and to exercise control over one's life contributes to positive health outcomes. Patients have the right to make decisions about their lives and to be responsible for the consequences. Nurses must respect the individual's values and rights and facilitate self-determination even if the patient's values conflict with those of the nurse.

Power in decision-making depends on knowledge and an ability to exercise choice. Some older people may need legal services to protect their rights, assets and eligibility for various services. Some older people delegate power of attorney to another individual who then has power to act on the older person's behalf and make decisions regarding assets and legal affairs. This can be for a specified period of time or indefinitely. Court of Protection is another method by which an individual's powers of decision-making are given over to a named representative of the client appointed by the court. These are used in the cases where the court judges an individual to be in need of protective services.

All nursing activities carry legal implications as nurses owe a legal duty of care to their patients. Every nursing activity carries the potential for a charge of negligence. Negligence can also result from mismanagement, wrongful delegation, failure to observe residents and clients, and so on. If a resident or client suffers harm from a nurse's actions or omissions, they could be personally sued by that person. Fortunately, the law does not expect nurses to be superhuman. If a negligence case was brought to court, the nurse's actions would be judged against what could have been expected from an ordinarily skilled nurse in the same speciality – not the very best, most perfect nurse, but an ordinary one. Nevertheless, nurses should make sure they are up-to-date, skilled and knowledgeable.

Advance Statements

Advance statements or living wills are a means by which individuals can express their wishes regarding their care in acute illness and in dying. The most common use of advance statements is to register views about particular medical treatments particularly life-prolonging treatments such as antibiotics, tube feeding or being kept on a life-support machine indefinitely. It is difficult to draft a living will that is clear and unambiguous. Nurses should encourage patients or clients who wish to write one to use one of the many sample living wills which are available (RCN, 1994a). A formula recommended by the Patients Association is to write and have witnessed the following:

> I do not wish to have active or invasive interventions to prolong my life if I become terminally ill and there is no likelihood of my regaining my ability to decide for myself. I consent to have care and treatment which is designed to keep me comfortable and free from pain and distressing symptoms.

> (Patients Association, 1996)

Patients who have an illness that goes through clearly predictable stages may want to refuse specific types of treatments in advance or to nominate someone formally to act as their proxy. The proxy, who is aware of the person's general views and life philosophy, would discuss matters on their behalf with the multidisciplinary team as required. A living will cannot be a direct request for assistance to commit suicide (RCN, 1994a). Without an advance statement, those patients who do not possess the capacity to give or withhold consent for a particular therapy can be treated under English law in their 'best interests'. Under English Law, a relative or next of kin does not have the legal authority to consent for another adult.

Since the 1970s, US legislation has been developed permitting the use of advance statements whereby a competent person can make anticipatory decisions about future health care or can nominate another to take such decisions on his or her behalf. Studies by Emanuel et al. (1991) showed that about 70% of individuals decide against life-sustaining treatments if they became incompetent and had a poor prognosis for survival. Danis et al. (1991) found that care followed the advance directives in 75% of the cases they studied retrospectively.

In the UK, there is currently no legislation governing the use of advance statements or proxies. Recent cases have, however, suggested that an advance statement indicating a refusal of therapy will be adhered to. Luttrell and Fisher (1997) point out that although a legally binding advance statement goes some way towards extending the autonomy of the patient, it cannot cover all the circumstances and decisions that often have to be made. In the USA, an attorney under durable power of attorney is entitled to make such decisions. In Scotland, a tutor dative can make decisions on behalf of incapacitated patients, but in England, Wales and Northern Ireland, medical decisions rest solely with the doctor. Both the Law Commission and the Scottish Law Commission recommend UK legislation which would enable a mentally competent adult to nominate an attorney who would be capable of taking health-care decisions on their behalf should they become mentally incapable. Both commissions are also in favour of clarifying the law on advance statements and setting it on statutory footing (Law Commission, 1995; Scottish Law Commission, 1995).

Euthanasia

The RCN and the BMA take the view that euthanasia is unethical. The RCN (1994a) is opposed to the introduction of any legislation that would make health-care professionals responsible for termination of life. In 1994, the UK government endorsed the House of Lords Select Committee's rejection of the case for legalising euthanasia (Government Response to the Report of the Select Committee on Medical Ethics, 1994). This position recognises concerns that older people form a vulnerable group who may be pressurised into considering euthanasia simply to avoid becoming a burden to their carers. It is considered, therefore, to be more important to develop adequate systems of social and palliative care. The RCN (1994a) states that giving drugs in order to relieve pain and suffering, and treatment limiting decisions, even if they have the secondary effect of shortening life, are not euthanasia.

Australia's first voluntary euthanasia bill became law on 1 July 1996. The Act allowed doctors in the Northern Territory to assist mentally competent adults who were terminally ill and suffering severe pain to end their lives. The Act caused tremendous controversy and was overturned 9 months after its introduction. Four people had been helped to die and two more were preparing to die.

Rationing

When the National Health Service was established, it was initially envisaged that the service would be comprehensive and free at the point of delivery. However, escalating costs have challenged these fundamental principles. Prescription charges were introduced in 1951 and charges for dental and ophthalmic treatment followed. The most radical and dramatic assault to these original principles has been the shedding of responsibility for continuing care. The introduction of the internal market has highlighted rationing as a major issue. Unfortunately, it has often been assumed that the needs of older people are less important than those of the young and that older people benefit less from treatment. Such assumptions do not take account of the heterogeneous nature of the elderly population and are not based on scientific evidence. Luttrell and Fisher (1997), for example, note that older people are rarely considered for renal dialysis and transplantation, or cardiological interventions, and are offered palliative rather than curative treatment for cancer although there is significant evidence that older people, if carefully selected benefit substantially from such interventions. Furthermore, Luttrell and Fisher suggest that accurate diagnosis and appropriate treatment of acute illness in older people improves outcome and reduces the inappropriate use of long-stay resources. Rationing on age alone is unjust (see Chapters 1 and 22 for further discussion of rationing issues).

CONSENT TO CARE, TREATMENT AND RESEARCH

Establishing Competence

Legally, everyone is presumed to have the mental capacity to make decisions until it is proven to the contrary. The relationship between patients and health professionals should be based on the concept of partnership. Before a person can be given treatment his or her valid consent is required, except where the law provides the authority to treat patients without consent.

Consent has been defined as the 'voluntary and continuing permission of the patient to receive a particular treatment, based on adequate knowledge of the purpose, nature, likely effects and risks of that treatment including the likelihood of its success and any alternatives to it. Permission given under any unfair or undue pressure is not consent' [British Medical Association (BMA) and Royal College of Nursing, 1995, p. 14].

Many frail and vulnerable older people have multiple problems which affect their ability to make decisions about care. Illness and impaired speech, hearing, sight, language, memory and other cognitive functions are common. The prevalence of moderate or severe cognitive impairment rises steeply with age, from 2.3% in those aged 65–74 years to 7.2% in those aged 75–84 years and 21.9% in those over 85 years of age (Ely *et al.* 1996). All too often, it is assumed that such patients are incapable of making their own decisions. Discussion with relatives is no substitute for discussion with patients. It is the responsibility of the doctor to judge whether the patient has capacity to give consent. A patient who lacks the capacity for one decision may be capable of consenting or withholding consent for another. Moreover, patients with fluctuating mental states may be capable of making a decision at one time but not at another (Luttrell and Fisher, 1997). Capacity for making decisions can be assessed using the checklist (**Box 14.1**) devised by the BMA and Law Society (1995).

It is always important to clarify why and from whom the question of competence has arisen. The family may have ulterior motives, the doctor may be distressed by noncompliant behaviours, the health-care system may be responding to difficulties in patient management, and the patient may be concerned about proving legal competence. Data gathering to establish competency will ideally include the following:
(1) Thorough neuropsychiatric evaluation.
(2) Physical functioning.
(3) Mental status examination.
(4) Depression assessment.
(5) Anxiety state assessment.

The source of the data, accuracy of informant, observational skills of the appraiser, and the time, place and pacing of the interview are of critical importance. The presence of depression or anxiety states has a significant influence on the quality

14.1 Checklist for Assessing Decision-making Capacity in Older People

- Does the patient understand what the medical treatment is, its purpose and nature, and why the treatment is being proposed?
- Does the patient understand its principal benefits, risks and alternatives?
- Does the patient understand the consequences of not receiving the proposed treatment?
- Has the patient been given a free choice?
- Has the patient had enough time to make an effective decision?

of patient response. Luttrell and Fisher (1997) suggest the steps shown in **Box 14.2** to enhance autonomy and self-determination in decision-making.

Nurses must seek the views of all patients concerning their care and treatment. Although some frail older people may have difficulty in communicating, hearing or understanding, this does not lessen the nurse's obligation to consult them and to gain their consent to nursing interventions. Particular attention and skill needs to be offered to older people with mental-health needs, or fluctuating mental 'capacity' to make decisions. **Box 14.3** lists considerations for assisting decision-making in older people with mental health needs.

Consent for Treatment

Health professionals should provide comprehensive understandable information prior to seeking a patient's consent

14.2 Enhancing Autonomy and Self-determination in Decision-making

(1) Identify and correct handicaps resulting from:
  - Disease involving hearing, speech, language and eyesight.
  - Anxiety and depression.
  - Memory dysfunction.
(2) Allow patients time for decision-making:
  - Give adequate information.
  - If necessary explain the concepts and issues more than once.
  - Back up explanations with written information if necessary.
  - Encourage discussion with relatives and friends.
  - If appropriate, use translators, ideally not always family members.

14.3 Assisting Decision-making in Older People with Mental Health Needs

- It is important to remember that very few people are totally incapable of making any decision.
- Remember that capacity to make choices can vary according to the environment, the people around, the time of the day, the person's physiological status or reactions to medication.
- Identify physiological, psychological, social or other factors which may be influencing the person's mood or decision-making capacity.
- Seeming inability to make a decision in one aspect of life does not mean that choice cannot be made in another. Choices can be offered on a decision-specific basis.
- Physically frail people, and particularly those with communication difficulties, may find it difficult to express choices in ways which are easily understandable. This does not mean that they are unable to make choices. Difficulty in expressing choices does not equate to mental incapacity.
- Use a range of skills to build relationships, support and communicate.
- Try to understand the person (e.g. their biography); if the nurse understands how the person has lived it is easier to know how they would like to live. Try to understand their values and what is important to them (e.g. work, family, prayer). This is particularly important for people from different cultures. Much of this information can be gained through daily interaction with the person and family/significant others.
- Give time for decisions and, if possible, defer the decision until the person is most able to make it (e.g. a lucid phase or a relative's visit).
- If appropriate, reinforce with written or other visual material.
- If necessary, offer a limited range of choices, so that the person can make a decision more easily and can succeed in the decision-making. If there is no other way, decisions can be gently guided. However, it is important that this 'assisted' decision-making is used as a means of maximising the person's control over their own life, rather than removing the decision from them or limiting their choices.
- Offer as many choices as possible in aspects of life about which the person can self-determine, such as what to wear, what to eat.
- Reinforce successful choices and behaviours but take care not to patronise or infantilise the person.
- The best efforts should be made to establish and adhere to the person's known values, views and preferences.

Source: Adapted from Heath H. Rights, risks and responsibilities. In: Ford P, Heath H, eds. *Older people and nursing: issues of living in a care home*. Butterworth Heinemann, 1996; British Medical Association and Royal College of Nursing. *The older person: consent and care*. London: British Medical Association, 1995.

and during treatment so the patient can decide whether to request the treatment to be altered or stopped (BMA and RCN, 1995). Treatment given to a competent person without his or her consent may be considered battery in law. The patient does not have to prove that he or she suffered harm from the procedure, they merely have to demonstrate that it was carried out without their consent. Usually, a person capable of giving consent can only be given medical treatment against his or her wishes in accordance with the provisions of Part IV of the Mental Health Act 1983, the 1984 Mental Health Act (Scotland) and the 1986 Mental Health (Northern Ireland) Order.

In emergencies, if the person is a serious danger to herself, himself or others they may be given the minimum treatment to prevent danger. Involuntary hospitalisation is governed by two principles: is the person dangerous to his or her self, or is the person dangerous to others? Usually the patient's wishes prevail if judged competent. When the patient is incompetent, a variety of factors will be considered and judges have frequently decided these matters based on the individual case rather than any overriding principle.

Consent for electroconvulsive therapy (ECT) must be given by the patient if he or she has the judgement or capacity to make such a decision. Since ECT is often used to treat severe depression, the capacity to think rationally may be questionable. If the patient is able to clothe, feed and take basic care of self, he or she is likely to be judged competent, but if not ECT may be given against the patient's expressed wishes. Relatives cannot consent on a patient's behalf and should not be asked to sign consent forms but of course should be involved in decisions about treatment wherever possible. Health professionals must ensure, however, that relatives have the patient's best interests at heart.

If an older person is not looking after themselves at home or not being looked after properly by carers and is causing a risk to the safety and wellbeing of others, public health doctors have compulsory powers under Section 47 of the National Assistance Act 1948 and an emergency procedure under the 1951 Amendment Act to transfer people into a residential care facility. In practice, however, these powers are used very rarely.

Consent for Research

Researchers, health professionals and local research ethics committees should ensure that agreement to participate in research is a free choice and that consent can be withdrawn at any time. Consent for research leads to another set of issues regarding consent, particularly since dementia is a major area of research interest to health professionals and drug companies. Ideally, a living will would designate the willingness of an individual to participate in research but realistically this is rarely the case. The following safeguards should be in place:
(1) Make the written material about the research readable.
(2) Tailor the information to the needs of the patient.
(3) Allow patients to review the material for a reasonable

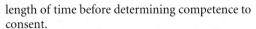

length of time before determining competence to consent.

(4) Use teaching, review and testing regarding patient's ability to understand material.

(5) Develop rapport with patient and encourage questions.

(6) Involve patient's family in consent process. They may use language more familiar to the patient and make the material more understandable to patient.

Testimonial and Contractual Capacity

Testimonial capacity involves an individual's capacity to testify in court. An issue may arise as to an older person's ability to accurately recollect significant data. Because of the long delay before a case reaches the courts, an elderly witness may no longer be a reliable informant or, perhaps, not be alive. Testamentary capacity regarding wills, marriages and other contracts may be questioned in cases that involve older people. Capacity to contract involves the ability to know the nature and effect of the transaction. Generally speaking, courts are loath to invalidate a marriage, although family members may be especially concerned when an elderly parent marries someone they suspect is a 'fortune hunter'.

Wills are used to express an individual's wishes regarding the disposition of his or her assets on death. Wills are sometimes disputed and lawyers may request a psychiatric examination concurrent with the making of a will by a very old person. The law does recognise the existence of 'lucid intervals' in which an otherwise impaired person may be capable of effectuating a will. Codicils, or subsequent additions to the will, may also be contested sometimes with devastating consequences for future family relationships if they benefit one relative over another. 'Undue influence' may be charged legally when a person has testamentary capacity but is so impaired that he or she is subject to manipulation.

Patients' Rights

Older people have the same rights to services and health care as any other members of society. Health professionals therefore have an obligation to ensure that the rights of older people are not eroded in the provision of health care.

(BMA and RCN, 1995)

Patients' rights in institutions of all types are effected by law, as are the rights of the general population. Legal rights vary according to the setting and individual competency. Nursing responsibilities are:

- To ensure that the patient has seen, read and understood the rights.
- To document explicitly when and why any rights may be temporarily suspended.

- To observe and record observations attesting to the individual's ability or inability to manage daily affairs.
- To be sure the patient's status is reviewed at appropriate time intervals and that he or she obtains legal assistance in presenting his or her defence. Nurses may sometimes have to act as patient advocates to ensure individuals' rights are upheld.

Health professionals are responsible to patients for the confidentiality and security of any information gained through the course of their work. There must be no use or disclosure of confidential information gained in the course of professional work for any purpose other than the clinical care of the person to whom it relates, unless the person has given explicit consent to its disclosure.

Advocacy

Advocacy is representing the interest of others by acting on their behalf or by attempting to influence the formulation of administrative, institutional and legislative policies that affect them. Instruments of advocacy include protest, disruption, representation, demonstration and argument appropriate to the protection of rights, entitlements and privileges of specified persons.

An advocate is one who maintains or promotes a cause, defends, pleads or acts on behalf of a cause for another, fights for someone who cannot fight, and often gets involved in getting someone to do something he or she would not otherwise do. Advocates may or may not be legal representatives of the individual. Citizen advocates are available in many areas. They are trained volunteers who act on behalf of people who may have difficulty in representing their own interests. They can be invaluable in helping an older person express his or her views. Such advocates are neither a relative nor associated with the health-care system and so can offer assistance without being influenced by conflicting interests. All nurses are required to be advocates for their patients and clients within the Code of Conduct [United Kingdom Central Council for Nursing, Midwifery and Health Visiting (UKCC), 1992] and for many older people, the care staff are their sole advocates. However, the nurse must use her professional judgement as to how and when to advocate. An advocate needs to be clear at all times whose position and needs are being met. The patient or client must always be the focus.

In some situations there may be a tension between the maintenance of standards and the availability or use of resources. Should nurses decide to take action regarding poor standards of care, an essential part of the process is accurate record keeping. Records should be completed at the time of the incident or problem and should detail the consequences for the residents or clients who have not been given the care they needed and deserved. Any deficit in the care given to an individual patient or client should be recorded in their nursing notes and a formal report made to the manager of the care area. Copies should be sent to the nurse's local professional organisation or union representative. The situation should also be discussed with the professional staff of the UKCC. If the nurse feels unable to complain to their line manager, they should sidestep them and go to the top.

The Code of Professional Conduct (UKCC, 1992) applies to all persons on the register regardless of the post held. It is intended to be a support to practitioners who are concerned about standards of care. However complaining about standards of care, or 'whistle-blowing' is fraught with difficulties. If nurses express concern at the situations which lead to poor care, they may risk censure from their employers. On the other hand, however, if they do not make their concerns known they are then vulnerable to complaint from the United Kingdom Central Council for Nursing, Midwifery and Health Visiting for failing to justify its standards and their registration may be in jeopardy. Nurses who choose to whistle-blow are also faced with a difficult balancing act concerning whether or not to reveal matters about patient care which are in the public interest against maintaining patient confidentiality and public confidence in the service. Making a complaint is never going to be an easy thing to do as it involves the difficult decision of balancing the potential personal, financial and professional costs against doing what is right. The protection of membership of a trade union and professional organisation is crucial. Whatever happens, going to the press should only be the very last resort. Many employers now include clauses in their contracts of employment forbidding employees to speak to the press or outside bodies.

The reports of the Health Service Ombudsman are an invaluable source of information about the National Health Service and provide important lessons as to how to improve service and care. In 1993–1994 there was an increase of 12.8% in the number of complaints to the Health Service Ombudsman. This increase has been attributed to a greater assertiveness in the population and willingness to complain supported by central policy initiatives such as the Patient's Charter (Department of Health, 1992).

PRINCIPLES OF WORKING WITH FRAIL AND VULNERABLE OLDER PEOPLE

Frail and vulnerable older people are frequently perceived as being 'at risk'. During the 1980s concerns about upholding the rights of older people came to the fore. Working with older people who are having difficulty in coping with their lives demands sensitivity. Older people because of reasons of pride or because of mental impairment may not state their problem or problems directly. Tolerance and patience may be required in teasing out the issues; often a great deal of trust must be present before a frail older person will confide in a nurse. Perhaps several visits will be needed. Working with this group of older people takes time and often the relationship which the nurse establishes with the older person is crucial. Reciprocity is important in such relationships in order for the older person not to feel totally dependent and needy,

14.4 Principles of Working with Frail and Vulnerable Older People

1. When interests compete, the adult client is the only person you are charged with serving. This principle reaffirms the traditional primary loyalty nurses have always had to their patients.
2. When interests compete, the adult client is in charge of decision-making until he or she delegates responsibility voluntarily to another or until the court grants responsibility to another.
3. Freedom is more important than safety; that is, the person can choose to live in harm or even self-destructively provided he or she is capable of choosing, does not harm others and commits no crimes.
4. In the ideal case, protection of adults seeks to achieve simultaneously and in order of importance: freedom, safety, least disruption of lifestyle and least restrictive care alternatives.

Source: Dunlap L. *Improving protective services for older Americans: a national guide series.* Portland, ME, USA: Center for research and advanced study, University of Maine, 1982.

and to maintain some control over the situation. It is important to remember always that these older people are survivors, people who have lived through major world wars, social upheavals and personal hardships.

A variety of private and public agencies may be involved with a dependent older person providing several services at one time. The need for coordination among the various service providers, that is, community nurses, social workers, doctors, practice nurses, discharge planners, lawyers, clergy members, family and friends, is crucial.

A useful theory of intervention with frail, vulnerable older people has been advanced by the Human Services Development Institute of the University of Southern Maine (Dunlap, 1982). See **Box 14.4**.

Risk Assessment and Management

When working with vulnerable older people fear of harmful consequences can lead staff to favour 'safe' options. An element of risk is part of everyone's life but it is important that risk is defined and management of risk planned in professional practice. Risk assessment and risk management are now key issues for all practitioners in health care. Many risk decisions are made in a context where philosophies and policies on risk minimisation and normalisation may be in conflict. Many agencies have policies to address issues around risk. Policies enable:

- Provision of a consistent service.
- Clear and accurate decision-making.
- Justification of decisions made.

- Promotion of openness and clarity about the values and principles underlying risk taking.
- Support to be given to those taking decisions (Lawson, 1996).

The law provides a foundation for professionals to work within and to utilise and justify their risks but it rarely provides direct answers. As nurses, we owe a duty of care to our patients and clients. Risk assessment involves evaluating and weighting consequences and their likelihood. Nurses can be disciplined or even dismissed for a risk decision which could have caused harm. Risk taking involves balancing likely benefits with likely harms (Kemshall and Pritchard, 1996). Each stage of the decision-making process should be documented, shared with others and monitored and reviewed regularly.

Information about the way risk decisions have been made should be available to assist relatives and carers understanding. Particular roles and responsibilities of individuals and agencies should be clearly specified. Older people have the right not to have their independence unnecessarily restricted due to the anxieties of others (Lawson, 1996). Nurses take risk decisions on a daily basis and need to take them in a manner that can be easily justified. A structured framework within which risk is assessed and managed is important and the majority of care settings now have explicit policies or guidelines on risk assessment and management. The dichotomy of 'safeguarding' versus 'promoting' is shown in **Figure 14.1**, and a brief risk assessment checklist in **Figure 14.2**.

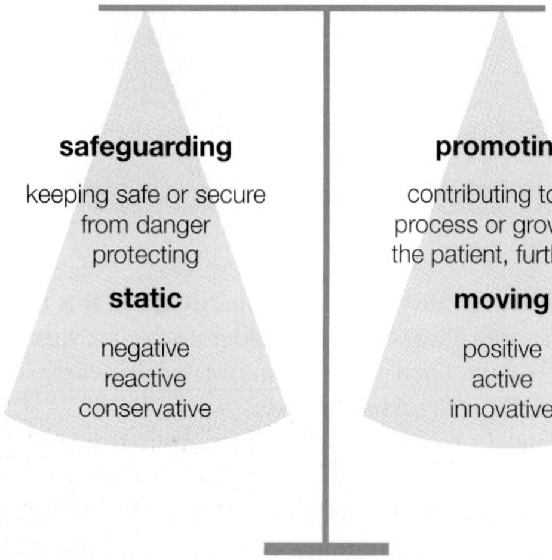

Restraint

In broad terms, restraint means restricting someone's behaviour to prevent harm, either to the person being restrained or to other people. The use of restraint is always an emotive issue. There are those who argue for its complete abolition and those who favour it as the only means to ensure control over the safety of a patient, the staff or other patients [Royal College of Nursing (RCN), 1992]. Nurses cannot remove all risks from a patient's life and it is not acceptable for example, to immobilise someone in a chair all day just in case they fall over. Restraint should only be used for short periods and only as a final resort when all other measures for preventing harm have been tried. Methods often used for restraining people include bedrails, sedative drugs, inappropriate use of night-clothes during waking hours, and arranging furniture to impede movement. It is important to make clear why a particular form of restraint is being used in a given situation. Use of restraints should be discussed by the whole healthcare team, fully documented and be reviewed regularly (RCN, 1992; BMA and RCN, 1995).

safeguarding	promoting
keeping safe or secure from danger protecting	contributing to the process or growth of the patient, furthering
static	**moving**
negative reactive conservative	positive active innovative

Figure 14.1 The dichotomy of 'safeguarding' and 'promoting' (Source: Adapted from Carson D. The Staff Nurse's Guide. London. Austen Cornish. 1990).

1. is the proposed action a gamble, a risk or a dilemma?
2. list all the possible benefits, for the patient, of acting
3. list all the benefits for other people
4. how likely are these to occur?
5. manipulate the risk by taking steps to make the benefits more likely to occur
6. list all the possible kinds of harm, to the patient, of acting
7. list all the possible kinds of harm to other people
8. how likely are these to occur?
9. manipulate the risk by taking steps to reduce the likelihood of harm occurring
10. list duties to risk
11. obtain the patient's informed consent
12. obtain the informed consent of colleagues
13. assess whether the risk should be taken

Figure 14.2 A risk-taking assessment strategy (Source: Adapted from Carson D. The Staff Nurse's Guide. London. Austen Cornish. 1990).

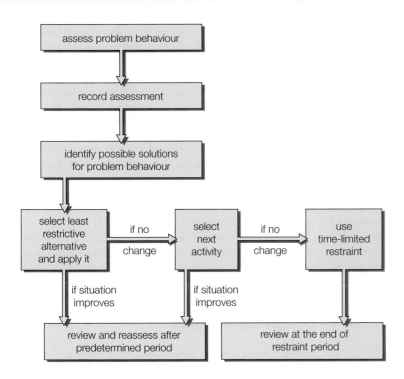

When considering the use of restraints the principles shown in **Box 14.5** are recommended by the RCN and BMA.

Older people with dementia who tend to walk around without obvious purpose are a significant cause of anxiety for nurses and carers. Locking doors may be one way of dealing with this problem as it then offers a safe area for the person to wander in. However, locked doors may also restrain others who have no wish to be restrained. Two alternative measures which have provoked a lot of debate recently are the use of electronic tagging and boundary crossing alarms which alert carers when the older person passes a certain point. Some people believe both are degrading and inhumanising. Electronic tagging should be used as a last resort and should not be used as an alternative to adequate supervision. The RCN (1994b) states that electronic tagging should be documented in the nursing notes and be subject to continuous assessment and regular evaluation. All institutions should have policies for the use of restraints that outline procedures for monitoring and reviewing the type and frequency of restraints used.

It is generally accepted by health and social-care professionals that people in need of help should not be intruded on any more than is necessary. This includes the personal care of persons as well as the handling of their material resources. In considering which service to use when assisting an older person, the least restrictive one should be the first choice. **Figure 14.3** depicts the decision-making process if restraint is being considered.

14.5 Recommended Principles for the Use of Restraints

- People should be permitted the maximum amount of freedom and privacy compatible with safety.
- The method used should always be the minimum possible in the circumstances and should be used only for as long as necessary to end or reduce significantly the threat to the older person or other people.
- Older people may wish to accept certain risks in order to enjoy greater freedom and nurses should be careful not to overprotect individuals by unduly limiting their activities.
- Restraint should not be used merely to aid the smooth running of the health-care facility, as a substitute for insufficient staff or as a punishment.

Assessment

Often, older people who find themselves in need of services are not happy about it. Furthermore, there may be others such as family and friends who are equally unhappy. Perhaps they are exhausted from trying to help the older person over a long period of time. Maybe the older person is demanding, even hostile. People in need of help may be confused, frightened, dependent and unwilling or unable to make decisions for themselves. Often, there is pressure on the worker to 'do something now'. Assessment is key to successful service provision. Of course, if there is an emergency such as a life-threatening illness, in-depth assessment will have to wait. Many agencies have developed standardised assessment tools.

Generally, assessment should proceed at the pace the client can tolerate. Developing a care plan takes considerable judgement and thought. Priorities have to be developed. If possible, it is important to work first on what the client sees as the problem before proceeding on to what the nurse thinks needs to be done. In this way, trust can be won. Working with frail older people can be a balancing act in so many ways – pacing of the work, how much to intrude, what to push and when to leave the person alone. If the client is mentally clear and understands the situation but still refuses a nurse's interventions, the nurse cannot legally intrude. In those cases, the only thing to do is to leave the person alone after first establishing a bond and making sure the person knows who to contact if he or she desires assistance. If the client is not mentally clear and is refusing interventions, it may be necessary to take legal action.

ABUSE AND NEGLECT OF OLDER PEOPLE

There has been increasing recognition in the UK, particularly since the mid 1980s, that older people are at risk of all forms of abuse. There is no system for the obligatory reporting of the abuse of an older person in the UK. The prevalence of abuse in the population over 65 years of age has been estimated to be approximately 5% (Ogg and Bennett, 1992). It has been identified that people with dementia are more likely to experience abuse, although their increased risk may be explained only partly by their cognitive impairment (Homer and Gilleard, 1990). The terms abuse and neglect of the elderly are used to describe situations in which individuals over the age of 65 years of age experience:

- Battering.
- Verbal abuse.
- Exploitation.
- Denial of rights.
- Forced confinement.
- Neglected medical needs.
- Other types of personal harm, usually at the hands of someone responsible for assisting them in their activities of daily living (Fulmer and O'Malley, 1987, p. 3.)

Abuse of older people has generated considerable interest in the last decade as the prevalence of the problem has been recognised. In Britain, a study was made of situations in which individuals were referred for respite care (Homer and Gilleard, 1990). Nearly half (45%) of the caregivers admitted to some form of physical or verbal abuse and neglect. Verbal abuse and neglect were significantly related to long-standing problems in the relationship and had occurred long before

care giving was necessary. Often the abuse was precipitated or augmented by alcohol abuse. The caregivers willingly talked about their difficulties but the older people would rarely do so. However, a recent evaluation of an elder abuse help line reported that a significant number of abused older people were using the service (Action on Elder Abuse, 1997). The best source of information in these cases, therefore, is apparently not the patient. None of the prevalence studies to date has included sexual abuse and it is only recently that professional awareness of the problem has been explored (McCreadie, 1994).

Recourse to the law may be required to protect the person. The Mental Health Act, 1983 (Sections 2 and 3) may be used to admit patients who are considered at risk from abuse. However, in most cases of suspected or actual abuse of people with dementia their need is usually for protection from abuse rather than compulsory treatment in a psychiatric facility as governed by the act (Coyne *et al.* 1993).

Dynamics of Abuse

Different types of abuse appear to arise for different reasons. Eastman (1994) suggests that the abused person is usually severely mentally or physically impaired; very old and usually female. Action on Elder Abuse (1997) reported that three times as many women were victims of abuse but perpetrators of abuse were carers in only 5% of all incidents. They tend to be abused by relatives, live with those relatives and experience repeated incidents of abuse.

Stress is a key factor whether associated with alcohol, long-term medical problems of the carer or financial difficulties. Pillemer and Finkelhor (1988) examined profiles of victims and abusers. Unlike other studies, which found that older women were the usual victims, this study found that men were just as likely to be abused as women although the abused or neglected women were more severely damaged both physically and emotionally. The abuser, as profiled in earlier studies, was most likely an adult child, but this study found that 58% of the abusers were spouses. This raises the hypothesis that wives who are caregivers are abusing their frail husbands, possibly in retaliation for past abuse. Elder abuse may be spouse abuse grown old and reversed. On the other hand, it must be acknowledged that the abuse or neglect could have commenced with old age and that older men are much more likely to live with a spouse than older women.

Frail older people are most often cared for in the home and the demands of such care on the family are thought to increase the incidence of abuse. Alzheimer's disease (AD) and other dementias are particularly intolerable. Paveza *et al.* (1992) found that the overall prevalence of severely violent behaviour toward family members with AD was 17.4%.

Anetzberger (1987) studied the perpetrators of elder abuse in a small sample of Ohioans who abused their elderly parents and identified certain predictive factors:

- Socialisation to abusive actions.
- Pathological or authoritarian personality characteristics

that increased tolerance for abuse infliction or decreased tolerance for stress.
- Inability to provide satisfactory care.
- Intolerance for the intimacy of caregiving.
- Vulnerability of the victim.

Although these individuals expressed love and filial obligation, they felt socially isolated and a lack of cooperation from the parent for whom they cared.

Anetzberger's study did not reveal whether the adult children had in the past been physically or psychologically abused by their parents. There is speculation that some abusive persons are abused in retaliation as they become old and frail. Carlse (1987) notes that more often the abusive person remains so and even when disabled may use manipulation and other forms of abuse.

Traynor (1994) warns that existing research on elder abuse is often inherently flawed. Definitions and language used to describe elder abuse are too loose to allow proper comparison. Sample sizes tend to be small and selective. Finally, because of the differences between the USA and the UK in levels of violence generally he urges caution in translating findings across the two countries.

Over the past few years throughout the UK, a number of organisations both statutory and voluntary including the Royal College of Nursing (1996) have published guidelines on how to tackle the issue of mistreatment of older people (**Box 14.6**).

Abuse and Neglect in Institutional Care

The nursing home sector is the largest single source of complaint to the United Kingdom Central Council for Nursing, Midwifery and Health Visiting (UKCC). Complaints reveal serious professional misconduct such as physical and verbal abuse as well as inadequate systems of drug administration, ineffective management systems, lack of systematic care planning or effective record keeping, and almost nonexistent induction or in-service training.

The continuing care sector has perhaps the most diverse group of practitioners employed within it. Some practitioners choose this speciality as an area where nursing is the key therapy and force for good, while others are perhaps attracted by convenience and a perceived association with a less demanding set of responsibilities. The softer management structures and reduced hierarchies are interpreted by some as refreshing, enabling autonomous practice and have encouraged significant innovation, yet these same freedoms make the establishment and monitoring of standards of care more difficult. There is often much less access to professional development and support. A 'policing' role is likely to be almost impossible and so any change is most likely to occur through education and socialisation.

Abuse of older people in hospitals, nursing homes and their own homes has been documented and discussed for

14.6 Checklist for Nurses in Situations of Suspected Abuse or Mistreatment

Assessment
- Safety of the older person: is the older person in immediate danger?
- What can be done immediately to increase safety?
- Are there barriers to reaching the older person (cognitive, family interference, emotional)?
- Are adequate physical, social, and financial resources available to properly care for the older person?
- What medical problems may make the older person particularly vulnerable to abuse and neglect?
- What type of mistreatment has occurred, how frequently and of what severity? What is your evidence for suspecting this?

Interventions
Preventive interventions include:
- Make professionals aware of potentially abusive situations.
- Educate the public about normal ageing processes.
- Help families develop and nurture informal support systems.
- Link families with support groups.
- Teach families stress management techniques.
- Arrange comprehensive care resources.
- Provide counselling for troubled families.
- Encourage the use of respite care and day care.
- Obtain necessary home health-care services.
- Inform families of resources for meals and transportation.
- Encourage caregivers to pursue their individual interests.

Reporting
A nurse who encounters abuse must:
- Report suspected cases to their managers, the client's general practitioner and social services department if appropriate.
- Ensure that an investigation will be conducted and action taken to protect the abused person if necessary.
- Keep accurate written records of the situation which are dated and signed (while still maintaining confidentiality).
- Record the content, date and time of telephone conversations with other professionals in the client's notes.

Nurses must be aware of and educated in issues around elder abuse and have knowledge of the definitions and reporting policies within their area of practice.

Source: ; RCN. *Combating abuse and neglect of older people*. London: Royal College of Nursing, 1996.

years yet it still exists in many situations. Poor wages, over-work, and lack of cooperation from management contribute to this mistreatment. The extent of abuse of patients in nursing homes has been largely speculative and often based on isolated incidences. Pillemer and Finkelhor (1988) conducted a telephone survey of 577 nurses' aides and nurses working in 31 nursing homes in New Hampshire. Those persons interviewed were asked firstly, if they had observed incidences of physical or verbal abuse of patients within the previous year and, secondly, if they had committed any such acts. The study recognised that even with the possibility of under-reporting the incidences were significant. Thirty-six per cent of the sample had observed physical abuse and 10% reported they had committed one or more physically abusive acts. Even more appalling, 81% had observed psychologically abusing incidents and 40% reported they had been psychologically abusive. The most frequent abusive actions were excessive restraints, pushing, grabbing, shoving, pinching, yelling and swearing at the patient. Based on the evidence of this study, it appears that maltreatment is a common part of institutional life. This study needs further replication but the implications are that in spite of regulation the quality of care may be deplorable.

Action on Elder Abuse (1997) reported that one-quarter of the abusers in their help line study were paid care workers and 20% of incidents took place in a care environment. Abuse prevention programmes must first attend to the quality of life of staff and the stresses of the work situation if more humane treatment is to trickle down to the dependent patient. A common form of institutional abuse, fortunately on the wane due to legal and moral pressures, has been that of restraining individuals. Restriction of movement may be one of the most devastating of abuses and has been so embedded in nursing care that only recently has the enormity of such disregard for human dignity become an issue.

Abuse and Neglect in Domiciliary Care

The home is the principal site of care for frail older people. Domiciliary care has changed radically because the needs of patients who have been discharged to the home are often complex. This is particularly true of the frail older person. Not only the treatment related to the disease from which he or she is recuperating but also the personal and human needs must be attended to if the individual is to recover necessary functions. In the arena of home care, reports of problems include the following:

- Inadequate supervision of patient care.
- Poor coordination of services.
- Inadequate staff training.
- Theft and fraud.
- Drug and alcohol abuse by staff.
- Tardiness and absenteeism.
- Unprofessional and criminal conduct.
- Inadequate record keeping.

Meeting Vulnerability Needs

Daisy has lived for over 50 years in a large Psychiatric Hospital but moved last year into a small community home with seven other people from the same hospital ward. She likes her room but does not particularly like the other residents and misses being able to walk around the rural hospital grounds. Her daily routine was to rise late in the morning, spend time curling her hair and putting on her best clothes and makeup. She would then walk the half mile to the local shopping centre, where she would browse around the local charity shops before heading for the George and Dragon, where she would spend the afternoon and early evening. All the regular customers knew her as Daisy and many would buy her drinks. Daisy is determined to continue her daily trips to the high street and the pub but is becoming less physically able to do so. Her gait is becoming more unsteady and she is less able to see the traffic on the main road, particularly as she refuses to wear her glasses. Daisy's only relative is a son who has been raised by Daisy's aunt from the time she went into the psychiatric hospital. He visits once a week and has strongly objected to the fact that the Registered Mental Nurse in charge of the home 'allows' his mother to go out. He is convinced that she is going to fall or be hit by a car when crossing the road. With her increasing vulnerability, he is now insisting that she be confined to the home.

- What subjective information could the nurse gather in order to make an assessment of Daisy's needs?
- What objective information would inform the nursing assessment?
- What strengths does Daisy exhibit that would assist in determining the plan of action?
- In this situation, how could the nurse balance the risks with the rights of all the individuals concerned?
- What strategies could the nurse use to assess Daisy's 'competence' to take decisions which could possibly involve her in risk?
- What considerations should the nurse use in developing a plan of care ?
- What would be the desirable outcomes of the plan of care ?
- How could the nurse evaluate whether these outcomes had been achieved?

The number and diversity of providers, both licensed and unlicensed, make monitoring of care extremely difficult (Institute for Health and Aging, 1989). Vilbig (1989) reports that home care workers hired to care for disabled older people are sometimes abusers and thieves. In a few recent cases, they have murdered their clients. Although the home care industry at large is appalled at these events, there seems no way to avert them. Theft of belongings seems to be the most common problem, and older people who have complained are often dismissed as 'confused' or 'paranoid'. Most agencies try very hard to monitor the quality of care they provide. Home care workers are often poorly paid and the turnover rate of employees is high. Many simply do not show up or do not do the work when they do show up. It is clear that even though it may be costly more care must be exerted in investigating the background of workers who are sent into the home to care for dependent older people and their work must be monitored more closely. In view of recent cases of elder abuse being perpetrated by nurses who have been struck off the UKCC professional register, there have been increasing calls by the public and professional organisations to set up a register for unqualified care workers.

Changing Perspectives on Elder Abuse

Elder abuse is still a relatively under-researched phenomenon. Trends in understanding the problem have changed. At first the tendency was to focus on the characteristics of and care for the abused. Then attention shifted to the characteristics of the abuser and now paid carers and professionals are receiving attention. Interventions to prevent and deal with elder abuse mirror these changes in perspective. Increasing attention for example is now being paid to the education and supervision of staff in caring environments as a means of reducing the incidence of abuse rather than training staff in such institutions to recognise the problem. Further work still needs to be done in terms of research and developing multi-agency strategies for prevention.

In 1994, Action on Elder Abuse surveyed all local authority social services departments, health authorities and National Health Service (NHS) trusts in England and Wales to determine how they were dealing with elder abuse. Surprisingly, only 24% of health authorities and 22% of NHS trusts who responded had a policy (some did not see the need to have a policy). Perhaps unsurprisingly given the so-called Berlin wall between health and social services post the operationalisation of the NHS and the Community Care Act 1990, very few policies had been written cooperatively with other agencies, although as Action on Elder Abuse point out, collaboration and cooperation by all agencies is essential.

SUMMARY

Using the demographic, social and economic trends as a background, this chapter has discussed key aspects which affect the lives of frail and vulnerable older people. Legal and ethical issues have been debated, and suggestions have been made as to how nurses can help to maintain and promote the rights of vulnerable older people to make their own choices and live their own lives as they would wish. To date, most of the existing theory about ageing has been based on cross-sectional data in which age cohorts have been compared despite evidence that the ageing experience of cohorts is affected by both their unique experience of historical events and such variables as their size relative to that of the population as a whole. Longitudinal studies are needed but have been infrequent because of the time, resources and commitment they demand (Wenger, 1992). It has been said that the progress of civilisation can be judged by the total number of human beings who achieve longevity while maintaining a life of meaning and purpose. In the care of the very old who are frail and vulnerable, subject to the whims of social policy and potential abuses and neglect, our human progress or lack of it is most visible.

The very old, however, are not simply an administrative or medical category, or a new problem group. They do not on our evidence threaten to overwhelm the health and welfare services with impossible demands for help. Nor should they run the risk of being blamed for the help they do need

(Bury and Holme, 1991, p. 164)

Nurses are perhaps the ideal advocates for frail and vulnerable older people. They have a key role in service provision and care planning. The need for help with daily activities increases sharply as people grow older. In the future, institutional costs and financial incentives to families may increase the number of frail and vulnerable older people cared for at home. The vast majority of care currently provided to the older people is given by informal caregivers, usually family members, but health and social policies have been consistently unsupportive of these families providing little recognition of their immense contribution to the care of the frail elderly in our society. As nurses we should be cognisant of the trends, the realities, and our place in influencing health and social policy.

KEY POINTS

- The oldest old are the most rapidly growing group in the population but very old persons are often much less vulnerable than they appear.
- The concept of frailty in older age has many aspects and interpretations.
- Aspects which may link to vulnerability in later life include gender, ethnicity and poverty.
- There are distinct legal and ethical considerations for nurses working with vulnerable people. These particularly involve promoting rights and choices.
- There is currently no legislation governing the use of advance statements or proxies in the UK.
- Although euthanasia is legal in some other countries, it is not in the UK, and key professional organisations take the view that it is unethical.
- In establishing a vulnerable person's ability to consent to care, treatment or research, the legal concept of 'competence' is central.
- Risk assessment and management is a key aspect of the role of the nurse with vulnerable people.
- Restraint should never be used unless all other options have failed.
- There has been increasing recognition in the UK that older people are at risk of all forms of abuse and neglect.
- Nurses have a key role in promoting the rights of vulnerable older people to make their own choices and live their own lives as they would wish.

 AREAS AND ACTIVITIES FOR STUDY AND REFLECTION

- What major economic and legal issues are a concern to you as you contemplate your own old age?
- Discuss with your colleagues the advantages and disadvantages of advance statements and how you would introduce the topic to an older person in your care.
- Reflecting on your practice as a nurse, what are your legal and ethical responsibilities to your patients and clients?
- Discuss with your colleagues the pros and cons of rationed health care. Is age a valid criterion for denial of certain services?
- Discuss the various legal mechanisms for protecting frail and vulnerable older people.
- How would you deal with a case of elder abuse in your place of employment?

REFERENCES

Action on Elder Abuse. *Everybody's business: taking action on elder abuse*. London: Action on Elder Abuse, 1994.

Action on Elder Abuse. *Hearing the despair: the reality of elder abuse*. London: Action on Elder Abuse, 1997.

Anetzberger G. *The etiology of elder abuse by adult offspring*. Springfield: Charles C Thomas, 1987.

Bengtson VL. Generational accounting doesn't add up. *Aging Today* 1992, **13**:10.

Bhalla A, Blakemore K. *Elders of ethnic minority groups*, Birmingham, 1981, All Faiths for one Race.

Blakemore K. Does age matter? In: Bytheway B *et al.* eds. *Becoming and being old*. London: Sage, 1989.

BMA/RCN. *The older person: consent and care*, London: British Medical Association, 1995.

Buchner D, Wagner E. Preventing frail health. *Clin Geriatr Med* 1988, **8**:1.

Bury M, Holme A. *Life after ninety*. London: Routledge, 1991.

Calder SJ, Anderson GH. Ethnic variation in epidemiology and rehabilitation of hip fracture. *Br Med J* 1994, 309:1124–1125.

Carlse J: The abusive relationship. *N Z Nurs J* 1987, 12:16.

Carson. *Nurs Standard* 1991, 5:30.

Coyne AC, Reichman WE, Berbig LJ. The relationship between dementia and elder abuse. *Am J Psychiatry* 1993, 150:643.

Danis M, Southerland LI, Garrett JM *et al*. A prospective study of advance directives for life-sustaining care. *N Engl J Med* 1991, 324:882.

Department of Health. *Patient's Charter*, London, 1992, HMSO.

Donaldson L. Health and social status of elderly Asians: a community survey. *Br Med J* 1986, 293:1079–1082.

Dunlap L. *Improving protective services for older Americans: a national guide series*, Portland, ME, USA. University of Maine: Center for Research and Advanced Study, 1982.

Eastman M. The victims: older people and their carers in a domestic setting. In: M. Eastman, ed. *Old age abuse: a new perspective*, 2nd edition. London: Chapman and Hall, 1994; 23–30.

Ely M, Melzer D, Opit L, Brayne C. Estimating the numbers and characteristics of elderly people with cognitive disability in local populations. *Research Policy and Planning* 1996, 14:13–18.

Emanuel LL, Barry MJ, Stoeckle JD *et al*. Advance directives for medical care: a case of greater use. *N Engl J Med* 1991, 324:889.

Evandrou M, Victor C. In: Bytheway B *et al*. eds. *Becoming and being old*. London: Sage, 1989.

Fenton S. *Race, health and welfare*. Bristol: University of Bristol, 1985.

Fulmer T, O'Malley T. *Inadequate care of the elderly: a health care perspective on abuse and neglect*. New York: Springer, 1987.

Gale BJ, Steffl BM. The long-term care dilemma. *Nurs Health Care* 1992, 13:34.

Government Response to the Report of the Select Committee on Medical Ethics, Com No. 2553. London: HMSO, 1994.

Grundy E. Demographic influences on the future of family care. In: Allen I, Perkins E, eds. *The future of family care for older people*. London: HMSO, 1995, 1–18.

Heath H. Rights, risks and responsibilities. In: Ford P, Heath H, eds. *Older people and nursing: issues of living in a care home*. Oxford: Butterworth Heinemann, 1996.

Hek G. Contact with Asian elders. *J Distr Nurs* 1991, (December),13–15.

Holden K. Poverty and living arrangements among older women: are changes in economic wellbeing underestimated? *J Gerontol* 1988, 43:22.

Homer AC, Gilleard C. Abuse of elderly people by their carers. *Br Med J* 1990, 301:1359.

Institute for Health and Aging. Home health services in California and Missouri. *Res Briefs* 1989, 6.

Jones SR. Infections in frail and vulnerable elderly patients. *Am J Med* 1990, 88:30.

Kemshall H, Pritchard J. *Good practice in risk assessment and risk management*. London: Jessica Kingsley, 1996.

Law Commission. *Mental Incapacity Law*, Com No. 231, London: HMSO, 1995.

Lawson J. A framework of risk assessment and management for older people. In: Kemshall H, Pritchard J, eds. *Good practice in risk assessment and risk management*. London: Jessica Kingsley, 1996; 51–67.

Luttrell S, Fisher F. Ethical aspects of quality care. In: Mayer P, Dickinson E, Sandler M, eds. *Quality care for elderly people*. London: Chapman and Hall, 1997; 17–36.

McCreadie C. Introduction: the issues, practice and policy. In: Eastman M, ed. *Old age abuse: a new perspective*. London: Chapman and Hall, 1994; 3–22.

McFarland E *et al*. Ethnic minority needs and service delivery: the barriers to access in a Glasgow inner city area. *New Community* 1989, 15:405–415.

Mays N. Elderly South Asians in Britain: a survey of relevant literature and themes for future research. *Ageing and Society* 1983, 3:71–79.

Newbern VB. Failure to thrive: a growing concern in the elderly, *J Gerontol Nurs* 1992, 18:21.

Norman A. *Triple jeopardy: growing old in a second homeland*, London: Centre for Policy on Ageing, 1985.

Ogg J, Bennett G. Elder abuse in Britain. *Br Med J* 1992, 305:998.

Office of Population Censuses and Surveys. *General Household Survey*. London: HMSO, 1992.

Office of Population Censuses and Surveys and General Register Office for Scotland. *1991 Census: persons aged 60 and over: Great Britain*. London: HMSO, 1993.

Patients Association. *Advance statements about future medical treatment: a guide for patients*, London: The Patients Association, 1996.

Paveza GJ, Cohen D, Eisdorfer C *et al*. Severe family violence and Alzheimer's disease: prevalence and risk factors. *Gerontologist* 1992, 32:493.

Perls T. The oldest old. *Sci Am* 1995, 272:50–55.

Phillipson C. The sociology of retirement. In: Bond J, Coleman P, eds. *Ageing in society: an introduction to social gerontology*. London: Sage, 1990.

Pillemer K, Finkelhor D. The prevalence of elder abuse: a random sample survey. *Gerontologist* 1988, 28:51.

Raleigh VS. The demographic time bomb will not explode in Britain in the foreseeable future. *Br Med J* 1997, 315:442–443.

RCN. *Focus on restraint, 2nd edition*, London: Royal College of Nursing, 1992.

RCN. *Living wills: guidance for nurses*, London: Royal College of Nursing, 1994a.

RCN. *The privacy of clients: electronic tagging and closed circuit television*. London: Royal College of Nursing, 1994b.

RCN. *Combating abuse and neglect of older people*, London: Royal College of Nursing, 1996.

Rosenthal CJ. Kinkeeping in the familial division of labor. *J Marriage Family* 1985, 47:965.

Scottish Law Commission. *Report on incapable adults*. Scotland: HMSO, 1995.

Sinclair I. Residential care. In: Sinclair I, Parker R, Leat D, Williams J, eds. *The kaleidoscope of care: a review of research on welfare provision for elderly people*. London: HMSO, 1990.

Social Trends. London: HMSO, 1995.

Stone R, Cafferata G, Sangl J. Caregivers of the frail elderly: a national profile. *Gerontologist* 1987, 24:616.

Stott D. Ethnic differentials in long-term illness reporting: a case study of South Bedfordshire. *Health Soc Care Commun* 1994, 2:119–125.

Traynor J. Lifting the lid on elder abuse: questions and doubts. In: Eastman M, ed. *Old age abuse: a new perspective, 2nd edition*. London: Chapman and Hall, 1994; 199–214.

Troll LE, Bengtson VL. The oldest-old in families: an intergenerational perspective. *Generations* 1992, 17:39.

UKCC. *Code of professional conduct, 3rd edition*, London, 1992.

Vilbig P. Elderly hiring caretakers often contract for abuse. *Senior Spectrum* 1989, 8:1.

Warburton RW. *Implementing caring for people. Home and away: a review of recent research evidence to explain why some elderly people enter residential care homes while others stay at home*, Department of Health. London: HMSO, 1994.

Wagnild G, Young HM. Another look at hardiness. *Image* 1991, 23:257.

Wells T. Major clinical problems in gerontologic nursing. In: Calkins E, Davis P, Ford A, eds: *The practice of geriatrics*. Philadelphia: WB Saunders, 1986.

Welsh Office. *Health Statistics Wales 1995*, Cardiff: Welsh Office, 1996.

Wenger C. *Help in old age – facing up to change*. Liverpool: Liverpool University Press, 1992.

Williams J. Elders from black and minority ethnic communities. In: Sinclair I, Parker R, Leat D, Williams J, eds. *The kaleidoscope of care: a review of research on welfare provision for elderly people*. London: HMSO, 1990.

Belonging

15 Intimacy and sexuality
Hazel Heath

LEARNING OBJECTIVES

After studying this chapter you will be able to:

- Discuss the views expressed by older people on the meaning and role of intimacy and sexuality within their individual lives.
- Analyse the components of the concept of sexuality.
- Discuss a range of influences on the expression of sexuality by older people, particularly concerning social attitudes and expectations.
- Describe biological and psychological changes which take place with ageing.
- Discuss perspectives on touch in the lives of older people, and the potential for nursing in this area.
- Evaluate a range of research studies into sexuality and its expression in later life.
- Discuss the expression of sexuality by older persons within a range of individual lifestyles.
- Discuss particular considerations for sexual health and functioning in later life, specifically related to chronic illness and sexually transmissible disorders.
- Describe in detail nursing roles and functions which may assist older people towards the achievement of fulfilment in the expression of sexuality in the ways in which they choose.

INTRODUCTION

Sexuality is a powerful issue. On one hand, we live in a 'sexualised society' in which sexual imagery is commercially successful in selling everything from cars to ice cream (Hawkes, 1996). On the other hand, a sexual act can be the most intimate and private sharing between two people. The expression of sexuality can be strongly influenced by generational, cultural or religious beliefs, and behavioural norms. It is a source of deep and powerful emotions from fear and embarrassment to infinite happiness and fulfilment, and it is an ever-present factor in our lives, whether we choose actively to associate with it or not (Hawkes, 1996). It is not surprising, therefore, that it is a complex and potentially difficult subject.

Sexuality is a fundamental aspect of being human that continues throughout life. The need for contact with other human beings, closeness or intimacy, or sexual satisfaction does not automatically diminish when individuals reach a certain age. In fact, sexuality and intimacy can become particularly fundamental in older age because Western societal attitudes often deny older people the right to express themselves as sexual beings and to show intimacy in the way they would choose. Contrary to the prevailing social stereotypes, older people are sexual beings, are sexually active, have sexual health needs, need sexual health education, may be HIV positive and should enjoy the same rights as all other citizens in respect of their sexuality (Ford, 1998).

On the progression through life, the emphasis of sexuality expression or sexual fulfilment may change. In early life, the focus may be on pleasure-seeking, relationship-building or procreation. In later years, companionship and sharing, intimate communication and physical nearness might assume greater priority. Some researchers have coined the phrase 'from procreation to recreation' to refer to this change in emphasis. Yet intimacy and sex can be of enormous benefit in old age; they can help to maintain a healthy self-image, provide psychological refuelling and re-energising, act as an outlet to diffuse personal anxieties, and help to prevent social disengagement and avoid depression. Sex can even be a means of promoting intergenerational understanding when both young and old share some of the same fears, insecurities and pleasures afforded by it. For example, older people have sought to learn more about HIV and AIDS because they are concerned about younger people being at risk (Beth Johnson Foundation, 1996).

Sex can be a safe and valuable form of exercise at any age, and Comfort (1977, p. 888) suggests that there is a clinical impression, unconfirmed by published statistics, that regular intercourse and orgasm are at least as effective as exogenous hormones in preventing the secretory and atrophic changes that occur with ageing. Kellett (1993) states that masturbation can be a helpful and healthy practice in later life, particularly for persons without partners or with partners who are ill or incapacitated by long-term health problems. Butler and Lewis (1988) similarly suggest that masturbation can provide an avenue for the resolution of sexual tensions, physical exercise and preserving sexual functioning in those individuals who have no other outlet for sexual activity and gratification of their sexual need.

Intimacy and sexuality may also help in facing some of the challenges of later life, such as negative societal stereotypes, the effects of ageing, the loss of friends or partners and chronic or multiple illnesses or disabilities. Greengross and Greengross (1989) state that:

Ben Bradgate is a 74-year-old ex-pitman who has been a widower for 5 years. He has led an active life, including his enthusiasms for rugby, cycling and singing in the local pubs. Mr Bradgate's wife Janey had been a miner's daughter. Her family were Primitive Methodists, but Mr Bradgate's were Catholics. Mr and Mrs Bradgate were obviously strongly drawn to each other, particularly to consider getting married in the religiously intolerant Lancashire of the 1930s. Mr Bradgate recalled, 'I fell in love with her and I liked her so much, I said "I'm not letting my ideas…" and of course it upset my family. And nobody – my father and mother didn't come to the wedding'. Mr Bradgate abandoned Catholicism.

Throughout their marriage, which 'waxed and waned', their sexual relationship was central to Mr Bradgate's understanding of intimacy. It had drawn them together in the first place, and both of them had enjoyed sex in the early days. At times, it may have been the best part of their relationship. Later on, when Mrs Bradgate did not want 'to be bothered', he took her acceptance of his more eager sexuality as a sign of loving. 'I was always on the sexual side, and she understood the position. Even if she weren't in fettle, she wouldn't worry if I said, "Let's have a bit of fun, come on lass".'

The most extraordinary moment of intimacy was their last night in bed together. Mrs Bradgate was about to go into hospital and was in pain from the cancer that was to kill her. 'She must have had this idea in her head that she would never see me no more. We had a cuddle that night. "Come on Ben, there might not be many more times in your life", she said. To her eternal credit she did do that … and it's never left me that, it's never left me'. That last intimate physical moment is a symbol of their mutual love which he holds on to. For Mr Bradgate, the worst thing in his life has been 'losing me friend, me pal and me bed partner'.

The one thing lacking for Mr Bradgate now is intimacy. 'I'm missing a lady to talk to. I'd like a lady friend, if it's only somebody to talk to, have a little cuddle now and again, even if nothing else happened. I think it brings some happiness to your mind'.

(Thompson *et al.*, 1991, p. 232)

At a time when we face multiple challenges, this aspect of our identity can give meaning to life and bolster security, belonging, and esteem. As we reach later life, some of us may believe that our physical sex life is over. Others know that this need not be true, and continue to enjoy happy and fulfilling sexual relationships, but many of us are trapped because we cannot consider sexuality positively and are unable to explore the wide range of possibilities that could be available. We feel inhibited by the whole subject and are afraid of anything new or different. We may need reassurance that it is normal to look at these aspects of our personality and our needs, in order to decide whether or not we wish to make changes in our lifestyle.

(Greengross and Greengross, 1989, p. 13)

Nurses potentially have a great deal to offer to older people in helping them to live fulfilled lives, particularly when illness, disability or changes in circumstances threaten fundamental aspects of their identity or lifestyle. A great deal of sensitivity, sound knowledge, skill, open-mindedness and flexibility is required in order to work effectively.

This chapter aims, in as far as this is possible, to present older people's views and perspectives. It discusses the concept of sexuality and influences on the expression of sexuality in later life. It acknowledges social, moral, biological and psychological dimensions and the effects of illness on the expression of sexuality. The chapter reviews the research-base on sexuality in older persons and discusses a selection of the lifestyles that older people may choose to adopt. It concludes with a detailed discussion of how nurses can work with older people in a sensitive and constructive way.

WHAT IS SEXUALITY?

The Concept of Sexuality

The term 'sexuality' has many dimensions and various meanings. There is no single understanding of the concept, and definitions differ in their focus and interpretations. For example:

- The terms 'sex' and 'gender' are commonly used interchangeably, e.g. 'this facility is open to both sexes' – does this mean both genders, and are there only two, some would argue not.
- The term 'sexuality' is used to describe a holistic expression of an individual's identity, or a particular sexual orientation or sexual preference,
- The terms 'sex' and 'sexuality' are used interchangeably, with the broader aspects of expression not always acknowledged.
- To many people, the words 'sex' or 'sexuality' bring to mind the physical or genital aspects – the sex act, but this is merely one aspect of the concept.

Concepts related to sexuality (adapted from Webb, 1985):
- Sexual self-concept: how one feels about oneself.

- Sexual identity: the person one believes and feels one is as a sexual being.
- Sexual orientation: the individuals or group of people to whom one feels attracted.
- Sexual preference: the individuals with whom one prefers to have sexual contact
- Gender identity: the gender with which one identifies one-self as a sexual being (male, female, male and female at different times, a distinct identity which is neither distinctly male nor female).
- Gender norms: the norms of rights, responsibilities or behaviour which a particular culture expects of, or imposes upon, individuals of a specific gender.
- Gender roles: the roles which a particular culture defines as appropriate for individuals who express themselves as a particular gender. These may be work or family-based, such as breadwinner, homemaker or in parenting.
- Gender stereotypes: a selection of traits ascribed to a gender.
- Intimacy: physical, emotional, intellectual or social closeness with another.
- Sensuality: that which arouses the senses.
- Eroticism: that which promotes sexual arousal or pleasure.
- Sex: concerning biological aspects, or a sexual act.

For this chapter, a composite definition is offered: 'sexuality is a quality of being human, all that we are, encompassing the most intimate feelings and deepest longings of the heart to find meaningful relationships' (Hogan, 1980). 'Sexuality is an energy force that is expressed in every aspect of a person's being' (Starr and Weiner, 1981). 'These multifaceted expressions communicate a person's individuality' (Webb and Askham, 1987) 'and identity' (Stuart and Sundeen, 1979). The ways in which persons perceive their sexuality is affected by many profound influences including self-identity, social and bodily functioning according to expectations, moral doctrines and perceived alliance to prevailing societal norms and values.

Dimensions of Sexuality

Sexuality is relevant at all levels within Maslow's hierarchy of needs. Like food and water, it is a basic biological need for most humans but it can also transcend the biological realm to potentially include all dimensions of an individual's life. **Figure 15.1** illustrates this as applied to later life.

Influences on Sexuality

The influences on an individual's sexuality are numerous. It could be argued that the constant interaction between these work to produce harmony.

The Social Influence on Sexuality

This is the sum of cultural factors that influences one's thoughts and actions related to interpersonal relationships as well as sexuality related to ideas and learned behaviour. Social sexuality is also influenced by the media, literature, and the more traditional sources of family, school and religious teachings. The belief of what constitutes masculine and feminine is deeply rooted in one's exposure to cultural factors.

The Moral Influences on Sexuality

These are the 'I should' or 'I shouldn't' type of influences on individual decisions. They may derive from beliefs inculcated in early years about 'right' and 'wrong', or from religious doctrines.

The Biological Influences

These arise from how we feel about how we look, function, react or seem to others. It links with personal development, particularly concerning puberty, reproductive functioning and ageing. It also links with personal identity in that physiological functioning will be at its best if one feels attractive

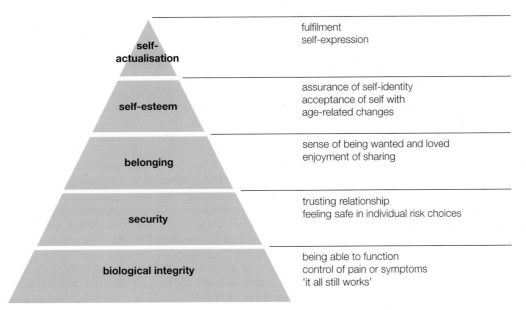

Figure 15.1 Dimensions of sexuality expressed within Maslow's hierarchy.

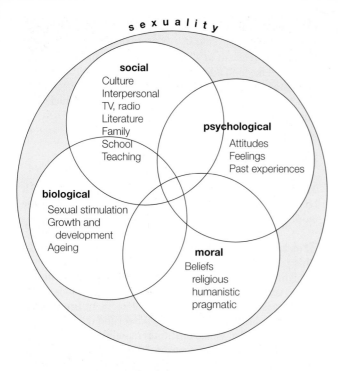

Figure 15.2 Interrelationship of dimensions of sexuality.

to others, desired, wanted and valued. Conversely physiological functioning may become problematic if the situation or the relationship does not meet one's needs in this respect.

The Psychological Domain of Sexuality

This reflects one's attitudes, feelings toward self and others, and learning from past experiences. This begins at the earliest stages of development. From birth, one is bombarded with cues and signals of how one should relate to others or deal with one's bodily needs. Self-identity is also shaped from the earliest days of life. **Figure 15.2** attempts to illustrate the interrelationship of the sexuality dimensions.

CONSIDERATIONS IN LATER LIFE

Societal Attitudes and Expectations

The expression of sexuality or a desire for intimacy in older people is influenced by a number of cultural, biological, psychosocial and environmental factors. Western societal images of sexuality and intimacy as the province of the young and physically beautiful are very powerful.

Images of Sexuality

In Western societal images, sexuality and sexual interest are linked with youth and physical attractiveness. As Ford (1998) highlights, 'The images of slender and muscular high cheekboned beauties confront us day and night on television, in magazines and on billboards. Older people may be used for

advertising (for thermal underwear, laxatives or insurance) but it is unlikely that they will be portrayed as sensual or sexual beings.'

The underlying message of much of the advertising is that ageing is negative and that, in order to increase sexual attractiveness, the ageing process must be avoided or suppressed (Pointon, 1997). Reporting on a US conference, *Women and Ageing: Bodies, Generations and Cultures,* Zeilig (1996) concluded that one of the more conspicuous topics emerging throughout the 3-day event was the interest in face lifts, cosmetic surgery and all the means by which women are induced to allay the ageing process.

Some of the images are particularly damaging, such as when older individuals who express sexual interest are portrayed as 'dirty' or 'impotent', over-sexed lechers or sexless, and 'preposterous in every way in which they express sexuality' (Gibson, 1992). Pointon (1997) suggests that the media images mirror the public's perception of sexual behaviour among older people, and thus the prevailing images are socially constructed.

The Social Construction of Sexual Self-image

Self-image is linked to being of use in society, and usefulness is a socially constructed idea (Phillipson and Walker, 1986). For men, social usefulness is defined for productiveness at work. Compulsory retirement removes this opportunity. For women, social usefulness has traditionally been linked to reproductivity, which ceases at the menopause, and child-rearing which may be largely complete by the time a woman reaches middle age. For women, therefore, menopause is widely presumed to herald the beginning of a reproductively useless phase of life. Alongside this, there is also a stereotype that women are only interested in sex for procreation, for example the English language has no equivalent term for virility to describe high levels of sexuality in women.

According to Ford (1998), there is a gender difference in the social construction of self-image. Victor (1987) suggests that growing old is easier for men than women because being male is associated with competence and autonomy and that these 'valued attributes' can withstand the ageing process. Woman, she argues, are desired for beauty and child-bearing abilities. DeBouvoir (1973) suggests that older men may be considered handsome but older women are rarely described as beautiful.

Older gay men experience similar problems to those of ageing people generally (Pointon, 1997), but older gay men tend to be stigmatised by age, lose people close to them and face further discrimination problems because of their sexual identity. Research shows that older male homosexuals tend to disengage from active participation in the gay community, due in part to the lack of hospitality afforded them by their younger counterparts who dominate the public gay community (Berger, 1982). Lacking role models of successful ageing, gay people often may be uncertain about what to expect as they grow older.

Older lesbians are often not subject to the double standard of ageing faced by heterosexual women or homosexual men.

Particularly in late older age, the proportion of men to women decreases and it becomes increasingly common for women to become companions. In addition, affection between women is more socially accepted (Raphael and Robinson, 1980).

Social Age-control Theory

Socially prescribed 'age' identities, with their norms and expectations, influence the ways in which people behave. Littler (1997) describes how sex is perceived as natural for the young and middle aged but that senior people are conceived as devoid of sexuality. She asks, 'Why is it that women who have dressed stylishly throughout their younger age, suddenly feel the need to dress in a sombre and unobtrusive fashion in their senior years?' Littler argues that societies which promote older age as decline have a very negative effect on an older person's ability to view this stage of life positively, particularly in the field of sexuality expression. However, despite such views, older people do get together as sexual partners and, as Robinson (1983) highlights, unlike physical problems, the constraints of societal attitudes and norms can be challenged simply by not conforming to expectations.

The following example is taken from interviews by Thompson *et al.* (1991) and illustrates the effects that social attitudes can have on older people:

Ben is very aware that an older man's sexuality is widely disapproved of. He risks being scorned as 'a dirty old man'. He argues that this is the wrong view. 'Well I don't treat it that way. There's no difference to me, older people doing what the younger people do, you've got the same ingredients to make it!' But then he cannot admit to his family that he has these longings. In the evening he plays music on his records, 'aye, aye, and I'm thinking about women. There's something wrong with me i'n't there – there must be, I shouldn't be thinking about women – my age'. He poured out his feelings in the interview, a confessional refrain to which he returned again and again.

Putting his wishes into practice had so far failed dismally. He has to be attracted by the woman, and 'there's one woman does. And I daren't look at her!' Ben has 'broached it' with her, and simply got the brush-off. 'Oh, she said, "Ger off with ye!" – and I don't blame her – I know we're old.'

(Thompson *et al.*, 1991, p. 234)

Family Influences

Societal prejudices that sexual interest is inappropriate in older age are often reinforced by younger families. Some adult children, even those who hold permissive standards concerning their own sexual conduct, cannot accept that their mothers or fathers would want to engage in sexual activity, especially with a partner other than the other parent (Pointon, 1997). They may resent the new partner being in the place of the other parent, or there may be other motives. An economic motive discourages parents from forming new relationships which may divide expected inheritance, or from spending money on a new partner which might have strengthened the inheritance. There may also be practical motives in that, once

Meeting Sexuality Needs

Donald Clark and Alice Wickham, who live in different wings of a large nursing home, have begun to show an attraction for each other. A jovial and outgoing man of 87, Mr Clark has been widowed for a few years and his children visit weekly. Of a much quieter disposition, Miss Wickham has never married and has no family. She spends her days reading novels, which she enjoys, but is not able to talk about the books as a stroke has left her unable to speak. Mr Clark has increasingly asked the staff to wheel him to sit beside Miss Wickham, and they then hold hands. The staff have encouraged the relationship as they can see the couple were growing fond of each other, and often leave them alone in a private room. One day recently, Mr Clark announced to the staff that he intends to propose marriage to Miss Wickham and would ask his son to buy a ring. He wants Miss Wickham and himself to move into a double room and to sleep in a double bed. On hearing this, his son was extremely angry and insisted that the staff must not encourage his father in this 'foolishness'. If it does not stop, he has threatened to move his father to another home, which, as he pays the bill, he believes he is entitled to do. The staff have met to discuss the dilemma.

- List the objective data that could assist the nurses in making a decision.
- List the subjective data that could assist them.
- List the thoughts and feelings of all the parties involved, including the nurses, and the factors that might be influencing these.
- If Mr Clark and Miss Wickham were to seek a sexual relationship, what help, advice or health promotion might be appropriate?
- Develop a plan of care for the support and help they might need, including how you plan to broach sexual health issues with the two residents.
- What outcome criteria could be used to evaluate the care, including those of the older people themselves.

a parent has a new partner, he or she is no longer so readily available for practical help such as child-minding.

Another reason suggested for resentment against a parent's new partner, that the lone parent is easy to exploit and control. The introduction of a new lover or spouse will give the parent an ally and protector, changing the whole relationship in terms of power. It is, therefore, perhaps in regard to sexuality that the power of ageism creates its greatest potential for intergenerational conflict.

Generational Influences

Those who are currently old were likely to have been brought up with values prevalent during Victorian times and strict religious morality when sex outside marriage, or even for pleasure, was considered sinful. Younger older people are likely to have been influenced by society's changing attitudes and have a more liberated view of sexual activity.

Erikson *et al.* (1986) found a large number of female octogenarians in their study to have been strongly influenced by the prudish, Victorian atmosphere of their youth. Many of them experienced difficult marital adjustments and serious sexual problems early in their marriages. Many of the couples found their old-age intimacy had transcended the painful differences they felt when they were young. Few elders acknowledged disharmony within their present marital relationship. Those who did were unhappy at the increased dependency of an ill spouse and in a sense were grieving the loss of the patterns and expectations that had become comfortable in the relationship, but were now disrupted by illness and incapacity.

TOUCH

Touch and intimacy are integral parts of sexuality, just as sexuality is expressed through intimacy and touch. Touch is an important, yet often neglected sense. Without it, humans can experience a whole range of responses 'from discomfort to complete psychotic breakdown' (Colton, 1983). 'Touch is a way to define self and experience the world; touch triggers a variety of responses that affect physiology, emotions and behaviour' (Miller, 1990, p. 3).

Touch is the first sensory system to become functional. Throughout life touch provides emotional and sensual knowledge about others. Skin texture influences sensation, appearance and the willingness of others for touch and intimacy. Although the desirability of an unwrinkled skin is promoted in media images, an old face can show the lines of experience. Sensations of old skin, clean, dry and powdered or cologned, linger in the remote memories of many of us who were held by a grandmother or grandfather. These can provide a foundation for closeness with older people.

Older people who do not have opportunities for physical closeness with others may experience a type of 'tactile hunger'. This is exacerbated by living in a care environment where limited touch is offered (Montagu, 1986). Colton (1983) suggests that touch hunger is analogous to malnutrition in that it results from the lack of adequate nutrients for bodily survival. Touch stimulates chemical production in the brain, which feeds blood, muscles, tissues, nerve cells, organs and other body structures. Without this stimulation, like nutrients in food, the individual could be deprived of sustenance and could starve.

Touch in Nursing

Touch is a fundamental and universal aspect of nursing (Fisher and Joseph, 1989). It may be instrumental (deliberate and initiated to perform an act such as a wash), or expressive (spontaneous and showing feelings such as an expression of comfort). Touch can be used as a skilled nursing intervention and to decrease sensory deprivation (LeMay, 1992). It can calm and reassure, comfort and soothe, and help older people to feel valued (Fisher and Joseph, 1989; Fraser and Ross-Kerr, 1993). In Moore and Gilbert's research (1995) older residents of a nursing home perceived greater affection and intimacy when nurses used comforting touch, but also that higher or lower levels of affection were communicated during nurse–patient encounters. Their research suggested that adults in general rely more on nonverbal cues and that visual and hearing loss may reduce an older person's ability to derive meaning from nonverbal behaviours such as a nod or a smile. They may depend more on what they can feel, rather than see and hear. At a time when their need for touch was the greatest, the older people had begun to think of themselves as untouchable. Touch was thus a way of reassuring them that they were still loveable, and raising their self-esteem.

Each person has feelings and predispositions about touch based on his or her own culture and life experience. Nurses should try to recognise the influence of these aspects on the ways in which they use touch. It is important to remember that some individuals do not seek touch and do not enjoy it.

RESEARCH INTO SEXUALITY IN LATER LIFE

Studies on Sexual Activity and Sexual Relationships among Older Persons

Since Kinsey's work in the 1940s and 1950s there have been a number of studies on the sexual habits and attitudes, but these are almost exclusively based in the USA. In considering the applicability of these works to the UK, it is important to appreciate the differences in the two cultures.

Critiquing research into sexual activity and relationships among older persons presents challenges:

- Many studies ignore the older population completely. For example, the recent large-scale survey in Britain was advertised as 'the most authoritative study ever made into the sexual habits of the nation' (Wilby, 1994, p. 5), but the upper age limit of the sample was 59 years.
- Some studies have very small samples of older people. For example, although Kinsey *et al.*'s work (1948, 1953) is still one of the most authoritative accounts of Western sexual behaviour, his conclusion that 75% of 80 year olds are impotent was, in fact, based on a sample of four people. Kinsey *et al.*'s (1948) total sample was 12,000,

but the number of people aged over 60 years was only 185 (Gibson, 1992). In addition, the Masters and Johnson study (1976), although hailed as a breakthrough in understanding of sexual functioning and the role of ageing, included only 31 individuals aged over 60 years out of a total of 694 (Robinson, 1983).

- There may be under-reporting, which may be due to reluctance or embarrassment on the part of the research subjects.
- In some studies the generalisability of the findings may be limited because the samples were invited from a very limited source (e.g. Brecher, 1984, respondents to a magazine) and therefore biased.
- Alternatively, single indices, such as the frequency of sexual intercourse, were used as a guide to overall quantity or quality of sexual activity, orgasms or libido (Seymour, 1990). Many sexually active people with high libido and who achieve regular orgasms may not have sexual intercourse in the conventionally recognised sense.
- Some studies which describe changes in sexual activity with ageing, particularly when cross-sectional data collection methods are used, make no allowances for generational or cohort effects. One study from Duke University (George and Weiler, 1981) recorded over 6 years, the sexuality activity of older people with a partner. They found that the generational effect was greater than the effect of ageing. The predictive validity of cross-sectional studies is questioned by Kellett (1993, p. 310) who emphasises that the age-linked decline in sexual activity suggested by cross-sectional studies is 'much greater than that which is found in practice'. (*See* Chapter 1 for background on the use of cross-sectional, as compared with longitudinal methods for studying the effects of ageing.)
- The bulk of the literature on sexuality comes from the USA and is, therefore, based within a culture different to that of the UK.
- There is very little literature which acknowledges the ethnic or cultural diversity of the UK.

Most studies suggest that a decline in sexual activity, or the ability to enjoy sexual activity, is not an inevitable consequence of ageing. Masters and Johnson used direct observation and physical measurement in laboratory settings to investigate the physical measurement in sexual response patterns. One of their findings was that there was no time limit drawn by advancing years to female sexuality and that, although there was a slowing in the male reaction pattern, this did not necessarily diminish satisfactory sexual activity with ageing. They concluded that: 'there is every reason to believe that maintained regularity of sexual expression, coupled with adequate physical wellbeing and healthy mental orientation to the ageing process, will combine to provide a sexually stimulating climate within a [partnership]. This climate will, in turn, improve sexual tension and provide a capacity for sexual performance that frequently may extend to and beyond the 80 year age level'.

The suggestion of inevitable decline has been dispelled in other studies. In 1968, Pfeiffer, Verwoerdt and Wang, from Duke University, found that 13% of their subjects aged 60 and over reported an increase in sexual activity during an eight year follow up. Pfeiffer *et al.* (1968) also reported that substantial proportions of older married persons continued sexual activity until at least their eighties. In Starr and Weiner's (1981) study, 75% of their questionnaire respondents aged 60 to 91 years said that sex in later life was the same or better compared to when they were younger. Thirty-six per cent said it was better in later years.

The most recent large-scale study into sexual activity which included older people (Janus and Janus, 1993) again in the USA, found that considerable numbers in the oldest age group (65+) were sexually active (53% of men and 41% of women). The study further reported that many of the respondents said that sex was at least as gratifying as in earlier years and often more gratifying because it was less hurried, they shared to a greater degree with their partners and had more time to spend on the seductive build-up. They also reported that they experienced more warmth and intimacy in the sex act. Janus and Janus (1993, p. 28) stated in their report that it had become very clear to them as they conducted their interviews 'that men and women over the age of 65 years did not want to be relegated to the rocking chair and were often as sexually driven as they were in their youth'. They also predicted that 'the greying segment of Americans may be leading the way to superior sexual experience' (p. 22).

THE SPECTRUM OF LIFESTYLES

Aloneness

The main constraints on sexual expression may be social or demographic, rather than biological. Demographically there are more older women than men, and this gender imbalance can create problems for older women. They may have had fewer opportunities for relationships with unmarried men of their own age. They may, therefore, choose partners from their own gender or from among younger men. They may elect for a life of celibacy, seek out professional sex workers or resign themselves to masturbation.

Widow(er)hood

The sexual life of widows is a matter of great concern because so many older women will be widowed. Beresford and Barrett (1982) found that sexually active widows tended to be younger, widowed for a longer duration, and more liberal in their attitudes than sexually non-active widows. Most widows indicated a desire for male companionship but possessed an ambivalent attitude toward remarriage. Widows report that they miss sexual relations with their husbands but that they have a great need for non-genital touching. These needs are not being met by friends and family (Beresford and Barrett, 1982). Older men tend to remarry sooner than do their female counterparts following the death of a spouse. Men marry on the average of 3 years following the death while women who remarry take an average of 7 years following widowhood (Burke and Knowlton, 1992).

In interviews by Thompson *et al.* (1991), a man widowed at 79 years of age had seriously thought about remarriage for a while.

> The Health Visitor said to me 'You know, Mr. Seldon, you don't want to worry. You're a marvellous man for your years and you look a lot younger. And for every man in your position, there are nine women'. And I said, 'I only want one!'. So then it comes down to a sort of shortlist. I'm giving you my innermost thoughts through these years.
>
> (Thompson *et al.* 1991, p. 234)

The death of a partner may remove the immediate opportunities for closeness and intimacy but also self-identity 'I am a husband or wife or partner'. Some people respond with periods of aloneness or increasing asexuality. The phenomenon of 'widower's impotence', which can result from guilt, depression, long periods of abstinence from sexual activity and the strangeness of a new sexual partner, may hinder a man from consummating a new partnership.

Marriage

When older people married, prevailing values dictated that marriage was for life. Indeed many marriages are extremely fulfilling for the partners.

> Those of us fortunate in having long-lasting and successful marriages will have outgrown the need to impress or try to change the other, having by now learnt tolerance of areas where we differ. A distinct advantage as we get older is to have someone with whom we can be totally honest. This can help us in accepting ourselves more easily as the people we are, rather than those we used to have hopes of becoming. A close relationship with our partner is for many of us the foundation stone on which we build the last part of our lives.
>
> (Greengross and Greengross, 1989, p. 12)

Many describe how they become closer to their partner following retirement. Among Thompson *et al.*'s (1991) interviewees were Mr and Mrs Mimms, who were 'just turning eighty' and who said that their present age was the best time of life. Sex was positively important to them, and their relationship was very close. Annie Mimms said:

> We're pleased with each other, and we like to have each other – you see, I suddenly think of something and I run down the garden, and have my little say, and then we'll have a walk 'round. We've got a very good relationship – oh yes, yes, very good, yes, very good, very good – we've had a really nice time, the last 14 years.
>
> (Thompson *et al.*, 1991)

However, it is important not to make assumptions and to remain non-judgemental. Married people may be happy or unhappy, fulfilled or unfulfilled. As with all aspects of life, the importance of sexual activities varies considerably.

In Thompson *et al's* work (1991), one wife described how she openly relished her husband's declining sexual powers.

> *She:* We are not interested in sex. I jist ken that he's a man and I'm a woman – this load of rubbish aboot the older the fiddle the better the tune, it's utter rubbish. And as for snow being on the rooftop and fire underneath - that's tripe!
>
> *He:* I wouldn't say ye'er not interested, the point is ye'er not able.
>
> *She:* We've had enough, let's fact it –I wouldna gie ye a bit o' steak and chips fir all the sex that wis ever thingmy. Let's face it, sex is no necessary if ye love a person.
>
> *He:* No that's true.
>
> *She:* Sex isna – it's an overrated pastime. I think it's mair attraction fir the men than what it is fir the women – ye ken I often torment ye aboot sex.
>
> *He:* Oh I ken.
>
> *She:* It would be a dull day if I didna. I've seen me saying Come on, lock all the doors an' we'll stay in bed all day. But he never takes it!
>
> (Thompson *et al.* 1991, p. 218.)

Gay and Lesbian Lifestyles

Societal attitudes towards gay and lesbian people have changed dramatically during the lifetimes of older generations. Indeed, homosexuality has been illegal during much of this century and equality in the age of consent for sex between two men has only now been addressed in the legislature. Therefore, if older individuals appear to display more restricted attitudes towards homosexuality than younger people, these may be embedded in the restricted attitudes prevalent in their formative years. Young people may be more accepting of peer variation but still intolerant of the same behaviour in the old.

The majority of literature of the lifestyles, sexuality and intimacy of gay and lesbian people is based in the USA and there is a limited amount which focuses on older people. Within the available literature, Berger's Gay and Gray: The Older Homosexual Man (1982) and Kehoe's study of lesbians (1988) provide useful insight into the lifestyles of gay males and lesbian woman in the USA. The work of Kelly (1980) found homosexual activity of aged men varied from a low to moderate degree, depending on individual desire. By 65 years of age sexual satisfaction was still maintained, but the number of friendships had diminished. Both gay and lesbian people used a self-selection process to establish friendships or friendship networks (Raphael and Robertson, 1980). Quam and Whitford (1992) noted that over half of the lesbians in their study reported most of their closest friends were lesbian, only 27.5% of the gay men reported that their closest friends were gay men. Sixty-five per cent of the study population indicated that their closest friends were a mix of gay and non-gay men and women; about one-third of the lesbian women described their friendships to be comparable.

In the absence of kinship bonds, gay and lesbian people develop homosexual friendship networks. Lesbians over 60 years old live with the triple threat of being women, older people and having a different sexual orientation (Deevey, 1990). An intensive study of 100 lesbians between 60 and 86 years of age found that most lived alone, were retired from helping professions, and had college or advanced degrees. Nearly half were overweight and considered themselves restricted by health problems, although 72% considered themselves healthy and 82% considered themselves emotionally healthy. Eighty-four per cent felt positive about being lesbian, and almost half had at one time been married. Many described themselves as lonely, presently celibate and desiring a relationship with a woman within 10 years of their own age. The majority desired special senior centres or retirement communities for lesbians (Kehoe, 1988).

Older lesbians often have practised serial monogamy throughout life and in late life continue to anticipate the finding of a new mate if the need arises. Until the age of 46–55 years, gay men have often been found to have had multiple liaisons but, in recent years, a decrease in multiple liaisons is becoming evident. Berger (1982) notes that sexual patterns tend to remain consistent over a lifetime. After 46 to 55 years of age partnerships are nearly nonexistent. The situation has been attributed to several factors: the death of a loved one and rejection of the idea of a single lifelong partner.

Problems that confront homosexual older people are similar to those that face any aged person: loss of important people, presence of a stigma associated with being aged and fear of losing independence. However, one problem distinct to older homosexual and lesbian people is the lack of the economic, emotional and physical security that occurs in relationships where the partners are legally married. Laws and regulations governing life insurance and estate benefits discriminate against the lover liaison. Even with a legally recorded will that states that benefits should go to the lover, family members may contest in probate hearings.

Health-care providers often lack sufficient information and sensitivity when it comes to caring for older homosexuals. This sensitivity is of utmost importance when attempting to obtain a health history. The use of open-ended questions such as 'who is most important to you' is much better than asking 'are you married?' This helps the nurse to look beyond the rigid category of family and to open the opportunity to real discussion.

Angie, a 72-year-old woman, sought therapy after the death of her 'room-mate' with whom she had lived for over 45 years. Troubled by her feelings regarding the room-mate's death, Angie stated that she needed support in managing concerns about her own future. Angie did not volunteer that her room-mate was also her lover.

(Altschuler and Katz, 1996)

SEXUAL HEALTH

The concept of sexual health has generated a great deal of discussion over recent years, and many professionals have had difficulty in finding a definition that captures the essential components of human sexuality in the context of health and illness. In addition, it is becoming increasingly difficult to define sexual health today, in a society where cultural and social boundaries and expectations change very rapidly (English National Board, 1994).

The World Health Organisation (WHO) defines sexual health as 'the integration of somatic, emotional, intellectual and social aspects of sexual being, in ways that are positively enriching and that enhance personality, communication and love'. The key elements of sexual health are:

- A capacity to enjoy and control sexual behaviour in accordance with a social and personal ethic.
- Freedom from fear, shame, guilt, false beliefs and other psychological factors inhibiting sexual response and impairing sexual relationships.
- Freedom from organic disorders, diseases and deficiencies that interfere with sexual response (WHO, 1986).

Older people will be confronted with adjustments to be made as a result of normal age-related changes, but can still be sexually healthy and fulfilled. Sexual health is individually defined and wholesome if it enriches the involved parties and leads to intimacy (not necessarily coitus).

The Physical Effects of Ageing on Sexual Function

The physical changes in sexual response within the four phases suggested by Masters and Johnson (1976) – excitation, plateau, orgasmic and resolution – are summarised in **Table 15.1**. In Masters and Johnson's (1976) study the oldest woman was 78 years of age and the oldest man 89 years.

Generally with ageing there is a decline in the intensity of sexual desire and the need for sexual release becomes less urgent than in a younger person. At the same time, it usually takes longer for an older person to become sexually aroused and to attain orgasm, the intensity of subjective sexual excitation is reduced and the process of resolution is accelerated. Sometimes one of the phases is omitted; for example the person may become aroused but not attain orgasm. The intensity of subjective excitation may then reduce and the process of resolution is accelerated. Some of the changes are significant in sexual functioning, some are clinically important, and others can be accommodated with personal adaptation.

It should be stressed, however, that sexual ageing is highly individual and there are many exceptions to the normal ageing patterns. Some older people claim that their sexual response is unaffected by ageing, although this may result from changed expectations in later life. In people who are interested in sexual activity, this never totally disappears, and orgasm in both men and woman has been observed into the ninth decade. Biological factors include:

- Adequate circulation to the genital area to support the vasocongestion that takes place.
- Functional neurological pathways to conduct motor, sensory and reflex impulses.
- Adequate and appropriate hormone availability to influence the integrity of the genital structure and function.
- Intactness of the genitalia.

Ageing individuals who do not understand the physical changes that affect sexual activity become concerned that their sex life is approaching its natural conclusion. For women, this may occur with the onset of menopause or, for men, when they discover a change in the firmness of their erection, the decreased need for ejaculation with each orgasm, or when the refractory period between ejaculations extends. Morning intercourse can be more satisfactory because many ageing men experience an erection early in the morning.

Changes in the Male

Masters and Johnson's (1976) research suggested that men experience the peak of sexual responsiveness and capacity at around the age of 17–18 years. Young males are usually intensely sexual, erections can be an instant response to mental or physical arousal and their sensations are genitally focused. The frequency of orgasm is at its peak [Kinsey (1948) suggests that 4–8 per day is not unusual]. Detumescence (shrinkage of the penis to its usual size) after orgasm is slow and a considerable portion of the erection may be retained for half an hour or so after ejaculating. The refractory period

	Physical Changes in Sexual Responses in Old Age	
	Female	Male
Excitation phase	Diminished or delayed lubrication (1–3 min may be required for adequate amounts to appear) Diminished flattening and separation of labia majora Disappearance of elevation of labia majora Decreased vasocongestion of labia minora Decreased elastic expansion of vagina (depth and breadth) Breasts not as engorged Sex flush absent Slower and less prominent uterine elevation or tenting	Less intense and slower erection (but can be maintained longer without ejaculation) Increased difficulty regaining an erection if lost Less vasocongestion of scrotal sac Less pronounced elevation and congestion of testicles
Plateau phase	Decreased muscle tension Decreased capacity for vasocongestion Decreased areolar engorgement Labial colour change less evident Less intense swelling or orgasmic platform Less sexual flush Decreased secretions of Bartholin glands	Decreased muscle tension Nipple erection and sexual flush less often No colour change at coronal edge of penis Slower penile erection pattern Delayed or diminished erectal and testicular elevation
Orgasmic phase	Fewer number and intensity of orgasmic contractions Rectal sphincter contractions with severe tension only	Decreased or absent secretory activity (lubrication) by Cowper gland before ejaculation Fewer penile contractions Fewer rectal sphincter contractions Decreased force of ejaculation (approximately 50%) with decreased amount of semen (if ejaculation is long, seepage of semen occurs)
Resolution phase	Observably slower loss of nipple erection Vasocongestion of clitoris and orgasmic platform quickly subsides	Vasocongestion of nipples and scrotum slowly subsides Very rapid loss of erection and descent of testicles shortly after ejaculation Refractory time extended (time required before another erection ranges from several to 24 hours, occasionally longer)

Source: Miller CA. *Nursing care of older adults*. Glenview, Illinois: Scott Foresman/Little Brown, 1990; Eliopolos C. *Gerontological nursing*. Philadelphia: JP Lippincott, 1987; Shippee-Rice R. Sexuality and aging. In: Fogel C, Lauver D, eds. *Sexual health promotion*. Philadelphia: WB Saunders, 1990.

Table 15.1 Physical changes in sexual responses in old age.

after orgasm (the time it takes to achieve another erection) is very short (seconds to minutes).

Masters and Johnson's work suggested that with ageing the sensations become more generalised. By the fifties, the frequency of orgasm and length of refractory period have usually changed significantly. Men between 50 and 60 years are usually satisfied with one or two orgasms per week. After 50 or so, more direct, more intense and longer stimulation is required to achieve an erection and ejaculation.

Other changes which may be experienced include that:

- The angle of erection (penis to abdominal wall) increases from 45 degrees in youth to 90 degrees after the age of 50 years or so.
- Retraction of the testes during orgasm also tends to disappear.
- The ejaculatory force diminishes, in some cases to seepage, and there may be fewer penile contractions. Some older men find that they are unable to ejaculate every time they masturbate or have intercourse but, because the need for ejaculatory release is less urgent, the inconsistency of ejaculation may not be felt to be an insurmountable problem.
- Detumescence after orgasm may be rapid.
- The refractory period following ejaculation increases, and may even extend to 24 hours.

Although these changes are commonly present by the age of about 60 years, it is suggested that they show little further advance after that age. An 80-year-old man can remain responsive to sexual stimulation, especially if active sexual functioning has been maintained. He is capable of experiencing orgasm and can have frequent and enjoyable erections when he is effectively stimulated. Fertility can also persist until the tenth decade.

If these changes can be acknowledged as normal consequences of ageing, this can diminish anxiety that the man is losing erectile functioning.

Changes in the Female

According to Masters and Johnson (1976) women attain their sexual peak in their late thirties and early forties, and thereafter decline at a relatively slower rate than men. Female sexuality appears to be subject to far greater variations than the male, and the middle-aged peaking of sexuality is usually seen in women who have a history of successful sex and relationships where accumulated reinforcement is derived from repeated pleasurable experiences. For the female, the changes in sexual anatomy and physiology that occur as a consequence of ageing are compounded by the effects of postmenopausal oestrogen deficiency. These may be reversed by hormone replacement. The World Health Organisation (1981) has defined the menopause as 'loss of ovarian follicular function. Menstruation ceases and as a result there is a loss of reproductive function'. The stages of the menopause are:

- Climacteric – a gradual waning of ovarian functions taking place between the ages of 35 to 45 years and which may continue until the age of 53 years or more.

- Perimenopausal – the stage prior to completed menopause when menstruation may become irregular but has occurred in the preceding 12 months.
- Postmenopausal – menstruation has not occurred for at least 12 months.
- Premature menopause – the menopause can also occur at an earlier age and this is viewed as the premature menopause or premature ovarian failure (POF). It affects 1% of women under the age of 40 years [Royal College of Nursing (RCN), 1997].

With ageing, the orgasmic and resolutions phases become shorter, genital blood flow tends to decrease as women age, leading to impairment of vasocongestive responses during arousal. This means inadequate cushioning for penile thrusting, which can result in urethral and bladder trauma, predisposing to urinary tract infection. The vagina becomes narrower and shorter, with a thinning of the vaginal mucosa. Vaginal secretions become more scarce and less acidic.

Both sources of genital moisture in women are oestrogen-dependent and are impaired after the menopause. The clitoris decreases in size and is particularly affected by decreased activity. The uterus decreases in size. Lack of secretions and thinning of the vaginal walls may result in painful intercourse (dysparenunia) as a result of lack of lubrications or infections. Women remain capable of multiple orgasmic responses, essentially without a refractory period, throughout life and women have been known to become orgasmic for the first time at ages in excess of 80 years (Comfort, 1977).

Psychological Aspects

A number of important psychological factors have been identified that seem to play an important role in determining the extent of sexual activity in older age. These include the individual's degree of sexual activity in earlier life and psychological resilience in adapting to altered physiological conditions influencing sexuality expression.

Individual psychological aspects affect sexuality considerably throughout life. Sexual urges in adolescents may lead some to be aggressive while others fall in love. Similarly, responses to changes in the physical aspects of sexual expression may lead some individuals in their fifties to withdraw, some to seek new young partners and erotic stimuli, and others to integrate the changes into their lifestyles and relationships.

Psychological influences should not be underestimated. These can include:

- Changed feelings about one's body.
- Doubts about physical and sexual attractiveness.
- Guilt about seeking sexual activity in later life.
- Guilt about masturbating.
- Guilt in seeking a new partner.
- Uncertainties about sexual performance.
- Monotony in a relationship.
- Unresolved grief.

The increased time taken in physical arousal may be misinterpreted as lack of interest in the partner, or lack of partner's ability to stimulate. This is particularly so if there is a large difference in age.

Retirement from paid work, or children leaving the 'family nest', can have a profound and far-reaching effect on relationship. After retirement or other profound changes in circumstances, couples who have led a fairly regular and stable sex life can experience sexual conflicts, and the difficulty of role adjustment can provide fertile ground for such conflicts. The identity of individual partners may be largely defined by work role, or by being the homemaker. Once these aspects are no longer strongly present, this may require considerable adjustment by one or both partners (Gibson, 1992).

Sexual Functioning

Under most circumstances, sexuality depends on the individual or couple's sex drive and psychological aspects, but is strongly influenced by general health. Illness, pain, fatigue or disability such as joint stiffness may interfere with sexual functioning, but need not curtail enjoyment of sexual activity entirely. In fact, sexual activity may enhance some therapies, for example in arthritis, because it stimulates the release of cortisone, adrenaline and other chemicals that are natural pain relievers. Sexual activity is also good exercise; it can assist in reducing physical and psychological tension, and help to raise self-esteem.

Sexual Dysfunction

Sexual dysfunction, which occurs in both men and women, may have a physiological or psychological base, but psychological dysfunction is more common than physical impairment (Ham, 1986; Butler and Lewis, 1988).

Sexual Problems in Men

A major problem confronting the ageing man is the fear of impotence or the actual occurrence of impotence, but Comfort (1977) claims with confidence that impotency is never a consequence of chronological age alone. Broderick describes the experience:

> There is nothing more recalcitrant than a recalcitrant penis. If you are trying to get it to perform, it seems the harder you try, the more difficult it is.
>
> (Broderick, 1978, p. 5)

What men generally call impotence may be diminished potency and frequency of sexual activity, or there may be a complete absence of erectile response. Causes may be psychological, lifestyle (such as the excessive use of alcohol, tobacco or drugs) or physical (such as damage to the nerve supply, disease of the blood vessels, problems with the muscle of the penis, hormone imbalance, radical surgery, trauma or drugs). Various medications that affect the sympathetic and parasympathetic nervous systems interfere with the capacity of the penis to erect or ejaculate. Adrenergic agents block impulses that affect contractibility of the prostate gland and seminal vesicles and depress or interfere with ejaculation. The anticholinergic preparations affect penis erection by vasocongestion in the venous channels. The ganglionic blocking agents possess properties of both the adrenergic and anticholinergic preparations and affect both penis erection and ejaculation (Sherman, 1992). A few medications have been found to increase sexual desire. The phenothiazines increase the libido in the older woman, and levodopa heightens sexual desire in the older man (Sherman, 1992).

Environmental agents, including industrial chemicals and exposure to electromagnetic fields used by some industries, can induce impotence. The effects of inadequate housing, lack of privacy and feelings of psychological inferiority are also contributory factors to impotence.

The British Diabetic Association (1995) suggests that all men experience impotence at some time in their lives, but the prevalence increases with age. Morley (1988) estimates that 8% of men aged 55 to 64 years will experience impotence. The percentage rises to 25% for men 65–74 years of age and to 55% for men 75 to 84 years of age. Approximately 75% of men over the age of 85 years experience impotence. As a result of negative societal views about sexual desires in older people, it may be difficult for them to discuss these issues openly.

Assessment of impotence includes a history, and open discussions to help identify any psychological influences from the man or his partner. Questions about whether the man experiences erections on waking, whether he masturbates and the nature of the erection when he does, are relevant in establishing whether the causes are primarily physical or psychological. Testing for levels of testosterone, luteinizing hormone, zinc, thyroid function, alcoholism and medication side effects is important. If appropriate, the penis can be injected in order to assess its erectile response and to introduce the man to the technique, should this be an option.

Available treatments include counselling and sensate focusing under the guidance of a sex therapy (a programme of encouraging physical stimulation and postponing intercourse which helps to focus on intimacy and enjoyment rather than 'performance').

Vacuum therapy uses a pump and cylinder to create a vacuum around the penis so that it engorges. The plastic cylinder is placed over the penis and against the body, using plenty of lubricating jelly to produce a seal. A hand or battery-operated pump is then used to draw air out of the cylinder. This relaxes the muscle and draws blood into the penis, causing it to enlarge. A rubber band is then slipped around the base of the penis to trap the blood and maintain the erection. This may be left in place for up to 30 minutes. Most people experience satisfactory results. There may be some bruising or colour changes in the penis while the band is in place, and the band may affect the ability to ejaculate. The device can be used frequently but one hour of rest between uses is recommended.

Potential Effects of Drugs on Sexual Function			
	Effect on		
Drug Category	Desire (psychological)	Arousal (physiological)	Orgasm
Alcohol	Initially increased	Reduced	Much reduced
Analgesics	Reduced	Reduced	Reduced
Anticholinergics	Often reduced	Erectile dysfunction	Reduced
Antidepressants	Often reduced	Reduced	Reduced
Antihistamines	Reduced	Reduced lubrication Erectile dysfunction	
Antihypertensives	Reduced	Reduced	Ejaculatory problems
Anti-Parkinson	Increased	Increased erectile function	
Antipsychotics		Reduced lubrication Erectile difficulties	Ejaculatory problems
Antispasmodics	Reduced	Reduced	
Beta-blockers	Reduced	Erectile dysfunction Breast tenderness	Orgasmic difficulties
Cimetidine		Erectile dysfunction	
Digoxin	Reduced	Erectile dysfunction Gynaecomastia	
Diuretics		Reduced lubrication Erectile dysfunction Breast tenderness	
Lithium	Increased		
Oestrogen		Increased lubrication	
Opiates	Reduced	Reduced	Delayed ejaculation
Tranquillisers	Reduced	Reduced	Reduced

NB: These drugs do not always cause problems and the effects vary from person to person

Table 15.2 Potential effects of drugs on sexual function.

Surgical penile implants can be used to make the penis sufficiently stiff for penetration. This is usually considered only when other methods have failed.

Hormone medication and reconstructive surgery to revascularise the penis are occasionally considered, but there are dangers with both treatments (British Diabetic Association, 1995).

Sexual Problems in Women

Research on sexual dysfunction has tended to concentrate on men. There is less knowledge of female sexual dysfunction, particularly drug effects.

Older women may experience pain on intercourse (dyspareunia) because of the thinning of the vaginal wall and the lack of lubrication. In many instances, use of a water-soluble lubricant can resolve the difficulty. For some time, hormone replacement therapy (HRT) has been an option for maintaining vaginal tissue integrity, but there is ongoing debate about the benefits versus the risks, particularly long-term, and there are some women for whom HRT is not recommended (RCN, 1997). In older women, prolapse of the uterus, rectoceles and cystoceles can be surgically repaired to facilitate continued sexual activity, and collagen injections are now being used to relieve urinary incontinence.

Illness/Disability and Sexual Functioning

Illness and disability, whether acute or chronic, can totally disrupt the expression of sexuality and sexual activity. Some examples are discussed below, although the list is not exhaustive, and some general principles are drawn.

Acute Illness

As the Stroke Association advises, 'sex is probably the last thing you worry about when you have just had a serious illness of any kind' (Duddle, 1996). In the early stages of an acute illness, mental and physical energy will be directed towards regaining and maintaining homeostasis rather than towards physical sex or the expression of sexuality in other ways.

As the individual recovers, there may be fear about engaging in sexual activity, either on the part of the patient or partner, in case this may exacerbate the health problem. It is vital at this stage that patients and partners are given accurate information and appropriately supported. Sufficient recuperative time must be allowed but this will vary according to the health of the individual and the illness experienced. Manual stimulation or masturbation can often be used early in the recovery period to maintain sexual function, if desired by the patient. It has been shown that masturbation makes less oxygen demand than sexual intercourse and is therefore less taxing on body systems, particularly the heart (Woods, 1983).

Older people are particularly susceptible to the effects of inactivity and disuse. Appropriate support in the early stages can help them, when they are ready, to re-establish their usual patterns of sexual activity, within any limitations imposed by their health. (*See* **Figure 15.3** for coital positions which may be useful to couples experiencing illness or disability.)

Myocardial Infarction (MI)

The most common impediment to sexual function following MI is fear. The strain of intercourse is estimated to be approximately equivalent to climbing a flight of stairs, with a mean peak heart rate of approximately 117.4 beats per minute (McCracken, 1988).

Intercourse can be resumed when comparable activities are able to be performed. For some this will be as early as 4 or 5 weeks after infarction, but for others the average will be closer to 13.7 weeks, depending on the severity of the infarction and anxiety of the person (Stein, 1980). If angina accompanies intercourse, the person should consult the physician. Advice on resuming sexual intercourse after MI is given in **Box 15.1**.

Sexual counselling is too often regarded as irrelevant to older patients, particularly older women. Energy expenditure by older people, having sex in familiar surroundings with their usual partner, is undoubtedly much less than that

recorded in young men. Patients can normally resume sexual function within 3 to 4 weeks after acute MI (Pathy, 1991).

Stroke (Cerebrovascular Accident)

In a Stroke Association leaflet *Sex after Stroke Illness*, Duddle (1996) advises that, as with other serious illness, sexual activity in the early stages may be difficult. It may be difficult to obtain a good erection because the nerves to the genital organs may be affected by the stroke but, because only one side of the body is usually affected, the nerves on the other side can usually take over. Tiredness and anxiety play a major role and Duddle suggests that 'the harder you try, the less you succeed'. Women may tend to lose interest in sex, or find it more difficult to become aroused.

One possible problem relates to blood pressure. Tablets can help but these may also affect sexual performance in some people. Duddle advises various measures (see chronic pain section below) and urges that 'sex is meant to be fun – to cement a relationship together, not a deadly serious affair or an exam you keep failing' (p. 3).

Chronic Pain

This may occur as a result or arthritis, or of other chronic conditions. It can be devastating not only to body image but also to enjoyment of sexual activity. Writing for the charity Pain Concern UK, Webster (1997) recommends 10 tips for people with chronic pain, and many of these could be helpful to people with other chronic illnesses (**Box 15.2**).

Diabetes Mellitus

It is not generally recognised that 50% of diabetic males experience impotence at some time and 1 in 10 has a continuing problem (British Diabetic Association, 1995). Females may

15.1 Resuming Sexual Intercourse after MI

- Plan the resumption of sexual activity to correspond to sexual activity before the heart attack.
- Encourage gradually increasing exercise.
- Familiar surroundings and familiar partner reduce anxiety.
- Temperature should be comfortable, not extreme (avoid hot or cold bath and showers just prior to intercourse)
- Foreplay is desirable to allow for gradual increase in heart rate prior to orgasm.
- Avoid a heavy meal, alcohol or becoming unduly fatigued.
- Different positions may help to decrease exertion and chest pressure.
- Nitroglycerine 15–30 minutes prior to sex may be recommended.
- Sexual activities are not advisable in chronic heart failure or unremitting chest pain.

also become inorgasmic. This is due to neuropathy and cardiovascular changes. These changes accompany maturity onset diabetes. It has been suggested that the development of impotence occurs 5 years or longer after the onset of this disease (Felstein, 1983) and may be preceded by retrograde ejaculation (often explained as dry orgasm, passage of sperm into the bladder rather than the penis. The first passage or urine after ejaculation is cloudy but this is physiologically harmless). Checking for nocturnal or early morning erections is of value in differentiating physiological from psychological causes. Female diabetics experience little interference with sexual functioning but they are more prone to monilial (candida) infections, which may result in painful intercourse (dysparenunia).

Prostate Disease

Both prostate cancer and benign prostatic hyperplasia (BPH) are increasingly prevalent as men get older. BPH affects 33%

of men aged 50 years and over (Garraway *et al.* 1993). In its review of the literature on men's health, the RCN (1996) described the current controversies surrounding the efficacy of screening and some treatments, especially radical surgery in the light of the common side effects including incontinence and impotence.

Most men who undergo surgical procedures such as transurethral resection and other types of prostatectomies, resection of the bladder neck, resection of the colon for cancer, or a sympathectomy may find to their dismay that they have retrograde ejaculations, the result of interference with autonomic innervation in the pelvis (Boyarsky, 1983). Particularly after a prostatectomy, a space remains where the enlarged prostate had been. The principle that fluid travels the path of least resistance applies here. At the point of ejaculation, the semen moves backward into the bladder rather than forward through increased resistance, which produces a retrograde, or dry, ejaculation. Lack of understanding

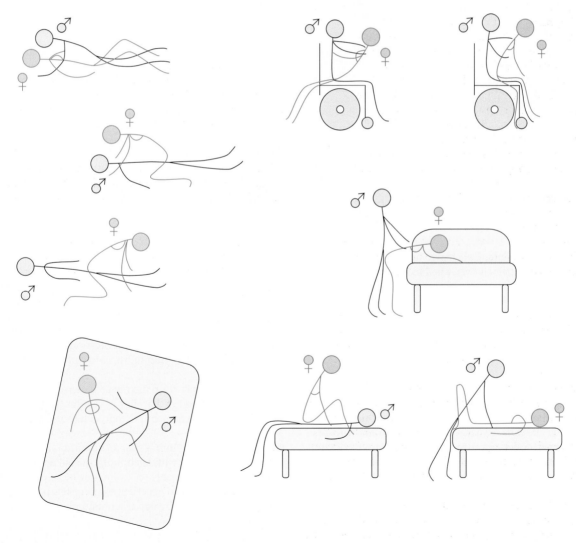

Figure 15.3 Coital positions which may be useful for couples experiencing illness or disability.

15.2 Advice to People with Chronic Pain

- Be totally honest with your partner. Most partners are afraid of having any physical contact with the pain sufferer for fear of hurting them. Do explain what hurts and what does not, where they can touch and where not, and just how much pressure to apply; for example, some pain is activated by light touch, others much deeper.
- If you are the pain sufferer, honesty extends to telling your partner that you feel you want sexual contact or intercourse, this may be difficult if you are not usually the initiator of the contact.
- Most people think of sexual contact occurring at bedtime. Chronic pain does lead to fatigue and many sufferers only want a mug of cocoa at the end of the day, not sexual activity! Work out when your pain is at its lowest level, could this be the time for sexual activity? Sexual activity during the day can be difficult if, for example, there are small children but the problem can be overcome with planning.
- Remember, hurt does not always mean harm, and relaxation does help pain. Relaxation techniques prior to sex, a warm bath or analgesia half an hour prior to sexual activities and the use of pillows to support body parts during sexual activity can be helpful.
- Do time your medication in order that it is having most effect when you make love. If you do not feel your medication is adequate, discuss this with your doctor. Changing to another drug may help.
- There is no reason why transcutaneous electrical nerve stimulation (TENS) machines cannot be used while lovemaking, but do be aware that with movement you could have an increase or decrease of stimulation from the electrodes, they may also be pulled off if the leads are not adjusted.
- Depending on the type of pain and disability, the 'traditional' positions for intercourse may be impossible to use, but there are many others that can accommodate most physical problems (see Figure 15.3).
- Most people think about intercourse but, if this is not possible, there are many ways to have a meaningful relationship without. Many patients describe finding other parts of their body which, when caressed by a loving partner, can give great fulfilment. Touch is very important.
- Masturbation is a way of exploring your own body and finding the areas that give you pleasure. Masturbation can also be a helpful technique to give pleasure to your partner if intercourse is not possible.
- The organisation SPOD (the association to aid the sexual and personal relationships of people with a disability) offers a counselling service and advice on a range of issues including differing positions for sexual activity, aids and services. (See list of useful addresses for SPOD).

Source: Adapted from Webster C. *Advice on sexual activity for people with chronic pain*. Canterbury: Pain Concern UK, 1997.

---

regarding this physiological change further convinces men that their sexual activity is over, when in fact it is not. Erection can be attained and orgasmic pleasure achieved.

It is vital that men, and partner if the patient wishes, are fully aware of the risks and possible long-term effects of undergoing radical surgery and that they make fully informed choices about their own bodies.

Hysterectomy

Following hysterectomy, the abdomen may feel sore for 3–4 months and may interfere with resumption of normal sexual activity. The woman may wish to abstain from intercourse for 6–8 weeks following surgery. A decrease in lubrication and sensation can occur in the lower genital tract. If the ovaries are removed with or without the removal of the uterus, sexual desire may be reduced. More long-term, the woman may experience changes in the orgasmic sensation as the uterus can play a role in reflecting orgasmic contractions and intensifying the sensations, described as acting 'like a sounding board on a piano'.

Dementia

There is a dearth of research on sexuality and people with dementia, and most of the studies tend to describe the problems (Archibald, 1997). People with dementia express sexuality in individual ways, as do all other people but, particularly in advanced dementia the person may behave in ways which can be problematic for carers or professional caregivers.

Archibald (1997) highlights some of the issues. For example:
- With loss of short-term memory the person with dementia may forget that they have recently had sex.
- They may misrecognise and approach the wrong person in a sexual way.
- Dementia can result in sexual disinhibition and, for example, a person with latent homosexual desires may for the first time openly seek someone of the same sex, or someone who has experienced no or few partners may actively seek partners and obtain pleasure from the interactions.
- Roles change as the carer increasingly takes on responsibilities.

- Reciprocity, an important aspect of any relationship, can be missing in dementia.
- The carer may no longer view the person as a sexual partner. They may feel distaste or see intimacy almost as akin to incest.
- The person with dementia may need and demand sexual intimacy which the carer is no longer able to provide.
- Due to their vulnerability, the person with dementia may be sexually abused, or may become an abuser.
- Which person's needs are paramount?
- What happens if the person with dementia goes into residential care and expresses sexual need towards the staff or other residents, or masturbates in public?

Archibald (1997) emphasises the importance of recognising that the person with dementia is an adult being with adult status and possibly sexual needs. Adult status, which includes the acceptance of the person as a sexual being, is symbolised by autonomy, self-determination and choice. The concept of personhood prevails, with its attendant full membership of society. These factors, central to the philosophy of person-centred care, are often missing in the life of someone with dementia (see below for further discussion of strategies for nurses to deal with 'problem behaviours'; *see* Chapter 18 for discussion of mental health needs).

Sexually Transmissible Infections and Older People

Societal views of older people as asexual have fostered assumptions that sexually transmissible infections (STIs), including HIV/AIDS are not an issue for older persons, even among health-care professionals. In fact, older people are affected by HIV and AIDS both directly and indirectly. Older people have become HIV-infected mainly due to transfusion with blood or blood products prior to 1985 (when screening was introduced), although sexual spread is also significant. Currently, 11% of people living with AIDS are over 50 years (Kaufman, 1993), but this may be an underestimation (Hinkle, 1991). In June 1993, 2% of people living with AIDS were aged over 60 years, as were 2% of those diagnosed as HIV positive (Public Health and Laboratory Service, 1993). In the USA, the number of reported cases of AIDS in the over 60 year group has continued to rise with the increasing total number of cases. There is also some evidence to suggest that these statistics may be higher in older age groups than reported.

The study by Rogstad and Bignell's (1991), although small, serves to illustrate the diversity of older people's lifestyles. They investigated the sexual practices of older adults attending two departments of genitourinary medicine by studying a historical review of case-notes. Sixty-nine per cent of men and 53% of women in the sample were sexually active. Casual partners were cited by 68 patients and the range of contacts was between one and 30. The use of professional sex workers overseas was cited by five patients and current or past gay relationships by 16. Six men were participating in casual anoreceptive sexual intercourse without condoms. Fifteen men were sexually participating in both their marital relationship and with other partners concurrently. Two women attended the clinic after rape. Sexually transmitted disorders were diagnosed in 47 men and 11 women. Anxiety regarding HIV was the prime reason for attendance in 22 men and six women, although none were tested positive.

There are distinct considerations concerning older people and HIV. They may have multiple illnesses yet still function and, when admitted to hospital, the possibility of HIV may not be considered. HIV-related illnesses tend to be more aggressive, and the time between acquiring HIV infection and the onset of AIDS may be shorter in older people (Kendig and Adler, 1990). HIV-related dementia is becoming more common (*see* Chapter 18).

Sexual Health Promotion

There has been little attention paid to sexual health promotion for older adults, compared with younger people and specific groups identified as 'at risk'. The Beth Johnson Foundation (1996) identified dilemmas caused by this lack of information to people in mid-life and beyond:

- Many do not have the baseline information they require in order to protect themselves from infection.
- The ageism in society and the view that older people are not sexual beings leads to people assuming they are not at risk.
- It can be difficult for people who are worried to actually seek out and ask for help.
- The older generation often have good relationships with grandchildren or other young people, which can allow them to be health educators if they have a baseline knowledge and understanding of the issues.

An awareness of these concerns led the Beth Johnson Foundation to produce a leaflet, with a grant from the local HIV/Sexual Health Unit. The leaflet was produced in partnership with various groups of older people. Key areas within the leaflet highlight that:

- HIV/AIDS can affect anyone regardless of age, background, race or culture, and is found in most parts of the world.
- Because of society's attitude to old age it is thought that people over a certain age don't have sex.
- Sometimes as people grow older the HIV/AIDS infection is mistaken for other illness, because older people do not believe it can happen to them.
- Older people find it helpful to have the facts about healthy sex not only for themselves, but because they worry about their grandchildren or young people.
- People who have HIV infection may feel and look well, many do not even know they have the infection but can still pass it on to others.
- AIDS can develop some years after catching HIV.
- HIV is not passed on by shaking hands, kissing and cuddling, toilet seats, coughing and sneezing, swimming pools, sharing crockery, towels or food, or blood transfusions given in Britain.

Clearly there is a need for sexual health services for older people, but there is some concern that the emphasis on HIV and AIDS will overshadow the recognition of AIDS-related dementia. The challenge will be to ensure that care workers recognise that older people may be sexually active and, as such, have sexual health needs just as other adults.

NURSING ROLES AND FUNCTIONS

Nursing and Sexuality

As was discussed at the beginning of this chapter, sexuality is a powerful subject which can generate deep and complex reactions within individuals. It can be particularly difficult to deal with in nursing. Everyday nursing practice involves intimate contact with patient's bodies, emotions, relationships and lives in general. It brings together the professional and the personal in a delicate interface. Nurses are required to work within their professional code, but they are also wives or husbands, lovers, partners, heterosexual, homosexual, bisexual, in love, out of love, celibate, sexually active, sexually inactive – and they have a whole range of individual beliefs, values, difficulties, fulfilments and sexual desires [English National Board (ENB), 1994].

Particularly since the introduction of Roper, Logan and Tierney's Activities of Living model (Roper *et al.*, 1983), which included a category on expressing sexuality, there has been an increasing awareness of this aspect of care, but nurses still find it a difficult area to confront. From a discourse analysis of the Nursing Times 1980–1990, Carr (1996) concluded that, while some of the decade's early papers remain a source of valuable information, there was overall little encouragement for the general nurse to become more involved in their client's sexual health. In the middle of the decade the papers largely reinforced the separateness of working within sexual health, and conveyed the impression that sexual activity and its consequences form aspects of care needing skills, education and training not available to the general nurse. The papers towards the end of the decade demonstrated a greater awareness of the nurse's potential role in working with sexuality issues.

Carr identified a number of themes in the literature, including:

- The nursing culture does not support discussion of sexual matters.
- The culture links sexual behaviour to stigmatised disease processes.
- The culture is unsure if this really is an issue that nurses should be involved with.
- Care is generally poor in this area.

The situation is compounded by a general lack of knowledge in issues relating to sexuality.

Even nurses who are generally comfortable with sexuality issues may find difficulty addressing them with older people. In Carr's review, older people were mentioned in only one of the 86 papers he examined. Nurses are often unsure of what to acknowledge regarding older people's sexuality and may write in the assessment box 'not applicable', 'retired' or 'daughter brings in his talcum powder'. The difficulties arise partly because of the societal stereotype that older people are asexual, and are compounded if the nurse identifies the older person with her or his parents or grandparents and is unable to accept them as sexual beings.

Particular difficulties may be encountered by nurses caring for an older person from a different culture, religion or ethnic group. For example, cultural norms might prescribe that a woman does not undress in front of men, or is only permitted to show her body to her husband or female members of her own sect. The difficulties are compounded if the older person does not speak English and an interpreter is not available. As discussed fully in Chapter 19, at present the number of older people from different races is small, but will increase in the years to come. It behoves nurses to learn about the range of people with whom they work and to remain open and sensitive to individual needs.

A recognition of the importance of sexuality and sexual health is an essential aspect of holistic care. Well-informed and skilled practitioners who recognise the importance of sexuality and sexual health will inevitably contribute to the effective management of a whole range of issues.

If nurses are to have a sound understanding of their role and responsibilities in this area of health care, they need to be helped to explore and discuss a whole range of ethical, moral and professional issues (ENB, 1994).

Nursing Education and Sexuality

Professional preparation has to address these issues and should aim to:
- Facilitate the personal exploration of feelings, beliefs and attitudes to sexual identity.
- Enable the professional carer to explore the relationship between personal experiences and beliefs and professional and personal behaviour (ENB, 1994).

The ENB has proposed a framework for sexual health education and training which can be used to develop learning programmes for qualified practitioners. It can be used to incorporate elements of sexual health into post-registration programmes or to build specialist programmes in sexual health. A framework is also offered for a learning unit on sexuality, sexual health and older people (**Box 15.3**).

The five-stage training and education model developed by Carr (1996) from his literature analysis is also useful in this respect (**Figure 15.4**)

The Nursing Role with Older People

Nurses have multiple roles in the area of sexuality and older people and sexuality is a vital aspect for nurses who care for older people to understand, regardless of the setting in which

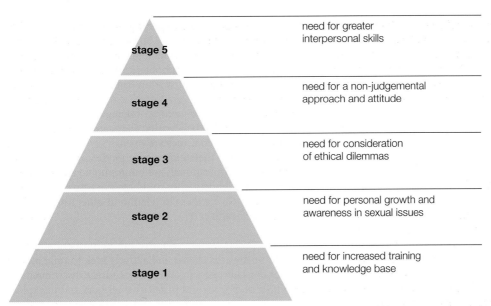

Figure 15.4 The five-stage training and education model (Source: Carr G. Themes relating to sexuality that emerged from a discourse analysis of Nursing Times during 1986-1990. *J Adv Nurs* 1996, 24: 196–212.)

they work. The nurse is a facilitator of a conducive milieu in which questions can be asked and in which older people's sexuality can be expressed. Most important is providing privacy and helping older people to retain control over their sex lives. The nurse should be an educator and provide information as well as guidance to older people who seek it. Anticipation of problems can ward off anxiety, misconceptions, and an arbitrary cessation of sexual pleasure. If the subject is difficult to broach directly, written information can be used, and this can also be useful to reinforce verbal explanations (**Box 15.4**). Validation of the normalcy of sexual activity may be needed, or a discussion of the physiological changes that occur with age, or the effect of illness and treatment that may interfere with sexual activity by altering the routine or interfering with physical performance. Counselling may be helpful for older people to adapt to natural physiological changes and image-altering surgical procedures.

Older people may or may not have difficulty discussing intimate areas with individuals who are comfortable and capable of dealing with it. The nurse has the responsibility to help maintain the sexuality of older people by offering the opportunity to discuss. Rarely are sex histories elicited from older people (Royal College of Psychiatrists, 1998), and physical examinations do not include the reproductive system unless it is directly involved in the present illness. However, when one does ask questions about sexual issues or when older people are examined, the nurse needs to be particularly cognisant of the era in which the individual has lived to understand the factors affecting conduct.

To assist and support older people in their sexual needs nurses should be aware of their own feelings about sexuality. They must question their attitude toward old people (single,

15.3 ENB Framework for Learning Unit on Sexuality, Sexual Health and Older People

Human growth and development
- Anatomy and physiology: ages and stages; menopause

Psychosocial aspects
- Psychosocial development and sexuality.
- Sexual abuse.

Health and ill health
- Body image.
- Disease.
- Safer sex.
- Sexual fulfilment.
- Loving relationships.

Promoting sexual health
- Strategies for sexual health promotion.
- Risk and needs assessment.
- Theories of behaviour.

Sexualities
- Sexual diversity and orientation.
- Sexual practices.
- Attitudes, prejudices and discrimination.

Policies and sexual health
- Pressure/lobbying.
- Groups (e.g. Age Concern).

Source: English National Board for Nursing, Midwifery and Health Visiting. *Sexual health education and training, guidelines for good practice in the teaching of nurses, midwifes and health visitors.* London: English National Board for Nursing, Midwifery and Health Visiting, 1994.

married or homosexual) who hold hands or caress or fondle each other. Only after confronting one's own attitudes, values and beliefs can the nurse provide support without being judgmental.

Attitudes and Anti-discriminatory Practice

Fundamental to offering appropriate care is an open, non-judgemental attitude, as well as a sound understanding of the distinct considerations influencing the expression of sexuality in later life. For example, caregivers have become surprised, angry or even moralistic with older people who are found in bed with another older person, either having sex or masturbating. Stevenson and Courtenay (1982) found that nursing assistants who were extremely religious had the most difficulty in accepting the sexual expression of older adults in nursing homes. It is not uncommon to hear a staff member talk to an older person who has committed an indiscretion (in the staff member's eyes) as if he or she were a child, reprimanding the elder for the behaviour. Sometimes the staff members themselves unknowingly provoke a sexual response from the resident or patient. Comments about looking handsome or, 'Are you going to be my date?' seem harmless and 'cute'. However, for older people (men) who still have sexual desires but little opportunity to express them, this may initiate behaviour that the staff finds offensive such as sexual statements or grabbing to fondle a staff member. This often results in a reprimand to, or punishment of, older people. The same is true with older people (women) in an institutional setting. Comments made by male staff members about appearance or about relationships with male residents can stimulate expressions of sexuality that are dealt with jokingly. Judgmental attitudes are not helpful and may remove the civil rights of older people.

Expressions of sexuality are considered, in many nursing home settings, to be a disturbing or behavioural management problem. To consider them so is a measure of the taboo against sex and older people. White (1982) interviewed residents in 15 nursing homes and found that 91% were sexually inactive, although 17% said they would like to be active sexually. His study seems to reinforce the concept that sexual interest in the institutionalised is related to prior levels of activity and interest. If it has been an important method of coping, it is likely to remain so. Sexual education and discussion groups should be provided for staff and residents to decrease the overreactions that are commonly seen and to determine policies that allow consenting individuals to engage in sexual activity in private.

Archibald's (1994) framework is helpful when there is perceived to be a 'problem' relating to sexual behaviour (**Figure 15.5**). It is important that nurses retain an awareness of any aspects of their practice which may be discriminatory to any individual patients or patient groups, whether this be on the grounds of age, gender or sexual orientation.

There is a growing awareness that lesbians and gay men are exposed to discrimination. Specifically, the Royal College of Nursing (RCN) (1994) highlights that:

- They experience homophobia, anti-lesbian and gay feelings, or even hostility from some health-care providers.
- Some fear the consequences of being open about their sexuality, but also believe that they cannot always get the relevant care even if they are open.
- Some fear that they may even be physically harmed if health-care professionals are homophobic and that a breach of confidentiality could have negative consequences for them in relation to other aspects of life or future health care.

The RCN (1994) recommends that nurses must examine their behaviour towards clients and actively seek to raise awareness among colleagues in order to discourage discrimination, unhelpful responses and insensitive services and to explore all possible ways of supporting and assisting lesbians and gay men using their service. Nurses undertaking research should develop studies of lesbians' and gay men's actual and perceived health-care experiences and should establish how nurses can best meet the needs of these patients. Nurses in education should recognise the need for the profession to be better informed and to have more positive attitudes in these areas. Pre and post-registration programmes should be alert to recognising these needs.

15.4 Guidance on Sexual Intercourse with a Urinary Catheter

- There is no need to avoid sexual intercourse if you have a catheter.
- It is possible to teach you or your partner to remove the catheter before intercourse and replace it afterwards.
- Alternatively intercourse can take place with the catheter in, as long as a few simple rules are followed:

1. In women, the catheter should be firmly strapped to the inner thigh or stomach.
2. Men need to bend the catheter over the tip of the penis once they have an erection and then hold the catheter with a condom.
3. Very rough intercourse should be avoided.
4. It may be necessary to find a new position which makes it more comfortable for the partner with the catheter.

Source: *Useful advice for those with a catheter.* Produced by the staff of Geffrye Ward, Homerton Hospital NHS Trust, Hackney, London E9 6SR.

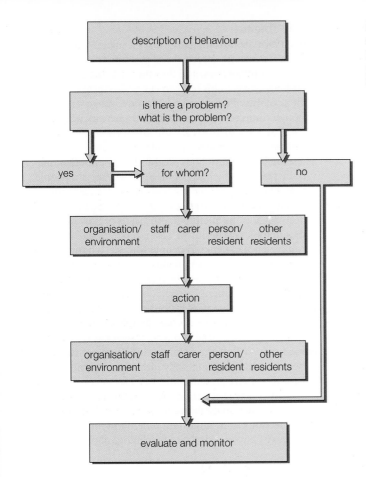

Figure 15.5 Framework for action when the expression of sexuality is perceived to be a problem (Source: Archibald C. Sex: Is it a problem? *Journal of Dementia Care* **1994, 2(4):16–18).**

Assessment

Discussion of sexuality and sexuality problems may be uncomfortable for both nurse and older person. Nurses should include this aspect, explicitly or implicitly, depending on the appropriateness of this to the individual, and recognise barriers to the expression of sexuality, such as environmental barriers, iatrogenic barriers, such as drugs, and the older person's willingness or reticence to discuss sexuality.

Environmental Factors

Environmental barriers result predominantly from the lack of privacy available to the older person. Lack of privacy can occur when older people live with adult children. It is rare that if a parent has a suitor in to visit they have a place to go by themselves without other family members around.

Some care homes still separate men and women and even married couples. There are specific places for mixed company to congregate, and there are rules about male residents going into women's rooms and vice versa. Environmental considerations include:

- Providing opportunities and facilities for privacy.
- Room doors kept closed.
- Staff knock and wait for permission to enter before doing so.
- Older people free to remain in rooms and stay undisturbed.
- Facilities for privacy between couples and partners.
- Consideration of the intrusion on privacy by members of the opposite sex, particularly in mixed-sex wards.
- Facilities to enhance personal presentation – mirrors, hairdressers and grooming aids.

Fortunately many care homes now offer accommodation and care to married couples, although rarely to gay or lesbian couples. However, horrific stories still hit the headlines:

At 14 they promised each other they would be together until their dying days. But 71 years on, social services chiefs look set to achieve what war, family, tragedy or the trials and tribulations of married life could not. They have ruled that Bill and May Hill can no longer live together. While Mr Hill, 85, qualifies for council-funded care, it has been decided that his wife, also 85, must move out of the private nursing home she shares with him to a cheaper residential home because she does not need intensive nurs-

ing care. No-one can bring themselves to tell the couple that they might soon be forced apart. 'It would be an absolute tragedy if they were to part' said the home manageress, 'I cannot imagine how they would cope without each other, it would break their hearts'. The couple's son has asked for his mother's health to be reassessed because her condition has deteriorated in recent weeks, and the Council has agreed to this.

(Hopkins, 1996)

Intervention

Interventions will vary depending on the identified needs from the assessment data. A variety of suggested interventions for the scope of the nurse's role in working with older people's expression of sexuality is offered in **Figure 15.6**. The maintenance of sexual function for older people with chronic conditions is described above.

McCracken (1988) recommends three areas which are particularly important for nurses who work with older adults in promoting the expression of sexuality and healthy sexual functioning:
- Sexual education in respect to normal ageing changes.
- Education relating to changes occasioned by chronic illness or treatment.
- Advocacy in dispelling the myths associated with age and sex.

Although all nurses should have a baseline understanding of sexuality and sexual changes in later life, some interventions require higher levels of education and skills. For example, the assessment and treatment of erectile dysfunction, described above, would require referral to a specialist, and there are some nurse specialists and practitioners now working in this area of care. The PLISSIT model can be used as a framework for nurses to evaluate the level of intervention which nurses can effectively contribute, and the point at which a specialist service is required (**Box 15.5**).

Assisting with Personal Presentation

Sexuality is expressed through grooming, clothes, hairstyling, fragrances, cosmetics, body care preparations and procedures, and bodily adornments such as jewellery or markings. This is so in every type of lifestyle and culture but there are specific aspects for older people, particularly those whose modes of expression have been limited by illness, disability and environmental limitations. The importance of personal presentation to older people has long been recognised. The study by Kaas (1978) of 85 older nursing home residents clearly demonstrated that 'the major mode of sexual expression, as seen by the residents, was trying to remain physically attractive. The majority of residents (61%) said they did not feel sexually attractive any more'. Kaas concluded that it is especially important that nursing home staff help residents to remain physically attractive so that they can maintain their sense of sexuality and that physical appearance should be stressed more as a means of sexual expression and identity.

Body Image

Price (1990a, 1990b) emphasises that the manner in which individuals are dressed, groomed and presented affects their perceptions of themselves, and thus their self-concept, through their body image. This body image is also intimately bound with sexuality. Price's model of body image care (1990), although conjectural, offers a helpful framework within which nurses can view their work with older people. Price suggests that three major aspects feed an individual person's body image. These are body reality, body ideal and body presentation:
- Body reality is the body 'spots and all'. Very old people have undergone many real body changes as a result of ageing, illness, progressive disability or illness treatment.
- Body ideal is the 'picture in our heads of how our body should look and perform'. This is a potential source of ambivalence in very old people who feel 'young' but whose bodies may be, in reality, of advanced age.
- Body presentation: how the body is presented to the outside environment.

Dissonance in these perceptions may result in what Price terms 'altered body image'. Older people are at risk, and this may affect how they feel about themselves as sexual beings. Price suggests that the detrimental effects of dissonance between body reality and body ideal can, to some extent, be balanced by body presentation.

Body image is dynamic and constantly changing. Each person evaluates image through the eyes of culture, era, trends and reflections from important others and mirrors. Internal messages of physiological and psychological origin form the

15.5 The PLISSIT Model

Level 1
Permits the older person to discuss sexuality and sex.

Level 2
LImited information to the concerns of the client. Work at dismissing myths and stereotypes. Discuss normal ageing changes or teaching basic anatomy and physiology.

Level 3
Specific Suggestions: guidelines for techniques which prevent or alleviate a specific sexual problem

Level 4
Intensive Therapy: this level involves a level of expertise at which few nurses are prepared to function. This means a referral to a qualified sex therapist.

Source: Anon J. The PLISSET model: a proposed conceptual scheme for the treatment of sexual problems. *J Sex Educ Ther*, 1976, 2:1–15.

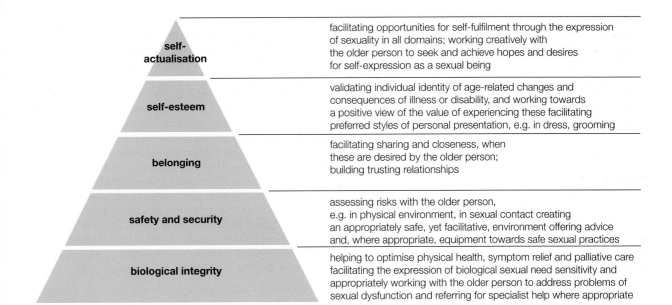

Figure 15.6 The scope of the nurse's role in working with older people's expression of sexuality expressed within Maslow's hierarchy.

depth dimensions of body image and self-concept. Body monitoring may require more attention as one ages. For instance, special diets, medication regimens, elimination and sleep patterns may intrude into daily schedules. When the body begins to limit valued activities, one's image of it changes.

Assisting older people to cope with the gradual and abrupt changes in body image that occur with ageing is a very individual process. Some persons hardly notice the gradual changes until confronted with a specific limitation, or a member of the same cohort they have not seen for years. Body image normally shifts gradually and abrupt changes are always traumatic.

Clothing and Self-esteem.

Clothing can be a demonstration of individuality and personality. Personal articles of clothing that express the individual's desires enhance self-esteem. When clothing must be worn for the convenience of institution or situation, the individual's needs are overlooked. Older people may have difficulty finding clothing that fits properly, particularly if there have been changes in body shape. Although the impact of clothing selection has been poorly investigated for older people living in care homes, there is no reason to assume that its importance diminishes. Nurses can greatly assist by helping them to go shopping, or inviting clothing manufacturers to come into the home.

Roles

Roles in life, be they work roles, family roles or friendship roles are means of expressing the masculine and feminine aspects of ourselves. Webb (1985) defines gender roles as those 'which a particular culture defines as appropriate for

people who are biologically women or men'. Webb and Askham (1987) argue that 'sex-role definitions are a part of sexuality and they are relevant to health care because professionals, like others, use them as standards by which to judge behaviour and may categorise as deviant those who do not conform to traditional expectations' (p. 77). Work, family and friendship-based roles are discussed to a lesser extent in the literature than other modes of sexuality expression but these roles can be a fundamental aspect of self-identity. For example, a woman's self-identity may be inextricably linked with her role as a mother, a man's self-identity may be inextricably linked with the physical strength he demonstrates in his work doing heavy manual labour, and a person's identity may be inextricably linked with the business acumen, sharp decision-making and leadership that they demonstrate in their director role.

These aspects are important for nurses to understand. When an older person's usefulness to society is questioned by others, when the ability to fulfil family, work or friendship-based roles is compromised, acknowledgement of the contribution one has made in any of these respects can help to bolster self-identify, self-esteem and the meaning of the life that has been lived.

Counselling and Advocacy

Old people do seek counselling on sexuality and sexual concerns, but we do not always hear them and many of us are not well enough prepared to help them. Successful and continuing sexual activity is but one sign of healthy ageing. The nurse can also act as an advocate for older people. It is important to look for ways to provide more home care to maintain the option of privacy and control over one's sexual life and to investigate possible directions to provide comfort without nursing homes and acute care hospitals exerting their authority over sexual expression.

Evaluation

Older people whose sexuality needs are fulfilled will consider their sexual life with satisfaction. This will be apparent through verbal and nonverbal expression, the individual's self-image, and involvement and concern about others.

SUMMARY

Sexuality is a complex and powerful issue. Prevailing Western societal stereotypes suggest that sexuality and sexual activity are not important to older people, but the documented research and the stories of older people themselves suggest exactly the opposite. There are strong influences on the expression of sexuality by older people, which may be psychological, social, moral or generational. There are also considerations to sexual activity and intimacy in later life which arise from the demographic trends, the processes of ageing, disability, illnesses and their treatment. There are also distinct considerations concerning the promotion of sexual health. The nurse has a variety of roles in assuring the sexuality of older people: facilitator, educator, confidante, supporter, counsellor and advocate, but it is vital that nurses are adequately prepared for these roles. The primary aim of nurses, doctors, clinical psychologists, social workers and, indeed, society as a whole, should be to work towards the creation of an environment for older people that is tolerant and conducive to the continuity of sexual expression and intimacy for those for whom this constitutes an important aspects of their lives (Gibson, 1992; Pointon, 1997).

KEY POINTS

- Intimacy and sexuality are fundamental aspects of being human which continue throughout life, as the stories of older people demonstrate.
- Sexuality can be a powerful, complex and potentially difficult aspect of life, and particularly for nurses working with older people.
- Western societal images and attitudes suggest that the expression of sexuality or desire for intimacy in older people is inappropriate. Older people can internalise these stereotypes and modify their behaviour to conform to them. In this way older people can be socially controlled.
- Touch is an important, yet often neglected, aspect of relationships and communication. Older people who do not have the opportunity for physical closeness may experience 'tactile hunger'. By touching older patients, nurses can reassure them that they are loveable and attractive, thus helping to raise their self-esteem.
- Much research on sexuality ignores older people, and particularly older people from minority ethnic groups.
- Research overwhelmingly demonstrates that sexuality and intimacy are important aspects of older people's lives.
- Sexual health has not been considered an issue relevant to older people. However, there are distinct considerations concerning the physical aspects of ageing, psychological aspects, and illness or disability.
- Older people have shown enthusiasm in developing health promotion materials, specifically on HIV/AIDS and on learning about healthy lifestyles.
- Nursing as a profession is just beginning to acknowledge its role in sexuality and sexual health, particularly where older people are concerned.
- Nursing education and continuing development should provide nurses with a sound knowledge base in sexuality and sexual health, alongside the opportunity for them to enhance their personal growth and awareness of sexuality issues, consider ethical dilemmas, develop a non-judgemental approach and develop greater interpersonal skills.
- Nurses have a vital role in promoting anti-discriminatory practice, assessment, creating an appropriate environment, assisting with personal presentation, helping achieve positive body image, counselling and advocacy.

AREAS AND ACTIVITIES FOR STUDY AND REFLECTION

- Talk with one or more older persons with whom you have developed a close relationship about sexuality and intimacy in their lives. What does it mean to them? How has this changed over the years? Were there any events or situations which had a major impact on their thoughts, feelings or behaviour? Have they ever experienced problems and how did they cope with them? Were there any particularly good times? How important do they consider sexuality and intimacy as an aspect of life?
- Select an older person you have nursed and for whom there was an issue concerning the expression of sexuality or sexual health. Write down what you felt were the key issues for the person and the factors which influenced these. Evaluate the care offered in the light of the contents of this chapter. Reflect on your own feelings when working with this person, and specifically the factors which influenced your reactions and the way in which you dealt with the situation.
- Review the care plans for all the older people in your work area. Evaluate their effectiveness in acknowledging, supporting and promoting the expression of sexuality or need for intimacy of the individuals. If you consider them inadequate, develop an action plan to enhance the care and documentation.
- Review the medication charts in your clinical area and identify all those which could affect sexual desire or functioning.
- Make a point of studying images of older people in the media. How does it present their sexuality, compared to that of younger people?

REFERENCES

Anon J. The PLISSIT model: a proposed conceptual scheme for the treatment of sexual problems. *J Sex Educ Ther* 1976, 2:1–15.

Altschuler J, Katz AD. Sexual secrets of older women: Countertransference in clinical practice. *J Clin Gerontol* 1996, 17:51–67.

Archibald C. Sex: Is it a problem? *Journal of Dementia Care* 1994, 2:16–18.

Archibald C. Sexuality and dementia. In: Marshall M, ed. *State of the art in dementia care*. London: Centre for Policy on Ageing, 1997.

Beresford JM, Barratt CJ. The widow's sexual self: a review and new findings. Paper presented to the Gerontological Society of America, Boston, November 1982.

Berger R. *Gay and gray: the older homosexual man*. Urbana: The University of Illinois Press, 1982.

Beth Johnson Foundation. *Healthy sex forever*, Stoke on Trent: Beth Johnson Foundation, 1996.

Boyarsky RE Sexuality and the aged. In: Steinberg FU, ed. *Cowdry's care of the geriatric patient, 6th edition*. St Louis: Mosby, 1983.

Brecher EM. *Love, sex and ageing*. Boston: Little Brown, 1984.

British Diabetic Association. *Impotence*. London: British Diabetic Association, 1995.

Broderick C. Sexuality and ageing: an overview. In: Solnick R, ed. *Sexuality and ageing*. California: The University of Southern California Press, 1978.

Burke MA, Knoulton CN. Sexuality. In Burke MM, Walsh MB (eds). *Gerontological nursing*. St Louis: Mosby, 1992.

Butler RN, Lewis MI. *Love and sex after 60*. New York: Harper and Row, 1988.

Carr G. Themes relating to sexuality that emerged from a discourse analysis of Nursing Times during 1986–1990. *J Adv Nurs* 1996, 24:196–212.

Colton H. *The gift of touch*. New York: Sea View/Putnam, 1983.

Comfort A. *A good age*. London: Mitchell Beazley, 1977.

DeBouvoir S. *The coming of age*. New York: Warner,1973

Deevey S. Older lesbian women: an invisible minority. *J Gerontol Nurs* 1990, 16:35.

Duddle M. *Sex after stroke illness*. London:The Stroke Association, 1996.

ENB. *Sexual health education and training, guidelines for good practice in the teaching of nurses, midwives and health visitors*, London: English National Board for Nursing, Midwifery and Health Visiting., 1994.

Erikson E, Erikson JM, Kivnick HQ. *Vital involvement in old age: the experience of old age in our time*. New York: Norton, 1986.

Felstein I. Dysfunctions, origins and therapeutic approaches. In: Weg R, ed. *Sexuality in the later years: roles and behavior*. New York: Academic Press, 1983.

Ford P. Sexuality and sexual health. In: Marr J, Kershaw B, eds. *Caring for older people: developing specialist practice*. London: Edward Arnold, 1998.

Fisher LM, Joseph DH. A scale to measure attitudes about non-procedural touch. *Can J Nurs Res* 1989, 21:5–14.

Fraser J, Ross-Kerr J. Psychophysiological effects of back massage on elderly institutionalised patients. *J Adv Nurs* 1993, 18:238–245.

Garraway WM. High prevalence of benign prostatis hypertrophy in the community. *Eur Urol* 1993, 24:313.

George LK, Weiler SJ. Sexuality in middle and later life. *Arch Gen Psychiatry* 1981, 38:919–923.

Gibson H. *The emotional and sexual lives of older people: A manual for professionals*. London: Chapman and Hall, 1992.

Greengross W, Greengross S. *Living, loving and ageing, sexual and personal relationships in later life*, London: Age Concern England, 1989.

Ham RJ. Sexual dysfunction in the elderly. In: Ham RJ, ed. *Geriatric medicine annual*. Oradell, NJ: Medical Economics, 1986.

Hawkes G. *A sociology of sex and sexuality*. Milton Keynes: Open University Press, 1996.

Hinkle K. A literature review – HIV seropositivity in the elderly. *J Gerontol Nurs* 1991, 17:12–17.

Hogan R. Nursing and human sexuality. *Nurs Times* 1980, 76:1299–1300.

Hopkins N. Couple facing the pain of parting after 71 years. *Daily Mail*, May 16 1996, p 14.

Janus S, Janus C. *The Janus report on sexual behaviour*. London: John Wiley, 1993.

Kaas MJ. Sexual expression of the elderly in nursing homes. *Gerontologist* 1978, 18:372–378.

Kaufmann T. *A crisis of silence: HIV, AIDs and older people*. London: Age Concern, 1993.

Kehoe M. Have you ever seen a lesbian over 60? *The Ageing Connection* 1988, 4:4.

Kellett J. Sexuality in later life. *Rev Clin Gerontol* 1993, 3:309–314.

Kelly J. Homosexuality and ageing. In: Marmor J, ed. *Homosexual behavior: a modern preappraisal*. New York: Basic Books, 1980.

Kinsey AC, Pomeray WB, Martin CE, Gehard PH. *Sexual behaviour in the human male*. Philadelphia: WB Saunders, 1948.

Kinsey AC, Pomeray WB, Martin CE, Gehard PH. *Sexual behaviour in the human male*. Philadelphia: WB Saunders, 1953.

LeMay AC. *Nurse-patient touch and the wellbeing of elderly patients*. PhD thesis, University of London, 1992.

Littler G. Social age-cohort control: a theory. *Generations Review* 1997, 7:11–12.

Masters W, Johnson V. *Human sexual response*. Boston: Little Brown and Co., 1976.

McCracken AL. Sexual practice by elders: the forgotten aspect of functional health. *J Gerontol Nurs* 1988, 14:13–17.

Miller CA. *Nursing care of older adults*. Glenview: Scott Foresman/Little Brown, 1990.

Montagu A. *Touching: the human significance of the skin, 3rd edition*. New York: Harper & Row, 1986.

Moore JR, Gilbert JA. Elderly residents: perceptions of nurses' comforting touch. *J Gerontol Nurs* 1995, 21:6–13.

Morley JE. Impotence in older men. *Hosp Pract* 1988, 23:139.

Pathy MSJ. Therapeutic advances in the management of acut MI. *Care of the Elderly* 1991, October:413–416.

Price B. *Body image, nursing concepts and care*. New York: Prentice Hall, 1990a.

Price B. A model for body image care. *J Adv Nurs* 1990b, 15:585–593.

Pfeiffer E, Verwoerdt A, Wang H. Duke longitudinal studies. Aged men and women, *Arch Gen Psychiatry* 1968, 19:753–758.

Phillipson C, Walker A. *Ageing and social policy. A critical assessment*. Hants: Gower, 1986.

Public Health and Laboratory Service. *AIDS/HIV Quarterly Service Tables*, No 20. Communicable Disease Surveillance Centre,June 1993.

Pointon S. Myths and negative attitudes about sexuality in older people. *Generations Review* 1997, 7:6–8.

Quam JK, Whitford GS. Adaptation and age-related expectations of older gay and lesbian adults. *Gerontologist* 1992, 32:367.

Raphael S, Robertson M. Lesbians and gay men in later life. *Generations Review* 1980, 6:16.

RCN. *Men's health preview: prepared on behalf of the Men's Health Forum*, London, 1996, Royal College of Nursing.

RCN. *The menopause, osteoporosis and hormone replacement therapy*, London, 1997, Royal College of Nursing.

RCN. *The nursing care of gay and lesbian patients: an RCN statement*, Issues in Nursing and Health 26, London, 1994, Royal College of Nursing.

Royal College of Pychiatrists. *Taking sexual histories from middle aged and elderly men: a survey*. London: Royal College of Psychiatrists, 1998.

Robinson P. The sociological perspective. In: Weg R, ed. *Sexuality in the later years, roles and behaviour*. New York: Academic Press, 1983.

Rogstad K, Bignell C. Age is no bar to sexually acquired infection. *Age Ageing* 1991, 20:377–378.

Roper N, Logan W, Tierney A. *Using a model for nursing*. London: Churchill Livingstone, 1983.

Seymour J. Sexuality in the elderly. *Care of the Elderly* 1990, 2:315–316.

Sherman D. Effects of medications on sexual function. *Contemp Long Term Care* 1992, 15:64.

Shipee-Rice R. Sexuality and aging. In: Fogel C, Laurer D, eds. *Sexual health promotion*. Philadelphia: WB Saunders, 1990.

Starr B, Weiner M. *The Starr–Weiner report on sex and sexuality in the mature years*. New York: McGrath, 1981.

Stein R, Sexual counselling and coronary heart disease. In: Leibium S, ed. *Principles and practice of sex therapy*. New York: Guilford Press, 1980.

Stevenson RT, Courtenay BC. Old people, orgasms, and God: a replication determining the relationship between religiosity and attitudes of nurses' aides toward sexual expression among older adults in nursing homes (abstract). *Gerontologist* 1982, 22:261.

Stuart GW, Sundeen SL. *Principles and practice of psychiatric nursing*. St Louis: Mosby, 1979.

Thompson P, Itzin C, Abendstern M. *I don't feel old*. Oxford: Oxford University Press, 1991.

Victor C. *Old age in modern society*. London: Chapman and Hall, 1987.

Webb C. *Sexuality, nursing and health*. Chichester: John Wiley, 1985.

Webb C, Askham J. Nurses' knowledge and attitudes about sexuality in health care: a review of the literature. *Nurs Educ Today* 1987, 7:75–87.

Webster C. *Advice on sexual activity for people with chronic pain, Canterbury*. Pain Concern UK, 1997.

White C: Sexual interest, attitudes, knowledge, and sexual history in relation to sexual behavior in the institutionalized aged. *Arch Sex Behav* 1982, 11:11.

Wilby P. Sex and the British – the survey they tried to stop. *The Independent on Sunday*, 1994, pp.5–8.

Woods NF. *Human sexuality in health and illness, 3rd edition*. St Louis: Mosby, 1983.

World Health Organisation Scientific Research Group. *Report on the menopause, Vol. 14*. Geneva: WHO Publications, 1981.

World Health Organisation Regional Office for Europe. *Concepts for sexual health*, EUR/ICP/MCH 521, WHO, Copenhagen, 1986.

Zeilig H. Woman and ageing-bodies, generations, cultures. *Generations Review* 1996, 6:9–11.

USEFUL ADDRESSES

Association of Sexual and Marital Therapists, Whitely Wood Clinic, Woffindon Road, Sheffield, S10 3LT. Tel: 0114 271 6310.

British Association for Counselling Information Line. Tel: 01788 578328.

British Menopause Society, 36 West Street, Marlow, bucks, SL2 2NB. Tel: 01628 890199

Relate: National Marriage Guidance, Herbert Gray College, Little Church Street, Rugby, CV21 3AP, Tel: 0178 857 3241.

DISCERN, Suite 6, Clarendon Chambers, Clarendon Street, Nottingham, NG1 5LN, Tel: 0115 947 4147.

Men's Health Helpline 01811 995 4448

National AIDS Helpline: Tel: 0800 567123 (Bengali, Gujerati, Hindi, Punjabi, Urdo 0800 28222445, Cantonese 0800 2822446, Arabic 0800 2822447).

SPOD (Sexual and Personal Relationships of people with a Disability), 286 Camden Road, London, N7 OBJ, Tel: 0171 607 8851.

Women's Health Concern, PO Box 1629, London W8 6AU. Tel: 0181 780 3007 (counselling line)

The Impotence Association Helpline. Tel: 0181 767 7791

16 Relationships, communication and social support
Irene Schofield

LEARNING OBJECTIVES

After studying this chapter you will be able to:

- Describe the relationships between an older person and their family and friends, and evaluate the contribution each makes to the health and wellbeing of the older person.
- Evaluate the role of different types of social support network in facilitating independent community living for older people.
- Describe the differences between aloneness and loneliness and relate these to clients you have cared for.
- Describe the concept of reciprocity as it applies to the caring relationships between older people and their carers.
- Discuss how various types of groups might be supportive to older people.
- Reflect on your own relationships with some older clients and assess your position within their relationship network.
- Discuss the barriers to effective communication with older adults and describe strategies to overcome them.

INTRODUCTION

This chapter will examine the many facets of belonging: relationships with family, friends, groups and community. Nursing interventions are included as they relate to each context. Two common myths relate to the concept of belonging in later life. One is that older people are neglected by their families and the second is that the majority of older people are lonely. In exploring relationships between older people and family and investigating the social world of older people in general, it is the intention of this chapter to demonstrate that there is little evidence to substantiate such beliefs. Communication is integral to the development of relationships. Whilst it is accepted that communication can be impaired by the effects of age-related physical changes (*see* Chapter 12), it is less frequently acknowledged that psychosocial aspects of ageing can also affect the interaction. Age-related psychosocial influences will be examined in the context of forming relationships.

It is now widely acknowledged that a caring relationship acts as a buffer against age-linked social losses. The maintenance of a stable intimate relationship is more closely associated with good mental health and high morale than a high level of activity or elevated role status. In other words, older individuals seem to be able to manage stresses if relationships are close and sustaining, and, if they are not, prestige and keeping busy may not prevent depression in later life. In the first major study of people over 75 years of age in Britain, Abrams (1978) asked respondents to give their own description of what makes a satisfying life for people like themselves. The biggest single group of replies concerned having good neighbours and good friends. This was rated above good health or enough money.

In contrast, Bowling and Browne (1991) in their study of over eighty-fives in a single socially deprived area found that emotional wellbeing was more closely associated with positive health status than a supportive social network.

The consensus view appears to indicate that a confiding relationship is a buffer against stress and illness and that a caring person may be a significant survival resource. Social bonding appears to increase health status though the process is poorly understood. This chapter will familiarise the reader with primary and secondary relationships as experienced in later life within generations and between generations. A network of family, friends and acquaintances can sustain older people and give life meaning. The distinction between primary and secondary affiliations is based on the intensity and importance of relationships. Primary relationships are intimate, face-to-face associations that provide a strong sense of sharing and belonging. The secondary relationships are more formal, impersonal and superficial.

PRIMARY RELATIONSHIPS

The maintenance of primary and secondary relationships within a person's own generation becomes more difficult with age. Cohorts die or age at such variable rates that they may be unable to provide the intimate exchange of earlier years. Territories shrink, and secondary networks are less available to an individual. The remaining relationships may become burdened. It is not uncommon to find ageing spouses or siblings living in relative isolation and struggling to maintain themselves with few supports.

Primary relationship possibilities might include a spouse, lover, friend or family member, while an acquaintance or someone who provides a service to the older person would constitute a secondary relationship.

Friendships

Friendships in Abram's (1978) survey of retired people were thought to be more important to psychological wellbeing than family. They often provide the critical elements of life-satisfaction that family may not, i.e. commitment and affection without judgement, personality characteristics that are compatible because they are chosen, availability without demands, and caring without obligation. Friends may share a lifelong perspective or may bring a totally new dimension into a person's life. Males and females engage in particular types of friendships which are learned in childhood and continue throughout the life span (Nussbaum, 1994). Women's friendships tend to be based on emotional intensity and self-disclosure, so that needs and problems are openly discussed. Men's friendships tend to be sociable but not intimate and connected with a shared activity. Men's close relationships are confined to immediate family, while those of women are more diverse. On the death of a spouse, women are better prepared to adapt to their single status, while men in the same position may not have confidant relationships to sustain them through widowerhood. In a UK study, Jerrome (1981) carried out in-depth interviews with 66 unattached older women and found that friendship was significant to them in the following ways:

- It acts as a buffer against social loss.
- It can provide socialisation for older age. Identity as an older person is less salient to those who have been friends throughout life, and grown old together.
- It enables people to share activities and services.
- It helps people to preserve self-image and a sense of worth.

In the USA, Adams (1987) studied the longitudinal patterns of friendship among older women and found that many changes occurred in the process of ageing. The friendship network tended to enlarge in the later years, but the frequency and intensity of the relationships diminished. Widows tended to reach out to a new set of friends and diminish contact with friends who had spouses. Widows interviewed by Thompson *et al.* (1991) described their predicament: 'I find it difficult now, you're always single and you find it difficult when there's couples' and 'you don't want to be gooseberry when there's couples'. Many developed new friendships in senior centres and retirement communities. The relative homogeneity in these settings may have contributed to the development of these relationships. On the other hand, many older individuals developed a sense of liberation from social constraint, and in turn friendships evolved that would never have been considered in their youth. In an earlier study, Adams (1985) found that few women over 70 years old have male friends without romantic notions. The lack of male friends may be attributed to early socialisation patterns and expectations. If they have no legitimate contact with men through spouse or work they may be reluctant to establish friendly relationships. On the other hand, the dearth of older men and their social-isation to sexual rather than platonic relationships with women, may be an equally strong factor, although not addressed in this study.

Male friendships are even less frequently studied than those of females. Reisman (1988) assessed the value of friendship to a group of ageing men and found that casual friends tend to increase in number during the leisure of retirement but close friendships remain few. Ongoing friendships were only mentioned as significant by 15% of married men, 12% of divorced men and 6% of single men. These data obscure the fact that many men believed their wife or children to be their closest friends. We do not yet know if for life-satisfaction women need a broader network of friends than do men, but it is certainly a field ripe for investigation.

Among women studied by Tate (1982) it was found that greater life-satisfaction was significantly predicted by number of friends, good health and having as few offspring as possible living in the same city. It has also been observed that for older women, friends tend to be physically separated, and neighbours are more likely to be casual friends but more constant companions. Friendship is more likely to occur within one's own age group among the youngest and oldest members of our population whereas the middle-aged group spreads ties across all ages. In addition, economic status in all of these three life periods influences friendship patterns. The least adaptive for an older person is relying on and identifying with only a few close friends.

Considering the obvious importance of friendship, it seems to be a neglected area of exploration and a seldom-considered resource of professionals assisting older people. Adams (1983) makes helpful points for service providers trying to assist an older person to remain living independently. It is important to consider the size, composition, and structure of the person's friendship network, the nature of the needed task and the person's feelings about receiving certain types of help from friends. Nurses may help older people to maintain and revive old friendships by assisting them in letter writing, taking care to deliver phone messages and discussing the nature of friendships. New friendships are facilitated by the opportunity for both closeness and distance.

Couple Relationships

The most significant and binding relationship is usually that of the couple. However, the chance of a male and female couple going through older age together is exceedingly slim. After 80 years of age, only 14% of women are living with a spouse (General Household Survey, 1991). Men who survive their spouse into later life ordinarily have multiple opportunities to remarry if they wish. It is less likely that a woman will have opportunity for remarriage in later life. Older men most often marry younger women, though there is an increasing trend for younger men to marry older women.

Long-standing Couple Relationships

Couples in late life may have needs, tasks and expectations that are different from those of their earlier child-rearing years. Couples married for 50 years or more describe a happy marriage as related to congruence of perception. This does not necessarily mean the couples agree, but rather that they know what to expect from each other. Askham (1995) suggests that in later life, the weight of investment in the relationship and a shared sense of history are more likely to sustain a marriage, rather than mutual feeling towards one another. People who stay together for a half-century or more are not necessarily happy doing so. In the past, couples may have been kept together through the solemn promises made as part of religious marriage vows. More recently, changes in the divorce laws and differing expectations surrounding the marriage partnership have made it much easier to dissolve a marriage and increasingly, older couples are becoming less likely to stay in an unsatisfactory marriage. Health-care professionals need to be alert to the possibility of marriage dissatisfaction in older age. In reviewing the literature, Jerrome (1993) warns of the need to interpret study results with some caution. The majority are cross-sectional design studies involving groups of couples at different stages of development. Studies of marriage have focused on marital satisfaction and marital role relationships. Marital satisfaction has been seen to increase in couples immediately post-retirement, to increase at the end of the child-rearing phase but not to the extent of the early years, and to decline with increasing age. Men were more likely to take on traditional female tasks, rather than the other way round. Keith and Wacker (1990) found that older men were more likely to take on traditional female tasks than younger men, but this did not lead to any increase in psychological wellbeing for the couple. Many of the following issues may put severe strain on couples in the last phase of life:

- Efficacy in task accomplishment.
- Finances.
- Health.
- Previous marriages.
- Relationships with children.
- Sexuality.
- Long-standing patterns of communication.
- Matching of personal needs for activity or disengagement.
- Ability to support each other through crises.
- Attitudes about ageing.

Spouse as Caregiver

Elderly spouses caring for disabled partners have special needs. Respite from continuous care is essential; often the spouse has significant health problems that are neglected in deference to the greater needs of the incapacitated partner. Life satisfaction tends to be limited when illness, low income, multiple demands, and the loss of intimacy and companionship converge on a conscientious mate. It is most difficult when the partner is aphasic or incontinent. In Wenger's (1987) small study of spouse carers, the men focused on the physical strain of nursing and doing household chores, while the women found the social and emotional needs of caring most taxing. Rose and Bruce (1995) cite a number of studies which suggest that men do well and make good carers, despite the traditional ideas regarding caring as women's work. Rose and Bruce found highly commendable examples of male carers in their own study of couples, however they construed quite different gender-related motivations between male and female carers. The caring performed by the men was conscientious and became a source of pride and self-esteem to them. In contrast, the women rather than taking pleasure in their accomplishments, grieved for the partner they had 'lost' and the diminished relationship.

Sibling Relationships

Although British studies on sibling relationships are sparse, it is suggested that siblings have the potential to give each other much support in later life (Jerrome, 1993). Siblings share a unique history, albeit with variable personal interpretations, and the same biological and cultural roots. They become particularly important when they are part of the support system, especially among single or widowed elders living alone; in terms of a hierarchy of potential carers they come third in line after spouses and adult children. In an earlier study of women's friendship, respondents who said that they didn't have close friends, admitted to being close to siblings, cousins and sometimes nieces. The nature of sibling relationships have been variously described as intimate, congenial, loyal, apathetic, hostile, advisory, competitive and envious. These relationships may be fraught with lingering resentments and competition for parental approval or they may be particularly close and comforting. Scott (1992) suggests that resolution of old hurts or conflictual relationships may be necessary between siblings before they can work together in providing for parents' needs or in developing supports among themselves. They may help each other modify and refine early experiences that were troublesome by reminiscing and gaining new perspectives with which to interpret earlier events.

Other Kin

Interaction with collateral kin (cousins, aunts, uncles, nieces and nephews) generally depends on proximity and preference. Often maternal kin are emotionally closer than those in the paternal line. These may provide a reservoir of kin from which to find replacements for missing or lost primary relationships.

Beware of the Myth of Family Neglect

It is common to hear people in general and health-care professionals talk about a past golden age when older people were part of a three generational household and lived out

Meeting Relationship Support Needs

Ivy and John Stone are childhood sweethearts. A few weeks before they celebrate their 50th wedding anniversary Ivy begins to notice that John is becoming very forgetful. He recently went to the local shop and came home empty-handed, as he had no idea why he had gone. Other changes in his lifestyle and personality are becoming apparent. He is careless in his grooming, whereas he has always been meticulous before now. His usual sleeping pattern is disturbed and he often wanders about during the night. Ivy wonders if these are normally expected changes due to ageing. Their three children live in opposite ends of the country, but when they come to the anniversary celebration they notice dramatic changes in their father's personality. He is irritable and easily angered, which is not at all the way they remember him. Upon the insistence of the children, Ivy agrees he should see a doctor. John refuses as he feels there is nothing wrong with him. Ivy has always complied with John's wishes so she persuades the children that she can manage alright and whatever is wrong is probably a temporary reaction to something.

After the children return to their homes and Ivy returns to her usual household routines she realises she is feeling tired all the time and it seems whatever she does makes John angry. There is just no pleasing him. She begins to lose weight and is unable to sleep. John's rambling worries her and now so do most things; however, she struggles through the days.

Somehow a year passes and John is getting more difficult and forgetful each day. She rarely leaves the house, as she is afraid he will do something dangerous or hurt himself. Finally, Ivy goes to her general practitioner as her own extreme fatigue makes her fear she has something seriously wrong. She is referred to the practice nurse for the collection of blood samples. When the nurse asks how she is feeling, she breaks down in tears saying, 'I feel like I'm carrying a sack of lead on my back'.

- What are Mrs Stone's comments that provide subjective evidence?
- What information can the nurse herself obtain from her observations and brief history taking that provide objective data for a holistic nursing assessment?
- Suggest two unmet needs that may be the most significant to Mrs Stone at this time.
- Suggest nursing aims for each unmet need, reflecting realistic outcomes and using concrete and measurable terms.
- Suggest one or more interventions for each area of unmet need justifying your choice of intervention.
- What other professionals or organisations are available in your area to help couples like Ivy and John Stone?

their lives in the bosom of the family. It has been called the 'classical family of Western nostalgia'. This is often compared with present British society where older people are perceived to be left to live alone or put into institutional 'homes'. It is important that nurses working with older people and their families are well acquainted with the evidence that explodes such myths and indicates that older people and their families have closer emotional ties than at any time in history.

Stereotypical beliefs about intergenerational family relationships are likely to adversely affect the way nurses relate to both parties, particularly at times of opening and closure of professional intervention. A historical perspective puts present day structures of family into a clearer perspective. Laslett's (1977) seminal work on the examination of English parish records challenges the myth of the nuclear family as a modern phenomenon. Laslett concludes that the nuclear family was probably the norm even in pre-industrial Britain,

where only 11% of households could be classified as extended family groups and only 6% lived in three-generational households. However, Laslett did find that older people had children living with them for longer than in present day society. This was most likely as a result of differences in population structure, due to patterns of marriage and family building, rather than differences in customs and sentiment. In pre-industrial England, the age of marriage for women was between 23 and 27. Many continued child-rearing into their late thirties and forties, so that there was a strong possibility of children still being at home when the parents reached older age. Any surviving grandparents tended to enter the homes of married descendants and generally lower life expectancy resulted in few older people in industrial society.

According to Victor (1994), there was little evidence to show that older people living with younger relatives were well cared for, and it was common practice to draw up legal contracts and wills in which property was exchanged for maintenance. During the industrial revolution, there was an increase in three-generational households in urban areas, as people migrated to towns and cities to find work in factories. There was an increase in family size, with over 50% of families having six to nine children. Grandmothers were needed for childcare, as both parents and all but the youngest children would be out at work. Also, older people were more likely to be cared for if they had property to bequeath or where their support was subsidised by poor law relief (Anderson, 1983). More recently, those who are now in mid-life will perhaps call to mind older people being cared for by unmarried daughters, sharing the same household. The extensive loss of young men during the First World War followed by mass emigration to New World countries shortly afterward resulted in a shortage of marriage partners. Thus, one-third of eligible young women at that time never married and were later available to care for ageing parents and other needy relatives.

Family Life Today

As in the past, the nuclear family remains the norm, and three-generational households are rare. Older couples occupy a single household, and when a partner dies (usually it is the husband who dies first) the remaining partner continues to live alone. Over 50% of people over 75 years of age now live alone, with the great majority valuing their independence to do so. This is evident from the studies which demonstrate older peoples' reluctance to go into institutional care, and a culture of fierce independence, which is characteristic of Western industrialised society (*see* Chapter 13). There is little support for the premise that family ties are any weaker than in the past. Longitudinal research spanning the 1970s and 1980s by Bengston in the USA suggests that despite structural changes in families over a 15-year period, there remains strong intergenerational bonds. Families, therefore, continue to be the source of a great deal of material and emotional support across generations. The shifting need for mutual support helps establish a solid reciprocity that is comfortable in the giving and the receiving. Too often we think of the older family members in terms of recipiency and dependency. However, recent research indicates that up to the age of 69 years, people are more likely to give help to children and parents than to receive help from them (Gerontology Data Service, 1996). Even into advanced age, older people often provide emotional and financial support, childcare and cultural and religious continuity. As the population continues to shift toward increasing numbers of frail older people with multiple problems, it is less certain that this situation will continue. Trends in mortality, fertility, marriage, divorce and alternative family styles will all affect the delicate balance of generational needs and services.

A long-running longitudinal study of a cohort is that of the Berkeley Growth Study Group of children in the USA, begun in 1928. These children are now entering older age and their parents, who are in advanced old age, form the sample for the Berkeley Older Generational Study. From a recent study of this group it was found that those in better health had greater contact with and felt closer to their families than those who were not well. Some feel that as parents' needs for assistance intensify the children's attitudes shift from affection to obligation. Women are in greater contact and feel closer in family relationships than men, although it appears from the study by Field *et al.* (1993) that widowhood may be a more important factor than gender in this observation. It is equally as important to know how changes in feelings toward family can influence health. It is usually assumed that family relationships are desirable for the older individual to promote a sense of belonging. Such a generalisation needs further examination. The quality, meaning and importance of relationships with family members are significant factors in maintaining morale and experiencing life satisfaction. In considering the future nature of family and concepts of intergenerational support, Jerrome (1993) examines several areas of change:

- **Demographic**. Falling fertility rates, reduction in family size and narrowing of the distance between generations means that there will be fewer persons available to provide social support.
- **Technological**. Change from a heavy industry based economy to commercial and service industry has provided more employment opportunities for women, particularly those in midlife, and at a time when older parents may begin to need more social support.
- **Legal**. More liberal legislation regulating marriage, divorce and homosexuality have increased the proportion of families that are divided, reconstituted and unconventional. Reconstituted families are often top-heavy with adults, with the result that there are fewer children with the potential for caring. Little is yet known as to how such changes will affect the social support of older people.
- **Ideological**. The emphasis on community care as social policy, as opposed to institutional care, relies on the continuing support of 'the family' for its success.
- **Economic**. State pension provision, occupational pensions and general rising levels of affluence have brought more choices in family relationships, so that ties are increasingly governed by sentiment rather than obligation.

Family History

A potent force, often overlooked in families with older members, is the influence of the family history. As mentioned earlier, sibling position in a family profoundly influences relationships with parents and other siblings. From these early roots, sibling rivalry flourishes. Motivation, socialisation, affiliation and aggression are all related in some way to family dynamics. Sibling relationships, parental expectations and parental favouritism, may influence future relationships with ageing parents. There has been little study in this area, but it is known that the history of these early beginnings is never totally discarded. In later life parents may depend on the eldest child to care for them just as they depended on that child to care for younger siblings decades before, or each parent may have a different 'favourite' child. Sometimes a 'rejected' child may attempt to gain love and recognition by caring for the older person or may unconsciously punish the parent for injustices experienced in the distant past. Nurses may help all family members understand the present situation as reflecting many conflicts from the past. Simple awareness of the many influences on interactions and recognition of the acceptability of feelings may provide sufficient reassurance. In more severe situations in which feelings are expressed in destructive ways, family counselling may be recommended.

Rivalry among family members for the approval of ageing parents is most common when there is awareness of a potential inheritance. Many people are reluctant to admit to themselves that such thoughts enter their minds. It is helpful to recognise the reality of such considerations and that it may be just as natural to entertain such feelings as it was to attempt to gain more than one's share of the parental love in the early stages of childhood. Most close relationships are fraught with ambivalence. Learning to accept this fact will ease feelings of guilt or shame. If the family has never been close and supportive, it will not magically become so when the parents are old. Resentments long buried may crop up and produce friction or psychological pain.

One of the tasks of middle age centres on ability to work through youthful feelings and attitudes toward parents. The mature adult begins to see parents as individuals rather than extensions of their own needs. However, submerged conflicts and feelings often return to surprise adult children. Mature acceptance of ageing parents with all their foibles and personal idiosyncrasies is an ongoing task. Nurses may help family members accept their own idiosyncrasies as meaningful and valid, even though the relationships are always complex, clouded with ambivalence and influenced by the past. Some families can be encouraged to express their feelings more openly, although if they have never done so, it may be difficult to break long-standing habits within the family relationships. Most important, each family member needs to be accepted and understood as significant to the family system.

Deference

Older people may play games with their children, perhaps ones they have always played or ones invented to avert fear and loneliness. Some manipulate, dwell on infirmities, belittle themselves, or use their money to wield power. Children may rightfully feel used and angry. Among health-care professionals it is common to believe that the old are maligned and neglected. Nurses can help people see their situation more clearly and recognise the validity of their view and also that it is preferable not to put up with games or avoid confrontation in deference to their parent's age. An open and honest approach is less likely to end in regret.

Scapegoating

We are aware of the detrimental effects of consistently being the scapegoat for others, although most people are given this role occasionally or cast it on others at times. Ageing parents may be seen as scapegoats. In these cases, the focus of energy is seen as flowing toward the younger generation as the bearers of unfulfilled dreams, whereas the elders are the carriers of disappointment and worn traditions. They may personify all the facets of life we are conditioned to avoid: death, illness, depression and uselessness. It may be easy to displace responsibility and project feelings onto an ageing parent who may, in fact, have already internalised their own feelings of social rejection. As nurses, perhaps the most useful approach to families who seem to scapegoat the failing parent would be to explore the adult child's fears and concerns related to their own ageing; for example, 'Having your parent with you must make you think a lot about growing old yourself'.

The dynamics of scapegoating older people have not been examined in the literature. It is recognised that when a family crisis occurs the sick and frail older person is likely to be removed from the family group and in some way seen as the source of the problem. If the older person has sapped family strength, the move may temporarily restore family balance even though solution of the real problem will only be deferred.

Crises

Losing a family member is a major crisis, particularly if by death or an abrupt undesired separation. This is the time when insidious scapegoating occurs. A middle-aged woman dying of cancer is trying to make peace with herself and her family. Her ageing mother has lived with the family for several years. She hovers over her daughter, as any mother would a dying child. The adult children of the dying woman are offended; the husband feels crowded out. Soon there is a spoken, or unspoken, desire: 'Why isn't it Grandma? She has lived her life'. Grandma is an object of resentment because she is surviving. It seems so unfair! Nurses in contact with such families may help the family verbalise the unspoken and accept those feelings. The family, including Grandma, needs to talk about the needs each feels in relation to the dying woman and to each other. Helping each other through such trying times is difficult. External support, such as a nurse can give, will help each accept his or her pain without blaming.

Role Reversal

Adult children are often said to reverse roles with parents when the parents become older and more dependent. This has a demeaning connotation, as if the elder becomes a child again. There is some evidence that adult children are shifted to the role of friend, companion and confidant to the elder (Connidis and Davies, 1992). In the event of illness and deterioration of the elder the adult child may at times feel parental but the inner child always remains in search of the protective and guiding parent. These dynamics often make the caregiving role very complex and difficult. If an older parent is beginning to need help, suggestions (**Box 16.1**) to family members may be useful.

16.1 Helping an Older Parent

- Involve the parent in all decisions that affect care.
- Assist the older parent to remain as independent as possible and provide assistance only for those things that are especially stressful or depleting.
- Seek resources that provide options for independent living.
- If the parent insists on promises never to be put in a nursing home, the family could promise that they will do everything possible to prevent it.

16.2 Types of Social Support Networks

Family-orientated (local family-dependent)
- Older person/couple live near or with family on whom they are dependent and other ties are unimportant.
- Most successful in enabling frail older people to remain in the community.

Fully-integrated (local integrated)
- Older person/couple are long-term residents of the area, family lives locally.
- Close relationships with friends and neighbours.
- They have an active network even if they are housebound.

Community-integrated (wider community-focused)
- More likely to occur among middle-class couples, single people, migrants and those who are rich.
- Family may be local but uninvolved or the family is geographically distant though supportive.

Attenuated (local self-contained)
- Family are distant but supportive.
- The older person/couple have little local contact, and are often migrants.
- Seen as vulnerable.

Detached (private, restricted support networks)
- Few ties of any kind.
- Seen as vulnerable.

Source: Wenger C. Support networks in old age: constructing a typology. In: Jefferys M, ed. *Growing old in the twentieth century*. London: Routledge, 1989.

Social Networks and Social Support Networks

Social networks are the vehicles through which social support is distributed and consist of family, friends and neighbours. It is suggested that being embedded in a social network is vital for general wellbeing, and that involvement in a social network appears to play a critical role in enabling frail older people to remain in their own home. Bowling and Browne (1991) summarise social networks as follows:
- Emotional support which leads the recipient to believe that they are cared for and loved.
- Appraisal and esteem which lead the recipient to believe that they are esteemed and valued.
- Personal contacts which lead the recipient to feel a sense of belonging to a primary social group.
- Material aid and instrumental (service) support.
- Information about the environment and new social contacts.

Types of Social Network

In general an individual's social network will consist of 16–50 persons, while the social support network of an older person will consist of between 5–7 members (Wenger, 1995). In addition to size, composition and geographical dispersion, the network can be assessed in terms of density. How many of these supportive individuals are known to each other, and can form collaborative links in the service of the older person being supported? Such a network can be described as being of high density. Wenger (1989) identified five distinctive types of support network on a continuum from family orientated to detached (**Box 16.2**). She has compared the characteristics of support networks in rural Wales with urban Liverpool (Wenger, 1995), and contrary to popular thinking that rural rather than urban areas would provide a more supportive environment, she found that the working class older people living in inner city Liverpool had more supportive informal networks than anticipated. She ascribes this to the greater stability of the urban population, which provided more family dependent types of network. Wenger's work has much to offer nurses in terms of providing a theoretical basis to underpin the nursing

assessment of social support. A nursing assessment based on Wenger's typology can help nurses to identify vulnerable individuals who could benefit from formal service support.

There are differences in the social networks of men and women with women having significantly larger and more diverse networks and more intimate relationships with female friends. Older men's friendships tend to be more sociable than intimate and based on shared activity. Men tend to feel more satisfied than women with spousal support and turn toward it more frequently, while women seek support from spouse and others.

Married persons tend to have larger and more diverse networks than persons separated, divorced, widowed or never married. Childless married persons tend to rely strongly on each other, while childless unmarried persons are more resourceful and have greater diversity in social networks. Widows generally have extensive support networks and the role of children, particularly of daughters, is critical. Single women have larger diverse networks but are less likely to have a relative to provide the required level of support with increasing dependency.

There are also social class differences. There is more migration among middle-class people, so that networks may be more widely dispersed but at the same time less constrained by distance because of access to transport. Older people from working class backgrounds tend to have smaller networks that consist mainly of family and also have more ties with neighbours. Although middle-class people may have a more diverse network, working-class supports may indeed be more reliable and available to provide regular practical help.

There is much interest by policy makers as to how the growing number of older people will be supported by social support networks in the future. Jarvis (1993) in an analysis of the British Social Attitudes Survey of 1986 concludes that older people tend to turn to people with whom they have a close relationship, and whom they see regularly, for social support. These may or may not be relatives but it is proximity and intimacy that count. Jarvis (1993) suggests that concerns about the availability of family, as being the main source of support may well be unfounded, when there are others who are able to fulfil the role. A longitudinal study of the Berkeley older generation in the USA showed that social supports beyond the family decrease over time for the very old and for men but not for women and the oldest old. The satisfaction with support from children tended to increase over time as the elders relinquished involvement beyond the family. These data are significant because they confirm the constancy of family in the support network of the old. Filial obligation toward parents is different than filial affection and seems to be somewhat related to proximity. The sense of obligation toward mothers tends to override role conflicts and even attenuated affections (Finley *et al.* 1988). Daughters involved in other roles seemed to feel less obligation toward fathers and in-laws, and the sense of obligation is somewhat related to affectional ties. The dynamics of filial obligation in this study were related to sex, proximity, education, income, culture and multiplicity of role demands. These factors need considerably more study before we will understand the complexity of issues that impact feelings about caring for older family members.

Older People and Nurses

Much has been written on nurses' attitudes toward older people, with many studies indicating that attitudes are predominantly negative. Stockwell's influential study on the unpopular patient (Stockwell, 1972), identifies patients with mental health problems, those in distress and those with the longest length of stay in hospital (characteristics which typify the older hospital patient) as being those who were perceived to be the least popular among nursing staff. Fielding's (1986) respondents described nursing older people, as 'depressing, dull and slow'. Respondents' beliefs reflected acceptance of negative stereotypes and demonstrated poor communication. The majority expressed their unwillingness to consider nursing older people as a career speciality. D'A Slevin (1991) cites professional socialisation processes as further negative contributory factors, and that nurses' negative attitudes to older people reflect those of society in general.

Pursey and Luker (1995) interviewed groups of community nurses in an attempt to identify attitudes towards working with older people in community settings. Most respondents turned towards past hospital experiences, rather than recent community-based encounters in order to cite examples of satisfaction and dissatisfaction in working with older people. Sources of satisfaction revolved around care given in the context of a close, respectful and mutually satisfying relationship, while sources of dissatisfaction mainly consisted of thwarted attempts at giving individualised care to heavily dependent individuals in environments which were rigid and routinised.

In comparison to how nurses regard caring for older people, very little attention has been given to how older people themselves view and relate to nurses. Ford (1996) describes a small study in which she elicits the views of patients in a continuing care ward. In addition to efficiency and effectiveness in giving technical care, patients valued intuitive acts of kindness and caring from their nurses. In return, patients wanted to be able to reciprocate in some way, for example with a gift or providing moral support to the nurse. Ford (1996) suggests that there is a need for more discussion on the concept of reciprocity. This is particularly relevant to continuing care settings where residents may be seen as having little left to give; yet personal self-esteem is dependent on being able to reciprocate in relationship with others. For some nursing-home residents and clients receiving domiciliary care, nurses may be the only 'others' with whom they come into contact. Nursing assessment which includes a biographical interview (Schofield, 1994; Wells, 1998) may reveal sources of shared experience and provide a basis for mutual regard. The nature of relationship between nurses and their patients cannot be considered without addressing the role of communication. Positive interaction must take place in order to achieve a mutually satisfying relationship. With little exception, studies highlight the paucity of nurses' communication with older patients, despite the claim that communication is a priority nursing role (Armstrong-Esther *et al.* 1994; Nolan, 1995a).

Pets

It is highly appropriate to include pets in the category of primary relationships. The strength of feeling and attachment a pet owner can have towards their pet is not always readily understood, particularly by those who are not themselves pet owners. Many older people have close relationships with a cat or a dog and this could be the longest relationship after that with a spouse. It is now well acknowledged that pets provide companionship to older people, a sense of purpose, help them to feel needed and loved, provide tactile comfort and act as a source of entertainment and humour. In addition, a dog may provide a sense of protection and safety. For stigmatised or isolated persons, pets may be even more important because they are always available and nonjudgemental. The unquestioning, uncritical and unconditional affection, seldom found in human relationships, may somewhat compensate for the lack of human contact. Lee and Lee (1992) suggest that people tend to be comfortable talking about their pets, and that this can be a way of opening up the channels of communication between patient and nurse. Much can be learnt about older individuals by listening to them talk about their pets.

A neglected area of concern is the grief experienced by the loss of a pet. This can occur through death of the pet – an older client commenting on the day he had to have a pet dog put down, said that it was one of the saddest days of his life. Loss also occurs on separation when the individual goes to live in a care home. Recognising the potential for distress, the Joseph Rowntree Foundation commissioned a study into pets and people in residential care (University of Warwick, 1993). The report found evidence that some people endured suffering themselves, yet avoided seeking help for fear of being parted from their pet. It highlighted the need to ask people about pets during routine admission and assessment procedures, and to have policies whereby pets are accepted or prospective residents are assisted to make mutually satisfying arrangements for the pet. Finally, the report addresses the difference between personal pets and communal pets and/or those which visit on a regular basis such as PAT (Pets As Therapy) run by the ProDogs organisation. Many people believe that occasional visits from animals or contact with a communal pet can ease the distress of loss of a personal pet. Many of the homes which reported having encountered residents affected by the loss of a pet were homes that kept communal pets. Guidelines on the development of policy and practice in this area were developed from comments collected during the study.

Cuddly Toys and Dolls

A somewhat controversial issue is the possession of cuddly toys and dolls, usually by older people who have dementia. It can be alarming to see an older adult cuddling a teddybear or attempting to hold food up to the mouth of a doll. The fear is that such behaviour appears to infantalise the adult person. Attachment to these objects may well be based on past life experiences, such as the loss of a pet, or a child through stillbirth or early death, or just simply their form and texture provide a source of tactile comfort. Francis and Baly (1986) found that if the plush animals (North American term for cuddly toys) were self-selected and made available but not recommended the results were positive. The older people who chose plush animals often became quite attached to them, named them and commented on how they enjoyed them. It was also observed that having a plush animal promoted interpersonal interaction, provided comfort and improved interest in social activities. Although all these things are useful, it has been suggested that in the absence of a comforting human interaction a cuddly toy may provide some small measure of comfort.

Families with Adult Children with Learning Difficulties

Older people may be primary caregivers to adult children who have learning difficulties. Adults with learning difficulties are increasingly likely to survive into older age, though average life expectancy remains less than the general population. Many of them suffer from Down's syndrome, with the risk of developing dementia as they grow older. The increase in longevity of parents and child can result in illness and dependency of both parties, and additional caring responsibilities for those involved.

Grandparenthood

Some discussion on the status of becoming or being a grandparent can increase nurses' appreciation of the opportunities for personal development, family relationships and intergenerational support in middle and later life. In the past, the stereotypical image of the grandparent was that of someone who looks old, however with the advent of earlier marriage, earlier and more closely spaced children, many more people become grandparents in their mid to late fifties. With this, it is becoming increasingly more common for older people to become great grandparents and even great great grandparents. The most remarkable feature of grandparents in modern society is the diversity in terms of age and roles undertaken. For example, a person might be aged from 30 to 80 years or even older when they first become a grandparent, whilst a grandchild could be a newborn or a retiree. Increasing divorce rates and remarriage may also influence grandparenting roles in ways which are as yet little understood.

Helen Kivnick (1982, 1983) an American psychologist in studies of grandparenthood, identified the following five major dimensions:
(1) Grandparents played a central role in the upbringing of the grandchild.
(2) Grandparents were viewed as wise esteemed elders.
(3) Grandparents promoted a sense of family history and continuity.
(4) Grandparents were able to relive or redo the past through their grandchildren.
(5) Grandparents indulged their grandchildren.

Most grandparents demonstrate a combination of these attributes. Though much of the literature on grandparenthood originates in the USA, there have been some attempts in the UK to describe the significance of becoming a grandparent (Cunningham-Burley, 1986) and the contribution of grandparents to the material wellbeing of grandchildren (Wilson, 1987). Roles have been discussed in terms of grandparents being 'detached' from their grandchildren, though visits had taken place within the last 1–2 months, and 'active' whereby grandparents had substantial involvement in the upbringing of their grandchildren; this accounted for almost half of the sample (Cherlin and Furstenberg, 1985). In a small qualitative study by Thompson *et al.* (1991, p. 178), becoming a grandparent was associated with biological renewal and a new sense of purpose: 'You just look back and say there's a part of me. A new generation, another branch of the tree' and 'A lot of people say "Oh I couldn't stand being a grandparent, I'd feel old!" And you don't. It's another lease of life, it is. You've got something to look forward to'. In Thompson *et al's* study there was a sense that those who did not have grandparents had missed out in some way. One father described this as follows:

> *I suppose they are missing something really, yes. Partly by seeing them so seldom and partly by not having much of a relationship with them. Because they really need some adults who understand their little ways and deal with them differently than us, which is what they don't have at the moment. They really only have us and people who are not in the family.*

(Thompson *et al.* 1991, p. 209)

When older clients talk to nurses about their children and grandchildren, careful attention to what is said can reveal sources of satisfaction or discontent and the potential for intergenerational support. It has also been suggested that children who grow up with close ties with grandparents are likely to have more positive attitudes to older people in general (Jerrome, 1993).

The Caring Relationship

With only approximately 5% of frail older people living in care homes, the majority of dependent older people who require care, receive this in their own homes, mainly from relatives. This continuing situation underpins the policy of care in the community. Typically, carers are often portrayed as women, in particular married daughters who have families of their own. However, evidence from the General Household Survey (Green, 1988) does not wholly support this view. Respondents were asked whether they carried out any extra responsibilities above those of normal household tasks on a regular basis on behalf of family members who were sick, elderly or handicapped. (The self-reported responses relied on individual interpretations of 'extra responsibilities', and there may also have been gender differences in interpretation.) However, on the strength of the data it was estimated that nationally over 6 million people had regular caring responsibilities.

The report confirmed that the majority of carers were women (3.5 million) yet a sizable minority consisted of men (2.5 million). However, there were variations in the gender of carer, with type of household and relationship to the person being cared for. Where the older person who required help lived with a spouse, then it was the spouse who took primary caring responsibility, and this divided equally between men and women. Where the dependent person lived alone, with a sibling or with younger household members, then the main carer was usually a younger female, normally a daughter. Nearly three-quarters of carers looked after someone who lived in another household. The issue of caring is very rele-

vant to all nurses who come into contact with older people, as 75% of carers were caring for a person over 65 years and 26% of people who spent over 20 hours caring were themselves aged over 65 years (Green, 1988). Most published texts and policy documents use the term 'informal' carers. The Carers National Association which has done much to highlight the needs of non-professional carers dislikes the use of the term, pointing out that there is nothing informal about caring and that somehow its use devalues the work of carers. The NHS and Community Care Act (1990) reinforced a commitment to support carers as well as the person being cared for. However, there was concern from many quarters that carers were not receiving support as promised, and additional legislation in the form of the Carers' (Recognition and Services) Act 1995 provides carers with a statutory right to have their needs assessed.

The Essence of Caring

Previous paragraphs address caring or more specifically caregiving in the light of numbers of people giving and receiving care. Such surveys are of interest to social policy makers and service providers. Definitions of caring used by social policy makers tend to revolve around helping people with activities of daily living, and are known as the instrumental aspects of caregiving. Some definitions clearly state that caregiving is not a reciprocal relationship, and that a feature of the relationship is that the person being cared for is incapable of reciprocating in kind. Failure to consider the wider dimensions of caregiving can result in nurses' missing opportunities to support carers. Consideration needs to be given to the motives behind caregiving. Nolan *et al.* (1995b) building on the work of Bowers suggests a typology of caring consisting of eight categories:

(1) **Anticipatory care** – is concerned with thinking about the need for care in the future, and can come from the person who may become the carer or the person who will require care either at the beginning or perhaps later when a more intensive type of care is needed. It may be unspoken or expressed, perhaps to the practice nurse during a routine health check for example. In this case, the nurse may recognise an opportunity to give information regarding support groups and the carer's statutory right to an assessment. In this way anticipation is informed rather than speculative.

(2) **Preventive care.** This occurs when the carer is monitoring from a distance, perhaps by a discrete enquiry about the adequacy of a diet or that medication is being taken.

(3) **Supervisory care.** This occurs for example when medication is put into special containers to aid compliance. At this point the cared-for person is likely to be aware of being given assistance. Again nurses can be of assistance if they are knowledgeable about resources.

(4) **Instrumental care.** This is reached when the carer is carrying out practical tasks. This category of caring features largely in the literature and is viewed as being

the greatest source of stress.

(5) **Preservative care.** Bowers (1988) suggests that protective care whereby the carer tries to minimise the failing abilities of the person being cared for, and maximise their independence is a far greater source of stress than instrumental care. She suggests that this desire to be protective is often the cause of conflict between carers and service providers, whose offers of instrumental care are rejected in an attempt to preserve protective caring. Nolan *et al.* (1995b) cite the example of withholding a diagnosis of cancer in order to protect the patient. In most cases, this is ill-advised as in the long term, such a paternalistic approach is more likely to lead to greater anxiety and stress for all concerned. Nurses can play their part in helping carers to see that an honest but gentle approach will be least detrimental in the long run.

(6) **Preservation care.** This is concerned with preservation of the cared-for person's sense of 'former self', in order to maintain self-esteem. Carers themselves may give high-quality instrumental and preservation care, and expect the same from service providers. Most hospital or care home nurses will have witnessed at some time, the displeasure or distress expressed by a relative that a seemingly small aspect of care has not been carried out as they themselves would have done it. A deeper understanding of the rationale underpinning such behaviour can help nurses to appreciate the importance of collecting detailed information, and using it to plan and deliver care in a way which models that of the carer. Only in this way can the preservation aspects of care which are of paramount importance to the carer be maintained.

(7) **(Re)constructive care.** Nolan *et al.* (1995b) suggest that there are limits to the concept of preservation care in that the notion of preservation of self-esteem on which it is based is closely linked with having valued roles in society. When these roles cannot be fulfilled because of deteriorating health, then reconstructive care based on past and new roles could be developed. An example springs to mind where two staff nurses working on an acute medical ward described how they would greet a particular patient who had dementia with an affectionate hug. His personal care skills were deteriorating but he was able to maintain self-esteem by showing affection towards others. The nurses recognised this and encouraged it.

(8) **Reciprocal care.** This underpins all other categories, and is perhaps the most complex aspect of caring. This might be out of love and affection, duty, altruism or the desire to give something in return for past acts and services by the person needing care. A relationship which encompassed some of these features was that of a very tiny Scotswoman who was the full-time carer of her husband who had dementia. The man seemed to tower above her and his challenging, often physically aggressive behaviour sometimes made it difficult for

her to cope. I asked her how she managed to carry on, and she replied that he had been a most loving husband and had been so kind and considerate towards her that there was no question that she would not continue to care for him.

Quereshi and Walker's (1989) study of carers in Sheffield describes a wide variety of relationships. Not all were based on mutual regard and help. Some of those who cared out of a sense of duty also harboured resentment towards the cared-for person, and such relationships were more prone to collapse. The quality of the relationship prior to the need for care is key to understanding the reasons for stress. There is now some evidence to suggest that older people would rather not have to rely on close relatives when they are in need of care. Rather than imposing themselves as a burden on younger relatives, they would prefer to rely on formal support (Salvage *et al.*, 1989).

Assessment

Nurses working in general practice are in a key position to point carers in the direction of appropriate help. A rapid initial carer assessment can be made by using the following three questions to explore the issues:

- Are you caring for someone on a regular basis?
- Are you able to do everything you want for them?
- Do you get time to yourself?

Assessment of the carer's needs, strengths and stresses, and quality of the relationship as well as any existing support systems will assist the nurse in gaining a holistic picture of the interventions that may be helpful. The Carers National Association has compiled an information pack for professionals that contains examples of assessment forms and self-assessment forms for carers themselves to complete. A reminder as to how carers define their needs is provided by a 10-point plan (**Box 16.3**).

Figure 16.1 illustrates an alternative form of assessment using a family diagram. A mutually constructed, written assessment of a carer's needs and coping capacities can be comprehensive and specific and becomes a document of their strengths in times of stress. Areas to be included are sources of stress, particular coping methods, resources that are used or can be used, and the rewards and problems of caregiving. Although staff are well aware of the need for written care plans and evaluation of patient progress, this may not be shared with or given to the carer. Inclusion in the development of a nursing care plan and periodic evaluation may help carers assess their effectiveness, even in the face of patient deterioration. Factors that are indicative of coping in the caregiving role include perceived wellbeing, perceived social support, promotion of functional ability of the cared-for person and positive relationship to cared-for person.

Older Gays and Lesbians

Increasingly, we will become aware of older people and the family relationships they have developed as gays and lesbians.

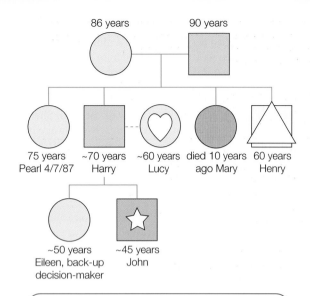

Notes

1. Patient has lived with husband in small room with shared bathroom and kitchen for 20 years.
2. Primary decision maker is grandson, John, who helped admit patient to programme, he handles finances.
3. 12/10/86 durable Power of Attorney of health wishes signed and John designated.
4. Henry has been a very close friend and wants to be informed if something significant like death occurs.

Guidelines for Notes

a. Documentation is to be objective versus impressions or subjective.
b. Include on diagram who would be the back-up decision maker.
c. If durable power of health-care wishes and/or finances have
   been assigned, indicate in this area as well as in progress notes.
d. any add-ons need to be initialed and dated.

Key

⬤ female	--- in-law relationship
⬛ male	♡ primary care-giver
△ non-blood informal support	☆ primary decision-maker
⬤ deceased	

children should be listed by birth order from left to right

Figure 16.1 Family diagram (sample). (Source: Stanford Geriatric Education Center: Ethnogerontology Conference, Jan 10, 1991, Stanford University, Palo Alto, California.)

Writing from a North American perspective, Kimmel (1992) believes gays and lesbians are often involved in three different

family structures simultaneously: the family of origin, the family of spouse and children, and the family of friends and lovers. Though it is not legal for same-gender couples to marry, many of them enter into marriage contracts. It is unknown how many of these involve older persons. We need much more knowledge of cohort and generational differences between age groups to understand the recent, dramatic changes in the lives of lesbians and gays in family lifestyles.

SECONDARY RELATIONSHIPS

Although family and friends seem to be most effective in acute, emergency situations, others are needed for long-term support, enjoyment and variety and to augment primary relationships. The development and maintenance of peer groups are important. The great advantage of group affiliations for older people is in the diffusion of relationship intensity and the constancy over time. A reliable group maintains its function despite the loss or addition of members. This is an important consideration when working with older people.

Group Affiliations

Group affiliations are secondary and complementary to primary relationships. Secondary supports may also be more durable than primary because they are not bound by conflicting feelings. They do not have long-standing intimate histories and rarely involve constant exposure. Secondary relationships are characterised by their parameters. Usually they are recreational or service orientated, somewhat superficial and constrained by specific needs or goals. Professionals are sometimes the instigators, facilitators or connecting link

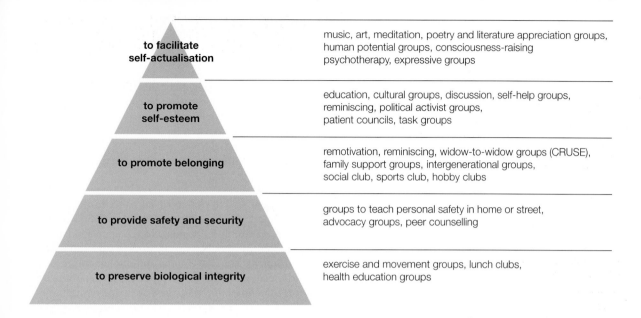

Figure 16.2 Maslow's hierarchical needs met in group work with older people.

to secondary networks. It is important that nurses working in primary care have knowledge of groups supportive to older people in the local community. Groups providing secondary support networks may be formal or informal, may either function well or poorly, depending on the needs of the older participants and the skill of the group leader.

Informal Groups

Informal groups are those that spontaneously arise and have few restrictions, expectations or goals. They are secondary networks by virtue of their low intensity and lack of demands. In fact, they could be called tertiary groups (or those at a third level of importance) because they cannot be relied on to provide interpersonal support, but they may be significant in a person's particular adaptation. Examples of such groups include informal groups of older people who meet at parks, shopping centres and cafes; senior citizen activities (these have formal and informal components); groups that form in care homes; or any group that occurs sporadically for the purpose of socialisation, discussion or participation in a particular activity.

Formal Groups

Formal groups are defined by their expectations, dependability and goals. The intensity of interpersonal exchange varies in accordance with the members' and groups' goals. Much has been written in the North American literature concerning goals and methodology of groups for older people; the most current is the work by Burnside (1994). Nichols and Jenkinson (1991) is a useful UK text for nurses proposing to set up a support group, although it does not relate specifically to older people.

Needs Assessment

Groups can be organised to meet any level of Maslow's hierarchy, and they often meet multiple needs. Using the assessment of social climate and human needs as basic guides, the nurse can select the type of group most suitable in a given situation. Groups may be formed to accomplish something tangible, such as the group set up by Culhane and Dobson (1991) to support older women who had received inpatient treatment for a depressive illness. The group served as a place to share the difficulties of living alone; several new members joined the group at the time of a recent bereavement. As the group developed, members were able to share painful memories and use each other to learn new coping strategies. Therapy groups imply some psychological deficit or conflict and should be led by qualified personnel. Nurses with training in psychotherapy are well equipped to lead such groups. The third type of group does not explore deep psychological needs, but rather in helping persons extend and grow they often remove some of the barriers to personal growth. It may be possible to help people discover latent growth potential by encouraging group membership and following hierarchical need (**Figure 16.2**).

The following 'curative factors' for group work were identified by the American theorist Yalom in the 1970s:

- **Altruism:** a chance to give to others.
- **Group cohesiveness:** loyalty and commitment to group.
- **Universality:** commonalities among members.
- **Interpersonal:** input (learning) – conversation.
- **Interpersonal:** output (teaching) – conversation.
- **Guidance:** developing awareness of options.
- **Catharsis:** emotional sharing and reliving painful experiences.

379

- **Identification**: role modelling by members and leaders.
- **Family re-enactment**: relating to members and leaders as to family members.
- **Insight**: gaining cognitive and emotional awareness of own needs.
- **Instillation of hope**: increasing ability to be assertive and autonomous.
- **Existential factors**: living and dying, loving, leaving.

In the USA, group work with older adults has often been based on Yalom's guidelines for group work with younger persons. However, it has been found that some modifications may be necessary when working with older persons if the group is to be successful. For example, Yalom's curative factors can be used as goals for the group work.

Group Structure

Implementing a group follows a thorough assessment of the environment, needs and potential for various group strategies. Major goal decisions are reached, and with those decisions several structural decisions are intrinsic. For instance, several older diabetics in an acute-care setting may need health-care teaching regarding diabetes. The nurse sees the major goal as restoring a sense of control and balance in each individual's lifestyle.

Guide for Evaluation of Group Meetings

Some factors used to evaluate group meetings:

- **Setting** – seating arrangement, room comfort, activities carried on in area, facilities; note movement of chairs, reseating, and objects that facilitate or distract.
- **Goal** – how is this established? Who is included in decision about goal? Flexibility of goal.
- **Participants** – list name, age, physical problems of importance to group, sex and mobility.
- **Interactions** – dyads, Triads, mini-conversations, monologues, effects of placement, role of leader and roles of members.
- **Process** – mood of group at beginning; unusual events in setting, community, nation; deaths; accidents; upset in ward or agency routines; new people in setting.
- **Themes** – outstanding themes expressed in group, usually not more than three or four; loneliness, power or lack of autonomy, rejection, universality and independence.
- **Problems** – how were they handled? Was the approach effective? If problems occur again, what could be done?
- **Significant content** – one intervention that was goal directed and worked; one intervention that was unsatisfactory. What would have been more helpful.
- **Evaluation of goal accomplishment** – portions of goal accomplished; serendipity, evaluation of group progress and plans for next meeting related to evaluation of previous group meeting.

Groups of older people have some unique aspects that require an extraordinary commitment on the part of the leader:

- They often need assistance or transport to the group.
- They may need more stimulation and are less self-motivating (this is, of course, not true of self-help and senior action groups).
- Many older people likely to be in need of groups are depressed. The depression can be contagious and leaders become depressed.
- Leaders must be prepared for some members to become ill, deteriorate and die.
- Leaders are continually confronted with their own ageing and attitudes toward it.

Group leaders need to plan in advance to incorporate a consistent support person in the group if possible. If not, someone must be available for planning and recapitulation of group sessions. Students should generally work in pairs and will need supervision. Skills in developing and implementing groups for older people improve with experience. Even though the effort is sometimes draining, there are many rewards.

Community Affiliations

Community networks may not be visible to a casual observer. Even the older person may initially state he or she has no one to turn to when in need. The nurse must be specific to discover an existing network. Such questions as these may elucidate a secondary network in the community:

- How did you get to the doctor the last time you went?
- Where do you get your hair cut?
- Where do you go shopping?
- How do you manage your washing?
- What did you do the last time you experienced a crisis?
- Have you called anyone for assistance recently?
- Have you been a member of any organisations?

Often shop assistants, hairdressers, bank clerks, doctors, pharmacists, bus drivers and clergy are a barely recognised part of the community network for isolated older people. Town centre shopping areas sometimes become the counterpart of the historical Village Square for older people who are alone.

ALONENESS

In the UK, a large percentage of older people, mainly older women, live alone. This reflects the affluence of our times, the likelihood of widowhood for women, the involvement of families willing to assist older people in maintaining an independent lifestyle and the cultural value of individual independence that is highly treasured in our society. There is little information on the effects of living alone as it pertains to survival and satisfaction. Males living alone or with someone other than spouse are thought to be at a disadvantage in terms of survival while it seems to make less difference to women. Both sexes are affected by income, race, physical activity and employment, but these are variable effects.

Many people have a strong need to be alone. Nurses need to assess whether clients are lonely or like to be alone. Nursing care plans will be distinctly different for the alone and the lonely. To make an adequate assessment it is important to understand the difference between loneliness and being alone.

- Loneliness is an affective state of longing, emptiness and feeling bereft.
- To be alone is to be solitary, apart from others and undisturbed.
- Lonely people may be alone or surrounded by others.
- People who are alone may be lonely or satisfied.
- Loneliness can be viewed as a condition of human life that sustains, extends and deepens humanity.
- Self-growth comes from a person's ability to recognise and cope with loneliness.
- Factors of loneliness and aloneness change as a person moves up Maslow's hierarchy of needs (**Figure 16.3**).
- Loneliness accompanies self-alienation and self-rejection.
- Loneliness is evidence of the capacity for love. The degree of attachment is directly correlated with the felt loss when detachment occurs.

Assessing the Need to be Alone

- Does the patient frequently close the door or turn toward the wall?
- Does the patient wear earplugs or eyeshades?
- Is the patient reluctant to engage in conversation?
- Is there any time allowed for total privacy?
- Does the patient seem absorbed in thought without agitation? Daydream?
- Does the patient lie or sit with eyes closed frequently?

Interventions

- Share your observations of behaviour with patient.
- Ask about the meaning.
- Assure patient certain time of privacy.
- Attempt to assign room with a quiet patient.
- Minimise disturbances as much as possible.
- Discuss the needs and perceptions of the patient in regard to being alone.

cause		intervention

detachment related to realisation of impending death
extrasensory experiences
 	
desire for solitude
	trans-cendence	allow time to be introspective
		  with quiet human contact
		exploration and acceptance of
		  meaning, validation
		protect privacy

loss of social relevance uselessness waning capacities relinquishment of work role loss of economic status	**self-esteem**	voluntary work develop latent talents modify expectations act as consultant based on expertise prioritise budget to maintain some areas of satisfaction
loss of intimates loss of spouse extremes of behaviour socially unacceptable behaviour	**belonging**	attend senior centres join support groups
sensory losses crime-ridden environment fear of crime	**safety and security**	use hearing aids and optical aids have a companion when going out burglar-proof home, guard dog
pain illness dying stigma of cancer or AIDS	**biological integrity**	alleviate pain provide comfort measures reassure that person will not be alone acceptance, touch, attendance to basic needs allow time alone as desired

Figure 16.3 The hierarchy of isolation and loneliness (Source: Idea from Ravish T. *J Gerontol Nurs*. 11(10):10, 1985.)

LONELINESS

Loneliness in Later Life

It is a common belief that the majority of older people are lonely, especially as so many older people live alone. These may be attitudes of youth and middle age that change in the realities of the later maturing process. It is imperative that nurses do not equate living alone or being alone with feeling lonely. Widowhood is a common and inevitable status for the majority of older women who have married. At the same time there is strong evidence that independence, albeit in a single occupancy household, is the overwhelming desire of the majority of older adults. Loneliness can be experienced by older people who live with adult children due to lack of company from their peers, between marriage partners (Jerrome, 1990), and living in a care home, where opportunities for the development of friendship between residents are poorly facilitated. Friendship in later life provides opportunities for intimacy and shared activities, as well as mutual support with age-related life transitions, such as death of a spouse.

It is important for nurses to recognise that frail older people, living alone, with little social support are perhaps at increased risk of experiencing loneliness and social isolation, and that these may impact on health and wellbeing. Tornstam (1990) studied loneliness among Swedish people and identified three types of loneliness:
(1) Intensity or quantity (how often and how painful).
(2) Inner (personality introversion).
(3) Positive (isolation sought).

The degree of inner loneliness is higher in older people than among the young, although overall younger people experienced more feelings of loneliness than did the old. These findings merit further investigation as they relate only to one country and may reflect certain cultural artifacts. Early developmental experiences and present situations remain important factors in the loneliness experienced by older people. The important contribution of Tornstam's is the attempt to show loneliness as a complex and multidimensional affect. It is not a categorical condition of being older. For nurses, this indicates the need to discuss loneliness in depth rather than simply identify it as a possible factor in the existence of clients. Loneliness is a passive, possessive and painful emotion, whereas aloneness, solitude and isolation may be actively sought, enhancing and creative.

Assessing Loneliness

It is important that nurses assess whether their clients are lonely and discuss with them appropriate interventions.
- Does the patient initiate contact?
- Is the patient anxious, withdrawn, apathetic or hostile?
- Does the patient cling to others or attempt to detain them?
- Is the patient unable to articulate his or her own needs?
- Is the patient eager for visitors and distressed when they leave?
- Does the patient exhibit contempt for his or her condition or self?
- Has there been a major disruption in number of contacts with the patient?
- How often does the patient feel lonely and under what circumstances?
- Does the patient provoke to gain attention?

Interventions

Donaldson and Watson (1996) put forward the view that nurses can intervene to alleviate loneliness among older clients, and that research is necessary to point the way forward. They suggest that investigation based on older people's feelings about loneliness (cognitive approach) or absence of an attachment figure and significant social network (interactionist approach) as being appropriate frameworks for research by nurses. These approaches have already been used in studies by other disciplines. The General Household Survey (Office of Population Censuses and Surveys, 1991) reveals that over two-thirds of all older people report seeing relatives or friends at least every week or more often and over one-third saw friends or relatives daily (**Figure 16.4**). By 1991, daily contact with friends and relatives had fallen to a quarter of respondents. This partly reflects the tendency of older people to remain in their own homes, after widowhood for example, rather than moving in with younger relatives (Grundy, 1996). An appreciation of older people's lives, and knowledge of the types of social and supportive networks and their strengths and weaknesses can assist nurses in taking a meaningful social history. As a result, supportive persons can be involved from the very beginning in planning care, gaps can be uncovered and action taken to provide friendship and support, depending on local conditions. An intervention might be giving assistance to apply to a voluntary visitor scheme such as those run by Age Concern. A study by King and MacMillan (1994) on discharge planning for older patients highlights gaps in social history taking, whereby nurses failed to detect important sources of social support prior to discharge.

Bowling et al. (1988) in a study which included all people aged 85 years living in an East London borough, found that only 12% of the respondents wanted voluntary visitors to alleviate feelings of loneliness. The questions used by the research team to measure the quality of social support could also be used or adapted by nurses in the process of making an initial assessment:
(1) If you needed the help of a relative or friend do you know one who would help?

(2) Do you have at least one friend or relative who understands you?

(3) Do you have at least one friend or relative who shows they care about you?

Practical approaches might be as follows:
- Ask about loneliness.
- Spend time with patient in silence or in conversation.
- Assist in keeping contact with people important to patient.
- Let patient know when you will be available.
- Explore the nature of the loneliness with the patient; also, the phenomenon of loneliness.
- Guide person in reviewing life experiences related to loneliness to gain insight (for patient) and data (for you).
- See or call client frequently for brief periods.

COMMUNICATION

Communication is key to the formation of successful relationships throughout life. Earlier in the chapter, the significance of friendship and supportive relationships have been discussed in relation to the maintenance of self-esteem, social support and general wellbeing in later life. It is important that nurses are fully aware of the effects of ageing on communication so that wherever possible, modifications can be made to facilitate more effective communication. It is intended in this section to briefly review the literature on nurse-patient communication, which on the whole tends to indicate that communication is poor. The underlying reasons for this will be explored and will be followed by some strategies to promote more effective communication. In addition, the burgeoning research by sociolinguists which focuses on older people, and from which nurses can learn a great deal will be discussed.

Communication in Nursing

Older people are a most heterogeneous group and between them they demonstrate a wide range of ability in regard to communication. There are those who are in good health, alert and receptive, and at the other extreme there are those with severe impairments. It is the latter who challenge to the full nurses' communication skills. If we accept the premise that communication with people is central to nursing, it follows that those with impaired ability, however small, should receive more attention from nurses. Sadly, this tends not to be the case, as a number of studies reaching back 20 years or more, indicate that people with impairments are stigmatised or left with little attention (Armstrong-Esther and Browne, 1986, Armstrong-Esther et al. 1994). Furthermore, nurses' communication with patients in general (Audit Commission, 1993) and older people in particular (Wells, 1980; VanCott, 1993) leaves much to be desired. Successive research studies into how

nurses communicate with older people suggest that interactions tend to be infrequent and limited to the routines of providing physical care. There is little exploration of the older person's feelings regarding their present condition, reason for referral to the health services or planning for the future.

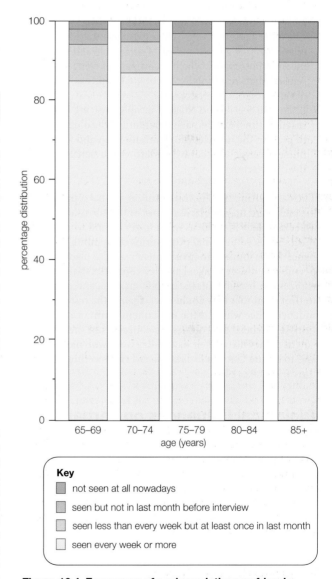

Key
- ☐ not seen at all nowadays
- ☐ seen but not in last month before interview
- ☐ seen less than every week but at least once in last month
- ☐ seen every week or more

Figure 16.4 **Frequency of seeing relatives or friends. (Source: General Household Survey, 1986. In:** *The health of elderly people: an epidemiological overview.* **London: Central Health Monitoring Unit, HMSO, 1991.) Crown copyright is reproduced with permission of the Controller of Her Majesty's Stationery Office.**

Barriers to Communication with Older People

In a seminal paper on the power of language as a means of social control, Lanceley, (1985) draws upon the work of socio-linguists in an attempt to explain why the language of nurses working in a rehabilitation setting appears to be predominantly controlling. She describes the traditional nurse and patient relationship which is still (even today) mostly perceived by both parties to be one of inequality, with the nurse wielding the power of the professional. Contributory factors to this imbalance of power might be:

- Lack of reciprocity in terms of social exchange.
- The older person is seen as being disadvantaged in the relationship as a result of loss of social role and the material possessions which accompany earning-power.
- Ageist beliefs resulting in stereotyped impressions and devaluation of older people.
- Biological age-related changes in sight, hearing and reaction time, which make it harder for the older person to pick up the nuances of communication and for the nurse 'receiver' to accurately interpret the signals from the older 'sender'.

The care setting itself is constraining, in that a person in a hospital ward may not have control of the taken-for-granted aspects of daily life such as when to get up and when to eat a meal. A lack of personal possessions or 'symbols of dominance' in the immediate environment may also place the older person at a disadvantage. Lanceley concludes that often the expressions used by nurses are discouraging and restrictive, to the extent that they could work against the restoration of independence which is the fundamental aim of rehabilitation. It is crucial that nurses are conscious of the power of language they use in their day-to-day work with older clients, and to ensure that it is facilitative and empowering wherever the caring takes place.

Biological Influences on Verbal and NonVerbal Communication

The ageing effects of sight, hearing and speech on communication have already been addressed (*see* Chapter 12). Less commonly mentioned is the slowing of reaction time as a result of degeneration of neuronal tissue. This can cause minor delays in receiving or initiating a message and may have the effect of conveying lack of interest, understanding or feeling to the nurse. In addition, although it is known that older people retain a wide knowledge of vocabulary, they may be less able to produce complex sentences of their own and have difficulty interpreting those of others, particularly if the sentence is poorly organised (Hummert, 1994). Fatigue and frailty as a result of acute or chronic ill health can also inhibit the communication process. **Box 16.4** contains some of the conditions which can prevent effective nonverbal communication. These could have the effect of slowing down the inter-

16.4 Influences on Nonverbal Communication

Facial movement
Fatigue
- Lack of spontaneity of facial expression.
- No response.
Parkinson's disease (PD)
- Blank facial expression.
Cerebrovascular accident (CVA)
- Lack of response due to paralysis.
Poor hearing
- Blank or inappropriate response.

Gaze and eye contact
Partially sighted
- Prolonged gaze.
Fatigue
- Decline in spontaneity.
- May look away.
- May close eyes signalling end of interaction.
Ptosis
- Drooping eyelid partially obscures eye

Gesture and body movement
Fatigue
- Decline in spontaneity and response.
Discomfort and pain
- Becomes restless.
- Fidgets with bedcovers.
Paralysis

Body posture and body contact
Arthritis
CVA
Fatigue
Osteoporosis
PD
- Reduced mobility and sitting posture which in turn affects range of expressive behaviours.

Use of personal space
Poor hearing
- Undesirable proximity as personal space is breached.

Smell, appearance, clothes
Affective disorder
Arthritis
CVA
Dementia
Fatigue
- May affect ability to care for self and clothing.
- Presentation of self is compromised.

16.5 Ways to More Effective Communication

- Seek out a quiet place or turn off televisions and radios in the vicinity.
- Close the bed curtains (in hospital) to aid concentration.
- Choose time when patient appears most alert and receptive.
- Listen intently and concentrate on what is being said.
- Give increased attention to patient's non-verbal cues.
- Attend to pacing and clarifying of issues. Give more time.
- Attend to loudness, pitch, articulation, sentence structure and complexity and speed of delivery.
- Use appropriate vocabulary.
- Use touch and monitor response.

action, could lead the nurse to believe erroneously that communication is breaking down or could signal the end of the interaction. Age-related changes may affect speech in the following ways:

- **Quality.** Consonants may be less precise and articulation slowed by changes in the muscles used to create speech. Ability to make rapid repetitive movements of the tongue and lips may be reduced. Ill-fitting dentures exacerbate these changes.
- **Loudness.** Changes in the respiratory organs result in a decrease in the amount of expired air, reducing volume.
- **Pitch.** Changes in the length and tension of the vocal cords result in a higher pitch.

Box 16.5 gives some suggestions as to how circumstances and communication skills can be modified to bring about more effective communication.

Use of Touch

Touch can be used as an additional form of nonverbal communication, so long as this is acceptable to the recipient. If the older person quickly draws back on being touched, it suggests that touch is an unwanted form of contact on that occasion. Le May and Redfern (1987) in reviewing the literature on touch and older people suggest that appropriate use of touch can enhance communication. Touch such as holding a hand can communicate empathy and a nurse's willingness to listen or just be with the person, when they may no longer have the strength and energy to talk. A single touch on the arm or hand may encourage and extend concentration, particularly for people with mental impairment, or provide orientation for those with sensory impairments. Touch and intimacy are discussed in detail in Chapter 15.

Stereotyping Older People through Use of Language

Beliefs and attitudes held by other age groups about older people can lead to instances of inappropriate and inaccurate communication. Biggs (1993) suggests three factors that contribute to intergenerational misunderstanding:

- Older people's lives are accorded less status and communication with them is perceived as a waste of time.
- The age-graded society in which we live affords little opportunity for interchange between age cohorts.
- Lack of empathy with older people because it is impossible to have direct experience of what it is like to be old.

Biggs discusses the findings of intergenerational sociolinguistic studies. Uncharacteristic of usual conversational norms, some of the older subjects on the first encounter, talked readily of health-related problems (termed painful self-disclosure) and revealed their age. The younger listeners responded to the former with politeness but judged these revelations to be socially insensitive and self-centred. They reacted positively and enthusiastically to the revelations of advancing age with such expressions as, 'Gosh, you don't look it!' The 'gift of praise' is the acceptable intergenerational response that rewards in the short-term and provides a ritualised negotiation of an otherwise problematic encounter (Biggs, 1993, p. 77). While both of these topics are highly appropriate to nurse and patient communication, younger nurses at the beginning of their career may have already formed stereotypical views as a result of experiences akin to the study group. Younger people also tend to make ageist assumptions about the language competence of older people, denigrating older speakers as 'doddery', 'vague' and 'rambling'. These assumptions influence their expectations and the ways in which they interact with older people (Giles, 1991). As a result, younger people may over-accommodate speech to meet stereotypical communication deficits in older individuals. Such speech is slow, of low grammatical complexity and consists of overly simple vocabulary. Articulation is unnecessarily slow, the voice tone in which it is delivered is demeaning or too familiar and overall the quality of talk is low (Hummert, 1994). Alternatively, communicators may choose to distance themselves from the negatively stereotyped individual and under accommodate their speech to the needs of the older adults. They may use unfamiliar vocabulary such as slang words and speak more softly or more rapidly than normal.

An extreme form of patronising speech, known as secondary baby talk, is delivered in a high pitched voice and has wide pitch variations. It is commonly addressed to older people in institutional settings. In one study, the older people reported a preference for this type of speech because it conveyed a sense of caring and nurturing, even though the content was demeaning. The constant use of patronising speech

16.6 A Sociolinguistic Model for Analysis of Discourse

In any interaction there is a sender, a receiver and a message. Communication breaks down because of problems in the following areas:

Acoustics
- It is noisy.
- The receiver has a hearing deficit.

Phonology and syntax
- One of the parties has an unfamiliar accent or dialect.
- Neurological or physiological problems affecting formation of speech.

Lexicon
- Participants do not share same vocabulary.
- Medical jargon or abbreviations are used.

Conceptions
- The meaning of the message in conceptual terms is not shared by sender and receiver.

Intent
- The reasons underlying the sender's statement or question have been misinterpreted by the receiver.

Credence
- Refers to the belief that one speaker places in the other's words.
- Does the speaker have the knowledge and authority to say that and are they correct?

Source: VanCott ML. Communicative competence during nursing admission interviews of elderly patients in acute care settings. *Qual Health Res* 1993, 3: 184–208.

---

by carers, particularly in institutional settings, may reinforce age-stereotyped behaviours, constrain opportunities for communication and psychological development, and result in loss of personal control and self-esteem; the older individual is never allowed to achieve true self-expression. The effects of such talk are often insidious and go unrecognised, yet caring organisations which fail to address training needs in the domain of communication cannot claim to be providing individualised care.

Working Towards More Effective Communication

The communication needs of older people are little different from those of other people needing care. However, to communicate effectively and without bias nurses must first examine their own attitudes towards older people and ask themselves whether any prejudices are revealed in their day-to-day communication with older clients. A sound knowledge base and confidence in their own communicative abilities will enable them to make a rapid assessment of each client's communication needs. VanCott (1993) applies a sociolinguistic model (**Box 16.6**) to analyse hospital admission interviews with older patients. The model can be applied to any verbal interaction and students on a post-registration course have used it to assess their own interview skills. This could be done by having a trusted third party sit in to assess competence in the designated areas, or by tape recording the interview. The latter course of action obviously requires that the older person give their permission. In this instance, approval from the local nursing ethics committee was also required.

SUMMARY

Throughout this chapter the intention has been to convey the sustenance derived from thriving primary and secondary relationships. Nurses often develop close ties with older people because they are with them during their most vulnerable moments. They have a privileged position in relation to older people and must be aware of the quality of their relationships. Often they become like family, particularly to patients in care homes. Their role is to help support existing relationships and attempt to find ways in which older people can find substitutes for those lost or no longer available. We might view nurses as providing transitional caring relationships that sometimes evolve into personal attachments of great significance to the nurse and the older person.

KEY POINTS

- The majority of older people have sustaining social networks, though an increasing number of very old people are at risk of social isolation.
- Families are supportive to their older members and take on complex caring roles.
- Friends and peer groups provide mutual support and self-esteem for older people.
- It is important for nurses to differentiate between loneliness and the client's wish to be alone.
- Communication is key to the formation of successful relationships throughout life. Barriers may stem from client and nurse.

AREAS AND ACTIVITIES FOR STUDY AND REFLECTION

- Are there any types of social support network particular to the area where you practice? Select a client who illustrates this and describe their social support network.
- Select a client with dementia who is receiving intensive family care and support and reflect on the caring relationship in the light of Nolan's typology.
- What facilities and services exist in your area to support carers?
- Reflect on your own communicative competence with older clients by applying VanCott's sociolinguistic model to an initial nursing interview.

REFERENCES

Abrams M. *Beyond three score years and ten*, First Report, London, Age Concern England, 1978.

Adams RG. Service support of elderly women by friends. *Gerontologist* 1983, 23:221.

Adams RG. People would talk: normative barriers to cross-sex friendships for elderly women. *Gerontologist* 1985, 25:605.

Adams RG. Patterns of network change: a longitudinal study of friendships of elderly women. *Gerontologist* 1987, 27:223.

Anderson M. *What is new about the modern family: an historical perspective*, British Society for Population Studies, The Family, Office of Population Censuses and Surveys Occasional Paper 31, London, 1983, OPCS.

Armstrong-Esther CA, Browne KD. The influence of elderly patient's mental impairment on nurse-patient interaction. *J Adv Nurs* 1986, 11:379–387.

Armstrong-Esther CA, Browne KD, McAfee JE. elderly patients: still clean and sitting quietly. *J Adv Nurs* 1994, 19:264–271.

Askham J. The married lives of older people. In: Arber S, Ginn J, eds. *Connecting gender and ageing*. Buckingham: Open University Press, 1995.

Audit Commission. *What seems to be the matter: communication between hospitals and patients*. London: National Health Service Report No. 12, 1993.

Biggs S. *Understanding ageing. Images, attitudes and professional practice*. Buckingham: Open University Press, 1993.

Bowers BJ. Inter-generational caregiving: adult caregivers and their aging parents. *Adv Nurs Sci* 1988, 9:20–31.

Bowling A, Browne PD. Social networks, health and emotional well-being among the oldest old in London. *J Gerontol Soc Sci* 1991, 46:20–32.

Bowling A, Leaver J, Hoeckel T. *A survey of the health and social service needs of people aged 85 and over living in city and Hackney*, Department of Community Medicine, City and Hackney Health Authority, 1988.

Burnside I. *Working with older adults: group practices and techniques*. Boston MA: Jones and Bartlett, 1994.

Central Health Monitoring Unit. *The health of elderly people: an epidemiological overview*, London, 1992, HMSO.

Cherlin A, Furstenberg F. Styles and strategies of grandparenting. In: Bengston V, Robertson J, eds. *Grandparenthood*. London: Sage, 1985.

Connidis IA, Davies L. Confidants and companions: choices in later life. *J Gerontol* 1992, 47:115.

Culhane M, Dobson H. Groupwork with elderly women. *Int J Geriatr Psychiatry* 1991, 6:415–418.

Cunningham-Burley S. Becoming a grandparent. *Ageing and Society* 1986, 6:453–470.

D'A Slevin O. Ageist attitudes among young adults: implications for a caring profession. *J Adv Nurs* 1991, 16:1197–1205.

Donaldson JM, Watson R. Loneliness in elderly people: an important area for nursing research. *J Adv Nurs* 1996, 24:952–959.

Field D, Minkler M, Falk RF *et al*. The influence of health and family contacts and family feelings in advanced old age: a longitudinal study. *J Gerontol* 1993, 48(1):18.

Fielding P. *Attitudes revisited: an examination of student nurses' attitudes towards older people in hospital*, London: Royal College of Nursing, 1986.

Finley N, Roberts D, Banahan B. Motivators and inhibitors of attitudes of filial obligation toward aging parents. *Gerontologist* 1988, 28:73.

Ford P. What older people value in nurses. In: Ford P, Heath H, eds. *Older people and nursing: issues of living in a care home*. London: Butterworth Heinemann, 1996.

Francis G, Baly A. Plush animals. *Geriatr Nurs* 1986, 7:140–142.

George LK, Gwyther LP. Caregiver well-being: a multidimensional examination of family caregivers of demented adults. *Gerontologist* 1986, 26:253.

Gerontology Data Service. *Getting around after 60: a profile of Britain's older population*. London: HMSO, 1996.

Giles H. 'Gosh, You Don't Look It!' A sociolinguistic construction of ageing. *Psychologist* 1991, 3:99–106.

Green H. *Informal carers*. Office of Population Censuses and Surveys Social Survey Division Series GH5 No. 15, Supplement A, London, 1988, HMSO.

Grundy M. Population review: (5). *The population aged 60 and over*, Population Trends No. 84, London, 1996, OPCS.

Hummert ML. Stereotypes of the elderly and patronising speech. In: Hummert ML, Wiemann JM, Nussbaum JF, eds. *Interpersonal communication in older adulthood*. London: Sage, 1994.

Jarvis C. *Family and friends in old age and the implications for informal support: Evidence from the British Social Attitudes Survey of 1986*. London: Age Concern Institute of Gerontology and Joseph Rowntree Foundation, 1993

Jerrome D. The significance of friendship for women in later life. *Ageing and Society* 1981, 1:175–197.

Jerrome D. Intimate relations. In: Bond J, Coleman P, Peace S, eds. *Ageing in society*. London, Sage, 1993.

Keith P, Wacker R. Sex roles in the older family. In: Brubaker T, ed. *Family relationships in later life*, 2nd edition. London: Sage, 1990.

Kimmel DC. The families of older gay men and lesbians. *Generations* 1992, 17:37.

King C, Macmillan M. Documentation and discharge planning for elderly patients. *Nurs Times* 1994, 90:31–33.

King's Fund Centre. Carer's needs – a 10-point plan for carers. *Community Care* 1989, 30:

Kivnick H. Grandparenthood: A overview of meaning and mental health. *Gerontologist* 1982, 22:59.

Kivnick H. *The meaning of grandparenthood*. Ann Arbor, Michigan: UMI Research Press, 1983.

Lanceley A. Use of controlling language in the rehabilitation of the elderly. *J Adv Nurs* 1985, 10:125–135.

Laslett P. *Family life and illicit love in earlier generations*. Cambridge: Cambridge University Press, 1977

Lee L, Lee M. *Absent friend: coping with the loss of a treasured pet*. Henston Press, 1992.

Le May A, Redfern S. A study of non-verbal communication between nurses and elderly people. In: Fielding P, ed. *Research in the nursing care of elderly people*. Chichester: John Wiley & Sons Ltd, 1987.

Nichols K, Jenkinson J. *Leading a support group*. London: Chapman & Hall, 1991

Nolan M. Busy doing nothing: activity and interaction levels amongst differing populations of elderly patients. *J Adv Nurs* 1995a, 22:528–538.

Nolan M, Keady J, Grant G. Developing a typology of family care: implications for nurses and other service providers. *J Adv Nurs* 1995b, 21:256–265.

Nussbaum JF. Friendship in older adulthood. In: Hummert ML, Wiemann JM, Nussbaum JF, eds. *Interpersonal communication in older adulthood*. London: Sage, 1994.

Office of Population Censuses and Surveys, General Household Survey. London: HMSO. 1991.

Pursey A, Luker K. Attitudes and stereotypes: nurses'work with older people. *J Adv Nurs* 1995, 22:547–555.

Quereshi H, Walker A. *The caring relationship: elderly people and their families*. London: Macmillan, 1989.

Reisman J. An indirect measure of the value of friendship for aging men. *J Gerontol* 1988, 43:109.

Rose H, Bruce E. Mutual care but differential esteem: caring between older couples. In: Arber S, Ginn J, eds. *Connecting gender and ageing*. Buckingham: Open University Press, 1995.

Salvage AV, Vetter NJ, Jones DA. Opinions concerning residential care. *Age Ageing* 1989, 18:380–386.

Schofield I. A historical approach to care. *Elderly Care* 1994, 6:14–15.

Scott JP. Sibling interaction in later life. In: Brubaker TH, ed. *Family relationships in later life*. Newbury Park: Sage Publications, 1992.

Stockwell F. *The unpopular patient*. London: Royal College of Nursing, 1972.

Tate LA. Life satisfaction in elderly women. *Gerontologist* 1982, 22:89.

Thompson P, Itzin C, Abendstern M. *I don't feel old*. Oxford: Oxford University Press, 1991.

Tornstam L. Dimensions of loneliness. *Aging* 1990, 2:259.

University of Warwick. *Pets and people in residential care*, Social Care Research Findings No. 44, Joseph Rowntree Foundation, 1993.

VanCott ML. Communicative competence during nursing admission interviews of elderly patients in acute care settings. *Qual Health Res* 1993, 3:184–208.

Victor CR. *Old age in modern society*. London: Chapman & Hall, 1994.

Wells D. Biographical work with older people. In: Barnes E, Griffiths P, Ord J, Wells D, eds. *Face to face with distress*. London: Butterworth Heinemann, 1998.

Wells TJ. *Problems in geriatric nursing care*. Edinburgh: Churchill Livingstone, 1980.

Wenger C. Support networks in old age: constructing a typology. In: Jeffery S, ed. *Growing old in the twentieth century*. London: Routledge, 1989.

Wenger C. A comparison of urban with rural support networks: Liverpool and North Wales. *Ageing and Society* 1995, 15:59–81.

Wenger GC. Dependence, independence and reciprocity after 80. *J Aging Stud* 1987, 1:355–377.

Wilson G. Women's work: the role of grandparents in intergenerational transfers. *Sociological Review* 1987, 4:703–720.

USEFUL ADDRESSES

Pro-Dogs grief counselling scheme for pet owners
Rocky Bank,
4 New Road,
Ditton,
Kent ME20 6AD.
Tel: 01732 848499

Pets As Therapy (PAT Cats and Dogs),
Sue Gaywood,
General Manager,
6 New Road,
Ditton,
Aylesford,
Kent, ME 20 6AD.
Tel 01732 872222.

Carers National Association,
Ruth Pitter House,
20/25 Glasshouse Yard,
London EC1A 4JS.

The Relatives Association,
5, Tavistock Place,
London WC1H 9SN.
Tel 0171 916 6055.
A forum for relatives and friends of older people in care homes.

Self-esteem

17 Transitions
Diane Wells

LEARNING OBJECTIVES

After studying this chapter you will be able to:

- Explain the nature of psychosocial transition and utilise theoretical frameworks in order to explain the transitions characteristic of later life.
- Discuss the nurse's role in caring for people in transition.
- Compare the differences you might expect in adaptation to retirement between an individual who was encouraged to take early retirement and one who chose to work until statutory retirement age.
- Appreciate the complexity of reaction to grief.
- Appreciate the significance of 'home' and discuss the psychosocial issues surrounding a move in later life.
- Discuss how older people might manage the change from independence to dependence, as a result of bodily changes.

INTRODUCTION

In this chapter five transitions which frequently occur in later life will be considered.

- Retirement.
- Bereavement.
- Widowhood.
- Moving home.
- Transitions of the body.

Before considering these five transitions, the theoretical frameworks underpinning the chapter will be reviewed briefly.

- The biographical approach to assessment.
- Maslow's theory of development
- Parkes Theory of psychosocial transition.
- Stress.

Transitions are perceived as times that offer opportunities for personal development, although the process may be difficult and sometimes very painful. Feelings aroused during transitions are usually normal and serve a function of helping the necessary changes take place (Nichols, 1993).

There is often a sense of loss and grief during transitional phases. Even when there is no grief experienced, the change and newness of situations may lead to uncertainty. Many nurses expect to support clients who are bereaved, facing widowhood, coping with body changes or those moving to new accommodation. The idea of supporting people who face retirement may be less obvious as a nursing role. However, retirement is a powerful experience which has important implications for health. Many clients seeking help with other issues around the time of retirement may benefit from a prac-tice nurse (for example) offering to discuss the retirement experience. Further, if nurses are involved in preventive health care this could usefully include preparation for retirement.

A transition is a period of time when change is taking place, and yet 'transition' suggests much more than 'change'. A change may occur very quickly but the term transition suggests a process which may take a long time: it may take weeks, or months or years. For example, when changing jobs, moving house or making new relationships, the experience for the individual at this time is much more than 'seeing new faces' and 'travelling to new places'. There are usually many aspects to learn about and new skills to develop, whether the change has been chosen or not. There are gains and losses, and perhaps unexpected feelings. New situations, even when planned for, may bring surprises. These new demands are opportunities for personal development. The concept of personal development is preferred here to adaptation, as the former emphasises the effort made by the individual and potential for positive outcomes. Adaptation is unfortunately, often understood as a passive process, of fitting in or conforming to constraints. In later life, most people experience many transitions related to their experiences of the following:

- Employment.
- Retirement.
- Relationships, particularly bereavement.
- Residence.
- Health and dying.

Personal development is as much a feature of later life as it is of other adult years. When so many demands for change are made upon the individual at this time, we cannot, as has often been the case, regard later life as a time of inevitable stasis.

A Biographical Approach to Assessment and Understanding Older People

This is the most important framework for the chapter because transitions are best understood within the context of the life span. The life a person has lived, the values and meanings developed over time, all have an impact upon the way in which transitions are managed. Such an understanding can help the nurse to perceive reasons for behaviour, and can provide the necessary information to support the sense of continuity during times of change.

Taking a biographical approach to the care of older people has been an important development in social gerontology (Gearing and Coleman, 1996; Johnson, 1991), and is increasingly identified in nursing (Schofield, 1994; Wells, 1998) as offering methods to improve assessment, understanding, therapeutic practice and possibly generating theory. Listening to the patient's story, or pieces of the story which are offered, can help the nurse relate the care she gives to the patient's needs. Also, telling the story can be therapeutic for the patient, and can help to create a partnership between the patient and nurse. Finally, and perhaps most importantly, hearing the patient's story can help the nurse perceive the world as a particular patient sees it.

Whatever changes are taking place, whatever transitions people are experiencing, past, present and future are all important: as we experience new situations we are often flooded with powerful memories. Parkes' theory of psychosocial transitions (see below) reiterates the point, and fits easily with a biographical approach to care. When the nurse and patient together can recognise what has been valued by the patient and what is being lost, then it is more likely that feelings can be explored and a sense of continuity can be maintained.

Some of the changes that are experienced by older people occur very quickly when, for example, illness or bereavement precipitates a move into a residential home. If an older person were asked at that point 'What would you like?' it may be difficult to gain a clear expression of their wishes. It may be a time of crisis and as Johnson (1991) points out, the answer to such questions rarely lies on the surface. Practitioners need to use any time they have to anticipate likely decisions and transitions by building up 'an authentic picture' (Johnson, 1991) of the person. The real picture is the one given by the client themselves. Telling and listening to stories about the patient's life is often enjoyable for both nurse and patient, but it may also be difficult. Getting close and being involved with any patient poses questions such as:

- How close is close enough?
- Might it hurt her or me?
- Might I get in deep water?
- How do I get out?
- Am I doing the right thing?

This will be discussed below in the section on stress.

Maslow's Theory of Development

Since this is the organising framework for this book, it is pertinent to look for features of Maslow's theory that reflect issues addressed in this chapter. (The reader is also recommended to read the section on Erikson's (1980) theory of psychosocial development in Chapter 2).

Maslow's theory is concerned with personal growth. In his elaboration of this idea he makes two statements which are very relevant for nursing older people:

No psychological health is possible unless (the) essential core of the person is fundamentally accepted loved and respected by others and himself.

Capacities clamour to be used and cease their clamour only when they are well used.

(Maslow, 1968.)

The first statement may be particularly significant for elders with few social contacts, or during times when relationships are disrupted. The second statement concerning the use of capacities is particularly relevant for health promotion activities with more active elders.

If we accept Maslow's idea that psychological health is only possible when a person is given and gives to themselves acceptance, respect and love then practitioners have a responsibility to assess whether a client is in receipt of these and able to feel worthy of such. If the answer is 'no' to any of these, then there is responsibility to consider the appropriate action. This is not to suggest that these requirements for health (acceptance, respect and love) can or should be provided at all times and in all situations. Usually acceptance and respect are present, but in stressful situations staff may admit to finding that their acceptance of and respect for a particular person is under strain. Furthermore, relationships between practitioners and clients do not always include 'love'. Many clients receive love from other sources, but among older clients the socially isolated are often over-represented, so it is likely that some older people do not receive the love that Maslow suggests is necessary for health. Some older people survive on memories of love and some manage with stoicism, but the distress sometimes observed in older people may be an indication of their feeling unloved and unlovable. Erikson considers later life to be a time for review and evaluation. Those who dislike what they perceive of their own lives may end their days feeling disgust and despair, or in Maslow's terms in a state of ill health.

When Maslow wrote 'Capacities clamour to be used and cease their clamour only when they are well used' (Maslow, 1968) he seems to have unwittingly indicated some of the health needs of those facing retirement (see Savage, 1995, p. 58–63, for a discussion of love in nursing).

For many people, later life, especially the early years following retirement, is a time for growth and development. Many in their fifties, sixties and seventies demonstrate Maslow's idea of people searching for developmental opportunities, or are relieved that they can at last engage in activities which had alluded them while in full time employment.

A Theory of Psychosocial Transition

Parkes (1993) describes a theory of psychosocial transition (PST) to explain how the developmental process referred to above takes place. He says it is the sense of 'grief' which can stimulate change. Parkes' examples of PSTs are bereavement following the death of a spouse, loss of sight or loss of a limb. It is, however, not the specific event that distinguishes a PST, since not all bereaved people have the same sort of experience and not all grief is caused by bereavement. 'Grief' he explains is an emotion that draws us toward something or someone that is missing. It happens when there is a 'discrepancy between the world that is and the world that should be'. This 'should be' is the model or internal construct created by an individual while relating to the situation that is now lost. This explains so well those experiences of, for example, the bereaved spouse who 'hears' her husband's key turn in the lock.

The internal world that has to change consists of all the assumptions made about daily life, in relation to this now absent person, part, bodily function or home. It takes time for the assumptive world to change, and during this time the sense of grief draws the emotions towards that which is lost. Although painful this serves a function: it is this which stimulates the change. The old ways of relating are eventually extinguished because they do not fit. As a person finds appropriate ways to relate to the changed situation so a new assumptive world is created.

Stress

Psychosocial Care and Stress

If times of transition are developmental opportunities which involve a sense of loss and pain then a nurse who gets to know such a client and their life and values, may experience some stress from being close. The closeness suggested here takes time and is only appropriate if the client wishes it.

Training and support are essential, and need to be built into the framework of the organisations concerned with patient care (Nichols, 1995). The experience of being listened to and respected in one's endeavours can sustain the nurse to return to the patient and offer to listen as a patient expresses her needs, wishes, desires and distress. Maslow's ideas about the requirements for mental health hold good for nurses as well as patients! Some patients prefer to contemplate alone but still require skilled nurses to make the offer of help and understand the response.

A nurse who regularly has the experience of being listened to herself is more likely to be able to listen to others as they work out how to manage their transitions.

RETIREMENT

Retirement traditionally marks the time when work ceases, and a new phase which is characterised by increased rest and leisure starts. For as long as there has been a state retirement pension, men at the age of 65 years and women at the age of 60 years could, after about forty years of employment, look forward to around 10 years of doing what they wanted. Within this generalisation there have always been variations. Some of this variation is individual and some according to gender. For many women the distinction between 'work' and 'not work' was less clear cut, firstly because many had been in part-time work, and secondly, having taken more responsibility for home care, 'work' is more continuous whether in employment or not.

Whatever the variations, there was a general pattern of retirement occurring at around 60 to 65 years, and the preceding employment time usually far exceeded the retirement period. The ratio was about 4:1. Now the pattern has changed dramatically. As unemployment increases, so the phenomenon of early retirement increases also. Since the 1970s, older members of the workforce have been made redundant, offered incentives to take redundancy, or offered early retirement, sometimes with financial inducement or sometimes without. It is not uncommon in the 1990s for a person to leave work in their early fifties, having completed thirty years work, and looking forward to probably thirty years of active life. The ratio of work to retirement, counted as decades, has changed from 4:1 to 3:3.

At the same time, the working life is changing for many people. Those in work have a less secure position, with more part-time jobs than the previous generation, and so work and retirement are evolving as different things with changed meanings. It may be that with less availability of work more people will have lives that are a mosaic of part-time jobs, education and leisure. When that becomes a common experience the transition between employment and retirement may be replaced by a transition between employment and reduced employment, thus easing the process. In the meantime, many who are leaving work early are those who have given most of their energies to work, and for whom work has provided a major source of identity. As long as the life span is segmented according to age and economic activity (by which is meant work which is paid for), this transitional period will be important.

The conventional retirement which coincided with the state pension was often seen as a reason to give a party and review the working life to mark the event. That may make some contribution to acknowledging the transition, but it is likely that people need also the time and attention to consider what this event means for them. For the person it is not just an 'event', it takes longer than the party, it is a 'process', which requires psychological work.

When early retirements occur, colleagues often seem uncertain about what to do. It is a good idea to start, as in other health promotion activities, with asking the individual concerned. The offer needs to be made. The retiree may well want to review her or his working life, even if they plan to continue working. Ceasing to be a full-time employee and taking part-time work within the same organisation changes the working relationships, and so it is important to explore what this means for the individual and the group.

The long retirement phase, often spanning 30–40 years, has prompted a distinction to be made between third and fourth ages (Laslett, 1996). The third age is defined as the time following full-time employment, when people have the interest, energy and commitment to fulfil many important roles, and also probably involve themselves in a variety of leisure pursuits. The fourth age is the time of increased frailty when a degree of dependence is inevitable, and many of the roles and pastimes will probably have to be relinquished. Laslett (1996) has written extensively about this, and sees the third age as a time of personal fulfilment (which could be equated with Maslow's 'self-actualisation') as well as a time of community responsibility. Laslett thinks that many older people are willing to offer their skills to ensure that features of the heritage are protected and passed on. He would like to see libraries, historic houses and galleries kept open for longer hours by older people.

The success of the university of the third age (Laslett, 1996) is already a testament to the willingness of some retired people to give to the community, albeit in that case a community of other older people. Providing a workforce to extend the opening hours of libraries and galleries is also an intergenerational activity and so would mitigate against the separation of the generations. Many high streets, whose commercial life is placed in jeopardy by out of town supermarkets, are already being kept alive by the contribution of elders in charity shops. Such contribution of elders is frequently voluntary, but by no means peripheral: the jobs they do for free are important supports to the community life. Economic production, which measures only paid employment, is misleading.

Helping the Psychosocial Transition of Retirement

Times of change are usually times of continuity and discontinuity, or as Marris (1986) explains when considering 'loss and change' there is a need 'to preserve the threads of meaning'. Sudden changes involving many aspects of life are usually difficult to manage. If just some things change and some remain constant then there is time to change the 'assumptive world' (Parkes, 1993). Discussion with a respective retiree might usefully focus on:
• The experience of the working life.
• What has been valuable?
• What was felt to be difficult or a waste of time?

When this work is completed then the prospective retiree can consider questions such as:
• What is going to be different?
• What is going to continue?

Each of these could be related to, firstly, interests, secondly, commitments and thirdly, roles. The discussant does not need to ask all the questions, as often the retiree will raise their own ideas and interests.

The topics that seem to be important will vary enormously. Books on retirement tend to have chapters on money, health, leisure, part-time work and voluntary work. These are the things that can be written about more easily as information can be given. As either a nurse or as a colleague, the important things to offer are time and skill, which enable the retiree to know that someone is interested in the retirement experience. However creative and energetic a person is about the opportunities available in retirement, a feeling of being 'dismissed' is hard to avoid, and the 'feeling' is often based on fact.

There is often a feeling within the retiree of identity disruption. Although this term has been used by sociologists to describe the experience of people managing their lives in the midst of a chronic illness, there are some similarities, in particular the feeling of being stigmatised, set apart and marked as someone outside the work group. One person observed 'It is interesting how quickly the expertise of a retired person is ignored. I know an expert farmer whose views were often sought until he retired, but then he was quickly de-skilled because people no longer wanted to listen to what he had to say'. Encouraging the prospective retiree to reflect on their career seems to be a crucial activity. Such a review allows the person to evaluate their work role and other aspects of the employment experience such as friendships at work. Many retirees will quickly make connections with the future looking at the continuities and discontinuities.

For those wanting to support future planning for retirement, Coleman and Chiva's (1991) 'coping with change' model offers a framework. This approach is suitable for situations where the prospective retiree has asked for this kind of help or agreed when it has been offered. If uninvited, these ideas might seem intrusive. The authors suggest that prospective retirees 'identify their experiences of change and transition in life and focus on their needs concerning yet another change called retirement'. The intention is to help both individuals and groups to:
• Analyse their understanding of change and transition by exploring their feelings and reactions to change.
• Identify the key issues of their retirement.
• Consider their choices and options.
• Assess their skills and the resources available to them to put their plans into action.

The implicit message in this is that although feelings may be at the beginning of the process, it is thoughts, plans and cognitive processes that are the likely or desired outcomes. This may not be desirable and may not be the reality. The plans may be 'hopes' that are full of emotional investment. Although Coleman and Chiva's outline is a useful framework to start with, each person using it needs also to test it and adapt it for their own and the client's needs (**Figure 17.1**). Although the authors suggest a review of changes and transitions as the starting point, as suggested above, this could be preceded by a review of the retiree's career.

Young and Schuller (1991) studied the experiences of a group of retirees. Some had taken retirement at the state retirement age and others had retired early. Many who were made redundant in their fifties, but were then unable to find further work, felt themselves to be in a limbo situation. Employers often did not want to employ people of this age and so they were effectively 'retired' from the workforce, but this freedom from work did not lead to a freedom to do what they desired which was to work again. Also, many were not free to enjoy life because they were short of money and were ineligible for retirement benefits such as a state pension, a bus pass, or free National Health Service prescriptions. The sense of ambiguity experienced by the individual is well expressed by Mr L.

(Schuller, 1990.)

The date for Mr L's departure was fixed well in advance and the redundancy payment reasonably generous. He had no material worries. Why then was he thoroughly discontent? In part it was because of a lack of occupation. As a gardener and a handyman, Mr L could not fill his time with these activities. Attempts to serve as a volunteer for a charity dealing with the handicapped had not been successful, as he and his friend Mrs E had felt exploited by the professionals involved, who had allowed them to work while they themselves had drunk coffee in their own little clique. These experiences could happen to anyone (which is not to downgrade their importance to Mr L). The particular source of Mr L's unhappiness was his uncertainty about his own place in society. Being about the same age (60 years), Mrs E. had at least passed the official age of retirement. and although she was dissatisfied with the lack of outlet for her energy she had her own business as a part-time reflexologist. Mr L had no such structuring to his days or weeks. As he saw it, he was in a complete limbo from which he would not escape until he reached formal retirement age. This was symbolised by his yen for a free bus pass. It was not the money to be saved on the fares that mattered, nor was he particularly keen to be classed as a pensioner. But the mere fact of having a bus pass would have let him know where he stood in society's eyes and released him from his liminal state.

(Schuller, 1990.)

Young and Schuller found that those who were better paid when in work and those who owned their own houses were more likely to avoid the constraints of poverty. Having enough money to live on, however, is not the only measure of a satisfactory retirement, as the story of Mr L demonstrates. The lack of fit between being considered too old to work, but not old enough to receive the advantages of later life, may create an ambiguous status and feelings of uncertainty that the working life is over. One solution suggested by the researchers is for the government to make benefits available when the working life is over, rather than leaving people in the limbo land suffered by Mr L. This does not mean, however, that we accept the current trend to discard older workers at an increasingly early age. There is evidence that

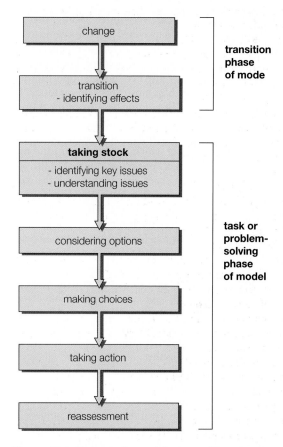

Figure 17.1 Coleman's model of transition.

employers take this option of discarding elders because it seems easy. More part-time jobs and retraining for older people would be ways of retaining their skills and put a brake on the ageism and segregation of older people. For every one person in the Greenwich study (Young and Schuller, 1991) who expressed a positive view of the retirement experience two expressed a negative view. It could be argued that granting the state pension at an ever-earlier age only reinforces the idea that older people are a passive group in society.

BEREAVEMENT

Bereavement in Later Life

In later life those with many close relationships among friends and family are likely to experience many losses. Only those who have avoided loving can avoid the sense of grief following bereavement. Older people are usually rather resilient following bereavement and this is probably because they have learned much from earlier losses. Even if the older person seems to manage the bereavement process without too many outward signs of turmoil that may belie the intense emotional impact following the death of a partner.

A widow said several months after her husband died, 'I

think people think I don't care very much because they see me coping but ... (her voiced quavered and tears came to her eyes) I do care, I did love him and miss him so much'. Perhaps she was indicating that, as she seems to cope, her friends no longer ask her how she is or give her enough opportunity to talk about how she misses him most. She went on to say, 'It's those times – I might just be coming back from the shops – it's hardly a thought it's more like a feeling... "Oh I'll tell him that ... oh of course he's not there ... so I can't."' This is an example of a 'pang' of grief which is so common, and may continue for months, or years or perhaps the rest of life. It is often brought on by some experience shared with the partner such as (here) daily conversation. We cannot know exactly how another person feels, but such stories have a poignancy which usually gets through to the listener.

A friend of this widow had herself been widowed twice, once at the end of the Second World War, after just a few years of marriage. Her second marriage was about 20 years later, and came to a rather abrupt end 10 years after that, when her husband died after a short illness. Observing her friend bereaved after nearly 50 years of marriage she said, 'I used to think, when I heard someone talk about their sadness after such a long marriage, "What are they complaining about? They've had all that time together." Now I realise when they've been together for so long, and done so much together, it's very hard to be alone again'.

It is almost inevitable to compare one's own plight with that of a friend, particularly when there are some similarities. This widow was, however, also ready to see that her own feeling of 'You are lucky to have had so long with your husband,' served to separate her from her friend. She gave up her old viewpoint and learnt to stand in a new place, to give more support.

Grieving

Following bereavement, multitudes of feelings are usually experienced, often shock and numbness first, even if the death is expected. One cannot be prepared in the sense of arranging one's feelings. CS Lewis captured some of his experience in A Grief Observed (recently made into first a successful stage play and then a film Shadowlands).

No one ever told me that grief felt so like fear. I am not afraid, but the sensation is like being afraid. The same fluttering in the stomach, the same restlessness the yawning. I keep on swallowing. At other times it feels like being mildly drunk, or concussed. There is a sort of invisible blanket between the world and me. I find it hard to take in what anyone says or perhaps hard to want to take it in. It is so uninteresting. Yet I want the others to be about me. I dread the moments when the house is empty. If only they would talk to one another and not to me.

Lewis had been close to H throughout her illness, and here he is talking about his own process, working through in his own unique way. No two people are the same in their response to death, but feelings often include:

- Numbness.
- Shock.
- Anger.
- Sadness.
- Despair.
- Loneliness.
- Regret.
- Frustration.
- Guilt.
- Anxiety.
- Self pity.
- Bitterness.

As noted by Lewis above, the experience is not confined to the brain; the whole body often suffers, with symptoms such as 'exhaustion, tension, restlessness, insomnia, apathy, loss of appetite and loss of weight' (Scrutton, 1995).

Individuals Who May Be Especially Vulnerable

The nature of grief, its length and possible complications are likely to be related to the personality of the bereaved, the nature of the relationship with the deceased and the context, which would include social support and other experiences of loss. One of the most difficult grief experiences is that following secret love, for example a gay relationship that has been kept secret or an extramarital relationship.

For those who love in secret ... grief must be hidden. There won't be any of those letters of sympathy, which mean so much, and there can be no talking about the loss to colleagues at work or to neighbours. We heard of a bereaved man whose cover was so good that the neighbour's only reaction to his friend's death was to ask if there was a room to let. Those who love in secret must mourn alone.
(Cave, 1993, p. 294.)

A man took his seriously ill partner to hospital. The two men had been lovers and lived together for over 20 years, but in the hospital, according to records, they were 'friends' and not 'next of kin'. Therefore, although one of them was dying in the accident and emergency department, the other was kept outside and not allowed to express his love at the most important time. Afterwards, the surviving partner told this story repeatedly, as if he could not come to terms with being prevented from comforting his lover for the last time.

One of the reasons for remaining at home during a terminal illness is to maintain relationships for the benefit of both the dying person and the circle of friends and family. The corollary of this is that when working in institutions, nurses have a particular responsibility to work with the family group and the patient group. This approach is well developed in some areas of practice, such as hospices, but even experienced workers readily admit there are many difficulties involved. It takes time to build up the team and the skills for this work (Saunders, 1990) but there are benefits for staff, clients, their families and friends.

Friends and relatives often rally round to offer emotional and physical help, and it all may be accepted, but also the bereaved person may choose not to accept all the offers. One woman said, 'After my husband died, I just wanted to be on my own, for a while – people seemed to find that difficult to understand, but that's how I felt'. People who do not have many friends or family are the most vulnerable, and most likely to need social and health-care services (Wenger, 1994). Wenger's research shows that older people who have few friends restrict their interactions with attitudes such as, 'I've always kept myself to myself' or 'I've always been a bit of a loner' are the ones most likely to need help (not just in relation to bereavement). Even if some of these people are very private and resist offers of help until absolutely necessary, nurses working with them can, over time, build up an 'authentic picture' (Johnson, 1986) and this may facilitate the offer of appropriate help.

Mourning, 'Gifts' and Continuity

It is often said that in twentieth-century Britain death is avoided and the bereaved are often left to manage as well as they can with little support. It is argued that the lack of formal mourning and for many the reduction of ritual practices means that 'life goes on' almost as if the death has not taken place, and those experiencing grief are expected to be private about their feelings. Although this is true for many people, nevertheless families and friends usually arrange a funeral with great care, and this activity can in itself give some comfort. Ensuring that the details of burial or cremation, a service and provision of food and drink for those who attend are all carried out 'as he would have wanted' can be the beginning of the healing process. It's as though the family and friends are saying 'he is not here ... but we are trying to do this as he would have wanted it to be done. We can continue to "be" and to behave with a sense of his "being" still with us'.

An increasing number of people want to arrange burials and memorial events which are devised and conducted by the friends and family of the deceased, or perhaps devised during the life of the deceased. *The Natural Death Handbook* (Albery *et al.* 1993) has extensive advice and accounts of experiences for those wishing to make individual arrangements; for example, a 'green burial' in a garden without a wooden coffin, or for relatives who wish to lay out a body themselves, as their last act of love. The information and stories in this handbook are proof that the conventional methods of burial or cremation orchestrated by undertakers and ministers of religion represent just some of the options available.

While arranging a funeral and for some time afterwards there is, for those who were close, usually a wish to remember the attributes and values of the person who has died. The memories may be sad, but contain also a sense of gratitude for the life that was lived and shared. These ideas of gratitude for the life are evident also in formal memorials whether they are in stone (statues) or in scholarship (awards or books), but they are also the material used in letters of condolence. This idea of wanting to acknowledge what one has gained from knowing the deceased is both commonplace and of some comfort.

In a book written for children, Varley (1985) explains this very well. She tells of how Badger lives in the wood with his friends. They have a happy life and enjoy each other's company. Badger is getting old and he tells his friends that he will probably be going down the 'long tunnel' soon. When he dies all his friends are so sad and wonder how they are going to manage without him. They sit together talking about their sadness, but then they begin to remember the things they have learnt from him; for example, frog says, 'Badger helped me to learn to skate'. As each remembers they tell the others of the 'gifts' given by badger. The author says, 'He had given them each a parting gift to treasure always'.

Friends and family often remember in a similar way and find it healing to treasure the 'gifts'. Marris (1986) explains this phenomenon as the search for 'threads of continuity' in the face of loss. The healing process cannot be forced: the bereaved person can derive comfort from knowing how others valued their loved one but each person finds their own way of recovery through grief. If someone else such as a professional suggested to a crying relative that remembering the good things would be helpful it might sound like a failure to recognise and respect the current sadness and distress. If, however, the bereaved can have the experience of feeling understood then they are more likely to remember the positive aspects.

Scrutton (1995) describes how, although he is an experienced manager of a residential home, it was only when depression was evident among residents and staff that he began to realise what might be the cause. During the previous few weeks three residents had died, and although superficially everything had been dealt with, it had been Christmas and staff had felt it necessary to carry on with the festivities. In discussion with the staff, everyone agreed this depression that was hanging over them was probably related to the three deaths, and the fact that very little time had been spent acknowledging the losses or helping people to grieve.

Once staff realised this they went to the residents to ask how they felt. The residents agreed they did not like the way things had been dealt with. When no one discussed the deaths, they said, they feared that when they died it would be the same – they would be gone and forgotten. When everyone had a chance to discuss the deaths, the memories, the feelings and the whole experience the atmosphere improved, the depression began to lift and people felt better. An alternative approach is to conduct a memorial service and invite all staff and relatives. This needs careful planning not only in relation to all the 'things' that need to be done, but also to prepare the staff psychologically: they will need time to 'think through' before the event about how they will respond to expressions of grief (Costello *et al.* 1996).

Providing Care for a Family

Information is a start, but it may not be enough, and a nurse may find herself in the midst of someone's response to bereavement.

A woman was being investigated for a heart condition in a medical ward. Her condition deteriorated and the ward doctor explained to her husband that his wife was quite ill, but the exact cause was not known. One evening unexpectedly she died. The staff attempted to resuscitate her, but failed. The woman's brother, not knowing what had happened, arrived to see her during the resuscitation attempt. On being told what had happened he was very upset. Also he was worried that other members of the family, including her husband, might be coming to the ward to see her. He seemed to want to prevent this from occurring, and so the ward sister asked if he would like her to phone the other family members. He thought this was the best thing to do, and wanted to speak to them on the phone also. The sister made the phone call and spoke to the husband first. He had other members of the family with him in the house. When the ward sister explained to him what had happened the husband shouted, 'You let her die how could you? You should have looked after her better. You had a day off on Monday'. The sister did not know what to say. She was not surprised by the upset, but she had thought that she, the doctor and other staff had done all they could and had kept the husband informed of what was happening in relation to his wife's care. She felt very troubled that evening and in the night. By the following morning she began to think, 'If someone close to me died, I suppose I might look for someone to blame, especially if it was unexpected'.

The following morning the sister was in the ward, working with patients, when suddenly she saw a large bunch of flowers had been placed on a table in the centre of the ward. They were to her, from the family of the woman who had died the night before. The ward sister wished she could have met with the family again to discuss the situation, but clearly the family did not want that. The situation seemed so incomplete, and that is probably how the family felt about the death. Nurses, and others working with terminally ill people and bereaved people, frequently 'feel the things which others are finding intolerable'. In psychological language this is called a 'projection'. All of us need people to hold our unwanted feelings at times, but in the midst of working life it is often very difficult to understand what is happening, and that is why the ward sister went over her actions wondering what she had done wrong. The accusation did not seem to 'fit'. Of course it did not 'fit' in any rational sense, but this was not rational it was a massive feeling from the husband of 'How could you let this happen?' This perfectly 'understandable' feeling on the part of the husband does not make it much easier for the ward sister or other person 'receiving the projection'.

Speck described a situation that was similar, but this time with a dying person who was very angry with him for being able to go on holiday. In conclusion Speck says, 'I, in my role as chaplain, needed some space in order to regain my ability to think'. He gained this having a discussion with the ward sister, but he urges, 'Such situations cry out for consultation for the staff group,' so that people can tolerate the ambivalence and carry on with the work (Speck, 1994, p. 100).

What is often called 'reassurance', which usually means saying such things as 'It will be OK', 'Try not to worry', or 'Don't upset yourself so', can be experienced as 'I don't want to know about all this'. These 'reassuring phrases' can leave people isolated rather than offering comfort. Fabricius (1991) quotes a tutor as saying, 'Giving "reassurance" is rather like throwing a fire blanket over the patient. It stops the nurse from catching fire whilst the patient is left burning inside'.

Clichés like 'Don't worry', are often said because the nurse feels overwhelmed and wonders when this sad despairing state is going to end or how the bereaved person is going to manage for the rest of that day. Having listened and shown interest, concern and if one feels it empathy, it may be helpful to ask, 'What are you going to do for the rest of the day?' or 'How is it going to be when you get home?' This does not deny the feelings, and nor does it take away the responsibility for self-care, but it does offer a discussion to consider how these feelings are going to be managed for the rest of the day.

Although we talk of 'thinking through' the event to prepare oneself, a crucial part of this work is *feeling through* the situations. That is what makes it such difficult work, and why much of this work in skill development has to be with people, not just texts.

THE WIDOWED LIFE

Becoming a widow or widower is, like other transitions, a time of change that relates closely to the past and the future. Wilson (1995) points out that widows and widowers face major changes relating to images of themselves, roles and relationships. The three issues are intertwined. The self does not stand alone but is closely associated with roles and relationships. Being a widow or widower means no longer being a husband or wife who relates to a spouse. To say this is stating the obvious, but it serves as a reminder when working with someone who has been widowed that it is important to consider what the marriage relationship has meant to that individual person, and what being a wife or husband has meant.

The loss of such an important relationship is usually one of the most traumatic events in a person's life. Also it brings with it major changes in a person's sense of identity. A telling example is the use of the word 'we'. In a couple relationship, people often talk of shared activities, shared ownership and shared ideas. In widowhood, frequently the sense of a shared life seems to continue in speech at least.

Several months after her mother's death a woman gently reminded her father that 'I' and not 'we' had been out, 'my' and not 'our' house was being painted. He tried to speak as a single person, but it usually came out as 'we' and 'our'. Eventually he found it too difficult and said, 'I've talked about life like this with your mother for so long, I can't change it now. I give up – does it matter?'

A widow who lives alone in a house which she has never shared with her husband often refers to matters relating to the house and garden as if she shared them with someone. Is this habit or a protection against feeling lonely?

Social networks are crucial to the wellbeing of older people, particularly those who are alone perhaps for the first time.

Women do have an advantage in this sphere at present. Throughout their lives, men tend to have less contact with family members and smaller social networks than do women (Wilson, 1995, p. 108). Often marriage has provided the husband with an entrée to friends and social events (Wilson, 1995, p. 105). Thompson's (1993, p. 689) study showed that widowed women look to their close friendships with other women for emotional support, and often do not feel a need to remarry. Men seem to look for similar features in their relationships with women also, and wish to marry them! As the numbers of women are much greater than the numbers of men among older people at present, it is perhaps fortunate that women are less keen on remarriage.

When widowhood follows a period of caring for a spouse it may be seen as an opportunity to increase social activity. Again it is easier for women than men. The mutual support so important among women is at present not an accepted norm for men in our culture (Scott and Wenger, 1995), and as men's life expectancy is shorter than women's, a man who has already cared for a terminally ill wife is likely to be quite frail himself. Additionally, the social network is usually smaller and often consists of his wife's friends (Wilson, 1995, p. 105).

Older people who are retired and married seem to rely quite heavily on the marriage for a sense of identity. When the identity of the wife or husband is no longer there, the task of creating a new identity may be taken on with energy and interest. The paucity of accepted roles in our society is, however, at times a block to this energy and interest. The marginal position of all retired people discussed in the section on retirement is of particular relevance for widows and widowers. Since society does not recognise and support many roles, especially for the oldest old, the creation of new roles in widowhood is not just an individual project, it is also a societal project. Those who are successful at the personal level may also have an opportunity to make an impact on wider groupings in society. Unfortunately, the picture at present is often not very hopeful at a micro level. Wilson (1995) states that people in her study often remarked on the constraints placed upon them by their own families:

> Widows and widowers who had the chance to alter the way they lived when no longer constrained by a partner often found that any attempt at a change was stopped or criticised by families. Children were recorded as disapproving of new relationships or constantly requesting parents not to take the risks involved in travelling to visit friends or going on holiday. Women were requested not to do their own housework and not to become vegetarian. Children were reported as generally controlling, and anti change.
>
> (Wilson, 1995, p. 111.)

If this is the prevalent pattern, or when this pattern is prevalent, widows and widowers may need to gain support from one another when seeking new ways and new roles. Wilson (1995, p. 113) herself suggests a 'new collectivity' may be a more fruitful approach to later life because she sees it as more attainable than the 'individual project' (involving reflection and self-fulfilment) often put forward as a way to live, especially in later years. The 'new collectivity' could also be a way of escaping the constraints of over-solicitous offspring. Maria Bengston (1997), an American gerontologist, is currently undertaking a research project to study shared living arrangements for older people, and she is looking particularly at projects set up by the elders themselves. In one she visited, 15 older women together purchased a block of 16 flats so that one flat could be used as communal space where the residents could meet and where communal domestic equipment, such as for laundry, could be sited. Such living arrangements recognise the individual's wish for privacy, autonomy, sharing and probably much support. The most important feature of this is that the living arrangements are devised by the people who are going to live together. Such projects may need particular private and state support, and possibly changes to financial, legal and attitudinal practices. For the elders it would be like setting up a new company and allow for a wide range of skills to be used or developed, and for new roles and relationships to emerge.

The commitment to the 'individual project' is now so well established in our society, it seems unlikely that it will be dropped and replaced with collectivity. Instead, the two principles of self-fulfilment and collective concern could coexist.

MOVING HOUSE? MOVING HOME? OR MOVING TO A 'HOME'?

One of the questions frequently asked of the recently bereaved is, 'Are you staying in the house?' Given what has already been said about the importance of continuity during a time of transition, clearly the decision to move house needs, if possible, to be left until the grief process is complete. 'Not that you ever get over it,' said one widow, 'but you learn to live with it'. Recovery from grief or 'living with it' can be defined as the time when the bereaved person has re-established an independent life.

Many people have no wish to move, and therefore stay in the house previously shared with others for as long as possible. At any one time, about 5% of people over 65 years of age are in institutions; but 60% die in institutions, so it seems most stay in their own homes, but are cared for in a hospital or home before they die. The wish to 'stay put' is often expressed in the words 'It's my home'. Clearly this means not only that 'This is where I live,' but also it suggests feelings such as 'It is right for me to be here, and not to be anywhere else'.

Whether older people remain where they have been for years, move to more convenient and smaller places, or relinquish their independence and go into a home, the word 'home' is bound to be used in discussion about the decision, and it will be said with considerable emphasis. A relative might ask 'would you want this to be your new "home"?' An older person may say, 'Are you suggesting that I make this my "home"?' A staff member of a nursing home might say, 'This is your "home" now'. Each person uses the same word but the meanings may be very different.

Meeting Transitional Needs

James Haskin had been a civil servant for more than 40 years. During the early years of his working life he stayed around in the North East of England. That's where he had grown up, and although most of his friends had moved away, he stayed and visited his parents every few weeks. He married Alison in his late twenties and moved to Sheffield, where they both worked, shared many interests and had some good friends. In their early fifties they decided to take early retirement and to move back quite close to where they both used to live, only a few miles from Alison's mother. She was the only one of their parents still alive.

They had only been in their new home a few months when Alison had a car crash. She was driving her mother to see an old friend one wintry day, when the car skidded, and crashed into an oncoming lorry. Alison was killed, and her mother survived, but was unable to walk again. James found it almost intolerable. He managed all the funeral arrangements, but hardly knew what he was doing. He looked after himself in a meticulous but heartless manner. He felt that if he could maintain the standards of housekeeping and cooking that he and Alison had shared, it might be alright. He had feelings, but they did not seem to be connected to anyone alive. His feelings, and his thoughts led always to the same questions, 'Why did it happen? What might I have done differently to prevent the accident?' and 'If we had never come to live here maybe, it would not have happened.'

Several weeks after the funeral, Alison's sister Hilary called, mainly it seemed to tell him she had arranged for her now disabled mother to go to a nursing home. James did not seem very interested, which caused his sister-in-law to remark on this. Then he started to shout and swear, until he felt little beads of perspiration were standing all over his face. Next, he seemed to crumble in pain, and sat down exhausted. 'I'm sorry,' she apologised. 'I'm sorry,' he said, 'and I feel awful, awful. I think something is happening to me. Can you get the doctor?' She dialled 999. The ambulance took him to hospital, where a myocardial infarction was diagnosed. James's pain settled, but he talked and talked, especially to his nurse. He was prescribed medication for any recurrence of cardiac pain, but while in hospital he had hardly needed it. He told the staff that he would like to get back home as soon as possible, and added, 'So much has happened recently, and I know this heart attack is another thing to cope with, but I think I better go home and see what I can do.' The staff agreed, but said they wanted him to attend a rehabilitation programme.

As a cardiac rehabilitation nurse you are contacted and asked if you can visit James before he leaves hospital. The ward nurse is able to give you this story because James said he wanted you to know why he has been in such a state recently.

- What are Mr. Haskin's comments that provide subjective evidence?
- What other information would you want to obtain in order to provide support to Mr. Haskin during this rehabilitation stage?
- Suggest two unmet needs that may be the most significant to Mr. Haskin's at this time.
- Suggest the nursing aims for each unmet need, reflecting realistic outcomes and using concrete and measurable terms.
- Suggest one or more interventions for each area of unmet need, justifying your choice of intervention.

Sixsmith (1990) is one of the few researchers who has conducted research to find out what a group of older people meant by 'home' and how this differed from the views of employed younger people and unemployed younger people. He found that some 'meaning categories' were common to all three groups such as they all felt that home meant 'comfort', 'family', 'do what you want', and 'it's what you make it'. Other ideas such as 'memories' and 'good neighbours' were important only to the older group, whereas 'self' and 'possessions' were important to younger people only. Looking at older people's ideas about home in more depth he found three themes:

- Home focus.
- Independence.
- Attachment to home.

Home focus meant that the home becomes more important in later life because an individual's activities are more restricted and the home is a secure place of refuge.

Independence is far from being an abstract idea; Sixsmith explains that it is actually 'grounded in the material world'.

The home plays an important part in framing the experience of independence and identity in the world through affordance of control.

(Sixsmith, 1990, p. 8l.)

Attachment was related to memories that have at least two functions: remembering can be a process of re-evaluating (Butler, 1963) or it may be a way of expanding the experience. When lives seem humdrum and superficial, memories can release people from the present. He quotes Rowles who thinks that fantasy and remembering can make you free. Some feel that their home is essential to preserve continuity with the past and to leave it would be like leaving the past behind.

Many older people, with their partners, or alone, do move house and usually satisfactorily, but Sixsmith's research gives some important pointers for consideration. To reiterate – among the group of older people studied, firstly, the home was extremely important as the basis for independence and, secondly, memories and good neighbours were greatly valued.

A widow stayed in the family home for about 4 years following the death of her husband. Then she moved to a smaller, more convenient house. After the move, thinking about the gains and losses she said, 'There were so many memories in the old house, but nothing has happened here'. When she had been there for a few weeks it was coming up to her birthday, so, rather unusually for her, she decided to have a birthday party. Afterwards she said, 'Everyone knows where I am now, and I have now at least one event to look back on here'. Myerhof (1984) has pointed out that there are few rituals associated with later life. Often older people assume that little notice will be taken of them, but when celebrations are suggested they may be quite glad to be the focus of attention for a while.

The decision to move from one's own home to a home organised by professionals, or to be part of someone else's household, for example moving in with a relative, is likely to involve all kinds of feelings. It is often one of the most important decisions in later life, especially since it is so often irreversible. Making such a decision, when feeling unable to sustain an independent existence is likely to arouse within the older person a wish to review the past, and consider how the idea of home can be sustained or if it is actually going to be relinquished. Such consideration, however, is often absent, as Nolan's study showed. He found that clients, carers and professionals all seem to avoid acknowledging the possibility of the client moving to a home. Planning was prevented partly because anticipatory thinking made the carers feel guilty. The value of making a biographical assessment (Johnson, 1986; Gearing and Coleman, 1996) is evident again here. Those nurses who are in contact with older people could, as explained in the introduction, observe and listen to their clients to gain 'an authentic picture' (Johnson, 1986),

perceiving the world as they see it and understanding what has been important throughout their lives and in the present. By observing and listening it is possible to:

- Elicit older people's attitudes to a broad range of things.
- Understand family relationships.
- Find out about relationships between carers and the older person.
- Discover various kinds of help and services which would be acceptable and unacceptable.
- Relate to, and understand, people labelled as 'difficult'.
- Hear how people coped with past difficulties and hardships with a view to how they might cope in the future.
- Understand and relate to people who suffer dementia'(Gearing and Coleman, 1996).

Gearing and Coleman describe the use of this approach in relation to community care packages for people remaining in their own homes, but it is just as relevant for supporting the decision-making of those who are leaving their homes. With this complexity of understanding and empathy nurses may find themselves supporting more people to stay in their own homes. A carer (Waddington, 1996) described how he managed to procure an intensive package of care for his mother to remain in her own home, among all that she loved, until she died. Knowing what has been important, supporting an elder to clarify her needs, wishes and desires, can create a state of readiness to make a choice. Although such choices are often made in a hurry, the greater the clarity concerning wishes the better. Then options can be considered and choices made.

Unfortunately, the information is not always available for people to make the choices. Nolan states that his studies like their predecessors show that 'sufficient, clear and understandable information' continues to be unavailable (Nolan *et al.*, 1996, p. 270). It could be argued that this state of affairs is allowed to persist partly because the demands for this information have not been strong enough. Clarity concerning the wishes of potential residents may increase the pressure for improved information. In the meantime, when there is already a tendency to avoid thinking about the need to move, this lack of appropriate information can only make things worse. The preparation is so important. Nolan considers:

The processes preceding admission and the perceptions that these processes engender will influence and partly determine the quality of that admission and subsequent adjustment.

(Nolan *et al.*, 1996, p. 271.)

He distinguishes four perceptions of clients that interacted to shape the experience of admission:

- Desirability.
- Legitimisation.
- Reversibility.
- Continuity.

In other words, it is important whether or not a patient perceives the admission to a home or sheltered housing as:

401

- What they want.
- Appropriate.
- Able to be altered.
- Familiar – as a place, a group of people and the patterns of daily life.

This idea of perceived 'continuity', as in other psychosocial transitions, is crucial. Most of those studied by Nolan had not been involved in a positive planned choice for reasons explained above, but nevertheless were able to rationalise the move because they could see the reasons: 'it was possible to construct a personally coherent explanation of the move into care.' The most unhappy situations were those in which the client had no opportunity to explore options, the decision was taken out of their hands and was irreversible, and emotional care was absent.

It is sometimes difficult to know what 'emotional care' is, especially when much of the writing is focused on individuals, and much of the nursing experience is with groups. A recent study (Reed and Payton, 1996) of how residents 'construct familiarity', to ease the transition process when entering a home could be helpful. Even before admission the information that was important was concerned with linking biographies. One lady whose daughter had chosen the home for her said of it:

She (the daughter) told me that the matron knew me from when I worked in (a local shop), and I thought, well, that's nice, it doesn't feel so bad. I can't think who she is, of course, but I'll probably know her when I see her.

(Reed and Payton, 1996.)

The researchers were interested to find out how the residents took action to discover features of the home and people within it to create a sense of familiarity. Once there, the process continued, in a rather careful manner.

The development of special friendships is often but not always related to the initial social exchanges in the early days of residency. When talking about special friends in later interviews, participants will sometimes trace the history of the friendship to their first days in the home and it seems as if there is a limit to the numbers of people that they construct familiarity with.

Another said:

I got talking with a couple of people that I recognised from around the village, and that helped, then when I'd found my feet I got to know some more people that I didn't know before.

(Reed and Payton, 1996, p. 554.)

One resident found himself always placed between people with whom he was unable to converse, and although he mentioned this to the researchers it seemed not to be noticed by the staff, and he did not like to complain. So here again there is place for observing and trying to be in tune with what older people would like. Carers continue to be important for residents and vice versa. The transition to care means so many different things for carers too. There may be feelings of guilt, relief, confusion, anger and often great concern about whether the new arrangement is satisfactory. Frequently, the carers do not feel cared for during their transition. Family care needs skilled practitioners, teamwork and time. When in the midst of change and perhaps traumatic change the feelings of one member of the family may quite unconsciously engage a staff member in a relationship which is unhelpful to the wellbeing of others. For example, a new resident may express relief at getting away from her relatives which may be understood by staff as a complaint about the carers. It may then be difficult to hold a critical feeling at bay when seeing these carers again. In **Figure 17.2**, Maslow's hierarchy is used as a framework to explain the transition from home to a care home.

Working with the family group is a very skilled activity. As workers listen to each one they can find themselves feeling sympathetic to one and perhaps angry with another, yet aware of wanting to do the best for the client, *and* work with the family.

Nurses in an assessment ward were feeling quite worn out trying to work with a patient and her family. The patient was quite ill but was receiving medical and nursing care which was effective. She needed many hours of care each day which the nurses were happy to give. The strain they felt was from the family. The patient's three daughters and a son all telephoned, or visited separately each day and wanted to discuss their mother's care in detail with each contact. The named nurse explained that if the son and daughters could choose one liaison person that would be preferable. Having many people to relate to creates unnecessary complexity and takes time, which was in short supply. The response was 'Impossible, we don't all talk to one another'. The nurses began to realise that whilst working with the family, they were being drawn in to a long-standing family feud. Realising this they took great care not to 'fuel' it, and did manage to persuade the family to reduce the number of contacts.

The complexities of family relationships sometimes become painfully clear when one member falls ill.

BODY TRANSITIONS

Body Changes in Later Life

The bodily changes that are liable to occur with ageing are very variable, but most people find their activity restricted to some extent. Giving up driving a car or riding a bicycle are major losses, since private transport is often associated with a sense of autonomy. This is particularly important in Western societies, where friends and family members often live outside the neighbourhood. Waiting for a bus, taxi or kind friend's offer of a 'lift' to a social event or the shops can signify 'dependence'. Most older people resist this for as long as possible.

Body transitions are, similar to other transitions discussed in this chapter, likely to create psychological work – they are psychosocial transitions. As shown in the example

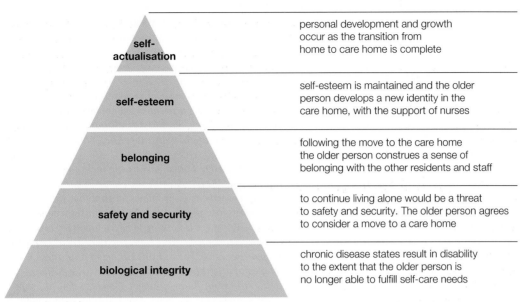

Figure 17.2 Maslow's hierarchy used as a framework to explain the transition from home to a care home.

below, as the body changes there is often a requirement for physical and social change and alongside this new 'meanings' are created.

A woman who had always been very active found, in her eighties, that she could not move as easily as she used to because of the arthritis in her joints. This did not stop her from doing most of the things that she was used to doing, as she discovered ways of adapting her movements to situations. In department stores, for example, she would take the escalator as usual, but getting off required extra effort. She was not able to step smoothly off, but instead, threw her weight and gave a small jump. This was quite alarming to others, but quite effective. She had no wish to go in the lift and so her companions had to remind themselves that she had not fallen yet, and it was her choice to continue using the escalator. When asked about her method, she said that it was rather like lots of things in life, 'You just have to launch yourself and hope that you'll arrive safely!' This worked for her, for as long as she was able to go to department stores.

This example demonstrates that a change in bodily functioning is not just an individual experience, important as that is, but it is also a social experience. The adaptation on the part of this woman was excellent; it achieved the required result, but that was not enough. Since the 'new behaviour' stimulated concern and anxiety in her companions, she had to contend with this response and convince them. She rose to the occasion taking the opportunity to express her adaptation as a philosophy of life:

You have to launch yourself and hope that you will arrive safely.

Body Changes in Chronic Illness

Sociologists studying chronic illness, for example Bury (1988), are urging us to try to understand how those living with illness manage their lives, not by superimposing our ideas or concepts but by listening to their stories. Bury's (1988) own study of arthritis sufferers demonstrates clearly the social significance of his informants' disability. When hands can no longer grasp and hold there may be a need for help, but the request for help changes relationships. If the help is given freely then the person with arthritis is likely to feel a sense of dependency, thus changing the relationship. The sense of equality and reciprocity previously enjoyed is often in jeopardy, and might be lost. That is bad enough, but the alternative could be worse. What if the help requested is refused, or given grudgingly? That situation could herald the beginning of a deteriorating relationship. Bury points out that having a chronic illness can put the sufferer into a state of continual anxiety as they struggle to negotiate new ways of life – experiencing the world differently, doing things differently and relating differently.

Pinder has studied how people with Parkinson's disease (PD), together with their spouses, managed; she called her study *Striking Balances*, as she found that when living with PD, although the drugs provided some relief, sufferers were always alert to the fact that symptoms could reappear. They got to know by careful study how long they were likely to remain symptom free and during this time would fit in the most crucial activities, then perhaps hope to do a little more but with the knowledge that their bodies might crumble and feel useless again. Each sufferer and each couple developed expertise from careful study of the symptoms.

Experiencing Body Transitions

There is now a growing literature on illness narratives (Frank, 1995; Sacks, 1986). All of these writers make the point that there is an urgency to tell the story and for the story to be heard. It is in the story that meanings are recreated, as they need to be, when illness has disrupted the coherence of the life-story. It is sad that psychologists and sociologists have to alert practitioners to these phenomena which have been under the practitioners' gaze all the time, but the patient's wish to tell his or her story has often been seen as an interruption to the (medical) practitioner's task. Frank describes the physician's 'history taking' as a way of suspending 'normal conventions of politeness and thus (legitimising) interruptions'. Frank is, however, hopeful as he says one doctor has written to him acknowledging the difference between history taking and the patient's story. 'Until recently the medical history was considered to be the story.'

Listening to the patient's story can help practitioners to relate the care they offer to the patient's needs; it can be therapeutic for the patient, and can help to create a partnership between patient and nurse. Finally, and perhaps most importantly, this willingness and interest in the patient's story can help practitioners to perceive the world as a particular patient perceives it.

As explained in other sections of this chapter it is not always easy, and requires appropriate training and support. Nevertheless, there are benefits. Frank argues:

Through their stories, the ill create empathic bonds between themselves and their listeners. These bonds expand as the stories are retold. Those who listen then tell others, and the circle of shared experience then widens. Because stories can heal, the wounded healer and wounded storyteller are not separate, but are different aspects of the same figure.

(Frank, 1995.)

Another 'wounded storyteller' tells of the comfort provided by one who is skilled and brave enough to be close to an old lady's pain:

It's Monday and Louise is working tonight and she sits on my bed chatting quietly. She seems to understand the suffering and fear that ageing forces us to endure. She doesn't try to cajole me or make light of the effort required to keep myself going. She has a gentle humour and somehow makes me laugh at my infirmities; laughter is a fine medicine.

'One day nearer,' Louise says as she tucks me into bed, and she says the words with such hope in her voice, not in a morbid way as if she knows for sure that something better waits just ahead of me. And she makes it sound so natural, as if there is nothing to be frightened of and her words comfort me because I am frightened, but beyond the fear lies hope, beyond this tunnel of pain there is a wonderful bright future and I just have to be patient.

Louise strokes my hair soothingly. 'God bless you,' she says as she switches off the light. And I wonder is that what death will be like, as if someone has switched off the light, and as I lie in bed I pray that God in His infinite mercy does that but I pray that He does it gently, tenderly...without pain because I am bone weary and all that was once strong in me is crumbling and there is little left to support me. I am exhausted by this world.'

(Dean, 1993.)

SUMMARY

Psychosocial transitions are as common a feature in later life as at any other time in the life span. Older people will have developed skills and strategies for managing transitions during the course of their lives. Nurses have a crucial role to play in encouraging older people to use their capacities and strengths to adapt and attain personal growth in the face of loss and change. Nurses who listen and try to understand their patient's experiences are liable, through empathy, to experience stress. Nurses can be supported in this important work through the process of work supervision.

KEY POINTS

- In later life, as at any other life stage, psychosocial transition brings opportunities for personal development and growth.
- Nurses have a crucial role in helping older people negotiate transitions.
- Work supervision, either singly or in groups, can sustain nurses while they support clients through psychosocial transition.
- Early retirement, often with financial inducements, decreased job security and more part-time working have led to dramatic changes in the pattern of retirement.
- Widows and widowers may appreciate support in exploring new identities.
- Widowers are less likely to have supportive networks.
- A move from home into an institution is often unplanned and the older client and family are left to negotiate their own transitions.
- A major transition for an older person is moving from health to illness and at the same time endeavouring to achieve some semblance of normality in the face of bodily change.

AREAS AND ACTIVITIES FOR STUDY AND REFLECTION

- Consider a patient who has recently been admitted to a hospital or a home, or added to a caseload for community care. Write down what you know about his or her feelings. How often did you remember the patient's own words? Reading this back to yourself what were the feelings aroused in you as you wrote about the patient? Were your feelings similar to the patients or did you find yourself reacting, perhaps wishing some feelings would disappear?
- Consider and discuss how the process of retirement might be facilitated in the work place? What are the roles of (a) the manager (b) the colleagues (c) the retiree in this process? What action can be taken in their private life with friends and family?
- How often is the death of a resident or a patient acknowledged and an opportunity for discussion given in an institution, or with friends and family? What action might be taken to help the friends with the bereavement process?
- A man aged 82-years-old is dying in hospital. How might his wife be involved in his care? What might the advantages and disadvantages be?
- You visit a man who has recently been discharged from hospital. The referral requests monitoring of diabetes. In conversation he says his wife died only 3 months ago and he is still finding it difficult to manage on his own. How would you like to conduct the discussion?
- Imagine you are anticipating the arrival of a new resident in a home. How would you like to prepare for their arrival?

REFERENCES

Albery, Nicholas, Elliot G, Elliot J. *The natural death handbook*. Virgin Books, 1993.

Bengston M. Conference presentation at Annual Conference of British Society of Gerontology, Bristol, 1997

Bury M. Meanings at risk: the experience of arthritis. In: Anderson R, Bury M, eds. *Living with chronic illness*. London: Unwin Hyman, 1988.

Butler RN. The life review: an interpretation of reminiscence in the aged. *Psychiatry* 1963, 26:65–76.

Cave D. Gay and lesbian bereavement. In: Dickenson D, Johnson M, eds. *Death, dying and bereavement*. London: Sage Publications, 1993.

Coleman A, Chiva A. *Coping with change-focus on retirement*, 1991, Health Education Authority, London.

Costello J, Atkins A, Edwards V, Hughes S. Acknowledging loss. *Elderly Care* 1996, 8:35–36.

Dean E. Sitting it out. In: Dickenson D, Johnson M, eds. *Death, dying and bereavement*. London: Sage Publications, 1993.

Fabricius J. Running on the spot or can nursing really change? *Psychoanal Psychother* 1991, 5:97–108.

Frank AW. *The wounded storyteller: body illness and ethics*. Chicago: Chicago University Press, 1995.

Gearing B, Coleman P. Biographical assessment in community care. In: Birren JE, Kenyon GM, Ruth J, Schroots JJF, Svenson T, eds. *Aging and biography*. New York: Springer Publishing Company, 1996.

Johnson M. The meaning of old age. In: Redfern S, ed. *Nursing elderly people, 2nd edition*. Edinburgh: Churchill Livingstone, 1991.

Laslett P. *A fresh map of life, 2nd edition*. London: Macmillan Press, 1996.

Lewis CS. A grief observed, Faber and Faber, London, 1961.

Marris P. *Loss and change*. London: Routledge and Kegan, 1986.

Maslow AH. *Toward a psychology of being, 2nd edition*. Van Rostrand Reinhold, New York, 1968.

Myerhof B. Rites and signs of ripening: the intertwining of ritual, time and growing old. In: Kertzer DI, Keith J (eds) Age and anthropological theory, London, Cornell University Press, 1984.

Nichols KA. *Psychological care in physical illness, 2nd edition*. London: Chapman & Hall, 1993.

Nichols K. Institutional versus client-centred care in general hospitals. In Broom A, Llewelyn S (eds) *Health Psychology. Processes and application*. London: Chapman & Hall, 1995.

Nolan M, Walker G, Nolan J *et al*. Entry to care: positive choice or fait accompli? Developing a more proactive response to the needs of older people and their carers. *J Adv Nurs* 1996, 24:265–274.

Parkes CM. Bereavement as a psychosocial transition: processes of adaptation to change. In: Dickenson D, Johnson M, eds. *Death, dying and bereavement*. London: Sage Publications, 1993.

Pinder R. Striking balances. In: Andersom R, Bury M, eds. *Living with chronic illness*. London: Unwin Hyman, 1988.

Reed J, Payton VR. Constructing familiarity and managing the self: ways of adapting to life in nursing and residential homes. *Ageing and Society* 1996, 16:561–578.

Sacks O. *A leg to stand on*. London: Pan, 1986.

Saunders C. *Hospice and palliative care: an interdisciplinary approach*. London: Edward Arnold, 1990.

Savage J. *Nursing intimacy: an ethnographic approach to nurse patient interaction*. London: Scutari Press, 1995

Schofield I. A historical approach to care. *Elderly Care* 1994, 6:14–15.

Schuller T. Work ending: employment and ambiguity in later life. In: Bytheway B, Keil T, Allat P, Bryman A, eds. *Becoming and being old*. London: Sage Publications, 1990.

Scott A, Wenger GC. Gender and social support networks in later life. In: Arber S, Ginn J, eds. *Connecting gender and ageing in later life: a sociological approach*. Buckingham: Open University Press, 1995.

Scrutton S. *Bereavement and grief: supporting older people through loss*. London: Edward Arnold and Age Concern, 1995.

Scrutton S. "What can you expect my dear, at my age?" Recognising the need for counselling in a residential unit. *Bereavement Care* 1996 15(3):28–29.

Sixsmith AJ. The meaning and experience of 'home' in later life. In: Bytheway B, Johnson J, eds. *Welfare and the ageing experience*. Aldershot: Avebury, 1990.

Speck P. Working with dying people: on being good enough. In: Obholzer A, ed. *The unconcious at work*. Routledge, London 1994

Thompson P. Comment: "I don't feel old": The significance of the search for meaning in later life. *Int J Geriatr Psychiatry* 1993, 8:685–692.

Varley S. *Badger's parting gifts*. London: Picture Lions, 1985.

Waddington P. Towards care in the community. *Br J Nurs* 1996, 5:1

Wells D. Biographical work with older people. In: Barnes E, Griffiths P, Ord J, Wells D. *Face to face with distress*. London: Butterworth Heinemann, 1998.

Wenger GC. *Support networks of older people: a guide for practitioners*, Bangor, Wales, 1994, Centre for Social Policy Research and Development, University of Wales.

Wilson G. I'm the eyes and she's the arms. In: Arber J, eds. *Changes in gender roles in advanced age*. Buckingham: Open University Press, 1995.

Young M, Schuller T. *Life after work: the arrival of the ageless society*. London: Harper Collins, 1991.

18 Mental health
Lynne Phair

LEARNING OBJECTIVES

After studying this chapter you will be able to:

- Differentiate mental health from mental illness in older people.
- Differentiate the various types of mental disorders in older people.
- Discuss the role of the nurse in the care of an older person with mental-health problems.
- Identify the role of the multidisciplinary team in the care of older people with mental-health problems.
- Evaluate interventions aimed at promoting mental health in older people.
- Identify the appropriate use of different therapeutic interventions.
- Understand the theoretical framework of the person-centred model of dementia care.
- Evaluate the use of normal life activity as a therapeutic intervention with older people.

INTRODUCTION

Nurses who work with older people will at some point in their practice come across someone who has a mental-health problem. With the implementation of the over seventy-fives' health check this could mean that the practice nurse may be the first health-care professional to notice any symptoms of a mental-health problem. Whether identified at a screening interview by a generic nurse or identified through an in-depth specialist assessment by a mental-health nurse, the outcome and needs of the older person will remain the same. All older people are vulnerable to mental illness just the same as any other group of the population. All nurses wherever they work should then ensure that they at least recognise when a person is having some difficulties and know the appropriate action to take. At last the myth that mental impairment is inevitable is being destroyed. This chapter is designed for nurses who work both in the specialist field of mental health and for those who do not but who may meet someone who requires special intervention. The chapter will examine the most common forms of mental illness in old age and will then concentrate on the particular role the nurse has in the care of that person. The text will highlight not only the psychological aspects of the person's care needs but also physical and social care requirements. The nurse is uniquely placed to care for the person's physical consequences of any multiple pathology, the maintenance and monitoring of any consequences of pharmacological treatment and also offer specialist therapeutic interventions using both a puristic and an eclectic approach.

The specialist field of mental-health services for older people is a recently recognised speciality within psychiatry. Traditionally, older people would be cared for or treated within a generic service. Alternatively, the person with mental-health needs would be treated in a psychogeriatric service. In 1966, there was only one consultant for older people with mental-health problems; this number had risen in 1995 to 350 (Melzer *et al.* 1995). Within some district's health areas there are still no specialist services for older people; however, the development over the past 30 years should not be underestimated.

It is within the context of this relatively new speciality that this chapter is written. The text will enable the reader to understand medical diagnoses and treatment regimes of specific mental-health problems of old age. For nurses, the emphasis should be on assessment and implementation of a care programme which will enhance the wellbeing of the older person and consequently enable active treatment. The role of the nurse is an integral part of any health-care team and their unique contribution will be highlighted in this chapter.

THE CONTEXT OF MENTAL HEALTH CARE DELIVERY IN THE UK

The social policy and health-care provision service in the UK is discussed in Chapters 1 and 22. For mental-health clients, however, there is also another emphasis of care which is superimposed on the care delivery system in the form of the Care Programme Approach (CPA). This approach was introduced in 1991, but did not receive broad acceptance until 1996, when health authorities and NHS trusts were required to ensure that it had been implemented [Department of Health (DoH) and Social Services Inspectorate (SSI), 1994].

407

In order to understand the importance of this approach, the history of its development should be acknowledged.

Achieving a Seamless Service

In the 1980s, there was a change in the social security laws which enabled the development of private and independent residential care. At the same time, it was becoming acknowledged that people with mental-health problems should not be kept in hospital for many years simply as an asylum from the outside world. The revolution of mental-health care began. In some areas this included developing community services and strong links with social services. While in others, people with severe and enduring mental-health problems were discharged into the community or residential care, with little or no resources to assist them in this transition.

Over the next decade, community services developed in an unstructured way, and the needs of this client group were seen differently in different health and social service departments. Despite some areas of excellent service development, there were a number of tragedies involving people with severe mental-health problems. The most publicised of these was the death of Jonathan Zito. He was murdered by Christopher Clunis on an underground station for no apparent reason. The enquiry identified very poor communication between health and social services and a lack of coordination of care and treatment for this very ill man. It was concluded that a major shift in attitude and approach to people living in the community was required. The emphasis of local joint services caring for people in the community wherever possible became the government priority (DoH and SSI, 1994).

Thus, the CPA was implemented and has now become obligatory in all mental-health services. The emphasis is that all mental-health clients in the community:

- Have a key worker (either health or social service worker).
- Have regular reviews of their package undertaken by a multidisciplinary team.
- Are all care-assessed, implemented and reviewed in a systematic way.

The additional emphasis is in respect of client involvement. This should be conducted from a needs-led perspective, thus involving the client and their carers in any plan of treatment or care. Any development of mental-health services would automatically include older people and so this shift in culture is now central to any mental-health care delivery for this client group.

Within mental health, an enduring mental illness may not only cause physical or psychological disablement but may also cause social disablement leading to stigma, a low standard of living and demoralisation (Thornicroft et al. 1992). Thus, any needs-led assessment must consider all of these aspects and develop a package of care which will both prevent deterioration of the person from their illness and promote health and wellbeing through assessment and

management of all areas of the person's life and experience. Thornicroft et al. (1992) defines need in terms of 'a type of impairment or other factor causing social disablement, or of the model of treatment or other intervention required to meet it'.

Just because a need has been identified does not automatically mean that the skills or resources are available to meet that need. However, mental-health professionals must acknowledge the effect of their mental illness on the older person at every level of their functioning. They must listen to the client and learn to help him or her identify what they see as their needs, thus enabling a true partnership approach to be achieved.

THE CONCEPT OF MENTAL HEALTH

Maslow's hierarchical needs model is not ideal for understanding people with mental-health needs as it might be assumed that the higher one rises in terms of needs met, the more likely one is to be mentally healthy. Theoretically, this view is useful. The rationale is humanistic. If anyone is underrated then expectations of mental health are reduced, feedback is modified, and a danger of instigating a self-fulfilling prophecy exists. Some older people fear they will lose their intellectual powers as they age and are particularly vulnerable to any implication that confirms their fear.

Mental health, like general health, is a continuum concept. The absence of mental illness does not mean one is mentally healthy, nor does the presence of psychological symptoms mean one is mentally ill. The continuum of mental health and mental illness is more complex and dynamic than can be illustrated in **Figure 18.1**.

This concept is a guide for organising care with the expectation that the individuality of each client will always be the uppermost concern. Mental health for adults, and particularly for older people, is difficult to define because the differentiation of personality throughout the life span results in idiosyncratic and sometimes eccentric adaptations in later life. In fact, many health-care professionals are quick to classify and attribute negative personality characteristics such as 'cantankerous', 'crusty', 'disagreeable', 'grouchy', and 'grumpy' to older individuals as a part of their character, without investigating any possibility of a mental-health cause.

THE ROLE OF THE MENTAL-HEALTH NURSE

A nurse who has specialised in the care of older people with mental-health problems will have developed an expertise in all aspects of gerontological care. The special emphasis will be in respect of their knowledge and skills in interpersonal and communication skills. The use of themselves as a therapeutic tool is heightened as nursing techniques centre around observation and understanding of the intricacies of nonverbal and verbal communication. The nurse will also be skilled

health								illness
feelings and thoughts	normal clear sufficient open clear	personality disorders distorted impulsivity lack of caring not socially acceptable	paranoid disorders selective over-control defended blocked	anxiety disorders blocked rigid controlled ruminative unwanted intrusions	substance-induced disorders distorted diminished dulled or released impaired	mood disorders acute/dulled little/passive angry/ helpless grandiose/ slowed	somatoform disorders narrowed through illness diverted to body focused on body	organic mental disorders fragmented lost primitive hallucinations delusions

Figure 18.1 A simplistic representation of a continuum of mental health and illness.

in managing serious mental illness, in assessment and management. They should also be able to identify, manage and treat the more common physical problems of ageing or physical complications due to ill health.

The mental-health nurse who works with older people must learn to use subtle skills to enhance a person's wellbeing, and their action is often not obvious to the untrained eye. This in itself has caused problems for nurses who choose to work in this field and skills in articulating their unique contribution need to be learned (Ford *et al.* 1997).

An expert mental-health nurse will carry out his or her work within the philosophy of a person-centred approach to care. A nurse is uniquely placed to bridge the divide between the traditional medical model of care and the totally psychological aspects of care. Meeting the needs of a person through a person-centred approach, and emphasising an older person's personhood through the care delivery will be discussed later in this chapter. It is presumed, however, that the nurse reading this work will at all times view the older person as an individual, while looking at all aspects of their care needs.

Psychological Assessment of Older People

Traditional methods of assessing older people revolved around the person's physical health and any mental illness identified through using medical diagnosis. Today a nurse should undertake a comprehensive assessment of an older person by assessing the mental health, physical health, social status and environmental characteristics of the person. General issues in the psychological assessment of older people involve distinguishing between normal and diverse characteristics of ageing and pathological conditions. Baseline data is often lacking from the individual's middle years, and few standardisation samples include any old subjects. The use of standardised tools and functional assessment is valuable, but the data will be meaningless if not placed in the context of the person's past life, and their hopes and expectations for the future. Distinguishing normal from pathological ageing in a particular individual depends on these factors.

Obtaining data from older people is best done during short sessions after some rapport has been established. Performing repeated assessments at various times of day and in different situations will give a more complete psychological profile. It is important to be sensitive to the person's anxiety, special needs and disabilities. The interview should be focused so that attention is given to strengths and skills as well as deficits.

Cognitive function and mental status have overlapping characteristics and the terms are often used interchangeably in the literature. However, they are not the same (**Table 18.1**). The terms are used interchangeably because some of the concepts come from screening instruments measuring cognitive functioning, while others come from the psychiatric evaluation or mental status examination.

Many clinicians and health-care providers use the patients' level of orientation to time, place and person as a quick indicator of cognitive functioning; however, this is grossly inaccurate (Palmateer and McCartney, 1985). After administering the Cognitive Capacity Screening Examination (CCSE), Palmateer and McCartney found that clients can be oriented during administration of the CCSE but they have deficits in other areas of cognitive functioning, such as abstraction, concentration and memory. Differences in level of orientation and non-orientation responses were observed, after conducting mental status examinations on patients with and without dementia. The level of orientation evaluation consisted of ability to identify the day of the week, month, year, city and hospital. The results concluded that screening examinations were unacceptably insensitive. The two non-orientation items examined were serial seven's, and recall of three items, which demonstrated high diagnostic sensitivity but low specificity.

Assessment of cognitive functioning includes attention span, concentration, intelligence, judgement, learning ability, memory, orientation, perception, problem solving, psychomotor ability, reaction time and social intactness. Even though these categories were determined from published studies of cognitive function and impairment they were not defined (McDougall, 1990). Definitions of 12 domains can be found in **Table 18.1**.

Common tests which give an indication of a person's

Domains of Cognitive Function	
Domain	Definition
Attention	The ability to focus, in a sustained manner for a period of time, on one activity or object.
Concentration	The ability to concentrate is manifested by the individual's ability to answer questions, ignoring unimportant or irrelevant external stimuli.
Intelligence	Broadly defined, intelligence is the ability to comprehend or understand. General intelligence usually includes verbal aptitude, calculation skills and spatial relationship skills. There is evidence that as people age, non-cognitive factors such as motivation, response speed and sensory deficits play increasingly significant roles in intellectual performance. When referring to older adults, a distinction must be made between the terms 'intelligence' and 'competence'. Intelligence is described as an inference of underlying traits, based on observations in many situations. Competence is a more situation-specific combination of intellectual traits that with adequate motivation will permit adaptive behaviour. Intelligence is usually determined by similarities and vocabulary tests, and mathematical tests, e.g. calculations that require the individual to add or subtract using serial sevens or serial threes and digit span forwards and backwards. The individual is required to add or subtract three or seven from 100 five consecutive times.
Judgement	Judgement is the mental ability to perceive and distinguish the relationship between two objects. An individual is evaluated for appropriate and realistic behaviour that is based on an awareness of the environment and the consequences of his or her behaviour. Parameters usually assessed include physical and psychological needs, ability to form appropriate goals and plans, and ability to act on these goals and plans. Other important indicators of judgement are the individual's ability to handle financial matters or drive a car.
Learning ability	Learning is a sustained, highly deliberate effort to acquire knowledge or a skill. An important learning difference for older adults is the increasing time required for acquisition of knowledge or skills and retrieval of information from memory. Older adults' ability to learn may be improved with a longer acquisition and response period, with a particular emphasis on a self-paced approach. The amount of material and the number of task demands presented during instruction may also influence learning ability.
Memory	In a broad sense, memory implies the ability to recall previously experienced ideas, impressions, information and sensations. It is clinically helpful to differentiate between immediate retention (memory for the recent past) and recall (memory for the remote past). Memory is usually assessed by an individual's ability to remember and recall specific words during an interview.
Orientation	Orientation usually consists of an individual's knowledge of person, place and time. Orientations evaluated from an individual's ability to answer self-referent questions, i.e. questions with the who, what, where and when of a situation. Does the person recognise the function of and awareness of those around him or her?
Perception	Perception generally refers to the processes involved in the acquisition and interpretation of information from the individual's own environment. There is a relationship between quality of the sensory apparatus and cognitive functioning. Assessment is usually accomplished through observation of an individual's capacity to accurately reproduce the design drawn by the examiner and to do this with a reasonable degree of coordination and speed.
Problem-solving	Problem-solving comprises the set of cognitive activities required to transform one state or condition into another. Reaching a solution involves three steps: analysing the given set or condition, determining what new condition is desired and generating and weighing alternative strategies for getting from a given condition to the desired condition. A naturalistic example of problem-solving would be to ask grocery shoppers to determine the best buys on a particular set of products.
Psychomotor ability	Psychomotor behaviours pertain to motor effects of cerebral or psychic activity that lead to purposeful or goal-directed behaviours.
Reaction time	Reaction time in the purest sense is the time that elapses between the application of a stimulus and the resulting reaction. Reaction time is assessed by determining response time to abstract shapes, letters, visual stimuli and words.
Social intactness	Socialisation is a process of individual integration into society and learning to have in socially acceptable ways. Social intactness as an adult includes a narrow range of skills and attitudes that are necessary to perform social roles such as occupational skills. Social intactness is usually determined by assessing the quality and quantity of an individual's social support network and the appropriateness of their social interactions.

Adapted from: McDougall, 1990.

Table 18.1 Domains of cognitive function.

cognitive abilities include the Mini-Mental State Examination (MMSE) and the Clifton Assessment Procedures for the Elderly (CAPE). Both of these can be completed quickly and the scores used to inform a judgement (Alzheimer's Disease Society, 1995). It is important that the nurse does not rely on any psychological test alone but combines the results with their observations and intellectual understanding of the person's behaviour and situation.

The Nurse's Role in the Assessment of Mental-health Needs

The nurse's assessment of mental-health needs should consist of a systematic process of collecting information about an individual, the physical health and the world in which they live. The nurse would include any information obtained from the person, their family and any significant others. Assessment is the baseline for future investigations as well as being the basis from which care is prescribed or suggested. The Royal College of Nursing (1994) have developed some useful guidelines which outline the essential components of a mental-health assessment (**Box 18.1**).

Any assessment should ascertain the person's 'needs'. The assessment should be based on their perspective, that of any relative or carers, and from the professional perspective. The skill is then to meet these needs while keeping the older person's wellbeing central to any plan of care.

ORGANIC DISORDERS

In view of the number of seemingly unrelated terms used to search the literature, definitions are necessary for clarification. The definitions used are significant in the diagnosis, assessment and treatment of a person's presenting mental-health symptoms. If a patient is misdiagnosed, the treatment prescribed may be grossly inadequate or the patient may be written off as a hopeless or untreatable case.

Dementia

Dementia is a term that is used to describe a set of different diseases, all of which have the same result. The definition, therefore, reflects this.

Dementia is a set of symptoms where there is evidence of a decline in memory and thinking which is of a degree sufficient to impair daily living, present for 6 months or more (Alzheimer's Disease Society, 1995). For some, this diagnosis only reflects the medical approach to the disease. Psychologists such as Kitwood tend to look at how the intervention of the carer will affect the person with dementia. Yet even he acknowledges that the person with dementia will show some decline in memory, the ability to make judgements and other cognitive functions (Kitwood, 1997). Others who view dementia from an environmental perspective tend

18.1 Guidelines for Assessing Mental Health Needs in Older Age (Royal College of Nursing, 1994)

Assessment is an ongoing continuous process that aims to identify positive factors that can be used as a stepping stone for further care planning. Assessment is not a 'once only' act and should not be seen as an end product in itself.

The principles of mental-health assessment by nurses are:
• Selecting the right tools for the job.
• Good interpersonal skills and relationships.
• Where to make the assessment.
• Identifying individual needs, strengths and assets upon which to base nursing intervention.

The three broad categories of mental health that serve as useful markers for considering what is normal are mood, cognition and behaviour.

Mood: relates to the way in which they feel at any particular time.
Note if the mood is appropriate to what is happening to the person, and whether their mood hinders them from carrying out activities.
Cognition: relates to understanding and being able to respond appropriately to information. Types of cognitive ability include memory, perception, thinking, learning and decision-making.
Behaviour: relates to how the person responds to a situation. It would be important to establish if the behaviour was in keeping with the person's culture and the social context.

A mental-health assessment will use information gathered by :
• Interviewing the individual.
• Observing behaviour, reactions and body language.
• Observing environment and looking retrospectively at life events.
• Examining physical changes and mental processes that may indicate problems with lifestyle.

to speak of the disease as a disability. This, it is felt, will also then help to change the view from a medical disease to that of a problem in the social context (Marshall, 1997). It is important that a nurse looks at the problems of dementia from all perspectives and the expert nurse will then be able to draw on relevant viewpoints at appropriate times in order to ensure appropriate clinical, psychological or social care.

Dementia is a disease consisting of loss of intellectual abilities of sufficient severity to interfere with social or occupational functioning. The essential feature of dementia is impairment in short-term and long-term memory. These diseases are multifaceted and involve memory, judgement, abstract thought, higher cortical functions and changes in behaviour and personality.

Dementia is the decline of memory and other cognitive functions in comparison with the patient's previous level of function as determined by a history of decline in performance, abnormalities noted from clinical examination and neuropsychological tests. The diagnosis of dementia is based on behaviour and cannot be determined by CT scan, EEG or other laboratory instruments, although specific causes of dementia may be identified by these means. When consciousness is impaired by delirium, drowsiness, stupor, coma, or when other clinical abnormalities prevent adequate evaluation of mental status, a diagnosis of dementia cannot be made.

It is inevitable that with the number of older people living longer there will be proportionately more people suffering from dementia. It is estimated that there are 650,000 people in the UK with dementia in 1996 (Alzheimer's Disease Society, 1995). Of these, just over half suffer from Alzheimer's disease. That figure makes up about 5% of the population of people over 65 years of age. Although it may feel at times that most people with dementia are residing in some form of residential care, this is a misconception. Eighty per cent of people with dementia live at home whatever the extent of their impairment and 23% live at home alone. Dementia also affects 3% of people under 65 years of age. The Alzheimer's Disease Society (1995) identify that this group has a disproportionately high morbidity and also create more dramatic social consequences.

There are a number of different types of dementia, which often become acknowledged just as 'Alzheimer's disease'. It is important to acknowledge that there are some significant differences in the most common types of the disease.

Alzheimer's Disease (AD)

AD was described by Alzheimer in 1906 and is a cerebral degenerative disorder of unknown origin. It is not just a disease of the old, but the incidence increases concomitant with ageing. In younger people it is called presenile dementia, and in older people it is called senile dementia of the Alzheimer type or SDAT. The characteristic changes (found at autopsy) in the brain are neurofibrillary tangles in cellular matrix, senile plaques (depositions in cerebral cells), atrophy of cortical tissue (brain shrinks in size) and a loss of cholinergic neurones in the limbic system. Plaques are focused most densely in the hippocampus and the cortex (Tobiansky, 1994a).

The course of this disease ranges from 1 to 15 years, with death usually occurring because of pulmonary infections, urinary tract infections, decubitus ulcers or iatrogenic disorders. AD is diagnosed on the basis of tests ruling out other disorders that may mimic dementia and the globally progressive nature of the disease.

AD destroys proteins of nerve cells of the cerebral cortex by diffuse infiltration with non-functional tissue called neurofibrillary tangles and plaques. The disease is progressive and is accompanied by increasing forgetfulness, confusion, inability to concentrate, personality deterioration and impaired judgement.

Vascular Dementia

The term 'vascular dementia' has only relatively recently been used to describe this particular type of dementia. Vascular dementia used to be described as 'arteriosclerotic' dementia. It was identified, however, that arteriosclerosis is not often present in vascular dementia (Tobiansky, 1994a).

Vascular dementia is responsible for 20% of all types of dementia in western Europe and not surprisingly occurs more commonly in older age. Contributing factors correspond with risks associated with a stroke. These include smoking, heart disease and excessive alcohol intake. Vascular dementia is caused when small clots are carried into the cortical areas of the brain. These cause a lack of oxygen to the brain and ultimate death of those particular brain cells. Obviously this damage can occur in any part of the brain and the resulting presenting symptoms would depend on this. The normal pattern of symptoms is that the person may present with transient ischaemic attacks, visual loss, falls, confusion, dysarthria and dysphasia. Hypertension is also often evident (Tobiansky, 1994a)

When testing people for dementia, Villardita identified that patients with vascular dementia had increased emotional lability and worse attention to fine coordination tasks (Tobiansky, 1994a). The presentation is therefore a changing one, but diagnosis can be made on occasions by a CT scan. If this type of dementia is diagnosed and the underlying cause identified, it is possible to improve the person's condition, although it is not possible to repair cognitive damage that has already occurred.

Lewy Body Dementia (LBD)

This type of dementia has not had general recognition, although it was discovered in 1912 by Lewy as part of the cortical changes in Parkinson's disease (PD). Lewy bodies are pink staining structures found in the cytoplasm of neurones. They occur in the brain stem and cortical areas of the brain. They are present in PD and so are often found when dementia is not present. As methods of investigation have improved, more researchers have identified the presence of Lewy bodies at autopsy examination.

People who have diffuse LBD show marked impairment of parietal lobe functions, this includes difficulties with hand-to-eye tasks, dyspraxia and reasoning skills. The usual loss of memory expected in dementia is not so common. The most significant difference between LBD and other types is that the presentation can be variable. This frequently includes visual or auditory hallucinations, fluctuating episodes of confusion or lucidity, and unexplained falls. Despite the fluctuating pattern, the clinical features persist over a longer period (weeks or months), unlike toxic confusional state which varies daily.

Patients who suffer with LBD often have mild forms of parkinsonism with the associated symptoms. The most significant difference in treatment is that a person with LBD is often very sensitive to psychotropic drugs, which can cause mild spontaneous extrapyramidal features. The course of the disease is also variable but it does show a pattern of deterioration and then plateau over a period of about 8 years (Tobiansky, 1994b).

Creutzfeldt-Jakob Disease (CJD)

This type of dementia has a rapid progression and the prognosis is poor. It is a dementia caused from small, infected proteins known as prions. In cattle the infected protein causes bovine spongiform encephalitis (BSE) and in sheep it causes scrapie.

The clinical features are of dementia and the brain shows spongy change on autopsy examination. CJD can affect anybody at any age. The speed at which the disease becomes apparent and causes the person's death is particularly traumatic. At present there is no treatment or cure (Livingston, 1994).

Pseudo Dementia

Pseudo dementia is a syndrome in which dementia is mimicked or caricatured by functional psychiatric illness. The most common psychiatric illness presenting in this manner is a major depressive episode. While pseudo dementia can occur at any age, it is most often seen in elderly patients. The prognosis for patients diagnosed correctly with a pseudo dementia or a depression-induced organic mental disorder is reversible, according to Baldwin (1997), and appears to be good.

Pick's Disease

Pick's disease is a rare progressive degenerative brain disorder involving atrophy of the frontal and temporal lobes of the cerebral cortex. Pick's disease is an uncommon type of progressive dementia with clinical features similar to AD. It was discovered by a Czechoslovakian physician, Arnold Pick, in 1892, and has a distinctive histopathology of degenerating neurones that contain globular intracytoplasmic filamentous inclusion bodies. The clinical distinction between AD and Pick's disease is often difficult; however, it is suggested that frontal lobe changes are the earliest signs, hence diminished drive, tactless and insensitive behaviour, a vacant expression and disinhibition. These symptoms will be identified before impairment of memory, although this does follow (Thompson, 1997). Pick's disease shows a more rapid progression than AD (Uhl *et al.* 1983).

HIV-related Dementia

HIV-related dementia refers to the neurological impairment that occurs in up to 75% of people with AIDS. Neurological impairment may soon be the dominant aspect of the clinical presentation of AIDS. HIV-related dementia is of two types, depending on whether it is the result of direct or indirect involvement of the central nervous system (CNS). Indirect effects on the CNS are the result of tumours, malignancies and abscesses that occupy cerebral space. Symptoms include lethargy, confusion, headaches, focal neurological deficits and seizures. However, recent studies indicate that the HIV can infiltrate the CNS directly and produce a distinctive AIDS–dementia complex. It is thought to do so early in the disease or even before onset of other symptoms and may be the earliest and only sign of HIV infection (Navia and Price, 1987).

AIDS–dementia complex is characterised by cognitive, motor and behavioural changes. Only rudimentary intellectual and social functioning remains intact, and psychomotor retardation is evident. Depression, agitation, delusions, hallucinations, grandiosity and paranoia are common symptoms. The end result of AIDS–dementia complex closely resembles AD (Adams, 1988). Nurses must be aware in cases of dementia which progress more rapidly than is typical of AD, the AIDS–dementia complex must be considered. There have been several cases of mistaken diagnoses of AD that at autopsy were found to be AIDS-related dementia. HIV infection should be considered as a possible cause of dementia in older people even when they are not initially thought to be in any high-risk group for AIDS.

COMMON TERMS USED WHEN DESCRIBING MENTAL-HEALTH SYMPTOMS

Confusion

Confusion is the term used to describe a person who is disorientated to time and place, has incongruous conceptual boundaries, paranormal awareness and seemingly inappropriate verbal statements that indicate memory defects. Confusion is a clinical term used for assessment of a patient's behaviour. However, it is often used by nurses as a diagnostic term synonymously used with the medical diagnosis of dementia. This imprecision of meaning among nurses often leads to inconsistent reporting of patients' behavioural presentation.

Cognitive Impairment

Cognitive impairment is a term used to describe a disturbance in cognitive functioning. Cognitive functioning is a broad construct that includes a number of categories:
- Attention span.
- Concentration.
- Intelligence.
- Judgement.
- Learning ability.
- Memory.
- Orientation.
- Perception.
- Problem solving.
- Psychomotor ability.
- Reaction time.
- Social intactness (McDougall, 1990).

Assessment of cognitive function and a complete mental status examination are essential components in the diagnosis of delirium, dementia, Alzheimer's disease and Parkinson's disease.

CARING FOR A PERSON WITH DEMENTIA

Many people with organic illness are cared for in the community by members of their families. All aspects and principles of care and management should be applied equally whether a person is receiving support in the community, in a day care environment, or in a residential or nursing setting. The role of the nurse will depend on the environment and situation, thus requiring the nurse to be either an educator, a facilitator, a manager or a direct caregiver, depending on the circumstances of the older person. (Setting standards in

dementia management for primary and secondary care are listed in **Box 18.2**).

Person-centred Dementia Care

There has been for many years a traditional approach to caring for people with dementia, based on the medical approach to care. The person with dementia has been diagnosed and viewed as a person who is neurologically impaired and is damaged by the disease. The staff have been trained to manage the problem behaviour of such people and to ensure that their essential care needs are met. This has been undertaken within an institutional environment, or at least with an institutional ethos of managed and structured days and routines. The staff held the control and thus the power over the lives and activity of the person with dementia. The staff had few problems and 'knew what was best'.

 18.2 Setting Standards in Dementia Management for Primary and Secondary Care

Changes that indicate possible dementia
- Memory loss, predominantly for recent events.
- Difficulties with learning and retaining new information.
- Difficulty in handling complex tasks.
- Impairment of reasoning ability.
- Impairment of spacial and visuoperceptual ability.
- Language deficits.
- Changes in behaviour.

Assessment to assist with the initial diagnosis and exclude reversible causes
- Brief assessments of cognitive impairment [e.g. Mini-Mental State Examination (MMSE)] as an adjunct to other assessments.
- Health history.
- Review of treatments.
- Tests including blood count (including erythrocyte sedimentation rate or viscosity), urea and electrolytes, liver function, calcium and bone biochemistry, vitamin B_{12}, serology for syphilis, thyroid function and urine examination.
- Consider red cell folate test, gamma GT, chest X-ray, computerised tomography (CT) scan, if clinically indicated.

Treatment recommendations
- Determining the stage of disease severity is a clinical decision which may be assisted by using the MMSE.
- Before prescribing drug treatment, identify contraindications from the manufacturer's specific

product characteristics.
- It is strongly recommended that a carer be identified to assist with treatment and continuous informal assessment.
- Clinical impression and assessment must be used to determine the benefits of treatment to the individual and family group. The patient's quality of life is important.
- The initial prescriber should assess the patient's requirements for additional medical support.

The use of support services
- Support and services should be available to all patients, regardless of whether treatment is prescribed.
- Services available vary but could include memory clinics, needs assessments, clinical diagnostics, treatment for coexisting illnesses, management of vascular risks and use of antidepressants, neuroleptics and anxiolytics for non-cognitive symptoms.
- Care and support could include CPN monitoring, psychiatric care programme, carer/patient counselling/support/stimulation, day hospital, social worker assessment, respite care.
- Information, education and advice should be offered.
- Follow-up services will change as the person's needs change.

Adapted from: GM Clinical Bulletin, 1997.

In 1976, Williams defined a culture as 'a settled patterned way of giving meaning to human existence in the world and of giving structure to action within it. A culture has three norms; social power through the institution, standards of behaviour, and thirdly the beliefs about what the culture is and what it ought to be.'

(Kitwood, 1995).

This approach to care has been challenged by innovative practitioners (Phair and Good, 1989). Over recent years, a new attitude to dementia care and a new culture of dementia care has been slowly developing. The new attitude argues that there is little difference between the staff who offer the care and those with the dementing illness (Kitwood, 1995). Kitwood argues that everyone is damaged in some way by their own biography, and all people have some deficiencies. For care staff they still have the ability to protect themselves by denial and collusion. Within normal communication people without a neurological impairment use many skills to hide their true feelings or to communicate using nonverbal methods, or traditional defence mechanisms. Often it is the incongruency between verbal and nonverbal messages which will indicate that the person is denying their true feelings or opinion (Kitwood, 1995). For a person with dementia, it is argued that they have lost the ability or the desire to play games and hide their true feelings, and so their feelings are true and authentic to that moment in time. The fundamental philosophy underpinning the new culture of dementia care is, therefore, that there is little difference between the cared and the cared for, and if care staff understood more about themselves they would be able to understand the clients for whom they care better.

The person-centred approach to care effected by Kitwood introduces the concept of personhood. A person is accorded the status of personhood when it is acknowledged that every human being:

- Has unique subjectivity.
- Has a place in the human group.
- Has needs.
- Is valued for no instrumental purpose but simply as a person.
- Has rights.

Everyone needs to feel wanted and so should have personal worth, be able to make choices, be able to trust those with whom one lives and have hope. This combination of personhood and personal worth are human values of the Western culture and should be aspired to for all citizens, regardless of any disease or disability.

The medical model has traditionally concentrated on the neurological damage caused in a dementing illness. This is also challenged by Kitwood. He believes that the presentation of dementia in any one person will be caused by a combination of factors; namely the person's personality, their biography, their physical health and their social psychology. When these factors are combined with the neurological impairment, the person will present with the disease in a discrete way. Within the person's life experience and the disease process, the care staff will then either add or detract from the person and their individual needs depending on the understanding and approach that is adopted with the person with dementia.

The needs of everyone whether or not affected by dementia can be described as being either physical or psychological. The two are intertwined and thus should be respected within that context. Kitwood identifies five key elements to a positive approach to a client with dementia.

(1) **Validation.** The person should have their experience acknowledged as real at that time. Acknowledge the feeling that the person is experiencing. Denial of the person's feelings is denying the experience.

(2) **Facilitation.** The person should be enabled to do what they can do. Staff should only intervene when the person cannot manage.

(3) **Celebration.** Every one should consciously work towards a partnership with the clients, working as equals and they should openly show that enjoyment.

(4) **Stimulation.** All the senses should be stimulated in a pleasurable way. The environment should smell, look and sound encouraging with a positive ambience.

(5) **Relaxation.** The atmosphere should be relaxed. Staff should at the very least give the impression of being unrushed. Staff should take opportunities to be with the clients even when undertaking administrative work.

It is considered by Kitwood that with every positive action there is a negative element to mirror it. Thus, with every positive intervention made by staff, damage can be done to a client by negative psychological approaches or a malignant psychology. These key elements have also been identified under main headings:

- **Disempowerment** – the staff undertake personal care tasks that the person could carry out for themselves.
- **Infantalisation** – the staff imply that the person has the mentality of a child or are patronising.
- **Treachery** – the use of dishonesty or deception to obtain compliance from the person.
- **Condemnation** – blaming the client for their actions.
- **Intimidation** – the use of threats and the abuse of power by the staff.
- **Objectification** – the staff talk over the person for whom they are caring, or they deal with the person as if they are an object.
- **Stigmatisation** –the staff treat the person with dementia as if they were different to other people.
- **Out-pacing** – the staff give information too quickly to the person and do not adjust their methods of communication to meet the ability of the person.
- **Invalidation** – the staff ignore the feelings demonstrated or expressed by the person.
- **Banishment** – the staff remove the person either physically or psychologically from the main living area.

The effect of the staff on the person with dementia should be considered within the context of how a person unaffected by a disease is influenced emotionally by those around them. Within an average person's life, if they receive positive acknowledgement of their achievements, have people around them who understand how they feel, and are able to express themselves, any negative psychology they experience will be dealt with within their supportive environment and it will not do any lasting damage. For people who live within a malignant environment, perhaps suffering constant abuse or receiving degrading acknowledgement, they will respond within the expectation of that abuse, as they have no way of receiving compensatory influences. A person with dementia will not necessarily have the facility within themselves to know where to find positive support and so will be vulnerable to respond to the communication that they receive from care staff. Thus, if the care staff offer a positive psychological approach to the person, the person's emotions will be supported. If, however, the staff do not value the person and use a malignant psychological approach, the person will become more damaged and will not be able to compensate from within themselves.

Kitwood extends the theory of a person-centred approach even further by looking at the positive and negative psychology within the context of 'wellbeing' and 'ill being'. As already stated, everyone regardless of their mental state will be affected by their own state of wellbeing. This, Kitwood argues, has twelve points:

(1) The assertion of willpower.
(2) The ability to express a range of emotions.
(3) Initiation of social contact.
(4) Affectional warmth.
(5) Self-respect.
(6) Social sensitivity.
(7) Acceptance of others who suffer.
(8) Humour (though not necessarily understood by others).
(9) Self-expression.
(10) Showing pleasure.
(11) Helpfulness (even if the person being helped does not recognise it as such).
(12) Personal relaxation.

Conversely, the person can experience ill being if certain negative effects or attributes, which may occur in normal life, are allowed to continue unabated or unsupported. For example:

• Unattended distress.
• Sustained anger.
• Anxiety.
• Fear.
• Boredom.
• Cultural alienation.
• Apathy and withdrawal.
• Despair.
• Physical pain.
• Oppression.

Thus, the total philosophy of the person-centred philosophy of care is combining all of these influencing factors and ensuring that staff have a depth of knowledge and the appropriate combination of skills to enable the person with dementia to live their life in a fulfilled way.

The Nurse's Role in a Person-centred Approach to Care

Wherever nurses care for people with dementia, the most fundamental part of their practice is to reflect on their own attitudes about the disease. To try to find ways of really 'seeing' the person with special needs, and not just to 'see' the disease and its resultant problems which are consuming that person, is also of vital importance.

The King's Fund publication *Living Well into Old Age* (1986) provides a set of values for care professionals which should serve as the basis for any service:

• People with dementia have the same human value as everyone else irrespective of their degree of disability or dependence.
• People with dementia have the same varied human needs as anyone else.
• People with dementia have the same rights as other citizens.
• Every person with dementia is an individual.
• People with dementia have the right to forms of support that do not exploit family and friends.

Incorporating these values with the principles of the person-centred approach to dementia care will ensure staff have a positive philosophy of care. This underpinning value system can then act as a thread through which all aspects of care can run. An overview of the nurse's role in the care of people with dementia can assist the reader to develop further knowledge from other sources.

The environment of an institution makes a statement about the value placed on the residents by the professionals and wider society. There are two types of environment; the physical and the social; the former being the sum of the potentially changeable factors and the latter referring to communication factors (Gravell, 1988). It is important, therefore, that the physical and social factors do not mismatch.

The Environment

Specific aspects within the environment have been identified as causing psychological stress to patients.

The Atmosphere of the Unit

If there is a generally run down feeling in the unit with poor decoration and inadequate maintenance it can contribute to an air of neglect. This in turn can affect the person by lowering their spirits and thus their self-esteem and feeling of self-worth. This could easily be interpreted as a mild depression or even progression of their dementia.

The Furnishing and Accessories

These should be chosen with care. The domesticity of the furniture will assist in the overall objective to create a positive environment and will help to make people more relaxed, thus reducing antisocial behaviour and the need for sedative medication.

Responding to the Person's Behaviour and Conversation

The Older Person Who Walks Around

People are naturally inquisitive; this is not necessarily different for people with dementia. 'Wandering' is a negative label as it really reflects the observer's perception of the activity. The person may be investigating or searching for someone or something. Locked doors often cause agitation as the person may believe that what they want is behind that door. If there is no danger to the person or others, they should be left to continue their exploring, being diverted or shown a route away from danger when necessary. Restraining in any shape or form will only cause more frustration and can very easily become an abusive act or an act of false imprisonment (Phair, 1990; Royal College of Nursing, 1992).

Conversation and Communication

The quality of the conversation is often more important than the quantity. The verbal content, the tone and speed of the interaction all influence the messages that are important. The message being given by the nurse will carry additional information, including anger, compassion, power or frustration. They must be aware of their own body language as the energy and intonation of the communication will have possibly more impact on the older person than the actual words spoken. Phair and Good (1995) identify some key pointers to assist with communicating with people with dementia (**Box 18.3**).

One of the most frustrating aspects of communication for staff is the older person who repeats him or herself, constantly perseverating and asking repetitive questions. Staff must remember that if the person has not retained the answer to the question, for them, it will be the first time they have inquired. There is no point in expressing frustration, accept it is the first time they have heard the answer and offer the information respectfully. While doing so, ascertain if the person is repeating themselves because of other reasons, perhaps anxiety or boredom.

Purposeful Activity

Every person has their own organised approach to activity in their life. For some that may be physical, it may be work or it may be keeping a family. There is very clear evidence that encouraging people with dementia to undertake activity is part of the nurse's role. There is a real danger that people with dementia in institutional settings may suffer from sensory deprivation. Restricted stimulation caused by limited visual stimulation, limited conversation and physical activity can

18.3 Communicating with People with Dementia

- Always assume that the person with dementia can understand. Never say anything within hearing distance that you don't want them to hear.
- Use short sentences to ensure that the person does not forget the beginning of the sentence before the end is reached.
- Avoid the use of jargon that is not contemporary to the person; also avoid the use of expressions that should not be taken literally.
- If the person does not understand be prepared to repeat the question in a different way, but try not to introduce too many new words.
- When giving instructions, break down the actions into simple steps.
- Ensure that the environment is conducive to imparting important information.
- Maintain eye contact and give the same message with your body and face as you are giving with the words.
- Some people have more success than others at communication with certain older people, use this if it helps.
- Watch for signs of restlessness and withdraw, do not pursue the conversation if the person is not ready.
- Immediate reassurance or reward is important, reality for some people with dementia is often immediate.
- Try to state things positively rather than reinforcing the persons failure.

Source: Phair and Good, 1995.

all add to their problems and how they present their frustration (Hallberg *et al.* 1990).

Involving people in activity reduces what is felt as disruptive behaviour (Smith-Jones and Francis, 1992), and it is an essential part of an individualised package of care. Up to 80% of interactions in a residential setting will be related to physical care, with most being restricted to informing or questions (Salmon, 1993).

Encouraging dependence, however well intentioned and however unconsciously conducted, will only devalue the person's self-worth and increase, in the long term, the care professional's workload. Encouraging involvement in activity assists with the person to remain physically active, and prevents stiffness, muscle spasm and wasting. Activity can improve cardiac output and enable the person to psychologically feel valued, motivated and have a sense of dignity (Phair and Good, 1995).

It is important that the identified activities have either a purpose for the older person or have a therapeutic reason to assist in maintaining the person's level of functioning. The stereotypical view of activity is Bingo on Monday, sing-along on Tuesday, fluffy ball making on Thursday and so on. It is important to discover from the person or their carer what is a valuable activity to them, it may be something simple, e.g. watching football on television or doing some knitting. Some people may not have any activities or hobbies that they can still manage to undertake, or indeed they may not have had an active life in the past. If the nurse can identify the value of a certain activity, they will probably be able to explain to the older person about its value to them.

Enabling the person to feel part of the society in which they live will enhance their wellbeing and encourage relationship formation. This feeling of wellbeing will stay with the person even if they are unable to remember the activity which has caused it. Any involvement in domestic work, gardening or discussion about new fabrics, or even the choice of channel on the television should not be excluded from the person who has dementia.

More structured activity may have a health promotion initiative which is not obvious to the older person or their family. Dementia of any type causes complex deterioration of many physiological and psychological aspects of the person. Thus, any activity should reflect the physical, psychological and social health promotion needs of the older person. Short mat bowls, for example, can offer a variety of therapeutic uses to somebody with dementia. The cardiovascular system is exercised promoting oxygenation, and muscle activity is encouraged assisting in the prevention of muscle wasting. The mobilising immediately relieves pressure risk areas and hand–eye coordination is important to maintain as it is a skill used in eating. The conversation, if facilitated appropriately by the nurse, can be encouraging, while offering camaraderie and praise in a failure-free environment is psychologically supportive. The simple arithmetic encourages the person to think actively and assists in stimulating the person's ability to concentrate. The movement, although gentle, will help to stimulate the appetite and the gastrointestinal tract, particularly in respect of peristaltic movement. Finally, the activity can help the person to feel more rested and relaxed and so aid a more restful night's sleep. The success or failure of the implementation of such activity will depend on the skills of group dynamics and the interpersonal relationship skills of the nurse facilitating the group.

Normal life activity should be promoted with exactly the same rationale as described in the group activity. Arguably, assisting a resident in continuing a personal hobby should be promoted before any organised group activity.

Physical Aspects of Care

A person with dementia will have a varying level of physical care needs depending on a number of factors. The nurse will need to assess the current level of care and also anticipate the effect of any particular aspect of their needs in relation to how the dementia or organic illness is affecting the individual person.

Essential Physical Care

The type and approach to essential care will depend on the person's current mental health state and how it is affecting them. For some, the nurse may only need to assess the person and then instruct other care staff to carry out that care. This may be just supervising and advising the person about where their washing implements are or giving total person hygiene care to the person. The level of personal care should not only reflect their mental state but also the person's personal expectations and their cultural needs and requirements. A man who only shaved once a week, for example, may be perceived as being difficult if he is shaved every day and expresses some resistance to this. Alternatively, a person who has particular religious rules may require very strict hygiene requirements. The skill of communication and understanding of the older person is just as important in personal care as it is in any aspect of the person's mental-health care.

If a person is objecting to an aspect of personal care, the question should always be asked 'is this care essential and if so why?' The nurse should be constantly aware of the impact of staff on the person and their own standards and expectations. If the care is not essential, then perhaps it could be left on that particular occasion.

The Care of Medical Conditions and Conditions of Old Age

A person who is suffering from an organic illness may still have any other condition that can affect older people in general. The management of these conditions may be complicated by the organic illness because of the possible difficulty the older person has in understanding instructions and complying with any treatment plan.

It may also be difficult for the older person to express their needs or pain, or explain the symptoms they are experiencing. The nurse, therefore, has not only to be skilled in understanding and identifying symptoms of medical conditions but also to have communications skills which enable them to extract the presentation of symptoms from a person who is not expressing them in a normal fashion.

Any management programme should be followed within the context of the person's organic illness and will require skilled intervention. The person is entitled to the same access to assessment, however, and the nurse may need to employ aspects of advocacy in order to ensure the older person has accurate representation and access to treatment.

Prevention of Physical Complications

As the person's organic illness progresses, the potential complications of any debilitating and terminal illness will need to be managed. The nurse must ensure that assessment and management of the person will include accurate health promotion in respect to:

- Pressure damage risk.
- Nutrition.
- Lifting and movement.
- Muscular contraction.
- Problems of constipation.
- Sleep disturbance.
- Hypostatic chest conditions.
- The danger of falls and complications associated with them.

Once again, the management of these possible complications and their prevention has to be undertaken within the context of the person's failing mental state and their ability to understand instruction or health management advice.

Psychological Support

The psychological support of a person with an organic illness will extend to the support of their carers and significant family members. It is important to try to recognise the feelings that have generated from them. People with dementia retain an essential awareness regardless of whether or not they can put it into words (Frank, 1995), and their expressed emotion will affect the carer and how they are able to manage the situation.

In order to recognise and support the emotions expressed by the older person, it is important to remember that the most vital skill is to firstly acknowledge and skilfully respond to the emotion that is being demonstrated. In order for this to be achieved, the nurse must have formed a relationship with the person. The respect and dignity required in supporting the expression of emotions of somebody with dementia require all the skills of good communication and counselling techniques. The nurse must use their expertise, however, to read and understand the feelings the person is trying to express, and not just rely on the words being spoken. Helping people express their feelings or responding to expressions may need to be undertaken on a number of occasions before the person is familiarised with the reassurance and support. Dealing with this aspect of a person's wellbeing requires a combination of patience, understanding, and professional expertise.

People with dementia sometimes become distressed by events that have happened in the past, but which for them are very real now. That emotion needs to be supported slowly through the nurse's expertise so that the person can be calmed and reassured and then gently brought back to the present day.

The psychological support of a person with an organic illness can be undertaken through informal approaches from a nurse using counselling and supportive skills or in more formal structured individual or group settings. It is a relatively recent development that people with organic illness can work with their emotions. Work undertaken by Feil (1992) developed a unique approach to enabling older people with dementia to explore their feelings through validation

therapy. There are mixed views on its effectiveness, but arguably the person would improve and be able to express themselves through skilful group work techniques or a positive environment (Bleathman and Morton, 1992). Nonetheless, this work has highlighted the need for validation of feelings through which psychological support can be achieved.

Structured groups of reality orientation were popular in the 1980s. However, there is little evidence to support the anecdotal view that it is beneficial to continue to bring someone back to the present day (Hanley, 1986). Similarly, reminiscence therapy has not been proven to offer psychological support or assist in restoration of a person's memory (Brotchie and Thornton, 1987). If used with skill, however, reminiscence does enable the person to use the skills they still possess. Their self-esteem can be raised and relationships do develop. The outcome of the memory is essentially irrelevant, and the group should be considered a success if the people are able to enjoy conversation and interaction, thus diverting ruminating thoughts, improving communication skills and raising self-esteem (O'Donovan, 1993).

More recently, memory clinics have been established in order to support people with dementia in the early stages. Although there is little evidence to show that the groups prevent any deterioration in the person's memory or indeed restore memory, the groups act as a positive outlet for carers and the person with dementia in enabling them to express their feelings and views in a supportive environment. Management hints can also be discussed within this scenario (Allen, 1996).

Any psychological support systems established must be undertaken with the knowledge and skills that are required by nurses working with any client group. The significant difference is that the needs of a person with organic illness and their family may require a very eclectic approach, and may require the nurse to use their skills at very short intervals in informal as well as formal settings. Other therapeutic activities and groups will be discussed briefly later in the chapter.

MEASURING THE QUALITY OF CARE

Quality assurance is now a requirement in any service. Methods of auditing care have been developed, but there are relatively few that attempt to capture the perceived reception of that care. It is also rare to find a method of audit that attempts to examine the impact of the care staff on the person receiving care from the point of view of the person with dementia.

Recent publications have identified that the opinion of the person with dementia can be obtained. Phair undertook a study to collect the opinions of people with dementia using the critical incident technique. This formed part of the quality assurance programme for a mental health unit (cited in Goldsmith, 1996). Goldsmith himself identifies how people with dementia can give useful opinion about the quality of their care, and about how that care is delivered. The fundamental principle must be that the professional observer must find methods of audit and quality assurance that the person can manage. Questionnaires and long interviews may not be appropriate but short one-to-one discussions under controlled conditions can offer extremely useful information. Communicating with a person with dementia has begun to be seen as a useful and fulfilling occupation. Poetry is now being written by people with dementia and by poets using the words of people with dementia (Goldsmith, 1996; Killick, 1997). For care staff, the challenge is to listen with an open mind to the opinion that is being expressed.

More systematic approaches to quality assurance are available. These usually present the perspective of quality from the provider's point of view and use quantitative data to support any quality measure. Kitwood and Bredin (1992) developed a method of measuring the quality of the care received by the person with dementia from (it was hoped) their point of view. The research was carried out in social care settings, and thus it could be acknowledged that acute physical problems would not have been evident in some of the clients involved in the study. The technique is, however, an extremely useful audit tool and so deserves discussion. Arguably, the method would be suitable for any care environment where older people are in receipt of care. The technique has not, however, been validated in these areas and so cannot formally be recommended for all care environments.

Dementia Care Mapping

The process named dementia care mapping is becoming acknowledged as a validated and reliable method of recording the type of care, the approach to care and the quality of the care of people with a dementing illness. The process is labour intensive, but is able to paint a clear picture of the care patterns in a communal area over a period of time. The method is behavioural in its approach, and records activity, how long each activity lasts and the client's apparent response to that interaction. The scoring is designed to show how the client responds to the activity rather than how the care is offered; thus, the technique should be able to identify individual approaches to a client's needs.

Dementia care mapping is conducted by two mappers who record data on individual clients. The data collected is then compared to ensure some level of objectivity. For experienced users of the system the information will also convey the culture of the unit, the attitude of the staff, and how well the physical psychological and social needs of the person are being met. Care plans can be examined within the context of the information gathered, and staff development and training programmes can be drawn up, thus ensuring accurate targeting of the development needs of that unit. The technique should not, however, be seen as a panacea for a total quality approach to the care of people with dementia. Any treatment plans, quality of hygiene or the quality of intimate procedures cannot be measured by this technique and thus would still need to be reviewed independently.

SUPPORTING CARERS

The needs of carers are discussed in Chapter 16. The families of people with dementia require both practical and psychological support. There is now evidence to challenge a stereotypical view that carers do so out of guilt and duty. Nolan *et al.* (1997) offer a view that there are many different types of caregiving. These are:
- Anticipatory.
- Preventative.
- Supervisory.
- Instrumental.
- Protective.
- Preservative.
- Reconstructive.
- Reciprocal.

Family caregivers will give different types of care at different times. In their work they also clearly identify that family caregivers travel a distinct journey when caring for a person with dementia. The nurse, then, has to be able to acknowledge this journey and be able to adjust the type and nature of support required. Supporting the complex needs of the family are an integral part of the role of the nurse and require clear skills if support is to be offered successfully for the care of the person with dementia.

The Admiral Nurse Service was set up in response to a growing demand for support from carers. Admiral nurses have a caseload of about 100 carers, ranging in age from 30–90 years. They offer support from the time the relative is diagnosed with dementia and throughout the stages of the illness.

FUNCTIONAL ILLNESS IN OLDER PEOPLE

Depression

It is only relatively recently that depression has been recognised in older people as a real and debilitating illness. Many older people have felt symptoms of depression were just part of ageing and as a consequence have not received appropriate treatment. This has been compounded by a lack of assessment skills and screening by health professionals (Wade, 1994; Hughes, 1997; Armstrong, 1996). Depression in old age is common. In Liverpool, a study found that 11.3% of older people living in the community were diagnosed as suffering from depression (Copeland *et al.* 1987). Other studies identified 10–14% of older people suffered from depression, however not every study identified if the depression was primary or secondary to another disease (Baldwin, 1997). In 1990, the suicide rate for people over 65 years of age was over 50% higher than the average for the population as a whole, and older men were particularly at risk (Wade, 1994). Older people are less likely to visit their general practitioner with symptoms of depression and it is common for the symptoms to be mistaken as a physical illness or the beginning of dementia.

The Causes of Depression

It is now recognised that the cause of depression is often a combination of physical, psychological and social factors. Research does suggest that it is more common in people living in urban areas and among women rather than men (Wade, 1994).

Bereavement, and in particular the loss of a partner, is a significant factor in depression, and is more common in those who have been widowed for less than 3 years (Wade, 1994). This may be a factor combined with other significant factors such as ill health, financial hardship, social isolation, severe life events, lack of social support and medication (Hughes, 1997; Wade, 1994; Murphy, 1988).

Living in a residential environment has also been identified as a precipitating factor in depression. It is not clear if this is because of the social factors of the institution, the routines, rituals and loss of control of the older person or because of the loss of other factors in their lives and an increased physical dependency. There is evidence, however, that older people living in a care home are less likely to be treated for depression (Hughes, 1997; Wade, 1994).

The Signs and Symptoms of Depression

A diagnosis of depression is usually made if the person is experiencing at least four of the symptoms listed below for more than 2 weeks [World Health Organisation (WHO), 1993]:

- Depressed mood to a degree that is abnormal for that person, present for most of each and almost every day sustained for at least 2 weeks.
- Loss of interest or pleasure in activities that are normally pleasurable.
- Decreased energy or increased fatigue.
- Loss of confidence or self-esteem.
- Unreasonable feelings of self-reproach or excessive and inappropriate guilt.
- Recurrent thoughts of death or suicide.
- Complaints or evidence or diminished ability to think or concentrate, such as indecisiveness or vacillation.
- Change in psychomotor activity with agitation or retardation.
- Sleep disturbance.
- Change in appetite (increase or decrease) with corresponding weight change.

Traditionally, depression was further classified as endogenous or reactive. This supposedly clarified whether the depression has a social cause (e.g. bereavement). This is now considered irrelevant as the social context of the person will affect how the depression affects the person suffering the illness.

For older people, the effects of depression have a very significant effect on their overall health. Older people are more likely to be preoccupied with somatic symptoms, which will increase with depression. If someone has arthritis, the pain will become more severe and their tolerance threshold is lowered. They may also succumb to other minor ailments as their immunity decreases. This could lead to severe problems of malignancy as depression can cause depressed T-lymphocyte function (Mottram *et al.* 1996a; Murphy, 1988). Evidence suggests that depression is recognised as a prodrome of certain types of carcinoma, in particular cancer of the lung, pancreas and stomach (Murphy, 1988). Labelling their presenting symptoms as hypochondria is both incorrect and stereotypical. Other symptoms will develop as the depression continues. The physical presentation of depression includes palpitations, headaches, shaking, stomach discomfort and general aches and pains. As the depression continues the loss of appetite, sleep disturbance and lack of concentration can cause increased joint stiffness, constipation, mild confusion, decreased skin turgor and increased likelihood of infection. The complications which may easily follow may include, increased risk of pressure sores, increased risk of falls increased dependency and thus increased feelings of worthlessness and loss of control. Depression then in older people will have very dramatic effects on the whole life of the older person and so must be considered a serious mental illness.

There are other physical illnesses that have an associated depression including pernicious anaemia, renal dysfunction, Addison's disease, hypothyroidism, some malignancies and cerebral vascular accident. Some medications also have a side effect of depression. Common drugs include steroids, beta-blockers, methyldopa, nifedipine, non-steroidal anti-inflammatory drugs, digitalis and levodopa. The nurse should ensure that every aspect of the person's current health status is examined in order to establish if there are any other physical causes which may be exacerbating the presenting symptoms (Mottram *et al.* 1996b).

The psychological symptoms can easily be mistaken for early signs of dementia if a detailed recent history is not obtained. The picture should then become clear of the sequence of events and presenting symptoms, thus enabling a clearer diagnosis. Of course as with any physical illness the older person could suffer from dementia and also become clinically depressed. In this situation, the skills of assessment are particularly expert as the differential between the two illnesses may be marginal to the observer.

The most dangerous aspect of depression in older people is the effect the disease has on the person's total being. As described, the physical deterioration can be rapid. Psychologically, the person's feelings of unworthiness may escalate into suspicion and paranoid ideation. In severe depression, a person may present with psychotic symptoms of visual and auditory hallucinations and persecutory delusions. They are commonly of a very negative nature and usually distressing. The person may believe the food is poisoned or that some one is trying to kill them or their family; others have an overwhelming feeling of doom and then become very agitated and frightened. For some older people, the symptoms become so severe they become a danger to themselves as they begin to express suicidal thoughts either to act out the instruction of the voices or to free themselves of the trauma. It is at this time that emergency treatment for the depression is required

The Treatment of Depression

Methods of treating depression have developed over the past 50 years. There are very clear reasons why different types of treatments should be used, depending on the presentation of the illness. The severity of the depression will dictate how dramatic the treatment needs to be.

Electroconvulsive Therapy (ECT)

Since its introduction in 1938, ECT has remained the most controversial and yet the most effective treatment for depression. In modern practice, it is only used if the person's life is threatened because their depression has become so severe they have stopped eating, drinking or have profound retardation or suicidal behaviour (Baldwin, 1997). It is also considered the treatment of choice for older people who have delusional depression.

ECT involves passing an electric current through the brain. The passage induced a grand mal-type seizure. The carefully regulated procedure will now only visibly show a small twitch of an eyebrow or register of the activity on a monitor. The procedure no longer creates broken limbs or bitten tongues as believed from the past.

Despite many controlled trials, it is still unclear exactly how ECT works. The evidence of the outcome is, however, that older people do recover from very severe life-threatening depression with relatively few side effects. The short-term memory deficit is believed to be short lived and is argued by some to be usually present before the ECT.

A course of six to eight treatments over 3–4 weeks will in 80% of cases ensure a full recovery from depression (Baldwin, 1997). For older people, it may also be the treatment of choice if the person cannot tolerate antidepressant drugs. Contraindications for this treatment would reflect those for any treatment requiring a general anaesthetic. The risks are often outweighed by the danger to the person's life of not having their severe depression treated.

The Role of the Nurse in Managing Depression

The role of the nurse is both practical and psychological. The older person will require full pre and postoperative care, along with skilled psychological support for their depression and their disorientation and short-term memory problems after the treatment.

Nurses should be mindful that the person may recover from their motor retardation after two or three treatments, yet their morbid thoughts may remain for a while longer. This is a particular time of caution, especially if the person was expressing suicidal thoughts. Anecdotal opinion is that some find the energy at this time to carry out the action which they still believe to be correct when previously they did not have the energy or volition to do so.

If there is concern that the older person will experience some memory problems following the ECT, it may be administered unilaterally. That is, the paddles are placed on one temple only. However, some believe that bilateral ECT is more effective and successful treatment is achieved more quickly (Benbow, 1989).

Pharmacological Treatment

Older people will respond successfully to drugs prescribed for depression providing their effects are monitored carefully. Clinical depression is accompanied by a reduction in amines, particularly 5-hydroxytryptamine (5-HT or serotonin) and noradrenaline at neurosynaptic junctions in the brain (Gould, 1997). Many of the drugs used to treat depression raise the level of these chemicals in the brain.

The problem for older people is the side effects of many of the drugs. Tricyclic antidepressants, for example, have the anticholinergic adverse effects for some older people of blurred vision, retention of urine, cardiac problems, constipation and delirium. Antihistamine side effects of over-sedation and weight gain may also occur. Postural hypotension is also a common side effect of these drugs. For people who already suffer from glaucoma, cardiac or parkinsonian-type problems these drugs will only exacerbate the problems.

A newer group of drugs, selective serotonin reuptake inhibitors (SSRIs), have fewer side effects of a less dramatic nature. These may include nausea, anxiety, headache, diarrhoea and insomnia (Baldwin, 1997). There are other groups of antidepressants that are used less frequently with older people. These are the groups of drugs which include monoamine oxidase inhibitors, reversible inhibitors or monoamine oxidase agents, and serotonin noradrenaline reuptake inhibitors (Baldwin, 1997).

For the nurse caring for someone who is prescribed antidepressants the most important action would be, as with all drugs, to familiarise themselves with the specific side effects of that drug and the recommended dosage. There are some principles, however, which the nurse should follow when an older person is prescribed antidepressants. Good practice would recommend that the lying and standing blood pressure is taken twice daily for at least 2 weeks, while the person becomes accustomed to the drug. Many antidepressants have a sedative side effect. They should, therefore, be taken in the evening or when sleepiness for some hours will not affect the person. The drug should be prescribed in small doses at first, in order to assess the tolerance of the person. When the treatment is over, the drug should then be withdrawn just as slowly. This will enable an accurate assessment of the brain's ability to continue to produce the chemicals without the support of the drug. Antidepressants can take up to 3 weeks before the therapeutic levels are felt to have a positive effect. For a person suffering from severe depression that time can be endless. The nurse should ensure that appropriate psychological support this given, while monitoring the person's dietary intake and their bowel activity. It is when someone is suffering for the most severe effects of depression that their physical as well as their psychological needs have to be proactively managed.

The problem of sleeplessness for people who are suffering with depression is common. People can easily be prescribed sleeping draughts that they then become dependent on. The nurse should ensure that every other approach to aiding restful sleep is assessed before sleeping draughts are used. This symptom of depression could easily become a long-term problem because reactive treatment with drug intervention becomes the first and only intervention. Hospitals and institutions have been found to use more sedatives than is necessary, with the resultant dependency of the older person. This in itself then brings difficulties that have to be managed (Gould, 1997).

For people who are living in the community, the nurse must be aware that antidepressants are potentially lethal drugs, and have been taken as an overdose with lethal effects. The nurse should work with the doctor and the older person to ensure the risk of attempted suicide is lessened (if that is a risk). Medicines should be prescribed in small quantities and the person's mood level monitored closely, with regular supportive visits and practical help as required.

Psychosocial Interventions

As it has already been illustrated, depression will affect every aspect of a person's health. Any physical illness they have will be exacerbated, or at the very least, their tolerance of that illness will be lowered. The depression itself will bring a feeling of low esteem and poor concentration and for many there is the fear and belief that they will never improve. There is also emerging evidence that a single treatment approach whether pharmacological or psychotherapeutic will not succeed if the person as a whole is not offered care and support.

The psychosocial approach to the care of depression is, therefore, well suited to the role of the nurse. As described throughout this book, Maslow's hierarchy of needs should be addressed in all aspects of health and illness. For a person with acute depression, their motivation and concentration will be affected along with their appetite and desire and ability to carry out the most mundane of everyday activity.

For older people living in the community, it may be apposite to arrange for the person to receive domestic help. This help should be facilitative in nature and not overbearing. For people who are not eating or who have a poor appetite, the temptation may be to arrange meals-on-wheels. Although this will meet the nutritional needs, the lack of social contact may mean that the person does not have the desire to eat. This is supported by methods of encouraging the appetite, the smell of cooking, the vision of food prepa-

ration and the company of the home help will all support the person in their difficulties in trying a diet. Obviously a delivered meal would be better than no food at all; however, the desired outcome may not be achieved so easily. It is also important that the person is encouraged to have some company. This may be arranged at the day centre or day hospital. Again the exercise of getting up and getting organised for the trip will assist in establishing some purpose to the day. The transport should be of an appropriate type and all care staff involved should understand the possible anxiety of the older person who may be fearful of going out, meeting new people, etc. It should also be recognised that the person may need assistance in getting ready and this may take more time than usual. Once at the day unit, the activity and interaction should be positive in nature. An anxiety-provoking effect for someone with depression is to see other older people with severe mental-health problems, or with the residual effects of a stroke; this may again cause increased anxiety because of their already lowered mood and motivation. Support in meeting those other people and perhaps groups and activities that are failure-free but not demeaning should be undertaken.

If the person is admitted to hospital with depression or indeed is living in a residential setting, the principles will remain the same. The relationship with the nurse will be paramount in the care and recovery. The physical needs of the person can be met by facilitation and support. Automatically undertaking care will not necessarily help the person, but nagging or becoming very authoritative will also only lower the persons feeling of self-worth.

The environment of the unit should be examined to establish that it is communicating a positive message. Is it tidy and clean, with a positive aroma? Can the pleasant aroma from the kitchen be smelt by the person, thus stimulating the appetite? Is the person given time and support to get up in the mornings, and is the person encouraged to stay up in the evening, rather than go to bed and then require sleeping tablets at 10 p.m.

The motivational aspect of the person needs very careful management. Activity should be in keeping with the person's premorbid interests, and should be for duration that they can manage. If the person is very depressed and can only concentrate for a few minutes, a short but meaningful discussion is better than trying to engage the person for a great length of time. A programme of purposeful activity with conscious times of inactivity can be agreed with the person. Some activity may be new to the older person but with careful explanation of the therapeutic rationale compliance can be achieved (Phair, 1990). An example of this would be in encouraging the person to participate in a game of short mat bowls in the unit. They may not have the motivation or desire or may be too agitated to partake. The nurse may encourage them to passively watch on the first occasion. This would enable distraction (for a short time) from their ruminations and enable passive social contact with others. This in itself may sew seeds or relationship development in a non-threatening way. On the second occasion, the person may be encouraged to participate for a short time. The rationale may be explained: the gentle activity will assist with the stimulation of appetite, muscular exercise and thus bowel stimulation. The exercise will also assist in promoting sleep, while the contact with others and the sense of camaraderie will offer support to the person. The concentration will also be assisted by the hand–eye coordination, and again provides a diversion from any ruminations.

The nurse should then see any activity that was traditionally seen as the role exclusively of the occupational therapist as part of their nursing role. They can use this psychosocial intervention as observable evidence of the improvement of the older person. Television can also be used as a therapeutic activity if the person is enabled to watch a programme that they enjoy. Watching something the person likes initially may show the nurse that after a few minutes they become agitated showing nonverbal signs of distress (Ford *et al.* 1997). The focus for the nurse and the person can be used as the common foundation for the development of their relationship. As the person progresses, observing their ability to concentrate on a programme they enjoy can be used as a measurable observation for the positive effects of any other treatment (Phair and Good, 1995).

The level of noise in a unit, the 'business' of the staff and the general atmosphere will affect how well or badly the person responds to any formal treatment. Isolation in a single room can be just as damaging as insisting that the person participates in a wholly inappropriate and demeaning activity. The milieu and the relationship of the nurse and patient are vital components in any treatment of depression (Phair and Good, 1989). The interpersonal, counselling and active listening skills of the nurse coupled with their understanding and knowledge of the physical complications of depression do place the nurse in a key position in the treatment of a person with this illness. The most skilled practitioner will be able to use all of these skills in a seemingly effortless way, and often the drugs prescribed will be perceived as the reason for the person's recovery.

Psychotherapeutic Techniques

Another approach to the treatment of depression is to work with the person in respect of their cognition. For some older people who have never been used to discussing their feelings and emotions, these methods may need to be used sensitively. For others, the depression is so severe that the psychomotor retardation disables the person and they are unable to work through their feelings and thought processes in a positive way. In these circumstances, the person with depression may require one or a combination of the previously mentioned therapeutic interventions in order to raise their mood enough for them to begin to explore their innermost feelings.

All psychotherapeutic techniques should only be undertaken by professionals with an acknowledged expertise in managing people's emotions. Although it may be relatively simple to open dialogue with a person, the skill is immense when handling the emotions, thoughts or experiences that the person has had. Leaving the person unsupported at the end of a session is perhaps more dangerous than not commencing the therapy. It is for this reason that all of the therapies now mentioned should not be undertaken lightly.

Counselling
Specific types of counselling may be appropriate depending on the identified cause of the depression. Bereavement counselling, for example, is a good example of this. If a person is unable to move through the stages of bereavement, counsellors trained in this field can facilitate this providing the depression is also treated.

Psychotherapy
Group and individual psychotherapy will benefit some older people. The most common type is cognitive behavioural psychotherapy. There is little evaluation of its effectiveness as opposed to other methods of treatment (Baldwin, 1997), however in one study, clients being treated with this method responded more positively that a control group who were only being treated with placebos. The aim of this type of treatment is to assist people in shifting the way they think about situations and thus affect how they feel about them. Negative thinking is targeted and the emphasis is focused on social issues thought to be relevant to the depression (Baldwin, 1997). Specialists qualified in this field have to consider the added complications of old age, namely that the person may or may not have and adjust to any treatment accordingly. The person's age should not be considered a reason for not offering this very specialised type of treatment.

Hypomania and Manic Depression

Some episodes of depression are followed or superseded by episodes of elation. This series of mood swings, which may be rapid or slow to manifest, may indicate a bipolar mood of the older person demonstrating an affective disorder. The depressive episodes will present in a very similar way to that already described. The hypomanic state may, however, be far more dramatic in its presentation. The main symptoms identified by WHO (1993) in ICD-10 include:
- Elevation of mood.
- Increase in general energy and libido.
- Increased sociability, irritability and familiarity.

Sleep decreases and the person's ability to reason will also be affected. The person may be over-talkative and there will be grandiosity, often with financial overspending. The ICD-10 states that it should only be classified as 'mania' if delusions and hallucinations are present. Most people who are suffering from manic depression will have a history stretching back into younger adult life (Jacoby, 1997). Jacoby states that it is very rare for older people to develop unipolar manic illness in later life, however unipolar depressive illness is more common.

The Nurse's Role

This illness draws on the nurse's ability to assess every aspect of the person's life. Hypomanic illness affects the physical, social and psychological aspects of the older person, possibly more acutely that many other illnesses. The nurse must be aware of the physical consequence of overactivity, lack of sleep and often a poor diet. The grandiose ideas can cause arrogance in the person sparking off confrontations with others, while the overspending can cause severe financial hardship for the person and their family. Treatment should be a combination of managing all of those clinical aspects while managing the illness. It is best to reduce the stimulation experienced by the person if at all possible. If the person is admitted to hospital, this may mean giving them a side room, keeping noise levels low and having all sensory stimulation kept to a minimum. The drug regime will depend on the severity of the hypomania, that is, how acutely ill the person is and how much there are dangers of physical complications of the psychiatric illness.

The most common drugs used are still neuroleptics. These also carry side effects, the most common being extrapyramidal effects increasing the risk of falling. Anticholinergic drugs should then also be prescribed to counter-balance these. The nurse has a role in monitoring not only the effect of these drugs but also the common side effects. It is a balancing act between the drug regime and the effects of the hypomania, and intensive care by experienced nurses is advisable.

Prophylactic treatment of affective disorders is effectively managed by the use of lithium carbonate. This drug levels the mood and has been found to be effective in people who experience recurrent depression as well as manic illness. Again the drug needs to be monitored closely. Before prescribing the drug the doctor should undertake a full screen to ensure the person has adequate kidney and thyroid function. This should then be reviewed every 6 months for the duration of the treatment, which may be many years. When nurses are taking a blood specimen they should record when the drug was taken and try to take the blood specimen 12 hours after the tablet; this will ensure an accurate reading of the blood levels. The nurse should also be aware of the doctors preferred therapeutic range, as there are variations. However, it is usually 0.4–0.8 mmol/litre. If the level of lithium carbonate rises above 1.0 mmol/litre there is a danger of toxicity. In this case, the drug should be stopped and advice sought from the doctor immediately.

The nurse will also have a role in supporting the person and their family after the episode of hypomania. There may be some financial debts to deal with in respect of the person's activities while they were unwell. Practical as well as psychological help is vital at this time in order for all concerned to accept and come to terms with the events which may have occurred during the illness episode.

Anxiety States

The acknowledgement of a presenting anxiety state in older people is still considered by many to be an illness that is ignored by health-care professionals. The symptoms are common, distressing and treatable. The older person may present with a collection of physical problems: backache, headache and bowel disturbance, to name but a few. The symptoms of anxiety are classic and yet so often ignored when presented by an older person. The physical treatment of these symptoms will only compound the problems and not deal with the underlying anxiety causing the symptoms. It is also common for older people to be labelled as attention seeking or play acting, as this particular mental-health problem is neither tolerated nor understood.

The person may become entrenched in their own anxiety state, as their own management of it becomes an integral part of their life. This may include behavioural changes, for example avoiding what they perceive as the trigger or not eating correctly as they suffer dyspepsia. For others, the constant cry for help may alienate them from their families and health professionals. Many then become stigmatised and when a physical illness not connected to the anxiety becomes evident the symptoms are missed.

Common symptoms of anxiety in older people will include sleep disturbances, daytime tiredness, bowel and back problems, headaches and a feeling of doom.

The Role of the Nurse

It is important that a thorough physical investigation is conducted to ensure that there are not any physical illnesses causing the problems. The older person will then need to feel that they can trust the nurse. A positive relationship with someone who has an unconditional positive regard and a non-judgemental approach is vital for people with this illness. A structured programme of anxiety management would then be the action of choice. It is also important to uncover the underlying cause of the anxiety and within the anxiety management programme look for solutions to the causative factor. For some, there may not be one single cause and this can lead to a more complicated approach to care and treatment. The reason for the anxiety and subsequent fear may be very realistic. It is important that the nurse supports the person in their decisions and promotes an approach that is the most appropriate for that person.

Certain drugs can also be given to assist the older person with their symptoms. Benzodiazapines have proved to be very effective in dampening the symptoms but they only lead to avoidance of the real issue. They are also addictive and can cause many complications for the older person. They should, therefore, be used very sparingly.

It is increasingly acknowledged that older people may also suffer from post-traumatic stress. A lot of work has been undertaken with young people; however, the effects of the Second World War are for some older people still causing many inner problems. When caring for someone who has an anxiety state, it is important to consider the possibility of a post-traumatic stress response. If this is considered a possibility, assistance should be sought from an expert in this area of practice.

Meeting Mental Health Needs

A 91-year-old lady, Ivy Edwards, lives alone in a large block of flats in an inner city. Her family has moved away and her husband died some 30 years ago. Ivy has always had a 'nervous disposition' and she worries about money and the increased crime rate. As a result of this, she has stopped going out of the flat. A neighbour brings food and she has a private home help for 1 hour a week. She is worried about falling and being on her own and Ivy regularly calls the doctor to visit. She is very independent and reluctant to go to a day centre. On one of the doctor's visits, he notes that she is not sleeping well and is losing weight. Her conversation is a little more negative than normal, although nothing very dramatic. He feels that she is beginning to show some signs of depression and asks the community psychiatric nurse (CPN) to visit. The CPN undertakes an assessment over a number of weeks. Ivy tells the nurse that she has a number of things wrong with her, a pain in her hip the cause of which she does not know, occasionally wetting the bed at night and intermittent constipation. Eventually, when the nurse has gained her trust, Ivy says that she is 'terrified of falling, not being able to call anyone and dying alone'. She is eating less and is becoming a little muddled. The CPN helps Ivy understand the need for more social contact and support and explains the physical effects of her anxiety and depression. She agrees to talk to a social worker who undertakes a social care assessment.

A multidisciplinary meeting is held with Ivy and her son, the doctor, the CPN and the social worker. Through careful explanation and health education, as well as an explanation of the services, Ivy agrees to have a home help visit daily, to visit a day centre twice weekly, and to have meals-on-wheels and a telephone lifeline system. She also agrees and enjoys 2 weeks respite care every 2 months in a residential home. The CPN monitors her psychological and physical health, both of which have improved dramatically as the social involvement and human contact improved.

The mental and physical-health needs of Ivy were set to become acute and probably life-threatening. Because of the skilled approach of all disciplines involved and their professional acknowledgement of everybody's role, she is now able to stay in her own home and receive a less expensive yet more appropriate type of care. The health needs are met with a social care solution, and her good health is maintained in the same manner.

- What information did Ivy give to the nurse in the home that offered subjective data for the nursing assessment?
- What information did the nurse collect that provided objective data for the assessment?
- What strengths does Ivy demonstrate that could be used as a basis for his plan of care?
- What interventions could the nurse make regarding her specific problems?
- What particular contribution would each member of the team be likely to make to the care of Ivy?
- List possible outcome criteria for the plan of care for Ivy? Her own desired outcomes, and assessment of the achievement of these, should be included.
- How could the care plan be evaluated?

Schizophrenia, Paraphrenia and Paranoid States

Schizophrenia is possibly the most commonly used word to describe people with mental illness by the general public, and yet is very often completely misunderstood. For older people, there are two different groups of people who suffer from schizophrenia. The first are those who developed the illness at a young age and have grown old. The second are a rare group who develop late-onset schizophrenia, usually referred to as paraphrenia.

Schizophrenia is a severe and enduring mental illness in which the person has difficulty in judging and interpreting reality. The person's emotional and thinking processes may also be altered. It is a psychotic disorder consisting often of delusions and or hallucinations. A delusion is a belief held by the person which is not consistent with the evidence available, yet the person cannot change their view. These may be in the form of grandiose delusions whereby they believe they have special powers, or through ideas of reference. This can be observed if a person believes that there are special messages being transmitted, perhaps every time they see a red car, or when certain music is played. It is fairly common for people to experience ideas of reference from the television and radio.

A hallucination is when the person experiences the stimulation of one of the senses which is not real or triggered by true external stimuli. These are most commonly auditory, but may be visual, olfactory or gastultory. The person may also experience thought disorders whereby they have difficulty in language production. Their speech may become incoherent or very slow, or even rapid. They may also use words that are apparently meaningless (neologisms) (Morley and Sellwood, 1997).

The effect on the person experiencing these symptoms may be seen in other aspects of their life and ability to function. They may experience behavioural difficulties, including apathy, loss of enjoyment and pleasure, flatness of affector motor retardation, impoverished speech and poor self-care (Morley and Sellwood, 1997). The person may only experience one or two episodes of psychosis in their life, while others experience several severe relapses which affect their ability to maintain their own lifestyle and social integration in the community. As a person grows older, the effect of these severe symptoms will potentially have a greater impact on their physical health and their ability to maintain their independence. There is debate among specialists about the true occurrence of paraphrenia. There has been no international coding for it as the debates centre around whether the older person really develops the symptoms at a later age, or whether they were always there but just well controlled (Howard and Levy, 1997).

The marked difference for people who are thought to be suffering from paraphrenia is that they do not have such behavioural difficulties as those developing schizophrenia at a younger age. Their affect is not dampened and they often have some social awareness and abilities. However, the effect of psychotic episodes and the difficulty in management remain the same.

The Nurse's Role

A relationship of trust is essential when caring for an older person with a psychotic illness. The person may not come to receive services until there has been an exacerbation of their symptoms and this may have involved upset neighbours or even the police. For community psychiatric nurses, they are well suited to supporting the older person and helping them to manage their delusions or other symptoms. The older person must be able to trust the nurse. This does not mean that the nurse should collude with the older person, however developing a positive relationship without constantly confronting the older person may enable essential care to be administered. Diet, hygiene and management of any physical health needs must form the priority for the nurse; through this there may be some improvement in an understanding of what the person is experiencing and thus an ability to help.

Recent work advocates that the person's hallucinations should be respected and lived through. If the person is assisted in understanding their hallucinations and learns to live with

them they will in turn be able to take control of them (Allen, 1997). The use of antipsychotic drugs may be unavoidable. The nurse's role in the management of any drug therapy is integral in its success or failure. For older people the common side effects of extraparamidal symptoms may compound other problems of old age. The naturally ageing kidney will also mean that dosages of neuroleptics must be carefully calculated in order that a dose for a younger person does not become a lethal drug for someone who is older. The choice of neuroleptic must be carefully made by the doctor. The nurse should ensure an accurate description of the presenting symptoms is given so that specific drugs can be administered and bland classic neuroleptics are not given simply to 'calm someone down'.

Any drug regime will carry added complications of possible sedation, which will increase the risk of falls, increased risk of pressure sores and hypostatic pneumonia. Nurses working in mental health units should, therefore, ensure that all care plans reflect the holistic needs of the older person, even if the presenting problem is a very classic psychiatric illness.

ACUTE REVERSIBLE MENTAL DISORDERS

Acute Confusional State

Acute confusional state (ACS) or 'delirium' is a commonly occurring global cognitive disorder in older people. The causes of ACSs usually lie outside the nervous system. Acute organic mental disorders are so labelled because they are not chronic conditions, are organic in origin and are potentially reversible. 'Acute' in these cases has no connotation of abrupt onset. The onset of disturbance may be rapid or gradual. Reversible organic brain dysfunction is characterised by fluctuating levels of consciousness, orientation, mood and memory. At times this can be disconcerting to the nursing staff. One may enter the patient's room and find an alert, oriented individual, and a short time later the same person will be grossly disoriented. The onset of an ACT is often the result of a physical illness or drug toxicity.

The two most common features of an ACT were found by Foreman (1990a) to be poor concentration and inattention. Other symptoms include overwhelming anxiety, florid delusions, frightening illusions, and tactile, visual and olfactory hallucinations, but these are less common. The severity of delirium is related to the level of physiological disturbance and degree of cerebral oedema, and of pre-existing cognitive impairment. Illusions are often evident in conjunction with ACS and may be the most obvious signals of toxic states. Frightening misinterpretations of the environment when under physiological stress and in unfamiliar situations are common for many older people.

In addition to psychological manifestations of acute cerebral impairment, physical symptoms such as the following are often present:

- Vasomotor instability.
- Elevated pulse and respiration.
- Temperature fluctuations.
- Tremors of fingers, hands, lips and facial muscles.
- Headache.
- Generalised weakness.

An individual with acute toxic confusion is physically ill as well as mentally impaired. Any condition that compromises the cellular function of the brain will cause an acute organic brain disorder.

An ACS is a common psychiatric complication of physical illness and of treatments for physical illness in older people. It is often a more common signal of physical illness than body symptoms such as fever, pain or tachycardia (Lipowski, 1986). Older people with some degree of dementia are particularly susceptible to developing toxic confusion in response to physical illness, drug intoxication and psychosocial stressors. It is typically of abrupt onset and brief duration. It can also present as a 'pseudo delirium', a toxic confusional-like state that occurs as a result of psychosocial stressors, depression, mania or severe anxiety. It is estimated that 50% of persons over the age of 65 years who are admitted to medical or surgical units will display toxic confusion on admission or in the course of their stay in hospital.

The toxic state results from a combination of reduced cerebral oxidation and cholinergic activity, and is exacerbated by physical or psychosocial stress. It usually ends in either full recovery or death, although it may result in some degree of permanent dementia if the causal factors go unattended.

Although acute confusion is generally considered transient and self-limiting, its presence is concomitant with illness and is associated with higher mortality rates and longer hospital stays (Foreman, 1986). Immediate attention is therefore critical. Identifying and removing the underlying causes and providing supportive and symptomatic care is essential.

The nurse has a responsibility to ensure that the person comes to no physical harm and is helped to maintain their self-esteem during any episode of confusion. It is important that the nurse recognises the seriousness of the situation and adjusts the environmental influences, deals with any physical cause and uses appropriate interpersonal skills to support the person at this time, thus ensuring continuity of care (Schofield, 1997a). Attempting to control apparently disruptive behaviour by administering major tranquillisers, chastising or attempting to control the person will exacerbate the situation.

In a small study, Schofield talked with people who had experienced a toxic confusional state. Most viewed the episode with bewilderment, surprise and curiosity. It was important, therefore, to discuss the episode with the person afterwards, with a great deal of skill and sensitivity, in order to help the person place the experience within the context of their overall illness (Schofield, 1997b).

ACS should not be dismissed as an inevitability of later life. Furthermore, the management of ACS requires a great deal of skill and understanding.

STRUCTURED THERAPEUTIC ACTIVITY

There are many types of therapeutic activity which could be described in this section. Also, there is evidence which supports some pychologists' view that psychological therapies have been left by psychologists for others to do and that the direct involvement of psychologists as clinicians with older people has been rather limited (Hanley and Gilhooly, 1986). Because of this, some 'therapies' have been undertaken by well-intentioned but poorly trained care professionals and many of the psychological benefits of the intervention have been lost.

This section can offer no more than an overview of the most common types of therapeutic intervention. Information about how to undertake such activity should be obtained from literature specialising in the topics described.

Reality Orientation (RO)

As with many therapies, RO can be traced back to 1958 in the USA. Over the following 30 years it has spread throughout the world. There are three major types of RO: basic RO, or 24-hour RO, RO classes and advanced RO. Twenty-four hour RO is a continual process whereby staff present information constantly reminding the person of the time and place. Confused speech is not reinforced, and there are always large, rather unfriendly signs to tell people where they are. RO classes usually support 24-hour RO but are sometimes done in isolation. The third type, advanced RO, is where wide-ranging topics are discussed (Holden and Woods, 1982). There is limited evidence on the long-term effects of RO, but it is acknowledged that, provided the staff continue to follow a positive approach throughout the day, RO can be useful and cost-effective (Hanley, 1986).

Reminiscence Therapy

Reminiscence therapy is very different from RO. It has the key aim of using people's life experience to highlight the older person's remaining skills and abilities rather than highlighting their deficits. Everybody reminisces; it is normal activity for people of any age. Using reminiscence as a therapeutic intervention has become popular, but staff must be aware that it can have negative effects in some situations.

There are three main ways that reminiscence therapy can be used: firstly as a social tool in a large group, perhaps as a sing-along, or watching a film; secondly, on an individual basis to help develop relationships and improve interpersonal communication; and thirdly as a group activity to improve communication skills, raise self-esteem and channel ruminating thought patterns. Reminiscence therapy is not a history lesson; it is irrelevant to the outcome of the session whether or not the information discussed is chronologically correct. The session should encourage the client to be the person who is in control, they have the knowledge and the experience and the care professional should not be didactic in their approach. The main benefits for the staff must be a better understanding of the client and their life; the benefit for the older person should be a feeling of a positive energy that leaves them content and at peace. Although the therapeutic value of reminiscence is in doubt (Brotchie and Thornton, 1987), anecdotal evidence shows that if older people are given the opportunity to use their life experience in a positive way it can raise their self-esteem and make them feel valued (Phair and Elsey, 1990).

Validation Therapy

For 20 years, Feil has been developing an approach to communicating with elderly disorientated people. The method she feels is unique and is based on the theory that very old people struggle to resolve unfinished life issues before death. Their behaviour reflects this in four specific progressive stages:

- Malorientation.
- Time confusion.
- Repetitive motion.
- Vegetation.

There are, in turn, very specific techniques to help with individuals at each stage (Feil, 1992). These techniques include:

- Empathy.
- Reminiscing.
- Polarity.
- Touch.
- Mirroring.

In stage 3 and 4 of the deterioration, the objects that the disorientated older person talks about become symbols; a sock may represent dressing a small child, rocking may represent motherhood and safety.

Some studies carried out to assess the benefits of this therapy were conducted by Feil herself. Not surprisingly, it was found that after 5 years of validation, 30 organically brain-damaged people had become less incontinent, their speech had improved and they showed greater contentment (Feil, 1989). There was no control group, however, and little discussion in the research account of how much change was due to the pathological changes of the disease process or the extra attention these people had received.

A study in the UK noted some improvement in interaction; however, it was not established how much of this improvement was due to the validation therapy and how much was due to the structure of the group (Bleathman and Morton, 1992). Kelly (1995) points out that the evidence for the success of validation therapy remains largely anecdotal and still needs to be tested.

Music Therapy

The general aim of music therapy with people with mental-health problems is to meet emotional, social and spiritual needs of the clients. It should also be used to improve their self-esteem and improve their quality of life. Music therapy can be used for different reasons within a clinical setting. It can also be beneficial within somebody's own home if the type of music is appropriate to the client's taste. It can be used by a qualified music therapist to assess memory and general knowledge, to stimulate movement and even rekindle feelings. However, this should be done with great sensitivity, as music can provoke a range of negative and positive feelings (Brooker, 1991). It may also help in a small group to rebuild social bridges, emphasising the person's positive attributes and giving them the opportunity to take control by choosing the music.

The Use of Pets

For people who live at home, having a pet can offer companionship. It is also thought to both relieve stress (by stroking) and encourage exercise in those people who may not otherwise go out. The 'Pat-a-Dog' service is now operating in many parts of the country. To have a dog in a unit may be very comforting for some and offer a focus for their affections. The benefits of having an animal, particularly a dog, should be considered quite seriously before embarking on obtaining an animal. It will undoubtedly assist in creating a domestic atmosphere (if a dog has previously been part of the person's life) and is thought to improve communication and counteract some of the negative consequences of institutionalisation. One study in Australia, however, found that the perceived benefits of the dog were greater that the actual benefits and, although the dog acted as a catalyst for conversation, after 6 months the residents had got used to the animal and the benefits disappeared. The staff, however, remained more enthusiastic about the benefits of the dog than the residents (Winkler *et al.* 1989) (*see* Chapter 16 for further discussion of pets).

Activities for Pleasure

The list of activities that can be used to bring pleasure to somebody with a mental-health problem is endless and many are already in regular use in a care setting. The key issue to consider is, however, whether the intervention to be offered (which should not be patronising) is in keeping with the person's social and cultural lifestyle, and also their cognitive ability. The therapeutic intervention that is initiated for pleasure should therefore follow the guidelines given in **Box 18.4**.

Careful choice of appropriate activity will then also become part of any programme of rehabilitation. Goals may

18.4 Guidelines for Activities for Pleasure

These should:

- Be appropriate to the person's level of ability or concentration span, but sufficiently challenging for the person to feel they have succeeded.
- Be appropriate to the premorbid ability of the person.
- Offer variety.
- Be more than a means of 'killing time'.
- Focus on the remaining abilities of the person, however small they may be.
- Avoid too much choice, as this will cause confusion if the person has a dementing illness (Sheridan, 1992).

be set around activities that the person enjoys. Equally pleasurable activity can be used as an objective measurement tool for the person's progress. If a person never watches football it would be meaningless to assess their level of concentration based on this. If, however, the person was an avid fan, their ability and desire to follow the match would be a clear indication of their level of functioning.

Organised Exercise

Physical activity should be encouraged for any one suffering from a mental-health problem. Apart from the advantage of being a diversion for the person, the physiological benefits are obvious. Gentle exercise, whether as assisted walking, regular keep-fit, indoor bowls, swimming or EXTEND classes, will improve the circulation, contract and extend the muscles, increase the blood supply to the periphery and increase the oxygen to the brain. This in turn will assist in preserving the homeostasis of the muscles and also help to prevent tissue deterioration and pressure sores. Any hand–eye coordination or mental arithmetic will help concentration and cerebral activity. Any programme of physical exercise that was not generally accepted as normal life activity should be reviewed by a doctor or physiotherapist before implementation (Phair and Good, 1995)

Encouraging the person to participate will usually be successful with careful explanation of the health benefits. Even for older people who cannot actively participate, they may gain benefit from passive participation in watching others.

SUMMARY

The beginning of this chapter describes how recent legislative changes have been made to ensure that all people suffering from a serious and enduring mental-health problem are monitored and offered the appropriate level of support and supervision. This has been described as the Care Programme Approach (CPA). It is important for all health-care professionals to ensure that the philosophy of CPA is taken with any older person suffering from a mental-health problem. Multi-agency and multidisciplinary working must be accepted as fundamental to the proper care and support of any older person experiencing difficulties. Managing the risk of supporting someone in the community who is suffering from dementia is not the unique role of any one service, yet in so many areas communication between the two major providers, health and social services, is commonly described as, at best, patchy and, at worst, nonexistent. Examples of joint working do exist where services have looked to offer shared solutions to problems and also to develop services that will meet all the needs of older people with mental-health problems. These 'one door' point of access services were both popular with users and capable of providing innovative, high-quality care, the essential component being that traditional professional boundaries were ignored and the older persons needs were seen as the pivotal point.

The most common mental-health problems of older people have been described in this chapter and the needs that arise from these difficulties described. The nurse who has specialist knowledge of mental-health problems is uniquely placed to assess and ensure that the care offered meets every requirement of the older person. It is important, however, that the nurse does not begin to presume that because of their position in being able to assess all of those needs, that they are the person who is best placed to deliver them.

Skilled mental-health care should, like any other field of nursing, involve health promotion, risk assessment and therapeutic intervention as core components of care. For many mental-health needs, the older person may be able to avoid a serious episode of mental illness or physical illness as a consequence of their mental health if the nurse is proactive in their intervention.

Mental-health care of all older people is the business of every nurse who comes into contact with an older person. Physical problems may be a manifestation of a mental-health need or a consequence of a mental-health need. Similarly, pure mental-health symptoms may be a serious mental-health problem or simply the manifestation of a physical health problem. Whatever the combination, the mental health of older people must become central to all nurses who believe and want to offer a high quality service to their client.

KEY POINTS

- The Care Programme Approach requires that all mental-health clients in the community have a key worker, regular multidisciplinary reviews of the care package, and are all care assessed, implemented and reviewed in a systematic way.
- The continuum of mental health and mental illness is complex and mental health, particularly for older people, is difficult to define because the differentiation of personality throughout the life span results in highly individual adaptations in later life.
- The role of the mental-health nurse with older people encompasses all aspects of gerontological care, with special emphasis on communication and the use of self as a therapeutic tool.
- Cognitive functioning is an aspect of mental health status but the two are distinct.
- A nursing assessment of mental health encompasses cognitive functioning (including memory, perception, thinking, learning and decision-making), mood (in the context of what is currently happening to a person) and behaviour (how a person responds to a situation). It should be based on the older person's perspective and encompass that of relatives and carers.
- The term dementia is used to describe a range of conditions in which organic changes take place. The most common of these is Alzheimer's disease and vascular dementia.
- 'Personhood' and the 'person-centred approach to care' is underpinned by the acknowledgement that each person has unique subjectivity, has a place in the human group, has needs, has rights and is valued for no instrumental purpose but simply as a person.
- The new culture of dementia care promotes the notion that all individuals are damaged in some way by their biographies, and all have deficiencies. The difference for someone with dementia is that he or she may have lost the ability to hide their true feelings or 'play' games.
- Depression is more common in older people than is generally recognised, and nurses have a key role in recognition, treatment, and offering psychosocial support.
- The range of psychosocial interventions and structured therapies available to nurses include reality orientation, reminiscence, validation, music, pleasure activities, exercise and the use of pets.

AREAS AND ACTIVITIES FOR STUDY AND REFLECTION

- How effectively are the mental-health needs of physically ill older people met within your practice area?
- What are the mechanisms for assessing the mental-health needs of the older people in your practice area and how effective are these?
- What tools are used to assess mental-health needs? Are these effective, for example, in distinguishing between cognitive change and emotional health?
- What level of expertise (knowledge, skills, experience, specific education and training) do the staff undertaking mental-health assessments in your area possess? How could this be enhanced?
- If the majority of the older people with whom you work have mental-health needs, how effectively are their physical needs met?
- How often is the term 'confusion' used as a general label, without identifying the specific manifestations of this, or the behaviours which might indicate it?
- How effective is multidisciplinary and interdisciplinary working in your practice area and how could this be improved?

REFERENCES

Adams T. HIV-related dementia. *Nurs Times* 1988, 84:45.

Allen C. GP based memory aid group benefits clients and carers. *Nurs Times* 1996, 92:42–44.

Allen D. Finding a voice. *Nurs Stand* 1997, 11:21–23.

Alzheimers Disease Society. *Dementia in the community*, London, 1995, Alzheimers Disease Society.

Armstrong E. Depression: moving on. *Nurs Stand* 1996, 11:10.

Baldwin R. Depressive illness. In: Jacoby R, Oppenheimer C, eds. *Psychiatry in the elderly, 2nd edition*. London: Oxford Medical Publications, 1997.

Benbow SB. The role of electroconvulsive therapy in the treatment of depressive illness in old age. *Br J Psychiatry* 1989, 155:147–152.

Brooker E. Just a song at twilight. *Nurs Times* 1991, 87:32–34.

Bleathman C, Morton I. Validation therapy: extracts from 20 groups with dementia sufferers. *J Adv Nurs* 1992, 17:658–666.

Brotchie J, Thornton S. Reminiscence: a critical review of the empirical literature. *Br J Clin Psychology* 1987, 26:93–111.

Copeland, J, Dewey M, Wood N *et al*. Range of mental illness among the elderly in the community: prevalence in Liverpool using the GMS-AGECAT package. *Br J Psychiatry* 1987, 150:513–516.

Department of Health and Social Services Inspectorate. Mental illness. *The health of the nation key area handbook, 2nd edition*, London, 1994, HMSO.

Feil N. Validation the Feil method. How to help disoriented old. Ohio: Edward Feil Productions, 1989.

Feil N. Honesty, the best policy. Nursing the elderly. *SCP* 1992, 4:10–12.

Ford P, Heath H, McCormack B, Phair L. *What a difference a nurse makes*, London, 1997, Royal College of Nursing.

Foreman M. 1990a. Acute confusion states in hospitalized elderly: a research dilemma. *Nurs Res* 1990, 35:34.

Foreman MD. 1990b. The cognitive and behavioural nature of acute confusional states. *Sch Inq Nurs Pract* 1990, 5:3–16.

Frank B. People with dementia can communicate if we are able to hear. In: Kitwood T, Benson S, eds. *The new culture of dementia care*. London: Hawker, 1995.

GM Clinical Bulletin. *Setting standards for the diagnosis and management of Alzheimer's disease in primary and secondary care. The views of the expert panel of the primary and secondary care faculty*. Sevenoaks: Medipress Ltd, 1997.

Goldsmith M. *Hearing the voice of people with dementia. Opportunities and obstacles*. London: Jessica Kingsley, 1996.

Gould D. Pharmacological treatments and electroconvulsive therapy (ECT). In: Norman I, Redfern S, eds. *Mental health care for elderly people*. London: Churchill Livingstone, 1997.

Gravell R. Communication problems in elderly people. Beckenham; Croom Helm, 1988

Hallberg I, Norberg A, Eriksson S. A comparison between the care of vocally disruptive patients and that of other residents at psychogeriatric wards. *J Adv Nurs* 1990, 15:410–416.

Hanley I. Reality orientation in the care of the elderly patient with dementia. In: *Psychological therapies for the elderly*. London: Croom & Helm, 1986.

Hanley I, Gilhooly M (eds). *Psychological therapies for the elderly*. London: Croom & Helm, 1986.

Howard R, Levy R. Late-onset schizophrenia, late paraphrenia, and paranoid states of later life. In: Jacoby R, Oppenheimer C, eds. *Psychiatry in the elderly, 2nd edition*. London: Oxford Medical Publications, 1997.

Holden V, Woods R. *Reality orientation psychological approaches to the confused elderly*. London: Churchill Livingstone, 1982.

Hughes C. Depression and mania in later life. In: Norman I, Redfern S, eds. *Mental health care for elderly people*. London: Churchill Livingstone, 1997.

Jacoby R. Manic Illness. In: Jacoby R, Oppenheimer C, eds. *Psychiatry in the elderly, 2nd edition*. London: Oxford Medical Publications, 1997.

Kelly JS. Validation therapy: a case against. *J Gerontol Nurs* 1995, 21:41–43.

Killick J. Communication: a matter of life and death of the mind. *J Dement Care* 1997, (September/October):14–15.

King's Fund Centre. *Project paper No. 3. Living well into old age*, London, 1986, King's Fund Publishing Office.

Kitwood T. Cultures of care tradition and change. In: Kitwood T, Benson S, eds. *The new culture of dementia care*. London: Hawker Publications, 1997.

Kitwood T, Bredin K. Towards a theory of dementia care: personhood and well-being. *Ageing and Society* 1992, 12:269–287.

Lipowski Z. A comprehensive view of delerium in the elderly. *Geriatric Consultant* 1986, 7:26.

Livingston G. Understanding dementia. The rarer dementias. *J Dement Care* 1994, (May/June):27–29.

Marshall M (ed) State of the art in dementia care. CPA London, 1997.

McDougall GJ. A review of screening instruments for assessing cognition and mental status in older adults. *Nurse Pract* 1990, 15:11.

Melzer D, Hopkins S, Pencheon D, Brayne C, Williams R. Health care needs assessment. In: Stevens A, Rafferty J, eds. *Epidemiologically based needs assessment review, Vol. 2*. Oxford: Radcliffe, 1995.

Morley M, Sellwood W. Schizophrenia in later life. In: Norman I, Redfern S, eds. *Mental health care for elderly people*. London: Churchill Livingstone, 1997.

Mottram P, Hamer C, Williams J, Wilson K. Declining blues. *Nurs Times* 1996a, 20:24–26.

Mottram P, Hamer C, Williams J, Wilson K. Distress signals. *Nurs Times* 1996b, 20:26–28.

Murphy E. Increased mortality rates in later life. *Br J Psychiatry* 1988, 152:347–353.

Navia B, Price R. The AIDS dementia complex as the presenting or sole manifestation of HIV infection. *Arch Neurol* 1987, 44:65.

Nolan M, Grant G, Keady J. *Understanding family care*. Buckinghamshire: Open University Press, 1997.

O'Donovan S. The memory lingers on. *Elderly Care* 1993, 5:27–31.

Palmateer LM, McCartney JR. Do nurses know when patients have cognitive deficits? *J Gerontol Nurs* 1985, 11:6.

Phair L, Good V. *Dementia a positive approach*. London: Whurr Publications, 1995.

Phair L, Good E. People not patients. *Nurs Times* 1989, 85:42–44.

Phair L, Elsey I. Sharing memories. *Nurs Times* 1990, 86:50–52.

Phair L. George, an elderly depressed patient. *Nurs Times* 1990, 86:64–66.

Royal College of Nursing. *Focus on restraint, 2nd edition*. London: Scutari, 1992.

Royal College of Nursing. *Guidelines for assessing mental health needs in old age*, London, 1994, Royal College of Nursing.

Salmon P. Interaction of nurses with elderly patients: relationships to nurses attitudes and to formal activity periods. *J Adv Nurs* 1993, 18:14–19.

Schofield I. Patient-centred care in the management of postoperative orthopaedic patients with an acute confusional state. *J Orthopaedic Nurs* 1997a, 1:71–75.

Schofield I. A small exploratory study of the reaction of older people to an episode of delirium. *J Adv Nurs* 1997b, 25:942–952.

Sheridan C. *Failure free activities for the Alzheimer's patient*. London: Macmillan, 1992.

Smith-Jones S, Francis G. Disruptive institutionalised elderly: a cost-effective intervention. *J Psychosoc Nurs* 1992, 30:21–25.

Thompson H. Biological approaches to ageing and mental health. In: Norman I, Redfern S, eds. *Mental health care for elderly people*. London: Churchill Livingstone, 1997.

Thornicroft G, Brewin C, Wing J. *Measuring mental health needs*. London: Royal Gaskel, 1992.

Tobiansky R. Understanding dementia. The clinical course of dementia. *J Dement Care* 1994a, (September/October):26–28.

Tobiansky R. Understanding dementia. Diffuse Lewy body disease. *J Dement Care* 1994b, (March/ April):26–27.

Uhl GR, Hilt DC, Hedreen JC *et al*. Pick's disease (lobar sclerosis). Depletion of neurones in the nucleus basalis of Meynert. *Neurology* 1983, 33:1470.

Wade B. Depression in older people: a study. *Nurs Stand* 1994, 8:29–35.

WHO. *ICD-10 classification of mental and behavioural disorders*, Geneva, 1993, World Health Organisation.

Winkler A, Farnie H, Gericeuich F and Long M. The impact of a residential dog on an institution for the elderly: effects on perceptions and social interactions. *The Gerontologist* 1989, 29(2)216–223.

USEFUL ADDRESSES

African-Caribbean Mental Health Association, 35-37 Electric Avenue, Brixton, London SW9 8JP. Tel: 0171 737 3603

Alzheimer's Disease Society - England, Gordon House, 10 Greencoat Place, London SW1P 1PH. Tel: 0171 306 0606, Fax: 0171 306 0808

Alzheimer's Scotland, Action in Dementia, Drumsheugh Gardens, Edinburgh EH3 7RN. Tel/Fax: 0141 339 7177. 24 hour helpline: 0800 317 817.

Alzheimer's Society of Ireland, 43 Northumberland Avenue, Dun-Laoghaire, Co. Dublin. Tel: 00 353 1 288 1282, Fax: 00 353 1 284 6030

British Association of Counselling (BACS), 1 Regent Place, Rugby, CV21 2PJ. Tel: 01788 578328.

Depression Alliance, PO Box 1022, Lonodn SE1 7QB, Tel: 0171 721 7672.

Fellowship of Depressives Anonymous, 36 Chestnut Avenue, Beverely HU17 9QU. Tel: 01482 860619.

Manic Depression Fellowship, 8-10 High Street, Kingston-on-Thames, KT1 1EY. Tel: 0181 974 6550.

Manic Depression Fellowship (Scotland), 7 Woodside Crescent, Glasgow G3 7UL. Tel: 0141 331 0344.

Manic Depression Fellowship (Wales), Belmont, St Cadoc's Hospital, Caerleon, Newport NP6 1XQ. Tel: 01633 430430.

MIND - National Association for Mental Health, Ganta House, 15-19 Broadway, Stratford, London E15 4BQ. Tel: 0181 519 2122.

Scottish Association for Mental Health, Atlantic House, 38 Gardner's Crescent, Edinburgh, EH3 8DQ. Tel: 0131 229 9687.

19 Cohorts, gender and ethnicity
Karen Rawlings-Anderson

LEARNING OBJECTIVES

After studying this chapter you will be able to:

- Identify factors that contribute to the diversity of life experiences of older people.
- Relate how major historic events can affect each cohort of older people.
- Specify some of the gender characteristics that have been shown to affect the lives of older women.
- Distinguish between the concepts of culture, race and

ethnicity, and discuss how these relate to the ageing population in Britain.
- Discuss the implications of recent research findings relating to the health-care needs of older people from minority ethnic groups.
- Utilise knowledge gained to enhance care delivery for older people from minority ethnic groups.
- Outline areas for further research in relation to caring for older people from minority ethnic groups.

INTRODUCTION

Our ageing population is diverse and heterogeneous; older people in today's society not only come from a variety of ethnic backgrounds, but gender and cohort position may also create significant differences within and between individuals and groups. Demographic trends suggest that the future holds yet more changes for the makeup of the older population. Are nurses adequately prepared to provide sensitive and meaningful care to present and future cohorts of older people? If nursing care is to be appropriate, nurses require knowledge of the diversity of backgrounds that older people come from and need to be able to explore how these experiences have shaped the way they view the world. The aim of this chapter is to investigate how cohort; gender and ethnicity frame the experiences of older people and how nurses can utilise this information to plan care that is sensitive to their needs. The diversity of life experiences that have affected the older people in their care must also be acknowledged. While the life experiences of all older people are important, this chapter will focus primarily on those who have traditionally been ignored or marginalised in society. Thus, the chapter will briefly discuss the effect of cohort position and how this can be used to understand historical influences on the lives of older adults; the section on gender will primarily focus on the experiences of women. However, the major emphasis of the chapter will be on the experiences and needs of minority ethnic groups who form a growing section of our older population. It is the nurse's skills in listening to the spoken and unspoken histories of older people that will provide a basis for the assessment of need and identification of health problems in older people.

COHORTS

In gerontology, a cohort is a group of people born within a certain time span, usually a decade. For example, all the people born in Great Britain between 1910 and 1919 would form a cohort. Differences between cohort characteristics have been used to explain trends, make predictions and develop policies in response to such trends in a population. These trends are influenced by a number of factors, for example legal changes, medical advances and political and historical influences, all of which can have significant implications for different birth cohorts within the population.

Clarke (1995) highlights the significance of the Divorce Reform Act in the 1970s on different birth cohorts and discusses the tendency for the proportions of divorced men and women to rise from one birth cohort to the next. This can influence the number of older people living alone and can have an impact on spouses being available as carers for dependent partners in later years. She also examines changes in cohabitation and marriage in recent years. The impact of such a trend is significant in the changing structure of the family between cohorts, and can have a considerable influence on care provision within families. For example, an increasing number of grandparents may take on childcare responsibilities for divorced or lone-parent children than in previous birth cohorts.

Epidemiologists may use cohort studies to link changing disease patterns among cohorts to historical or medical events, for example the reduction in the incidence of rheumatic fever can be explained for the most part by the discovery and use of antibiotics. This in turn could explain a reduction in heart valve disease in successive cohorts of the population. The use of vaccines to decrease or eradicate certain infectious diseases has also affected cohorts differentially in their experiences of many diseases, and the consequent effects on family life. Other medical advances, such as the availability of the contraceptive pill, made a significant impact on the lives of a whole generation of women and men relative to previous birth cohorts.

Major historical and political events can also have considerable cohort effects – the effects of the two world wars are still having an impact today. These effects can have implications for care provision for certain cohorts that should not be ignored. For example, Bender (1997) outlines the possibility of traumatised cohorts, following the Second World War. He discusses the sequelae of living through highly stressful life events and states that many older adults' war experiences deleteriously affected their lives immediately after the event, while others may become distressed later in their lives as a result of such experiences. Bender suggests that this may have influenced the high frequency of depression among today's older adults and that perhaps depression is not a feature of old age in general, but a feature of a whole generation traumatised by war. It is also important to consider the age of a cohort when significant life events occurred; for example, the two world wars had an impact not only upon adults who lost spouses and family members during wartime but also on those who were children at the time and were evacuated or lived with grieving families.

The implications for nursing practice are profound when considering interventions such as reminiscence therapy. Are nurses adequately skilled to facilitate the recounting of painful and distressing memories or are older adults forced to recount only simplistic and emotionally trivialised accounts of their experiences, leading to what Bender (1997, p. 343) terms as 'inauthenticity of the interaction'? Conversely, some individuals have survived the horrors of a war by not discussing it, and might welcome discussing a more sanitised account of historical events. It is imperative that nurses recognise the possible effects that such events can have on cohorts and consider the implications for individualised care and planning appropriate therapeutic interventions.

Individuals within a cohort may experience very different life events. Consider the differences between two women born in the same year and country, one of whom remains in her country of origin, the other who emigrates to another country where the climate, language and customs are very different to that of her homeland. These two women's life experiences will influence how they view life, their expectations and the way that they live. Thus, cohort effects can differ according to individual circumstances in some instances, but nurses should be able to recognise the significance of birth cohort effects and have knowledge of the historical events that may have affected an individual. It is imperative, however, that the multifaceted experiences of older people are not merely related to cohort affect alone, as factors such as gender, social class and ethnicity all influence the individual in a significant way.

GENDER

Currently most research that identifies gender characteristics in later life is epidemiological research which focuses on differential morbidity and mortality rates. Arber and Ginn (1991) outline how sociological research has, in the past, ignored older people in research about the family and also how the political economic approach has failed to examine the ways in which productive and reproductive roles within the family influence available resources in later life. Issues relating to gender in later life have been further complicated by the debate relating to how women and older people can be brought into research about social stratification. Additionally, it has been noted that feminist research has tended to focus on the lives of younger women and is in its infancy in exploring the lives of older women (Bernard and Meade, 1993). However, there is now a growing body of literature and research which focuses upon aspects of older women's lives. It is reasonably easy to examine the available data to determine the effects that gender may have in later life, although it is difficult to unravel the coexisting influences that cohort, class and ethnicity have on older women.

The Gender Gap and Marital Status

At every age females outlast males, and so not surprisingly the older population is dominated by females. This is due to a variety of reasons, but mainly due to reductions in mortality and differing increases in life expectancy. In Britain, life expectancy has increased considerably throughout the last century, especially among older age groups. At the age of 60 years, life expectancy has increased by approximately 4 years since 1900 for males and by 7 years for females. At the age of 70 years, male life expectancy has increased by 2 years and female life expectancy by almost 5 years (Coombes and Kalache, 1996). In the UK, there is a marked imbalance between the sexes at all ages, but this imbalance increases with age and is particularly significant in the over 85-year-olds (**Table 19.1**). Between the ages of 60 and 65 years, there are 108 females to every 100 males; this increases to 298 females for every 100 males in the over 85-year-olds.

The faster reduction in female mortality has resulted in what Arber and Ginn (1991) have termed 'the feminisation of later life', and nurses are likely to be caring for a greater number of older women than men. It is important that nurses recognise this as a demographic trend and look at the implications of this for their practice. For example, are nurses able to articulate their assumptions about the health-care needs of older women and challenge stereotypical views of them?

The marital status of the older population also shows marked differences between the sexes. Men are more likely to be married than women. In 1990, 73% of men over 65 years of age were married, compared to 38% of women of the same age (Arber and Ginn, 1991). This is influenced by cohort effect to a certain extent, in that many men were killed

Gender of the Older Population in the United Kingdom, 1991 (Thousands in each Age Group)						
AGE	60–64	65–69	70–74	75–79	80–84	85+
Male	1386	1278	980	720	422	224
Female	1490	1482	1288	1130	839	668
Sex ratio (Females per 100 males)	108	116	131	157	199	298

Adapted from: Victor, 1994.

Table 19.1 Gender of the older population in the United Kingdom.

in the two world wars, which limited the availability of marriageable men (Victor, 1994). The greater longevity of women also influences the percentage of widows between the sexes. In 1990, 17% of men aged 65 years and over were widowed, compared to 49% of women of the same age. In the same age range, 7% of men were single compared to 10% of women. Three per cent of older men and women were divorced or separated at this age (Arber and Ginn, 1991). It can be expected that the number of divorced or separated older people will increase significantly in the future. The implications of these statistics are that older women are more likely to live alone than men and this, in turn, has implications for health and social-care provision in the community.

Contemporary Attitudes and Older Women

Ageism does not affect men and women equally; women bear the double burden of both ageism and sexism. Historically, older women in popular culture were portrayed as witches and evil crones and these negative images are perpetuated today in the continuation of the stereotypical image of the nagging mother-in-law.

Itzin (1990) suggests that there is a double standard of ageing, which arises from conventional expectations of age-related roles for each sex. Individuals are expected to fulfil certain roles at different times of their lives and transgression of these prescribed roles results in disapproval and lost opportunities. Itzin conceptualised these as male and female 'chronology' – male chronology hinging on employment and female 'chronology' focusing on reproduction. Thus, women are devalued as soon as their useful reproductive life is seen to be over regardless of the number of children they have produced or how many productive working years they have left. From this perspective, older women are seen to have little value in a patriarchal society that values youth and economic activity.

Interestingly, research carried out by Evers (1984) over a decade ago demonstrated that in a small sample of lone women aged 75 years and over, those women who had pursued interests and employment outside the home (active initiators) were more likely to feel independent and able to cope on their own than those who had centred their lives on home and family (passive responders). Thus, it seems that there is some evidence, albeit limited, to suggest that women who are able to challenge the accepted norms earlier in life may reap the benefits in later years. However, most of today's older women have followed traditional roles in relation to family and employment, which has had a marked effect on their position in society in later life.

The Working Lives and Income of Older Women

Women are at greater risk of poverty in later life than men due to differential employment opportunities, marital status and family roles (Groves, 1993). Earlier in this century most women who were in paid employment were not married, partly due to the assumption that they would give up work after marriage, but also due to formal marriage bars which required women to leave their jobs upon marriage. 'Career or marriage' was the choice that many women had to make. During the First World War many women entered the labour market, but most were not retained in the post-war period. Many more married and some single women entered into the paid labour force during the Second World War and employment opportunities for women generally expanded at this time. By the 1960s it had become acceptable for married women to work prior to the birth of their first child, with many returning to work when their children were in full-time education. This, in turn, led to the rise of part-time employment for many women. Beechey and Perkins (1987) note that this increase in part-time opportunities was convenient for women, but was not associated with the same pay conditions and occupational benefits as full-time employment and this has adversely affected many older women's pensions today.

During this increase in women's employment outside the home, traditional expectations of the role of women in domestic life did not alter dramatically. Thus, women in general have not been able to build up pensions over a working lifetime of full employment, nor must it be said, has this been an expectation of them. This has left the majority of married women dependent on their spouse's income and pension and single women with lower pensions, due to a history of sex discrimination in relation to pay and inclusion in occupational pension schemes. Arber and Ginn (1991) confirm that the major source of gender differences in income in older people is non-state provision associated with occupational and private pensions.

In summary, although it is difficult to disentangle the influence of class and ethnicity from the equation of current financial status, older women's financial status is generally poorer than that of older men. This is due to employment patterns, discriminatory pay structures and family commitments in earlier years, which will affect the financial status of older women for some years to come.

Health Issues and Older Women

While many older people enjoy good health and lead independent and active lives, the predominant image of old age as being a time of health problems reflects the preoccupation of policy makers with ensuring that service provision will be able to meet the demands of an increasingly ageing population (Arber and Ginn, 1991). It also reflects older people's concerns with their own health status, their worries about being a burden to others and their wish to remain independent for as long as possible (Sidell, 1993).

While the fact that women generally live longer than men has already been established, it is worth noting the work of Jarvis *et al.* (1996) in relation to functional ability. They have summarised data from a variety of sources and report that older men consistently rate their health as better than women and that women are more likely to report physical impairment than men. For example, 85% of men aged 60–79 years reported no difficulty with getting out and walking down the road, compared to 80% of women in the same age range. However, in the 80 years and above age range, the figures decreased to 60% for men and 47% for women. When using a measure of overall disability, 25% of women over the age of 80 years are 'severely' disabled compared with 11% of men (Arber and Ginn, 1991). Interestingly, given these difficulties, 11% of men and 4% of women over the age of 80 years reported themselves as having some caring responsibilities. This suggests that men are more likely to be caring for someone at this age than are older women (though numerically, there are far more women than men carers).

Gender differences are also noted in general practitioner (GP) consultation rates. Although the gender differences between men and women narrows with age, older women make up a substantial proportion of GP consultations. It has been postulated that although women live longer, they are more likely to be afflicted by a variety of chronic and highly symptomatic conditions such as osteoporosis and arthritis, which could account for differential consultation rates (Sidell, 1993).

It is important that nurses take these factors into consideration when assessing and planning care for older women. For example, it is common for older women to be told by (mainly male) GPs that the painful symptoms of arthritis are to be expected as they get older. Blaming age for symptoms reinforces negative stereotypes and low expectations of obtaining symptom relief (Sidell, 1992). The nurse must assess older women's main concerns with their health problems and ascertain which members of the multidisciplinary team may be best suited to provide interventions of therapeutic value for them. For example, aids in the home to ease household tasks may be more helpful than ineffective analgesia. Nurses also have a role to play as advocates for older women in verbalising their needs to the medical profession when they feel ill-equipped or reluctant to do so themselves.

In summary, there are a variety of influences on the status and health of older women. It is imperative that nurses are aware of how these have shaped the health needs of older women in their care and how they may also have influenced their own perceptions about the role and status of older women in our society.

ETHNICITY, CULTURE AND RACE

The National Health Service (NHS) was established in 1948 to meet the health-care needs of a fairly homogenous population. However, over the last 50 years the population of Britain has become more ethnically and racially diverse. At both government and professional levels, guidelines have been developed and initiatives designed to promote equity in care delivery for an increasingly heterogeneous population (Department of Health, 1991, 1997; UKCC, 1992), yet there is mounting evidence to demonstrate that individuals from minority ethnic groups do not receive care that is appropriate to their needs. Before discussing the evidence and ways of overcoming inadequate service provision, it is first necessary to outline the meaning of the concepts of ethnicity, culture and race in order to understand their meaning, how they are utilised in the literature and their relevance to discussions about older adults.

Ethnicity

Ethnicity is a term often used interchangeably with race; however, ethnicity is a concept based more on cultural, linguistic and religious criteria than physical characteristics. Blakemore and Boneham (1994) state that ethnicity comprises of some, if not all, of the following:

- Ideas of 'peoplehood', whereby individuals identify with a common homeland, shared history or political struggle.
- Language – either a language distinct from the majority or a distinctive use of a common language such as dialect.
- Attachment to a particular religion that fosters group cohesion.
- A distinctive culture.

Defining one's ethnic identity is obviously subjective, but a feeling of belonging to a particular ethnic group can be a resource for individuals to make sense of their world. It should be noted that we all belong to an ethnic group and identify to a certain degree with others from the same ethnic background. However, a minority's racial and ethnic identity does not emerge in isolation, but from the interaction which takes place between the minority and the majority.

Culture

Culture is not as broad a concept as ethnicity. It has been variously defined over the years (Peacock, 1986; Leininger, 1991; Helman, 1994), but is generally understood to refer to a distinctive way of life that encompasses common understandings (both implicit and explicit) that are learned and shared by a group. Cultural beliefs and values guide behaviour in terms of accepted norms and taboos within a community and are often linked to adherence to a particular religion. These beliefs, values and behaviours are dynamic as some aspects of culture are retained and passed on unaltered from one generation to the next, while other aspects fall by the wayside depending on social, political and economic forces. However, culture affects all individuals in a powerful and often subconscious manner.

Race

Racial distinctions are made on stereotypical beliefs about the innate characteristics of a group (Blakemore, 1993). Although race is socially constructed, it is based on superficial biological differences such as skin colour, bone structure and hair type. Racist beliefs are grounded in the view that some races are superior to others. However, there will always be differences in opinion about who belongs in which racial category, both in academic debate and among individuals from differing racial groups themselves. For example, should British Asians be categorised under the umbrella term 'Black' to reflect a shared experience of oppression from discriminatory practices or separately as 'Asian' to reflect the uniqueness of their situation? It can be seen that racial categories are neither fixed nor mutually exclusive, and while discriminatory practices at both an individual and institutional level can explain inequalities in access to and uptake of health services, they are not always helpful as the sole explanation for differences in care provision.

Thus, while not wishing to diminish the significance of racial discrimination, it is suggested that when trying to discover and explain differences in health-care provision and delivery, the concept of ethnicity is a useful tool in examining reasons for those differences. It is a concept commonly used in the literature and has been used in much of the recent research related to older people. However, the terms 'ethnic minority' and 'minority ethnic groups' can be contentious and problematic at times, since much of the recent research uses the ethnic classifications used in the 1991 census (**Table 19.2**). While this classification provides useful information on the main ethnic groups in Britain, it does not include 'invisible minorities' such as Irish, Jewish or Cypriot people who could be classified either as 'white' or 'other'. These groups of people have significant communities in a variety of geographical areas and often identify themselves as a distinct ethnic group with particular needs. Though many from these groups may not be of pensionable age at present, they will be part of our older population in the not too distant future. It is also important to note that there can be as much diversity among ethnic groups as between ethnic groups, as individuals have different histories, settlement patterns and lifestyles. For example, older people who class themselves as Caribbean may come from different islands that are thousands of miles apart and which have quite distinct cultures, although they may share some common elements.

Patterns of Migration and Settlement in Britain

Throughout history, Britain has seen the arrival and settlement of many groups of people from other countries. In more recent years there is a traceable history of migration that has shaped the current older population in Britain (Young and George, 1991; Age Concern, 1995). It has already been discussed in Chapter 2 that historical influences help to shape the motivations and aspirations of individuals throughout their life span. For most people, having to leave their country of birth to resettle in a foreign country is a major life event. For some, the circumstances which caused them to leave will have been even more traumatic. An appreciation of the reasons for resettlement is more likely to enhance the nurse's understanding of the older client's outlook on life.

The reasons for migration are as varied as the ethnic groups themselves and older people from minority ethnic groups live in all parts of Britain. Data from the 1991 census demonstrates significant differences between ethnic groups in terms of their respective numbers and the degree to which they are concentrated in selected areas (Balarajan and Soni Raleigh, 1992). The main concentrations of minority ethnic groups are in Greater London (44.6% of all people from ethnic minorities), the West Midlands (14.1%) and Greater Manchester (4.9%). Some districts and boroughs have much larger proportions of minority ethnic groups than others. For example, 44.8% of the population of Brent is made up of people from minority ethnic groups and this has major

Ethnic Origin of the Older Population in the United Kingdom, 1991

Ethnic origin	Population aged 60 years and over	Females aged 60 years and over	Males aged 60 years and over
Black-Caribbean	54,308	24,139	30,169
Black-African	5682	2192	3490
Black (other)	3696	1856	1840
Indian	57,396	27,741	29,655
Pakistani	17,568	6644	10,924
Bangladeshi	5298	1215	4083
Chinese	8904	4787	4117
Other: Asian	8047	4414	3633
Other: Other	14,566	7450	7116
Total (Ethnic minorities)	175,465	80,438	95,027
White	11,459,522	6,659,513	4,800,009
Ireland	256,468	144,717	111,751
TOTAL (Ethnic minorities and white population)	11,634,987 Excluding Ireland	6,739,951 Excluding Ireland	4,895,036 Excluding Ireland
	11,891,455 Including Ireland	6,884,668 Including Ireland	5,006,787 Including Ireland

Source: Adapted from *Age Concern*, 1995.

Table 19.2 Ethnic Origin of the Older Population in the United Kingdom

implications for service provision in health and social care in this area, such as provision of appropriate catering and interpreting services. It is imperative that health authorities are aware of both the ethnic mix of the client population they serve, but also the age distribution among those groups. This will directly impact on the planning of future services for a growing number of older adults from minority ethnic groups.

On an individual level, nurses should include an exploration of an older client's personal migration history in their assessment. It is wrong to assume that all older people from minority ethnic groups were born in another country, some older people have migrated here themselves, while some from more established communities are second generation. The length of time a person has lived here can affect their expectations and knowledge of the availability of health services and the social support that they have available. An older person who has recently arrived to join their family may be dependent on their family and have had little opportunity to develop other social networks, whereas someone who has lived here for over 30 years may have well-established social networks outside of the family. Ill health may have had a profound effect on individual hopes and plans for the future; for example, a chronic disability may have thwarted plans to return to their country of origin or their ability to live independently. These issues can all be ascertained by sensitive questioning and can contribute significantly to the holistic assessment of individual needs of the older person from a minority ethnic group.

Demography of Older People from Minority Ethnic Groups

Table 19.2 sets out the ethnic origins of older people in Britain according to the 1991 census definitions. As previously mentioned the census classification of ethnic origin does not include hidden populations and so available data on the Irish community has also been included.

It can be seen that minority ethnic populations vary in size and in the gender distribution among groups. In the Caribbean, African, Indian, Pakistani and Bangladeshi communities, older men outnumber women. This is in contrast to the Chinese and Irish communities, which reflect a similar pattern to the dominant White ethnic group where older women outnumber men. The main reason for this appears to be due to migration patterns among the Indian, Pakistani and Bangladeshi communities whereby dependent families of male immigrants have remained in their homeland. However, it is not so clear why Caribbean and African groups are distributed in this manner.

The age profile of minority ethnic groups is shown in **Figure 19.1** and demonstrates the fact that generally, minority ethnic groups are younger than the indigenous White population. There are also differences between minority ethnic groups which reflect migration patterns. The implications of these profiles are that in the next 20–30 years, the ageing population will consist of much greater numbers of minority ethnic older people. As time progresses and second and third generation British make up the bulk of the older community within minority ethnic groups, it is likely that generational depth will affect their needs, which will differ to those of their parents and grandparents (Tripp-Reimer, 1983).

Contemporary research indicates that current service delivery in health and social care does not adequately meet the needs of older people from minority ethnic groups, which has major implications for future provision of services.

Contemporary Research on Service Provision

In the last 15 years a growing body of empirical research related specifically to the health and social needs of older people from minority ethnic groups in Britain has emerged. A discussion of this research will highlight areas for service development and the need for strategic planning in relation to the future needs of our ageing minority ethnic populations.

Double and Triple Jeopardy?

The concepts of double and triple jeopardy have become an integral part of the debate on the experiences of older people from minority ethnic groups. Notions of double jeopardy were first hypothesised by the National Urban League in the United States, who suggested that older people from minority ethnic groups were handicapped by the cumulative disadvantages of ageism and racism. In subsequent American research, inequalities related to income, life expectancy and

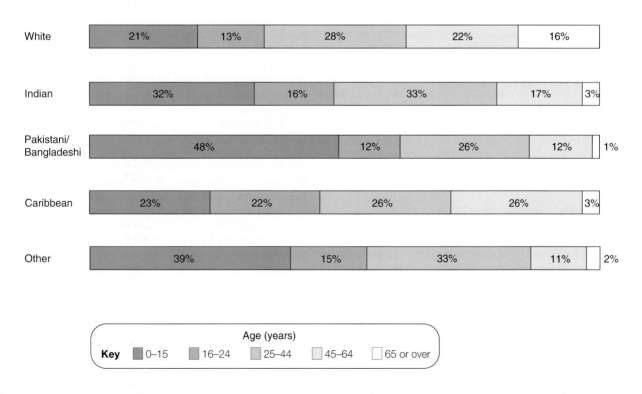

Figure 19.1 Age distribution by ethnic group, Great Britain 1986–1988 combined (Source: Adapted from Help the Aged, 1991).

disease, social support and life satisfaction have been highlighted (Blakemore and Boneham, 1994). In Britain, the notion of double jeopardy was extended to that of triple jeopardy by Norman:

> Older people from minority ethnic groups are not merely in double jeopardy by reason of age and discrimination, as has often been stated, but in triple jeopardy, at risk because they are old, because of the physical conditions and hostility under which they have to live, and because services are not accessible to them.
>
> (Norman, 1985, p. 1.)

While the concepts of double and triple jeopardy are useful frames of reference there are some difficulties with their use. They convey a notion that distinct types of discrimination affect the lives of older people that can somehow be added together in a mathematical formula (Butt and Mirza, 1996). Additionally, in the British literature the notion of double or triple jeopardy has been assumed to be fact rather than being rigorously tested or used to develop a more sensitive recognition of the heterogeneity of the minority ethnic population (Blakemore and Boneham, 1994). It is difficult for researchers to control for cohort, socioeconomic status, sex and other characteristics that confound notions of 'multiple hazard'. In Britain, studies related to the health status of older people from minority ethnic groups have not set out to test for double jeopardy but rather to describe the inequalities that exist.

Finally, the concept of double jeopardy has not always been borne out in some of the American studies, and the idea that age may in some instances have a levelling effect has been postulated. Although differences in material conditions such as income and housing tend to widen in later life, the evidence that psychological wellbeing and family integration is worse for older people from minority ethnic groups is mixed. Similarly in Britain, Blakemore and Boneham (1994) contend that further longitudinal studies comparing differences between different cohorts of minority ethnic groups and the indigenous population need to be carried out to disentangle inequalities of living in inner cities from inequalities primarily due to issues of race and ethnicity.

The British Evidence

Three main themes can be drawn from British studies of older people from minority ethnic groups: socioeconomic position, health and social-care needs, and access and uptake of services. Many of the early studies in the 1980s were small community based projects and it has only been in recent years that larger national surveys have been carried out. However, there is a general consensus of opinion emerging from this work, which will now be discussed.

Many studies paint a picture of financial hardship and poverty among older people from minority ethnic groups. Jadeja and Singh (1993) state that there are three main categories of immigrants who are now financially compromised: refugees, parents who have joined their families and economic migrants. Many in the first two categories have not had the opportunity to work and build state or private pensions. Economic migrants often came to Britain from countries where no state provision for pensions was made and they were only able to start contributing towards their pensions once they gained employment in this country. Additionally, due to widespread discriminatory practices many were in the lowest paid jobs and low wages lead to relatively lower contributions toward pensions. Unemployment is also higher among minority ethnic groups.

In a small local survey of older Asians in Leicester, Jadeja and Singh (1993) found that only 14% had worked for more than 20 years in Britain and 70% existed purely on income support. Evidence from previous local surveys on minority ethnic groups in Birmingham (Bhalla and Blakemore, 1981), Nottingham (Berry *et al.* 1981) and London and Manchester (Barker, 1984) all suggest that state pension and means tested benefits were the only source of income for the majority of older people.

Another theme has been that although older people from minority ethnic groups are comparatively young in comparison to their White counterparts, they report more long-term chronic illnesses and difficulty with self-care and domestic tasks than the majority of the population (Bhalla and Blakemore, 1981; Blakemore, 1982; Greenslade *et al.* 1991; Bowling *et al.* 1992). This may be due to differential morbidity between groups, but may also be a reflection of poorer housing, employment and poverty in their younger lives.

There is also a growing body of evidence to suggest a greater use of GPs by minority ethnic groups than is the case for older people from the ethnic majority (Fenton, 1987; Balarajan *et al.* 1989; McCormick *et al.* 1990). The reasons for higher than average GP consultation has not been systematically explored. Pharoah (1995) suggests that although higher consultation rates do not necessarily mean greater frailty or illness among older people from minority ethnic groups, it certainly lends weight to this contention.

It is interesting to note that despite higher than average GP consultation rates, there is evidence to suggest a low level of contact with health visitors and district nurses among older people from minority ethnic groups (Blakemore, 1982; Cameron *et al.* 1989; Hek, 1991). This suggests that GPs are not acting as a source of referral to other services and Pharoah (1995) found that GPs reported very little liaison with other agencies over older patients from minority ethnic groups. This contrasts to her findings that link-workers reported extensive liaison with a wide range of agencies and that practice nurses were more likely to have liaised over individual patients.

Askham *et al.* (1995) examined the provision of statutory services to older people from black and minority groups, paying particular attention to the provision of mainstream, specific or separate services. They carried out a postal survey of social service departments (SSDs) and district health authorities (DHAs) with significant minority ethnic populations, interviewed a range of staff from these areas, and also interviewed middle aged and older Asian and Caribbean people who resided in these areas. There was great variation between SSDs and DHAs in terms of service provision for older people from minority ethnic groups and when they did cater for specific needs the provision was patchy and on a very small scale. The existence of completely separate services was very low in all areas. Specific services within mainstream provision were found particularly in home help and meals services. Services least likely to provide either separate or specific facilities were residential care, personal care, mental-health services and community health services. Proposed service changes tended to be toward separate or specific facilities. Only 10% of staff interviewed said they thought that needs could be accommodated solely within mainstream services. However, hardly any of the Caribbean people interviewed expressed a desire to be treated in a special way when receiving social or health care. This compares to nearly half of the Asian respondents. When this evidence was analysed in more depth, the study revealed that respondents felt that they should be treated fairly, kindly and effectively, and stressed the importance of equality of service for all. However, many respondents demonstrated a lack of knowledge about the services provided in their area, commented on poor interpreting services, and saw provision of appropriate food as lacking in both health care and social service facilities. It is also noteworthy that one in six staff mentioned low uptake of services by older people from minority ethnic groups and this was attributed to lack of knowledge of services, low referral by GPs, and fear of discrimination or of services being inappropriate. Thus, a complex picture of service needs and provision emerges and Askham *et al.* (1995) recommend that priority should be given to interpreting and link-worker services, improving information about service provision, and to staff training and guidance. They also note that residential care is a problematic area that requires further development and provision.

Patel (1990) has reviewed many of the smaller scale studies of older people from minority ethnic groups and concludes that an overall pattern of lack of uptake of domiciliary services, day centre places and residential housing reflects concerns over language difficulties, provision of appropriate food and fear of racist abuse. It also demonstrates a certain lack of information about services available to this group of older people.

Enduring Myths

Much of the literature revealed a number of commonly held beliefs about minority ethnic groups among service providers which serves to perpetuate the status quo.

Many authorities saw low take-up of services as a reflection of lack of need (Bowling, 1990; Morton,1993). This leads to a 'Catch 22' situation whereby services cannot be developed until a need is demonstrated and it is difficult to demonstrate a need until an appropriate and accessible service is provided.

This state of affairs is further exacerbated by a commonly held belief that minority ethnic communities 'look after their own' and that extended families prefer to provide care for their elderly relatives (Pharoah, 1995; Butt and Mirza, 1996). However, Bowling (1990) did not find evidence that minority

ethnic communities had the necessary resources, expertise or commitment to care for their own elderly without the support of the voluntary and statutory sectors. Although a higher rate of multi-generational households is found among Asian older people in general, this may have resulted from economic necessity rather than desire (Butt and Mirza, 1996). Furthermore, there is some evidence to suggest that older people living with their families can feel isolated or lonely, particularly if the younger family members are out at work (Lewando-Hundt and Grant, 1987; Chiu, 1989).

Many service providers also assumed that people from minority ethnic groups would return to their 'homeland' in later life and so there would be little demand for services in the future. This may well have been the intention of many migrants in the early years after their arrival in Britain; however, many who hoped to return either cannot afford to or realise that they would no longer fit in. Also, many have been here for most of their lives and see Britain as their home where most of their family and friends live.

Blakemore and Boneham (1994) suggest three images of older people from minority ethnic groups can be seen in the literature: the self-reliant pioneer, the gradually adjusting migrant and the passive victim. While they suggest there are some reflections of reality in these images, they warn that uncritical adoption of these concepts will only serve to stereotype older people from minority ethnic groups and lead to service provision that does not take account of individual need.

Mainstream or Separate Provision?

There is a demonstrable need for health and social-care services that are appropriate for older people from minority ethnic groups; however there is little evidence that this is currently being provided. Many areas that have specific services for minority ethnic groups are run by the voluntary sector or by local self-help groups. While these projects are meeting the needs of their local populations, they are often run on shoestring budgets with short-term funding which is problematic (Askham *et al.* 1995) and provides only short-term solutions (Patel, 1990). These separate services also assume there is already access to statutory mainstream provision and further marginalise older people from minority ethnic groups.

In order to maximise the freedom of choice for individuals from all ethnic groups, the consensus of opinion from recent research suggests that services for older people from minority ethnic groups should be incorporated into mainstream service provision. In order for this to be achieved, additional investment needs to be made into support services such as interpreters, link-workers and catering. There also needs to be investment in staff training at all levels and a continuing need to recruit staff from minority ethnic groups (Askham *et al.* 1995). Pharoah (1995) suggests that commissioning of services be based on local needs assessment and be tailored to fit the demographic makeup of the local population. However she stresses that this should not be at the expense of providing appropriate services now. Patel states that 'Black elders are part of this society and hence entitled to mainstream services' (Patel, 1990, p. 58). This is reflected by recommendations from a European conference which advocates that service provision should not be a monopoly of the State, but by a plurality of agencies and that staff should be recruited into mainstream rather than separate, marginal initiatives (Soulsby *et al.* 1994). The recommendations also advocate consultation with minority ethnic communities on the future pattern of services.

Patterns of Health and Disease among Minority Ethnic Groups

The Government's health strategy, *The Health of the Nation*, pointed out the importance of addressing the health needs of the population of Britain, identifying the health of minority ethnic communities as a specific group (Department of Health, 1992). Calman also stated that people working within the health service should be aware of ethnic differences in disease patterns and provide services that are appropriate and modified to take account of cultural variations (HMSO, 1991). Unfortunately, epidemiological data for some ethnic groups is sparse due to lack of pertinent research and the fact that ethnic origin has not routinely been recorded in health information systems. This state of affairs should improve as information on ethnicity is now being recorded in the census and ethnic monitoring has been introduced within the health service.

In general, people who migrate tend to be fitter than those who stay behind. In first generation migrants, patterns of health and morbidity tend to resemble that of their country of origin (McKeigue, 1991). Minority ethnic populations do not suffer from more 'exotic' diseases than the majority of the population, but they do have different patterns of morbidity and mortality to the majority. Balarajan and Soni Raleigh (1995) have identified that in relation to the Health of the Nation targets minority ethnic populations have quite different morbidity patterns to the population as a whole.

Coronary Heart Disease (CHD) and Stroke

Death rates from CHD are higher in people from southern Asia and the African Commonwealth (McKeigue and Marmot, 1988), yet the usual risk factors of smoking, plasma cholesterol and hypertension are generally not higher in southern Asians. There is now increasing attention on the role of diabetes and insulin resistance in Asians who develop CHD. Mortality from stroke is higher in people from the Caribbean, the Indian subcontinent and the African Commonwealth. Balarajan (1991) estimates that death rates from stroke in Caribbeans were about double the average in England and Wales. Caribbeans and Asians also have a higher than average propensity for hypertension.

Cancers

Information relating to the incidence of cancers in minority ethnic populations is sparse because ethnic origin is not routinely recorded in data. There is some evidence to suggest that mortality from cervical cancer is raised in Caribbean women and the incidence of this is high in some Asian countries.

The Irish have a higher than average incidence of cancers of the mouth, throat and lung (McKeigue, 1991). However low uptake of screening services among minority ethnic groups is evident.

Diabetes

The prevalence of diabetes and associated mortality is several times higher in Asians, Caribbeans and Africans than in the indigenous population. Diabetes is about five times more common in Asians than in non-Asians and it goes largely undiagnosed. It is estimated that about one-third of Asians are diabetic by the time they reach the age of 65 years (Balarajan and Soni Raleigh, 1995).

The differential disease patterns in minority ethnic groups suggest that groups with higher incidence of certain diseases should be targeted for screening and that preventative measures and health campaigns must be developed that are appropriate for these groups.

MEETING THE NEEDS OF OLDER PEOPLE IN THE COMMUNITY

It has become apparent that many differences in the older population attributed to cohort, gender and ethnic variation may in reality be indications of educational differences, socioeconomic factors, language differences, unawareness of potential resources and wariness of racial discrimination at both an organisational and an individual level. Health-care programmes at both organisational and individual level should always take account of the specific needs and circumstances of different communities by recognising the social, economic and ethnic background of their client population. While at an individual level Maslow's hierarchy may not be relevant to all ethnic and cultural groups, at a macro level it can be used to demonstrate the type of services needed by older people from minority ethnic groups in the community in order to lead fulfilling lives. **Figure 19.2** shows what services may be required at each level if older people are to achieve their greatest health and social potential. It also highlights areas that require urgent attention from health authorities, social service departments and the voluntary sector if the needs of older people from minority ethnic groups are to be met. These services may be required to support families in the care of their relatives or as the sole resource for older people living on their own.

As discussed in previous sections, it is apparent that many older people from ethnic minority groups are not having their basic needs met and until service provision is tailored to meet these needs then higher order needs such as self-fulfilment will not be achieved.

Arber and Ginn (1991) argue that three key types of resources are required to maintain the independence of older people in the community and that these resources interrelate to form a 'resource triangle'. The three types of resource they

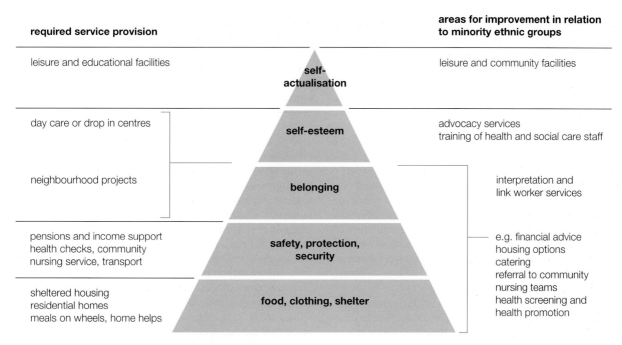

required service provision

areas for improvement in relation to minority ethnic groups

leisure and educational facilities — **self-actualisation** — leisure and community facilities

day care or drop in centres — **self-esteem** — advocacy services / training of health and social care staff

neighbourhood projects — **belonging** — interpretation and link worker services

pensions and income support, health checks, community nursing service, transport — **safety, protection, security** — e.g. financial advice / housing options / catering / referral to community nursing teams / health screening and health promotion

sheltered housing, residential homes, meals on wheels, home helps — **food, clothing, shelter**

Figure 19.2 Provision of health and community services for older people in relation to Maslow's hierarchy.

identify are material, health and caring resources, which themselves are influenced by gender, class and race. In outlining these triple requirements for independence, they suggest that in combination the lack of a number of these key resources can result in a loss of autonomy and independence for older people, which results in lower life satisfaction. While Arber and Ginn discussed this 'resource triangle' in relation to gender, it could equally be applied to ethnicity and could be used as a checklist for care providers (whether for health or social care) when they are ascertaining the resources available to older people from minority ethnic groups in their care.

NURSING PERSPECTIVES

A review of the literature shows a paucity of studies that directly investigate how well nurses are able to care for older people from minority ethnic groups on an individual level. However, there are a few related to caring for patients from minority ethnic groups in general that reveal that nurses are not adequately prepared to deliver care in our multicultural and multiethnic society.

In a small study to elicit health visitors' perceptions of working with minority ethnic clients, Foster (1988) interviewed random samples of health visitors from a London inner city area and from a health authority in the Home Counties. Both sets of health visitors identified cultural differences and language as major issues in their dealings with minority ethnic groups. Racism was an issue discussed mainly by the London respondents. Only two health visitors discussed socioeconomic disadvantage as a factor in the health status of

their clients. Very few of the London health visitors felt that the health services responded adequately to the needs of the minority ethnic population, while over half of those from the home counties believed this to be the case. Foster suggested that the views of the Home Counties' health visitors about the adequacy of services might be due to the fact that proportionally more interpreters were available to them. The author also suggests that there is a danger of health visitors with relatively few minority ethnic clients assuming there are no problems generally in working in a multiethnic society.

In contrast to this, a study of ward based nurses in Oxford to determine their experiences of caring for patients from minority ethnic groups revealed several problems from the nurses' perspective (Murphy and Macleod Clark, 1993). They identified difficulties with:

- Communication.
- Approaching the client in the presence of relatives.
- The number of visitors.
- The smell of their food.
- A lack of knowledge about cultural issues.
- The inability to give psychological care.
- Establishing a relationship with the client.

Interestingly, many of the nurses interviewed (who worked in an area with relatively few minority ethnic patients) assumed that nurses who worked in areas with significant numbers of minority ethnic clients would be much better prepared and not experience the same problems that they had experienced. Rawlings-Anderson (1992) explored this idea by replicating the study in an inner-London hospital where a significant percentage of the population were from minority ethnic groups. The results revealed that the nurses' experiences were strikingly similar to those in Murphy and Macleod Clark's study, with communication difficulties being experienced by all respondents. Many nurses described feelings of frustration at not being able to deliver appropriate nursing care, but some of them seemed to accept this as being inevitable and made little attempt to improve the situation. This supports claims that lack of effective communication with minority ethnic patients serves to increase their feelings of vulnerability and alienation at a very stressful time (Pearson, 1986a). The findings in the London study did indicate that although many nurses could highlight cultural differences in health practices, there was a tendency for them to interpret behaviour from their own cultural perspective. This ethnocentric perspective can seriously hinder the delivery of care that is sensitive to patients' needs. It is also interesting to note that not all of the nurses in this study were aware of the services that were available to improve the care delivered to patients from minority ethnic groups.

Although this research has revealed that nurses are not always able to deliver sensitive and appropriate care to their patients from minority ethnic groups, there are limited guidelines that identify good practice aimed at improving patient outcomes. It is imperative that nurses develop their awareness of their own cultural beliefs, improve their knowledge base in relation to the minority ethnic groups they care for and advance their skills of individual assessment in order to be able to ascertain the needs of older people from minority ethnic groups and to improve the quality of care that they deliver.

Cultural Awareness

There are two main schools of thought in relation to improving cultural awareness in nurses – the 'culture specific' and the 'culture general' approach.

The culture specific approach is based on the assumption that lack of knowledge about different cultures is the main cause of inappropriate care provision, and it seeks to redress this knowledge gap. In the USA, the 'transcultural nursing' movement has developed as a means of addressing these issues. The pioneer of this movement, Madeleine Leininger, has written on this subject since the 1960s and has developed a theory of 'culture care diversity and universality' which seeks to advance nursing research into the variety of health beliefs and caring practices that distinguish different cultural groups (Leininger, 1991). Leininger has studied more than 54 cultures in Western and non-Western countries and has identified 172 care constructs with specific meanings, usages and interpretations. She claims that there are more diversities than universalities and that if nurses are aware of these they will be able to give 'culture-specific' care.

In Britain, the transcultural nursing movement has not influenced nursing theory and research as it has in the USA. Since the 1980s, there has been a growing body of literature that focuses on the differences in health beliefs and practices among a variety of minority ethnic groups, but this has not always been based on research findings (Dobson, 1991). One of the major reasons that this culture specific approach has not been popular in Britain is the growing body of literature that criticises the transcultural or multicultural approach in health care generally. The criticisms of the culture specific approach are that it can ignore structural issues that affect people's health, such as race, class and gender (Bruni, 1988; Culley, 1996), and that ignoring political and structural aspects of society can lead to 'victim blaming' of minority ethnic groups themselves (Pearson, 1986b; Patel, 1990). A further criticism is that cultural groups themselves are not homogenous and that research that purports to provide an understanding of a particular culture may not be representative of a whole cultural group (Mason, 1990). The advantages of this approach are that it can provide a point of reference for nurses who have little knowledge about particular religious or cultural groups and can help them to interpret information gathered from patient assessments. However, it must be noted that the knowledge gained from this type of literature must be used in conjunction with individual assessment, otherwise it will only serve to perpetuate the ethnic stereotyping it seeks to redress (Baxter, 1988).

The culture general approach advocates that nurses cannot hope to understand other peoples' cultures if they are not able to understand and articulate their own cultural beliefs. Nurses need to explore their own cultural orientations and recognise how their own attitudes and values can have an impact upon their behaviour towards people who are perceived to be different (Lynam, 1992; McGee, 1992). Thiederman (1986, p. 52) states that, 'Lack of knowledge about one's own culture can distort the caregiver's perception of the ethnic patient just as easily as ignorance about the patient's culture can'.

It is often very difficult to express how cultural beliefs affect lifestyle and health practices and nurses should explore their own cultural practices and discuss these with others. If they are able to determine how their own culture affects their health practices, they are in a better position to discover how culture can determine behaviour in others. For example, are there certain foods that they eat when ill, are there any activities that they do not undertake if suffering particular ailments?

The exploration of culture and its attributes has been postulated by some as a means of providing nurses with a conceptual framework with which to improve their assessment skills (Glynn and Bishop, 1986; Giger and Davidhizar, 1995). This approach can assist nurses in understanding the general components of cultural practices, but can leave them without any idea about common practices that their clients may engage in. However, a sound understanding of what constitutes culture and cultural practices can guide the type of questions a nurse might use when assessing patients' needs.

It can be seen that the culture specific and culture general approaches both have advantages and drawbacks and it is suggested that nurses can best improve their practice if they draw on both approaches to improve the quality of care they deliver to older people from minority ethnic groups. This can be achieved by nurses utilising frameworks that incorporate the assessment of cultural practices relevant to health and also by building up a knowledge base of health-related practices of the communities they care for. See Appendix 11 for examples of cultural status asessments.

Nursing Older People from Minority Ethnic Groups

If nurses are to provide individualised and appropriate care to older people from minority ethnic groups, it is crucial that they are able to identify their needs following an assessment. Facets of both the culture general and culture specific approaches and an understanding of the wider structural variables that affect older people from minority ethnic groups are required in order to carry out a comprehensive assessment and to plan appropriate care.

Perhaps the most important factor to consider before assessment commences is to ascertain if interpretation and advocacy services are required and available. Not all older people from minority ethnic groups have a good understanding of English and this needs to be taken into consideration. A proactive approach to the utilisation of interpreters needs to be taken and assessments planned to coincide with availability of interpreters. If health service interpreters are not available, nurses must consider very carefully who else can be used to interpret. It must be remembered that it is not always appropriate to use members of the family to discuss personal details, especially if the family member is very young and may not have the required vocabulary or knowledge related to medical issues. Some health authorities also employ advocates or link-workers who are able to explain the patient's problems and any nursing interventions from the cultural perspective of the patient. Even if an older person from a minority ethnic group does speak English, the nurse should be mindful of their perceived vulnerability and use language that is simple and direct without being patronising.

Once the assessment has begun, the nurse needs to ascertain the patient's understanding of their health status and the factors that they believe have influenced this. It is also useful to try and find out how the older person's community views ill health and the role of the sick person. Not all cultures share the Western view of the 'sick role' and this can lead nurses to view patients as noncompliant if they do not seem interested in participating in their own care. This will enable the nurse to plan care that is congruent with the patient's beliefs or help them to identify health promotion strategies that might improve their health status. It is also important that the nurse is aware of any particular disease patterns that might affect that particular ethnic group in order that appropriate health screening can be mobilised and pertinent questions relating to early indications of disease can be elicited. For example, an older Asian patient might not have a known history of hyperglycaemia, but a nurse might detect the early warning signs of diabetes if a history of increasing thirst and lethargy is elicited through focused questions.

Meeting Cultural Needs

Dilvinder Kaur, a Sikh woman in her seventies, is admitted to the unit where you work as a primary nurse. She is in a weak state and has been diagnosed as having a chest infection; she is also very dehydrated. She is accompanied by her daughter who plans to stay with her mother until she is settled and sleeping. Dilvinder Kaur speaks little English herself and she tells her daughter that she is fearful about being left on her own in hospital. She is especially anxious about being asked to undress and also expresses concern about how she will prepare herself for early morning prayers. Dilvinder Kaur's immediate care includes the siting of an intravenous infusion. Based upon this care study, and using your knowledge of culture general and culture specific approaches, develop a nursing care plan as follows:

- **What are Dilvinder Kaur's comments that provide subjective evidence?**
- **What is the objective evidence?**
- **Suggest two unmet needs that may be the most significant to Dilvinder Kaur at this time.**
- **Suggest the nursing aims for each unmet need, reflecting realistic outcomes and using concrete and measurable terms.**
- **Suggest one or more interventions for each area of unmet need justifying your choice of intervention.**

It is also important to find out what the patient believes will help them to improve their health or recover from illness. Many older people from minority ethnic groups utilise folk healing practices and these should be discussed and where practicable included in their planned care. Folk healing practices are often complementary to and certainly not incompatible with Western medicine and their inclusion in planned care can demonstrate an acceptance and respect of those aspects of a persons identity that are most important to them. However, it is equally important to determine if any health practices are, in fact, detrimental to wellbeing so that appropriate education can be planned. Linked to this is the importance of religion to older individuals. Many older people find comfort in religious activity and those from minority ethnic groups may not have the expectation that their religious needs can be catered for within a health service that reflects the values of the ethnic majority. Asking simple questions about any religious requirements such as needing time and space to pray may reduce anxiety considerably, as can arranging for suitable religious personnel to visit the patient. It is also important to ascertain if the older person's religion affects the type of food they might find acceptable or unacceptable, or whether they have got any objects of religious significance that the nurse should know about.

Nurses should be mindful that some older people from minority ethnic groups may well have experienced discrimination and abuse in previous encounters with health service personnel or other patients and may lack confidence in stating their needs. This should not be interpreted as indifference, but rather considered as a self-protective mechanism learnt from years of being an outsider in a hostile environment. Thus, the assessment should not be a one-way process, but a mutual sharing of knowledge and patients should be encouraged to ask about any issues they are unsure of. A confident, yet non-patronising approach should indicate to the patient that the nurse is competent to plan appropriate care and is interested in determining any particular needs they may have. It is also important to focus on nonverbal cues that may give some indication of personal preferences or misunderstandings as some older people from minority ethnic groups may not have any experience of the health-care system and may not understand what is expected of them. For example, an older Chinese woman who had recently moved to England to join her family was admitted to a medical ward for investigations into anaemia. She agreed to have a series of tests suggested by the doctor as she believed him to be in a position of authority and that she could not refuse. When the time came for her to have an endoscopic examination she was asked to starve prior to the procedure. She said she would comply with this request, but later confided in her daughter that she had, in fact drunk some water prior to the procedure. She believed that the procedure would make her condition worse. This was because she believed her condition was caused by an excess of Yang, which can cause dehydration, and not being able to drink prior to the procedure had caused her great distress. Not only had this woman not felt that she could ask questions or discuss options for care, no one had ascertained her beliefs about the cause of her health problem and the nurses were unaware of the reasons for her distress. Drinking prior to the procedure had also compromised her safety. In this case 'culture specific' knowledge about Yin and Yang forces in Chinese philosophy would have been helpful to the nurses, as would 'culture general' knowledge that health beliefs and practices are an important aspect of cultural identity.

During the initial assessment of an older person from a minority ethnic group it is also important to ascertain what family support is available to them. It is wrong to assume that extended family networks will be able to look after their older relative without additional support. In a hospital setting this is vital for effective discharge planning and in the community it is important to ensure that appropriate referrals to other services are made.

Financial status also needs to be assessed and referral to a social worker may be necessary to determine if they are claiming all the benefits to which they are entitled. It is also of importance to determine gender roles within the family unit. For example, a widowed woman who has had little previous contact outside the family may have no idea how to claim benefits or how to access community support.

All of the above should be part of the assessment of any older person, but given the evidence discussed in previous sections regarding poor uptake and knowledge about services, it is especially important in older individuals from minority ethnic groups. Once a detailed assessment has been undertaken, care can be planned that is appropriate to the patient's needs and wishes. Again, this should be the case for any patient, but there may be some aspects of care that nurses should be aware of with regard to minority ethnic groups. For example, if a patient is to have an intravenous infusion it would be appropriate to know if they follow the right hand or left hand rule of hygiene in order to ascertain which side it would be most appropriate to site the cannula. It is also a good idea to discover if all religious rules are required to be followed during times of ill health. For example, although fasting is usually required during Ramadan, this may be waived during periods of ill health and so the individual's views must be sought in order to plan appropriate care.

Evaluation of care is paramount if lessons of good practice are to be learnt. Determining if mutually set goals have been met and whether the care delivered met the patient's cultural needs can be ascertained by asking about satisfaction with care and observing for nonverbal cues. Nursing interventions that have been noted to be particularly useful when caring for older people from minority ethnic groups can then be shared with others. For example, leaflets outlining healthy eating regimes that include preferred food of a particular minority group could be prepared and utilised by others. This may then lead to other initiatives, such as providing information in a variety of languages or producing audio-visual material for older people who may not speak English and are not literate in their mother tongue.

Overall, nurses need to utilise knowledge about specific ethnic groups, general knowledge about cultural determinants of health practices and their understanding of the structural variables within society in order to provide care that is both appropriate and sensitive to the need of older people from minority ethnic groups.

SUMMARY

This chapter has explored how cohort, gender and ethnicity can affect the lives of older people. A complex interconnection between these concepts makes it difficult to determine exactly how strong an influence each one has on individuals. However, if health-care professionals are aware how cohort position, gender and ethnicity can have profound effects on the life experiences of those older people that they care for, they should be able to plan services at both an organisational and at an individual level that will meet their needs. The challenge now is to plan services that will be appropriate for future cohorts of older people.

KEY POINTS

- Britain's older population is heterogeneous: cohort position, gender and ethnicity create significant differences in the life experiences of our ageing population.
- Cohort effects have a dramatic influence on individual life chances and experience.
- Differences in morbidity and mortality between men and women, together with marital status, family roles and employment history, influence the position of older women in our society.
- Differential migration patterns have determined the geographical and social position of older people from minority ethnic groups in Britain. The age profile of minority ethnic groups demonstrates that they are generally younger than the indigenous population. This has major implications for future service delivery.
- Recent research indicates that the health and social-care needs of older people from minority ethnic groups are not being met within mainstream service provision. This situation is perpetuated by several enduring myths about the nature of minority ethnic groups.
- Health-care providers must take into account the diversity of backgrounds of Britain's ageing population if service delivery is to be appropriate and sensitive to needs.
- Nurses must develop their skills of assessment if they are to deliver care that is culturally sensitive.

AREAS AND ACTIVITIES FOR STUDY AND REFLECTION

- How have older people described their younger life to you? How have they related major historic events and the impact that these have had on their lives?
- What characteristics of older people are specific to gender?
- What ethnic groups do you mostly come into contact with in your daily work? What do you know about their migration patterns, language, religious and cultural beliefs?
- In your experience, how does an older person's ethnic origin affect their beliefs about health and ill health?
- What specific services are provided in your place of work to meet the needs of minority ethnic groups?
- Have you identified any areas of service provision in your place of work that could be improved in relation to meeting the needs of older people from minority ethnic groups? How would you go about establishing these improvements?
- Would you be able to discuss with another health-care worker the specific health-care needs related to your own ethnic origins?
- What areas of personal development do you need to focus on in order to improve the care you deliver to older people from minority ethnic groups?

REFERENCES

Age Concern: *Age and race: double discrimination. Life in Britain today for ethnic minority elders*, London, 1995, Commission for Racial Equality and Age Concern.

Arber S, Ginn J. *Gender and later life: a sociological analysis of resources and constraints*. London: Sage Publications, 1991.

Askham L, Henshaw L, Tarpey M. S*ocial and health authority services for elderly people from Black and minority ethnic communities*, London, 1995, HMSO.

Balarajan R. Ethnic differences in mortality from ischaemic heart disease and cerebrovascular disease in England and Wales. Br Med J 1991, 302:560–564.

Balarajan R, Soni Raleigh V. The ethnic populations of England and Wales: the 1991 census. *Health Trends* 1992, 24:113–116.

Balarajan R, Soni Raleigh V. *Ethnicity and health in England*, London, 1995, HMSO.

Balarajan R, Yuen P, Soni Raleigh V. Ethnic differences in general practice consultations. *Br Med J* 1989, 299:958–960.

Barker J. *Black and Asian old people in Britain*, Mitcham, 1984, Age Concern.

Baxter C. Culture shock. *Nurs Times* 1988, 84:36–38.

Beechey V, Perkins T. *Women, part-time work and the labour market*. Cambridge: Polity Press, 1987.

Bender M. Bitter harvest: the implications of continuing war-related stress on reminiscence theory and practice. *Ageing and Society* 1997, 17:337–348.

Bernard M, Meade K, eds. *Women come of age: perspectives on the lives of older women*. London: Edward Arnold, 1993.

Berry S, Lee M, Griffiths S. *Report on a survey of West Indian pensioners in Nottingham*, Social Services Research Section, Nottingham, 1981, Nottingham City Council.

Bhalla A, Blakemore K. *Elders of the minority ethnic groups*. All Faiths For One Race (AFFOR), Birmingham, 1981.

Blakemore K. Health and illness among the elderly of minority ethnic groups. *Health Trends* 1982, 14:68–72.

Blakemore K. *Ageing and ethnicity*. In: Johnson J, Slater S, eds. Ageing and later life. London: Sage Publications, 1993; 68–75.

Blakemore K, Boneham M. *Age, race and ethnicity. A comparative approach*. Buckingham: Open University Press, 1994.

Bowling A, Farquhar J, Leaver J. Jewish people and ageing: their emotional well-being, physical health status and use of services. *Nursing Practice* 1992, 5:5–16.

Bowling B. T*he development, co-ordination and provision of services to elderly people from ethnic minorities: a report on four innovatory projects*, London, 1990, Age Concern Institute of Gerontology.

Bruni N. A critical analysis of transcultural theory. *Aust J Adv Nurs 1988*, 5:26–32.

Butt J, Mirza K. *Social care and Black communities*, London, 1996, HMSO, London.

Cameron E, Badger F, Evers H. District nursing, the disabled and the elderly: who are the Black patients? *J Adv Nurs* 1989, 14:376–382.

Chiu S. Chinese elderly people: no longer a treasure at home. *Soc Work Today* 1989, 2:15–17.

Clarke L. Family care and changing family structure: bad news for the elderly? In: Allen I, Perkins E, eds. *The future of family care for older people*. London: HMSO, 1995.

Coombes Y, Kalache A. Demographic characteristics. In: Shukla R, Brooks D, eds. *A guide to the care of the elderly*. London: HMSO, 1996.

Culley L. A critique of multiculturalism in health care: the challenge for nurse education. *J Adv Nurs* 1996, 23:564–570.

Department of Health. *The patients charter: raising the standard*, London, HMSO, 1991.

Department of Health. *The health of the nation: a strategy for health in England*, London: HMSO, 1992.

Department of Health. The new NHS modern, dependable. London: HMSO, 1997

Dobson S. *Transcultural nursing: a contemporary imperative*. London: Scutari Press, 1991.

Evers H. Old women's self-perceptions of dependency and some implications for service provision. *J Epidemiol Community Health* 1984, 38:306–309.

Fenton S. *Ageing minorities: Black people as they grow old in Britain*, London, 1987, Commission for Racial Equality.

Foster M. Health visitors perspectives on working in a multiethnic society. *Health Visitor* 1988, 61:275–278.

Giger J, Davidhizar R. *Transcultural nursing: assessment and intervention*, 2nd edition. St Louis: Mosby, 1995.

Glynn N, Bishop G. Multiculturalism in nursing: implications for faculty development. *J Nurs Educ* 1986, 25:39–41.

Greenslade L, Pearson M, Madden M. *Irish migrants in Britain: socio-economic and demographic conditions*, Occasional Paper in Irish Studies No. 3, Liverpool, 1991, University of Liverpool.

Groves D. Work, poverty and older women. In: Bernard M, Meade K, eds. *Women come of age: perspectives on the lives of older women*. London: Edward Arnold, 1993; 43–62.

HMSO. *On the state of the public health for the year 1991*, Annual Report of the Chief Medical Officer (Calman), London: HMSO, 1991.

Hek G, Contact with Asian elders. *J District Nurs* 1991, 10:13–15.

Helman C. *Culture, health and illness*, 3rd edition. Oxford: Butterworth Heinemann, 1994.

Help the Aged. *An ageing population*, Factsheet 2, London, 1991, Family Policy Studies Centre.

Itzin C. As old as you feel. In: Thompson P, Itzin C, Abendstern M, eds. *I don't feel old: the experience of later life*. Oxford: Oxford University Press, 1990; 107–136.

Jadeja S, Singh J. Life in a cold climate. *Community Care* 1993, 963:12–13.

Jarvis C, Hancock R, Askham J, Tinker A. *Getting around after 60: a profile of Britain's older population*, London, 1996, HMSO.

Leininger M. *Culture care, diversity and universality: a theory of nursing*. New York: National League for Nursing Press, 1991.

Lewando Hundt G, Grant S. *Studies of Black elders: an exercise in window dressing or the groundwork for widening provision (Coventry survey)*, Social Services Research, Coventry, 1987, No. 5 and 6: 1–9.

Lynam M. Towards the goal of providing culturally sensitive care: principles on which to build nursing curricula. *J Adv Nurs* 1992, 17:149–157.

McCormick A, Rosenbaum M, Fleming D. Socio-economic characteristics of people who consult their general practitioner. *Popul Trends* 1990, 59:8–10.

McGee P. *Teaching transcultural care: a guide for teachers of nursing and health care*. London: Chapman and Hall, 1992.

McKeigue P. Patterns of health and disease in the elderly from minority ethnic groups. In: Squires A, ed. *Multicultural health care and rehabilitation of older people*. London: Edward Arnold, 1991; 69–77

McKeigue P, Marmot M. Mortality from coronary heart disease in Asian communities in London. *Br Med J* 1988, 297:903

Mason C. Women as mothers in Northern Ireland and Jamaica: a critique of the transcultural nursing movement. *Int J Nurs Stud* 1990, 27:367–374.

Morton J, ed. *Recent research on services for Black and minority ethnic elderly people*, London, 1993, Age Concern Institute of Gerontology.

Murphy K, Macleod Clark J. Nurses' experiences of caring for ethnic-minority clients. *J Adv Nurs* 1993, 18:442–450.

Norman A. *Triple jeopardy: growing old in a second homeland*, London, 1985, Centre for Policy on Ageing.

Patel N. *A 'race' against time? Social services provision for Black elders*, London, 1990, The Runnymede Trust.

Peacock J. *The anthropological lens. Harsh light, soft focus*. Cambridge: Cambridge University Press, 1986.

Pearson M. Fitting in. *Senior Nurse* 1986a, 4:14–15.

Pearson M. The politics of ethnic minority health studies. In: Rathwell T, Phillips D, eds. *Health, race and ethnicity*. London: Croom Helm, 1986b; 100–116.

Pharoah C. *Primary health care for elderly people from Black and minority ethnic communities*, London, 1995, HMSO.

Rawlings-Anderson K. Registered nurses' experinces of caring for patients from ethnic minority groups, unpublished MSc dissertation, King's College, London, 1992.

Sidell M. The relationship of elderly women to their doctors. In: George J, Ebrahim S, eds. *Health care for older women*. Oxford: Oxford University Press, 1992; 179–196.

Sidell M. Health issues and the older woman. In: Bernard M, Meade K, eds. *Women come of age: perspectives on the lives of older women*. London: Edward Arnold, 1993; 63–84.

Soulsby J, Halpin E, Patel V. Race, migration and older people in Europe, recommendations and report arising from a conference in Preston, 13–15 September 1993, University of Central Lancashire, Preston, 1994.

Theiderman S. Ethnocentrism: a barrier to effective health care. *Nurse Pract* 1986, 11:54–59.

Tripp-Reimer T. Retention of a folk-healing practice (Matiasma) among four generations of urban Greek immigrants. *Nurs Res* 1983, 32:97–101.

UKCC. *Code of professional conduct*, 3rd edition, London, 1992, United Kingdom Central Council for Nursing, Midwifery and Health Visiting.

Victor C. *Old age in modern society*, 2nd edition. London: Chapman and Hall, 1994.

Young J, George J. History of migration to the United Kingdom. In: Squires A, ed. *Multicultural health care and rehabilitation of older people*. London: Edward Arnold, 1991; 17–27.

FURTHER READING

This section is related to minority ethnic groups. While some of these books appear somewhat dated, they do describe many aspects of cultural and religious beliefs that may be helpful. As with all literature of this nature, they are intended to give general information only and are no substitute for individual assessment.

Chan J. Dietary beliefs of Chinese patients. *Nursing Standard*.1995, 9:30–34.
This article gives an overview of Chinese philosophy and how this influences dietary preferences.

Douglas J. *Caribbean food and diet*. Bristol: Training in Health and Race, 1987.
This book covers the background of the Caribbean community in Britain, looks at dietary patterns and discusses how to give dietary advice.

Department of Health, Social Care Group. They look after their own, don't they? Inspection of community care services for black and ethic minority older people. London: HMSO, 1998
This publication summarises the findings of an inspection to evaluate the extent to which Social Service Departments addressed the needs of ethnic minority older people. It also includes good practice checklists.

Gunaratnamy Y: *Checklist health and race. A starting point for managers on improving services for black populations*. London: Kings Fund Centre, 1993.
This provides guidance for managers in Regional Health Authorities, purchasing authorities and provider units. It aims to enable managers to make services more appropriate and accessible to black populations.

Henley A.. *Caring for Muslims and their families : religious aspects of care*. London: DHSS/ Kings Fund, 1982.
Henley A. *Caring for Hindus and their families : religious aspects of care*. London: DHSS/ Kings Fund, 1983.
Henley A. *Caring for Sikhs and their families : religious aspects of care*. London: DHSS/ Kings Fund, 1983.
These books were written in conjunction with representatives from relevant communities. They cover the basic tenets of religion; practical care; dietary restrictions; naming systems; and rituals related to birth, marriage and death.

Karmi G. *The ethnic health handbook. A factfile for health care professionals*. London: Blackwell Science, 1996.
This book gives information on major religious and ethnic groups. It also has a list of national contacts for each group.

Mares P. *The Vietnamese in Britain : a handbook for health workers*. Cambridge: Health Education Council / National Extension College, 1982.
This covers the history of migration from Vietnam and has sections on both health and diet.

Mares P, Henley A, Baxter C. *Healthcare in multiracial Britain*. Cambridge: Health Education Council / National Extension College, 1985.
A comprehensive book covering explanations of health inequalities, health needs and expectations and health services.

Neuberger J. *Caring for dying people of different faiths*. 2nd edn, London: Mosby, 1994.
This book focuses on religious beliefs and how this may impact on caring for the dying.

Sampson C. *The neglected ethic: religious and cultural factors in the care of patients*. London: McGraw-Hill, London, 1982.
An overview of the main world religions and practices.

Spitzer J, Vyras N. *A guide to the Orthodox Jewish Way of Life for Healthcare Professionals*. The Joint Academic Department of General Practice & Primary Care, St Bartholomew's and the Royal London Hospital Medical School and East London & the City Health Authority, London, 1996.
A pamphlet discussing the Jewish way of life and how this can impact on health and health-care practices.

Care Concern
20 Pentonville Road
London
N1 9XB

Care Concern is an independent day care provider, specialising in the provision of day care facilities to frail older people from minority ethnic groups. Care Concern believes in working in partnership with local authorities, health authorities and community or voluntary user groups.

1990 Trust
South Bank Techno Park
90 London Road
London
SE1 6LN

This organisation provides research, administrative and technical support to Black organisations and networks. They have established a Black Elders project and are preparing a national directory of organisations working with the black elderly.

Self-actualisation

20 Achieving self-actualisation through learning and creativity
Bernie Arigho

LEARNING OBJECTIVES

After studying this chapter you will be able to:

- Provide a comprehensive definition of self-actualisation and identify several of the qualities that may be found in self-actualised older people.
- Describe the fundamental differences in activities and capacities between self-actualised people and those who are not, and suggest reasons why these differences arise.
- Describe several learning opportunities that are available to older people, and the special developmental factors predominant in each.
- Specifiy several types of creative self-expression achieved by older people, including those less often in the public eye. Relate creativity to self-development and show how the nurse can assist this process.
- Discuss the role of the nurse in relation to the self-actualisation of older people.

INTRODUCTION

Self-actualisation, as defined by the humanistic psychologist Abraham Maslow (1954), is regarded as the highest level of human functioning. Each individual is viewed as being motivated through life to achieve their full potential as a unique human being. This perspective offers a relatively optimistic appraisal of human nature, one that focuses upon the highest and noblest motives and aspirations of human beings. We each have the potential for continual self-development towards a level at which the self is eventually transcended and the individual becomes more concerned with wider global issues of ethics and problem-solving.

Maslow (1954) believed that only a few special people actually succeed in reaching the ultimate goal of self-actualisation. Other lower-level needs must be satisfied before an individual can attain complete fulfilment of potential. The common human experience is to be restricted and blocked at different levels of achievement by various internal and external inhibitions, such as defence mechanisms and oppressive social circumstances. The important point is that the basic drive towards development is an essential and universal human need, one that gives meaning to life at every stage. This model of human motivation is, therefore, particularly relevant to the nursing care of older people since it conceptualises the ageing process as one of development and growth.

Maslow believed that only older people were capable of self-actualisation, the very pinnacle of personal development, because it requires the wisdom and maturity that can only be acquired by facing all the difficulties and challenges of life and still being true to oneself. This is similar to Erikson's recognition of ego-integrity versus despair as the final and

highest developmental challenge facing an individual (Erikson, 1987). This is not something that comes naturally to us: it is something towards which we work as we get older. Moreover, it is something which can be facilitated by a healthy social environment and helpful behaviours by other people.

The Characteristics of Self-actualised People

The concept of self-actualisation is by its very nature not susceptible to rigorous definition. It relates to abstract ideals such as the search for truth and beauty, about which we can never have absolute agreement. However, such concepts are capable of being systematically and qualitatively investigated by objectively studying and describing the lifestyles of older people. Maslow (1954) studied the lives of eminent historical figures to arrive at a composite picture of the distinguishing characteristics of self-actualised people (**Box 20.1**). He believed these traits to be so attractive that everyone must essentially aspire to achieve them.

Maslow (1967) believed that such complete examples of self-actualised people were extremely rare, but that many people experience transient moments of self-actualisation, which he called peak experiences. These are moments of intense happiness and a sense of fulfilment, that occur sometimes during creative work, contact with nature, appreciation of the arts, intimate relationships or acts of great physical achievement. The attempt to accumulate more peak experiences is a realistic way of trying to reach what is an ultimate ideal state.

The question we are exploring is no less than what are the highest goals of human existence. What is good, better

20.1 Traits of Self-actualised Persons

- **Time competent**: uses past and future to live more fully in the present.
- **Inner directed:** source of direction depends on internal forces more than on others.
- **Flexible:** can react to new situations without unreasonable restrictions.
- **Sensitive to self:** responsive to own feelings.
- **Spontaneous:** able to and willing to be oneself.
- **Values self:** accepts and demonstrates strengths as a person.
- **Accepts self:** approves of self essentially despite weaknesses or deficiencies.
- **Positively views others:** accepts others as essentially good and constructive.
- **Positively views life:** sees the opposites of life as meaningfully related.
- **Capable of intimate contact:** establishes deeply satisfying interpersonal relationships with a few, rather than many, people.

characteristics of maturity and wisdom, if these are indeed valued as the highest personal goals? Maslow's model has been chosen because ageing is not viewed as decline or withdrawal into oneself, but rather as the opportunity for fulfilment and transcendence of the self. Moreover, the view of life as the gradual satisfaction of needs by means of problem-solving is particularly applicable to the practice of nursing.

The model can be viewed as the evolution of an individual within society. As people develop they become more active self-determining agents of their development. A child's first need is to be given food, shelter, safety, security and love. Their need is fulfilled by an adult, who has moved to sufficient levels of self-esteem and mastery to give to the child. In adolescence, the focus on self intensifies and development is powered by the need to be accepted. As one experiences love outside the family, goals enlarge. World concerns and ethics may eventually transcend self, family, community and nation.

Maslow's model of human needs is often presented diagrammatically as a pyramid, tending to over-emphasise the importance of the lower level needs, and making self-actualisation appear like the unnecessary icing on the cake. However, in Maslow's conception, it is the drive towards self-actualisation that motivates all development. Lower level needs are important in that they underlie and make possible further development, such development involving an enlarging of concerns beyond narrow self-interest and a gradual flowering of maturity. The higher the stage reached, the higher the achievement. True human development might thus more appropriately be viewed as an inverted triangle, showing a process of expanding interests outside of oneself and one's immediate circles (**Figure 20.1**).

The different levels of development all depend on the meeting of lower level needs, and regression as well as further development is possible at every stage. People may have

and best in human activity? The relevance to nursing care is that these issues also relate to the question of what is a healthy and well-adjusted individual at any particular stage in life. Clearly there are different views as to what these may be. We are engaged in a moral as well as an intellectual debate. If we accept the perspective of the possibility of development throughout the life course, then another way to look at this is to ask what does it mean to age successfully. What are the

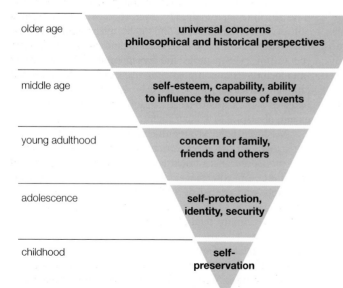

Figure 20.1 The inverted pyramid: development as an expansion of interests.

older age	universal concerns / philosophical and historical perspectives
middle age	self-esteem, capability, ability to influence the course of events
young adulthood	concern for family, friends and others
adolescence	self-protection, identity, security
childhood	self-preservation

temporary or fleeting experiences of self-actualisation, but find that their outlook becomes constricted again because of difficulties with the satisfaction of their underlying needs. Various kinds of illnesses, mental and physical, can be both causative and symptomatic of these difficulties. It is interesting to note that as a person ages, and self-actualisation becomes more attainable through life-experience and learning, it becomes more likely that help will be needed from others for some aspects of care. The new threat to these needs and the loss of independence may not only hold back development but also actually cause regression. On the other hand, some older people come to accept such losses as inevitable, and can trust others to give them the help they need while they continue to grow spiritually and emotionally. Carers have a vital part to play in enabling such people to feel confident, free from fears concerning their basic needs, and free to develop. Some of the challenges and crises that sometimes accompany older age would seem to require and prompt the kinds of strengths of character that are encompassed by the concept of self-actualisation. For older people, self-actualisation is not only a possibility borne out of the lessons and endeavours of a long life, it may also be the response to the particular experience of being old.

For some, a sense of not fulfilling their potential may create feelings of low self-worth or even depression, thus putting at risk the more fundamental needs of self-care and calling for the help of others. It might simply be argued that such people are not and never will be completely self-actualised and self-transcendent. According to Maslow (1967) few people are. Self-actualisation presents as an ideal state of human existence, one to which we all are driven, but few achieve in an enduring and comprehensive way. We will not find perfect quintessential examples of the ideal, but we are all capable of achieving some aspects of it. Self-actualisation consists of many different qualities, some of which we may develop to greater or lesser extents. Moreover, it does not occur in individual isolation; it is an individual and a social phenomenon and as such it can be recognised and facilitated by an appreciative outside world. Some of the qualities of self-actualisation will now be explored, with particular reference to the experience of later life.

Courage

Courage may be defined as that quality of mind or spirit that enables a person to face difficulty, danger or pain with firmness and without damage to their self-esteem, their integrity or their continuing development. It is a core quality that lies at the heart of all of the characteristics of self-actualised people as described by Maslow. In old age (though certainly not exclusively or universally) there may be many trials requiring courageous responses. For example:

- Death of loved ones.
- Loss of physical powers.
- Constant niggling physical complaints.
- Financial difficulties.
- Enforced moves into care settings.
- Awareness that one's own death is approaching.

Ill health, physical weakness and relative material poverty may be the circumstances in which people discover resources of courage and deeper meanings to existence beyond conventional measures of success. Such spiritual strength is often testified to in the appreciations of older people by their carers. Carers have a role to play in not only recognising and appreciating such strong qualities, but also in providing physical and emotional support (through sensitive and appropriate nursing interventions) to sustain development.

Altruism

Self-esteem, high morale and meaning in life are derived from helping others and generally helping to make the world a better more caring place, for the sake of the present and the future. The emphasis in this highest stage of moral development is on what is right for humanity, not on what is right for oneself at this moment. This is a crucial element in continuing development in later life, and is one that may be threatened by illness, disability or enforced retirement. The caring relationship may become so unbalanced in the perceived exchange of rewards that it reinforces a growing sense in the patient that they are not fulfilling their need to care properly for themselves or others. Opportunities to care and help can be provided, and instances of such behaviour can be recognised and appreciated. The self-actualised person does not become introspective to the extent of wanting to be remote from the world. On the contrary, at last the world becomes valuable for its own sake rather than for what the self can obtain from it, and such a person will want to do whatever they can, given their limitations, to aid the growth and the wellbeing of others. Such activities may be as simple as stroking a cat, watering a plant, feeding birds, and sharing a confidence, a friendly joke or a smile with a nurse.

Humour

A certain kind of humour is transcendent because it momentarily removes one from an isolated ego state to join in surprise and warm acceptance with others at the ludicrous situations of human beings. This is not a disparaging or derisive type of humour, but rather one that engages with other people on the same level, and is respectful of their concerns and feelings. It requires the ability to step back from oneself and see the total context of an event. As such it requires a high level of awareness and some degree of self-transcendence, including the ability to laugh good-naturedly at one's own limitations. The benefits of good humour are social, psychological and physiological. The care setting can be one in which older people feel confident that their natural and personal expression of good humour will be appreciated. Caring relationships can be informal and equal enough to acknowledge the older person's strength of character in being able to laugh at the common human difficulties.

Snapshots of Self-actualisation

I would not like to stay the same age all my life, as to grow old is to expand, to gain knowledge and understanding, and to learn from experience.

When you get to my age, you'll probably look back as I do, and you'll see it all spread out. Marvellous, isn't it really?

When you stop to look back you realise how one thing has led to another, and it has sort of made a pattern. What do they say, 'there's a divinity which shapes our ends'? I think there probably is.

I believe firmly in the afterlife and I believe our loved ones go on living and I believe that they help. I'm often conscious of them you know. And that has helped me a lot, that faith and the knowledge that when I do pass they'll be there waiting for me. People might laugh, but that's my faith. And it's helped me go through all sorts of things.
(Coleman, 1986)

SUCCESSFUL AGEING

Success in life is evaluated very differently by people depending on their background, temperament and values. Theories about successful ageing are based on particular views about what seems to be appropriate or desirable for a certain stage in life. We may not all agree on the characteristics of success, but Maslow's model allows for more flexibility in that the ultimate goal of self-actualisation is a lifelong pursuit that will have an infinite number of variations, strengths and difficulties. Many people tend to define success in old age in terms of retaining physical powers for as long as possible – 'cheating the clock' as it were. Physical strength and vigour are not special characteristics of self-actualisation; they may be found if only some of the lowest needs are met. If one is self-actualised, then one will put as much energy into life as one can, will be motivated to work hard at everything and will appreciate what is important to continuing good physical health. This does not mean that biological and genetic realities can be defeated. Self-actualisation is primarily an advanced state of mind and moral development requiring advanced years and experience, rather than an ability to seem biologically younger for longer.

While being positive about what can be achieved in old age, it is important to guard against reacting to negative images of older people with equally unrealistic positive images. There are no guarantees that old age will bring wisdom and self-transcendence; it is something that has to be worked at. Maslow examined the lives of famous people for his examples of self-actualised role models, but there is no need to become famous or conventionally successful in order to have achieved the goal. Indeed, a lifelong preoccupation with worldly ambitions and conventional success is an indication that the drive towards self-actualisation has been sidetracked. We are more likely to find living examples of self-actualised states of being in the unpublicised lives of older people whom we encounter for the first time in our work as nurses.

Behaviours and Activities Leading to Self-actualisation

The drive towards self-actualisation is a lifelong pursuit, and the experience of old age, which has been hypothesised as the most likely stage of its enduring achievement, represents the culmination of the coming together of a unique individual with a unique set of life circumstances. How the individual has interacted with these circumstances will determine their stage of development.

When nurses encounter older people in a care setting, they meet somebody who has expended a lifetime's effort and energy into their development. They will be at different stages of development (though these cannot be rigidly measured), and they will have travelled along different routes. They will have been creative, altruistic, good-humoured and courageous to varying extents. Maslow's model of human needs and continuing development does not conceive of a point in life when there is nothing left to do but regress and decline. This attitude represents a block to growth and is therefore a symptom of ill being. It tends to be bred by societies that overvalue material commodities in relation to spiritual values, and youth in relation to age. If lower level needs cannot be completely met by the individual because of illness, then these can be partially met or assisted by others. If death is imminent and inevitable, then the ultimate achievement is to accept this with courage and understanding, not apathy or despair. There is always realistic hope, if we have the resources to see it. Whatever has been achieved and whatever the present and future material limitations, there is always a stage further on which to develop. The fact that older people may need to be helped to some extent with their development is not a derogatory comment nor contradiction of the self-actualisation principle; the whole concept of lifelong development must be seen in terms of a helpful social system as well as the driven individual.

Learning and Growing in Later Life

Maslow believed that certain kinds of behaviours could help people in their natural tendency towards self-actualisation.
- Experience life as a child does, with full absorption and concentration.
- Experiment with new ways of doing things.
- Be true to your own inner feelings rather than follow the voice of tradition, authority or the majority.
- Be yourself, not an act, in your interactions with people.
- Stand up for what you believe, and be prepared to be unpopular if necessary.
- Take responsibility for yourself.
- Work hard at whatever you decide to do.
- Be aware of your unhelpful defences and have the courage to release them.

These kinds of behaviours are associated with learning and growth, and as such they can be facilitated by appropriate educational opportunities of a formal and informal nature. This section will examine some of the ways in which older people can learn new skills or rediscover old ones, become involved in broad humanitarian issues and work towards personal self-development. These are opportunities that give people chances to continue their development towards self-actualisation. They may also provide the arena in which self-actualised behaviour can be expressed. It may be argued that without a sense of individual direction and purpose in life one's quality of life is undermined. In recent years in adult education there has been a move towards approaches that aim to be more empowering for older people (Davies, 1993). In such approaches, older people are recognised as a heterogeneous group of people capable of identifying their individual needs and how to achieve them. Tutors become less 'subject experts' and more enabling facilitators.

Learning is crucial at every stage of development, and **Figure 20.2** illustrates some examples of learning activities that are relevant to different levels of need. The nurse's role is to be informed and to assist the older person to find what is the appropriate learning opportunity for their individual needs.

Further Education

Universities and colleges of further education offer courses at certificate, diploma and degree level that have reduced fees for people of a pensionable age. More flexible pathways towards degrees are now encouraged by the credit accumulation transfer scheme, enabling people to choose courses at different colleges over a number of years, and gradually build up the required number of credits towards an academic qualification.

In many cases, places are available to older students who do not wish to study for a formal qualification and who are participating purely for reasons of self-development. Some courses are aimed particularly at older learners, such as return to study skills, pre-retirement training, computing skills, health promotion, creative reminiscence work and volunteering activities. Other courses have demonstrated the value to all concerned of a broad intergenerational range of learners (Scholz, 1993); for example, combating ageist attitudes, emphasising the intrinsic value of scholarship and the exchange of life-experience across the generations. Colleges now offer a wide variety of distance learning packages to help meet the educational needs of people who cannot commit themselves to full-time intensive study. The Open University has developed expertise in providing methods of learning that enable people to study wherever they live and in their own time. Their supported open learning methods, backed up by study packs and audio-visual materials, have enabled many older learners to achieve academic success.

The University of the Third Age

The University of the Third Age is an educational self-help organisation of growing size and importance in the UK. It describes itself as a learning cooperative, a collective of people devoted to learning for its own sake, outside of any search for academic or professional advancement. It is run by and for older people, requiring no formal academic qualifications and giving none. Tutors are unpaid older people, and all members are acknowledged as having valuable life-experience and skills to offer one another. Members in local centres organise their own activities and study groups according to their interests, skills, knowledge and resources. For a small

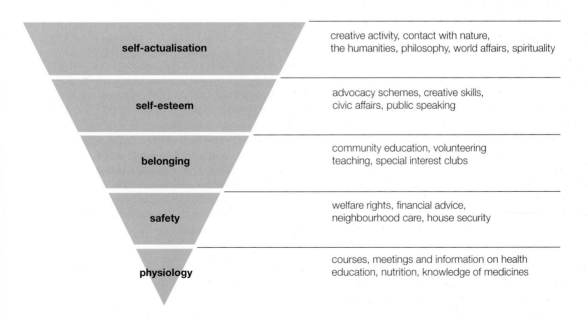

Figure 20.2 Learning activities according to level of need.

annual membership fee members can join any of the local centres' many study groups. At U3A South London, for example, learning groups are available on languages, geology, writing workshops, rambling, social studies, art, outings and social occasions. At present there are over 160 centres in the UK with almost 20,000 members. The National Office in London (*see* Useful Contacts) can be contacted for information about how to join a local centre or how to start a new one.

Community Colleges and Adult Education

Local authority community education services provide a wide range of low-cost educational programmes for older people who live within their boundaries. Some of these colleges also do outreach work in residential homes, sheltered housing units and day centres. Issues of accessibility and equal opportunities are critical to the success of such programmes, and consultation with representatives of older people's groups helps to ensure that a convenient and practically useful service is provided. The National Institute of Adult Continuing Education helps to coordinate a network of agencies concerned with education for older people. They offer information, publicity and in some cases grant support for innovative projects by local providers of adult education. Each year an adult learners week focuses on the educational needs and achievements of older people. Many projects were initiated and developed during the 1993 European Year of Older People and Solidarity Between Generations. Some of these projects have successfully forged links with local voluntary organisations and self-help groups. Many projects are aimed specifically at older people from ethnic communities. Local authorities provide directories of all such active groups.

Intergenerational Projects

There is special value in inviting older people to participate in educational activities with children and young adults. The older people are given the opportunity to share important cultural knowledge and lifetime experience with the generations to follow. An active concern about the future of society is a mark of self-actualisation, and intergenerational projects can enable this concern to be put into effect. Such work can also help to promote more positive attitudes towards older people and ageing in general. Preparation for later life and continuing development is best begun early in life. The exchange thus aims to be a mutually beneficial one. By focusing on both younger and older people's shared humanity and joint interest in development and learning, the superficial differences and socially created strangeness between generations can be overcome. There are many examples of successful formats and methods for such projects (Schweitzer, 1993; O'Connor, 1993; Adams and Gowland, 1994; Hewitt and Harris, 1992). Age Exchange specialises in intergenerational theatre projects and visits by older people to classrooms to make links between reminiscence and the school curriculum. Magic Me develops partnerships between schoolchildren and older people in residential homes. Other groups focus on the involvement of older people in school oral history projects.

Library Services

For many older people reading has been a lifelong pleasure and source of enlightenment, providing an opportunity for quiet, individual engagement with subjects and writers of interest. It may be a time for the extension of knowledge of an author, for the revisiting of much-loved works or for the discovery of new perspectives. Libraries in the UK offer special services for older people living in the community and for those in care settings. As well as providing books, records and cassettes, some arrange clubs and creative activities programmes. They are also a good source of information on where to go for further advice and information. Large print and talking books are available, as well as reading machines and other aids to converting text into sound. There are also homebound and community library services that provide resources and training for staff in residential homes, nursing homes and day centres. Museums and Art Centres also often provide special educational and creative activities at concessionary rates for older people.

Collective Political Action – Elder Empowerment

Closely related to the concept of individual self-actualisation is the aim of 'empowerment' for older people. Being empowered suggests being self-determining, self-expressive and having an influence. Social and political groups who aim to improve the social status of older people are concerned with fundamental issues of human rights and equal opportunities. They seek to identify and counter examples of negative discrimination against older people. One such example is the relative lack of educational opportunity in later life, and the underlying failure to recognise its importance for older people. Progress in the political sphere is thus relevant to greater numbers of older people being given opportunities for continuing development. Organisations campaigning at the political level for rights and equal opportunities for older people include Age Concern, Help the Aged, The Beth Johnson Foundation, the Centre for Policy on Ageing, Development Education Centres and many local and regional pensioners' groups (*see* Useful Contacts). The Pre-Retirement Association and the Association for Educational Gerontology are particularly concerned with educational opportunities and quality of life for older people.

As an example of an active campaigning organisation, Counsel and Care are particularly concerned with the quality of life experienced by older people who require forms of health and social care. They provide a free advice and information service for older people and their carers with regard to many different aspects of quality of care. They have published reports on such issues as restraint and risk-taking, privacy, hearing loss, recreational and leisure activities, and older people's expectations and experiences of residential care and nursing homes. They have assembled a database of all registered private and voluntary homes in the Greater London area, and make suggestions about homes for people based on individual needs and requirements.

Elder empowerment is now recognised as an international and multicultural issue, though there are national and regional variations on the problems facing older members of societies (Thursz *et al.* 1995). In so far as political action by older people represents a genuine concern about rights and improved social conditions for all, then it is related to the kind of self-transcendence characteristic of self-actualisation. Pressure group politics can be a very effective means of influencing social policy, and with growing numbers of older people there is the hope that their collective voice will be heard. However, it must be remembered that they are a very diverse group, and that some are more relatively disempowered than others across a number of dimensions; for example disability, wealth, education and ethnicity (Norman, 1985).

CREATIVITY

Malsow regarded high levels of creativity as one of the indicators of the self-actualised person. The evidence shows that not only is continuing creativity possible in old age, but that it may be a time for the development of new original creative styles. Some of the services and types of care provided for older people are influenced by views of what are appropriate activities for people at that stage of life. Such views are often based merely on stereotypes of older people, or on narrow studies of certain groups of older people at particular times in history. Gerontological research has helped to debunk many myths about what is inevitable or socially desirable in old age, and has emphasised the importance of individual life histories and social opportunities for older people. Lehman's study (1953) of the creative contributions of famous people fails to take into account the influence of social conditions on behaviour and development – such factors as health, health care, social opportunities and social attitudes. Negative attitudes towards the capabilities and contributions of older people are a form of social discrimination akin to sexism and racism. Such discrimination has been, and continues to be, a block to creative work and personal development in our society. Simonton (1990) has studied creativity among older people and concludes that creative activity is not tied to chronology or biological ageing but to successive acts of self-development along the individual life course. As people become more self-actualised over time, there is reason to believe that increased independence of mind and greater freedom from practical cultural concerns will release more creative imagination for the older person.

Creative responses have been observed in relation to emotional crises such as life-threatening illnesses. They can be a way of dealing with and mastering various existential challenges at any stage of life. Ageing, the awareness of life approaching its end and the experience of multiple age-related disease processes are challenges that older people receiving nursing care may be confronting. The motivation to be creative, once stimulated and empowered, can go to extraordinary lengths in order to find a means of expression. There can be no strict division between learning and creativity; the arts, education and indeed health are by definition interconnected. This section will look at ways in which the

Meeting Self-development Needs

Tom was born in 1915. His family had been hill farmers in Wales for several generations. At the age of 82 years he is retired and living in Southeast London with his wife. Their son, David, lives nearby with his family, and they are in daily contact. When David suggested that his parents move to London so that the family could be closer together, Tom was insistent that they find somewhere near green open spaces. One of his favourite sayings is that 'God made the country, and man made the town.' Tom left school at 14 years of age to follow in his father's footsteps on the farm. He has always had a sharp brain and been quick to learn. Talking about his work on the farm, he describes it as 'hard work, but good work; work is good'. He has always been a practical man who needed things to do in order to be content. He had a deep respect for the animals on his farm, and has always kept dogs. He is a man of few words, but always has a comment to make about everything. His life and work are clearly a source of pride to him, though he spends little time sharing reminiscences about them. He attends church service every Sunday morning, and regularly goes for walks with his dog in the local parks. He likes to go for a pint in his local pub about twice a week. He has been married for 57 years, and for the last 5 years has been the main carer for his wife, who has Alzheimer's disease. 'She always stood by me, and I'll always stand by her,' he says. Tom has never had any serious illnesses requiring hospitalisation.

One morning when his son came to visit he found Tom half-conscious in his chair. Despite Tom's protestations, David took him to the hospital. It was determined that he had had a mild stroke that left him weakened on the left side.

Based upon this case study, develop a social and recreational nursing care plan using the following procedure:

- What are Tom's comments that provide subjective evidence?
- What is the objective evidence?
- Suggest two unmet needs that may be the most significant to Tom at this time.
- Suggest nursing aims for each unmet need, reflecting realistic outcomes and using concrete and measurable terms.
- Suggest one or more interventions for each area of unmet need, justifying your choice of intervention.

motivation for creativity can be fostered and freed. It will also include ways in which older people can more generally be encouraged to develop their appreciation of the arts.

Creativity can be the means by which we fully express ourselves as individuals, free from the restraints of social expectations and internal defences. This is the highest goal, but creative activities also help us to move forward at every stage of development and level of need. The lower four levels of need must be met to some degree before one is ready for highly creative acts. Plans for creative activity must take into account the person's needs at every level, as well as the person's particular interests, talents and wishes. Activities that are imposed upon us for other people's benefit play no part in our development. Our genuine interest must be engaged if we are to take anything valuable from the experience. The creative endeavour involves the risk of trying something new and unfamiliar, the attempt at positive change in ourselves and in the making of something new in the world. The stages of creativity are preparation, frustration, incubation, illumination and elaboration. For some, the perceived risk of failure can be a powerful deterrent. For many people the stimulus of an interested and supportive person will help them to explore new avenues of creative self-expression and uncover latent talents and interests. People may need gentle support and encouragement in order to overcome inhibitions caused by low self-confidence or fears of rejection by others. The creative attitudes and processes are more important to development than the final product itself. The world may judge for itself (rightly or wrongly) whether or not the product is an artistic or financial success. The person has reached a high level of development if they have shown curiosity, craving for understanding, innovation and original expression.

The Importance of the Subjective Experiences of Older People

In keeping with the use of a humanistic model of development, we encourage nurses to employ humanistic methods of assessing older people's needs and personalities. This involves focusing on their experience of life, and in particular their experience of care, as they perceive it. It is not enough to observe the external picture, we must also try to gain access to their inner world of thoughts and feelings. This is a process that enables people to re-create their own self-image for other people and for themselves. Some people are more willing to disclose than others, and some are more self-reflective and analytical than others. Whatever their background, personality or intelligence they will be trying to find and create meaning and purpose in their life at present, and this is a process that can be encouraged, respected and sometimes enhanced by a creative medium beyond conversation.

One way in which this can be achieved is through the keeping of a journal of daily or occasional thoughts and reflections about life as the older person sees it. For some people this may have been a regular or temporary activity during their earlier years. For others it may be something that they previously felt that they never had time to do. It can be a helpful way to chart development and to see developing patterns and recurrent themes as time goes by. Such personal records may be highly confidential, or they may be a deliberate attempt by the person to communicate vital information to carers and the outside world about new experiences and new needs. As carers, this information about insights and understandings is crucial to our providing the appropriate assistance. As people who are ourselves becoming older, we have a great deal to learn from the richness of each person's individual experience. As with all aspects of development and health affecting older people there are lessons to be learned by health carers for their own development: charting one's progress through life does not have to begin in old age.

In recent years we have seen the emergence of a national movement for the provision of arts in health care, seeking to humanise health-care settings in which the individual can become lost amid an overriding concern with institutional demands and medical models of care (Senior and Croall, 1993). The work of writers-in-residence in National Health Service Trusts makes direct links between writing as an arts activity and as a form of health care in the broader sense of personal self-development.

It provides an opportunity (for the client) to take up the role of narrator, perhaps hitherto assumed in group members' lives by care staff.

(Sampson, 1997.)

Such projects require few facilities or special equipment, and no special literary abilities by participants. People are helped and given skills to take narrative control of their experiences, so giving them the opportunity to participate more in their health-care community.

Reminiscence, Life Review and Life History Work

The attitude we have towards our past lives is an important determinant of our levels of development and self-esteem. To simplify a complex question, our past life-experience may be something solid on which we can build, or there may be many unresolved areas that are hindering our growth. The use of reminiscence as a social, creative, educational and therapeutic method with older people has become very popular in the UK and the USA among specialist nurses, care assistants, social workers and occupational therapists. It is important to be clear as a practitioner about what is trying to be achieved for different people through the encouraging of reminiscence. Studies of the effects of reminiscence have tended to obscure individual attitudes and also the different social experiences which reminiscence may occasion. Recent research applies a more differential approach, indicating the types of reminiscence that are helpful for individual people at certain times (Bornat, 1994; Webster and Haight, 1995). Reminiscence is a highly complex activity, serving many different possible functions, varying from intense and painful self-criticism to light-hearted joke-telling. Webster and Haight (1995) have attempted to clarify the conceptual uncertainty by exploring four different types of recall: life review, reminiscence, autobiography and narrative. All the different types are a form of creative activity, because to some extent they involve a reconstruction and new presentation of the self. Some types particularly lend themselves to specific creative activities.

Life Review

Butler's elaboration of the process of the life review (1963) was the signal for new positive attitudes from health carers to the reminiscences of older people. It was seen as the means whereby older people might be able to find overall satisfactory meaning and purpose in their lives, and so face the latter part of life with equanimity and enhanced integrity. The suggestion that this was an essential natural process that could be facilitated by a therapist has been taken up by clinical psychologists and mental-health nurses. Haight *et al.* (1995) have argued for a format that is structured across the key stages of the life course, that includes guidance towards evaluating one's life and that is done on a one-to-one basis. There are clearly similarities between the concepts of a successful life review, self-actualisation and Erikson's final developmental stage of ego integrity (Erikson, 1987).

Reminiscence

Reminiscence has become a well-known activity in care settings for older people. It often lacks the structured approach and the guided evaluative component of the life review, but for many this is its attraction. Many practitioners emphasise the recreational aspects of the process rather than any therapeutic possibilities. However, for individual people taking part there are many possibilities for meeting important personal and social needs through their reminiscences. Gibson (1994) has summarised some of the vital functions of reminiscence in care settings for older people as follows:

- Making links with the past.
- Changing the perceptions and attitudes of others.
- Expressing a range of emotions.
- Increasing one's sense of identity and self-worth.
- Transmitting cultural heritage across generations.
- Reversing the gift relationship between the carer and the person cared for.

These functions may meet people's particular needs from their reminiscences, and can be considered and enabled by the facilitator. Different kinds of reminiscence work can stress the artistic, recreational, therapeutic or educational objectives of the activity. It should depend on what the individual wants to achieve for themselves, with the worker acting as a sensitive and interested supporter. Reminiscence informs all of the arts – visual, literary, musical and dramatic – and different people will have preferred forms of self-expression (**Box 20.2**). Group work skills (Bender *et al.* 1987) and creative skills will enhance the experience for the participants, and a comprehensive range of training courses in

20.2 Creative Reminiscence Ideas

Ideas for writing
- The important things in life – a list or a poem.
- Things my mother used to say – an anthology (individual or group).
- Advice to a young couple – in the form of a letter.
- What a day that was – a journey through the highlights of a memorable day.

Ideas for drawing
- Design a card to mark the occasion of a special festival.
- My smartest clothes – sketch of the clothes someone use to wear when they wanted to be really smart.
- Dressing for work – a sketch of work clothes.
- Seaside collage – a collage based on the sights, sounds, textures, smells and tastes of the seaside.

Ideas for music
- Songs that are connected with the places people come from.
- Desert Island Discs – pieces of music you would like to take with you to a desert island.
- Dance music – memories of going dancing, different types of dances.
- Songs our parents used to sing – make a songbook.

Ideas for drama
Re-enactments of these scenes:
- Getting into trouble at school.
- Getting ready to go out, and being told when to come back by parents.
- Being interviewed for a job.
- Teaching someone how to do your job.

reminiscence work and training manuals (Osborn, 1993) are provided by Age Exchange Theatre Trust (London), which also publishes an international journal of reminiscence work. More information about reminiscence aids is included in the Useful Contacts section.

Autobiography

Autobiography is the comprehensive writing up of the life lived to date, while narrative is more like storytelling and information giving about life history details. Whatever form life history details take, they are particularly important to the quality of care when radical changes in lifestyle for the older person become likely. Helping means assisting people to achieve their objectives, and in order to do this we have to uncover what these objectives are. Looking back on our lives helps us to decide what is important to us, and what kind of a person we are. It is the basis for our self-esteem and self-image. Johnson (1986) has written about the need for biographical approaches to care, and has offered some ground rules for biographical interviews:

> First, establish a clear interest in the interviewee for their own sake. Second, approach the interview without introducing the subject of the person's 'problem'. Third, express a real interest in their life and what they see as its major themes and events.
>
> (Johnson, 1986.)

The importance of a biographical perspective on the patient is now emphasised in nurse training courses, and is exemplified by The Nursing Times Open Learning Programme (Adams, 1991). To work with and care for older people in the most mutually satisfying way, knowledge of life history is an essential part of the picture.

Self-actualisation requires an honest appraisal of oneself and one's past so that reorganisation and development are possible. It can be seen that reminiscence and life review are activities that will from time to time become essential to this process. The lows in life are as important as the highs in providing opportunities for growth.

The Creative Arts

The creative arts can perform many different types of developmental functions for older people. For some it may become a serious second career after retirement, important in terms of remaining independent and financially solvent, as well as providing a creative satisfaction that may have been missing from earlier employment. Involvement in the arts may widen people's social contacts and influences and so broaden their outlook. It may be a way of achieving a sense of belonging to a group, or it may lead to new friendships and loves. The soul of art is the expression of inner thoughts, feelings and experiences: if something is true to these, then it has succeeded at the highest level for the individual, and this can be assisted and appreciated by others. Even when not directly setting out to do autobiographical work, the artist's personal world, life history and self-concept will inform all creative expression. Some artists find that autobiography is the most effective way of initiating and developing the creative act. Once confident in this medium, they may move on to treat other subjects.

It has been stressed that simply being involved in creative activity does not demonstrate necessarily that the person is self-actualised. Artistic expressions provide opportunities for growth and high-level development, and may lead to the meeting of needs that enable progress towards self-actualisation. Some of these higher-level achievements are:

(1) Conflict resolution.
(2) Clarification of thoughts and feelings.
(3) Creation of balance and inner order.
(4) A sense of being in control of the external world.
(5) The creation of something positive out of seemingly negative experiences.
(6) The sustenance of human integrity.

Maslow's view was that the lower four levels of need must be met to some extent before an individual is ready for creative acts of a self-actualised nature. If a person is struggling with problems with regard to physiology, safety, love or esteem then they are disabled from further advance. This is something to consider for nurses who are planning creative activities programmes. It must also be considered that dissatisfaction at one of the higher levels may adversely affect the fulfilment of lower level needs. For example, an individual in spiritual crisis or who has lost an important personal relationship may lose interest in taking care of physiological needs. Nurses must work with the whole person at every level of need to establish their readiness for certain kinds of creative expression, challenges and change.

In recent years, there have been some excellent examples of arts projects that specifically aim at encouraging the creativity of older people in a variety of settings – day centres, community centres, residential and nursing homes, and sheltered housing units. Such projects also aim to utilise the creative skills of older people so that they are enabled to make their contribution, and the rest of society is enabled to benefit from the late flowering of too often neglected talents. In the UK at present, arts funding for older people comes from a collaboration between different statutory, private and voluntary organisations. It is a complex picture of provision with many regional and local variations. Some of the most successful projects have involved joint work between voluntary agencies such as Age Concern, local statutory providers and local freelance arts workers (Kaye and Blee, 1997). While there have been encouraging pockets of such activities around the UK, the great majority of older people with nursing care needs have poor access to arts services that help them to develop their creative ability. The recent consultation exercise by Age Concern England to map existing arts provision for older people (one-fifth of the population) concluded that they are presently excluded from national, regional and local arts policy planning.

Supporting Creativity

The establishment of a safe and supportive structure is vital to creative development. The facilitator works towards an atmosphere of trust in which the person can develop the confidence to cultivate their own individualistic creativity. There is no absolute right or wrong action to be approved or disapproved. We help the person work towards a perfect expression of their unique experience. Such perfection is indeed rare. Self-belief can be low at the onset, and the fear of failure can paralyse the will to attempt any form of creative expression. Individual encouragement and support, followed by involvement in group activities, can be the pathway to a more individualistic personal achievement in line with the characteristics of self-actualisation. The same is of course true for creative work with all age groups. Improving services for older people may simply involve giving them the same opportunities that other age groups have. It seems that society

20.3 Awakening and Nurturing the Creative Spirit

1. Carry out an individual assessment of each level of need.
2. Consider activities that are structured to meet the needs of people dealing with the first three levels of need.
3. Explore individual needs, talents, interests, vocations, and hobbies that promote self-esteem and self-actualisation.
4. Invite to group activities that encourage people to develop their interests.
5. Encourage individual activities and projects that develop from the group activities.
6. Provide materials and the supportive atmosphere in which people may try new means of self-expression.

encourages people to fully express themselves when younger, and then takes away the opportunity for optimal growth just when it is most likely to be possible – in later life. **Box 20.3** gives some suggestions for bringing about an atmosphere in which the creative spirit can be awakened and nurtured.

Music

Music is a universal form of human expression, and a highly personal experience with infinite room for individual variation in taste. Music can soothe and relax, or it can impassion and dynamise. It can reach our deepest and most intense feelings, and so stimulate our motivation for life, purposeful activity and development. It has a primitive quality of rhythm and tone that is at the root of our humanity and all forms of expression. There is a sense of being transported away from physical limitations that comes from playing or hearing the music we like – a liberation of the spirit. In a powerful way we can be connected with times, places and people that have important meanings for us. Our preferences for certain kinds of music will be related to life experience and personality. As with all aspects of ageing, mere age is not the determinant of the kind of music or musical activity that the person wants. Music is used as a therapeutic tool by trained therapists, but it can simply be used as a means of enjoyment and personal expression. A wide variety of activities are offered:

- Listening and meditating.
- Movement.
- Exercise.
- Dance.
- Exploring different types of music.
- Singing.
- Studying music.
- Going to concerts.
- Reviewing pieces.

- Learning an instrument.
- Reminiscing.
- Rediscovering and redeveloping old musical skills.
- Percussive accompaniment.
- Instrument-making.
- Composing songs or instrumental pieces.

The patient's personal history can include a special file on musical tastes, interests and skills. The Council for Music in Hospitals emphasises the energising value of performance by musicians of a professional standard for severely disabled older people. The Tibble Trust and Living Arts in Hospitals involve older people in social and creative activities that utilise their past musical preferences.

RECREATION AND LEISURE

Leisure has been defined as 'relatively self-determined, psychologically pleasant activities providing opportunities for recreation, personal growth and service to others' (Kaplan, 1972). It is not something that must be done for financial reasons, but something we choose to do for our own benefit and for its own intrinsic value. We may work very hard at it, or it may be a rest from work. The concept of leisure covers a broad area of human activity that relates to all levels of human need. It is not so much what you do, but the way that you do it, that determines the level of need met. For some people a meal is a basic necessity, while for others it may be a social event and a work of art.

Social changes since the 1950s have resulted in an increase in the leisure time available for people and an increased interest in different leisure pursuits. However, opposed to this there are factors that can make it difficult for older people to take advantage of the many developmental possibilities offered by leisure activities. For some people, their professional working career may have become so important as to constitute for them their raison d'être. Initially, large amounts of leisure time may threaten their need for self-esteem; they may simply not know how to start constructively using all this new spare time, or they may have been brought up to believe that such activities are worthless in themselves. There may be some hope that as a society we are starting to change our attitudes as to what constitutes valid and valuable activity. Nurses have a role to play in this continuing values shift.

For the older person who has worked hard all their adult life, and has looked forward to sharing more leisure time with their partner in retirement, the death of their partner can take away for them the love and companionship that they needed in order to enjoy this time. Some common forms of leisure activity – bingo, betting shops, television (watched by the over 65s on average 36 hours a week according to the Carnegie Inquiry into the Third Age) – may not provide sufficiently for affection and self-worth. These services are energetically marketed by commercially driven organisations and can become major interests for older people. Such leisure services do not tend to have personal self-development as their main aim, though some social and educational needs may be met through such activity.

There may be more time available for leisure activities, but this can be accompanied by less money with which to pursue them. People need realistic suggestions that are affordable as well as appropriate to their individual needs. In short, we as a society need a greater number, variety and availability of services and opportunities that have personal self-development as their sole aim.

Carpenter's (1987) suggestions (**Box 20.4**) are aimed at older people who do not have much money to spend on leisure activities. It has to be recognised that the author is reflecting his own personal way of solving the problems, and that needs fulfilment is very much an individualistic pursuit within a particular cultural context. Nevertheless, his ideas reveal the imagination, creativity and freshness of attitude that are the hallmarks of continuing development.

Contact with Nature

The natural landscape is important as a source of relaxation, reminiscence and inspiration for older people. This is not an aspect of life that we become more remote from as we become older. On the contrary, older people often feel a special intimacy with the wonder and beauty of plant and animal life. It involves a sense of the immortal and the transcendent that is akin to self-actualisation. Visits to parks or nearby countryside will gently stimulate thoughts, memories and feelings. Some participation in gardening activities can help an interested person to meet needs such as:

- Pleasurable sensory stimulation.
- The reassurance of a return to familiar activities.
- Stress relief.
- Growing one's own food.
- Taking care of the plants.
- Learning and teaching about how to keep the garden.
- A spiritual feeling of being part of a benign and purposeful universe.

Horticultural therapists specialise in this area of work, and can be approached for consultancy, training and information (see Useful Addresses).

Exercise

This again is a vital basic need that can be developed so that it becomes more creative, social and therapeutic. Older people will vary greatly in their general levels of fitness and in their lifelong methods of keeping fit and taking exercise, such as domestic tasks, physical work, sporting activities or social outings. If a new form of exercise is to be embraced then a gradual increase in activity should be encouraged. It is particularly inspiring to see such large numbers of older people taking up long-distance running late in life. A 74-year-old participant in the London Marathon of 1996 said, 'I don't go fast, don't overdo it. But I go for a 20-mile run a few times to get used to it, perhaps 50 miles in the week. It's a lot, but I'm not working, I've got time' (Arigho, 1996). Running and jogging clubs are now more open and encouraging towards older runners, and in this more enlightened atmosphere older runners are constantly pushing back the boundaries of achievement. The organisation Extend provides recreational movement to music for the over-sixties in the community and for older people in residential homes and day centres. Their workers must pass courses in anatomy, physiology and kinesiology, as well as a practical course in Music and Movement. The guiding principle behind the organisation is that movement and exercise is essential to the maintenance of function, but that beyond this there are social and psychological benefits to be gained for the participants (*see* Chapter 6 for further discussion on the benefits of exercise).

Social, Therapeutic and Recreational Nursing

Nurses usually meet older patients for the first time because problems have arisen that prevent the person from indepen-

20.4 Leisure Activities for People with Limited Money

How to make time a pleasure for myself and others while staying within my budget:

1. Accept invitations, even for unfamiliar activities. It may open new interests.
2. Go with a younger person, possibly a grandchild, to an arts event and discuss it with them (a good way to bridge the years and gain a different perspective).
3. Go to a food market, buy some unusual produce, and invite someone to come round and conjure up a meal.
4. Develop an interest in community affairs or local politics. Take an active part in campaigning for the party or pressure group of your choice.
5. Become a volunteer for a local action group of your special interest.
6. Take advantage of the social and creative activities offered by your church.
7. Give a party, and involve friends in the planning and preparation.
8. Make contact with old friends. Arrange a trip to meet them.
9. Go fruit and vegetable-picking with friends.
10. Arrange special outings with young relations.

Source: Carpenter, 1987.

dently meeting some of their needs, causing symptoms of ill health. The common physical problems of sensory loss, reduced mobility and various underlying medical disorders can disrupt creative and leisure activities and so threaten needs at all levels. As well as these there may be social and psychological factors which are resulting in the manifestation of symptoms of unmet needs: poor income, loss of job, lack of perceived role, bereavement, enforced move to a new home, lack of autonomy, routinisation of life, and social devaluation. Using recreational activities as a means of solving these problems can be justified as a legitimate and vital nursing intervention.

Social, Therapeutic and Recreational Nursing (STAR Nurses) developed as a special interest group of the Royal College of Nursing. Their aim was to develop the work of member nurses by raising the awareness and understanding among fellow professionals and clients that these activities form a normal and essential part of life. Much of the focus was on promoting the use of social and recreational therapy in nursing services for older people. Their particular concern was for those care settings in which older people are suffering from sensory deprivation and absence of enjoyable and creative activity. They published fact packs and newsletters, and organised conferences, workshops and study days. Although the group is no longer active, it has been instrumental in highlighting the need for nursing development in this area. All nursing posts are subject to budgetary constraints, and so the work of such organisations has taken on a campaigning nature, arguing the need for the creation of special Activities Nurses or Recreation Coordinators in nursing care settings for older people. There remain great regional and local differences in the extent to which such work is prioritised by health-care organisations.

Holistic Health Care

It is now recognised that in order to help a person with a particular set of problems, the whole person must be taken into account in all their individual needs. A large number of complementary therapies are now available that aim at increasing wellbeing in holistic and non-pharmacological ways. Such methods as massage, aromatherapy, reflexology, yoga and meditation help many to achieve raised levels of relaxation and physical functioning, where more conventional approaches do not seem to work. Extravagant claims that ageing can be reversed and that a particular approach has discovered the secret of perfect fulfilment should be received with caution. It is a mark of self-actualisation to be aware of one's limitations, and not to exaggerate one's abilities. There is also something ageist about wanting to avoid ageing, which should be viewed as an opportunity for development rather than as a disease in itself.

The Nursing Role in Relation to the Self-actualisation of Older People

This chapter has aimed to counter the pessimism that sometimes pervades attitudes to old age and the care of older people. The last years of life can become a satisfying culmination of hopes and beliefs. The interventions that carers make can have a great impact on the person's experience of old age. There are a number of factors at work in the outcome, and these are all subject to positive influence from the person, their carers and the wider society. There is now increased awareness of the malleability of the life course, and the consequent heterogeneity of older age groups. The possibility of lifelong learning and continuing development at every stage of life has been established beyond doubt. There has been an upsurge of interest in complementary therapies and spiritual approaches to healing and growth. More and more nurses are realising that the concept of health must include the aesthetic and spiritual dimensions. This is not to recognise the problems facing development and growth; it is to emphasise that a hopeful approach is justified.

The role of care workers appreciating and recognising the possibility of self-actualisation is to:

- Support and encourage people to seek what is possible and desirable for their development.
- Assist people in finding the resources to help themselves.

Sometimes this can be best facilitated by recourse to outside agencies who specialise in a particularly suitable method.

The involvement and full understanding of the individual in their chosen way forward is essential to their progressing through the levels of affiliation and self-esteem. Self-actualisation is impossible without having control, self-determination and self-efficacy. Nurses, along with other members of the multidisciplinary team, can assist people to obtain a sense of mastery. To do this effectively the nurse must be sensitive to the person's needs and knowledgeable about the relevant resources and materials. The level of assistance required may range from simple information giving to full provision and organisation of all booking and transport facilities.

The nurse–patient relationship can be seen in the light of two people each trying to achieve their developmental potential. The interaction between them is crucial to their individual drives for self-actualisation. The emphasis in this chapter has been on how older people can be helped to meet their needs through the nurse's support and acknowledgement. It is clear that the demands and challenges posed by such an individualised and humanistic approach to nursing care require and stimulate high-level achievements by the nurses themselves. As with all positive interactions, there are roles of supporter and personal achiever for each participant in the exchange.

20 Self-actualisation

REFERENCES

Adams J. *Different lives, different perspectives*. The Nursing Times Open Learning Programme, Vol. 87, No. 26, 1991.

Adams T, Gowland D. *Challenging images: exploring attitudes to ageing with pupils preparing for cross generational projects*. London: CSV LinkAge, 1994.

Arigho B. They run against our expectations. *Generations Review* 1996, 6:2–5

Bender M, Norris A, Bauckham P. *Groupwork with the elderly*. London: Winslow Press, 1987.

Bornat J, ed. *Reminiscence reviewed*. Buckingham: Open University Press, 1994.

Butler R. Life review: an interpretation of reminiscence in the aged. *Psychiatry* 1963, 26:65–76.

Carnegie Inquiry into the Third Age. *Leisure: new opportunities in the third age*, 1992, The Carnegie United Kingdom Trust.

Carpenter L. *Getting better all the time*. New York: Simon and Schuster, 1987.

Coleman P. *Ageing and reminiscence processes: social and clinical implications*. Chichester: John Wiley, 1986.

Davies M. Theories of ageing and their implications for pre-retirement Education. *J Educ Gerontol* 1993, 8:67–74

Erikson E. *Childhood and society*. London: Paladin, 1987.

Gibson F. *Reminiscence and recall*, London, 1994, Age Concern England.

Haight B, Coleman P, Lord K. The linchpins of a successful life review: structure, evaluation and Individuality. In: Webster J, Haight B, eds. *The art and science of reminiscing*.

Hewitt M, Harris A. *Talking time! A guide to oral history for schools*. London: Tower Hamlets Education, 1992.

Johnson M. The meaning of old age. In: Redfern S, ed. *Nursing elderly people*. Edinburgh: Churchill Livingstone, 1986.

Kaplan M. *Implications for gerontology from a general theory of leisure*, Conference on Leisure and the Third Age, Paris, 1972. International Centre of Social Gerontology.

Kaye C, Blee T. *The arts in health care: a palette of possibilities*. London: Jessica Kingsley, 1997.

Lehman H. *Age and achievement*. Princeton University Press for the American Philosophical Society, 1953.

Maslow A. *Motivation and personality*. New York: Harper and Row, 1954.

Maslow A. Self-actualization and beyond. In: Bugenthal J, ed. *Challenges of humanistic psychology*. New York: McGraw-Hill, 1967.

Norman A. *Triple jeopardy: growing old in a second homeland*, London, 1985, Centre for Policy on Ageing.

O'Connor M. *Generation to generation: linking schools with older people*. London: Cassell, 1993.

Osborn C. *The reminiscence handbook*, 1993, Age Exchange.

Sampson F. Some questions of identity: what is writing in health care? In: Kaye C, Blee T, eds. 1997.

Scholz W. New prospects at the third stage of life: older people at university. *J Educ Gerontol* 1993, 8:

Schweitzer P. *Age exchanges*, 1993, Age Exchange.

Senior P, Croall J. *Helping to heal: the arts in health care*, London, 1993, Calouste Gulbenkian Foundation.

Simonton D. Creativity in the later years: optimistic prospects for achievement. *Gerontologist* 1990, 23:182.

Thursz D, Nusberg C, Prather J, eds. *Empowering older people: an international approach*. Casell, 1995.

Webster J, Haight B, eds. *The art and science of reminiscing*. Taylor and Francis, 1995.

USEFUL ADDRESSES

Learning in Later Life
National Organisation for Adult Learning (NIACE),
21 De Montfort Street,
Leicester LE1 7GE.

The Open University,
Centre for Continuing Education, PO Box 188,
Milton Keynes MK7 6 DH.
The University of the Third Age,
1 Stockwell Green,
London SW9 9JS.

The Pre-Retirement Association,
Nodus Centre,
Dept. of Education Studies,
University of Surrey,
Guildford GU2 5RX.

The Association of Educational Gerontology,
Mrs Lesley Hart (Secretary),
Senior Studies Institute,
Graham Mills Building,
Strathclyde University,
Glasgow GB1 1QE.

Intergenerational programmes
Age Exchange Theatre Trust,
Age Exchange Reminiscence Centre,
11 Blackheath Village,
London SE3 91A.

The Kensington and Chelsea Community History Group,
1 Thorpe Close,
London W10 5XL.

Magic Me,
33 Stroudley Walk,
London E3 3 EW.

Creativity and Leisure in Later Life,
Artability,
St James Centre,
Quarry Road,
Tunbridge Wells TN1 2EY.

Horticultural Therapy,
Goulds Ground,
Vallis Way,
Frome,
Somerset BA11 3DW.

Jessica Kingsley Publishers,
116 Pentonville Road,
London N1 9JB.

Living Arts,
c/o Alison Mc Morland,
75 Clouston Street,
Glasgow G20 8QW.

The Council for Music in Hospitals,
74 Queens Road,
Hersham,
Surrey KT12 5LW.

Nottingham Rehab,
Ludlow Hill Road,
West Bridgford,
Nottingham NG2 6HD.

The Tibble Trust,
25 Fryerning Lane,
Ingatestone,
Essex CM4 0DD.

Winslow Press,
Telford Road,
Bicester,
Oxon OX6 0TS.

The University of the Third Age
1 Stockwell Green
London SW9 9SP

Towards the end of life: dying and death, transcendence and legacies
Sheila Goff

LEARNING OBJECTIVES

After studying this chapter you will be able to:

- Identify mechanisms which older people use to find meaning in illness and death.
- Discuss spirituality including religion.
- Identify mechanisms useful in assessing and discussing spirituality.
- Define the concept of legacy, and name several types of legacies and what can be done to facilitate their expression.
- Define some special needs of older people who are dying in relation to the general death and dying literature.
- Define the cultural influences on the management of death generally in Britain and specifically relate these to older people.
- Discuss the current arguments for and against assisted death.
- Describe and discuss the apparent gender differences in bereavement reaction

INTRODUCTION

For some people, the totality of life exists within what can be perceived and experienced by each individual within his or her life span. Others envision a totality of life that transcends the limitations of what can be perceived by finite human senses. Religion, spirituality and the power of the mind can help humans to transcend the pain of illness or adversity. This chapter deals first with some of the conscious and unconscious processes that older people may go through in preparing for death. Part of this preparation is the search for meaning in life and death. The different ways in which people prepare for this are explored as well as ways in which nurses can assess and help these complex processes. Legacies as part of this preparation are explored here. The next section of the chapter deals with the social contexts and management of death in later life in Britain. Research on death and dying is examined for its relevance to older people. The special needs of people who are going through a 'timely' death are considered. Issues of grief and bereavement in later life are examined in the last section of the chapter.

TRANSCENDENCE

This chapter deals with the meanings of life and death: the culmination of experience and various mechanisms by which one transcends the purely physical limitations of existence. The way one perceives time, experiences extensions of the self and copes with the sure knowledge that death is inevitable may be the ultimate victory or defeat.

The thesis of Maslow's writings is that the mystic, the sacred and the transcendent experiences frequently arise from the ordinary elements of one's life. Asceticism, self-denial and rigorous rituals may be used by some to reach the peaks of human experience; many others find more prosaic approaches just as effective.

An 86-year-old widow seemed to blend with her world of plants, birds and flowers. Each new blossom or bird call excited her as she mused in her small garden. Her conversation was sprinkled with minute discoveries, each of which thrilled her. She became so close to nature that some thought her eccentric. In her last years of life, her interest in the living and growing things consumed her. Hours were spent gazing at leaves, grass, ants and twigs. The cycles of nature seemed to become a part of her being as she experienced her own limited existence. She was found dead in her garden one morning. It was then learned that her breasts were eroded with cancer. She had not gone to a doctor and had never given evidence of pain; rather a sense of mild euphoria filled her last months of life.

Peak Experiences

A peak experience is when one momentarily transcends self in love, wisdom, insight, worship, commitment or creativity. It is the time when restricting boundaries seem to vanish and one feels more aware, more complete, more ecstatic or more concerned for others. Peak experiences include many modes of transcending one's ordinary limitations. Spiritual and paranormal experiences, creative acts, courage and humour are all potentially peak experiences. They are the extraordinary events in one's life that clearly demonstrate self-actualisation and personal authenticity.

This portion of the chapter examines mechanisms that move humans beyond the boundaries of visible, concrete reality and toward a wholly integrated 'self'. The 'self' as used by Jung means the supreme oneness of being: aspects of self that are highest and lowest, light and dark, conscious and unconscious, male and female. The ability to embrace the possibility of every potential behaviour as native of self instils compassion and a sense of oneness with the world.

Time Transcendence

Life is the passage of time. Conscious experience alters our time perception, and the subconscious destroys it. Therefore, the release of the subconscious transcends the limitations of time that conscious life experience imposes on us. If we conquer time, we conquer annihilation and the dimensions of time that lie within the mind. Recognising the importance of time perception, particularly in old age, we explore this fertile field more fully.

Influences on time perception include age, imminent death, level of activity, emotional state, outlook on future and value attached to time. Conclusions from studies of older people generally support the view that they perceive time as passing quickly and favour the past over the present or the future. In a study of community dwelling older Americans, the respondents were present-orientated and valued past, present and future equally, although they viewed the past as the most important time of their lives and derived most enjoyment out of reviewing the past.

Newman (1987) studied changes in time perception that occur in the process of ageing and found that as one grows older there is an expanded sense of time. Newman found that time perception expands in relation to one's quality of life. The emphasis is on the inner experience as crucial to expanding consciousness. The implications of this study are profound and reinforce the necessity of providing older people with validation of the need to rock, meditate, fantasise and perform many other 'passive' activities that may, in fact, be consciousness expanders.

Transcendence through Illness or Adversity

In his powerful account of his experiences in a Jewish concentration camp, Frankl (1987) maintains that physical and emotional suffering can be endured if the meaning and purpose are evident. Serious illnesses influence how one perceives the meaning of life. There is often a distinct shift in goals, relationships and values among those who have survived serious illnesses and endured suffering. Serious illness and approaching death may provoke a heightened awareness of beauty and of caring relationships.

Steeves and Kahn (1987) found from their work in hospice care that certain conditions facilitate the search for meaning in illness. They noted the following:

- Suffering must be bearable and not all-consuming if one is to find meaning in the experience.
- A person must have access to and be capable of perceiving objects in the environment. Even a small window on the world may be sufficient.
- One must have time free of interruption and a place of solitude to experience meaning.
- Clean, comfortable surroundings and freedom from constant responsibility and decision-making free the soul to search for meaning.
- An open, accepting atmosphere in which to discuss meanings with others is important.

The following nursing actions may facilitate the search for meaning in suffering:
- Give the patient an opportunity to talk about changes in values.
- Help the patient realise these changes are part of a growth process.
- Listen and facilitate expression of feelings about death.
- Recognise the importance of the rebirth of a sense of beauty. Often there has been a 'peak experience' the patient may wish to share.

The Potential for Self-healing

Healing may occur in the search for meaning. Healing emanating from the mind/soul is an ancient method that has generally been neglected and denigrated by the scientific community until recently. Other traditions have considered the power of the mind as being instrumental in the healing process in that it opens the potential for self-healing. Self-healing may be experienced in many ways. The result may or may not be the eradication of a disease but may bring about the integration of a condition or situation into a sense of wholeness and wellness. To do so, 'we will need a rapprochement between ancient wisdom and modern science, between mystery and mastery' (Cole, 1992, p. 17).

Transcendence through Religion and Spirituality

Nurses often interpret a patient's spiritual needs in terms of religious affiliation, rites and rituals. Burnard (1997) distinguishes between religion and spirituality. Religion, he suggests, usually refers to a set of beliefs about a higher being or a transcendental quality.

Religious teachings can help formulate a meaningful philosophy through a system of beliefs, practices and social controls having specific values, norms and ethics that vary between religious groups. Religion is one aspect of spirituality, and it may or may not fill spiritual needs.

Spiritual needs are broader and more individual than any particular religious persuasion. Watson-Druee (1995) describes spirituality as follows:

Spirituality is a state of awareness of one's eternal being which is formless, timeless and not confined to space at any particular time. Spirituality is a feeling of infinite worth in which 'the higher self' transcends human perceptions of religion and human limitations, and taps into the collective consciousness of humankind. Through spirituality, people find the inner strength to cope with adversity in life. Spirituality is about unconditional love for one's self and others; a commitment to working in harmony with life's purpose; recognising that every event and circumstance is an opportunity for growth and learning. Spiritual experiences enable one to find meaning and insight to life.

(Watson-Druee, 1995, p. 173.)

Nurses may avoid dealing with spiritual needs because they feel they are too personal. The issue of who is the most appropriate person to work with the spiritual needs of someone who is dying is addressed by Walter (1997). He argues that the simplest solution is that spiritual care should be left to the chaplain or other religious leader, and this is the view taken by the UK Patient's Charter. Walter points out several problems with this approach. Firstly, it implies that only some patients have a spiritual dimension, and equates spiritual needs with religious beliefs. Secondly the approach is incompatible with the practice of holistic care. Walter sees an anomaly in nurses who claim to offer holistic care and who definitely regard emotional and social care within their realm and yet refer spiritual issues to the chaplain. He highlights the recent identification of the spiritual with the search for meaning and argues that exploration of this with the patient is the responsibility of any member of the multidisciplinary team.

How can one begin to assess and discuss spiritual matters? Ross (1997) points out that the form of assessment has not been determined. Some would favour a formal assessment such as Stoll's (1979) guidelines for spiritual assessment while others would advocate an ongoing discussion at appropriate times and with which ever member of the caring team the patient feels most comfortable. Some questions that may be helpful in addressing spiritual issues are:

- Ask the individual his or her source of strength and hope.
- Ask if the individual sees any connection between physical health and spiritual beliefs.
- Discuss sources of spiritual strength throughout life.
- Enquire who or what has been most influential on a person's thinking during their life.
- Interventions may involve calling religious leaders, and sharing spiritual readings, poems and music.

We humans are spiritual animals who need love and meaning no less than food, clothing, shelter and healthcare. Religious beliefs and practices are often regarded as reflections of more basic realities, such as psychological need or economic and political power.

(Cole, 1992, p. 17)

The religious impulse, as conceptualised by Maslow, resides within each person and in its highest fulfilment integrates the life experience rather than splitting life into the sacred and the profane. Maslow believes the organisational and ritual aspects of religion can be expressions of meaning and only become empty gestures when one separates self from the source of spirituality.

Throughout history and in all cultures, sacraments, symbols and metaphor have been used to organise and understand human experience, and even cognitively impaired people have been found to respond positively to faith rituals and symbols. Shared purpose and shared preparation using appropriate materials brings individuals into contact with others and with the transcendental. In addition to the comfort and security of these rituals, our sense of connection with others is enhanced by ceremonies. It is thought that new ceremonies are needed to integrate the shifting experiences of ageing (such as retirement, relocation, health care and inter-generational exchanges) in a positive manner.

Jung proposes a natural religious energy that in the current age has often been channelled into 'isms' rather than religious expressions. He believes religion must unite the inner and outer man in equal degree. No completely rational approach can do this, but art, dreams, fantasies and other intuitive expressions may assist the scientific soul to become whole. There are many ways one can touch religious energies within and outside of formalised religion.

Religion as a Coping Resource

The prevalence and importance of religious beliefs and activities in later life have been investigated with various conclusions. A large American study of more than 1000 individuals between 55 and 94 years of age living in the same geographical area revealed the following:

- Religious activities and attitudes are very common among older adults.
- A large proportion of older persons claim that religion helps them to cope. This response occurred both when asked directly about religion as a source of strength in difficult times and when asked indirectly how they coped with or survived stressful life events.
- There is a strong correlation between wellbeing and religion even when controlling for health, wealth and social support. This is particularly true for women aged 75 years and over.
- Correlations between wellbeing or adjustment and religion tend to increase over time, suggesting that as other sources of wellbeing decline, religion may become even more important.

Courtney *et al.* (1992) studied the correlation between religiosity and adaptation in a group of centenarians. They found a significant relationship between religiosity and physical health and successful coping. The very old are more likely to be interested in the non-organisational aspects of religion than in active participation. The church is the social institution with the greatest potential for reaching older people with needed service. In the USA, typically 40–60% of congregations are composed of retired persons and 'parish nurses' are becoming visible nationwide as churches and hospitals join forces to provide health maintenance and monitoring activities for parishioners.

In British society, Davie (1994) found belief in God to be growing even though levels of practice in terms of church attendance are decreasing. Davie argues that this evidence is contrary to an underlying assumption that British society has become more secular. This is important when considering the influences on people who are dying since it may be that even though religion is not practised in an overt way, when it comes to facing their own mortality, religious traditions offer some comfort and meaning.

Spiritual Needs and Resources

Gerontologists are aware of the significance of religion and spirituality in the adaptational capacity of older people. Life satisfaction, happiness, morale and health have all been studied in relation to religion. However, spirituality has not achieved a central focus in the study of ageing and it could be argued that, although the basic mysteries of life are the essence of existence with meaning, they have eluded researchers. Remembering, identifying meanings and grasping one's own connection to the universe are the realities of the human spirit, 'temporal transcendence' (Brewer, 1986) and the blending of past with present and future. This may be why the real self never feels old until the spirit is crushed. Frankl (1990) wrote most eloquently of facing the transitoriness of human existence that is ageing: 'Being old is not the centrality of the self – spirit is. Spirit synthesises the total personality, provides integration and energising force.'

There is debate as to how nurses can best be prepared to give spiritual care. In an important study Bradshaw (1994, 1997) argues that the best way to teach this aspect of care is by example and not in the classroom. She feels that delivering satisfactory spiritual care depends on being a certain kind of person able to establish a relationship of trust with the patient. As Peberdy (1993) points out, the life experience of the nurse influences the way in which this trusting relationship develops. She also emphasises that spiritual care is not only about relationships but that the spirituality of the institutions in which patients are looked after should be taken into account. The atmosphere and physical environment created by the staff and managers reveals much about attitudes to the total care of people.

Haase *et al.* (1992) have developed a conceptual model useful in understanding spirituality (**Figure 21.1**). This model clarifies the components of spirituality.

Dreams – Personal and Collective

Jung saw the goal of the last half of life as reconciliation of one's various repressions by the use of dreams, myths and symbols to become a whole person. To discover the hidden and embrace the unconscious is the process of individuation and transcendence, which may occupy one intensely after midlife. To explore the hidden, one may analyse dreams. They are the windows of the unconscious.

To fully use dream material for self-transcendence, the concept of collective unconscious must be explored. Jung views the collective unconscious as composed of archetypal images or symbols. They include powerful, collectively carried, instinctual reactions:

- **Anima**: feminine principle.
- **Animus**: masculine principle.
- **Wise old man**: king, hero, medicine man, saviour.
- **Great mother**: infinite love, understanding, help, protection, and tyranny over the dependent.

In dreams for a brief time we possess qualities 'beyond ourselves' – we are phenomenally courageous, infinitely wise and forgiving, not ego-centred but intimately aware of all life and feel oneness with life.

Jung believed each person could best analyse and interpret his or her own dreams by meditating on them and examining them in great detail. To understand the meaning, several steps are employed. Establish the context of the present life situation, then examine each image or symbol carefully for all the possible meanings. He suggests a series of dreams may be a most satisfactory basis for interpretation, since important images occur repeatedly in dreams.

Following is an example of a dream an older woman had following the death of her roommate.

I have dreamed of her every night since she died. She sometimes sings to me and she is waiting for me on an island and says she won't go on without me. She's holding a big bowl of soup.

She talked about the dream, about death and about the fear of dying alone. She spoke of how her roommate knew she loved soup and also mentioned that her roommate was deaf. The dream seemed to give her assurance that she would not be alone in death (a compensatory aspect of the dream because so many do die alone) and that physical limitations were conquered through death (the singing of her deaf roommate). In a symbolic sense the soup could mean nourishment, love, a blending, an offering or it could be from the present context of her life, in which she seldom got the kind of soup she enjoyed. The old woman died 2 weeks after her roommate. Jung might call this a 'prospective' dream because it prepared her for a future place and time.

Dreams provide access to the unconscious of the individual or the collective unconscious. The individual may express desires, conflicts, fears, prophecies, hidden aspects of personality, compensation, or modifications of recent or distant experiences. Dreams that connect one with the collective unconscious may be very vivid, seem highly significant, and include surprising or incomprehensible symbols that seem to have no relationship to the dreamer's life. Jung believes these dreams are especially significant in transcending the personal and deepening one's experience by connection with remote people through symbols significant to many.

Jung believed that dreams function to promote growth and individuation and that they are sources of information and creative power. Nurses can express interest in the dreams of their older clients and explore meanings with them. Sharing a dream can be a revealing and intimate gesture.

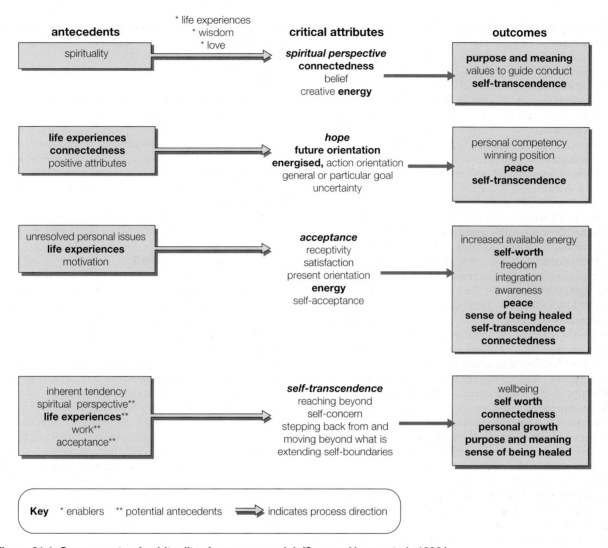

Figure 21.1 Components of spirituality: A process model. (Source: Hasse *et al.*, 1992.)

Fantasies and Daydreams

Most studies indicate a decreasing importance and intensity of daydreams and fantasies in old age. However, we must remember cohort effects and realise that those born 75 years ago were culturally conditioned in a way that put little importance on dreams and fantasies. We might assist the older person to value their self-exploratory activities by giving credence to them.

Memories could well be included with dreams and fantasies because they become so intertwined in the later years. The conscious and unconscious seem to merge in a more holistic manner as the very old move back and forward in time with ease, weaving recurrent dreams, hopes and fantasies into their memories. Often we mistakenly label this fluidity as confusion or inaccuracy if we hold strict boundaries and a segmented personal reality. We might take lessons from older people who have learned to make peace with their multiple realities.

LEGACIES

Extending one's meaning to others can be a gratifying activity in the last years. Throughout life, shared experiences provide satisfaction, but in the last years this exchange allows one to gain a clear perspective on how his or her movement on earth has had impact.

The legacies that people leave in the world can be very important to the individual in giving meaning to the life lived. To believe they will leave nothing can reinforce their mortality. A legacy is one's tangible and intangible assets that are transferred to another and may be treasured as a symbol of the bequeather's immortality. Older people should be encouraged to identify that which they would like to leave and whom they wish the recipients to be. This process has interpersonal significance and prepares one to leave the world with a sense of meaning. It can provide a transcendent feeling of

continuation and tangible or intangible ties with survivors. Legacies are diverse and may range from memories that will live on in the mind of others to bequeathed fortunes. Examples of legacies include:
- Oral histories.
- Autobiographies.
- Shared memories.
- Taught skills.
- Works of art and music.
- Publications.
- Human organ donations.
- Endowments.
- Objects of significance.
- Written histories.
- Tangible or intangible assets.
- Personal characteristics such as courage or integrity.
- Bestowed talents.
- Traditions and myths perpetuated.
- Philanthropic causes.
- Progeny: children and grandchildren.
- Methods of coping.
- Unique thought: Darwin, Einstein, Freud and others.

The list is as diverse as individual contributions to humanity. Erikson's seventh stage of man identifies the generative function as the main concern of the adult years and the last stage (eighth) as that of reviewing with integrity or despair what one has accomplished. We propose that legacies are generative and are identified and shared best as one approaches the end of life and that this activity establishes integrity.

Autobiographies/Life Histories

Oral histories are an approach to immortality. As long as one's story is told, one remains alive in the minds of others. Doers leave their products and live through them. Powerful figures are remembered in fame and infamy. The quiet, unobtrusive person survives in the memory of intimates and in family anecdotes. Everyone has a life story. The quest for immortality grew out of words, the human ability to articulate meaning and personality to others. Without words, experience would contain no past or future. The short span of one's days would amount to only a series of sensory impressions, not even rising to the perceptual level, since percepts are formed through internalised concepts and words spoken to the self.

Autobiographies and recorded memoirs can serve a transcendent purpose for those who are alone, and for many who are not. Nurses can encourage older people to write, talk or express in other ways the meaning of their lives. The human experience and the poignant anecdotes bind people together and validate the uniqueness of each brief journey in this level of awareness and the assurance that one will not be forgotten. Dying patients can express and order their memories through audiotapes that are then bequeathed to families if the older person desires. Sharing one's personal story creates

bonds of empathy, illustrates a point, conveys some of the deep wisdom that we all contain, and connects us with our deepest human consciousness.

A real story touches not only the mind, but also the imagination and the unconscious depths in a person, and it may remain with him or her through many years, coming to the surface of consciousness now and then to yield new insights.

Nurses can also assist older people and their families to compile biographies. A loose-leaf folder or photograph album can be used to collect photographs, artifacts such as an old tram ticket or ration book, and accounts of particular events or periods of life, such as schooldays. These compile into vivid accounts of a person's life that serve as valuable records and a legacy after the person has died.

Collective Legacies

Each person is a link in the chain of generations and as such may identify with generational accomplishments. An older man may feel himself a significant part of a generation that survived the two world wars. A middle-aged man may identify with the generation that walked on the moon. Those years of youthful idealism are impressed in one's memory by the political or ideological climate of the time. That is the stage when one searches for a fit in the larger society.

The importance of this to nurses lies in how they use this knowledge. For instance, the nurse may ask, 'Who were the great men of your time? Which ones were important to you? What events of your generation changed the world? What were the most important events you experienced?' Sometimes it is helpful to mention certain historic events and ask about individual reactions (see Chapter 1 for further discussion of biographical work).

Legacies Expressed through Others

There are many ways that one's legacy is expressed through the development of others: in a teaching and learning situation, or through mentorships, patronage, shared talents and organ donations. In other words, one's legacy may be a product of his or her own brought to fruition through someone else who may also become an intermediary. Thus, people and generations are tied in sequential development. Some examples may illustrate this type of legacy:
- An older man cried as he talked of his grandson's talent as a violinist. They shared their love for violin, and the grandfather believed he had genetically and personally contributed to his grandson's development as a musician.
- A professor emeritus spoke of watching his son give a lecture and hearing him expound ideas that had been partially developed by the professor and his father before him.
- One older lady worried about preserving the environment for future generations, so she took her great-niece's young children on nature walks to stimulate

their interest in birds, plants and animals. She also donated land for a natural park.

People who amass a fortune and allocate certain funds for endowment of artists, scientific projects and intellectual exploration are counting on others to complete their legacy. The following are suggestions for assisting elders to identify and develop their legacy:
• Find out lifelong interests.
• Establish a method of recording.
• Identify recipients, either generally or specifically.
• Record legacy.
• Distribute as planned.
• Provide for systematic feedback of results to older person.

It is gratifying to the old if a legacy can be converted into some tangible form, ensuring that it will not readily be dismissed or forgotten. The following vehicles convey legacies:
• Summation of life work.
• Photograph albums and scrapbooks.
• Written memoirs.
• Taped memoirs (video or audio).
• Artistic representations.
• Memory gardens.
• Mementoes.
• Genealogies.
• Pilgrimages.

Living Legacies

Many older people wish to donate their bodies to science or donate body parts for transplant. This is one mechanism to transcend death. Parts of the body keep another alive, or, in the case of certain diseases, the deceased body may provide important information leading to preventive or restorative techniques in the future. Donation of body parts in older age may not be encouraged, since they are often less viable than those from younger people. Persons interested in providing such a legacy should be encouraged to call the nearest university biomedical centre and obtain more information. The nurse then has a postmortem obligation to the client to assist in carrying out his or her wishes.

Property and Assets

Many people have considerable assets to leave to their families, philanthropic foundations, or on occasions to friends, pets or strangers. Yet many older people die each year leaving inheritances with no specified beneficiaries. Many of these are retained until someone successfully substantiates claims to them. Wealth may be viewed as a means toward power more often than transcendence; therefore older people are often reluctant to disperse material goods before their death and frequently never make out a will. The nurse's responsibility in this regard may be limited to advising older people

to obtain legal counsel while they are healthy and competent and plan how they would like to distribute their worldly goods. Families often consider wills a taboo subject and refuse to discuss them.

There are certain ways to plan estates that are decidedly advantageous in terms of control and taxation. Since these laws are complex and ever changing, it can be helpful to use the services of a financial adviser (*see* Chapter 14 for further discussion).

Personal Possessions

One's personally significant items are highly charged with memories and meaning, and transferring them to friends and kin can be a tender experience. They should never be dispersed without the individual's knowledge. It is vital that people approaching death be given the opportunity to appropriately distribute their important belongings to those whom they feel will also cherish them. Nurses may encourage them to plan the distribution of their significant items carefully. Some choose to distribute them before dying, and in those cases nurses often need to help family members accept these gifts, recognising the significance.

The Nurse's Role

We have dealt with several mechanisms that may be used to establish a legacy. Often this becomes a major concern before one's death, but some persons may avoid any such concern, particularly when angry, in pain or denying their own mortality. Nurses need not push the individual to accomplish this task but should be available to assist the patient and family members. Certain questions allow the older person to consider a legacy if he or she is ready to do so. For example:
• Have you ever thought of writing an autobiography?
• If you could leave something to the younger generation, what would it be?
• Have you ever thought of the impact your generation has had on the world?
• What has been most meaningful in your life?

These suggestions may stimulate ideas for spontaneous statements, which are far more valid in an interpersonal context. When discussing meanings of life, it is possible a client will become despairing and find no meaning. In those cases, life review may be in process and the nurse can assist with this.

DYING AND DEATH

Birth, dying and death are universal, uncontestable and individually unique events of the human experience. The fact of death remains unchanged, but the experience of death (the age, place and manner of death) has been profoundly altered in the twentieth century. Death has become associated with older people. In England and Wales in 1990, 80% of deaths were of people aged 65 years or over and over 20% were 85 years or more (Office of Population Censuses and Surveys, 1992).

Two important comparable surveys of the needs of nationally represented samples of about 700 adults dying in 1969 and 1987 provide interesting and useful information about social and demographic change in the care of the dying, particularly relevant to issues around older people. The methods of these studies are described in Cartwright *et al.* (1973) and Cartwright and Seale (1990), while the results are summarised in Seale (1993) and Cartwright (1993). In both surveys, the principal carer of the person who had died was interviewed in order to find out as much information as possible about the last year of that person's life. A major change between 1969 and 1987 was that people were living longer. This brought different problems. Physical needs were greater and yet changes in social and family organisation have meant less care from family and more dependence on formal services. Older women were more often found to be living alone. These women had themselves frequently cared for others who had died.

Since most deaths in Western societies are of the old, and as life expectancy continues to increase, the problems of older people have much in common with the problems of the dying and vice versa (Seale, 1993). Yet very little of the death and dying research and literature specifically focuses on death in later life. This neglect has largely arisen because most of the recent research and thinking about dying has centred around the work of hospice care, which has traditionally focused on people dying from cancer who are comparatively young (Walter, 1993; Cartwright, 1993). One of the reasons for this focus may be that the process of dying from cancer is usually predictable and has recognisable stages, particularly in a younger person who is otherwise fit. It is much more difficult to define when an older person who may have a multitude of different illnesses is actually dying. Seale (1993) feels that the implication of this is that those caring for older people should also consider themselves to be caring for the dying and that this role cannot be left solely to those who specialise in palliative care.

While there is no doubt about the great advances that have been made in the care of the dying in terms of better pain and symptom control, it is important to reflect that these may not be generally relevant to everybody. As Seale (1993) points out, the well-researched and resourced areas of pain control and bereavement support may not be at all relevant for a slowly dying older widow living alone whose needs are for long-term care and who has no carers to require bereavement support. The particular needs of people dying in later life are important to consider when policy decisions are made about palliative care service provision.

Process of Dying

The work of Kübler-Ross was instrumental in providing better care for the dying and helping them realise that the behaviour and feelings they experience are normal. She has also been responsible for sensitising and helping the health-care professionals to realise that there is more to dying than just physical manifestations.

Everyone may or may not pass through the five stages of dying identified by Kübler-Ross (1969). The progression through the stages may be kaleidoscopic rather than sequential. Several pitfalls affect those who use the stages of dying as a panacea for dealing with dying. Persons using the framework are prone to stereotype the dying person, 'He's in the denial stage,' or 'She's in the depression stage.' Health professionals should not force terminally ill people into pre-established stages; rather they should take into account the actual experiences of the individual (Lindley, 1991). One tends to forget that all involved in and with the care of the individual's dying may be experiencing different aspects of the same process simultaneously, which can lead to misunderstanding, confusion and withdrawal. Yet, the stages provide a useful vehicle to facilitate sharing information and experiences about dying. The phases or stages one experiences in dying, as discussed earlier, are not as definitive as they seem on paper (**Figure 21.2**).

Kübler-Ross's benchmark work is another example of the way in which death in older people has been neglected because it focused on untimely deaths. Those persons in the study were middle aged, and confronted with an abrupt cessation of careers, relationships and tasks that had been planned. Her framework continues to serve as a helpful cognitive grid or guideline of possible mood and coping mechanisms for death rather than a fixed sequence that determines a 'good death'. Retsinas (1988) points out that model responses such as that of Kübler-Ross may not be appropriate for older people.

There is evidence that older people have the least fear of death and think and talk about it more readily. Kalish (1985) suggests that this can be explained because older people:
- Place less value on their lives and recognise that they have a limited future.
- Have lived their fair share of years.
- Become socialised into accepting their own death by the more frequent deaths of their own peers.

These suggestions are to some extent confirmed by the work of Young and Cullen (1996) concerned with people actually facing death. Their case studies of dying people of all ages in East London incorporate conversations with patients, families and the health professionals looking after them. They found that older people generally found death easier to accept. Several of the informants were explicit in stating that they were not afraid of dying. Some seemed to no longer have a strong wish to live stating loneliness since the death of spouses and friends as one reason for this. However, one older woman with whom they spoke is a reminder not to automatically equate later life with the acceptability of death, but to consider individuals in the context of their complex past and present influences. She was a woman of 74 who was not at all tolerant of what was about to happen having recently embarked upon a new and fulfilling relationship (Young and Cullen, 1996, p. 27).

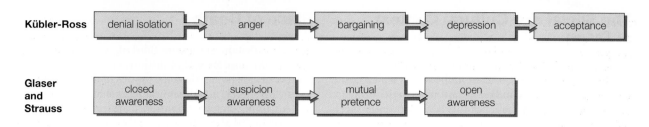

Figure 21.2 Theories of the stages of dying (Source: Kübler-Ross, 1969; Glasser and Strauss, 1963).

In another account of the dying process of an older person, Leviton, an American theorist, explained the behaviour of his dying father using stressors in response to dying:

- Loss.
- Deprivation.
- Separation
- Unwanted changes.

The stressors and stress responses are self-explanatory. Mediating variables (the second factor) influence whether one will react with a positive or negative outcome, which in a sense is similar to the fight-or-flight response used in other stress theories. Mediating factors take into account life experiences, history and other influences that are significant in predicting the response to stress. One of the most important variables is perception. The meaning derived from the social and physical environment will affect adaptation. Mediating variables are:

- Age.
- Sex.
- Religiosity.
- Culture.
- Style and type of dying.
- Environment.
- Personality.
- Life's experiences.
- Experiences with death.
- Meaning given to past life, dying and death.
- Perception of social and physical environment.
- Awareness of nearness to death.
- Forewarning, knowledge, control.
- Positive stress responses.
  - Contentment.
  - Growth.
  - Learning.
  - Problem solving.
  - Challenge.
- Negative stress responses.
  - Chronic anger, hatred.
  - Acute fear.
  - Agitation.
  - Inappropriate death.

Returning to the problem of the difficulty in defining when an older person is dying, the focus has tended to be on physical deterioration as the prime indicator of dying. The less visible, subtle and frequently misinterpreted indications of an older person's terminal process are based on psychological clues. For example, someone without perceptible physical changes that indicate dying may have a sudden and abrupt change in thought and behaviour. Coded communication such as saying goodbye instead of the usual good night, giving away cherished possessions as gifts, urgently contacting friends and relatives with whom the person has not communicated for a long time, and direct or symbolic premonitions that death is near are indications that the individual is approaching or is experiencing death.

Anxiety, depression, restlessness and agitation are behaviours frequently categorised as manifestations of confusion or dementia but in reality may be responses to the inability to express feelings of foreboding and a sense of life escaping one's grasp. Botwinick *et al.* (1978) were among the first to show that significant psychological decrements in cognitive performance appear within a 5-year period before death ('terminal drop'). Initial studies were conducted on older people in long-term care. Studies of those living independently in the community also have shown similar significant changes in performance ability. A concomitant factor in predicting death was the degree of functional ability, not chronological age.

White and Cunningham (1988) examined the concept of 'terminal drop' and found it to be a phenomenon chiefly demonstrated by decline in vocabulary and verbal abilities. The time period when it was noticeable was 2 years before death rather than the 5 years previously proposed by Botwinick *et al.* More recently, Lentzner *et al.* (1992) found decline in the year prior to death was largely predictable based upon previous lifestyle and functional capacities. Many individuals, regardless of advanced chronological age, showed no detectable terminal drop before death if their lifestyle and functional capacities had been generally satisfactory.

In later life, the dying trajectory may not be as clearly marked as in younger people. Older people may become accustomed to chronic disorders and repeatedly make adaptations in their lifestyle to remain active and defy death.

The Social and Cultural Context of Dying

Western societies have been described as death-denying. A recent surge of academic interest in the way in which death is thought about and handled in various societies (Walter, 1994) would seem to challenge this label. However, there still seems to be a general trend for people to be less open about death than in previous generations. The process and aftermath of dying has been largely taken out of the family and community domain and handed over to professionals, be they doctors, nurses, undertakers or bereavement counsellors.

The privatisation of death in Western societies has been considered by a number of writers. Mellor and Schilling (1993) argue that the secularisation and medicalisation of death has resulted in the event being removed from the public space. They see this as related to the shift which has occurred in the significance of death from the social body to the individual body. There is now less concern about the continuation of the social body when a death occurs and more focus on a good death for the individual.

Walter (1994) argues that death has been revived in the public domain with a public discourse in, for example, the media, medicine and life insurance debate. However, he argues that as public rituals around death are decreasing in the West, there is an increase in the individualisation of death and funerals, with people being encouraged to plan their own funeral or memorial service.

Cultural Issues in Palliative Care

There has been a recent increase in awareness and interest in cultural issues related to palliative care. Some of the resultant research has produced surveys of uptake of palliative services by ethnic minority groups (O'Neill, 1994; National Council for Hospice and Palliative Care Services, 1994). Other studies have been of a descriptive nature, mainly aimed at assisting health professionals involved in caring for the dying (Firth, 1993; Neuberger, 1994; Green, 1993). The emphasis of such studies has been on providing a useful guide to certain 'exotic' cultural customs among Britain's ethnic minority groups. For example, Firth notes the importance for some Hindus of dying on the floor, while for Sikhs it is important that they have 'the five K's symbols of faith' nearby at all times (Firth, 1993, p. 30–31).

While these are useful descriptions, they need to be treated cautiously to avoid the danger of stereotyping individuals from a certain cultural background. Neuberger (1993) warns against a tendency to put the other into categories and speculates that this makes their differences easier to deal with for the professional. As people from Britain's diverse ethnic groups grow older and approach death, these issues will become highly relevant and demand a knowledgeable as well as a sensitive approach to the complexities of dying in a different culture where attitudes and practices around death may be quite unfamiliar.

Place of Death

Overall in Britain, about one-third of people die at home. The rest die in some sort of institution, such as a hospital, hospice or care home where the process of dying is managed by doctors, nurses and other health professionals.

An important contribution to research and understanding in this area is Hockey's anthropological account of how death is managed in Britain today (1990). She describes ethnographic studies of three organisations dealing with death: a residential home, a hospice and a bereavement organisation. One of the central themes of her argument is that the major strategy used by Western society to manage death is the careful maintenance of a boundary between life and death. She argues that such a boundary creates an exclusion of the living from the experience and has contributed to the loss of meaning of death in Britain. She suggests that whereas the spatial arrangement and organisation of the residential home conform to a death-denying mode of management, the whole philosophy of the hospice is aimed at breaking down the boundary between life and death. The environments of the two institutions are seen as indicative of their different approaches, with the wards being hidden away out of sight in the residential home and very visible from the reception area of the hospice which is itself approached through glass doors. Everything is symbolic of a blurring of the boundary between life and death including the symbols of water and valleys that pervade this particular hospice. In contrast, she sees the manipulation of metaphors, the use of symbols and all the activities of the residential home as masking the literal function of the organisation and attempting to distance and separate out the process of dying.

Hospice

The hospice movement has been tremendously important in altering and shaping attitudes and practices around death. In Britain, it has a religious basis although many hospices are non-denominational. Central to the philosophy of hospice care is a commitment to holistic care taking account of the emotional, social and spiritual needs of the patient as well as their physical requirements. Such holistic care should be delivered by a multidisciplinary team of professionals who work with the patient and their informal carers involving them in decisions about their care and management (Saunders, 1978).

Since the opening of St Christopher's Hospice in Sydenham, South London, in the 1960s, there have been many developments in the area of palliative care. The principles developed in the hospices were taken out into the wider community when home care teams were set up in the 1970s. Many of these were funded by Macmillan Cancer Relief and are widely referred to as 'Macmillan teams'. Other services such as day care and hospital support teams who help patients who are dying in the hospital environment have since developed. Palliative medicine has been a recognised speciality since 1987 and there is now a National Council for Hospice and Specialist Palliative Care Services (details are given at the end of this chapter).

The modern hospice movement developed to help those people dying from cancer and as such the principles and surroundings have not been so relevant to the care of the dying older person. Cartwright (1993) reports from her survey that the older people get the less likely they are to die at home and the more likely they are to die in residential care. In her sample, none of the people who were 85 years of age or over died in a hospice and over a third died in a residential or nursing home.

Nursing the Dying

Institutional settings tend to dissect an individual into component parts, dealing with segments rather than with the living whole. Nurses are caught up in the biological and physical aspects of patient care. It is easy and non-threatening to relieve physical symptoms associated with dying, but to permit oneself to become involved in meaningful interpersonal relationships to support the dying older person can be more difficult.

Relevant here is the seminal work done by Menzies in the 1950s. As a psychoanalyst, Menzies was asked by a London teaching hospital to assist them in making organisational changes to the system of nursing. She suggests that some of the activities of nursing could provoke unsustainable anxiety in the nurse by replicating certain primitive, unconscious, unpleasant and infantile fantasies in consciousness. Menzies argues that nursing has been organised in the hospital setting, to contain this anxiety by evading it rather than confronting and thereby reducing it. To do this, rituals and symbols have been established which help to defend and distance the nurse from anxiety. According to Menzies, these included 'splitting up the nurse–patient relationship' through task allocation of the workload of the ward so that the nurse repeated the same task for all patients rather than nursing an individual patient which would require closer involvement. Performance of nursing through a series of ritual tasks is considered by Menzies to be a method used by the nursing service to spare nurses anxiety by minimising the number and variety of decisions that must be made. Further protection for the nurse against anxiety was provided by 'denial of the significance of the individual', which refers to both nurse and patient, and is achieved by depersonalising symbols such as the uniform of the nurse, and reference by nurses to patients by diagnosis rather than by name. This strategy also helped another defence mechanism, that of detachment, achieved by encouraging the nurse to deny upsetting or disturbing feelings that arose out of their interactions with patients. Menzies work is of course now dated and nurse education and organisation have changed.

The philosophy guiding the practice of palliative nursing and changes in general nursing practice such as the instigation of the 'named nurse' concept have aimed towards a more holistic approach. However, perhaps new rituals such as some activities around the completion of written care plans and other paper work have developed and may act as a defence against the distressing and demanding work of

Meeting Spiritual Needs

Jimmie cannot believe that his wife Lorna is dying. The doctor tells him she is in the early stages of multiple myeloma and she could die in less than a year or she might have remissions and live another 10 years. The couple have worked hard all their lives and brought up two sons. Neither Jimmie nor Lorna have yet reached 65 years of age. They have retired early and are financially secure. They thought that the best years of their lives were ahead of them. Both Jimmie and Lorna are the type to confront a problem head on and they gather all the relevant material they can find and assiduously study it to find out as much as they can about the condition. Lorna says that she does not want to mention the problem to others as she, 'can't deal with their pity'. She also stresses that she expects to have long remissions and to live to be at least 75 years old, so why trouble friends and family. As a result, Jimmie cannot share his fear and grief, as he has promised to respect Lorna's wishes in this respect.

Lorna begins a course of chemotherapy and friends begin to notice her lethargy. They worry about her but she insists, 'I'm fine'. Six months pass with a steady downward course in Lorna's condition. Her two sons begin to suspect that she isn't well and Rab, the youngest, says to her, 'We're worried about you mum, is there something you're keeping from us?' She denies it, but Rab also notices that his father is withdrawn. He knows something is wrong but is at a loss. Rab just happens to visit when the community nurse is leaving the house. He insists that she tell him what is going on.

Based upon this case study, develop a nursing care plan using the following procedure:

- **What are Lorna's comments that provide subjective evidence?**
- **What information can the nurse herself obtain from her observations of the family and discussion with Rab which provide objective data for a holistic nursing assessment?**
- **Suggest two unmet needs that may be the most significant to Lorna and her family at this time.**
- **Suggest nursing aims for each unmet need, reflecting realistic outcomes and using concrete and measurable terms.**
- **Suggest one or more interventions for each area of unmet need, justifying your choice of intervention.**

nursing in general and particularly looking after people who are dying.

There is now more recognition within organisations and individuals that those working with dying people need a structured support system to enable continued effective practice. Reflective practice is encouraged within clinical supervision (Johns, 1996). The difficulty is that once again while such systems are encouraged for those working in specialist hospice or oncology units, the needs of those staff working in the hospital or residential home settings where most older people die are perhaps not so well acknowledged or met.

Death as Growth

The awareness of dying can be an instrument of growth and fuller appreciation of living. Indeed, many older people say they awake each day feeling just glad to be alive. Given the limited time left for an older person to remain in this plane of existence, it is ever more important that the last days of life hold full significance to the degree desired by the individual. Fry (1991) found that older people were able to cope with death and dying if they had internal control, social support, prayer and were preoccupied with objects of attachment. It is important to look at approaches that will allow the older person to die with dignity and comfort and perhaps achieve final growth.

Impediments to Growth

In many cases, imposed indignities begin when dying individuals are admitted to a hospital. Control is surrendered over the remainder of life and death. Hospitals dictate rules, regulations and patient protocol, which are enforced by the caregivers – the nurses and others. Stereotyping of older people may occur, as they are labelled 'confused', 'stubborn' or 'cantankerous', and assumed to be 'helpless'. Privacy and individuality are eroded. For the remainder of the person's life (which may be in a hospital), decisions will be made *for* them, not *with* or *by* them. Such loss of control over decisions precipitates fears of helplessness, loneliness and pain. These fears threaten the older person's self-worth, integrity and identity.

Needs of the Dying

It is difficult to separate the physical and psychological needs of the dying older person to identify specific interventions and approaches because they are interwoven. Freedom from pain, freedom from loneliness, conservation of energy and maintenance of self-esteem are four major needs that are most often neglected in the dying older person. When unfulfilled, these impede the ability to reconcile the remainder of life.

The needs of the terminally ill individual in hierarchical order are shown in **Figure 21.3**. Interestingly, as Bradshaw (1997) points out, Frankl would argue for the turning upside down of this hierarchy of needs according to Maslow, insisting from his experience that if man has found meaning, he can indeed endure almost any amount of physical pain and discomfort.

Freedom from Pain

Pain is not merely a physical phenomenon: depression, anxiety, fear, and other unresolved emotional concerns of the dying induce pain. When emotional needs are not met, the total pain experience, physical and psychosocial, may be exacerbated or intensified. Medication alone cannot relieve this pain. Instead, empathetic listening and allowing the dying person to verbalise what is on their mind are important interventions that must be based on the energy level of the one who is dying. (*See* Chapter 9 for further discussion of pain and a summary of the World Health Organisation analgesic ladder system for the step-wise and regular approach to the management of terminal malignant pain.)

Freedom from Loneliness

Loneliness can come from within as well as without. Those dying in later life have sustained many losses: loss of friends through death, perhaps loss of spouse, loss of control by institutionalisation, loss of meaningful possessions and loss of physical abilities (sight, hearing and body functions). Language barriers and cultural differences can also generate loneliness.

In the hospital setting the nursing staff can easily intensify loneliness by caring for the older person with detachment, by surrendering to the mechanical technology of the profession and by avoiding the death situation. In these ways, the nurse truly isolates the old person. Offensive odours emanating from the patient's room or body keep people away. Unrelieved pain, physical or psychological, intensifies loneliness. Behaviour meant to attract attention may in fact distance people. The dying person is frequently placed in a single room or curtained-off as it becomes more apparent that death is approaching; care is reduced with decreased tactile and audio stimulation. Lighting in the room is dim, curtains or blinds may be drawn, and people speak in hushed tones or not at all. The dying person may perceive this as abandonment, the ultimate loneliness. The person may be wishing for companionship or human presence; yet knowingly or unknowingly nurses may foster this loneliness and aloneness.

Room location and environment are important considerations to reduce or eliminate loneliness. It is critical to assess the rationale for isolating the dying person in a single room. For whose benefit is it: the patient, the staff or to protect the uncomfortable visitors to the hospital unit? For some people, it is reassuring to see activity when one is confined to bed. Placing the dying older person in a room with several other persons can provide the opportunity to share conversation and companionship and security that he or she will not die alone. The patients who remain in the room after a death have the support and solace of each other. When there are only two persons in a room, the remaining occupant is left alone, a situation that can be frightening and a negative

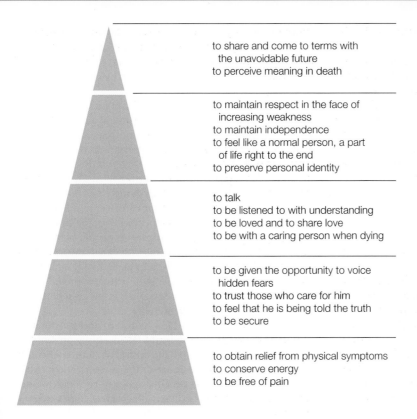

Figure 21.3 Hierarchy of the dying person's needs.

to share and come to terms with
   the unavoidable future
to perceive meaning in death

to maintain respect in the face of
   increasing weakness
to maintain independence
to feel like a normal person, a part
   of life right to the end
to preserve personal identity

to talk
to be listened to with understanding
to be loved and to share love
to be with a caring person when dying

to be given the opportunity to voice
   hidden fears
to trust those who care for him
to feel that he is being told the truth
to be secure

to obtain relief from physical symptoms
to conserve energy
to be free of pain

experience. These considerations are very individual and must be based upon patient preference.

If the energy level of the dying person allows ambulation, he or she should be free to leave the confines of his or her room and associate with other patients, visitors and staff. When physical tolerance is limited to sitting in a chair, a wheelchair can provide mobility and accessibility to the larger environment with the least energy expenditure. Sitting by the nurses' station or desk is sometimes preferable to sitting alone in one's room. If possible, the patient should be encouraged to wear his or her own clothing.

A pleasant room atmosphere with bright colours and diffuse, high-intensity lighting not only protects older people from visual discomfort but also affords a clearer visual contrast of objects. It has been noted that in the last hours of the dying process individuals turned toward light. Perhaps this supports the value of using bright colours and adjusting lights to keep the patient in touch with life until the end of living.

Live plants and flowers are a way of bringing the outside world in. Memorabilia, pictures, cherished objects, or anything that brings solace should be recognised as important in the care of the dying. These tangible objects are a means of coping with anxiety and furnish a modicum of security and familiarity in an alien environment. A portable radio is easy to reach, conserves energy, staves off loneliness and provides contact with the outside world. Television, if available, can also be a beneficial outlet. Visitors should be allowed to be with the dying person any time of the day or night.

Night can be the most lonely and painful time for those who are dying. It is a time of least attention, a time when one thinks and reviews the sorrows and joys of life past and what is to be. It is a time of fear of dying alone and no one will know. When a friend or relative cannot stay with the dying person, a nurse may be able to spend a little time sitting with the patient. Not all dying patients want this attention, but if they do, it should be available.

A little time spent listening relieves some of the loneliness of impending death. When caregivers cut the patient off as he or she begins to recall days of long ago, an avenue that helps relieve loneliness has been deliberately blocked. Reminiscence is a means of putting one's life in order. It is a valuable way for the older person to evaluate the pluses and minuses of life. It is a means of achieving closure to life by resolving conflicts, giving up possessions and making final goodbyes. It can create a new meaning in life.

Everyone who cares for the dying should be aware of the potential for isolation and loneliness evoked by the dying process. Some older people may welcome physical contact, so that the nurse may hold a hand or put an arm around the patient's shoulder that says, 'I care' and 'You're not alone.'

Conversely, some older people have developed a lifestyle around aloneness. These individuals do indeed prefer solitude. Thrusting any of the nursing care approaches just suggested at them would only serve to aggravate the patient and the care situation. It is important to be sensitive to the patient's cues and to assess and act on them accordingly (see

Chapter 16 for further discussion on loneliness or the desire to be alone).

As a result of the interwoven nature of loneliness and pain (pain may precipitate loneliness and loneliness can exacerbate pain), the nurse may need to deal with physical and psychological discomfort separately or together, depending on assessment of the situation.

Conservation of Energy

Older people facing death use great amounts of energy in attempting to cope with the physical assault of illness on the body and in the emotional unrest that dying initiates. Nursing interventions should be directed toward the conservation of patient energy. How much can the individual do without becoming physically and emotionally taxed? What activities of daily living are most important for the older person to do independently? Would it be best to bathe the person so he or she could eat alone or feed the patient so he or she could wash or receive visitors? How much energy does the patient need to talk with visitors or staff without becoming exhausted? The older person should be involved in answering such questions and making these decisions. The emotional turmoil and anxiety produced when the patient is cared for without explanation or inclusion in the decision sap the energy that might have been conserved by manipulating the patient's physical requirements.

Anxiety binds energy. Energy can be spared and anxiety reduced by listening, touching and providing rest and an environment that permits the patient to be dependent as it becomes necessary. Perhaps conservation of energy is the most tangible patient need the nurse faces when caring for the dying older person. By meeting the needs for freedom from pain, freedom from loneliness and conservation of energy, the nurse has already begun to intervene on behalf of the maintenance of self-esteem.

Maintenance of Self-esteem

Pride in oneself is a composite of the physical and psychological attributes of one's years of living. For the older person, it is difficult to watch self-image dissolve through loss of independence, loss of the potential for doing (a result of physical disabilities) or loss of body functions such as hearing, seeing, eating, urinating, defecating or cleaning self. The older person may begin to feel ashamed, humiliated and like a 'burden'.

By their approach and attitude towards older people, institutions and caregivers can erode self-esteem. The older person's privacy and dignity are invaded by a number of physicians and others who come to look, prod and poke in search of diagnoses and learning. Additional insults may be imposed by inappropriate use of first names or other terms such as 'dearie' or 'love'. Behaviour such as this by caregivers compounds the situation for the older person who is dying. Withdrawing from the dying reinforces the older person's feeling of worthlessness.

When self-esteem is at an ebb, other factors such as psychological and physical pain, aloneness and depletion of energy are intensified. Depression aggravates pain and further isolates the individual. One cannot deny that the way people respond to dying is influenced by their background, past experiences, religious and philosophical orientation, and the prior degree of life involvement. If experiences have been negative, the lack of care and attention by caregivers creates a pathetic state of affairs.

Self-esteem and dignity complement each other. Dignity involves the individual's ability to maintain a consistent self-concept. Caregivers frequently take control and dignity away from the dying and impose their expectations on the patient. Essential to the facilitation of self-esteem is the premise that the values of the patient must figure significantly in the decisions that will affect the course of dying.

The important concept for the caregiver to master is that the dying individual is a living person with the same needs for good and natural relationships with people as the rest of us have. If this concept can be fully accepted, incorporation of the value of the patient to him or herself will significantly affect the course of the person's dying process. Including the person in decisions about care encourages the patient to control the most important event in life.

What can be done to help maintain and bolster self-esteem of the dying older person? Focus on the present and the opportunities that exist in the immediate future. Attention must be paid to the appearance of the person's body: cleanliness, lack of odours and personal appearance. Physical comfort is vitally important because with comfort comes security. Caregivers must become good listeners to allow the dying to express their fears of pain, aloneness, and the struggle with the separation and grief over losses. Caregivers may assume the management of necessary body and ego functions for the older person. This requires emphasis on respect and helpfulness rather than encouraging dependency, guilt or conflict. Human contact is vital. One quickly falls into the confusional syndrome of human deprivation: loneliness. As early as 1967, it was shown in sensory deprivation experiments (i.e. touch) that a disintegration and loss of ego integrity (dignity) occurred. It is therefore of utmost importance for the caregiver to use auditory, visual and tactile stimulation appropriately to nurture and foster self-esteem in the dying older person. Verbal and nonverbal communication are necessary to convey positive messages. Appropriate and sensitive use of touch can be powerful ways of conveying to the dying person that the nurse or caregiver is prepared to meet the person on his or her own terms and that the person is an individual unique unto self and appreciated.

Communication

Central to meeting the needs of the dying is the quality and the manner in which caring professionals communicate with patients. There is now much useful literature to assist doctors and nurses in the business of breaking bad news to dying patients and their families and in ways to handle and not avoid difficult questions (Buckman, 1988; Lugton, 1988). Much of the work has focused on cancer patients but many of the issues relating to loss, fear and the difficulties of disclosing feelings and emotions are relevant to caring for dying people in general. Nurses in palliative care and oncol-

21.1 Assessment of the Dying Patient and Family

Patient
- Age.
- Gender.
- Coping styles and abilities.
- Social, cultural, ethnic background.
- Previous experience with illness, pain, deterioration, loss, and grief.
- Mental health.
- Intelligence.
- Lifestyle
- Fulfilment of life goals.
- Amount of unfinished business.
- The nature of the illness (death trajectory, problems particular to the illness, treatment, amount of pain).
- Time passed since diagnosis.
- Response to illness.
- Knowledge about the illness/disease.
- Acceptance/rejection of the sick role.
- Amount of striving for dependence/independence.
- Feelings and fears about illness.
- Comfort in expressing thoughts and feelings and how much is expressed.
- Location of the patient (home, hospital, nursing home).
- Relationship with each member of the family and significant other since diagnosis.

Family
- Family makeup (members of family).
- Developmental stage of the family.
- Existing subsystems.
- Specific roles of each member.
- Characteristics of the family system.

- How flexible or rigid.
- Type of communication.
- Rules, norms and expectations.
- Values, beliefs.
- Quality of emotional relationships.
- Dependence, interdependence, freedom of each member.
- How close to or disengaged from the dying member.
- Established extrafamilial interactions.
- Strengths and vulnerabilities of the family.
- Style of leadership and decision-making.
- Unusual methods of problem-solving, crisis resolution.
- Family resources (personal, financial, community).
- Current problems identified by the family.
- Quality of communication with the caregivers.
- Immediate and long-range anticipated needs.
- Family rules, norms, values and past experiences that might inhibit grief or interfere with a therapeutic relationship.

Source: Hess, 1994.

ogy settings are encouraged in their education programmes to develop their communication skills but there is evidence that despite the theoretical awareness, the actual communication remains superficial and non-therapeutic (Wilkinson, 1991). The difficulty in recognising the actual dying process that can occur in later life, which was described earlier in the chapter, has implications for communication practice. Maintaining hope and an acceptable understanding of the illness, pain, fear, anxiety or other stressful emotions (Benner, 1984) becomes more difficult for nurses to sustain over a longer time period.

Assessment

Few tools exist for assessing the dying. The nurse must depend on knowledge and understanding of the dying process, behaviours identified by various theorists of dying, and glean information from various studies that cite dying behaviour. **Box 21.1** provides assessment guidelines that address the psychosocial aspects of the dying client as well as the family. The physical assessment of dying uses the same assessment techniques with attention to specific systems that are used with all other patients in collecting patient care data.

Intervention

Interventions have many facets and range from the simple act of hand holding to dealing with a multitude of emotions. The core of interventions focuses on communication, pain and symptom relief, knowledge of available resources, and fostering involvement in and control of decision-making by the patient as long as possible. In the days and hours before death, specific signs and symptoms of physical and spiritual needs draw more attention. These are shown in **Tables 21.1** and **21.2**.

Dehydration and the Dying Patient

This is an issue which has attracted a considerable amount of recent debate. Much of this stems from the hospice argument against the usual practice in acute care setting of artificial rehydration with intravenous fluids when patients are unable to take adequate amounts of oral fluid. Craig (1994, 1996) argues that the approach of sedation without hydration or nutrition as used in certain circumstances in palliative care is dangerous ethically and legally. She is concerned that not everyone referred for 'terminal care' proves in fact to be dying. She cites older people as being commonly admitted to

Physical Signs and Symptoms Associated with the Final Stages of Dying, Rationale and Interventions		
Physical signs and symptoms	Rationale	Intervention (if any)
Coolness, colour and temperature change in hands, arms, feet, and legs, perspiration may be present	Peripheral circulation diminished to facilitate increased circulation to vital organs	Place socks on feet; cover with light cotton blanket; keep warm blankets on person but, *do not use electric blanket*
Increased sleeping	Conservation of energy	Spend time with the patient; hold the hand; speak normally to the patient even though there may be a lack of response
Disorientation, confusion of time, place, person	Metabolic changes	Identify self by name before speaking to patient; speak softly, clearly and truthfully
Incontinence of urine and/or bowel	Increased muscle relaxation and decreased consciousness	Maintain vigilance, change bedding as appropriate, utilise body-worn pads, try not to use an indwelling catheter
Congestion	Poor circulation of body fluids, immobilisation, and the inability to expectorate secretions causes gurgling, rattles, bubbling	Elevate the head with pillows and /or raise the head of the bed; gently turn the head to the side to drain secretions
Restlessness	Metabolic changes and decrease in oxygen to the brain	Calm the patient by speech and action; reduce light; gently rub back, stroke arms, or read aloud; play soothing music
Decreased intake to food and fluids	Body conservation of energy for function	Do not force patient to eat or drink; give ice chips, soft drinks, juice, popsicles as tolerated; apply petroleum jelly or lip salve to dry lips; if patient is a mouth breather, apply protective jelly more frequently as necessary
Decreased urine output	Decreased fluid intake and decreased circulation to kidney	None
Altered breathing pattern	Metabolic and oxygen changes of respiratory system	Elevate the head of bed; hold hand, speak gently to patient *Additional general interventions* Learn to be 'with person' without talking; a moist washcloth on the forehead may be soothing; eye drops may help soothe the eyes

Source: Hess, 1994.

Table 21.1 Physical signs and symptoms associated with the final stages of dying, rationale and interventions

hospital in a dehydrated condition due to multiple pathology, being regarded as terminally ill when hydration could alleviate the immediate situation and allow time for proper physical and psychological assessment.

There are advantages and disadvantages to hydrating dying patients, which are well described by Sutcliffe (1994) and Dunphy *et al.* (1995). The literature gives conflicting reports as to the physical discomfort caused by dehydration and whether the use of intravenous fluids actually relieves discomfort or provides an additional burden to the patient. Those working with the dying express concern that the use of intravenous fluids gives mixed messages about medical intervention at this stage of a patient's illness (Dunphy *et al.* 1995). Whichever choice is made with regard to the use of artificial hydration demands careful explanation and discussion with the patient and family if possible. Withdrawing hydration can seem a harsh decision if families are not carefully prepared for it.

Emotional/Spiritual Symptoms of Approaching Death, Rationale and Interventions		
Emotional/spiritual symptoms	Rationale	Intervention
Withdrawal	Prepare the patient for release and detachment and letting go of relationships	Continue communicating in a normal manner using a normal voice tone; identify self by name; hold hand, say what person wants to hear from you
Vision-like experience (dead friends or family, religious vision)	Preparation for transition	Do not contradict or argue regarding whether this is or is not a real experience; if the patient is frightened, reassure them that it is normal
Restlessness	Tension, fear, unfinished business	Listen to patient express his or her fears, sadness and anger associated with dying; give permission to go
Decreased socialisation	As energy diminishes, the patient begins making his or her transition	Express support; give permission to die
Unusual communication: out of character statements, gestures, requests	Signals readiness to let go	Say what needs to be said to the dying patient; kiss, hug, cry with him or her, if it feels appropriate

Source: Hess, 1994.

Table 21.2 Emotional/spiritual symptoms of approaching death, rationale and interventions

Assisted Death

The Institute of Medical Ethics considered the following issue:

The lives of an increasing number of patients, predominantly but by no means elderly, are now being prolonged by modern medicine in states of coma, severe incapacity or pain they consider unrelievable and from which they seek release. Doctors in charge of such patients have to decide not only whether they are morally bound to continue with life-prolonging treatment but also if no such treatment is being given, whether and in what circumstances it is ethical to hasten their deaths.

(Dickenson and Johnson, 1993, p. 149.)

The working party concluded that a doctor is ethically justified in assisting death if the need to relieve intense and unceasing pain caused by an incurable illness outweighs the benefits to the patient of further prolonging life.

There continues to be much debate about this issue, with the palliative care specialty, in general completely opposing any change in law to assist death and believing that most suffering can be relieved by good palliation (Twycross, 1993; Roy, 1990). Objections to assisted death related to the older person include the fear that older, frail people may request their doctors to end their life simply to relieve what they may perceive as their burden on their family. Any change in the law which allows assisted death in those that request it may open the way for unrequested assistance particularly in those unable to communicate, such as people who suffer dementia in later life.

While the debate continues, there is no doubt that in Britain there is more concern about the use of excessive medical intervention when people are dying. One response to this has been the introduction of the advanced directive or living will. This is not a valid legal document in Britain at the moment but it is a means by which an individual can communicate their wishes about treatment should they become seriously ill with no prospect of recovery.

Cardiopulmonary Resuscitation (CPR) Decisions

In 1989, an outraged relative complained to the Health Service Ombudsman that his 80-year-old mother had been designated not for CPR in the event of cardiac arrest during an admission to hospital. The decision had been made without any consultation with his mother or himself. He said that notwithstanding his mother's admission to hospital for treatment of pneumonia, she normally had a very good quality of life. He was determined to find out on what basis such a decision had been made. The consequences following this event triggered the publication of a letter by the Chief Medical Officer, which was circulated to all hospitals requesting that they draw up policies on the making of CPR directives. The incident subsequently generated a great deal of discussion and research interest. This covered, for example, criteria on which such a decision should be based (Dautzenberg *et al.* 1993), guidelines for the formulation of policies Royal College of Nursing (RCN) and British Medical Association (BMA), 1993; Doyal and Wilsher, 1993), and studies canvassing the views of older people and their relatives (Mead and Turnbull, 1995; Bruce-Jones *et al.* 1996). Although efforts are being made to determine which patients are most likely not to survive CPR, so as to inform a DNR policy, it is yet by no means clear that any one single factor can be predictive of survival. So far single factors such as advanced age, malignancy, respiratory disease, renal failure, dementia, housebound status and cerebrovascular accident have been independently associated with a poor CPR outcome. However, a combination of variables in the form of a 'pre-arrest morbidity index' has been shown to give a better prediction of outcome (Dautzenberg *et al.* 1993).

Studies indicate that older people are becoming much more knowledgeable about CPR, possibly as a result of popular television drama. The majority are willing to discuss what might be thought a sensitive issue and to make a decision in hypothetical cases. In addition, they tend to have unrealistic expectations of the CPR outcome, in that it is largely successful (Mead and Turnbull, 1995). While it is generally agreed that people should make decisions concerning their own bodies, very many older patients are not in any fit state to make the decision at the time of hospital admission. This being the very time that cardiac arrest is likely to occur. Unlike in the USA, the advance directive does not yet have legal force (*see* Chapter 14), and in such instances of mental and physical incapacity, a team approach to decision-making is advocated (RCN and BMA, 1993). In a small study, Sayers *et al.* (1997) found that even when patients were screened for mental competence prior to being asked for their decision on CPR, few patients' decisions met set criteria for giving informed consent. With time, an increasingly well-informed older population will expect to be asked for their wishes concerning CPR. While they may still ask the doctor to do what is best, nurses can play their part by always noting patients' CPR status (Aarons and Beeching, 1991), clarifying patients' understanding of the procedure and supporting them through the decision-making process.

BEREAVEMENT

Bereavement is a universal phenomenon. Its associations with increased mortality and morbidity have been well documented. Studies have shown that the mortality rates for widowed people are higher than those for married people (Bowling, 1987). Furthermore, there is evidence of a difference between the sexes. Young *et al.* (1963) studied a cohort of widowers of 55 years of age or older and found that the mortality rate was 40% higher than in married men, during the first 6 months following the death of their partners. This sharp increase was followed by a gradual decrease in mortality back to the level of married men.

In a Swedish study, Berg *et al.* (1981) found a 48% increase in mortality among widowers compared to a 22% increase in widows in the first 3 months of bereavement. They found that an excess in mortality at a lower level continued

for 11 years post-bereavement. Bowling (1987) puts forward several possible explanations for these findings including:
- Stress of the bereavement.
- Lack of social support.
- Role change.

She concludes that the physiological consequences associated with the stress of a bereavement in combination with change in role is most likely to account for this increased mortality. Roles within marriage possibly protect against health problems and when this married role disappears the protection goes with it. Bowling proposes that this is more evident in men who generally have less support networks to compensate for the gap than do women.

In terms of morbidity, there are indications that women find it harder to adjust to bereavement in the long term, although data is conflicting. In a detailed exploration of widowhood, Bowling and Cartwright (1982) found that generally those who had the most difficulty in adjusting to bereavement were more likely to be female, comparatively young and in poor health themselves. They suggested the reason for the increased morbidity in widows could be linked to loss of role in that being a wife is more important for self-identity than being a husband.

Phases of Mourning

In an attempt to understand the grieving process and so help those who are having difficulty with it, various phases of mourning have been suggested (Parkes, 1970; Worden, 1991). Worden's four tasks of mourning (Worden, 1991) are:
1. To accept the reality of the loss.
2. To work through the pain of grief.
3. To adjust to the environment in which the deceased is missing.
4. To emotionally relocate the deceased and move on with life.

As with proposed stages of dying referred to earlier in the chapter, it is important to note that the phases or tasks of mourning are not compulsory and people may experience all or some of them in a variety of orders or simultaneously. Within these phases many reactions and behaviours may be seen. Common bereavement reactions (Baro *et al.* 1986) are:
1. Shock and emotional numbness.
2. Total or partial disorganisation.
3. Hallucinations.
4. Aggressive reactions.
5. Feelings of guilt.
6. Feelings of shame.
7. Ambivalent behaviour – simultaneous or alternating searching and avoiding.
8. Maintenance (sometimes obsessive) of memories.
9. Idealisation of the dead person.
10. Identification with the deceased, e.g. taking on their beliefs and wishes directly or through a third person.

Effect of Age on Bereavement Reactions

Assumptions that it is easier to cope with the death of a loved one in later life are probably incorrect. Parkes (1986) cites his own work with 44 widows from London in which he found less morbidity in bereaved women under the age of 65 years than those aged over 65. He also reviews other studies in which he finds inconclusive results on this issue.

Bowling and Cartwright (1982) carried out a large study of the older widowed people in Britain. They interviewed over 350 recently widowed older men and women, their GPs and their families and friends to find out what their needs were and how well they were met. They comment on the effect that demographic changes over recent decades have had on the way in which older people cope with bereavement. Many more old people now live alone and a long way from family. Daughters and other female relatives are now more likely to be working and so are less able to care or spend time with their older widowed relative. The researchers found that people bereaved in later life appreciated sympathy, relief from loneliness and help with the practicalities of day-to-day life which were made more difficult with their own declining physical and financial reserves.

In later life people are much more likely to have to face multiple losses not only related to the deaths of spouse and friends but also of familiar housing, finances and the loss of self-esteem that may be associated with their own failing health.

Normal Grieving

Bereavement is a natural process and the majority of people deal with it using their own coping mechanisms and do not require professional help. Sometimes people find it difficult to resolve certain feeling about their loss and can exaggerate, mask or get stuck in one of the phases of mourning. As Worden (1991, p. 13) explains, 'it is necessary to acknowledge and work through the pain or it will manifest itself through some symptoms or aberrant behaviour'. Counselling or therapy may be needed to help resolve such a situation.

In considering what is a normal grief reaction it is essential to take account of cultural background as part of the individual assessment of the bereaved person. Practices around death vary greatly among different cultural groups. They often have a very important function in completing the rite of passage between life and death and health professionals should be sensitive to behaviours and beliefs which are outside their own experience or cultural biography. For example, it is regarded as part of normal grief in the West for the bereaved to have dreams and talk to the dead for a few weeks after the death. In some cultures such as that of the Hopi, dialogue with the deceased goes on for many years after the death and is regarded as completely normal and actually beneficial to settle old disagreements. Baro et al. (1986) question how helpful some Western bereavement support is for other cultural groups. Bereavement counselling and groups may be completely inappropriate for people from other cultural groups where death is perhaps handled in a very different way.

Anticipatory Grief

It has sometimes been assumed that an opportunity to rehearse for bereavement during the period of illness prior to death can help older people to adjust better to the actual bereavement. In fact, studies of older widows by Dessonville et al. (1983) showed the reverse in that an anticipatory grief period was associated with poorer psychological adjustment. Another study by Hill et al. (1988) found no difference in the adjustment of widows who were 'prepared' for the death of a spouse and those who were not. Significantly, those widows with recent disabilities, with few friends and not feeling close to their children were predictive of the need for counselling 6 months after bereavement (Goldberg et al. 1988). These data can alert nurses to widows at risk of impaired bereavement.

Studies that look at which pre-death factors influence the course of bereavement in older people are few. In one American study that monitored older widows during the initial 13 months after the bereavement, there was less depression in the surviving partner when one or all of the following had occurred:

- Shared social activities between partners.
- Financial preparation made.
- Involvement of the surviving partner in help with daily activities during the final illness.

Conversely, factors that seemed to predispose towards more depression in the survivor were:

- Sudden, unexpected death.
- Unease about the management of the death by the survivor.
- Inability of the survivor to find work.

A surviving spouse may convey a sense of relief when the partner dies following a long and painful illness or one in which the individual's personality had been greatly changed for an extended period before death. One woman merely touched her husband's face and said, 'At last, we can be at peace.' In another case, a woman was out shopping when her husband suffered a massive heart attack. She blamed herself for not being there and felt sure she could have saved his life.

Caring for the Bereaved Older Person

Attitudes about the death of older people need to be kept in mind when considering the needs of the bereaved. As Baro et al. (1986) point out it is important that accepted views about the natural timing of death in old age do not in any way devalue or negate the unique grief of the survivors.

Most grief reactions are normal and uncomplicated.

During the initial period of bereavement older people are usually helped by some sort of support network which may be family, friends or church members and may be supplemented by health professionals. Practical help with daily living and finances is often needed at this time. The danger is that a lot of this help is crisis orientated and disappears after a few weeks. An ongoing support network is helpful and the health professional has a responsibility to inform of other community resources. Self or mutual help groups may be useful for some people in providing a forum for talking about practicalities and their feelings with people who have all experienced a bereavement. Such groups tend to be used more by women than men, possibly as a result of the accepted cultural view that men prefer to talk less about their feelings and 'get on with things' alone (Baro *et al.* 1986).

Organisations that offer bereavement counselling exist nationwide and are usually run by volunteers who have had some basic counselling training. Most people are helped through the process of grief by these interventions but occasionally where grief is complicated, as described earlier, further help may be required from a professional counsellor and medical opinions explored as to the advisability of medication use.

Effects on Sexuality

The absence of a sexual partner following the death of a spouse temporarily cancels an important expressive role of feelings and of femininity or masculinity. The intimacy and closeness of a mate provide strong self-affirmation. The loss of this important role results in asexuality for many older people. Seldom are they thought to be full sexual beings even when married. When widowed, most older women are effectively neutered. Men may seek and find new sexual partners but are vulnerable to 'widower's impotence' a result of guilt, depression, long periods of abstinence from sexual activity and the strangeness of a new sexual partner. All these factors may hinder an older man from consummating a new partnership.

Coping with the Death of a Child

It is often thought the death of a child may be the most difficult grief an older person must bear. A small study of 12

Jewish and 17 non-Jewish older people whose children died seemed to indicate that the Jewish mothers could not let go of their grief whereas the non-Jewish women accepted and went on with their lives (Goodman *et al.* 1991). While this interpretation is questionnable, the study pointed out that the manner in which one integrates the death of a child has to do with the centrality of that child to one's existence, the ability to express grief, aspects of generativity in the lifestyle, general health and wellbeing.

Sibling Death

Deaths of siblings are particularly hard to integrate as the close affiliation and identification threaten one's own mortality to a greater degree than most relationships. In addition, the death of each sibling removes one more member of childhood: those that can confirm youth and energy. On the other hand, the first sibling who dies may teach the others more about death and coping.

Planning for the Care of Survivors

Outliving those one loves may create an emptiness that can never be fully assuaged. **Table 21.3** provides a nursing care plan for survivors with suggested interventions, but nurses must be prepared for this most difficult of all tasks.

SUMMARY

It is clearly true that death is inevitable and as has been discussed in this chapter, there is evidence that this certainty perhaps predisposes older people to think and talk about the subject more than other age groups. However, it is important that this does not tempt health professionals into glossing over or minimalising the very special and individual needs of dying older people and their carers.

It is questionable how much of the wealth of research into dying and specialist palliative care services is relevant to those dying or bereaved in later life. The complexities of this whole area have been demonstrated in this chapter. They warrant further consideration and research.

Nursing Care Plan for Survivors		
Nursing need	Expected outcomes	Interventions
Depression, loneliness, social Isolation related to loss of spouse, sexual partner, friend, companion or confidante		
Manifestations: anger, nervousness, palpitations, increased perspiration, face flushing, dyspnoea, urinary frequency, nausea, vomiting, restlessness, apprehension, panic, fear, headache	*Short-term/intermediate goals:* the survivor will develop or use immediate support systems, express feelings of security, exhibit meaningful social relationships and show decreasing signs of depression *Long-term goal:* the survivor will demonstrate readiness to build a new life as a single person.	Attempt to develop a therapeutic relationship through touch, empathy, and listening Listen to perceived feelings Help person realise that grief is a painful but normal transitional process Encourage use of other women, daughters, widows, men and friends as support systems Encourage balance between linking phenomena (mementoes, photographs, clothes, furniture) associated with the deceased and the bridging phenomena (new driving skills, evening classes, new job) Establish contact with CRUSE for counselling if appropriate Refer to appropriate agencies
Anxiety related to increased legal, financial and decision-making responsibilities		
Manifestations: tearful, crying, sleep disturbance, weight pain, compulsive eating, weight loss, anorexia, fatigue, confusion, forgetfulness, withdrawal, disinterest, indecisiveness, inability to concentrate, guilt feelings: displays feelings of detachment, inferiority, rejection, alienation, emptiness, isolation; unable to initiate social contacts; seeks attention	*Short-term intermediate goals:* the survivor will demonstrate adequate decision-making skills in financial and legal matters as evidenced by seeking legal aid, writing or calling appropriate agencies, formulating a realistic budget *Long-term goals:* the survivor will cope with legal, financial, and decision-making responsibilities with only a moderate degree of anxiety, and make rational decisions about singe life	Assist in obtaining lawyer if necessary Encourage to contact social security and/or spouse's employer to assure receipt of all benefits Encourage to contact insurance agencies if applicable Discourage immediate decision-making regarding assets (e.g. home, stocks, etc.) Encourage to seek advice from individuals who are trusted Contact proper social agencies if indigent or in need Assist in seeking employment if health permits and client so desires Offer alternatives for decision-making Refer to any other proper community agencies that offer needed assistance

Source: Alexander and Kiely, 1986.

Table 21.3 Nursing Care Plan for Survivors

KEY POINTS

- Towards the end of life, some older people may achieve a sense of being which transcends the material and physical limitations of existence.
- Older people sometimes discover new insights on the meaning of life as a result of illness and approaching death.
- Older people may find strength through religious or spiritual beliefs. It is the role of any member of the multidisciplinary team to address these aspects of support as part of providing holistic care.
- Legacies can consist of tangible and intangible assets and represent an individual's contribution to the world.
- Phases of dying, such as those suggested by Kübler-Ross, may not be so relevant to death at the end of the natural life span.
- The hospice and palliative care movement are gradually influencing care of the dying, in a wider context.
- Euthanasia is illegal in the UK and the law is unlikely to change. Concern centres round the excessive use of medical treatment at the end of life and inappropriate resuscitation decisions.
- Phases of grief and tasks of mourning can increase our understanding of the grieving process. Loss of a loved one is made no less acceptable by its occurrence in later life.

AREAS AND ACTIVITIES FOR STUDY AND REFLECTION

- Reflect on if and how the spiritual and religious needs of older people are assessed and addressed in your own working environment. How could the team take this on?
- Consider your own feelings about looking after older people who are dying. What helps you with this complex process?
- What factors in your own cultural background do you think influence your beliefs about death? How might these relate to your practice?
- How might you respond to an older person who asks if he is dying?
- Are advanced directives being discussed or used in your own practice area? What are your own feelings about these issues and how might you begin to discuss them with the team.
- When would you consider it appropriate to refer an older person for further help with their bereavement?

REFERENCES

Aarons EJ, Beeching NJ. Survey of "do not resuscitate" orders in a district general hospital. *Br Med J* 1991, 303:1504–1506.

Alexander J, Kiely J. Working with the bereaved. *Geriatr Nurs* 1986, 7:85.

Baro F, Keirse M, Wouters M. Spousal bereavement in the elderly. *Health Promotion* 1986, 1:1.

Benner P. *From novice to expert: Excellence and power in clinical nursing practice*. California: Addison-Wesley, 1984.

Berg S *et al*. Loneliness in the Swedish aged. *J Gerontol* 1981, 3:342.

Botwinick J *et al*. Predicting death from behavioural test performance. *J Gerontol* 1978, 33:755.

Bowling A. Mortality after bereavement: A review of the literature on survival periods and factors affecting survival. *Soc Sci Med* 1987, 24:117–124.

Bowling A, Cartwright A. *Life after death*. London: Tavistock, 1982.

Bradshaw A. *Lighting the lamp: the spiritual dimension of nursing care*. London: Scutari Press, 1994.

Bradshaw A. Teaching spiritual care to nurses: an alternative approach. *Int J Pall Nurs* 1997, 3:51–57

Brewer EDC. Researching religion and aging: an unlikely scenario. In: Oliver DB, ed. *New directions in religion and aging*. New York: Haworth Press, 1986.

Bruce-Jones P, Roberts H, Bowker L, Cooney V. Resuscitating the elderly: what do the patients want? *J Med Ethics* 1996, 22:154–159.

Buckman R. *I Don't know what to say*. London: Macmillan, 1988.

Burnard P. Why care? Ethical and spiritual issues in caring in nursing. In: Brykczynska G, ed. *Caring: the compassion and wisdom of nursing*. London: Edward Arnold, 1997.

Cartwright A, Seale C. *The natural history of a survey: an account of the methodological issues encountered in a study of life before death*, London, 1990, King's Fund.

Cartwright A. Dying when you're old. *Age Ageing* 1993, 22:425–430

Cartwright A, Hockey L, Anderson JL. *Life before death*. London: Routledge, 1973.

Cole TR. The aging spirit: agism and the journey of life in America, *Aging Today* 13(4):17, 1992

Courtney BC, Poon LW, Martin P *et al*. Religiosity and adaptation in the oldest-old. In: Poon LW, ed. *The Georgia centenarian study*. Amityville: Baywood, 1992.

Craig GM. On withholding nutrition and hydration in the terminally ill: has palliative medicine gone too far? *J Med Ethics* 1994, 20:139–143.

Craig GM. On withholding artificial hydration and nutrition from terminally ill sedated patients. The debate continues. *J Med Ethics* 1996, 22:147–153.

Dautzenberg PLJ, Broekman TCJ, Hooyer C, Schonwetter RS, Duursma SA. Review: patient-related predictors of cardiopulmonary resuscitation of hospitalized patients. *Age Ageing* 1993, 22:464–475.

Davie G. *Religion in Britain since 1945: believing without belonging*. Oxford: Blackwell, 1994.

Dessonville CL, Thompson LW, Gallagher D. The role of anticipatory bereavement in the adjustment to widowhood in the elderly. *Gerontologist* 1983, 23:309.

Dickenson D, Johnson M, eds. *Death, dying and bereavement*. London: Sage, 1993.

Doyal L, Wilsher D. Withholding cardiopulmonary resuscitation: proposals for formal guidelines. *Br Med J* 1993, 306:1593–1596.

Dunphy K, Finlay I, Rathbone G, Gilbert J, Hicks F. Rehydration in palliative and terminal care: if not- why not? *Pall Med* 1995, 9:271–228.

Firth S. Approaches to death in Hindu and Sikh communities in Britain. In: Dickenson D, Johnson M, eds. *Death, dying and bereavement*. London: Sage, 1993.

Frankl V. *Man's search for meaning*. London: Hodder & Stoughton, 1987.

Frankl V. *The unheard cry for meaning: psychotherapy and humanism*. New York: Simon and Schuster, 1990.

Fry PS. A factor analytic investigation of home-bound elderly individuals' concern about death and dying and their coping responses. *J Clin Psychology* 1991, 46:737.

Glaser B, Strauss A. *Awareness of dying*. Chicago: AVC, 1963.

Goldberg E, Comstock G, Harlow S. Emotional problems of widowhood. *J Gerontol* 1988, 43:206.

Goodman M, Rubinstein RL, Alexander BB, Luborsky M. Cultural differences among elderly women in coping with the death of an adult child. *J Gerontol* 1991, 46:321.

Green J. *Death with dignity: meeting the spiritual needs of patients in a multi-cultural society*. London: Macmillan Press, 1993.

Haase JE, Britt T, Coward DD *et al*. Simultaneous concept analysis of spiritual perspective, hope, acceptance and self-transcendence. *Image J Nurs Sch* 1992, 24:141.

Hess PA. Loss, grief, dying. In: Beare P, Myer J, eds. *Principles and practices of adult health nursing, 2nd edition*. St Louis: Mosby, 1994.

Hill C, Thompson L, Gallagher D. The role of anticipatory bereavement in older women's adjustment to widowhood. *Gerontologist* 1988, 23:792.

Hockey J. *Experiences of death. An anthropological account*. Edinburgh: Edinburgh University Press, 1990.

Johns CC. Developing a reflective model for nursing. *Nurs Times* 1996, 92:39–41.

Kalish RA. The social context of death and dying. In: Binstock RH, Shanas E, eds. *Handbook of ageing and the social sciences*. New York: Van Nostrand Reinhold, 1985.

Kübler-Ross E. On death and dying. New York: MacMillan, 1969.

Lentzner HR, Pamuk ER, Rhodenhiser EP *et al*. The quality of life in the year before death. *Am J Public Health* 1992, 82:1093.

Lindley DB. Process of dying. Defining characteristics. *Cancer Nurs* 1991, 14:328.

Lugton J. *Communicating with dying people and their relatives*. London: Austen Cornish, 1988.

Mead GE, Turnbull CJ. Cardiopulmonary resuscitation in the elderly: patients' and relatives' views. *J Med Ethics* 1995, 21:39–44.

Mellor PA, Shilling C. Modernity, self-identity and the sequestration of death. *Sociology* 1993, 27:411–431.

Menzies I. The functioning of social systems as a defence against anxiety. (A report on a study of the nursing service of a general hospital.) 1959: Reprinted in: Menzies I. *Containing anxiety in institutions. Selected essays*. London: Free Association Books, 1988.

National Council for Hospice and Specialist Palliative Care Services. Open doors: improving access to hospice and specialist palliative care services by members of the Black and ethnic minority communities, London, 1994.

Neuberger J. Cultural issues in palliative care. In: Doyle D, Hanks GWC, Macdonald N, eds. *Oxford textbook of palliative medicine*. Oxford: Oxford University Press, 1993.

Neuberger J. *Caring for people of different faiths, 2nd edition*. London: Austen Cornish, 1994.

Newman M. Aging as increasing complexity. *J Gerontol Nurs* 1987, 13:16.

Office of Population Censuses and Surveys. *Mortality statistics*, London, 1992, HMSO.

O'Neill J. Ethnic minorities-neglected by palliative care providers? *J Cancer Care* 1994, 3:215–220.

Parkes CM. The first year of bereavement: a longitudinal study of the reaction of London widows to the death of their husbands. *Psychiatry* 1970, 4:444–467.

Parkes CM. *Bereavement. Studies of grief in adult life, 2nd edition*. Harmondsworth: Penguin Books, 1986.

Peberdy A. Spiritual care of dying people. In: Dickenson D, Johnson M, eds. *Death, dying and bereavement*. London: Sage, 1993.

Retsinas J. A theoretical reassessment of the applicability of Kübler-Ross's stages of dying. *Death Studies* 1988, 12:207.

Ross L. The nurse's role in assessing and responding to patients' spiritual needs. *Int J Pall Nurs* 1997, 3:37–42

Roy DJ. Euthanasia: taking a stand. *J Pall Care* 1990, 6:3–5.

Royal College of Nursing and British Medical Association. *Cardiopulmonary resuscitation*, A statement from the RCN and the BMA, London, 1993, Royal College of Nursing.

Saunders CM. The philosophy of terminal care. In: Saunders CM, ed. *The management of terminal disease*. London: Edward Arnold, 1978.

Sayers GM, Schofield I, Aziz M. An analysis of CPR decision-making by elderly patients. *J Med Ethics* 1997, 23:207–212.

Seale C. Demographic change and the care of the dying, 1969–1987. In: Dickenson D, Johnson M, eds. *Death, dying and bereavement*. London: Sage, 1993.

Steeves R, Kahn D. Experience of meaning in suffering. *Image J Nurs Sch* 1987, 19:114.

Stoll R. Guidelines for spiritual assessment. *Am J Nurs* 1979, 79:1574.

Sutcliffe J, Holmes S. Dehydration: burden or benefit to the dying patient? *J Adv Nurs* 1994, 19:71–76.

Twycross R. Assisted death: a reply. In: Dickenson D, Johnson M, eds. *Death, dying and bereavement*. London: Sage, 1993.

Walter T. Sociologists never die: British sociology and death. In: Clark D, ed. *The sociology of death*. Oxford: Blackwell, 1993.

Walter T. *The revival of death*. London: Routledge, 1994.

Walter T. The ideology and organisation of spiritual care: three approaches. *Pall Med* 1997, 11:21–30.

Watson-Druee N. Culture, ethnicity and religion. In: Heath HBM, ed. *Foundations in nursing theory and practice*. London: Mosby, 1995.

White N, Cunningham WR. Is terminal drop pervasive or specific? *J Gerontol* 1988, 43:141.

Wilkinson S. Factors which influence how nurses communicate with cancer patients. *J Adv Nurs* 1991, 16:677–688.

Worden JW. *Grief counselling and grief therapy*. London: Routledge, 1991.

Young M, Cullen L. *A good death: conversations with East Londoners*. London: Routledge, 1996.

Young M, Benjamin B, Wallis C. The mortality of widowers. *Lancet* 1963, 2:454–456.

FURTHER READING

Forster M. Have the men had enough? An account of the care and death of an older family member through the eyes of several generations. 1994

Shields C. *The stone diaries*. London: Fourth Estate, 1993.

USEFUL ADDRESSES

Information for Health Professionals

National Council for Hospice and Specialist Palliative Care Services
59 Bryanston Street
London W1A 2AZ
Tel. 0171 611 1153
Coordinating and representative organisation for hospice and palliative care services in UK (except Scotland).
Publishes quarterly newsletter and occasional papers.

Hospice Information Service
St Christopher's Hospice
51 Lawrie Park Road
Sydenham
London SE26 6DZ
Tel. 0181 778 9212
Maintains directories of palliative care services in the UK and abroad. Collects statistics on palliative care provision.

Help the Hospices
34-44 Britannia Street
London WC1X 9JG
Tel. 0171 278 5668
Provides grants for hospices for education and training. Supports courses and conferences in all fields related to palliative care.

National Association of Bereavement Services
20 Norton Folgate
London E1 6DB
Tel. 0171 247 0617
Support organisation for bereavement services. Publishes the National Directory of Bereavement and Loss Services.

Information and Support for patients and carers

Macmillan Cancer Relief
15/19 Britten Street
London
SW3 3TZ
Tel. 0171 351 8711
National charity working to help improve the quality of life for people with cancer. Funds professional posts and education and provides grants for patients in financial need.

Marie Curie Cancer Care
28 Belgrave Square
London SW1X 8OG
Tel. 0171 235 3321
Provision of hospice services through centres throughout the UK. Marie Curie nurses provide nursing care to people with cancer at home. The service is free to the patient.

CRUSE Bereavement Care
Cruse House
126 Sheen Road
Richmond
Surrey TW9 1UR
Tel. 0181 940 4818
National organisation for anyone bereaved by death. Offers a counselling service and practical advice. Local branches exist throughout the UK.

The development of nursing with older people
Hazel Heath and Pauline Ford

LEARNING OBJECTIVES

After studying this chapter you will be able to:

- Discuss key demographic and social changes which influence the development of nursing older people.
- Discuss changes taking place in the structure of the nursing workforce, and the implications of these.
- Discuss how nurses can effectively seek the views of older people as consumers of health care.
- Discuss health and social policy developments concerning long-term care, technological and pharmaceutical advances, and healthy lifestyles, and the opportunities for nursing within these.

- Discuss key issues for education in order to prepare the nursing workforce of the future.
- Discuss how nurses can develop their research-base for practice and clinical effectiveness, and influence the research agenda for the future.
- Discuss the key themes within the newly emerging roles for nurses working with older people.
- Discuss the potential for gerontological nurse specialists and practitioners.
- Discuss the strengths, weaknesses, opportunities and threats within the current situation and suggest an agenda for action.

INTRODUCTION

Major changes in British society, social policy, health-care systems and consumer expectations influence the evolution and development of nursing and nursing roles with older people. This chapter examines the influences on those changes, the emerging trends in the demography of the older population, the shifting of societal expectations, the characteristics of the nursing workforce and developments in health and social care In particular it examines emerging opportunities for nurses working with older people. It highlights new roles developed by individual nurses who have revised and refined their ways of working in response to trends, or as a result of innovative, imaginative forward thinking. The chapter also examines the implications of current and projected changes for nursing education and research.

DEMOGRAPHIC CONTEXT

Demographic patterns relating to older people are discussed in Chapters 1, 14 and 19, but the main features of current population projections can be summarised as follows (House of Commons Health Committee, 1996):

- The older population is ageing. In the immediate future, while there is expected to be a slight fall in the numbers of younger elderly people, there are parallel rises in the numbers aged over 75 years and over 80 years.
- The total older population is expected to continue to grow, particularly during the first two decades of the next century.

- Between 2020 and 2030 a further increase of 20% is projected.

Reflecting on the biographies discussed in Chapter 1, in 2030, when the oldest old population is reaching its peak, a person born in 1940 will be 90 years of age and a person born in 1975 will be 55 years of age. As consumers of health care, people from these generations will be influenced by their own unique life histories and experiences. They will be different to those who currently are old. It is often said that future generations of older people will be more aware of their rights, but conversely they may have adopted a philosophy of taking responsibility for their own health, and be more willing to contribute financially.

Demographic and social changes are also impacting on the nursing workforce. One major shift in the profile of the population of nurses on the United Kingdom Central Council for Nursing, Midwifery and Health Visiting (UKCC) register is that the nursing profession has 'aged' rapidly in recent years. A survey conducted by the Institute of Employment Studies (IES) showed that more than 1 in 10 of those on the register are aged 55 years or over, including 4% who are aged 60 years and over (Seccombe & Smith, 1997). In the next 5 years the number of registrants aged over 55 will nearly double. The authors of the survey suggested that many of these older practitioners are unlikely to be available for nursing employment and should be discounted from the potential pool.

Another IES Survey (Seccombe & Smith, 1996) highlighted that a large proportion of nurses aged 45–49 years come within the scope of early and normal retirement ages for nurses. This survey concluded that up to one-quarter of nurses currently working could retire by the millennium (**Figure 22.1**). The statistical analysis of nurses on the effective register of the UKCC as at 31st March 1997 shows that 46% are aged 45 years

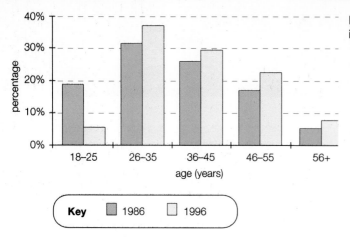

Figure 22.1 Age profiles of NHS nurses in 1986 and 1996.

Key   1986   1996

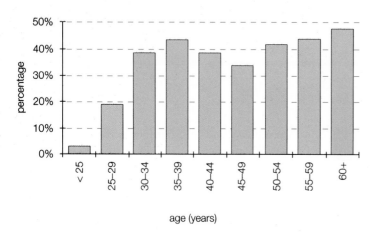

Figure 22.2 NHS nurses working part-time, by age group. (Source: Seccombe and Smith, 1996, p. 5)

and above. A high proportion of older nurses work part-time (**Figure 22.2**).

Simultaneously, initial entries to the register from education in the UK have reduced by more than 11.1% between the years 1990–1991 and 1995–1996. This reflects both the falling level of intakes into nursing education and the cessation of intakes into enrolled nurse education. Over the next 2 or 3 years the level of initial entries will reduce even more sharply, reflecting cutbacks in the number of nurse education places commissioned in recent years. At the same time, the number of nurses not renewing their registration has more than doubled. The inflows of nurses from abroad are comparatively small and tend to fluctuate, but the number applying for admission from nurses qualifying abroad has all but halved over the last 5 years (IES, 1997).

Comparing the projected demographics of older people with those of the nursing workforce, it seems clear that nurses will always be in demand to work with older people. In fact, the statistical analysis of the professional register of the UKCC for November 1997 shows that the major area of practice for nurses working both full-time and part-time, and in both the National Health Service and the independent sector, was the care of older people (UKCC, 1997) (**Figure 22.3**). In addition to the nursing of older people being the main area of practice, it should be remembered

that a high percentage of patients in the other main areas, such as community nursing, general medical, general surgical and mental health will also be pensioners.

As populations and health-care systems change, the one constant is the consumer of the service – the person whom the system claims to serve. The key to 'getting it right' is to truly understand the needs, wishes and aspirations of the older person who is receiving the care. We believe that the most logical way of planning and evaluating current and future services for older people is to ask the older people themselves.

SEEKING THE VIEWS OF OLDER PEOPLE

The 'Consumer Movement'

In recent years, there has been a steadily growing emphasis on the quality of information being given to patients and the public in order that they become more involved in planning and evaluating health-care services. Throughout the UK, there are varied schemes that seek to obtain the views of older people. Many of these emphasise that older people are the largest section of health service users.

(A) Full-time practice

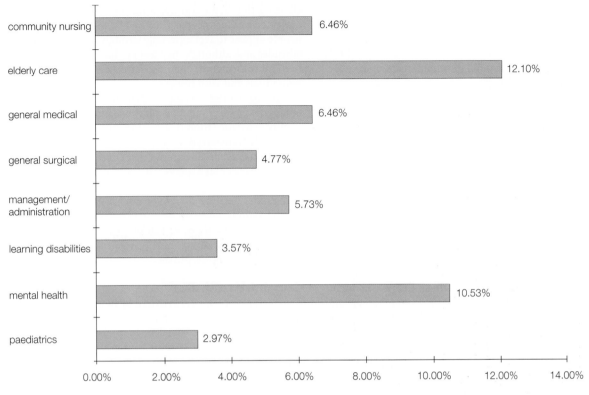

(B) Part-time practice

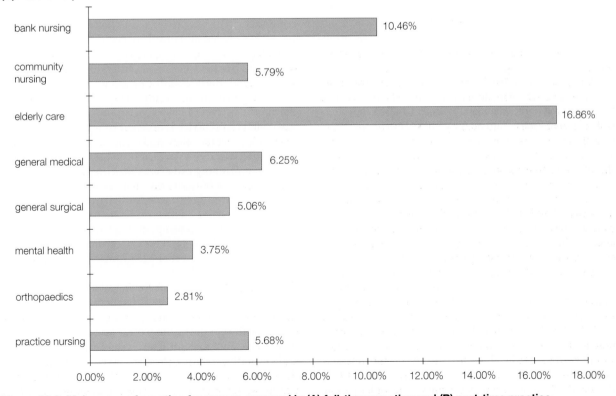

Figure 22.3 Main areas of practice for nurses engaged in (A) full-time practice and (B) part-time practice (Source: UKCC, 1997).

Recent reports have recommended a range of consumer measures. Farrell and Gilbert (1997) suggest consumer health information centres at regional level, in trusts and general practitioner surgeries and strengthening of consumer health councils in their role of consulting local people. Hope (1997) calls for patients to be given full information about the effectiveness of different medical treatments so that they can participate in decisions about their care, and also for patients to be involved in setting the agenda in medical research. Entwistle *et al.* (1997) conclude that information about how treatments work should be available through telephone helplines, health information shops, community health councils and libraries.

Citizens' juries are an area of particular interest. These are small groups of people, selected through market research techniques to represent a cross-section of the community. They meet to discuss questions posed by local commissioning authorities and consider evidence presented by witnesses. At the end of the session, the jury draws conclusions and, although these are not binding, the commissioning authorities usually agree in advance to publish the jury's conclusions, respond to recommendations within a set time and either follow the suggestions or publicly explain why they do not intent to do so. Citizens' juries have, as yet, no official status in the UK but the Institute of Public Policy Research (IPPR) is developing a British model to be a regular part of the decision-making process. There are concerns as to whether juries could truly represent all sections of the population, particularly people who are disadvantaged by physical disability, mental vulnerability or not understanding the English language.

A group comprising representatives of consumer organisations has also been set up to advise the Central Research Development Committee (CRDC) on how patients could be more involved in influencing the research and development programme of the National Health Service. The group includes representatives of the National Consumer Council, the Carers' National Association, and the Alzheimer's Disease Society.

Older People as Consumers

The concept of consumerism implies that the user of the service has freedom of choice and the necessary information to exercise an informed choice. Whether all older people, and particularly those who are vulnerable, or who are disadvantaged in their contacts with society, such as those in care homes, are actually consumers is arguable (Nazarko, 1997). For example, the literature clearly demonstrates that only a minority of older people have any choice in which home they enter (Reed and Payton, 1996).

The most common method of service evaluation is the patient and customer satisfaction survey. Many studies have shown that the older the respondents, the higher the satisfaction levels (Bartlett, 1995; Fitzpatrick, 1991; O'Leary, 1992), but the results are not merely related to the age factor. The method of eliciting older people's views has a profound effect

on how those views are expressed. The attitude of the person eliciting the views also has a marked effect on the views expressed by older people. Cornwell (1989) reports that older people appear to feel especially strongly about professional attitudes and, although they seem to have intense feelings of need for information, they also have a desire to be treated as individuals and with respect.

Brooker (1997) suggests that often the tools used to obtain the views of older people are inappropriate, and often quality assurance tools developed with younger age groups are simply transferred to older people without reference to their special needs. She argues that consideration should be given to particular aspects when obtaining older people's views:

- The older person's current health status.
- Expectations.
- Reluctance to criticise or fear of repercussions.
- Cognitive functioning.
- The use of carers as proxies.

Current Health Status

The health problems experienced by older people can affect their ability to participate in interviews or focus groups and to read questionnaires (Bartlett, 1995). For example, 96% of people over the age of 80 years have great difficulty in reading 12 point print, even with spectacles (Royal College of Optometrists, 1995). Other challenges may include hearing impairment, breathlessness or pain that prevents a person sitting comfortably for the required time. However, the influence of an older person's poor health status, low mood or low self-esteem on their expressed satisfaction is unclear and more research is needed into this (Brooker, 1997).

Expectations

Expectations about health care are a key determinant of degree of satisfaction (LeBow, 1983), and high satisfaction may be an artefact of low expectations (Brooker, 1997). As highlighted in Chapter 1, different cohorts of older people may have different values and expectations. This is a result of differing experiences in their formative years (particularly so for people whose early years were lived in poverty), their present criteria of need and what gives them satisfaction. People born from 1948 onwards will have lived all their lives in the welfare state and their expectations will be free health care as a right of citizenship, although these perceptions are now beginning to change. Research on different expectations of health care in differing age groups is sparse (Medical Research Council, 1994).

Bartlett (1995) suggests that for older people, and particularly the oldest old, their expectations of institutional life may be very low indeed and possibly influenced to some extent by images of the old workhouse system and consequent reluctance to depend on 'welfare'.

Older people may not be accustomed to being asked their opinion (O'Leary, 1992). For example, in Ford's (1995) research one woman in her nineties said that throughout her life no-one had ever asked for her views. Older adults may also be more inclined to wish that their health-care decisions would be made for them.

Reluctance to Criticise or Fear of Repercussions

The power balance between a health and social-care professional and an older person within the health and social-care system, particularly one who is ill or feeling vulnerable, can profoundly influence an older person's willingness to comment critically about the services being received. The reluctance may be compounded by feelings of dependence or the fear of repercussions.

Older people in care homes are highly dependent on the staff. Fear of repercussions is likely to be a greater inhibitor of negative responses in older people than other age groups (Brooker, 1997; Bartlett, 1995). Clark and Bowling (1989) concluded that the older people in their study, older residents in long-stay care, were reluctant to reveal their feelings, probably due to low expectations and fears of repercussions if they expressed criticism. Typical expressions were, 'It isn't for me to say', 'It's alright', 'I'm thankful there are people to take care of me', 'I don't have any likes, I just take what I get. If people do things for you, you can't grumble' (p. 128).

Assumptions about Cognitive Functioning

One of the common stereotypes which influences research with older people is that their attention span may be limited or their memory unreliable. This assumption is unfounded in reality. In addition, useful insights can be gained even from people whose cognitive functioning is impaired (National Consumer Council, 1990) and observational tools have now been developed which can provide a holistic and patient-centred way of monitoring a person's responses to the care and environment (Brooker, 1995). An example of this is dementia care mapping (*see* Chapter 18).

Seeking the Views of Carers or Significant Others

When there are perceived to be difficulties with obtaining feedback from older service users, the views of relatives or carers may be sought. Carers can offer valuable insight into the views and experiences of an older person. However, the views of the older person and carer may be different and it should not automatically be assumed that the views of a carer can be used as a proxy for those of an older person (Epstein *et al.* 1989). Feedback from relatives or carers will naturally be influenced by their own experiences and feelings, and collecting feedback from carers is important and valuable in its own right (Brooker, 1997).

Methodological Considerations

The King's Fund Centre (1991) emphasises that self-completion questionnaires and similar type of survey do not work with older people and state that older people often find it much easier to talk about their experiences in an interview situation than to respond to the impersonal format of a questionnaire.

Brooker (1997) concludes that the most effective way in which to achieve reliable results from older people is a one-to-one structured interview, as many of the misunderstandings that might otherwise occur can only be dealt with in this context. She suggests that:

- The interview should take place in a setting that is physically comfortable for the older person, remembering chair heights, lighting and temperature, and freedom from background noise.
- Verbal communication can be reinforced by large-print visual prompts.
- The skills and attitude of the interviewer are important.
- Special attention needs to be paid to privacy, and to assurances regarding the confidentiality of the feedback.
- Jargon or terminology, which the older person may misunderstand, should be avoided.

A particularly effective method of obtaining an older person's feedback is to invite them to relate their experiences. As the older person describes their experiences, and the narrative unfolds, the reality of each situation becomes clear. Observation can also be a useful method for accessing the reality of a health-care situation (King's Fund Centre, 1991), and focus groups of older people can be used to develop research tools.

Reliability of Research with Older People

Assumptions may be made about the reliability of feedback given by older people, particularly those who are physically or mentally frail. In reviewing literature on research with frail older people, Phillips (1992) suggests that an assumption underlying the discussions is that older respondents may be impaired or under-educated. However, older people can and do give accurate and valuable feedback. Rogers and Herzog (1987) found that people aged 70 years and over were more accurate on survey interviews than younger respondents.

Successive studies have demonstrated that even the most vulnerable or frail older people in care homes are able to effectively give their views. Ford (1995) concluded that 'older people who are patients in continuing care settings are some of the most highly dependent and disadvantaged members of society'. Despite this, her study demonstrates that they have a clear view of what nurses and nursing mean to them. 'They know what they want and what they value' (p. 64).

Validity of Research with Older People

Phillips (1992) states that 'currently, the single most important measurement challenge facing nurse researchers who study frail elders is the validity of measurement'. She suggests that validity has been addressed in a very limited fashion, and that three types of validity are of special importance for measuring the findings of research involving frail older people. These are construct validity, content validity and norm-referenced versus criterion-referenced validity.

Construct validity concerns the meaning of the concepts or key ideas being investigated in the research. Attention needs to be paid to terminology as different generations may interpret the same word differently, particularly a very old person and a much younger researcher. For example, when asked if she would be prepared to take part in some research, one woman interpreted the term 'research' to mean 'being experimented upon'.

Content validity difficulties arise when the aspects covered by the research tool are not those most relevant to the research informant. These are particularly likely to occur when research tools or instruments are borrowed from younger age groups to be used with older people. For example, a survey asked a range of questions to establish patients' satisfaction with the service offered during the first 24 hours of their admission to hospital. One patient responded positively to all the questions because aspects such as the politeness of staff, food and noise levels were to his satisfaction. Unfortunately, the questionnaire did not allow him to say that his first 24 hours had been very difficult because he did not have his hearing aid or usual analgesia and he was therefore in pain from his arthritis. The content of the research tool was not valid in identifying the reality of his experiences and was, therefore, not a valid measure of his satisfaction. Content validity difficulties can be overcome to some extent by rechecking the results with an older person in a subsequent interview.

Considerations of whether results are norm-referenced or criterion-referenced can also be important. Norm-referencing is when results are compared with standards or test scores from a large, representative sample which is considered to be the 'norm'. Results collected from a group of older people measured against a 'norm' obtained from a sample of much younger people will not produce valid results as they are not comparing like with like. In criterion-referencing, scores on a particular research instrument are correlated with some external criterion. Again, the criterion being compared to results obtained from a group of older people needs to be valid for that specific group.

HEALTH AND SOCIAL POLICY FOR OLDER PEOPLE

The health and social-care agenda for older people is substantial, as almost every aspect of health and social-care policy development impacts on older people. The millennium has provided a focus for debating the future of health and social policy. For example, for 'The Debate of the Age', Age Concern England has established a number of groups who are charged with various tasks. The health and social-care group, which comprises key organisations, representatives and 'stakeholders' in health and social care for older people, has determined three areas which it considers to be those of

prime importance for the future (Age Concern, 1997):
- Long-term care.
- Health futures and rationing health care.
- Healthy lifestyles and health promotion.

Current policy and emerging trends in each of these areas will now be discussed, together with the implications for older people and the nurses who work with them.

Long-term Care (LTC)

In addressing LTC a broad range of services must be considered. Essentially, the focus should be on older peoples' needs for care in the long-term, wherever that care is provided. LTC includes personal and nursing care and other forms of support that may be required, such as domestic help. It does not include acute medical and nursing care.

Current policy in this area was set out in the 1989 White Paper *Caring for People* and was enacted in the subsequent National Health Service (NHS) and Community Care Act, which took effect in 1993 (Secretaries of State, 1989).

The White Paper had three central objectives:
1. Enabling people to live as normal a life as possible in their own homes or in a homely environment in the community.
2. Providing the right amount of care and support to help people achieve maximum possible independence.
3. Giving people a greater say over how they live their lives and the support they need to help them to do so.

Such values as independence and autonomy gained considerable support in both the policy community and among users of social care services. However, for the specific objective of 'supported independence' to be achieved, a major barrier needs to be overcome (Harding *et al.* 1996; Joseph Rowntree Inquiry, 1996).

The division between health and social-care services is considered by many to be both artificial and unhelpful. Health services are funded from general taxation and are generally free at the point of use. Social services are the responsibility of the local authority and are subject to means testing and charging. The continual dialogue regarding definitions of 'health' or 'social need' is generally unhelpful for the user who just needs the service. The outcome, however, is all important to the user who, if his or her needs are defined as 'health', will be offered care free of charge but, if they are deemed to be 'social', will be means tested and may be charged.

Such boundaries are not static, and it is clear that redefinition of certain health services such as social care is set to continue. Such developments are considered to be particularly controversial. Older people in particular regard this process as a change to the principles of care from the 'cradle to the grave' to which they have contributed and to which they believe they are entitled. Currently, older people report difficulties in accessing services which are fragmented and uncoordinated. Despite some considerable effort to resolve such problems they remain unresolved for those who have long-term and complex needs. The community care reforms have not resolved the structural problems of coordinating health and social services. Both older people and the nurses who work with them report that increasing numbers of users, who hitherto would have been assessed as requiring nursing care, are having their needs redefined as 'social'. There is also the fundamental issue that, as a result of these redefinitions, some older people who need nursing care are not receiving it.

The current Government focus on how health and social services should and could function will undoubtedly lead to significant changes. We would hope that any changes will reflect the need for:

- Transitional arrangements for people who are currently old.
- Coverage of carers (in terms of protected contributions and entitlement to an insurance based income replacement benefit).
- Coverage of services to ensure that LTC needs are addressed in domiciliary, residential and any other settings.
- The pattern of incentives arising from any given funding structure, and ways of influencing these, to achieve desired outcomes.

The virtues of integrating services has been considered (Kings Fund, 1997), and it remains to be seen whether the government will support such developments. Pooled budgets (Downey, 1997), locality commissioning and Health Action Zones all provide opportunities to support innovative developments focusing on a more integrated way of working. As a starting point, if we can achieve the prime consideration of the needs of individual older people, rather than the structure of the service, there will be greater opportunity for developing care services that are appropriate and flexible. In turn, the workforce will become more adaptable and creative.

The Single Registration Care Home

The provision and regulation of residential and nursing homes are governed by the Registered Homes Act 1984 for England and Wales, the Registered Establishments (Scotland) Act 1987 and the Registered Homes (Northern Ireland) Order 1992. For England, Wales and Scotland, residential care is defined as residential accommodation with personal care. Personal care is generally considered to be of the type that could be provided by a competent and caring relative. Residential homes are registered with local authority social services departments. Nursing and mental-nursing homes must, at all times, be in the charge of a person who is a registered nurse or registered medical practitioner. They register with the local health authority.

There is currently much debate surrounding the emergence of a single registration care home. As yet there is no widely agreed definition of what is meant by a single registration care home. There is some agreement that the current policy of insisting that people move if their needs change, for example from a residential to a nursing home, does not reflect a true focus on the needs of the older person.

There are many issues yet to be resolved before the single registration care home becomes a reality. These include the definition of such a home, how needs will be assessed, how the homes will respond to changing need, the staffing levels and skill mixes within the homes, how re-enablement approaches to care will be addressed, and quality assurance.

Various proposals have been offered. The Royal College of Nursing (RCN) suggests that a single registration care home is one within which 'all individuals have a nursing assessment undertaken by a skilled, expert nurse with that client group. Those residents who are assessed as having nursing care needs will have those needs planned, managed, taught, supervised and sometimes directly delivered by registered nurses' (RCN, 1997a). The RCN has also called for an independent nationally-trained single regulation inspection framework. Along with many others, the RCN believes that a single registration care home would offer flexibility of services along with a continuum of care, and would thus offer greater choice to people needing LTC. It would make the best utilisation of the valuable scarce resources of skilled nursing and social-care professionals, and would offer the opportunity to genuinely develop holistic care for people with complex needs.

Opportunities for Nursing

Demonstrating the Value of Nursing

In the current climate of LTC, the need to demonstrate the value of nursing through the measurement of outcomes from practice is receiving a new and important level of interest. When purchasers of care consider the cost-effectiveness and value for money elements of services provision, they need to be clear that nursing is both cost-effective and good value for money. A number of studies have now been undertaken which demonstrate this (Audit Commission, 1991; Bagust and Slack, 1991; Buchan and Ball, 1991; Carr-Hill et al. 1992; Buchan et al. 1996).

Clearly if nurses wish to argue that older people benefit from the interventions of expert and skilled nurses, then it is important that nurses are able to articulate what it is that they do which may make a difference to the health and wellbeing of an older person. Nurses have to identify the 'indicators' for nursing care, as distinct from those for trained and competently delivered personal care. Nurses then need to identify the knowledge, skill and experience used in any care scenario. The concept of expert practice encompasses clinical skills, knowledge and experience, along with an ability to problem solve (Benner, 1984).

All nurses should have core skills which maintain a safe standard of care for older people. Because of the complexities of older age, nurses need specific knowledge, skills and expertise to work with older people. Such knowledge, along with a positive approach to health in older age, should help nurses become skilled in understanding and responding to: age changes, psychological adjustment to growing older, altered presentation of disease, multiple pathology and adverse drug reactions.

An Example 'Indicator for Nursing'

The nurse's story

Although Mary had only lived in the home for about 2 months, I felt quite close to her. She had moved into the home because her daughter was no longer able to cope with both her and her husband, who had early dementia. They were a very close family and her daughter used to bring her dad to see Mary once a week, but seemed to feel particularly guilty at having to 'let mum go into a home'. Because Mary wasn't able to do very much for herself, she needed a great deal of care, and this gave us the opportunity to talk. She told me about her family life and how much she enjoyed working in a local shop, which she'd done for many years.

On the morning I came back from my days off she seemed different. It's difficult to put my finger on exactly what had changed but she seemed more sleepy, yet restless and a bit agitated. I just had a feeling that she was deteriorating. I kept a close eye in her. She was on a pressure relieving mattress and her skin was in good condition. Despite her difficulties with drinking and eating, we'd managed to keep her fairly well hydrated and nourished. We'd also got her analgesia sorted out with the general practitioner, and had managed to keep her pain free most of the time.

Towards the end of the afternoon I decided to ring Mary's daughter and let her know that her mother was unwell. She was very distressed and said she would come in the morning. By the following morning, Mary was obviously dying but she seemed peaceful and comfortable. When husband and daughter arrived I talked with them before they went into see Mary. They were reassured by how peaceful she looked and I encouraged them to talk to Mary, and to say what they felt they wanted to. Mary's husband didn't seem to take on board what was happening but talked to his wife and intermittently stroked her head.

It was way past the end of my shift but the daughter wanted me to stay. I don't think the evening staff particularly liked it, but I felt that Mary's daughter needed the support and that she had specifically asked me to stay.

Mary died peacefully later that evening, with her husband and daughter beside her.

The daughter was particularly grateful for the way her mother had died.

She rang the following day and we were able to advise her on some of the practical arrangements that needed to be made, and some of us went to the funeral. We still hear from Mary's daughter from time to time.

Table 22.1 An example 'indicator for nursing'.

In its publication *What a Difference a Nurse Makes*, the RCN (1997b) offered a framework of outcome definition for nurses to use in their practice areas. The framework assists with the identification and articulation of what it is that the expert nurse offers in relation to the care of an older person. It also identifies the specific knowledge, skills and experience that a nurse brings to a specific care scenario, thus enabling distinctions to be made from the intervention of someone without that specific knowledge, skills or experience (**Table 22.1**)

Assessing Older People

In a climate where the drive for cost containment results in health and nursing need being redefined as social, the role of assessment, and particularly the assessment of nursing need, is crucial. The lack of a tool that specifically assesses the nursing needs of an older person has exacerbated the difficulties. Nursing encompasses both health and social care but, in the current climate of division between these two, the value of nursing is often minimised. Because the health and social needs of older people are so interrelated, the divisions between health versus social care remain arbitrary and unworkable for nurses. Older people's needs for nursing can-

not easily be separated into a list of care tasks or activities, some 'health' and some 'social'. In fact, it is argued that such division undermines the holistic nature of professional nursing care (RCN, 1993; RCN, 1997c).

Building on the outcome indicator work, the RCN (1997c) developed a tool for assessing the nursing needs of older people and, uniquely, the type and amount of registered nurse (RN) care. The tool enables a nurse to make an assessment of:

1. An older person's abilities and need for care.
2. The stability and predictability of their health status, through which the need for a RN can be determined.
3. The level of nursing intervention required (i.e. management, supervision, directive care, actual care or no nursing care).
4. The amount of time each older person needs from the RN in any given category of care.
5. A consideration of the evidence needed to assist in illustrating the rationale for the decision-making.

Such an assessment tool could also contribute to the development of an integrated health and care service. If nurses can

An Example 'Indicator for Nursing'

Analysis of the contribution of the registered nurse to the care of Mary Edwards and her family

KNOWLEDGE – empirical
- The physical and psychological processes of adjustment to living in a care home, increased dependency and the end of life.
- Family dynamics and the importance of relationships. How to support families.
- How to maintain maximum health status and functioning, despite illness or disability.
- How to prevent health problems, or recognise them when they occur.
- The physiology and psychology of dying, and the potential effects of this on a family.
- How to promote comfort and rest.
- Pharmacology in pain relief, e.g. drugs combined for maximum palliation, delivery methods and adverse drug reactions.
- The scope of the role and accountability of the qualified nurse.

SKILLS
- Assessment skills, recognising the needs of Mary, her husband and family, and the other staff (particularly listening and observation skills).
- Skills of decision-making, weighing up the options of the situation.
- Interpersonal skills to support the patient in the expression of her wishes, and her husband and daughter. 'Being with' skills.
- Clinical nursing skills to help Mary achieve maximum physical and psychological comfort.
- Skills in using equipment e.g. for pressure relief, moving and handling, pain relief.
- Negotiation skills to work with, and support, other staff during difficult times.
- Intrapersonal skills to appreciate the effects of such a situation on self, and to seek help when appropriate.
- Coping skills.

EXPERIENCE
- Experience of such situations in the past, enabled the nurse to look at all the cues, including the subtle ones, and to prioritise, respond and act accordingly.
- Experience of practical steps to take after a death has occurred.

KNOWLEDGE – tacit
The instinctual appreciation of, for example:
- The changes which herald deterioration and/or death.
- How to be sensitive and supportive to someone who is dying.
- The importance of supporting Mary's husband and daughter.
- To do what feels to be right for Mary and her family, despite personal difficulties.

The outcome of the intervention of the registered nurse

- Mary had a peaceful and pain-free death.
- She died in the way in which she had wished, with her family around her.
- With support, Mary's daughter was able to accept the situation, and to support her father in his understanding.
- With advice, Mary's daughter was able to make funeral arrangements and to feel content that she had done her best for her mother.

The indicator for nursing

The registered nurse (RN) caring for complex health and psychosocial needs will perform an assessment in order to reveal the complex factors that may cause an altered health state. The RN understands the significance of presenting symptoms and how these might be relieved. The RN understands various combinations of interventions/treatments/therapies and their effets and drawn from a range of options for the relief of distress and the promotion of comfort. In each of these elements, the RN prioritises, balances and works with the needs of the patient, the family/significant others and other health/social care staff.

Table 22.1 An example 'indicator for nursing' (continued).

feel confident that they can identify and articulate their contribution to the care of an older person then they are more likely to feel positive about working in an open and collaborative way. The tool has been developed for use in the care homes sector, although it is anticipated that it may have uses in other settings.

Health Futures and Rationing Health Care

Technological Advances
Increasingly sophisticated and high-cost equipment is constantly being developed and improved. Medical technology and telematic interventions are both areas of rapid advancement impacting significantly on the provision of health and social-care services of older people. Such innovations increase the scope for diagnosis and for intervention. However, as the boundaries of what is technically possible are extended, questions inevitably arise both about whether such interventions are either economically justifiable, or ethically defensible. This is complex territory in which the debate as only just begun.

Technological developments will also facilitate more flexibility in the location of care. Benefits will include:
- More care in people's own homes.
- Direct access to care information and advice.
- Direct links with emergency services and support.
- Direct links with specialist knowledge and support.
- Two-way communication facilities.

As Laing and Buisson (1996) observed:
Telemedicine will accelerate the move towards hospital-at-home in various ways. It will enable current hospital-at-home procedures to be monitored more closely by specialists, so that those procedures are less dependent on the participation of the patient's general practitioner. The development of medical equipment which can communicate directly with the hospital will enable new treatments to be carried out at home.

(Laing and Buisson, 1996, p. 38)

Opportunities for Nursing
Nurses can utilise the developing technology in innovative and creative ways to enhance their practice, particularly in the context of an ageing population. Community Nurses are particularly well placed to be at the frontier in terms of developing new approaches to care. Technology could facilitate quicker discharge from hospital. It could also prevent or reduce hospital admissions as problems could be identified and communicated more instantly.

Pharmacological Advances
Advancements in drug treatment are being achieved at a steady pace, and there are predictions of imminent breakthroughs. In 1997, a new drug Aricept was the first to be licensed in Britain for the treatment of mild-to-moderate Alzheimer's disease (AD), and the potential benefits are being heralded as particularly exciting. Similar breakthroughs with other drug therapies for any number of chronic conditions can be anticipated, as can the debate regarding the cost of such treatments. It is estimated that Aricept would cost £80 per person per month, and considerable concern is being expressed about the feasibility of such expenditure. What is interesting is the comparison of £80 per month with the cost of alternative treatments for other client groups, or indeed with a comparison with the cost of residential care for the person with AD.

These are challenging decisions with which society must deal. It is surely appropriate that an elected Government take the lead in establishing some form of decision framework, rather than leaving such decisions as the responsibility of individual clinicians. The Government should produce the framework within which the clinicians can operate and apply clinical judgement and documented evidence to support their decision on whether an intervention is prescribed or not prescribed.

Integrated Acute Services
Linked to debates about rationing has been the development of integrated acute services for older people. Integrated units have resulted from the merger of specialist services for older people, generally with acute medical services. As all age ranges (other than children) are cared for in the same unit, it is argued that this prevents discrimination on the basis of age. However, it is hard to see how this in itself could prevent decisions regarding treatment being made on the basis of age rather than on the basis of clinical need.

In April 1998, the first wave of Trust mergers took place in England, Scotland and Northern Ireland. By April 1999, all trusts in Wales will have merged, and a further wave of mergers is planned for the following year. Mergers are central to the Government's vision for a new health service on the basis that joining services produces efficiency savings that can be diverted into patient care. When trusts merge, clinical and support services are reconfigured. The RCN has argued that patients' needs must be at the centre of merger plans and that:
- There is a demonstrable benefit for patients.
- Rationalisation is cost-effective (rather than cost cutting) and evidence-based where appropriate.
- The consultation process is adequate and in line with legal requirements; consultation must involve the local population, community health councils and professional organisations and unions.
- Within primary health-care service development, a public health focus should be maintained in order to meet national objectives relating to maximising health gain.
- The reduction in inequalities in health must be a key aim of any service development.
- Any reconfiguration of the workforce must be done with reference to accurate and up to date research and evidence, must retain a core professional identity for nurses. It must also safeguard the senior nurse and clinical specialist posts necessary to promote professional leadership for nurses in clinical care.

Clearly the merger of services will continue and, with the majority age group residing in hospital likely to be those aged over 65 years, there are strong economic arguments for integrated services. However, it is essential that the specific and special needs of older people are not overlooked in such services. The RCN has issued guidance on the provision of services for older people (**Box 22.1**)

22.1 RCN Guidance on Mergers: Principles of a Good Service for Older People

Older people have specific health needs which can be distinct, and additional, to those of the younger population. In order that these are met, older people require a range of services. The RCN believes that local services for older people must include:

- Health education.
- GP and primary health-care team intervention.
- Clinics for specific needs, e.g. memory clinic, falls clinic, pain clinic.
- Accident and emergency services that offer an explicit focus on the special needs of older people.
- Transportation services which are appropriate and responsive.
- Acute diagnostic services (delivered on one site to reduce the transfer and escort of older people while they are ill).
- Acute medical and surgical care.
- Rehabilitation/re-enablement services (which operate across primary–secondary care boundaries, especially on 'discharge' from acute care, and are delivered in whichever environment is appropriate to individual need).
- Multidisciplinary team assessment and review.
- Hospice/palliative care.
- Continuing health care.

The setting in which a service is delivered may change over time, but the overriding principles of the service should remain.

Essential characteristics of a good service for older people
A service for older people must have:
- A policy ensuring older people have equal access and priority to health care.
- An appropriate philosophy of care that encompasses the needs of older people.
- Standards and audit procedures which recognise the special needs for older people.
- An organisational structure that provides the most effective care and the most efficient delivery of that care, while making the best use of available resources in response to the local needs of older people.
- Access to skilled multidisciplinary carers, who can

recognise and meet the needs of the older person.
- The provision of a suitable environment that enables older people to reach and maintain their optimum physical and psychological functioning.
- An educational policy with adequate resources, that allows staff access to studying the care needs of that older person at an advanced level.

Criteria for good practice in units and services for older people
It is recommended that:
- The needs of older people are explicitly included in the service agreements and all quality specifications of contracts.
- Each unit or service develops policies and philosophies which reflect the special needs of the older person.
- Quality initiatives and audits, nursing and medical, meet the special needs of older people.
- Changes to the environment or organisation take account of the special needs of older people.
- Units and services demonstrate commitment to multidisciplinary working.
- Opportunities are available for the study of older people for all staff at appropriate levels, and for the professional updating and development of registered nurses to at least diploma or degree level.
- The skill mix reflects the needs of older people and includes specialist or advanced practitioners in caring for older people.
- Nursing practice reflects current research in relation to the care or older people.
- Further multidisciplinary research takes place into admission policies and outcomes of care in a variety of settings where older people are cared for.
- In acute care units, the recommendations in the Audit Commission report Lying in Wait – The Use of Medical /Beds in Acute Hospitals, 1992, Appendix iii are considered.
- Specialist units for older people act as resource centres for the development and dissemination of specialist skills and knowledge.
- Specialist units for older people aim to become centres of excellence and demonstrate a commitment to the enhancement and development of the speciality of caring for older people.

Rationing Health Care

The need to ration health and social-care service expenditure will continue to concentrate the minds of many and to dominate many debates relating to the older members of our population. Such debates tend to view older people in negative terms as the passive receivers of services and resources. This view overlooks the contributions that older people have made throughout their lives and presupposes that older people cannot contribute in any positive way, either now or in the future. It ignores any concept of reciprocity and disregards the valuable roles that older people play in society as well as in smaller social groups such as families. It also perpetuates the ignorant perspective of all older people as sick and in need of expensive treatment and care.

Rationing on the basis of age alone is thought by Roberts *et al.* (1996) to be immoral. In their view it is not a defensible position for a civilised society, particularly in the context of debates about 'wasted millions' in the health service. Roberts *et al.* do not accept that there is underfunding. Rather they consider the problem as one of pricing and resource management which, if addressed, would 'release enough resources for redeployment to eliminate any need to ration effective health care in the short to medium term future'.

The rationing of health and social care on age-based criteria is a highly emotive issue. The very notion that some people should be excluded from access to care is seen by many as anathema within a system which supposedly attaches value to principles of equity. It is likely, however, that there will be an increase in the tendency to restrict access to services and treatments. We believe that a clear framework is necessary, and that this should be developed at Government level. Such a framework would facilitate greater public debate, greater clarity in the debate and greater visibility in the decision-making.

Healthy Lifestyles

Perhaps one of the best ways of resolving some of the potential challenges of an ageing population would be to consider the impact of healthy lifestyles on the population generally and on older people in particular. Unfortunately, research into the prevention, or indeed reversal, of age-related disease and disability has been largely ignored, particularly in comparison to other areas of health research [Medical Research Council (MRC), 1994]. The reason for this is not clear but cynics might argue that if prevention increases longevity then it does so at the risk of an extended period of disability and suffering. As the MRC (1994) points out, there is no evidence to support such views. In fact, the evidence demonstrates that the later the onset of disease, the higher its fatality and therefore the shorter on average survival of its victims. The MRC also highlights the scope that now exists for reducing ill health in later life, particularly in areas such as cardiovascular disease and stroke (*see* Chapter 3 for further discussion of health and wellness promotion).

In 1996, the Health Education Authority commissioned a review, which was undertaken by the Centre for Policy on Ageing (CPA) (Dalley et al, 1996). This review distinguishes between approaches to healthy ageing and health promotion for those who are already old.

> *Healthy ageing can be seen as a legitimate goal of health promotion activities irrespective of age. It is an aspect of the benefits conferred by lifelong health promotion and is relevant, therefore, to the whole population. If we were to ask what activities or interventions do most to promote healthy ageing, we should have to consider the opportunities for health promotion across the whole course of a human life – from foetus to very old age – with the goal of healthy ageing in mind.*
>
> (Dalley et al, 1996)

This kind of life span approach would seem highly relevant, appropriate and fair. The review highlights the well-established concept of 'successful ageing' which is generally characterised by the preservation of functional ability. Maintaining physical and mental activity is seen to be the key to successful ageing. If we could truly develop a positive approach to ageing then the potential to reduce discomfort, distress and disability is significant. As the report suggests:

> *The 'dividends' that could be yielded by effective health promotion for older people include not only health benefits. However, if it is possible to shorten the period of time for which expensive medical services are required or postpone the kind of loss of independence which usually requires long-term nursing or social care, then there will also be major cost savings, some of which will accrue to older people themselves.*
>
> (Dalley et al, 1996, p. 9)

A new emphasis on recuperative care, rehabilitation and public health has arrived with the change in Government. As a result, it may be possible to approach health promotion in relation to older people in a more creative and visionary manner. A Green Paper with new targets to replace some of the *Health of the Nation* objectives was issued in the spring of 1998 and a review of public health functions and inequality took place in the winter of 1997 as part of the work on the NHS.

We believe it is vital that the health and wellbeing of the older members of society should be seen as integral to any new debate about reducing health inequalities. We would also argue that any approach to healthier lifestyles should take a life span approach, so that while we need to focus on those who are currently ageing, we should at the same time look at prenatal health and the health of children as a way of investing in the health of our nation in the longer term.

The following levels of action have been suggested:
- Individuals' self-care among older people themselves; informal care; formal care.
- Local agencies, local authorities (housing, education, social services and transport).
- National agencies, central government departments, appointed bodies, voluntary agencies and private sector organisations (Dalley et al, 1996).

Opportunities for Nursing

The opportunities for nurses and health visitors to contribute towards healthier lifestyles in people of all ages are vast. These are discussed in detail in Chapter 3. Particular opportunities are now arising for nurses to promote health and wellbeing in areas that have traditionally been neglected, such as the continuing care of older people (Masterson, 1997).

EDUCATION OF NURSES TO WORK WITH OLDER PEOPLE

Current Education Programmes

The appropriateness of the preparation and ongoing development of nurses who work with older people has been a fundamental concern to many in the field for years, and this concern is shared by other countries in the European Community. Both pre and post-registration programmes are felt to be largely inappropriate and inadequate, particularly in areas such as the long-term care for people with mental-health needs (Nolan and Keady, 1996). It is therefore timely that the United Kingdom Central Council and National Boards are reviewing the needs.

In their survey of curricula for both pre and post-registration programmes for the English National Board (ENB), Davis *et al.* (1997) found:

- A lack of coherence and logical structure within some curriculum documents, with no clear relationship between course philosophy, objectives and content.
- Very little evidence that older people are involved in developing programmes or teaching students. When this did happen, it was generally via advocates and specific interest groups, rather than service users themselves. Only one of over 70 programmes involved patients in the assessment process in the validation of students' work.
- Those programmes which appeared to focus more explicitly on the needs of older people for self-determination had an emphasis on challenging attitudes, encouraging participation, and had content specifically aimed at developing the skills to challenge and change practice.
- Although it appears that practitioners are given opportunities to participate in programme development and delivery, many course leaders identified barriers to collaboration; for example, pressures of work and the speed at which curricula need to be developed.
- Apart from the focused courses, few curricula specify content related to the autonomy and independence of older people, rather they form 'threads' through the curriculum without explicit reference to how course members might be encouraged to apply these ideas in caring for older people.
- Some problems with terminology. Use of the phrase 'the elderly' is common and was noted in more than half of the curricula. A number of curricula also suggested a gender bias.

A similar educational evaluation commissioned by the National Board for Scotland is also being undertaken, and it will be interesting to see how the results correlate with those of the ENB study.

Preparing the Workforce of the Future

The current challenge is to prepare a nursing workforce to work in both specialist and non-specialist arenas. Older people are receiving care in all areas of health and social-care services and, in the light of emerging trends, fairly speedy work is currently being undertaken to develop programmes to prepare the future nursing workforce.

At the time of writing, some providers are looking at multidisciplinary education. Others are focusing on advanced nursing roles and a number of organisations now offer programmes for gerontological nurse specialists and practitioners at both first degree and Masters level. However, due to the lack of a clear national framework for specialist or advanced practice, or what defines a nurse practitioner, there is little consistency in what these courses offer. Additionally, nurses are creating and developing new roles, particularly specialist roles but, because the specific education needed by them does not exist, they are supporting their development in an ad hoc way by extensive reading, peer support, clinical supervision, attending conferences or using single relevant modules from more generic courses.

There is an urgent need for flexible programmes at appropriate level urgently need to be developed in order to support nurses in clinical practice, and particularly in the many newly emerging nursing roles.

RESEARCH INTO NURSING OLDER PEOPLE

A variety of methodologies have been used to research nursing with older people and there remains much to learn to ensure the research agenda facilitates best future practice. In particular, we need to learn from the evidence relating to the heterogeneity of older people as a research population, informed consent, conceptual clarity and developing appropriate methodologies for nursing.

Acknowledging the Heterogeneity of Older People

There are specific considerations in sample selection with older people and particularly in ackowlding the heterogeneity of older people (Bowsher *et al.* 1993; Phillips, 1992). Older people are highly diverse individuals with highly diverse abilities and needs. In order for research to be credible, individual differences must be acknowledged. Older people with mental-health needs are a major group within health care and it is unfortunate when research studies ignore or exclude them because their contribution may be considered 'unreliable'. Creative methodologies can be used to access the experiences and realities of older people, even those who are particularly vulnerable; for example, dementia care mapping can be used to assess the activity levels and degree of engagement of people with dementia.

Informed Consent

The British Medical Association and Royal College of Nursing (RCN) (1995) emphasise that older people have the same rights as all other adults to consent or to refuse to participate in research projects. However, they stress that people who are hospitalised, residing in an institution, or who otherwise find themselves to be in a situation of dependency may feel under pressure to conform with the wishes of others. It is, therefore, essential that they are given adequate advice and information, in accessible language, to enable them to make a valid, independent decision. They should also be offered the choice to withdraw their consent at any time (*see* Chapter 14 for issues concerning an individual's mental 'capacity' to consent).

Greater Conceptual Clarity

Researching older age can be complex and it is vital for nurses to be clear about exactly what they are researching. For example, many of the previous studies into nurses' attitudes to older people could have benefited from greater clarity on the concept of 'attitude'. Distinctions need to be drawn between attitudes, values and beliefs. The potential components of attitudes are cognitive, emotional and behavioural intention. This is particularly important in nursing because how nurses say they think and feel about something does not necessary predict how they will behave. In addition, the research has generally failed to make the distinctions between attitudes towards older people, as individuals and collectively, between the process of ageing, and the state of being old. Also, much of the research has failed to separate out the attitudes of nurses to older people as patients, and their attitudes to the organisation and structure of work with older people.

Seeking Appropriate Methodologies

Nursing practice is not straightforward to investigate because, even in one single interaction, there can be an enormous range of processes taking place. Methods, such as critical incident technique (CIT) and storytelling, have produced vivid narratives of nursing practice which have provided valuable insights into the processes of nursing. Future analyses of nursing practice can be based on such frameworks (Benner, 1984).

Reed (1994) attempted to use CIT to investigate concepts of expertise in nurses in long-term care settings for older people but her research was curtailed 'by the apparent inabil-

ity of nurses in the study to identify any significant incidents' (p. 336). Reed gained the agreement and apparent enthusiasm of nurses in a long-term care ward in a small hospital for older people to work with her on identifying 'significant incidents'. She gave them guidelines adapted from Benner. Her interviews with the nurses were preceded by a short period of semi-participant observation during which she observed the activities of the nurses, noting down any incidents that she could identify as incorporating skills such as communication and relationship skills. She found it very difficult to identify anything other than relationship skills but presumed that it was likely that the 'expertise' would be hidden from an observer. After three interviews, she had been unable to uncover any incidents which demonstrated expertise, or indeed any incidents at all. Reed believed that the nurses did not, and could not, see their work as a series of incidents but would talk about general approaches, general principles and general philosophies of care. Having successfully completed some work on critical incidents with nursing students, Reed questioned whether this indicated a limited expertise in the nurses who worked with older people or whether the differences were due to different ways of thinking and reasoning.

Reed (1994) questions the usefulness of critical incident technique in situations where the work is not so clearly episodic. She also questions whether the identification of incidents by an observer may impose an inappropriate structure. Reed believes that the problem is compounded by the possibility that some expert practitioners do not recognise their own expertise and this may be particularly the case when their area of practice has been consistently seen as one which involves few skills, as in the care of older people. She concludes that 'there are no foolproof ways of doing research which will gain us access to the essential nature of experience' (p. 341).

The difficulties which expert nurses experience in describing 'everyday practice' have been clearly demonstrated. One of the difficulties is that they do not think in terms of systems and structures, nor do they address problem-solving from a mechanistic linear approach. Instead they think holistically. Expert practice is embedded in tacit knowledge, which cannot be identified through observational methods, or even easily through reflection. By acknowledging intuitive thought, expert practitioners engage in holistic problem solving. If research methodologies are to articulate the intricate processes involved in nursing practice, they must be able to access these dimensions.

Expert nurses have demonstrated that it is possible to access and articulate these dimensions and thus to illuminate a whole range of aspects of nursing not visible using other research methodologies (RCN, 1997b).

Nursing Research in Practice

Although arguably research has now become accepted as integral to nursing practice and education, Kitson *et al.* (1997) suggest that we face particular challenges in that:

- The scope of research in nursing tends not to be focused beyond that of local need.
- There is a lack of consolidation to promote the development of a research-based body of knowledge relevant to nursing.
- The high levels of expertise required to respond to all research and academic opportunities is restricted through a lack of agreed professional objectives and defined aspirations.
- The scale of research undertaken has tended to be small and the methods employed limited. Consequently the findings of the research are difficult to generalise.

Despite these challenges, Kitson *et al.* (1997) believe that nurses are enthusiastic about research-based activities, and suggest that many initiatives have been established to disseminate and implement research-based knowledge and practice. This has been supported by the report of the Department of Health Taskforce (1992) and an evaluation of how the recommendations had been implemented (Read, 1994).

Nurses who work with older people face particular challenges, in achieving clinical effectiveness through working towards evidence-based practice, in undertaking their own research and in influencing broader research agendas. There are challenges in obtaining adequate information and support networks for nurses who want to become involved in research or who wish to implement research findings. These challenges are particularly acute for nurses who work in isolation; for example, those in small care homes in rural areas. Even those in larger organisations may have no access to library facilities. Ensuring access to appropriate databases, particularly direct access from clinical practice areas, presents a further challenge.

Additionally, nurses who wish to undertake studies using the type of naturalistic methodologies described above, may face resistance from managers, researchers or commissioning and funding bodies who favour quantitative research, and particularly randomised controlled trials. Nevertheless, there is a great deal that nurses can achieve in developing the information collection methods they use in their everyday work, such as audit information, quality-of-care measures, accident reports, infection notifications, or risk assessments. If collected and analysed rigorously, these can provide a very useful basis for evaluating clinical effectiveness and developing nursing practice.

Clinical Effectiveness

The drive to address the uncertainty of clinical interventions by uncovering the best available evidence is increasingly filtering into practice. Walshe and Ham (1997) review how clinical effectiveness has permeated everyday practice in the UK and describe a number of approaches to identifying evidence and implementing it, the most comprehensive being the comparison of existing patterns for the provision of clinical services with available evidence in order to identify and address any mismatch.

Another initiative to support nurses in clinical practice by offering evidence-based solutions to clinical and practical problems has been the development of clinical guidelines. As a result of a priority setting exercise by nurses in practice, research, education and management identified areas for the development of new clinical guidelines (McClary, 1997). The rehabilitation of older people was identified as a priority area.

Critics of the evidence-based movement describe it as naive reductionism and cookbook medicine. Counter argument is that it resolves legitimate conflicts over values in order to choose between priorities of courses of clinical action (Kitson *et al.* 1997).

Clinical effectiveness can be achieved when practice is based on the best-available clinical knowledge, information and evidence. Obtaining this can be a daunting task but databases such as the Cochrane Databases of Systematic Reviews of Effectiveness, Controlled Trials and Protocols are very useful. As part of its strategy to promote clinical effectiveness in health care, the Department of Health has funded a nursing and midwifery information service to provide help and support to nurses in enhancing their clinical effectiveness. The service helps nurses to locate and appraise the research, guidelines, systematic reviews, journals, newsletters, patient groups and professional organisations. The service also provides information and assistance in standard setting and clinical audit, and can put nurses in touch with other projects developing audits, standards, tools or methodologies in a particular area of interest.

Influencing the Research Agenda

Research priorities are set at various levels including national government, regions and local areas. Some of these are highly relevant to older people; for example the priorities in the research and development (R&D) strategy for the National Health Service in Scotland include:

- Ageing and quality of life.
- Preventing, delaying and coping with dependency.
- Physical and mental disability assessment.
- Stroke and related disorders.

The United Kingdom Central Council and National Boards for Nursing, Midwifery and Health Visiting also determine research priorities and commission and fund research.

A national initiative was set up jointly by the RCN and the Centre for Policy in Nursing Research (CPNR) established at the London School of Hygiene and Tropical Medicine. Its principle aim was to establish a coordinated and systematic method for identifying development priorities in the nursing profession, thereby informing the process of commissioning new research and advising other research funding agencies of the priorities in research relevant to nurses. The initiative identified a key role for the RCN in setting R&D priorities, conducting and commissioning research, facilitating effective dissemination and implementation of research, and building a suitable infrastructure to support these activities.

Through the RCN project team and working groups involving a variety of experts, four themes were identified as priorities: care and caring practices, health-care environment, organisation and management, and health-care workforce. Further work on the care and caring practice theme identified key topic areas for research, including:

- Patients' perspectives of care and how they are assessed.
- The role of informal carers and how health and social care are and will be integrated.
- Nursing interventions, including preventative care, treatment and support, and nurse-led services.
- Access to, and exit from, health services, and nurses' role in this process.
- Chronicity and how to facilitate coping with chronic illness.
- Evaluating the effect of nursing practice of new technologies, including those developed by other disciplines and those used by nurses to improve clinical effectiveness.

All of these priorities are highly relevant to older people.

It can be extremely difficult for individual nurses to feel that they can influence research agendas, and the RCN/CPNR priority setting exercise offered an example of how nurses can work together to achieve a more united voice. The more explicitly that nursing older people features in the R&D agendas, the more evidence there will ultimately be for nurses to use towards ensuring that their practice is effective.

THE VALUE OF NURSING WITH OLDER PEOPLE

The role of nursing with older people has overcome many challenges in its development (*see* Chapter 1) and it is important to appreciate that, as a speciality, it is relatively young. It is also important to appreciate that these challenges have been overcome in the context of a largely ageist society and despite ageist professionals, poor education, chronic underfunding, second-class hospital accommodation, ritualistic practice and poor skill mix, with particularly low numbers of registered nurses. Of key importance was the absence of staff who actively chose to work with older people, with the result that much of the workforce were placed within the speciality because they were considered unfit to work anywhere else. Alternatively, it was the only service where vacancies existed and certainly in the experience of one of the authors there was no choice but to accept a job working with older people.

While acknowledging these challenges, some commentators remain particularly critical of nurses' work with older people. Although it is accepted that nursing must take responsibility for its own practice, it is important to view the progress of gerontological nursing alongside these challenges, not as a way of excusing current poor practice, but in order

that practice development and educational programmes can be cognisant of the very specific needs within the speciality. In this way, the very real achievements can be celebrated. Despite the historical disadvantages, some of nursing's most innovative work originated among nurses working with older people; for example, National Health Service nursing homes (Wade *et al.* 1983; Bond and Bond, 1987; Bond *et al.* 1989), primary nursing (Pearson, 1983,1988), and intermediate care (Wilce, 1988).

To some extent, it could be argued that the speciality's legacy of disadvantage has stifled the articulation and recognition of the enthusiasm and pioneering work that has, albeit slowly and patchily, been developed. Rather than continuing to reflect on historical circumstance, particularly in relation to criticising current practice, we believe that what the speciality now needs is for gerontological nurses to focus on current and future practice opportunities, thereby providing leadership and identifying the pathway.

The RCN has argued (1993) that older people's needs are 'among the most complex encountered within any health or social-care setting, and nurses who work with older people have developed highly specialised understanding and skills to meet these needs'. As contributors to that specific piece of work, we would now argue that it is expert nurses who have developed the specialist understanding and skills, and we acknowledge the challenge of ensuring that all nurses develop a degree of specialist knowledge. In recognition of the need to test some of its assumptions, the RCN has offered a framework for nurses to identify and record their own outcome indicators. Such a framework, therefore, offers the potential for researching expert practice (1997b).

The 'Distinct' Elements of Nursing with Older People

As with any other age group, older people are unique individuals but arguably the culmination of a lifetime of individual experiences, alongside the complexities of individual physiological, psychological, sociological ageing, create older age as the epitome of individuality (*see* Chapters 1 and 19).

Alongside this individuality, older people as a group have distinct needs, which form the basis of the distinct body of knowledge which specialist nurses need to master. These distinct needs derive from:

- Distinct genetic and lifestyle factors, survival factors and generational and cohort characteristics.
- The ageing processes, both physical and psychosocial, the effects of which are totally individual. In each person, systems of the body age at different rates and in individual ways, and the physical processes interact with the life experiences.
- Multiple pathology, the older an individual is, the more disease processes he or she is likely to experience. It is not uncommon for 80 and 90-year-olds to have upwards of four medical diagnoses. Partly because of the interaction between individual ageing processes and multiple

pathology, diseases may be difficult to recognise and diagnose.

- Altered presentation of illness. Disease can present differently in older age. This altered presentation most often takes the form of some kind of physical instability, mental instability, immobility or incontinence. These manifestations have become known as 'the Four Is', and were previously termed 'the giants of geriatrics'. An example of this would be that a chest infection would probably cause a raised temperature in a younger adult, whereas in an older adult the first sign of an infection might be an acute mental confusion.
- Polypharmacy and adverse drug reactions. When drugs are prescribed, particularly for multiple pathology, they tend to cause more adverse drug reactions, and these may be difficult to identify in the context of all the relevant factors.

Undertaking a Nursing Assessment of an Older Person

When assessing an older person, therefore, an expert nurse is trying to unpick the complexities of individual ageing (both physical and psychosocial), multiple pathology, altered presentation of illness and drug reactions. Assessing an older person is, therefore, a complex activity, requiring high levels of skill and knowledge. For example:

- Because of the 'altered presentation of illness', atypical or vague symptoms such as lethargy, incontinence, increased mental confusion or agitation, reduced appetite, weight loss, sleeping disorders and falls, can indicate problems such as infection (particularly chest or urine), metabolic disorder (e.g. hypothyroidism), organ failure (e.g. cardiac), or mental change (e.g. depression).
- The consequences of deterioration in one function (e.g. hearing loss) may be most evident in the emergence of another problem (e.g. paraphrenia).
- The prognosis of one problem (e.g. depression) may be dependent on the progress of another (e.g. physical illness).
- Judgements about action to be taken may be a matter of balancing priorities, as that which improves one aspect of health may aggravate another, particularly during drug treatment.
- Because older people have fewer adaptive mechanisms, one problem tends to exacerbate another. Health or social breakdown can start a 'domino effect', leading to decline or even death. Once breakdown has occurred health can deteriorate quickly.
- There are distinct challenges in communicating with older people, particularly those who have sensory impairment. There may also be generational characteristics which create barriers, for example in values, priorities or language.
- There is a lack of generally agreed health and illness norms for older people, e.g. optimum blood glucose levels, or when to treat high blood pressure.
- Many older people who come into contact with nurses

have 'informal' carers. Their needs and involvement create an additional dimension to nursing practice that is not present in all areas. This situation needs special consideration; for example, the needs and views of an older person and carer may differ, and both may be under considerable stress.

- Nursing older people with mental-health needs, such as dementia, requires distinct knowledge and nursing skills, for example in obtaining 'consent' to care or treatment.
- To an older person, how they are functioning within their chosen lifestyle priorities and towards the achievement of life goals will generally be more important than a specific medical diagnosis. When assessing an older person's function, the nurse needs to understand that she or he may function differently according to the environment, time of day, people around, physiological state or medication reactions. Functional impairment can indicate that there is an underlying health need.
- There is a need for nurses to maintain and promote a positive view of older age and older people, despite societal and professional prejudices. This requires an approach that focuses on abilities and strengths, as well as disabilities and needs, and factors that have helped to maintain the older person's abilities and coping. The older person's goals for quality of life should be kept in focus, particularly as these may conflict with 'standard health advice'.
- Gerontological nurses must maintain a positive view of the potential effects of health promotion, which, often contrary to expectations, can be effective even into very old age. Potential outcome indicators can be an increase in general wellbeing, delayed disability and premature death. We consider that re-enablement approaches are fundamental.

GERONTOLOGICAL NURSING

Terminology changes over time, partly as a response to its social and professional context, but also in an attempt to influence those contexts. At this point in the chapter, it feels important to explain what we mean by gerontological nursing. The term itself is to us dynamic and creative. It captures the view that practice is both responding to changing circumstances but also that it is moving towards the future, developing in a proactive way, i.e. it moves nursing forward into the next millennium. The term gerontological nursing captures for us what we consider expert practice to be. To be truly expert, nurses must move beyond nursing and indeed beyond health care. By this we mean that nurses must expand their knowledge and consider the plethora of life influences. This can be achieved in a number of ways:

- Adopting a life span perspective.
- Exploring the impact of ageism.
- Acknowledging the meaning of poverty and of disability.

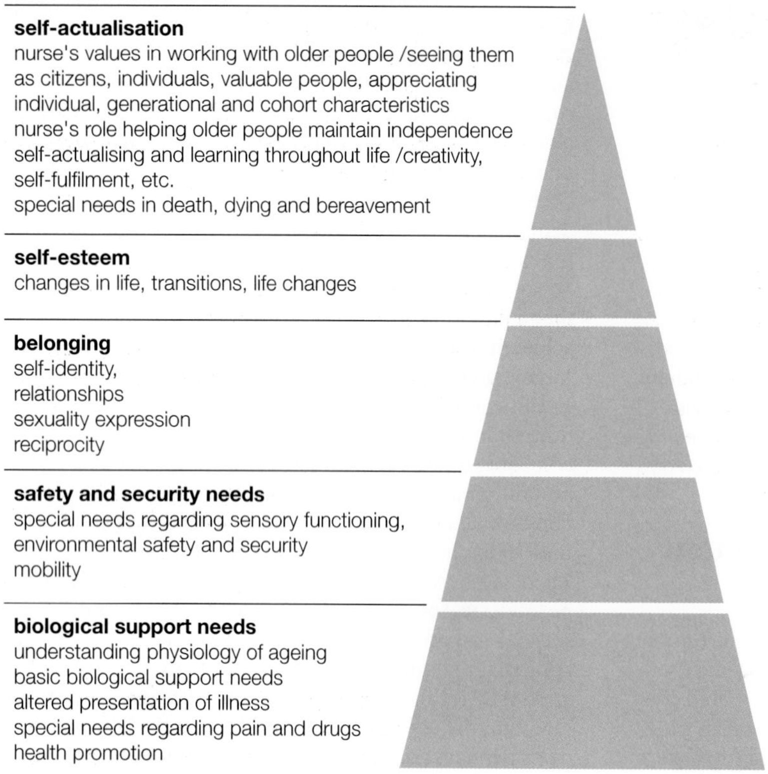

self-actualisation
nurse's values in working with older people /seeing them
as citizens, individuals, valuable people, appreciating
individual, generational and cohort characteristics
nurse's role helping older people maintain independence
self-actualising and learning throughout life /creativity,
self-fulfilment, etc.
special needs in death, dying and bereavement

self-esteem
changes in life, transitions, life changes

belonging
self-identity,
relationships
sexuality expression
reciprocity

safety and security needs
special needs regarding sensory functioning,
environmental safety and security
mobility

biological support needs
understanding physiology of ageing
basic biological support needs
altered presentation of illness
special needs regarding pain and drugs
health promotion

Figure 22.4 Aspects of the role of gerontological nurses, expressed within Maslow's hierarchy.

- Considering the impact of housing, transport and diet.
- Recognising the relevance of social networks.

If a nurse can achieve all of this in addition to advanced knowledge, skill and expertise in the health, social and nursing needs of older people, then we would consider that nurse to be expert in a gerontological sense.

For example, a woman (aged 87 years) visits the health centre for her over seventy-fives' check, during the course of which she tentatively explains to the nurse that she has concerns about her developing friendship with a man because, although she feels she would like the relationship to be intimate, she has never experienced intimacy with a man. In this situation, the nurse needs not only skill and sensitivity in discussing the subject with the older woman, but also an understanding of the distinct influences of the older woman's life experiences, such as the values she may have been taught as a young woman, the education she may have received on the practical and relational aspects of intimacy. The key here is to be aware that different cohorts of older people will have had different experiences. It is likely that this woman was brought up in an era where sexual intimacy was never discussed, and the impact of the First World War and subsequent social change may have severely curtailed her social experience of the opposite sex. As the relationship develops, the nurse may feel it appropriate to offer ideas from her broad gerontological knowledge of the particular needs of the older woman within the local area in terms of transport, driving regulations, social centres, travel advice. She may feel it appropriate to draw on her understanding of the psychological aspects of relationships in later life, of the impact of life transitions or of the physiological age-related changes affecting sexuality and sexual activity in older age (*see* Chapter 15 for further discussion).

In the first major UK text describing gerontological nursing, Wade (1996) states:

A gerontological perspective moves away from an illness-dependency model of care towards a biographical, developmental, positive approach. That is not to say older people are not ill, but the focus of nursing is to assist the individual to maximise and adapt according to their own potential, with varied settings. This approach recognises the older person as a consumer of care, requiring varied skills from nursing. Gerontological nursing frameworks focus upon the person and the environment, and the process between the two that produces health and wellness.

Additionally, Nolan (1994) emphasises the need for gerontological nursing to recognise that older people are not a homogenous group and that nursing older people needs to be open to outside influences and that the necessary skills go beyond the confines of a model of nursing (**Figure 22.4**).

EMERGING ROLES AND OPPORTUNITIES FOR NURSING

In preparation for this section of the chapter, we surveyed a number of nurses who we consider to be expert practitioners with older people. This was achieved by the circulation of questionnaires and individual interviews. We asked questions relating to job titles, key role components and responsibilities, clients and colleagues. We gathered information about line management, funding for the post and ways of working utilised by the respondents, which facilitated the gathering of older people's views and opinions. Finally, we asked the respondents to tell us what they saw in the future for nursing in terms of individual and professional opportunities. This data collection was then analysed for themes, which were subsequently tested among a small group of close colleagues, all of whom work with older people. As such, we offer the personal views, experiences, and opinions of nurses who are actively involved on a daily basis in services for older people.

A Sample of Emerging Nursing Roles – a Thematic Analysis

The responses were from nurses undertaking vastly different roles in a wide range of settings. Some are working at UK level, and others in single units. The respondents included directors of care services, directors of nursing, health strategy nurses, project managers, clinical leaders, and unit/home/locality managers. Despite the variety of posts, there were strong themes.

User Focus

The older person and their significant others were central to service planning and provision for this was achieved by:
- Keeping in touch with older people's views and the reality of their experiences, even though the nursing role may not involve direct clinical involvement.
- Personal involvement with clinical care.
- Developing and utilising skilled communication strategies.
- Making time to 'hear' the voice of the patient and their significant users.
- 'Demonstrating how nurses respond to patients views and suggestions and continuing the involvement.'
- Planning care in a way which fully utilises the involvement of patients and significant others.
  'Care planning should therefore state patient objectives, what is important to them, and includes measures of satisfaction and dissatisfaction.'

This latter point can be addressed in a variety of ways such as:
- Interviews with clients and carers.
- Questionnaires related to service provision.
- Groupwork.
- Focus groups.

- Carers support groups.
- Clients community meetings.
- Advocacy service.

Other forms of communication which are used as particular management strategies include:
- Formal complaints procedures.
- Listening to anecdotal evidence.
- Developing user-led strategies (with Social Services departments and other stakeholders) for older people.
- Open days (users and carers involved).
- Working with user representatives such as Age Concern.
- Working with pensioners' action groups and community health councils.

One comment received captured this:
> *'A culture of open, honest and robust communication with each other and encouraging all those in touch with our service to be open in the interaction with us.'*

The Nursing Context

Changing the Culture
All of the respondents referred to the need to move away from an illness culture towards a health model. This was best achieved by placing health into a social-care context. Nurses should focus on the new public health agenda, which aims to address social and economic deprivation and social exclusions. This should drive many of the nursing elements of care and a new strategy for working with population groups.

Change – Working with it and Seeing it as an Opportunity
Respondents referred to the need to maintain a broad base of knowledge, skill and expertise to facilitate a flexible and creative way of working. They also talked about the importance of using change as an opportunity to improve client and carer health and social care.

Cost-consciousness
The need to be increasingly creative in response to doing more with less in terms of human and financial resources was a strong theme particularly related to the need to capture the Trust business ethos and translate this into the provision of an effective quality services for the client group. Reference was made to the need for commitment and energy, and one of the key challenges was recruitment and retention of staff.

The Scope of the Nursing Role

Cross-boundary Working
Throughout the responses it was clear that collaborative working was viewed as the only viable way of working, particularly if services were to be further improved or developed. Respondents mentioned the need to '*ensure that boundaries don't become barriers*' and '*health and social services need to work collaboratively*'. There was an emphasis on the value of both lay and professional views and opinions.

513

Nurses are working across and within all the sectors. The most successful had developed integrated working to maximise health potential and independent living for older people.

Some respondents talked about their involvement in interagency and inter-professional training.

Working beyond 'Traditional' Boundaries

Many advocated the importance of nurses being involved in commissioning and purchasing services and the importance of developing needs assessment and health gain management skills.

Some are working where there is no specialist service, for example in general practitioner practice, ensuring priority for special needs of older people within other priorities such as continence promotion, diabetes and asthma clinics.

Working Collaboratively

A long list of close working colleagues was given in all responses, with nurses developing new partnerships in an effort to reduce professional boundaries and protectionism within the professions. The need for collective approaches and action for health-care needs assessment was clearly identified, as was a strong user focus which *'facilitated collaborative working as it seems to help professionals overcome territorial behaviour'*.

Complex and Multidimensional/Multi-level Working Structures

These structures involved the nurses relating 'upwards' and 'downwards' and 'sideways' within management structures, working within a matrix and broad networking. It was felt that, to be truly effective, nurses needed to work at all levels and across all boundaries.

The respondents also linked with many different individuals in the organisational structure: service receivers, other professionals, other organisations, other statutory bodies, professional organisations, professional networks and professional colleagues.

Multidimensional and Multi-level Roles

Most of the respondents were taking on many different roles within the complex structures and highlighted that this reflected the need to be flexible in their day-to-day working:

> *'I wear a number of hats each day – the skill is knowing which hat to wear.'*

The range of roles covered clinical care to strategic planning, often within the same week.

Quality – Implementation and Evaluation

Work involved closely monitoring the service. Even at more strategic levels of working, it involved being in close touch with the realities of the day-to-day delivery of the service for both the receivers and service deliverers. It also involved spending time in service areas, such as wards, nursing homes and day care, and delivering direct-contact care and support to the older people, their families and carers, and the nurses and other staff involved. The roles involved setting up systems that will objectively evaluate the quality of the service delivered and involve patients and their significant others in audit and the development of standards of care.

The Place of Nursing

Valuing Nursing

All emphasised the importance of nursing skills and developing nursing-led services:

> *'So much is held in the balance by nurses – let's quantify it, illustrate how effective it is, use our skills to lead teams, provide expert knowledge and opportunities within nursing for enthusiastic and effective people – let's not lose them to general management posts.'*

They highlighted the need for professional networking, which helped them develop their knowledge and confidence. They referred to the need to *'seize the ground and retain it by demonstrating the value of their contribution'* to the overall wellbeing of patients and families along with the benefits to the service in general.

The current focus on articulating the benefits of skilled nursing was captured well in this quote *'ensuring that nursing does not lose sight of the important issues of care. Increasingly there are pressures to move into increased technology and leave the essential aspects of nursing behind. Technical work may offer apparent prestige and status but it is ultimately only technicians' work.'*

The respondents also mentioned undertaking and using research to demonstrate the effectiveness of qualified nurse interventions was a common theme reflecting the recognition that nursing must identify and articulate their benefits.

Developing Nursing

There was a strong emphasis on the need for education to ensure skill development for current and new roles. Lifelong learning, work-based learning and using technology for learning were cited as being particularly appropriate. Utilising current trends such as clinical effectiveness, outcome measures, evidence-based practice and specialist training were recognised as providing opportunities which nursing should not ignore as they in effect could provide 'pathways for development'.

Overall their was a consensus of the need to ensure that nursing is articulated, recognised and valued for its contribution to effective health care.

Personal Ways of Working

Personal and Professional Responsibility

The respondents mentioned:
- Personal and professional commitment and integrity.
- Keeping sustained.
- 'Preparing myself' – motivation and drive, political awareness, strategic thinking and action, reflection and evaluation, own philosophy beliefs and values.
- 'Developing and using my skills tool kit.'
- Always following through systematically.

- Being personally as well trained as possible on whatever field of work we are in.
- Flexibility and being able to adapt.

Being Proactive

Interestingly, roles at all levels involve some degree of strategic planning which all of the respondents acknowledged.

Influencing

- They mentioned being 'political' – having an awareness of the opportunities to influence at all levels from the Government to the individual person.
- Influencing 'non nurses'.
- Nurses using their ability to effect change, provide leadership, maintain standards and liaise effectively with other disciplines.

Being Positive

A number of examples of positive working were cited. There seemed to be a view that expert nurses should remain in a position to impact on practice and this clearly affected several of the respondents career choices.

The need to utilise advocacy skills to ensure that older people remained on any agenda was key, with examples ranging from allocation of new furniture to staffing resources and provision of new services. This seemed to be very much a case of fighting the corner for older people, but doing it in a positive way. There was a recognition of the risks in developing a paternalistic approach.

Maintaining an awareness of ageism and the many ways in which it can manifest was also a key point.

NURSING OLDER PEOPLE: A SWOT ANALYSIS

In order to identify where gerontological nursing currently stands, and how the speciality can best position itself for the future, a SWOT analysis was undertaken by five nurses who are working at national level in a variety of posts including strategic and operational management, education, policy analysis and practice development. They were asked to consider the strengths, weaknesses, opportunities and threats in relation to the nursing of older people currently, and in the future. They identified the following:

Strengths

- **The policy agenda.** There is a clear focus on older people. A number of health and social policy initiatives are addressing the needs of older people, e.g. the Royal Commission into long-term care, the Health Select Committee work on long-term care and on health and social needs, various White Papers on registration and inspection of care homes. There also now seems to be more coherence in terms of policy and a common voice in the policy agendas.
- **Interest in older people.** Many organisations and bodies are becoming interested in 'older people' issues. Several national newspapers have run campaigns. The United Kingdom Central Council has undertaken a project on nursing for the continuing care of older people and another including older people with mental-health needs. Ageing issues now appear to be on the agenda of most health-care research programmes. Millennium celebrations will include focus on older people.
- **Involvement of organisations.** There has been a slow but gradual increase in interest in older people's needs among nurses generally. This is evidenced by nursing journal campaigns and companion articles. Ageing has been a recent theme in over 30 international journals. The number of nurses belonging to the 'older people' membership forums in the Royal College of Nursing (RCN) has recently increased drastically. A number of organisations want to work with nursing at a national level and several actively promote the benefits of working with expert nurses.
- **Shift of service emphasis.** With the downsizing of secondary care, and shortened lengths of hospital stay, there are more highly demanding throughputs but also recognition of the need for ongoing re-enablement towards independence. This has opened new doors for nursing practice, for example in intermediate care settings, accident and emergency nursing, integrated services and long-term care. In addition, the recognition of the need for gerontological nurse specialists is gradually emerging.
- **Consumer and user involvement.** There is greater recognition of the need for user involvement as evidenced by the increasing literature base developed within nursing, which adopts a nursing focus. All of the respondents to our surveys talked at length about strategies used to involve users in service planning and evaluation.
- **Academic basis of nursing.** There is a more sound academic base that strives to be person-centred and empowering of older people.
- **Nursing practice.** The ability to form good relationships with patients and significant others and the communication abilities which facilitate multi-agency working. Nurses are often cited as being the member of the team who assumes responsibility for liaison and coordination. Nurses have a broad knowledge base, alongside a specific specialist knowledge, which makes them a flexible workforce. A number of organisations and professions related to nursing are supporting the developments in nursing. Nursing has always had huge public support.

Weaknesses

- **Health and social policy.** The division between health and social care, particularly as nursing falls between the two.

- **Services to older people**. Older people paying for nursing care. Inequality in access to services and in the type of services offered. Limited choice in some areas, such as when entering a care home. Age-based rationing.
- **The independent sector**. There are weaknesses because the independent sector is such a disparate set-up. At present, there are no national standards or a common regulatory body. There is a need for one authority to pull together all the issues relating to the independent sector and its development, particularly continuing preparation and education of nurses.
- **Nursing education**, particularly pre-registration preparation. There is usually insufficient emphasis on the needs of older people, and there is a lack of practice-based education and practice-based facilitation to learn the real art of working with older people. Few education leaders and teachers are particularly interested in the needs of older people.
- **Recognition of nursing**. There is generally a lack of recognition of what nurses can offer, particularly nursing in continuing care. This is rife among nurses themselves. Nurses lack assertion and articulation skills, with the result that they do not communicate their own value.
- **Ageism**. There are powerful influences of ageism among the general public and fellow health-care professionals. If people who have power in health service organisations recognise that specialist skills and knowledge are needed to care for older people, older people are more likely to receive good care. Ageism can be recognised in most areas of service provision and nursing colleges.

Opportunities

All of the strengths, weaknesses and threats have the potential to create and present opportunities.

- **Health and social policy**. The current Government has a stated agenda to reduce social inequities and social exclusion. This creates opportunities for the voices of older people to be heard.
- **Creativity**. Because nursing works in such a creative way it can maximise opportunities for influencing at all levels.
- **Gerontological nursing**. Opportunities exist for gerontological nursing, and specifically in continuing care, to demonstrate the false divide between health and social care and to demonstrate that nurses really cross the boundaries. The RCN Assessment Tool illustrates this. There are opportunities for gerontological nurse specialists to undertake skilled assessment and recognition of need and planning care for ongoing re-enablement.
- **International working**. There are international opportunities because of the globally ageing population. This needs to be captured and taken forward. There are also many opportunities for international collaboration with other countries and cultures through research and education.

- **Nursing development**. Nurses have opportunities to create practice-developing methods, clinical leadership and practice-based education and learning. Technology, and in particular the introduction of telemedicine, is likely to result in nurses working more autonomously in areas which were hitherto the remit of the medical profession, as is nurse prescribing. There is a real opportunity to look at how nurses can work in a patient-centred way with older people and break down professional barriers.
- **Consumer and user involvement**. There are now increasing opportunities for greater user involvement. There are increasing expectations and expressed need for a quality service by older people themselves. This will be enhanced as care providers gain understanding through education.

Threats

- **Future services**. There is the potential for disparate service development as district general hospitals downsize and services go out into the community. Without a clear strategy there is a risk that service providers in the community may merely reinvent the institution. Such dispersed service provision may result in greater loss of consistent approaches to care.
- **Funding**. If the government doesn't address this, then older people's opportunities for genuine consumer power are unlikely to be achieved.
- **Secondary care**. This is becoming excessively technology-focused resulting in a renewed emphasis on the importance and prestige of technological care. This mitigates against services for groups such as older people, who require a service which is more therapeutically intensive rather than technologically focused. Inevitably a repeated debate on skill and skill mix will emerge. There are threats from fast tracking people through the system often referred to as 'discharging them sicker and quicker'.
- **Specialist knowledge**. In hospital, the disappearance of specialist services for older people has posed significant challenges to the quality of service that can be given. Many centres of good nursing practice have disappeared. As a result, the need for skilled nursing intervention based on specialist knowledge and practice has been lost and nursing teams now working in new settings (general) are again having to develop the arguments for specialist knowledge and practice. This is particularly hard in the face of ageist attitudes and service provision, which concentrates on those who have the most acute needs. The current debate on specialist gerontological nurses may well be seen as only necessary in care homes.
- **Nursing**. There are significant threats to nursing, for example that nursing in continuing care will disappear.
- **Good practice**. The ongoing development of health and safety and fire regulations could mitigate against all that

is considered good practice (e.g. scones which the care home residents think they have made but, due to regulations, have to be thrown away while professionally prepared scones are served!)

- **Education.** The continuing placement of education within universities. The threat is that we end up with only an academic base in gerontology, which remains divorced from the realities of clinical practice.
- **Professional understanding.** Nursing being understood, i.e. anybody can do it. Evidence, education and assertion are needed.
- **Cost of nursing.** Therefore, we need to demonstrate the difference between expert and non-expert.
- **Social service driven purchasing.** Where this undervalues the nursing contribution.
- **Awareness.** Nurses not recognising their responsibility in relation to lifelong learning
- **Attitudes to development.** The mental mind-set of some nurses who are unable to question, challenge and develop presents a problem. In particular, the mind set of the nurse who starts most sentences with 'I've been doing it like this for 15 years so why should I change now' or the nurse who says 'Five years experience is definitive evidence of skill and expertise'.

GERONTOLOGICAL NURSE SPECIALIST/PRACTITIONER

The practitioner of the future must, for reasons already discussed, develop an extensive gerontological knowledge base and, for this reason, there is real potential for specialist gerontological nurses.

Our vision for nursing older people of the future is a band of expert, skilled and knowledgeable gerontological nurses who transcend any care boundaries and move in and out of a care location anticipating and responding to need. Such nurses can be employed by any employer, health or social, independent or statutory. What will matter is that the nurses are able to practice at an advanced level in an autonomous way. There is a growing band of nurses currently working with older people who are ready and waiting to take up the challenge.

As a way of overcoming some of the problems relating to specialist knowledge, expertise and skill, it is likely that pre-graduate nurse education will be reconsidered to ensure that all nurses who graduate have some knowledge and skill of working with older people.

A new emphasis on the recently lost clinical nurse's specialist role is likely as the nursing profession considers how best to respond to the needs of the ageing population and the loss of specialist services within specialist units and teams. While clinical nurse roles are likely to emerge in both the long term and acute sector, it is likely that we shall see the emergence of a gerontological nurse practitioner, who will work at an advanced level utilising diagnostic and assessment skills and knowledge. It is envisaged that such practitioners will be employed to work in limited numbers in a variety of settings.

These nurses could well develop their roles in accident and emergency, general practice, rehabilitation services and some long-term care establishemnts. In such settings, the gerontological nurse practitioner will be the first point of referral by nurses and informal carers who want expert and skilled assessment. The gerontological nurse practitioner would then refer on for specific specialist assessment by doctors and physiotherapist, etc. Such developments may seem exciting. However, it is the view of the authors that nurses in the UK should retain their clinical involvement and resist the developing trends to concentrate on the more technical aspects of care at the expense of maintaining and further defining the highly skilled, complex therapeutic interventions that expert nurses working with older people specialise in.

Gerontological nurse specialists would ideally:

- Develop a user-focused approach.
- Work with, and alongside, the patient and significant others.
- Be accessed directly by members of the public and health and social-care professionals.
- Work creatively and flexibly across all sector boundaries.
- Be aware of the community facilities and constraints, e.g. housing and transport.
- Work closely with other health and social-care professionals, particularly specialist physicians, social workers, physiotherapists, occupational therapists, speech and language therapists, psychologists and dietitians.
- Have ready access to podiatrists, ophthalmologists, dentists.
- Provide care based on best available research evidence.
- Receive information from, liaise with, and give feedback to representatives from drug companies and equipment suppliers.

The role should encompass:

1. **Working with individuals and their families**

The focus of the nurse's work is the individual person, with all their needs and wishes, in the context of their lives and relationships, and helping them to live life as close as possible to the way in which they would choose. The nurse could provide:

- Health assessment, care and information.
- Advice on how to manage the illness and symptoms. Particularly important in this respect is the balancing of medications. The specialist nurses could teach patients:
  - how to take their drugs, the effects and side effects.
  - how to store and take the drugs.
  - how to re-order and obtain drugs.
  - the importance of having the right drug.
  - how to simplify regimes [in conjunction with the general practitioner (GP)].
- Help to balance chosen lifestyle with the problems which arise from the illness (such as fatigue, pain, insomnia, constipation, incontinence or sexual difficulties).
- Advice on maximising health generally, such as exercise and nutrition.

- Advice on maximising life generally (e.g. driving, working).
- Advice on safety (e.g. exercise with chronic pulmonary disease or cardiac failure).
- Emotional, psychological and social support.
- Advice at times of crisis.
- Expert nursing care.
- Practical help (with adaptations, equipment, services or benefits).
- Specialist nurses could also run a helpline service which patients could use at any time.
- Patient support groups and networks could also be set up.
- Services could be delivered in a wide variety of settings, including individual homes, health centres, GP premises, day care centres, special units, hospital wards, hospital clinics and care homes.

2.   Fostering links between sectors and care providers
Specialist nurses could act as the link:
- Between the various providers of services.
- With other organisations and agencies, including housing departments, social services, education departments, schools, day centres, social groups, disability and appliance services, voluntary agencies and voluntary groups.
- Between patients/GPs and pharmacists/drug companies, updating on new drugs and how these can be obtained, side effects (**Figure 22.5**).

3. Educating health and social-care professionals
Specialist nurses could also:
- Teach nurses on pre and post-registration programmes.
- Teach nurses in various settings.
- Speak at conferences.
- Work through networks of specialist nurses.
- Teach other health-care professionals.
- Publish their work.
- Be involved in promoting and supporting research into nursing older people.

4. Educating the public at large
- Nurses could be involved in public awareness-raising activities, such as roadshows. These could be run in conjunction with a voluntary sector organisation.
- Specialist nurses could also develop a key role in public health, adopting a locality approach to the overall wellbeing of an ageing population.

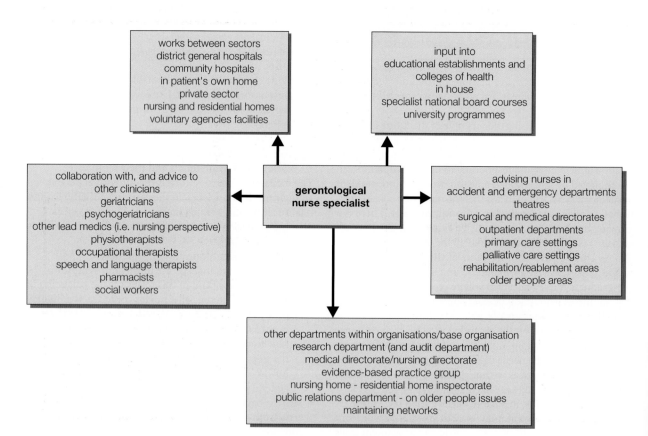

Figure 22.5 An example service model showing the working relationships of a gerontological nurse specialist (developed by Tina Wills).

The Education of Specialist Nurses

As discussed earlier, specialist educational programmes are under-developed. This is also the case with nursing older people. Various Masters level modules exist, either in gerontology or nursing older people, but gerontological nursing programmes which assist nurses to develop their clinical skills, alongside their knowledge base, are urgently needed.

Until such programmes are widely available, the specialist knowledge and skills will tend to be acquired by:
- Learning 'on the job'.
- Basing new learning on their previous valued experience, e.g. as a community nurse.

- Learning from working alongside experts, such as consultants or specialist nurses.
- Reading about each new aspect they come across.
- National and local networks.
- Major conferences.

AN AGENDA FOR CHANGE

The best framework within which to build an agenda for the future, we believe, integrates the essential elements of policy, practice, education and research (**Figure 22.6**). Through this integration, nurses can develop practice which:

policy
long-term care
regulation of long-term care
health versus social care
acute care
rehabilitation/reablement
intermediate care (including respite,
community hospitals and enhanced
primary care services)
primary care
health promotion

practice
organisational and practice
development programmes
in all sectors
valuing and promoting the
nursing role with older people
developing nursing practice with older
people in non-specialist settings
multidisciplinary practice development

older people
(and significant others where appropriate)
driving the service
involvement in planning and evaluating services
stragies which actively seek and facilitate the
involvement of all older people, particularly those
who may be excluded on the grounds of their
'vulnerability', e.g. 'with mental health needs',
'homeless'. or in 'a minority'

education
preparing the workforce for the future
with portfolios of skills to meet
changing needs, flexible and able to adapt
reviewing pre-registration nursing education
programmes, particularly experience with well,
independent older people and opportunities
for practice-based learning
continuing development opportunities for all
nurses working with older people through
flexible programmes, clinical supervision,
local programmes
multidisciplinary development programmes
emphasis of gerontological aspects, clinical
knowledge and skills, and psychosocial aspects
of care in all programmes

research
promoting research which articulates the value
of nursing, particularly in neglected areas
developing research partnerships, e.g. gerontology
and rehabilitation
developing multidisciplinary research
incorporating a nursing perspective into health-care
studies (e.g. the lifestyle impact of drug
trials undertaken by doctors)
utilising systems of information collection already in
place towards research studies
(e.g. audit information)
influencing and responding to the broad
research agenda

Figure 22.6 An agenda for change.

- Anticipates and responds to changes in policy.
- Builds and works from the foundations of sound research.
- Feeds and is fed by the education of both nurses and the older people with whom they work.

Central to any agenda for the future must be the older person and his or her significant other persons. We genuinely believe that all nurses working with older people should strive to develop strategies that result in older people, or their representatives, driving the service and the way in which it is delivered. The future agenda must also actively strive to incorporate the contribution and needs of all older people, and particularly those who, both historically and currently, have been undervalued and overlooked. This includes older people with mental-health needs, people from minority ethnic groups, older people who have often been disenfranchised, such as those who are homeless or live in nursing homes, and the carers who support older people.

Nursing must also actively seek to work collaboratively with multi-agency colleagues. Of necessity, this requires us to step back from the traditional ways of working and the 'norms' of current practice. It also requires that we reconsider the contribution of nursing – how we can work to capture opportunities and respond to the changing needs and constraints, both of the older person and the service providers. As this chapter has demonstrated, this may involve working across the boundaries which have traditionally been barriers, particularly the historical divisions between health and social care, and developing our work through multidisciplinary and multi-agency education, research and practice development projects.

Policy and Practice

Nurses have opportunities to work with older people and influence policy for the future in all of the key areas shown in **Figure 22.6**. Due to the increased emphasis on the provision of long-term care, nurses have a new opportunity to develop models of service provision, and participate in service planning and commissioning. In particular, long-term care offers considerable potential for nurse-led services such as:

- 24-hour resource centres.
- User-referred drop-in centres.
- Nurse practitioner clinics.
- Outreach nursing.
- Working with homeless people.
- Models of long-term care which look beyond health-care need and genuinely strive to support the older person in a community care model of service that they have chosen.

Fundamental changes are taking place in the regulation of long-term care provision, including that traditionally regulated by social services. This will impact on the nursing role in inspection and regulation, and how nurses will work within care homes. Nurses working nationally and locally need to develop strategic responses to these developments which, of necessity, confront the boundaries and require nurses to seriously consider working in a more dynamic and proactive way. In our view, the opportunities this presents should not be underestimated.

The current trend for mergers and the reconfiguration of services presents opportunities for nurses to advocate for older people to have right of access to the acute services they need when they, like all other age groups, experience acute illness. Particularly considering the context of cost-containment and age-based rationing, this cannot be taken for granted. In addition, nurses should be actively involved in influencing and shaping services which offer the expertise to meet the distinct and special needs of older people experiencing acute illness or undergoing surgery. Nurses are leading and actively contributing to projects which could ultimately enlighten the debate about what are the components of effective acute services for older people. These include the work of the HAS 2000 (which supersedes the former Health Advisory Service).

The potential human and financial benefits of effective acute services for older people are obvious:

- Shorter lengths of stay.
- Quicker 'throughputs', with fewer beds becoming 'blocked'.
- Reduced 'failed discharges', when people are readmitted and 'discharged' so regularly that it creates 'the revolving door syndrome'.

The opportunity exists to create responsive, highly skilled and specialist services, in which a re-enablement approach to care is implemented at the outset. The result is that older people will not be disempowered and deskilled, but will be able to maintain or regain their self-care abilities, their self-efficacy, and to live the lives they choose once they have reached their maximum potential following the acute illness.

Primary health care has been in seemingly relentless evolution for some years now, and will continue to do so under current government initiatives. Within this evolution, nurses have the opportunity to develop services with and for older people which:

- Help them to remain as healthy and possible.
- Respond quickly and effectively in order to identify change in health or 'ability to cope' at an early stage.
- Offer to older people services that meet their needs and help them to remain healthy and independent at home.

Developments in the constructive use of the over seventy-fives' health assessment, nurse-led clinics and advice on specific health issues such as travel advice, are now widespread. There are also currently opportunities for nurses to influence national policy initiatives in health promotion.

As this chapter has highlighted, growing numbers of nurses are now developing new roles or working in new areas such as social services or commissioning. In such roles, their understanding of the realities of older people who are ill or disabled and their understanding of how to meet health and social needs can considerably enhance the basis on which commissioning or purchasing decisions are made and services are developed. The indication is that these roles will continue and new opportunities will be created.

Research

Opportunities to develop the research on which nursing practice, education and policy with older people is based, and the opportunities that exist for influencing research priorities have been discussed in the chapter. The key to the future agenda lies in nurses developing their confidence in dealing with research, seeking help when they recognise that skills are lacking or that they are confronting barriers, finding support that will facilitate the development of their skills and support rigorous studies, and having the courage and tenacity to grasp the agenda in order to 'move forward'.

Education and Continuing Professional Development

Education to prepare the future nursing workforce must be addressed as a priority. Particularly in view of the age profile of the health and social-care populations of the immediate future, it is vital that all nurses have an understanding of the special considerations necessary to work effectively with older people.

Educationalists who teach about nursing older people should critically review their own expertise. The following questions are offered as a starting point for teachers to personally reflect on.

- How actively are older people involved in the planning, teaching and evaluation of your programs?
- What is the basis of your clinical knowledge and experience of nursing older people?
- Is it based within current nursing practice?
- Is it underpinned by research in which older people participated?
- What is the basis of your 'claim' to understand the distinct and special needs of older people?
- How sound is your gerontological knowledge. For example, how in touch are you with current gerontological literature (often non-nursing) such as research on intergenerational working, the role of leisure in the lives of older people, citizen advocacy, or the needs of widows in the first year of their bereavement?
- Have you considered the biographical approach (see Chapter 1) as a basis for your practice as a teacher and curriculum planner? If so, how does your teaching enable older people to tell their own stories to the individuals you teach and for the students and course participants to hear them?

Pre-registration curricula can build on the positive experiences that students, and particularly young students, may have had with older people in their personal lives by offering them opportunities to engage with older people who live independently and contribute actively to their social circle, as well as those who experience illness or disability and whom nurses most commonly encounter.

It is vital that education programmes offer sufficient emphasis on later life. Older people are now the major client group in all sectors of health care and all nurses will work with them. It is also important that programmes engender positive, open and constructive attitudes to working with all age groups, and that they raise awareness of age-discrimination. It is also important that student nurses develop an understanding of their potential contribution towards creating appropriate, healthy and facilitative environments for the future care of older people.

The Nursing Workforce and Leadership

Some nurses will become leaders in their work and in moving forward the agenda with and for older people. Leadership is a key determinant of how effective nurses will be in creating and shaping services for older people in the future. Personal leadership qualities include:
- Being an effective communicator.
- Management skills – management of yourself and others.
- The ability to be creative and flexible.
- Influencing skills.
- Skills to be proactive, opportunistic, flexible and assertive.
- Negotiation skills.
- Team-building and motivating skills.
- The ability to think logically, critically and analytically and to problem-solve.
- Empathy, and the skills and commitment to work with older people and their significant others.
- The skills to work collaboratively with multiple agencies.
- The courage and skills to work across boundaries and move through 'barriers'.
- The ability to remain focused, feel in control, to function and to give time to others if appropriate, even when under pressure.

In addition, if the agenda for older people and the nurses who work with them is to reach its full potential, gerontological nurse leaders must identify, nurture, develop, support and promote the leadership qualities of other nurses with whom they work. Leaders of gerontological nursing are vital in all spheres and at all levels. There is currently a re-emergence of specialist nursing roles with older people in all areas of care, and these are beginning to redress the balance of the large number of posts which were lost when specialist older people services were disseminated. These nurses will continue to develop and influence the future agenda.

SUMMARY

The emerging policy agenda heralds a brighter future for nurses working with older people. Key to this is the extensive and growing interest within society about how Britain can respond to the needs of an ageing population. As a result, there is intense policy development and media interest relating to the needs and care of older people. Simultaneously, nurses who work with older people have undertaken significant work with the key emphasis being on identifying and articulating what it is that nurses contribute to health and social care. The motivation for this work derives not from professional protectionism, but from the lived experience of nurses who have witnessed older people at their most vulnerable and who have known that when expert nursing has been available, the patient's quality of life and power to direct their own destiny has been considerably enhanced by the nurse's input.

As this chapter has demonstrated, the current scenario offers opportunities for nurses to promote health, and to influence and create a positive future for health and social-care services for older people in all sectors and at all levels. Gerontological nurses recognise that the majority of older people live independent lives and that older individuals contribute to all 'levels' of life, be that national Government or individual families.

For the most part, nurses spend their working time with older people whose contribution to life is daily modified by illness or disability. That does not mean that their contribution is any less valuable – quite the contrary. In fact, by not actively seeking and facilitating that view, we risk losing a perspective rich in lived experience that could potentially help each of us to learn about life.

(The sections on pages 513–517 were developed through the contributions of: Alan Crump, Jan Dewing, Ursula Gallagher, Gillian Granville, Annette Hanny, Jim Marr, Liz Matthews, Brendan McCormack, Helen Peace, Lesley Potter, Irene Schofield, Karen Smith and Tina Wills. Sincere thanks for their views and their willing participation.)

KEY POINTS

- Nursing older people is a major and developing speciality, particularly in the context of the projected demographics of the older population.
- The views of older people should be central to the planning and evaluation of current and future services, but there are particularly considerations when seeking these views.
- The health and social-care agenda for older people is substantial, as almost every aspect of health and social-care policy development impacts on older people. Key areas include long-term care, health futures and rationing, healthy lifestyles and health promotion.
- In long-term care, key areas of development in demonstrating the value of nursing have been new tools to assess nursing need and to measure the outcomes from nursing practice.
- In order to prepare the nursing workforce to work with older people, the appropriateness of the preparation and ongoing development of nurses who work with older people need to be addressed.
- Research on nursing older people must acknowledge their heterogeneity and seek methodologies that will illuminate the whole range of aspects within nursing.
- The role of nursing with older people has overcome many challenges in its development but, despite these, some of nursing's most innovative work has originated among nurses working with older people.
- There are many distinct and special aspects to nursing older people which require nurses to develop additional knowledge, skills and experience.
- A thematic analysis of emerging nursing roles with older people revealed increasing emphasis on a user focus, challenging the culture, working with change, cost-consciousness, cross-boundary working, working beyond 'traditional' boundaries, working collaboratively, complex and multidimensional/multi-level working structures and roles, quality implementation and evaluation, valuing and developing nursing, personal and professional responsibility, being proactive, influencing and being positive.
- A SWOT analysis offered key pointers to where gerontological nursing is currently, and how the speciality can best position itself for the future.
- A key emerging role is that of gerontological nurse specialist or practitioner, and the chapter described a framework within which the role could develop.
- An agenda for change should integrate the essential elements of policy, practice, education and research, and maintain the older person (and significant others) at the centre.
- The emerging policy agenda heralds a bright future for nurses working with older people but, if this is to reach its full potential, gerontological nurse leaders must identify, nurture, develop, support and promote the leadership qualities of nurses with whom they work.

REFERENCES

Age Concern. *The debate of the age: health and care interim report*, millennium paper, London, 1997, Age Concern England.

Audit Commission. *The virtue of patients making the best use of ward resources*, London, 1991, HMSO.

Bagust A, Slack R. *Ward nursing quality*, York, 1991, University of York, Health Economics Consortium.

Bartlett H. Consumer evaluation as a quality indicator. In: Bartlett H, ed. *Nursing homes for elderly people: questions of quality and policy*. Switzerland: Harwood Academic Publishers, 1995.

Benner P. *From novice to expert*. Menlo Park: Addison Wesley, 1984.

BMA and RCN. *The older person: consent and care*, London, 1995, British Medical Association.

Bond J, Bond S. Developments in the provision and evaluation of longterm care for dependent old people. In: Fielding P, ed. *Research in the nursing care of elderly people*. Chichester: Wiley, 1987.

Bond J, Bond S, Donaldson C *et al. Evaluation of continuing care accommodation for elderly people*, Report No. 38, Vol 7, Newcastle upon Tyne, 1989, Health Care Research Unit, School of Healthcare Sciences, University of Newcastle upon Tyne.

Bowsher J, Bramlett M, Burnside IM, Gueldner SH. Methodological considerations in the study of frail elderly people. *J Adv Nurs* 1993, 18:873–879.

Brooker DJR. Looking at them, looking at me: a review of observational studies in the quality of institutional care for elderly people with dementia. *J Mental Health* 1995, 4:145–152.

Brooker DJR. Issues in user feedback on health services for elderly people. *Br J Nurs* 1997, 6:159–162.

Buchan J, Ball J. *Caring costs: nursing costs and benefits*, Brighton, 1991, Institute of Manpower Studies.

Carr-Hill R, Dixon P, Gibbs I *et al. Skill mix and the effectiveness of nursing care*, York, 1992, Centre for Health Economics, University of York.

Clark P, Bowling A. Observational study of quality of life in NHS nursing homes and a long-stay ward for the elderly. *Ageing and Society* 1989, 9:123–148.

Cornwell J. *The consumers' view: elderly people and community health series*, London, 1989, King's Fund.

Dalley G, Howse K, Killoran A, Seal H. *A framework for promoting the health of older people: a discussion document*, London, 1996, Health Education Authority/Centre for Policy On Ageing.

Davis S, Ellis L, Lanker S. *Promoting autonomy and independence among older people: an evaluation of educational programmes in nursing*, London, 1997, English National Board for Nursing, Midwifery and Health Visiting.

Department of Health. *Report of the taskforce on the strategy for research in nursing, midwifery and health visiting*, London, 1992, HMSO.

Downey R. Minister's counsel for care. *Community Care* 1997, (June).

Entwistle V, Watt I, Herring J. *Information about health care effectiveness: an introduction for consumer health information providers*, London, 1997, King's Fund.

Epstein AM, Hall JA, Tognetti J, Son LH, Conant L. Using proxies to evaluate quality of life. *Med Care* 1989, 27:91–98.

Farrell C, Gilbert H. *Health care partnerships: debates and strategies for increasing user involvement in health care and health services*, London, 1997, King's Fund.

Fitzpatrick R. Surveys of patient satisfaction 1: designing a questionnaire and conducting a study. *Br Med J* 1991, 302:1129–1132.

Ford P. What older people value in nurses. In: Ford P, Heath H, eds. *Older people and nursing: issues of living in a care home*. Oxford: Butterworth Heinemann, 1995.

Harding T, Meredith B, Wistow G. *Looking to the future*, London, 1996, HMSO.

Hope T. *Evidence-based patient choice*, London, 1997, King's Fund.

House of Commons Health Comittee. *Long term care: future provision and funding*, Vol 1, third report, HSC 59-1, London, 1996, HMSO.

Joseph Rowntree Foundation Inquiry. *Meeting the costs of continuing care*, London, 1996, Joseph Rowntree Foundation.

King's Fund Centre. *Information on obtaining the views of the elderly: consumer feedback resources*, London, 1991, King's Fund.

King's Fund Centre. *The future organisation of community care:*

options for the integration of health and social care, London, 1997, King's Fund.

Kitson A, McMahon A, Rafferty AM. High priority. *Nurs Times* 1997, 93:26–30.

Laing W, Buisson M. UK domiciliary care market report, London, 1996,

LeBow JL. Client satisfaction with mental health treatment: methodological considerations in assessment. *Evaluaton Review* 7:729–752.

Masterson A. The Nursing and Health Visiting Contribution to the continuing care of older people. United Kingdom Central Council for Nursing, Midwifery and Health Visiting, London. 1997

McClary M. Identifying priorities for guideline development as a result of nursing need. *DQI Network News* 1997, 6:4–5.

MRC. *The health of the UK's elderly population*, London, 1994, Medical Research Council.

National Consumer Council. *Consulting consumers in the NHS: a guideline study. Services for elderly people with dementia living at home*, London, 1990, National Consumer Council.

Nazarko L. Choice of compulsion? The growth of consumer in health care for the elderly. *Nurs Management* 1997, 3:18–21.

Nolan M. Geriatric nursing: an idea whose time has gone? A polemic. *J Adv Nurs* 1994, 20:989–996.

Nolan M, Keady J. Training in longterm care: the road to better quality. *Rev Clin Gerontology* 1996, 6:333–342.

O'Leary A. Patient satisfaction as a measure of quality in the care of the elderly. *Br J Nursing* 1992, 1:470–472.

Pearson A. *The clinical nursing unit*. London: Heinemann, 1983.

Pearson A, ed. *Primary nursing: nursing in the Burford and Oxford nursing development units*. London: Croom Helm, 1988.

Phillips LR. Challenges of nursing research with the frail elderly. *West J Nurs Res* 1992, 14:721–730.

Read S. The strategy for nursing in nursing, initial impact. *Nurs Res* 1994, 1:72–84.

Reed J, Payton VR. Constructing familiarity and managing the self: ways of adapting to life in nursing and residential homes. *Ageing and Society* 1996, 16:561–578.

Rogers WL, Herzog AR. Interviewing of older adults: the accuracy of factual information. *J Gerontology* 1987, 42:387–394.

RCN. *The value and skills of nurses working with older people*. Royal College of Nursing, London, (pp. 508, 516), 1993

RCN. *Single registration care homes*, London, 1997a, Royal College of Nursing.

RCN. *What a difference a nurse makes: an RCN report on the benefits of expert nursing to the clinical outcomes in the continuing care of older people*, 1997b, London, Royal College of Nursing.

RCN. *The RCN assessment tool: nursing older people*, London, 1997c, Royal College of Nursing.

RCN. *Mergers: good practice for older people. Principles in a continuum of health care*, London, 1998, Royal College of Nursing.

Roberts C et al. The wasted millions. *Health Services Journal*, 10th October, 15, 1996.

Royal College of Optometrists. *The ageing eye*, Factsheet No. 7, London, 1995, Royal College of Optometrists.

Seccombe I, Smith G. *In the Balance: Registered nurse supply and demand*, 1996, Report 315, Institute of Employment Studies and Royal College of Nursing, IES, Brighton. 1996.

Seccombe I, Smith G. *Taking Part: Registered nurses and the labour market in 1997*, Report 338, Institute of Employment Studies and Royal College of Nursing, IES, Brighton. 1997.

Secretaries of State. *Caring for people: community care in the next decade and beyond*, CM 849, London, 1989, HMSO.

UKCC. *Statistical analysis of the UKCC's professional register, 1 April 1996–31 March 1997*, London, 1997, United Kingdom Central Council for Nursing, Midwifery and Health Visiting.

Wade B, Sawyer L, Bell J. *Dependency with dignity: different care provision for the elderly, occasional papers on social administration, No. 68*. London: Bedford Square Press, 1983.

Wade L. New perspectives on gerontological nursing. In: Wade L, Waters K, eds. *A textbook of gerontological nursing: perspectives on practice*. London: Balliere Tindall, 1996.

Wilce G. *A place like home: a radical experiment in healthcare*. London: Bedford Square Press, 1988.

Appendices

Normal Physical Assessment Findings in Older People

Cardiovascular Changes

Cardiac output	Heart loses elasticity; therefore, decreased heart contractility in response to increased demands
Arterial circulation	Decreased vessel compliance with increased peripheral resistance to blood flow resulting from general or localised arteriosclerosis
Venous circulation	Does not exhibit change with ageing in the absence of disease
Blood pressure	Significant increase in the systolic, slight increase in the diastolic, increase in peripheral resistance and pulse pressure
Heart	Dislocation of the apex because of kyphoscoliosis; therefore, diagnostic significance of location is lost
Murmurs	Diastolic murmurs in over half of older people, the most common heard at the base of the heart because of sclerotic changes of the aortic valves
Peripheral pulses	Easily palpated because of increased arterial wall narrowing and loss of connective tissue; feeling of tortuous and rigid vessels
Heart rate	No changes with age at normal rest

Respiratory Changes

Pulmonary blood flow and diffusion	Decreased blood flow to the pulmonary circulation; decreased diffusion
Anatomic structure	Increased anterior-posterior diameter
Respiratory accessory muscles	Degeneration and decreased strength; increased rigidity of chest wall; muscle atrophy of pharynx and larynx
Internal pulmonic structure	Decreased pulmonary elasticity creates senile emphysema. Shorter breaths taken with decreased maximum breathing capacity, vital capacity, residual volume and functional capacity. Airway resistance increases; less ventilation at the bases of the lung and more at the apex

Integumentary Changes

Texture	Skin loses elasticity; wrinkles, folding, sagging and dryness
Colour	Spotty pigmentation in areas exposed to sun; face paler, even in the absence of anaemia
Temperature	Extremities cooler; decreased perspiration
Fat distribution	Less on extremities; more on trunk
Hair colour	Dull grey, white, yellow or yellow-green
Hair distribution	Thins on scalp, axilla, pubic area, upper and lower extremities; decreased facial hair in men, women may develop chin and upper lip hair
Nails	Decreased growth rate

Genitourinary and Reproductive Changes

Renal blood flow	Because of decreased cardiac output, reduced filtration rate and renal efficiency; possibility of subsequent loss of protein from kidneys
Micturition	In men: possibility of increased frequency as a result of prostatic enlargement
	In women: decreased perineal muscle tone; therefore, urgency and stress
Incontinence	Increased nocturia for both men and women. Possibility that polyuria may be diabetes related
	Decreased volume of urine may relate to decrease in intake but evaluation needed
Incontinence	Increased occurrence with age, specifically in those with dementia
Male reproduction: testosterone production	Decreases; phases of intercourse slower, lengthened refractory time
frequency of intercourse	No changes in libido and sexual satisfaction; decreased frequency to one or two times weekly
testes	Decreased size; decreased sperm count; diminished viscosity of seminal fluid

Appendix 1 Normal Physical Assessment Findings in Older People.

Normal Physical Assessment Findings in Older People (continued)

Genitourinary and Reproductive Changes (continued)

Female reproduction:	
oestrogen	Decreased production with menopause
breasts	Diminished breast tissue
uterus	Decreased size; mucous secretions cease; possibility that uterine prolapse may occur
vagina	Epithelial lining atrophies; narrow and shortened canal
vaginal secretions	Become more alkaline as glycogen content increases and acidity declines

Gastrointestinal Changes

Mastication	Impaired because of partial or total loss of teeth, malocclusive bite, and ill-fitting dentures
Swallowing and carbohydrate digestion	Swallowing more difficult as salivary secretions diminish
Oesophagus	Decreased oesophageal peristalsis. Increased incidence of hiatus hernia with (gaseous distension)
Digestive enzymes	Decreased production of hydrochloric acid, pepsin and pancreatic enzymes
Fat absorption	Delayed, affecting the absorption rate of fat-soluble vitamins A, D, E and K
Intestinal peristalsis	Reduced gastrointestinal motility, Constipation because of decreased motility and roughage

Musculoskeletal Changes

Muscle strength and function	Decrease with loss of muscle mass; bony prominences normal in older people, since muscle mass decreased
Bone structure	Normal demineralisation, more porous, shortening of trunk (a result of intervertebral space narrowing)
Joints	Become less mobile; tightening and fixation occur. Activity may maintain function longer. Normal posture changes; some kyphosis. Range of motion limited
Anatomical size and height	Total decrease in size as loss of body protein and body water occurs in proportion to decrease in basal metabolic rate. Increased body fat; diminished in arms and legs, increased in trunk. Decreased height from 2.5 to 10 cm from young adulthood

Nervous System Changes

Response to stimuli	All voluntary or automatic reflexes slower. Decreased ability to respond to multiple stimuli
Sleep patterns	Stage IV sleep reduced in comparison to younger adulthood; increased frequency of spontaneous awakening. Stay in bed longer but get less sleep; insomnia a problem, which should be evaluated
Reflexes	Deep tendon reflexes responsive in the healthy older person
Ambulation	Kinesthetic sense less efficient; may demonstrate an extrapyramidal Parkinson-like gait. Basal ganglions of the nervous system influenced by the vascular changes and decreased oxygen supply
Voice	Decreased range, duration and intensity of voice; may become higher pitched and more monotone

Sensory Changes

Vision			
peripheral vision	Decreases	retina	Observable vascular changes
lens accommodation	Decreases, requires corrective lenses	stimuli threshold	Increased threshold for light touch and pain. Ischaemic
ciliary body	Atrophy in accommodation of lens focus		paraesthesias common in the
iris	Development of arcus senilis		extremities
choroid	Atrophy around disc		
lens	May develop opacity, cataract formation; more light necessary to see	Hearing	Less perceptible high-frequency tones; hence, impaired language
colour	Fades or disappears		understanding
macula	Degenerates	Gustatory	Decreased acuity possibly due to
conjunctiva	Thins and looks yellow		decline in sense of smell; may
tearing	Decreases; increased irritation and infection		increase the amount of seasoning
pupil	May differ in size		on food
cornea	Presence of arcus senilis		

Appendix 1 (cont.) Normal Physical Assessment Findings in Older People.

Katz Index of Activities of Daily Living

1. Bathing (washdown, shower or bath)

I: Receives no assistance (gets in and out of bath, if bath is the usual means of bathing)
A: Receives assistance in bathing only one part of the body (such as the back or a leg)
D: Receives assistance in bathing more than one part of the body (or not bathed)

2. Dressing

I: Gets clothes and gets completely dressed without assistance
A: Gets clothes and gets dressed without assistance except in tying shoes
D: Receives assistance in getting clothes or in getting dressed, or stays partly or completely undressed

3. Toileting

I: Goes to 'toilet room', cleans self and arranges clothes without assistance (may use object for support such as stick, walking frame or wheelchair and may manage night bedpan or commode, emptying it in the morning)
A: Receives assistance in going to 'toilet room' or in cleansing self or in arranging clothes after elimination or in use of night bedpan or commode
D: Doesn't go to room termed 'toilet' for the elimination process

4. Transfer

I: Moves in and out of bed as well as in and out of chair without assistance (may be using object for support such as stick or walking frame
A: Moves in and out of bed or chair with assistance
D: Doesn't get out of bed

5. Continence

I: Controls urination and bowel movement completely by self
A: Has occasional 'accidents'
D: Supervision helps keep urine or bowel control; catheter is used, or is incontinent

6. Feeding

I: Feeds self without assistance
A: Feeds self except for getting assistance in cutting meat or buttering bread
D: Receives assistance in feeding or is fed partly or completely by using tubes or intravenous fluids

ABBREVIATIONS
I = Independent A = Assistance D = Dependent   Source: JAMA 1963,185:915.

Appendix 2 Katz Index of Activities of Daily Living.

Stretch your arms and legs; take a deep breath.

Fold your hands on your stomach; raise your arms over your head toward the headboard.

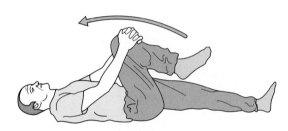

Grab each leg with both hands below the knee and pull toward your chest slowly.

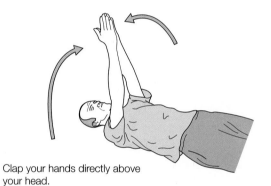

Clap your hands directly above your head.

With your arms at your sides, bend at the elbow and curl your arms as if "making a muscle."

Lift each leg off the bed, but try not to bend your knee. Use an arm to help.

Appendix 3 Exercises: (a) lying down.

Bend forward and let your
arms dangle; try to touch the
floor with your hands.

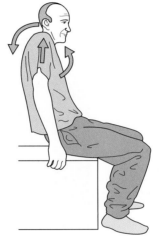

Shrug your shoulders forward,
then move them in a circle,
raising them high enough to
reach your ears.

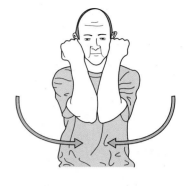

Touch your elbows together
in front of you.

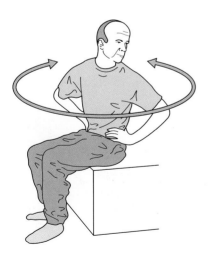

Twist your whole upper body
from side to side with your hands
on your hips.

While still sitting, move each
of your knees up and down as
if you are walking; each time
your right foot hits the ground,
count it as one. Lift your knee high.

Appendix 3 Exercises: (b) sitting.

Using your arms, push off from the bed and stand up; if you get dizzy, sit down and try again.

Hold your arms out and turn them in big circles.

With hands at your sides, bend at the waist as far as you can to the right side, then to the left.

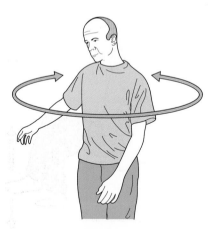

Keep your feet planted on the ground and twist your upper body at the waist from side to side with your arms swinging; when you twist to the right, count it as one.

While holding onto the edge of the bed or back of a chair, bend your knees slightly.

Appendix 3 Exercises: (c) standing up.

Walking is good exercise. It helps in toning muscles, maintaining flexibility of joints, and also is good exercise for the heart and circulatory system. Walking briskly for 20 minutes a day, 3 times a week can be as effective a heart conditioner as jogging, but it does take a longer time to achieve the same effect as jogging. For those who cannot walk rapidly for long periods, walking to the point of muscular fatigue also helps maintain good muscle tone.

There are signs your body may give you to indicate you are overdoing exercise. Stop, rest, and if necessary call your doctor if you experience any of these symptoms:

- Severe shortnesss of breath
- Chest pain
- Severe joint pain
- Dizziness or faint feeling
- Heart flutters

In all walking exercises, go only as fast as you are able to walk and still carry on a conversation. If you cannot, slow down.

Inside

It is important to maintain walking ability. Determine how far you can walk and each day walk to 75% of that distance, building endurance. Wear supportive shoes and use whatever aids are necessary.

Outside

Wear soft-soled shoes with good support, i.e., jogging shoes. When walking, push off from your toes and land on your heels. Swing arms loosely at your sides. Begin with 10-minute walks and build up to 20 to 30 minutes.

Walking upstairs requires effort. Place one foot flat on a step, push off with the other and shift your weight. Use a railing for balance if necessary.

Appendix 3 Exercises: (d) walking places.

Braden Scale for Predicting Pressure Sore Risk

PATIENT'S NAME	EVALUATOR'S NAME		Date of Assessment	
Sensory Perception Ability to respond meaningfully to pressure- related discomfort	**1. Completely Limited** Unresponsive (does not moan, flinch or grasp) to painful stimuli, due to diminished level of consciousness or sedation OR Limited ability to feel pain over most of body surface	**2. Very Limited** Responds only to painful stimuli Cannot communicate discomfort except by moaning or restlessness	**3. Slightly Limited** Responds to verbal commands but cannot always communicate discomfort or need to be turned OR Has some sensory impairment which limits ability to feel pain or discomfort in one or two extremities	**4. No Impairment** Responds to verbal commands Has no sensory deficit which would limit ability to feel or voice pain or discomfort
Moisture Degree to which skin is exposed to moisture	**1. Constantly moist** Skin is kept moist almost constantly by perspiration, urine, etc Dampness is detected every time patient is moved or turned	**2. Moist** Skin is often but not always moist Linen must be changed at least once a shift	**3. Occasionally Moist** Skin is occasionally moist, requiring an extra linen change approximately once a day	**4. Rarely Moist** Skin is usually dry; linen requires changing only at routine intervals
Activity Degree of physical activity	**1. Bedfast** Confined to bed	**2. Chairfast** Ability to walk severely limited or nonexistent Cannot bear own weight and must be assisted into chair or wheelchair	**3. Walks Occasionally** Walks occasionally during day but for very short distances, with or without assistance Spends majority of each shift in bed or chair	**4. Walks Frequently:** Walks outside the room at least twice a day and inside room at least once every 2 hours during waking hours
Mobility Ability to change and control body position	**1. Completely Immobile** Does not make even slight changes in body or extremity position without assistance	**2. Very Limited** Makes occasional slight changes in body or extremity position but unable to make frequent or significant changes independently	**3. Slightly Limited** Makes frequent though slight changes in body or extremity position independently	**4. No limitation** Makes major and frequent changes in position without assistance
Nutrition Usual food intake pattern	**1. Very Poor** Never eats a complete meal. Rarely eats more than a third of any food offered. Eats two servings or less of protein (meat or dairy products) per day Takes fluids poorly Does not take a liquid dietary supplement OR Is NPO and maintained on clear liquids or IV for more than 5 days	**2. Probably Inadequate** Rarely eats a complete meal and generally eats only about half of any food offered. Protein intake includes only three servings of meat or dairy products per day. Occasionally will take a dietary supplement OR Receives less than optimum amount of liquid diet or tube feeding	**3. Adequate** Eats over half of most meals. Eats a total of four servings of protein (meat, dairy products) each day Occasionally will refuse a meal, but will usually take a supplement if offered OR Is on a tube feeding or TPN regimen, which probably meets most of nutritious needs	**4. Excellent** Eats most of every meal; never refuses a meal. Usually eats a total of four or more servings of meat and dairy products Occasionally eats between meals; does not require supplementation

Braden Scale for Predicting Pressure Sore Risk

Friction and shear	1. Problem	2. Potential problem	3. No Apparent Problem	
	Requires moderate to maximum assistance in moving. Complete lifting without sliding against sheets is impossible Frequently slides down in bed or chair, requiring frequent repositioning with maximum assistance Spasticity, contractures or agitation leads to almost constant friction	Moves feebly or requires minimum assistance. During a move skin probably slides to some extent against sheets, chair, restraints or other devices. Maintains relatively good position in chair or bed most of the time but occasionally slides down	Moves in bed and in chair independently and has sufficient muscle strength to lift up completely during move. Maintains good position in bed or chair at all times	

Total score

NPO = Nothing by mouth   IV = Intravenous
TPN = Total parenteral nutrition

Source: Braden B., Bergstrom B. A conceptual scheme for the study of the aetiology of pressure sores. *Rehabilitation Nursing* 1987, 12:9.

Appendix 4 (cont.) Braden Scale for Predicting Pressure Sore Risk.

Decision-Making Guide for the Selection of Pressure-Relieving Equipment *						
Risk factors	No risk/ minimal risk	Low risk	At risk/ compromised	Compromised/ tissue break down	Compromised/ extensive tissue breakdown	Complications of immobility
Skin integrity	Intact skin	Small reddened areas on bony prominences that blanch/may have skin sensitivities	Reddened areas but skin intact	One or more areas of superficial breakdown Some areas may have full involvement Wound care is necessary	One or more areas of full thickness and deep tissue damage Needs improved cutaneous circulation	Any of previous categories
Mobility	Ambulatory/ short hospital stay anticipated	Limited mobility: may require assistance with turning and walking	Limited mobility	Limited mobility	Limited mobility	Severely limited mobility or immobile
Nutrition	Adequate nutritional status	Adequate nutritional status	Inadequate oral intake; questionable nutritional status	Malnourished	Malnourished	Any of previous categories
Continence	Continent	Continent or indwelling urinary catheter	Frequent or total incontinence; no urinary catheter	Incontinent	Incontinent	Any of previous categories
Sensory factors	Normal	Normal	May have decreased sensation	Altered	Altered	Any of previous categories
Mental status	Normal	Normal	May be receiving sedatives, narcotics, barbiturates, psychotropic medication	Altered	Altered	Any of previous categories
Weight	Normal	Normal	May be over or under weight	May be over or under weight	Altered	Any of previous categories
Suggestions for support surface	Good quality standard foam mattress	Static mattress overlay and frequent risk assessment	Dynamic mattress overlay	Specialist pressure relieving system	Air fluidised surface	Ask for specific advice from company representative

* This guide should be used in conjunction with clinical judgement, a risk assessment score and advice from a company representative.

Source: Simpson A, Bowers K, Weir-Hughes D. Pressure sore prevention. London: Whurr Publishers Ltd, 1996

Appendix 5 Decision-making Guide for the Selection of Pressure-Relieving Equipment.

Selecting Wound Dressings

Product	Yellow/brown slough		Granulating wound				Epithelialising wound		Black necrotic wound		Clinically infected wound		Malodorous wound
	small and dry	small and moist	deep cavity	cavity	medium to high exudate	low to medium exudate	clean medium to high exudate	clean low to medium exudate	small and superficial	extensive and deep	small cavities	shallow and open	
Allevyn						●		●					
Bactigras												●	
Bioclusive								●					
Clorhexitulle												●	
Comfeel hydrocolloid	●	●				●		●	●	●			
Cutifilm								●					
Duoderm								●					
Fucidin Intertulle		●										●	
Granuflex	●	●				●			●	●			
Granugel		●	●	●					●	●			
Inadine	●	●							●	●		●	
Intrasite				●				●					
Jelonet								●					
Kaltostat			●	●	●						●	●	
Kaltogel		●	●	●	●						●	●	
Lyofoam					●		●						
Lyofoam Extra					●		●						
Melolin							●	●					
NA Dressing							●	●					
NU-Gel	●	●	●	●				●	●	●			
INA Ultra								●					
Opsite Flexigrid								●					
Paratulle								●					
Release								●					
Seasorb				●	●						●	●	
Serotulle								●				●	
Skintact								●					
Sofra-tulle												●	
Sorbsan		●	●	●	●		●				●	●	●
Spyrosorb		●				●		●					
Sterigel	●	●						●	●	●			
Tegaderm								●					
Tegagen		●	●	●	●			●				●	
Tegasorb Advanced	●	●				●		●	●	●			
Tielle						●		●					
Tricotex								●				●	
Unitulle								●					

Source: MIMS Monthly Index of Medical Specialities, February 1997, p. 344.

Appendix 6 Selecting Wound Dressings (darker dots indicate appropriate products).

Weak Opioids and Common Non-Prescription Analgesics

COMMONLY USED WEAK OPIOID PREPARATIONS

Generic Name	Contents Weak Opioid	Contents Non-Opioid
Co-codaprin	Codeine 8mg	Aspirin 400mg
Co-codamol 8/500	Codeine 8mg	Paracetamol 500mg
Co-codamol 30/500	Codeine 30mg	Paracetamol 500mg
Co-dydramol	Dihydrocodeine 10mg	Paracetamol 500mg
Co-proxamol	Dextropropoxyphene hydrochloride 32.5mg	Paracetamol 500mg

COMMON NON-PRESCRIPTION ANALGESICS

1. Containing aspirin and paracetamol. Other major ingredients listed, but minor additives (e.g. caffeine) omitted

Brand Name	Contents	Brand Name	Contents
Actron	Aspirin, Paracetamol	Disprol	Paracetamol
Alka-Seltzer	Aspirin	Hedex	Paracetamol
Anadin	Aspirin, Quinine	Panadeine	Paracetamol, Codeine
Andrews Answer	Paracetamol	Panadol	Paracetamol
Aspro	Aspirin	Paraclear	Paracetamol
Aspro Clear	Aspirin	Paracodol	Paracetamol, Codeine
Aspro Paraclear	Paracetamol	Paramin	Paracetamol
Coda-med	Paracetamol, Codeine	Paramol	Paracetamol, Dihydrocodeine
Codanin	Paracetamol, Codeine	Phensic	Aspirin
Codis 500	Aspirin, Codeine	Solpadeine	Paracetamol, Codeine
Disprin	Codeine	Veganin	Aspirin, Paracetamol, Codeine

2. Containing Ibuprofen

Anadin Ibuprofen, Cuprofen, Migrafen, Novaprin, Nurofen, Proflex, Reclofen

Source: British National Formulary

Appendix 7 Weak Opioids and Common Non-Prescription Analgesics.

A Guide to Using the Equianalgesic Chart

Equianalgesic means approximately the same pain relief. Onset, peak, effect and duration of analgesia for each drug often differ and so may vary with individual people.

Variability among individuals may be due to differences in absorption, organ dysfunction, or tolerance to one drug and not to another.

An equianalgesic chart is a guideline. The individual patient's response must be observed. Doses and intervals between doses are then titrated according to the individual's response.

An equianalgesic chart is helpful when switching from one drug to another or switching from one route of administration to another.

Relative potency of various routes of morphine administration: (Hanks et al. 1996)

Oral morphine	to Ratio
Rectal morphine	1:1
Subcutaneous morphine	1:2
Intravenous morphine	1:3
Subcutaneous diamorphine	1:3

Appendix 8 A Guide to Using the Equianalgesic Chart

Approximate Oral Analgesic Equivalence to Morphine

Analgesic	Potency ratio with morphine	Duration of action (h)[b]
Codeine } Dihydrocodeine	1/10	3–5
Pethidine (meperidine USA)	1/8	2–3
Tramadol	1/5 [c]	5–6
Dipipanone (in Diconal UK)	1/2	3–5
Papaveretum	2/3 [d]	3–5
Oxycodone	4/3 [c]	5–6
Dextromoramide	[2] [e]	2–3
Methadone	[3–4] [f]	6–12
Levorphanol	5	6–8
Phenazocine	5	6–8
Hydromorphone	8	3–5
Buprenorphine (sublingual)	60	6–8
Fentanyl (transdermal)	150	72

a   multiply dose of opioid by its potency ratio to determine the equivalent dose of morphine sulphate

b   dependent in part on severity of pain and on dose; often longer lasting in very elderly and those with renal dysfunction

c   tramadol and oxycodone are both relatively more potent by mouth because of high bioavailability; parenteral potency ratios with morphine are 1/10 and 3/4 respectively

d   papaveretum (strong opium) is standardized to contain 50% morphine base; potency expressed in relation to morphine sulphate

e   dextromoramide: a single 5 mg dose is equivalent to morphine 15 mg in terms of peak effect but is shorter acting; overall potency ratio adjusted accordingly

f   methadone: a single 5 mg dose is equivalent to morphine 7.5 mg. Has a variable long plasma halflife which leads to cumulation in many patients when given repeatedly; overall potency ratio adjusted accordingly.

Source: Twycross R. *Symptom Management in Advanced Cancer*, 2nd edn. Oxford: Radcliffe Medical Press, 1997.

Appendix 9 Approximate Oral Analgesic Equivalence to Morphine.

Neural Blockade Procedure and Examples of their Applications

Sacral intrathecal block
For perineal pain due to rectal or pelvic cancer with sacral nerve involvement

Coeliac plexus block
May help upper abdominal pain due to cancer involving the stomach, liver or pancreas

Lumbar sympathetic block
For painful peripheral vascular disease of lower limbs

Lumbar psoas block
For chest wall pain due to lung cancer or bone disease

Stellate ganglion block
For facial or opthalmic pain. For example, intractable post-herpetic neuralgia

Epidural catheter
Used for postoperative pain, end-stage peripheral vascular disease and intractable cancer pain

Single epidural injection
Sometimes helpful for nerve root pain with a benign (e.g. osteoarthritis) or malignant cause

Source: Latham, 1993

Appendix 10 Neural Blockade Procedure and Examples of Their Application .

Cultural Status Assessments

Pfeifferling Model

1. How would you describe the problem that has brought you here?
NOTE: The clinician may need to identify others who can facilitate the discussion of the client's/patient's problem.
A. Who in the community and your family helps you with your problem?

2. How long have you had this problem?
A. Do you know anyone else with it?
B. Tell me what happened to them when dealing with this problem.

3. What do you think is wrong with you?
A. What might other people think is wrong with you?
B. Tell me about people who don't get this problem.

4. Why has it happened to you, and why now?
A. Why has it happened to the involved part?
B. Why do you get sick and not someone else?

5. What do you think will help clear up this problem?
A. If specific tests or medications are listed, ask what they are and what they do.

6. Apart from me, who else do you think can make you feel better?
A. Are there therapies that make you feel better (some discipline) that I don't know about?

Kleinman Explanatory Model

1. What do you call your problem? What name does it have?
2. What do you think caused it?
3. When do you think it started?
4. What does your sickness do to you?
5. How severe is it? Will it have a long or short course?
6. What do you fear most about your sickness?
7. What are the chief problems your sickness has caused you?
8. What treatment should you receive? What are the most important results you hope to receive?

Source: Pfeifferling, 1981; Kleinman, 1981.

Appendix 11 Cultural Status Examinations.

Index

Index